For Gemye,

An amazing colleague

and friends.

Frank

Developmental Psychology

Developmental Psychology

The Growth of Mind and Behavior

Frank Keil
YALE UNIVERSITY

W. W. NORTON & COMPANY NEW YORK · LONDON

To Kristi, Derek, Dylan, and Martin

W. W. NORTON & COMPANY has been independent since its founding in 1923, when William Warder Norton and Mary D. Herter Norton first published lectures delivered at the People's Institute, the adult education division of New York City's Cooper Union. The firm soon expanded its program beyond the Institute, publishing books by celebrated academics from America and abroad. By midcentury, the two major pillars of Norton's publishing program—trade books and college texts—were firmly established. In the 1950s, the Norton family transferred control of the company to its employees, and today—with a staff of four hundred and a comparable number of trade, college, and professional titles published each year—W. W. Norton & Company stands as the largest and oldest publishing house owned wholly by its employees.

Editor: Aaron Javsicas
Developmental Editor: Sandy Lifland
Manuscript Editor: Janet Greenblatt
Project Editor: Rachel Mayer
Electronic Media Editor: Callinda Taylor
Editorial Assistant: Shira Averbuch
Marketing Manager, Psychology: Lauren Winkler
Production Manager: Eric Pier-Hocking
Photo Editor: Michael Fodera
Photo Researchers: Donna Ranieri and Julie Tesser
Permissions Manager: Megan Jackson
Permissions Clearing: Bethany Salminen
Text Design: Lissi Sigillo
Art Director: Rubina Yeh
Composition: Jouve
Manufacturing: Courier—Kendallville

Library of Congress Cataloging-in-Publication Data

Keil, Frank C., 1952–
   Developmental psychology : the growth of mind and behavior / Frank Keil. — First edition.
      pages cm
   Includes bibliographical references and index.
   ISBN 978-0-393-97885-8 (hardcover)
   1. Developmental psychology.   I. Title.
   BF713.K443 2014
   155—dc23
                                                                    2013034957

W. W. Norton & Company, Inc., 500 Fifth Avenue, New York, NY 10110-0017
wwnorton.com

W. W. Norton & Company Ltd., Castle House, 75/76 Wells Street, London W1T 3QT

1 2 3 4 5 6 7 8 9 0

About the Author

Frank C. Keil is the Charles C. and Dorathea S. Dilley Professor of Psychology and Linguistics and chair of the Psychology Department at Yale University. Keil received his B.S. in Biology from M.I.T. in 1973, an M.A. in Psychology from Stanford University in 1975, and a Ph.D. in Psychology from the University of Pennsylvania in 1977. He was a faculty member at Cornell University from 1977 to 1998 and has been at Yale since 1998. For over 35 years, he has taught an undergraduate lecture course in developmental psychology, as well as advanced seminars at the undergraduate and graduate level on topics in cognitive development and cognition.

Keil has published extensively on topics concerned with many areas of the development of cognition and language. He wrote two books on aspects of conceptual development and, with the philosopher Robert Wilson, he edited the *MIT Encyclopedia of the Cognitive Sciences*, which was selected as the Outstanding Book in Psychology by the Association of American Publishers in 1999. Keil served as president of the Society for Philosophy and Psychology and has received numerous awards for his scholarship, including the Boyd R. McCandless Award (Developmental Psychology), the Distinguished Scientific Award for an Early Career Contribution to Psychology, a Guggenheim Fellowship, a fellowship at the Center for Advanced Study in the Behavioral Sciences, a MERIT Award from the National Institutes of Health, and the Ann L. Brown Award for Excellence in Developmental Research. Keil served as Master of Morse College at Yale University from 2001 until 2012. Keil and his wife Kristi Lockhart, a clinical and developmental psychologist, are parents of three sons who are now in their twenties and thirties.

Contents in Brief

PART I Framing Psychological Development

Chapter 1 Approaching Psychological Development 2

Chapter 2 The Biology of Development 33

PART II Origins

Chapter 3 Coming to Perceive the World 76

Chapter 4 The Emergence of Action 115

Chapter 5 Coming to Understand the Physical World 145

Chapter 6 Connecting with the Social World 187

Chapter 7 The Origins of Emotion, Temperament, and Personality 227

PART III Developing Competencies

Chapter 8 Language Development 260

Chapter 9 The Growth of Knowledge 303

Chapter 10 The Growth of Cognitive Skills 343

Chapter 11 Intelligence and Schooling 385

PART IV The Self and Others

Chapter 12 Morality in Thought and Action 426

Chapter 13 Knowing Ourselves, Knowing Others 467

Chapter 14 Becoming Part of the Family 503

Chapter 15 Becoming Part of the Community 543

PART V Broader Developmental Context

Chapter 16 Psychopathology in Childhood 586

Chapter 17 Development after Childhood and Adolescence 629

Contents

ABOUT THE AUTHOR v

PREFACE xvii

PART I Framing Psychological Development

CHAPTER 1

Approaching Psychological Development 2

Why Study Development? 4

Development as a Key to Understanding Children's Capabilities 4

Development as a Means for Insight into the Mature Form 5

Development and Social Policy 6

The Nature of Development 6

Categorizing Developmental Phenomena 7

Periods of Development

Areas of Development

Basic Questions about Psychological Development 9

Is Development Stage-like or Continuous?

Is Development Global or Local?

How Do Nature and Nurture Shape Development?

Perspectives on Development 14

Empiricist and Nativist Perspectives 14

Empiricism

Nativism

Comparative and Evolutionary Perspectives 17

Cross-Cultural Perspectives 18

Neuroscience Perspectives 19

Behaviorist Perspectives 19

Psychoanalytic Perspectives 20

Cognitive Science Perspectives 20

Studying Psychological Development 22

Observational Studies 22

Experimental Studies 23

Longitudinal Approaches 26

Cross-Sectional Approaches 27

Converging Methods 28

Designing a Sound Study 28

Reliability and Validity

Within-Subjects and Between-Subjects Designs

Conclusions 30

Summary 31

CHAPTER 2

The Biology of Development 33

The Basis of Development 35

Inputs to the Biological System 36

The Genes

The Environment

Interactions between Genes and Environment

Constraints on Development 38

Viability

Differentiation of Cells and Structures

Timing and Sequencing

The Beginnings of Development 41

Meiosis and Fertilization 41

Meiosis and Mitosis
Fertilization

The First Patterns of Differentiation 43

Anatomical Development 44

Structures and Systems in the Embryo and Fetus 44

The Embryonic Period
The Fetal Period

Preterm Births 47

Why Does Anatomical Development Progress
As It Does? 49

Diversity out of Uniformity 49

Sexual Differentiation 52

Adverse Influences on the Developing
Embryo and Fetus 53

Brain Development 56

Major Changes to Brain Structures 57

Neurons and Neurotransmitters 58

Development of Neurons 60

Proliferation
Migration and Synaptogenesis
Consolidation
Myelination

Experience and Brain Development 63

Puberty and Brain Development 64

Behavioral Genetics 67

Heritability 67

Behavioral Genomics 68

Conclusions 70

Summary 72

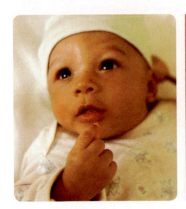

PART II Origins

CHAPTER 3
Coming to Perceive the World 76

Vision 78

Perceiving Differences in Brightness and Acuity 79

Visual Acuity
Visual Experience and Brain Development

Color 84

Perceiving Hue and the Clustering of Hues
Categorical Perception of Color

Depth Perception 86

Cues to Depth
Which Depth Cues Predominate? Gibson's Visual
Cliff Studies
Functional Significance of the Depth Perception System

Perceiving Patterns and Recognizing Objects 91

Pattern Perception in Other Species
Plasticity in Perceptual Development
Perceptually Grouping the World

Face Perception 95

Development of Face Perception: A Two-System Model
Facial Attractiveness

Hearing 100

Noticing and Remembering Sounds 100

Locating Sounds 101

Perceiving Complex Sound Patterns 104

The Chemical Senses: Taste and Smell 107

Taste 107

Smell 109

Intermodal Perception 109

Conclusions 112

Summary 112

CHAPTER 4
The Emergence of Action 115

Foundations of Motor Development 116

Reflexes in Infancy 117

Theories of Motor Development 118

The Maturational Account
Dynamic Systems Theory

Perception and Action 122

Coordination in Changing Bodies 122

Reaching 123

Empiricist View of Eye-Limb Coordination

Constraints on Links between Eye and Limb

Navigating Space 125

Active versus Passive Visual Experience and Action

Walking and Seeing

Learning to Engage in Specific Actions 131

Early Imitation 131

The Process of Imitation

The Development of Birdsong: Variations on the Imitation Theme

Imprinting, Action, and Critical Periods 135

Conditioning 136

Classical Conditioning

Operant Conditioning

Constraints on Learning

Conclusions 142

Summary 143

CHAPTER 5

Coming to Understand the Physical World 145

Piaget's Approach 146

Piaget's Theory of Cognitive Development 147

The Sensorimotor Period in Infancy 149

Stage 1: Use of Reflexes

Stage 2: Emergence of Primary Circular Reactions

Stage 3: Appearance of Secondary Circular Reactions

Stage 4: Coordination of Secondary Circular Reactions

Stage 5: Appearance of Tertiary Circular Reactions

Stage 6: Invention of New Means through Mental Combinations

Key Aspects of Piaget's Theory 154

Examining the A-Not-B Error 155

Infant Knowledge and Understanding 157

Thinking about the Unseen 158

Studies of Object Permanence and Solidity

Principles That Guide How Infants Understand

Comparative Considerations

Understanding Causation 164

The Use of Number 166

Spatial Knowledge in Infants 169

Categorization in Infants 171

Distinguishing the Physical World from the Social World 175

Action at a Distance and Social Contingency 176

Goal and Belief Attribution 177

Conclusions 183

Summary 184

CHAPTER 6

Connecting with the Social World 187

Developing Bonds between Infants and Caregivers 189

Early Perspectives on Infants' Bonds with Others 190

Psychoanalytic Approaches to Infant-Parent Bonds 190

Learning Theory Approaches 191

Bowlby's Ethological Approach 192

The Underpinnings of Attachment 194

Components of Attachment 194

Smiling

Clinging and Touching

Cuteness

Bases of Social Interactions 199

Contingent Responding

Social Referencing

Joint Attention and Gaze Following

Individual Differences in Attachment Style 201

Studying Attachment Styles in the Strange Situation 202

Causes of Different Attachment Styles 203

Parent Effects on Insecure Attachment

Child Effects on Insecure Attachment

Interactions of Parent Effects and Child Effects

Consequences of Different Attachment Styles 208

Correlations between Infant Attachment Styles and Children's Social Interactions

Long-Term Links between Infant Attachment Styles and Adult Relationship Styles

Cross-Cultural Differences in Attachment Styles 210

Effects of Early Social Deprivation 214

Social Deprivation in Humans 214

Deficits in Socially Deprived Infants

Untangling Causation

Deprivation Studies in Nonhuman Primates 218

Tactile Stimulation and Physiological Needs

Peer-Raised Infants

Critical-Period Effects? 222

Conclusions 223

Summary 224

CHAPTER 7

The Origins of Emotion, Temperament, and Personality 227

Emotional Development 228

Approaches to Emotional Development 229

Differentiation of Emotions in Infancy 230

Basic Emotions

Complex Emotions

Moral Emotions?

Perceiving and Thinking about Emotions 236

Recognizing Emotions in Others

Emotional Contagion

Emotional Regulation in Infancy 237
  Situational Factors
  Attentional Deployment
  Response Modification
Evolutionary Preparedness and Emotional Development 242
  Preparedness for Acquiring Certain Fears
  Preparedness and the Development of Disgust
  Preparedness and the Development of Other Emotions

Temperament and the Origins of Personality 247

Temperament-Based Components of Personality and Early
Development 248

Determining Differences in Temperament 249
  The New York Longitudinal Study
  Modern Approaches to Studying Temperament
  Linking Temperament to Personality Development
Child–Environment Interactions and Goodness of Fit 252
  Environments for "Squeaky Wheels"
  Parental Influences on Temperament

Conclusions 255
Summary 256

PART III Developing Competencies

CHAPTER 8

Language Development 260

The Structure and Complexity of Language 262
Components of Language 262
Universal Constraints on Language 263

Acquiring a First Language 263
Developmental Patterns 263
  Prelinguistic Perception and Communication
  One-Word Utterances
  Multiword Utterances
  Linguistic Rules
Child-Directed Speech 267

Theories of Language Acquisition 268
Behaviorist Approaches 269
Connectionist Approaches 270
Statistical Learning Approaches 270
Nativist Approaches 272

Discovering the Meanings of Words 273
Linking Words to Concepts 273
Constraints on Word Meanings 275
  Perceptual Constraints
  Conceptual Constraints
  Pragmatic Constraints
  The Nature of Constraints on Word Meanings
Developmental Changes in Word Meanings 278
  Overextensions and Underextensions
  Linking Features with Meanings

The Growth of Grammar 280

Effects of Age on Language Acquisition 281
Acquiring Language after the Critical Period 282
Acquiring American Sign Language after the
Critical Period 283
Inventing a New Language 283

The Domain Specificity of Language 284
Neural Dissociations 285
  Aphasias
  Williams Syndrome
  Specific Language Impairment (SLI)
Species Specificity 288
  Chimp as Child
  Nonhuman Primates and Sign Language
  Bonobos and Joint Attention

Language and Thought 290
Linguistic Relativity and Linguistic Determinism 290
  The Sapir-Whorf Hypothesis
  Color and Number
  Other Influences of Language on Thought
Language as an Amplifier of Thought 292
Influences of Cognitive Development on Language 294

Language and Communication 295

Conclusions 299
Summary 300

CHAPTER 9

The Growth of Knowledge 303

Dimensions of Cognitive Development 305
Qualitative versus Quantitative Development 305
Global versus Local Patterns of Development 306
Foundational versus Emergent Constraints 306

A Closer Look at Piaget's Theory 308
The Preoperational Period 308
The Concrete Operational Period 311
The Formal Operational Period 311
Alternative Explanations of Piaget's Theory and Results 313
  Seriation
  Thinking about Classes
  Conservation

Domains of Knowledge 320
Spatial Relations 321
Number 324
Biology 327
Other Domains of Thought 334
  Beliefs about Physical Mechanics
  Beliefs about Substance
  Beliefs about Cosmology

Sociocultural Views of the Development of Knowledge 337
Vygotsky's Views 337

Conclusions 339
Summary 340

CHAPTER 10

The Growth of Cognitive Skills 343

Memory 344
Components of Memory 345
Types of Long-Term Memory 346
  Explicit Memory versus Implicit Memory
  Procedural Memory versus Declarative Memory
  Semantic Memory versus Episodic Memory
Memory Strategies 349
Development of Metamemory 350
Memory and Expertise 352
Infantile and Early Childhood Amnesia 353
  Memory Format Change Hypothesis
  Neural Change Hypothesis
  Cueing Hypothesis
  Culture, Gender, and Early Childhood Amnesia
Emergence of Long-Term Autobiographical Memory 356

Attention 358
Attention as an Active Exploratory System 359
Three Components of Attention 359
  Orienting
  Alerting
  Executive Functioning

A Developmental Disorder in Attention: ADHD 363
  Biological Bases of ADHD
  Misdiagnosis of ADHD

Reasoning and Thinking about Knowledge 366
Analogical Reasoning 366
Scientific Reasoning 368
Metacognition and Accessing Knowledge 370
  Illusions of Knowing
  Evaluating Others' Knowledge

Three Specific Skills 372
Reading 372
  Learning to Read
  Teaching Reading
  When Reading Is a Challenge: Dyslexia
Mathematical Reasoning 376
  Growth of Mathematical Skills
  Teaching Mathematics
  Developing Problem-Solving Strategies
Using Symbolic Representations 378
  Using Maps and Models
  Children's Drawings

Conclusions 380
Summary 381

CHAPTER 11

Intelligence and Schooling 385

What Is Intelligence? 387
The Psychometric Approach 387
  Interpreting Test Scores
  Correlates of Intelligence Test Scores
Psychometric Theories of Intelligence 390
  Spearman's Theory of General Intelligence
  Carroll's Three-Stratum Theory of Intelligence
  Cattell's Theory of Fluid and Crystallized Intelligence
Alternative Views of Intelligence 393
  Gardner's Theory of Multiple Intelligences
  Sternberg's Theory of Successful Intelligence

Origins of Intelligence 396
Infant Indicators of Intelligence Test Performance 396
The Heritability of Intelligence 397

Group Differences and Intelligence Tests 400
Sex Differences 400
Ethnic and "Racial" Differences 402
Explaining Group Differences 402
  Are Group Differences Irrelevant?
  Genetic Factors
  Socioeconomic Factors
  Sociocultural Stereotypes
Group Differences over Time 406

Environmental Influences on Intelligence Test Scores 407
Enhancing Early Environmental Influences: Head Start Programs 408

Schooling 409

Characterizing Schools 409
Two Prominent Models of Education

What Schools Do 411
Schools as Socializing Agents
Schools as Cultural Institutions
Schools as Vehicles of Values

Schools and Thought 412
Cognitive Science and Teaching
Three Cognitive Science Themes for Education

Implementing Cognitive Science Ideas in the Classroom
Aptitude-Treatment Interactions

Creativity 417

Measures of Creativity 417

The Development of Extraordinary Creativity 420

Conclusions 421

Summary 422

PART IV The Self and Others

CHAPTER 12

Morality in Thought and Action 426

The Development of Moral Thought 427

Debating the Origins of Moral Thought 428

Evolutionary and Cultural Psychology and Morality 429

Characterizing the Basis of Moral Thought 430

Piaget's Theory of Moral Development 431

Piaget's Stages of Moral Reasoning 432
Stage 0: Premoral Development
Stage 1: The Heteronomous Stage
The Transition between Stage 1 and Stage 2
Stage 2: The Autonomous Stage

Evaluating Piaget's Account 434
Distinguishing Morality from Conventions
Accounting for Intentions
Immanent Justice across Cultures

Kohlberg's Theory of Moral Reasoning 437

Kohlberg's Stages of Moral Reasoning 437

Evaluating Kohlberg's Theory 438
Unclear Stages
Cross-Cultural Variations
Possible Gender Biases

Alternative Theories of Moral Development 440

Gilligan's Theory of Moral Development 440

A Pluralistic Approach to the Development of Moral Thought 441
Contributions from Personality Psychology
Contributions from Cultural Psychology
Domain-Specific Moral Reasoning

The Development of Moral Behavior 444

Consistency of Moral Behavior 444

Antisocial and Prosocial Behavior 448
Antisocial Behavior
Prosocial Behavior

Temperament, Personality, and Moral Behavior 452
Self-Regulation
Arousal Level and Positive Emotionality
Empathy

Social Influences on Moral Behavior 456
Punishment and Learning Theories
Modeling Theory and Moral Behaviors
Parent-Child Interactions and the Development of Conscience

Conclusions 463

Summary 464

CHAPTER 13

Knowing Ourselves, Knowing Others 467

Self-Concepts and Self-Representations 468

Senses of Self 468
Neisser's Five Senses of Self

The Mirror Test and Self-Concept 471
Variations on the Mirror Test

Gender Identity 472

Developing a Sense of Self-Worth 474

Self-Esteem 474

Self-Efficacy 476

Self-Regulation 477

Brain Maturation and the Development of Self-Regulation 480

Contextual Influences on Self-Regulation 481

Developing a Theory of Mind 482

Early Aspects of Theory of Mind 483

Comparative Perspectives on Theory of Mind 484

Understanding False Beliefs 487

Evaluating the False-Belief Task

A Theory of Mind Module? 490

Beyond False Beliefs 492

Making Attributions about Ourselves and Others 493

Emerging Explanations of Behavior 493

Traits and Optimism 496

Attribution, Motivation, and Creativity 497

Conclusions 499

Summary 501

CHAPTER 14

Becoming Part of the Family 503

Parenting 505

Parenting Styles 506

Parenting Contexts 508

Parenting across Cultures

Parenting across Socioeconomic Groups

The Ecological Systems Approach

Interventions to Improve Parenting 510

Parent Effects in Relation to Other Influences 511

Child Effects

Genetic Effects

The Interactionist Approach to Family Dynamics 514

Gender Socialization in the Family: A Web of Interacting Influences 515

Siblings and Family Dynamics 518

Birth Order Effects 518

An Interactionist Approach to Birth Order Effects

Sibling Relationships and Socialization 520

Jealousy and Conflict between Siblings

Siblings and Social Understanding

Sibling Relationships within the Family

Changes in the Family 525

Changes in Parents' Age 525

Changes in Family Size 527

Working Parents and Child Care 529

Changes in Family Structures 530

Single-Parent Families

Same-Sex Parents

Divorce

Blended Families

Child Abuse 536

Effects of Abuse 537

Explaining the Cycle of Abuse 537

Foster Care 538

Conclusions 539

Summary 540

CHAPTER 15

Becoming Part of the Community 543

Levels of Affiliation 544

The Changing Nature of Social Interactions 545

Developing Relationships 546

Friends

Imaginary Companions

Bully-Victim Relationships

Enemies

Dating and Romantic Relationships

Social Groups 553

Cliques and Crowds

Sociometric Status and Social Interaction

Developmental Patterns in Levels of Affiliation 558

Social Network Effects 558

Media Influences on Development 559

Television 560

The Pervasiveness of Television Watching

Changes in Television Watching with Age

Positive Effects of Television

Negative Cognitive Effects of Television

Negative Social Effects of Television

Responding to the Influences of Television Violence

Stereotyping in the Media

Video Games, Computers, and the Internet 569

Video Games

Internet Communities

Roles in the Larger Culture 574

Distinctive Cultural and Subcultural Roles 574

Gender Roles and Stereotyping 576

Conclusions 581

Summary 582

PART V Broader Developmental Context

CHAPTER 16

Psychopathology in Childhood 586

Autism 588
Features of Autism 588
Diagnosis of Autism 589
Incidence of Autism 589
Causal Factors 590

Anxiety Disorders 592
Incidence of Anxiety Disorders 592
Causal Factors 593
Cognitive Factors
Biological Factors
Obsessive-Compulsive Disorder 595
Types of Obsessive-Compulsive Disorder
Incidence of Obsessive-Compulsive Disorder
Diagnosis of Obsessive-Compulsive Disorder
Causal Factors

Eating Disorders 598
Anorexia Nervosa 598
Incidence of Anorexia
Cognitive Distortions in Anorexia
Genetic and Environmental Causal Factors
Bulimia Nervosa 602
Incidence of Bulimia
Causal Factors

Depression 603
Unipolar Depression 604
Biological Causes
Social Causes
Cognitive Causes
Bipolar Disorder 607
Causal Factors
Diagnosis of Bipolar Disorder

Conduct Disorder: The Case of Psychopathy 609
Features of Psychopathy 610
Diagnosis of Psychopathy 611
Causal Factors 612

Schizophrenia 614
Features of Schizophrenia 614
Causal Factors 616
Early-Onset Schizophrenia 619

Treatment of Childhood Psychopathologies 619
Behavioral Therapies 619
Cognitive-Behavioral Therapy 620
Psychoanalytic Therapies 621
Family Therapies 622
Pharmacological Treatments 622
Evaluating Therapies 624

Conclusions 625
Summary 625

CHAPTER 17

Development after Childhood and Adolescence 629

Physical and Physiological Changes in Adulthood 630

Cognitive Changes in Adulthood 635
Reaction Time and Speed of Processing 635
Memory, Higher Cognitive Functions, and Reasoning 635
Daily Activities and Cognitive Aging 639
Circadian Rhythms, Cognition, and the Lifespan 641

Changes in Personality in the Lifespan: Individual and Group Changes 643
Changes in Individuals 643
Stressful Life Events 644
Group Changes 645

Stages of Life? 648
Erik Erikson's Approach 648
Stage 1: Trust versus Mistrust
Stage 2: Autonomy versus Shame/Doubt
Stage 3: Initiative versus Guilt
Stage 4: Industry versus Inferiority

Stage 5: Identity versus Role Confusion
Stage 6: Intimacy versus Isolation
Stage 7: Generativity versus Stagnation
Stage 8: Integrity versus Despair
Understanding Stages of Adult Development 652

What Does It Mean to Be Old? 652
Stereotypes and Ageism 654
Cultural Variation in Stereotypes and Ageism? 655

Conclusions 656
Summary 657

EPILOGUE 659
GLOSSARY G-1
REFERENCES R-1
CREDITS AND ACKNOWLEDGMENTS C-1
NAME INDEX N-1
SUBJECT INDEX S-1

Boxed Features

Development and Social Policy

What Kinds of Experimental Research Are Justified? 25

Visiting Nurses, Prenatal Care, and Child Development 51

Legislating Early Stimulation 106

Can a Toddler's Motor Development Be Accelerated? 137

The Myth of the First 3 Years 181

Day Care and Attachment 212

The Causes and Consequences of Problems in Emotional Regulation 244

The Cognitive Effects of Bilingualism 296

Sputnik and Intuitive Science 328

Children as Witnesses 360

Computers and e-Learning in the Schools 418

At What Age Should an Offender Be Treated as an Adult? 457

Potential Drawbacks of Self-Esteem 478

China's One-Child Policy 522

Free Speech and Children's Rights 570

Prescribing Psychoactive Medications to Young Children 623

When Is It Acceptable to Deprive the Elderly of Some Rights? 650

New Directions in Developmental Research

Measuring Infants' Brain Function: Near-Infrared Spectroscopy (NIRS) 21

Repairing Brain Damage Later in Life? 66

Cochlear Implants and the Question of Critical Periods for Auditory Processing 102

Mirror Neurons and Early Imitation 134

Advances in Infant Eye-Tracking Methods 172

New Insights into the Role of the Father 204

The Effect of Parenting on Emotion Processing in Children 240

A Language Gene? 287

Biological Knowledge and Exposure to Nature 333

The Genetics of Dyslexia 375

A *g* for Emotional Intelligence? 395

Moral Dumbfounding: Judgment or Intuition? 446

Theory of Mind in Dogs? 486

Epigenetics and Families 512

The Development of Racial and Ethnic Occupational Stereotypes 578

Co-rumination, Gender, and Depression 608

Why Do We Age and Why Do We Live as Long as We Do? 632

Scientific Method Boxes

Diet and Methylation 40

Intersensory Perception at Birth 111

The Genetics of Early Handedness 124

Agents and Order 182

Internal Working Models and Attachment Styles 209

Inferring Actions from Emotions 238

Early Use of Syntax to Guide Learning New Words 276

Early Motivation to Learn about Kinds over Individuals 318

Maternal Reminiscing and Children's Autobiographical Memories 357

Direct versus Inquiry-Based Methods of Instruction 414

Instrumental Helping in Toddlers 450

Gaze Following in Human Infants and Great Apes 485

Training Parents to Moderate Sibling Conflicts 524

Effects of "Minimal" Group Affiliations 580

Psychopathy and Fear Processing 613

The Positivity Bias in Older Adults 647

Preface

have been deeply involved in teaching introductory courses in developmental psychology since my first year as a teaching assistant at Stanford University in 1973. And I have taught my own lecture course since joining the faculty of Cornell University in 1977. While there have always been a range of available textbooks for this course, I have always felt the need for a book that comes closer to my own vision of how developmental psychology should be taught. I thought that there should be a book celebrating the beauty and incredible complexity of psychological development while also offering clear and compelling accounts of why development occurs as it does. Equally important, I wanted a book that showed how an understanding of development is essential to understanding psychological processes in adults and how a developmental perspective offers unique insights into mature psychological functioning. I believed a textbook on developmental psychology should illustrate common developmental themes across all areas of psychology while also explaining how trajectories within broad domains can each take on their own special characteristics. And I thought that a textbook should discuss commonalities and contrasts across cultures and even across species, as well as considering how psychological development fits into a broader context of biological and neurobiological development. Moreover, I believed that to fully illuminate the study of development, a textbook should situate psychology within a larger set of disciplines—including anthropology, computer science, linguistics, neuroscience, philosophy, and sociology—that intersected with psychology. Different texts touched on some of these ideas, but none covered all of them, and many did not seem to have a single voice that wove topics and themes into an integrated whole.

Finally, and perhaps most immediately compelling, the birth of our first son in 1981 made me want to dive much more deeply into the broad literature on all aspects of psychological development. But this also created an unanticipated challenge. As any parent knows, a newborn child is an instant lesson into just how much we don't know about development, a lesson that keeps expanding in scope as that child grows up. Moreover, as soon as I thought I was making some progress in linking scholarly work to my own personal experiences, our second son was born, and then our third son. And each child offered dramatic new insights and perspectives into development. Many years later, after our youngest son finished college and was out in the world, it was finally time to finish writing this textbook.

I have worked on various drafts of this book for over 30 years, writing and rewriting as my insights changed and the field of developmental psychology itself has undergone dramatic changes. I have also used drafts of the text in my courses at Yale for over a decade, constantly refining it in response to feedback from my ever gracious and helpful students. Throughout this entire process, which has continued throughout most of my academic career, I have written and rewritten three or four drafts of the entire book, finally winnowing down the material into the book that you have before you. In the course of writing the book, I have gained an immense appreciation for all of my colleagues in the field who have contributed so spectacularly to the flowering of the discipline over the past few decades. Developmental psychology today is an incredibly vibrant and exciting field that is far more closely connected to the rest of the psychology and other disciplines than ever before, and my excitement and pleasure in writing about it has increased every year. I hope that some of that excitement and pleasure is contagious to readers of this text. I deeply appreciate how this first edition is only the beginning of an evolutionary process that will continue in future editions, but after three decades of immersion in this project, it finally seemed time to take it out of my classroom and share it more widely.

Overarching Themes and Principles

There are fascinating themes and principles that keep recurring throughout developmental psychology and that help to show how different threads of research mutually reinforce each other. These themes and principles serve as constant touchstones for organizing the material in the book. Seven themes stand out as recurring most frequently.

One key theme is the *centrality of feedback loops, both positive and negative.* Development is rarely, if ever, a one-way process in which one factor causes another to happen without some kind of feedback. Parents influence their children, who in turn influence their parents, in cycles of interaction that can reinforce desirable outcomes or aggravate undesirable ones. The simple acts of learning to walk and successfully reaching toward objects involve constant feedback loops between what a child sees and how she acts. Even at the neural level, the growth of neural circuits can depend on feedback from experience, which in turn can change how future events are experienced. In all areas of development, we will see the central importance of feedback loops.

A second major theme is that *development is a dynamic exploratory process in which the child is more than a passive recipient of experiences and information.* When children are viewed as actively engaging with the world, it is much easier to understand development, whether it is development of perception, cognition, motivation, or morality.

A third theme is to see that *development is constrained by factors that arise both internally from within the child and externally from the environment.* While constraints may seem to somehow hinder development they may actually foster development by acting as scaffolds and guiding frameworks that make otherwise overwhelming problems of learning and skill development manageable. We will see the value of constraints and how they can guide development in many areas, while still allowing for enormous diversity of outcomes. Discussions of constraints also allow for a balanced treatment of the tradeoffs between nativist and empiricist views of development and the related, often needlessly contentious, nature/nurture debate.

A fourth theme is to focus on *what children can do and how their basic capacities emerge and serve as foundations for later development, as opposed to focusing on what children cannot do compared with older children and adults.* While younger children and infants certainly have limitations that are not found in later years, it is almost always more fruitful to avoid "deficit models" of development and instead ask how children progress as they grow.

A related fifth theme that occurs in all areas of development is that *infants and children usually have some viable version of a skill throughout development; they rarely go "offline" as they retool or improve on a system.* Just as the human heart must beat continuously as it goes through remarkable anatomical and physiological changes from its early embryonic stages to birth and beyond, most perceptual, cognitive, emotional, and social systems must have some working functional capacity throughout development. For example, infants'

emotional states have functional values both for themselves and for their interactions with others, and while their emotions change considerably in the first year of life, infants cannot simply shut down their emotional systems when transitioning to new kinds of emotions or emotional interaction patterns. The same is true for everything from language to friendship and is closely related to the idea that the most functionally vital aspects of systems often appear earliest in both development and in the evolutionary history of organisms.

A sixth theme is the *ever-present links and interdependencies between different areas of development.* It simply isn't possible to consider cognitive development without also considering social and emotional development, just as understanding social development depends on related changes in cognitive development, and a full account of emotional development depends on understanding both social and cognitive development. We will often focus primarily on one area at a time, but we will always take into account how the different areas of development also interact and must be understood in their entirety to obtain a full picture of what develops.

A final theme is that *developmental psychology is not just a human-based process.* All organisms with significant behavioral components grow from immature states to mature states and show fascinating patterns of change and constancy. Comparisons across these organisms and especially with humans are not just interesting in their own right, they can also greatly help us to understand what is unique about human psychological development, as well as telling us about what kinds of developmental problems tend to converge on one common class of solutions and what kinds of problems embrace an enormous diversity of possible solutions. This comparative perspective also highlights the ways in which evolutionary considerations can inform thinking about development. These seven themes and principles recur throughout this book and provide a way of weaving together all of the book's content to create an integrated and more memorable whole that reveals larger developmental patterns.

Linking Theory and Evidence

Developmental psychology has emerged robustly in the past few decades as a full-fledged science in which scholars propose theories and models and then test them rigorously. This book celebrates the ways in which ideas, many of which have been with us for centuries, are now being tested in carefully designed experiments or through powerful new statistical analyses of large data sets. It is fascinating to see how classic issues are now coming into much clearer focus as a result of clever new studies. Throughout this text, we will encounter theories, sometimes conflicting theories, and ask how they can be tested and what the current evidence tells us. In many cases, the debate continues with more than one view remaining viable, but also with a much better understanding of the research path forward.

I am convinced that even the most complex and intricate theories of development, ranging from neural growth patterns to changing social network analyses, can be explained in such a way that any introductory student can appreciate their key dimensions and how to evaluate them in light of the right kinds of studies and evidence emerging from those studies. All the theories and studies in this text have been written up, reviewed, and rewritten several times to ensure that they are clear and accessible and that the links to empirical research are compelling. I want all the readers of this text to be able to step into the shoes of leading investigators in developmental psychology so that they can understand what drove the researchers both in terms of theory and their passion to design and execute studies to answer developmental questions.

Integrated Treatment

As already is clear from the way our themes and principles cut across diverse areas, a hallmark of this text is the way it integrates material across all the chapters and keeps illustrating how certain patterns and ideas keep recurring. There are several forms of such integration throughout the book. Some themes recur across all the different times of development, from the prenatal period to the period of old age. Some themes recur across domains, ranging from perceptual to cognitive to social to moral domains. Some themes recur across cultures and even across species. The child develops as a whole person in which many different psychological systems are linked together and depend on each other and which have strong continuities with earlier and later periods of development. This book reflects that integration both in terms of how it has been organized and written and in terms of my own perspective. The book is topically organized within a chronological framework, which serves to provide maximum integrations in distinctive developmental periods, as well as providing more coherent treatments of each area of development. As a single author of this book, an increasingly vanishing breed of introductory text authors, I have been able to develop a voice and lines of thought that are woven throughout every chapter and that mutually reinforce each other. After reading a chapter or two, students should have a constantly building feeling of familiarity with ideas and approaches that helps make everything hang together. Near the end of the book, I offer a different kind of integration through a discussion of psychopathology in development. More than just a review of the psychopathology literature, Chapter 16 shows how aspects of development that are covered in earlier chapters, ranging from brain development to cognitive executive functioning to socialization, come together in an interwoven manner to contribute to the emergence of various forms of psychopathology. Students will see how all that they have learned bears on powerful and compelling problems. They will then experience a different form of integration of the same range of topics in the final chapter, which considers development after childhood and in which there is a fascinating set of questions that can have some striking resonances to earlier developmental questions and themes. I have taken great pains to present the full spectrum of theories and approaches but always with an eye toward how they relate to each other and to larger developmental issues that transcend any one school of thought. In doing so, I have immersed myself in reading the literature on different aspects of development, as well as engaging in many conversations and corresponding with experts across many disciplines, far more deeply than I ever could have imagined I would do when I first started on this project. The entire process has fed back into this book, and it has been great fun as well!

Distinctive Pedagogical Features

To best convey the themes and principles, to set forth the relations between theory and evidence, and to provide the most integrated treatment possible, this book has several distinctive pedagogical features. Throughout every chapter, there are comprehension checkup questions, a pedagogical tool that enables readers to immediately know if they have mastered the key issues they have just encountered. In each chapter, there are also highlighted key terms that are defined in the Glossary of the book. Each chapter ends with a conclusion that brings together the key ideas and often offers a novel integrative insight. The summaries that follow the conclusions are comprehensive digests of the entire chapter in a bulleted format. Any students who can clearly recognize and elaborate on each bulleted point will have a good sense of how well they have mastered the chapter. Finally, at the end of each chapter, for more in-depth consideration of the material, there are sets of extended thought questions that challenge students to consider a problem more thoroughly.

Every chapter has a box that is concerned with a social policy issue connected to material in the chapter so that students can see how basic research can be linked to important and socially relevant real-world issues. A second box in each chapter is concerned with an example of an exciting new direction of developmental research so students can see how the field continues to evolve through innovative research initiatives. It is an important way of illustrating how developmental psychology is a dynamic, active field. A third box in each chapter illustrates in more detail the methodology of scientific research relevant to the topics of that chapter. The purpose here is to show in a manner closely analogous to posters at scientific conferences how an experiment is organized in terms of hypothesis, method, results, and conclusion, and to include illustrations of the experimental setup and results. These boxes are somewhat simpler than most posters at meetings, but they very much capture their spirit.

Throughout the book, there are brief historical discussions of research topics that make clear how current ideas and research emerged from older traditions. There is also careful documentation of cutting-edge research that serves not only to ground the research in particular studies but also serves as a rich source of references for further explorations by students, references that are also available on the instructor Web site and in prepared LMS materials available free of charge to every instructor using the book.

In the end, these pedagogical devices all serve the overarching goal of this book, which is to get to the heart of developmental psychology. My aim is to expose readers to developmental psychology's big questions in an engaging and compelling way that invites students to join researchers in one of the most lively and fascinating areas of intellectual inquiry that also has immense personal relevance and social importance.

Supplementary Materials

Our supplements package was developed based on data from a survey of 60 instructors currently teaching developmental psychology at a wide variety of schools. Our book-specific resources are easy to access in one place through wwnorton.com/instructors. They are also searchable on the *Interactive Instructor's Guide*, making lecture planning easy.

Presentation Tools

- *Lecture PowerPoints* offer images and instructor-only lecture notes that include additional examples and teaching suggestions, which will help ease the transition to using a new textbook. Each chapter also includes an optional set of slides that cover the research behind a concept covered in the chapter to illustrate how the science

of developmental psychology leads to the theories students are learning about in class.

The *Developmental Psychology Lecture PowerPoints* were written by David Barner and Jessica Sullivan, both of whom are at University of California, San Diego.

- All of the art in the book is available as PowerPoints and JPEGs to make creating custom presentation materials easy.
- Presentation tools are downloadable at wwnorton.com/instructors.

Videos

- Chapter Opening Videos from Frank Keil himself serve as an introduction to the chapter topics and help convey his enthusiasm and voice to the reader.
- Classroom Videos with discussion questions feature enactments of classic experiments and demonstrate a variety of characteristics from varying developmental periods, showing developmental psychology as a science in action. The *Developmental Psychology* videos were curated by Tasha Howe of Humboldt State University.
- Videos are available at wwnorton.com/instructors as part of the Interactive Instructor's Guide and as part of our LMS-ready materials.

Interactive Instructor's Guide

- The searchable *Interactive Instructor's Guide* offers classroom activity suggestions with print-ready handouts, chapter opening videos, and classroom videos with discussion questions. The *Developmental Psychology* videos were curated by Tasha Howe of Humboldt State University, and the activities were written by Melissa Barnett at the University of Arizona.
- The *Interactive Instructor's Guide* is downloadable from wwnorton.com/instructors.

Test Bank

- The *Test Bank* for *Developmental Psychology* is designed to help instructors prepare their exams. The *Test Bank* has been developed using the Norton Assessment Guidelines, and each chapter of the *Test Bank* consists of five question types classified according to the first five levels of Bloom's taxonomy of knowledge types: remembering, understanding, applying, analyzing, and evaluating. Questions are further classified by section and difficulty, making it easy to construct tests and quizzes that are meaningful and diagnostic.

- The *Test Bank* questions were written by Thompson Davis of Louisiana State University and Lisa Rosen of Texas Woman's University, with Tasha Howe of Humboldt State University.
- The *Test Bank* is available in paperback and on disk; it is also downloadable in PDF, RTF, or ExamView formats from wwnorton.com/instructors.

Norton Coursepacks: Our Content, Your Course

- Easily add high-quality Norton digital media to your online, hybrid, or lecture course—all at no cost. Norton Coursepacks work with and leverage your existing Learning Management System, so there's no new system to learn, and access is free and easy. Comprehensive coursepacks are ready to use, right from the start, but they are easy to customize, using the system you already know and understand. The *Developmental Psychology* Coursepack includes classroom videos with discussion questions, Quiz+ review questions, and flashcards available for the students (or assignable as instructors see fit), as well as the Test Bank.
- Quiz questions were written by Thompson Davis of Louisiana State University and Lisa Rosen of Texas Woman's University, with Tasha Howe of Humboldt State University.
- All of these materials are downloadable in Blackboard, Moodle, D2L, Angel, and Canvas formats.

eBook

- Same great book, a fraction of the price.
- An affordable and convenient alternative to the printed textbook, Norton eBooks retain the content and design

of the print book and allow students to highlight and take notes with ease, print chapters as needed, and search the text. Norton eBooks are available online and as downloadable PDFs. They can be purchased directly from our Web site, or with a registration folder that can be sold in the bookstore.

Acknowledgments

My deepest debt goes to my wife Kristi Lockhart, who was assigned to the same office as me on our first day of graduate school and who has been my one true love and colleague ever since. Kristi has made major career sacrifices for the sake of our family and my career and has always done so with great generosity and good humor, spreading that spirit of generosity and good humor to our children as well. As a parent and partner she has been loving, supportive, and playful in ways that have sustained and inspired all of us. I am infinitely fortunate that she is the love of my life and marvel every day that she was willing to spend her life with me. She has taught me more about children, parenting, and family dynamics than all other sources combined and has been the best parent ever. Through countless discussions with her about almost all the topics in this book and through listening to her many observations about children, I have been a most grateful recipient of her wisdom. I owe her everything. I have also shared with Kristi in the delight of watching our three sons grow, each in their own ways, into remarkable young men. From their first moments as newborns to their lives as young adults, Derek, Dylan, and Martin have taught us both many volumes about development and continue to do so, as well as providing us with the most rewarding and meaningful experiences of our lives. Kristi, Derek, Dylan, and Martin have also been incredibly patient and tolerant of my obsession with this book and the ways it has hovered over all of us for decades. These two photos of our

family cover only part of the entire period of writing this book, but they show the passage of time during which I was writing it. The many hours I have spent working on this book have been all too evident to every member of my family, and they all have been tremendously gracious about its intrusions into their lives. I thank all of them from the bottom of my heart for their support, their inspiration, and their forbearance and I thank the heavens that I was lucky enough to be part of this family.

Certain people at W. W. Norton also deserve extraordinary thanks, starting with Don Lamm and Don Fusting, who originally signed me up to write the book years ago. I appreciate the support I have received from the Acquisitions Editors Sheri Shavely, Roby Harrington, Jon Durbin, Cathy Wick, and, especially recently, Aaron Javsicas, who made sure the whole project met critical deadlines and who has been very helpful in selecting art. I have also been blessed with brilliant copy editing by Janet Greenblatt and project editing by Rachel Mayer. I thank Vanessa Drake-Johnson, who served as an early Developmental Editor of the book, and Photo Editor Mike Fodera, Photo Researchers Donna Ranieri and Julie Tesser, Media Editor Callinda Taylor, Editorial Assistant Shira Averbuch, Production Manager Eric Pier-Hocking, and Marketing Manager Lauren Winkler. I also would like to thank Jonathan Kominsky who worked on the art manuscript in New Haven.

But I must especially acknowledge the massive contributions made by two Developmental Editors, Sarah Mann and Sandy Lifland. Sarah became involved in the project in 2007 and went through the entire text and asked me probing questions about what I really wanted to say and if I was saying it in the best and briefest ways possible. She helped enormously to shape what had become a far too long body of text into something much more workable. Even more critically, Sandy Lifland has had a profound influence. She is a legendary editor who early on gave me challenging feedback on the crude first drafts of this book and made me realize just how much more I had to do if I wanted to write the book I really envisioned. She then rejoined the project in 2011 and worked full time on the book until its publication. We studied, considered, and often extensively discussed every word of text, every line in every figure and graph for ways that they could be clearer, better connected to the big ideas of the book and to the basic scientific literature. Sandy herself read hundreds of original articles to understand more deeply what I had in mind and to ensure that I was getting across to the reader exactly what I really intended. She also kindly pointed out to me several cases where I still wasn't clear in my own head about what I actually wanted to say. I honestly cannot imagine a better editor who cared more about creating a product of real intellectual and aesthetic value.

This book has been reviewed through the years by many scholars who have been involved in all stages of its evolution, sometimes sending me extensive comments on earlier drafts, other times providing confirmatory reviews to Norton editors about the near final drafts. I have included the affiliations of the reviewers at the time that they wrote their reviews, and some may since have moved on to other colleges and universities. I deeply appreciate all the work that the reviewers have done and thank the following:

Joseph Allen, University of Virginia
Richard Aslin, University of Rochester
Terry Au, University of Hong Kong
Melissa Barnett, University of Arizona
Kymberley Bennett, Indiana State University
Paul Bloom, Yale University
Amanda Brandone, Lehigh University
Sara Broaders, Northwestern University
Gwen Broude, Vassar College
Jean Burr, Hamilton College
Joseph Campos, University of California, Berkeley
Carol Cheatham, University of North Carolina
Judith Danovitch, Michigan State University
Daniel Dickman, Ivy Tech Community College of Indiana
Ann Edworthy, Swansea Metropolitan University
Leanne Franklin, Cardiff Metropolitan University
Janet Frick, University of Georgia
Jeffrey Gagne, University of Texas at Arlington
Susan Gelman, University of Michigan
Gilbert Gottlieb, University of North Carolina, Chapel Hill
Joan Grusec, University of Toronto
Amy Halberstadt, North Carolina State University
Jacqui Harrison, University of Bolton
Brett Hayes, University of New South Wales
Fay Julal, Southampton Solent University
Robert Kavanaugh, Williams College
Rachel Keen, University of Massachusetts, Amherst
Debby Kemler Nelson, Swarthmore College
Susan Kemper, University of Kansas
Katherine Kinzler, University of Chicago
Kristin Lagattuta, University of California, Davis
Alan Leslie, Rutgers University
Robert Lickliter, Virginia Tech
Gary Marcus, New York University
Ellen Markman, Stanford University
Lori Markson, University of California, Berkeley
Carol Murphy, National University of Ireland, Maynooth
Simone Nguyen, University of North Carolina, Wilmington
Bjorn Nilsson, Skovde University College
Samuel Putnam, University of Oregon
Philippe Rochat, Emory University
Lisa Rosen, Texas Women's University
Karl Rosengren, Northwestern University
Paul Rozin, University of Pennsylvania
Jenny Saffran, University of Wisconsin, Madison

Rose Scott, University of California, Merced

Meghan Sinton, College of William and Mary

Susan Sonnenschein, University of Maryland, Baltimore County

Hiroko Sotozaki, Western Illinois University

Caroline Stanley, Wilmington College of Ohio

Michael Steele, University of Utah

Catherine Tamis-LaMonda, New York University

Ross Thompson, University of Nebraska

Elliot Turiel, University of California, Berkeley

Eva Twetman, Halmstad University College

Mike vanDuuren, University of Winchester

Kristy vanMarle, University of Missouri

Peter Vishton, William & Mary College

Maria Wong, Idaho State University

Fei Xu, University of California, Berkeley

I am also grateful to those scholars who have written the ancillaries: Tasha Howe, Humboldt State University, who worked on the *Test Bank, Student Study Quizzes, and Video Curation;* Thompson Davis III, Louisiana State University, and Lisa Rosen, Texas Woman's University, both of whom worked on the *Test Bank and Student Study Quizzes;* Melissa Barnett, University of Arizona, who worked on the *Classroom Activities;* and David Barner, University of California, San Diego, who with the help of Jessica Sullivan, worked on the *Lecture PowerPoints.*

Finally, I thank those many colleagues at Cornell and Yale who have inspired and educated me on a daily basis.

Frank Keil
August 2013

PART I

Framing Psychological Development

1

Approaching Psychological Development

Why Study Development?
- Development as a Key to Understanding Children's Capabilities
- Development as a Means for Insight into the Mature Form
- Development and Social Policy

The Nature of Development
- Categorizing Developmental Phenomena
- Basic Questions about Psychological Development

Perspectives on Development
- Empiricist and Nativist Perspectives
- Comparative and Evolutionary Perspectives
- Cross-Cultural Perspectives
- Neuroscience Perspectives
- Behaviorist Perspectives
- Psychoanalytic Perspectives
- Cognitive Science Perspectives

Studying Psychological Development
- Observational Studies
- Experimental Studies
- Longitudinal Approaches
- Cross-Sectional Approaches
- Converging Methods
- Designing a Sound Study

Conclusions

Summary

A baby is born and seems totally helpless. He can't feed himself or warm himself or move to avoid danger. Does he know anything that will help him get what he needs? Can he do anything that will draw the attention of those who can help him?

Consider some of the perceptual challenges a baby faces in the first week of life (see Figure 1.1). It's the middle of winter, and a 3-day-old baby boy is leaving the hospital with his parents. In the morning, he is moved rapidly from the nursery, where he has been looking up at the white ceiling with its blinking red light and hearing the intermittent cries of other infants and the muffled conversations of nurses. He is wheeled in a nursery cart into a noisy hallway where many large people bustle past on both sides of him, occasionally looming over and cooing at him. On arrival in his mother's room, she scoops him up and embraces him, as she has many times in the past 3 days. As she nurses him, he feels her warmth and hears her voice as he tastes and smells sweetness. He is then rushed down the busy hall again, this time held in his mother's lap as she sits in a wheelchair—and outside into a blast of cold air and a 100-fold increase in brightness. He is buckled into an infant seat in a rumbling older car and driven home over bumpy roads, with trees and telephone poles whizzing by the windows. When the car stops, he is carried into a house where a dog is barking, two children are shouting excitedly, and a telephone is ringing. Finally, he is brought into a quiet, darkened bedroom and laid in a crib for a nap. All of this takes about 1 hour.

Many observers would consider this infant a completely helpless creature with no behavioral or perceptual abilities and a brain like a blank canvas, waiting for experiences to be painted on it in his encounters with a richly structured environment. This view is the basis for the seventeenth-century philosopher John Locke's famous statement that the child's mind is a tabula rasa, or "blank slate," upon which knowledge and perceptual skills will be "written" through experience (Locke, 1690/1964). The great psychologist and philosopher William James described this view more colorfully when, at the turn of the twentieth century, he wondered if all the newborn saw was a "blooming, buzzing confusion," a meaningless collage of fleeting images, colors and sounds (James, 1890).

Newborns' behaviors might seem to reinforce the notion that they are completely helpless and passive, waiting to gain understanding and meaning through experience. They sleep a great deal, and even when they are awake, they do not clearly attend to any one stimulus. In fact, their eye movements often seem uncoordinated, and they seem unable to track moving objects visually. In addition, there is no easy indication that they recognize anything they see. In casual observations of young infants, Locke's

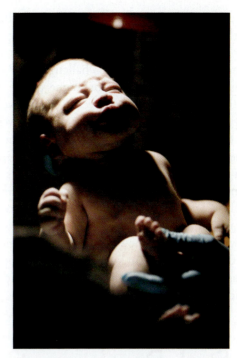

FIGURE 1.1 **A newborn baby.** William James, the philosopher/psychologist, described the newborn's first perception of the world as encountering a "blooming, buzzing confusion."

comparison of the newborn's mind to a blank slate appears to be warranted.

Moreover, when it comes to making sense of the world, the infant faces remarkable perceptual challenges. How could our 3-day-old boy possibly understand his trip home? He typically sees only the top half of people's bodies, and those people often appear and disappear too rapidly for him to recognize them as individuals. How could he form an impression of the body as a whole? As he is brought to his mother in her hospital room, how does he know that she is getting closer rather than staying the same distance away and blowing up in size like a balloon? And how does he link his experience of seeing her face as she approaches with his completely different experience of her when nursing? At home, when he hears a dog barking, children shouting, and a telephone ringing, how can he tell which sounds come from which objects?

If babies did not have any perceptual abilities to help them make sense of the world's patterns, these challenges might overwhelm them. In fact, they are born remarkably well equipped to begin making sense of the world they perceive. Indeed, even newborns make interpretations that go far beyond seeing the world as a blooming, buzzing confusion.

Understanding what newborns can see or hear or understand and how they add to their knowledge and abilities as they age is an area of great interest to developmental psychologists. Developmental psychology can be viewed as a scientific way to address our intrinsic fascination with

similar developmental questions throughout the lifespan. It looks at the challenges that confront the growing child and asks how the child or adolescent or young adult is able to master these mental and physical challenges.

In this chapter, we will explore some of the strategies used in the scientific study of psychological development. We will present several reasons for examining development. We will then discuss the nature of development, looking first at periods of development (the child at different ages) and then at domains of development (the spheres in which development occurs, such as perception and cognition). We will briefly address some basic questions about development before going into different perspectives on development. Finally, we will consider how to study psychological development, discussing different kinds of studies and approaches and the criteria for sound studies that give us valid, reliable, and replicable results.

Why Study Development?

A child is born and grows from infant to toddler to school-age child to adolescent and to adult, regardless of where he is born or who his parents are. In the course of development, he acquires a wide range of perceptual and motor skills as well as cognitive and social abilities. Developmental patterns are intrinsically interesting, since we all have faced the challenges of acquiring skills and knowledge and fitting into a family, a peer group, and a community. These patterns are the key to understanding what changes over the course of development, what stimulates and what constrains development, and what problems may develop along the way. Knowing what occurs in infancy or early childhood or adolescence can give us clues to understanding adult mental states and behaviors as well. Finally, studying development can also give us insight as we make decisions and formulate social policies that affect children.

Development as a Key to Understanding Children's Capabilities

The process of psychological development is a remarkable story, informed by sophisticated scientific methods and theories. This story is animated by the problems that children confront at different ages and the ways they tend to solve them. Many of these problems are universal, faced by children in all cultures throughout the world, as in the perceptual challenges faced by a newborn, as described at the beginning of the chapter. For that reason, many aspects of the development story follow a similar arc regardless of where and how children live. All children,

for example, must learn how to talk, to walk, to find their way home, to count, to catch an object, and to know when others are mistaken. Developmental psychologists ask how skills and knowledge are acquired by children. They look at how children master motor skills, cognitive skills, and social skills. They examine the universal commonalities that affect the development of children throughout the world. And they study how developmental constraints can affect the age at which particular skills and knowledge are acquired.

Consider two key components of this story in a bit more detail. For one, children throughout the world must learn to decode and respond to communication from others. In just a few short years, virtually all children master much of their culture's language, even though languages vary widely. As they come to understand and produce new and complex linguistic expressions, they must refine several skills—from decoding speech sounds to making inferences about a speaker's meaning. As a second example, all children must form a sense of themselves as individuals within their own family and community. Even very young children weave together several skills and forms of understanding in the course of developing a sense of self. As an adult, this self-knowledge—seeing yourself as distinct from others and possessed of particular abilities and traits, as well as having a sense of the choices and goals that direct your journey through life—is easy to take for granted. In fact, this kind of understanding depends on a rich array of early accomplishments, ranging from controlling the movement of your limbs to knowing which parts of your knowledge are private and unavailable to others. Over the course of childhood, these abilities and many others become integrated into a unified sense of self.

The problems facing the developing child require complex solutions far beyond the capacities of even the most advanced computers, yet all children either solve them completely or are well on their way to a solution within the first few years of life. The course of development is a fascinating story in which a limited range of abilities and behaviors starts the infant on a developmental pathway leading to a variety of remarkable achievements, including social collaborations, problem solving, and acquisition of specialized expertise. One major goal of this book is to explain how that success is possible.

As the story of development unfolds, parents do not simply mold their children into a desired form. Instead, if things go well, they work as mentors, coaches, and partners with their children, helping them develop in optimal ways. Studying development is one way to better understand children—to appreciate them as individuals in their own right and to see their nobler goals and beliefs. In addition, each child's development takes place within many different communities, including family, peers, school, town, and the entire culture, each of which exerts its own influences.

Understanding these developmental patterns can also grant each of us a new perspective on our own developmental journey. To appreciate these common developmental stories, as well as their individual variations, is to gain insight into a new world of remarkable complexity and wonder. Put differently, all the intriguing questions about the adult's mind and behavior apply to development as well; and in the field of development, these questions are enriched by a host of new ones about origins and changes. Successful psychological development is one of the great wonders of modern science.

Development as a Means for Insight into the Mature Form

At some point in our lives, almost all of us stumble across clues about what our parents were like as children or as much younger adults—an old photo album, a grainy home movie, a saved drawing from preschool, or a surprising story from someone who knew them many years ago. These records of the past seem to hold answers to all kinds of nagging questions: Was my mother always so outgoing and friendly? Was my father always so concerned about tidying up? Did something happen early in their lives that made both of my parents so thrifty? Knowledge about someone's origins and background often offers clues into that person's thoughts and behavior in the present.

Studying development offers unique insights into some of psychology's oldest and most intriguing questions. For example, are our personalities the same both as children and as adults? What are the roots of our moral intuitions? How does language change the nature of thought? And how does conscious experience differ from mental life that occurs outside of consciousness? Researchers in both biology and psychology are increasingly discovering that they can sometimes answer questions about mature organisms by considering how they emerge and change in the course of development.

A surprising discovery from the field of embryology helps to illustrate this principle, though the question that motivated the research might appear obviously—or even ridiculously—unanswerable: Are zebras white animals with black stripes or black animals with white stripes? Those who studied adult zebras for the answer concluded that zebras must be white with black stripes, because the adult underbelly was often white (see Figure 1.2). But a different answer emerges when considering how the stripes develop (Gould, 1983): zebras actually seem to be black animals with white stripes. Studies of the developing fetus revealed a process of inhibiting the skin's dark pigment in particular areas to lay down a series of white stripes on a black background (Bard, 1977). This example not only shows how studying development can sometimes resolve seemingly unanswerable ques-

FIGURE 1.2 Studying development to understand adult structures. Even the closest examination of an adult zebra does not clarify whether it is a black animal with white stripes or a white one with black stripes. But prenatal developmental analyses suggest an answer to this question.

tions; it also provides insights into why that coloring might have evolved, how skin patterns relate to embryonic growth, what might go wrong in deviant cases, and so on. The developmental context greatly enriches our understanding of the final form.

Leaving biology and returning to psychology offers many similar examples. Understanding how psychological skills develop—such as recognizing faces, handling threatening situations, or even understanding that a multicolored thing is one object rather than two—is central to understanding the mature form of these abilities in adults. Studying development can allow us to see subtle distinctions that become blurred in adults, but it can also allow us to see the foundational framework for a behavior as it emerges. For example, for hundreds of years, scholars have debated whether people are basically selfish but learn from society's constraints how to behave appropriately, or whether they are, at their core, caring and altruistic but become "corrupted by society." Developmental studies are enormously revealing here, as they can suggest whether one aspect of morality or the other is truly foundational. This particular developmental story is still unfolding, but recent work suggests that both facets of morality, self-interest and altruism, may appear very early as equally intrinsic components of human nature (Bloom, 2013; Warneken & Tomasello, 2009). These findings certainly do not mean that infants and young toddlers hold fully formed moral beliefs, but they make strong suggestions about the nature of humans' deepest moral impulses.

Q: Give an example of how patterns of development provide insight into a mature form.

Development and Social Policy

As citizens in a democracy and as decision-making adults and potential parents, we are also in a position to put developmental insights to practical use (see Figure 1.3). Just a sample of today's headlines shows that we will all need to make choices concerning children's education and welfare: When should a child be tried as an adult if he or she commits a crime? What is the appropriate age to start sex education? Are preschool programs for disadvantaged children effective? Is joint custody best for children of divorced parents? Should birth parents always have access to the adopted child? We owe it to the younger generations to make these decisions based on sound information.

Although we will not resolve these difficult questions in this book, we will see how developmental psychology bears on them and how to interpret and use information about these issues. This kind of critical thinking is one of the most valuable aspects of education—and one important way of putting this skill to use is in the decisions we make, as individuals and as a society, about our children. In that sense, studying development provides tools for evaluating the kind of nuanced information you will encounter, and often have to act on, for the rest of your life.

Knowledge of psychological development also affects how each of us relates to those who depart from behavioral norms, how we value them as individuals, and how we make decisions about their welfare. Some of the most challenging social policy decisions concern individuals with special needs. These include children with learning disabilities, social deficits, or emotional problems. All of us have encountered or heard about children who struggle with anxieties, ranging from a mild fear of dogs to paralyzing distress about almost everything outside the home. An understanding of anxieties and how they develop in children requires considering how the child perceives and thinks about the world and how these perceptions and thoughts change as the child matures. Knowing more about how thoughts and emotions interrelate in development can also help you understand children with emotional problems, such as depression or uncontrollable anger.

When a school district decides how to teach children with special needs, when there are debates about expanding children's health care coverage to include treatment for emotional difficulties, or when a community establishes a program to help children recover from a natural disaster, it is critical to understand the nature of both normal and abnormal psychological development. Without an appreciation of how both normal and abnormal thoughts, feelings, and behaviors develop, it is difficult to effectively support those who are affected by these decisions. Such an appreciation also reduces social stigma and prejudice, as it brings to light all that we have in common with those who are impaired.

> Q: Name a social policy question involving children, and explain how basic research in developmental psychology might help to answer it.

FIGURE 1.3 **Child labor.** Basic research in developmental psychology can have important implications for social policy. A better understanding of psychological development can help support arguments against the use of children as laborers. Although most people consider child labor a thing of the past, as depicted in this photo, the practice is still common in many parts of the world.

The Nature of Development

When we study development, we are interested in the patterns of change that occur in an organism as it progresses through its lifespan. In this book, we will focus on patterns of change between birth and young adulthood, but it is possible to extend the idea of developmental change to include adulthood and older age. Indeed, midlife and later life changes—including some faculties that come only with advanced age, such as wisdom (Baltes & Staudinger, 2000)—are discussed in Chapter 17.

Psychological development includes patterns of change in mind and behavior that occur as an organism progresses through its lifespan. The mental changes involve the growth of processes such as perception and reasoning, as well as changes in emotion and motivation. Behavioral changes over the lifespan range from young children's toilet training or learning to avoid temper tantrums to adolescents beginning to date. Psychological development is one of the most challenging and rewarding areas of psychology because it explains how we come to be who we are. There is a popular misconception that studying young children might be simpler because young children have fewer abilities than adults. As we will see, however, understanding psychological development requires careful consideration of both the child's early abilities and the mature mind toward which a child is progressing.

Categorizing Developmental Phenomena

To study the rich, vast scope of a lifetime of changes, psychologists group developmental patterns in several ways. We will consider how development can be divided into periods and domains before turning to some of the broader questions that developmental psychologists ask and the diverse perspectives that inform their search for answers.

Periods of Development One way of categorizing developmental patterns involves dividing the lifespan into a series of developmental periods based on age—most commonly these are the *prenatal period, infancy,* the *preschool period, young school age, later school age,* and *adolescence.* Researchers who consider the entire lifespan would add *young adulthood, middle adulthood,* and *late adulthood* to this list (see Figure 1.4). One reason for dividing development into these periods is that each one shows unique patterns of change in mind and action, so it makes sense to treat each period as a distinct area of study. A second, more practical reason is that certain periods require their own specialized research methods. Most researchers who study infancy, for example, use the same set of techniques.

Considering these periods in a little more detail, the *prenatal period* covers development from the moment of conception to birth some 9½ months later. The study of early prenatal development focuses largely on anatomical and physiological development. Considerations of psychological development usually do not enter the picture until shortly before birth, at which point some researchers ask how experiences in the womb might influence behaviors after birth. As we will see, research in this area has revealed that infants prenatally develop a preference for some of the sounds of their mother's language such that, at birth, they already prefer to listen to her language over others. The developmental psychology of the prenatal period also involves understanding the psychological effects of substances that can harm the developing fetus. For example, children whose mothers drank excessive amounts of alcohol during pregnancy are more likely to have a host of cognitive and emotional problems.

Infancy usually refers to the first year to year and a half of life. The most notable feature of this period is that infants are largely preverbal. The absence of language has led some researchers to propose that the infant's mind works differently from the minds of older children, hypothesizing that the infant may lack the ability to think about anything that is not present. Infants' behavior also shows many differences from the behavior of older children, ranging from young infants' sleep patterns, to crawling, to the pronounced fear of strangers that emerges at around 8 months of age. Studying infancy also requires a specialized set of research methods, since infants can't say in words what they like or dislike.

The *preschool period,* from roughly age 1½ to 4, includes changes on several fronts. Language appears and flourishes such that most 4-year-olds can chatter away on any number of topics. During this period, children clearly show the ability to think about things that are not present, and their memory skills often improve considerably. Socially, children improve in their ability to understand other people's minds, and they develop the capacity for much more complex social interactions.

Young school age, from roughly age 5 to 7, is a period in which children's social and cognitive skills expand considerably. Their memory strategies become much more effective, their mathematical skills become more sophisticated, and they usually learn to read. They can understand more complex discussions and seem to follow more elaborate lines of reasoning. Socially, one of their most significant changes is the child's experience in the world outside the family, most notably in school. Another major socialization tool in many cultures, the television, becomes ever more influential.

In *later school age,* from roughly age 8 to 12, children continue to make clear advancements as they improve their ability to express complicated thoughts and solve complex problems. As self-control improves, they appear increasingly able to inhibit impulses and delay gratification. Their real-world knowledge increases greatly as they come to understand their community and its place in the world. At the same time, their social networks expand and tend to focus on friendships with peers of the same sex.

Adolescence, from roughly age 13 to 20, is another period of salient changes. Some are physical, as the differences

FIGURE 1.4 Periods of development. The members of this extended family represent many developmental periods, from infancy and the preschool period through adolescence and late adulthood.

between the sexes become more distinct during puberty. At the cognitive level, adolescents are increasingly able to consider hypothetical situations and to see how two people can disagree without either being mistaken. There is also a surge of risk taking in this period that may involve underestimating some risks, thrill seeking, and difficulty in controlling impulses, representing both cognitive and emotional changes. Other more purely social and emotional hallmarks of adolescence involve entering romantic and sexual relationships and establishing independence from one's parents.

Young adulthood, from roughly age 21 to 30, is a period of consolidation of the many changes that have occurred in earlier years. The wildness or volatility of adolescence typically diminishes, and this period's cognitive changes may mostly involve gaining more detailed knowledge and applied skills. In most cultures, adults in this age group commit to a particular role in life, either in a career or as a homemaker.

Characteristics of *middle adulthood*, roughly age 31 to 60, vary considerably across cultures. It is important to keep in mind that a century ago, members of most communities in the world had an average lifespan of 40 years. Even today, the average lifespan of a man in Sierra Leone is 37 years, while that of a woman in Japan is 86 (CIA World Factbook, 2010). Given such an enormous range in life expectancies, it is difficult to generalize about experiences during this period. In specific cultures, such as the United States, more consistent patterns take shape. For example, most adults in the United States and other developed countries are likely to reach their career peak during this period and enter the period when their own children reach adulthood and leave home.

Late adulthood, from the late 60s onward, encompasses a gradually increasing age range in many cultures as lifespans increase. Like middle adulthood, late adulthood is characterized by huge individual variations. Some people show a substantial decline in cognitive and motor skills, whereas others show only modest changes even in very old age. Moreover, performance in some tasks that draw on large amounts of stored knowledge can continue to improve well into old age. In terms of social and emotional change, older adults show a strong tendency to experience the present and remember the past more positively than younger adults.

This brief chronology merely serves as a reminder of the enormous amount of change that occurs from birth through childhood and adulthood and into old age. These nine periods are also somewhat arbitrary; the lifespan could potentially be divided into either fewer periods or more, depending on what kind of developmental changes serve as a basis for the divisions.

Areas of Development Our overview of the hallmarks of different periods helps to illustrate the full sweep of development, but developmental psychologists usually pose specific questions, focusing on changes in particular kinds of psychological processes. Thus, besides dividing the lifespan into chronological periods, developmental psychologists also categorize developmental phenomena into the different types of psychological processes that undergo developmental changes—including *perception, action, cognition, morality, social behavior,* and *emotions* (see Figure 1.5).

Perceptual development involves the ways people grow in their ability to pick up information from the world by using their senses and by processing sensory information. We will see, for example, that infants may perceive faces and speech sounds in quite different ways from older children and adults, raising profound questions about how people transition from one way of perceiving to another. Perceptual development also involves changes in the ability to integrate information from different senses, such as hearing and vision, and to use that information to guide action.

Development of action is concerned with how people change in their ability to move about in the world and purposefully guide their bodies and limbs. It also includes the development of reflexes and conditioning, a particular type of learning that focuses on behavioral changes in response to positive and negative reinforcements. Developmental changes in this area are often most obvious among young children—for example, as a child progresses from crawling to walking or from being unable to catch a ball at age 2 to catching a ball while running at age 5.

The study of *cognitive development* focuses on how people change over the lifespan in the ways that they understand and use information. Research in this area usually involves observing changes in behavior in order to make inferences about the changes in a person's thoughts and beliefs. Thus, when a 7-year-old first demonstrates that she understands multiplication, researchers will ask how that child's mental representations of mathematical concepts have changed in accordance with her new understanding. Cognitive development includes not only gaining particular types of knowledge, such as understanding the characteristics of physical objects or the biological world, but also developing mental abilities such as memory and attention that support many kinds of thought and behavior.

The study of *moral development* asks how a child's sense of values emerges as well as how moral and immoral behaviors develop. Examining the development of values can include studying how children reason through moral decisions and also exploring their particular beliefs about whether behaviors like cheating or physical aggression are ethical under various circumstances.

The field of *social development* looks at how a wide range of relationships between people form and change. Psychologists in this area may investigate how an infant forms

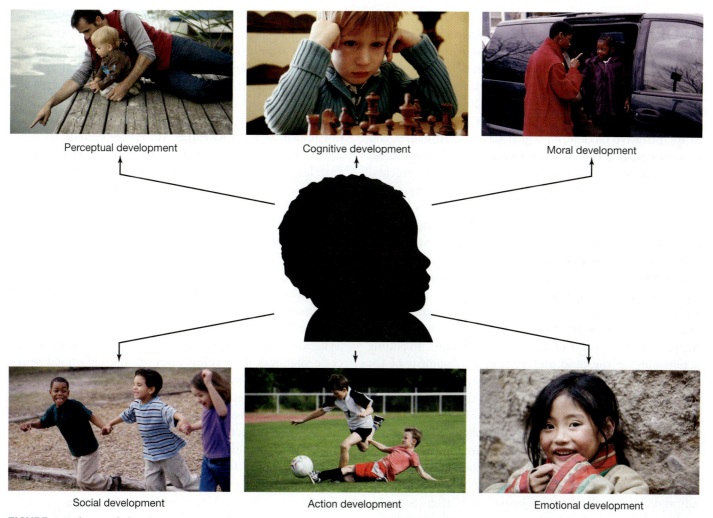

Perceptual development

Cognitive development

Moral development

Social development

Action development

Emotional development

FIGURE 1.5 Areas of development. The different areas of development interact constantly throughout the lifespan. Nonetheless, researchers tend to focus on a particular areas—such as changes in perceptual, cognitive, action, social, moral, or emotional processes.

a special attachment to a caregiver and shows distress at separation. They may examine how teasing and bullying in middle school affect both the bullies and the victims. Studying social development in adolescence might focus on how teens' first romantic relationships differ from earlier close relationships. Other topics of interest within social development include how particular social qualities, such as shyness or leadership, emerge.

Research on *emotional development* examines how the full range of emotions takes shape, beginning in infancy. Its concerns range from which basic emotions are present in a newborn to the way complex emotions, such as guilt, emerge out of simpler ones, such as sadness and fear. Because psychologists often construe motivation in emotional terms—that is, behaving in a particular way to feel better (or to avoid negative feelings)—the field of emotional development may also study motivational changes that occur with increasing age. These include the disillusionment that often emerges in adolescence or the more positive outlook that can come with older age.

Basic Questions about Psychological Development

Clearly, psychological development is not a monolithic concept; changes over a lifetime happen in several different dimensions. Furthermore, specific periods and psychological processes show their own distinct patterns in the ways that developmental changes unfold. These differences lead to questions about which patterns happen in what circumstances. We will consider three broad questions about dimensions of development that pertain to many developmental periods and processes.

Is Development Stage-like or Continuous? Are there points in development when children gain a new capacity that is completely different from what they previously were able to do? Or is development more of a continuous process in which thoughts and behaviors slowly become more elaborate and complex? **Qualitative change** takes place when a new kind of structure or process emerges that was not present before. In developmental psychology, discussions of qualitative change often refer to different **stages of development**; a child is said to be in one stage before a qualitative change occurs and in a different stage after the change. Stages involve relatively discontinuous changes in thinking and behaving, resulting in new kinds of accomplishments and patterns of thought that were not present before that stage. This stands in contrast to **quantitative change**, in which the same structures and processes remain but show differences in their magnitude. Discussions of quantitative change focus on incremental expansions to a mental or physical process or capacity.

In physical development, we can easily see both qualitative and quantitative patterns of change. For example, a tadpole's body undergoes qualitative changes as it develops into a frog (Gilbert, 2010). A series of interactions between genes and hormones causes the tadpole's body to break down and resorb the tail that it used for swimming and then to use the resorbed material to generate new structures that distinguish the frog's body from the tadpole's. This tail resorption happens in the context of many related changes, including a reshaping of the head and massive development of the tongue, a shift from the tadpole's herbivorous digestive system to the frog's carnivorous one, and the development of a middle ear that allows the frog to hear in the air. Thus, a whole constellation of interconnected changes in structure and function serve the developing organism's needs. Each of these physical developments can be considered a qualitative change in its own right, as each bodily system has structurally and functionally distinct "before" and "after" states.

The difference between qualitative and quantitative changes is especially clear in the tadpole's case because we can contrast the qualitative changes that transform the tadpole into a frog with the very different outcome that results when a tadpole undergoes purely quantitative change: blocking the action of thyroid hormones can create a developmental path in which the tadpole can reach enormous dimensions (see Figure 1.6). When a tadpole retains its same basic structure and grows ever larger without undergoing the normal transformation of its anatomy or physiology, then it exhibits quantitative change.

In the course of normal development, we typically see a mix of qualitative and quantitative patterns of change in the same organism. Animals that undergo metamorphoses (for example, tadpole to frog, caterpillar to butterfly) exhibit especially dramatic qualitative changes, but more typically the two kinds of change are both apparent. Thus, when a deer grows its first set of antlers, it makes a clear qualitative transition from its earlier antler-free period; yet other aspects of its anatomy, such as its skeleton and muscles, grow larger in a more quantitative fashion at the same time.

In human development, the most obvious patterns of qualitative physical change occur during adolescence. After a period of relatively incremental change in childhood in which the body gradually increases in size on most dimensions, patterns of change during puberty take on a different character (see Figure 1.7). In girls, these changes include a broadening of the hips relative to the rest of the body and the development of breasts as new functional organs. The reproductive system changes as well. At the biochemical level, the onset of menses represents a major new hormonal cycle that was not taking place in the childhood years. For boys, a different set of qualitative changes occurs. The upper body develops more extensively relative to the lower body, and facial hair grows from previously hairless skin. The male reproductive system also changes substantially.

Keeping in mind the case of the supersized tadpoles, it is easy enough to picture how a pattern of exclusively quanti-

FIGURE 1.6 Qualitative versus quantitative development. It can be difficult to tell whether a pattern of psychological development is qualitative or quantitative, but the contrast is often clearer in biological change. **(A)** The tadpole's dramatic qualitative change into a frog (from eggs to tadpoles to adults) is caused by a rise in thyroid hormone production that occurs in the tadpole's normal development. **(B)** Quantitative change, but not qualitative change, occurs when a tadpole lacks thyroid glands and hence cannot produce thyroid hormones. As such, it cannot metamorphose from a tadpole into a frog (qualitative change). Instead, the tadpole continues to grow (quantitative change), resulting in a giant tadpole (bottom) compared to a normal tadpole (top).

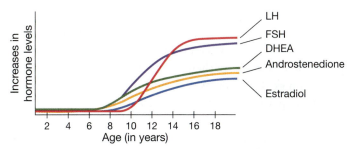

FIGURE 1.7 **Increases in hormone levels and qualitative changes during puberty.** There is a surge of blood hormone levels during puberty in both girls and boys that produces dramatic qualitative physical changes in their bodies. LH (luteinizing hormone) stimulates ovulation in girls and growth of testes in boys; FSH (follicle-stimulating hormone) stimulates the formation of ova in girls and sperm in boys; DHEA (dehydroepiandrosterone) and androstenedione are involved in the production of testosterone and estrogen; estradiol is produced as estrogen and affects breast development and body shape in girls and bone maturation and growth in boys. Adapted from Gordon and Laufer (2005).

tative changes would differ from one involving qualitative changes. Imagine a child who simply grows larger and larger, never changing in body proportions and never acquiring any of the secondary sex characteristics that develop during puberty. In an extreme case of purely quantitative change, this child would continue growing at the same rate throughout his lifespan and never show other signs of aging.

This distinction between qualitative and quantitative change also applies in the psychological realm. Consider, for example, the consistent finding that infants who are younger than 6 months old are unable to see the depth relations conveyed in pictures, but after the first 6 months of life, they perceive these relations easily (Yonas et al., 2002). Their visual systems change qualitatively at around 6 months of age, acquiring a whole new kind of functional capacity in a

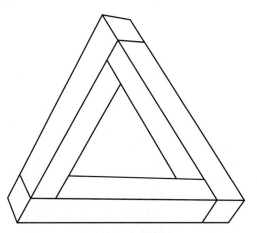

FIGURE 1.8 **Qualitative change in depth perception.** Because 3-month-old infants cannot yet see depth as it is depicted in two-dimensional pictures, they would not find this "impossible" figure troubling. In contrast, a 7-month-old can see depth in pictures and might well find this illustration odd.

short period of time (see Figure 1.8). By contrast, the ability to see patterns in high resolution, which is called visual acuity, gradually sharpens from birth through the first year of life and seems to be a clear case of quantitative change.

As we consider developmental patterns during particular periods of life and within different domains, we will often ask if the changes seem to be continuous and quantitative or if they seem more qualitative and therefore suggestive of distinct developmental stages. In some cases, as you will see, experts disagree about which kind of change is occurring, and a series of experiments can often help us choose between the alternatives. These debates are important not just for understanding what kind of change is happening; they can also, for example, help teachers design strategies that suit children's emerging abilities.

Q: What is the difference between stage-like and continuous change?

Is Development Global or Local? In some cases, developmental change sweeps across many types of processes or abilities at once. When such **global changes** occur, similar developments occur at roughly the same time in very different areas of thought. Global changes are therefore general changes that apply across all situations or domains. For example, during middle childhood, children seem to show strong improvement in the ability to focus on the information most relevant to a task and ignore irrelevant or distracting information (Houde et al., 2010). This new ability to sustain attention could support improvements in a variety of areas where the ability to stay focused is critical. Thus, a child at this age might show gains in making moral judgments, reasoning about video game puzzles, and solving math problems.

Other times, particular skills and mental competencies each show their own unique sets of developmental changes. When development is characterized by such **local changes**, different kinds of psychological capacities develop relatively independently of each other. Local changes are therefore specific changes that occur in restricted areas or domains. In this case, a change in patterns of moral judgment would not necessarily coincide with or resemble a change in understanding mathematical concepts. Consider an example in which a researcher carefully tracks a child's patterns of both moral and mathematical reasoning from age 5 to 10. During this period, the child seems to undergo a major shift in how she thinks about moral dilemmas. Perhaps in the early years she has difficulty understanding immoral acts that cause no physical harm but may cause psychological harm, but in later years she becomes attuned to the psychological consequences as well. During this 5-year period, her mathematical skills also show great changes. Initially, she can only do the simplest addition, while by age 10, after some training with the researcher, she can easily do long division.

This child has shown strong changes in moral reasoning and mathematical skills during the same period, but these would still be considered *local changes* if there were no relationship between the two patterns of change. For example, by taking frequent measurements, the researcher might discover that the two domains showed different developmental trends (see Figure 1.9). Perhaps the improvements in moral judgment started off rapidly at age 5 and then gradually slowed down by age 10, while changes in mathematical ability showed the opposite pattern, changing slowly at first, then showing steep gains. We would have further evidence for local change if, after additional training in math, the child improved at solving a broad range of similar mathematics problems but showed no gains in moral reasoning. Taken together, these findings would clearly indicate that the changes in these domains took place independently of one another, in the form of local changes. By contrast, if the changes in both moral and mathematical reasoning seemed tightly linked in their patterns and timing, and if training in one of these areas also helped in the other, those results would suggest more global change.

In reality, global changes and local changes happen together and often affect the same processes and skills. Development in capacities such as memory, which contributes to a variety of psychological processes, can support broad, global changes that affect many different areas. At the same time, more specific, focused patterns of change can take shape within local areas. If, for example, general improvements in memory over the course of development affected every area of thought, those improvements would need to be taken into account in such diverse areas as language acquisition, mathematical reasoning, and conflict resolution skills—even as each one of these areas showed its own local patterns of change as well.

How Do Nature and Nurture Shape Development?

Few aspects of developmental psychology are as prominent in popular culture as the "nature/nurture" debate. In these discussions, patterns of thought and behavior that emerge in much the same way regardless of experience are considered the results of "nature," whereas "nurture" is said to describe psychology and behavior that result from specific experiences. This basic "nature/nurture" distinction can be fruitful in discussing development—but it must be applied carefully. It makes little sense to talk about any behavior or psychological process as *exclusively* a product of either nature or nurture.

Consider two physical developments that might seem to illustrate either pure nature or pure nurture. Beard growth in men seems like a development rooted completely in "nature," the unfolding of a genetically predetermined process. In reality, however, the environment is also important, as an extreme environment that disrupts hormonal output can prevent beard growth. Hundreds of years ago in Italy, preadolescent boys who were talented singers were sometimes castrated to preserve their high voices (Peschel & Peschel, 1986). Castration is obviously an extreme circumstance, but strictly speaking, it involves an environmental, or "nurture"-related, influence. Similarly, although a person becomes sunburned from exposure to ultraviolet light, the influence of "nature" also plays a role. Different individuals burn to differing degrees in the same sunlight in the same environment because of genetic differences in pigmentation and other light-sensitive molecules in the skin. Thus, even traits subject to very strong and specific genetic influences cannot emerge without the support of a particular range of environments. And even the most experience-associated traits can develop only within constraints that are heavily influenced by genes.

Because all development, whether physical or psychological, involves an interplay of nature and nurture, it can be tempting to assume that the entire nature/nurture debate is misguided—an argument about a dichotomy that does not

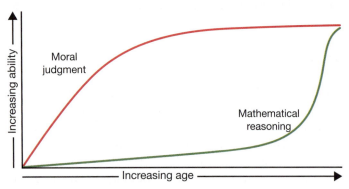

FIGURE 1.9 Local developmental change. If two developmental processes show their own distinct patterns of change, their development would be considered local rather than global. Here we see different developmental trends for two hypothetical processes. Note that both processes start at the same lower level and end up at the same higher level, but moral judgment changes rapidly at an early age and then levels off, while mathematical reasoning increases slowly at an early age but increases rapidly at an older age. It is implausible that these two processes would reflect different aspects of changes in the same underlying system.

really exist. According to such accounts, all development is a mixture of both, and it makes no sense to ask how a particular trait, behavior, or psychological process is influenced by nature or nurture. There are, however, good reasons why the debate has been a topic of fascination for millennia.

While it is true that all psychological development involves interactions between nature and nurture, there are real differences in developmental patterns that can be understood by asking about the relative influences of genes and environment. For example, we can ask if across a wide range of "normal" environments (that is, environments that do not involve such unusual occurrences as brain surgery, hormone disruption, or extreme trauma and deprivation) a child will develop the ability to mentally fuse the separate images seen by the right and left eyes. This capacity for binocular vision requires repeated experiences in a lighted environment with both eyes at the same time; if such environmental conditions are met over time, the vast majority of children will acquire binocular vision in essentially the same manner. In contrast, quite specific environmental experiences are needed to be able to learn how to read—for example, being taught to recognize groups of letters and to associate them with what they represent. This ability does not develop automatically in any environment.

In this book, we will consider the nature/nurture question in many different contexts and at several periods in development. We will see that scientists have disagreed about the roles of nature and nurture in areas ranging from language, to morality, to spatial navigation. These debates are worthwhile, and they can often be illuminated by the data patterns produced by careful research. For example, if some aspects of language development happen in the same way worldwide, regardless of the particular language spoken and regardless of whether parents speak to their children often or just a little, those linguistic developments might be considered more a function of nature than a function of nurture. If, however, those same aspects of language are closely linked to the particular language a child is exposed to, and if they vary greatly, depending on how parents speak to their children, nurture would seem to be more central. Even in cases like these, however, it is important not to oversimplify the question into a matter of "either/or," in which one kind of influence completely excludes the other. We will see that carefully designed studies can be essential to disentangling the relative contributions of nature and nurture to many aspects of development.

One way of thinking about how nature and nurture contribute to some aspect of development involves imagining how a range of different environments might affect these developmental changes (Chomsky, 1975, 1988). Figure 1.10 depicts a situation in which a particular initial state (say, the way a newborn mentally represents human faces) develops in different environmental conditions, shown in the figure

as different colored lines. The upper panel represents a more nature-biased account, where environmental variations have little effect on the development of face perception. The outcomes at the right fall quite close together, signifying, in this scenario, that the mind comes to represent faces in much the same way, regardless of the environment an individual experiences. On the other hand, the lower panel represents a nurture-biased account. Here, the triangles representing outcomes are widely dispersed, signifying that quite different ways of representing faces develop, depending on differences in the environment.

Of course, Figure 1.10 is an idealized representation; in practice, it is much more challenging to determine how the influences of nature and nurture affect development. Moreover, individuals do not really begin life at exactly the same "initial state." Nonetheless, this illustration helps to convey what is often at stake in nature/nurture debates; accounts of development may predict different patterns of change, and even different outcomes, depending on which kind of influences they emphasize.

Up to this point, we have considered nature and nurture largely in terms of whether a particular psychological process or structure tends to develop in the same way regardless of the environments experienced or whether the developmental outcomes vary widely, depending on particular kinds of experiences. A different angle on nature/nurture tends to focus less on such qualitatively different outcomes and instead looks at how genes and the environment each contribute to individual differences (Plomin, 1989). For example, there are intense debates about the extent to which an individual's intelligence is more a product of nurture (including education) as opposed to nature (including genes). It is important to keep in mind that even if the *qualitative aspects* of a skill emerge the same way in most environments, individual differences in the *degree* of the skill could still depend on how the environments differed. For example, in humans, the anatomy and structure of particular muscles develop in the same way across most environments—but when we compare two individuals, the strength of each muscle is significantly related to experience. We will need to keep in mind these different ways of framing nature/nurture discussions as we explore psychological development.

Q: What are some ways in which scholars might disagree about the initial mental state of the newborn infant?

The three questions that we posed in this section—concerning qualitative and quantitative change, global and local change, and nature and nurture—are relevant in each

FIGURE 1.10 Envisioning the "nature versus nurture" debate. This diagram shows one way of depicting the differences between developmental accounts that emphasize nature's influences and those that emphasize nurture. Think of tracing developmental changes from an initial state, as shown on the left, across a range of different environments. (These developmental paths are shown as different colored lines.) In the strong nature account at the top, development that takes place in a wide range of environments results in very similar outcomes. In the strong nurture account, development that takes place in different environments leads to quite different outcomes due to the influences of distinct environmental factors and experiences.

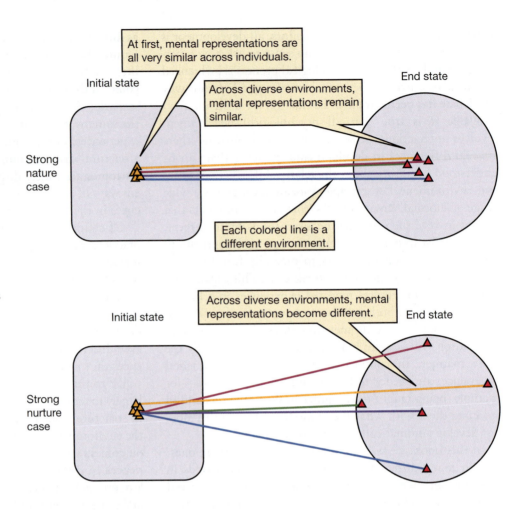

Perspectives on Development

The fundamental questions just described are usually posed within a particular psychological perspective on the process of development. These different perspectives—which include *comparative and evolutionary perspectives, cross-cultural perspectives, neuroscience perspectives, behaviorist perspectives, psychoanalytic perspectives, cognitive science perspectives,* and more broadly *empiricist* and *nativist* perspectives—are each based on specific intellectual traditions. They are each associated with certain research methods, styles of argument, and theoretical positions. Thus, each perspective tends to approach developmental questions somewhat differently.

Rather than contradicting each other, these perspectives usually offer complementary approaches. Each one

and every chapter that follows. In studying development, it is always useful to consider how these three questions reflect on a particular aspect of development. The answers are not always easy to determine, but just posing these questions can guide further exploration of developmental phenomena.

helps to frame a set of phenomena in a manner that emphasizes some aspects over others. When different perspectives are applied to the same phenomena, they often raise different kinds of questions and therefore yield different answers. Because each perspective invariably leaves out some aspects of a problem and emphasizes others, you might think of them as different lenses for examining patterns of change, each one bringing certain issues into sharp focus. For these reasons, we will often find it useful to consider how multiple perspectives provide their own unique insights into a developmental pattern. It is also important to keep in mind which perspectives are in play as you pose questions about psychological development. We start by considering a pair of broad philosophical perspectives on development commonly known as empiricism and nativism.

Empiricist and Nativist Perspectives

By the time psychology emerged as a separate discipline in the late nineteenth century, philosophers, biologists, and others had been actively discussing many of its central issues for centuries, and some of the most persistent, intriguing questions focused on the origins of human perceptions and knowledge. Two philosophical perspectives on development, empiricism and nativism, helped to shape these discussions, which often led to inquiries about how knowledge originates and takes shape in the mind of an infant or child (Spelke & Newport, 1998).

Empiricism Empiricism is a view of development that emphasizes the idea that a general, all-purpose learning system, with few or no biases toward acquiring particular kinds of information, is present at birth. Empiricists' proposals and speculations can be traced back thousands of years, but they are best exemplified by three remarkable seventeenth- and eighteenth-century philosophers (see Figure 1.11). John Locke (1632–1704) laid out the general idea that all human knowledge is built up by forming links, or mental associations, between the phenomena we experience. George Berkeley (1685–1753) incorporated this idea of association-based knowledge in his explanation of how we perceive and interpret the visual world. And David Hume (1711–1776) used this same association-based view of knowledge to develop a theory about how complex mental processes work, including how humans understand cause-and-effect relationships.

"All knowledge through the senses" is perhaps the best-known slogan associated with the empiricist movement. It simply means that the content of all knowledge and thought—an elaborate web of learned associations—could only be gained from experience. This slogan, however, hardly does justice to the empiricist position. The empiricists were committed to the idea that the mind (and the

brain) made sense of the world by linking together any bits of information that co-occurred frequently enough in experience. Any piece of information, such as the sound of the word "no," could become associated with any other, such as an angry facial expression, provided that an individual experienced that particular combination—in this case, a word and an expression—sufficiently often. In this way, the empiricists argued, sensory experiences that were relatively meaningless on their own became meaningful over time through learned associations.

Nativism Nativism is a view of development that emphasizes the idea that a set of different learning systems is present at birth, in which each system is biased to acquire particular kinds of information better than others. The roots of nativist philosophies go at least as far back as the ancient Greek philosopher Plato, and their influence continued into the sixteenth and seventeenth centuries with scholars such as René Descartes and Gottfried Leibniz. Unlike the empiricists, nativists believed that human knowledge could never be understood solely in terms of an increasingly complex web of associations. Their early discomfort with the empiricists' view arose from the observation that different breeds of domesticated animals, such as dogs, showed distinct dispositions and abilities; for example, Labrador retrievers retrieve and sheepdogs herd (see Figure 1.12). Since empiricism could not explain these differences in other species, the nativists asked, why should it be considered plausible for explaining differences in humans? Other arguments against empiricism arose from the sense that it

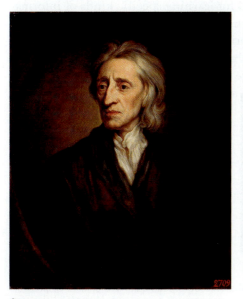  

A   B   C

FIGURE 1.11 The early empiricists. Empiricist philosophers **(A)** John Locke, **(B)** George Berkeley, and **(C)** David Hume supported the idea that all knowledge is based on learned associations. This view of how the human mind comes to perceive the world, understand causality, and have new ideas is still with us today.

was impossible to account for the enormous differences in people's specific talents, like musical talent, mathematical ability, or athleticism, only in terms of their prior "associative" experiences.

Instead, the nativists held that certain aspects of mental life were intrinsic to being human and that these capacities were present at birth. The nativists also agreed that these inborn capacities were more specialized and more complex than the general associative mechanism proposed by the empiricists. Beyond these points of agreement, however, there was—for good reason—enormous diversity among the nativists about the nature of the human mind. Without the insights of modern experimental psychology and cognitive science, they could only speculate based on dissatisfaction with the empiricists' much simpler model.

The empiricist and nativist perspectives still influence the study of development today, but at a much more sophisticated level (Carruthers et al., 2007; Pinker, 2002, 2004). The nativists no longer have to rely on intuitions that certain kinds of knowledge—of God, or morals, or mathematics—seem inborn. Instead, they now have experimental data that they can analyze. They propose specific models of mind that make different predictions about such experimental data than do the models proposed by the empiricists.

Empiricist models of psychological development typically involve general learning mechanisms that apply in pretty much the same way to all sorts of content and experience. In these models, the mind's only specializations for handling different kinds of information occur at early stages in the process, such as in the way we perceive the initial input from our different sense organs. Nativist approaches, on the other hand, focus on learning mechanisms tailored for processing particular kinds of information, such as learning language or retaining a mental map of your neighborhood in memory. These nativist approaches suggest that we use specialized capacities for processing much more than just sensory input and that these specializations may include higher mental functions that are far "downstream" from the perceptual system.

Nativism is commonly focused on the influences of "nature" on development, while empiricism is linked to "nurture" (Cowie, 1999), but these links can be misleading. In fact, both empiricism and nativism are based on the idea that organisms must be born with initial capacities that help them perceive and understand their physical and social environment (see Figure 1.13). Sensory organs such as the eyes and ears gather and process information right from birth, and they relay that information about the world to the brain, which processes and interprets that information. Thus, both traditions emphasize that nature endows the newborn with sensory organs and a brain with the capacity to process information from the start.

Empiricists and nativists disagree, however, on the relative roles of nature and nurture in the particular ways we process and interpret information as it moves "downstream" from the sensory organs to the highest levels of thought. For empiricists, once sensory information has undergone some initial perceptual processing, nature's only role is to provide for a general, all-purpose associative mechanism that allows the mind to link together any kind of inputs—whether they are visual or auditory, social or physical, or of any other sort—based on how often they co-occur.

In contrast, a nativist perspective tends to favor preexisting specializations not just for the simplest processing of incoming information but for all levels of the mind. Nativists believe that infants come into the world with mental structures tailored for learning specific kinds of information, such as language, moral principles, or number concepts. These theories consider the brain's specializations

A   **B**   **C**

FIGURE 1.12 Intrinsic behavioral tendencies. People have recognized for centuries that different dog breeds can have distinct dispositions and reasoning capacities in areas like **(A)** retrieving (as in this Labrador retriever), **(B)** herding (as in this sheepdog), and **(C)** attacking (as in this Doberman). These kinds of strong, intrinsic behavioral differences among animals provided early support for a nativist view of development.

FIGURE 1.13 The initial state. Watching a newborn observe the world immediately raises questions about the human mind's initial state. Clearly, the newborn's brain already differs in important ways from those of other creatures, yet the newborn also clearly has a great deal to learn through experience. Developmental psychologists are intimately concerned with questions about how a baby's biological nature interacts with input from the environment.

for capacities like language use and social interactions to be "built in" or heavily influenced by nature in much the same way that particular parts of the brain are specialized to process visual input from the eyes and other parts of the brain process auditory information from the ears. It is important, however, to remember that just because a particular specialization is strongly influenced by nature does not necessarily mean that it is evident at birth. Remember that male facial hair, which is largely driven by nature, usually doesn't manifest until after puberty. If a particular specialized mechanism is typically present at birth, that often suggests a dominant role for nature in the mechanism's development; but later developments

(for example, the growth of a beard) can still be more a product of nature than of nurture.

We will often find it more useful to consider whether a line of experimental research fits better with a nativist or an empiricist view rather than thinking in terms of a simple nature-versus-nurture dichotomy. These debates between empiricist and nativist views are less about whether or not something "built in" or something "learned" enables perception or cognition to develop. Instead, they focus on whether the mind is initially specialized only at the lowest levels of processing different types of sensory information or whether specialized mechanisms exist at all levels of information processing. Nature and nurture are part of this story, but they are not enough on their own.

Comparative and Evolutionary Perspectives

Questions about developmental psychology have never been confined to humans. Many other species have offspring that grow and develop more elaborate behaviors. Indeed, more than most psychological questions, inquiries about development naturally seem to lead to comparisons across species, which are the main focus of the *comparative perspective*. Even a casual observer of a dog nuzzling her puppies or a baby monkey clinging to its mother cannot help but be struck by the close bonds between parents and offspring and wonder why they exist, how they came about, and what they mean to the animals (see Figure 1.14). In fact, an extraordinary diversity of organisms seems to confront similar challenges during development, such as coordinating visual and motor skills with changing body size and ensuring that

FIGURE 1.14 Comparative and evolutionary perspectives. These perspectives often examine a comparable developmental process across several species, as shown in these examples of mothers caring for their young. Researchers may then ask if these behaviors are alike at a deeper psychological level—perhaps because they have evolved to serve similar functions.

FIGURE 1.15 Cross-cultural perspectives. Developmental researchers often ask if developmental patterns unfold in the same ways across cultures. For example, do friendships form in similar ways in all these groups of children? Are the roles of boys and girls the same in all cultures?

fragile young survive to an age of self-sufficiency. A true appreciation and a genuine understanding of developmental psychology must keep in mind the common problems that many organisms confront, even as they sometimes solve them quite differently.

Closely related to comparative perspectives, *evolutionary perspectives* ask how and why a particular trait, whether it is a body part or a behavior, emerged over successive generations of a population through the process of natural selection. **Ethology** is the study of traits from an adaptive evolutionary perspective that usually involves comparisons across species. Thus, ethologists examine how certain traits improve a species' fitness within its specific environment, conferring advantages that make members of the species that have these traits more likely to survive and produce viable offspring. Understanding how particular traits affect a species' ability to reproduce in its environment also requires closely analyzing the local environment itself in terms of its physical features and the other organisms that inhabit it.

Evolutionary and comparative perspectives, however, do far more than describe the range of patterns of development and how they relate to a population's particular environment. Using these perspectives, we can pose specific questions about the origins of various psychological capacities, including our earliest emotions. For example, feelings of disgust at bodily excretions do not seem to be present at birth, but they emerge in all cultures during the third year of life. From an evolutionary perspective, minimizing contact with bodily excretions makes sense, since this would reduce the spread of disease. But perhaps there are also evolutionary reasons that disgust doesn't appear until an age when the child is actually able to do something to avoid the contamination by means of toilet training and hygiene. Researchers are currently trying to learn whether both factors—the desire to avoid contamination and the inability to do so before about the age of 3—affect the way the emotion of disgust develops. Comparative analyses often pose similar questions about the roots of particular human tendencies, such as the tendency to value things you

already own more than things you are about to acquire, a bias known as the endowment effect. Comparative research has demonstrated that monkeys show similar biases even without observing similar behaviors in others (Lakshminaryanan et al., 2008). Those results suggest that future developmental studies of the endowment effect in humans may find its earliest traces even before culture has much of an influence.

Cross-Cultural Perspectives

Before making general statements about the development of any process, whether it is a child's attachment to a parent, the concept of self, or almost any other aspect of psychological development, it is crucial to gain a sense of how that process develops in different cultures (see Figure 1.15). All too often, we take our own culture's patterns as the obvious default options, only to be surprised that these familiar tendencies actually may be quite rare in other cultures.

The *cross-cultural perspective* on development focuses on two main issues. First, how do cultural variations influence patterns of development? Research addressing this question has become increasingly sophisticated in recent years, demonstrating how development in such diverse areas as moral reasoning, folk biology (intuitive patterns of reasoning about the living world), and religious beliefs differ between cultures. The most insightful approaches have developed models in which specific aspects of cultures, such as cultural values or norms, are thought to have distinct psychological outcomes. For example, some cross-cultural researchers have argued that growing up in a collectivist culture, where the group is considered more important than the individual, results in different patterns of reasoning than growing up in a more individualist culture (Nisbett et al., 2001).

The cross-cultural perspective's second main concern is with consistency across cultures: What aspects of behavior or mind, if any, develop in the same way throughout the world? Whereas some kinds of psychological development differ systematically across cultures, others show little variation and reflect universal patterns of psychological development. For example, the way children come to learn about rules of etiquette or religious practices may vary dramatically as a function of culture, but the way they learn to walk or to perceive visual depth develops in much the same way regardless of culture. Some of the more interesting and controversial questions within cross-cultural perspectives involve how culture contributes to the development of morality, spatial abilities, and interpretations of events.

Neuroscience Perspectives

Neuroscience perspectives focus primarily on the neurobiological systems that give rise to psychological development. One way to do this is to consider the maturation of the brain. For example, between birth and age 2, extensive changes occur in brain size and physiology, raising questions about how those changes relate to the psychological developments taking place during these years. Thus, the hippocampus, a brain structure centrally involved in forming new memories, was once thought to be fully mature late in infancy—so that older infants would likely form memories in similar ways to older children and adults. However, more recent work suggests that between birth and 3 years, hippocampal structure changes substantially at the neural level, and these changes may help explain how memory abilities change in the first 3 years of life (Ghetti et al., 2010). Because of this neuroanatomical research, psychological views of early memory are changing. In recent years, neuroscience researchers have claimed similar linkages between specific aspects of brain development and the emer-

gence of various capacities, such as learning language, delaying gratification, searching for hidden objects, and perceiving faces. As the methods of measuring the developing brain's structures and patterns of activity become more refined, it will be possible to study how brain growth influences psychological development in greater detail (see Figure 1.16).

A second way the neuroscience perspective informs the field of psychological development has to do with how the nervous system changes as a result of experience. Experience modifies the brain in many different species, and it is essential to keep in mind that the causal relationships between changes in the brain and psychological development run in both directions: brain development can cause psychological changes, and experiences—including their psychological components—can also change the brain. For example, as mentioned earlier, experience with visual information that reaches both eyes simultaneously is essential to the development of normal binocular vision, raising the question of how early visual experiences cause changes to individual brain cells.

Behaviorist Perspectives

In the history of psychology, the great challenge of studying internal events and mental states in a scientific, unambiguous way has fueled some major disputes. In the last few decades, some researchers have developed innovative and increasingly precise techniques for inferring mental states. Others, however, find it more prudent to focus on observable behaviors and how they are shaped by external factors over the course of development. Proponents of this behavior-focused approach favor *behaviorist perspectives*, which have a long history in North American psychology (Watson, 1913). As we will see in Chapter 4, behaviorists developed particular methods that enabled researchers and animal trainers to shape behaviors through carefully controlled patterns of reinforcement (Skinner, 1938). Despite severe limitations to behaviorism that emerged in the 1960s, some of its techniques for modifying behavior are still commonly used with both humans and nonhuman animals. A behaviorist perspective can be helpful in some clinical situations, as in modifying the behavior of an aggressive child who is hurting others in the classroom. Because the child's aggression may arise from several factors that are difficult to tease apart, a clinical psychologist might focus initially on trying to change the child's behavior through positive, and possibly negative, reinforcements (see Figure 1.17). Behaviorist perspectives can have severe limitations when they deliberately ignore all information about mental states and processes, but by emphasizing relationships between changes in the environment and changes in behavior, they can bring into sharp focus aspects of psychological development that might otherwise be neglected.

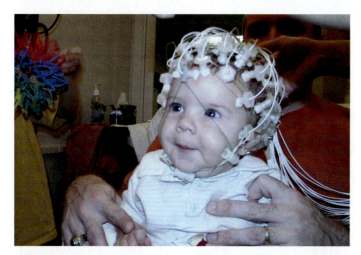

FIGURE 1.16 Neuroscience perspectives. This infant is hooked up to an EEG (electroencephalogram). Neuroscience perspectives on psychological development ask how biological changes in the brain (here measured as electrical waves picked up on the head's surface) relate to psychological changes over the course of development.

FIGURE 1.17 **Behaviorist perspectives.** Behaviorist perspectives on development ask how various external reinforcements, such as rewards and punishments, can shape a child's behavior. Here, stickers seem to be a strong reward for a recent behavior.

FIGURE 1.18 **Psychoanalytic perspectives.** Psychoanalytic perspectives often ask how an emotionally powerful early experience, such as toilet training, might relate to later personality development.

Psychoanalytic Perspectives

In contrast to behaviorism, *psychoanalytic perspectives* focus on understanding internal mental states and processes. Psychoanalytic perspectives, which originated from Sigmund Freud's psychoanalytic theory, cover several different ways of talking about mental life, but they tend to share a few key features. Their proponents see the mind as having distinct components that exert different kinds of influences on behavior. Among these components, they emphasize the power of the unconscious—thoughts and emotions occurring outside awareness—to affect behavior. They also view many kinds of psychological problems as a result of conflicts between different components of the mind, such as between conscious and unconscious desires.

Psychoanalytic views of development tend to see early childhood experiences as having important and lasting influences later in life (see Figure 1.18). Sometimes those early experiences are thought to set up internal conflicts or provoke strong emotional reactions that can stay unresolved and outside of awareness until a skilled therapist unearths them. Most psychoanalytic perspectives also view development as a series of stages, thereby emphasizing patterns of apparent qualitative change. The process of moving through those stages could also give rise to unresolved internal conflicts. In this view, if a child fails to make a complete transition from one developmental stage to the next, he can remain partially "trapped" in a psychological stage that conflicts with other, more mature aspects of himself.

Many aspects of psychoanalytic perspectives have been criticized in recent years, including psychoanalytic accounts of infants' attachments to their parents, the development of moral beliefs and behaviors, and the nature of toilet training, among many others. These challenges often seek to refute specific psychoanalytic proposals, very often those of Freud himself, which seem to make incorrect predictions about parent-child relations or to propose developmental psychological processes for which there is no evidence. It can therefore be tempting to dismiss all psychoanalytic perspectives as quaint historical curiosities. Yet, in a broad sense, these perspectives highlight several important aspects of psychological development that are still of great interest, such as the influence of processes outside of consciousness, the role of early experiences, the idea that the mind develops distinct components with different characteristics, and the presence of developmental stages.

Cognitive Science Perspectives

Late in the twentieth century, the *cognitive science perspective* on studying the mind emerged in universities and research centers. This approach to developmental psychology draws on methods and models from several disciplines—psychology, computer science, philosophy, neuroscience, and linguistics—to ask how specific skills or kinds of knowledge emerge and change. These perspectives involve more than just embracing different fields' approaches, however. In particular, cognitive science perspectives focus on questions about how our ways of representing and using information

Measuring Infants' Brain Function: Near-Infrared Spectroscopy (NIRS)

Across fields of psychology, researchers are studying brain activity to shed light on the processes underlying thought and action. One commonly used set of techniques, called functional neuroimaging, involves taking precise measurements of neuronal activity and representing them as images that show different levels of activation in specific brain regions. In studies of older children or adults, a technique known as functional magnetic resonance imaging (fMRI) has become the dominant method of brain imaging. This method takes advantage of the finding that when neurons in a specific area of the brain are active, the amount of oxygenated blood flowing to that area increases. Thus, fMRI scanners work on the principle that at a molecular level, oxygenated blood reacts differently in a magnetic field than deoxygenated blood. By measuring this difference in the brain of a volunteer while he performs a particular mental task, researchers are able to see which brain areas receive greater blood flow—and to infer that those areas are the most active. This kind of neuroimaging can capture detailed images of activity in particular brain areas, but it requires that the participant be very still inside a scanner, usually for 15 minutes or longer. During the scan, the machine's powerful magnets also cause sudden, loud pulsing noises. For these reasons, the technique is difficult to use with young infants.

Recently, a new silent brain-scanning technique known as near-infrared spectroscopy (NIRS) has been developed that can tolerate substantial head movements without compromising the resulting images, and it seems to be safe for use with infants (see Figure 1.19). NIRS involves shining a low-energy band of near-infrared light through the infant's scalp and skull and measuring the infrared light that is reflected back. Based on the reflection patterns, researchers can determine blood oxygenation levels in different areas of the brain (Aslin & Mehler, 2005; Hoshi, 2007; Meek, 2002; Sakatani et al., 1999; Villringer & Chance, 1997). Thus, like fMRI, NIRS is a way of measuring which brain regions are more active based on the increased flow of oxygenated blood to those areas. Using precise sensors, these measurements can be taken with relatively low levels of infrared light, comparable to a few minutes of bright sunlight. This technique offers an important new way of addressing

critical questions about early changes in brain functions and psychological processes (Minagawa-Kawai et al., 2011; Wilcox et al., 2005).

One interesting use of NIRS has been to explore whether infants' brains have regions specialized for processing numbers long before the child can speak. Researchers monitored infants' brain activity with NIRS as the infants repeatedly viewed groups of objects. Most of these groupings had 16 items, but occasionally the infants saw an "oddball" array with a different number. Intriguingly, 6-month-olds reliably showed increased activation of a particular region of the brain's right hemisphere when a deviant number appeared in the display (Hyde et al., 2010). Further research will be needed to determine whether this pattern of results is specific to observing a change in number. By helping researchers to address questions like this and to make inferences about the mental capacities of preverbal infants, NIRS is likely to be an especially useful tool for studying early brain development.

FIGURE 1.19 Near-infrared spectroscopy (NIRS) and brain activity. This infant's brain activity is being measured with NIRS. Low-energy near-infrared pulses of light are transmitted through the scalp and skull onto brain regions, then reflected back onto sensors near the light transmission points. This procedure, which is as harmless as a few minutes of bright sunlight, allows researchers to measure blood flow changes in various parts of the infant's brain.

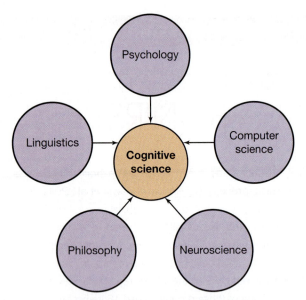

FIGURE 1.20 Cognitive science perspectives. Cognitive science perspectives often ask about how people represent and use information. Cognitive scientists draw on the theories and methods of several disciplines to see how each one offers unique insights into common questions.

change over the course of development (see Figure 1.20). To fully address these questions, they seek to integrate many ways of studying information processing, including formal computation (computer science), biological bases (neuroscience), logical consistency (philosophy), expression in language (linguistics), and the way these different types of information processing take place in a real organism in real time (psychology).

In practice, a cognitive science researcher may focus within one discipline, but will nonetheless consider how the progress in other relevant disciplines informs her work. For example, a cognitive scientist interested in how language is acquired might conduct experiments on language acquisition in children (psychology), but when designing experiments, she might also look at formal descriptions of language capacity (linguistics), conceptual analyses of the relationship between language and thought (philosophy), models of language acquisition in computer systems (computer science), and relations between brain development and language development (neuroscience). In the study of development, questions about the origins of thought and knowledge and about the ways that skills and abilities change over time naturally lead to considerations of what kinds of information processing the developing organism is doing.

We will frequently consider the cognitive science approach in this book—not only in areas of development traditionally associated with it, such as visual perception and logical reasoning, but also in areas such as social and emotional development. In almost all areas of psychology, it is useful to consider how people represent and use relevant information.

Studying Psychological Development

Not surprisingly, it takes a wide range of approaches to study topics as diverse as a newborn infant's ability to see color and an adolescent's ways of relating to her peers. Throughout this book, we will encounter various methods of investigating particular questions about development. At the outset, it is useful to survey the range of research techniques that we'll encounter to provide a methodological road map and to explain some key terms.

Observational Studies

The oldest, and seemingly simplest, method of research is the **observational study**, in which children are simply observed in a natural setting and their behaviors are carefully recorded (see Figure 1.21). These records may take the form of trained observers' written notes or collections of audio or video recordings. But this method is not always as simple as it sounds. Suppose you are interested in researching how children's personalities develop between ages 3 and 5. Perhaps you plan to observe a classroom of 20 preschoolers to test some ideas about how the traits of shyness, aggression, and leadership develop and how they relate to the child's preschool experiences. (For example, shy children may seek out different environments within the classroom than extroverted children.) What observational data would you collect? You could potentially measure thousands of different variables: the number of seconds between each conversation for each child, the direction and duration of each eye gaze, a vast array of facial expressions or body postures, the objects a child

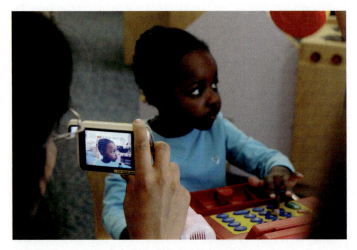

FIGURE 1.21 Observational studies. Videos of children in everyday settings offer rich opportunities for data collection, but coding and interpreting the footage also create challenges.

holds, the size of the group a child is in, each child's proximity to the teacher, and so on.

To focus on their research questions and keep from being overwhelmed by information, observational researchers must decide which variables to measure among a vast set of possibilities and how frequently to measure them. Suppose, for example, that a theory of emerging friendships suggests that shy children take longer to establish friendships than outgoing children because the shy children make less eye contact with peers whom they have just met. A researcher might measure durations of eye contact every 5 minutes after some shy children and some outgoing children first meet other new children. Later on, when analyzing the data, the researcher would see whether the amount of early eye contact was systematically related to later measurements of the time required for a friendship to develop. In addition, the observational setting itself may be critical. Perhaps a key aspect of personality must be examined across several situations to be understood. Thus, the researcher must decide whether to observe the children in the preschool classroom, in the home (at a particular time or day of the week), or in a less familiar setting, such as a new mall. Observational studies require a specific model or theory to help guide these decisions, specifying which variables should be of interest and why.

New observational technologies open exciting possibilities for observational research, but these developments may also muddy the research issues at stake. When tape recorders became commonplace, they were soon used in many studies. Video recording represented the next major change, and soon researchers were collecting thousands of hours of videos of children in a wide range of situations. Today, the decreasing cost of digital video and increasing computational abilities to automatically search video frames will likely contribute in important ways to developmental research. Another exciting technological innovation allows some aspects of video scenes to be automatically coded based on researchers' specifications, making it quicker and easier to analyze very large data sets of children's behaviors in natural settings (Roy et al., 2009). But these technologies are valuable only when researchers use them carefully and strategically to zero in on critical variables. Researchers must decide which recorded behaviors to observe and how to categorize and quantify them.

Observational studies play an indispensable role in developmental research despite their limitations. In many situations, they allow researchers to assess children's behavior under natural, normal circumstances—without the distortions caused by bringing children into a lab to study their behavior under carefully controlled conditions. In addition, observational studies allow for the possibility of unexpected discoveries outside the immediate research question. Such surprises are a common source of inspiration in scientific research, and observational studies can suggest many new possibilities to pursue.

One intrinsic limitation to observational studies is that they uncover correlational patterns, not causal ones. This limitation is important to keep in mind because the goal of most scientific research is to identify causal relationships. For example, if a researcher wants to know whether children play more aggressively after watching violent cartoons, she is asking whether the cartoon violence somehow *causes* the kids to treat each other more aggressively. An observational study might show a strong correlation between these behaviors, such that children who watch more violent shows also favor more aggressive play. But these observations would not help the researcher determine whether one of these behaviors caused the other. It might be true that watching violent cartoons makes children more likely to play rough, but the correlation could also be driven by a different causal relationship. One possibility is that children who are aggressive choose to watch more violent cartoons. In that case, being aggressive would cause the television watching, rather than the other way around. Another possibility is that a third variable, such as lack of parental control, could cause children to both behave aggressively and watch more violent television. In this case, aggression and viewing violent TV could be closely correlated, even without being directly linked.

Some scientists use complex statistical techniques to try to infer causality from observational data (MacKinnon, 2006). While such approaches can strengthen a particular causal interpretation of the data, it remains difficult to rule out the possibility of other influences on the data (Pearl, 2010). We will see, in contrast, that well-designed experimental studies can clearly demonstrate specific causal relations. This is just one example of the tradeoffs involved in choosing between research methods. Observational studies may often yield exciting new ideas, but they typically do not produce firm conclusions about cause and effect.

> **Q:** What are some strengths of observational studies?

Experimental Studies

To answer developmental questions about cause and effect—such as whether watching violent cartoons *causes* aggressive behavior or whether participating in after-school programs *causes* better academic performance—researchers often design an **experimental study**. The goal of these studies is to manipulate a single variable while holding all other aspects of the experimental situation constant. By changing only one variable at a time in the course of an experiment, researchers are better able to pinpoint exactly which change caused any differences they observe in the experiment's outcome.

To return to our earlier example, if a researcher wanted to determine whether watching violent cartoons *causes* aggressive behavior, she might recruit two groups of children for a study in which she would manipulate the amount of time the children spent watching violent cartoons. She would be careful to randomly assign children to each group to ensure there were no initial differences between the groups. If the children who watched the cartoons for many more hours subsequently showed an increase in aggression while the other children did not, this would support the claim that watching violent television can cause children to behave more aggressively.

In most developmental psychology experiments, a researcher presents some sort of stimulus or event to a participant (usually a child or nonhuman animal) and then measures the participant's pattern of behavior. It is common to speak of the **independent variable**, which is the variable manipulated by the experimenter, and the **dependent variable**, which is the variable being measured to see whether or how it changed in response to manipulation of the independent variable. For example, in an experiment designed to test children's verbal memory, you might be interested in finding out how the child's age (the independent variable) affects the percentage of words from a list the child can recall correctly (the dependent variable). In this scenario, age would be the independent variable because you are interested in the way differences in age affect another measure (memory). In this case, you would "manipulate" age by presenting the memory task to children of different age groups. To be sure that any differences in performance were due to the children's ages and not to some other aspect of the testing situation, it would be crucial to carefully control, or hold constant, all other variables. Thus, you would want to make sure that all the children were tested in equally quiet environments that were free of distractions, and at the same time of day so that they would be equally alert. Finally, you would want to ensure that all the children were similar to each other in terms of socioeconomic status, cultural background, and other possible differences and that they were drawn from the same broader group, or population, that you wish to study, such as middle-class elementary school students.

One advantage of experiments is that they allow researchers to examine highly specific effects of stimuli and events on participants. For example, suppose a researcher wanted to know if kindergartners were able to use transitive reasoning—that is, if stick A is longer than stick B, and if stick B is longer than stick C, do kindergartners realize that stick A must be longer than stick C? It is unlikely that kindergartners do much observable transitive reasoning in their daily lives. Some aspects of everyday situations may involve this kind of thought, but all the complexity and variety of these real-life

problems would make it impossible to tell for sure whether a child is using transitive reasoning to solve them.

But when an experimenter poses carefully designed, age-appropriate questions that require transitive reasoning, he is able to assess the children's abilities more clearly. In the context of an experiment, the researcher could present transitive reasoning problems of various difficulty that deal with some topics familiar to kindergartners (such as comparing the heights of children) and some topics that are unfamiliar to them (such as comparing the costs of hotel rooms). Those systematic manipulations would help the researcher determine whether young children failed at certain transitive reasoning tasks primarily because of a difficulty with this type of reasoning or whether their failures were actually due to other factors (such as difficulty remembering all the components of the problems or unfamiliarity with the material used in the problems).

Of course, experimental approaches also have their limitations. Perhaps the biggest challenge is **ecological validity**—whether a study faithfully captures a pattern of behavior that would occur in the normal circumstances of childhood. An experiment that lacks ecological validity may be elegantly designed and carefully controlled, but its results may be irrelevant to the real world. To take an extreme case, imagine that you wanted to experimentally examine the development of sharing in children between the ages of 5 and 10. In your experiment, a group of children are brought to the lab—where digital cameras and note-taking researchers will record how often they share—and put in pairs. One child in each pair is shown a basket of several types of candy and asked to point out her favorite. An assistant then gives many pieces of that same candy to the other child in the pair, who is sitting across the table. As the cameras record and the experimenters take notes, the children with candy almost always share it with the other child, regardless of their age. You could hastily conclude that there are no developmental changes in sharing between ages 5 and 10, but there would be clear problems with this conclusion. Surrounded by adult observers and confronted with a blatantly unfair distribution of candy, almost any child would be compelled to share. In a more natural setting, children might behave very differently, depending on their age. Although the problems are clear in this example, similar issues lurk in most experimental studies. The more a study departs from everyday situations, the more it risks failing to measure variables of real interest. Yet, such departures from real-life circumstances can also confer great advantages by allowing researchers to elicit specific behaviors and closely control their measurements.

More broadly, experimental research requires certain idealizations from real-world settings (Strevens, 2009). All scientists try to isolate the phenomena they study—which is why physicists think about "frictionless" inclined planes and "ideal" gases and biologists think about hypothetical,

What Kinds of Experimental Research Are Justified?

Experimental techniques are invaluable in developmental research, but unlike observational studies, experiments bring children and infants into environments they would not otherwise encounter. How do researchers justify manipulating children's experience?

Clearly, not all experiments are justified. Few would approve of an experiment that caused children to feel intense shame and discomfort in order to study their coping strategies. It strikes us as simply wrong to purposely upset children or make them uncomfortable, regardless of the value of the scientific insights that such an experiment might yield. But what about a more benign experiment in which an infant stares at a stimulus for 10 minutes until he is bored? And is it acceptable to pay a 6-year-old a large sum of money to participate in an extremely tedious task? Researchers must carefully consider the risks and benefits for participants in their studies—especially when working with children and infants, since they are much less able to advocate for themselves than are most adults. The researcher's goal, as in all research on humans, is to minimize any risks to participants and to directly benefit both society at large and the participants themselves to the greatest extent possible.

In most countries with large-scale human research programs, every university, hospital, or other institution that undertakes such research is legally required to have an institutional review board, commonly called an IRB. An IRB typically consists of researchers from a wide range of fields who are engaged in studies of humans, and it often also includes members of the community outside the research institution. On behalf of the research institution, IRB members scrutinize all research proposals that involve human subjects to ensure that the planned studies do not pose unreasonable or unnecessary risks for those who participate.

Ideally, researchers should always analyze the costs and benefits of their own studies and strive to ensure that their benefits outweigh their potential risks. Risks to participants might range from discomfort in doing an experimental task to self-esteem problems if a child finds out that her peers outperformed her. On the other hand, participants can also benefit from taking part; in fact, some tasks might be intensely engaging for young participants. More broadly, a study's benefits to society include any information the research yields that furthers understanding of development, so as to better inform decisions about children's education, care, and welfare.

Another critical issue in the IRB's review, and one that is especially important in studies involving infants or children, is the participants' ability to consent to take part. Before they consent, potential participants should be told as much about the experimental procedures and goals as possible without compromising the research. The researcher must also be sure that all participants understand that they are free to discontinue the study at any time and are under no obligation to finish a session or a task. In the United States, a child under age 18 is not considered fully capable of consenting to participate in research. Along with the child's own consent, a parent or legal guardian must give written consent as well. In addition, researchers who work with children must watch them carefully throughout the experiment for any signs that they would like to discontinue the study, and their wishes must be honored. During and after a study, researchers typically are also obligated to protect participants' privacy, and the records are usually coded to make sure no one reading about the research can identify the participants.

Because experiments involve studying people outside of normal daily circumstances, they often raise the clearest questions about potential risks, but concerns about costs and benefits to participants are also relevant to observational studies. Many observational studies risk intruding in children's lives, as the observers may be in plain view, unintentionally influencing the children just by being present. Even so, most researchers assume that children who have (with parental approval) consented to participate will fairly quickly become accustomed to being observed and will behave normally. Concerns about confidentiality are as important in observational studies as they are in experimental studies—maybe more so, since the natural behavior being observed may be more revealing of the child's true nature. A child who cheats in a contrived laboratory card game may not be nearly as stigmatized as one observed cheating in the classroom. For all these reasons, observational studies usually require participants' consent, but researchers may opt not to reveal the focus of their research until after the observation is complete to avoid influencing children's behavior.

Many important research questions in developmental psychology, such as how children deal with failure, are particularly difficult to study because of ethical concerns. Children are an especially vulnerable group, so it is only reasonable that developmental research should be conducted extremely carefully.

simplified ecological systems. Likewise, psychologists sometimes focus on individuals without accounting for all the social influences that affect each person. But does the effect of isolation from a normal, social context undermine conclusions about the individual? This question—how much are you influencing the processes you're researching just by isolating them?—is important to keep in mind for all psychological research, but many contend that it is especially relevant to questions of development.

There are certainly tradeoffs between focusing on the developing organism outside the context in which development takes place, as experiments typically do, and accounting for the developing child's many complex interactions with other people and the broader culture. Developmental researchers think carefully when designing their studies about which emphasis is best for the question they are addressing. In some cases, often in the initial stages of exploring a topic, observational studies may be more appropriate. In other cases, such as pinning down cause-and-effect relationships more precisely, experimental designs may provide more insight. Experimental researchers therefore constantly attempt to simplify the situations that they study in ways that allow them to understand what is going on without distorting the circumstances too much from everyday experiences. Psychologists continue to wrestle with questions about which aspects of psychological development can be studied with relatively little attention to such contextual issues and which ones are inextricably linked to those issues.

> **Q:** What are some of the tradeoffs between naturalistic-observational methods and experimental methods when asking research questions about psychological development?

Longitudinal Approaches

In choosing between observational and experimental studies, all research psychologists must consider their available resources, their research questions, and the advantages and drawbacks of different types of study. When developmental researchers are interested in how children change over time, they typically must decide between two different approaches to studying change over time—namely, longitudinal and cross-sectional approaches. Each of these approaches has its own strengths and weaknesses, and each can be used in designing either an observational or an experimental study.

One appealing way to learn about a developmental pattern is to study a single group of children repeatedly, over a time period that includes the aspects of development you wish to research. This method of measuring the same children's abilities or behavior on a regular basis over time is known as a **longitudinal approach**. For example, you might want to study how children come to understand the concept of fractions by looking at how their ability to solve various fraction-based math problems changes from ages 5 to 15. Taking a longitudinal approach to this study would involve tracking the progress of the same group of children over this 10-year period, perhaps assessing each child's understanding of fractions at the beginning of every school year (see Figure 1.22A).

Longitudinal approaches are well suited to uncovering developmental differences between individuals. By taking repeated measures of each individual child over time, the researcher essentially documents each participant's specific developmental trajectory—which can then be compared with those of other participants. Thus, if some children first understand fractions by visualizing sections of a figure, while others begin to learn about them by following steps in a calculation, a longitudinal study might reveal how these different patterns unfold. Longitudinal studies can also help researchers ensure that many of the variables that could influence their results are held constant. There is no need to worry about whether separate groups of participants are truly comparable, since the same set of participants is studied over the course of developmental change; whatever is distinctive about a child at one age will tend to remain distinctive at later ages. Finally, longitudinal studies allow a special kind of research known as **microgenetic analysis**, in which the researchers assess participants every few days or weeks rather than every few years (Cheshire et al., 2007; Siegler, 1995). This approach documents the details of developmental transitions at a scale much closer to real-time change in skill or cognitive structure. For example, one might do a microgenetic analysis of a child overcoming an error in mathematical calculation.

Longitudinal studies also have several drawbacks. A major limitation is that they often require an enormous commitment of time and expense. Some studies can take 15 to 20 years to complete. If, for example, you wanted to test a theory about whether the strength of infants' bonds with their mothers predicted their romantic relationship styles as adults, you would have to wait for the infants to reach young adulthood. Such long time frames cause additional problems beyond the research team's extended commitment to a single study. Because of the need to maintain consistency throughout the study, a researcher can get stuck asking participants the same questions in the same way for many years, even if advances in the field suggest new, preferable approaches. Likewise, in long-term longitudinal studies, researchers run the risk that their measures may seem

A

B

FIGURE 1.22 Longitudinal versus cross-sectional approaches. (A) In a longitudinal study, the same group of people is studied at various time intervals. **(B)** In a cross-sectional study, a different group of people is studied at each age of interest to the researchers.

outdated or flawed by the time the study is over. Retaining a large enough group of participants over time is also challenging, as families move or no longer want to participate.

Finally, a subtle problem can confound the more experimental longitudinal studies. Suppose you assessed understanding of fractions by repeatedly presenting children with a series of problems to answer. If you do this every 6 months for 6 years, the experimental assessments themselves can become a form of training that affects how the participants' understanding of fractions develops. In this case, you would be studying the *effects of participating in the experiment* rather than the natural course of development. For that reason, experimental longitudinal studies are often used to study the effects of training on the development of particular skills or capacities.

Q: What are some drawbacks of longitudinal studies?

Cross-Sectional Approaches

A study that examines developmental change by comparing groups of children at different ages is known as a **cross-sectional approach** (Figure 1.22B). To use this approach to study how children learn fractions, you might select six groups of 20 children each, taking a group of kindergartners, a group of second-graders, and so on, through a group of tenth-graders, and then test each group's abilities to solve problems using fractions. With sufficient research staff, the entire study could be conducted in just a few weeks, rather than the 10 years that a longitudinal design would require. The cross-sectional approach provides another advantage when it comes

to experimental studies. Unlike the longitudinal approach, which requires the same participants to repeat the experimental tasks at different ages, the cross-sectional approach involves studying a different group of children in each age group. As a result, each child is assessed only once, and there is no need to worry about the experimental tasks accidentally becoming a form of training. Most of the experimental studies discussed in the chapters that follow will be cross-sectional.

The largest drawback of cross-sectional studies concerns their inability to follow specific individuals' development over time, which makes them much less sensitive than longitudinal studies to individual differences in developmental paths. For that reason, psychologists who are interested in how individual differences develop over time, such as how personality traits emerge, tend to use longitudinal approaches. Nonetheless, cross-sectional studies can shed light on other kinds of individual differences, such as how a behavior manifests at particular points in development. For example, a researcher might be interested in how shy children cope with large groups at the ages of 5, 10, and 15. A cross-sectional observational study could enroll 20 shy children at each of these ages and then observe the children's interactions within large groups to see how the behaviors of each age group differed. By comparing the coping methods of the 5-year-olds, the 10-year-olds, and the 15-year-olds, the researchers could learn how those behaviors varied with age.

Aside from these specific strengths and weaknesses, a different sort of factor related to broad historical patterns can also influence whether a researcher uses a cross-sectional or longitudinal design. If the changes within a culture over time significantly alter children's experiences, research that compares children of different ages can be subject to **cohort effects**, in which a given age group (or cohort) might differ in important ways from people in the same culture who are somewhat older or younger. Suppose you were interested in how and when children first become aware of their peers' interests and activities. If you simply used a cross-sectional design to examine four different groups of children, in grades 4, 6, 8, and 10, you would likely get distorted results. With the rapid rise of online social networks, today's fourth-graders probably know more details about the daily activities of distant acquaintances than their older siblings did at the same age. This cohort effect might suggest another approach and a slightly different research question—perhaps a longitudinal study of how the increasing availability of social networking sites influences what children know about their peers over the course of childhood and adolescence.

> **Q:** What are some drawbacks of cross-sectional studies?

Converging Methods

Developmental psychologists, like other psychologists, often use several different ways to explore a particular problem. As we have seen, each method has its own advantages and limitations. As researchers apply more methods to the same problem, the different approaches tend to complement each other in ways that create a more accurate overall picture. This process is known as using **converging methods**. As researchers use various approaches to probe a phenomenon from different vantage points, the results of the different types of studies tend to converge on a more accurate, objective answer than any single method could produce. For example, we might observe that certain forms of parent-child interactions are correlated with the children having earlier autobiographical memories when they grow up. But to be more confident that the interaction is having a causal effect on earliest memories, we might also conduct an experimental study in which we taught randomly assigned parents to interact in a particular way with their young children and then later asked those children if they had earlier memories than those of the children in a control group whose parents had not been taught to interact in this particular way. Similarly, if we perform a cross-sectional study of children between the ages of 2 and 7 who are sampled 1 year apart and observe that the correlation emerges at around age 7, we might then do a longitudinal study to see how early parent training has to occur to have a maximal effect. Consider, therefore, the ways in which the advantages and disadvantages of observational and experimental studies and longitudinal and cross-sectional approaches overlap. Table 1.1 illustrates the main strengths and weaknesses of each and how they intersect in different types of studies. These tradeoffs illustrate the importance of using converging methods.

Throughout this book, we will see how converging methods can give rise to new insights into specific developmental questions. For example, researchers who study infants' understanding of physical objects use a number of different methods to figure out what is happening in babies' minds. Some measure how infants react when their expectations are violated; others examine infants' reaching patterns in response to different objects; and still others study the details of infants' eye movements as they examine an object or event. When these different methods all tend to tell the same story, their separate measures tend to support one another. On the other hand, when various methods tell very different stories, this raises important questions for researchers about how to interpret each measure.

> **Q:** What is the value of using converging methods?

Designing a Sound Study

Beyond the tradeoffs involved in different types of developmental studies, several concerns about research methods apply to almost all psychological studies. These concerns are relevant regardless of whether the research participants are adults or children. At the most general level, researchers need to make sure their findings are as *reliable*, *valid*, and *replicable* as possible.

Reliability and Validity The issue of **reliability** refers to whether researchers would obtain consistent results if they or others repeated the research study in the future using the same types of participants. More precisely, researchers often talk about the reliability of a specific way of measuring behavior, such as a test or an experimental task, rather than the study as a whole. A highly reliable measure will consistently yield the same pattern of results, as long as investigators have controlled for other possible influences. Such a measure is analogous to a tool that works the same way every time rather than working only sometimes.

Suppose researchers are testing a theory that young children remember events they see in videos more accurately than events described in words. The researchers develop a way of testing both kinds of memory, and they design a study using this memory test at several different ages. The measure has reliability problems if it yields different results when repeatedly used with children in the same age group who have the same demographic characteristics.

There are two forms of reliability: test-retest reliability and interrater reliability. *Test-retest reliability* is an indica-

		Longitudinal Approaches	Cross-Sectional Approaches
		+ Document individuals' developmental transitions. − Participants may drop out as study progresses.	+ Easier to ensure that the same number of participants take part at all ages. − Do not track individuals' developmental trajectories.
Observational Studies	+ Rich data may allow for unanticipated insights. − Support correlational arguments but cannot determine causal relationships. − Behaviors of interest may not appear without experimenter intervention.	+ May uncover long-term patterns of change in individuals. − Require a long time commitment from research staff.	+ Reveal distinctive patterns for each age group. − Questions about individual differences are more difficult to address.
Experimental Studies	+ Allow exploration of cause-and-effect relationships. + Researchers can design focused assessments of specific variables. − Create possibilities of ecologically invalid measures.	+ Good for studying long-term effects of training. − Repeated assessments may become an unwanted form of training.	+ Enable quick assessment of hypothesized differences between age groups. − May miss key transitions as well as individual developmental patterns.

TABLE 1.1 Tradeoffs of different developmental research methods. The advantages (+) and disadvantages (−) of each kind of study and each kind of approach are shown here, as well as the advantages (+) and disadvantages (−) of using converging methods—longitudinal observational studies, cross-sectional observational studies, longitudinal experimental studies, and cross-sectional experimental studies.

tion of how consistently a measure yields the same result when it is used by the same researcher. If a given researcher finds large variability in results when repeatedly measuring the quality of children's memories, that would be a case of low test-retest reliability. *Interrater reliability* describes how consistently two different researchers get the same results when they use the same measure with the same child. To have high interrater reliability on a test of children's memories of videos and verbal descriptions, it would be important for the test to provide scoring guidelines describing how much detail is required to consider a child's recall fully "accurate." Otherwise, individual researchers could make different judgments of what constitutes an "accurate" memory. In a well-designed study, the measures should show both test-retest reliability and interrater reliability.

Reliability is a necessary part of research in developmental psychology, but reliability alone is not enough to conclude that research findings are sound. Even highly reliable measurements can be misleading if it turns out that you are not really measuring what you intended to measure. The criterion of **validity** refers to whether measurements accurately reflect what a researcher means to study. Returning to the example that compared visual and verbal memory, suppose the researcher develops a set of measures showing very high test-retest and interrater reliability. Thus, different researchers using these methods to test the accuracy

of children's verbal and visual memories could easily get consistent results, which would also closely resemble the results obtained from using the same methods with new groups of similar children. Nonetheless, these highly reliable measures may be assessing something very different from what the investigators intended to measure—if the measures themselves are flawed. That is, children's memory scores may not really reflect their ability to recall the videos and verbal descriptions. Perhaps the younger children are more easily distracted, which causes them to underperform unless they are tested in an especially quiet, focused setting. In this case, this particular memory measure would consistently suggest that young children have poorer memories than they actually do. The study would have reliability, but it would not be valid for the skill that the researchers intended to measure.

Like reliability, validity comes in different forms: internal validity and external validity. *Internal validity* is especially relevant to experimental studies. It concerns whether the changes observed in the dependent variable are really due to the experimenter's manipulation of the independent variable or whether the changes are caused by other extraneous influences. If, for example, a young child performed poorly on a memory test because she was distracted (rather than due to an inability to remember), the study would lack internal validity. *External validity* refers to whether the research findings are truly generalizable, or broadly relevant, to a wide range of situations. Perhaps children from particular backgrounds or cultures are more accustomed to remembering events seen on video and therefore are better able to recall them. If so, this would represent a limit on the study's external validity. Issues related to validity can be subtle and complex, but they are extremely important to consider.

We will see that the most compelling and exciting studies are those that carefully consider both internal and external validity while also achieving high reliability. Studies with reliable and valid measures also tend to have high **replicability**, which is simply the ability for others to easily reproduce the study and find the same results. Replicability is ultimately the hallmark of all good studies. Even if a study uncovers an interesting developmental phenomenon, if its measures are too difficult or intricate for most researchers to use, the usefulness of the research might be quite limited. Scientists want their pioneering studies to be easily replicated in other laboratories so that the findings can serve as a solid foundation for follow-up studies.

> **Q:** How can a study have high reliability but low validity?

Within-Subjects and Between-Subjects Designs In designing a developmental study, researchers must make one last major decision: whether to assess all children in a study in the same way or whether to divide children into groups and assess each group in a different way. In studies that use a **within-subjects design**, each child participates in all experimental conditions, and therefore all children are assessed in the same manner. This design allows researchers to compare the same subjects' responses to each experimental condition. For example, suppose you wanted to know whether children are more likely to believe a new piece of surprising information when they hear it from an adult or when it comes from a peer. In a within-subjects design, you might show each child in the study two videos: one in which a child of their same age describes a remarkable fact (for example, "Did you know that kangaroos can't walk backward?") and another in which an adult relays another equally remarkable fact (for example, "Did you know that some fish can live for more than 200 years?"). Each child would then be asked to rate the likelihood that each piece of information was true, perhaps on a 5-point scale. In contrast to this setup, a **between-subjects design** would involve assessing a different group of children in each experimental condition. You might divide the children into two equivalent groups. One group would watch the video of the child and then rate its truthfulness, while the other group would do the same with the video of the adult.

Both kinds of designs involve tradeoffs that must be taken into account when choosing which one to use in a specific study. Within-subjects designs have the benefit of requiring fewer children, since each child takes part in all experimental conditions. On the other hand, between-subjects designs have the strong advantage of ruling out any unintentional effects of assessing each child more than once. For example, if children become more skeptical about unusual facts the more often they hear them, a within-subjects design might not be well suited to the study just described. The children might give a harsher judgment of whichever video they viewed second. (This effect can be partially controlled by showing half the children the video of the adult relaying the fact first, while the other half sees the video of the child relaying the fact first, but it would still be a concern.) In addition, being presented with the two different videos and asked to evaluate each one could subtly suggest to participants that they should rate the facts differently, even if they seem about equally believable. In designing a study, an experimenter needs to keep these kinds of concerns in mind. In the spirit of using converging methods, some investigators will examine a single research question using a series of studies that includes both within- and between-subjects designs in an attempt to benefit from the strengths of both.

In summary, developmental psychology uses a wide array of methods to highlight many aspects of how people's minds and their behavior change over time. Choosing the best methods for investigating a particular problem requires careful consideration, and throughout this book we'll see how these issues play out in many areas of developmental research. Moreover, when it comes to studying certain kinds of abilities, the specific methods that researchers choose can affect how capable children seem to be, creating controversies about how to interpret the measurements (Cohen & Cashon, 2003). Taken together, however, the wide variety of methods now available allows researchers to discover and verify fascinating developmental patterns that would have been impossible to study even a few decades earlier.

Conclusions

A full explanation of the child's developing mind easily rivals the complexity and beauty of the cellular machinery explored by molecular biologists or the origins of the universe investigated by astrophysicists. Developmental researchers strive to build coherent models and theories of psychological development and then test them in rigorous ways, using both experimental and observational studies. Together, these theories and research methods enhance our understanding of the growing and changing mind.

Some of psychology's most challenging and fascinating problems focus on development—and their answers promise deep insights into who we are. Questions about the nature of developmental change have fascinated laypeople and researchers alike for thousands of years. In the last few decades, developmental psychologists have begun to address these millennia-old questions in a much more focused manner, as new methods and techniques have given researchers clearer insights into what develops and how. Patterns in the development of perception, cognition, and social skills are among the most complex in the natural sciences, and the details of these processes are often breathtaking in their elegance and beauty. The study of developmental psychology becomes ever more fascinating as research continues to reveal richer interrelations between the theories and the evidence. Just like reading an intricate mystery novel or appreciating a beautiful piece of art, studying development helps us all appreciate the wonder of what it means to become fully human.

STUDY AND REVIEW

SUMMARY

Why Study Development?

- Developmental psychology is a complex, elegant, and intrinsically fascinating scientific study of how children's minds and behaviors grow over time.
- Studying development offers insights into psychological structures and processes in adults by describing how those processes originate and take shape.
- An understanding of psychological development is critically relevant to many decisions about social policy, ranging from changes to local elementary schools to questions concerning children's legal rights.

The Nature of Development

- In considering the nature of developmental change, we want to know whether a developmental change is stage-like or continuous and whether change occurs globally or in a more local manner.
- Nature and nurture always work together to shape development. In looking more closely at interactions between nature and nurture, we can consider which kinds of development are more heavily influenced by nature and which are more influenced by nurture.

Perspectives on Development

- The various perspectives employed by researchers in developmental psychology function much like different lenses on development: each one brings certain issues and questions into sharp focus and de-emphasizes or even ignores others.

- Empiricist and nativist perspectives propose different models of how the mind processes information once that information has passed through our sensory and perceptual systems. Empiricist views emphasize the idea that a general system for learning associations based on experience is present at birth. Nativist views emphasize the idea that various learning systems are present at birth and that each system acquires particular kinds of information more readily than others.
- Evolutionary and comparative perspectives start with the premise that many organisms other than humans confront similar challenges in development. These perspectives use cross-species comparisons, as well as long-term historical considerations, to ask about how and why humans develop as they do.
- Cross-cultural perspectives compare patterns of developmental change across several different cultures; they ask which aspects of development remain relatively consistent across cultures and which ones vary dramatically.
- Neuroscience perspectives ask how brain development guides or constrains psychological development.
- Behaviorist perspectives focus on observable behaviors and ask how they are shaped by reinforcement over the course of development.
- Psychoanalytic perspectives are concerned with internal states and processes and their influences on behavior. They also focus on early experiences and unresolved conflicts and their effects later in life.
- Cognitive science perspectives consider how developmental changes in the mind relate to ways of acquiring, representing, and using information. These perspectives draw on

several different disciplines, including psychology, linguistics, philosophy, computer science, and neuroscience.

Studying Psychological Development

- Developmental psychologists take advantage of a rich array of research methods, each of which has advantages and drawbacks. Collectively, these methods can be used to gain objective views of what develops and how.
- In observational studies, researchers track developmental patterns over time by documenting various aspects of behavior, often in a naturalistic setting. In experimental studies, researchers manipulate variables to see how those changes affect specific behaviors.
- Longitudinal and cross-sectional approaches are two ways of studying developmental change over time. Using a longitudinal approach involves studying the same children at repeated intervals over the course of their development. Using a cross-sectional approach involves studying separate groups of children at different ages—for example, a group of 7-year-olds, a group of 9-year-olds, and a group of 11-year-olds.
- Reliability measures the degree to which a pattern of results would be consistently found when the same assessments are done in the same way with similar participants.
- Validity refers to the extent to which a set of measures actually reflects what the researcher is interested in studying and the extent to which that measure will continue to reflect that phenomenon in other settings.
- Replicability refers to the ability for other researchers to reproduce a previously documented pattern of results when they perform the same study with similar participants.
- In between-subjects designs, researchers assign separate (but equivalent) groups of children to different experimental conditions to compare the effects of the different conditions. In within-subjects designs, researchers assign all children to the same set of tasks to compare individual participants' performance across the different tasks.

THOUGHT QUESTIONS

1. It has been argued that just as people need to take driving lessons before learning how to drive a car, future parents should be required to take courses in developmental psychology so that they might be better equipped to make decisions about raising their children. Discuss the appropriateness and feasibility of such a view.
2. Design a study to explore the effects of violent video games on children's behavior, using three distinct converging methods. Discuss the tradeoffs of each method and how, in the aggregate, they offer insights that go beyond the benefits of any one study.

KEY TERMS

between-subjects design (p. 30)

cohort effect (p. 27)

converging methods (p. 28)

cross-sectional approach (p. 27)

dependent variable (p. 24)

ecological validity (p. 24)

empiricism (p. 15)

ethology (p. 18)

experimental study (p. 23)

global change (p. 11)

independent variable (p. 24)

local change (p. 11)

longitudinal approach (p. 26)

microgenetic analysis (p. 26)

nativism (p. 15)

observational study (p. 22)

qualitative change (p. 9)

quantitative change (p. 10)

reliability (p. 28)

replicability (p. 30)

stages of development (p. 10)

validity (p. 29)

within-subjects design (p. 30)

2

The Biology of Development

The Basis of Development
- Inputs to the Biological System
- Constraints on Development

The Beginnings of Development
- Meiosis and Fertilization
- The First Patterns of Differentiation

Anatomical Development
- Structures and Systems in the Embryo and Fetus
- Preterm Births

- Why Does Anatomical Development Progress As It Does?
- Diversity out of Uniformity
- Sexual Differentiation
- Adverse Influences on the Developing Embryo and Fetus

Brain Development
- Major Changes to Brain Structures
- Neurons and Neurotransmitters
- Development of Neurons

- Experience and Brain Development
- Puberty and Brain Development

Behavioral Genetics
- Heritability
- Behavioral Genomics

Conclusions

Summary

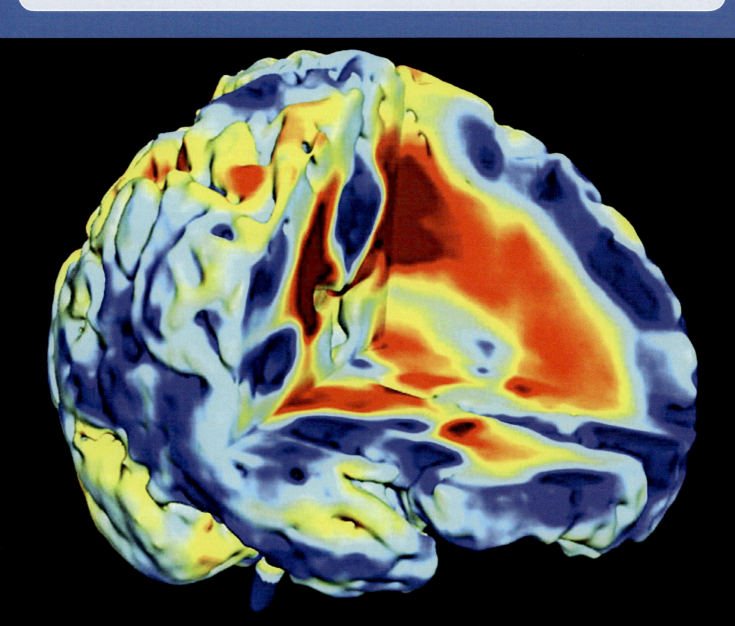

n 1989, a girl named Madeline Mann was born severely premature. Her gestational age was only 27 weeks, and she weighed only 280 grams (9.9 ounces); at that time, she was the smallest baby ever to survive a premature birth. There are only 110 recorded cases of newborns who weigh less than 400 grams, and the vast majority of these have serious medical complications. In fact, of all the newborns born weighing less than 500 grams, fewer than 1 percent reached 18 months without some kind of complication, often quite serious brain impairment (Muraskas et al., 2012). Yet, because of extraordinary medical care and some unique biological features relating to her situation, 22 years later, in 2012, Madeline was a senior honors student in a liberal arts college.

As seen in Figure 2.1, an almost impossibly small baby became an accomplished adult. These two photos vividly illustrate the biology of development and the extraordinary changes that occur. They also illustrate how normal development is a complex interplay of biological programming and environmental support. Just a decade earlier, Madeline would have been very unlikely to survive. She had to be mechanically ventilated for 65 days and could not leave the hospital until 122 days after her birth. She had some bleeding in the ventricles of her brain and immune system problems, both of which could have caused massive complications or death without constant vigilance and superb medical attention. Madeline may also have done so well because of a phenomenon in which the fetus, when it senses environmental stresses and drops in nutrition (as happened in Madeline's case), is sometimes able to slow down the rate of growth until the stresses are removed. This "thrifty phenotype hypothesis" may be a form of evolved adaptation

for fetuses in times of famine or other stresses that might impair maternal nutrient support (Hales & Barker, 2001). When those stressors are removed, the newborn baby can display rapid "catch up" in terms of physical and behavioral growth, apparently because of some genetic signaling that accelerates rates of growth once the child is in a more benign environment. In addition, whatever damage Madeline's young body did suffer early on, it was able to recover from those early insults, showing an important flexibility to the developmental process.

As impressive as our technology is in many areas of biology, it is remarkable how difficult it is to mimic the natural support of a mother's womb. Despite heroic technological efforts, the vast majority of extremely premature infants experience complications. Thus, the wonder of all development starts with biological development, which will illustrate several important themes for understanding psychological development.

In this chapter, we will consider how biological changes, including genetic and environmental influences, prenatal development, and brain development, bear on the study of developmental psychology. We will survey the biology of development, looking for principles and patterns that will help us understand psychological development—for example, how orderly patterns of change, involving precise timing and sequencing, are necessary for normal adult forms.

A closer look at development from the moment of conception onward reveals breathtaking patterns of change. From an initial cluster of seemingly identical cells, there emerges an organism with thousands of different cell types. From that initial ball of cells, a rich array of structures devel-

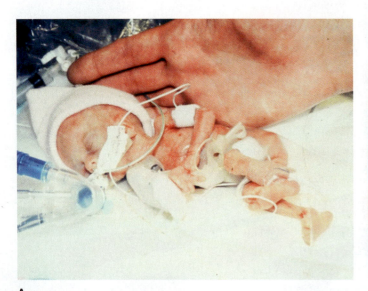

A

B

FIGURE 2.1 **Extreme premature birth and development. (A)** Madeline Mann was born at 27 weeks and had an extremely low birth weight because of complications of her mother's pregnancy. After her birth, she was hooked up to a breathing tube and kept alive through extraordinary measures. **(B)** Madeline survived and today is a college student without the physical or neurological impairments suffered by most infants born at extremely low birth weights.

ops, forming the organs and the general body shape. Limbs sprout and continue to grow for years; bodily structures change their size, shape, and proportions. All these changes must occur in an ordered sequence and at appropriate times for normal development to take place.

This chapter has two goals. First, it aims to examine the biological underpinnings of psychological development. How are developmental changes in the brain and other body systems related to psychological changes? Are children's brains physically immature in ways that limit their capacities to perceive, think, or feel? How do physiological changes, such as those that occur during puberty, influence thoughts and feelings? This chapter explores these issues by considering biological development both in the womb and after birth.

We will consider how relatively unspecialized cells develop into brain cells prenatally—that is, before birth—and how these cells grow and interconnect, giving rise to the brain's major anatomical structures. In studying postnatal development—that is, development that occurs after birth—we will focus on how aspects of the environment (such as various forms of deprivation) and major physiological changes (such as those that happen during puberty) exert distinct influences on brain function. Examining some key anatomical and physiological changes to the brain helps us see how neural development supports the psychological changes described in later chapters.

We will end by discussing a different kind of link between biology and behavior, that of behavioral genetics. Rather than asking how brain maturation influences psychological functioning and behavior, behavioral genetics asks how differences in the genes relate to variations in behavior. Researchers are beginning to understand how variations in genetic information are linked to differences in brain structure and function and how those neurological features are in turn linked to behavior.

The second goal of this chapter is to characterize some of the patterns common to both biological and psychological development. For example, both types of development involve **critical periods**, time frames in which certain kinds of experiences are essential for normal development. At the biological level, for example, a fetus develops normal sex organs only if it is exposed to particular hormones at a specific point in prenatal development. Similarly, at the psychological level, which is grounded in biological mechanisms, an infant's early visual experiences are crucial to developing the mental ability to fuse the separate images seen by each eye into one integrated visual experience.

Another developmental pattern in both the body and the mind is the tendency for vital systems to develop earlier than those that are less important for survival. In biological terms, the organs necessary for breathing and eating are functional at birth, whereas those supporting reproduction are not functional until puberty. Psychologically, infants learn to avoid dangerous ledges to keep from falling long before they can tell whether an object is balanced. Thus, development at any level of analysis, from individual cells to cognitive processes, shows some common patterns. This chapter offers just a brief glimpse into the rich fields of developmental biology and neurobiological development, but even this brief glimpse will yield powerful insights in later chapters.

The Basis of Development

Virtually every complex organism begins life as a single fertilized egg and develops into a creature with interacting anatomical systems and a broad range of behaviors. Starting before birth and continuing over the lifespan, the organism's environment exerts a critical influence on the way that it develops. At the same time, environmental influences interact continuously with the organism's biological makeup. As the organism matures, these interactions must allow it to progress toward the adult state in a way that supports its survival at every point in its development.

To understand how these complex processes take place, it is useful to think about development as a systems problem in the sense that developmental changes to the biological system must interact and build on one another in a way that supports the organism's needs at every stage. Imagine for a moment what the adult members of a new species would look like, but also the processes that would give rise to all their properties over the course of the lifespan. There would need to be a sequence of emerging structures and processes to yield the largest number of healthy, mature members of the species.

Examining an organism's needs in its environment and the developmental challenges it faces often suggests why that organism's development unfolds as it does. For example, newborn kangaroos, which are born blind, would have little use for functional eyes during the first days in the mother's pouch. But to get from the birth canal to the pouch, where its physical development continues, it needs forelimbs strong enough to crawl up its mother's belly on its own. Similarly, it is far more important for human newborns to have a functional sucking system for nursing than to be skilled at recognizing faces. Development proceeds as an ordered sequence of interdependent events, in which the more complex aspects of an organism depend on the essential, simpler systems that emerge earlier.

Considering the process as a systems problem leads us to focus on two main influences on development: the inputs that influence the process and the constraints that both limit and channel how development occurs (Newell, 1986). The *inputs* consist of an organism's genes, its environment, and the resulting patterns of gene-environment interactions. The *constraints* consist of the need for viability throughout development, the need for specialized cells to serve particular functions in the body, and the need for certain sequential processes to occur at just the right times.

Inputs to the Biological System

The interacting influences of genes and environment vary considerably across different kinds of organisms. Some animals are able to function in a nearly mature way from the moment they are born, while others mature gradually, developing systems that depend heavily on environmental inputs after birth. Such variations can happen even between relatively similar organisms. Thus, Australian brush turkeys are completely functional and self-sufficient right after birth, while many kinds of songbirds are born with closed eyes, without feathers or down, and lacking the ability to eat on their own. These sorts of differences arise because of the different local environments, or **environmental niches**, into which these birds are born and for which these birds have evolved special adaptations. Brush turkeys are born on the ground and must immediately fend for themselves, while songbirds are born in nests in trees and can safely remain helpless for quite some time after birth. These variations reflect the ways in which the different species' genetic codes were modified through natural selection, resulting in organisms adapted to their particular environmental niches.

The Genes Genes are the inherited instructions for producing the proteins that make up cells or for regulating whether other genes will be turned on or off. A gene is made up of a section of **DNA** (deoxyribonucleic acid), a long, double-stranded molecule consisting of specific sequences of just four different chemical bases (adenine, thymine, guanine, and cytosine—abbreviated as A, T, G, and C) that encode the specific instructions for cellular construction and development. The molecular structure of these four chemicals allows them to link up as **base pairs** (A with T, and C with G) to attach the two strands of the DNA molecule together in a twisting structure called a double helix, much like the way the rungs of a ladder link the two sides of the frame (see Figure 2.2). Because of these base-pairing rules, every occurrence of C on one strand of DNA corresponds to the site of a G on the other strand, and every A corresponds to a T. Thus, the two strands are said to be complementary.

Molecular biologists refer to the sequence of bases that makes up a gene as having two main parts. The *structural sequence* directs the assembly of particular proteins (or parts of proteins), which can then give rise to traits in several ways. For example, the proteins may become body structures, such as muscle, or they may become enzymes that trigger chemical reactions, like the digestive chemicals in

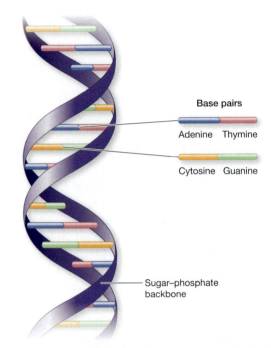

FIGURE 2.2 The double helix. The genetic material of all animals shares the same fundamental structure, a sequence of pairs of four chemical bases: adenine paired with thymine, and guanine paired with cytosine. These pairs are linked in a twisting structure called a double helix. The order in which these pairs occur on the double helix is the basis for all genetic differences between animals.

saliva. Adjacent to the structural sequence, most genes also have a *regulatory sequence* that acts like a switch to determine whether (and how much) the protein-coding genes will be active. Entire genes can also serve a regulatory function by coding for a type of protein that can "flip the switch" in the regulatory sequence that adjusts another gene's activity level. It is estimated that well over 95 percent of human DNA sequences is nonstructural and probably regulatory.

Sometimes, news reports or magazine articles describe genes "for" language, leadership, or aggression, suggesting that there is a single biological unit of information that directly and specifically produces these traits or behaviors. The reality is more complex and far more interesting. Instead of a simple link from one gene to a single trait or behavior, a complex web of interactions take place between multiple genes and environmental factors that together give rise to traits and behaviors.

In most organisms, the long DNA molecules are stored in the cell nucleus as tightly wound, highly compact **chromosomes**. In this form, roughly 3 billion DNA base pairs can fit inside a cell nucleus only 6 millionths of a meter across. The entire set of chromosomes in an individual organism is sometimes known as its **genome**. But the term can also be used to describe the typical genetic profile for a species or subspecies. Estimates of the precise number of genes in the human genome vary considerably, but at least 20,000 genes are packed inside our 46 chromosomes (Pennisi, 2007). Some have argued that this relatively low number means that most human brain structures, which involve trillions of cells, are too complex to be specified by genes. But this argument overlooks the power of gene interactions and the ways in which the interplay of a relatively smaller number of genes can yield many distinct proteins (Marcus, 2004).

Chromosomes normally occur in pairs, with each of the individual's parents contributing one chromosome in each pair. The two chromosomes in each pair contain corresponding genetic information about the same overall bodily structures or functions, but each chromosome may contain different variants of those genes, depending on the genes of the contributing parent. Biologists use the term **alleles** to talk about all the variations of a particular gene that can exist at a particular location on a chromosome. Thus, a single gene is said to be associated with a set of alleles.

For example, in humans, the ABO gene for blood type has several different alleles—for blood types A, B, AB, and O. Each individual receives two alleles for blood type—one from each parent—and the relations between those alleles then determine the child's blood type. When both parents contribute the same allele of a particular gene, the individual is said to be **homozygous** for that gene. If both parents contribute a type A allele, the child is homozygous (*AA*) and will have type A blood.

When each parent contributes a different allele of a particular gene, the individual is considered **heterozygous** for the gene. In these cases, the interactions between the alleles determine the outcome. Often one allele in a heterozygous pair is **dominant** over the other, meaning that its properties will be expressed preferentially over the properties of the other allele. For example, if a woman inherited one allele for type A and one allele for type O (*AO*), she would have type A blood because the allele for type A is dominant. The allele that is not expressed is known as the **recessive** allele. In this case, *O* is the recessive allele. (Recessive alleles are not expressed unless the individual is *homozygous recessive*, having received the recessive allele of that gene from both parents.) In other heterozygous cases, the alleles may be **codominant**, in which case both alleles are expressed simultaneously. This is the case when a person inherits one allele for type A and one for type B (*AB*), resulting in type AB blood. Blood type provides an unusually straightforward example of how traits are inherited, but most traits result from the interactions of multiple genes, contributing to the complex patterns of inheritance we see between parents and offspring.

Although most chromosomes come in pairs that contain matching genes, one important exception concerns the sex chromosomes, a special pair of chromosomes that determines the sex of many animals. In most mammals, there are two types of sex chromosomes: X chromosomes and Y chromosomes. Females have two X chromosomes, while males have an X and a Y chromosome. Females can therefore contribute only X chromosomes to their offspring, while males can contribute either an X or a Y chromosome. Thus, in humans, the sex chromosome contributed by the father determines the sex of the child.

The Environment Along with genes, the other main inputs to the biological system are the influences of all the environments in which an organism develops. Here, too, a seemingly simple concept can be examined at many levels. We often think of the environment as the physical world in which an organism develops, and although this is an important source of environmental influences, there are many other components of the environment to consider. In the first moments after conception, for example, the fertilized egg is bathed in a rich mixture of chemicals, including hormones secreted by the mother and, before long, additional hormones produced by the developing fetus. A male fetus experiences a very different hormonal environment than a female fetus, largely due to the fetus's own genetically triggered biochemical outputs. This sort of interaction of genetic and environmental influences—in this case, a genetic influence on the prenatal environment, which then triggers additional interactions—illustrates a complex relationship between genes and the environment.

The prenatal environment is also influenced by the mother's external environment, as it includes chemicals that the mother has ingested and passed on to the developing fetus. These might include chemicals that the mother has intentionally consumed, such as nutrients, caffeine, or alcohol, as well as chemicals that have entered her body without her knowledge, such as food additives or contaminants, air pollution, or compounds that contact her skin. Other aspects of the biological environment within the mother's body can also affect the fertilized egg. For example, when the mother contracts an illness that causes a high fever, her increased body temperature has the potential to cause birth defects (Czeizel et al., 2007; Hashmi et al., 2010). As we will see later in this chapter, the effects of each of these kinds of environmental influences also depend on the point in the developmental timeline when the fetus is exposed to them.

As the developing fetus approaches birth, other environmental factors can have an influence as well. These can include sounds in the outside world, as well as tactile sensations created when the mother's abdomen is touched. After birth, environmental influences proliferate as the baby experiences the world through all the senses, through the nutritional content of new foods, and through early social interactions. Through their behavior, babies also shape certain environmental influences. Thus, a baby who frequently cries and shows distress receives different environmental inputs, in terms of parental behavior, than a calm baby.

Interactions between Genes and Environment We have seen that genes and the environment constantly interact in complex ways, such that it rarely makes sense to consider them as completely separate inputs to the biological system. At the broadest level, environmental influences help us understand why differences may arise between the genotype of an organism and its phenotype. The **genotype** is the genetic information encoded as particular alleles in an organism's DNA (in contrast, the term *genome* is more often used for the genetic information that typifies a whole species). The organism's **phenotype** refers to the ways that the genetic information is expressed or manifested in an organism, including its anatomical structures, its biochemical processes, and its behaviors.

Environmental influences are an important clue to explain differences between genotype and phenotype because a particular allele's unique characteristics may only be expressed in certain contexts. For example, a child might inherit a genotype that predisposes him toward obesity, but he may only become overweight if he grows up in an environment with abundant food. Likewise, certain genetic variations related to lighter skin pigmentation can make an individual more vulnerable to skin cancer—but this increased susceptibility would be dangerous only in relatively sunny climates. Thus, a person with this genetic vulnerability who grows up in cloudy Astoria, Oregon, might not be any more likely to get skin cancer than other people from Astoria. But growing up in the desert sun of Tucson, Arizona, may make that same person much more likely to get skin cancer than other people in Tucson.

Other genes that have harmful effects in most environments can be rendered harmless in highly specialized environments. For example, some children are born with an allele that makes them unable to break down the amino acid phenylalanine, which is found in artificial sweeteners and other foods. If these children eat foods that contain phenylalanine, they will develop phenylketonuria (PKU), a condition in which phenylalanine builds up in their bloodstream, causing severe brain damage if left untreated. But if the same children grow up on a special diet without phenylalanine, they develop normally.

Different environments not only influence phenotypic features; they can also affect the activity levels of genes. It became clear only about 50 years ago that aspects of the environment could change genes' activities in this way (Jacob & Monod, 1961). Since that discovery, researchers have found that much of the information in the human genome is regulatory—that is, affecting when other genes are expressed and which genes can be activated by environmental factors such as hormones. Moreover, genes' intricate interaction patterns can form elaborate branching chains known as **regulatory cascades**. In these series of interactions, small changes in the activity of one gene can influence

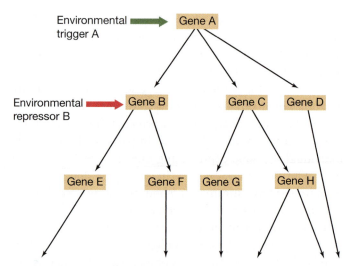

FIGURE 2.3 Regulatory cascades. This simplified diagram illustrates how genes can interact in complex patterns, where turning on one gene creates the products that turn on several other genes in a cascade. Environmental factors can also affect these cascades by turning genes on or off. (Real gene regulatory cascades involve many more interactions between intermediate stages and higher stages and between genes and their products.)

several other genes, which in turn can influence many more genes (see Figure 2.3). At the same time, these genes continue to be subject to environmental influences—from the biochemical surroundings of a particular cell to the features of the organism's external world.

Constraints on Development

We have seen how genes, the environment, and their interactions act as inputs that influence development. Development is also shaped by three key constraints: the *viability* of the developing organism, the *differentiation* of cell types and anatomical structures, and the *timing and sequencing* of developmental events. These factors interact in crucial ways during biological development. Here we consider each factor in turn.

Viability From the moment an egg is fertilized until the baby is born, that rapidly growing and changing mass of cells must stay alive by metabolizing nutrients and eliminating wastes. It must have some way of circulating nutrients, and to do so, it needs muscle activity, such as the heartbeat. By contrast, a complex machine like a passenger jet might not have a functional engine system until other critical control mechanisms are installed, moments before completion. Thus, the need for viability in living organisms places constraints on development, requiring that certain essential structures and functions develop before others, but such constraints do not necessarily apply to nonliving entities.

What does the constraint of viability require of the developing organism? The answer depends on the environment in which the organism must survive. Thus, a fetus receiving oxygen via its umbilical cord is a very different being from the breathing newborn it becomes. This remarkable transformation occurs by means of an intricate set of triggers, including constricted blood flow in the umbilical cord, the physical pressures of contraction during birth, and changing maternal hormones. These events empty the baby's lungs of fluid before birth, changing the circulatory path of blood flow to take in oxygen from the lungs (rather than via the placenta) and activating the breathing reflex (Wyllie, 2006). Despite the complexity of this near-instantaneous transition, only a small percentage of newborns need resuscitation. Thus, over the course of development, both prenatally and postnatally, the constraint of viability can impose radically different requirements.

Differentiation of Cells and Structures The fertilized egg splits into two cells, then each of those cells divides, yielding four, then those four become eight. Though the eight cells seem identical, each will become specialized for a different function. What controls this differentiation into cell types, and what patterns does the process follow? Many researchers have devoted their careers to these questions, since cell differentiation is the key to understanding how the complexity of an organism emerges.

The biologist Conrad Waddington (1957) vividly depicted the process of specialization during development using the visual representation of a landscape (see Figure 2.4). He described changing cells undergoing a process of **canalization** through which they get committed to becoming certain types (Salathia & Queitsch, 2007). He compared the differentiating cell to a ball

FIGURE 2.4 The landscape of canalization. Conrad Waddington envisioned the canalization process as a terrain with ever-deepening valleys and ridges. Like a ball rolling down this landscape, a developing cell becomes ever more entrenched in a certain fate. Adapted from Waddington (1957).

rolling down a surface with ever-deepening valleys and ridges, which represent different cell outcomes. As the valleys deepen and the ridges grow higher, the likelihood of the ball "jumping" to another valley diminishes. Likewise, after a cell begins a particular developmental path, it will be increasingly difficult for it to change course and become a completely different cell type. Several researchers have used this concept of canalization to describe how behaviors and abilities develop (Bishop, 2009; Gottlieb, 2007). Some scholars focus on the initial possibilities of many alternative developmental paths, while others focus on the valleys and ridges that represent increasingly limiting constraints on what develops.

These complementary views of the developmental process emerge frequently in later chapters as we consider aspects of behavioral and cognitive development. When we examine perceptual development in Chapter 3, we will see how certain cells become attuned to receiving simultaneous visual input from both eyes and how after starting down that path, it is ever more difficult to reverse course and become responsive to input from only one eye. When we consider social development in Chapter 6, we will see how children's early parental attachments become ever deeper and stronger, making these attachments difficult to extinguish even in abusive situations. This pattern of increasing commitment to a particular developmental path pervades biological and psychological development.

Cell differentiation is controlled by an intricate set of genetic interactions that specify how and when cells specialize. One striking process involves **epigenetic regulation**, which leads to changes in gene expression without changes to DNA sequences (Dolinoy, 2007). Epigenetic regulation occurs when a particular cell type has some genes turned off and others turned on by its surrounding chemical environment and then "freezes" that pattern of on-and-off genes. When the cell divides, the genes of all the cells that it creates have the same on-and-off pattern. Thus, environmental influences can fix cells to be of a certain type, so that when they divide, they will produce cells of that same type. One of the most common mechanisms for epigenetic regulation involves **methylation**, in which methyl groups (specific carbon-hydrogen configurations) become attached to certain DNA base pairs, usually with the result of turning off the activity level of a gene or affecting other genes that follow that gene in a regulatory sequence.

Even the kinds of foods that a pregnant woman eats may influence the activity of the fetus's genes and in turn affect the way its cells differentiate. This phenomenon is the focus of a rapidly growing field known as *nutrigenomics* (Ross, 2010; Waterland & Jirtle, 2004). It is thought that certain effects of dietary variation in the pregnant woman are linked to high levels of certain maternal hormones in the womb, causing changes in gene regulation that may contribute to diabetes (Drake et al., 2005). Low-protein diets during pregnancy have also been associated with changes in fetal gene regulation that may lead to diabetes later in life (Burdge et al., 2007; Langley-Evans, 2007; Lillycrop & Burdge, 2011). As one researcher put it, it now appears that "you are not only what you eat, but what your mother and grandparents ate as well" (Dolinoy, 2007, p. 7).

Timing and Sequencing In biological systems, changes in timing can have major effects on what develops. We have seen that genes turn on and off in response to regulatory signals; in addition, some genes are active only during certain periods in an organism's development. How does the timing of gene activation influence development? More generally, when the timing of an important event—like activating a gene or forming an anatomical structure—changes, how does the change influence other developing structures and patterns of genetic regulation?

It appears that the timing of major anatomical developments is governed by the same set of genes in all species. They are known as **heterochronic genes**, and they seem to operate by regulating the activity of other genes (Banerjee &

Slack, 2002; Hada et al., 2010; Pasquinelli & Ruvkun, 2002). In humans, errors in the timing of when specific genes turn on and off may result in anatomical defects, such as the abdominal cavity being unable to enclose the internal organs (Brewer & Williams, 2004). During normal development, the thin film of cells that initially covers the abdominal cavity is later replaced by thicker layers of skin and muscle cells. If this secondary set of layers doesn't develop at the right time, the organs may push out of the cavity, stretching the thin film into a large bulge. If the secondary layers of skin and muscle then start growing in after this delay, some of the organs may be trapped outside the body (Beckett & Baylies, 2007; Rochlin et al., 2010; Sun et al., 2007).

Closely related to timing is the issue of the sequence in which structural developments take place. For example, to build a house, some structures, like the foundation, must be completed before others, such as the walls—and those, in turn, must precede the roof. For other structures, sequencing is less important: the wiring can go in either before or after the plumbing. In a developing person, some structures or processes sequentially depend on others, and some can proceed independently. We will see several cases where cor-

SCIENTIFIC METHOD: Diet and Methylation

Hypothesis:
Paternal diets in mice can cause epigenetic changes, via methylation, that are inherited.

Method:
1. Male mice were fed control (20 percent protein) or low-protein (11 percent protein) diets, with the remaining mass of food made up of sucrose, from weaning until sexual maturity.
2. Mice on either diet were then mated with females reared on the control diet.
3. Twenty-six pairs of offspring (an offspring of a control mother and a control father paired with an offspring of a control mother and a low-protein father) were reared with their mothers until 3 weeks, when their livers were analyzed for gene expression.
4. DNA microarrays were used to explore global gene expression differences in the offspring from the two kinds of matings.

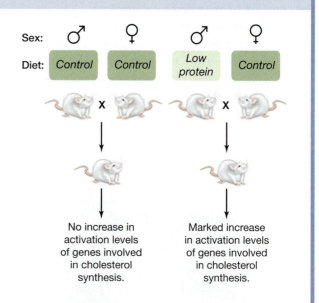

Results:
There was an extensive increase in activation levels of genes related to cholesterol synthesis in the offspring of males fed a low-protein diet. In general, there was more methylation of many genes in the low-protein groups, especially of a gene that regulated fatty acid synthesis. When methylation led this gene to be turned off, it may in turn have led to the increased

levels of activity of cholesterol synthesis genes, which might possibly be related to increases in heart disease.

Conclusion:
Feeding males a low-protein diet from birth to maturity can result in gene-regulated metabolic changes in their offspring.

Source study: Carone et al. (2010).

rect sequencing is vital. In the developing brain, for example, some kinds of nerve cells can develop only within a framework of other kinds of cells. These framework cells emit chemical signals that guide the growing nerve cells to their correct locations.

The Beginnings of Development

Considering development in detail reveals how the main inputs (genes and the environment) and the key constraints (viability, differentiation, and timing) interact throughout the process. In this section, we start with the processes that generate egg and sperm cells for reproduction and follow those cells from conception to the beginnings of differentiation.

Meiosis and Fertilization

Every human being starts with the fusion of two cells. The mother's egg and the father's sperm combine physically and genetically to create the new individual. We therefore start our discussion with **meiosis**, the unique process of cell division that produces the egg and sperm cells (see Figure 2.5A). We'll also see how meiosis differs from another type of cell division called mitosis, which gives rise to other kinds of cells throughout the body.

Meiosis and Mitosis In adults, most cells have two of each type of chromosome, with one chromosome in each

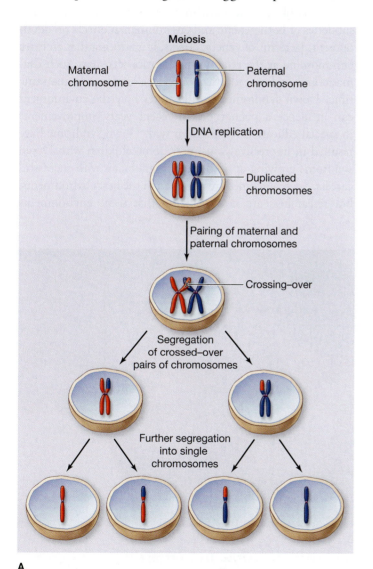

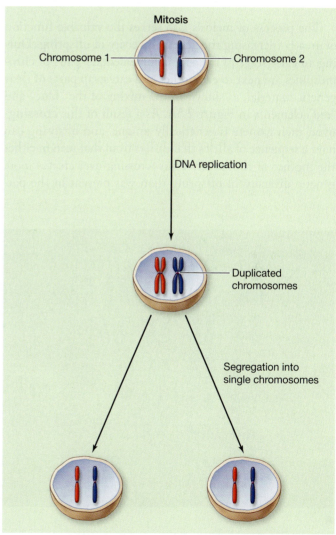

A

B

FIGURE 2.5 Meiosis and mitosis. (A) Meiosis is a special kind of cell division that prepares cells for sexual recombination. Normal human cells have 23 pairs of chromosomes. One chromosome of each parent goes to the sperm and egg cells that will be part of reproduction. **(B)** Mitosis is the process in which cell division occurs, but the chromosomes from both parents are copied and appear in all the new cells.

pair contributed by each parent. (The exception is the sex chromosomes: recall that males have an X and a Y chromosome, and females have two X chromosomes.) Typically when a cell divides, all of its genetic material—two copies of each type of chromosome—is reproduced in the new cells through the process of **mitosis** (see Figure 2.5B). However, the specialized **sperm cells** of the father and the **egg cells** of the mother are produced by meiosis. These specialized cells, known as **gametes**, have only one of each type of chromosome, or half the genetic material contained in the body's other cells. As a result, when the egg and sperm fuse during fertilization, the new cell has the normal, complete number of chromosomes—half from the egg and half from the sperm.

> **Q:** How is meiosis different from mitosis? What functional role does meiosis serve?

The process of meiosis also serves the valuable function of greatly increasing the genetic diversity of offspring. During an early stage of meiosis, complementary pairs of chromosomes are next to each other and can swap parts of their genetic material, as shown in the mixing of the "blue" and "red" elements in Figure 2.5A. As a result of this **crossing-over**, each gamete is genetically unique, and offspring can have a sequence of alleles that differs from that seen in either the mother or the father. Thus, crossing-over creates more genetic diversity in offspring than was present in the parents. This diversity is advantageous, as it increases the odds that the offspring's genotypes will make them well suited for new environmental challenges.

Yet, meiosis may not proceed correctly; imperfect crossing-over may result in genetic disorders, including a genetic condition known as **trisomy 21**. A child with trisomy 21 has three chromosomes rather than two in what is normally the twenty-first chromosome pair (see Figure 2.6A). This anomaly is easy to see when a biologist constructs a *karyotype* in which all the chromosomes in an individual's genotype are stained with dye and the chromosome pairs are aligned and photographed through a microscope. When it isn't lethal, trisomy 21 leads to the most common form of Down syndrome, a disorder whose effects include delays in cognitive functioning and motor skills. In addition, people with Down syndrome tend to have distinctive facial features (see Figure 2.6B) and are at high risk for certain heart defects.

The problems that occur in cases of trisomy 21 reveal the subtleties of both genetic and environmental effects on development. In terms of genetic effects, it is striking that an extra chromosome at the twenty-first location can have such dramatic and widespread effects on development. At the same time, Down syndrome also illustrates how the environment can influence a phenotype. In recent years, improvements in special education for children with Down syndrome have resulted in impressive gains, with some children with Down syndrome growing up to be college graduates with successful careers. Such outcomes are rare even in the best environments, but researchers are now realizing that some environments

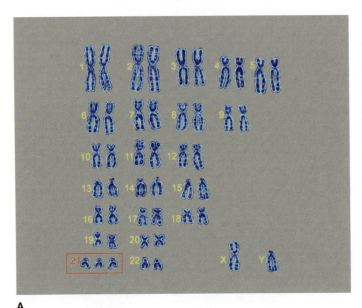

A

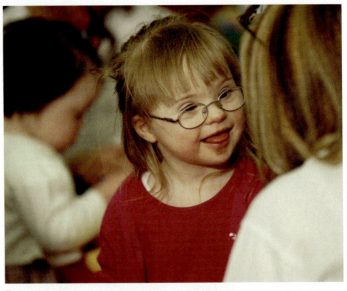

B

FIGURE 2.6 Trisomy 21 and Down syndrome. (A) A normal karyotype and a trisomy 21 karyotype. The upper panel shows a karyotype in which there is a pair for each of the 23 chromosomes. The lower panel shows a karyotype leading to Down syndrome, in which there are three copies of chromosome 21. **(B)** People with Down syndrome often have characteristic facial features that make them visually identifiable. A small amount of extra genetic material in part of the twenty-first chromosome causes a large set of effects, ranging from these facial features to heart defects and a variety of cognitive problems.

clearly can improve the future of such children far more than was thought possible a few decades ago (Pueschel, 2001).

Other errors during meiosis may result in extra or missing sex chromosomes. These anomalies can cause a number of problems involving sex-specific characteristics, such as breasts or facial hair, as well as other problems unrelated to sex differences. For example, women with Turner syndrome, which occurs in roughly 1 in 3,000 live births, have only one X chromosome (a condition known as monosomy X), and they are infertile. In addition to having reduced (or absent) female sex characteristics, individuals with Turner syndrome often are quite short, and they have webbed skin at the neck and drooping eyelids. Men with the rare condition of Klinefelter syndrome (roughly 1 in 1,000 live births) have an extra X chromosome (XXY). In addition to reduced male sex characteristics, they may also have abnormally long legs and show language impairments and excessive shyness.

Q: What are some examples of the effects of having extra or missing genetic material in the human genome?

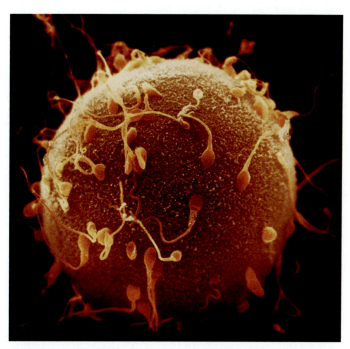

FIGURE 2.7 **Fertilization.** In the process of fertilization, 50 to 100 sperm, out of an original group of millions, finally reach the egg. The thread-like projections are the tails of sperm trying to enter the large, spherical egg.

Fertilization During sexual intercourse, many millions of sperm are released and swim in search of an egg to fertilize. Out of the millions that start the journey, only 50 to 100 sperm reach the egg and attempt to penetrate it (see Figure 2.7). When one sperm finally penetrates the egg, it triggers a series of chemical events that prevent all other sperm from entering, as well as allowing the penetrating sperm to move farther into the egg and fuse with the egg's genetic material (Gilbert, 2010). At this point, the fertilized egg is known as the **zygote**. If the zygote has an X chromosome and a Y chromosome, a male is created; if the zygote has two X chromosomes, a female is created.

Conception can result in twins or other kinds of multiple births. If the fertilized egg splits into two separate cells, each of which continues to develop into individuals, identical twins result. They are also known as **monozygotic (MZ) twins** because the two babies came from the same zygote, which is also the reason for their nearly identical genotypes. Biologists used to think that MZ twins had exactly the same genotype, but it turns out that subtle epigenetic effects can arise during in utero development and affect one or more sections of DNA, which can cause differences in the twins' susceptibility to certain diseases or subtle physical differences (Bruder et al., 2008; Ollikainen & Craig, 2011). By contrast, when two different sperm fertilize two different eggs, **dizygotic (DZ) twins** (or twins from two zygotes; also called *fraternal* twins) result. Because DZ twins develop from two separate conceptions involving genetically different sperm

and eggs, they are only as genetically similar as any two siblings—that is, they have half their genes in common.

The First Patterns of Differentiation

Around 2 hours after fertilization, the zygote makes the first of many cell divisions. Initially, as the cells divide rapidly by mitosis, they get smaller with each division, such that the overall mass of the zygote does not increase. When the cell divisions result in a 16-cell body at day 4, this compact, solid ball of cells is known as a *morula*, and it shows the first signs of cell differentiation: its outer cells are larger than its inner ones. At around day 5, the larger outer cells of the morula become clearly distinct from the inner ones. These outer cells (the *trophoblast*) will eventually become part of the **placenta** (an organ that will make possible the transfer of nutrients and oxygen from the mother and wastes and carbon dioxide from the fetus). The encircling outer cells trigger a group of the smaller inner cells to cluster in a ball-like structure, which eventually will become the embryo (see Figure 2.8). This overall structure—the outer ring of cells and the inner cell mass—is known as the *blastocyst*.

In humans, about 16 days after fertilization, the blastocyst's inner cell mass undergoes an important cell differentiation process known as **gastrulation**, which is oriented relative to the point where the sperm entered the egg. During

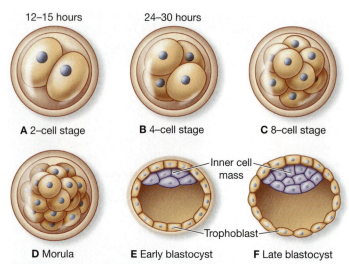

12–15 hours   24–30 hours

A 2–cell stage   **B** 4–cell stage   **C** 8–cell stage

Inner cell mass

Trophoblast

D Morula   **E** Early blastocyst   **F** Late blastocyst

FIGURE 2.8 The formation of the blastocyst. In the earliest stages of growth, the fertilized egg progresses from apparently undifferentiated cells to the beginnings of specialization.

gastrulation, a cascade of changes in chemical concentrations relative to this orientation point soon leads to **bilateral symmetry**, a hallmark of most complex organisms. An organism that shows bilateral symmetry has identical structures on both sides of a center line (right and left kidneys, arms, legs, eyes, ears, and so on).

In the process of gastrulation, cells and cell clusters move within the blastocyst to form three distinct layers (see Figure 2.9). The outermost layer of cells, the **ectoderm**, eventually forms the skin and, perhaps more surprisingly, the nervous system. The middle layer, the **mesoderm**, becomes internal tissues, such as the skeleton, internal organs, and muscles. And the blastocyst's innermost cell layer, the **endoderm**, develops into some of the glands, such as the thyroid, and the specialized tissues lining organs such as the lungs. A matrix of fine fibers within the blastocyst directs the cells' migrations, much like a set of guide rails along which the cells move. A great deal is happening during these migrations. Specific sequences of genes become activated and deactivated as cells in the different layers start to develop specialized features. The identities of these cells soon become nearly irreversible (Cyranoski, 2007; Jackson et al., 2010; Verfaillie, 2002).

How do the cells on the inside of the blastocyst, which eventually become parts of the embryo, differentiate from the blastocyst's external cells, which will form the placenta? The relative positions of these cells in the blastocyst seem to trigger different sets of genes within them, leading the cells to specialize for different functions. Presumably, the cells in the inner layer and outer layer receive different kinds of chemical signals (Surani et al., 2007; Thomas et al., 2004). If an outer-layer cell is moved to an inner position at an early enough point, it will genetically and functionally develop like an inner-layer cell, becoming part of the embryo rather than the placenta. The

same kind of functional transformation happens if an inner cell is relocated to an external position (Hillman et al., 1972).

Anatomical Development

So far, we have focused on changes at the cellular level, many of which are visible only with a microscope. Within just a few weeks after conception, however, noticeable anatomical features start to appear, and they change very rapidly in the following months.

Structures and Systems in the Embryo and Fetus

After fertilization and cell divisions that make the zygote into a multicelled organism, rudimentary nervous and circulatory systems and body structures appear and grow rapidly, becoming specialized for particular functions (see Table 2.1). We will briefly discuss the development of systems and structures from 2 to 8 weeks after conception (during the embryonic period) and from 9 to 36 weeks after conception (during the fetal period).

The Embryonic Period At about 2 weeks after conception, the fertilized egg attaches to the uterine wall (see Figure 2.10). After this implantation, it becomes more common to refer to the fertilized egg as an **embryo** (the embryonic period lasts from the middle of the second week until the end of the eighth week after conception). The first signs of legs and arms are visible at about the third week. The heart starts to beat at around 18 days, pumping blood around a rapidly expanding circulatory system. Limb buds appear as small bumps in the arm region, and similar buds emerge later in the leg region, following the head-to-toe principle of development in which structures tend to develop earlier in the more anterior regions of the embryo (situated toward the head or front). Development in which the more anterior structures of an organism mature earlier than structures in the posterior sections is known as **cephalocaudal development** (cephalo = head, caudal = tail).

In humans and all other mammals, as well as birds and other reptiles, the key event in gastrulation, during which the blastocyst starts to develop distinct layers of cells, is the formation of the **primitive streak**, which occurs at the end of week 2 in humans. The primitive streak is a ridge on one side of the blastocyst through which cells pass to become the mesoderm and endoderm. Where and when they pass through the streak influences whether the cells in each layer will become part of the head, the gut, or the tail (if the species has a tail). Cells within the streak itself appear to produce chemical signals that guide other

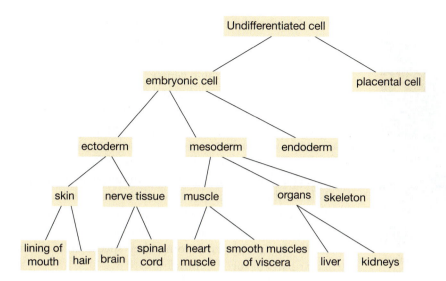

FIGURE 2.9 **Cell differentiation.** Cells differentiate in a pattern of hierarchical specialization, starting with cells that can become any sort of cell at all. Once a cell has progressed far enough down one path, it becomes extremely difficult to go back and revert to a less differentiated state.

cells to migrate toward the streak (Alev et al., 2010; Keller, 2005; Spagnoli & Hemmati-Brivanlou, 2008). Early-entering cells migrate toward one end of the streak, which may produce stronger signals, and become the head. Later-entering cells, as well as those that pass through the streak farther down, become other types of structures. Thus, the streak, which is one of the first signs of bilateral symmetry, also triggers a very early bias toward development in the head (see Figure 2.11). This head-to-toe progression is a powerful organizing principle of embryonic development.

Some cells that migrate into the streak end up forming the *notochord*, which signals ectodermal cells above it to form the *neural plate*, which lengthens and drops down into the surface to form a *neural groove* (at around day 18 in humans) with ridges on the sides. Eventually, these grooves fold in toward each other, join, and form a hollow **neural tube**.

Weeks after conception	Size (inches)	Weight	Hallmarks
2	0.01	< 0.25 oz	Embryo is soundly implanted on uterine wall.
4	0.125	< 0.25 oz	Limb buds appear; heart starts to beat.
6	0.5	< 0.25 oz	Fingers start to appear; some neural activity occurs; four-chambered heart is present.
8	1	0.5 oz	First elements of most body parts—for example, ears, fingers, toes—are present.
10	2.5	1.5 oz	Some movement occurs; fingernails appear.
12	3.5	2 oz	Kidneys start to make urine; blood is now made in bone marrow.
14	4.5	4 oz	Fetus may suck thumb; begins to make larger movements.
16	5.25	6 oz	Mother feels movements; some hair may be present.
20	10	1 lb	Fetus may hear sounds.
24	12	2 lb	If born at this time, 50 percent of babies survive with intensive care.
28	15	3 lb	Lungs can breathe air; eyes are open.
32	17	4.5 lb	Sleep and waking states are observed.
36	19	6.5 lb	Lungs are fully mature.
38	20	7.5 lb	Baby is full term.

TABLE 2.1 **Milestones of prenatal development.** The timetable of gross anatomical and physiological development of the human embryo and fetus is highly regular in normal cases. Although many structures are present in the first 5 months, not until well into the sixth month are babies at all likely to survive birth.

ANATOMICAL DEVELOPMENT **45**

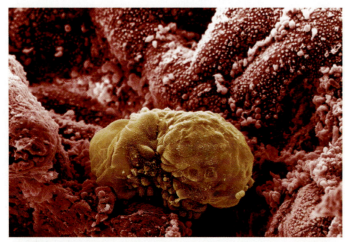

FIGURE 2.10 **Implantation of the embryo.** At 6 days, the blastocyst starts to implant on the uterine wall, as shown in this image. By 2 weeks, it is fully implanted and is about 0.01 inch long and is now known as the embryo.

This process of initial brain formation, called **neurulation**, is completed in week 4. The neural tube eventually becomes both the brain and the spinal cord. The notochord acts as a guiding framework for the spinal cord, with its cells eventually becoming parts of the vertebrae of the spinal column in humans. If the neural tube does not close properly, however, neural tube defects (for example, spina bifida, in which part of the spinal cord protrudes) will result.

After 3 weeks, the embryo's cells begin to differentiate. Cells that have identical genetic material take on different roles that support the development of a well-formed body. How can cells with the same genetic sequence become fingers, kidneys, brain cells, and muscles?

One key principle is that of successive differentiation. As specific cells develop, they narrow down their functional specialization in a step-by-step fashion, as shown in Figure 2.9. Thus, certain cells might first differentiate into three general groups: cells that can form muscles, organs, or the skeleton (bones). At first, the cells in the muscle group can become any kind of muscle, but at a later stage, most of those cells further differentiate into one of two main types of muscle. At an even later point, they specialize to form particular parts of specific muscles.

Dramatic changes in body structure occur between 4 and 8 weeks. At 4 weeks, the embryo is about 3 millimeters (about 0.125 inch) long. By the end of week 8, the embryo is well over 25 millimeters (about 1 inch) long. Even though it is only a little over an inch long, it already can be clearly seen as having human form.

The Fetal Period From the ninth week until birth, the growing human organism is referred to as the **fetus**. Over the next several weeks, the fetus changes dramatically (see Figure 2.12). It shows increasingly well-articulated fingers and toes. At 9 weeks, its four-chambered heart is clearly seen

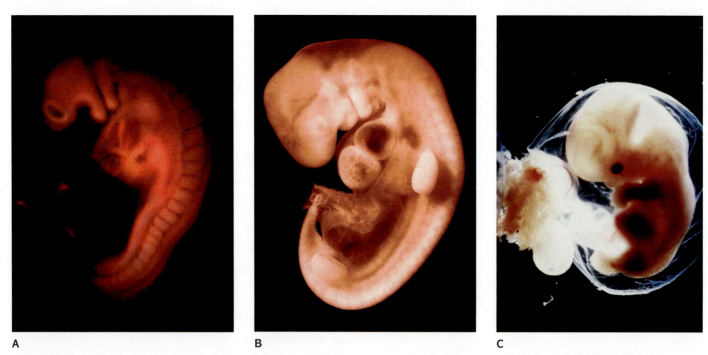

A   B   C

FIGURE 2.11 **The embryonic period. (A)** A 3-week-old embryo. The embryo's anterior structures, such as the head, tend to develop sooner than the posterior areas. **(B)** A 4-week-old embryo. By 4 weeks of age, the human embryo has a visible beating heart and the beginnings of limb buds, as well as a distinct head region. The heartbeat can be detected through ultrasound. **(C)** A 6-week-old embryo. The principle that structures near the head develop before those near the tail is complemented by the principle that structures near the body's midline tend to develop before those farther out to the sides.

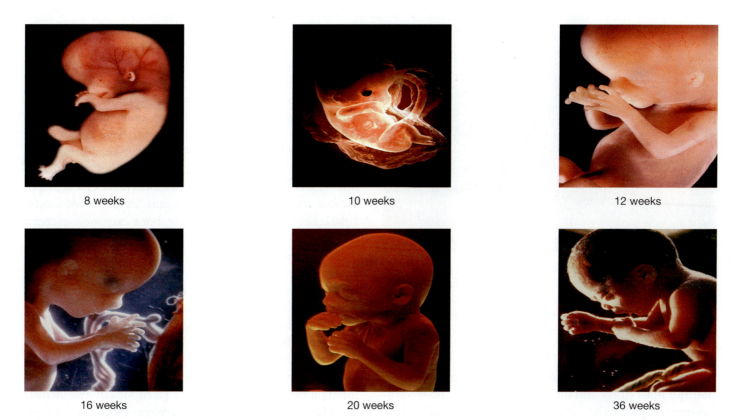

| 8 weeks | 10 weeks | 12 weeks |
| 16 weeks | 20 weeks | 36 weeks |

FIGURE 2.12 Prenatal development from 8 weeks to 36 weeks. From 8 weeks, both external and internal anatomical structures become further differentiated and more human in appearance. Development typically occurs earlier in the head region than in regions closer to the toes.

in ultrasound, as are visible facial features. Some of its neural connections are functioning, allowing it to show some reflexes.

By 12 weeks, it is quite easy to see most of the same anatomical features in the fetus that are visible in newborns. The fetus at this point is physiologically much more sophisticated than it was as an embryo, and most of its major bodily systems are partially functional. The fetus swallows, its muscles cause joint movements, and its kidneys now make urine. After 16 weeks, the fetus weighs 6 ounces and its external body parts are much more distinct. At 20 weeks, the fetus weighs about 1 pound, its hair is more evident, and its heartbeat can be detected with a stethoscope.

At 22 weeks, the fetus weighs about 1.25 pounds; this is the earliest stage at which a small number of premature newborns may survive birth, although this is possible only with the intensive medical care available at major hospitals, and the child is still likely to face many long-term disabilities. At 28 weeks, the fetus weighs close to 3 pounds. Its lungs typically have developed enough to be able to breathe air if birth is premature. By 6 months, the fetus is sufficiently well formed and physiologically mature that roughly 50 percent of infants born at that stage will survive if given intensive medical care. By 8 months, most infants will survive birth without major medical interventions. Once the fetus can survive on its own in the outside world, it is often called a baby.

At 36 weeks, the baby weighs about 6.5 pounds and is nearly full term. At this point, its movement in the womb is restricted because the baby is so tightly packed into the space. After its birth at 38 weeks of development, a newborn baby immediately breathes, cries, shows a range of behaviors and reflexes . . . and starts to learn about the world.

Preterm Births

A significant number of babies are born less than 38 weeks after conception. When babies are born 3 or more weeks early, they are known as **preterm** (or premature) **infants** and typically weigh less than 5.5 pounds, or 2.5 kilograms (see Figure 2.13). In the United States, roughly 12.5 percent of births are preterm, while in Europe, the rate is approximately 7 percent (Goldenberg et al., 2008). About 5 percent of preterm births occur before 28 weeks gestational age and are known as extremely preterm births.

Several forms of physical and psychological stress can increase the likelihood of a preterm birth. One major cause appears to be infections in either the mother or the fetus, which can indirectly cause either the onset of early labor or breaks in the membranes protecting the fetus (Goldenberg et al., 2008). Even infections far removed from the uterus, such as dental and gum infections, can increase the chances

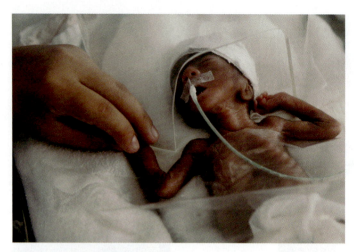

FIGURE 2.13 Extremely premature infant. Recent medical advances have made it possible for premature infants to survive at ages considered impossible a few decades ago. As younger and younger babies are able to survive, however, the incidence of severe, lifelong complications rises.

of a premature birth (Jeffcoat et al., 2001). Smoking, alcohol, and illicit drugs also increase the chances, and in combination they raise the odds still further (Dew et al., 2007). In addition to possible toxic effects, smoking, drinking, and drug abuse may put infants more at risk simply by exposing them to the increased odds of being born very early. Along the same lines as these physical stressors, mothers who experience intense stress and hardship are more likely to have preterm infants. Psychological stress may cause inflammation and immune responses, which in turn increase the odds of preterm birth (Wadhwa et al., 2001).

Preterm infants, and especially those that are extremely premature, are a cause of concern for physicians and psychologists because these infants are at increased risk for a host of complications later in development. As we consider the consequences of preterm birth, however, it is critical to keep in mind that these problems take the form of increased risks— not certainties. Preterm infants may have no negative medical or psychological conditions at any point in their lives, as we saw in the unusual case we described at the beginning of the chapter, but the closer to full term an infant is at birth, the smaller the chances of these kinds of problems occurring.

The more immature the preterm infant is at birth, the higher the risk of medical and psychological problems, not just in infancy but also in childhood and beyond (Korvenranta et al., 2010). At the level of neuroanatomy, preterm birth is associated with greater risk of a number of irregularities in brain development (Allen, 2008; Chuang et al., 2007; Volpe, 2009). This damage appears to happen in two ways: (1) premature birth seems to disrupt patterns of neural growth that normally occur in the last few months before birth, and (2) the problem that may have triggered a premature birth, such as an infection, can damage the brain directly

(Volpe, 2009). The many mechanisms of damage are not well understood, making it difficult for physicians to reduce the rate of complications associated with extreme preterm births, even as infants are increasingly able to survive them.

Preterm births are also associated with a range of cognitive difficulties in memory, attention, and language skills, as well as with mental retardation in very severe cases (Allen, 2008; Anderson & Doyle, 2008; Rijken et al., 2007). These problems can persist long after infancy. School-age children who were born extremely preterm show a higher incidence of mild or severe cognitive impairments (Anderson & Doyle, 2008). Even among adults, those born extremely preterm show, on average, lower rates of school completion, lower levels of employment, and greater difficulty living independently (Allen, 2008; Moster et al., 2008).

How can the negative effects associated with preterm births be reduced? Interventions can aim to either reduce the rate of preterm births or minimize their negative effects. Reducing the preterm birthrate turns out to be a challenge. As doctors become better able to recognize the need to induce early labor, preterm birthrates are rising. Technologies such as in vitro fertilization for couples with fertility problems can also increase the odds of multiple fetuses and preterm births (Goldenberg et al., 2008). Nonetheless, medical advances are enabling doctors to prolong the gestational period without harming the mother or the fetus. Such interventions can range from convincing mothers to stop smoking, to screening for and treating infections promptly, to careful monitoring of the mother's diet and nutritional supplements (Iams et al., 2008).

Even with the most attentive prenatal care, however, preterm births still occur, and so the second form of intervention aims to help children who are born preterm. Studies suggest that among these children, those who experience more parental involvement and stimulating, active play in infancy and educational support in the early school years show cognitive and motor improvements (de Kieviet et al., 2009; Koldewijn et al., 2010). Preterm infants and preschool children have also shown early benefits from additional practice with motor skills and supportive educational programs, but these gains do not seem to be sustained through elementary school (Orton et al., 2009). Health care professionals, teachers, and psychologists still have much to learn about what kinds of interventions can provide long-term benefits for children born preterm. At this point, improving prenatal care to reduce the number of extremely preterm births is likely to be the most effective form of intervention.

Q: What difficulties reduce survival, and what long-term complications are likely when a fetus is born preterm?

Why Does Anatomical Development Progress As It Does?

What determines which body parts develop first? One nineteenth-century hypothesis suggested that the development of an embryo followed the same course as the species' evolutionary history. This idea is summed up in the phrase "ontogeny recapitulates phylogeny," where *ontogeny* refers to the development of an organism and *phylogeny* refers to the evolutionary lineage of a species (Haeckel, 1874; see also Gilbert, 2006; Gould, 1977). Researchers have cited some striking patterns in human embryonic development that seem to support the hypothesis. For example, structures vaguely resembling gills emerge early on, only to transform later into facial muscles, middle ear bones, and other structures. Later, a tail-like structure emerges that is then reabsorbed into the body.

Despite these observations, however, the idea that a species' embryonic development follows its evolutionary history is based on a misconception about evolution. In truth, evolution *does not* proceed in a straightforward path that starts with the simplest one-celled organisms and, over time, yields increasingly complex creatures. Species evolved not through a direct, linear progression but in branching patterns, such that organisms on different branches each acquired their own properties that differed substantially from the features of earlier species (see Figure 2.14).

Keeping that important caution in mind, the hypothesis that "ontogeny recapitulates phylogeny" still has some value when you consider how it relates to the develop-mental constraint of viability. Some of the earliest evolving structures were those necessary for an organism's basic functioning. These same necessary structures and processes are likely to emerge early in development to ensure that the organism is viable. The systems that support the most basic survival functions must emerge early in development—both in an individual organism's lifespan and in a species' evolution. In later chapters, we will see that this same principle applies to many aspects of cognitive and social development as well.

Diversity out of Uniformity

In considering how such a diversity of anatomical structures eventually develops from the zygote's undifferentiated cells, we have already seen how certain early developing features, such as the primitive streak, guide cells' specialization. In addition, some general patterns of body development are common to a wide range of species. These patterns can shed more light on the mechanisms of cell differentiation that support the formation of specific parts of the body (Larsen et al., 2001; Moore & Persaud, 2003). For example, how does the genetic material in the zygote's cells give rise to a developing hand or an ear? How do these structures emerge in the right place on the body? And what directs more detailed developmental patterns, such as the development of a five-fingered human hand instead of one with four or six fingers?

Much mystery still surrounds these questions. Nonetheless, recent discoveries have dramatically changed our

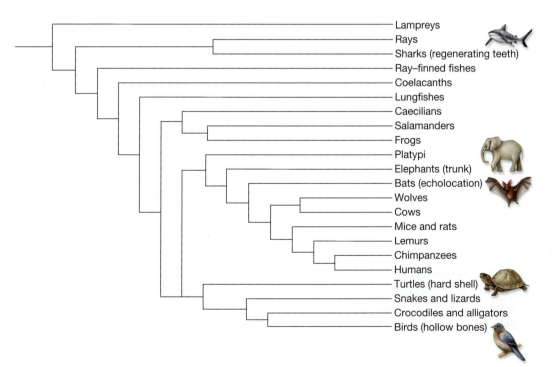

FIGURE 2.14 **Evolution as a branching tree.** At each branch in an evolutionary tree, a species acquires distinctive new traits, as shown in this small section of the evolutionary tree covering many vertebrates. As the branching structure shows, human development does not involve a progression through the properties of so-called "lower species." Adapted from C. Loeb, Macalester College.

understanding of how the body's overall structure develops, as well as how specific features, like limbs, emerge (Gilbert, 2010; Marcus, 2004; Mark et al., 1997). Special kinds of ordered clusters of master-switch genes known as **homeobox genes** activate or repress gene expression and thereby play an important role in defining the body plan. These homeobox genes contain the **homeobox**, a 180-base-pair sequence in the DNA of many different species of animals—from fruit flies to mice to humans. The homeobox encodes homeodomain proteins, which regulate genetic switches affecting the general structure and organization of certain body sections. First, the homeobox genes regulate the processes that lead to the formation of the anterior (front) and posterior (rear) sections of the organism's body (see Figure 2.15). Then, acting as switches at the top of large gene regulation cascades, they interact with other genes to code for species-specific appendages and other features. More specifically, when a homeobox gene is switched on, it sends chemical signals that reach many sections of the developing body. In response to these signals, genes throughout the body turn on or off as necessary to direct the growth of species-specific body parts, such as legs. The homeobox genes that govern the body plan in vertebrates are often called *Hox* genes.

> Q: What are homeobox genes? In what ways are their functions similar across a wide range of organisms?

Once the body's sections and major parts have been specified, how do the genes specify the fine-grained patterns of development, such as the appropriate number of fingers on a human hand? There is no gene sequence that codes for five fingers. Instead, various genetic influences trigger an intricate interaction of several chemicals. At critical points in development, these chemicals diffuse across the tissues from which the limbs later develop. The exposure of these tissues to specific concentrations of chemicals seems to trigger the appropriate number of fingers to develop (see Figure 2.16). The *Hox* genes also play a role in this process. Chemical signals turn these genes on and off in patterns that trigger limb growth in the appropriate region of the body.

The story of genes and body development involves both remarkable specificity and extraordinary generality. Each species' genome, interacting with a normal range of environments, results in that species' unique characteristics—and individuals' genes also cause clear differences within a species. Yet, the same basic genetic framework guides development

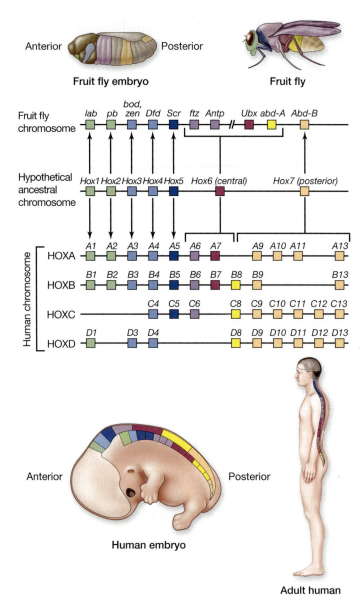

FIGURE 2.15 Homeobox genes. Homeobox genes are ordered clusters of genes that turn on and off genes that affect the general body plan in many species. In this drawing, squares of the same color indicate genes of the same type. Thus, the homeobox genes in the fruit fly also appear in humans, arranged in the same order. For example, genes of the same color code for comparable structures at the front (anterior) of the body across species, even though the particular types of structures differ radically. Adapted from Veraksa et al. (2000).

in a broad range of species as different as insects and mammals. Apparently, very early in evolutionary history, survival depended on body parts developing in the right sequence (for example, heads before front legs, front legs before hind legs) and in the right number (just one head, please!). The solution that emerged in the genes that encode the general body plan was so effective and reliable that these genes remained an active part of the genome in most later-evolving species, with relatively little change in their function.

Visiting Nurses, Prenatal Care, and Child Development

The city of Elmira, New York, sits near the Pennsylvania border in a region that has been economically depressed for decades, as its manufacturing economy has withered. Elmira's economic peak was in the late 1940s and early 1950s. Today, its population is half of what it was 60 years ago, and almost one-third of Elmira's children under 18 live in poverty. In the 1970s, David Olds, a graduate student at nearby Cornell University, set out to make a difference in the lives of Elmira's children, who at that time had the highest rates of abuse and child neglect in the state (Boo, 2006). Olds started the Nurse-Family Partnership Program, a program in which nurses visited disadvantaged pregnant women to advise them during their pregnancy and then after the birth of their child. Since that time, Olds's program has been extended to sites throughout the United States.

Nurses in the program visit first-time mothers in their homes, beginning during pregnancy and continuing through their child's second birthday. During their visits, they offer guidance about prenatal health and infant care in a nonthreatening, nonjudgmental way. They provide information about prenatal nutrition, explain the threats that smoking and alcohol pose to the fetus, and convey to the mothers the importance of avoiding behaviors that could compromise their own health or harm their infant (Olds, 2006; Olds et al., 2007). They often emphasize the immense promise and potential of the child—if only he or she receives the right kind of care and support (Boo, 2006).

The nurse's job can be extremely challenging. Members of the household, sometimes including the mother, may be hostile about taking an outsider's advice. One account of so-called "swamp nurses" who visited pregnant mothers in rural Louisiana discussed the challenges of an African-American nurse visiting white teenage mothers who often faced a host of problems, ranging from drug addiction to sexual abuse (Boo, 2006). To work well with these mothers, the nurses had to have an extraordinary combination of compassion, sensitivity, and firmness.

The Nurse-Family Partnership Program is evaluated repeatedly to make sure it is effective. Wherever possible, Olds has used *randomized assignment designs*, meaning that some mothers in a particular area are randomly selected to receive nurse visits and others in similar circumstances in the same area receive no visits. By randomly assigning mothers in comparable situations to either participate in the visiting nurse program or not, it is possible to compare outcomes between the groups to see whether the visits are effective. (Without random assignment, there would be no way to know whether group differences were due to the nurses' visits or to other factors, such as higher levels of motivation among mothers who seek the nurses' help.) In general, these careful studies often show positive effects for newborn infants. The effects are not always large, but the number of successes has encouraged agencies throughout the country to fund such programs.

Several studies have shown that nurse-visited mothers, especially the youngest mothers, have fewer medical complications during pregnancy and are less likely to have premature babies (Baldwin et al., 1998; Olds, 2006). In one study, the babies of nurse-visited mothers were almost a full pound heavier than the babies delivered by mothers in the control group, who were not visited by nurses (Olds et al., 1986). Nurse-visited mothers also tended to have fewer episodes of high blood pressure while pregnant and lower rates of cigarette smoking (Olds, 2006). Given the negative effects of fetal nicotine exposure on later brain development (Ernst et al., 2001; Thomas et al., 2000), these changes in the mothers' behavior represent an important medical treatment for the growing fetus.

The benefits of these programs extend far beyond the direct impact on brain growth. Nurse-visited mothers interact with their babies in a host of more positive ways and are less likely to abuse their children (Olds et al., 2007). After working with a nurse named Luwana, a mother named Alexis observed of her new son Daigan, "He's not as cranky as he was. And one thing I learned already is how he cries different when he's hungry than when he's wet." As Luwana explains to Alexis, "Making that distinction is important. . . . You're listening to him, and in his own way he's explaining what he needs" (Boo, 2006). Children of nurse-visited mothers show continuing benefits on into adolescence (Fisch, 2005; Kitzman et al., 2010; Olds, 2006). In many cases, these effects arise from a continuing pattern of positive interactions between mother and child (Leckman & Mayes, 2007).

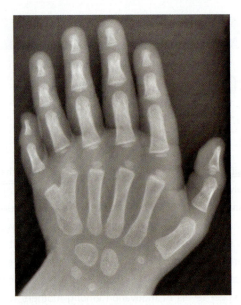

FIGURE 2.16 **Finger number.** Although infants are occasionally born with extra toes or fingers, as shown here, it is impressive how often the gene sequence results in the standard number. There is no specific part of the genome that codes for five digits per hand and foot. Instead, interactions between many genes result in overlapping chemical gradients that, together, usually result in this number.

Sexual Differentiation

So far, we have examined normal developmental processes common to all humans. But humans and many other animals also show different development patterns, depending on their sex. Differences between males and females are complex and occur not only in major anatomical structures, but also in physiological systems and, to some extent, in the brain (Austin & Edwards, 1981; McCarthy et al., 2009; Parker et al., 1999). Initially, the cells of the embryo do not show sex differences, but **sexual differentiation** starts very early, most likely in the first few weeks after conception. External sexual differentiation—the development of genitalia—occurs earlier in males than in females.

Although sexual differentiation is controlled by the X and Y sex chromosomes, genes do not directly code for sexual differentiation. Instead, these differences are controlled by exposure to particular sex-specific combinations of hormones, which are triggered and regulated through complex interactions between genes (McCarthy et al., 2009; Park & Jameson, 2005). If these genetic interactions trigger the embryo to produce higher levels of the male sex hormone testosterone, the cells exposed to testosterone will specialize to form structures with male characteristics. Likewise, if the embryo produces higher levels of the female sex hormone estrogen, this will trigger differentiation into cells that form structures with female characteristics. If an embryo with two X chromosomes (genetically female) is exposed to higher levels of testosterone before

the cells have begun to differentiate along female lines, that embryo can acquire many aspects of male anatomy, including sex-specific brain differences. The same kind of effect happens when undifferentiated embryonic males are exposed to higher levels of estrogen.

One example of early sexual differentiation can be seen in Figure 2.17. Initially, the human embryo has both Wolffian ducts and Müllerian ducts in the lower abdomen, as well as bipotential gonads (gonads that could develop into female or male structures). At this point, either male or female urogenital structures could emerge, but this changes as soon as the tissues are exposed to higher levels of a particular sex hormone. High testosterone and low estrogen cause the Wolffian ducts and testes to grow into a male urogenital system and cause the Müllerian ducts to wither away. High estrogen and low testosterone cause the Müllerian ducts and follicle cells in the ovary to grow into the female urogenital system and cause the Wolffian ducts to degenerate (see Table 2.2).

The adults of some species retain the capacity to change their phenotypic sex as a function of social dominance.

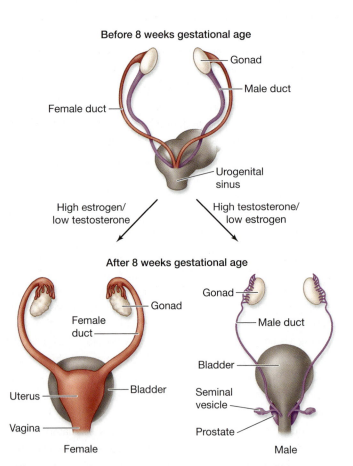

FIGURE 2.17 **The emergence of biological sex differences.** The early embryo has both the Müllerian ducts and Wolffian ducts. The urogenital system that develops from these ducts depends on which sex hormones contact the relevant tissues. Adapted from Matzuk & Lamb (2008).

Weeks after conception	Males	Females
6 or less	No anatomical differences; embryo is sexually bipotential.	No anatomical differences; embryo is sexually bipotential.
7	Testes start to form.	Ovaries start to form and develop functional subunits.
8	No obvious external differences; testosterone triggers growth of Wolffian ducts and withering of Müllerian ducts.	No obvious external differences; estrogen triggers growth of Müllerian ducts and withering of Wolffian ducts.
10	All internal sexual structures are present.	All internal sexual structures are present.
12	External sexual differences are visible.	External sexual differences are visible.

TABLE 2.2 **Changes in sexual characteristics in early prenatal development.** The presence of higher levels of testosterone or estrogen affects the development of sexual structures in males and females.

This phenomenon is most prevalent among reptiles, amphibians, and fish. There may be only one phenotypic male in the group whose role is stimulating ovulation in the phenotypic females. When that male dies, the dominant female undergoes a variety of changes that make her a phenotypic male, both behaviorally and anatomically. In these cases of environmental sex determination, all group members usually have the same genotype, and the specific male or female gene pathways are triggered by changes in the social environment (Francis & Barlow, 1993; Fricke & Fricke, 1977; Godwin, 2009; Robertson, 1972; Ross, 1990).

In humans, social context may cause much more subtle changes in hormonal balances, and if these changes occur during pregnancy, they could potentially have long-term effects on the fetus. For example, many studies of prenatal development have demonstrated that during pregnancy, maternal stress levels can affect the timing of the fetus's exposure to different levels of testosterone. One potential effect of these shifts in timing is to cause less sexual differentiation of the male brain; indeed, some researchers have claimed that this effect may be a biological basis of homosexuality (LeVay, 1993), although these claims remain controversial. The extent to which maternal hormones and the prenatal environment influence human sexual orientation remains unclear (Gooren, 2006).

A different aspect of the environment—namely, the number of older male siblings a male has—also seems to influence the frequency of homosexuality among men (Gooren, 2006; Puts et al., 2006). One controversial theory hypothesizes that the more older brothers a male child has, the greater the probability that child will develop homosexual attractions (Dawood et al., 2009). Because this effect only holds for older siblings with the same mother, not stepchildren or adopted children, it may be due to an immune response in the mother against some aspect of the Y chromosome or the hormones that trigger male characteristics. This theory suggests that the mother's immune response builds over the course of multiple pregnancies with male children, so that later sons would more likely be affected than earlier sons. Yet, since many firstborns can be homosexual and many lastborns are not, this pattern is only a small part of any account of how homosexual and heterosexual choices emerge in development. Much more research remains to be done before we can have a clear sense of the many factors contributing to homosexuality.

Sexual differentiation continues well after birth and on into puberty, and changing concentrations of hormones continuously influence the process. During this process, genes also interact with many kinds of environments, ranging from the hormones in the womb to the child's experiences after birth. All along, interactions between genes and the environment contribute to the ways that biological and behavioral traits emerge.

Adverse Influences on the Developing Embryo and Fetus

Given the complexity of development, it is remarkable that all of the body's structures form and grow normally and at appropriate times in the vast majority of cases. But sometimes problems do appear, often because of harmful environmental influences. Between 1957 and 1962, thousands of pregnant women in Europe and North America were given what appeared to be a new wonder drug for morning sickness: thalidomide. The drug has since become infamous for its adverse effects on developing fetuses. Its most obvious effects involved severely stunted limb growth and sometimes an absence of limbs (see Figure 2.18). It also caused serious defects in internal organs, genitalia, and the nervous system. More recent research suggests that thalidomide probably interfered with the activity of genes

FIGURE 2.18 Thalidomide and pregnancy. The tragedy of the babies whose mothers were prescribed thalidomide led to increased sensitivity to the dangers of teratogens and how the timing of exposure influences their effects.

that code for normal limb growth or perhaps with the *Hox* genes' timing signals (Marcil et al., 2003; Wolpert, 1999; Zeller, 2010).

Since the thalidomide disaster, doctors and the public have become more aware of possible negative influences on embryos and fetuses and better able to guard against them. Called **teratogens**, these hazardous internal or external environmental factors can potentially cause problems with development during the prenatal period. They can be classified into the categories shown in Table 2.3.

Teratogens illustrate a developmental theme discussed earlier: the importance of timing and sequencing in the developmental process. Specific teratogens tend to have especially strong harmful effects during specific times in prenatal development (see Figure 2.19). Thalidomide, for example, usually had its disastrous effects from 2 to 8 weeks after conception. Because of the sequence of anatomical development, the specific effects of thalidomide depend on the point during pregnancy when it is used. Using it only during a brief, early period in prenatal development, say at 3 to 6 weeks, might have impacts mostly on the arms and other anterior structures, whereas using it at a later period, say at 7 to 8 weeks, would more likely impair growth of the legs and more posterior structures. Generally, teratogens have the worst effects during the embryonic period, from about 2 to 8 weeks after conception, when the most dramatic qualitative changes take place. The central nervous system tends to be most vulnerable in the first few weeks after fertilization, fol-

lowed by the heart, then the limbs, the eyes, and finally the external genitalia, which do not seem to be influenced until after 6 weeks.

Thalidomide was a new, poorly understood drug when it was widely prescribed to pregnant women, as was diethylstilbestrol (DES), which was used to prevent miscarriage and led to increased risk for cancer in adolescents and adults who had been exposed to DES in the womb. In addition, some common drugs can also act as teratogens. For example, several anti-acne medicines are part of a family of chemical compounds known as retinoids. If a pregnant woman takes even a small amount of these medications, a wide range of birth defects become more likely. Depending on when in her pregnancy she takes the medication and for how long, it can cause hydrocephaly (swelling of the fluid-filled areas of the brain), microcephaly (undersized brain), heart defects, ear and eye defects, and cleft lip and palate (Durston et al., 1989; Maden, 2000). Vitamin A in its various forms is also a retinoid, and high doses of vitamin A during pregnancy can cause comparable defects—even though low doses are essential for normal development (Collins & Mao, 1999). A different drug, valproic acid, which is used to treat convulsive disorders (and sometimes bipolar disorder), can also cause birth defects ranging from neural problems to facial, heart, and skeletal malformation (Duncan, 2007; Finnell & Burn, 2001; Finnell et al., 2002). Even some drugs with minimal or no apparent side effects in adults can endanger a fetus.

Q: How does the timing of exposure to a teratogen affect its consequences for the developing fetus?

Teratogens are not limited to drugs; they can be part of the mother's diet as well. It is well known that drinking alcohol during pregnancy can be hazardous to the fetus, and its effects can be extensive. Depending on the age of the fetus, alcohol can cause smaller brain volume (see Figure 2.20) and impaired development of neurons and supporting cells (Archibald et al., 2001; Riley & McGee, 2005; Sowell et al., 2008; Spadoni et al., 2007).

Hazards posed by foods are often less obvious than the risks of drugs and alcohol. In some cases, foods can be contaminated with a trace amount of a teratogen that, while mildly harmful in adults, might be devastating for prenatal development. Many fish that are high in the food chain, such as swordfish and tuna, retain relatively high concentrations of mercury in their tissues from eating mercury-contaminated fish lower in the food chain. Because mercury can have strong teratogenic effects,

Teratogen type	Examples	Effects
Prescription drugs	Thalidomide	Underdeveloped limbs and organ problems
	DES (synthetic hormone)	Increased risk of various cancers in daughters
	Streptomycin (antibiotic)	Auditory impairment
	Retinoids (often prescribed for acne)	Brain defects, heart defects, eye and ear defects
Illegal drugs	Cocaine/crack	Stunted growth, microcephaly
	Heroin	Reduced neuron populations, memory deficits
Normally ingested substances	Alcohol	Fetal alcohol syndrome (mental retardation, microcephaly, anatomical defects in head and face)
	Nicotine	Anatomical defects, structural and functional impairments of the nervous system
	Aspirin	Amplifies effects of alcohol, bleeding problems
Environmental toxins (can enter via mother's diet)	Lead	Central nervous system damage
	PCB (industrial chemical)	Skin discoloration
	DDT (insecticide)	Impaired learning, neurotoxicity
	Petroleum distillates	Internal and skeletal malformations
Malnutrition	Iron deficiency	Impaired physical and cognitive growth
	Protein deficiency, insufficient calories	Increases negative effects of many teratogens
Infectious diseases	Rubella (German measles)	Deafness, blindness, heart defects, microcephaly, growth retardation, mental retardation
	Toxoplasmosis	Blindness, hydrocephaly, mental retardation
	AIDS	Possible growth retardation, microcephaly
	Herpes	Microcephaly, seizures
	Syphilis	Mental deficiency, hydrocephalus, deafness, blindness, bone malformations
Physiological disorders and immune incompatibilities	Blood incompatibilities	Neurodevelopmental disorders, possibly schizophrenia
	Diabetes	Congenital heart defects, neural tube defects, limb defects
	PKU (an inability to use an amino acid)	Mental retardation, heart defects
	Hypothyroidism (underactive thyroid gland)	Heart defects, reduced brain and body growth

TABLE 2.3 Teratogens and development. Teratogens are internal or external hazardous environmental factors that can affect the developing organism in utero and can result in birth defects. They are diverse both in kind and effects. Some of the effects can be remarkably specific, while others can be more global.

expectant mothers should limit their consumption of fish. Even more subtly, under some conditions, prenatal diets free of known teratogens can still have harmful effects on some fetuses. For example, during pregnancy, diabetic mothers must manage their blood level of insulin even more carefully than usual. Abnormally high or low blood insulin levels may lead to a kind of misprogramming of the fetal systems that regulate weight and metabolism (Plagemann, 2006). In addition, some maternal alleles appear to increase the risk of miscarriage or birth defects unless the expectant mother takes a certain dietary supplement, such as vitamin B_{12}, to offset the problem (Stover &

Garza, 2006; Tamashiro & Moran, 2010). Once again, genetic and environmental influences interact to produce developmental outcomes.

Although this book focuses on developmental psychology, a brief survey of biological development of the body as a whole has brought to light many principles that also pertain to neuropsychological development, ranging from canalization to the importance of when an organism encounters particular environments or events. We have also seen how prenatal development can affect postnatal functions and development, a theme we will carry forward in our discussion of brain development as well.

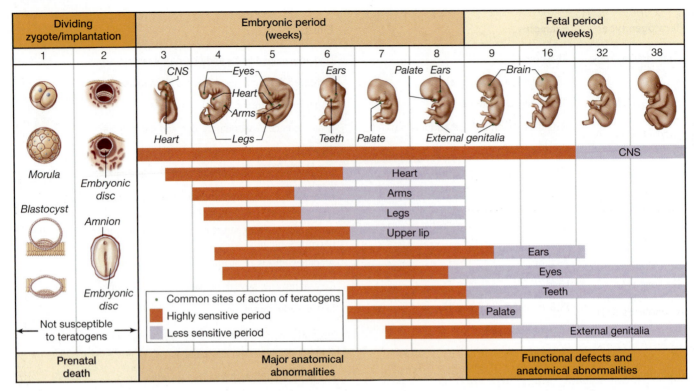

Dividing zygote/implantation		Embryonic period (weeks)						Fetal period (weeks)			
1	2	3	4	5	6	7	8	9	16	32	38

Morula

Blastocyst

Embryonic disc

Amnion

Embryonic disc

Not susceptible to teratogens

- Common sites of action of teratogens
- Highly sensitive period
- Less sensitive period

CNS

Heart

Arms

Legs

Upper lip

Ears

Eyes

Teeth

Palate

External genitalia

Prenatal death	Major anatomical abnormalities	Functional defects and anatomical abnormalities

FIGURE 2.19 Timing and teratogens' influences. This chart shows the periods in which different body systems and organs are most susceptible to teratogens and other external influences, as well as the periods when they are less sensitive but when exposure to teratogens can still cause damage. Adapted from Moore et al. (2013).

Brain Development

The development of the brain is an intricate process in which many structures develop in a tightly choreographed manner. During the prenatal period, some early-developing brain structures provide necessary frameworks for later ones, and spatial relations between these structures guide further development. Furthermore, the brain continues to grow and change dramatically after birth: the adult brain is roughly four times larger than the newborn brain. As we consider how the brain develops, it helps to keep in mind four themes that describe what is happening and why.

The first of these themes is a familiar developmental principle: vital structures and systems develop first. In the body, the heart is one of the first organs to function; indeed, the circulation of nutrients through the bloodstream is necessary for an organism's survival. In the brain, structures that support such life-critical functions as heartbeat, breathing, digestion, and blood pressure emerge very early. Similarly, structures that enable basic motion and sensing of stimuli tend to develop earlier than those that involve more complex coordination of actions or interpretation of information. The last structures to develop tend to be those involved in reasoning about choices and different patterns of information. Likewise, brain structures mature at very different rates, and brain

development tends to follow the "ontogeny recapitulates phylogeny" pattern. That is, brain structures that are evolutionarily older tend to mature earlier than regions that evolved more recently (Turner, 1950). The same pattern

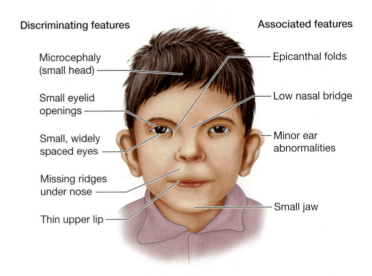

Discriminating features

Microcephaly (small head)

Small eyelid openings

Small, widely spaced eyes

Missing ridges under nose

Thin upper lip

Associated features

Epicanthal folds

Low nasal bridge

Minor ear abnormalities

Small jaw

FIGURE 2.20 The effects of high alcohol consumption during pregnancy. The child with fetal alcohol syndrome is born with low birth weight, microcephaly (abnormal smallness of the head), a low nasal bridge, a thin upper lip, and small but widely spaced eyes. Adapted from Riley & McGee (2005).

described earlier also holds in the brain: the structures and systems most essential for an organism's survival tend to appear earlier, both in evolution and in an individual's development.

The second important theme of brain development is that the later-developing brain structures tend to inhibit earlier-developing ones. In this case, inhibition is not simply a new system blocking the activity of an earlier one. Rather, as a new system develops, it tends to bring the existing systems under more refined and nuanced control. In later chapters, we will encounter various ways in which this pattern in brain development affects behavior; for example, some reflexes that are strong in newborns disappear as older infants become increasingly able to control and direct their movements (see Chapter 4). Similarly, we will see how development in the frontal areas of the brain during childhood underlies children's ability to inhibit a first impulse in favor of a more considered and effective response (see Chapter 13).

Third, sometimes "less is more" in brain development. That is, in contrast to most other body systems, several brain regions mature and become more sophisticated through processes of trimming away rather than proliferation and growth. Just as a gardener prunes a fruit tree to create a structure that is better suited to bearing fruit, brain regions undergo a *pruning* process to create more streamlined structures for the growing child or adolescent. Pruning brain regions may cause psychological changes in which a previously malleable behavior becomes less varied and more ingrained.

Fourth, the speed and amount of communication between different brain regions increases over the course of development. Many of the main thoroughfares of nerve cell communication can show as much as 100-fold increases in speed between birth and adulthood. These increases in speed and capacity allow different psychological systems to work together more efficiently.

As we look closely at brain development, we will also consider how environmental factors, including the prenatal maternal environment and the variety of environmental influences the child encounters, affect the developing brain. Does an extremely enriched or deprived environment affect an infant's brain? If an organism fails to have an experience before a certain age, what happens to the brain region responsible for processing that kind of experience? While it is obvious that brain development would influence our psychology, we will also see that psychological development influences the brain.

Major Changes to Brain Structures

The mature human brain has several distinct regions with specific functions. Most important for our developmental discussion are the regions shown in Figure 2.21. The brain

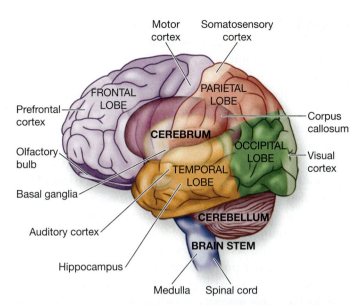

FIGURE 2.21 Basic structure of the human brain. The brain has three major parts and four lobes. Brain structures mature at different times and rates. Evolutionarily old structures required for survival, such as the spinal cord, medulla, and basal ganglia, mature early. Areas of the cortex that process sensory information, such as the visual cortex and the somatosensory cortex, mature earlier than the areas that process abstract information, such as the prefrontal cortex.

has three major parts. The **brainstem** is concerned with regulating heart rate, breathing, swallowing, blood pressure, digestion, and other automatic nonvoluntary processes in the body and is evolutionarily very old. The **cerebellum** is involved in coordination of voluntary movement and integration of some sensory information with action. The third and largest part, the **cerebrum**, includes the basal ganglia (involved in both voluntary and involuntary movement), the olfactory bulb (which processes information about smell), and the cerebral cortex.

The **cerebral cortex** is the most recently evolved region of the brain; it is most developed in humans and other primates and is usually associated with high-level thought. The cerebral cortex is divided into right and left hemispheres, which communicate with each other largely through a central pathway known as the **corpus callosum**.

Each hemisphere is further divided into four lobes that are primarily responsible for different functions. In general terms, the **frontal lobe** is involved in planning, problem solving, and regulating thoughts and emotion. The posterior parts of the frontal lobe are also involved in aspects of motor activity and understanding the grammar of languages. The **parietal lobe** has several functions, including processing and interpreting touch sensations, integrating visual and spatial information, and processing some aspects of the meanings of words. The **temporal lobe** processes auditory information and other aspects of language meaning, and it supports crucial components of memory. Finally, the occipital lobe processes visual information. These descriptions of the different functions of the lobes are approximate; in fact, the lobes interact extensively with one another and with other brain regions.

Brain structures and the pathways between regions mature at different times and rates. As we have seen, evolutionarily more ancient structures that are required for basic survival, such as the spinal cord, medulla, and basal ganglia, tend to mature earliest because they support such activities as breathing, heart rate, and appetite. Areas of the cortex that process sensory information, such as the visual cortex and the somatosensory cortex, mature somewhat later and continue to mature for some time after birth as higher and higher levels of processing become more refined. Finally, areas that process more abstract information and regulate other areas, such as the prefrontal cortex, tend to mature last. This sequence is only a crude characterization of a much more complex interplay between brain regions over the course of development, an interplay that also helps drive development. Thus, a circuit of mutual interactions between two areas may foster development of both.

Thinking about the brain in terms of regions with specific functions is helpful for understanding some aspects of its structure and capacities. But when it comes to understanding brain development, it is important to keep in mind that the brain is a highly interactive system in which each area depends on inputs from the others. When you recall the flowers at your cousin's wedding, you access and integrate memory traces from many different parts of the cerebral cortex. In this process, you use each of the four lobes in operations such as knowing where the wedding was held, constructing a mental image of the bouquets, remembering their sweet smell, visualizing how they were displayed, and knowing the names of roses, lilies, and orchids.

How does the embryo develop this rich array of brain structures and abilities? As mentioned earlier, in the first few weeks after conception, part of the ectoderm starts to form a groove, which will become the neural tube. By the time the ectoderm starts to close into a tube at 4 weeks, the structure has three distinct bumps: the forebrain, the midbrain, and the hindbrain, also known as cerebral vesicles. At 5 weeks, the forebrain and hindbrain vesicles split and form several distinct brain regions. Three of the most important regions are the *telencephalon*, the *diencephalon* and *midbrain*, and the *brainstem*.

The telencephalon eventually becomes the cerebral hemispheres, the areas that support the highest levels of psychological functioning. The diencephalon and midbrain give rise to the basal ganglia and other structures that reside between the cerebral hemispheres and above the brainstem. These include structures that integrate sensory information, as well as the cerebellum. By 10 weeks after conception, most of the brain's major regions are visible without use of a microscope.

At 20 weeks, the cerebral hemispheres are clearly visible, but they are smooth rather than fissured. This begins to change at around 24 weeks. At that point, the cortical surface develops the folds and fissures that are essential for supporting the complex processing of the human brain. These changes are summarized in Table 2.4 and Figure 2.22.

As noted earlier, the infant's brain grows quite a bit after birth. Weighing roughly 350 to 400 grams at birth, the brain's weight more than doubles in the first year of life, and it weighs about 1,250 grams (a little under 3 pounds) by 5 years. These large increases in brain mass in the first 5 years of life are assumed to increase its processing capacity. After age 5, brain volume stays relatively constant until some shrinkage begins in old age.

Neurons and Neurotransmitters

Along with these large-scale changes, the brain also changes dramatically at the microscopic level, both before and after birth. Since much of the change centers around

Weeks after conception	Event
3	Neural tube starts to form.
4	Three brain regions are now distinct: forebrain, midbrain, hindbrain; neural tube is almost completely closed.
5	Cerebral vesicles are now present.
10	Major central nervous system structures are now visible.
20	Brain weighs about 100 grams; cortical surface appears smooth.
24	Programmed cell death (apoptosis) begins.
28	Cortical surface has clear folds.
38 weeks–birth	Brain weighs 350 to 400 grams.

TABLE 2.4 Timetable of prenatal brain development. Major neural changes occur in a regular sequence of steps representing an extraordinary amount of change in a short period of time.

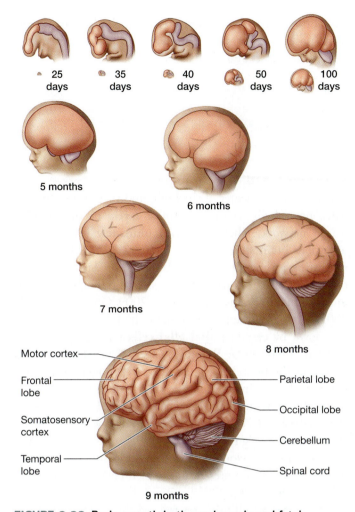

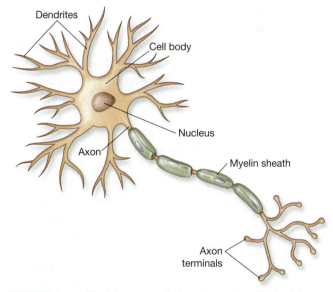

| 25 days | 35 days | 40 days | 50 days | 100 days |

5 months

6 months

7 months

8 months

Motor cortex

Frontal lobe

Somatosensory cortex

Temporal lobe

Parietal lobe

Occipital lobe

Cerebellum

Spinal cord

9 months

FIGURE 2.22 Brain growth in the embryonic and fetal stages. The brain structures are shown from 25 days through 9 months. The size of the developing brain from 25 days to 100 days is enlarged to show the details that would not be apparent at the actual sizes (which are indicated below the enlarged depictions). Note the relatively late appearance of cerebral fissures and the relatively late maturation of the frontal lobe. Adapted from Cowan (1979).

the brain cells known as **neurons**, we will briefly review what neurons are and how they work before considering how they develop and form connections. Like the body's other cells, each neuron is surrounded by a membrane that partitions the cell interior from its surrounding environment. As in other cells, the neuron's cell body contains the structures that support its basic functions as well as the nucleus, which contains its genetic material (see Figure 2.23). Neurons differ from other cells, however, in the specialized structures that enable them to transmit information to one another. Branching out from the neuron's cell body are the **dendrites**, which have receptors that receive chemical signals from other neurons. The number of receptors on a single neuron varies widely and can be as high as several hundred thousand. Many dendrites are also covered with small protrusions known as

dendritic spines, which also house receptors. Each neuron also has an **axon**, a tube-like projection that, in adults, can range from over a meter long (more than 3 feet) to less than a centimeter (under half an inch). Neurons typically have many dendrites and only one axon, although the axon may have several branches. Each branch ends in axon terminals, which have small bulbs at the tips that contain chemical **neurotransmitters**, which transmit signals across gaps between neurons.

Communication between neurons occurs at **synapses**, which are the small gaps between the axon terminals of one neuron and the dendrites of another. Neurons can be chained together in elaborate networks, with each neuron's axon terminals ending in synapses that separate them from the dendrites of other neurons—whose axon terminals, in turn, end in synapses that separate them from yet other neurons' dendrites. When the small bulbs at the end of an axon of the presynaptic neuron (the neuron sending the signal) release neurotransmitters into the synapse, these chemical signals cross the synapse and are received by the receptors at the ends of the adjacent dendrites on the postsynaptic neuron (the neuron receiving the signal). There are several types of neurotransmitters, and each neuron's receptors respond to particular types. These chemical signals can cause the receiving neuron to "fire," creating an electrical signal called an **action potential**. When the neuron fires, the action potential travels down the axon to the ends of the axon terminals. There, the resulting electrochemical changes trigger the ends of the terminals to release neurotransmitters into the synapse.

Dendrites

Cell body

Nucleus

Axon

Myelin sheath

Axon terminals

FIGURE 2.23 The structure of the nerve cell. Although nerve cell structures vary, most nerve cells have a cell body with a nucleus, dendrites, an axon, and axon terminals. The axon of many nerve cells is covered with a myelin sheath, which speeds transmission of the electrical impulse along the axon.

The speed with which the action potential travels down the axon partly depends on whether the axon is wrapped with **myelin**, a fatty substance that acts somewhat like the rubber insulation that directs electrical conduction along a wire. **Myelination** occurs when the axons are enclosed in a myelin sheath, which speeds the movement of the action potential along the axon. Myelin is produced by **glial cells**, which, generally speaking, serve to support the neurons by providing nutrients, producing myelin, and providing other kinds of structural support. The glial cells' importance and number are often underappreciated. In the human brain, there are roughly 100 times as many glial cells as neurons.

Although electrical signals play a key role in communication between neurons, it is important to remember that the action potential is *not* the same as an electrical current passing through a wire, which can travel at 300 million meters per second. In contrast, the action potential involves a series of electrochemical charges that travel down the axon much more slowly, ranging from 100 meters per second to a relatively sedate 1 meter per second. In development, neurons gradually become myelinated at different times and rates. As we will see shortly, the myelination process is thought to play a significant role in the development of various psychological capacities.

Development of Neurons

The four main processes involved in the development of neurons are proliferation, migration, consolidation, and myelination. *Proliferation* involves the creation of nerve cells and dendritic branches at different times of development. *Migration* refers to the remarkable ways that developing neurons move through brain tissue to their final positions. *Consolidation* refers to reducing the number of connections between neurons as a way of fine-tuning their structure and function. Finally, *myelination* helps speed up the transmission of information along the axonal shaft of a neuron.

Proliferation During the prenatal period, the production of new neurons, or **neurogenesis**, occurs on a massive scale. After the neural tube forms, roughly 250,000 new nerve cells are produced every minute until 100 billion are present. For many years, researchers thought that no new neurons were produced after birth, but postnatal neurogenesis has been documented in several brain areas, including the hippocampus, which is involved in memory and spatial knowledge (Abrous et al., 2005; Gould, 2007; Pujadas et al., 2010; Rakic, 2002; Richardson et al., 2007; Zhao et al., 2008). Although many fewer neurons are produced after birth than during the prenatal period, the neurons generated after birth can become fully integrated into existing circuitry (Zhao et al., 2008). While postnatal neurogenesis

has not yet been shown definitively in the human cortex, some positive reports suggest that with better measures it may be demonstrated there as well (Gould, 2007).

Q: Is there growth of new neurons after birth?

Migration and Synaptogenesis New nerve cells develop near the center of the brain and then move through older nerve cells to the outermost layers of the growing neural network, where they will ultimately become parts of various brain structures (see Figure 2.24A). Most of this **migration** is thought to happen either before birth or around the time of birth, but some migration is also thought to occur in adult human brains (Cayre et al., 2009; Ghashghaei et al., 2007). Nerve cells appear to migrate by following the paths laid down by certain **radial glial cells** that serve as guides (Hatten, 1990, 1999; Rakic, 1972, 1981, 1988). Chemical signals in the brain also guide nerve cell migration by providing different "instructions" for different cell groups about where in the brain to go and when to stop (Dodd & Jessell, 1988; Ghashghaei et al., 2007; Tessier-Lavigne & Goodman, 1996; Tessier-Lavigne & Placzek, 1991). Indeed, researchers can predict where axons will grow within tissue clusters based on which tissues are present and which chemicals they emit (Heffner et al., 1990).

After a nerve cell migrates toward the brain's outermost level, its axon starts to grow and interconnect with other neurons. As the axon grows, it finds its way to its appropriate destination, which can be more than a meter away. The end of the growing axon has a **growth cone**, which enables it to push its way through other tissues and track chemical signals that tell it in which directions to move (see Figure 2.24B and C).

When the branching ends of the axon arrive at their destination, they form the bulb-like structures that release neurotransmitters across the synaptic gaps between cells. The neuron also grows thousands of smaller dendritic branches from its cell body. This is where the brain's intricate interconnectedness becomes clear. Each dendritic branch can make synaptic connections with different neurons, so that just a few neurons can make hundreds of thousands of connections in a very small space. Across the entire human brain, the total number of connections is truly massive, somewhere around 10^{15} (that's 1,000 trillion, or a quadrillion!).

Q: What factors influence the direction in which individual neurons grow?

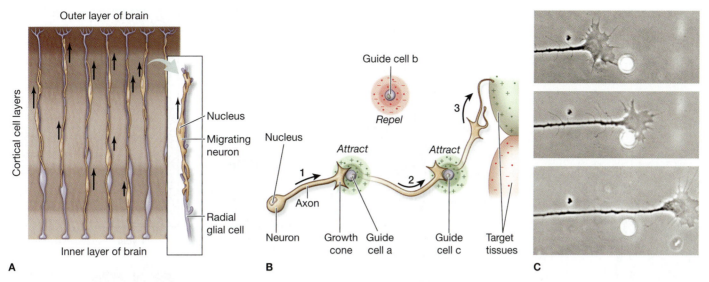

FIGURE 2.24 Nerve cell migration and axonal guidance toward target cells. (A) New nerve cells migrate from the inner layer of the brain through other layers of the cortex toward the outermost layer of the brain, traveling along radial glial cells that act as guides. Adapted from Rakic (1972, 1990). **(B)** Once a nerve cell reaches the outermost layer, it extends its axon by producing growth cones that are guided toward the target cell by chemical signals. These signals, made up of proteins, come from guide cells. Some proteins spur the axon to grow toward them by emitting attractant chemicals (as shown by guide cells a and c); other proteins repel the axon by emitting chemicals that trigger the axon to grow in the other direction (as shown by guide cell b). These signals affect the growing axon, causing the growth cone to twist and turn toward its target. **(C)** This series of three photomicrographs shows the path of a single axon as its growth cone moves toward the circular guide cell, reaches it, and then moves beyond it.

Synaptogenesis, the process of forming new synapses, creates the vast number of connections between neurons; each of our 100 billion neurons is associated with 10,000 synapses. In contrast to neurogenesis, which mostly takes place in the prenatal period, synaptogenesis remains an important process throughout the lifespan. Functionally, synaptogenesis seems to be involved in fine-tuning neural networks during learning. It creates new synapses in the course of certain experiences and eliminates synapses in the course of others (Waites et al., 2005), and it can be quite sensitive to variations in experience and environment (Flavell & Greenberg, 2008). In other mammals, such as rats, just a few days of experience can create new synaptic connections (Ge et al., 2007; He et al., 2010; Waites et al., 2005).

Although newborns do have neurons and synapses, their neurons are simpler in structure and make far fewer interconnections. In addition, around the time of birth, some neurons' growth cones are still seeking their target locations within the brain. Newborns' neurons are also much less myelinated than adult neurons (see Figure 2.25A). In fact, myelination continues well into adulthood in some areas of the brain. Development therefore proceeds both at the cellular level of individual neurons and in terms of their interconnections with other neurons (see Figure 2.25B and C).

Consolidation During development, the number of synaptic connections does not steadily increase. Instead, both prenatally and postnatally, there are periods of considerable pruning, a process that reduces the number of neurons and synaptic connections. Early on in childhood, the human brain has approximately 100 billion (10^{10}) nerve cells and as many as 1,000 trillion (10^{15}) synapses, but through the pruning process, both numbers decrease after childhood. This developmental pattern of an early excess of connections is sometimes called "initial overexuberance."

Neural structures can be pruned through programmed cell death, or **apoptosis**. In apoptosis, cells do not simply die randomly; instead, they die in highly specific patterns that help shape the resulting neural circuits. This type of cell death is first observed at around 24 weeks after conception. Cell death is a natural pattern of development in which neurons are pruned out of a system as a consequence of less use, less environmental stimulation, or less internal stimulation or because a maturational instruction shuts down cell function. When a neuron undergoes apoptosis, it necessarily eliminates all of that cell's synaptic connections. But another, more fine-grained form of **synaptic pruning** is also possible. In this case, the neuron stays alive, but some of its synapses are selectively eliminated. Both forms of pruning seem to be completed by adolescence (Huttenlocher, 1979, 2002). It is not yet clear whether these two forms—apoptosis and synaptic pruning—serve different functions. It seems plausible, though, that apoptosis is associated with larger-scale changes in neural circuits, while synaptic pruning may be more specifically localized and more sensitive to environmental factors.

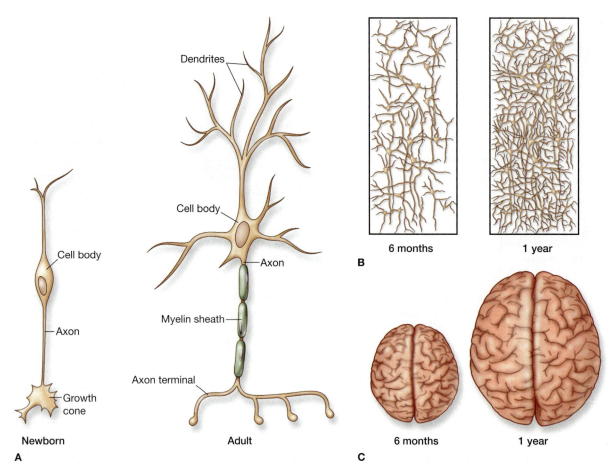

FIGURE 2.25 Increasing neuronal complexity. (A) Individual neurons become more complex and increasingly interconnected during the period after birth, as shown in these examples of a newborn and mature neuron in the cerebral cortex. Using growth cones, the newborn neuron is still growing toward target cells, where it will form axon terminals to communicate with other neurons, and it is not yet myelinated. **(B)** Between 6 months of age and 1 year of age, complexity of synaptic connections increases significantly, as does **(C)** the size of the brain. Adapted from Conel & Le (1941, 1967).

Q: How do connections between neurons change after birth?

Both environmental and genetic factors influence the complex processes that govern which cells and synapses get pruned (Blakemore, 2008; Hill et al., 2010; Thomas & Johnson, 2008). One classic study of how vision develops in newborn cats dramatically showed the effects of the environment—and specific experiences—on pruning. When the cats had one of their eyes covered up, and thus deprived of visual input, during the first 2 weeks after birth, the researchers observed striking changes in the cats' brains. The neurons that normally fire only when they receive visual input from both eyes at once actually died off (Wiesel & Hubel, 1963). As a consequence, while the kittens could see well with each eye independently, they lost the ability to mentally fuse the images seen by both eyes, a process that considerably enhances depth perception.

Genetic influences can also cause cells to die or connections to disappear, but the reasons for these kinds of pruning are less clear (Fox et al., 2010; Jacobson et al., 1997; Pettmann & Henderson, 1998). One possible explanation may be that an initial excess of neurons and synapses, which is followed by pruning, simply may be the most efficient growth mechanism early in brain development. As an analogy, consider the way to build a snow sculpture: First you make large balls of snow because it is the easiest and fastest way to get started and perhaps the mass helps link the balls together. Then you carve out the desired form from the large mass. Similarly, it may be especially efficient for the brain to grow large networks of neurons and interconnections as rapidly as possible at first and then to eliminate the excess cells and connections, resulting in a network shaped by both experience and genetic instructions.

Myelination Another remarkable pattern of postnatal neural development is myelination, the process of enclosing axons in the fatty material called myelin, which provides an insulating cover (Yakovlev & Lecours, 1967; see Figure 2.26A). As we have said, the myelin sheath increases the speed at which nerve impulses travel along the axon, making the process up to 100 times faster. Heavily myelinated bundles of axons in the brain are commonly called *white matter*, while the brain tissue that consists of unmyelinated cell bodies and dendrites is called *gray matter*. White matter often forms the connections between clusters of gray matter, where the more intricate circuits exist. The process of myelination begins before birth and continues well into middle age (Bartzokis et al., 2003; Westlye et al., 2009). The earliest structures to be myelinated are the spinal cord and lower brain structures. Myelination then proceeds toward the higher structures of the cortex and from the back of the brain toward the front.

Figure 2.26B shows how different brain regions become myelinated at different ages. Areas that process sensory information tend to be myelinated before birth and shortly thereafter. Areas that direct motor activity start being myelinated shortly before birth, and then myelination of these regions continues through the first year of life. Finally, myelination supporting integration of cortical association areas begins after birth and continues all the way into adulthood. In the cortex, myelination tends to slowly progress forward so that the last steps of myelination occur in the frontal cortex. Some researchers argue that the relatively late myelination of the frontal lobes in the mid-20s helps explain why some adolescents and young adults are especially prone to recklessness and risk taking (Casey et al., 2008; Kelley et al., 2004; Steinberg, 2010).

Experience and Brain Development

As we have seen, the environment influences developmental processes at multiple levels, ranging from its effects on cells and gene regulation to influences on larger bodily systems. Now let's consider environmental influences on the brain in more detail. We have already seen that depriving the brain of visual input from one eye affects the development of vision by causing pruning of nerve cells and synapses designed to receive input from both eyes. Similarly, research suggests that rats that develop in a deprived environment will have fewer and less complex neurons than rats that experience a normal environment (Black & Greenough, 1986).

These examples show that neurons deprived of a specific type of input may die off or show stunted development—but sometimes, they can thrive on a new type of input. **Compensation plasticity** refers to the capacity for an area of the brain that is deprived of its normal inputs and processing routines to become devoted to other functions instead. In some cases, this change results in a heightening of the remaining abilities to help the organism compensate for the loss. Thus, if a child is born deaf, the brain area typically devoted to the processing of auditory information may be repurposed to process visual information. As a result, the child's visual perception may be unusually acute and compensate for the auditory loss (Bavelier & Neville, 2002; Bavelier et al., 2006). In fact, on tasks that require sensitive peripheral vision, adults who were born deaf show distinct advantages over those with normal hearing (Dye et al., 2009). Evidence of compensation plasticity seems especially apparent in the

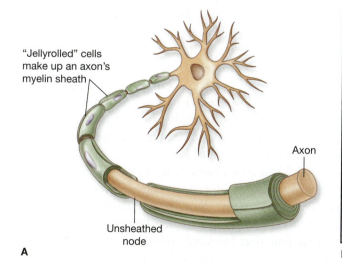

"Jellyrolled" cells make up an axon's myelin sheath

Axon

Unsheathed node

A

	Gestation	First year	Years 1–10	Years 10–30
Sensory systems				
Optic nerve	▬			
Initial stages of sensory processing	▬			
Motor systems				
Cerebellum		▬▬▬		
Major motor neuron tracts		▬▬▬		
Integrative systems				
Connections between midbrain and cortex			▬▬▬	
Cortical association areas			▬▬▬▬▬▬	

B

FIGURE 2.26 Myelination. (A) The wrapping of a fatty substance known as myelin several times around an axon is a critical developmental process that speeds up the conduction of nerve impulses along the axon. **(B)** The myelination process continues into early adulthood. Sensory areas are myelinated before birth. Myelination of the motor systems also starts before birth and continues past the first year of life. Finally, the integrative systems show little myelination until after birth, and the process continues into adulthood.

brain's association areas (Amedi et al., 2005; Merabet & Pascual-Leone, 2010; Röder et al., 2002).

We have considered the effects of a specific type of deprivation, such as loss of vision, in an otherwise normal environment. What happens at the neural level when a child grows up in a much more problematic environment with massive deprivation of all forms of inputs? Several studies have looked at orphans and abandoned children who grew up in deprived and highly stressful conditions—similar in some respects to conditions that inhibit neurogenesis and synaptogenesis in animals (Chu & Lieberman, 2010; Gunnar, 2001; Gunnar & Quevedo, 2007). A variety of measures suggest that such deprivation can cause changes in brain development. The deprived children showed differences in overall brain size and physiological activity (Nelson, 2007) as well as indications of lesser myelination of the connections between major brain regions (Eluvathingal et al., 2006). Some scholars have suggested that extremely deprived children may experience excessive pruning and have less organized synaptic connections (Nelson, 2007). As noninvasive measures of brain structure improve, it should be possible to document these differences more precisely and to determine whether they are sometimes irreversible.

Since deprivation can cause apoptosis and pruning of synapses, many have wondered whether an enhanced environment could have the opposite effect on brain development. Could engaging stimulation lead to more complex synaptic connections and dendritic branches? Many eager parents have attempted to accelerate their baby's brain development through such environmental "enhancements" as classical music, visually challenging mobiles, and intensive language exposure. In a broad sense, this question remains open, but it cannot be addressed experimentally in humans given the obvious ethical problems of assigning infants to "deprived," "normal," or "enriched" environments.

By posing more focused questions, however, researchers have found some effects of enrichment (Kempermann et al., 1997), many of which result from the learning experiences that take place in an enriched environment. Of course, when an organism learns, the brain changes. If rats are required to learn a new skilled task, that challenging experience will cause them to grow new synapses in the cerebellum (Black et al., 1990). Similarly, when monkeys are taught to use a new tool, their neurons in the brain region involved in grasping and tool use become more interconnected (Hihara et al., 2006).

Aside from growing new synapses, another subtle but important effect of learning is the strengthening or weakening of existing synaptic connections, a process that happens continuously in adult organisms. As we have already begun to see, experience can also affect the number of synapses, the neuronal patterns of connection, and the birth or death of neurons. These kinds of changes demonstrate the brain's **experience-dependent plasticity**, the ability of the brain to

be malleable, or "plastic," and physically change as a result of experience (Greenough et al., 1987).

In humans, it is not possible to directly measure experience-dependent changes in the number of dendritic branches or synapses. Indirect measures using neuroimaging suggest that these changes may occur during the process of acquiring and honing a skill. For example, when people learn to juggle, there is an increase in gray matter (where most neural interconnections occur) in the brain region associated with the visual processing of motion (Draganski et al., 2004). Similarly, years of intensive music performance training is associated with increased myelination of the relevant motor neuron pathways (Bengtsson et al., 2005; Hyde et al., 2009). Finally, compared with other adults, veteran taxi drivers have been shown to have enlarged hippocampal regions—areas involved in spatial reasoning and maintaining mental maps (Maguire et al., 2000). Together the findings from human and nonhuman animal studies strongly suggest that the brain restructures itself as a result of focused activity (Dayan & Cohen, 2011; Johansen-Berg, 2007). It remains controversial, however, whether commercial infant enrichment programs are any more beneficial than normal (nondeprived) infant experience.

Puberty and Brain Development

As children enter puberty, their behavior often changes significantly. Even the ancients took note. According to the Greek philosopher Aristotle, "Youth are heated by Nature as drunken men by wine" (Dahl, 2004, p. 8). His observation is borne out by statistics concerning reckless driving, unprotected sex, substance abuse, and a host of other dangerous behaviors carried out by adolescents (Steinberg, 2007). Besides risk taking, adolescents show a variety of behavioral changes, including a surge of interest in sex and romantic relationships, changed sleep patterns, and increased appetite. Several kinds of psychopathology are also much more common among adolescents than among younger children. Many of these changes will be discussed in the book's final chapters. Here we focus on some of the changes in the brain that relate to the upheaval of adolescence.

As mentioned in Chapter 1, puberty is a time of pronounced qualitative biological change. Males develop facial hair and broader shoulders, and females develop breasts and wider hips. Male voices become lower pitched, a phenomenon that led some overzealous medieval choir directors to castrate choirboys shortly before puberty, preserving their ability to hit very high notes (Rosselli, 1988). Given these dramatic bodily changes, it is natural to ask about corresponding changes in the brain—especially since brain signals trigger puberty's hormone surges (Dahl,

2004). Growth hormones increase height and size; adrenal hormones lead to pubic hair, acne, and other changes; still other complexes of hormones cause the sex organs to mature. Brain signals set off these anatomical changes, but what about the brain itself? Do changes in brain structure occur during puberty?

In fact, a number of dramatic changes in the brain occur late in childhood and during the teenage years (see Figure 2.27). Some of the most remarkable, well-documented changes take place in the frontal lobes. This brain region, which is associated with planning, problem solving, and regulating thoughts and emotions, undergoes significant pruning of synaptic connections during adolescence. It shows a 40 percent drop in the total number of synapses from late childhood to adulthood (Andersen, 2003; Huttenlocher, 1979). This decrease is thought to streamline the region's neural circuits to support faster and more efficient performance. At the same time, the amount of white matter in the frontal lobes substantially increases, perhaps supporting better communication and integration between the frontal lobes and other brain regions (Casey et al., 2008; Somerville et al., 2011; Yurgelun-Todd, 2007). In general, the section of the frontal lobes called the prefrontal cortex, which lies below the forehead at the front of the brain, matures the latest. It shows growth into the 20s.

One possible explanation for increased risk taking in adolescence involves interactions between systems in the frontal lobes and another group of brain structures called the limbic system (Somerville & Casey, 2010; Steinberg, 2007). The limbic system is concerned with emotion and memory, among other functions, and it is closely related to a structure called the *striatum*, which is involved in the detection of and response to rewards. For years, adolescents' risk taking was attributed to flaws in their reasoning about risks and consequences. Many experts believed that if ado-

lescents were better informed about the true nature of risks, their behavior would improve. But despite decades of driver's education courses, sexual education courses, and media campaigns about drug abuse, none of these approaches have worked very well in reducing risky behavior. At the same time, other studies have shown that adolescents are just as good as adults at estimating risks when asked to do so in judgment tasks (Steinberg, 2007). Why, then, do they still take more risks?

One clue comes from the finding that among adolescents, risk taking is much more likely in groups. Some researchers suggest that the social nature of this behavior relates to specific changes that take place during puberty in the connections between limbic system structures (the amygdala and nucleus accumbens, which regulate emotions), the striatum (which is concerned with rewards and motivation), and parts of the frontal lobe (the prefrontal cortex, which is concerned with planning and control) (Somerville et al., 2011). One result may be that during adolescence, the emotional arousal system is especially active during social interactions with peers and overrides the control system of the still maturing prefrontal cortex. At the same time, the emotional arousal system seems to undergo neural changes during puberty that make adolescents prone to pursuing greater immediate rewards, even when it means taking bigger risks. One theory suggests that these changes may actually help adolescents to take the risks associated with achieving independence from their parents (Casey et al., 2008). It may also be that the lure of rewards (detected in the striatum) tends to exert much greater influence on teenagers' planning and self-control systems (in the prefrontal cortex) and that only after adolescence do the prefrontal systems develop a stronger influence on regulating the brain's reward systems (see Figure 2.28).

As adolescents mature, the emotional arousal system becomes more regulated and less likely to overwhelm the brain's planning and self-control systems in the frontal and parietal lobes. The increasing myelination of these frontal and parietal regions may allow them to communicate more effectively with the emotional arousal and reward areas. At the same time, the pruning of neuronal

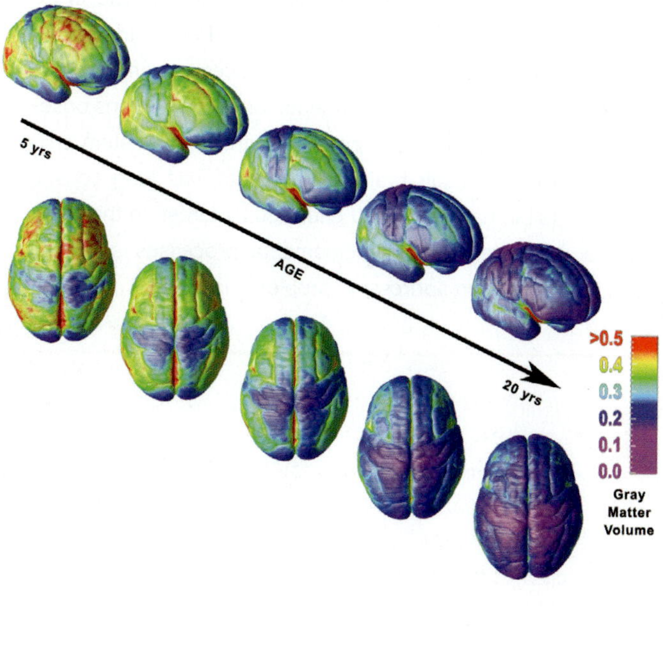

FIGURE 2.27 Changes in gray matter from early childhood through puberty and young adulthood. This set of computer images of right lateral and top views of the brain shows the changes in the distribution of gray matter in the cortex between ages 5 and 20. Red areas indicate high gray matter volume, whereas blue and purple areas indicate striking gray matter loss. Gray matter volume increases in areas associated with sensory and motor functions at earlier ages, but it decreases in these areas as the child grows older. Loss of gray matter volume in areas associated with integrating information and planning begins in late childhood and accelerates during adolescence. The loss of gray matter volume during adolescence may reflect a form of synaptic pruning. From Gogtay et al. (2004).

Repairing Brain Damage Later in Life?

Many of us know someone who has suffered the effects of brain damage as an adult. The damage can range from a shrapnel wound that impairs speech, a stroke that hampers vision, or the more widespread neuronal death that causes the motor problems involved in Parkinson's disease. For many years, research suggested that humans couldn't develop new nerve cells after birth, so these conditions were considered incurable. In the last decade or so, however, considerable evidence has shown that even adult brains sometimes generate new nerve cells (Arvidsson et al., 2002; Bjorklund & Lindvall, 2000; Muir, 2010). It appears that the different types of myelin cells that ensheathe many axons play a critical role in either inhibiting or promoting regrowth of nerve cells, depending on the type of myelin involved. In rats, the myelin cells that normally ensheathe the optic nerve inhibit nerve cell regrowth. But in one study, researchers cut the optic nerves of adult rats and then ensheathed the severed optic nerve cells with myelin cells transplanted from the olfactory bulb, because they were thought to promote nerve regrowth (Li et al., 2003; Raisman & Li, 2007). Indeed, the transplanted myelin cells promoted the growth of new cells in the severed optic nerves. Researchers have not yet managed to bring about enough nerve regrowth to restore the rats' vision, but that eventual outcome seems likely. In similar experiments aimed at regrowing motor neurons that have been cut, researchers are making progress restoring the cut nerves' functionality.

Myelin appears to affect nerve regrowth in interesting ways. In the central nervous system, the glial cells that produce myelin also produce three distinct proteins that become embedded in myelin and then directly inhibit nerve growth. These growth-inhibiting proteins may help set normal limits on healthy nerves' growth—but they also block regeneration when nerves are damaged (Woolf & Bloechlinger, 2002). Changing the material that ensheathes nerve cells by transplanting glial cells from olfactory nerves that have growth-promoting proteins could become a valuable method of repairing nerve damage in adults. Researchers are actively trying to understand how and why some glial cells promote nerve cell regeneration and others block it (Muir, 2010).

An especially effective way to repair nerve cell damage would be to have a population of cells in the adult brain that could differentiate into particular kinds of neurons. They could then take over functions that were disrupted by the death of other nerve cells. Such cells are known as adult **stem cells**. It was previously thought that the adult brain did not contain stem cells and that the only means of nerve regeneration was to regrow parts of existing neurons. Recently, however, it has become clear that the brain does have adult stem cells capable of becoming new, functional nerve cells, especially when they are surrounded by an appropriate scaffold of cells that doesn't inhibit nerve growth (Ma et al., 2009; Teixeira et al., 2007; Teng et al., 2002).

Moreover, some investigators have suggested that the brain's stem cells are part of an inherent developmental program that allows the brain to adapt to injury (Imitola et al., 2004). This capacity seems to diminish with age, however, which is why children tend to recover from brain damage more easily than adults do (Sun & He, 2010). Nonetheless, adults with brain damage can experience some recovery and neural adaptation, and adult stem cells may be part of this process.

Along similar lines, animal research into many neurodegenerative diseases, including Parkinson's disease, Lou Gehrig's disease (amyotrophic lateral sclerosis, or ALS), and multiple sclerosis (Rice et al., 2003; Silani & Corbo, 2004; Singec et al., 2007), has demonstrated that neural stem cells can repair brain damage and sometimes restore function (Akerud et al., 2001; Arenas, 2010; Isacson et al., 2003; Redmond, 2002). Of course, many questions about these processes remain unanswered, and adapting these treatments for use in humans poses significant risks. Even so, the possibility that neural stem cells could be used to repair brain damage that was long considered irreversible has generated enormous interest. In this case, a deeper understanding of developmental processes is yielding valuable progress on addressing problems in adults.

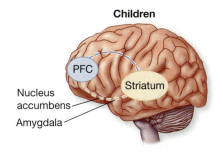

Children

Nucleus
accumbens
Amygdala
PFC
Striatum

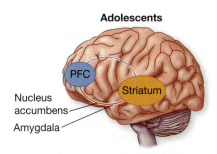

Adolescents

Nucleus
accumbens
Amygdala
PFC
Striatum

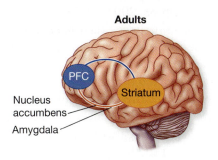

Adults

Nucleus
accumbens
Amygdala
PFC
Striatum

FIGURE 2.28 Changes in reward and control circuits. One key change in adolescence may concern the extent to which the prefrontal cortex (PFC) feeds back on the circuits related to rewards (the striatum). In children, reward circuits from the striatum and control circuits from the PFC are both immature (as shown by the light-colored structures and dashed circuit lines). In adolescents, there is increased sensitivity to reward cues from the striatum (shown by the darker structure and the solid line for the circuit), which overrides control circuits from the PFC, which has not yet fully matured. In adults, both structures and circuits are mature, and the PFC is better able to control the striatum. Adapted from Somerville & Casey (2010).

connections in all of these areas may allow more precise regulation of emotions (Steinberg, 2007). Thus, changes at the neural level may result in better integration of the cognitive control system, reward system, and emotional arousal system.

> **Q:** What are some patterns of brain change that seem to occur in childhood, puberty, and young adulthood?

Behavioral Genetics

The influence of genes on emerging neural structures and subsequent behaviors is a major theme of this chapter. Much of the research beginning to explain these genetic influences has been conducted in the past decade, and research relating gene expression to changes in the brain and behavior promises to remain one of the most active areas of neuroscience. But a line of work with a much longer history, known as **behavioral genetics**, examines how

differences in behavior relate to genetic differences between individuals or populations. Because this kind of research predated our fairly detailed biochemical understanding of DNA, behavioral geneticists have historically used statistical techniques to infer the degree to which individuals are related genetically—that is, the proportion of their genes that are the same. Researchers can then compare and correlate this level of genetic similarity with variations in behavior.

One of the most common research techniques in behavioral genetics involves studying monozygotic (MZ) and dizygotic (DZ) twins. Studying twins allows researchers to keep either the participants' genes (in the case of MZ twins) or their environment (twins raised together) relatively constant across experimental conditions. Because monozygotic twins have nearly identical genetic material, many researchers have studied MZ twins who were raised apart in attempts to examine the effects of experiences or environment while holding genes as constant as possible. Dizygotic twins, on the other hand, are only as genetically similar as any two siblings. Researchers have often studied DZ twins raised in the same household as a way to minimize environmental differences in the children's experiences while examining the effects of their genetic differences.

Heritability

Behavioral geneticists often talk about the **heritability** of a trait as a way of describing the extent to which variations in that trait, within a particular population, are due to genetic differences rather than environmental differences. If, in a particular group, all of the individual variations in a given trait were due to differences in individuals' genes, that trait would have a heritability of 1 for that population and environment. Likewise, if all individual differences in a trait were due to environmental variations, the trait would have a heritability of 0. Of course, genetic and environmental influences constantly interact, so no trait has perfect heritability. But the closer a trait's heritability comes to 1, the more that trait's variations—*within the group and environment in question*—are caused by genetic influences.

When heritability measures are applied to behavior, they are used to describe the degree to which behavioral differences among individuals in a population, such as variations in the traits of shyness or excitability, are due to those individuals' genetic differences. As an example of a trait with low heritability, consider the particular language that individuals speak. Our native tongue is solely a consequence of the language (or languages) we are exposed to while growing up, not the genes inherited from our biological parents. On the other hand, a trait with a very high heritability in most environments is height, which runs strongly in biological families. Still, it is critical to remember that heritability measures pertain only to populations, not to individuals. A heritability of .9 for height does not indicate that 90 percent of a specific person's height is caused by his or her genes. Rather, it means that across the whole population being measured, the differences in height are 90 percent attributable to genetic variations between that population's members. A single person's height reflects a complex interaction between his genotype and many environmental factors, including diet, exercise, and even stress. It doesn't make sense to try to describe "how much" of a single person's height is attributable to genes. A heritability measure is meaningful only in describing a population.

Heritabilities depend not only on the range of genotypes in a population but also on the environment in which a population is studied. In certain environments, heritabilities can be greatly reduced. For example, some forms of diabetes have substantial heritabilities, but if a population tends toward a diet that minimizes sugars and carbohydrates, it is likely that fewer people in that population will become diabetic. Thus, in that population, the heritability for the disease would be correspondingly lower, reflecting a stronger environmental influence.

The environment's influence on heritabilities has significant consequences when it comes to interpreting or comparing these measures. Even when the heritability of a trait is high for two separate populations, each in its own environment, it's important not to assume that *differences between the two populations* are also due to genetic influences. Suppose, for example, that height is highly heritable in two groups of children, one in suburban New York and another in a famine-stricken area of the Sudan. Even if height has a heritability of .9 in both groups, this does not mean that differences in height between the two populations are largely genetic. The Sudanese group would likely be shorter than the New Yorkers on average for reasons having nothing to do with genetics. Instead, malnutrition due to famine would likely decrease heights in the entire Sudanese population—even though, as a heritability of .9 tells us—differences in height *within that group* mostly could be explained by its members' genetic differences.

This point is often overlooked and can lead to false and inflammatory claims about the genetic bases for differences among groups. As we will see in several later chapters, the behavioral genetics approach has helped researchers understand the relative contributions of genetic and environmental factors to a wide range of traits, although complex gene-environment interactions can often make interpretations difficult.

Behavioral Genomics

Behavioral genetics still has a role in helping us understand individual differences (Plomin et al., 2000). But the field is rapidly changing in light of new knowledge about various species' genomes and increasingly sophisticated ways of measuring differences in phenotype (Haworth & Plomin, 2010; Kendler & Greenspan, 2006; Plomin & McGuffin, 2003; Toga & Thompson, 2005; Visscher et al., 2008). This new perspective is sometimes called **behavioral genomics** to emphasize the role of understanding a species' genome and its effects at the molecular level.

One way to understand this change in methodology is to see the shift that has occurred historically, starting with the early approach to human differences (Galton, 1883), when researchers could only compare the behaviors they saw with the levels of genetic variation they inferred by comparing twins, siblings, and other individuals. In the 1960s, this approach to research had shifted only modestly. Researchers knew that differences in DNA were responsible for all variances in genotype, but they did not understand how the DNA molecule gave rise to particular physical features, let alone its mechanisms for affecting behaviors. Over the next few decades, researchers began to understand how genes direct the production of proteins and how multiple genes can interact. Finally, in the last 10 years or so, an extraordinary surge of technology has made it possible to construct *gene expression profiles* in which a gene's expression (whether it is turned on or off) can be measured in thousands of tissue samples at various times and under different conditions. In addition, researchers can investigate how one gene's expression influences other genes. It is now also possible to study how changes in gene regulation affect the proteins that cells make.

Taken together, these molecular approaches have begun to suggest mechanisms for linking genetic variation to behaviors (Plomin & McGuffin, 2003). For example, when a certain gene is expressed, or "turned on," it may direct cells to create a protein that causes another gene to be expressed at several locations in the brain. That second gene may then direct the assembly of proteins that form receptors for neurotransmitters. Some of the neural circuits that influence human emotions may work in this way. Thus, regulatory interactions between several genes may make the receptors for certain neurotransmitters more sensitive, resulting in better emotional regulation. On the other hand, if some alleles of the initial gene don't fully "turn on" the cascade of regulatory interactions, individuals with those alleles may find it harder to regulate their emotions under stress (Schloesser et al., 2008). Environmental factors can also affect these complex processes of gene regulation. High levels of stress during development may change the activity levels of the genes that trigger whole sets of genetic interactions. The stress-induced changes could result in different patterns of synaptic connections within emotion-related brain areas (Champagne, 2010; Isles & Wilkinson, 2008; Schloesser et al., 2008).

Figure 2.29 illustrates a simplified model of how such networked effects might work. As this figure clearly shows, the effects of genes on behavior are quite indirect. They involve changes in cell membranes, nerve growth, neural circuits, large-scale physiological systems, and interactions among all of these. Moreover, the behaviors themselves can "feed back" on these systems and affect neural processes and structures. A particular genetic change does not "cause" a behavior as much as it is part of a rich network of causal interactions involving events within the organism and in its external environment.

As researchers develop more sophisticated ways of understanding the effects of gene variation at the cellular level, they are also developing more powerful ways to study how those variations give rise to different features and traits (Visscher et al., 2008). One new method combines the older twin study approach with neuroimaging that allows researchers to measure the size of specific brain regions. Researchers measure corresponding structures in both twins' brains and compare the similarities in the structures' size with the proportion of genes the twins share. The researchers can then calculate heritabilities of different brain regions' sizes by looking at patterns of variation across a large sample of twins (Peper et al., 2007; Toga & Thompson, 2005). Of particular interest is the gray matter in the cerebral cortex, where much of the most sophisticated processing of information is thought to occur. As Figure 2.30 shows, some brain regions, such as frontal areas of the cortex, seem to have much higher heritabilities for gray matter than posterior regions. This, in turn, suggests that cognitive functions associated with the frontal cortex, such as decision making and regulating conflicting thoughts, might also have high heritabilities. Comparable studies have also shown high heritabilities for some regions of white matter, suggesting that the degree of connectivity between certain brain regions may also be heavily influenced by genes.

In behavioral genetics, many genes are highly **pleiotropic**, meaning that one gene affects many traits. One way that genes can have these pleiotropic effects is through the kind of regulatory cascades discussed earlier, in which one

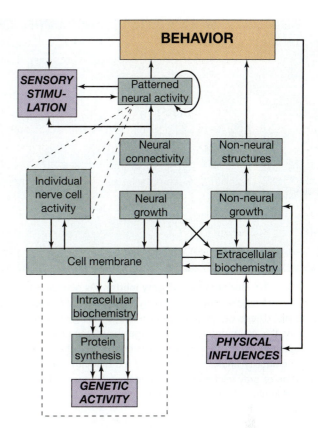

FIGURE 2.29 A model of gene effects. The new behavioral genetics, or "behavioral genomics," is not limited to inferring the differences between genotypes based on familial relatedness. Instead, researchers study the effects of gene expression both within cells and across cells. This diagram shows one model of how genes' actions can be linked to brain activity and how experiences can also influence brain and gene activity. From Johnson & Edwards (2002).

gene affects the activities of many others. Another way for a gene to affect multiple traits is in the way it is expressed differently within various tissues because of interactions with other tissue-specific genes. The opposite of pleiotropy (one gene affecting many traits) is evident when a single trait is **polygenic**, or affected by multiple genes. When different genes exert an overlapping influence in shaping a particular trait, that trait is considered polygenic. Both types of genetic influence are common in discussions of behavior, and they are also closely related. If a gene affects many different traits rather than just one, it is more likely that this pleiotropic gene's influences will "overlap" with the influences of other genes. For example, the same "generalist genes" may affect several different cognitive abilities (Kovas & Plomin, 2006).

A pleiotropic gene can affect several traits through quite different mechanisms. Figure 2.31 shows three possible mechanisms for how a gene might influence three separate cognitive functions. In the simplest case, the gene influences one brain region and consequently (in this simplified version) one cognitive function, such as improving an aspect of memory. Changes in that cognitive function would, in

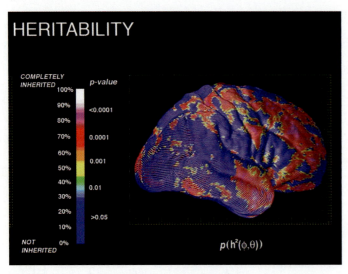

HERITABILITY

COMPLETELY
INHERITED

p-value

FIGURE 2.30 **Heritabilities of gray matter.** As neuroscientists develop more precise ways of studying the brain, they can ask how individuals' differences in gray matter relate to their genetic differences. As this computer-generated image shows, the proportion of gray matter in the frontal cortex (shown on the right) has a much higher heritability (indicated by pink and red shading) than the proportion of gray matter in posterior regions (shown on the left and indicated in blue). From Toga & Thompson (2005).

turn, influence related functions, such as attention and reasoning: with better memory, the outputs of attention and reasoning systems could be held in mind longer. In the most complex cases, a pleiotropic gene affects *several* different brain regions, and these regions also interact with each other. Most researchers who examine relations between genes and behavior think that the most complex case is also the most common (Visscher et al., 2008).

In short, researchers are working "bottom-up," starting from the molecular level, and "top-down," starting from the behavioral level, to go beyond correlating genotypic variations directly with behavioral variations. Their goal is to eventually explain all the specific interactions between genes and behaviors and the results of those interactions. Rather than simply asking which genes are "responsible for" particular behaviors, researchers are exploring the richly interconnected system of relationships between genes, proteins, various neural structures, and many facets of cognition, perception, and emotion—as well as their interactions with a wide range of environmental factors, from diet to visual stimulation.

Conclusions

Developmental biology is one of the most exciting and rapidly changing areas of research in the life sciences. Genetic mechanisms and anatomical structures are being more

closely linked than ever before. While a great deal of work remains to be done, researchers have already uncovered patterns in the way structure and function develop. These patterns of change are informative at one level as the necessary underpinnings for behavioral and psychological changes. At another level, they illustrate how developmental systems emerge while simultaneously, and continuously, solving problems of growth and form.

Perhaps the fundamental principle of the biology of development is that the most basic functions for survival tend to mature first. Initially, this means that the growing embryo must be able to receive nourishment and eliminate waste. Before long, though, the emerging organism needs more structure and function to survive, including a basic circulatory system and early segmentation of the body into compartments, which promotes further cellular differentiation. More broadly, the different tissues must be able to communicate so that cell migration, specialization, and other patterns of change can proceed. As we have seen, these lines of communication are set up by chemical changes triggered by the cells themselves.

The clearest pattern in biological development is the hierarchical nature of cell differentiation by which cells that are initially similar can become different kinds of specialized cells at later stages. The pattern is clearly sequential; cells pass through stages that are mostly, but perhaps not strictly, irreversible. Very early in the blastula stage, cells show considerable flexibility in terms of their function; when certain cell groups are moved at an early stage, the organism can adjust to continue normal development. Thus, a cell's final fate is not prespecified in its first few steps of differentiation. Instead, specializations emerge later, as a function of the cell's surrounding anatomical and physiological context.

These patterns in biological development suggest some similar principles for how psychological processes develop and differentiate. As you will see in later chapters, simpler emotions, such as joy, fear, anxiety, and anger, are thought to provide a necessary context for the development of more complex emotions, such as guilt and pride. Similarly, some argue that a child's early emerging understanding of her physical and social worlds influences the way she later comes to understand the biological world.

As researchers seek to understand the origins of psychological systems, they must confront questions about the different kinds of influences that shape those systems. The powerful influences of "nature" and "nurture" have been discussed for millennia, and in the past few decades, the "either/or" arguments about them have given way to an account of their interactions. Genes are one component of interrelated biological processes that are also subject to environmental influences at many levels. The local environment of a particular cell in the body, for example, might activate a

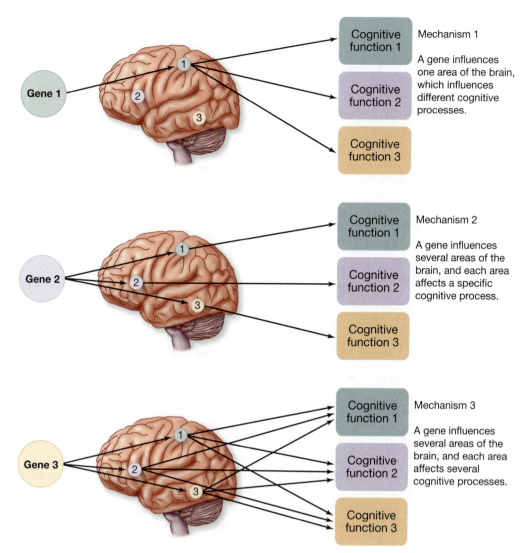

FIGURE 2.31 Three ways for a pleiotropic gene to affect behaviors. In mechanism 1, a gene might influence one brain region, which in turn would influence three different cognitive functions. In mechanism 2, a gene might influence three different brain regions, each of which would influence one cognitive function. In mechanism 3, a gene might influence three different brain regions, each of which would influence three different cognitive functions. The most complex case, mechanism 3, is also considered the most common. Adapted from Kovas & Plomin (2006).

Mechanism 1

A gene influences one area of the brain, which influences different cognitive processes.

Mechanism 2

A gene influences several areas of the brain, and each area affects a specific cognitive process.

Mechanism 3

A gene influences several areas of the brain, and each area affects several cognitive processes.

gene in that cell, causing it to produce a new protein. When the new protein becomes part of the cellular environment, it can cause chemical changes that subsequently turn other genes on or off. In this manner, one gene can interact with many others. A more global environmental factor, such as a toxin in drinking water, might also affect gene activities, often causing harm. Likewise, a deprived environment or one that is especially stimulating may affect brain growth through gene regulation pathways.

In all of these interactions, timing—as they say in vaudeville—is everything. We have seen how timing influences many patterns of development. During the blastula stage, even the timing of an individual cell's migration through the primitive streak influences its differentiation and development. During embryonic development, the length of a critical period can determine whether a neck like a giraffe's or a neck like an antelope's will result. Likewise, the effects of a teratogen depend on when it is introduced into the prenatal environment.

Sequencing, which is intimately related to timing, also exerts its own powerful influences. If, for example, the sequence of development of the basic body plan specified by homeobox genes is disrupted, we can see a proliferation of incoherent structures in the first most anterior compartment. The sequence of development is also crucial when particular structures, such as the neural plate, must serve as the foundation or the scaffold for later-developing structures. The earlier structures guide growth of what comes later and even influence patterns of cell specialization.

STUDY AND REVIEW

SUMMARY

The Basis of Development

- All living organisms go through systematic changes in anatomical and physiological systems across the course of development from conception to maturity. In recent years, major advances have been made in understanding the mechanisms that underlie these changes and how there are biological underpinnings of psychological development.
- Biological and psychological development both are characterized by common patterns, including critical periods and the tendency for vital systems to develop earlier than systems that are less important for survival.
- The inputs to the biological system are the genes, which contain the inherited instructions in the form of DNA for producing proteins and regulating expression of other genes, and the environment, which influences gene expression. The genotype is the full set of genes of an organism, while the phenotype is the expression of anatomical structures, biochemical processes, traits, and behaviors. Genes and environment constantly interact in complex ways to produce the phenotype.
- DNA is stored in the organism's chromosomes, which are found in the cell nucleus. In humans, chromosomes normally occur in pairs, with each parent contributing one chromosome containing gene variants known as alleles. If the offspring inherits the same allele from both parents, the child is homozygous for the gene; if the offspring inherits different alleles from the two parents, the child is heterozygous for the gene. A dominant allele is expressed when both alleles are dominant or when the other allele is recessive; the recessive allele is only expressed when both alleles are recessive.
- There are three constraints on development: the continuous need for viability of the developing organism, the differentiation of cell types and anatomical structures as development progresses, and the timing of when genes are switched on or off to produce developing cells and structures in particular sequences.

The Beginnings of Development

- The first stages of development are quite similar across most sexually reproducing organisms and involve formation of specialized cells called gametes for reproduction by meiosis, followed by fertilization of the female egg by the male sperm to produce the zygote.
- Once fertilized, the zygote makes a series of splits by mitosis. The first cell divisions initially produce what looks like an ever more fine-grained bumpy sphere. At a critical point, however—about 4 days in humans—the apparent spherical symmetry disappears as parts of the sphere fold in on itself, becoming the morula, and then, at day 5, becoming the blastocyst, which has an outer and inner ring of cells.
- Through a process called gastrulation, cells and cell clusters form three distinct layers—the ectoderm, the mesoderm, and the endoderm—that ultimately lead to formation of inner organs and structures, including the brain and skeleton.
- Cells that are initially undifferentiated become ever more specialized as sets of genes are turned on and off as a function of the local environment of surrounding cells.

Anatomical Development

- The embryonic period is from 2½ weeks to the end of 8 weeks after conception; the fetal period is from 9 weeks after conception until birth. From about 4 weeks after conception, the human embryo has features, such as a head and limb buds, which begin to visually resemble their adult counterparts.
- Initial brain formation is called neurulation and is completed in the fourth week after conception. There is a very early bias toward development in the head; embryonic development follows a head-to-toe progression known as cephalocaudal development.
- When babies are born 3 or more weeks early, they are known as preterm (or premature) infants, and they may be at increased risk for medical or psychological problems. The likelihood of preterm birth can be increased by infection in either the mother or the fetus or by smoking, drinking, or drug abuse by the mother.
- During the prenatal period, it is tempting to see development as obeying the principle of ontogeny recapitulating phylogeny. A closer examination, however, reveals the fallacies in this argument and shows that it is better understood as the idea that functionally important systems tend to emerge earlier both in development and in the evolutionary history of organisms.
- At a very broad level concerned with the order in which large body segments develop, there is a strikingly universal genetic code made up of clusters of genes known as homeobox genes (*Hox* genes in vertebrates) and shared by a wide variety of species. Within this framework, however, cascades of regulatory genes determine when genes are switched on or off, which provides for the enormous variations seen within and, most importantly, across species.
- Sexual differentiation is controlled by the X and Y chromosomes and by exposure to sex-specific combinations of hor-

mones. Higher concentrations of testosterone in male fetuses and higher concentrations of estrogen in female fetuses result in different genital structures in males and females and sex-specific traits and brain differences.

- The order in which body segments develop helps explain why hazardous compounds cause highly specific effects at certain times in development. When a particular segment is in its most active period of formation, internal or external hazardous environmental factors known as teratogens are most influential. Another body segment, usually farther away from the head, might not be as vulnerable until several weeks or months later.

Brain Development

- Brain development is dramatic during the prenatal period, when brain structures most essential for an organism's survival appear earlier than other brain structures and when later-developing brain structures inhibit earlier-developing brain structures. Extensive change occurs both in anatomical terms and in terms of patterns of cell growth.
- Brain cell growth includes not only the production of new nerve cells (neurogenesis), but also the tremendous elaboration of connections, wherein new synapses are formed between neurons (synaptogenesis). In addition, later pruning of connections, or synaptic pruning, and forms of programmed cell death, or apoptosis, seem to be used to sculpt efficient neural pathways in response to patterns of experience and neural firing. Myelination, the enclosing of axons with myelin, speeds the conduction of the nerve impulse.
- New nerve cells develop near the center of the brain and migrate to outer layers of the brain. Individual neurons "find their way" to remote locations in the brain using chemical gradients that guide them to their targets. When the growing neuron reaches its destination, chemical gradients trigger the growth cone at the end of the axon to interconnect with other neurons.
- Brain structure changes considerably after birth, primarily from the formation of new neuronal connections rather than from the production of new neurons. Moreover, neurons deprived of specific input may die off, but compensation plasticity may lead a brain deprived of normal inputs and processing routines to form new connections and become devoted to other functions instead.
- Puberty is a period distinguished by changes not just in the anatomy and physiology of the body as a whole, but also in the brain in particular. Neural circuits involving emotions, reward systems, and cognitive control become interconnected in ways that shift the degree to which adolescents and young adults engage in a range of behaviors, such as taking risks.

Behavioral Genetics

- A classic technique for studying links between genes and behavior, behavioral genetics typically uses twins with different degrees of genetic relatedness (MZ and DZ twins) and asks about the extent to which variations in phenotype are related to variations in genotype.
- The more recent field of behavioral genomics examines variations in individuals' genomes and the ways that those variations relate to gene interaction and protein synthesis, physiology, neuroanatomy, and ultimately behavior.

THOUGHT QUESTIONS

1. What constitutes an enriched environment? We have seen that severely impoverished environments, such as those caused by sensory deprivation or extreme stress, can psychologically affect a developing infant or child and even influence brain development. Some have argued that the reverse might also be true: that extremely enriched environments might accelerate and enhance brain development. If you wanted to test this possibility, what would the maximally enriched environment look like, and why?

2. Although the nineteenth-century notion that "ontogeny recapitulates phylogeny" is no longer accepted, what kernel of truth to this idea still has value today?

3. Should parents be allowed to "design" their babies? As researchers are increasingly able to link specific human genes to developmental outcomes, it may soon become possible for parents to specify, in cases of in vitro fertilization, which sperm should be allowed to fertilize which egg. How much control should parents have over specifying the kind of baby they want?

KEY TERMS

action potential (p. 59)

allele (p. 37)

apoptosis (p. 61)

axons (p. 59)

base pair (p. 36)

behavioral genetics (p. 67)

behavioral genomics (p. 68)

bilateral symmetry (p. 44)

brainstem (p. 57)

canalization (p. 39)

cephalocaudal development (p. 44)

cerebellum (p. 57)

cerebral cortex (p. 57)

cerebrum (p. 57)

chromosome (p. 36)

codominant (p. 37)

compensation plasticity (p. 63)

corpus callosum (p. 57)

critical period (p. 35)

crossing-over (p. 42)

dendrite (p. 59)

dizygotic (DZ) twins (p. 43)

DNA (p. 36)

dominant (p. 37)

ectoderm (p. 44)

egg cell (p. 42)

embryo (p. 44)

endoderm (p. 44)

environmental niche (p. 36)

epigenetic regulation (p. 39)

experience-dependent plasticity (p. 64)

fetus (p. 46)

frontal lobe (p. 57)

gamete (p. 42)

gastrulation (p. 43)

gene (p. 36)

genome (p. 36)

genotype (p. 38)

glial cells (p. 60)

growth cone (p. 60)

heritability (p. 67)

heterochronic gene (p. 40)

heterozygous (p. 37)

homeobox (p. 50)

homeobox genes (p. 50)

homozygous (p. 37)

Hox genes (p. 50)

meiosis (p. 41)

mesoderm (p. 44)

methylation (p. 39)

migration (p. 60)

mitosis (p. 42)

monozygotic (MZ) twins (p. 43)

myelin (p. 60)

myelination (p. 60)

neural tube (p. 45)

neurogenesis (p. 60)

neuron (p. 59)

neurotransmitter (p. 59)

neurulation (p. 46)

occipital lobe (p. 58)

parietal lobe (p. 57)

phenotype (p. 38)

placenta (p. 43)

pleiotropic (p. 69)

polygenic (p. 69)

preterm infant (p. 47)

primitive streak (p. 44)

radial glial cell (p. 60)

recessive (p. 37)

regulatory cascade (p. 38)

sexual differentiation (p. 52)

sperm cell (p. 42)

stem cell (p. 66)

synapse (p. 59)

synaptic pruning (p. 61)

synaptogenesis (p. 61)

temporal lobe (p. 57)

teratogen (p. 54)

trisomy 21 (p. 42)

zygote (p. 43)

PART II
Origins

3

Coming to Perceive the World

Vision
- **Perceiving Differences in Brightness and Acuity**
- **Color**
- **Depth Perception**
- **Perceiving Patterns and Recognizing Objects**
- **Face Perception**

Hearing
- **Noticing and Remembering Sounds**
- **Locating Sounds**
- **Perceiving Complex Sound Patterns**

The Chemical Senses: Taste and Smell
- **Taste**
- **Smell**

Intermodal Perception

Conclusions

Summary

On the northwest coast of India, outside the city of Ahmadabad, there is a small village. Many of its inhabitants live in extreme poverty with minimal access to health care. In one family that lived together in a 10-by-12-foot room, a baby girl was born with dense cataracts in the lenses of both eyes, which prevented her from seeing patterns of light; instead, she could see only the kind of diffuse light and shadowy forms that might be visible through a dirty, frosted windowpane. From her birth in 1972 until the age of 12, she lived as a blind person who could tell only general differences in dark and light. She needed a guide to help her walk about or to identify objects. When she was 12, her parents received a government subsidy that allowed doctors to remove the cataracts and provide her with glasses, which allowed her eyes to receive patterned light for the first time.

The critical question was whether, at age 12, she would still be able to learn to see. Would she come to recognize faces, places, and objects that she had never experienced visually? Could she use vision to find her way around in the world? For vision, is there a critical period in which certain kinds of experiences are necessary for normal visual development? Some 20 years after her surgery, researchers visited the woman and addressed these questions in great detail (Ostrovsky et al., 2006; see Figure 3.1).

The researchers discovered that it is possible to be able to learn to see surprisingly normally, even after spending the first 12 years of life essentially blind. The woman now used her vision to recognize faces and facial expressions, and she perceived depth well enough to judge objects' locations.

FIGURE 3.1 Restored vision and ability to see. The 32-year-old woman seated at the computer is being tested for her visual skills by researchers who are studying whether there is a critical period to learn to see. The woman was born with severe cataracts that prevented her from seeing more than light and dark as a child. After she had an operation to remove her cataracts at age 12, she was able to acquire the perceptual visual skills that enabled her to recognize shapes and faces and to judge depth, although she did have some subtle deficits in facial processing.

Although her ability to see fine details seemed permanently degraded and she made more face recognition errors than normal viewers would, the consensus was that she had made a striking recovery. Moreover, she seemed to have acquired these perceptual skills gradually, learning ways of seeing shapes and patterns.

Her experience raises some central questions about perceptual development. How does the newborn perceive the world, and how do perceptual capacities change in the first years of life? How much of perceptual development is based on learning from experience, and how much depends on the biological maturation of perceptual systems? Does vision or any other sense have a critical period, such that certain kinds of perceptual experiences must happen during a particular time frame for the perceptual ability to mature normally? How does information from different modalities, such as vision and hearing, interact in the course of development? These questions, along with others raised later in this chapter, frame the study of perceptual development.

Recall the newborn that we discussed at the beginning of Chapter 1. Remember the perceptual challenges that he was faced with during his first week of life—blinking lights, loud noises, people looming over him. Remember his apparent helplessness when he was assailed by sounds and sights as he was moved from the hospital nursery, put into a car, and driven home by his parents. Yet, despite their seeming helplessness, newborns actually come prepared to recognize some visual patterns and voices and tastes. In this chapter, we will see that infants are not like formless clay, waiting to let experience leave its mark on them. Nor are they fully mature perceptual creatures. A great deal of perceptual development and learning occur in the first year of life. The mechanisms of developmental change often involve **feedback loops** between the infant and the environment, in which an experience causes a change in the infant's state, which in turn influences how the infant's next experiences are processed. For example, early experience with visual patterns helps foster growth of areas of the visual cortex that support pattern perception. Growth in the cortex supports higher-resolution pattern perception, which in turn causes further development in the visual cortex. This constant interplay between organism and environment is an essential theme throughout this book.

In addition, we will see that a fundamental developmental challenge is to be able to categorize different stimuli into groups, whether it is a color category, such as *red*, or an object category, such as *dogs*. That essential ability to categorize makes perception and cognition more efficient by allowing us to apply some of what we learn to whole categories of things, rather than having to learn about each instance separately. In this chapter, we will see that several kinds of categorization play fundamental roles in perceptual development.

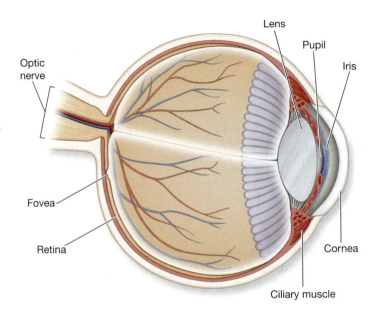

FIGURE 3.2 Innate specializations in the eye. More than 300 years ago, it was obvious that the eye contained specializations at birth for the kind of information (light) that it processed. Long before the invention of the camera, people were aware that the eye was "designed" to project images of light on the retina in such a manner that it could be "read" by the mind within. Such specializations included a lens and cornea to focus the light, an iris to control the amount of light, a ciliary muscle to adjust the focal length of the lens, a retina for receiving the focused light, a fovea for processing the most important information, and an optic nerve for transmitting information to the brain. All these specializations were clearly present at birth and were tailored for information in light, as opposed to sounds or smells.

We begin our discussion of perceptual development with vision, often thought to be the most complex perceptual system in development. Vision also nicely illustrates the contrast between sensation and perception. Sensation involves registering sensory information as it is initially taken in—for example, by the retina of the eye, the hair cells of the auditory system, or the taste buds of the tongue. Perception involves interpreting sensory input, such as understanding that certain shapes and contours make up a face, knowing that one object appears farther away than another, or recognizing particular sound patterns as a voice. We will examine such topics as the sharpness of vision, color vision, depth perception, and face perception.

From vision we move on to hearing, asking how infants notice and locate sounds and how they pick up on more complex patterns, such as those of speech. We then consider the chemical senses of taste and smell, asking whether newborns seem to distinguish different tastes using the same categories that adults do and whether smells help them respond more effectively to the world. Finally, we consider how infants integrate information across these different avenues of perception—for example, how a baby links his sister's voice with her face. In all these explorations, we will return to the questions raised earlier about the blind girl whose sight was restored and the newborn arriving home.

Vision

Thinkers in several fields have long been interested in our understanding of the visual world and how it develops from infancy. In fact, seventeenth-century scholars already had a fairly detailed understanding of the anatomy of the visual system. They knew that from birth, the human visual system consists of two eyes, each with a cornea, a lens, an iris, a retina with a two-dimensional, light-sensitive surface, and an optic nerve that seems to carry visual information from the retina to the brain (see Figure 3.2). In short, they realized that the visual system has extensive anatomical specializations tailored to receiving information in the form of light.

Given the easily observable structures and specializations of the eye, an empiricist would argue that these are simply *sensory* constraints that affect the initial processing of visual information. In this view, these sensory specializations are largely separate from the more impressive *perceptual* abilities—such as seeing objects in depth, differentiating colors, and recognizing patterns and objects—which are thought to arise from an all-purpose associative learning system. By contrast, the nativist would argue that specializations similar to the eye's facility for processing light might well occur at every level of perceptual processing—from the most peripheral sensory receptors in the eye all the way "upward" to the highest-level conscious impressions of visual perception. Over the centuries, both points of view flourished and attracted many adherents, largely because there was no experimental evidence that seemed to strongly favor one view over the other.

Starting in the 1960s, however, a rapidly growing body of research on young infants' capabilities started to reveal the extent to which visual perception requires specialized processing capacities. One way to approach the current state of this research is to consider the sensory and perceptual capacities of the young infant as we move "upstream" from the most peripheral, basic, and sensory visual input to more central, complex, and perceptual visual experiences. For example, at a peripheral, sensory level, much of the ability to register light at different levels of brightness involves processing that takes place in the retina, at the back of the eye. The more "midstream" level of visual processing, which involves much of the processing of color, happens in midbrain structures.

Finally, the highest levels of visual perception, which include processing patterns, such as faces and distinctive shapes, heavily involve the brain's visual cortex. Nativists and empiricists agree that specialized processing is crucial at the peripheral, sensory level; but as we move "upstream" from sensation to perception, specific research findings are needed to help us determine whether higher-level visual processing is based on a general learning system or specialized processing capabilities. We will therefore start by considering some of the earliest, "downstream" visual capacities that involve perceptual understanding: the ability to see differences in brightness and the ability to see the contrasts between light and dark that represent lines and edges. Working our way "upstream," we will then explore more complex aspects of visual perception, such as the ability to perceive colors, depth, and finally patterns.

Perceiving Differences in Brightness and Acuity

Virtually all theorists would grant that the newborn's ability to detect different levels of brightness provides an important foundation for more sophisticated perceptual activities, such as understanding patterns. If newborn infants couldn't even distinguish between different levels of brightness—to perceive, for example, a dark line on a light background—it is difficult to imagine how they could learn anything else about the visual world. For this reason, asking about the different levels of brightness that an infant can perceive serves as a common point of departure for researchers with different views, rather than a source of controversy.

Over an enormous range of brightness levels, a typical adult can perceive changes in brightness of as little as 1 percent. Young infants do not consistently perceive this full range of differences, but even newborns have brightness discrimination abilities that are sufficient to form a basis for higher-level perceptual skills (Aslin, 1987). For example, infants as young as 2 days old perceive differences between lamps of different brightness (Hershenson, 1964). Even more impressively, by at least 4 months of age, infants can judge relative levels of brightness in an image by comparing two adjacent areas (Chien et al., 2003; see Figure 3.3). Perceiving such relationships is a critical part of figuring out the actual brightness of an object seen under different lighting conditions. Thus, if you see a pure white square in low light, it may appear darker than a gray square lit with bright light. But if you see the white square next to the gray one and compare them, the white one clearly looks brighter, even under different levels of illumination.

> Q: Do young infants see differences in brightness?

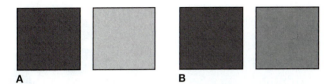

FIGURE 3.3 Brightness perception in infants. (A) Although young infants can see differences in brightness levels, **(B)** they may not be able to see the subtle differences that adults can see.

Visual Acuity The ability to distinguish levels of brightness within a field of view is typically not enough to know what that visual field looks like. Even when you can discern subtle differences in brightness through a frosted windowpane, you still may be completely unable to discriminate any patterns or to tell what kind of thing you are seeing. Thus, a crucial precursor to higher-level pattern perception must be **visual acuity**, the sharpness of vision based on the ability to see the contrasts in the world that represent lines, shapes, and shadows. Does the newborn view the world as if through a frosted window, seeing nothing more than blurs of varying levels of brightness? Such a world of undifferentiated dark and light blotches would severely limit the infant's visual experiences and, at least in the realm of vision, would strongly resemble William James's "blooming, buzzing confusion."

Since infants aren't able to report what they see, researchers have devised indirect methods for investigating their visual and perceptual abilities. One of the oldest of these techniques is called the **preferential looking method**. The idea behind this method is that infants might prefer looking at some displays (for example, striped patterns) more than others. When infants are presented with two types of displays at once and they reliably prefer to look at one rather than the other, this suggests that they can detect a difference between the two. Researchers have used this technique to explore whether infants see only undifferentiated areas of light and dark or more detailed patterns and whether they have expectations about certain events.

To measure an infant's visual acuity using the preferential looking method, a researcher could place two circles—one with wide black and white stripes and the other entirely gray—side by side where the infant can see them and then monitor the infant's eye- or head-turning patterns (see Figure 3.4). If the infant sees the difference and prefers to look at, say, the circle with stripes, the experimenter might then replace that circle with another that has thinner stripes and therefore requires greater visual acuity to distinguish it from the gray circle. As long as the infant continues to show a preference for the circle with stripes, the experimenter continues to substitute new patterns of finer and finer stripes to show along with the gray circle, until the infant shows no preferential looking. At that point, the researcher assumes that the infant can no longer detect a difference between the

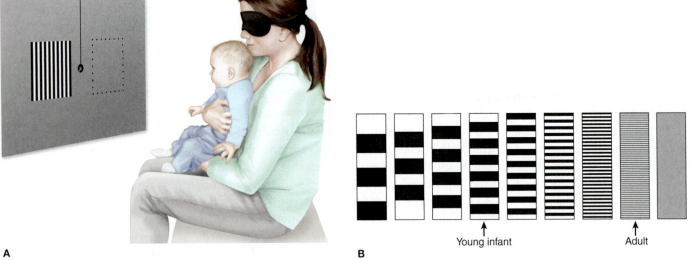

A

B

Young infant   Adult

FIGURE 3.4 Testing visual acuity in infants. (A) This setup for assessing visual acuity has a rectangular panel containing a square with gratings (thick or thin stripes) and a gray square (indicated by the dots) that cannot be distinguished from the background. To assess whether the infant can detect the square with the stripes, researchers monitor where the infant prefers to look, as indicated by fixation of his gaze. Adapted from Courage & Adams (1990). **(B)** Ever finer gratings are used until the infant is not able to discriminate between the horizontal lines and a gray square that is matched for the same overall level of brightness. At some point, all of us can no longer tell the difference between a very fine set of lines and gray; for newborns that point seems to come quite a bit sooner. Although newborns certainly do not see a formless blur, their visual world is considerably less sharp, and a 1-month-old's acuity is far below the adult level of performance. From Teller & Bornstein (1986).

circles. If this procedure were repeated with many infants of a particular age, the aggregated results would suggest a threshold for visual acuity at that age, which could be compared with the threshold values for adults.

As simple as it sounds, there are several challenges in making this technique work reliably. Researchers must be vigilant that some other factor besides acuity isn't causing infants to look at one pattern more than another. For example, researchers must ensure that the panels differ only in the acuity level required to see a difference between them, and not in other ways, such as overall brightness. In addition, if the infant sits in a parent's lap (which is common) and the parent can see the stimuli, the parent might unknowingly hold the infant a bit differently when the infant looks at the gray panel. (This can be overcome by blindfolding the adult.) Moreover, the researchers collecting the data must be "blind" to the experimental condition—that is, they should be unaware of which panel the infant is viewing. Otherwise, their own biases might influence the process. Finally, a challenge involved in interpreting data from preferential looking paradigms is the possibility that an infant who can easily tell two displays apart visually might not always show a preference for one over the other.

A second approach to measuring infants' visual acuity involves the **habituation method**. Rather than hoping that infants' preferences will be strong enough to provide evidence that they can discriminate between stimuli, as the preferential looking method does, the habituation method,

in essence, creates preferences. Most of us become bored if we see the same thing again and again. The habituation method purposely creates this kind of boredom as a way to create a preference for a new stimulus. At first, a gray panel might be interesting enough to an infant that she would look at it for some time. But if it is shown and removed repeatedly, even an infant reaches a point when she would rather look at almost anything else. When the infant seems completely bored with the panel, so that she hardly looks at it when it is presented, she is said to experience **habituation** to that stimulus. Habituation is used to study not just vision, but also audition, olfaction, and taste.

The experimenter then starts the critical second phase of the habituation method by introducing a second panel and watching to see whether the infant shows **dishabituation**—that is, renewed interest in response to the new panel. In a study of infants' visual acuity, this new panel might have very fine-grained black and white stripes. If the infant doesn't perceive the new panel as different from the original gray one, then she should not dishabituate—that is, her looking time should not increase in response to the new panel. But if the infant does see a difference, she should initially look much longer when the new panel is presented, followed by a gradual decline in looking at the panel as she becomes bored with it. To find a threshold measure of acuity, an experimenter might start with the second panel with the finest-grained pattern and then gradually substitute panels with more coarse-grained patterns until dishabituation occurs. Changes in

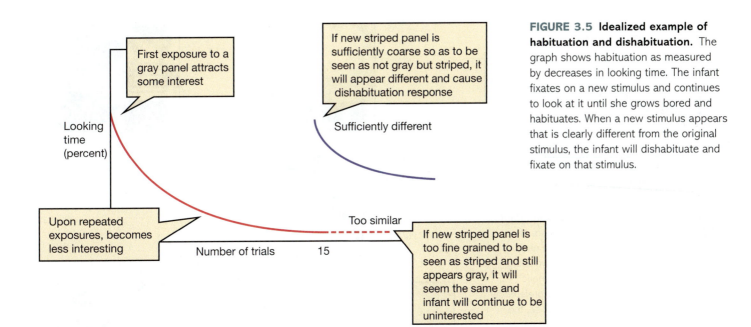

First exposure to a gray panel attracts some interest

If new striped panel is sufficiently coarse so as to be seen as not gray but striped, it will appear different and cause dishabituation response

Looking time (percent)

Sufficiently different

Upon repeated exposures, becomes less interesting

Number of trials   15

Too similar

If new striped panel is too fine grained to be seen as striped and still appears gray, it will seem the same and infant will continue to be uninterested

FIGURE 3.5 **Idealized example of habituation and dishabituation.** The graph shows habituation as measured by decreases in looking time. The infant fixates on a new stimulus and continues to look at it until she grows bored and habituates. When a new stimulus appears that is clearly different from the original stimulus, the infant will dishabituate and fixate on that stimulus.

looking times at a stimulus in a standard habituation/dishabituation sequence are shown in Figure 3.5.

A third way of testing acuity is by the **optokinetic nystagmus method**. Optokinetic nystagmus is the jumping of the eyes as they track a continuous succession of objects that stream by, such as watching telephone poles stream by while looking out of a moving train. In this method, researchers drag a panel of vertical stripes from right to left in front of an infant to determine how fine-grained the stripe pattern must be before the infants' eyes stop jumping from stripe to stripe and behave as if it were one homogeneous gray pattern moving from right to left.

Finally, acuity can be tested by measuring the electrical activity in the infant's brain that is evoked by visual displays. This method, known as the **visually evoked potential (VEP) method**, involves attaching electrodes to the baby's scalp to measure brain activity and to determine at what point the changing striped patterns that the infant is watching on a screen no longer cause corresponding changes in the brain's electrical activity. Thus, as an infant watches the screen, the researcher might present a sequence of patterns, alternating between the same all-gray screen and different black and white striped patterns, while monitoring the electrical activity in the infant's brain. At the beginning of the sequence, the striped pattern would be coarse-grained with a few wide stripes. As the sequence progressed, the infant would be shown finer and finer-grained stripes. Initially, every time the image on the screen switched from gray to striped, the researcher would measure a related change in brain activity. But when the striped pattern became too fine-grained for the infant to tell it apart from the solid gray pattern, the brain activity corresponding to the switch to the striped pattern would not occur.

In young infants, VEP measurements reveal sharper levels of acuity than preferential looking or habituation methods do. This discrepancy raises a fascinating question: Do some parts of the infant's visual system start to detect fine-grained patterns before the infant is able to act on such information? That is, the infant's brain may be registering a certain level of acuity during initial perceptual processing, but it may not be able to translate that information into actually "seeing" at that level of acuity and using it as a basis for action. It may take time for those initial stages of perceptual processing to become fully integrated with higher levels of perception. The difference between VEP measures of acuity and those from habituation or preferential looking highlights an important point about studying preverbal infants. Older children and adults can describe how they are experiencing a visual display, but even with careful, well-designed measurement techniques, it is still much more difficult to know exactly what preverbal infants are experiencing.

Even if we assume that measures based on habituation and preferential looking are the best indicators of what very young infants actually see, they still show that infants have enough acuity to perceive some lines, edges, and outlines. Over the first year of life, acuity improves considerably (Norcia et al., 2005). Figure 3.6 summarizes the changes in acuity in the first 3 years, based on average measurements from visually evoked potentials, optokinetic nystagmus, and preferential looking techniques (Courage & Adams, 1990; Kellman & Banks, 1998; Teller & Movshon, 1986). Averaging across these measures, by age 6 months, the infant has nearly 20:100 vision, meaning she can see patterns at a distance of 20 feet about as well as an adult with normal vision could see the same patterns at 100 feet. Many nearsighted

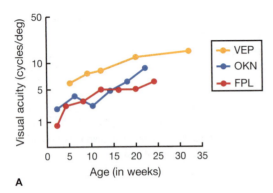

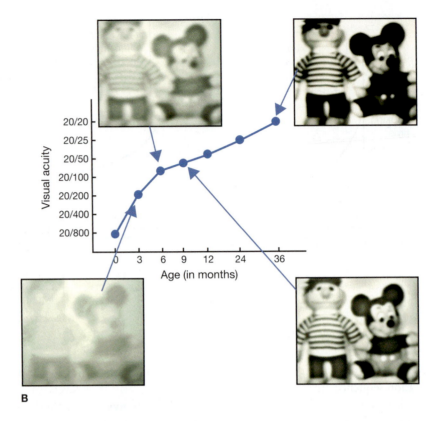

A

B

FIGURE 3.6 Changing visual acuity in infants. Acuity clearly improves in the first 3 years of life regardless of the particular measure used. **(A)** Here increased visual acuity is shown using visually evoked potentials (VEP), optokinetic nystagmus (OKN), and (forced choice) preferential looking (FPL) methods. By 6 months or so, the infant's acuity is sharp enough that it would rarely limit other perceptual tasks. Adapted from Kellman & Arterberry (2006). **(B)** The same photo is superimposed on a preferential looking methods curve to show how it would look to the infant at different ages as acuity increases.

adults without glasses cope with this kind of modest difference in acuity throughout their lives.

> **Q:** What are three different ways of measuring visual acuity in the human infant?

Many other acuity-related factors also change during the first year of life, especially **astigmatism**. In astigmatism, stimuli at different orientations are perceived with different levels of acuity. Thus, a vertical line might be in sharp focus while an otherwise similar horizontal line would be blurry. The perceptual differences caused by astigmatism are dramatic in very young infants, but only minor in most 1-year-olds and adults (Mutti et al., 2004). When adults experience astigmatism, it is typically due to distortions in the lens of the eye or the cornea, but in young infants astigmatism is normal. It happens because the eyeball is irregularly shaped in early infancy, and consequently, the retinal surface is irregular as well. As a result, only a small portion of the light that reaches the retina can be in focus at one time. As the infant matures, the eyeball grows and develops a more spherical form, which reduces the astigmatism. Soon after the infant is 1 year old, his eyeball has become roughly spherical, such that the light passing through the lens now lands, in focus, on the whole retina.

These changes in the eye's shape do not happen automatically according to a timetable of biological maturation. Instead, the eye's growth depends on whether it receives focused input—that is, whether the light patterns falling on the retina are sharply focused by the lens of the eye. If the light patterns on the retina are out of focus, the eye continues to grow until the patterns become more focused (see Figure 3.7). Apparently, the eye "assumes" that if the pattern is out of focus, it is because the eye is too small and the image is falling behind the retina, so the eye grows to adjust. This is generally true; a newborn's eyes are almost always too small to project images optimally on the retina.

Humans are not the only species in which the growth of the eyes depends in part on how sharply the retinal images are focused. Researchers have found that manipulating the degree of focused input to the retinas of newly hatched chicks affects the growth of the chicks' eyes. If, from birth, a baby chick wears contact lenses that keep its retinal images blurry, its eyeball and retina will continue to grow far larger than normal as the visual system keeps trying to expand to the size that will properly focus the image. Conversely, if the chicks experience sharply focused light on large regions of the retina unusually early in their development, the eyeball and retina will stop growing at a smaller size than normal. These environmental effects on the growth of the chicks' eyes start to happen almost immediately after the image on the retina goes either out of or into focus (Judge, 1990; Wallman et al., 1987; Zhu et al., 2005). Of course, there are

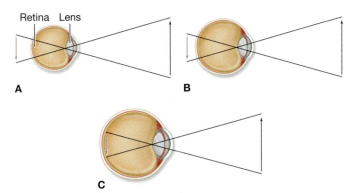

FIGURE 3.7 Growing the eye into focus. (A) In the more immature eye, the focused image would fall behind the retina. **(B)** The defocused image that falls on the retina causes the eye to grow until the image gets closer to the retina. **(C)** When the image is finally focused on the retina, feedback from that focused input tells the eye to stop growing. This pattern of eye growth is yet another illustration of the feedback loops that exist between structures in the organism and the ways in which the organism interacts with its environment, in this case with the surprising result of sensation influencing anatomy. Adapted from Zhu et al. (2005).

many important differences between the visual systems of chickens and humans, but the similar findings in monkeys (Hung et al., 1995; Smith et al., 2009; Troilo et al., 2000; Wiesel & Raviola, 1977) make it seem likely that such an effect would also be found in humans.

These findings in the visual system, in which biological maturation and environmental experience complement each other, also illustrate how development can advance by way of a feedback loop. If incoming visual information from the environment is being processed at a low level of acuity, the brain directs the eyeball and retina to keep growing. When the eyeball and retina get large enough to properly focus the incoming light, the brain senses an adequate level of acuity in its visual perception and directs the eye to slow its growth. Thus, environmental experience modifies the internal system, which then modifies the organism's experience.

> **Q:** How can different environmental experiences change the structure of the eye?

Visual Experience and Brain Development Both the eye itself and the visual processing areas of the brain grow in ways that depend not only on biological maturation but also on input in the form of visual experience. These two levels of growth can be best understood by considering the distinction between *optical acuity*, the sharpness of the image on the retina, and *processing acuity*, how well the brain's visual cortex (near the back of the brain) processes

the information received from the retina. If you think of the visual system as a video camera, its optical acuity would be a function of how well the lenses focus the incoming light; its processing acuity would depend on the sophistication of the software—namely, how well it is able to process and integrate the information from incoming light to assemble a complete image. The development of processing acuity in infants is not a simple maturational matter in which the relevant neural networks develop on a set schedule regardless of visual inputs. Instead, similar to the development of the eyeball and retina, the infant's visual cortex also requires increasingly focused input to develop the elaborate neural connections that enable higher and higher levels of acuity.

When the optical acuity of the eye itself is impaired, it sends degraded inputs to the visual cortex, which can directly lead to impairments in processing acuity as well. This is why, in many species, including humans, depriving the visual cortex of focused input inhibits the development of processing acuity in the brain, even when the eye's optical acuity is restored later. As described earlier in the case of the girl in India, people born with cataracts who receive corrective surgery after childhood never seem to regain full acuity (Ostrovsky et al., 2006). Regions of the brain require "practice" with certain kinds of visual experience and input to develop their normal processing capacity.

The effects of experience on acuity vividly illustrate the concept of critical periods, those developmental "windows of opportunity" during which specific sorts of inputs can profoundly affect the organism in ways that are largely irreversible after the period is over. Thus, if the visual cortex doesn't receive appropriately focused input in the first few years of life, no compensating experiences later—even 20 years of wearing perfect corrective lenses—can fully restore some forms of processing acuity in the visual cortex (Lewis & Mauer, 2005, 2009). At the same time, processes of biological maturation are also crucial to processing acuity and the ability to benefit from the necessary kinds of visual stimuli and experience. For example, preterm babies show some early developmental delays in visual acuity compared with full-term babies, even when they have the same amount of visual experience (Dobkins et al., 2009). The preterm babies' visual systems simply need some time to mature before the babies can fully benefit from their visual experience.

> **Q:** What sorts of critical-period effects are found in cases of deprivation of early visual experience?

Color

Color is a vivid part of most people's lives and may have important uses in all cultures, such as picking out a brightly colored object from a cluttered background, determining the ripeness or poisonousness of various fruits, and perceiving changes in the weather. Newborn infants have quite impressive color vision. They not only are able to tell apart different wavelengths of light (called **hue**), but also can cluster wavelengths into categories very much like the ones that adults use. Although it might seem that hue is simply a formal word for color, it actually refers only to the aspect of color that depends on wavelengths of light. Our impressions of color are also influenced by the ratio of color to white light (saturation) and the display's overall brightness. For the most part, when researchers discuss color vision in infants, they are talking about hue.

Perceiving Hue and the Clustering of Hues Early on, researchers used the techniques of preferential looking and habituation to test infants' color vision. In many of these experiments, the investigators showed the infants pairs of different-colored panels of equal brightness and then observed whether infants could distinguish between them. The studies suggested that infants have color vision very early and that it improves significantly in the first 4 weeks of life as infants develop the ability to distinguish ever-smaller differences in hue (Peeples & Teller, 1975; Teller, 1998). These improvements are thought to result from increases in the processing abilities of the whole visual system, not just from parts specialized for color (Kellman & Banks, 1998).

Perceiving differences between hues is one thing; clustering sets of hues into color categories is quite another. When you look at Figure 3.8A, it seems to have red bands, yellow bands, and green bands, among others—but these bands of color are actually psychological constructs. The light pattern depicted in the figure, like the patterns created by prisms and rainbows, is actually a smooth continuum of hues that runs from reds (with wavelengths of approximately 700 nanometers, or 0.0000007 meter) to blue-purples (with wavelengths of about 400 nanometers). All the colors of the rainbow are situated at different points along this continuum of wavelengths. As observers, however, we do not experience a world of gradually shifting colors; instead, we tend to see classes of colors that seem to have distinct boundaries. This is in marked contrast to how we see a continuum of different levels of brightness, as in the panel shown in Figure 3.8B. If shades of gray were perceived in the same manner as hue, we would see bands reflecting different classes of grayness from white to black.

This process of clustering wavelengths of light into familiar colors is one aspect of **categorical perception**. In its broadest sense, categorical perception refers to a tendency

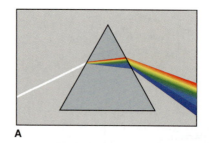

A

B

FIGURE 3.8 Light categories and continua. (A) The light coming out of a prism (or rainbow), which is a smoothly varying continuum of light frequency, appears to have "bands" corresponding to such easily labeled colors as "red," "blue," and "green"; these bands are the consequence of the categorical perception of color. **(B)** By contrast, light intensity for continuously varying shades of gray varies in a smooth, gradual manner from dark to light with no obvious "bands."

to cluster stimuli that vary along a continuum into discrete categories. Even though the stimuli differ only in small, consistent increments, those that are grouped together in a category seem highly similar to each other, while those in different categories seem markedly different (Goldstone & Hendrickson, 2010; Harnad, 1987).

Figure 3.9 illustrates the process of categorical perception of color. The difference between the wavelengths of blue 1 and blue 2 is the same magnitude as the difference between the wavelengths of blue 2 and green 1. Yet, blue 2 and green 1 appear much more distinct from each other than do blue 1 and blue 2. The same pattern holds for other color boundaries, such as green/yellow and yellow/red. Even when we're looking at identical differences in physical wavelengths of light, we don't always perceive the same degree of difference between hues. Across most of the continuum of wavelengths, a difference of 35 nanometers between hues is hardly noticeable. But at certain critical boundaries—compare 470 and 505 nanometers—the 35-nanometer interval appears to separate quite different shades of blue and green (Boynton, 1979; Wandell, 1985).

These differences in our discrimination abilities simply mean that we cluster groups of light wavelengths into classes, which we know as familiar colors such as red, green, blue, and yellow. One benefit of this perceptual tendency to categorize is that it simplifies our interactions with the world and with others. Communicating the color of an object is much easier if a relatively large range of wavelengths can be treated as roughly equivalent—as members of the same class. Consider how much simpler it is to convey a color than a specific shade of gray on the smooth continuum between black and white.

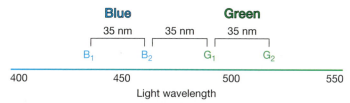

FIGURE 3.9 Categorical perception of color. This section of the light spectrum shows the transition between blue and green light. There is a constant continuum of increasing wavelength from 400 nanometers to 550 nanometers. B_1, B_2, G_1, and G_2 represent particular wavelengths of light along the continuum. Categorical perception occurs because B_1 and B_2 are put in the same category and are seen as quite similar to each other, as are G_1 and G_2, while B_2 and G_1 are seen as more different, even though the difference in wavelength between each of the pairs is the same (35 nanometers). These subjective differences in similarity create the bands that we see in a rainbow. The critical developmental question is whether these categories emerge as a consequence of visual experience and possibly exposure to language or whether they are part of how infants see the world right from the start. Adapted from Boynton (1979).

Categorical Perception of Color Where do our color categories come from? Do we come into the world with perceptual capacities that lead us to group hues into certain color categories, or do we learn color boundaries from our elders through language and experience? Could repeatedly hearing "red" in reference to a certain range of wavelengths instill in the child a sense of how to perceptually group different reds together? In fact, no such experience seems to be necessary.

Using the habituation method introduced earlier, researchers have shown that even 4-month-olds perceive color in categories. The infants are first habituated to a certain wavelength of light projected on a screen. Once habituated, the infants are tested to see how they respond to two other hues of light, which are equidistant from the first in terms of wavelength. The crucial difference between the two new hues is that one falls within the same color category as the first (habituated) hue, and one falls outside this color boundary. For example, the infants might be habituated to an intermediate blue (blue 2 in Figure 3.9) and then tested to see whether they dishabituate more to green (green 1) or to a different blue (blue 1), both of which are 35 nanometers away from blue 2 on the spectrum.

These studies have found that the infants dishabituate more strongly to wavelengths that fall outside the color boundary of the hue to which they were habituated (Bornstein, 1975; Bornstein et al., 1976; Franklin & Davies, 2004). Evidence for categorical perception of color in infants younger than 4 months of age is somewhat controversial, but some studies suggest that even newborns show categorical perception (Jones-Molfese, 1977). Demonstrations of categorical color perception in young infants provide strong evidence that the color categories we perceive are not just the result of experience and cultural exposure.

Studies of color perception across cultures further support the idea that we do not learn color categories solely from older members of our society but are instead endowed with perceptual color categories long before culture has had much influence. It is true, however, that different languages can help create the categories we perceive. Older children and adults sometimes show patterns of categorical perception that are closely linked to the color categories of their primary language (Reiger & Kay, 2009). Nonetheless, multiple studies have also found some cross-cultural commonalities. For example, people from a diverse range of cultures and linguistic backgrounds tend to select the same hues as the "best" examples of color categories (for example, "the reddest red"; Berlin & Kay, 1969; Goldstone & Hendrickson, 2010; Heider & Olivier, 1972; Reiger & Kay, 2009).

How is it possible that preverbal infants tend to categorically perceive colors in the same way, but older children and adults tend to intermix such cross-cultural consistencies with differences linked to language and culture? It now appears that there may be two systems that influence the categorical perception of color. The first one, in the brain's right hemisphere, seems to be largely language free, is present in early infancy, and probably develops largely through a process of biological maturation. The other is housed in the left hemisphere, where language is typically most active, and it tends to emerge during the preschool years (Franklin et al., 2008a). In fact, toddlers will categorically perceive colors that they don't yet have words for with their right hemisphere, but they will categorically perceive colors that they can name with their left hemisphere (Franklin et al., 2008b). In most contexts, if language-based color categories conflict with preverbal ones from infancy, the language-based categorical perceptions will tend to dominate. These findings suggest that infants initially experience universal, common color categories that are shaped and constrained by the early development of the first, preverbal system. Within a few years, the second system's language-derived categories gain a predominant influence. Even adults can learn new, artificial color names for categories not represented in their own language—and when they do, categorical perception of these colors is lateralized in the left hemisphere (Kwok et al., 2011; Zhou et al., 2010). Some scholars think that the left hemisphere may have a broader ability to acquire new color categories and categorically perceive them such that it can do so even when the process is not mediated by language (Holmes & Wolff, 2012). There are still clearly two systems, with the right hemisphere being more maturation driven and the left hemisphere more experience driven, but language may be only one way of gaining such experiences.

Q: What evidence supports the claims that very young infants can see color and that they perceive colors categorically?

An important principle emerges here that will extend to our later discussions of cognitive development as well: the ability to perceive and understand the world requires categorization. There is simply too much raw information for any organism to master unless it simplifies and treats the members of some large classes of stimuli, such as colors or shapes, as equivalent for certain purposes. The ability to categorize is one of the most important ways in which infants and young children gain early footholds in perceptual and cognitive development.

Depth Perception

When a mountain goat is born in an especially steep area of the Sierra Nevada Mountains, it needs to be able to tell the difference between a small step down and a deep abyss as soon as it can walk. Likewise, it is highly uncommon for a baby squirrel to leap too far and miss the next branch in its sights or for a puppy to fail to catch the ball you've tossed. Animals that move about on their own would not survive long if they could not sense the distance to objects and surfaces. As adults, we use depth information whenever we reach out and grasp something and whenever we move through the world; we use it to drive, walk through crowds, and avoid dangerous drop-offs. But despite the obvious evidence that mature members of most visual species can perceive depth, the question of whether human infants can do so proved difficult to answer.

Cues to Depth Adults perceive depth with the help of three types of cues: *dynamic cues, binocular cues,* and *pictorial cues.* Researchers have explored the question of whether infants have depth perception by designing experiments that test whether infants perceive each of these kinds of depth cues.

Dynamic cues to depth are most active when either the observer or the observed objects are moving, and they work equally well when seen with just one eye or with both eyes. They do not require much acuity to be effective, which is one reason they can work so well even in low light or in a visually cluttered scene, such as when glimpsing objects through the branches of a tree. Dynamic cues seem to be the first depth cues that infants can use; even newborns use them to some extent. They are also clearly used by other species.

One of the simplest dynamic cues seems to be *looming*—namely, the perception that a rapidly expanding object is mov-

ing closer. When infants as young as 1 month observe such expanding patterns, their reactions indicate that they perceive depth. For example, if the looming object appears to be on a trajectory to collide with them, they will pull their heads back. Alternatively, if the looming object is a doorway-like opening, they will not try to move out of its path but instead will seem to anticipate moving through the opening (Carroll & Gibson, 1981; Schmuckler & Li, 1998; Yonas, 1981). Thus, not only are very young infants able to use looming as a depth clue, they are also able to interpret looming objects differently from similarly sized looming openings.

Another type of dynamic cue, called **motion parallax**, tracks the different ways that near objects and far objects appear to move relative to the motion of the eye. As Figure 3.10 shows, when an observer sees an object, an image of the object falls on the observer's retina. When the observer's eyes move, the images of those objects on the retina move

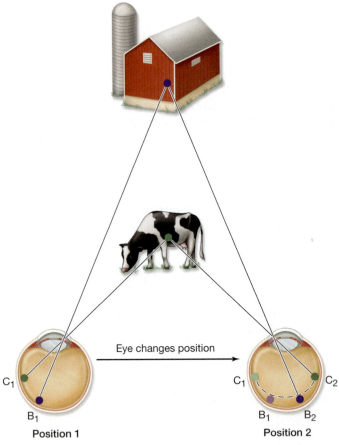

FIGURE 3.10 Motion parallax. Dynamic cues to depth work when either the observer, aspects of the scene, or both are in motion. Motion parallax cues to depth are based on the relative movement (or apparent movement) of objects based on their distance from the observer. When an observer moves, near objects and far objects move at different rates. Here, the near object (the cow) seems to move the longer distance (from C_1 to C_2), while the far object (the barn) appears to move the shorter distance (from B_1 to B_2). These differences can be used to infer the relative distances of the objects.

at different rates, depending on how close up or far away the objects are. In this particular example, the near object is initially seen to the right of the far object. As the observer moves from left to right, the near object appears to shift to the left of the far object. These differences in relative rate of movement allow us to perceive the relative distances of the two objects.

Motion parallax can be difficult to measure in young infants because it requires that they continuously track the motions of multiple objects while also keeping track of their own movements. Nonetheless, at least by age 3½ months, infants do seem to use motion parallax to perceive depth. By this age, they dishabituate when they view a screen in which depth relations between two objects appear to change in ways that would be highly unexpected or impossible looking to someone using motion parallax cues (Nawrot et al., 2009). At about the same age, they show a tendency to preferentially reach for objects that motion parallax cues indicate are closer (von Hofsten et al., 1992). Other researchers have inferred the use of motion parallax even in newborns. For example, when newborn infants have one eye covered and are presented with side-by-side stimuli consisting of a three-dimensional display and a two-dimensional photograph of that display, they will prefer to look at the three-dimensional version (Slater et al., 1984). The researchers argued that with one eye covered, the only major depth cue the infants can use is motion parallax.

In short, infants begin using dynamic cues to perceive depth as early as the first moments after birth and begin using them to guide their actions as early as 1 month of age. Experimental evidence suggests that they may not use some dynamic cues, such as motion parallax, across the full range of settings until somewhat later, possibly not until the third month of life. However, given that a wide range of species use motion parallax cues in their earliest moments, including many insects that move their heads from side to side to gauge how far to jump toward an object (Kral, 2003), it seems plausible that some early versions of motion parallax cues may be present at birth in humans as well.

Binocular cues rely on subtle differences between the two eyes to gauge how far away an object is. Two kinds of binocular cues are most important to consider: binocular parallax and convergence. **Binocular parallax** (also known as **binocular disparity**) refers to the slight disparity between the two eyes' views of any object. As Figure 3.11 shows, the right and left eyes always view any object from slightly different vantage points, and the difference between their views can be used to predict how close the object is to the eyes. The greater the disparity between the two retinal images, the closer the object is. The effect of binocular parallax is easy to observe by simply moving your fist closer and closer to your face while alternately viewing it through just one eye, then the other. As your fist gets closer, the difference between the images that each eye sees becomes larger,

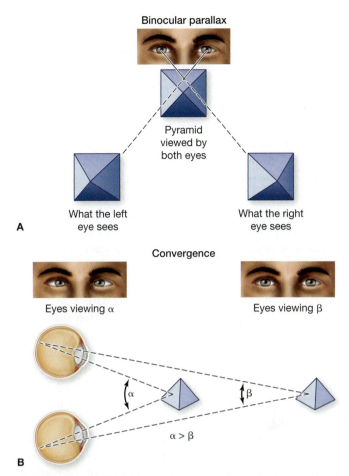

FIGURE 3.11 Binocular cues to depth. Binocular cues to depth require both a three-dimensional world and a viewer with two eyes. Distance is based on **(A)** binocular parallax, which is the disparity between two images (shown here as two different top views of the same pyramid), or on **(B)** the sensation of convergence of the eyes as they become less and less parallel for closer and closer objects (angle α is greater than angle β). These cues tend to lose their effectiveness for objects that are not nearby, as the relative difference between the eyes becomes negligible for faraway objects.

and the perceptual system interprets that disparity as information about distance. The process of using these binocular parallax cues to perceive depth is called **stereopsis**, which involves fusing two images into one image with depth.

The second binocular cue, **convergence**, is similar to binocular parallax, but rather than using the disparity between the two eyes' retinal images, convergence relies on the way the two eyes move—becoming increasingly crosseyed in order to focus on closer and closer objects. If you focus both eyes on your finger while holding it very close to your nose, you can feel a sensation of muscle strain; this is also illustrated in Figure 3.11. Convergence cues allow us to estimate the distance of an object by using the sensations of muscle tension in our eyes that correspond to pulling them into various angles of convergence.

The seventeenth-century empiricist George Berkeley proposed that convergence cues are a key component of the way infants learn to perceive objects in depth (Berkeley, 1709/1901; Pastore, 1965). More specifically, Berkeley suggested that the infant is born with only two simple depth-related sensations—the convergence feedback from the eye muscles when focusing on the object and the sensation of the degree of reaching or movement required to touch the object—and an ability to associate these two sensations. Simply put, infants would begin to associate a strong sense of binocular convergence with a near reach and weaker feelings of convergence with longer reaches.

Berkeley's empiricist model of learning to perceive depth makes some general predictions. First, if this model is correct, the very young infant should simply be unable to perceive depth, since she has not had time to learn the sensory associations that Berkeley describes. Second, depth perception should emerge gradually, based on the amounts and kinds of visual experiences the infant has had. The biggest problem with Berkeley's view is the evidence that many species, including humans, have excellent depth perception abilities in the absence of any learning experiences. Infants' eyes will converge automatically to fixate on a close object as early as 1 month (Hainline & Riddell, 1996), and infants between 5 and 8 months old can use convergence information as a cue to depth.

It is more difficult to tell whether infants use binocular parallax to perceive depth with normal objects because this ability involves a precise mental comparison of the tiny differences in the images that the two eyes see. But it is possible to artificially generate images that can only be seen when they are fused by the two eyes using parallax cues. (With each eye individually, the viewer sees only a seemingly random pattern of dots.) To see whether infants use binocular parallax cues, researchers present such images to infants on a computer screen. When the images are set in motion on the screen, the researchers monitor whether the infant's eyes track the images' movements. This technique has suggested that stereopsis emerges in about the fourth month of life and becomes increasingly sophisticated over the next few months (Fox et al., 1980; Granrud, 1986; Wattam-Bell, 2003). One possible reason that younger infants do not use stereopsis is that it may require greater visual acuity than they have yet developed (Brown & Lindsey, 2009). If young infants can't see patterns below a certain level of resolution, as shown in the blurriest images in Figure 3.6B, they may not be able to detect disparities in highly similar images.

The development of stereopsis presents another example of a critical-period effect. Some children are born with eye muscles that make their eyes excessively converge or diverge, resulting in either a "cross-eyed" or "wall-eyed" condition. As a result, the separate images that their right and left eyes see are too different for the brain to fuse them into a single image or to use the disparity between the images to provide depth information. If this situation persists for several years,

the inability to fuse the right and left eyes' images becomes irreversible, even if the problem with the eye muscles is later surgically corrected (Fawcett et al., 2005). Thus, a child as young as 6 years old who has surgery to correct a cross-eyed condition is unlikely to fully recover stereopsis, even after several years of normal visual experience. In such cases, the child often comes to rely on one eye much more than the other to avoid seeing double. This critical-period effect is thought to apply to stereopsis in particular, and not to convergence, because children with misaligned eyes might still register the muscle sensations associated with eye movements toward greater or lesser degrees of convergence.

> **Q:** What is some evidence for a critical period for binocular vision in humans?

The critical period for developing binocular depth perception has been documented more precisely in monkeys and cats. Like humans, monkeys and cats have certain neurons in the visual cortex that fire only when both eyes receive input simultaneously. These cells seem to be involved in computing the disparity between the two images and fusing them into one image. In a newborn kitten or monkey, however, these binocularly driven cells tend to be less responsive than they are in older animals. They become more fine-tuned only with considerable experience. If the animal wears eye patches on alternating sides to prevent that experience, the number of binocularly driven cells starts to diminish and eventually die off (Freeman & Ohzawa, 1992). When this happens, no amount of binocular visual experience later on can resurrect them (Crawford et al., 1996). This level of neural analysis concretely illustrates how critical-period effects are manifested in the nervous system. It shows how some neural circuits are attuned to certain stimuli during a critical period and then become much less changeable, allowing them to operate more efficiently (Hensch, 2004; Wang et al., 2010).

Pictorial cues can convey depth even in two-dimensional scenes like paintings and photographs and can do so even when seen with only one eye. Figure 3.12 illustrates three different types of pictorial cues: interposition, texture gradients, and convergence in the distance. *Interposition* occurs when one shape overlaps another, suggesting that it must be in front of the other. *Texture gradients* serve as cues to depth when a repeating pattern on a surface, such as the rough grid of a brick path, gets smaller and smaller the farther away the surface is. *Convergence in the distance* describes the way parallel lines, such as straight railroad tracks, seem to meet as they extend toward the horizon and thus show linear perspective, or the appearance of distance as the lines converge. Adults in all cultures

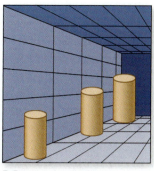

A Interposition   **B** Texture gradients   **C** Convergence in the distance   **D** Perspective illusion

FIGURE 3.12 Pictorial cues to depth. Pictorial cues to depth are those that indicate distance from the viewer by means of patterns on a two-dimensional surface or picture. They work equally well with one or two eyes. **(A)** Some, such as interposition, in which one object covers part of another object, appear in some of the earliest drawings in history. **(B)** Others, such as texture gradients, in which objects are depicted as smaller as they become more distant, appeared later in art history. **(C)** Still others, such as convergence in the distance, which provides linear perspective, appeared relatively late in the history of art and represented a major revolution in how to depict depth in paintings and drawings. Pictorial cues require fairly high levels of acuity to be effective and also have the potential to be misleading, as shown in **(D)**, where the cylinder farthest to the right appears much bigger than the one farthest to the left, even though they are the same size. The apparent difference in size is caused by pictorial cues to depth that suggest that the rightmost cylinder is farther away than the leftmost one.

can use these pictorial depth cues, but infants younger than about 6 months do not seem to use them (Kellman & Banks, 1998). Thus, only humans older than 6 months are likely to be fooled by the illusion in Figure 3.12D, in which identical-size cylinders in fact look very different in size because of surrounding pictorial cues.

One technique that researchers have used extensively to investigate when infants use pictorial depth cues relies on the simple fact that when young infants are presented with two objects, they consistently reach for the nearer one. A clever experimenter can use this reaching preference to find the conditions under which the infant sees a difference in depth. In one study, researchers showed 5- and 7-month-old infants a "window" like the one in Figure 3.13, which contained several pictorial cues to depth (Yonas et al., 1978). They then observed whether the infants more often reached toward the side of the window that would appear closer if the infants were relying on pictorial depth cues. The 5-month-olds showed no preferential reaching for the edge that would seem nearer based on pictorial cues. Instead, they responded to the surface as if it had no patterns on it at all, reaching for various parts seemingly at random. In contrast, the 7-month-olds consistently reached for the edge that would have looked closer to someone using pictorial cues. Recall from the visual acuity studies discussed earlier that 5-month-olds could easily see the lines and shadows that serve as the pictorial cues. Nonetheless, they did not use them to see depth.

Studies of many other pictorial depth cues have found this same time frame to be significant: 5-month-olds typically do not use pictorial cues effectively, but 7-month-olds do (Hemker et al., 2010; Kellman & Banks, 1998; Yonas

et al., 2002). These findings suggest that at around 6 months of age, a capacity emerges for using and integrating different kinds of pictorial cues. It is interesting that in some tasks, 5-month-old infants can readily see depth with two eyes by using binocular cues, but they cannot see it with one eye when only pictorial cues are available (Hemker et al., 2010). This pattern of results does not necessarily mean that the ability develops solely as a consequence of maturation;

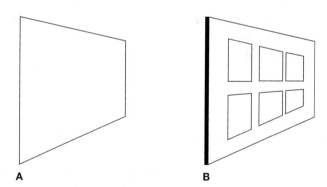

A   **B**

FIGURE 3.13 Sensitivity to pictorial depth. (A) A simple trapezoid conveys an illusion of depth, but it is not as compelling as **(B)** the illusion conveyed by an Ames window, where the right side seems farther away because of pictorial cues to depth. These cues are convergence in the distance (the top and bottom lines of the window become closer to each other) and texture gradients (the window panes become smaller in the distance). Young infants who cannot use pictorial cues to depth will reach equally for the right and left sides of the Ames window or in the middle, while older infants will reach more for the left side, thinking it is closer. This is one case where younger infants are more accurate; they are not misled by an illusion of pictorial depth. Adapted from Ames (1951) and Yonas et al. (1978).

learning experiences could be important as well. It is not yet clear why the ability to use pictorial cues develops later in infancy than the ability to use dynamic cues or binocular cues. One possible reason is that getting depth information from pictorial cues may require more learning or cognitive interpretation than the other types of cues. Another possibility is that pictorial cues may require more advanced levels of visual acuity.

Which Depth Cues Predominate? Gibson's Visual Cliff Studies Several research projects have also shown which kinds of depth cues dominate when different types are pitted against each other. Generally, the earlier-emerging cues tend to trump those that develop later. The best-known research techniques to explore these questions were developed by Eleanor J. Gibson, the twentieth century's most influential researcher in perceptual development. Gibson had an extraordinary talent for devising ways of studying infant behavior that could yield remarkable insights into their perceptual development. She developed numerous experiments that explored infants' perceptual abilities in circumstances that resembled their natural interactions with the world.

In the 1950s, while studying perception in newborn goats, Gibson was inspired to create a new experimental technique for studying infants' depth perception. She noticed that the busy handlers in the lab often had trouble keeping track of the baby goats, since even the newborns were able to wander around. The handlers solved this problem by placing restless baby goats on a raised surface, such as a stool or countertop. At the edges of these surfaces, the young goats would freeze, apparently because they immediately perceived the difference in depth and feared falling. Gibson realized that the newborn goats perceived depth without any prior experience. She devised the visual cliff technique to explore this phenomenon systematically in several species, including humans.

Figure 3.14 shows the **visual cliff** that Gibson developed. It consists of a large, transparent, and nonreflective pane of glass with two similar checker-patterned displays below it. One-half of the glass pane had a checkered pattern directly beneath it, so that the surface appeared solid. The other half of the glass pane had the same checkered pattern roughly 3 feet below, giving the impression of a sudden drop-off, or "visual cliff." A wooden plank across the pane's surface divided the two halves. The studies performed with this apparatus usually began with placing a 6-month-old on the wooden "bridge" between the two sides of the glass surface and observing where the infant crawled. Gibson and her team were especially interested in how the infants would respond to the "cliff" side of the pane. Their findings were clear and dramatic. The infants were quite reluctant to move onto the glass above the apparent drop-off, even when the infant's mother was on the other side

FIGURE 3.14 The visual cliff. Despite attempts by his mother to induce him to cross the visual cliff, this infant is clearly hesitant. The glass that covers the deep side of the cliff is nonreflective and illuminated such that the infant sees only the sudden drop-off.

smiling and enticing the baby with a favorite toy (Gibson & Walk, 1960).

How do we know which kind of depth cues the infants primarily used to avoid the "deep" side of the cliff? To check for use of pictorial cues, Gibson and her associates compared infants' performance on the two cliff setups shown in Figure 3.15. Cliff A was carefully designed so that the drop-off could not be seen by using pictorial cues to depth. On the deeper side of the cliff, the size of the checkered pattern was larger than the pattern on the shallow side. The pattern sizes differed by precisely the right amount to project identically sized squares on the retinas of infants crawling across the glass surface; based on pictorial cues alone, the whole

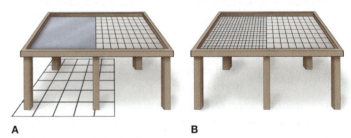

A   B

FIGURE 3.15 Dynamic clues to depth and performance on the visual cliff. Infants were tested on visual cliffs in which there were **(A)** motion parallax cues (dynamic cues produced by the different rates at which the two surfaces were seen to move when the infant moved his head) without pictorial cues to depth (larger squares below appeared on the infant's retina as the same size as the smaller squares above) or **(B)** pictorial cues (smaller squares on the left grid making it appear as if these squares were farther away than the larger squares on the right grid) without motion parallax cues to depth (no differences in perceived rates of movement, since both grids were on the same surface). The infants resisted crossing the visual cliff when dynamic cues indicated that there was a drop-off but not when pictorial cues indicated a drop-off. Adapted from Gibson & Walk (1960).

surface would appear level. Based on dynamic depth cues induced by motion, especially motion parallax produced by the different rates at which the upper and lower surfaces were seen to move when the infants moved their heads, the visual cliff would be obvious. The results were clear. The infants fearfully stopped at the "edge" even when the pictorial cues indicated a level surface, suggesting that they were relying on dynamic cues. This finding gained further support when the experimenters altered the visual cliff setup so that pictorial cues indicated a drop-off while dynamic cues indicated a level surface. In this case, the infants happily crawled across (Gibson, 1969; Gibson & Walk, 1960). To rule out use of binocular cues, researchers have conducted similar studies in which the infants wore an eye patch over one eye. In these cases, infants using only monocular cues were just as likely to avoid the cliff's edge, indicating again that they were very likely relying on motion parallax cues (Walk, 1968).

Q: In what ways does depth perception in young infants differ from depth perception in older children and adults?

Functional Significance of the Depth Perception System

As we have seen, the development of depth perception reveals a consistent pattern (see Figure 3.16): The use of dynamic cues emerges possibly as early as the first month of life. Then the effective use of binocular cues develops around 4 months, followed by the effective use of pictorial cues around 6 months. From an evolutionary perspective, what might account for this sequence?

One important advantage for the early emergence of dynamic cues such as motion parallax is that they are almost always reliable in the natural world. By contrast, later-developing pictorial cues can be misleading in many optical illusions that show contradictory representations of depth (see Figure 3.17). In addition, dynamic cues do not require good visual acuity, but both pictorial cues and binocular cues do. Under blurred conditions and with only one eye, it is still possible to use dynamic cues such as motion parallax or looming to infer depth relationships, even while it is not possible to use the other sorts of cues. Thus, dynamic cues are most useful to infants who initially have poor acuity and who have to judge depth in conditions of reduced acuity, such as in low light or with tears in the eyes. The key point is that natural selection favors the most robust and reliable early system for depth perception, the dynamic cues, and these are the dominant cues in young infants of most species. We will see that these sorts of evolutionary considerations, especially in comparative research across several species, can often provide meaningful inter-

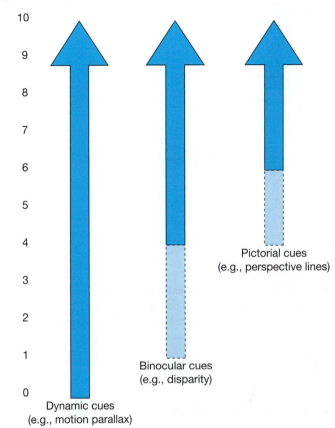

Age (in months)

FIGURE 3.16 Three different sets of cues specify depth for the infant. Dynamic cues such as motion parallax appear to be used first, probably right at birth. Binocular cues start to emerge as partially effective at around 1 month (as depicted by the dashed lines), becoming much more effective at 4 months. Pictorial cues are not effectively used until around 6 months of age, although some sensitivity to pictorial relations may appear as early as 4 months (as depicted by the dashed lines).

pretations of developmental patterns. Ideally, they also help predict new patterns and motivate new research.

Q: Why might infants be able to use dynamic cues to depth before binocular and pictorial cues?

Perceiving Patterns and Recognizing Objects

Do infants perceive meaningful patterns in the same ways that adults do? Do they, for example, devote more attention to human faces than to other recurring patterns in their

unrelated to language, such as preferring the musical meter that is typical of their own culture (Soley & Hannon, 2010).

Of course, infants, like the rest of us, do not pay equal attention to all the sounds they hear. Certain classes of sounds seem to stand out, even if they are not any more dramatic in terms of their physical properties. In particular, very young infants and even newborns seem to be especially attentive to human speech (Minagawa-Kawai et al., 2011; Vouloumanos & Werker, 2004, 2007). But here, too, a form of perceptual narrowing takes place early in infancy. Newborns are more attentive to monkey sounds than to synthetic sounds created to resemble speech. In contrast, 3-month-olds do not show this preference; they only prefer human speech sounds over the synthetic sounds (Vouloumanos et al., 2010).

In addition, infants are maximally attentive not just to any speech, but especially to the sort most likely to be directed at them. Researchers previously used the term "motherese" for the style of communication that people typically use with babies and young children (Newport et al., 1977), although it is also used by fathers and just about anyone else talking to an infant or young child. Such child-directed speech (more widely known as "baby talk") usually involves a higher-pitched voice, rising intonations at the ends of phrases, and longer pauses between sentences, among other properties. This kind of speech seems somehow more appropriate for interacting with infants—and research confirms this. Four-month-olds prefer to hear an unfamiliar adult's child-directed speech rather than the same person's normal adult speech pattern (Fernald, 1985), and this preference may be present as early as the first month of life (Cooper & Aslin, 1990; Cooper et al., 1997). Additional research suggests that child-directed speech helps infants detect boundaries between words by making them more salient (Thiessen et al., 2005).

Infants as young as 6 months are also able to pick up on some universal properties of communication; they can discriminate intonation patterns that indicate approval from those that indicate disapproval, regardless of the language of the speaker. Furthermore, they seem to be somewhat aware of the emotional meanings of the intonations, smiling more when the tone indicates approval and less in response to disapproval (Fernald, 1993). These findings show that infants not only attend to the speech around them, but also extract important meaning from it.

Locating Sounds

When we hear a sound, we often know its approximate location immediately, even when we are in the dark without visual clues. Only when a sound is extremely muffled, very low pitched, or heavily echoed do we become unable to locate its source. Even though we typically locate the source

of sounds automatically and effortlessly, this is actually a complex task, especially given the great speed at which it is carried out. Such a skill takes considerable time and experience to develop. As we saw with face perception, infants may develop two systems to support sound localization: a crude early system and a more sophisticated later-developing system that provides a richer sense of auditory space (Muir & Clifton, 1985).

Newborns show some capacity for sound localization (Braddick & Atkinson, 1988; Muir & Clifton, 1985; Muir & Field, 1979; Wertheimer, 1963), but this early ability seems to be based on a fairly crude mechanism in the brainstem that does not provide a sense of objects' locations in an auditory space. Instead, newborns seem to rely on a simple system that registers differences in sound intensity between the two ears and then causes a reflex-like turn of the head toward the more intense sound. In this response, the infant does not seem to have a higher-level, perceptual expectation of finding an object near the location of the sound, and he does not seem surprised if he finds nothing there. At around 2 months of age, the head-turning response to sounds disappears, only to reappear at around 4 months. But at this point, the localization response has a different character. It becomes more accurate and precisely directed toward the sound's source rather than simply turning the head toward the correct side.

Sound localization abilities, then, present another instance of a U-shaped developmental curve. The infant shows a crude initial ability to localize sounds, which seems to decline briefly before reemerging in a more sophisticated form (Muir & Hains, 2004; Muir et al., 1989). Unlike the newborn, when the 4-month-old localizes a sound, he seems to have a clear expectation that something is "out there" in a particular location in space (Muir & Clifton, 1985). The development of this second, more accurate system depends not only on maturation of the relevant structures in the infant's brain but also on experience. Over time, feedback from touch and vision helps the infant to fine-tune the processing of incoming information about sounds' locations. Compared with the first system, the second system offers the benefit of increased accuracy and more explicit awareness; its costs include the additional time and experience it requires to become more accurate.

Both sound localization systems develop in close connection with infants' other perceptual abilities. In newborns, even simple, reflex-driven localization provides tremendous help in gathering information about the world. By triggering an immediate look in the general direction of a sound, this rudimentary ability enables even the youngest baby to begin learning which sights go with which sounds even before the system is fine-tuned by experience. Thus, right from the start, the infant starts to learn about objects by using several senses at once to achieve a unified perceptual experience, rather than focusing on one sense at a time. As we will see shortly,

Cochlear Implants and the Question of Critical Periods for Auditory Processing

Although it has been known for some time that aspects of the visual system show critical-period effects, it has been more difficult to document such effects in hearing. Thanks to improving technology, researchers are now making advances in understanding critical-period effects on hearing. At the forefront of this research is work involving cochlear implants for very young children.

In response to incoming sound, the organ of corti within the inner ear stimulates the nerve cells that initially process auditory information. In most cases of total deafness, the organ of corti has been damaged. Cochlear implants are electronic devices that can be implanted in the ears to bypass the damaged organ of corti and cause stimulation of the auditory nerve fibers. The implant creates a form of hearing, the nature of which varies, depending on the age of the recipient.

As implants have been approved for younger and younger individuals, researchers have begun to ask whether there is a critical period for developing the ability to interpret the firing patterns of neurons as meaningful auditory input. Older recipients of implants are able to detect sounds through those implants, but can they learn to interpret those sounds in as sophisticated a manner as younger recipients? Or, analogous to the case of the girl whose vision was restored following cataract surgery, when the ability to receive auditory input is restored after early deafness, are there permanent effects of being deprived of auditory experience early in life?

In studies of cats that were born deaf, cats that received cochlear implants early in development showed better results than those that received implants when they were older. Those that got early implants gained higher levels of functioning in the auditory cortex, the brain area that processes sounds (Kral et al., 2002). Similarly, people who get cochlear implants in the first years of life can better distinguish between sounds than those who get the implants several years later.

Children who receive cochlear implants at younger ages usually have better outcomes (Pulsifer et al., 2003; Teoh et al., 2004a). "Younger" initially meant around 2 years of age, but more recent studies of children who get implants before age 1 suggest even better results than with 2-year-olds (Colletti et al., 2005; Dettman & Dowell, 2010; Niparko et al., 2010), suggesting a critical period in the development of some aspects of auditory perception. This critical-period effect may be largely caused by the brain's compensation plasticity (see Chapter 2). Recall that in blind people, areas of the cortex used for visual processing can become devoted to other sensory processes instead, resulting in more acute sensation in other modalities (such as hearing) to help compensate for the loss of vision. Or the visual cortex will show activation when subjects who were blind from birth or who became blind at a very early age read Braille by touching their finger to the letters (Gizewski et al., 2003). Similarly, if the auditory cortex does not receive auditory input, it can be "colonized" by other sensory functions, such as vision and touch, which help compensate for the hearing loss. By providing a different route for auditory input to reach the brain, cochlear implants may preserve the function of the auditory cortex for processing sounds (Teoh et al., 2004b).

Evidence is accumulating that the earlier the patient receives the cochlear implants, the more normal will be both her ability to distinguish between various speech sounds and her ability to articulate clearly; in fact, some neural circuits may show permanent declines in auditory and speech-processing abilities if implants are not present before roughly 4 years of age (Eisenberg et al., 2012; Kral & Sharma, 2012). (This connection between speech perception and articulation illustrates the kind of link between perception and action that we will see in more detail in Chapter 4.) Two concerns remain, however. First, the incidence of medical complications rises with implant surgery in younger and younger babies (Johr et al., 2008). Second, some members of the deaf community feel that any increased risk associated with the surgery is unacceptable, given that there is a rich and vibrant deaf culture that offers an alternative developmental path to many deaf children (Sparrow, 2010). Thus, even as the technology evolves and the critical-period effects are better documented, not all parents choose surgery for their infants.

Even adults who receive cochlear implants show some improvements that suggest an expansion of neural functioning in the auditory cortex. This pattern has been found both in adult cats (Klinke et al., 1999) and in adult humans (Teoh et al., 2004a). Thus, although it remains ideal to receive the implants as early in development as possible, they can still confer benefits to adults.

uniting the perceptual experiences from different senses may be one of the most basic ways that even the youngest infants begin making sense of the world. It is also intriguing that the second, higher-level localization system emerges around the same time that the infant becomes better able to visually perceive depth using stereopsis. As the visual ability to locate objects in depth improves, the auditory localization system seems to undergo a comparable shift.

> **Q:** How is the sound localization ability of the newborn different from that of the 5-month-old infant?

To fully understand how sound localization systems become fine-tuned with experience, researchers need to systematically manipulate those experiences and measure the effects on a young organism's behavior and neural functioning. For ethical reasons, these sorts of experiments are not possible with human infants, which is why some of the most revealing work on the development of sound localization has been done in other organisms. For example, by studying barn owls, which are excellent at precisely locating sounds, researchers have constructed a detailed biopsychological model of the development of sound localization (Bergan & Knudsen, 2009; Knudsen, 1988, 2004). These owls localize sounds more accurately as they grow older, but even the youngest owls turn their heads in a roughly appropriate direction. This early ability suggests that they have an innate ability to infer the approximate visual location that corresponds to the sound's source. As we have seen in a number of systems, these innate abilities act as frameworks within which extensive fine-tuning of the skill occurs. For the owls, fine-tuning the sound localization system requires simultaneous experience in both vision and audition. This is the case even at the level of neurons; specific cells can respond to both auditory and visual inputs.

The fine-tuning process also demonstrates the importance of plasticity in the young owl's localization system. If the baby owl's visual or auditory experiences are distorted, either by plugging one of its ears or by placing prisms over its eyes that shift the visual world to one side (see Figure 3.27), the owl will gradually adapt and start localizing correctly again despite the distortion. When the earplugs or eye prisms are removed within a certain critical period, the owl will then initially turn its head in the wrong direction before readapting to its undistorted perceptions. By allowing the owl to adjust to perceptual problems or injuries, a plastic localization system offers real advantages over one that is fully hardwired and less responsive to feedback from the environment.

The research on barn owls has shown that there are **sensitive periods** for calibrating the system (Knudsen & Knudsen, 1990). If an owl younger than 60 days of age has one ear plugged, it will adapt and adjust the localization system. If the owl is still young when the earplug is removed, it will initially localize incorrectly but then gradually readjust, as previously described. But if the plug is not removed until the owl is 200 days old, the owl's system will become permanently inaccurate and unable to readjust. Interestingly, the sensitive-period during which the owl is able to adjust to distorted sound perceptions ends much earlier than the critical period in which the owl can readjust to its own *unaltered* perceptions. At the age of 60 days, the owl loses the ability to adjust to distorted inputs, but it can still recover from those distorted inputs for another 140 days. Readjustment becomes impossible only after around 200 days of distorted perception. The difference in these periods reflects a default bias toward the owl's unaltered perceptual experience. Owls show comparable sensitive-period effects in adjusting their visual perceptions to distortions from prisms, except that the ability to adjust to visual deviations declines more gradually than the ability to adjust to auditory distortions.

FIGURE 3.27 Effects of visual distortion on sound localization in owls. The owl uses vision to interpret auditory cues and adjusts its perception of where a sound is coming from based on what it sees. This baby barn owl is wearing prisms that make the world seem 20 degrees to the right of where it really is. If the owl wears these prisms beyond a critical period of roughly 200 days, it will have permanently "retuned" its localization of sounds based on the distortions caused by the prisms. If the prisms are then removed, the owl will forever mislocalize by 20 degrees. Because the barn owl's localization has been studied in great detail and has been linked to underlying changes in neural responses, it offers an excellent model of developmental change within a constraining framework.

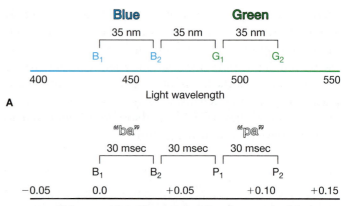

A

B

FIGURE 3.28 **Categorical perception of speech.** The categorical perception of speech can be understood the same way as the categorical perception of color **(A)**, except that, in this case, the physical continuum for perceiving speech **(B)** is the amount of time delay between lip release and voicing, called the voice onset time (VOT). Equal intervals of 30 milliseconds along this auditory physical continuum are not seen as the same psychologically. B_1 and B_2, both in the "ba" category, and P_1 and P_2, both in the "pa" category, are seen as much more similar to each other than B_2 and P_1, since they straddle the "ba" and "pa" categories. Even though physical distances are the same, the psychological distances are much shorter when they stay within categories rather than cross them. Even newborn infants show these categorical effects in their perception of speech.'

Q: How does the development of auditory localization in the barn owl demonstrate both constraints on the development of this perceptual skill and its plasticity?

Perceiving Complex Sound Patterns

Some sounds, such as a bell or a snap of a finger, are relatively simple in acoustic terms. Others, such as human speech, are remarkably complex. A simple empiricist view of auditory development might propose that babies learn to perceive the sounds that are acoustically simplest first. If this were true, then to young infants, all speech sounds would initially sound the same: just an overwhelming confusion of sound components. Several decades ago, however, researchers learned that young infants seem to perceive quite a large amount of structure in speech sounds. Most dramatically, infants do not treat every different nuanced speech sound as unique. Instead, they tend to perceive discrete categories of sounds. Even though sounds' physical properties vary smoothly along a continuum, infants regard all the sounds within a category as very similar to each other and very different from the sounds in different categories. In short, infants are capable of categorical perception of speech.

Many elements of speech primarily differ from one another in terms of their values on a single dimension. For example, the sounds "ba" and "pa" only differ in terms of voice onset time (VOT), which describes the time lag between releasing your lips to define the sound and the beginning, or onset, of voicing the sound. A speaker saying "ba" voices the "ah" sound almost immediately after releasing the lips, but for "pa" there is a longer delay before voicing occurs. The average VOTs for "ba" and "pa" are shown in Figure 3.28, which also shows the similar wavelength continuum for color vision that we considered earlier.

The VOTs range along a continuum—from negative VOTs, with voicing before lip release, to positive VOTs, which occur as much as 0.2 second after lip release—but psychologically, we do not perceive these sounds as varying gradually. Instead, we group similar sounds into categories and treat the sounds within each category as basically the same. This means that to differentiate between "ba" and "pa," we hear a fairly large range of VOTs as "ba" and then, past a certain point on the continuum, we hear a large range as "pa." As Figure 3.28 shows, sounds that are within the "ba" region sound very similar despite having voice onset times 30 milliseconds apart. Yet, if two sounds on opposite sides of the "ba"/"pa" boundary are 30 milliseconds apart, they sound very different, at least to adults.

Q: How does the categorization of speech sounds help infants to perceive speech?

Studies of infants of all ages have attempted to understand more clearly how categorical perception of sound emerges and changes over the course of infant development. The first breakthrough study on the topic repeatedly presented the infants with an artificially synthesized "ba" sound (with a consistent VOT) whenever they sucked hard enough on a special pacifier that measured sucking intensity (Eimas et al., 1971). Over time, their sucking for that particular "ba" sound declined, presumably because they had become habituated to it. The infants would then hear one of two artificially synthesized sounds that were identical to the original "ba" sound except for differences in VOT. The two sounds differed from the original "ba" by an equal amount of VOT, but in opposite directions as shown in Figure 3.28. To adults, the sound with a shorter VOT would still sound like "ba," while the sound with the longer VOT would sound like "pa" because it falls on the other side of the category boundary. If infants had no preexisting biases to categorically perceive speech sounds, then both would sound equally distinct from the original "ba" and they would dishabituate equally to either of the new stimuli. But if the infants perceived speech sounds categorically, they would perceive the new, short-VOT sound as a second "ba," essentially the same as the first, and they would show little dishabituation to it. In contrast, they would perceive the new, long-VOT sound as "pa," and they would dishabituate more strongly. In fact, they tended to dishabituate, suggesting that very young infants do tend to cluster together speech sounds into categories, just as adults do (Eimas et al., 1987). They do not simply take in sensory data; they actively interpret sensory experience and group similar perceptions into classes, treating similar perceptions as essentially equivalent. Like adults, infants categorically perceive various sounds in the speech stream, including contrasts such as "d" versus "t" and "b" versus "g," as well as differences between vowels.

These studies were initially interpreted as indicating an innate language-processing capacity, since the infants categorically perceived speech sounds in particular. But two other lines of work soon expanded on these findings. First, researchers showed that infants also categorically perceive nonspeech sounds (Jusczyk et al., 1980, 1983). Second, researchers found that other species, such as chinchillas and macaque monkeys, also categorically perceive human speech, even though they obviously don't have brain structures specialized for it (Kuhl & Miller, 1978; Kuhl & Padden, 1982). The debate over how to interpret these findings is ongoing (Aslin et al., 1998; Gerken & Aslin, 2005; Goldstone & Hendrickson, 2010). Some researchers have proposed that infants' categorical perception of speech results from general properties characterizing most species' hearing systems (Kuhl, 1986, 2004; Samuels, 2012). Others have suggested that additional aspects of human infant speech perception support the argument for an innate speech-processing mechanism in humans, such as a special sensitivity to perceiving certain contrasts that are found only in human speech (Eimas et al., 1987).

It is clear that infants' early experience with a particular language heavily influences the way their categorical perception of speech develops. Initially, very young infants will categorically perceive a wide array of distinctions between sounds in all languages. Typically by around age 8 months, however, they lose the ability to make most of the sound discriminations that are not considered meaningful in their own native language (Kuhl, 2004; Werker, 1989). English-speaking infants, for example, lose the ability they once had to distinguish two different versions of "d" sounds that are meaningful in Hindi, while infants in Hindi-speaking cultures further sharpen that perceptual skill. Intriguingly, not all abilities to distinguish contrasts in unfamiliar languages disappear; the reason that some remain is a topic of active research and discussion (Aslin et al., 1998).

In general, experience in a given language fine-tunes the auditory perception system, so that the particular boundaries and categories that are meaningful within that language become most salient (Eimas et al., 1987; Gervain & Mehler, 2010; Werker & Tees, 2005; Werker et al., 2007). In many ways, this pattern is similar to the fine-tuning that we have seen in the development of abilities to recognize visual patterns and to localize sounds. The infant is not born with a fixed and unalterable set of categories and ways of processing them, but rather is endowed with a set of biases that are selectively fine-tuned by experience.

Above and beyond these biases, there may also be a component of speech perception that accords with a very general tendency to learn associations between stimuli that frequently occur together. For example, a critical accomplishment in the first year of life is to be able to pick out and recognize specific words in the speech stream. To see how difficult this is for the untrained ear, simply listen to a native speaker of a completely unfamiliar language; it is nearly impossible to count the number of words in any utterance. Yet, one line of work shows that by at least 8 months of age, infants start to pick out words from the speech stream solely on the basis of how often certain syllables occur together in the same order (Saffran et al., 1996a, 1996b, 2006). In these studies, infants listen to a steady stream of nonsense syllables separated by consistent time intervals and without stresses or larger sound patterns to emphasize syllable clusters. They nonetheless seem to perceive "words" in that stream if certain triads of syllables (for example, "bidaku") repeatedly occur in the same order ("bidakubidakubidakubidaku"). Quite remarkably, it only takes a few minutes of listening to such patterns for an infant to start picking out the three-syllable regularities. Moreover, they show the same ability to pick up on the syllable sequences that make up actual words in a real, but unfamiliar natural language (Pelucchi et al., 2009).

More broadly, we can see three distinct developmental patterns in the development of speech perception: (1) infants learn sensory patterns, (2) they develop universal aspects of speech perception, and (3) they develop language-specific elements of speech perception, starting at around 6 months (Kuhl, 2004). All infants start with the same general framework for interpreting speech, one that imposes considerable structure on the information in the speech stream. But soon they modify this original structure in ways that reflect the properties of their native language.

Categorical perception is not an oddity of perceptual development; instead, it may be the mind's normal way of handling an otherwise overwhelming amount of information. Even though our sensory receptors filter out vast amounts of information about the physical world, the information we do pick up varies in an extraordinary number of ways. Without

Legislating Early Stimulation

I n 1998, following Governor Zell Miller's enthusiastic recommendation, Georgia's state legislature voted to supply a free recording of classical music to every child born in the state (Sack, 1998). The policy aimed to improve children's intellectual development through early stimulation. Miller was responding to research findings interpreted as showing that exposing infants to Mozart's music increased their intelligence and cognitive functioning (Rauscher et al., 1993, 1995). As other states took an interest in adopting similar programs, it became clear that these programs offered suppliers of the recordings substantial opportunities to profit. As a result, several companies sprang up offering musical recordings allegedly designed to enhance an infant's or toddler's intelligence with repeated listening. One enterprising company even trademarked the name "The Mozart Effect"—a reference to the research that inspired the trend—in an attempt to dominate the market.

The so-called Mozart effect had considerable intuitive appeal. It seemed appropriate that classical music, which most people view as cultured and sophisticated, would actually be good for the developing brain. Proponents of the effect even offered an explanation for the mechanism of improvement. Mozart's pieces had a rich mathematical structure (Hetland, 2000; Rauscher et al., 1993, 1995), and hearing the music's complex rhythms and patterns "exercised" brain circuits associated with spatial reasoning during a critical period of brain development. If these theories were correct, parents who deprived their children of such rich perceptual stimulation might be impairing their children's cognitive development, while parents and states that supplied Mozart recordings to all infants might have noticeably smarter children in later years. Even many years later, a cursory Internet search turns up all sorts of products making claims along these lines.

It might sound like a developmental psychologist's dream to see a policy designed and implemented in accord with developmental research. This research, however, was far less convincing than its advocates claimed. If listening to classical music has any effect on infants' cognition, it is small and short-lived, and it likely works through simply increasing the infant's alertness and attention—a property shared by lots of other stimuli, musical and otherwise. In fact, the claim that classical music, especially Mozart's, was unusually effective at enhancing intelligence was undercut by enthusiastic supporters of the effect. They claimed to find it even after exposing infants to sentimental popular music (Rideout et al., 1998), even though pop music does not seem to share the rich mathematical structure that supposedly boosts aspects of reasoning. Even worse, other researchers' attempts to replicate the initial findings of a "Mozart effect" generally have not succeeded (Chabris, 1999; McCutcheon, 2000; McKelvie & Low, 2002; Nantais & Schellenberg, 1999; Steele et al., 1999). These simple failures to replicate the findings, as well as demonstrations of a number of problems with the initial studies' experimental procedures, have repeatedly raised questions about whether the effect ever existed at all (Pietschnig et al., 2010; Schellenberg, 2005).

Although several U.S. states and some other countries proposed programs of distributing free classical music to newborns (see Figure 3.29), the proposals were rarely implemented, and Zell Miller's vision seems to no longer be part of Georgia's official activities. Yet, sales of music and videos touting the Mozart effect remain brisk, and many people firmly believe in the phenomenon. It might seem harmless, but from a public policy point of view, such misunderstandings incur real costs. Funds used to provide these materials to infants and toddlers might be better spent on more proven ways to improve their health. In addition, attempts to improve children's abilities through such "quick fixes" tend to give short shrift to educational problems that actually require much more long-term, structural support (Jones & Zigler, 2002).

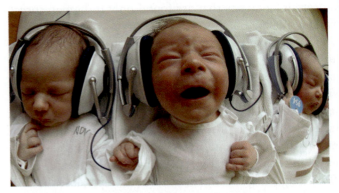

FIGURE 3.29 **Newborns and music.** Newborns listened to classical music over headphones as researchers tested whether hearing music would stimulate the newborns' cognitive development. But early exposure to classical music did not lead to a significant increase in cognitive abilities.

sorting stimuli into groups that allow us to treat some inputs as roughly equivalent, we would never be able to generalize based on limited experience, recognize new but familiar instances, or otherwise process information effectively. Our perceptual systems have evolved to impose certain types of clustering that help the developing person notice important real-world differences.

> **Q:** Why are young infants able to distinguish between some speech sounds that adults cannot?

The Chemical Senses: Taste and Smell

Although the visual and auditory senses dominate our perceptual world (as well as dominating the attention of researchers on infant perception), the chemical senses of taste and smell are also important to the way that infants perceive the world. Taste and smell are among the earliest emerging senses in the history of life, and in humans they may be functional even before birth.

Taste

Studies of the neuroanatomy and neurophysiology of fetuses in the womb suggest that taste perception functions well before birth (Beauchamp & Mennella, 2011). These studies, some of which involve physiological measures of the nerve bundles arising out of taste receptors, show that the fetus tastes the mother's amniotic fluid. The functional value that this ability serves is less clear, although it might be a way of starting to learn some distinctive things about that culture's diet, since fairly large taste-related molecules can pass from the mother's digestive system to the amniotic fluid. Thus, in some cases, the compounds that a fetus is exposed to in utero may make certain tastes more acceptable after birth. One study showed that newborn rats were more accepting of alcohol-laced liquids and other bitter compounds if their mothers were fed ethanol while pregnant (Youngentob & Glendinning, 2009). Thus, human infants whose mothers abuse alcohol may be more willing to ingest harmful compounds.

Adults are often said to have at least four basic taste categories: sweet, sour, salty, and bitter (Erickson & Covey, 1980), but infants may be less richly endowed. The ability to perceive all four of these basic tastes may take time and experience to develop. To assess taste perception in infants, researchers have adopted several strategies, which seem to converge on the finding that sweet substances play an especially important role in the life of the young infant.

Newborns and infants show a clear preference for sweet substances—not only sugar but also synthetic sweeteners such as saccharin—over other flavors. Infants can learn to suck in response to a sweet taste (Bartoshuk & Beauchamp, 1994), and sugar has a strong calming effect on very young infants, even acting as a kind of painkiller. Indeed, in the Jewish faith, it is common to have the infant suck on a rag soaked in sweet grape wine as a way of calming him during the ritual of circumcision. The practice dates back thousands of years and may reflect folk awareness of sugar's soothing effect (Blass & Hoppmeyer, 1991). As infants get to be about 1 month old, the effects of a sweet taste are amplified if the person providing the nutrition also makes eye contact with the infant (Zeifman et al., 1996). Since breast milk is quite sweet, this pattern suggests that infants' preference for sweet substances is closely linked to behaviors that calm them while nursing, which are obviously of great adaptive value.

Some assessments of early taste perception rely on correlations between facial expressions and sets of tastes. Adults clearly show distinct responses to sour, sweet, salty, and bitter (Steiner, 1979), and some evidence suggests that very young infants respond similarly (see Figure 3.30). Although we cannot know what these infants are experiencing, the relations between the substances they have tasted and their facial expressions imply that their experiences may resemble those of adults. Infants' facial responses to the four basic tastes also seem to emerge at different points in development. In line with the findings mentioned earlier, adults find it easier to identify newborns' responses to sweet substances than to bitter or sour substances (Rosenstein & Oster, 1988). It is not yet known whether newborns' less distinct responses to bitter and sour tastes reflect less ability to discriminate between these tastes or whether the infants fully sense the difference but respond with less taste-specific expressions.

The links between facial expressions and specific tastes may be evolutionarily quite old. When a wide range of primates are presented with sweet, sour, and bitter substances, they show facial responses similar to those shown by human infants (Steiner et al., 2001). It would be noteworthy enough if the great apes showed such expressions, but it is far more impressive that primates much more distantly related to humans, such as tamarins, also do. Primates more closely related to humans show more similarity to humans in their facial responses, but the overall pattern of resemblance is unmistakable.

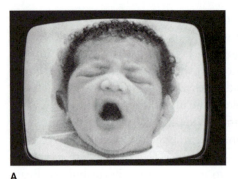  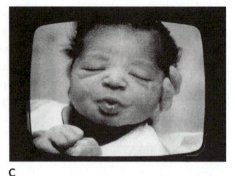

A   B   C

FIGURE 3.30 Facial responses to different tastes. Newborn facial responses to **(A)** bitter, **(B)** sour, and **(C)** sweet liquids. From Rosenstein & Oster (1988).

Even in the context of these evolutionary similarities, however, newborns' different facial responses to tastes should not be interpreted as evidence that links between tastes and expressions are fixed from infancy. Young infants can acquire new tastes just as adults can after experiencing new flavors. Thus, infants who drink a bitter form of synthetic formula in the first few months of life are likely to show a normal facial expression when they drink it at 7½ months. By contrast, infants who encounter that formula for the first time at 7½ months show a strong bitter reaction (Mennella et al., 2004; see Figure 3.31). Babies' ability to acquire new tastes from early experiences also suggests one possible consequence of feeding infants synthetic formulas. These formulas tend to have only one distinct taste, while breast milk has many tastes. As a result, formula-fed babies may become far less tolerant of alternative tastes (Mennella et al., 2004). Similarly, babies who are fed more fruits early on show much more tolerance for sour juices in their second year (Blossfeld et al., 2007). Above and beyond experience, babies also have some genetic dispositions either to tolerate or to reject some bitter substances such as alcohol or quinine. These dispositions interact with experience and may also be reflected in some cultural differences in diet (Mennella et al., 2005). Once again, now in the realm of taste, the complex interactions between initial genetic predispositions and the environment are essential to understanding development.

> **Q:** To which of the basic tastes do infants seem especially responsive? Why might this preference have adaptive value?

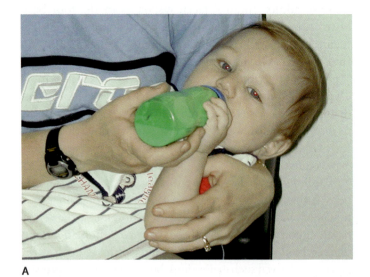 

A   B

FIGURE 3.31 Acquired tastes. Quite young babies can come to have acquired tastes through early exposure. Beginning when they were 2 weeks old, infants were fed either a bitter-tasting synthetic protein formula or a milk-based formula. They were both given the bitter-tasting formula in a test procedure when they were 7 months old and had clearly different reactions. **(A)** The infant who had been fed the bitter-tasting formula over 7 months accepted the bottle without a problem. **(B)** The infant who was encountering the bitter formula for the first time made a face and pushed the bottle away.

Smell

Because there are many thousands of distinct smells, systematically studying infants' olfaction is much more difficult than studying their taste perception. Nonetheless, very young infants do seem to show clear sets of olfactory preferences (Porter & Winberg, 1999; Schaal, 1988). Within minutes after birth, newborns are particularly attracted to odors associated with their lactating mother's breasts (Porter & Winberg, 1999). Newborns also prefer the odor of breast milk to that of formula, and they show the preference by orienting more strongly to the breast milk (Marlier & Schall, 2005). Infants younger than 3 days old also clearly habituate to a wide variety of odors. One common method of studying infants' ability to differentiate smells looks at changes in their breathing patterns when they smell a novel odor and the reversion to a normal breathing pattern with habituation. Other studies have used near infrared spectroscopy (NIRS) to show that the newborn's olfactory cortex, a brain region that processes odors, is more active when the newborn smells an odor such as vanilla than when it is presented with an odorless liquid (Bartocci et al., 2000).

Taste and smell also interact powerfully during eating and drinking. For example, even though cherry Kool-Aid clearly seems to taste like cherry, it becomes indistinguishable from sugar water when its odor is blocked. Clearly, the integration of taste and smell is so automatic that it is common to misattribute the source of sensory information (Enns & Hornung, 1985). Research on the ways that taste and olfaction work together in infants is not yet far enough along to confirm the strong expectation that even newborns would seamlessly integrate information from these two senses. One intriguing study, however, potentially lends support to this idea. In adults, it is not only sweet *tastes* that have a painkilling effect; it turns out that sweet *smells* do also. The evidence that sweet smells have a similar analgesic effect on infants raises the possibility that infants also perceive sweetness with both taste and smell and, like adults, experience increased tolerance for pain in both cases (Prescott & Wilkie, 2007). These effects of sweet smells have yet to be studied directly in infants, however.

It seems likely that with further research, the sensory systems of taste and smell, which evolved long before vision and audition, will show many of the same powerful themes of perceptual development. First, the role of very early experience cannot be overlooked. Several investigators suggest that prenatal experiences with tastes and odors in the womb may heavily influence preferences at birth (Beauchamp & Mennella, 2011; Mennella & Beauchamp, 1997; Mennella et al., 2001; Youngentob & Glendinning, 2009). Furthermore, as with localization of sounds, increasing evidence at the neurophysiological level shows that experiences early in infancy serve to fine-tune taste and olfaction to different environments (Hill & Mistretta, 1990). The findings in perceptual research in other modalities also suggest some likely directions for future research in this area. With further study, categorical perception effects on early abilities to perceive tastes and smells are likely to be found. As we will see shortly with other senses, integration across sensory modalities, including taste and smell, is also likely to be found to emerge early.

Intermodal Perception

Much like the ability to visually locate a sound's source, the interactions of taste and olfaction in eating and drinking raise the more general question of how we come to perceive an object as the same thing regardless of which senses we use. When we simultaneously see and touch a hairbrush, how do we know we are acting on the same thing with both senses?

The empiricists' classic, associationist accounts would say that we gradually learn specific links, or associations, across the sensory modalities through experience (Helmholtz, 1884/1968; Spelke, 1987). According to this view, we would have to learn how the textures and contours associated with touching sharp-edged or flexible objects correlate with their visual features. The ability to use several senses to perceive a single, enduring object would take time and learning to develop—and until it did, the infant's experience of seeing an object would have no relation to the experience of touching that object. The feel of the hairbrush bristles would not lead the infant to expect a bristly appearance. By contrast, a nativist would embrace the idea that right from the start, infants might have specialized abilities to link up inputs from multiple senses to create integrated mental representations of objects.

It now seems that nativist views are more accurate and that **intermodal perception**, which fuses and integrates information across sensory modalities, may be as basic as perception itself. A newborn who turns his head to look at a novel sound is engaged in the simplest form of intermodal exploration. His response relies on neural circuits that are simultaneously tuned to visual and auditory inputs specifying location. A more dramatic demonstration of intermodal perception involves experiencing an object in one sense modality and then recognizing it using a different modality. After seeing a hairbrush among other objects on a dresser, you could easily pick out the brush from the other objects, even in total darkness. Since newborns do not tend to explore objects with their hands, they might seem likely to fail on this sort of task (Spelke, 1987). In fact, infants seem to integrate touch and vision quite well—even though they use their mouths as their primary means of touch-based exploration.

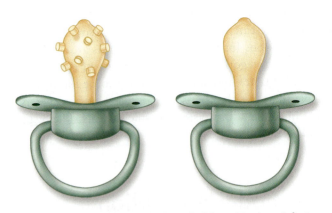

FIGURE 3.32 Integrating touch and vision. Newborn infants who mouth a particular object without seeing it, such as a nubby as opposed to a smooth pacifier, will then prefer to look at the same object they had previously mouthed when they see it for the first time. Adapted from Meltzoff & Borton (1979).

Anyone who has spent time with infants knows how quickly objects disappear into their mouths, a behavior that requires constant vigilance from parents and caregivers. This tendency may also serve as the basis of the infant's earliest intermodal perceptions. Researchers tested this possibility by having newborns suck on two textured spheres with pacifier-like handles (Figure 3.32). One sphere was smooth and the other was covered with bumps. Newborns were given one of these spheres or the other to suck on for a few minutes, but they were not allowed to see them. When researchers showed the objects to the infants and monitored their preferential looking, the infants looked longer at the object that they had previously explored with their mouth (Meltzoff & Borton, 1979). There are even some indications that despite their crude grasping abilities, newborns can integrate the feelings of objects in their hands with how those objects look (Streri & Gentaz, 2003). Interestingly, though, they may be more capable of visually recognizing an object that they previously held than of recognizing an object by touch that they previously saw (Sann & Streri, 2007). It takes several months before infants can "translate" accurately in both directions between touch and vision.

Q: Give an example of how infants use intermodal perception.

Using an experimental setup similar to the one with textured spheres, researchers found that when infants orally explore objects, they also develop expectations about how those objects move. In this case, the infants were allowed to suck and chew on disks that were either rigid or flexible and sponge-like. The researchers then showed the infants dynamic displays of two objects side by side, one moving without bending and the other flexibly deforming. Infants as young as 1 month looked longer at the object whose movement contrasted with the one they had explored earlier tactilely (Gibson & Walker, 1984). Note that unlike the study involving textured spheres, infants in this experiment looked longer at the novel object than at the familiar one. We will see that these sorts of shifts—infants sometimes looking longer at the novel object versus favoring the familiar one—are common in research on infants. Though they are curious, the infants' particular preference turns out to be less important than the finding of a clear, reliable relationship between the first experience and the preferential looking. This study also demonstrates that young infants can understand objects' different dynamic properties, such as rigidity or flexibility, even when their shape and texture visually appear identical.

Auditory-visual intermodal perception also has been explored extensively (see Scientific Research box). Many studies rely on infants' tendency to respond to a sound by looking at an object associated with that sound, even when the sound is actually coming from somewhere else. (Adults also do this; ventriloquism exploits this property of perception.) Infants turn out to be surprisingly sensitive to whether the sound they are hearing, such as a rattling sound, could plausibly be coming from the object they can see, such as a shaking glass with marbles in it. This is no small achievement considering the possible ways in which an event can be construed (Spelke, 1987).

The correspondence between sounds and their sources is not the only sound-vision relationship that interests infants. When they are as young as 5 months, infants look longer at happy faces than sad ones when a happy sound track is playing, and they look longer at sad faces while hearing sad sounds. This tendency is intimately related to sophisticated face perception; if the faces are inverted so the infants can't interpret the expressions, the infants no longer show the preference (Walker, 1982). Infants also seem to associate sounds with particular kinds of objects. When infants as young as 3 months were shown two clear cylinders side by side (Figure 3.33), they were able to link each one with the appropriate sound—the cylinder with one object making a "clunking" sound and the cylinder with multiple objects making a "clattering" sound—even though the cylinders were both turned at the same rate (Bahrick, 1988). Similarly, when infants as young as 5 months hear two qualitatively different sounds coming from behind a barrier, they expect to see two distinct objects; but when they hear two identical sounds, they have no clear expectations about one versus two objects (Brower & Wilcox, 2012). More subtle intermodal integrations, such as pairing a "clacking" with two wooden blocks banging together and a "splishing" with two sponges slapping

SCIENTIFIC METHOD: Intersensory Perception at Birth

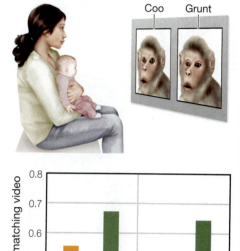

Coo   Grunt

Hypothesis:

Newborn infants can integrate sights and sounds for stimuli that they would not naturally encounter.

Method:

1. Newborn infants (1 to 3 days old) sat on an experimenter's lap and watched two videos of monkey faces without sound.

2. Infants then saw each of the videos with either the sound made by the monkey in that video (sound matched the video) or the sound made by the monkey in the other video. The sound came from a speaker between the two videos.

3. Experimenters recorded the infants' looking preferences when looking at the silent videos and when looking at the videos with one or the other monkey's vocalization patterns.

Results:

In experiment 1, newborn infants showed no significant looking preferences for either video without sound. But with sound, they looked longer at the video that matched the sound they heard. In experiment 2, they heard artificial sounds that were in synchrony with the facial expressions of one monkey and matched those as well.

Conclusion:

From the moment of birth, infants are able to map facial expressions onto sounds made by those expressions, even when they are nonhuman, suggesting a very general mechanism for matching visual events to sounds.

Source study: Lewkowicz et al. (2010).

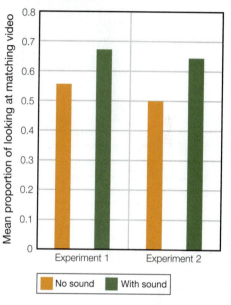

together, take much longer to develop. They often do not appear until near the end of the first year of life (Bahrick, 1983). With more meaningful stimuli, however, such as the mother's face and voice, even newborns seem to engage in intermodal perception. Thus, when a mother's voice accompanies her own face as opposed to the face of an unfamiliar female, after just a few minutes of seeing and hearing the face, an infant will orient more to the image in which the mother's face and voice match (Sai, 2005).

Q: When do infants first seem to be able to link emotional expressions in faces to the corresponding emotional sounds?

From the broad range of examples given here, we see that even newborns integrate information across sense modalities. Based on the information they receive, they form expectations about how objects' properties go together and how an object perceived in one modality should seem when it is perceived in another. This initial integration ability also provides an essential foundation for learning more complex relations across senses. By the time they are 6 months old, for example, infants seem to know which kinds of noises an aggressive-looking dog might make as opposed to a nonaggressive dog (Flom et al., 2009). In some ways, newborns do understand and use aspects of the intricate relationships between touch and sight or between sight and sound, yet they clearly cannot perceive all of these relationships. A key question for future research is to specify the range of these earliest abilities more precisely and to learn how they are amplified and extended during early development.

Q: What is the value of intermodal perception in newborns?

FIGURE 3.33 Integrating sound and vision. Even when both cylinders are turned back and forth at the same rate, 3-month-old infants know which one corresponds to a certain sound track. Adapted from Bahrick (1988).

Conclusions

We have consistently seen that infants have innate specializations within the different senses for perceiving patterns in the world, including those that integrate across the senses. These specializations do not emerge fully developed at birth. Rather, infants do a great deal of learning in order to perceive the world more accurately. One way to think about early perceptual development is that the newborn has a "head start" on understanding the informational patterns that exist in the world. This head start seems to affect all levels of processing, from experiencing sensory inputs to interpreting and integrating those experiences; but that innate capacity is not the same as having prior knowledge of the sorts of things we perceive. We are not like chickens with built-in hawk detectors, but neither are we blank slates. A basic, skeletal set of perceptual expectations guides further learning and development.

Perhaps the simplest way to characterize early perceptual development is to imagine that vision, hearing, taste, and the other perceptual systems function like curious individuals who first encounter the world with general hunches about what it is like. Since they recognize that their hunches are fallible, they initially hold only vague, sketchy expectations, and they constantly test those expectations to see how well they fit with aspects of the world. As time goes by, they adapt their hunches if they turn out to be incorrect, but they still show a bias to revert back to those hunches if information is unclear. Finally, the initial hunches are not infinitely flexible. They can be adapted to accord better with experiences of the world, but they cannot be changed in every way, shape, and form. For that reason, we and other animals are fortunate that the initial hunches capture enough of what is real about the world that they can become workable and useful. This metaphor of imagining perceptual systems as active agents helps us realize that from adults down to the tiniest infants, we are not passive perceivers of the world but active explorers. In the next chapter, we will look more directly at how the infant physically explores and interacts with the world.

STUDY AND REVIEW

SUMMARY

Vision

- Debates between nativists and empiricists in the realm of perceptual development can be understood in terms of the degree to which there are innate specializations for information beyond the processing of perceptual primitives such as brightness differences and lines and edges in the case of vision. Where specializations exist for more complex perceptual processing, such as for perceiving facial patterns, there is more support for nativist positions.

- To be able to explore questions about perception in preverbal infants, several important techniques must be used, most notably looking preferences and habituation/dishabituation paradigms.

- Even newborns have brightness discrimination abilities that serve as a foundation for higher-level perceptual skills. Their visual acuity is poor at birth, but it improves with age as the eye grows and focuses light on the retina and as the brain areas' processing acuity become more sophisticated.

- Newborn infants have a "head start" at developing complex visual perceptual skills, such as perceiving color in terms of categories and perceiving objects in depth. This is because infants are born with a preverbal system that matures quickly to enable them to perceive universal, common color categories. They also are born with the ability to use some dynamic cues—for example, motion parallax—to perceive depth in the first month of life.

- As the early stages of depth perception illustrate, newborns undergo a great deal of developmental change as their perceptual abilities become more sophisticated. They begin to use binocular cues and then pictorial cues to more accurately perceive depth. Much of this development involves feedback loops between the developing organism and its environment. Flexible systems show plasticity and enable the organism to respond to its environment and to its own changing state over the course of development.

- Among the different types of perceptual development, the perception of visual patterns is perhaps the most complex, requiring a great deal of learning. At the same time, even newborns seem to have some basic expectations about certain visual patterns, especially the human face. A U-shaped developmental curve characterizes infants' face-tracking abilities. Some see this as evidence for an early rudimentary system of face perception in newborns that declines and then is replaced by a more sophisticated system.

- Infants prefer certain faces because they perceive them as more attractive than others, a behavior that may reflect a genetically predisposed awareness of average facial values.

Hearing

- Development of the ability to perceive sounds has many parallels to vision. Very young infants do not start out perceiving only the simplest, most basic auditory "primitives" and then combining them to perceive complex patterns, such as speech. Rather, infants can process complex speech sounds from the start, and their perceptual abilities become increasingly attuned to the types of sounds they typically hear.

- At birth, infants also have a crude system for localizing the sounds they perceive. This rudimentary early system is later supplanted by a much more precise system in yet another instance of U-shaped developmental changes.

The Chemical Senses: Taste and Smell

- Young infants can clearly distinguish between various tastes and odors, but the research in these areas has been less extensive than for vision or hearing.

- Taste perception begins in the womb and may affect infants' preference for certain tastes after birth. Newborns and infants show a clear preference for sweet substances, which calm them and can have painkilling effects.

- Newborns show preferences for certain smells, especially the odor of their mother's breast milk.

Intermodal Perception

- Right from the start, infants are able to integrate information across the senses. They seem to know how something that looks a certain way, such as bumpy, will feel. They also have been found to integrate sights and sounds. These findings provide strong evidence against extreme empiricist accounts of perceptual development because even very young infants show capacities for intermodal perception before they could have formed associations between specific sensory experiences.

THOUGHT QUESTIONS

1. What is the function of critical periods? Why should there be critical periods at all rather than continuous environmental sensitivity? Are there any functional advantages conferred on the developing organism, or are they incidental consequences of other aspects of development?

2. How does being born blind versus being born deaf affect a developing child? How do the developmental implications and challenges of being born blind differ from those involved in being born deaf? Compare both the immediate and long-term implications for the developing child.

3. What is the basis for a preference for attractive faces? Why might newborn infants have a preference for faces that adults regard as more attractive? What does such a finding tell us about how face perception develops?

KEY TERMS

astigmatism (p. 82)

binocular cues (p. 87)

binocular disparity (p. 87)

binocular parallax (p. 87)

categorical perception (p. 84)

convergence (p. 87)

dishabituation (p. 80)

dynamic cues (p. 86)

feedback loop (p. 77)

Gestalt principles (p. 94)

habituation (p. 80)

habituation method (p. 80)

hue (p. 84)

intermodal perception (p. 109)

motion parallax (p. 86)

optokinetic nystagmus method (p. 81)

perceptual narrowing (p. 97)

pictorial cues (p. 88)

plasticity (p. 94)

preferential looking method (p. 79)

sensitive period (p. 103)

stereopsis (p. 87)

U-shaped developmental curve (p. 98)

visual acuity (p. 79)

visual cliff (p. 90)

visually evoked potential (VEP) method (p. 81)

4

The Emergence of Action

Foundations of Motor Development
- Reflexes in Infancy
- Theories of Motor Development

Perception and Action
- Coordination in Changing Bodies
- Reaching
- Navigating Space

Learning to Engage in Specific Actions
- Early Imitation
- Imprinting, Action, and Critical Periods
- Conditioning

Conclusions

Summary

There has been a surge of attention to the prevalence of obesity not only in children but also in infants. In 2010, U.S. First Lady Michelle Obama launched a national campaign to address what has been called an epidemic of childhood obesity. Around this time, the government of China also began voicing concerns about rising rates of childhood obesity. And in Europe, high obesity rates in infants and preschool children in some locales highlighted the large disparities among countries. Spain, for example, reported that up to 16 percent of 2-year-olds were severely overweight, while in Sweden, the rate was closer to 2 percent (Cattaneo et al., 2010).

There are many health problems linked to early childhood obesity. For example, overweight infants are more likely to eventually have diabetes, gallstones, fatty liver disease, sleep apnea, bone and joint problems, as well as a whole range of psychosocial problems (Lee, 2009). Most of these effects, however, gradually accumulate over many years and are not manifested until adulthood. It was not normally thought to be a problem if a baby was overweight; in fact, it was often seen as a sign of good health.

In one somewhat surprising way, however, researchers have found that obesity can influence an important aspect of infants' lives directly and quite dramatically—namely, their motor development. In one study of children between 3 and 18 months who were in the 90th percentile in terms of being overweight, researchers tested the infants' motor skills at frequent intervals. The overweight babies were almost two times as likely to show motor delays compared with normal-weight infants (Slining et al., 2010). For example, overweight babies tended to first walk at later ages than normal-weight babies, and the overweight babies had other delays in motor skills and coordination continuing for several months thereafter.

How could something as seemingly trivial as a little extra body fat cause substantial motor delays? Motor development is not simply a matter of a central motor control program maturing; instead, it involves interactions between central control patterns, physical properties of the limbs, and learning experiences. And as we will see, cyclical patterns and feedback loops play a critical role in these developmental processes.

In this chapter, we will explore the foundations on which early motor abilities are built, discussing such topics as reflexes, coordination of perception and action, imitation, critical periods, and conditioning. We will ask how infants progress from involuntary, reflexive actions to increasingly controlled and voluntary actions—for example, examining how infants become increasingly adept at reaching for objects and navigating space. We will explore how perception and action become increasingly integrated, asking such questions as: How do even the simplest acts of coordination develop in the infant, and how does the interplay between

biological maturation and learning in infancy support the development of the fluid, effortless actions typical of older children and adults? In what ways are infants sensitive to feedback from the environment and from their own bodies as they attempt to act on the world? How do infants adjust their actions in response to feedback, and how do these adjustments occur within a set of guiding constraints? We will also see how changes in the body, such as the weight of the arms and legs, affect the emergence and coordination of motor skills. The intricate interactions between these factors enable infants to begin organizing their actions right from the start. And yet, just as we saw in the previous chapter, these rudimentary capacities are flexible enough to allow for fine-tuning, so that infants can develop their motor skills based on how their changing bodies are able to respond to what is happening in the world around them.

As we discuss each approach to the development of action, we will see that familiar themes emerge. We will consider the tradeoffs between specialization and plasticity, we will examine the extent to which different aspects of motor development depend on both innate maturation and external environmental influences, and we will discuss how feedback loops are central to the fine-tuning of behaviors.

Foundations of Motor Development

Even before birth, babies engage in clear and unmistakable actions. Virtually every mother feels her unborn child kick and move about, sometimes so dramatically that the movements are visible simply by looking at the mother's abdomen. At birth, an infant's behaviors are already quite rich and varied. A newborn can cry in a variety of ways that seem to suggest different levels of distress. He can also nurse from a nipple or bottle, albeit initially a bit clumsily. As we saw in Chapter 3, he can turn his head toward a sound and blink in response to a bright light, as well as show a variety of facial reactions to different tastes and smells. He can also imitate others' facial expressions, an ability explored in depth later in this chapter. At the same time, a newborn human infant is strikingly helpless compared with the newborns of many more precocious species. Whereas many newborn animals can walk immediately after birth, human infants cannot walk until they are around 1 year old. A human newborn cannot even roll over or lift up his head when lying on his stomach. How does a newborn progress from such an apparently helpless state to become an active toddler? What are the foundations of motor development? To begin with, infants are born with reflexes that enable them to react before they are capable of more directed action.

Reflexes in Infancy

Some of the most noticeable actions performed by the young infant are built-in **reflexes**, which are automatic responses to particular forms of stimulation (see Figure 4.1). Normal infants exhibit these reflexes so reliably that physicians routinely use them to monitor the development in the baby's nervous system and to diagnose possible problems. Some of the most common reflexes are the **patellar reflex**, or "knee jerk reflex," in which tapping a tendon below the kneecap causes the lower leg to kick; the **rooting reflex**, in which brushing an object against the face causes a newborn to move his mouth toward the object and attempt sucking; the **grasp reflex**, in which touching the newborn's palm causes him to grasp tightly; the **stepping reflex**, in which gently lowering the baby feet-first to a surface triggers automatic stepping movements; and finally the **Moro reflex**, in which experiencing a lack of support causes a baby's arms to move out to the sides (Moro, 1918).

These reflexes make adaptive sense for getting infants through their first year or so of life. The patellar reflex is thought to be essential for maintaining balance and posture by triggering a quick response when a tendon is suddenly stretched. When the doctor's tap—or more naturalistically, a quick change in leg angle—suddenly stretches the tendon, the leg muscles compensate for the stretch by contracting. The elbow and other joints show the same kind of reflex, which is common to most vertebrates. The rooting reflex helps the newborn "home in" on his mother's nipples and is widely shared among mammals. Without rooting and sucking reflexes, a newborn would have difficulty eating and surviving. The grasp reflex triggers newborns to wrap their fingers around an object after sensing contact, and many infants' grip is strong enough to support their own weight. This reflex is found early on in many mammals for which such a holding action is important to survival. In human infants, it disappears after a few months. The stepping reflex supports the development of the rhythmic alternation of the limbs for walking, not just in humans but also in species that walk on all four limbs. The Moro reflex is one of the newborn's more complex reflexes. One well-known way of eliciting it involves initially holding the newborn firmly with one hand under the center of his back and the other hand under his head, then dropping the hand under the baby's head. When the hand under the baby's head is abruptly dropped downward (but only a small drop so as not to injure the baby), the baby's arms fly out to each side and then return to the centerline of his body. A common interpretation of this action is that it causes the infant to reflexively grasp his caregiver if he feels himself suddenly falling. Although some reflexes may be just vestiges of responses that were adaptive to our evolutionary ancestors, most still serve important functions.

A distinctive feature of many reflexes in newborns, such as the Moro reflex and the stepping reflex, is that they gradually disappear in the first few months of life. In the first half of the twentieth century, some researchers interpreted this disappearance of inborn reflexes as evidence that key aspects of motor development depend entirely on changes in the brain. They proposed that as specific regions of the cortex mature, these regions increasingly inhibit the activity of lower-level brain structures, which they believed are responsible for early reflexes. In support of this view, they cited evidence that the brain grows considerably larger and its neuronal branching becomes more complex over the first year of life (Conel, 1939–1959). In particular, growth in the brain's frontal cortex and the increasing interconnectedness of regions such as the motor cortex and other structures related to reflexes were all cited as evidence that motor development is a matter of increased inhibition and greater control of reflexes.

But does motor development in infants actually consist of little more than bundles of reflexes waiting to come under the control of higher-level mental functions? There are several reasons to believe that this is not the case. As we will see in more detail in the next section, the reasons

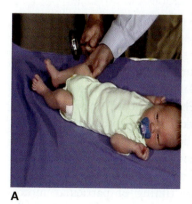 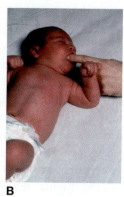 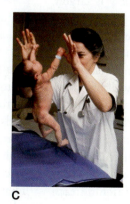  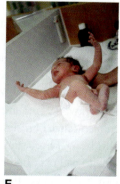

A   B   C   D   E

FIGURE 4.1 Reflexes in newborns. Healthy young infants show a wide range of reflexes. Some of these reflexes appear to vanish after the first few months of life, but in many cases they are still present in altered forms that are the result of changing anatomy. **(A)** Patellar reflex. **(B)** Rooting reflex. **(C)** Grasp reflex. **(D)** Stepping reflex. **(E)** Moro reflex.

that many early reflexes disappear have less to do with centralized developments in the brain and more to do with peripheral or bodily factors, like muscle strength or the size of the limbs, and the environment in which the infant is functioning. Furthermore, some reflexes may only seem to disappear, when they actually are still present but are being manifested in a different way, as we will see when we consider the effects of the changing weight of an infant's limbs as he matures. For example, researcher Esther Thelen demonstrated that contrary to the long-held belief that the stepping reflex ceases to exist, it actually becomes manifested in a different form as a "kicking reflex." By careful analyses of videotapes and measures of muscle actions in kicking and stepping by infants, she showed that they are essentially the same actions and that the movements change as a function of changes in the muscles and bones in the legs (Thelen & Fisher, 1982). We now turn to a discussion of theories of motor development to see more on how different researchers explain how infants become capable of various kinds of directed movement.

FIGURE 4.2 **Emerging motor skills.** The infant's first steps are a highly precarious enterprise with failure and discomfort from falls being commonplace. That babies continue to try to walk suggests a powerful underlying motivation that overrides immediate negative consequences.

> **Q:** Describe three reflexes that are present at birth, and explain how they change over the first few months of development.

Theories of Motor Development

Imagine a 13-month-old toddling about her parents' house, carrying various objects—sometimes alarmingly heavy and fragile ones (see Figure 4.2). Two weeks earlier she couldn't take a single unsupported step. This dramatic change may appear to resemble a tadpole-to-frog metamorphosis in the sense that it seems to be driven by an internal timetable of maturation that is relatively uninfluenced by practice or experience. In reality, however, this classic view is largely incorrect.

One of the earliest endeavors in developmental psychology was to construct charts and tables showing the average ages at which children meet common motor development milestones, such as sitting up, crawling, and walking (Bayley, 1935; Dennis & Dennis, 1940; Gesell & Ilg, 1949; McGraw, 1943; Shirley, 1931). Traditional charts showed the sequence of milestones as pretty much the same across all children. Thus, they indicated that almost all children are able to roll over before they can sit up, and sit up before they can walk. They also showed all children as reaching each milestone at roughly the same average ages (for example, sitting with support at 4 months, sitting alone at 7 months, creeping at 10 months, and walking alone at 15 months;

Shirley, 1931). More recent descriptions take care to show the age range in which particular motor skills normally appear in order to provide a sense of the typical variations, as well as the mean ages of these motor milestones (see Figure 4.3). They also recognize that not all motor developments necessarily unfold on the same, set timeline. A relatively late walker might not be a relatively late grasper of objects, because different factors, such as overall body weight (as noted in the opening to the chapter), might cause delays in development in walking but not in grasping.

> **Q:** What is the normal sequence of motor milestones in the first 18 months of life?

The Maturational Account Even the early studies of motor development in the late nineteenth century showed that experience has relatively little effect on when motor skills first appear; certain skills always seem to emerge at around the same points in development. At that time, the explanation for this consistency closely resembled the brain-based interpretation of infants' "disappearing" reflexes. That is, the highly reliable timing of particular motor milestones suggested that motor development depends entirely on the increasing sophistication of the cortex and its ability to orchestrate the timing and intensity of muscle

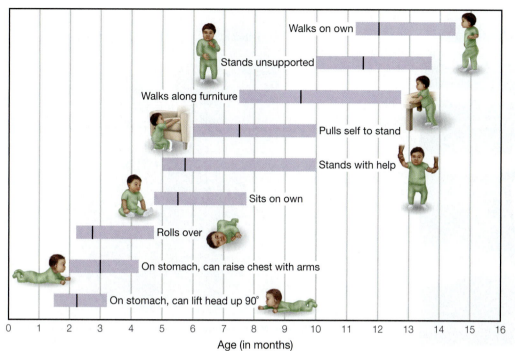

FIGURE 4.3 **Motor milestones.** Recent depictions of motor milestones show normal ranges within which each behavior appears. Each bar begins with the age at which the behavior has appeared in 25 percent of infants and ends with the age at which the behavior has appeared in 90 percent of infants; the vertical bar indicates the age at which the behavior has appeared in 50 percent of infants. In contrast to earlier views, these ranges reveal considerable variation in when a skill, such as walking alone, first appears. Adapted from Frankenburg et al. (1981).

movements. The first report along these lines was made by William Preyer, who, like many overeager parents, spent a great deal of time trying to teach his own son to walk before his son was a year old. Unlike most parents who have made similar attempts, Preyer wrote up the results of his labors, sadly reporting that not only did his son not walk any earlier than normal, but his final date of walking was actually a bit later than that of most other children (Preyer, 1888).

The proponents of the **maturational account** of motor development generally held that motor development depends on the increasing sophistication of the brain's motor programs for guiding more and more complex actions. They argued that a baby cannot walk before 1 year of age because the brain structures involved in guiding motor action are still too immature to coordinate the movements that enable walking. Training supposedly doesn't have much of an effect before a certain age because it has no functional cortical circuits to rely on.

The most influential advocate of the maturational account was Arnold Gesell. His landmark study involved the emergence of stair climbing ability in identical twin girls (Gesell & Thompson, 1929; see Figure 4.4). At the age of 46 weeks (about 11 months), one twin began daily practice at climbing five stairs. She made little progress for the first few weeks, but at around 50 weeks she quickly became able to climb the stairs, and by 52 weeks she could do it in less than half a minute. During this same period, the other twin had no practice. She was introduced to stairs for the first time at the end of 52 weeks—at which point she immediately climbed the stairs unaided, almost as rapidly as her sister. Similar studies on other early motor skills showed that

extensive training before a child was "ready" had little or no effect. These sorts of findings led many researchers in the 1930s and 1940s to assume that motor development was largely a preprogrammed affair governed by maturational timetables and unaffected by experience.

Q: What was the conclusion drawn from Gesell's stair climbing studies with infants?

Additional evidence for the maturational account came from observational studies of infants who showed relatively normal motor development despite their **motor deprivation**—that is, their limited motor experience. One well-known study examined motor development in Hopi infants who were bound to a cradleboard for parts of the day, especially when they were asleep (Dennis & Dennis, 1940; see Figure 4.5). Although these infants had less motor experience than others, they showed almost no motor development delays. Subsequent to those studies, researchers have found that truly devastating environments, such as understaffed orphanages where infants are left lying in cribs all day (see Chapter 6), can cause extensive delays in motor development (Dennis & Najarian, 1957), but even these early impairments are typically reversible. In fact, there are some indications that tightly swaddling infants, a practice found across an enormous range of cultures over the course of history, may help them to sleep and protect them from the cold without negatively affecting motor development (van Sleuwen et al., 2007).

FIGURE 4.4 **Learning to climb stairs.** Gesell's twin studies suggested that the age at which children learn a new motor skill, such as climbing stairs, is mostly a consequence of maturation rather than learning.

FIGURE 4.5 **Motor deprivation and motor development.** Native American infants were believed to spend much of their early lives immobilized on "cradleboards," raising questions about the importance of experience to motor development. Although they were immobilized during parts of the day, they were actually not immobilized most of the time and did not experience delays in their motor development.

Dynamic Systems Theory Since the 1970s, a new wave of research has largely replaced the maturational account. The new research was partly inspired by two new perspectives on movement. The first of these was developed by Eleanor Gibson (whose visual cliff studies were discussed in Chapter 3) and her husband, James Gibson. The Gibsons emphasized the constant interplay between perception and movement and the importance of this link for carrying out real-world actions. Thus, they believed that perception provides a context and a goal for an action, and the action then leads to the modification of a perception. You perceive your environment and then walk with the goal of maneuvering through that environment, so negotiating the environment is the action to be explained, not simply walking for the sake of walking. Similarly, you perceive a person who is running, and whether you are fleeing or pursuing that person significantly affects your own running. The Gibsons put motor development into the larger context of related changes in perception, attention, and the physical body, which work together to support more sophisticated actions.

The second perspective that helped launch the new wave of research arose from the work of the Russian researcher Nikolai Bernstein (Bernstein, 1967). Bernstein suggested that our actions are complex and orderly not just because of the brain's well-calibrated control of the body, but also because of the physical properties of our body parts and their interactions, including the size of the limbs, the way the

joints work, and how different parts move together. In this account, the changes that occur in the shift from walking to running involve more than just implementing a different set of instructions from the brain. Instead, Bernstein argued, as the limbs move faster, the pattern of movements used to walk becomes unstable while the pattern of movements in a typical run becomes stable. There are strong constraints on the nature and organization of limb motion and on the speeds at which particular kinds of motions can stably occur. Notice, for example, the difficulty of running very slowly or walking very fast.

These two perspectives on movement led to a series of innovative experiments designed to explore how perception and action might be interwoven into one "dynamic system," in which each continues to affect the other, and how the parts of the body itself physically constrain and organize actions. Some developmental psychologists have therefore come to embrace what is known as **dynamic systems theory**, the idea that the development of complex behaviors should be understood in terms of the interactions among all the changing components involved in executing the behaviors, and not just as sets of instructions sent from the cortex and carried out by the body. Thus, we need to take into account anatomy at the levels of individual muscles and bones, limbs, and the body as a whole, as well as the involvement of the peripheral and central nervous systems, and finally the broader context in which an action is occurring, such as whether an infant is wearing bulky clothes, is lifting a heavy object, or has a particular goal. Taken together, all these components make up a dynamic system, which can result in seemingly rapid and qualitative changes in behaviors as small components of the overall system change.

One set of studies by Esther Thelen had a particularly dramatic effect on the view that emerging central motor programs are the prime determinants of walking (Thelen, 1995, 2001; Thelen & Fisher, 1982; Thelen et al., 1984). As mentioned earlier, Thelen focused on the disappearance of the stepping reflex a few weeks after birth. Traditionally, this disappearance had been attributed entirely to brain development. Recall that earlier researchers theorized that the reflex is governed by a simple, lower-level motor program and that as more complex, higher-level brain structures develop, they inhibit the initial reflex. Then, as the higher-level cortical structures become more sophisticated, they reorganize the stepping reflex and cause it to reemerge later as a component of normal walking.

In line with dynamic systems theory, Thelen wondered if physical properties of the limbs themselves also contribute to the reflex's apparent disappearance and whether the stepping reflex might actually have a connection with later, voluntary stepping. To see how the weight of the limbs might affect infants' stepping reflex, she conducted several studies that involved changing the weight of the limbs. One study involved 1-month-old infants, whose stepping reflex had disappeared. When the infants were gently supported in a walking position in a small tank of lukewarm water (see Figure 4.6), the buoyancy supported the weight of their legs, and they made reflexive stepping motions.

In addition, when younger babies who still showed the stepping reflex had tiny weights attached to their legs—

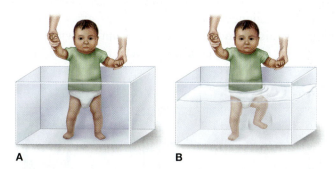

A   **B**

FIGURE 4.6 Physical constraints and motor skills. (A) When 1-month-old infants whose stepping reflex had disappeared were put in an empty tank and supported in an upright position, they did not make stepping movements. **(B)** When these same infants were supported in a tank of water, the buoyancy of the water lightened their limbs, and stepping and walking actions appeared spontaneously. These results suggest that physical constraints of the limbs, rather than central motor programs, may be a primary factor in the developmental changes of many motor skills.

approximating the additional weight of the limbs of older infants who lose the stepping reflex—these infants lost the reflex as well. This finding suggested that the reflex normally disappears as a result of changes in the physical dynamics of the limb, not because of changes in brain development. More specifically, Thelen discovered that the legs of older infants gained weight in fat without corresponding muscle increases. This line of research also explains the finding mentioned at the beginning of this chapter that obese infants walk considerably later than infants of normal weight. Even though the additional weight may seem inconsequential, an infant's motor development depends on just the right proportions of muscles and joint weights, so a little extra baby fat can cause substantial delays in walking.

Thelen analyzed the infants' dynamic patterns of leg movements, both during the stepping reflex and when they kicked their legs while lying on their back. In both cases, the timing and pattern of movements across muscle groups were nearly identical, suggesting that these two actions emerge from a common motor system, rather than granting the reflex a separate status.

Q: How does the weight of the limbs influence the development of motor skills?

Thelen's studies demonstrated that a complex action can be made to appear or disappear at many different times in infancy by simply changing the weight of the limbs. This finding makes the earlier maturational account—that an early reflex is inhibited by higher-level cortical developments only to reemerge when it is incorporated into a cortically controlled action—less plausible.

Following Nikolai Bernstein's thinking, Thelen felt that central motor programs are less important for explaining developmental change than the growth of the body parts that perform the actions (the bones, joints, and muscles) and their stable, coordinated patterns of motion. Thelen argued that babies incorporate particular motions into their voluntary actions if and when the timing pattern of the components is especially stable for a limb and its joints (Thelen, 1995). Just as it is difficult to run very slowly, Thelen argued that it is difficult to add certain motions to one's repertoire of voluntary actions until the various muscles are the right strength, the limb parts are the right weight, and the pattern of the movement is at the right speed.

Of course, Thelen's studies and others like them don't do away with the need for cortical structures that help guide actions. They just broaden the focus to include the developing body as well as the brain within a larger dynamic system. More generally, dynamic systems theory emphasizes the development of motor skills as a result of different interacting constraints: brain-based motor programs, physical properties of the body, features of the environment, and goals of the task at hand (Bertenthal & Clifton, 1998; Spencer et al., 2011; Thelen & Smith, 1998). In the development of action, the coordinated movements of muscles comprise just one part of a larger, integrated system.

Perception and Action

We have seen how the development of increasingly sophisticated motor routines involves the integration of several components involving both the brain and the body. In most cases, such actions are also integrated with perception of the environment and of oneself in that environment. An infant has to coordinate her actions with what she sees. Ultimately, she will become quite accurate at, for example, quickly putting her finger on a small object that she sees. Action and perception are intimately interwoven, and the infant has to learn to guide her voluntary actions by her perceptions and then to modify her perceptions based on her actions. Striking achievements in **perceptual-motor development**, which requires coordinating actions with perceptual information, depend on sophisticated systems to address complex developmental challenges. Perceptual-motor skills develop from the earliest moments of infancy and may continue to be refined to the highest levels of expertise, as in the dexterity of a concert pianist. Development and refinement of motor skills always involve feedback loops between actions and perception. You perform an action, perceive the result, and adjust your next action accordingly. Through this cycle, the action is refined and tuned. Even a single action, such as picking up a squirming puppy, can involve cycling feedback loops, as you adjust your hand position and arm motion to keep hold of the puppy.

Coordination in Changing Bodies

The squirrel jumping from branch to branch in a tree, the frog capturing a fly in midair with its tongue, and the child catching a ball in one hand have all developed a rapid, effortless coordination between vision and action (see Figure 4.7). All of them have developed these systems in bodies whose dimensions have changed dramatically over the course of their development. Consider a typical 13-month-old boy. He has yet to master many aspects of motor coordination, but he can quickly touch objects that he sees, no matter how his head is oriented or his body is turned. When he sees an object that is straight ahead of him, he moves his arms directly out in front of his body to touch it. When he looks over his right shoulder and spots another object, he does not move his arms in front of his body, but instead naturally and without hesitation reaches to his side and slightly behind his back to touch it. Infants engage with the world this way so often that we hardly stop to think about it. Yet, it involves coordination of the position of the eyes in the head, the head on the torso, and the torso with respect to the rest of the body. Meanwhile, all body parts must constantly update their locations with respect to the other body parts, and that information must be coordinated with information about objects' locations in space.

Infants successfully face the challenge of using their vision to rapidly locate objects in space and then use that information to direct motor actions at those objects. But infants accomplish an even more daunting feat: they coordinate vision and action while all their body parts continuously change. Think back to your clumsiest moments as a growing teenager. The challenge of coordination for infants is many times worse. Figure 4.8 shows how the proportions of the human body change from before birth to maturity. The adult's legs are three times longer than the newborn's. At the same time, the size and position of the head change considerably. A vast array of developing organisms must integrate perception with action under such changing conditions; very few, if any, main-

 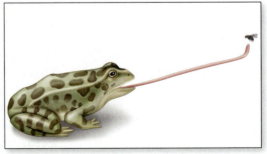 

A   B   C

FIGURE 4.7 Perceptual-motor coordination. (A) A squirrel jumping from branch to branch in a tree, **(B)** a frog catching a fly with its tongue, and **(C)** a toddler catching a ball are all examples of perceptual-motor coordination.

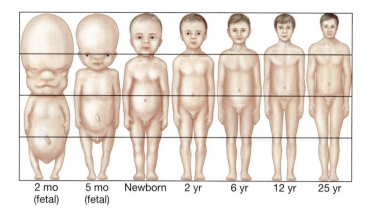

| 2 mo (fetal) | 5 mo (fetal) | Newborn | 2 yr | 6 yr | 12 yr | 25 yr |

FIGURE 4.8 Changing bodily proportions. The relative lengths of body parts change dramatically with increasing age. An adult human's legs are one-half of the total body length, while a newborn's legs are about one-third of the total body length. A newborn human's head is more than twice as big relative to its body as is the adult head. In other animals, even more dramatic ratio changes can occur. Adapted from Robbins et al. (1928).

tain constant body proportions throughout development. To further examine the perceptual-motor system and the changing body, we now turn to a discussion of reaching and the development of eye-limb coordination.

> **Q:** Describe the changes in relative size of body parts from before birth to adulthood.

Reaching

Many newborns do not touch much besides their own bodies, their clothes, and the bodies and clothes of their caregivers. Most of the time, both in experiments and in daily life, newborns fail to touch the objects they are trying to reach. These mostly failed attempts to touch objects are sometimes called **prereaching**. For example, infants younger than 2 months have trouble moving a hand horizontally across the front of their body (for example, moving the left hand to the body's right side). Researchers used to think that infants could not reach across the middle of the body because of an immature central nervous system or spinal cord (Provine & Westerman, 1979). But closer examination of infants who were reaching for objects with both hands suggested that infants start to reach across the middle of the body when they begin using both hands to try to hold onto larger objects, not because of a change in brain systems (Savelsbergh et al., 2003). That is, the goal of holding objects with both hands may provide a context for practicing and improving reaches across the body. Only at around 17 weeks are infants able to easily grasp an object with both hands at once. By 18 months, however, they are favoring one hand over another as they reach for objects based on genetic handedness biases (see Scientific Method box).

Empiricist View of Eye-Limb Coordination How do infants develop eye-limb coordination? The empiricist

account would suggest that the infant starts out with no such coordination and develops it by learning from experience. In this view, infants would initially move their limbs without regard to what they saw. Then, gradually, learning through trial and error, infants would come to associate certain sensations in the muscles and joints with certain patterns of visual input and would start to be able to move their hands toward what they saw. This same idea underlies Berkeley's (1709/1901) account of depth perception described in Chapter 3, in which he proposed that infants learn to see depth by forming associations between different sensations of eye convergence and the particular muscle and limb sensations required to touch objects at different distances.

As mentioned in the previous chapter, if you casually observe a young infant, the empiricists would seem to be right. The infant's limbs seem to move completely independently of what she sees, and coordination seems to emerge gradually as if she were learning associations between perceptions and actions. But a closer look reveals subtle ways in which innate constraints influence perceptual-motor development.

Constraints on Links between Eye and Limb Although the limitations on infants' early actions make their arm and hand movements appear haphazard, there may be some structure to the seeming randomness. Researcher Claus von Hofsten has conducted some of the most elegant explorations of infant reaching by painstakingly observing infants' hand movements toward objects (von Hofsten, 1980, 1983, 1984, 2004; see also Chen et al., 2010). He found that infants' hand and arm movements are sometimes quite slow rather than the rapid jerks that we are prone to notice. Some of his experiments used a standard fishing lure—without the hooks of course!—which the infants found especially attractive. The lure was moved slowly back and forth in front of the infant, and the infant's hand movements were videotaped and carefully coded.

When researchers interpreted these experiments with infants' early coordination difficulties in mind, they found that infants as young as 4 or 5 months, and possibly younger, moved their hands to track and often anticipated the paths of moving objects (von Hofsten, 1980, 1984, 2004; see also Robin et al., 1996). Thus, 4-month-old infants clearly anticipate the path of a lure as they reach out to catch it on arrival (von Hofsten, 1980; see

SCIENTIFIC METHOD: The Genetics of Early Handedness

Hypothesis:

Genetic influences on handedness can be seen at 18 months of age.

Method:

1. Nineteen pairs of 18-month-old twins participated. Five twin pairs were MZ, six were DZ same sex, and eight were DZ opposite sex.

2. Infants were invited to retrieve attractive objects (A) from a tube (B) that encouraged use of just one hand.

3. Three different tube positions (C) were used relative to the infant's body: left, middle, and right.

4. Researchers recorded which hand was used.

Results:

Although there was a preponderance of right-handed reaching in all three groups, there was also some left-handed reaching, especially for tubes in the left and middle locations. Significantly higher correlations for the use of the same hand were found between MZ twins than between DZ twins in either same-sex or opposite-sex groups, especially when the tube was in the middle position (see Table 1).

Conclusion:

Handedness biases that are influenced by genetic factors can be found at 18 months of age, at which point more closely genetically related infants show higher correlations in the use of the same hand in a reaching task.

Source study: Suzuki et al. (2009).

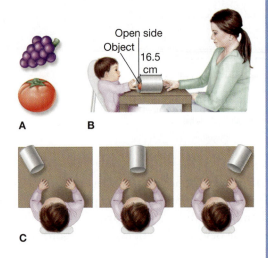

TABLE 1 Correlations between members of MZ and DZ twin pairs and handedness biases

	Left	Middle	Right	All Positions
MZ	.17	.66*	−.07	.64*
Same-sex DZ	−.54	−.45	.14	−.38
Opposite-sex DZ	−.41	−.15	−.22	−.18

MZ, monozygotic twin; DZ, dizygotic twin.
*significant correlations

Figure 4.9). In reaching for stationary objects, even newborns seem to have a sense of where to move their hands. They reach in roughly the right direction, although they very rarely touch the object and are not able to easily grasp it (Bertenthal & Clifton, 1998).

While newborn infants may have difficulty grasping objects, they nonetheless can guide their arms in an intended direction. In one study, researchers passed a beam of light in front of infants in a darkened room. The light source was arranged so that each infant could see the beam only if her hand passed in front of the light, revealing a well-illuminated hand (van der Meer, 1997). The infants initially moved their hands into the ray of light at random, but they quickly learned to adjust the direction and speed of their hand movements to bring their hands into the light and keep them there. Similarly, newborns will move their arms toward objects they find appealing, even if they cannot grab them (von Hofsten, 1984).

If even newborns are able to guide their limbs toward the objects they perceive, then simple empiricist accounts appear to be in trouble. These very early abilities suggest that links between eye and limb that are already present at birth serve as a framework that guides learning during perceptual-motor development (von Hofsten, 1980, 2004). The critical question concerns how those links are influenced by experience.

Q: To what extent are newborns capable of guiding their limbs toward a desired object? How does that ability change in the first few months of life?

Within a perceptual-motor framework that is present from birth, one powerful way that human infants show

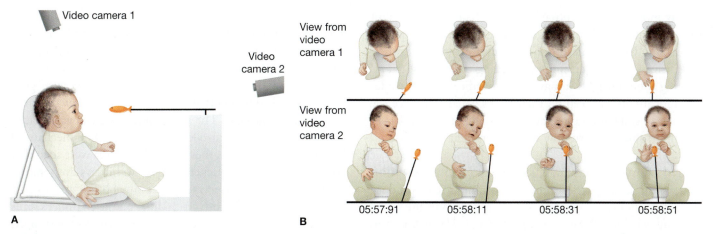

Video camera 1

Video camera 2

View from video camera 1

View from video camera 2

05:57:91   05:58:11   05:58:31   05:58:51

A   B

FIGURE 4.9 **Reaching in young infants. (A)** The setup in which an infant sits in a chair as an attractive object on a rod swings back and forth in front of him. Video cameras from above and straight ahead record the infant's reaching patterns, as well as his gaze and head movements. **(B)** Views of the infant recorded over time from above and from straight ahead as he reaches for the object when it moves in front of him. In this example, the infant is reaching in anticipation of making contact with the moving object. Adapted from von Hofsten & Lindhagen (1979) and von Hofsten (1980).

learning involves coming to understand that objects beyond a certain distance are not worth reaching for. Infants seem to understand this by the time they are at least 4 months old, as they are less likely to reach for more distant objects (Yonas & Granud, 1985). By 5 months of age, infants also modify the shapes of their hands to fit best with the shapes or orientations of objects that they are about to grasp (von Hofsten & Fazel-Zandy, 1984; see Figure 4.10). The purpose of reaching—to retrieve an object—is therefore integrated into an infant's perception and action from an early age. Another link between reaching and perception of distance also occurs with hearing. By 6 months, infants will reach less for objects they hear (in the dark) that are too far away (Clifton et al., 1991). Even more impressively, 10-month-old infants will adjust how they move their hands toward an object, depending on what they plan to do with it. Thus, they will reach faster to grasp a ball they want to throw than a ball they are going to stuff into a tube. Presumably the difference arises because the stuffing requires more dexterity and a more precise initial grip (Claxton et al., 2003).

Developmental improvements in reaching clearly are related to two kinds of changes in the brain: (1) changes to the neural circuits that directly enable action to become more sophisticated as the circuits mature, and (2) changes to the brain in response to learning new forms of actions. In addition, changes outside the brain are also important. In some cases, the infant's own body and posture may impose limitations, a pattern that fits with the tenets of dynamic systems theory. For example, 5-month-olds, who are not able to sit on their own, also seem to be quite poor at reaching for objects. But when these infants are propped up carefully with cushions, suddenly their reaching abilities become more sophisticated (Rochat & Goubet, 1995).

Later, we will see that these kinds of peripheral limb-based constraints, so called because they involve bodily features rather than instructions to the body by the brain, may be especially prominent in learning to crawl and walk.

Navigating Space

Parents are often surprised at just how fast an infant can move, especially, it seems, when they look away for a moment. As infants grow older, they become increasingly adept at getting around, usually progressing from creeping to crawling to various stages of walking. During this progression, just as in the development of reaching, their movements are con-

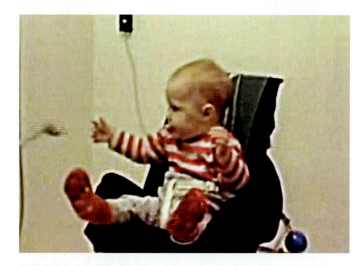

FIGURE 4.10 **Reaching in older infants.** This 8-month-old has become quite adept at both anticipating the trajectory of this rapidly moving object and also at adjusting her hand orientation and grasp width in such a way as to make effective contact with the object.

stantly guided by perceptual feedback. It is also important to note that not all infants go through the same sequence of learning to move around. Some never do much crawling and instead go from creeping to holding themselves up and moving about upright. It may be that medical recommendations for infants to sleep on their backs (so as to reduce the chances of sudden infant death syndrome) give them less of an opportunity to learn how to crawl on their stomachs.

Active versus Passive Visual Experience and Action

In learning a new action, how important is it to produce the action alone, as opposed to having someone else guide your movements? When a young baseball player learns to hit, how important is it for her to keep attempting to connect with the ball, rather than resting her hands on a bat swung by a coach? In both cases, she sees the ball moving toward the bat, then feels her arms move through space. Is the initiation of the action that important? To understand how perceptual-motor skills are best acquired, it is important to understand the different roles of active and passive visual motor experience and which kind of feedback most effectively supports the development of action. Only then can we make informed decisions about the kinds of activities that most benefit infants and young children.

An elegant approach to studying the role of feedback in perceptual-motor development was designed by Richard Held and Alan Hein (Held & Hein, 1963; see Figure 4.11). The researchers divided newborn kittens into two groups, active and passive. Both groups spent most of their time in darkness, where they were free to wander about as they pleased,

and both groups were treated identically when in the dark. They saw an illuminated world only for the few hours each day that they spent in a special environment—a cylindrical chamber with identically spaced vertical lines on the wall. In this environment, the passive kittens were placed in a "gondola," a small container that carried them just a few centimeters above the ground. The active kittens were always placed in the harness that controlled the gondola. The mechanical linkages between the harness and the gondola were such that the passive kitten experienced the active kitten's every move. Thus, if the active kitten moved rapidly, both it and its passive partner would see the vertical lines on the chamber's walls rushing by at the same speed. When the active kitten stopped or turned, the passive kitten would also stop or turn, so that both kittens' visual experience would change in the same way.

In short, the combination of this special environment and the gondola arrangement eliminated all the differences in the perceptual-motor experiences of the two groups of kittens except for one. The passive kitten's visual experiences were never a consequence of its own self-produced motion; instead, they resulted from the motions of the active kitten.

After experiencing these conditions for 3 hours a day over the course of 2 months, the two groups of kittens were tested with several different tasks to see if being an active as opposed to a passive participant had any effect on perception or action. The researchers tested whether the kittens would put their paws out to land on a table as they were lowered toward it, as normal kittens do. As experimenters lowered the active kittens, they would put out their paws to meet the table's surface at just the right time. By contrast, the passive kittens were unable to link their perception of the approaching table to their own actions; they did not stretch out their forelegs to meet the surface. Instead, they usually let their forelegs hang until their paws grazed the surface, and then they would step up on the table, just as they normally did in the dark.

FIGURE 4.11 Active versus passive experience. The active (A) and passive (P) kittens in the Held and Hein study. The two kittens had nearly identical visual experiences due to the yoking of the passive kitten's gondola to the movements of the active kitten. Nonetheless, perceiving movement that is not the result of one's own actions resulted in many perceptual motor deficits for the passive kitten. Adapted from Held & Hein (1963).

> **Q:** How did the passively and actively reared kittens in the Held and Hein studies differ?

Passive kittens also seemed less sensitive to depth relations in other situations. When an object rapidly approached their faces, they were much less likely to blink, which was the active kittens' (and normal kittens') automatic response. The researchers also observed the kittens on a visual cliff like the one Eleanor Gibson used to test infants' depth perception (see Chapter 3). The passive kittens would wander off onto the deep side of the visual cliff, showing no ability to avoid the apparent drop-off (see Figure 4.12). Indeed, Held and Hein noted that if a passive kitten was placed on a

FIGURE 4.12 The visual cliff and active experience in kittens.
Unlike this kitten, passively transported kittens in the Held and Hein studies were much more likely to wander off on the deep side of the visual cliff.

lab table for a moment, they would often have to rush over and catch it as it blithely walked off an edge. It is not clear whether the passive kittens were completely insensitive to these "cliffs" or whether they realized that a drop-off was imminent but did not know how to coordinate their actions with what they saw.

These studies and similar studies with other species, such as monkeys, show that it is not enough for the developing organism to have both unrestricted movement and unobstructed vision. The two must occur simultaneously so that the developing organism immediately sees the actions it produces and receives concurrent visual feedback; passive mimicry is not sufficient to support full-fledged perceptual-motor development. In the previous chapter, we saw that there seemed to be critical periods for the acquisition of some aspects of pattern recognition and auditory-visual localization. In contrast, there is no obvious critical period for establishing links between motion and vision. When the passive kittens were allowed to freely explore a normal, illuminated world, they quickly came to respond like the active kittens.

For obvious ethical reasons, no one has conducted a study like Held and Hein's with infants or children. But the importance of self-produced movement and concurrent visual feedback has been demonstrated in adults. In a version of Held and Hein's kitten study, an active participant and a passive participant both wore prisms, but only the active participant's visual experiences were directly correlated with self-produced movements. The passive participant rode along in a stand-up cart, seeing the same prism-distorted visual input as the active participant, but

not experiencing visual feedback from his own actions. When both participants were later tested, the active person showed an adaptation to the prisms, while the passive person was relatively unaffected (Held, 1965). There are many other studies showing these results. For example, it is possible to learn to trace the path through a maze using only a mirror image for visual feedback, but only if you yourself do the drawing. Passively following the maze with your hand while someone else draws has little or no effect (Bedford, 1989; Held, 1965).

One study with human infants has interesting parallels to Held and Hein's (1963) study. Infants between 2 and 3 months of age were outfitted with mittens, some of which had Velcro that stuck to toys and some of which did not have Velcro and so did not stick to toys. The infants with Velcro mittens would touch the toys, which would stick to their mittens, and then transport them about as shown in Figure 4.13A. The infants with mittens that did not have Velcro watched as a parent moved the toys around in a manner that followed the infants' arm movements, without allowing them to actively transport the toys themselves (see Figure 4.13B). These two groups of infants had the same experiences for just a few minutes a day for 2 weeks.

Over subsequent weeks, researchers measured how much time the infants spent spontaneously grasping and reaching, both in the laboratory and at home. As Figure 4.13C shows, the active infants did much more grasping and reaching, suggesting that their early experience in short sessions of actively reaching and manipulating objects helped jump-start their learning about these motions (Libertus & Needham, 2010).

More broadly, these studies suggest that organisms can best learn about their environments in active, exploratory ways. They learn very little when they are forced to passively receive a stream of information. Even when the passive experience involves nearly equivalent information, an active, self-initiated experience seems to have a dramatically different effect on both the level of motor activity and on the ability to use vision to guide action. In later chapters, we will examine just how broad the benefits of active experience are. For example, most theories of education conclude that students learn more effectively when they actively practice new skills rather than being passively guided by teachers.

Q: How has active and passive experience been shown to differentially influence perceptual-motor coordination in humans?

Walking and Seeing Like most other motor activities—such as reaching and grasping—walking has important links to perception. Blind children who are otherwise healthy in

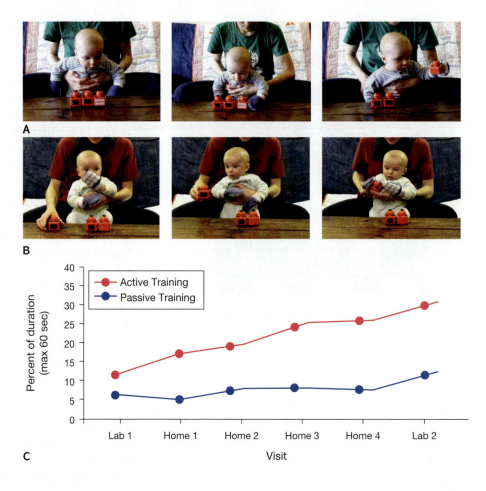

FIGURE 4.13 Active versus passive reaching and grasping. (A) Young 2- to 3-month-old infants who were given "active training" wore sticky mittens with Velcro and were able to "grasp" and transport toys. **(B)** Young 2- to 3-month-old infants who were given "passive training" wore mittens without Velcro and could not grasp or transport toys, but could only observe their parents doing so. **(C)** Infants given active training showed marked improvements in later weeks in time spent grasping and reaching, both in the lab and in the home, while infants given passive training did not show such improvements. Adapted from Libertus & Needham (2010).

all respects tend to start walking several months later than their sighted peers. Interestingly, the blind children's development of other motor behaviors before walking, including the ability to crawl, is not nearly as delayed (Adelson & Fraiberg, 1974). This suggests that vision is even more important to walking than to other motor activities.

> **Q:** Why might blind children be delayed in walking?

One important way in which vision helps us walk is by providing us with information about how our body is moving through the environment. When we walk at different speeds, we come to expect certain visual patterns known as **visual flow fields** to stream past at appropriate speeds, and we use this visual feedback to adopt a well-balanced posture. Vision, in particular the visual flow fields around us, provides us with what amounts to visual "hand rails" that make it easier to get about in a steady and sure-footed manner. These flow fields can work even when children and adults do not fixate on any objects in particular and just observe the overall stream of the environment passing

by them, as assessed by having wireless eye-tracking systems attached to their heads as they walk and run about (Franchak & Adolph, 2010). We are normally not aware of using this visual support while walking, but it quickly becomes obvious when we walk with our eyes closed. A series of studies vividly illustrated the extent to which toddlers depend on information from the visual flow field to maintain balance. In the studies, an unsuspecting new walker was placed in a room and allowed to stand for a few moments, at which point, even though the floor remained stationary, all the walls started to move in one direction as shown in Figure 4.14. Quite remarkably, even though the infant himself did not move, slow movements of the walls could "knock" the infants over by disrupting the coordination between their actions and their visual information (Bertenthal & Bai, 1989; Lee & Aronson, 1974; Stoffregen et al., 1987). Thus, if the wall was moving toward them, they felt as if they were moving toward the wall, tried to compensate by leaning backward, and lost their balance, rather than literally being knocked over by the walls. The same effect can be produced if an infant is walking instead of just standing still and the surrounding walls start to move in a manner no longer concordant with the walking. (Older children and adults are susceptible to these effects, too.)

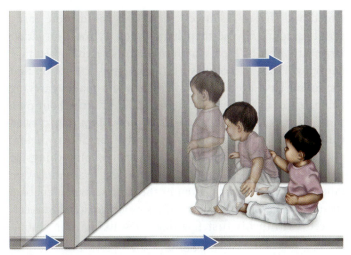

FIGURE 4.14 Visual flow fields and balance. Toddlers can be easily "knocked over" if the room around them moves in such a way as to suggest that they are moving when they are not. They rely on appropriate correlations between visual flow patterns in the environment and their own movements to help them balance. Here the walls are shown as moving toward the toddler, who feels as if he is moving toward the wall because of the visual flow patterns and compensates by leaning backward and falling over. Adapted from Bertenthal et al. (1997).

These studies demonstrate that visual information is not just a helpful support for walking. Rather, it is an intrinsic part of maintaining balance and therefore tremendously helpful in beginning to walk. Quite remarkably, this ability to use visual flow fields to control balance and posture is present in babies long before they have much capacity to use it. A newborn's head posture is responsive to the visual flow changes around her as early as three days after birth, even though her head still has to be carefully supported (Jouen et al., 1993; see Figure 4.15), and it becomes ever more responsive to small changes as the child grows older (Baumberger et al., 2004).

Besides guiding posture and balance, visual information is also critical for navigating the environment—and not just for avoiding large objects. Subtle changes in the visual flow allow us to adjust to dips and bumps in the walking surface (Vishton & Cutting, 1995; Warren et al., 1986). Watching a new walker manage to pick up on and adapt to irregular terrain makes it clear that visual information is used from the moment the toddler first starts to walk.

> **Q:** How does the visual world we move through function as virtual hand rails?

A final way in which moving through the world is linked to perception is evident in studies in which Eleanor Gibson and her colleagues tested how readily infants would traverse novel surfaces (Gibson et al., 1987). The researchers arranged an experimental setup similar to the visual cliff in which infants were placed on a starting platform and encouraged to cross the surface in front of them (see Figure 4.16). The researchers tested responses in two conditions. In the first condition, the surface was a rigid plywood plank covered with black velvet. In the second condition, the surface was a soft water bed, also covered in black velvet.

Young infants who could crawl but not yet walk were about equally likely to venture out on both surfaces. They certainly perceived the differences in rigidity, but because they were already down on the surface and wouldn't be risking a fall, the consequences were relatively unimportant. In contrast, infants who were just learning to walk were much more reluctant to step out onto the water bed than onto the wooden plank. One common response was to explore the surface tentatively with one hand, and upon confirming that it was not rigid, to stay put. Even before having any direct experience, the young toddlers held back from crossing the water bed. If the experimenters dropped a ball on its surface or tapped it lightly to show that it was not rigid, this information was more than adequate to inhibit these early walkers.

Thus, young infants perceive the **affordances**, or possibilities for action based on the properties of the objects or surfaces on which the action will be performed. A nonrigid surface does not inhibit all kinds of movement across

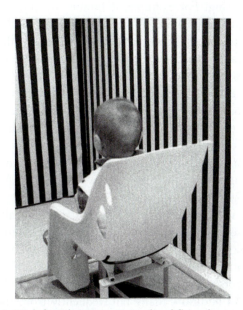

FIGURE 4.15 Infants' responses to visual flow changes. Babies will subtly move various parts of their bodies (for example, changing the position of their head and lower back) to compensate for movements in their environment. In this study, the room around the baby oscillated back and forth at different rates (based on movements of the side walls), and the 9-month-old baby showed corresponding back-and-forth oscillations of his body. Adapted from Bertenthal et al. (2000).

FIGURE 4.16 Perception and traversing novel surfaces. Gibson used a variant of the visual cliff to see how infants assessed traversability of a surface as a function of whether they were walkers or crawlers. The infant started down a ramp and then moved onto the main surface, which was either rigid or undulated like a water bed (as shown here). Crawlers happily ventured out on either surface, while walkers avoided the water bed. Adapted from Gibson et al. (1987).

it, only those that require maintaining upright balance to avoid falling. This is just one more way that the interaction between perception and action allows infants to respond flexibly to changes in their environment. Further studies have shown that infants are remarkably adept at adjusting their manner of locomotion, depending on the surface that they seek to traverse and taking into account the environment in many more ways than whether a surface is rigid or undulating. For example, if infants are put at the top of a downward-sloping ramp, the crawlers will proceed down it in much the same manner as they would cross a level surface, whereas young walkers will change their pattern of movement, often switching from walking to sliding (Adolph et al., 1993, 2003). More broadly, infants adapt their locomotion in highly flexible ways that are exquisitely sensitive to the particular environment in which they are put and to the ways that the environment poses specific biomechanical constraints on their actions, constraints that change as the toddler grows (Adolph, 2008; Adolph & Kretch, 2012).

These studies also highlight the finding that walking initially poses more risks and challenges than crawling. Given that walking is initially much slower and more difficult, what motivates expert crawlers to want to do it? After all, new walkers often drop to all fours when they need to move quickly. In addition, many fall frequently from the standing position, accumulating lots of bruises and bumps in the process of learning to walk. If walking is both slower and more painful at first, what motivates it?

One possibility is related to speculations about how walking evolved in the human species. Some theories suggest that the driving factor may have been the need to carry objects. As early hominins formed social groups in which they coop-

erated and shared resources, those who could more easily stand upright and use their hands to carry tools or gather larger amounts of food may have had a selective advantage (Lovejoy, 1981). Although still controversial, the notion that the infant first attempts to walk because it makes carrying things easier has considerable appeal. As I watched our own toddlers walk about, I was struck by how often they carried things from place to place with great delight. Shortly before taking their first steps, they attempted to carry things in their mouths, but this rather uncomfortable technique often failed. Walking upright, even in the earliest stages, enabled them to carry much heavier things much greater distances. Indeed, within his first few days of walking, our youngest son was discovered lugging a 5-pound jug of laundry detergent!

Infants are often able to carry or move objects even when crawling; for example, crawlers will support themselves with one hand while carrying an object with another, will use their mouth, or will slide an object along (see Figure 4.17). When they finally start to walk, however, their carrying behavior expands in important ways; they can more easily move large objects about and tend to do so more often and with greater speed (Karasik et al., 2012).

Q: Why should infants ever want to walk, given how uncomfortable and slow it is compared with their ability to crawl?

FIGURE 4.17 Carrying objects while crawling. Even before they can walk, infants have a strong drive to move things about and do so through several methods. When they start to walk, however, they tend to carry larger objects and do so with greater frequency. Adapted from Karasi et al. (2012).

Overall, early perceptual-motor development clearly illustrates that perception and action are part of an integrated system that enables infants to act on and get around in their world. Right from the start, there is a rough correspondence between what a newborn sees and hears and how she acts, and the integration of perception and action becomes much more refined in the months and years that follow. These refinements arise from several factors: the development of increasingly sophisticated neural circuitry, the growth and change in the size and proportions of the body, and the infant's ability to perceive the consequences of her own actions. This last factor is an excellent demonstration of the importance of feedback loops to the development of action. All these factors must be taken into account to understand how perceptual-motor skills develop.

Learning to Engage in Specific Actions

Up to this point, we have considered perceptual-motor skills such as walking, reaching, and grasping. These skills enable an infant to respond quickly to his environment and to begin navigating within it. Other kinds of actions require more specific and precise patterns of motion. These action sequences may require considerable learning, either by observing recurrent patterns in the environment or by experiencing environmental contingencies in response to one's own behavior. These sequences can range from an infant imitating a sequence of facial expressions to a dog learning a series of tricks.

The many ways of mastering such specific sequences illustrate the impressive range that organisms have for learning about the world while remaining subject to strong constraints and embedded in various feedback loops. We have already seen how cycles of action, perception, and adjusted reaction create the feedback loops that guide perceptual-motor coordination. Alternatively, an organism can learn about the consequences of its actions through feedback that involves being rewarded or punished. In the next sections, we will consider how these feedback systems, along with constraints on learning, guide the development of specific behavior patterns. To do this, we will examine three ways of learning specific action patterns: imitation, imprinting, and conditioning.

Early Imitation

Imitating others seems to come naturally—sometimes even unintentionally—whether it is imitating someone's gestures or even their manner of speaking (Pardo & Fowler,

1997). As we will see, even newborns can imitate simple facial expressions. Young toddlers often imitate older children and adults and, as many parents will admit, not always in desirable ways. Imitation is a part of all our lives, but its earliest manifestations in development were, until relatively recently, a mystery.

The Process of Imitation Much like reaching or walking, imitation might seem simple, but it is actually an intricate perceptual-motor achievement. To imitate a facial expression of another person involves perceiving the complex, dynamic patterns of facial movement, interpreting those movements in terms of your own facial muscles, remembering the pattern of facial changes after the model has stopped, and finally reenacting the neuromuscular event. Considering all these requirements, it is all the more remarkable that infants younger than 1 hour old can imitate the facial expressions of others.

Although researchers long believed that older infants could imitate facial expressions (Piaget, 1962), in 1977 Andrew Meltzoff and Keith Moore demonstrated the ability in newborns. The experimenters repeatedly made several different faces at newborns, in some cases within the first hour after birth, and videotaped the infants' facial responses. Observers then watched the videotapes, without knowing which expression the experimenter had been showing, and described the infant's expression. One of the acts the infants imitated most clearly was sticking out the tongue. As Figure 4.18 shows, the infants also imitated several of the experimenter's other acts, including opening the mouth in

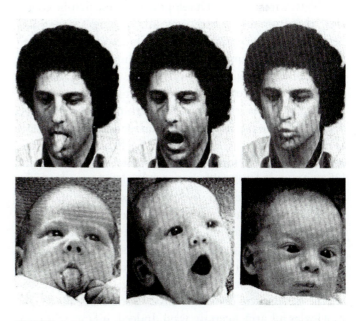

FIGURE 4.18 Imitation by infants. Infants between 2 and 3 weeks of age will imitate particular facial expressions (tongue protrusion, mouth opening, and lip protrusion) of an adult model. Normally, the adult must repeat the expression several times in succession with clear pauses between each display. From Meltzoff & Moore (1977).

a wide O shape and puckering the lips (Meltzoff & Moore, 1977).

These results were so remarkable that they were initially met with skepticism by those who thought that the accounts were exaggerated or perhaps had actually involved older infants. How could a newborn, who appears to be so helpless and, more specifically, so limited in terms of perceptual and motor abilities, possibly engage in something as sophisticated as imitating a facial expression? Although not all newborns imitate expressions consistently (or at all), and the imitation can often be subtle, their ability to imitate has since been confirmed in many carefully controlled studies (Abravenel & Sigafoos, 1984; Field et al., 1982; Meltzoff & Moore, 1989; Reissland, 1988; Vinter, 1986).

Q: What is necessary for infants to be able to imitate facial expressions?

FIGURE 4.19 Brain activity and reaching in human infants. Infants show similar brain activation patterns when they are reaching for an object and when they observe others reach for an object. Southgate et al. (2009).

The fact that imitation is possible almost immediately after birth naturally raises questions as to its underlying mechanisms. Meltzoff and Moore suggest that for many human actions, including both facial expressions and hand gestures, the ability to perceive the action and the ability to produce it might be mentally represented in the same neural code. Thus, when an infant perceives an action, the code for the related motor sequence is activated as well. Although this specific proposal is still being investigated (see New Directions in Developmental Research box), it is clear that from a very early age, infants have a strong link between their perceptions and their ability to reproduce certain kinds of actions. This has been shown in studies that measure brain activity while infants are reaching and while perceiving others reaching for an object (see Figure 4.19).

Early imitation is not restricted to things that infants see, of course. They also frequently imitate sounds, in some cases as early as 10 weeks of age (Kuhl & Meltzoff, 1996). Moreover, imitation is a form of social activity; 5- to 8-week-old infants are much more likely to imitate humans than inanimate objects (Legerstee, 1991). For example, infants are more likely to imitate an adult sticking out her tongue than a long red object moving out of a white tube. Meltzoff and Moore (1994, 1999) argue that the various forms of imitation may also help infants recognize people, as if by imitating the other person the infant is saying, "I know you. You are the person who does this" (that is, sticks out his tongue or wiggles his arm a certain way). Indeed, infants will reenact an imitated action shown by a specific model when encountering that model in the future or when exposed to a cue (for example, hearing the model) that reminds them of the model (Meltzoff, 2005). Even 6-week-old infants seem

to associate imitative actions with particular individuals. In one study, infants imitated an action by a specific adult whom they had seen performing that action 24 hours earlier. They readily imitated the familiar model, but were much less likely to imitate a new model. This is quite remarkable, given some claims that infants cannot recognize individual faces at that age. It also displays an impressive memory skill, which extends to several weeks in older infants (Meltzoff & Moore, 1994).

Newborns' ability to imitate facial expressions and actions is not uniquely human. Rather, imitation has a long evolutionary history in primates as a way of interacting that tends to bring individuals into similar emotional states (for example, feeling afraid). Thus, like human mothers, mothers of newborn macaques engage in making and imitating facial expressions with their infants (Ferrari et al., 2009a). This mother-infant facial feedback loop may help regulate their emotions so they can experience a shared emotional state and thus sense what the other is feeling. As Figure 4.20 shows, newborn macaque monkeys can also imitate human facial expressions, such as sticking out the tongue or showing a wide open mouth (Ferrari et al., 2006). This result is striking, given that the macaque newborns must be perceiving a representation of the human face that is generalized and abstract enough that they can use it to know which of their own facial muscles to move. Other studies of rhesus macaque newborns have shown that those that imitate most often also tend to develop more sophisticated motor skills later, such as those involved in grasping and reaching (Ferrari et al., 2009b). **Mirror neurons** are neurons in the brain that are activated both when performing actions and when perceiving them being performed by others. They are thought to support imitation and may be involved in the

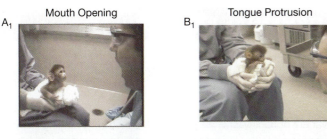

Mouth Opening   Tongue Protrusion

FIGURE 4.20 Imitation of facial expressions in newborns of other species. Newborn macaque monkeys will imitate the facial expressions of humans. From Ferrari et al. (2006).

process of learning new actions right from birth onward in monkeys (Ferrari et al., 2012).

> **Q:** How have infant imitation studies influenced views of infant memory?

One of the most puzzling questions about the development of imitation concerns the boundaries that define what kinds of behaviors infants are likely to imitate. Even if we narrow the focus to actions made by human agents, infants clearly do not imitate everything they see. Part of what drives their imitative tendencies may be whether they perceive an action as intentional. They seem to require several repetitions of an action to want to imitate it—not because they fail to notice it, but perhaps because they need to know it was not simply an accidental action, like a sneeze. No one thinks that young infants fully understand others' intentions, but infants may find some aspects of intentional behavior especially salient, a topic we will return to in Chapter 5.

The Development of Birdsong: Variations on the Imitation Theme Humans and other primates are not the only creatures that attend to others' actions in order to reproduce them. In fact, the imitative feats of developing songbirds seem to exceed the imitative capacities of human infants. There can be large lags between when a bird first hears a song and when the bird first reproduces it. Unlike human verbal memory, immediate rehearsal is not necessary for birds to remember what they have heard. For example, starlings will sometimes reproduce for the first time songs that they have not heard for over 15 months (Chaiken et al., 1994). Many birds come to sing complex and beau-

tiful vocalization patterns, using the songs to demarcate territory, attract mates, and identify themselves. But none sing full-fledged songs from birth, raising the question of how they develop these abilities. The answers have come from ethologists in the fields and meadows of the world and from neurophysiologists in their laboratories. Their findings illustrate some of the many different ways in which complex motor behaviors develop.

Among different types of songbirds, there are several different developmental pathways for learning to sing. Most birds imitate songs sung by older birds of their species. They hear a song, remember the patterns, and reproduce them. In addition, juvenile birds frequently are in a phase of overproduction of song components (somewhat like human infants' babbling), producing more "syllables" of songs than they will ever show as adults; they limit the components of their songs as they learn from older models. But songbirds also tend to be somewhat inventive and improvisational. They don't simply copy models' songs; they improvise in the specific style of the song they have heard. In most species, hearing good model songs enhances the quality of the songs that develop. For centuries, birdsong lovers in Japan would pay to have their young birds "tutored" by older prize-winning singers (Konishi, 1985; see Figure 4.21).

In some species, songs will emerge in relatively full form, even if the birds are reared in isolation, but the songs will typically be less rich and less tightly structured than those of birds reared in the company of older singing birds. Other species of birds, such as swamp sparrows, do much worse when they are reared in isolation. Although these birds do not simply stay silent, they only are able to develop a skeletal song that has the overall structure of the normal songs but that lacks details, including those that normally distinguish local groups of birds (Marler, 1991a, 1991b). Moreover, even more than listening to older singers, young songbirds must be able to listen to themselves. In general, if birds are deafened after they are born, their songs usually degenerate terribly. The feedback gained through hearing their own songs seems essential.

Finally, some songbirds, such as the zebra finch, show an innate bias to learn the songs of their own species, but if they are only exposed to the songs of a related species, they are also able to learn those songs. Nonetheless, learning another species' song tends to take longer than learning their own. In this way, the acquisition of birdsong by the zebra finch illustrates both learning within a set of guiding constraints (the framework songs of their own species) and also a flexibility in the learning process that allows them to transcend those constraints when the environment demands it (that is, when only other species' songs are available). This kind of pattern is often described as guidance by "soft constraints," which are said to provide a default bias toward a certain developmental pathway.

Mirror Neurons and Early Imitation

The remarkable ability of even newborns to imitate the actions of others has led many researchers to investigate the mechanisms that could support these surprisingly sophisticated behaviors. A recent series of findings in neuroscience on mirror neurons has resulted in some provocative suggestions about the neural basis of imitation (Lyons et al., 2006; Meltzoff & Prinz, 2002; Nakahara & Miyashita, 2005; Rizzolatti & Craighero, 2004). Some of the most intriguing findings initially came from studies of the neural basis of imitation in monkeys. Neuroscientists implanted electrodes in the monkeys' premotor cortex, the brain area involved in guiding actions, to monitor the firing of individual neurons. They recorded the firing patterns of premotor neurons, both when monkeys performed object-directed actions (including grasping, placing, and manipulating objects with their hands) and when they observed other monkeys performing similar actions. In several cases, the same neuron fired both when a monkey was performing a specific action on an object, such as grasping a block on a table, and when the monkey was watching another monkey engaging in the same action (Gallese et al., 1996, 2004). The neurons that fired when the monkey grasped the block did not fire when the monkey saw the block when it was not being grasped by a hand or when the monkey watched the experimenter simulate grasping the block when it was not present. Because these same neurons fired when the monkey either performed or observed a particular action on an object, they came to be called mirror neurons.

Interestingly, while the mirror neurons associated with a particular object-directed action did not fire when the action was performed in the absence of the object, they did fire when the monkey watched a robot perform the action. This suggests that the activity of mirror neurons is associated with the overall goal of the action rather than with the necessary limb movements (Gazzola et al., 2007; Rizzolatti & Sinigaglia, 2010). There may be a common code both for perceiving and for performing many kinds of actions. Researchers have documented what seem to be different populations of mirror neurons for hand movements, for facial movements, and for eating (Rizzolatti & Craighero, 2004).

It is relatively easy to document the activity of mirror neurons in monkeys, but it is far more difficult to do so in humans, because implanting electrodes in human brains solely for the purpose of experiments is unethical. Nonetheless, evidence from a variety of noninvasive measures of brain activity, ranging from electroencephalograms (EEGs; Altschuler et al., 1997) to functional magnetic resonance imaging (fMRI; Grèzes et al., 2003), suggests that the same brain regions responsible for object-directed actions are also active when people observe similar actions being performed by others. Studies involving people with intractable epilepsy have also offered more direct confirmation. These individuals already had deep electrodes implanted in regions of their cortex to help guide neurosurgeons attempting to treat the epilepsy. They were shown to have mirror neurons in several locations, some of which were analogous to the brain areas where they have been found in monkeys (Keysers & Gazzola, 2010). Other studies with 9-month-old infants used a net of scalp electrodes to detect mirror neuron–like processes in the motor control regions of the brain. These areas show similar electrical activity patterns when infants grasp an object themselves and when they anticipate that someone else's hand is about to grasp the object (Southgate et al., 2009, 2010). Thus, the motor region is activated when thinking about another's goal of grasping, not just by observing actual grasping.

It has been argued that the sort of imitation found in humans and higher primates is unique and that it represents a highly advanced evolutionary achievement (Rizzolatti & Craighero, 2004). Mimicry in other sorts of animals is argued to involve different kinds of processing and no mirror neurons. If this claim is correct, it raises the question of whether newborns' ability to imitate might arise from the presence of functional mirror neurons at birth. This question can only be answered with a detailed understanding of mirror neuron function, which can then be contrasted with other systems that might support mimicry. The more precise functions of mirror neurons remain a topic of considerable debate. Besides their role in imitation (Jeannerod, 1994), they may contribute significantly to attending to the details of others' actions (Wilson & Knoblich, 2005), to understanding the meanings of those actions (Gallese et al., 2004), and to social understanding and empathy (Baird et al., 2011; Meltzoff & Decety, 2003). It remains unclear, however, whether the activity of mirror neurons provides a basis for inferring others' thoughts, feelings, and intentions by neurally "simulating" their actions (Saxe, 2005). Thus, imitation may be the mirror neurons' core purpose or only a kind of side effect of their activity.

FIGURE 4.21 Imitation of birdsong. For centuries, songbirds have been prized in Japan, and juveniles were often exposed to "expert" adults for "tutoring" in the nuances of particular songs.

The zebra finches also illustrate an intriguing interaction between critical periods and environmental input. Most songbirds have a critical period in which they are best able to learn from listening to older singers. These periods can vary in length from a few months to over a year, depending on the species (Hensch, 2004). The start and stop times of the periods can also be environmentally influenced. Thus, if zebra finches do not hear good model songs during the normal developmental time frame for this period, they are able to postpone the critical period's onset by several weeks. Then, if an appropriate model comes along a bit later, they can learn just as easily. The length of the critical period for this species does not change; its start and stop dates simply seem to get postponed in the absence of a good model (Mooney, 1999).

The development of birdsong illustrates that there are many developmental paths for learning complex motor behaviors from models. Among songbirds, the particular role that songs play for a given species likely influences which developmental course is favored (Slater, 1989). The development of birdsong also draws together many of the themes of this book. Most songbirds show critical or sensitive peri-

ods for learning the skill from their elders. Perceptual-motor feedback is also essential, as most species will develop inadequate songs if they cannot hear their own efforts. In addition, a framework of biases toward learning and producing species-typical song elements, such as certain patterns of vocalization and repetition, is usually present at birth and guides further inputs. Moreover, the more complex the species' song patterns are, the more likely that the birds will depend heavily on input received from others and not just on a set of rote singing routines. Many of these same patterns also characterize imprinting, another behavior in young birds that has revealed important developmental principles.

> **Q:** What are some different patterns of birdsong development and what do they tell us about different ways of learning to imitate others?

Imprinting, Action, and Critical Periods

Young organisms sometimes learn in a powerful and seemingly irreversible manner known as **imprinting**. Imprinting is most common in birds, such as chickens, ducks, and geese, and its main function seems to be to ensure that young birds learn to stay close to their mothers. Newly hatched chicks will initially approach a wide range of objects. If they repeatedly encounter a particular object during the appropriate critical period, normally during the first few days after birth (Nakamori et al., 2010), however, they will continue to approach and follow it eagerly, often for the rest of their lives. In the natural world, this object is almost always their mother, but in the laboratory, young birds have imprinted on a host of other objects and even on the researchers themselves (see Figure 4.22).

A key aspect of imprinting is that the size, shape, and contrast of the object, as well as the manner of movement and many other factors, all influence the ease with which the chick will imprint on it (Honey & Bateson, 1996; Horn, 1990; Sluckin, 1972). Thus, as one researcher put it, the chick's brain is not "a tabula rasa on which experience makes it mark" (Horn, 1990). Outside the lab, where a newborn chick would likely encounter other chicks and perhaps the chicken coop itself during the critical period for imprinting, these innate biases greatly improve the chances that it will still imprint on its mother. A second feature of this kind of learning is that even when the chick simultaneously encounters two objects that are equally likely to cause imprinting, the chick will not imprint to both; instead, it will come to follow only one. The imprinting system does

FIGURE 4.22 Imprinting. A group of goslings swimming in a pond with ethologist Konrad Lorenz. Ducklings and goslings can imprint on a person (or on some part of the person, such as his boots) and will follow that individual as if he were a parent. These unusual imprintings require unusual environments in which the real mother is not present or only minimally so. The human would never win out over the real mother if they were both amply present in the environment, reflecting a natural bias to imprint on the mother, all things being equal.

not seem to allow imprinting on two distinct objects. This feature of the system also makes excellent sense for survival. Since no wild chick would need to imprint on two mothers, a double imprinting could become dangerously confusing for a young bird.

In the chick's brain, imprinting seems to occur in a region known as the intermediate medial hyperstriatum ventrale (IMHV), which is in the chick's forebrain. If the IMHV is lesioned before imprinting occurs, the chick will be unable to imprint. Moreover, lesioning this area after imprinting will erase what was learned with the imprinting. The same lesion will not block forms of learning unrelated to imprinting (Horn, 1990). And yet, while an IMHV-lesioned chick can no longer imprint on an artificial object such as a moving block, it will still follow a chicken about. How can we resolve this contradiction?

It turns out that in chicks, two independent systems are involved in behaviors like following, imprinting, and recognition. One system, which is present throughout the lifespan and does not involve the IMHV, consists of a general tendency to notice and follow other chickens. This system does not allow the chick to recognize another chicken as an individual. Rather, it is more like a general chicken detector that tends to make the chick orient toward others of its species and follow them.

The second system, which is in the IMHV region, governs the ability to recognize specific individuals rather than categories. This system, which is most receptive to learn-

ing during a critical period spanning the first few days after birth, is where the phenomena of imprinting occurs. It can support imprinting on an enormous range of objects and individuals, including many that do not look like chickens. Yet, in the natural environment, the coordination between this system and the other, earlier-emerging chicken detector system almost inevitably results in the chick imprinting on its mother (Bateson & Horn, 1994). We see here yet another example of the coordination of perception and action in development. The chicken-detecting-and-following system influences the chick's imprinting system and greatly increases the odds that the chick will imprint on the appropriate target.

As we saw in Chapter 3, this two-system model has inspired a similar model of infant face perception. In that model, the initial system orients the infant toward human faces as a general category. Then the experience the infant gains by attending to faces helps get the second system—the one for recognizing individuals—up and running. Imprinting in chicks and face perception in human infants demonstrate how the challenge of learning to attach to a specific individual might be solved in strikingly similar ways in two very different species. They also illustrate how the ability to recognize a general category and the ability to recognize a single individual both play important roles and can work together.

Imprinting is a highly constrained learning process involving a sequence of actions and perceptual discriminations that almost always emerges in the same way within a set time frame. In contrast, conditioning is a more flexible form of learning that can result in a variety of complex and variable behaviors. We will see, however, that these dramatic variations in conditioned learning still occur within a framework of constraints.

> **Q:** What is the evidence for two distinct systems in the development of imprinting?

Conditioning

Two of the most powerful and best-studied ways to elicit actions in infants involve classical and operant conditioning. The general theory of conditioning attempts to explain how organisms learn to respond to environmental events. In this theory, learning involves three components: awareness of stimuli, awareness of the environment, and awareness of consequences of actions. In the simplest kind of learning, the organism becomes aware of a stimulus. This is typically observed in instances of *habituation* and *dishabituation* (see Chapter 3). In the next level of learning, the organism must

Can a Toddler's Motor Development Be Accelerated?

Some affluent parents worry about how to give their children a competitive edge at the earliest age. In response to these kinds of concerns, enrichment programs for preschoolers, including programs to boost motor skills, have become commonplace in many cities and towns. But can these programs really deliver on their promises?

Imagine that a nationwide chain called Power Toddler claims that its 2-year program enhances the athletic skills of children aged 1 to 3 years old through early practice with motor skills. For a hefty fee, retired gymnasts, basketball players, and other athletes coach the toddlers for 2 hours each day, training the children to balance on beams, perform simple gymnastic movements, catch and throw balls, and do a variety of other simple athletic activities. Power Toddler's brochure says that perceptual-motor development largely depends on prior experience and that by enriching this experience for its students early on, its program confers a lifelong athletic advantage. It even cites some studies in which perceptual-motor skills seemed to be influenced by training (Boucher & Doescher, 1991; Laszlo & Sainsbury, 1993). The brochure goes on to refer to studies in Kenya that suggest that certain kinds of parenting practices might boost children's early motor development (Super, 1976). It even mentions some research arising from Esther Thelen's studies that shows that changes in muscles and other physical properties of the limbs can bring dramatic changes in motor abilities (Thelen, 1995; Vereijken & Thelen, 1997). On this basis, Power Toddler argues that through early exercise, toddlers can strengthen their muscles, which will enable them to achieve impressive new levels of motor activity.

As Power Toddler centers spring up across your state, the Consumer Protection Agency becomes concerned that the chain may be fraudulently promising parents more than it can deliver. The agency then turns to developmental psychologists for advice about the effects of intensive perceptual-motor instruction for children aged 1 to 3. It wants to know whether the Power Toddler program could really provide long-lasting benefits. Based on the information in this chapter, what does research on the development of action suggest about whether Power Toddler is using false advertising?

In considering this question, think back to Gesell's classic studies, such as the 11-month-old twin sisters who learned to climb stairs. These experiments involved younger children and far shorter durations of training than Power Toddler's 2-year program, but their findings suggested that extra training made no difference—all that seemed to matter was maturation (Gesell & Thompson, 1929). Here the question is: Do findings like Gesell's extend to later ages and longer periods of training?

Also consider how the evidence cited in Power Toddler's brochure relates to its promises of lifelong athletic benefits. While those studies and others—including the one described earlier that utilized Velcro mittens to accelerate infants' grasping and reaching (Libertus & Needham, 2010)—may well show how specific perceptual-motor experiences can improve early motor skills, this is not the same as providing evidence of more general, long-term benefits. Perhaps Power Toddler's program temporarily speeds up the development of perceptual-motor abilities but then other children catch up within a few months. Or perhaps Power Toddler's students regress back to normal levels when the program of constant practice ends.

This imaginary case is not far from real ones, and it illustrates how research on motor development might influence legal decisions about certain advertisements. In the hypothetical case of Power Toddler, the value of the program for physical prowess is probably quite modest. As long as young children have ample opportunities to engage in a variety of gross and fine motor activities, it is unlikely that special programs provide any additional and lasting athletic advantage. Participating in group activities with other children may confer some social benefits, but as a general rule, there is no evidence that toddlers who receive professional coaching are more likely to become skilled athletes.

FIGURE 4.23 Classical conditioning in sleeping newborns. Newborns can be classically conditioned to associate a tone with a puff of air to their eyes. They soon learn to blink when they hear the tone alone. **(A)** By monitoring sleeping infants' eye movement responses (EMRs) during this kind of classical conditioning, **(B)** researchers have found that sleeping infants who were conditioned show more EMRs than infants who were not conditioned. Those who experienced the classical conditioning also showed more brain activity suggestive of learning the association compared to infants in the control group. Adapted from Fifer et al. (2010).

A

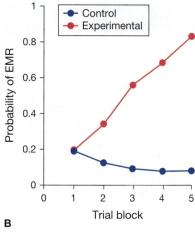

B

learn how stimuli are related; this level of learning is seen in *classical conditioning* (or Pavlovian conditioning). In the final level of learning, the organism learns about the consequences of its actions, where the stimulus usually takes on the role of a positive or negative reinforcer. This level of learning is known as *operant conditioning*. Let us now turn to classical and operant conditioning in more detail.

Classical Conditioning For over 100 years, since Pavlov's groundbreaking studies on dogs, it has been known that an enormous range of organisms can be classically conditioned. In **classical conditioning**, an initially neutral stimulus that does not normally elicit a response comes to do so through the repeated pairing of the neutral stimulus with a stimulus that would naturally elicit the response. To begin with, an **unconditioned stimulus (UCS)** has a preexisting relationship to an **unconditioned response (UCR)**. In Pavlov's dogs, meat powder (UCS) led to salivation (UCR). In a young infant, a puff of air to the face (UCS) will elicit an eyeblink (UCR) without any prior learning. If a tone is repeatedly paired with the puff of air, infants as young as 10 days will learn to blink (**conditioned response, or CR**) when they hear the tone by itself (**conditioned stimulus, or CS**), having learned the association between the two stimuli through classical conditioning (Little et al., 1984). Similarly, when infants are given a sweet solution (UCS), they will automatically show increased sucking (UCR). If a gentle stroking of the forehead, the conditioned stimulus (CS), is repeatedly paired with a sweet solution, even newborns will soon start to engage in anticipatory sucking (CR) in response to stroking alone (Blass et al., 1984), just as Pavlov's dogs came to salivate (CR) at the sound of a bell (CS) alone after the bell had previously been repeatedly paired with the meat powder (UCS).

Interestingly, infants can learn from classical conditioning even when they are asleep. (It is not uncommon for newborns to sleep 18 hours a day, which would leave less than 6 hours for learning if the infant needed to be wide awake to learn.) When a tone is consistently paired with an air puff delivered to sleeping newborns (see Figure 4.23), they will soon show more eye movement in response to the tone than other newborns who hear tones at random that are not paired with air puffs. In addition, only the infants who experience the air puff–tone pairings show increases in cortical activity that suggest that they are processing new memories (Fifer et al., 2010). The ability of infants to be classically conditioned whether they are awake or asleep enables them to learn as much as possible about important patterns in their world. In contrast, sleeping adults are not thought to be capable of classical conditioning. The ability to learn this way while sleeping may be a special adaptation of infancy because of the enormous amount of time infants spend asleep. Forming associations through classical conditioning is one way that infants begin adapting to their environments right from birth.

Q: What are some examples of classical conditioning in infants?

Early in the study of classical conditioning in infancy, J. B. Watson and his associates conducted a dramatic demonstration of this form of learning (Watson & Raynor, 1920). A 9-month-old infant referred to as "Little Albert" was brought into the laboratory, where he eagerly approached furry animals, such as rabbits. The child was then shown

FIGURE 4.24 The Little Albert study. The demonstration of classical conditioning in a child with the pseudonym "Little Albert" was used by James Watson to argue for an entire program of child rearing. Here Watson is pictured wearing a mask to see if Albert's fear of rats would generalize to a person wearing a furry mask.

a white lab rat. Initially, he seemed interested and unafraid as he reached toward it. In later trials conducted over 2 months, just as Albert touched the rat, a researcher behind him hit a steel bar with a hammer to make a sharp, loud noise (the UCS), which startled Albert and made him cry (UCR). After Albert had experienced several pairings of the rat with the noise, the researchers found that the rat alone (CS) could elicit a fearful response (CR). Whenever Albert saw it, he crawled away from it. This fearful response was then shown to generalize to other furry objects, such as rabbits (see Figure 4.24). Clearly, the current ethical restrictions would forbid this sort of study on infants or young children. The study has also raised considerable controversy over the years among those who disagree not only with its ethics but also with its methods (Paul & Blumenthal, 1989). In addition, it appears that contrary to Watson's claims that Albert was a normal healthy infant, he in fact had neurological impairments that raise questions about the extent to which the specific findings would extend to healthy infants (Fridlund et al., 2012).

The conditioning of fear, as in Albert's case, is interesting because it starts to illustrate some of the hidden complexity of classical conditioning (Rescorla, 1988). In the traditional view of classical conditioning, the conditioned response and the unconditioned response are supposed to be quite similar, with the conditioned response perhaps a bit weaker—for example, less salivation (CR) when the bell rings (CS) in the case of Pavlov's dogs, or not quite so active sucking (CR) by a human infant when her forehead is stroked (CS). But in the case of conditioned fear, the conditioned response is quite different from the unconditioned response (LeDoux, 1998). After Albert had been conditioned to fear the rat, he didn't startle and cry when he saw it as he had in response to the loud noise. Instead, he tried to avoid the rat in anticipation of hearing the loud noise. The conditioned behavior was clearly

adaptive and, in a sense, purposeful, rather than being limited to a simple association of a conditioned stimulus with an unconditioned one. Classical conditioning also relies on developing aspects of memory (Rovee-Collier, 1986) and on emerging expectations about future events (Fagan, 1993).

As we saw in Chapter 1, **behaviorism** is the notion that all behaviors can be instilled through conditioning, using combinations of punishments and rewards in association with sets of stimuli. Such conditioning makes certain actions more likely and others less likely. For many years, behaviorism and different forms of conditioning were thought to be the only scientific way to discuss learning, both in adults and throughout development. Behaviorists believed that infants come into the world as a **tabula rasa**, or blank slate, with little or no innate associations, and that any association can be conditioned through experience. Because they focused on the overt behaviors—that is, the *actions*—that resulted from the conditioning of these associations, behaviorists viewed most variations in behavior as a consequence of differences in the ways individuals were conditioned to act.

Classical conditioning models of learning were the first wave of behaviorism, with Watson being one of the strongest proponents of this point of view. The second wave arose with B. F. Skinner, a dominant figure in psychology in the mid-twentieth century. Skinner worked out the details of another way of modifying behavior known as operant conditioning (Skinner, 1938).

Operant Conditioning Compared with classical conditioning, **operant conditioning** (also known as **instrumental conditioning**) is more directly concerned with the way an organism learns to operate on its environment in response to either positive reinforcements that reward that behavior or negative reinforcements that punish that behavior. Skinner developed highly efficient methods for getting a wide range of species to exhibit specific behaviors. In one of the processes he used, called **shaping**, the researcher begins by rewarding spontaneous actions that resemble the desired behavior and then continues rewarding only behaviors that are increasingly similar to the desired response. As a result, the responses gradually change to become the desired behavior.

This technique was often used on pigeons in tightly controlled learning environments known as Skinner boxes (see Figure 4.25). Suppose an experimenter wanted the pigeon to peck a certain button whenever a green light in the box was illuminated. She might carefully observe the pigeon in the box and provide a reward, such as food pellets, whenever the pigeon happened to be facing toward the button while the green light was illuminated. After several trials, she would up the ante and only reward the pigeon when it was both oriented toward the button and standing near it while the green light was lit. When the pigeon had

FIGURE 4.25 Skinner boxes and pigeons. A "Skinner box" in which a pigeon's behavior is shaped through operant conditioning. Many researchers saw the Skinner box as promising a technological revolution in behavior modification—a revolution that was thought to ultimately provide a full explanation of human behavior as well.

learned this response, the reward might become contingent on actually touching the button while the green light was on—and so on, until the pigeon learned that it could earn a reward only by pecking the button while the green light was on.

What role does operant conditioning play in infant development? It can be a useful way for infants to learn to adapt to changes in their environment. It can be as simple as learning to change lip movements while nursing in response to positive reinforcement from the improved flow of milk. Likewise, 3-month-olds can learn to vocalize more in response to parents' smiles and other positive cues (Rheingold et al., 1959; Weisberg, 1963). Other studies have shown how infants at 6 weeks and older can learn to smile more often and more intensely through operant conditioning (Brossard & Decarie, 1968; Zelazo, 1971) and how infants who are at least 2 months old can be operantly conditioned to kick their legs more often when it causes a mobile (loosely tethered to the baby's leg) to move, providing a rewarding visual stimulus (Rovee & Fagan, 1976; Rovee-Collier & Giles, 2010; Watson & Ramey, 1972). In all these cases, the infants learn to adjust their actions to make a pleasant event occur more often. The infants are more likely to repeat these learned actions later in contexts highly similar to the ones in which they originally learned them (that is, in situations with the same stimuli and in the same setting). Infants will also make similar adjustments to reduce occur-

rences of unpleasant events (Sajwaj et al., 1974), though for obvious ethical reasons, there have been more studies of positive reinforcement of human infants than negative reinforcement.

Yet, most contemporary infant researchers have not used operant conditioning to shape desired infant responses. Instead, they have taken an easy, well-established infant action, such as sucking, and taught infants to associate it with a stimulus, such as a visual pattern, through operant conditioning. The researchers can then measure the infant's operant sucking response to see whether he can discriminate between the learned visual pattern and another one. (This technique is similar to the use of sucking as a measure of habituation, which was discussed in Chapter 3.)

Hundreds of studies have now shown that from birth on, infant behavior can be modified through both classical conditioning and operant conditioning. Infants can come to associate some stimuli with other stimuli, and they can alter their actions as a result. They also can be shown to change their actions as a result of positive and negative reinforcements. But those capacities do not necessarily support the behaviorists' key contentions about development: (1) that the infant comes into the world with few or no preformed associations, (2) that any pattern of associations can be learned from experience, and (3) that actions are simply learned responses to environmental contingencies. While learning and environmental influences clearly matter in infant development, several lines of research have greatly refined our understanding of both their contributions to development and their key limitations.

> **Q:** What are some examples of operant conditioning in infants?

Constraints on Learning It has now become abundantly clear that neither humans nor other animals associate all stimuli equally easily and that some stimuli can become associated in particular contexts but not in others. Thus, if a rat repeatedly sees a light and hears a noise at the same time prior to receiving a shock, it will respond fearfully to either the light or the noise. If a rat is repeatedly presented with a light prior to a shock and then later the noise is added, however, the noise alone will not cause a fearful response (Rescorla, 1988). Intuitively, it seems obvious how this **blocking** of the noise-to-shock association occurs; the formation of the first association interferes with the formation of the second association. The rat that has received light alone first has learned that the light is the critical determinant of the shock and therefore regards the subsequent noise when paired with the shock as redundant and uninformative. In effect, a decision is made about the likely informative value of the noise. The rat seems to engage in some form of cognition that goes beyond association.

Studies of human infants suggest that they experience similar blocking effects as early as 6 months of age (Sobel & Kirkham, 2006, 2007). The first association can be construed as a form of context that then influences the learning of a second association. Infants learned to look at either sequences of visual events in certain locations or visual events followed by sounds in specific locations. When the researchers measured infants' anticipatory eye movements to each location in response to these series of patterns, they found that the initial associations influenced the infants' later associative learning in ways that the classical laws of association could not explain, but which were quite similar to blocking phenomena found in other species.

A second important constraint on conditioned learning is that for particular species, some associations are easier to form than others. That is, considerable evidence across many species shows that organisms are **prepared** (through natural selection) to learn some associations and not prepared to learn others (Seligman, 1970). In Pavlovian conditioning, this can be seen where an animal will tend to associate some stimuli more strongly with certain outcomes than with others. Thus, a rat can more readily be classically conditioned to associate a sound (or a visual stimulus) with the pain of a shock than to associate a particular flavor with a painful shock. On the other hand, the rat is prepared to associate feelings of nausea with a prior flavor rather than with a certain sight or sound that preceded the feeling. The likelihood of associating nausea with a flavor tasted earlier remains high even when the rat experienced the taste several hours before feeling ill and the sound directly preceded the nausea (Garcia et al., 1974, 1985; Rozin & Kalat, 1971). The effects of preparedness on learning can be just as striking in operant conditioning. Thus, it is easy to train a pigeon to peck a button to get food or to flap its wings to

avoid shock (see Figure 4.26). But trying to shape it to perform the opposite associations—pecking to avoid a shock or flapping its wings to get food—will try the patience of even the most dedicated experimenter.

The pigeon and rat examples offer intuitive examples of why associations aren't formed in an unbiased manner. Many behaviors, especially those that appear earliest in an organism's life, are organized in ways that make functional sense for an organism in its normal environment. Thus, pigeons have evolved a set of escape behaviors that involve flapping their wings when they are in unpleasant or painful situations. Likewise, they have evolved a set of behaviors in seeking food that involve pecking at the ground (Woodruff & Williams, 1976). An animal's behavior is therefore intimately related to its typical environment, resulting in behaviors that are adapted to that environment, just as physical adaptations, like an animal's fur or webbed feet, are adapted to that environment. Thus, action is rarely arbitrary, but rather is directed by an organism toward solving certain problems in a particular environment.

We will see in Chapter 7 that the development of fears in human infants fits the idea of having prepared responses to certain stimuli. Human infants seem predisposed to develop a fear of snakes and spiders, but not of flowers or frogs (DeLoache & LoBue, 2009; Rakison & Derringer, 2008). These fears can form rapidly in infants who have never had negative experiences with snakes or spiders. In addition, monkeys reared in controlled settings where they never saw any snakes show a similarly strong bias to learn to fear them. In short, human infants seem very much like other primates in the ways they are prepared to associate some creatures with fear.

These constraints on conditioning—on both the context in which conditioning takes place and the ease or difficulty of forming particular associations—serve as a reminder that all actions, even those motivated by negative and positive

FIGURE 4.26 Prepared learning. Pigeons' tendencies to flap their wings and to peck are "prepared" to be associated much more strongly to some classes of events than others. It is much easier to train pigeons to flap their wings (and attempt to flee) to avoid shock than it is to get food, while the opposite is true for pecking.

reinforcements, develop within a framework of constraints. Those constraints do not necessarily specify which actions will develop. But they do make some kinds of associations, and therefore some kinds of behavioral responses, far easier to learn than others.

> **Q:** How are both classical and operant conditioning constrained such that not all associations are treated as equal?

Conclusions

Action does not develop in infancy either as a purely internal set of motor control programs or as a passive reflection of the pushes and pulls of various environmental contingencies. Instead, it arises from an interplay between dynamic properties of the body, the environment, and some elements of motor planning. The physical properties of a baby's limbs interact with specific environments, such as a tank of water or a ramp, in ways that become more than the sum of the individual elements. More broadly, action is an example of how much of development consists of dynamic interactions between distinct subsystems, whether they are perceptual and motor systems or different forms of information, such as spatial layout and number.

Across a wide range of approaches and topics, we have seen that the infant is constantly coordinating action with perception in ways that are critically dependent on the simultaneous feedback of self-produced movement. The feedback loop between a developing organism and its environment is an essential part of the developmental process and perhaps most easily seen and understood in cases of the development of action. As we saw in the discussion of perception and neural development in Chapter 3 and as we will see in later chapters, infants, children, and other developing organisms are often best understood in terms of their continuous cycles of interaction with their environment. We have also seen that an animal's actions are tailored for particular interactions with its specific environment, as in the linking of pigeon pecking to food-acquiring behavior. We have begun to think about constraints on development, leading to the idea that human infants (and infants in other species) are often endowed with preexisting frameworks that make certain actions more likely but do not predetermine them. This was particularly vivid in the development of birdsong, but it applies to many other cases as well. In Chapter 3, we saw some signs of preexisting frameworks in perceptual development, such as a schema for perceiving faces, but in this chapter we have gone beyond the perception of information to see how behavior itself conforms to different types of constraints. In later chapters, we will broaden this idea further to look at constraints on cognitive structures, on language, and on social behavior and emotions. In general, this chapter paints a picture of the infant as a dynamic, exploring, willful agent who is trying to make sense of and gain mastery over the world, much as we saw in Chapter 3. In Chapter 5, we turn to closely related questions about how the infant tries to make sense of that world.

SUMMARY

Foundations of Motor Development

- Newborn infants are endowed with many reflexes right from birth, including the patellar reflex, the rooting reflex, the grasp reflex, the stepping reflex, and the Moro reflex. Some of these reflexes disappear in the first few months of life. This is no longer thought to be solely a consequence of their inhibition by higher-level cognitive control, but rather is thought to reflect the changing properties of infants' muscles and limbs and the features of the environment in which they act.

- Psychologists have long documented various milestones in motor development, such as a sequence that proceeds from rolling over, to sitting, to crawling, to standing, and finally to walking, regardless of experience. It used to be thought that these sequences were merely consequences of increasing brain maturation. This view is now replaced by a view that emphasizes ranges and variation as to when normal behaviors appear, based on dynamic systems.

- Dynamic systems theory emphasizes the interactions between many components involved in executing behaviors and not just instructions being sent as one-way messages from the brain. Feedback loops are a central part of such an approach. The components include the physical environment, the physical properties of the body (especially the limbs), the properties of the brain and nervous system, and how the environment is being perceived.

- Dynamic systems theory has been supported by studies showing that minor changes in the limbs (for example, small weights attached to the limbs) or in the environment (for example, a ramp or a tank of water) can cause radical changes in motor behavior in the developing infant.

Perception and Action

- Action is often linked to perception, as in the case of reaching for an object. There are considerable challenges here, as the infant's body is undergoing dramatic changes while she is learning to guide her hands to an object.

- Through careful video analysis, it is possible to show that even newborn infants can crudely move their arms to reach in the direction of an appealing object or display. Their very early abilities serve as a framework that guides learning during perceptual-motor development.

- As infants grow older, they are able to use feedback from their perception of their own actions to fine-tune their movements to more and more accurate actions. But to do so, infants must perceive the consequences of their self-produced actions in real time. If they are made to be passive observers of actions made by others, they will not learn to fine-tune their actions. This effect has been well documented in kittens and increasingly in human infants.

- Walking might seem to be a skill that develops merely because of increasingly sophisticated signals coming from the brain. It is instead dependent on visual feedback of how the world is flowing by and on feedback from the infant's muscles and touch receptors. It also depends on the properties of the limbs, such that heavy babies take longer to walk because the walking system is so fragile that a little extra baby fat is enough to interfere with early walking.

Learning to Engage in Specific Actions

- One of the most dramatic early actions is imitation. Newborn infants will imitate several different facial expressions, as will newborn monkeys. Remarkably, the monkeys will imitate faces of another species, namely humans. Imitation requires a sophisticated mapping between perception, memory, and action, and it may involve a special set of neurons known as mirror neurons.

- The development of birdsong showcases several important patterns pertaining to the development of action. The variation across different species of birds shows that there are many possible developmental pathways for learning complex motor behaviors from models. Birdsong development illustrates critical periods and the great importance of perceptual-motor feedback in learning songs. The different patterns of birdsong development also illustrate how a framework of innate biases guides learning species-specific song elements.

- Imprinting is learning that seems to occur during a special time period, after which it becomes irreversible. It is most notable in many birds that normally imprint on their mothers but can be tricked into imprinting on a wide variety of other moving objects. It seems to involve an initial tracking system that makes moving objects of roughly maternal size the most salient, and an independent system known as the IMHV that leads the chick to imprint onto a particular individual, usually its mother, during a critical period.

- In conditioning, organisms learn to produce actions in response to environmental contingencies. Through classical conditioning, an organism learns how stimuli are related; through operant conditioning, an organism learns the consequences of its actions.

- Classical conditioning consists of identifying a preexisting stimulus-response relationship and then associating a new stimulus with the first stimulus, such that the new stimulus now produces an action similar to the original response. Originally demonstrated in dogs by Pavlov, it has been demonstrated many times in infants from birth onward, and it can occur even when infants are sleeping. John Watson used the phenomenon of classical conditioning, as demonstrated with Little Albert, to make broad claims about child rearing from the viewpoint of behaviorism.

- Operant conditioning is concerned with how organisms learn to operate on their environments in response to positive and negative reinforcements. Through the technique of shaping, in which the researchers reward spontaneous actions that come closer and closer to resembling a desired behavior, it is possible to get animals to produce chained sequences of novel behaviors, a technique that was greatly refined by B. F. Skinner, another proponent of behaviorism.

- Both classical and operant conditioning occur within a framework of constraints that can sharply limit what associations are learned and what behaviors are elicited in response to a stimulus. Organisms are prepared by natural selection to make certain associations and certain stimulus-response pairings that have adaptive value for those organisms in their environmental and ecological niches.

THOUGHT QUESTIONS

1. How can imitation be related to empathy? Infant imitation has often been described as a way of setting up feelings of empathy with another. Empathy, however, can have several forms, ranging from simple emotions to understanding another's point of view. Consider what forms of empathy would and would not likely be facilitated by infant imitation.

2. Why would imprinting behavior be selected for in the evolution of some species but not others? How might a species' developmental growth patterns, its relations to other members of the same species, and its niche be relevant?

3. Why are prepared associations useful? You have read how rats and pigeons are "prepared" to make certain associations more than others and that humans may be "prepared" to associate certain organisms with fear. What other associations might humans also be more prepared to form?

4. Can infants display early indications of exceptional motor skills? In several countries that have strong government support of Olympic development programs, scouts try to find evidence of extraordinary motor skill at younger and younger ages. If you were such a scout, what evidence, if any, would you use to identify infants under 1 year of age who are gifted with such extraordinary motor skills?

KEY TERMS

affordances (p. 129)

behaviorism (p. 139)

blocking (p. 140)

classical conditioning (p. 138)

conditioned response (CR) (p. 138)

conditioned stimulus (CS) (p. 138)

dynamic systems theory (p. 120)

grasp reflex (p. 117)

imprinting (p. 135)

instrumental conditioning (p. 139)

maturational account (p. 119)

mirror neuron (p. 132)

Moro reflex (p. 117)

motor deprivation (p. 119)

operant conditioning (p. 139)

patellar reflex (p. 117)

perceptual-motor development (p. 122)

prepared (p. 141)

prereaching (p. 123)

reflex (p. 117)

rooting reflex (p. 117)

shaping (p. 139)

stepping reflex (p. 117)

tabula rasa (p. 139)

unconditioned response (UCR) (p. 138)

unconditioned stimulus (UCS) (p. 138)

visual flow fields (p. 128)

5

Coming to Understand the Physical World

Piaget's Approach
- Piaget's Theory of Cognitive Development
- The Sensorimotor Period in Infancy
- Key Aspects of Piaget's Theory
- Examining the A-Not-B Error

Infant Knowledge and Understanding
- Thinking about the Unseen
- Understanding Causation

- The Use of Number
- Spatial Knowledge in Infants
- Categorization in Infants

Distinguishing the Physical World from the Social World
- Action at a Distance and Social Contingency
- Goal and Belief Attribution

Conclusions

Summary

ell before the end of their first year of life, each of our three sons had made many dozens of trips to the lake near our house. By the lake, we would throw stones that skipped along the surface and then sank and disappeared. The small waves lapping at their feet, the bobbing driftwood near the shore, the trees' leaves fluttering in the wind—all were objects of great fascination. What crossed their minds as they watched the world so avidly? Did they think that the stones that disappeared under water ceased to exist? Did they have a sense that the lake water was anything like the water in which they bathed? Did they understand why the leaves fluttered or that they even needed a cause to move? When they saw a duck out on the water or waddling on the bank, did they think of it as a living being with different capacities from an inanimate object? When they saw two pieces of wood drift under the dock, did they expect to see two pieces emerge on the other side? More broadly, as young infants, did they think about the world in qualitatively different ways than older infants or children think about it; or was there much more continuity to their cognitive development? These same kinds of questions pertain to the mental lives of infants throughout the world. This chapter examines how developmental psychologists have explored such questions scientifically.

In Chapters 3 and 4, we considered how the infant comes to perceive and act on the world. Coming to understand that world and hold specific beliefs about it is quite another task, even as it intimately depends on perception and action. In this chapter, we will consider infant cognition—that is, the capacity of infants to think, reason, and use knowledge about the world. We will see that considerable complexity lies beneath an infant's cognitions. But because infants can't explain their thought processes to us, developmental questions about their minds often revolve around whether their thoughts and knowledge are explicit or implicit. **Explicit cognition** involves having an awareness of knowledge or of a thought process, usually in a way that can be described in words, such as knowing that Paris is the capital of France or knowing the rules for solving a crossword puzzle. **Implicit cognition** works outside of awareness and may be difficult to describe in words. It might include the thoughts underlying the sense that an animal is sick, even if you can't say why, or the knowledge that helps you ride a bicycle, even though you can't fully explain the skill. We will see that recognizing the difference between explicit and implicit cognition plays an important role in understanding early cognitive development, often with the initial assumption that the cognition of young infants and other animals is mostly implicit.

We will explore cognition in several areas of infant development. In particular, we will consider how infants understand an object's physical properties (for example, its solidity or its continued presence when out of sight) and the causal

relationships between interacting objects, as well as how they understand different numbers of objects. We will also look at how infants think about physical space and how they come to view objects as members of categories (for example, knowing that a poodle is a dog and that a dog is an animal). Finally, we will consider how infants distinguish social agents that act (and react) on their own from inanimate objects.

Throughout the chapter, we will draw on some familiar developmental themes. We will investigate whether infant cognition is just a simpler version of older children's or adults' thinking or whether it is qualitatively different. Moreover, when infants show marked cognitive change, does that change seem to occur globally, affecting all kinds of thought and understanding, or does it seem limited to one kind of cognition, such as thinking about spatial relationships or understanding numbers? And in what ways is the infant's mind adapted, or receptive from the start, to think about the world in particular ways?

We will begin by exploring the work of Jean Piaget, the twentieth century's most influential developmental psychologist. In this chapter, we will discuss Piaget's general approach and his theory of infancy, along with the recent surge of research that suggests that infants have greater cognitive capacities than Piaget believed possible. In later chapters, we will consider Piaget's theories of childhood.

Piaget's Approach

It is impossible to fully understand Jean Piaget's approach to development without knowing a little about who he was (see Figure 5.1). Born in 1896 in Neuchâtel, Switzerland, Piaget showed an early scientific bent and was particularly fascinated by biology. His first publication came early—at the age of 10—and was followed by more than 20 additional biological papers by the time he was 21. When this impressive record earned him an offer to become a curator at a Geneva museum, he surprised the museum officials, who had assumed he was much older, when he declined the job because he had not yet finished school (Flavell, 1963; Piaget, 1952a).

In the following years, Piaget became increasingly interested in psychology, always taking what he considered a biological perspective. He did not focus on the inner biological mechanisms that lead to behavior but instead used biological concepts such as adaptation to the environment, relationships between the structure and the function of particular adaptations, and the developmental unfolding of structure over time to explore cognitive development. When he was roughly 24, he began working in Paris in the laboratory of Alfred Binet, a researcher whose studies of school-age children led him to develop the first workable standardized intelligence test. In Binet's lab, Piaget began interviewing large groups of children

FIGURE 5.1 Piaget. Jean Piaget (1896–1980) is the undisputed giant in the history of the study of cognitive development. His work over a span of several decades revolutionized the study of the developing mind.

and became fascinated with the kinds of mistakes on experimental tasks that children commonly make at different ages. To Piaget, these changes suggested a series of stages in normal cognitive development. Piaget returned to Switzerland, where he held a variety of academic posts and remained actively engaged in research until his death in 1980.

The scope of Piaget's work is breathtaking. He wrote more than two dozen major books and hundreds of articles on topics ranging from children's understanding of time, space, and number to topics in biology and philosophy, and he inspired an extraordinary range of studies in developmental psychology. Especially in the 1960s and 1970s, as the influence of behaviorism declined and researchers began reincorporating the workings of the mind into their explanations of behavior, there was a renewed interest in Piaget's work. It offered a way to bring cognition back into developmental psychology. Because his body of research is so vast, our goal here is to outline its most important trends and their place within developmental psychology. We will then present some of the more recent research that has challenged some of Piaget's assumptions and explanations.

Piaget's Theory of Cognitive Development

Piaget's theory describes several processes of cognitive development. To characterize those processes, Piaget thought of the child's knowledge and behavior in terms of schemes. A **scheme** describes a child's pattern of interacting with her environment; it includes the child's internal knowledge and interpretations

and also the behaviors that arise from them. Children are constantly engaging in a process of **adaptation**, by which the child better fits her schemes with new experiences in the environment. The two most basic forms of adaptation through which the child tries to achieve a better fit between her schemes and the world are known as *assimilation* and *accommodation*.

Assimilation is the process in which the child interprets something new and unfamiliar in terms of preexisting schemes—that is, behaviors and concepts that are already familiar to her. The result can often be a distorted or severely narrow view of that aspect of the world. Thus, if a 1-year-old has talked to relatives on a cell phone, she might first think that a television remote is somewhat like a cell phone, and after pushing its buttons, she may try talking into it. She has assimilated the remote control into the richer knowledge she already has about cell phones, but she has distorted her understanding of the remote control in the process. In contrast, **accommodation** occurs when the child alters her schemes—that is, her behavior or understanding—to better fit something new she has encountered. If our 1-year-old adjusts her knowledge of cell phones and how to use them in a way that incorporates the differences between the remote control and a cell phone, she has used accommodation. Through this process, she may realize that she does not need to speak into the remote, but it does help to point it at the television. As a result, she has differentiated her understanding of the cell phone and the remote.

Piaget suggested that we rarely see pure cases of accommodation or assimilation; rather, the two almost always work in concert to achieve the best fit between the child and the environment. There may be cases where assimilation dominates, but usually some small adjustments of behavior and knowledge are also needed. Similarly, there may be cases where accommodation dominates, but in order to relate the new scheme to the world as we know it, some assimilation must also occur.

This process in which both accommodation and assimilation work together to foster a better cognitive fit with the environment is known as **equilibration** (see Figure 5.2). We can think of equilibration as the child's tendency to achieve a dynamic balance between her schemes and her environment. Piaget conceived of a continuous and active interplay between the child's schemes and the phenomena in the world. In Piaget's terms, equilibration describes the process of achieving a closer correspondence between the environment and the child's thoughts and behaviors. This correspondence is never perfect, but for Piaget, improving it is the motivating force behind cognitive development. Thus, the 1-year-old girl who has never before seen a TV remote control has a mismatch between her existing cognitive structures and processes, or schemes, and how well they can be used to understand the remote control—so she strives to find a better match. This is equilibration.

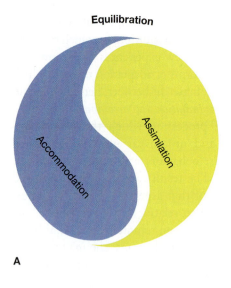

Equilibration

Accommodation

Assimilation

A

B

C

FIGURE 5.2 Equilibration and its two components: assimilation and accommodation. (A) Equilibration is seen as composed of two complementary processes of assimilation and accommodation. With assimilation, the child interprets new and unfamiliar things in terms of existing mental structures and concepts. With accommodation, the child adjusts her behaviors and concepts to better fit the environment. **(B)** When an infant first encounters a TV remote control, she may cognitively assimilate it into the more developed mental representation that she has for a wireless phone. **(C)** Somewhat later, she may accommodate her mental structures and behaviors for the remote control in ways that more closely relate to the unique properties of the remote control.

> **Q:** What is equilibration? What are the two processes that make up equilibration?

In Piaget's view, infants and children use various schemes to interact with their environment. Since these schemes are never perfectly matched with the aspects of the environment that they seek to interpret, children use equilibration to bring their schemes into closer alignment with the world they encounter, doing so through the complementary processes of assimilation and accommodation. As the schemes are adjusted through accommodation, their structure changes, perhaps modestly at first, but over time they may be completely reorganized.

A distinctive aspect of Piaget's theory is its emphasis on discrete periods and stages of development. Piaget is known as a stage theorist because he believed that assimilation and accommodation of many schemes lead to qualitative changes in cognition, which is evident in children's major leaps in understanding at certain points in development. In contrast, some approaches view development as a more gradual process of continuous, incremental change—quantitative change—as described in Chapter 1.

Piaget envisioned four periods of development across the lifespan: the *sensorimotor period*, from birth to roughly 2 years; the *preoperational period*, from roughly 2 years to 7 years; the *concrete operational period*, from roughly 7 years to 12 years; and the *formal operational period*, from roughly 12 years on. Table 5.1 outlines these four periods. We will discuss each of these periods in the appropriate chapter. Here we will discuss more general aspects of the stage theory before exploring the sensorimotor period in depth.

By dividing cognitive development into four periods, Piaget was proposing distinct, qualitative changes in the child's thinking about the world. During each period, the child acquires many new schemes—until she accumulates enough new understanding to trigger a transformation in her thought processes, leading her into the next period. Piaget believed that each period operates in a domain-general way; that is, during each period, the child uses certain characteristic ways of thinking to develop schemes about all aspects of the world—not just about one specific area, such as social agents. The only way to proceed from one period to the next is to accumulate enough new knowledge from experience to cause a reorganization of the schemes. Piaget observed that the specific ages associated with each period vary from child to child. By contrast, he believed that the order of the periods never changes, since each period provides a necessary foundation for the next one.

> **Q:** Describe Piaget's four periods of cognitive development and the distinguishing features of each.

Period of Cognitive Development	Age	Hallmark
Sensorimotor period	Birth–2 years	Infants learn to distinguish their own bodies and actions from the external world around them.
Preoperational period	2–7 years	Children can use symbols to mentally represent objects, but they fail to use mental operations that enable them to see the quasi-logical relations governing phenomena.
Concrete operational period	7–12 years	Children can apply quasi-logical operations to concrete information, but they fail to think abstractly or in hypothetical terms.
Formal operational period	12 years on	Children are able to think logically about things that are not immediately present and about abstract and hypothetical ideas.

TABLE 5.1 Piaget's four periods of cognitive development. Each of Piaget's four periods describes a qualitatively distinct way of understanding the world. The associated ages provide rough guidelines and can vary considerably across children.

Where would Piaget fall along the nativist/empiricist continuum? His view of infants and children as striving to understand the world better through assimilation and accommodation stresses an active, exploratory developmental process. While he clearly disagreed with the empiricist view of the infant as a passive vessel or blank slate, his emphasis on the domain generality of cognitive development and his notion that all knowledge is built up through experience made him an empiricist. Although he certainly was concerned with the mind (unlike a behaviorist) and with complex cognitive structures (rather than the simple networks of a classic associationist), he was nonetheless deeply at odds with the nativists' central tenets. Unlike the nativists, he never proposed that the mind has any innate biases toward particular areas of thought. Thus, while Piaget believed in innate schemes that work in ways that go beyond mere associations, he did not believe in the nativist view that there are innate domain-specific constraints for understanding such areas of knowledge as spatial layout, number, or the properties of physical objects. To better understand the details of Piaget's approach to infancy, we will turn to his description of the sensorimotor period.

Q: Is Piaget's approach more compatible with nativism or empiricism?

The Sensorimotor Period in Infancy

Piaget called the first 2 years of life the **sensorimotor period**. As he did for each of the four periods of cognitive development, Piaget further divided the sensorimotor period into smaller stages that give it texture and depth. He proposed that there are six distinct stages within the sensorimotor period (Piaget, 1952b). His evidence for these stages was especially personal, coming almost exclusively from detailed observations of his own three children.

Piaget saw a great deal of activity going on in infants during each of the six sensorimotor stages. This overview briefly characterizes each stage, focusing on the infant's understanding of physical objects, a form of understanding that Piaget called the **object concept**, an idea central to his overall theory of the sensorimotor period. Piaget's account of the object concept focuses on **object permanence**—how the infant comes to think of objects as things that still exist even when they are out of sight and not being used or acted on.

Stage 1 (Birth to 1 Month): Use of Reflexes Piaget believed that the very young infant interacts with the environment by means of relatively fixed, innate routines, or reflexes, which Piaget viewed as the simplest early versions of schemes. Among Piaget's examples of these infant reflexes, the most commonly mentioned are those related to breastfeeding, such as the sucking reflex, which is present from birth. In Piaget's view, these reflexive behaviors are not completely fixed, however. Rather, by interacting with the world, infants learn—through the processes of assimilation and accommodation—to modify the simple schemes that influence their reflexive behaviors. For example, Piaget repeatedly observed that his own children became increasingly proficient at finding their mother's nipple and at maintaining active sucking while nursing (thus modifying the sucking reflex through accommodation). The sucking reflex changed in ways that were directly related to the object it acted on, the breast. Thus, the infant "fine-tuned" the preexisting sucking reflex to make it more optimal for recovering milk from the breast. Similarly, one of our sons initially had trouble breathing while he was nursing, since he would bury his face in the breast and cover up his nose while sucking vigorously until he would come up for air. As the days passed, however, he began to show accommodation as he learned to breathe while nursing by turning his head to the side and by not pressing so hard. Through these kinds of modifications of schemes related to early reflexes, infants are able to change their behaviors and eventually integrate them into more sophisticated actions. In this way, according to Piaget, the infant's reflexes form the building blocks for more complex behaviors.

Piaget believed that the infant experiences the world in a radically different way than older children and adults do. In Sensorimotor Stage 1, infants have no awareness of objects as being "out there," independent of their own actions (see Figure 5.3). Instead, they understand objects only in the context of their own ways of routinely interacting with the world. In the breastfeeding example, the infants are focused on sucking and have little awareness that the breast itself is a distinct object; if the infants saw the breast from another angle rather than the close-up nursing position, they would not recognize it as the same object involved in nursing. This concept of the infant's experience is at odds with the research on intermodal perception described in Chapters 3 and 4, in which infants showed very early abilities to integrate information from different perceptual systems, such as vision and touch. As we will see, Piaget's view is also at odds with the more recent research on infant cognition.

> Q: What role do reflexes play in Piaget's first sensorimotor stage?

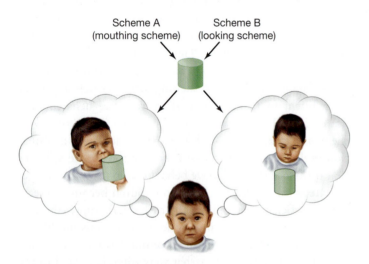

FIGURE 5.3 Multiple schemes and understanding objects.
According to Piaget, the young infant can have very different impressions of the same object when understood through different schemes. In this case, looking at a cylinder from one particular angle confers a distorted perspective, whereas mouthing the cylinder distorts it by focusing attention on its edge. According to Piaget, an infant would not even realize that the same object was involved, but later research raised doubts about this notion.

Stage 2 (1 to 4 Months): Emergence of Primary Circular Reactions

In Sensorimotor Stage 1, infants begin modifying their reflexes into more effective behaviors, or motor schemes. In Sensorimotor Stage 2, Piaget saw infants using and modifying their schemes in increasingly flexible ways to get better at stimulating themselves. The hallmark of this stage is the **primary circular reaction**, in which the infant discovers by chance that she can use her motor schemes from the first stage to interact with "new objects"—specifically, new parts of her own body (see Figure 5.4). If the infant finds that new action pleasing, she will try to reproduce it. Then, as these attempts lead to small adjustments in the original behavior, she will accommodate her original scheme to include the new body part and the new action. Since schemes cannot be changed completely, her original scheme partly shapes her understanding of the new behavior, so assimilation also occurs.

Infants can also create new schemes through primary circular reactions, but only schemes discovered accidentally and directed toward parts of their own bodies. Piaget offered an example in which his son, in the process of sucking, happened to have his tongue protrude beyond his mouth and touch his lower lip. He discovered that this was a pleasing sensation and attempted to repeat it. As he gradually became better at quickly licking his lower lip, he built a new scheme for lip-licking. Accommodation occurs here because as the licking scheme develops, it changes in ways related to the sensations of the lip. Assimilation is also involved because the infant's understanding of his lip is heavily influenced by learning about it through his lip-licking scheme.

The schemes developed by primary circular reactions are therefore routines in which infants learn to stimulate themselves better and better. In this context, Piaget argued that infants' understanding of objects remains largely unchanged from Sensorimotor Stage 1 to Stage 2. The infants still do not understand objects (including parts of their own bodies) as existing independently, but rather they see them as embedded in particular behavioral schemes. Thus, as infants in Stage 2 learn to interact with their own bodies in new ways, they remember only the actions and the effects they produced, not the objects that the actions involved.

Piaget recognized that even the most careful observations of his own children were not enough to build a theory of the sensorimotor period, so he developed predictions based on his observations and set out to test whether they held true for other infants. Some of his most interesting predictions concerned the object concept. For instance, as we have seen, Piaget believed that infants in Stages 1 and 2 cannot represent objects as existing independently and that the infants can only understand objects as parts of an ongoing scheme. The objects would vanish when the scheme was no longer being used. Piaget thus predicted that infants in Stages 1 and 2 would not search for an object once it was out of

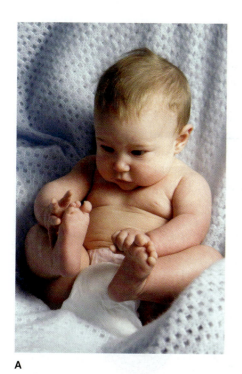
A

B

C

FIGURE 5.4 The developing object concept. As seen in these photos, young infants will scrutinize with apparent concentration many objects, including parts of their own bodies. Researchers on infant cognition are trying to understand how the infant thinks about those objects, such as whether he thinks that they are whole enduring entities that exist when out of sight.

sight. For example, if an infant playing with her favorite rattle accidentally dropped it between the folds of a blanket, she would not search for it, since she would not realize that the rattle continued to exist when she lost sight of it. For the same reason, Piaget believed that infants would not understand that an object's properties can change. For example, if an object is moving, the infant would watch it with a "tracking scheme"; but if the object suddenly stopped moving, the infant would continue tracking along the path the object would have taken if it had continued to move. Piaget based this prediction on the idea that because a moving object and a stationary object require different schemes, the infant is unaware that the stationary object is the same one that was moving a moment before.

> **Q:** According to Piaget, how do infants in Sensorimotor Stage 2 understand objects?

Stage 3 (4 to 9 Months): Appearance of Secondary Circular Reactions In Sensorimotor Stage 3, the infant further expands and modifies his set of schemes, most notably through the process of **secondary circular reactions**. Secondary circular reactions represent a major advance over the primary circular reactions of the previous stage because they involve applying new schemes to external objects, not just to

the infant's own body. Although younger infants do act on objects other than their own bodies, Piaget held that in Stage 3 they develop new schemes specifically for interacting with external objects. This is the first small step toward developing limited notions of an external world. But at this point, infants still recognize objects only in terms of the schemes in which they are embedded, rather than viewing them independently.

Like the primary circular reactions, secondary circular reactions initially happen by chance; then, if the behavior is pleasing, the infant reproduces it. The key advance in Stage 3 is that the infant acts on something other than his own body (see Figure 5.5). He might shake a rattle and find the noise interesting, then shake it again to repeat the sound. Over time, he would become more efficient at making the sound, producing a new rattle-shaking scheme. All three of Piaget's children showed secondary circular reactions to mobiles suspended over their bassinets. Each one discovered by chance that leg movements caused the mobile to move. As they sought to repeat this effect, they became increasingly efficient at integrating schemes: moving their legs while simultaneously watching the mobile. With time, such schemes become increasingly sophisticated. For example, an infant might modify the scheme of the mobile by performing an abbreviated and simplified version of the full scheme as a kind of shorthand way of recognizing it. Thus, an infant might give a brief perfunctory leg shake on recognizing a mobile, a leg shake that is a shortened and smaller version of the original that actually moved the mobile and made it exciting.

A   **B**

FIGURE 5.5 Secondary circular reactions and interactions with external objects. Infants in the 4- to 9-month-old age range start to explore objects, such as **(A)** the rattle and **(B)** the mobile, with ever more attention to the objects' unique properties. The infant in Sensorimotor Stage 3 initially discovers the sound of the rattle or the movement of the mobile by chance and then uses secondary circular reactions (shaking the rattle, setting the mobile in motion) to act purposefully on the object.

Q: How can a Sensorimotor Stage 3 infant develop actions tailored for an object but not really know that the object exists in its own right? Give an example.

As he did for Stages 1 and 2, Piaget tested predictions about how Stage 3 infants would respond to particular ways of manipulating objects. For example, he predicted that in Stage 3, objects completely out of sight are still "out of mind." But he thought that infants in Stage 3 would sometimes retrieve an object that had been partially covered, because their schemes were sophisticated enough to act on just part of an object, such as a rattle's handle. Piaget also predicted that if a blanket were placed in front of a Stage 3 infant's face, she would push it aside to reach for an object, but if the same blanket directly covered an object that she wanted, she would not remove it. Piaget maintained that the infant would move the blanket away from her face not to get at an object that she couldn't see, but rather to allow the looking scheme to operate. Once the looking scheme could again operate, seeing the object would then trigger a reaching scheme, and the infant would reach for the object. On the other hand, when the blanket covered an object, the infant could still use her looking scheme, but there would be no object visible to elicit it.

Stage 4 (9 to 12 Months): Coordination of Secondary Circular Reactions Stage 4 is perhaps when the most significant transitions in the sensorimotor period occur. Although there are no new behavioral hallmarks, such as the circular reactions, the infant is now integrating his vast array of relatively independent schemes into a smaller number of more complex and flexible schemes (see Figure 5.6). A key process for the infant in Stage 4 is interacting with the same object in various ways or, in Piaget's terms, applying multiple schemes to the same object. Through this process, the infant

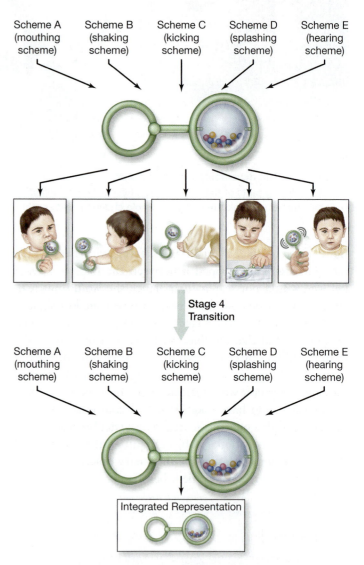

FIGURE 5.6 Integration of secondary schemes. As infants enter Sensorimotor Stage 4, they transition from seeing each object differently, depending on their schemes for using it, to a more integrated set of schemes that can support a more objective, scheme-independent understanding of the object. Thus, in Stage 3, each scheme involves a different representation of the object. After the transition to Stage 4, the schemes are unified into an integrated representation, and the infant's understanding of the object is no longer "embedded" in any one scheme.

begins to get a sense that the object has enduring properties and that it exists independently of his actions. "Viewing" the same object from the contrasting vantage points of several different schemes starts to bring the objective qualities of the object into relief. Consider again the infant's rattle. If an infant starts to put together the rattle-shaking scheme with a rattle-mouthing scheme, a rattle-hearing scheme, and a rattle-splashing scheme, she will start to understand that certain properties of the rattle persist across these different schemes. These properties start to emerge as ways of characterizing the rattle independently from any particular scheme. Thus, infants in Stage 4 undergo a dramatic transition as they start to integrate schemes and come closer to realizing that distinct objects exist "out there" in the world.

Even though infants at Stage 4 are beginning to use more integrated schemes to understand objects, they still do not truly appreciate objects existing apart from schemes. Infants in this stage will now retrieve a fully hidden object, but according to Piaget, they will not fully represent the object when it is out of sight (see Figure 5.7). In support of this idea, Piaget showed that although infants at this stage will retrieve a fully hidden object, they tend to make a particular type of mistake in their searching, known as the **A-not-B error**, or the **place error**. Infants make this error when an object has been repeatedly hidden for them to discover in the same spot (place A), but then the object is hidden in a new spot (place B) while the infant watches. Infants making the A-not-B error will again search for the object in place A, where it was previously hidden, even when other cues, such as a bulging cover, strongly suggest the new location. Piaget believed that by repeatedly finding the object hidden in the same spot, Stage 4 infants develop a particular scheme for retrieving that object at a particular location. He interpreted the A-not-B error as a consequence of the infant's inability to apply a new scheme to the object in its new location, since the object is still embedded within the older scheme.

A   **B**

FIGURE 5.7 The A-not-B error. The Stage 4 infant searches for the hidden object under cover A, where it was initially hidden and recovered several times, even though it was last hidden in location B. (In the actual experiment, the hidden object is not at all visible.)

cases where his children would experiment with different ways of acting on objects. For the first time, a baby might play with a bath toy by looking for the effects that dropping has on the object rather than focusing on the dropping action itself. Thus, while a Stage 4 baby might release the toy after holding it in the air and focus on the releasing action, the Stage 5 baby would drop the toy so as to make the biggest splash or to make it sink. Piaget referred to this as "the discovery of new means through active experimentation"(Piaget, 1952b), meaning that the child is constantly and intentionally discovering new ways of learning about objects.

There is, however, one critical way in which Stage 5 infants still have an immature object concept. Although they no longer commit the A-not-B error (they can find objects that were hidden while they were watching), they are unable to think about the objects as changing location while out of sight. This inability comes to light in their failure to understand **invisible displacement**, in which a hidden object is moved to a new hiding spot. In the simplest kind of invisible displacement, commonly known as a "shell game" (see Figure 5.8), an infant is shown an object being put under a cover, which is next to another cover of the same type. The two covers are then moved very slowly, in full view of the infant, so that they trade places. When the infant is asked to find the hidden object, she will usually reach for the cover at the location where the object was originally hidden. Apparently, she is unable to mentally keep track of the object's movement while it is hidden.

> **Q:** What is the A-not-B error, and why is it also known as the place error?

Stage 5 (12 to 18 Months): Appearance of Tertiary Circular Reactions An important new milestone in Stage 5 is the appearance of **tertiary circular reactions**, in which infants use schemes intentionally. In this stage, infants begin intentionally coordinating their use of schemes in innovative and creative ways to actively explore the world. And unlike infants in earlier stages, infants in Stage 5 finally understand objects as existing independently from their schemes. Piaget commented on several

> **Q:** What are invisible displacements, and why doesn't the infant in Sensorimotor Stage 5 understand them?

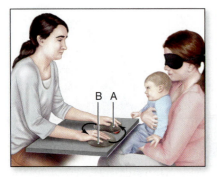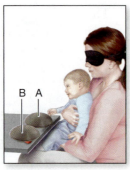

FIGURE 5.8 Invisible displacements. The error of invisible displacements occurs when an infant watches an adult hide an object under a cover and then watches the adult move the cover so that it slowly changes places with another cover. The infant searches where the object was initially hidden (place A) rather than at its new location (place B). (In the actual experiment, the hidden object is not at all visible.)

period. Most notable is the emergence of language, which Piaget took to be the most easily observable manifestations of a new competence in symbolic thinking—namely, the ability to use structured sounds (words) and relations (sentences) to stand for real-world things. For Piaget, language does not emerge as an independent skill following its own developmental course; it is inextricably linked to the ability to think symbolically, which also signals the transition out of the sensorimotor period.

Table 5.2 summarizes the six stages of the sensorimotor period and the significant developments found at each stage. As with Piaget's broader stages, the ages can vary across children. But Piaget believed that the stages themselves emerge only in one order. The significant developments focus on the object concept, which is where Piaget put his primary emphasis and where the most empirical support for his ideas is found.

Stage 6 (18 Months to 2 Years): Invention of New Means through Mental Combinations In Stage 6 of the sensorimotor period, the child can flexibly use schemes and can more powerfully represent objects and their relations. She knows that objects continue to exist apart from schemes and regardless of whether they are hidden or moved. And she can solve invisible displacements because she not only can represent an object in her mind, but can also manipulate her mental representation. The emphasis on more powerful cognitive representations and thought processes is also linked to a much broader array of changes in children during this

Key Aspects of Piaget's Theory

Piaget's theory of cognitive development in infancy is an extraordinary account for several reasons. First, it offers a dramatic view of infants as experiencing a very different world from the rest of us. In this view, younger infants cannot differentiate between objects and the actions they perform on those objects, and thus they do not understand that there is an external world separate from themselves. Quite unlike adults, young infants have no awareness beyond the schemes they are currently using.

Sensorimotor Stage	Age	Significant Developments
1. Use of reflexes	Birth–1 month	The infant's actions are mostly reflexive, but even at this stage, the infant learns to modify actions that began as reflexes.
2. Emergence of primary circular reactions	1–4 months	The infant discovers by chance the application of motor schemes to self and modifies schemes. The first acquired adaptations appear.
3. Appearance of secondary circular reactions	4–9 months	The infant now applies schemes more directly to other objects and modifies schemes accordingly. The infant discovers procedures designed to make interesting sights last.
4. Coordination of secondary circular reactions	9–12 months	The infant now links schemes together and starts to get a more objective sense of objects, but still interprets objects in terms of each specific scheme and not as objects per se. The infant now applies schemes to new situations.
5. Appearance of tertiary circular reactions	12–18 months	The infant now uses schemes intentionally to actively explore the world, and schemes are now truly subordinate to objects. The infant discovers new ways of acting on objects through active experimentation.
6. Invention of new means through mental combinations	18 months–2 years	The child can symbolically represent objects and their relations.

TABLE 5.2 Piaget's six stages of the sensorimotor period. Piaget's theory of six sensorimotor stages forms an essential backdrop for all later research in infant cognitive development. His ideas motivated many studies on infant cognition, the majority of which focused on infants' understanding of objects, and much of that work eventually challenged Piaget's theory.

Second, this view offers a detailed model of development that was one of the first to explain the mental states and processes underlying behavioral changes. Piaget theorized that higher-level cognition develops out of an inevitable progression of structures. Starting with reflexes, infants begin modifying those behaviors, allowing them to develop even more flexible schemes. These schemes are used first in self-directed actions, then applied to external objects, then gradually integrated into increasingly complex schemes that help the child gain an objective sense of what is "out there." This is a more sophisticated empiricist account than the early ones described in Chapter 3, in which infants begin life with only basic sensory capabilities and the ability to form associations. In Piaget's view, infants also have modifiable reflexes through which they begin learning about the world.

Third, this view stresses domain generality, in which stage changes affect everything that the infant does and thinks about. Thus, regardless of the cognitive domain, the transition to a new stage influences thinking and reasoning on all tasks in which a child is engaged. Whether the domain is number, spatial representations, or language, changes in a stage will fundamentally change how a child thinks in each case.

Finally, Piaget left us with lots of observational and experimental data. Much of his data revolved around the infant's object concept, which Piaget used to illustrate many aspects of his theory of sensorimotor development. Piaget's studies suggested that young infants can think about objects only in terms of currently active schemes and not as objects in their own right. Only by gradually elaborating and integrating schemes can infants finally become able to understand independent objects well after the first year of life.

Piaget's account of infancy is so comprehensive and compelling that it was considered mostly correct for many decades, and his work continues to motivate many studies. Since Piaget's time, however, researchers have come to question significant aspects of his theory, and clever experiments have revealed new insights about how infants think. Building on our exploration of Piaget's sensorimotor theory, we next turn to more current views of how infants understand the world, beginning with a new look at the object concept.

Examining the A-Not-B Error

Many studies have challenged Piaget's idea of the object concept. As early as 1971, researchers asked whether there were alternative explanations for the errors that Piaget observed young infants making. They hypothesized that infants might be aware of objects' independent existence but have other cognitive limitations that cause the errors (Bower, 1971, 1974).

The A-not-B error is one observation that has been explained differently in more recent research. Recall that infants make this error when, after repeatedly finding an object hidden in the same place, they then watch it being hidden in a new place but still search for it where they had found it before. Piaget considered this a failure to apply a new scheme to the object. But some researchers believe that infants' diligent searching for the unseen object may be evidence that infants are indeed mentally representing the object, in spite of their failure to correctly locate it (Ruffman et al., 2005). In one study, experimenters used the standard procedure, repeatedly hiding an object at place A, then obviously moving it to place B. But instead of using the infants' reaching to assess their understanding, experimenters observed the infants' reactions when they saw the object that had clearly been hidden in place B retrieved either from A, the "impossible" location, or from place B. They found that even infants who reached for the object at place A were more surprised when the object was found there, indicating that, despite their reach, they had expected to find it at place B (Ahmed & Ruffman, 1998). In other studies that used more hiding places, a similar pattern of results emerged: although they reached for the object at the wrong location (A), infants would also look at the correct location (B) more than at another location (C) (Cummings & Bjork, 1983; Diamond et al., 1994). These studies pointed out difficulties with Piaget's account, but they still did not fully explain what causes the errors.

Studies in both humans and other primates suggest a different account of the place error, one that suggests that infants can understand an enduring external world but are not yet fully competent in certain cognitive and motor skills to act successfully on the external world. As we have seen, Piaget believed that infants make this error because they cannot fully mentally represent unseen objects. The most prominent alternative account focuses instead on the reaching action involved in retrieving the hidden object. As discussed in Chapter 4, several of the earliest reflexes appear to be more robust in younger infants. Two of these, the grasp reflex and the avoidance reflex (a tendency to pull a limb back from sharp objects or edges), may interfere with retrieval when the object is hidden next to a barrier or anything else that could brush against the infant's hand. Even brief contact can trigger the infant to either reflexively grasp the barrier itself or to withdraw his hand (Diamond, 1985, 1991). Frame-by-frame video analyses suggest that these reflexive actions, triggered by a barrier, typically prevent the infant from retrieving the object from its new hiding place. If the object is instead placed to reduce the infant's likelihood of accidentally touching a barrier, the infant is much more likely to succeed (Diamond, 1991).

These findings suggest that younger infants may know that the concealed object exists, but they may only be able to engage in successful retrieval actions for some object-barrier configurations. Thus, at this point in their development, their ability to retrieve hidden objects may depend on the specific object-barrier configuration. Put differently, covers and barriers pose obstacles to the goal of retrieving an object. Younger infants have difficulty overcoming these obstacles without being distracted by them. But by around 8 months of age, infants start to be able to inhibit these reflexes and to control their actions more voluntarily.

Another contributor to the A-not-B error seems to be infants' tendency to try to make sense of what they see as if it involved intentional acts of communication. In all the traditional versions of this task, the experimenters look at the infant and clearly indicate that they are demonstrating something to the infant. That intentional, communicative component may have a strong influence on the infant's reasoning. In one series of studies, 10-month-olds saw either an agent deliberately communicating with them while covering and uncovering the object, an agent who performed the same actions while clearly *not* communicating, or an inanimate object that performed the actions (Topál et al., 2008; see Figure 5.9). In the communicative condition, the demonstrator established eye contact, talked to the baby ("Hello, baby, look here!"), and then hid the object in location A while looking back and forth from the object to the baby to clearly draw the baby into shared attention to the object. When the adult provides these rich communicative cues, roughly 80 percent of 10-month-olds commit the search error, while only about 40 percent make the error in the other two conditions. The authors suggest that younger infants may interpret the communicative cues as a way of teaching, as if the adult is trying to convey that "this is the hiding place for this object." The infants may then internalize that message in a way that usually overrules the fact that the object was hidden elsewhere on the last trial. Some tendencies to perseverate, or to repeat past actions, may also be at work, since 40 percent of the infants in the noncommunicative condition still commit the error, but these tendencies may not be the primary reason infants look in location A in the normal task.

Performance on the A-not-B task depends not only on the infant's ability to inhibit his reflexive actions, but also on his memory. Although infants may stop making the A-not-B error as early as 8 months, when there is no delay at all, their ability to do so depends on the length of the delay between when the object is hidden and when the infant is allowed to retrieve it. After a delay of several extra seconds, infants who normally pass the A-not-B task will fail. Many studies have also found that the more times infants find the object at location A, the more likely they are to make the error (Markovitch & Zelazo, 1999).

> **Q:** What is an alternative way of understanding the A-not-B error?

It seems as if infants have difficulty "letting go" of the practiced action of searching in place A, which interferes with, and can even overwhelm, competing actions (Munakata et al., 1997). This observation suggests that younger infants may simply be less mature in the brain regions necessary to inhibit the practiced action, specifically the dorsolateral prefrontal cortex (see Figure 5.10). Support for this idea comes from several sources. First, anatomical studies of human infants demonstrate relative immaturity of the dorsolateral prefrontal cortex compared with more posterior brain regions. Second, adults with damage to this brain area exhibit similar errors. Even after correctly indicating which card they should select from a group, they may be unable to select it by reaching (Diamond, 1991; Milner, 1964). Finally, adult monkeys with lesions in the dorsolateral prefrontal

FIGURE 5.9 Pragmatic factors and the A-not-B error. Many infants who normally fail the A-not-B task in the communicative version pass it in the noncommunicative and nonsocial versions. This may be because in the communicative version, the infants believe that the adult is intentionally communicating to them that they should look for the hidden object in the location on the right. From Topál et al. (2008).

Communicative   Noncommunicative   Nonsocial

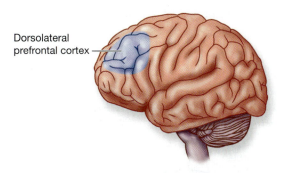

FIGURE 5.10 Inhibition of practiced actions. This view of a human brain (showing mostly the left side) shows the dorsolateral prefrontal cortex area that seems to be involved in inhibiting the tendency to produce previously practiced actions. This area is especially immature in infants relative to other brain regions and, when lesioned in adult monkeys, causes the monkeys to commit the A-not-B error.

cortex behave in precisely the same way on the A-not-B task as most 8-month-old infants and search in the wrong location, whereas adult monkeys with intact brains do not make the A-not-B error (Diamond & Goldman-Rakic, 1989).

It is quite remarkable that roughly 50 years and several hundred experimental studies after Piaget described the A-not-B error, researchers are still investigating its ultimate basis. The reflex inhibition accounts cannot fully explain why infants make the error when they merely observe the hiding and don't act; the memory-based accounts cannot explain why the infant looks at a second correct location more than at an incorrect alternative. Both motor control and memory are likely involved, and indeed we can imagine situations in which we, as adults, have acted similarly. Who hasn't lost their car keys, failed to find them where they normally are, and then after looking in several other spots, been unthinkingly "pulled" back to their usual spot to look there again? We don't do this because we cannot mentally represent hidden objects; we are merely defaulting to the most successful strategy. In short, recent research suggests that the A-not-B error has its basis in several cognitive differences between younger and older infants. No one specific difference may fully explain how infants understand the properties of hidden objects.

Infant Knowledge and Understanding

As we have seen, recent research has challenged Piaget's belief that infants have little or no awareness of objects and the broader world around them. It is now clear that infants are aware of the external world from a very early age, and they have some basic understanding of its highly regular and universal physical laws. In the rest of this chapter, we will consider what infants know about the physical world. Along the way, we will ask whether infants' impressive performance on many experimental tasks is evidence of high-level cognition or whether their seemingly sophisticated responses may be merely rigid, automatic behaviors, similar to the reflexes considered in Chapter 4. Do very young infants have intuitive belief-like theories that allow them to think flexibly about the physical world? What kinds of mental structures are minimally necessary to explain their behavior?

By way of framing the problem, consider the seemingly unlikely example of the kingfisher (Boden, 1989), which fishes for its underwater prey by diving toward it from the air. The kingfisher must strike at an angle to compensate for the distortion caused by looking down at its prey through the water, as shown in Figure 5.11. Although each dive can be described in terms of intricate geometric relations between the bird and its prey, kingfishers obviously do not "know" geometry. Instead, they automatically invoke a much more rigid and inflexible routine, outside of awareness, as they dive for fish. If a region of the kingfisher's brain computes geometric relations, it surely operates more like a "black box" module, giving the user access to its outputs but not to a conscious process of computing angles and distances (Dennett, 1991; Nagel, 1979). In considering the research that follows, it is helpful to keep the kingfisher in mind. Is the infant's performance simply an execution of automatic behaviors, or is a flexible understanding of the world truly present?

In observing infants' responses, it is difficult to tell whether we are witnessing flexible understanding or automatic

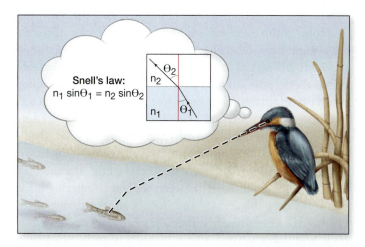

FIGURE 5.11 Inferring mental states underlying behaviors. Does the kingfisher deliberately and consciously calculate trigonometry in order to know how to dive after the fish? Clearly not, even if its behavior implies that such trigonometric calculations must be occurring. The same dilemma arises in trying to infer the mental states of a preverbal infant. Adapted from Boden (1989).

behaviors, and we often have to rely on intuitions about what sorts of behaviors seem to reflect something more than automatic routines (Bernal, 2005). We will see that some of the best evidence comes from the patterns in infants' errors as their understanding of physical objects develops. Some error patterns strongly imply a flexible, deliberative system rather than a preprogrammed "black box" response.

> Q: How might a preverbal infant's behavior be understood either in terms of a sophisticated internal set of theory-like beliefs or in terms of interactions "below" the level of beliefs?

Thinking about the Unseen

One way that researchers have tried to determine whether infants show flexible understanding has been to observe how they react to events that occur out of view. There are now several studies illustrating that infants as young as 4 months not only know that objects continue to exist while out of sight, but also seem able to think about unseen objects interacting in ways that conform to simple physics.

Studies of Object Permanence and Solidity Two properties of common physical objects are extremely reliable: permanence and solidity. Object permanence simply means that objects continue to exist over time. They don't exist for a while, blink out of existence, and then reappear. **Object solidity** means that rigid or hard objects cannot pass through other rigid or hard objects because they cohere (stick together) as single entities. Billiard balls, for example, bounce off each other; they don't pass through each other. Researchers have explored infants' knowledge of these two properties as a way of understanding how infants think about physical objects in general. One pioneering study on infants' understanding of solidity was conducted by Renee Baillargeon and her colleagues and is depicted in Figure 5.12. The experimental setup involved a solid screen attached with a hinge to the surface of a table. This study is typically described as "the drawbridge study" because the authors noted a similarity between the screen rotating back and forth over the surface and the action of a drawbridge. During the experiment, infants watched the screen swing back and forth several times through a full 180-degree arc, naturally stopping as it hit the table on either side (Baillargeon, 1987; Baillargeon et al., 1985). Infants as young as 3½ months soon habituated and lost interest in the event. Researchers then introduced a new object, placing a large box on the far side of the screen from the infant

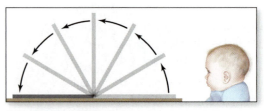

A Habituation event

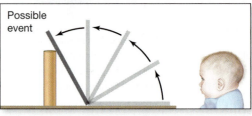

Possible event

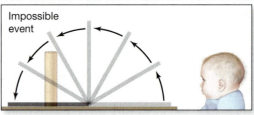

Impossible event

B Test events

FIGURE 5.12 Understanding permanence and solidity by 4-month-old infants. (A) In a habituation event, an infant sees a screen swing through 180 degrees several times. **(B)** An object is placed on the surface while the screen is down. The infant then observes the screen either moving through a smaller angle (a 112-degree arc) that would correspond to its stopping on top of the object (a possible event) or moving the full 180 degrees (an "impossible" event made possible by a hidden trap door through which the object moves while out of sight of the infant). Infants dishabituate more strongly to the 180-degree arc, even though the arc itself is much more familiar (due to the habituation event) than the movement through the smaller angle. Adapted from Baillargeon (1987).

in the path of the screen's arc. In one experimental condition, the infant watched the screen swing back and forth again, but only part of the way. The screen stopped where it touched the box, and at that point it also blocked the box from the infant's view. This is a perceptually novel event, but it is consistent with the law of object solidity (and so it is a possible event), and the infant showed only mild dishabituation. In a different experimental condition, the box was placed in the screen's path, but the infant then watched the screen swing through the full 180-degree arc, as in the original habituation trials. Because the screen should hit the box, this event is incompatible with object solidity. (The box dropped through a hidden opening in the table's surface to create the impossible event.)

Even at 3½ months of age, infants dishabituated much more strongly to the impossible 180-degree arc than to the partial arc that occurred when the screen was presumably blocked by the box. This response pattern seems to require the infants to understand some principles about object solidity and to apply them even to objects they cannot see (once the box is placed on the flat surface, the screen blocks it from view): (1) the infants must understand that both the screen and the box are solid objects; (2) they must know that both are rigid and do not change shape; (3) they must expect that solid objects cannot pass through one another; (4) they must assume that an object, even when it is out of sight, will stay where it was last seen unless something is seen to move it; and (5) they must assume that these properties remain consistent over time. It appears that infants as young as 3½ months are simultaneously using five or more principles to think about the objects around them and interrelating these principles to make reliable, correct predictions. As they get older, infants learn to apply these principles in more sophisticated ways. Thus, younger infants only notice significant mismatches between the screen's action and the box, whereas older infants can anticipate more subtle ways in which the size of the box should stop the screen at a certain angle (Baillargeon, 1995).

Before speculating on the details of how this knowledge might be represented and used, we need to explore in more detail the abilities of infants to make inferences about possible and impossible interactions between physical objects. In particular, can they reason about the physical interactions between multiple objects while the objects are out of sight?

After the drawbridge experiments, Baillargeon conducted a second series of studies that is perhaps the most remarkable exploration to date of infants' capacity for sophisticated reasoning about concealed objects (Baillargeon, 1986; Baillargeon & DeVos, 1991). In these studies, infants as young as 3 months watched a screen come down on a center section of a scene where there were no objects. They then watched a toy car roll down a ramp, continue on a marked roadway, go behind the screen, and emerge from behind the screen and continue rolling until it rolled "offstage" on the same path (see Figure 5.13A). After these habituation trials, the infants observed one of two new events involving a third object: a box or a small toy Mickey Mouse. In one condition, the box was placed behind the path before the screen came down (see Figure 5.13B). In the other condition, the box was placed directly in the car's path before the screen came down (see Figure 5.13C). In both conditions, the infants saw the car appear on the opposite side of the box at a time consistent with its previous speed of rolling.

Infants showed strong dishabituation only when the car seemed to have "passed through" the block placed directly in its path, an event that was physically impossible unless

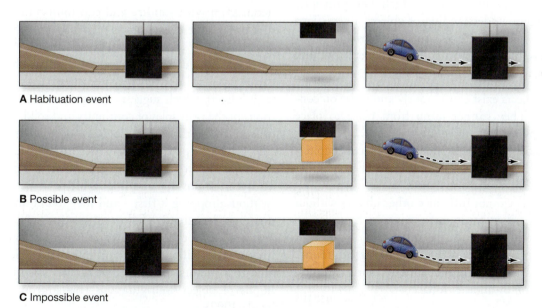

A Habituation event

B Possible event

C Impossible event

FIGURE 5.13 Thinking about interactions between objects that are out of sight. (A) In the habituation event, a screen is placed in front of a track and then is raised to show that there is nothing behind it. When a toy car is placed on the ramp, it rolls down the ramp and behind the screen until it emerges on the other side of the screen. **(B)** In a possible event, a box is placed behind the track so that when a car is rolled down the ramp, it is able to roll between the screen and the box and emerge on the other side of the screen. **(C)** In an impossible event, a box is placed on top of the track, but it appears as if the car is still able to roll to the other side of the screen. Yet even 3-month-old infants seem to understand that the car cannot pass through a box that is on the track, and thus they dishabituate if it reappears on the opposite side of the screen. They show much less dishabituation when the car reappears on the other side of the screen when the box has been placed behind the path of the car. Adapted from Baillargeon (1986).

there was external intervention to move the block. A second study showed that infants did not dishabituate longer when the block was placed in front of the path, showing that the effect was not simply caused when the block was closer. This dishabituation response may involve even more assumptions about objects' interactions than the drawbridge studies; in addition to their assumptions about object solidity and rigidity, infants appear to assume that an object traveling in a straight line will continue unless something interrupts it. Without this kind of assumption, they would not dishabituate so strongly, since the car could swerve around or hop over the box and appear on the other side without violating other assumptions about how objects interact.

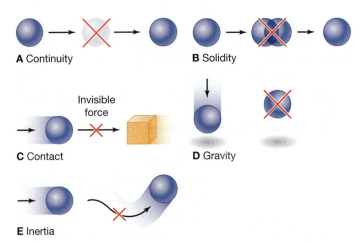

FIGURE 5.14 Intuitive physics. Depicted here are five principles that govern the behavior of most physical objects: continuity, solidity (cohesion), contact ("no action at a distance"), gravity, and inertia. The crossed-out drawing indicates a violation of the principle. Adapted from Spelke (1991).

Q: In what ways do infants seem to reason about the physical relations between unseen objects?

Principles That Guide How Infants Understand Studies of how infants understand object permanence and solidity suggest that it might be possible to codify the principles that they use to think about physical objects, what some have called the "intuitive physics of the young infant." Elizabeth Spelke has extensively investigated which key principles might guide infants' understanding of objects' interactions (Spelke, 1988a, 1988b, 1990, 1991). Spelke argues that young infants might use the five principles listed here to think about the physical world (see Figure 5.14):

1. *Continuity.* Objects exist continuously and move on connected paths. They cannot jump from place to place without occupying the intervening space.
2. *Solidity.* Physical objects are solid. Each object occupies a unique part of space; objects cannot interpenetrate other objects because all their parts cohere.
3. *Contact.* Objects cannot influence other objects without touching them; they must make contact; there is "no action at a distance."
4. *Gravity.* Unsupported objects will fall toward the ground.
5. *Inertia.* Objects do not change their motion abruptly unless they are acted on by another force.

Many of Spelke's studies exploring how infants become aware of these constraints involve an infant who watches as an object moves out of view behind a screen. When the screen is removed, the infant sees the object resting either in a position consistent with the constraints on physical motion or in a position that violates one or more of those constraints. Figure 5.15 shows how this technique has been used to explore infants' assumptions about continuity and

solidity. As an infant watches, a ball is held above a screen and then dropped behind it. When the screen is raised, the infant sees one of several configurations. In the initial trials for habituation, the ball is resting on the lowest surface. In the other two sets of trials, a new, higher surface is added to the display. When the screen is raised, the infant sees that the ball has either landed on the higher surface (consistent with solidity and continuity) or underneath it (an impossible event that is inconsistent with solidity and continuity).

Spelke found that 4-month-old infants dishabituate more strongly to the impossible event (measured in terms of looking at it longer), which suggests that they are surprised by violations of the principles of continuity and solidity. (To rule out the possibility that infants looked longer at the ball resting in the impossible position simply because they preferred this display, the researchers also showed the infants the ball resting in both the possible and impossible positions in the display without dropping it first—and they found no differences in looking.) In extensive follow-up studies, Spelke and her colleagues found that infants as young as 2½ months assume that objects will obey the continuity and solidity principles and that infants apply these principles broadly, across many kinds of object configurations (Baillargeon, 2004; Spelke et al., 1992).

Q: What are five principles governing the behavior of physical objects? Which ones do infants seem to grasp first, and why?

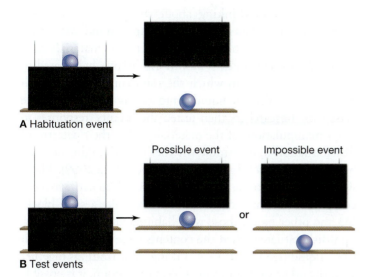

FIGURE 5.15 Testing principles pertaining to objects. (A) A habituation event shows the ball dropped behind a screen and coming to rest on a lower surface. **(B)** Test events show the ball being dropped behind the screen and either coming to rest on a higher surface that has been added to the display, which is a possible event, or coming to rest on the original lower surface, despite the addition of a higher surface above it, which is an impossible event. Spelke used this setup to explore whether infants dishabituated more to an impossible event in which the ball would have had to pass through another solid object, the higher surface. Adapted from Spelke et al. (1992).

By contrast, infants develop assumptions about the gravity and inertia principles somewhat later. For example, 4-month-olds do not seem to fully understand the gravitational relationship between a dropped object and a supporting surface that stops its fall. In some settings, 4-month-olds will not look longer at an object that stops moving in midair (an impossible event) than at an object that falls until it touches a surface (a possible event). Although other studies suggest that young infants may have some inklings of the importance of gravity—the tendency for unsupported objects to fall downward (Baillargeon & Hanko-Summers, 1990), these concepts are not sufficiently developed to make fully accurate predictions (Kim & Spelke, 1992). Concepts of inertia—the tendency of objects to continue the same motion unless acted on by another force—also take longer than the first several months to fully develop. There may be an early assumption that a moving object continues along the same path when unseen, as was found in Baillargeon's rolling car study, but if infants see a display indicating that a moving object must have abruptly changed direction while concealed behind a barrier, they will not look longer at this violation of the inertia principle until they are about 8 months old (Kim & Spelke, 1999).

Clearly, young infants are not fully aware of all the principles governing physical objects' interactions—not even prin-

ciples that are extremely prevalent in the natural world, such as gravity and inertia. They do, however, seem to have a very early knowledge of the principles of continuity, cohesion (solidity), and contact ("no action at a distance"). As a mnemonic, it may be helpful to remember that young infants use the three Cs to understand objects. Indeed, infants seem to be sensitive to these principles with little or no relevant experience. Why should infants' understanding of some principles, such as the three Cs, develop before others, like gravity and inertia? One possibility is that the early-emerging principles are more important to the young infant in anticipating the behaviors of a wide range of objects. Alternatively, perhaps inertia and gravity are best understood in a conceptual framework that already includes concepts such as continuity and solidity. This pattern fits with the hypothesis that earlier-emerging "core" beliefs may be more fixed and predetermined components in the infant's conceptual repertoire.

Other researchers have also questioned whether infants might be more proficient at using certain physical principles, such as inertia, in their own actions than they are while merely observing events. For example, infants who do not dishabituate to inertia-violating displays—such as when an object goes behind a barrier at one angle and emerges at another—show patterns of reaching toward objects in motion that clearly honor the principle of inertia (von Hofsten et al., 1998). Cognition linked to action may differ from cognition linked only to observation (Goodale & Milner, 1992). We saw in Chapter 4 that perception and action are intimately linked in an infant's attempts to learn about the world. In this case of thinking about objects, cognition and action may also be linked.

Finally, this pattern of results again raises challenges for the empiricist. By most accounts, the principles of inertia and gravity are just as salient in the young infant's life as principles of solidity and continuity. If infants simply built up associations through experience that eventually led to knowledge of physical laws, we would expect their understanding of different physical principles to develop at about the same time. There are some common exceptions to the later-developing principles of gravity and inertia, such as balloons that float and papers fluttering in the wind that change direction. But there are also exceptions to the earlier-emerging beliefs: clouds and liquids appear to violate solidity, and shadows seem to violate both solidity and continuity. The patterns that the young infant encounters do not seem to support learning about principles like solidity and continuity any more strongly than learning about gravity and inertia.

Even though the evidence doesn't seem to support a strong empiricist view, neither does it strongly support a strong nativist view in which a mature knowledge of physical objects and their behaviors is present at birth. It would be misleading to suggest that the young infant thoroughly understands the principles governing the physical world. Not only do some principles take longer for infants to understand; there are also extensive developmental changes to infants' use of the earliest-emerging principles within the first year of life. For example, although quite young infants seem to understand continuity and solidity in tasks that involve an object hidden behind a barrier, they take considerably longer to understand the same principles in tasks that involve an object contained inside of another. Baillargeon proposes that while solidity and continuity may be foundational principles that develop very early, it may take many months to learn how to apply those principles to different kinds of events, such as objects containing or covering one another (Baillargeon, 2004).

One way of thinking about the developmental changes is in terms of the principle of persistence, which states that objects do not change without a cause (Wang & Baillargeon, 2008). From a very early age, infants seem to assume that objects cannot (on their own) appear or disappear, break apart or assemble, or change their size, shape, or color spontaneously. For infants to be able to detect such impossible changes, they would have to be able to mentally represent the object's properties and remember them, abilities that develop considerably during the first year of life. Figure 5.16 shows two simple events that a 2½-month-old can detect as impossible because they violate the principle of persistence (Wang & Baillargeon, 2008). As the configurations of objects' properties and their changes become more complex, however, even 12-month-olds fail to detect some violations of the principle.

In addition to thinking about the properties of solid objects, young infants also start to understand the differences between solid objects and amorphous materials such as liquids. In one study, 5-month-old infants habituated to either a tilting glass in which the solid contents tilt as well or a glass in which the liquid contents stay horizontal as the glass tilts. Researchers then tested the infants' responses to other manipulations of the materials, using their patterns of dishabituation to determine whether they thought they had been watching a solid or a liquid (Hespos et al., 2009). Those who habituated to the liquid version dishabituated when the contents were emptied out and behaved like a solid block. On the other hand, those who habituated to the solid version dishabituated when the contents were then poured out like a liquid (see Figure 5.17). Taking these findings together with the other studies of solid object perception, it is possible that infants first master the properties of solid objects by as early as 2 months, but then take somewhat longer to start to understand the distinguishing properties of nonsolids.

Comparative Considerations When we study infants, it is natural to interpret much of their behavior by attributing to them adult-like beliefs and goals. Yet, as the kingfisher example showed, sophisticated behavior does not always require complex beliefs or knowledge. The experimental tasks investigating infants' reasoning about unseen objects seem to require sophisticated cognitions that we think of as human. But before we can make such statements with any confidence, we need to consider whether other species behave similarly (Weiss & Santos, 2006). If other species

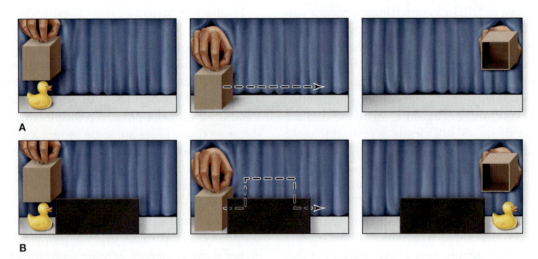

FIGURE 5.16 Early understanding of object properties. (A) A hand raises a cover to reveal a duck and then lowers the cover over the duck and slides it to the right. When the cover is lifted on the right, the duck has magically disappeared. **(B)** After lifting a cover to reveal a duck and then lowering the cover over the duck, a hand slides the duck behind a screen that is taller than the duck, lifts the cover when it is behind the screen (presumably leaving the duck behind), and then slides the cover out from behind the screen. When the cover is lifted, a duck has magically appeared. Infants as young as 2½ months are surprised at both event outcomes because of their assumptions about how objects interact with other objects. In particular, these event outcomes violate the principle of persistence. Adapted from Wang & Baillargeon (2008).

Habituation to Liquid

Habituation to Solid

FIGURE 5.17 Properties of solids and liquids. Five-month-old infants who habituate to a substance as a liquid that stays horizontal dishabituate when it comes out of the glass as a solid. Conversely, those who habituate to a substance as a solid that tilts with its container dishabituate when it comes out as a liquid. From Hespos et al. (2009).

Test trials

Solid

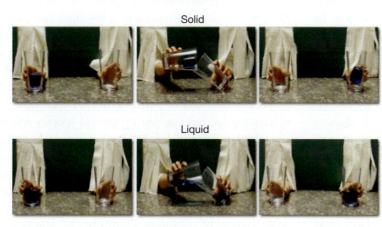

Liquid

act in the same ways on hidden objects, then we may need to deflate the level of cognitive sophistication that we attribute to human infants. We do not yet have a thorough, systematic comparison of how primates and other mammals perform on all the tasks previously used to assess reasoning about physical objects in young human infants, but some researchers have done comparative studies of related tasks. Their results are critical to understanding what sorts of beliefs about the physical world guide infants' behaviors—and if they should even be thought of as beliefs at all.

Consider the A-not-B task, which requires an understanding of object permanence. It turns out that a wide range of species can find the hidden object in the A-not-B task, and some, such as dogs and cats, never commit the A-not-B error. Figure 5.18 shows the age at which different species first pass the A-not-B task, as well as the age at which gorillas and humans pass the invisible displacements ("shell game") task (the other species never pass it). All the primates initially fail the A-not-B task but then later pass it. In contrast, dogs and cats always pass the A-not-B task but never

understand invisible displacements. Although the basis for this difference has yet to be fully explained, primates may share a particular way of encoding and remembering actions that differs from the way other species encode and remember actions and which, early on, causes the A-not-B error. Another factor that may differ across species is the influence of intentional communication (see p. 156). While many great apes, such as gorillas and chimpanzees, are able to understand when others direct their attention to an object (Pitman & Shumaker, 2009), humans may be the only species with a well-developed sense of when another person is explicitly demonstrating an action (Gergely, 2011). That is, when a person demonstrates an action to a human infant, the infant may automatically encode the action as something important that the other person wants to teach. That interpretation may cause human infants to fail the A-not-B task more often than other primates, despite being their cognitive equals or superiors in other respects.

Moreover, when we consider tasks like Baillargeon's and Spelke's for assessing knowledge of solidity, it seems that

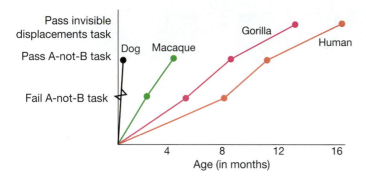

FIGURE 5.18 The object concept across species. Most primates fail the A-not-B task in early infancy and then pass it later. Members of the ape family also later come to pass the invisible displacements task. Dogs, cats, and some other animals always pass the A-not-B task and never pass the invisible displacements task. These results suggest that dogs, cats, and other nonprimate animals may be solving the A-not-B task in ways that don't create a foundation for being able to later solve the invisible displacements task. Adapted from Gomez (2005).

organisms quite distant from primates can take solidity into account. Consider, for example, a task devised for dogs that resembles Baillargeon's rolling car studies and Spelke's dropped ball studies mentioned earlier. Dogs watched a treat slide down a transparent tube and then were allowed to retrieve it from one of two doors (Kundey et al., 2010). In one condition, a highly visible wall was inserted between the two doors (see Figure 5.19). In the other condition, there was no wall. Dogs of many breeds and mixes seemed to be aware of solidity, searching for the treat in the "near door" when they could see the wall was present, but searching in the "far door" when there was no wall. This study illustrates that some aspects of the baby's understanding of physical objects, such as solidity, may have quite ancient evolutionary roots, since humans' common ancestor with dogs is evolutionarily much older than humans' common ancestor with primates. It also shows that nonprimates can solve solidity problems that are clearly different from those they would encounter in their natural environments, suggesting a quite general appreciation of solidity.

Research with nonhuman primates, as well as with some nonprimates, suggests that many species have some sense of the solidity and continuity of novel objects as well as some competence at object permanence tasks (Deppe et al., 2009; Gomez, 2005; Hall-Haro et al., 2008; Neiworth et al., 2003; Santos, 2004). They seem able to make inferences about the properties of objects that are out of sight, which take them far beyond the ways that much simpler organisms, such as insects, avoid collisions with objects or land on solid surfaces. Given that several of the species that manage to use these principles have brains of very modest size and complexity, we must be cautious about interpreting similar behavior in human infants as evidence of rich, sophisticated cognition. Further studies may demonstrate that the nuances of human infant responses are evidence of sophisticated thinking. But without that evidence, it is risky to think that infants' responses in these experiments are based on conscious, explicit, adult-like beliefs about objects.

The ability to reason about unseen events may be an important distinction between humans (and perhaps a few apes) and other animals. A monkey who passes the A-not-B task shows that it can think about an unseen object, but this task does not involve thinking about a dynamic event, such as two objects interacting. Even the invisible displacements task, which only humans and a few apes can pass, involves the simplest possible event: one object moving. By contrast, Spelke, Baillargeon, and other infant cognition researchers study events that involve reasoning about two objects' interactions while both are out of view. Very few studies have explored nonhumans' performance on such tasks, and only systematic studies comparing several species will help clarify whether human infants have a uniquely sophisticated capacity to think about the physical world. Given that only humans and the great apes (chimpanzees, bonobos, gorillas, and orangutans) can follow invisible displacements, including some intricate ones (Albiach-Serrano et al., 2010), some aspects of reasoning about objects' motions while out of sight may require certain higher-order cognitive abilities. Nonetheless, much of the object concept seems to fall within the abilities of a broader range of species.

> Q: How has comparative work with other species changed our views of the human infant's developing object concept?

Understanding Causation

When infants react to "impossible" physical events with dishabituation, it is difficult not to assume that they are reason-

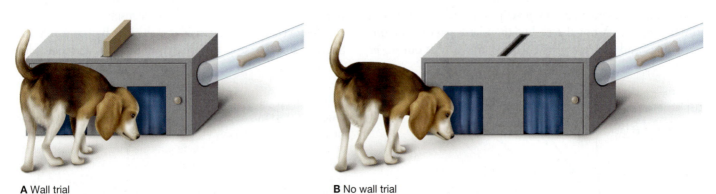

A Wall trial **B** No wall trial

FIGURE 5.19 **Dogs and object solidity.** In a task with striking similarities to the studies assessing concepts of solidity in human infants, dogs from a wide range of breeds preferred the "near" door when the wall was inserted **(A)** and the "far" door when it was not **(B)**. Success on such tasks by nonprimates suggests that human-like cognitive abilities may not be required to solve such tasks. Adapted from Kundey et al. (2010).

ing about what they have seen in terms of cause and effect. We see them as being surprised that their causal expectations have been violated. If we, as adults, put ourselves in their shoes, we explain the problems with the impossible events in causal terms. The drawbridge should have stopped *because* the box would have prevented it from swinging all the way. The car could not have rolled all the way down the path *because* it would have had to pass through the block. Our understanding of everyday objects is saturated with causal thinking.

As we have seen, infant responses to events that seem to violate physical laws strongly suggest that infants, too, are thinking in terms of causal relations. Nonetheless, to investigate infants' understanding of cause and effect in its own right, it is helpful to examine studies that directly address this centuries-old issue. Some have argued that causal ideas are as crucial for infants as for adults and that causality is a primitive conceptual building block that the infant needs from the first moments of awareness (Fodor, 1981). Others have maintained that an understanding of causality can develop only gradually through learning from experience, either from repeated association of events that regularly occur together over time and space (Hume, 1748/1910) or through active experience initially produced by the infant's own actions (Piaget, 1955).

One line of work tried to distinguish whether infants who observed simple events actually understood the causal relationship between them or whether they were merely noticing and remembering how often the two events (such as movement of a green object and movement of a red object) co-occurred in space and time—referred to as *spatial contiguity* and *temporal contiguity* (Leslie, 1982, 1984). The researchers set up experiments to investigate whether infants actually encoded that one event caused the other, such as movement of one object launching the other's movement through a collision. For example, in one set of studies, infants watched a film of events like those in Figure 5.20A, depicting movement of a green block and a red block. In one condition, they saw the red block move across the screen until it stopped next to the green block, at which point the green block started moving. In another condition, the direction of movement was reversed: the green block moved first, and when it stopped next to the red block, the red block began to move. To adults, the first condition would convey the impression that the red block caused the green block to move, while the second condition would suggest that the green block caused the red block's movement. These events were exactly the same except for the direction of movement and the order of the two blocks' movement. To notice that the two events are different, an infant would have to notice at least one of these features. Seven-month-old infants showed clear dishabituation when the event shifted from one in which the red block "caused"

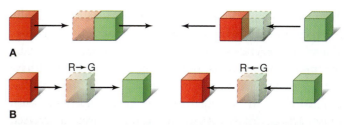

FIGURE 5.20 Perception of causality by 7-month-olds.
(A) The red block seems to push the green block on some trials, and the green block seems to push the red block on other trials.
(B) The same block changes color, first from red to green, then from green to red. Adapted from Leslie (1984).

the green block to move to one in which the green block "caused" the red block to move. Does this dishabituation mean that they understand that the two events are showing different causal relationships? On its own, it does not. Infants could simply be habituating to something like "red event" then "green event" and dishabituating when their order was reversed.

Another pair of conditions examined whether the infants were making causal interpretations rather than just temporal associations. These conditions used two films, each showing only one block that traveled at the same speed as the blocks in the first films. This time the block changed its color at the same time and place where one block previously seemed to push the other (see Figure 5.20B). As before, the films then showed the same actions reversed. In one, a red block changed into a green block, and in the other, a green block became a red block. This second pair of films was used to test whether the infants would regard the mere change of color as an apparent case of physical causation. If they were merely encoding "red event" followed by "green event," they might dishabituate just as strongly when the order of these events was reversed. In fact, they showed much less dishabituation between the two single-block color change films than they did between the two films of two-block "launches," where one block seemed to collide with the other block, apparently causing it to move. They showed much more awareness when the order of cause-and-effect relations changed in the "launching" films, and found a mere shift in the order of color changes much less surprising. Several other follow-up experiments helped to rule out other interpretations and strongly indicate that 7-month-olds see causation that goes beyond mere temporal and spatial contiguity (Leslie, 1984; Leslie & Keeble, 1987).

It is difficult to tell whether younger infants think in terms of causality or whether they merely react to causal patterns without explicitly coding one event as causing another (Carey, 2009; Goodman et al., 2011; White, 2009). Some researchers argue that infants need to learn the notion of causality in their first several months of life (Cohen & Amsel, 1998; Cohen & Oakes, 1993; Haith & Benson, 1998).

According to this view, the notion of causality gradually emerges out of noticing spatial and temporal contingencies. Those contingencies might be made especially salient by the infant's own actions. Indeed, one study found that having 4½-month-old infants wear sticky Velcro mittens that enabled them to pick up balls gave them experience with causal action. These infants later dishabituated to reversed causal events (that is, events in which the agent and recipient of an action were reversed from what the infants had previously observed) 1½ months earlier than infants who were not supplied with such mittens. This result was argued to support the claim that causality is learned through actions that facilitate attention to and encoding of relevant parts of physical events (Rakison & Krogh, 2012; see also Libertus & Needham, 2010, as described in Chapter 4).

An alternative view argues that there is a primitive perceptually driven way of detecting some forms of causality that does not need to be learned or built up through experience. In this view, infants may come into the world with a mental "module" that directly responds to certain perceptual sequences with an impression of causation (Scholl & Nakayama, 2002, 2004; Scholl & Tremoulet, 2000). The idea of a *module* refers to an innate biological structure that responds automatically to specific inputs (Fodor, 1983). If this second view is correct—if impressions of simple physical causality are the output of a module—then we should be able to see awareness of causality even in very young infants. In this view, infants may come into the world with a module that responds automatically to certain perceptual configurations, such as collisions, with a sense of causation. It may still take many months, however, for infants to be able to think about cause conceptually in situations that are not like those perceptual cases.

One piece of evidence for a module that detects physical causality comes from studies showing that 7-month-old infants see physical causality under almost exactly the same perceptual conditions as adults (Newman et al., 2008a). The temporal and spatial relations that convey a sense that one object has launched another (as opposed to their movements being causally unrelated) are so similar and unrelated to actual experience observing such launchings that it is very hard to see how they could be learned. Yet, even if there is a core module for perceiving physical causality under certain simple collision conditions, it may take months or years before all the forms of perceptual and conceptual causality are easily understood by young children.

The Use of Number

The infant's ability to appreciate physical causality is impressive, and it seems to relate to specific patterns in the world. The ability to think about number, however, seems quite different. In our culture, we count ages, minutes, days, years, money, and just about everything else of importance that can be quantified. Is this tendency specific to technologically advanced cultures, or is it a universal aspect of human nature? If number concepts are universally used across all cultures, that universality raises the question of whether such concepts are present in the young infant's mind. Although universal concepts are not necessarily present in infancy—they can arise from culturally universal experiences, such as the experience of going through puberty or being elderly—a concept's universality leads us to consider whether it might have very early developmental origins.

Older accounts of number concepts claimed that children and "primitive" peoples could not think about number conceptually and could only think about differences in quantity using configurations of objects (knowing, for example, that a group of three objects usually forms a triangle). More recently, however, researchers have found that every culture that is carefully studied does use number concepts (Lave, 1977; Pica et al., 2004; Saxe & Posner, 1983; Zaslavsky, 1973). Moreover, even other species show increasingly clear evidence of numerical competence, suggesting that number concepts do not depend on humans' language skills and the ability to use number words (Gallistel, 1990). The developmental question, then, is how these universal number concepts emerge. Are young infants predisposed to understand number concepts? Several studies strongly suggest that they might be.

We have seen that developmental psychologists have a relatively limited set of ways of studying infants' mental states, most of which revolve around habituation/dishabituation paradigms. This limitation poses a challenge when it comes to exploring whether infants show numerical competency. The most successful technique involves habituating an infant to a small number of stimuli, such as three, and then seeing if he dishabituates when he is exposed to a different number of stimuli. The difficulty is to control all the other variables that could influence the infant's response. For example, a visual display of three objects normally forms a larger, more complex visual pattern than a display of two objects. As a result, many kinds of perceptual contrasts between the displays, including their different contours or configurations or the differing amounts of visual space they take up, could cause the infant to dishabituate. If an infant who has habituated to a display of three objects shows renewed interest when he sees a display of two, any of these perceptual factors, rather than a conceptual awareness of the difference in number, could be the reason. In early experiments, when researchers attempted to control for these perceptual influences, their results suggested that infants were sensing number (Antell & Keating, 1983; Starkey & Cooper, 1980). Nonetheless, concerns remained about whether the infants were truly aware of abstract numerical differences as opposed to perceptual contrasts, such as the geometric patterns formed by specific numbers of objects.

One way that researchers attempted to determine whether the infants' responses were based more on numerical concepts or perceptual contrasts was to see whether they would dishabituate to differences in number even when these differences depended on widely varying perceptual experiences, such as sights and sounds presented in a cross-modal (across two sense modalities) study (Starkey et al., 1990). In one study, infants viewed two displays side by side, one showing two objects and the other showing three objects (see Figure 5.21). At the same time, a speaker hidden between the displays repeatedly played sets of either two or three drumbeats. In this paradigm, the researcher presented the visual and auditory patterns simultaneously to determine whether infants would match the number of individual elements across the two sense modalities. Infants as young as 6 months reliably looked longer at the display showing the number of objects that matched the simultaneously presented drumbeats (Starkey et al., 1990). The effect can even be found in newborn infants, who can recognize differences between such numbers as 4 and 12, as depicted by discrete sounds and visual dots (Izard et al., 2009).

Other studies examined whether infants would show such cross-modal number concepts if the sounds and sights were not presented together. These studies therefore asked if a representation of number could emerge from a stimulus set, be held in mind when the stimulus was removed, and then be applied to a new stimulus set in a different modality. This would mean that a number concept could

be held in memory apart from the actual stimuli. Researchers habituated infants to visual displays of either two or three objects; then, after turning off the visual display, they played a stream of randomly ordered two- and three-beat drum sequences. Infants as young as 6 months looked longer at the source of the sounds when the number of drumbeats matched the number of objects to which they had just been visually habituated (Starkey et al., 1983, 1990). This effect has been found repeatedly using a variety of methods (Jordan & Brannon, 2006; Kobayashi et al., 2005).

It is useful to try to understand what these experiments reveal about infants' subjective experiences. It appears that even infants experience a world in which number is an important and meaningful concept and that they may do so in some cases right from birth. They appear to be aware of abstract quantities and to be able to recognize similarities in "three-ness" or "two-ness" between stimuli that differ in virtually every other respect. Moreover, the experiments that presented visual and auditory stimuli separately suggest that infants can remember these number concepts and use them across modalities. The infants seemed to know that "three-ness" was repeatedly being presented in the visual display, they habituated accordingly, and then they showed a renewed interest when they recognized that familiar number in the drumbeats. Infants have also recognized number in similar cross-modal studies involving touch and vision (Feron et al., 2002), further demonstrating that their notion of number transcends any particular modality.

These studies on infant number concepts are only the beginning of our understanding of the early roots of the number concept in infancy. Major questions remain unanswered, especially those concerning what, if anything, infants do with this ability to infer number from the physical world. Do they use it, as other animals apparently do, to guide their actions even in infancy? Other animals use number to keep track of their young or of caches of food, yet comparable behaviors in infants are not obvious. Alternatively, is it simply a necessary building block in the later-developing structure of mathematical knowledge? No matter how (or whether) it is used from the start, even very young infants appear to have some abstract concept of number.

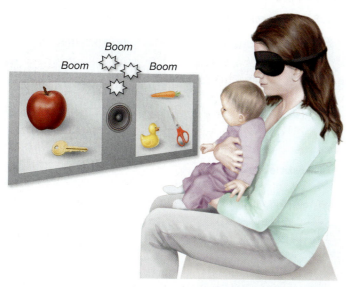

FIGURE 5.21 Intermodal sensing of number. When 6-month-old infants hear three bursts of sound (for example, a sequence of three drumbeats) from a speaker hidden between two photographic displays—one showing two objects and the other showing three objects—they typically look toward the display of three objects, which matches what they have heard.

Q: What is the evidence that infants less than 6 months of age have a concept of number?

One use of early number concepts may be to support a crude form of arithmetic. Indeed, infants can use their concept of number to understand changes in quantity, even doing simple subtraction and addition. In a seminal series of studies, 5-month-old infants were habituated to a toy mouse placed on a stage (Wynn, 1992). A screen then blocked the mouse, and the infant watched the experimenter take another, identical toy mouse and move it behind the screen. When the screen was removed, the infant saw either one or two mice on the stage (see Figure 5.22). In this "addition" test, infants looked longer when they saw only one mouse on the stage, despite the fact that they had just been habituated to a single mouse, since this violated their expectation of what the outcome should be after another mouse was added behind the screen. In another version of the experiment, the display started with two toy mice. The screen then concealed them, and the infant saw a hand emerge and remove one mouse from behind the screen. When the screen was lifted, the infants looked longer when the display showed two mice, because it violated the perceived "subtraction." These results have been replicated by other scientists in studies that rule out possible perceptual and conceptual confounds (Simon et al., 1995; Slater et al., 2010).

The meaning of these findings, which seem to show "subtraction" and "addition" by infants, has been actively debated. Do the infants' responses indicate an ability to manipulate numbers, or could infants be "solving" the task on other grounds? One proposal suggests that infants are simply remembering the individual objects they have seen. When the set of objects an infant remembers doesn't match the set of objects she perceives, she will appear surprised and look as if she had arrived at an expected result using addition or subtraction (Feigenson et al., 2002a, 2002b;

Uller et al., 1999). But she may simply be comparing the set of objects she remembers with the set of objects she sees and noticing the mismatch. This process would not require any specific numerical concepts or operations such as addition and subtraction. Other studies, however, suggest that infants can add and subtract with displays of numbers that are too large for the number of objects that infants can normally represent in their minds (McCrink & Wynn, 2004). Moreover, infants can add and subtract number of events, which are not tracked by remembering specific objects (Wynn, 1996). Thus, while object representations may be used on some occasions to guide inferences about addition and subtraction, they cannot be the sole basis for such abilities.

Hence, it seems that numerical abilities, including some basic arithmetic operations, may be present very early in life, long before the infant acquires language. This preverbal ability raises questions about the use of number concepts in other species. It was traditionally assumed that other species did not understand number in the sense of different quantities of countable objects, but these assumptions have since been challenged (Gallistel, 1990). One of the most dramatic demonstrations of numerical competence in other species involved testing monkeys in replications of the studies involving adding or taking away objects. It now seems clear that not just the great apes, but a variety of monkeys not only are aware of number but also have some notion of subtraction and addition (Flombaum et al., 2005; Hauser et al., 1996; Mahajan et al., 2009). Even pigeons seem

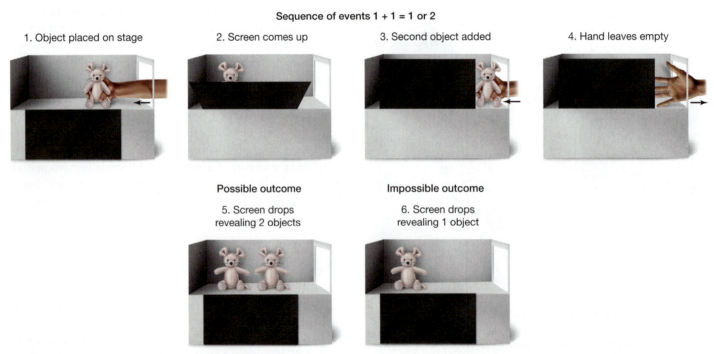

Sequence of events 1 + 1 = 1 or 2

1. Object placed on stage   2. Screen comes up   3. Second object added   4. Hand leaves empty

Possible outcome   Impossible outcome

5. Screen drops revealing 2 objects   6. Screen drops revealing 1 object

FIGURE 5.22 Addition in infants. A toy mouse is placed on a stage. The mouse is then blocked by a screen, and a second toy mouse is placed behind the screen. The screen drops to reveal either one or two toy mice. Five-month-old infants dishabituated when they saw just one mouse display but not when they saw two mice. Adapted from Wynn (1992).

to engage in simple forms of subtraction (Brannon et al., 2001), as do newborn chicks (Rugani et al., 2009).

Q: In what sense do infants have the ability to add and subtract?

Number awareness and mathematical skills in infants may not all arise from the same cognitive ability. There is growing evidence that numerical abilities depend on several distinct cognitive systems. One striking finding along these lines is that the ability to estimate differences in quantity involves separate areas of the brain from the areas of the brain involved in the ability to perform numerical calculations. In particular, estimation heavily involves the parietal regions of the brain, while calculations involve more frontal regions as well as areas that are also associated with language abilities (Cohen et al., 2000; Dehaene, 2009; Stanescu-Cosson et al., 2000). Different regions may be responsible for these abilities because the parietal regions emerged earlier in the course of evolution than the frontal regions, so that the abilities associated with earlier-emerging regions may be more common across species and more developmentally primitive. Thus, the estimation ability is thought to be evolutionarily very old, early to develop in the infant, and common to many species, whereas the calculation ability is possibly specific to humans, later to develop, and dependent on language (Cohen et al., 2000; Dehaene, 2009; Dehaene et al., 2004; Stanescu-Cosson et al., 2000). Considerable debate remains on just how important language is to the emergence of numerical skills (Brannon, 2005; Carey, 2001; Gelman & Butterworth, 2005; Wynn et al., 2002; Xu et al., 2005b).

In addition to an early estimation system, there is also evidence for an early-emerging system for processing discrete small numbers. When infants compare amounts such as two versus four, they may be using a distinct cognitive ability arising from a different brain region from that used for estimation. When electrical signals known as event-related potentials (ERPs) are measured on 6-month-old infants' scalps, distinct electrical patterns suggest that large-number estimations occur in different regions of the cortex from those associated with small-number operations such as addition and subtraction (Hyde & Spelke, 2011). This more primitive addition and subtraction ability, possibly one that involves mentally representing objects, does not involve language and may be shared with other species.

As one leading researcher in the field put it, "Our arithmetic intuition consists of a complex web of knowledge" (Dehaene, 2009, p. 254). Several distinct components to this intuition are present well before the first year of life and before the emergence of language, and they may function largely independently of each other. Over time, and possibly through language-based processes, these components become integrated and help create a more unified sense of number and arithmetic, although carefully designed tasks can reveal developmental vestiges of these distinct components (Dehaene, 2009).

Q: How is the preverbal infant's numerical ability different from that of a 5-year-old? How does comparative research across species shed light on this question?

Spatial Knowledge in Infants

Throughout this book, we have seen that infants are more likely to be proficient at skills that are needed early on. These skills include perceiving depth, perceiving faces, categorizing color, and tracking quantities. Another central skill involves knowing where one is. This ability requires creating mental maps of different environments, retaining them outside those environments, and being able to use those maps later to find one's way or to find an object. Spatial knowledge involves spatial representation—that is, knowing where objects are in relation to other objects or to the self and knowing where landmarks are so as to be able to find objects or to navigate from one place to another. For spatial knowledge to be used successfully, spatial representations must be abstract and flexible, going beyond simple storage of past action patterns.

The ability to use spatial knowledge might seem too complex and sophisticated for infants, and indeed a number of early researchers, including Piaget, proposed that children younger than about 1 year had no such abilities. Nevertheless, Piaget acknowledged that children younger than 2 could succeed at some spatial tasks. But recall that in his view, infants' spatial skills were based entirely on sensorimotor knowledge, which could only be used in motor schemes for performing simple actions (Piaget, 1952b, 1954; Piaget & Inhelder, 1967). One way to understand the limitations that Piaget attributed to infants revolves around how infants encode objects in relation to themselves and to other objects.

Spatial relations can be encoded egocentrically or allocentrically. An **egocentric representation** simply notes where things are relative to one's own body. A baby might remember that a chair last appeared on her right. An **allocentric representation** notes where things are relative to other landmarks in the world. You might remember that a chair was just below the right-hand corner of a window. Egocentric representations might seem simpler, but they are not reliable if the observer moves or turns her body. Perhaps young infants, who mostly sit still, can only encode spatial relations egocentrically until they have had ample experience in freely getting around on their own in the world.

Some early studies suggested that infants younger than 1 year are primarily egocentric, a finding that would be compatible with Piaget's theory that infants tend to encode the world in terms of sensorimotor representations (Acredolo, 1978, 1990; Acredolo & Evans, 1980). But other evidence indicates that even fairly young infants may have considerably more objective ways of representing spatial layout. By age 6 months, infants can keep track of changes in their own body position while making judgments about where objects are, even in featureless round environments (Tyler & McKenzie, 1990). They also seem to be able to track some geometric properties of their environment (for example, shapes and angles in the environment) and to use the angles as well as distances from landmarks to locate objects (Newcombe et al., 1998, 2005). One experimental technique involves hiding an object in a sandbox. The experimenter then retrieves it, either from the location where it disappeared or from a novel location. Infants as young as 5 months look longer when the object reappears in a new location (Newcombe et al., 1999, 2005). The infants' surprise when the object reappears in a novel location can then be used to test whether their perceptions are egocentric or allocentric.

To determine whether infants are using egocentric or allocentric representation to locate an object, experimenters habituated infants to a scene and then moved the infants to new locations or moved the object and observed where the infants expected the object to be. In one study, 4½-month-olds habituated to a pig puppet rotating in a wooden cage on one side of a table (Kaufman & Needham, 2011). The infant's view of the table was then blocked with a screen while the infant was moved, either to another side of the table or around the table and back to his original position. While the infant's view of the table was screened off, the puppet and cage were left in the same place or moved to a new position, diagonal to its original location. (In its new location, it was in the same position *relative to the infant* who had been moved to the other side of the table.) The key question was whether the infant would look longer at the puppet when it occupied its same location but stood in a new position relative to the infant himself, or whether the infant would be more surprised to find the puppet in a new location but occupying a constant position relative to his own body. In fact, the infants tended to look longer when the puppet changed its real, or allocentric, location rather than when it changed its position relative to themselves, or their egocentric location.

The finding that infants are capable of allocentric spatial representations well before age 6 months still leaves unanswered the question of why much older infants respond egocentrically in some tasks. The answer may lie in similarities between the tasks on which they respond egocentrically and the A-not-B task (Acredolo, 1990; Kaufman & Needham, 2011; Twyman & Newcombe, 2010). Remember that one explanation of the A-not-B error is that infants tend to get "stuck" repeating the same retrieval action that they have performed several times before, even when they know that the object is located elsewhere. In a similar way, some of the tasks that assess infants' representations of where objects are located train them to repeatedly turn their head to one side to look at an interesting sight. When the infants are then rotated in the same setting, they may have difficulty suppressing that earlier action, even if they don't really expect the interesting sight to be there. Of course, it is possible that infants' repeated actions are linked to their sense that the event or object really is where they are looking, but other evidence clearly indicates that they can also represent locations allocentrically. Thus, infants may have a single allocentric spatial representation that does not always correspond to their physical response bias, or they may have competing allocentric and egocentric spatial representations. Careful studies will be required to tease apart these two alternatives.

When young infants represent locations in an allocentric manner, what cues are they using? Among the distinct types of cues that infants could use, three especially prominent ones are beacons, landmarks, and the geometric shape of their environment. Using *beacons* seems to be the simplest technique, which simply involves noticing that an object is located directly under or right next to another salient and presumably permanent object (the beacon). Using *landmarks* involves somewhat more relational representations; it involves being able to use distance and direction from salient objects (the landmarks) to determine where another object is located, such as knowing that an object is located halfway between two landmarks. Thus, an infant might notice that a toy is halfway between a chair and a television. Finally, using *geometric cues* involves noticing that the environment has a particular shape—say, that it is an L-shaped room and that the object is located at the inner corner of the L.

It might seem that infants should first use beacons, then landmarks, then finally geometric cues, following our intuitions about the cues' complexity. But this conjecture should be tempered by the wealth of animal studies showing that an enormous variety of species use all three kinds of cues, sometimes without any apparent experience. Birds, rats, fish, and ants can, in some circumstances, use beacons and landmarks to find desired objects (Gray et al., 2005; Vallortigara et al., 2009), and they can also use geometric information (Brown et al., 2007; Cheng & Newcombe, 2005; Sovrano et al., 2007; Tommasi et al., 2012; Wall et al., 2004; Wystrach & Beugnon, 2009). In addition, some species reared in environments that lack unique geometric cues (for example, fish in a circular tank) will nonetheless use geometric information the first time they encounter it (for example, fish in a new rectangular tank) (Brown et al., 2007; Lee & Spelke, 2010). Thus, in at least some cases, the type of allocentric representation that seems most complex also seems to emerge without any prior experience.

Indeed, for animals and older children, geometric cues often trump landmark or beacon information when these cues are in conflict (Lee & Spelke, 2010; Spelke et al., 2010). There is no clear consensus on whether young children similarly prioritize geometric representations, let alone whether young infants do (Cheng, 2008; Twyman & Newcombe, 2010). Still, most researchers agree that infants seem to have access to all three allocentric representations by 6 months, and what may change with development is which ones serve as the default systems in specific contexts.

The simplest ways of measuring spatial knowledge, via locomotion, are difficult to use with babies, since they are so relatively immobile. But once a child can walk, the measures are easier and the evidence can be convincing. For example, although young children often get lost in strange places, they also show surprisingly impressive levels of performance. When one of our sons was barely a year old, he surprised us by very purposefully navigating a novel path through an unfamiliar shopping mall to return to a pet store that had fascinated him when we passed it a short while before. We had initially rushed our son past the pet store, and after carrying him through several turns, we had arrived at an ice cream shop in the mall. Upon being set down, he ignored the usually irresistible ice cream and immediately set off on a path for the pet store. We followed him in fascination as he wove through the crowds, taking a different path from the one on which he had been carried, until more than 100 yards later, he ended up with his face pressed against the window of the pet store. Considering that he had been walking for only a few weeks and that the mall was crowded with adults who frequently obscured his view, this navigational skill was extraordinary—and unlikely to have just emerged in his first few weeks of walking. Exactly how it developed, however, remains mostly unknown, a mystery for clever and creative future research. Infants may be endowed with an ability to use beacons, landmarks, and geometry, but with limitations on each and interference between them, as well as intrusions from egocentric responding, it may take several years after infancy to fully integrate all these cues into one coherent navigation system.

Q: Describe three different ways of knowing one's location in space. How are those different sorts of information used in development?

Categorization in Infants

In earlier chapters, we saw that infants categorically perceive color, speech, and possibly other kinds of stimuli, but such behavior is only the beginning of categorization. Going beyond perceptual categorization, infants also categorize objects, events, animals, and people—grouping them into classes based on shared features and later into classes based on shared functions or meaning. These more conceptual categories are internally processed by mental representations that are typically called "concepts" of those categories or of the objects that make up those categories. They enable an infant to both appreciate the category as a whole and to distinguish or individuate members within that category. Consider the mental representations involved in learning the categories "dog," "friend," or "truck," much less "Pokémon." How do infants come to understand categories of things that go beyond immediate perception (see Figure 5.23)?

The empiricists have a straightforward answer to this question: infants learn these categories by being exposed to many examples of objects and discovering the objects' shared properties through experience. As infants see more and more dogs, they will notice the features that these animals typically share, such as fur, barking, and particular body shapes. Over the course of many learning experiences, these common properties come to stand for the category of "dog" and enable children to recognize new dogs. In the empiricists' view, this learning process consists of strengthening the associations between certain categories and their properties through repeated experiences in which they occur together. By contrast, nativists hold that infants have predetermined

FIGURE 5.23 **Categorization in infancy.** When a 1-year-old plays with a truck, what sort of categorization is also at work? Does the infant realize that the truck is a kind of vehicle that is made by people? How is the 1-year-old's categorization different from that of a 9-month-old or a 2-year-old? Researchers hold various views of infant categorization and of the influence of language on categorization.

Advances in Infant Eye-Tracking Methods

For many years, researchers have been measuring eye gaze as a means of making inferences about infant perception and cognition (Salapatek & Kessen, 1966). Major changes in the technology of tracking eye movements have provided important new ways of conducting such studies with infants (Aslin & McMurray, 2004). Sophisticated eye tracking has been performed on adults for quite some time, but eye tracking in infants presents special challenges. In many cases, the tracking requires adults to sit still and keep their head immobile, resting their chin on a support and holding their forehead against a brace. Other systems allow somewhat freer head movements, but larger head and body movements will compromise accuracy. In addition, calibrating most adult eye-tracking systems requires the participant to look at a number of specific objects. Because infants can't be told to sit still or to focus intently on command, measuring infant eye tracking requires a way of compensating for frequent head movements.

Technological improvements and advanced software now make it quite easy to calibrate eye-tracking systems in preverbal infants and to compensate for some degree of head movement. In addition, some eye-tracking systems simply consist of having an infant wear special glasses that contain both a camera that records what she sees and infrared sensors that constantly track where she is looking within that scene. The systems are often calibrated by showing the infant bright dots that become larger at various locations on a screen. The dots naturally attract the infant's attention, so no explicit training is needed.

Eye tracking is increasingly being used to explore how infants think about objects and their properties. For example, when an infant sees an object go behind a barrier, eye tracking provides

suggestions about what he is thinking. Eye-tracking evidence suggests that when infants as young as 4 months old watch an object move for a few seconds, then disappear behind a screen, they actually visualize the unseen object moving behind the screen, as shown by their anticipatory eye movements toward where the object will reemerge (von Hofsten et al., 2007). Subtle factors may influence when infants can successfully show predictive eye movements that anticipate an object's reappearance, and here, too, eye tracking may help reveal how young infants' prior experiences—for example, repeated viewing of the object as it moves along a path before the screen is put in place to hide the moving object—facilitate this ability (Johnson & Shuwairib, 2009). By the time they are 6 months old, infants can accurately envision the object moving behind the screen and can even seem to envision one object hitting another behind a screen and this second object then moving out from behind the screen (Woods et al., 2010).

Eye tracking can go beyond exploring infants' understanding of objects' motions to probing their thinking about objects' functional properties—that is, knowing what an object can be used for. Infants usually do not show consistent, correct motor uses of simple everyday objects, such as hairbrushes, cups, and phones, until well after they are 12 months old. But do they encode objects' functional uses at an earlier age, before they are able to act them out? To measure this early ability, we can track infants' eye movements while they watch brief video clips of actors using objects either correctly or incorrectly. One study focused on infants at ages 6, 8, 12, 14, and 16 months while they watched adult actors use a brush, or a telephone, or a cup either correctly or incorrectly (Hunnius & Bekkering, 2010). For

biases to think about some categories—biases that can range from simply understanding a particular concept from the start to more abstract constraints on classes of concepts. For example, a nativist might claim that there is a bias to favor functional features (an object serves as a container) over perceptual ones (an object is a cylinder) when both are equally salient and in competition with each other. In Chapter 7, we will consider some special categories to which young infants seem to have fear responses, and in Chapter 9, we will consider in more detail how older children come to understand concepts, but we will begin here with a discussion of some work on young infants' abilities to think about categories.

We know from the research on number that infants are surprised when number changes. But what about when object properties change? Since infants base categories on their recognition of objects' shared properties, the stability of those properties is an important part of categorization. If a toy cat disappears behind a barrier and immediately thereafter a toy dog appears at the other end of the barrier, adults will assume that two objects are involved because they believe that objects' properties are stable and cannot change while moving briefly behind a barrier. Do young infants have similar ideas about what properties, such as size, shape, and color, remain stable over time (Xu, 2003; Xu & Carey, 1996)?

FIGURE 5.24 Eye tracking as a window into functional understanding. Infants as young as 6 months have strong expectations about the motor actions and targets associated with specific objects. Here infants look ahead to a person's mouth when she lifts a cup, even when the cup is moved to a location that would be more appropriate for a phone. The dot indicates where the infant is looking. From Hunnius & Bekkering (2010).

example, when the adult used the cup correctly, infants at all ages would look "ahead" from the moment the adult grasped the cup until it reached the adult's mouth, anticipating correctly that the cup would soon be at the adult's mouth. When the adult moved the cup to her ear instead, as if to use it as a phone, infants of all ages still looked expectantly at the mouth, having trouble anticipating this atypical action even as they saw the adult's hand continue to move toward her ear (see Figure 5.24). In contrast, adults quickly readjusted and tracked the object as it moved to an atypical location.

These results show that by 6 months of age, well before most infants show consistent use of such objects, infants have developed expectations about specific motor actions associated with these objects. These anticipations may not constitute a full functional understanding, but they are at least an important precursor. To be sure, eye-tracking systems, no matter how sophisticated, are only one window on infant cognition. The largest benefits of the new technology will lie in how information gathered from eye-tracking studies converges with data from other methods.

In one study that examined this question, 9-month-olds watched as a toy truck disappeared behind one side of a barrier, then saw a toy duck emerge soon after from the other side before going back behind the barrier. When the barrier was lifted to reveal only one object, the infants did not dishabituate. But when the raised barrier revealed both a truck and a duck, the infants dishabituated; they appeared surprised to see two objects. In another experimental condition, the infants saw both the truck and the duck at the same time on either side of the barrier before both disappeared behind it. In this condition, the infants seemed to expect to see both objects when the screen was raised (Xu & Carey, 1996).

These results suggest that 9-month-olds do not realize that objects, like the truck and the duck, keep most of their properties over time. Some researchers have suggested that as children's early language skills emerge (at about 1 year), their way of representing category knowledge changes, resulting in properties being more stably attached to objects (Xu, 2002; Xu et al., 2005a). The labels provided by words may help infants direct their attention to an object's properties so as to know how a category contrasts with other categories. An alternative interpretation is that younger children's memories of properties may fade more quickly in certain kinds of tasks, but that with categories that have more memorable properties or tasks that reduce the demands on memory (such as briefer disappearances behind the barrier), children might view the properties as being preserved over time (Baillargeon & Wang, 2002; Wilcox & Baillargeon, 1998; Wilcox & Chapa, 2004).

One piece of evidence supporting this second view is the finding that when researchers demonstrate a different function for each of two objects in advance (for example, pulling a handle on one object makes a light flash, while turning a knob on the other object makes a short melody occur), the 10-month-olds pass the task as easily as 12-month-olds, expecting that there are two objects (Futo et al., 2010). Further support has come from studies in which infants observe a self-moving, seemingly animate object (a moving toy caterpillar) go behind one side of the screen and an inanimate, inert object (a red cup) go behind the other side. When they are presented with such a large distinction between animate and inanimate categories, 10-month-olds again pass the task (Surian & Caldi, 2010; see also Bonatti et al., 2002). But younger infants may need more powerful indicators of distinctive object properties to remember them across different parts of the screening event (Baillargeon et al., 2012). Taken together, these studies illustrate that infants have some early sense of object types, but the studies also illustrate the great challenge of knowing how infants categorize the world before they can speak and whether their early categories are anything like the ones we associate with names like "dog," "cat," and "truck."

FIGURE 5.25 **Levels of categorization.** Despite very high perceptual similarity between the birds and the airplanes, infants as young as 9 months recognize the two categories as distinct in sorting and imitation tasks. These results have been taken to show that preverbal infants form categories on conceptual bases as well as on perceptual ones. From Mandler (2004a).

> **Q:** How do 9-month-olds and 12-month-olds differ in their abilities to track objects and their properties when the objects are out of sight? How have these developmental differences been explained?

In addition to exploring infants' use of categories by studying their understanding of objects' stable, physical properties, developmental researchers have also investigated the level of abstraction (that is, the generality) at which categories are first represented in the infant's mind. Some studies strongly suggest that infants as young as 10 months old tend to categorize at surprisingly abstract levels, using "vehicle" rather than "car," or "animal" rather than "dog" (Mandler 2004a, 2004b, 2012; Mandler & McDonough, 1993, 1998; see Figure 5.25). This may be because certain general properties (for example, being a self-moving entity) are easier to recognize than more specific properties (for example, number of legs or kind of tail). One method of studying the categories that infants use involves looking at the order in which infants touch a group of objects arrayed in front of them (Mareschal & Tan, 2007; Ricciuti, 1965). Researchers infer that objects touched one right after the

other, such as all vehicles, are seen by the infant as belonging to the same category. The same high-level categories have been found with other techniques involving imitations of taught properties about categories. Thus, if an infant sees an experimenter say "vroom vroom" while moving a truck, she will then make the same motion and sound not just with other trucks but also with other vehicles, such as cars and planes (Mandler & McDonough, 1996). Infants may not always categorize at the higher level, and researchers can prime them to categorize at lower levels by showing them multiple lower-level examples earlier (Mareschal & Tan, 2007), but the key point is that infants do not need to begin categorizing at a lower, "more concrete" level. Other studies suggest that infants as young as 6 months can form abstract categories such as "vehicle" and "animal." In those studies, after infants habituate to many members of a broad category, such as vehicles, they then dishabituate more to novel items that are not vehicles than to novel members of the habituated category (Bornstein et al., 2010).

Infants expect members of the same categories to have the same kinds of hidden features. Thus, when 9-month-olds are taught that a novel feature exists inside a kind of box, they expect all boxes of that type to have the same feature inside, but they do not expect that other types of boxes will have that feature inside (Dewar & Xu, 2010). Even more dramatically, infants develop hunches about which properties are essential to a category and which are more incidental. For example, we tend to think that inside properties of animals are more likely to indicate their category than surface, outside properties like a collar. Some have argued that this psychological bias toward inside, usually unobservable features is a human universal and is found in all children of early preschool age (Gelman, 2003; Keil, 1989). In fact, the bias may emerge even earlier. In one study, 14-month-old-infants watched two animated cats that each moved in their own way: one swayed side to side and the other jumped up and down. Each cat had either a red hat and a red stomach (indicated by a translucent image beneath the skin) or a blue hat and a blue stomach. Then, a new cat with a mismatched hat and stomach (either a red hat and a blue stomach or a blue hat and a red stomach) appeared and began to move like one of the original cats. The infants did not dishabituate when the new cat moved like the cat that shared its stomach color (since this is what they expected). But they did dishabituate, and look longer, when the cat moved like the cat that shared only its hat color (Newman et al., 2008b; see Figure 5.26). The infants seemed to find the inner property of stomach color more important for categorizing and forming expectations than the surface feature of hat color. Thus, not all features are treated equally in categorization, and infants favor some of the same ones that adults consider essential.

> **Q:** What is the evidence that children under 1 year of age sometimes more easily grasp higher-level categories than lower-level ones?

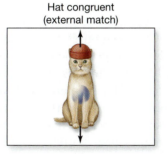

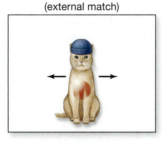

FIGURE 5.26 Categorization and essential features. One study sought to determine whether infants use internal or external information to categorize animated objects. **(A)** In a habituation event, animated cats with a blue hat and blue stomach moved side to side, while animated cats with a red hat and red stomach moved up and down. **(B)** In test events, the stomach color and hat color were mismatched, and the cat's movement either matched the motion of the cat with the same stomach color or with the same hat color. Infants expected the motion to be the same as that of the cat with the same stomach color (internal feature), and they dishabituated when it was the same as that of the cat with the same hat color (external feature). Adapted from Newman et al. (2008b).

Distinguishing the Physical World from the Social World

Much of the infant's understanding of the physical world involves having a clear sense that social agents behave in radically different ways from inanimate things. We have already seen that the difference between social and nonsocial categories may be one of the most fundamental conceptual distinctions that infants make. They do far more than make the distinction, however; they reason about social agents and nonsocial things in very different ways. For the most part, social agents are other people, but they can also be animals. Social agents have many observable properties that distinguish them from inanimate things (see Table 5.3). Social agents typically can move on their own, whereas inanimate objects need external agents to set them on their way. Social agents can change their own trajectories, whereas

Social Agents (People and Animals)	Inanimate Things
Can move on their own.	Require an external force to move.
Can change the direction of their own movement midpath without external influence.	Only an external force can change their direction of movement midpath.
Causal reactions can be immediate or delayed.	Causal reactions tend to be immediate.
Influence from afar ("action at distance") is common.	Influence almost always requires direct contact.

TABLE 5.3 Some easily perceivable properties that distinguish animates and inanimates. There are several properties relating to the behaviors of social agents that are markedly different from those relating to the behaviors of inanimate things and that appear to be known to young infants.

inanimate objects will continue on the same path of motion unless an external object or obstruction intervenes. Inanimate things and social agents also respond differently to causal influences. For inanimate objects, consequences tend to be immediate. Hit one ball with another, and it instantly responds to the collision. By contrast, a social agent might take some time to respond. A child who is pushed may not react at all, but after several pushes may erupt in a rage. In addition, inanimate objects cannot be influenced from a distance; they require direct contact. By contrast, social agents can be influenced from afar, a concept that can be described as "action at a distance." For example, a person can react to something she hears or sees from far away (Gelman & Spelke, 1981). Moreover, social beings are believed to have goals and intentions for their actions, whereas the movements of inanimate objects are not believed to be intentional. Many organisms pick up on these cues to divide the world into social and nonsocial categories. Even when newborn chicks are presented with two kinds of objects, one that moves on its own and one that moves only when it comes into contact with another object, the chicks prefer to associate with self-propelled objects, presumably because self-propulsion is a reliable cue indicating animate mothers and not inanimate objects (Mascalzoni et al., 2010).

Action at a Distance and Social Contingency

Infants can be quite sensitive to the ways that social agents, and not inanimate objects, can influence each other from a distance. In a study that investigated infants' expectations about "action-at-a-distance" causality, the infants watched animated videos of two 6-foot-high cylinders "interacting" in different ways (see Figure 5.27). In the first interaction, which showed action at a distance, cylinder A moved toward cylinder B and stopped near it, without touching it. After a moment, cylinder B then moved away. In the second video, which showed a "launching" event, cylinder A moved toward cylinder B, but the cylinders made direct contact before cylinder B immediately moved away. Infants as young as 7 months showed different reactions when watching similar events that involved either social or nonsocial pairs of objects (Spelke et al., 1995). When the moving objects were simple cylinders, infants dishabituated more strongly to the action-at-a-distance event than they did to the launching event, since they did not expect that one cylinder could cause another to move without touching it. Even at age 7 months, however, infants reacted quite differently when, instead of cylinders, the videos showed two people interacting in these same ways. Infants no longer dishabituated more strongly to the action at a distance than to the launching. It is as if they knew that social beings don't require direct contact to influence each other (Schlottmann & Surian, 1999; Schlottmann et al., 2009; see also Luo et al., 2009, for related findings with 5-month-olds).

In somewhat older infants, various cues that there is a social agent present will trigger inferences that the agent is perceiving and attending to information. One study asked if cues that there is contingent responding (where responses from one person or object are dependent on the responses from another) were sufficient to elicit expectations of a perceiving and attending agent. In that study, 12-month-old infants saw a featureless furry object in front of them on a table (see Figure 5.28). The object seemed to make beeping sounds contingent on the infant's own sounds (Johnson et al., 1998). (In fact, an experimenter was covertly pressing a button to make a sound each time the infant made one.) Even though the beeps did not sound human, the way the furry object's "responses" seemed to depend on the infant's sounds gave

FIGURE 5.27 **Action at a distance.** When infants saw cylinder A stop without touching cylinder B and then saw B move off on its own, they dishabituated more strongly than when they observed cylinder A make contact with cylinder B. When cylinders A and B were replaced with people, infants did not show stronger dishabituation to the action-at-a-distance event. They seemed to expect inanimate objects to act on each other through direct collisions but allowed for animate beings to act on each other at a distance. Adapted from Spelke et al. (1995).

Action–at–a–distance event

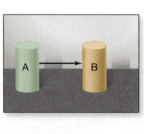

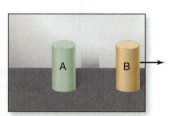

Launching event

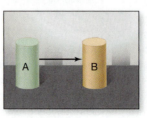
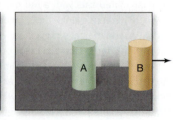

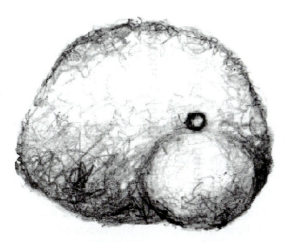

FIGURE 5.28 **Perceiving social contingency.** When confronted with a featureless furry object that made sounds contingent on their own sounds, 12-month-old infants seemed to regard the object as a social being. They even turned when the furry object turned in order to look where the object seemed to be "looking." From Johnson et al. (1998).

the infant a strong sense that he was interacting with a social agent rather than with something inanimate. This sense was powerful enough that when the furry object then turned 90 degrees, the infant also turned to look where the object appeared to be "looking" (Johnson et al., 1998, 2007, 2008; Shimizu & Johnson, 2004). Moreover, infants appeared to infer that if an object interacts contingently with a person, seemingly responding to his actions, then the object's attention-gathering side faces the person during the interaction (Movellan & Watson, 2002). Knowing that an entity is social leads to this kind of inference about the motives for its actions. In fact, adults respond similarly; in interactions with a robot that clearly looks mechanical but is programmed to respond contingently to them, adults also tend to overestimate its mental capacities (Scassellati, 2002).

Goal and Belief Attribution

We have seen that quite young infants can distinguish social agents from inanimate objects based on the social agents' capacity to respond to action at a distance and contingency information and that infants use this information to make inferences about what other social beings are perceiving and where they are directing their attention. Beyond the directly observable differences between social agents and inanimate objects, some of the most profound differences concern social agents' intentions, goals, and beliefs. Although these distinctions are not measurable the way a change in trajectory is, adults and older children can infer them immediately—and we often make inferences automatically about another person's goals and intentions. We seem to understand imme-

diately that a person reaching for a door handle intends to grasp it or that a person or animal that chases another may have negative intentions. Infants, like adults, seem driven to interpret the behaviors of social agents in terms of goals.

One line of research asked if infants tend to encode events in terms of goals as opposed to simpler physical attributes. In one study, 5-month-olds and 9-month-olds saw a small stage-like setup with one object—say, a ball—on the left and another object—say, a teddy bear—on the right (Woodward, 1998; see Figure 5.29). They then saw something move in from "backstage"—a hand in one experimental condition or a stick in the other condition—and remove the ball. Next, a screen came down to block their view of the stage, and when it was raised, the infants saw that the teddy bear and the ball had switched locations—the teddy bear was now on the left and the ball was on the right. Once again, they saw either a hand or a stick "enter" from backstage and remove one of the objects. The question was whether infants would

A Habituation event

B Same reach

C Same goal

FIGURE 5.29 **Interpreting actions in terms of goals.** After watching a hand reach for an object **(A)**, infants as young as 5 months are more surprised to see the hand move to the same location to retrieve a different object **(B)** than they are when the hand moves to a different location to retrieve the same object as before **(C)**. Apparently, they interpret the hand as having the goal of obtaining a specific object. By contrast, after seeing a stick "reach" for an object, the infant appears surprised to see the stick go to a new location to retrieve the same object. They appear to view the stick as simply moving to a set location without having a particular goal. Adapted from Woodward (1998).

assume that a person (represented by the hand) would have a goal related to a particular object, but a stick would not. Researchers would answer this based on how the infants reacted to where the hand or the stick moved after the objects changed location. If for all events the infants simply encoded the physical actions in front of them, they should be more likely to dishabituate when the action changed and the hand or stick went to a new location. If, however, they selectively encoded the hand in terms of the goal of its inferred actor, they might be more likely to notice when the hand reached for a new kind of object, even if it was in the same location. By contrast, even if infants did encode goals for hands, they should not encode any goals for the stick and should show stronger dishabituation when it went to a new location.

The results were clear. When infants had originally seen a hand remove the ball, both the 5-month-olds and the 9-month-olds dishabituated more strongly if the hand went to the ball's old location (on the left) and removed the teddy bear than if the hand once again found the ball, even though it was in a new place (on the right). By contrast, if they had originally seen a stick remove the ball, they dishabituated more strongly if the stick went to the ball in its new location (on the right) than if it went to the ball's old location (on the left) and ended up with the teddy bear instead (Woodward, 1998). The opposite patterns of results in the two conditions neatly demonstrate that the infants interpreted the actions of the hand as intentional but did not attribute intentions to the stick. The infants in these studies certainly seemed to think about social agents as being embedded in different patterns of causation than inanimate objects, and in some cases these results were even found in infants as young as 3 months (Luo, 2011; Luo & Baillargeon, 2005). Nonetheless, we must be careful in attributing adult-like beliefs to infants. More conservatively, we can say that the infants' responses make good sense to our adult intuitions.

For many years, it was assumed that infants, as well as young toddlers, might be able to think about others' goals and desires but not about their beliefs. This assumption arose from the ways in which children younger than about 3½ years old fail at certain kinds of laboratory tasks that require understanding that a person may have false beliefs—for example, a person's false belief that an object that was moved when she was not present is still in its original location (Wimmer & Perner, 1983). We will look at these false-belief tasks in more detail in Chapter 13, but the key point here is that these tasks that are failed by young children require the children to answer an explicit question about an individual's false belief—for example, they are asked where the person will look for the object that was moved in the person's absence (Baillargeon et al., 2010). But if a child's understanding of false beliefs is instead measured in terms

of the child's spontaneous responses, such as the child's reaction to a violation of expectations, then quite remarkably, infants as young as 13 months seem able to take false beliefs into account in interpreting others' actions.

In these studies, an infant might observe an actor watching a toy being moved from one container to another. Then a screen comes up, blocking only the actor's view of the containers. The infant watches as the toy is moved to the other container while the actor's view is still blocked. When the screen comes down, the infant observes the actor either reaching for the container where the toy was originally hidden or reaching for the container into which it was moved while out of sight (see Figure 5.30). Infants look longer when the actor reaches toward the toy's new location, even though it is where the toy really is (Onishi & Baillargeon, 2005; Surian et al., 2007). They seem to expect the actor to look for the toy at the original location, based on the assumption that the actor has a false belief that it is still there. If the same experiment is performed without a screen, the infants look longer when the actor reaches for the toy at its original location, because they assume that the actor watched as the toy was moved and formed new beliefs about where it is.

Infants appear to be surprisingly sensitive to the cues that indicate the particular goals of a social agent. If infants watch an animation in which a triangle moves around a screen in a way that suggests it is "chasing" a square, they will dishabituate when the shapes reverse their roles and the chaser switches from chasing to fleeing, indicating that the infants recognize that each now has a different goal (Rochat et al., 2004). These studies shed new light on decades-old research showing that adults also attribute goals to simple geometric figures. The infant studies clarified that these attributions were not a gradually acquired cultural convention but a foundational way of seeing social agents (Heider & Simmel, 1944).

Young infants even appear to understand social agents' goals in ways that lead to inferences about the agents' dispositions and future behaviors. In one study, 12-month-old infants watched an animation in which one shape (a triangle) "helped" another (a ball) to move up a hill while a different shape (a square) "hindered" the ball. Researchers then asked if the infants would make inferences about how the shapes would interact in a new task. Specifically, would the infants assume that the ball would more likely approach the shape that previously had helped it move up the hill rather than the shape that had hindered it (Kuhlmeier et al., 2003; see Chapter 7)? The results indicated that in a new context (one without a hill to climb), the infants looked longer when the ball approached the helping shape. They may have looked longer because they saw approaching the helper as the more coherent ongoing event and therefore wanted to keep monitoring it. (Although infants sometimes look longer at unexpected events, in other cases,

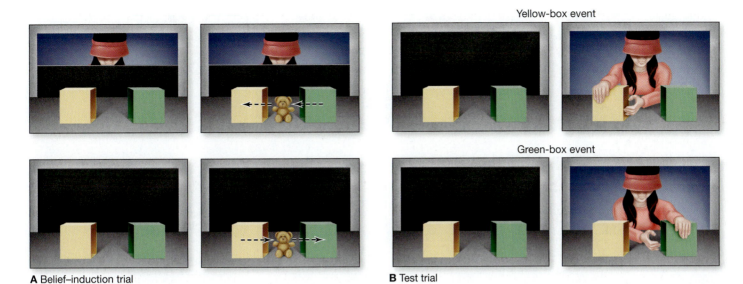

A Belief–induction trial   **B** Test trial

Yellow-box event

Green-box event

FIGURE 5.30 Understanding false beliefs. (A) In the belief-induction trial, infants observe the actor watching the toy being moved from the green box to the yellow box, and then the infants observe the toy being moved from the yellow box to the green box while the actor is out of sight and her view is blocked. **(B)** In the test trial, the infants watch the actor reach for the toy either in the yellow box or in the green box, and researchers measure the infants' reaction (based on looking time) to where the actor searches for the toy. Infants as young as 13 months look longer when an actor reaches for the object in the green box if it was surreptitiously moved from the yellow box while a screen blocked the actor's view. Adapted from Onishi and Baillargeon (2005).

such as this one, they look longer at expected events. The key finding is that they showed a clear difference in looking time between events in which the ball approached helpers versus when it approached hinderers.) Remarkable as this finding is with 12-month-olds, it was then replicated in an even more striking way with 6-month-olds (Hamlin et al., 2007). In this version of the task, infants watched as a display of real three-dimensional objects either helped or hindered another object's path up a ramp. The infants were then allowed to choose (indicated by reaching) which object they wanted to hold, the helper or the hinderer. They consistently preferred the object that helped. Attributing goals to social agents therefore leads infants to make further inferences about how those same agents will behave in the future and whether it is desirable to be in close proximity to them.

By 18 months, infants understand human actions in very different terms from those of objects, and they become increasingly able to differentiate between a true social agent with intentions and goals and an object that is merely behaving like one. For example, if infants watch someone repeatedly attempting an action, such as putting a ring on a hook or pulling the cap off one side of a bar, and failing, they will not imitate the failed action they repeatedly observed but instead will imitate the action they assume was intended (Meltzoff, 1995; see Figure 5.31; see also Johnson, 2000). By contrast, after watching an inanimate object produce the same "failed action," the infants do not infer a goal—they simply reproduce the action they saw.

> **Q:** How do studies on infant imitation reveal differences in how infants see social and nonsocial agents and their actions?

What is it about watching social agents' actions that triggers infants to attribute goals to them? Are human-like features, such as a face or a hand, essential? That view, although long popular, seems unlikely, given that infants will attribute goals to simple geometric shapes after watching them chasing and fleeing. In fact, just the appearance of self-propelled motion in any sort of object can trigger infants to attribute goals to the object.

In a study similar to one discussed earlier, in which a hand or a stick retrieved a teddy bear or a ball (Woodward, 1998), when 5-month-olds saw a small block seemingly move on its own toward an object, they assumed that it had a goal. Much as infants in the earlier study assumed that a hand moving an object was a social agent and that it had a goal, the infants in the second study assumed that the self-propelled block was also a social agent and that it would have the goal of "seeking out" and approaching the same object, even when that object was moved to a new location. In contrast, if the block had a long handle that seemed to be manipulated by something out of view, the infants inferred that it was an inanimate object and that it

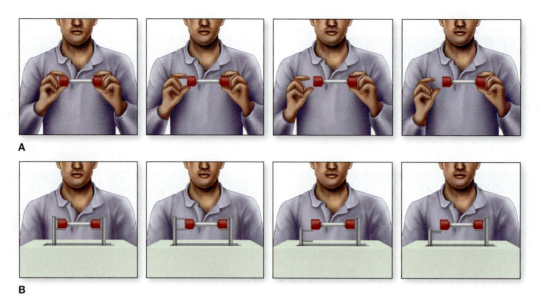

A

B

FIGURE 5.31 Imitation of intended goal. (A) When a social agent is viewed as engaging in an action, 18-month-old infants imitate the intended action (even if the agent is not able to achieve the goal) rather than the real action, inferring a goal to act on. In this case, the human actor is repeatedly trying to pull the cap off a small bar. The infant imitates actually taking the cap off instead of the failure to take it off. **(B)** When the same action is performed by a machine (which also is not able to pull the cap off the end of the bar), the infant does not imitate the goal. Adapted from Meltzoff (1995).

would return repeatedly to the same location, even when a different object was located there, since they assumed that an inanimate object would not have a goal (Luo & Baillargeon, 2005; see Figure 5.32). Thus, even before their first 6 months of life, infants attribute goals based on simple

perceptual cues of apparent self-directed movement (see also Luo, 2011). The more cues there are indicating that something is a social agent, such as action at a distance, contingent responding, and self-propelled movement, the easier it is for younger infants to infer that a social agent,

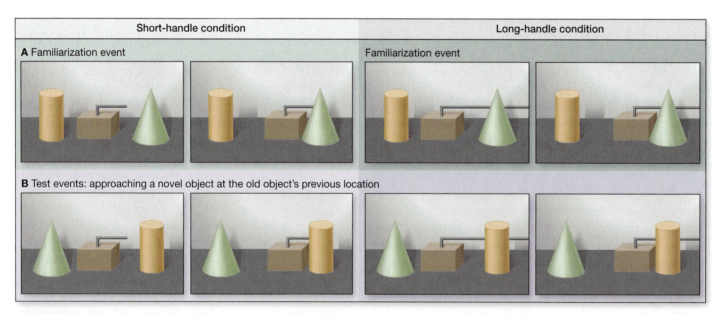

FIGURE 5.32 Context and goal attribution. When infants saw a block with a small handle as moving by itself, they attributed goals to it. During the familiarization event, the infants observed the block with the short handle contact the cone (and since it seemed to be self-propelled, they perceived the cone as its goal). When the location of the cone and cylinder were switched, the infants expected the block to contact the cone at its new location, and they dishabituated when the block seemed to have a new goal (approaching a new object—the cylinder—at the previous location of the cone). When they saw the block being moved by an off-screen agent holding a longer handle, they no longer attributed goals to the box and did not dishabituate when the box approached the cylinder at the previous location of the cone. Adapted from Luo & Baillargeon (2005).

The Myth of the First 3 Years

Do children's experiences in the first 3 years of life have an especially powerful impact on the development of brain structures and functions that then has long-term consequences for psychological abilities long after that period is over? Both proponents of early education and intervention programs and purveyors of products like "educational toys" that are said to maximize early learning experiences in infants frequently refer to neuroscientific evidence, such as the formation of an especially large number of synaptic connections in the first few years of life, to suggest that children must develop cognitive skills when these new neural circuits are forming or risk having insufficient neural growth later on to support rapid learning. These changes are described as evidence for developmental "windows," or critical periods, during which essential learning must take place if it is to happen at all. Other discussions refer to the pruning of synaptic connections, which starts to occur in toddlers, arguing that this process shapes the brain's architecture in particular ways. Certain forms of pruning are said to occur only in early development, so that if a young child misses out on certain early experiences, optimal pruning will not occur.

These neurodevelopmental patterns are used to argue that early intervention programs for disadvantaged children are especially important because early childhood is a time when environmental inputs sculpt the brain. Others outside of psychology, such as economists, have used these claims to support arguments for targeting most funding for disadvantaged children to the first few years because they believe it will have the greatest impact at that time (Doyle et al., 2009; Heckman, 2006).

Accepting such claims is tempting, given the many significant brain changes that occur during the first few years. But even though the patterns of brain change in early childhood are remarkable and widespread, anatomical development doesn't provide supporting evidence for benefits from a specific kind of early intervention program.

John Bruer, a philosopher of science with expertise in neuroscience, has examined how well the neuroscience data on development support the popular claims that there are critical learning periods in early development. It is especially important to put these claims to the test, as they are used to justify social policies that allocate vast resources for enriched experiences in the first 3 years of life (Bruer, 1999, 2006, 2008). In short, the strong neuroscientific claims about critical learning periods before age 3 do not hold up (with the important exception of cases in which children are severely neglected). As Bruer puts

it, "neuroscience cannot currently tell us much about whether we can, let alone how to, influence brain development" during the first few years (Bruer, 1999). Bruer has also pointed out several reasons to be cautious about neuroscience-based claims about critical learning periods: (1) Bruer says that most critical-period effects that have been clearly demonstrated pertain to quite focused abilities, such as binocular fusion of the eyes' separate images or the ability to see with high acuity. He states that there is no evidence for broad, general critical-period effects on perception and cognition. Even the critical periods for visual development can happen at different times, depending on the visual task involved. (2) Bruer points out that most of the patterns of synaptic overexuberance and pruning in the brains of infants and young children may be largely determined by genes in a way that is not influenced very much by the normal range of environmental experiences, even if there may be effects in cases of more extreme deprivation. (3) He argues that the detailed timing of major early brain developments, even in the areas of neural tissue that would be most relevant for such abilities as executive processes in memory and reasoning, doesn't closely coincide with the time frames or critical periods considered most important for psychological change (Bruer, 1999, 2002).

Clearly, popular claims about development can have a huge effect on public policy. To evaluate these kinds of claims, we need to have a detailed understanding of early cognitive development and how its patterns relate to what is known about early brain development, including experimental studies showing how experience might be related to changes in cognition and the brain. The kind of interesting, stimulating environments that Early Head Start and similar programs promote surely do provide experiences that are valuable for children's cognitive development. The problem lies in the policy choices that parents and politicians make when they are convinced that the first few years are all that really matters (Heckman, 2006). If all of cognitive development was constrained by such a powerful, fixed critical period, then communities would devote all of their resources and energies to infants and toddlers, leaving little or no resources for the later years. When bad science causes even modest changes in spending along these lines, older children may suffer. Advances in cognitive neuroscience are shaping how we understand cognitive development in infancy and early childhood. It is important to keep these exciting findings from being distorted in ways that might hurt rather than help most children (Goswami, 2006; Munakata et al., 2004).

rather than an inanimate object, is present (Biro & Leslie, 2007). Older infants and children will easily make such inferences with just one cue (see Scientific Method box).

The behavior of somewhat older, but still preverbal, infants shows that their inferences about social agents can be complex: they assume not only that agents have goals and beliefs, but that they will act reasonably. For example, if infants as young as 9 months old have been habituated to an animation of a shape hopping over a barrier to move next to another object, they will dishabituate if they see the shape perform the same hop when the barrier is gone. They will not dishabituate, however, when, in the absence of the barrier, the shape simply moves along the ground straight toward the object. Even though the shape takes a different path from the one they saw during habituation, the infants apparently recognize

that this is the only reasonable way to behave, in light of the shape's apparent goal (Gergely et al., 1995).

Given that young chimpanzees have similar reactions to these kinds of animated scenes (Uller, 2004), any interpretations we can make about human infants' social understanding based on these findings may also apply to some of the great apes as well. Thus, chimpanzees are believed to understand that social agents have goals and intentions. They may differ from human infants, however, when it comes to understanding false beliefs. Despite many attempts, it has not been possible to show that apes, such as chimpanzees, can consistently take into account false beliefs, even when using the spontaneous response methods that have revealed such abilities in human infants as young as 13 months old (Call & Tomasello, 2008; Krachun et al., 2010).

SCIENTIFIC METHOD: Agents and Order

Hypothesis:

Before they have language, infants will understand that only intentional agents are likely to create order out of disorder.

Method:

1. Twenty-four 12-month-old infants watched either a video of a disordering event, in which the blocks went from order to disorder, or a video of an ordering event, in which a randomly arranged group of blocks became neatly ordered.

2. For both kinds of events, infants saw (a) the blocks in the initial state, (b) a screen in front of the blocks, and (c) the blocks in the end state after the screen had been removed.

3. After the screen was in place, either an animated, self-moving object or an inanimate object went behind the screen and stayed there after the screen was removed.

4. Researchers recorded infants' looking times at the end state.

Results:

Infants looked longer at an ordering event that was accompanied by an inanimate agent than they did at a disordering event that was accompanied by an inanimate agent. They did not show a looking time difference between disordering and ordering events for animate objects.

Conclusion:

By 1 year of age, infants expect only animate agents to be capable of producing order from disorder. They expect that both animate and inanimate entities can produce disorder from order.

Source study: Newman et al. (2010).

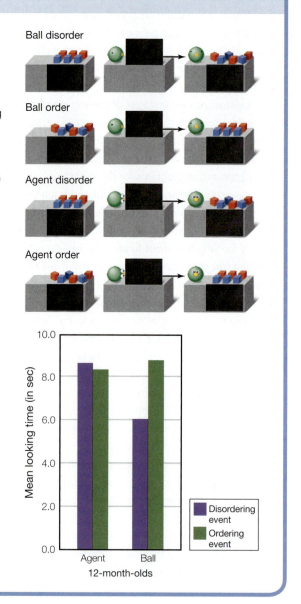

Finally, older infants start to infer that only social agents acting intentionally can cause certain kinds of changes, such as imposing order on a disordered scene. One study set up different conditions to observe infants' reactions to changes in the orderliness of a display. In one condition, a set of blocks formed a neat array (an ordered grouping of the blocks), which was briefly obscured by a screen. When the screen was lifted, the blocks were seen to have been scattered. In this condition, it is easy to imagine that either an intentional agent or an inanimate object, such as a rolling ball, could have caused the change. In a second condition, a disordered set of blocks was momentarily concealed by a screen. When the screen was removed, the blocks were seen to have been neatly ordered. In this condition, only an intentional agent could have caused the change. When 12-month-olds are shown similar events, they look longer when an inanimate object seems to have created order from disorder, as this violates their expectations about what inanimate objects can do (Newman et al., 2010; see Scientific Method box). In contrast, once infants determine that something is a social agent, they understand that it can cause specific kinds of changes that follow from having goals, such as imposing order. Similarly, infants as young as 9 months expect a hand, but not a claw, to be able to select two colors of balls out of a transparent container in a nonrandom manner and to put them in a display where the colors show a precisely repeating pattern (Ma & Xu, 2013). In short, well before the end of the first year of life, infants view inanimate objects as dramatically different from animate creatures. We will see in Chapter 6 that these expectations about the social world and the capabilities of social agents form a critical foundation for developing the earliest social relationships: attachments to caregivers.

Conclusions

Infants are clearly able to think about the world in ways that go far beyond merely having perceptions and engaging in actions. It seems likely that even at birth, infants have certain expectations about the properties and behaviors of physical objects and are surprised when their expectations are violated. We have seen that these expectations seem to be linked together as a coherent set of principles. These expectations also seem to involve a clear understanding of causation, although perhaps only the causes reflected in simple physical interactions. As a result, it is tempting to attribute to infants an intuitive grasp of basic physical mechanics even though

this is primarily known through their reactions to possible and impossible events. Based on fairly recent advances in developmental research, we have also come to see that infants in the first few weeks of life can use abstract principles—for example, that solid objects cannot interpenetrate—to reason about unseen events. And we have seen that years before they learn to count, infants can distinguish various quantities on the basis of number. In addition, we have seen that infants can recognize that there is a profound difference between animate and inanimate entities, a contrast that will be an important building block for the development of social relations. More broadly, infants may come into the world with evolutionarily quite old foundations of "core knowledge" that they can use early on to make rudimentary sense of areas such as physical mechanics, social agency, number, and spatial layout (Carey, 2009; Carey & Spelke, 1996; Keil, 1981; Spelke & Kinzler, 2007). The challenge lies in trying to better understand how this early knowledge is mentally represented and how it changes in the years that follow.

Because research on infant cognition is one of the fastest growing areas of psychology, it is especially important to take a step back and consider how the exciting advances in this area fit into the larger picture of our understanding of development. In recent years, researchers have repeatedly shown that infants previously considered essentially precognitive were capable of remarkably precocious performance on tasks that seemed to require impressive cognitive abilities. There were numerous strengths in this approach, especially to counter the many years of mistaken views that infants could only understand the physical world in terms of basic perceptions and actions. But the intense focus on infants' surprisingly sophisticated capacities has come with a cost as well, for we may sometimes forget that infancy is a time of enormous developmental changes that also affect cognitive capacities. A full story of infant cognitive development will have to explain how infants come to understand new concepts and how simple understandings can become more complex and richly connected. Answers to these questions, along with careful characterizations of infant capacities throughout the first year of life, are needed for a full account of how infants' understanding of the physical world emerges. We also see an important message in this chapter that will reappear in later chapters. Development doesn't just consist of perceptual skills feeding into cognitive ones. Advances in cognitive development, such as learning about categories, can also feed back on performance of more perceptual tasks, such as recognizing distinct objects. These two domains of development are intricately linked and often interdependent.

STUDY AND REVIEW

SUMMARY

Piaget's Approach

- Jean Piaget, the undisputed giant of developmental psychology, characterized a child's knowledge and behavior in terms of schemes, or patterns of perceiving, thinking, and interacting with the world. He described how these schemes were constantly adapting to the environment through the processes of accommodation and assimilation.

- Piaget argued that there is a distinct stage of development in infancy known as the sensorimotor period, which in turn consists of six substages. The main focus of this period is the developing object concept.

- Piaget did not view infants as really capable of seeing a world out there that is independent of their actions until after the first year of life.

- Piaget believed that for younger infants, out of sight is truly out of mind; he was convinced that they can only think about objects when they are acting on them and that their concepts of the objects are subordinated to those patterns of action.

- Piaget examined infants' developing object concept by testing how they respond to manipulations of objects. One task, known as the A-not-B task, which involves hiding an object and seeing where the infant will search for it, was thought to be a litmus test for whether infants can really represent objects in their own right and as enduring while out of sight. Infants fail this task until roughly 1 year of age.

Infant Knowledge and Understanding

- The last three decades have seen a revolution in the study of infancy, based in large part on studies using dishabituation or other violation-of-expectation paradigms. This research suggests very different developmental patterns and much earlier forms of understanding than Piaget had proposed.

- Even the youngest infants seem to know there is a world "out there" that is independent of their actions.

- Young infants also appear to have several interlinked expectations about the nature of physical objects and how they behave. These expectations suggest that infants may have an intuitive theory of the mechanics of bounded physical objects, but there is a great deal of uncertainty as to what it means for an infant to have such a theory.

- Studies seem to suggest that young infants understand that there is object permanence or continuity, that objects are solid and cannot interpenetrate other objects, and that objects must make contact to influence other objects.

- Quite young infants also have notions of causation that are not simply the result of associations of elements over time and space. They seem to be able to perceive physical causality in simple collision situations and show surprise when their causal expectations about such physical events are violated.

- Infants are not only able to differentiate different quantities of objects in terms of their number, but are also able to interpret events representing addition and subtraction. They do all of this without any spoken language, raising provocative questions about how their numerical knowledge might differ from that of older verbal children.

- Infants also have spatial knowledge of the world. They are able to construct representations of the layout of the world around them and then can use those representations to remember the locations of objects. From an early age, they may be able to use several distinct cues to spatial layout, including beacons, landmarks, and geometric properties of the environment, relying on different cues, depending on the context to locate objects.

- Perhaps the highest level of cognition is the use of abstract concepts that stand for classes and relations that go far beyond perception. Infants are often able to use quite broad categories, and the category-related knowledge does not invariably proceed developmentally from the most specific categories on upward to the most abstract, general categories.

Distinguishing the Physical World from the Social World

- Infants develop sharply contrasting expectations about the behaviors of animate creatures and inanimate objects. They recognize that social agents can move on their own and can be influenced from afar (action at a distance), whereas inanimate objects need an external force to move them or change their direction through direct contact.

- They see different patterns of contingent responding, different principles governing interactions, and are heavily influenced by inferences about goals when they believe that an entity is animate.

- There is increasing evidence that infants can also attribute false beliefs to social agents and use those attributions to anticipate different kinds of behaviors.

THOUGHT QUESTIONS

1. While chimpanzees and other great apes often appear quite close to human infants in how they reason about physical mechanical relations, there appears to be a major contrast

concerning their ability to think about false beliefs. Human infants as young as 13 months are able to take false beliefs into account, but adult great apes are unable to do so. What, specifically, is likely to be the cognitive difference between these two groups that can explain this difference?

2. What kinds of experiences might be most valuable to emphasize for a young infant's cognitive development, and what kinds of experiences might be least valuable? What are the social policy implications?

3. Preverbal infants seem to have very distinct expectations about the properties and behaviors of social agents and inanimate physical objects. Consider whether preverbal infants also have systematic distinct expectations about other contrasting categories, such as between naturally occurring and human-made objects, between living and nonliving objects, and between edible and inedible things. How might we test for whether preverbal infants do have different expectations about such objects?

4. Preverbal infants seem to appreciate physical causality in a collision and social causality in a situation in which one agent seems to frighten another. Is there a common concept of "cause" being evoked in both cases, or is each completely distinct in the mind of the infant, with no awareness that both instances can be described as one thing caus-

ing another? What experiments might distinguish these possibilities?

5. Dogs seem to pass the A-not-B task very early, but they never pass the invisible displacements task. What sort of cognitive or perceptual process might enable them to be more precocious than human infants in the A-not-B task but much worse at invisible displacements?

KEY TERMS

A-not-B error (p. 153)

accommodation (p. 147)

adaptation (p. 147)

allocentric representation (p. 169)

assimilation (p. 147)

egocentric representation (p. 169)

equilibration (p. 147)

explicit cognition (p. 146)

implicit cognition (p. 146)

invisible displacement (p. 153)

object concept (p. 149)

object permanence (p. 149)

object solidity (p. 158)

place error (p. 153)

primary circular reaction (p. 150)

scheme (p. 147)

secondary circular reactions (p. 151)

sensorimotor period (p. 149)

tertiary circular reactions (p. 153)

6

Connecting with the Social World

Developing Bonds between Infants and Caregivers

Early Perspectives on Infants' Bonds with Others
- Psychoanalytic Approaches to Infant-Parent Bonds
- Learning Theory Approaches
- Bowlby's Ethological Approach

The Underpinnings of Attachment
- Components of Attachment
- Bases of Social Interactions

Individual Differences in Attachment Style
- Studying Attachment Styles in the Strange Situation
- Causes of Different Attachment Styles
- Consequences of Different Attachment Styles
- Cross-Cultural Differences in Attachment Styles

Effects of Early Social Deprivation
- Social Deprivation in Humans

- Deprivation Studies in Nonhuman Primates
- Critical-Period Effects?

Conclusions

Summary

Anna Mae He was born in Memphis, Tennessee, in 1999. Her parents were Chinese immigrants who had recently fallen on hard times and had very limited income. Because of complications during the pregnancy, the hospital bill was quite large, and Anna's parents began looking for a way out of their financial crisis. When Anna was 27 days old, her biological parents put her into what they thought would be temporary foster care with another couple.

Anna's parents visited her once a week until her second birthday, when they had an altercation with Anna's foster parents. This incident resulted in a court order preventing Anna's biological parents from seeing her and terminating their parental rights. After a long series of subsequent court battles over custody, the original court ruling was finally overturned in 2007, and Anna was returned to her biological parents 8 years after she had been placed with her foster parents. Anna's foster parents adored her, and Anna's feelings toward them seemed equally positive. But the judge who overturned the case ruled that any harm that might come to Anna by being removed from her foster parents was outweighed by the rights of her biological parents (see Figure 6.1).

The custody battle over Anna Mae He drew intense interest in the national press because it seemed to pit two very powerful human impulses against each other. On the one hand, the rights of the biological parents should not be permanently terminated unless the parents pose a risk to the child. On the other hand, a child who has been raised, practically from birth, by loving foster parents should not be removed from the only family she knows and loves.

FIGURE 6.1 Anna Mae He case. For 8 years, Anna Mae He grew up in the United States with foster parents. But after a lengthy court battle, she was returned to her biological parents, who took her back to China. The case highlighted a tension between two competing principles: the rights of biological parents and the rights of those who bring up a child from early infancy. In addition, the rights of the child must also be taken into account.

Moving beyond the complexities of this particular case, it is easy to see how the broader issues it raises relate to all children and their families. How and why are bonds formed between children and their parents, and what are the costs of breaking those bonds? Do newborns bond with specific caregivers in the first few weeks of life, or do those bonds form later, when the infant is more psychologically sophisticated? Is the period of infancy and early toddlerhood especially important for establishing these relationships? How do early bonds with caregivers differ among children, and how do these differences arise? Do those social patterns established in infancy have irreversible effects on interpersonal relations later in life?

Building on Chapter 5's discussion of how infants seem to think differently about social beings than they do about inanimate objects, this chapter focuses on the earliest social bonds in infancy, especially those between parents and their children. We will first consider how these bonds typically develop and how they were explained by early theorists, providing a context for the more detailed examinations that follow. We will consider some early perspectives on parent-child bonds, starting with the work of Sigmund Freud, whose ideas continue to have reverberations today. We will then discuss learning theory approaches, which dominated the American psychological landscape for much of the twentieth century, yet were ultimately undermined by both theoretical and empirical considerations. We will then turn to the ethological approach, pioneered by the British researcher John Bowlby and one of his North American colleagues, Mary Ainsworth. This approach underlies most current theories of bonding and is the dominant framework for the study of **attachment**—the strong and enduring emotional bond between a child and a significant other and the processes that create and maintain this long-lasting social relationship.

We will look at the underpinnings of attachment, focusing on the behaviors that facilitate and maintain attachments for a species. In humans, we will see that smiling, cuddling, clinging, following, and "cuteness" may play particularly important roles. We will also look at analogous behaviors in other species to better understand the implications of these attachment behaviors that fit with the ethological approach. We will then examine two social and cognitive skills that help give human attachment its unique nature: social referencing and joint attention.

Not all attachments happen in the same way, however. There are pronounced individual differences in the ways that infants and young children relate to their parents. We will consider how researchers measure these differences and ask why they occur, examining the roles of parenting, children's temperaments, environmental stressors, and genetic factors. We will also ask whether particular attachment styles are associated with certain ways of relating to others later in life. For example, if a young toddler seems to show great insecurity in his attachments, does that behavior predict anything about how he will form intimate relations in college? We will also consider the important contributions of cross-cultural studies and ask if particular attachment styles and behaviors found in other cultures mean the same thing in terms of underlying attachments as they do when they are found in North American cultures.

Finally, we will focus on the ways that extreme social deprivation affects attachment. Its devastating consequences raise questions about how these effects develop and how long they persist after the children's circumstances improve. The ethological perspective, which underlies a variety of comparative studies of attachment in other species, has proved particularly useful for understanding the impact of deprivation. At the end of the chapter, we will return to the familiar theme of critical-period effects to ask whether there is a critical period for the formation of normal attachments.

Age	Behaviors That Set Up and Maintain Bonds between Caregivers and Infants
Newborn	Infants show a preference for looking at faces over other stimuli and attend to human voices, but they do not show clear bonds to specific people.
3 months	Infants smile at people more, but they still do not show specific bonds to particular individuals.
6 months	Infants have now formed bonds to specific individuals and smile most in their presence.
8 months	Most infants show separation distress when the individuals with whom they have formed specific bonds leave.

TABLE 6.1 Development of early bonds. Four behaviors related to forming and maintaining specific bonds between caregivers and offspring and the approximate ages at which they first appear in infancy. This is the most typical developmental sequence in humans from birth to approximately 8 months.

Developing Bonds between Infants and Caregivers

Virtually all human infants, like the young of many other species, form bonds to those who take care of them. These bonds are difficult to measure in their own right, but they can be inferred through certain sets of behaviors that serve to set up and maintain proximity between human caregivers and their children (see Figure 6.2). Disrupting these bonds or preventing them from forming can lead to devas-

tating and often lasting effects. The first such bond is generally between parent and infant, but infants also develop strong bonds with others, including siblings and other family members and caregivers. Nonetheless, much of the theory and research we will explore in this chapter involves the infant-parent bond and especially the infant-mother bond. The most typical sequence for developing bonds is summarized in Table 6.1.

A newborn does not seem to have **specific bonds**—that is, bonds to particular individuals. As we have seen in earlier chapters, this does not mean that newborns aren't sensitive to social stimuli as being somehow different, but they show no evidence of a strong desire to be around particular people. Even though very young infants may be able to recognize their parents through sound, smell, and sight and may find that recognition pleasing, they do not show distress if a parent is not there. Infants' lack of specific bonds early on has been a cornerstone assumption of adoption agencies for centuries. Those agencies typically would like an adoption to occur as early in the infant's life as possible to avoid separation pains in both the infant and the biological parents.

Infants first show specific bonds at around 6 or 7 months. Prior to that age, they may well prefer to interact with their parents over others, but this is largely because the parents know best what makes the baby happy. A socially adroit stranger can usually be just as effective. At 6 months, infants become more skilled at being social partners and seem to shift from being junior partners to full partners in the social interaction. As such, they are more sensitive to others' social and emotional states and are more adept at influencing and responding to those states.

FIGURE 6.2 The origins of attachment. Both parent and child display behaviors that any observer would recognize as the beginnings of an attachment. Here, for example, a Mongolian mother coos to her very young baby. But can a newborn infant have a specific attachment to her mother?

Q: When do specific bonds first seem to form, and why do they form at this age?

Developing social skills may well be involved in building a foundation for bonds between children and caregivers. Such social skills include recognition of and interactions with specific individuals and communication of distress when a caregiver leaves (see Figure 6.3). An infant younger than approximately 7 months might show distress when someone she is interacting with leaves, but this distress doesn't indicate a specific bond to that person because another person can reengage the infant and stop the distress. By contrast, true **separation distress**, which typically emerges at about 8 months and is also known as **separation anxiety**, does indicate a specific bond. In this case, the infant cannot be consoled by a stranger, no matter how skillful; the infant wants a particular person to come back, not just any social partner. This general sequence of developing specific bonds is seen in all cultures throughout the world and has been noted since the beginning of written history.

As infants develop over the first 2 years, a wider range of behaviors reflects the bonds between infants and others. These include crawling to maintain proximity to the caregiver and increasingly rich communication skills. The infant also gets better at coping with brief separa-

tions and at inferring exactly when a separation is likely to be brief or long lasting. In short, even though infants may recognize their parents very early in development, that recognition does not directly translate into specific bonds. Only after several months of life do infants seem to have strong bonds to particular people and show distress when those individuals are not near. We now turn to theories of how those bonds emerge over the course of development.

Q: How is separation distress related to the emergence of behaviors to maintain proximity?

Early Perspectives on Infants' Bonds with Others

Many theories have been proposed to explain the bonds that infants form with others, but most research has occurred in the context of three major approaches: psychoanalytic theory, learning theory, and the ethological perspective. Today, the ethological perspective is the dominant view in the field, but it is important to understand that perspective in terms of other approaches that preceded it.

Psychoanalytic Approaches to Infant-Parent Bonds

Early in the twentieth century, Sigmund Freud changed how we view our mental lives. Freud is best known for his theories of mental illness and the unconscious and for launching the discipline of psychoanalysis, but some of his most important contributions concern the emergence of social relationships and personality (Freud, 1905/1976, 1925/1976).

Freud's theory of bonds between infants and parents emerged out of a broader account of **psychosexual development**, a proposed series of stages of development related to drives, instincts, and sources of pleasure, with a particular focus on sexual desire. According to Freud, all boys and girls progress through these stages in ways that are intimately related to the kinds of bonds they form to others. Freud placed an extraordinary emphasis on the unique nature of the early mother-infant bond, which he believed stems from breastfeeding, a source of oral gratification that becomes associated with the mother. Although Freud's focus on breastfeeding has been criticized by later writers, it

FIGURE 6.3 Separation distress. At 6 months of age, babies begin to form specific attachments to their primary caregivers and within a month or two typically show distress at separation, often clinging to an attachment figure who is about to depart.

is important to remember that in Freud's time, breastfeeding was so widespread in all social groups that any other form of infant feeding would have seemed abnormal. Freud considered nursing to be the earliest and most basic pleasurable act for the infant. He believed that in performing that act, the infant forms a profound attachment to the mother (and to her breast). Freud maintained that the mother-infant relation is the prototype around which all later close relationships revolve.

Yet, Freud overemphasized the pivotal role of the mother-infant bond. Many studies have shown that given the right opportunities, father-infant bonds can be equally intense and important to the infant (Lamb, 2004, 2010; Parke, 1996). Thus, the amount of time spent with the infant is a much better predictor of the strength and quality of attachment than the sex of the caregiver (Clarke-Stewart, 1989). Similarly, the special place of breastfeeding comes under question, given that no differences in later attachment behaviors have been found between bottle-fed and breastfed babies. Although there may be some behavioral differences in breastfeeding versus bottle-feeding mothers, with the breastfeeding mothers sometimes reporting closer feelings to the infant, those differences do not seem to translate into differences in how infants bond to their mothers (Lawrence, 1994). Some of these errors in Freud's approach may have arisen because he never really engaged in any direct observations of children; his accounts relied much too much on adults' reports of their childhoods.

Q: Why, in Freudian theory, might bottle-feeding and breastfeeding have different consequences for the infant?

Freud's views were followed by several other psychoanalytic approaches that collectively contributed to recurring themes that have survived to this day. One issue that Freud considered was how children develop relationships to their parents that are linked both to their own sexuality and to the sex of the parent. Today, the question is whether fathers and mothers behave differently with children of different sexes, even when they are carefully trying to be evenhanded, and whether such differences affect gender roles and influence the nature of attachment itself. A second major issue concerns whether early relations between parents and the young child become powerful touchstones for all later relationships and whether anything like a critical period effect occurs. Finally, there is the question of how much the human infant's cognitions and beliefs come to shape attach-ments, as opposed to the more basic drives for affiliation seen in other animals. All of these issues were examined by Freud and his psychoanalytic successors and, as you will see shortly, are still actively researched today.

Learning Theory Approaches

Learning theory approaches to infant-parent bonds were defined by an attempt to focus exclusively on the infant's behaviors and the ways in which the environment reinforces them. Learning theorists believed that the drives of oral gratification and pleasure seeking are not well defined and therefore not easy to study and measure. They attempted to restate drives in terms of more clear-cut physiological constructs, such as thirst, hunger, and physical discomfort (Sears et al., 1957), which can be responded to by any caregiver. Learning theorists believed that bonds emerge by being associated with positively reinforcing stimuli. Initially, the stimulus might be the breast or bottle, but soon it would become the mother herself (or any other caregiver) because of her close association with breastfeeding or bottle-feeding. Learning theory tried to avoid all talk of an infant's internal mental states and tried to posit the simplest biological drives as motivating forces. The focus on behavior and positive and negative reinforcements led to assumptions that feeding schedules, the form of feeding (bottle versus breast), and the age of weaning might all heavily influence the nature of attachment (Gewirtz, 1961). After all, if bonds are forged by caregivers being associated with reinforcing stimuli, the schedule of reinforcement and its delivery system should matter greatly. Learning theory views of attachment enjoyed a period of great popularity, especially in the 1950s and early 1960s, when learning theory dominated many areas of psychology. These views promised a simple and perhaps even quantifiable set of rules for understanding how and when attachments occur.

The stark simplicity of learning theories, however, made it easy to see where the theories fell short in their ability to explain the formation and maintenance of infants' and children's bonds as they exist in the real world. One problem with learning theory approaches was that they neglected any cognitive components in the development of bonds. For example, if it is important to the development of bonds that infants understand that their mothers are unique beings who continue to exist when they are out of sight, learning theory has no way of taking into account an infant's or child's thoughts and how they relate to the formation of bonds. Similarly, if an infant's thoughts about a caregiver's intentions and goals are relevant to the nature of the bonds that are formed, learning theory is of no help in understanding how bonds might vary with differences in those thoughts.

Another major flaw of learning theories was their difficulty in explaining how an infant's bond could endure in the face of repeated and consistently negative interactions with a parent or caregiver. Normal learning theory would predict that abuse would lead to the "extinction" of a bond, but this is often not the case. In many cases, an abused child still desperately wants to be close to the abusive parent, even though the closer the child is, the more likely it is that painful interactions will occur. It is in these situations, where an infant is being repeatedly abused both verbally and physically, that the bonds can be most surprising.

> **Q:** What are some limitations of learning theory approaches to attachment?

Bowlby's Ethological Approach

The study of bonds between offspring and their parents underwent a dramatic shift largely because of the pioneering work of John Bowlby and Mary Ainsworth (see Figure 6.4). Bowlby described the bond between children and their caregivers as an attachment, and that term has come to dominate contemporary research on how infants and young children (and even adults) form bonds to others. Although the term *attachment* had long been used in literature to describe close social bonds (White, 1916), it was not commonly used for the processes of forming and sustaining these social bonds until Bowlby made it central to his theory. In developmental psychology, the term has now come to have a specific set of meanings arising from Bowlby's body of work. Bowlby emphasized the behaviors that created and maintained attachment, leading some to describe his view of attachment as "the infant's ability to seek proximity to a specific caregiver" (Pipp & Harmon, 1987).

In discussions of human attachment, affection and emotion are often mentioned. For example, Ainsworth defined attachment as "an affectional tie that one person or animal forms between himself and another specific one—a tie that binds them together in space and endures over time" (Ainsworth & Bell, 1970, p. 50). But if we take a comparative approach and consider attachment across a wide range of species, a more conservative definition focuses on the *behaviors* that set up and maintain bonds between offspring and parents (see Figure 6.5). It is difficult to know what emotions to attribute to other animals when they show attachment to their mothers by acting to keep the mother close, such as chicks peeping and following. In these cases, it is much easier to infer the attachment bond based on the behaviors that maintain contact between parents and offspring.

Along these lines, the ethological approach to attachment has become the dominant perspective in the field. It approaches the bond between offspring and parents from an evolutionary and comparative perspective, asking about its functional role in the development of organisms and groups of organisms. Ethology largely developed in Europe in the 1930s, when such major figures as Konrad Lorenz and Niko Tinbergen studied animals' social behavior in naturalistic contexts (Lorenz, 1965; Tinbergen, 1951). These studies gave rise to the notion that animals have repertoires of actions that are assembled into larger-scale behaviors. Ethologists paid special attention to animals' signaling systems and the species-specific "conventions" used to communicate threats, sexual availability, and the like. And they studied how these systems are then assembled into the more complex behaviors that govern mating, territoriality, and caring for offspring.

In this ethological context, Bowlby began studying attachment in human infants (Bowlby, 1969). Bowlby's major contribution was to describe attachment in evolutionary and comparative terms, focusing on the similarities and differences in the ways that various species' offspring

A　　　　　B

FIGURE 6.4 John Bowlby and Mary Ainsworth. (A) John Bowlby's studies on attachment and separation transformed how the psychological community thought about the bonds formed between child and parent. **(B)** Mary Ainsworth began working with Bowlby in the early 1950s, making many important advances in the study of attachment from an ethological perspective.

FIGURE 6.5 Attachment in different species. Many organisms form attachments to their parents, as seen in these examples across several species. The ethological approach stresses the functional role not only of attachment itself but also of the component attachment behaviors that set up and maintain attachments.

attach to caregivers. He saw complex attachment behaviors as being built up out of specific behavioral elements, such as smiling, crying, and clinging. Across species, the particular combinations of these elements varies considerably; what species have in common is the way they integrate these elements into coordinated behaviors that set up and maintain attachments. One of Bowlby's most important contributions was to focus attention on these attachment behaviors as an essential means of binding the caregiver to the infant—thereby creating attachment itself. For any species whose young are relatively helpless early on, attachment is a crucial way to make sure that parents take care of their infants. For Bowlby, attachment has the evolutionary function of protecting infants from threats to their survival, ranging from predators to physical hazards to starvation. Across a wide variety of organisms, it is adaptive for vulnerable offspring to engage in behaviors that increase the odds of staying in proximity to parents, and it is adaptive for parents (in terms of passing on their genes) to be responsive to those behaviors in ways that maintain proximity to the offspring. As such, caregivers become safe havens in situations that are threatening or frightening, thereby offering a **secure base** from which the young offspring can explore.

As noted earlier, the young infant does not appear to have a unique bond to a specific caregiver. Bowlby built on the observations of many others by noting four phases in the development of attachment (Bowlby, 1969; see also Ainsworth et al., 1978):

- *Preattachment phase* (birth to 6 weeks). Infants in this phase display attachment-related behaviors but do not seem to target them to particular individuals.
- *Attachment-in-the-making phase* (6 weeks to 6–8 months). During this phase, infants start to use signals such as smiling and crying to focus on specific people.
- *Clear-cut attachment phase* (6–8 months to 18 months–2 years). During this phase, infants more actively stay near

a particular person by using more effective signals (such as protesting if a particular person leaves) and by behaviors to maintain contact with that person (such as crawling toward her and clinging to her). Infants use the caregiver as a secure base for exploration.

- *Reciprocal relationships phase* (18 months–2 years and older). During this final phase, children are better able to take into account the parent's needs and adjust their behavior accordingly, such as being able to wait for the parent to return without protesting. Thus, the child and the parent become more like partners solving a problem to help them get to a common goal.

But Bowlby may have underestimated how even newborns can quickly recognize their mother based on her smell and can use that information to have specific kinds of interactions with her. Newborns may not really be attached, but they may begin tailoring interactions with specific people right from the start (Winberg, 2005).

Bowlby stressed that although attachment behaviors are crucial for creating and maintaining attachment, they should not be equated with attachment itself. He believed that careful analysis of attachment behaviors could yield insights into the nature of the underlying attachment but that assuming a simple linkage between attachment and attachment behaviors could be misleading. For example, he insisted that the strength of an attachment behavior does not necessarily indicate the strength of the attachment itself. Some of the strongest and healthiest attachments provide infants with such trust in their caregiver that they have no need to cling to the person constantly to guarantee that they will not be separated. If a child is anxious about whether the mother will always be there, however, he might show extremely strong attachment behaviors, such as clinging, crying, and following, in an attempt to stay near the mother at all times. The strength of attachment behaviors can also depend on the particular situation, whereas the nature of the underlying attachment does not. A child who shows very strong attachment behaviors in frightening or alarming situations may show very low levels of the same behaviors in safe situations, such as being at home among well-known people, even though the strength of the attachment itself remains constant across both situations.

Q: Why is it important to distinguish attachment from attachment behaviors?

Bowlby also wanted to distinguish attachment from **dependency**, which is reliance on another person for basic physiological needs, such as food and shelter, and for protection from perceived or real threats. Although most early attachment relationships between infants and parents involve the infant's high level of dependency on the parents, it is misleading to equate dependency with attachment. Dependency is not necessary for strong attachment, nor do all dependencies lead to attachment. Dependency also implies a passivity on the part of the infant that Bowlby felt underestimates the infant's capacities, as he instead saw the infant as actively engaging in behaviors that help create attachment.

Sometimes strong attachment develops between an infant and those who play relatively minor roles in satisfying the infant's most immediate needs for nutrition and comfort. Some infants whose parents have intense work demands may spend 50 hours a week in day care and have a caregiver at night who helps feed them and put them to bed. Those children may interact playfully with their parents only a few hours a day, yet they still seem to form strong attachments to them, often the strongest of all their attachments (Clarke-Stewart, 1989; Harvey, 1999).

Although Bowlby was influenced by psychoanalytic approaches, he disagreed with psychoanalytic views that linked attachment to the infant's feelings of gratification while breastfeeding or to some form of sexual drive. In the end, he rejected many details of the psychoanalytic perspectives on attachment, even though, in a broader sense, he was influenced by their emphasis on the importance of early bonds and the ways that disrupting those bonds could cause long-term problems in relationships (Bretherton, 1992). He also advanced the idea that infants develop cognitive models of their early attachments, which guide their interpretations of future interactions with caregivers (Bowlby, 1958). Although this notion has not been explored until quite recently (Johnson et al., 2010) it is, in many ways, a natural outgrowth of earlier psychoanalytic approaches.

The ethological approach has become the dominant perspective for understanding attachment because of its clear continuity across species and because it allows for integration of many other psychological processes, such as those involving emotions, social interactions, cognitions, and motivations. It is best understood as an approach or perspective rather than a precise theory, since its large reach allows for many different interpretations of the details. Because comparative studies of behavior have shown a resurgence in recent years, its relevance remains strong.

The Underpinnings of Attachment

Infants as young as 1 month are social beings and participate in one-on-one social interactions much of the time that they are awake. Soon after birth, infants engage in behaviors that initiate and maintain social interactions (Stern, 1985). Bowlby focused on these behaviors and how they contribute to the formation and maintenance of social bonds. Both in human infants and in infants of other species, components of attachment, such as smiling, clinging, and touch, as well as baby-like features, help form and maintain attachment so that parents will care for their helpless offspring. The ability to form human attachments builds on other abilities as well, including particular kinds of social skills and understanding. The more recent cognitive approach says that for infants to develop bonds with others, they must also have some grasp of the special tempo of interactions with others and the kinds of information that such interactions can convey. Without these underpinnings, the special nature of human attachments would not be possible. These underpinnings help support a large array of activities beyond attachment, including communication, feelings of empathy, and threat detection. But here we focus on the ways they contribute to the formation and maintenance of attachment.

Components of Attachment

We have seen that attachment behaviors bind caregivers and infants together, and for many developmental psychologists, these behaviors are the basis for inferring attachment itself. Nonetheless, the role of the particular components of the **attachment complex**, the set of behaviors and mental states that, when taken together, are responsible for setting up and maintaining attachment, can vary considerably across different species. These commonalities and differences are nicely illustrated by smiling and clinging and by their different roles in humans and monkeys. They also are seen in the juvenile features that make up "cuteness," which serves to trigger caregiving responses by adults toward infants.

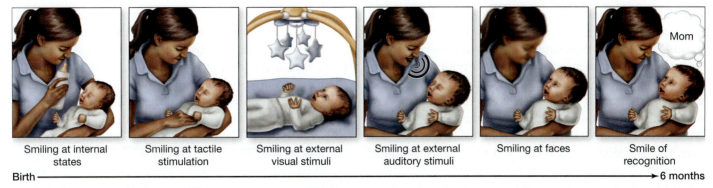

| Smiling at internal states | Smiling at tactile stimulation | Smiling at external visual stimuli | Smiling at external auditory stimuli | Smiling at faces | Smile of recognition |

Birth ——→ 6 months

FIGURE 6.6 Stimuli that elicit smiles. In Wolff's classic account, stimuli that elicit an infant's smile progress from internal states to external stimulation to social stimulation and finally to unique individuals. Today we regard the young infant as having greater sensitivity to social entities, but Wolff's general pattern does capture changes in smiling in the first months of life.

Smiling Infants' smiles are among their most endearing behaviors. The first smile clearly meant for a specific parent brings great pleasure. But smiling does not emerge as a mature behavior in the newborn (see Figure 6.6). Indeed, most parents quickly realize that they are very ineffective at making their newborn smile, no matter how many silly faces and sounds they make. It is not that newborns are incapable of smiling, but what makes them smile may be quite different than at later ages. The first researcher to study these developmental changes systematically was Peter Wolff, who investigated which stimuli elicit smiles most effectively at different ages in infancy (Wolff, 1963). He found that as infants get older, they increasingly prefer auditory and visual social stimuli.

The infant initially appears to smile in response to her own internal state, such as just after a feeding or after a particularly good burp. A little later, the best stimuli to elicit a smile are likely to be external, primarily those involving touch and motion, such as hugging and rocking—which give way to other kinds of external stimuli, such as interesting sights and sounds. Then, the most pleasing stimuli become specifically social, as the infant smiles at the sound of a person's voice or on seeing her face. Finally, at about 6 months of age, the best elicitor of a smile is the face of a particular known individual, producing the "smile of recognition." Countless parents would agree that at around 5 or 6 months, something changes: the infant starts to clearly look into your eyes and smile at you because she knows and likes you and not simply because some other stimulus has made her feel good. Those endearing first smiles of recognition often seem to appear just in the nick of time for parents who have been lurching through months of sleepless nights. In fact, this smile of recognition might serve an important adaptive function for the human infant. Just when caregivers feel completely overwhelmed and exhausted, the smile of recognition appears, and the invigorated parents suddenly

feel that they can withstand anything their adorable bundle throws at them.

The smile is a classic example of an attachment behavior that serves a signaling function in a feedback loop between parent and infant (see Figure 6.7). The mother rocks the baby gently, causing the infant to give a small smile. This

Mother smiles and rocks baby

Baby's smile produces more smiling and rocking in mother

Mother's smile and rocking produces larger smile in baby

Baby smiles

FIGURE 6.7 Contingent responding. The infant and the mother often become partners in a positive-feedback loop in which smiling and rocking on the mother's part produces more smiling in the baby, which in turn produces more smiling in the mother. Through such a loop, close bonds are developed and maintained between the two.

smile pleases the mother, causing her to smile back at the infant and continue rocking, which in turn causes the infant to smile more, and so on, until each partner is fully engaged with the other. This is an example of a positive-feedback loop, a system in which the actions of each component serve to escalate the actions of the other, so that the system quickly reaches a maximum level and remains there for as long as the system components can work without fatigue. In this case, the behaviors of the infant and the mother continue to escalate as each responds to the other until, eventually, either the infant or the mother gets tired and breaks off the encounter. Just watching a mother attending to her smiling infant can reveal the intensity of these interactions. The mother is often leaning forward and actively engaging the infant, while both mother and baby appear to completely ignore the rest of the world. And if the mother breaks out of this feedback loop too abruptly, the infant becomes distressed. These feedback loops become more and more effective in the first year of life as infant and caregiver become more sophisticated and perceive and produce effects in the other through their smiles and other signals of positive emotions (Mendes et al., 2009).

In short, an infant's smile prolongs the interaction with the target of the smile (Csibra, 2010), increasing the amount of time spent in close proximity to the caregiver. The infant's smile actively produces positive emotions in the caregiver (Fogel et al., 2000; Symons & Moran, 1994), motivating the caregiver to keep interacting with the infant. These effects can be demonstrated at a physiological level as well. For example, when most mothers view their infant's smile, the smile elicits high levels of neural activity in the reward regions of the mother's brain, such as in the ventral striatum, as well as in an area of the hypothalamus associated with the production of **oxytocin**, a hormone found in higher concentrations in the mother's saliva as a consequence of seeing her infant's smile (Strathearn et al., 2008). This effect is especially strong in mothers who are more sensitive to the moods and emotions of their infants (Strathearn et al., 2012). Oxytocin, in turn, is known to produce increased feelings of trust and affection toward others (Kosfeld et al., 2005), especially when they are part of one's "in-group" (De Dreu et al., 2010).

Q: How does the smile function as an attachment behavior?

Clinging and Touching Infants often cling to their caregivers while being held, and clinging may play a role somewhat comparable to that of the smile in the formation of human attachments, namely, to maintain proximity. For monkeys, clinging may be considerably more important

than smiles or other facial expressions to keep close to their mothers. Infant monkeys do show expressions similar to smiles that may reflect roughly similar internal states, but these expressions do not appear to be as closely linked to the mother's behavior as human infant expressions are. In contrast, clinging is essential to the welfare of infant monkeys. They will often hang on to their mothers for hours (see Figure 6.8). Clinging not only helps keep them near the mother and moving with her, it also seems to serve a signaling function, building a bond of attachment between the two. In humans, clinging may be less essential in its own right, because it is just one of several ways to help form attachments. Thus, human infants born with tiny or nonexistent limbs form perfectly normal attachments to their parents (Decarie, 1969); monkeys with similar afflictions may not fare nearly as well. For humans, touching between the caregiver and the infant is still important in the development of attachment, but this contact seems less crucial as a signaling behavior on the human infant's part, compared with its function in other species.

One way to understand the species differences in clinging and related behaviors comes from a model of how clinging emerged and changed over the course of evolution (Matsuzawa, 2006). Clinging first emerged in primates about 50 million years ago, as primates had a unique ability to grab fur with their hands. In its initial form, still seen in primates such as lemurs, the baby clung to the mother but she did not respond. Around 40 million years ago, however, higher-level primates started to embrace their offspring back, and a form of mutual clinging, or embracing, emerged. The next major leap occurred about 5 million years ago, with the emergence of great apes. In contrast to other monkeys, who find direct gaze threatening, the great apes started to hold each other stomach to stomach in ways that enabled mutual gazes. Those gazes were reinforcing, especially when accompanied by smiles, which reflect positive relations in both humans and chimpanzees. Finally, in humans a unique ability emerged to disengage more easily from direct clinging while maintaining contact through facial expressions, vocalizations, and more intermittent touches. Humans, therefore, have an especially powerful set of behaviors for forming and maintaining attachments without direct contact. Nonetheless, the decline in the necessity for direct physical contact does not indicate that clinging and other forms of touch are irrelevant to the formation of human attachments.

Humans share with many other mammals a long common history of the positive effects of contact. For example, there is an extensive literature on the effects of contact on rat pups, which shows that gentle stroking can calm stress responses and help develop positive bonds (Jutapakdeegul et al., 2003; Weller & Feldman, 2003). Touch can also

FIGURE 6.8 **Clinging in primates.** Normal infant monkeys of many species cling to their mothers. This not only helps the infant monkey hang on, but also seems to help the infant forge bonds with its mother and promote a feeling of security.

help pups learn whom to attach to. Touch of the sort normally received from a pup's mother can set up a positive bond with a smell that is experienced at the same time, presumably a mechanism through which infant rats learn to form bonds to their mother (Kojima & Alberts, 2011). In human infants, too, gentle touching seems to reduce stress. Thus, when infants are put in a situation in which their mothers do not respond to them, touching can reduce the infants' typical physiological stress response to the situation (Feldman et al., 2010; Jean & Stack, 2009; Jean et al., 2009; Moszkowski et al., 2009). Even in newborns, skin-to-skin contact has been shown to have an analgesic, or pain-reducing, effect (Gray et al., 2000). There are also indications that human infants who sleep in physical contact with their mothers breastfeed more often through the night and may have lower rates of sudden infant death syndrome as well as lower stress levels (McKenna et al., 2007). While this is not to suggest that this should be the only sleep pattern for an infant, it is yet another indication of the value of physical contact between mother and infant (Waynforth, 2007).

An infant's touch also helps to create responses in parents that strengthen the infant-parent bond. Much as infants' smiles lead to increases in oxytocin in their mothers, their touching and stroking of the mother's breast also increases the mother's oxytocin levels (Matthiesen et al., 2001). Moreover, it appears that affectionate contact between fathers and infants can also cause the father's oxytocin levels to rise (Gordon et al., 2010). These findings suggest that there are some common physiological pathways in both mothers and fathers for forming and maintaining attachments.

Comparing the ways that humans and other primates use touch and facial expressions to develop early bonds illustrates both common themes and species-specific adaptations. As we have seen, various forms of tactile contact play an important role in many species, and clinging is often especially significant among primates. Nonetheless, while touch remains very important for human infants, they often come to interact most richly with their caregivers through visual and auditory means, often several feet away from the target of affection. By contrast, most primates other than the great apes (who engage in direct eye contact as do humans) appear to need more immediate physical contact to build and maintain attachments. Thus, both of these systems help to develop and maintain social interactions, working through different routes in humans and most other primates.

> **Q:** Compare and contrast smiling and clinging in terms of their functions in setting up and maintaining attachments.

Cuteness Even "cuteness" seems to be a critical component of attachment across several species. The so-called "kewpie doll" configuration of more rounded faces, larger eyes relative to the face, and smaller noses, chins, and limbs is found in the infants of an enormous range of species and is thought to evoke affection from mature members of the species. Biological models of growth help to explain the developmental patterns that give rise to these features, which have been shown to be extremely appealing to humans (Alley, 1988). Even 5-month-old infants prefer looking at infantilized faces rather than looking at more mature faces (Van Duuren et al., 2003). Konrad Lorenz was one of the first ethologists to propose such a pattern, as shown in Figure 6.9. He suggested that certain juvenile features automatically activate a kind of "baby schema" in much the same way that other stimuli trigger responses.

It is intriguing how often toy developers, cartoonists, and other kinds of artists greatly exaggerate baby-like features in portraying older children to make the images more appealing. Although the effects of cuteness have not been studied systematically in many species, it appears that at least some species may share the human predisposition to respond positively toward members of their species with

FIGURE 6.9 Baby features that lead to the perception of cuteness. The ethologist Konrad Lorenz suggested that there might be features shared by the young of many species that elicit a "cuteness" response in adult members of those species, a response that inhibits aggression and encourages nurturance. Commercial artists frequently attempt to enhance the cuteness of a child or an animal in greeting cards by exaggerating the head and eye size. While the artistic merit of such a style may be debatable, the ethological manipulation of instilling "cuteness" tends to work on even the most jaded viewers. Adapted from Lorenz (1971).

infant-like anatomical features. For example, adult female rhesus monkeys are more likely to interact positively with monkeys whose facial fur and skin have been dyed to match the hues common in rhesus infants (Higley et al., 1987).

Human infant cuteness appears to arouse specific neurophysiological patterns of responses in adults, often based on quite subtle differences in perceived cuteness. One study involved digitally altering photographs of babies' faces to make them appear either more or less cute, using algorithms that subtly changed key facial features (Glocker et al., 2009; see Figure 6.10). Adult participants viewed three versions of each face: the unaltered face; the face that was artificially made cuter by showing such high baby schema features as a round face, high forehead, big eyes, and small nose and mouth; and the face that was made less cute by showing such low baby schema features as a narrow face, low forehead, small eyes, and big nose and mouth. In response to the images, the areas of the adults' brains typically associated with anticipating a reward showed activation levels corresponding to the degree of cuteness of the infant. The cuter the face (as validated by independent ratings), the more active the reward-anticipating

system was. The authors suggested that this bias might be an evolutionarily selected mechanism for eliciting mothers' caregiving responses toward their young. Other evidence suggests that women of reproductive age may be able to detect more subtle differences in baby cuteness than older women or men of any age, possibly because it is especially adaptive for women in that group to have a strong response to cuteness (Sprengelmeyer et al., 2009).

Although not yet studied systematically, it seems likely that infants don't just appear cute. They likely also behave in ways that increase their cuteness to relevant adults. These behaviors could range from vocalizations and facial expressions to body postures or motions that seem to elicit strong positive responses from adults. The proposal that infants play a more active role in displaying cuteness so as to maintain proximity to adults would be very compatible with Bowlby's perspective.

Q: How does cuteness play a role in ethological views of attachment?

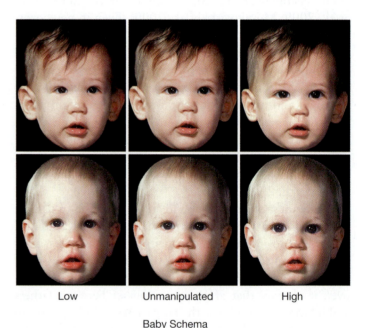

Low   Unmanipulated   High

Baby Schema

FIGURE 6.10 Variations in cuteness. Subtle variations in baby schema features, as shown here, lead not only to different adult ratings of cuteness but also to different levels of activation of brain regions associated with anticipation of reward. The photos were altered to change the baby schema features to low baby schema features (narrow face, low forehead, small eyes, big nose and mouth) or high baby schema features (round face, high forehead, big eyes, small mouth and nose) or were unaltered, and then these photos of the same infant with low, unaltered, or high baby schema features were rated for cuteness. From Glocker et al. (2009).

Bases of Social Interactions

For an infant to form attachments to people and not to stray items of furniture, there must be something different about social beings that the infant perceives as special. As discussed in previous chapters, certain social stimuli, such as the face, have a special status in the infant's perceptual development. We have also seen that young infants can distinguish social beings from inanimate objects and that they think about social and nonsocial entities in very different ways, understanding, for example, the causes and consequences of behaviors. With respect to attachment, we will see that these abilities to distinguish social agents from nonsocial objects also affect an infant's social interactions.

Contingent Responding Infants anticipate the behaviors of social beings and may experience quite powerful emotional reactions when those expectations are violated. For example, infants expect their parents to attend to them and respond in the rhythmic pattern of give-and-take that characterizes social interactions—that is, they expect contingent responding. If a parent looks at an infant with an impassive, straight face, known as a **still face**, infants as young as 1½ months of age become distressed at the lack of response and reciprocity in the social interaction (Adamson & Frick, 2003; Bertin & Striano, 2006; Cohn & Tronick, 1988; Field, 1977; Tronick, 1989; see Figure 6.11). It is easy to empathize with the infants' reactions; it is very rare and always uncomfortable to attempt a face-to-face interaction with someone who does not seem to react. Infants seem to share the expectation that social overtures will cause a response in the other person, and they show discomfort when there is no response. Reactions to a still-face task may also be indicative of the quality of an infant's future attachment to the caregiver. One meta-analysis of many still-face studies concluded that infants who showed fewer negative reactions to their mother's face during the task were more likely to show higher-quality attachments several months later (Mesman et al., 2009).

Local cultures can influence patterns of contingent responding between caregivers and infants early in the infant's life. For example, mothers' responses to infant vocalizations start to vary across cultures within the first few months after birth. In one study, infants from northern Germany and from small villages near Kumbo, Cameroon, in West Africa, were observed several times between the first and third month of life (Kärtner et al., 2010). At first, mothers in both cultures tended to respond to their infants' vocalizations in roughly the same manner. By 3 months, however, the German mothers and the Kumbo mothers were responding quite differently, reflecting differences in the way that older infants and mothers interact in each culture. The

FIGURE 6.11 Infant's reaction to the still face. (A) If an infant's mother stops interacting with her and freezes her face into a "still face" that she maintains for several seconds, the infant will start to disengage socially and will often show distress as well. **(B)** When the mother smiles and interacts with the infant, this will encourage the infant to reengage in social interaction with the mother.

German mothers showed more visually oriented responses, such as gazing, using facial expressions (for example, smiles, raised eyebrows, or wide open mouths), or pointing to an object roughly 2½ times more frequently than the Kumbo mothers, while the Kumbo mothers showed 50 percent more touch-oriented responses (for example, stroking, patting the infant's body, or kissing his face) than did the German mothers. Apparently, in just a couple of months, the parent-infant pairs start to pick up these cultural norms. This key contrast in attachment behaviors—namely, behaviors that can occur at a distance versus those that require close contact—seems to be quite modifiable across cultures.

Social Referencing Another fundamental social behavior that emerges very early in development involves relying on the expressions and behavior of others for important information about how to interpret various situations. For example, in an unfamiliar and potentially dangerous circumstance, it makes sense to watch the facial expressions and actions of those who know more about the situation. If they are panicking, your anxiety will likely increase as well. This phenomenon is known as **social referencing**, and its development has been extensively studied (Campos & Stenberg, 1981; Feinman et al., 1992; Hornik & Gunnar, 1988). These studies suggest that infants as young as 7 months use the facial expressions of others as an important source of information about how to react to ambiguous situations.

Studies of infants' reactions to the visual cliff situation, which we explored in Chapter 3, have shown that infants use social referencing as one source of information about whether to cross the transparent surface over the visual cliff. If the mother appears alarmed, the infant will be much more likely to avoid the deep side of the cliff, while an encouraging mother can often coax the infant to cross the transparent surface (Sorce et al., 1985). Similarly, older infants have been shown to use social referencing of their mothers' reactions to guide their walking on unfamiliar surfaces (Adolph et al., 2010). Moreover, a mother's emotional reaction to a new toy can influence whether her infant will choose to play with it; for example, an infant will carefully avoid playing with a toy for which the mother shows marked distaste (Hornik et al., 1987; Mumme et al., 1996). Regardless of whether a mother shows her anxiety or some other reaction in her voice or in her face, the emotion she expresses can strongly influence her infant's behavior (Vaish & Striano, 2004).

Social referencing can play a key role in the development of specific attachments. If infants observe someone showing fear or anxiety while interacting with a stranger, they are less likely to want to interact with that stranger. This increased wariness toward certain strangers will slow the process of forming an attachment to those individuals, which can have negative practical effects. For example, if an infant's parents are quite anxious about leaving their child with a new caregiver, the infant may pick up on that anxiety and thereby take longer to bond with the new caregiver. Conversely, if the parents show low anxiety and a welcoming attitude toward a new caregiver, the infant is more likely to be receptive to the caregiver as well.

Joint Attention and Gaze Following In addition to social referencing, infants show another crucial social behavior known as **joint attention**, in which the infant and another person simultaneously attend to the same object or event. When there is joint attention, both partners understand that pointing or some other indication is meant to focus the two of them on the same thing (Bruner, 1983, 1990; Scaife & Bruner, 1975; see Figure 6.12). Joint attention is not only a social behavior; it is also intrinsically communicative, and many have suggested that mastery of joint attention may be critical for the foundation of language skills (Bruner, 1976; Carpenter et al., 1998; Tomasello et al., 2005).

Some critical components of joint attention may be present as early as moments after birth, as newborns have been shown to follow the gazes of others at above-chance levels (Farroni et al., 2004). Gaze-following skill improves considerably in the following months, when infants become better able to follow gazes to increasingly distant objects. After 3 months or so, infants increasingly use their observations of others' hands and eye gazes as indicators of where to look (Amano et al., 2004; Csibra & Gergely, 2005). Well before age 1, they can interpret another person's gaze as indicating

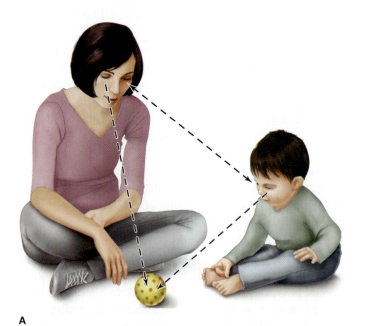

A

B

FIGURE 6.12 Joint attention. (A) In joint attention, a triangle is set up between two individuals and a referent in the world. The two individuals look at each other and at the object in a reciprocal fashion that suggests that each wants to make sure that the other knows they are referring to the same object. **(B)** Pointing often accompanies these interactive looking behaviors, as it focuses attention on an object in a way that is both a social act and a communicative one. Joint attention emerges at around 9 months of age and reflects a more sophisticated way for the infant to link to the social world.

that an object is behind a barrier (Csibra & Volein, 2008). In general, gaze following is a fragile skill before 2 months and then develops strongly between 2 and 8 months, at which time infants reliably follow the gazes of others (Gredebäck et al., 2010).

Q: How might gaze following help support the growth of human attachments?

At about 9 months, gaze following seems to develop into more full-fledged joint attention. Around this time, infants begin looking at things that an adult is looking at, seemingly in an attempt to gather information about what interests the adult (Bakeman & Adamson, 1984). In doing so, they may be more explicitly thinking of the other person as a being with goals and desires that are indicated by direction of gaze. These joint-attentional behaviors appear roughly at the same time as pointing and are used to include both the other person and the pointed-at object. Although younger infants may point to things, it seems to simply reflect the infant's own attention to an object, usually as a result of recently touching it, rather than an understanding of a shared focus with another person (Carpendale & Carpendale, 2010). At around 9 months, though, the infant starts to point to an object and then alternate her gaze between the object and the person, as if trying to track whether the person is "following" her (Bates, 1976). Similarly, when someone else points at an object, the infant is now much more prone to alternate her gaze between the indicated object and the person. These tasks require the infant to attend to both the object and the other person simultaneously, with the clear intention that the other person should likewise attend to both the object and the infant. This process seems to require the ability to understand that others have minds with their own goals and desires (Trevarthen, 1979).

Q: What is joint attention, and how is it relevant to the young child's understanding of social entities?

Joint attention typically becomes fully functional within 2 to 3 months after infants form their first specific attachments, and it may be critical for elaborating those attachments into richer and more meaningful bonds. Those bonds may be based, in part, on the interests and experiences the infant shares with others. This dimension of shared interests and experiences may well be uniquely human. Although a great many other species show gaze following (often based on head direction but sometimes also on eye direction), it is possible that only humans use gaze following as a window into others' minds and a way of building a sense of shared experiences (Rosati & Hare, 2009).

This discussion demonstrates that infants are sensitive to the special ways in which social beings can interact and the important information that those interactions provide (Dykas et al., 2011). Their attachments to social beings start quite early in development. Later in infancy, they develop even richer expectations about social creatures, especially those to whom they have formed attachments. The development of attachments to parents, caregivers, and peers occurs in a great variety of animals, but the nature of these attachments often differs from species to species. The differences may largely arise from variations in the way different species perceive and understand social beings.

Individual Differences in Attachment Style

Our discussion of attachment so far has focused primarily on developmental patterns that most children share. In particular, we have considered how an ethological perspective can illustrate the various component behaviors involved in forming and maintaining attachments. We have also noted how different cultures may rely on different kinds of behaviors and have mentioned that some attachments seem to be of higher quality than others. We now turn to the issue of individual differences in attachment style, which is the focus of most attachment studies.

Individuals show significant differences in **attachment style**—the pattern of relating to significant others that is based on expectations about how they will respond and that affects perceptions, emotions, thoughts, and behaviors in close relationships. In this section, we will explore some of the profound questions about what these differences mean for infants' relationships with others. We will examine some ways of measuring these variations in attachment and consider the challenge of determining what factors are responsible for them. Finally, we will consider some implications of different attachment styles: How should we understand cultural differences in attachment patterns? And do early attachment styles have any implications for intimate relationships later in life? First, however, we need to discuss ways of characterizing different attachment styles and measuring them.

Studying Attachment Styles in the Strange Situation

Some infants and children tend to show high levels of trust and confidence that a parent will be reliably available for comfort, support, and protection, while others are more anxious and insecure about whether this kind of support will be available. In developmental psychology, these kinds of expectations about close relationships, as well as the associated emotions and behaviors, are the basis of attachment styles. Comparing attachment styles requires a standardized method that can objectively pick up indications of different styles across a wide range of individuals. The oldest method, which is still the most prevalent one, was developed by Mary Ainsworth (Ainsworth, 1979). Inspired by the ethological approach, Ainsworth became interested in developing a method of measuring behaviors that reflect different attachment styles. Ainsworth's method is commonly known as the **Strange Situation** because it examines an infant's reactions in certain unusual and mildly threatening situations, both in the mother's presence and when the mother has left the room, as well as how the child responds when the mother returns (see Figure 6.13). In the Strange Situation, different children respond to the experience in different ways, but a particular child continues to show the same response pattern across repetitions of the same measure. This measure is most often used with infants between 1 and 2 years old.

Q: How is the Strange Situation used to measure different attachment styles?

The Strange Situation involves a sequence of eight episodes that vary in terms of the apparent level of "threat" to the infant, ranging from the mild unease of being in a strange room with the mother to the potentially greater discomfort of being left alone with a stranger (Ainsworth et al., 1978; Ainsworth & Wittig, 1969). Typically, the infant's behavior in each episode is filmed, and judges who are unaware of the infant's responses in other episodes are asked to rate the behavior in a given episode according to a scale developed by Ainsworth and her colleagues. On the basis of the infants' behavior in the Strange Situation, infants' attachments were initially classified into three categories:

- Type A infants showed an **insecure/avoidant attachment**, typical of approximately 20 percent of middle-class American children.
- Type B infants showed a **secure attachment**, typical of approximately 70 percent of middle-class American children.
- Type C infants showed an **insecure/resistant attachment**, also known as an **anxious attachment**, typical of approximately 10 percent of middle-class American children.

Type A infants, characterized as having insecure/avoidant attachments, tend to spontaneously explore more than the other types do when they are in a room alone with the mother. More important, they do not appear upset when the mother leaves, and they show much less concern toward strangers than other infants do. Most infants are at least cautious and watchful around unfamiliar people, and many become strongly agitated. In contrast, Type A babies tend to react less to strangers, sometimes even completely ignoring or avoiding them. One of the most distinctive behaviors of Type A babies occurs when the mother returns after a separation. At her return, Type A infants usually actively avoid contact with the mother by turning away or by appearing to ignore her. In some cases, it seems as if they blame the mother for the stressful separation and try to reduce the pain by withdrawing from her. Some Type A infants may simply be too preoccupied with play and unconcerned with whether the mother is there to notice when the mother returns after a separation. Several behaviors of Type A infants tend to cluster tightly together for members of that category. Thus,

A **B** **C**

FIGURE 6.13 The Strange Situation. In the Strange Situation, researchers assess the infant's attachment to the mother by watching **(A)** whether the infant plays with toys when the mother is in the room, **(B)** how the infant reacts to a stranger in the room, and **(C)** how the infant reacts when the mother returns to the room after having left it for awhile.

Type A babies are not only avoidant, but they also show less visible anxiety in the absence of the mother.

Type B infants show secure attachments and actively explore novel environments when the mother is present, presumably because they know they can trust and rely on the mother's help if the situation becomes frightening. These babies clearly show distress when the mother leaves and will be quite apprehensive toward strangers when alone with them. When the mother returns after a separation, Type B babies are delighted to see her. They clearly enjoy close physical proximity with the mother and interact with her in positive ways, such as hugging and smiling. These children also tend to be much friendlier to strangers when the mother is present, perhaps greeting a new person with a wave or smile or even approaching the stranger. They appear to be so confident in the mother that while she is present, they don't seem to worry about getting into a difficult social situation. Looking more closely at the Type B group reveals several clear subtypes, ranging from babies who reunite happily with the mother at a distance through smiles and gestures to those who need prolonged, close physical contact to reunite.

Type C infants, who show insecure/resistant, or anxious, attachments, somewhat resemble Type A infants in that both types of infants have insecure attachments. A key difference in these types is that Type C infants are much more likely to show their distress. They are less prone to explore than the other types, even when the mother is present; when the mother leaves, they show great distress, often more than Type B babies. They can initially be more clingy to the mother in unfamiliar situations. Yet, after a separation episode, they may appear angry with the mother, despite maintaining close proximity to her, unlike the Type A (avoidant) babies. Type C infants are uncomfortable around strangers, not only when left alone with them, but even when the mother is present. In short, they seem anxious about whether they can rely on the mother, but rather than dealing with the problem by avoiding her, Type C babies show greater distress than normal when she leaves and continue to indicate their unhappiness even after she returns.

Researchers have disagreed about whether the three types of attachment are the most appropriate categories and whether they are robust outside of middle-class America (Lamb et al., 1984). Later researchers developed a fourth category, Type D infants, who show another form of insecure attachment called **disorganized attachment**. Their behaviors seem far less consistent than those of the other types, and these infants appear to be insecure and unusually controlling with their parents at the same time (Barnett et al., 1999; Cicchetti & Toth, 1995; Main & Solomon, 1990; Solomon & George, 1999). Type D babies usually represent fewer than 10 percent of infants, and they are more likely to come from homes in which they have been maltreated. They are also more likely to show aggressive behavior

as preschoolers (Lyons-Ruth et al., 1993). Developmental psychologists have been especially interested in Type D babies because increasing evidence suggests that disorganized attachment in infancy predicts psychopathology in adolescence (Atkinson & Zucker, 1997; Cicchetti & Toth, 2005).

As you will see later in this chapter, there may also be another attachment style that is strongly associated with the severe deprivation that often occurs in institutions. Infants with this **indiscriminate attachment** style can be as affectionate and receptive to complete strangers as they are to their primary caregivers (O'Connor et al., 2000; Tizard & Ross, 1975; Zeanah et al., 2002). In many cases, they will rush up and hug and cling to virtually any adult in the same manner. Researchers have suggested that an indiscriminate attachment style can be quite unrelated to the security of attachment (Zeanah et al., 2005) and is therefore a different dimension on which attachment can vary. Indiscriminate attachment may also be measured in the Strange Situation (Lyons-Ruth et al., 2009), which enables researchers to more easily explore its occurrence in noninstitutionalized populations as well.

> **Q:** What are the four attachment styles associated with Type A, B, C, and D babies?

Causes of Different Attachment Styles

How do different attachment styles arise? To what extent are they influenced by an infant's initial disposition? To what extent are they influenced by the way the parents and other caregivers interact with the infant? Later in this chapter, we will see that severe social deprivation can have dramatic, albeit often not irreversible, impacts on later attachments. Here the central question is whether the differences between less extreme social environments can contribute to subtle differences in attachment style. We will also consider how infants' dispositions might foster certain kinds of social interactions and hence certain kinds of attachments, creating another example of how feedback loops can be so critical to understanding attachment. Researchers have been especially interested in disentangling the causes of insecure attachments because of concerns about how insecure attachment in infancy might affect children's later relationships (see, however, Ein-Dor et al., 2010). For that reason, we will focus primarily on the causes of insecure attachments.

Parent Effects on Insecure Attachment Even without realizing it, parents can sometimes behave in ways that might increase the chances of an insecure attachment.

New Insights into the Role of the Father

Until fairly recently, almost all attachment studies focused on mothers and infants, relegating fathers to a marginal or nonexistent role. Although the majority of attachment studies still focus on mother-infant bonds, research on father-infant relations is providing a more comprehensive account of attachment and a better understanding of how maternal and paternal roles often differ.

Historically, fathers have been less involved in child rearing than mothers (Barry & Paxson, 1971; Hewlett & Macfarlan, 2010; Munroe & Munroe, 1992). The question of why this is so has been considered extensively from an evolutionary perspective (Gettler, 2010; Munroe & Munroe, 1992). One evolutionary argument revolves around uncertainty about the paternity of a child—the notion that, unlike mothers, fathers can rarely be 100 percent sure that they are the child's biological parent. This argument suggests that fathers are less invested in child care because there is some doubt about whether their efforts would be promoting the survival of their own genes (Dawkins, 1976). Along these lines, some have suggested that even when fathers do devote time and care to their offspring, they could be doing so to curry favor with the mother and thereby increase the odds of future mating and more offspring (Geary, 2000; Gettler, 2010). Nonetheless, it is critical to remember that human fathers tend to spend far more time taking care of infants than the fathers in virtually any other primate species (Geary, 2000).

Research suggests that the differences in how human fathers and mothers bond with their children are primarily a consequence of dominant cultural practices rather than a result of intrinsic differences between fathers and mothers (Lamb, 2004; Russell & Saebel, 1997). In some cultural contexts, the differences can be very large. For example, while mothers and infants sleep in the same bed across many cultures, father-infant co-sleeping has never been a strong cultural tradition (Ball et al., 2000; Weisner, 2009). Yet, the more dramatic cross-cultural finding is the enormous variation in the level of father involvement with their children (Lamb, 2004). For example, Aka fathers, who are part of a nomadic hunter-gatherer culture in central Africa, stay within an arm's reach of their children roughly 50 percent of the time. In contrast, Kipsigis fathers, who are part of a pastoral culture in Kenya, spend very little direct time with their children until around the child's fifth year (Hewlett, 1991; Hewlett & Macfarlan, 2010). More broadly, fathers tend to be more involved in child rearing in hunter-gatherer cultures than in pastoral-agrarian cultures, although specific cultures deviate from this pattern (Gettler, 2010). This wide variation has led some researchers to argue that it is misleading to focus on differences between mothers and fathers as intrinsic and unchangeable (Lamb, 2004). Culture seems to have an enormous influence on how much time fathers spend with their children and the kinds of activities that they engage in with their children.

Fathering may be associated with certain biological changes in fathers, especially in those who spend more time with their infants and children. When they become fathers, males in many species show a drop in testosterone. Testosterone is thought to foster both mate seeking and competition between males for the best mate, while a reduction of testosterone may facilitate parenting, in that the males with lower testosterone levels may spend less time seeking mates and more time with their offspring (Muller et al., 2009; Wingfield et al., 1990, 2000). Just being a father does not necessarily lead to sustained low levels of testosterone; the kind of fathering matters as well. This was convincingly demonstrated in two groups living next to each other in Tanzania who came from nearly identical biological backgrounds (Muller et al., 2009). One group, the Datoga, was pastoral and mostly made up of herders, whereas the other group, the Hazda, consisted of foragers in the hunter-gatherer tradition. Following the general correlation that we noted earlier, the Hazda fathers were much more involved parents who spent more time than the Datoga fathers in close proximity to their infants. When researchers measured testosterone levels in the fathers' saliva, they found that the Hazda fathers had consistently lower levels of testosterone than did the Datoga fathers. In contrast, men in both groups who were not fathers showed higher testosterone levels and no group difference. Thus, dif-

What causes those behaviors? Early on, Ainsworth and her colleagues proposed that some parents may have difficulty understanding the infant's needs (Ainsworth et al., 1978). More recent research has supported the notion that parents' problems in perceiving and responding to social cues can lead to more insecure attachments (Belsky, 2005; Braungart-Rieker et al., 2001).

One set of studies in this area examined mothers' ability to accurately perceive negative emotional states, not only in their own 4-month-old infants, but also in their

ferent cultural roles for fathers can influence hormonal levels, which in turn feed back to support more intense fathering roles. Similar feedback loops also seem to occur with prolactin and oxytocin, two hormones associated with nurturance and trust, both of which have been measured at higher levels in fathers who are more in tune with their infant's social and emotional states (Gordon et al., 2010). It seems very likely that cultural differences will be found here as well.

One difference between mothers and fathers in some Western cultures concerns their role with respect to who is more playful and who is more authoritarian. Studies conducted in Mexico, the United States, and Australia have shown that fathers tend to spend more time playing with their children, while mothers more often act as the disciplinarian (Bronstein, 1999; Lamb, 2010; Parke, 1996; Russell & Russell, 1987). This finding runs counter to some stereotypes about parental roles, but it is important to remember that when the father spends less time with the child, it may be easier for him to ignore the child's transgressions. Fathers also tend to play in more physically active ways with both boys and girls. Finally, while fathers tend to spend more than twice as much of their time with children in play (see Figure 6.14), mothers have to divide their time between play and many other activities in which fathers tend to be less involved, such as feeding, bathing, and dressing.

Often, the differences in mothers' and fathers' relations with the child seem more related to the amount of time each parent spends with the child. Thus, fathers and mothers who are primary caregivers interact with their infants in similar ways, and secondary caregivers of different sexes also show similar interaction patterns (Field, 1978). In the past, most Western infants developed an attachment to the mother earlier than their attachment to the father, but as fathers have become increasingly involved in child rearing, differences as to when attachments are formed are diminishing (Sayer et al., 2004). Moreover, as more fathers become stay-at-home parents, it is likely that a considerably more detailed account of attachment in general will emerge, as well as a better understanding of how maternal and paternal roles may differ.

In contrast to popular stereotypes, when cultural practices and time spent with infants are factored out, mothers and fathers do not appear to be biologically different in their sen-

sitivity to infants. Despite the common belief that mothers are biologically better tuned to be sensitive to their infant's cries or facial expressions, empirical studies have not provided evidence for these differences (Field, 1978; Frodi et al., 1978). Mothers respond physiologically to crying in ways that fathers cannot (such as increased lactation in nursing mothers), but these physiological differences do not necessarily correspond to psychological differences. When men and women behave comparably with their infants, the outcomes appear to be much the same as well. Having parents of either sex who are sensitive and responsive to their infant's needs, desires, thoughts, and feelings is associated with more positive psychological outcomes in the children (Lamb & Lewis, 2010).

FIGURE 6.14 **Fathers and attachment.** Although traditional studies of parent-child bonds have focused on the mother, a more recent line of work has examined fathers. Some behavioral differences do seem to exist in how mothers and fathers interact with their children, such as fathers being more playful and mothers more authoritarian, but the largest difference is still a much greater amount of time that mothers typically spend interacting with their children compared to fathers.

partners and their own parents before the babies were born. The less accurate a mother-to-be was at perceiving distress-related emotions, the more likely her infant was to show insecure attachments at age 12 months or older (Braungart-Rieker et al., 2001; De Wolff & Van IJzendoorn, 1997).

Thus, a mother's ability to understand when another person is truly distressed, without being insensitive or oversensitive, is related to developing an appropriate interactive relationship with her infant. Although the precise mechanisms of the parent's influence may be complex and indirect

(Atkinson et al., 2005), the correlation between parental social perceptions and the quality of the child's later relationships is not surprising—especially in light of the essential reciprocal give-and-take that characterizes even the earliest infant-mother relations.

> Q: What is an example of how interaction patterns between parents might predict parent-child attachment relations?

As a second example of parental influence on attachment, high levels of maternal anxiety during the prenatal period can predict insecure attachments. Mothers who showed higher levels of general anxiety during their pregnancy with their first child had a higher incidence of insecurely attached infants at 12 months of age (Del Carmen et al., 1993; O'Connor et al., 2003). Other studies have shown that maternal depression before or during pregnancy is also related to difficulties in parent-child attachment (Atkinson et al., 2005; Bagner et al., 2010; Carter et al., 2001; Field, 2000; Toth et al., 2009).

The fathers' attitude toward the infant and his appropriate role as parent may also affect whether the infant has secure or insecure attachments. Fathers' views of infants and paternal roles, as measured when their infants were 3 months old, partially predicted the qualities of interaction in the Strange Situation at 12 months, as did patterns of interaction with the infant at 3 months. Thus, fathers who described their infants in more positive terms, who saw themselves as important in their infant's development, and who felt that time spent with their infant was an important life priority were more likely to have securely attached infants. Similarly, fathers who were more sensitive to their infant's states at 3 months, who were more animated in play, and who showed more reciprocal play were more likely to have securely attached infants. But fathers who had negative attitudes toward their infants and were not sensitive to their infants' needs when interacting with them at 3 months were more likely to have insecurely attached infants. On the other hand, mothers' attitudes and views of maternal roles did not predict attachment quality, although interaction patterns at 3 months did. Part of the effect may stem from the fact that maternal attitudes tend to be more similar across mothers, but the difference may also suggest that fathers' roles are more influenced by their attitudes (Cox et al., 1992).

In general, parents' social skills and other attributes—measured before their child is born—seem to correlate with the nature of infant-parent attachments. These correlations seem to suggest that parents' attributes can cause different attachment outcomes, but these causal inferences require a great deal of caution. A number of other factors may also explain the correlation, such as parents' and children's shared genotypes for social skills. That is, biological parents and their children may share genes that contribute to difficulties in perceiving or understanding social and emotional information. For example, Asperger's syndrome, an autism spectrum disorder in which individuals have difficulty understanding emotional and mental states of others, co-occurs more often in people who are genetically related (Campbell, 2010). If a parent has Asperger's, a child is more likely to have it as well and may have greater difficulties understanding social nuances in interactions, leading to insecure attachment styles. Similarly, there have been several arguments that genes may substantially affect individual differences in emotional regulation (Hariri & Holmes, 2006; Posner et al., 2010; see Chapter 7). A mother who has trouble regulating her emotions might be more likely to have a child with similar problems (because of the genes they share), and those difficulties might lead both mother and child to overreact to stressful situations, potentially increasing the likelihood of insecure attachment. Direct comparisons between parents and children are challenging, however, because the behavioral and physical manifestations of the same genotype can vary with age and often look quite different in a child and an adult. For example, the phenotype for an Asperger's genotype will look different in a 1-year-old than in an adult.

> Q: What are some ways in which father-child and mother-child interaction patterns differ?

Child Effects on Insecure Attachment Children themselves might contribute to the formation of insecure attachments. They may have traits that make them insecure, or they may behave in ways that cause their parents to respond in ways that then influence the child's attachment style, leading to a feedback loop between the behavior of the child and that of the parents. These child effects on attachment are of great interest to parents who wonder if they, as parents, are primarily responsible for their child's attachment style or whether the child is more responsible.

Some researchers have investigated child effects on attachment by examining whether infant temperament plays a role. As discussed more fully in Chapter 7, infant temperament describes how each infant tends to emotionally respond to specific situations; for example, some babies are highly reactive and fussy to loud noises, while others are hardly perturbed. At this point, there is not a clear consensus on precisely how much infant temperament affects attachment style. Among the researchers who suggest that it does not have an influence, some have pointed out that because the same child can show different attachment styles with different caregivers, a child's temperament does not *invariably* cause a particular style of interaction (Sroufe, 1985; Sroufe & Waters, 1982; Sroufe et al., 2010). Moreover, in twin studies comparing monozygotic and dizygotic twins' attachment styles, it has been difficult to consistently demonstrate a higher level of concordance in monozygotic twins, even though temperaments are more similar in monozygotic twins (Bokhorst et al., 2003; O'Connor & Croft, 2001; Roisman & Fraley, 2006, 2008). It can therefore be difficult to find a consistent association between a particular infant temperament and later attachment style.

Other research groups, however, have found some relationship between early behaviors associated with temperament and later attachment styles. For example, newborn infants who react more negatively to the interruption of sucking are more likely to be classified later as Type C babies (Miyake et al., 1985), as are infants who cry longer, more frequently, and more intensely than others (Calkins & Fox, 1992, 2002; Crockenberg & Leerkes, 2003). Some researchers suggest that both infant temperament and parents' behaviors contribute to attachment style but because those components strongly interact with each other, it can be difficult to consistently find simple temperament effects (Mangelsdorf et al., 2000).

Infants may have traits like extreme arousability or irritability or impulsivity that affect their reactions to people and situations (see Figure 6.15). These reactions, which are based on their ability to self-regulate, may in turn affect how their parents react to them. Thus, irritable infants can cause some mothers to be less responsive, which in turn may influence the quality of attachments (Crockenberg, 1981; Gervai, 2009).

For example, consider a "colicky" infant whose distressed crying wakes his parents every few hours, leaving them constantly sleep deprived. The exhausted parents, confronted with an infant who always seems upset, might be less sensitive to changes in the infant's emotional states than the parents of a child who shows distress only rarely, sleeps through the night, and regularly naps during the day. Children with respiratory illness or Down syndrome also more frequently show insecure attachments, presumably reflecting ways in which the baby's illness and communication problems might decrease the parents' ability to be sensitive to the infant's emotional states and needs (Cassibba et al., 2004; Sroufe, 1985).

While infants sometimes do have different attachment styles with different parents, in studies of families with two children and two parents, each child's attachment style typically stays constant across both parents instead of each parent's style staying constant across both children. Thus, in those families, the children's attachment styles are more consistent than those of the parents, suggesting that the children themselves may be shaping the styles they use more than their parents are (Schneider-Rosen & Burke, 1999). Furthermore, any parent of more than one child will attest that even young infants show distinct characteristics that inevitably color the parent's interactions with the baby. As we will see in greater detail in Chapter 7, these individual differences in how babies interact with caregivers may predispose them to different attachment styles.

A   B   C

FIGURE 6.15 **Child effects on attachment.** Some infants seem to be intrinsically less happy and more sensitive to adverse events than others. These differences in temperaments may well lead to different social interaction patterns with parents and caregivers that in turn help create different attachment styles. Parents are likely to react differently to **(A)** an irritated baby, **(B)** a neutral baby, and **(C)** a happy baby.

Interactions of Parent Effects and Child Effects The development of more sophisticated ways of assessing child effects has also helped clarify how interactions between child effects and parent effects shape attachments. Although there is an increasing belief that infant temperament does influence attachment, we must still look for feedback loops, wherein parental behavior affects the child's behavior, which in turn affects parental behavior. Temperamental differences may often interact with particular social dispositions of the child's caregivers (Kagan, 1998). These views are supported by more recent work looking at links between particular gene variants associated with infant temperament and particular kinds of parenting. For example, if caregivers communicate poorly with their infant, that difficulty can increase the infant's risk of showing a disorganized attachment style—but only among infants who have a particular allele of the dopamine-related gene known as *DRD4*. That particular allele of *DRD4* may help create a temperament that is particularly susceptible to the effects of parental communication problems (Gervai et al., 2007). In short, the effects of a certain temperament on attachment style may depend on whether it co-occurs with a particular form of parenting.

Interactional patterns may be greatly amplified by the infant's own beliefs about how caregivers are likely to behave. Bowlby clearly sensed this possibility when he proposed that infants have an **internal working model**—namely, a mental representation of the self and others and how they might interact in different circumstances (Bowlby, 1969, 1979). These models seemed plausible as ways of explaining how infants with different attachment styles might have different expectations about and responses to caregivers. Yet, the models were difficult to verify in their own right until studies directly looked for their presence using techniques that have successfully explored social cognition in infants. As described more completely in the Scientific Methods box, securely attached infants expected other infants to seek comfort from caregivers and for the caregivers to respond accordingly. In contrast, insecure/resistant infants also expected infants to seek comfort but thought that caregivers would not provide it; and insecure/avoidant infants thought not only that infants would avoid seeking comfort but also that caregivers would not provide it if requested (Johnson et al., 2010). The infants' expectations based on these models amplified the role of feedback, as the models might help to strengthen a particular kind of attachment style, which in turn would reinforce a particular class of models.

> **Q:** To what extent do infants' temperament styles influence later attachment styles?

Consequences of Different Attachment Styles

Does an infant's attachment style early in life have long-term consequences? And if it does, how stable are those effects? To address these questions, we turn to behaviors and other psychological variables that correlate with attachment styles in infancy. For example, researchers have studied whether infants' attachment styles affect such broad abilities as negotiating the environment by finding one's way successfully through toys and furniture, reaching for toys, and positioning oneself in a convenient position for interacting with those toys. Securely attached 18-month-olds show more skills in all these abilities than do insecurely attached infants (Cassidy, 1986, 2001). Securely attached infants therefore seem to have a more refined situational awareness and a better ability to orient themselves to those situations, even when they are not social. In the rest of this section, we will concentrate on the effects of attachment styles on later social interactions. As always, we will also ask about possible causal relationships and the presence of possible feedback loops. A final issue concerns the extent to which our later attachments are predetermined by what happens to us as infants—in particular, whether there is a sensitive period in infancy that results in infant attachment styles that exert effects on later attachments (Sroufe, 1978).

Correlations between Infant Attachment Styles and Children's Social Interactions In the past two decades, many studies have asked how different attachment styles influence an infant's ability to negotiate the social world. In general, secure attachments of Type B infants seem to lead to more successful social abilities. In contrast to insecurely attached infants, securely attached infants engaged in more reciprocal interactions in peer play, had more positive emotions, and were less withdrawn. Securely attached infants had smoother interactions with strangers when they were 3 years old, and they were rated more highly by teachers for competence in peer play (Lieberman, 1977; Lutkenhaus et al., 1985; Waters et al., 1979). Similarly, toddlers who were securely attached as infants were judged to be more sociable with peers and more attentive and interested in their playmates (Pastor, 1981). Many other studies also suggest relations between infant attachment styles and later social skills in toddlerhood and preschool years (Granot & Mayseless, 2001). For example, infant attachment styles seem to predict a 3-year-old's attractiveness as a potential playmate with peers. Children who were securely attached as infants were seen as more attractive to interact with than those who had been anxiously attached, suggesting that lower interaction skills may be partly caused by

SCIENTIFIC METHOD: Internal Working Models and Attachment Styles

Hypothesis:

Infants with different attachment styles have different mental representations about how infants and caregivers will interact in situations involving seeking and providing comfort.

Method:

1. Thirty-three 13-month-old infants watched animations in which a "baby" encountered difficulties and a "mother" responded.

2. Infants were habituated to a "separation" video in which the "mother" left the "baby" and the "baby" pulsed slightly and emitted human infant crying sounds (as indicated by the sound waves).

3. Infants then observed two test events in which the "mother" either responded by moving next to the "baby" or responded by moving farther away.

4. Researchers recorded infants' looking times and related these to infants' classifications in the Strange Situation.

Results:

Secure infants looked longer when the "mother" moved away from the distressed "baby," while insecure infants looked longer when the "mother" moved closer.

Conclusion:

Infants' cognitive models of how caregivers and infants interact vary with their attachment styles, suggesting that the models may further entrench those styles, which in turn reinforce those models. Other studies in this set show that infants also have different models of how babies will respond to caregivers, further supporting the idea of a feedback loop.

Source study: Johnson et al. (2010).

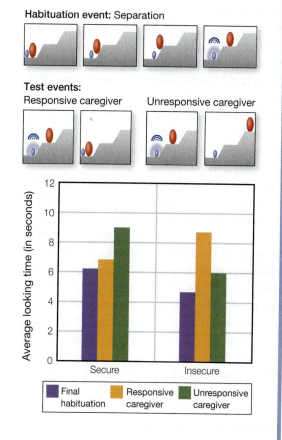

Habituation event: Separation

Test events:
Responsive caregiver   Unresponsive caregiver

others' perception that children with insecure attachment styles in infancy are less desirable (Jacobson & Wille, 1986).

Despite all the evidence of an association between infants' attachment styles and their abilities and social tendencies as children, these studies do not unequivocally show that attachment style differences in infancy directly cause those later abilities and social tendencies. There are two alternative ways of interpreting this evidence. First, some infants' temperamental features may elicit ineffective patterns of social interaction from others. These features might hamper the typical back-and-forth rhythms that help build ways for two individuals to come into better emotional and social synchrony. In infancy, these problems might lead to insecure attachments, and later they might cause more strained interactions with peers and other social difficulties. In this view, children's social difficulties are not caused by insecure attachment in infancy; instead, insecure attachment and later problems with socializing might share a common cause, arising out of infant temperament.

A second interpretation for the link between infants' attachment styles and the nature of their childhood relationships suggests that certain environmental conditions can foster insecure attachments and also affect later social patterns. For example, if a family is under extreme stress— say, from marital discord or poverty—the constant pressure could lead to insecure attachments that could last for several years. The effects could work through both children and parents. Stressed parents might be less able to fully engage with their infants and less sensitive to their needs, leading infants to see the parents as less reliable sources of comfort and safety. Infants in stressful environments might be poorly nourished or sleep deprived and less adept at communicating their states to their caregivers, which could lead to both less responsiveness from the caregivers and insecure attachment in infants and older children.

One study examined attachment patterns in families in East and West Germany shortly after the fall of the Berlin Wall. This was a stressful time: as the country was being reunited, many families were experiencing radical changes in their workplaces, homes, and networks of support. These social and political changes led to insecure attachments when parents had trouble adjusting to the changes (Ahnert & Lamb, 2001). In such cases, insecure attachment styles in infancy might be correlated with later social problems because both factors might result from the same environmental stressors. Similar effects may occur when one parent in a military family is deployed abroad. If the parent who stays with the children does not have adequate social support to handle the stress of the transition, the children may be at increased risk for insecure attachments (Posada et al., 2010).

It is also likely that these two explanations—one focused on the child's temperament and the other on the environment—interact to affect childhood patterns of social interaction. An infant with a difficult temperament can more easily trigger adverse behavior in most caregivers, which then exacerbates the infant's difficult behavior, and so on, in a downward-spiraling feedback loop. As these alternatives show, there is still much to learn about the development of insecure attachments and their effects later in childhood (Sroufe, 2002).

Long-Term Links between Infant Attachment Styles and Adult Relationship Styles Researchers have also explored whether adult relationship styles are related to infant attachment styles. While the connection is a complex one, some links between childhood attachment style and later relationship style as adults have been revealed with the help of sophisticated analytical models and methods (Cassidy, 2000; Fraley, 2002; Fraley & Roberts, 2005; Fraley & Shaver, 2000; Roisman, 2009). For example, one study revealed that styles of interaction between parents and their 13-year-olds were related to those children's styles of romantic relationships 8 years later, at age 21 (Roisman et al., 2001). Looking at infant attachment styles more directly, one longitudinal study has shown that the interactional style between a mother and her 18-month-old child does predict some aspects of the child's later relationship style with peers and partners (Zayas et al., 2011). In that study, researchers measured the mother's behavior toward the infant, rather than the infant's behavior in the Strange Situation, and found that the children whose mothers provided them with more sensitive care in infancy were less controlling at age 22. They also had less anxiety about partners rejecting or abandoning them and were less concerned about relying on those partners. Nonetheless, shared genotypes and environmental influences likely contribute to these links between infant attachment style and adult relationship style. For example,

infants whose mothers are more sensitive caregivers might share with their mothers a genetic predisposition for interpersonal sensitivity that makes them less likely to be controlling as adults.

Although unusual interactional styles in infancy can predict social problems in middle childhood, adolescence, and even adulthood (Brumariu & Kerns, 2010; Collins & Sroufe, 1999; Sroufe et al., 1999), these links may not result specifically from events in infancy. Instead, they may grow out of a consistent and sustained pattern of problematic interactions that started in infancy and continued throughout much of childhood. Had the difficulties stopped after infancy, the long-term effects might have disappeared. Thus, problems in infancy do not necessarily cause problems in adulthood. Indeed, when struggling families manage to leave acute poverty after the infant's first year, and when infants start to have much more rewarding interactions, they usually do not suffer negative long-term consequences. Unfortunately, effects can work in the other direction as well. Those families that enter poverty and its attendant chaos often show a rise of insecure attachments (Weinfield et al., 2000). It is thus quite difficult to support the notion that irrevocable patterns of relating to others are established during a specific sensitive period. In short, even if infants show some problematic social behaviors, these interactional patterns can be modified to produce more fruitful and productive interpersonal behaviors and relationships.

> **Q:** What are two possible explanations for the correlations between infant attachment styles and later social behavioral patterns?

Cross-Cultural Differences in Attachment Styles

Although Ainsworth conducted several studies of individual differences in attachment styles in Uganda (Ainsworth, 1967), most research on attachment styles has been conducted in Western countries, particularly on middle-class Americans. In this chapter, we have occasionally looked at effects in other countries and in other social classes, but it is important to more directly consider how attachment styles and patterns of child care can vary across cultures. This approach will enable us both to better understand what the common research techniques, such as the Strange Situation, are measuring and to understand the individual differences themselves. One strategy that can help shed light on the meaning of differences in attachment is to see whether they manifest similarly in different cultures.

Perhaps surprisingly, the relative incidence of different attachment styles, as measured using Ainsworth's Strange Situation, varies dramatically across cultures (Thompson, 1998; Van IJzendoorn & Kroonenberg, 1988). Consider, for example, the substantial cultural differences shown in Table 6.2. The majority of German infants studied were measured as insecurely attached (mostly avoidant, or Type A). Japanese infants showed no **avoidant attachments** whatsoever, and they were almost three times as likely as their American counterparts to show anxious (Type C) attachments. Finally, one group of Israeli children showed almost 10 times as many anxious attachments as Swedish children. Because the procedure used in the Strange Situation is relatively straightforward, it does not seem that these variations can be explained by simple methodological discrepancies in how the assessments were conducted (Harwood et al., 1995; Thompson, 1998; Van IJzendoorn & Kroonenberg, 1988). At the same time, it makes little sense to conclude that entire cultures are rearing most of their children in socially maladaptive ways.

Perhaps there are subtle ways in which the Strange Situation is inadequate as a measure of differences in attachment style across cultures. One possibility is that differences in child rearing across cultures influence the degree of "strangeness" that children experience in the Strange Situation. Consider, for example, that in most Japanese households, early separation of the mother from the child is strongly discouraged. Japanese infants are usually in close proximity to their mothers for longer periods of time than infants in other cultures. Similarly, some Israeli infants who live in a kibbutz community experience repeated contacts with familiar adults in the kibbutz and may hardly ever see strangers. Despite the differences in these experiences, both groups might be expected to show an increase in Type C responses in the Strange Situation because both Japanese and Israeli infants would develop expectations that caregivers would always be immediately available and responsive and therefore would show increased distress and anxiety when left alone with a stranger. On the other hand, in some parts of Germany, child rearing often emphasizes early independence from adults. If these children are more accustomed to separations and more frequently exposed to strangers, those experiences could easily lead to a greater incidence of Type A responses.

The problem, then, is that the Strange Situation conveys very different levels of anxiety, depending on a culture's child-rearing practices. Ideally, a more consistent measure would involve exposing children from different cultures to equivalent levels of subjective "strangeness" and then looking for differences in attachment style. Although no perfect technique along these lines has yet been developed, other evidence suggests that cultural differences in attachment style have been exaggerated. In fact, the differences appear much smaller when the full Strange Situation method is not used. For example, one analysis focused on the infant's initial reaction to the Strange Situation before separation from and reunion with the mother occurred (Sagi et al., 1991). The researchers hypothesized that the ways that infants first size up a novel situation might be less vulnerable to cultural differences than their responses to separations. The initial reactions were thought to reveal, among other things, the infant's level of trust in the mother in a way that might be robustly measured across cultures. When such an analysis was undertaken, cultural differences did indeed become greatly reduced and often became nonexistent (Sagi et al., 1991). In particular, when infants were coded in terms of initial reactions only, it was still possible to code them into clear attachment style categories; then when cross-cultural comparisons were made between infants from Germany, Holland, Israel, Japan, Sweden, and the United States, most of the typical differences across cultures disappeared, with only infants from Sweden and Israel having somewhat different frequencies of classifications from the other groups. Of course, even the initial reactions might not be perfect measures, as they, too, could be influenced by prior cultural experiences and how unfamiliar those experiences made the initial situation seem.

Cross-cultural comparisons using different methods for studying attachment therefore illustrate the problems that can arise in applying an assessment technique to different

	Type A (Avoidant)	Type B (Secure)	Type C (Anxious)
Sweden	22	75	4
Israel	8	57	34
Great Britain	22	75	3
Japan	0	68	32
Germany	49	33	12
Netherlands	34	6	0
United States	22	66	12

TABLE 6.2 Attachment style across cultures. The percentages of infants with particular attachment styles, as measured by the Strange Situation, vary dramatically across different cultures. Those differences, however, may be less a reflection of differences in underlying attachments and more a reflection of differences in the perceived "strangeness" of different situations. (Percentages do not sum to 100 because some infants' styles could not be reliably coded, and some infants were coded as Type D.) Adapted from Thompson (1998).

Day Care and Attachment

In many societies, the percentage of two-parent households in which both parents work outside the home increased greatly in the last few decades of the twentieth century. In 1975, 39 percent of American mothers with children under 6 years of age worked outside the home. That percentage increased continuously up to 59 percent in 1998, and in 2006 it was roughly 65 percent (Coontz, 2010; Cotter et al., 2008). These changes are coupled with other changes in Western families, especially because grandparents and other relatives are less likely to live nearby and so are not available to take care of the children when the parents go to work. In this context, day care can be viewed as either a liberating source of social support or a necessary compromise for dealing with economic necessity. Sometimes these views can coexist in the mind of a parent who is concerned about the impact of day care on his or her children.

It is important to understand that the range of day care settings and programs is enormous. Day care providers differ in their philosophies, caregiver-to-child ratios, training methods for staff, rates of staff turnover, and physical facilities. Given this wide variety of forms of day care and given the general trend toward increasing use of some form of day care in many cultures, the most pressing social policy questions revolve around what kinds of day care are associated with the most positive outcomes for children (see Figure 6.16).

Some researchers argue that spending a lot of time in day care, usually defined as being cared for by individuals other than the parents for 20 or more hours a week, poses some risks for children even when the care is high quality. The most consistently negative research assessments of the effects of long hours in day care initially came from the Pennsylvania Infant and Family Development Project (Belsky, 1986, 2001, 2005; Belsky & Rovine, 1987, 1988). In that project, researchers measured Strange Situation responses in 1-year-olds who spent large amounts of time in day care during their first year of life and found that 43 percent of the infants were classified as insecurely attached to their mothers, as opposed to 28 percent of infants who experienced little or no early day care. Other studies in the 1980s reported similar effects (Barglow et al., 1987; Gamble & Zigler, 1986).

These early studies treated day care as the same across all of the studies and did not take into account other factors, such as the quality of the day care (for example, the ratio of infants to caregivers and caregiver training) and the differences in the children (temperament and gender) and in their families (for example, sensitivity and responsiveness of the parents to the child and stressors experienced by working parents). Some researchers expressed concern that these other factors may have also played a role in attachments between mothers and their infants who were in day care (Clarke-Stewart, 1989). Moreover, using the Strange Situation in these kinds of studies may have introduced problems similar to the ones introduced in the cross-cultural studies. Children who have spent much of their infancy in a day care center with strangers coming and going might have quite different adaptations to what is "strange" than infants who spent more time close to a parent. Extensive day care can thus be thought of as a kind of "culture" quite different from extensive home care, so it is important to be cautious in interpreting these differences in Strange Situation classifications, especially in light of later studies.

In the early 1990s, a massive U.S. study was launched to look more systematically at how both the quality and amount of nonmaternal child care related to many aspects of development. That study, known as the NICHD Study of Early Child Care and Youth Development, started with over 1,300 infants and continued to study over 1,000 of those children well into adolescence (NICHD, 2005). Although the results are complex and nuanced, several general patterns have been found consistently and replicated in other countries.

FIGURE 6.16 **Effects of day care.** Many studies have examined the effects of day care on attachment style. The most investigated factors for links to attachment style are (1) the quality of the care itself, which can vary enormously across different day care settings, and (2) the amount of time spent in day care.

The researchers looked at the possible effects of both quality and amount of nonmaternal care in three areas: children's attachment style, their broader social functioning, and their cognitive and language development. They also asked if the effects varied depending on children's backgrounds. For example, would more at-risk children be more influenced by quality of care?

In this study, it was difficult to systematically link differences in children's attachment style to either the amount of time spent in day care or quality of care. Although low-quality care seemed potentially associated with insecure attachments at 15 months, the same link was not found at 36 months (NICHD, 2001). Moreover, while children who were in day care at an early age showed an initial advantage in self-confidence and social skills, these positive effects were relatively modest and tended to disappear with increasing age (Lamb, 1998; NICHD, 1998, 2001, 2003). With respect to broader social functioning, the amount of time a child spends in day care is associated with more aggression, more disobedience, and more challenges of adults in a child's early school years, but it is not related to higher incidences of psychopathology. This finding makes sense, given that children who spend much of their time with peers and away from their parents might well be less intimidated by adult authorities. Even into the teenage years, 15-year-olds who had been in more extensive day care as infants showed somewhat higher levels of risk taking and impulsivity (Vandell et al., 2010).

Nonetheless, these associations, while statistically significant, are not massive. More specifically, the correlations between amount of time spent in day care and variables like impulsivity levels or risk-taking tendencies are roughly at the 0.1 level. This means that the vast amount of variation across children is due to factors other than the amount of time they spent in day care. While any statistically significant correlations are of interest, it is important to keep their small size in mind (McCartney et al., 2010).

The effects of day care quality might seem to be easier to demonstrate, but they, too, can be hard to document consistently, especially with respect to attachment security and social behaviors. Better quality of care is, however, associated with higher levels of cognitive and linguistic development among children and even among adolescents (NICHD, 2001; Vandell et al., 2010). The higher the quality of care, the higher the children's scores on assessments of cognition and language. Moreover, children who spend more time in high-quality day care tend to score higher on cognitive and linguistic measures than do children who spend less time in such care.

Poor-quality day care has, unsurprisingly, been associated with more negative outcomes—but these relationships are not always easy to interpret. Some studies have found that kindergartners who had been in poor-quality day care showed more behavioral and social difficulties than those who had been cared for at home, whereas those who had been in high-quality day care showed no more difficulties than those cared for at home (Howes, 1990; Loeb et al., 2007). When children experienced poor-quality day care only after infancy, it still predicted later adjustment problems. It is also important to keep in mind that parents who seem least sensitive to their children's needs are also more likely to be less attentive to differences in day care quality. Some studies, such as the NICHD study, have tried to control for parent and child effects statistically, but there is still a strong possibility that these factors, as well as shared genotypes and shared environments, continue to influence the associations between day care quality and later outcomes. Without experimental studies that randomly assign children to different levels of quality care—which would obviously be unethical—it is difficult to tell.

As noted earlier, the amount of time that mothers spend at work does not predict attachment relations with their infants (Huston & Rosenkrantz Aronson, 2005). But the amount of *available* time a mother spends with her infant does predict the quality of the attachment relationship. Thus, when mothers have the time, whether they work or not, the extent to which they choose to use that time to interact in a high-quality manner with their child is related to the quality of the attachment. Even then, however, the causation appears to be that sensitive mothers who relate to their children well want to spend more time with them, not that the time spent itself causes the relationship to be better and makes the mother more sensitive.

A final question concerns whether the amount and quality of day care show different developmental associations for children from disadvantaged backgrounds. It now appears that these children benefit more than other children from high-quality care and large amounts of it and that they suffer more from lower-quality care (Anderson et al., 2003; Caughy et al., 1994; Dearing et al., 2009; Geoffroy et al., 2010). For these children, high-quality day care is most often related to higher levels of cognitive and linguistic skills rather than social skills.

Overall, high-quality child care is rarely associated with detectable long-term problems and is often associated with positive outcomes. These positive associations are especially strong for cognitive and linguistic development among children from disadvantaged backgrounds. The social policy implication seems clear. Poor families often have fewer options for child care, putting their children at higher risk for ending up in low-quality care. These patterns suggest that it is especially important to focus resources on making high-quality care available to the most disadvantaged children.

groups without considering whether they all interpret the technique in the same way. Failure to consider such culture-specific differences may lead to the belief that cultures show large differences in the incidence of different attachment styles, whereas a more culturally sensitive analysis might reveal deeper commonalities that suggest quite consistent ratios of the different styles across cultures. We should not underestimate the influences of culture on many aspects of a child's behavior, but in making cross-cultural comparisons, we cannot assume that a particular measure means the same thing to all participants.

The cross-cultural comparisons also highlight some of the limitations of the Strange Situation. Over its long history, it has produced many useful insights, but we must interpret it carefully, mindful of the setting. In addition to the problem of controlling for subjective impressions of strangeness, the measure tends to categorize children into one of three or four types, whereas many believe that differences in styles should be thought of as varying along a continuous dimension (Lamb et al., 1984). Researchers have developed other measures that try to avoid some of the limitations of the Strange Situation (Cassidy & Marvin, 1992; Thompson, 1998), but even these newer measures can be challenging to apply and interpret across all cultures. Variations in attachment styles certainly continue to be a topic of great interest; the challenge for future research in this area is to develop new ways of assessing attachment styles that are robust across all cultures and settings.

> **Q:** What are some cautions to keep in mind when using the Strange Situation to study attachment styles across cultures?

Effects of Early Social Deprivation

As we have seen, different species form and maintain attachments in similar ways, though many of the specific attachment behaviors differ. In this section, we will explore what happens when human infants and other primate infants are prevented from forming normal attachments. Although laboratory experiments on humans would be unethical, experimental studies on other primates have enabled researchers to compare the effects of social deprivation on those primates with human children's developmental outcomes in several tragic real-world settings. We will consider which aspects of social contact are most important for developing normal attachments and whether the effects of early social deprivation can be reversed.

Social Deprivation in Humans

When children are deprived of the opportunity to form attachments, the effects can be devastating. These effects have been discussed for many years (Bakwin, 1942; Durfee & Wolf, 1933; Lowrey, 1940; Provence & Lipton, 1962). René Spitz's research on infants in Latin America in the 1940s has been especially influential (Spitz, 1945, 1946). Spitz compared two groups of infants. One group lived in a foundling home that had roughly one nurse for every eight infants. The infants rarely had the same caregiver for very long, both because of rapid staff turnover and because the nurses frequently rotated assignments. The babies could not see one another or the bustle of activities in the ward because bed sheets were hung on the railings all around the cribs to reduce drafts. Instead, each infant saw a largely featureless, white world during most waking hours. As Spitz put it, "The result of this system is that each baby lies in solitary confinement up to the time when he is able to stand up in his bed" (Spitz, 1945, p. 63).

The infants in the second group that Spitz studied were raised in a nursery because their mothers had been imprisoned. These infants were able to see out of their cribs and interact freely with other infants and caregivers. The nursery had a better caregiver-infant ratio, and there was less staff turnover than in the foundling home. In addition, the imprisoned mothers were allowed to interact with their babies for roughly 20 hours each week. The infants in the prison nursery also had toys and more opportunities to crawl about, but the nursery environment was not kept especially clean and there was not careful medical supervision. In short, foundling babies lived in an environment that was sterile in every sense of the word (antiseptically clean and devoid of any meaningful social activities and objects; see Figure 6.17), whereas the babies in the prison nursery lived in a less clean but more stimulating environment.

Deficits in Socially Deprived Infants In the first few months of life, neither the foundling home nor the prison nursery environment seemed to make much of a difference for the infants. After 4 months, however, dramatic differences emerged: the prison nursery babies showed relatively normal reactions, while the foundling home babies showed massive deficits. Four classes of adverse effects were most frequently observed in the foundling babies:

1. The infants became progressively less likely to move about. Locomotion of all forms, including exploratory crawling, diminished, and the infants tended to sit or lie in one place for hours.

FIGURE 6.17 Social deprivation. Infants and children who grow up in orphanages with severe social neglect (as in this Romanian orphanage) often suffer devastating psychological and biological consequences.

2. The infants developed bizarre reactions to strangers and unfamiliar things, exhibiting terrified faces and gestures, screams, and wild rages directed at the unknown person or thing. The infants were extraordinarily unstable and hyperfearful. Sometimes, if a stranger remained present, the infants would suddenly frantically cling to the person.

3. The infants showed unusual, repetitive motor patterns, including incessantly rocking back and forth, biting or gnawing at parts of their own body, and banging their head against the crib. These sorts of behaviors are usually attributed to a need for stimulation, even at the cost of self-mutilation. Apparently, some situations can create such a need for stimulation that the obvious pain is not a deterrent.

4. Many of the deprived infants had disconcertingly vacant, expressionless faces. They had a faraway look in their eyes, seemed to look right through most people who approached, and seemed unaware of what was going on in their immediate environment.

The most disturbing difference between the groups, however, was the mortality rate. Over 37 percent of the infants in the foundling home had died by the end of 2 years. By contrast, not a single child out of the 122 who were in the prison nursery died, even though the foundling home had better sanitary conditions and more frequent professional medical visits (Spitz, 1945, 1946). Thus, the foundling babies, whose physical needs of nutrition, physical warmth, and shelter were all met, had a significant chance of dying, whereas children in the dirtier, less physically healthy prison environment showed lower mortality rates. The foundling babies died of a variety of causes, including a measles epidemic, but Spitz argued that since the prison nursery children were exposed to a similar range and frequency of diseases, the foundling babies' social deprivation must have somehow made them more susceptible to the illnesses. (This hypothesis anticipated the finding that intense stress can reduce the immune system's response, making stressed individuals more susceptible to a variety of afflictions; Cohen et al., 2007; Gunnar & Vazquez, 2006; Maes, 1997; Schleifer et al., 1999.) The cliché that "man does not live by bread alone" never had a more vivid and depressing demonstration.

In another study, institutionalized infants' showed delays in motor behavior and language, as well as failure to interact with their peers or to seek out adults when in distress. Those who were still institutionalized at 10 to 13 months also showed impairments in deferring gratification, generalizing, and problem solving (Provence & Lipton, 1962). In short, deprivation is devastating, and its effects seem to be linked to deficient exposure to other individuals (see also Goldfarb, 1943, 1945, for other early studies on the devastating effects of early social deprivation). Nonetheless, more detailed studies were needed to pin down the specific causes. Further studies in humans, as well as companion studies with primates, have greatly helped narrow down the possibilities.

> **Q:** What are some of the effects of long-term social deprivation in human infancy?

Untangling Causation After the Second World War, Freud's daughter, Anna, a major figure in psychoanalytic theory in her own right, and her colleague, Sophie Dann, published a paper about a group of six children whose parents had been killed in concentration camps during the war (Freud & Dann, 1951). The six children had each arrived separately at a concentration camp in Terezin, Czechoslovakia, when they were between the ages of 6 months and 1 year. It was unclear how much of an opportunity they had had to form specific attachments with their parents before arriving at Terezin, given the chaos in their families' lives shortly before they were sent to the concentration camps. The children remained at Terezin for almost 3 years and were cared for by various fellow prisoners, but they never had an opportunity to become attached to any of the adults, as the adults were constantly being relocated or killed or dying of disease and starvation at Terezin. The children survived through the efforts of many adults, and upon liberation in the summer of 1945, they were taken to England. There they remained in the care of Freud and her colleagues for approximately 1 year before being placed in foster homes (see Figure 6.18).

Despite the horrors of the camp and the lack of attachments to any adult figures, the children did form close bonds to each other. In fact, they were extraordinarily close

A   **B**

FIGURE 6.18 **The mediating factor of close peer bonds.** Anna Freud and Sophie Dann's studies of six children who had grown up in a concentration camp revealed that bonds formed among the children were able to mitigate many of the deleterious effects of being deprived of a constant set of caregivers. **(A)** Children behind barbed wire at a concentration camp in Auschwitz. **(B)** Children who had been separated from their parents during the war and brought to England to live in war evacuation residences, as were the six children in the Freud and Dann study.

and showed great distress when one of the six was absent. They also were quite wary of adults and took a long time to trust adults and show any attachments to people outside their group. Even with all their hardships, however, these six children seemed considerably better off than children who underwent more complete social deprivation. They were less withdrawn, did not show self-mutilation, and had relatively normal social relations among themselves except for being extremely "clingy" with each other. Apparently, the opportunity to interact and bond with peers was enough to protect these children from the intense emotional problems observed in more fully deprived infants. This study suggested that infants' need for nourishment might not be the most important factor motivating their attachments. It also showed that the role of nurturant older individuals in early social development is not as absolutely critical as most parents might think.

Later studies on deprivation have led researchers to suggest that in the first few months of life, interacting with any responsive social beings may be enough to put infants on a normal trajectory for attachment. Only later, after about 6 months, does the infant seem to need to form specific attachments to individuals. Thus, children isolated from their parents early on show few or no deficits as long as other responsive caregivers fill in during the first few months of life (Schaffer & Callender, 1959; Schaffer & Emerson, 1964). At that age, interacting with a variety of people is as beneficial for the infant as the same level of interaction with one person. Even if very young infants are able to recognize individuals and develop specific interaction patterns with them, they may not need such interactions with the same individuals at an early age. Instead, they simply need

opportunities for social give-and-take with willing partners. Although infants can attend to the special distinctive properties of some social stimuli very early on, it seems to take time and practice to learn the nuances of those stimuli that form the foundation for specific, focused attachments.

Unfortunately, children still suffer from social deprivation throughout the world, and its effects remain as devastating as they were in Spitz's time. In Romania, a large number of children were abandoned to state-run orphanages during a period when Nicolae Ceausescu headed the country. When he fell from power in 1990, foreign researchers started to visit the orphanages and found horrendous conditions. There were often more than 10 children for each caregiver, making meaningful interactions impossible. Children who were younger than 2 were left lying in their cribs without stimulation for up to 20 hours each day. In recent years, one group of Romanian infants has been studied extensively—not to document deprivation effects, but to understand how the children responded when they were removed from their harsh environment and adopted into loving families.

This group of severely deprived children showed the same tendencies toward vacant expressions and rocking back and forth that were seen in the deprived children in earlier studies. As American and Canadian families began adopting these children, researchers started to ask about the developmental outcomes and adjustment of the children who had been adopted. One relevant study followed three groups of infants in British Columbia (Mainemer et al., 1998). One group had been in Romanian orphanages for at least 8 months before adoption. A second group had been adopted from Romanian orphanages at an earlier age, in the first 4 months of life. A third group, which served as a control group, consisted of Canadian-born, nonadopted children who were matched with the first group in terms of age and sex.

The researchers examined many aspects of the adopted children's development and their adjustment to their new circumstances and found complex patterns of effects. But one clear finding stood out. In most cases, the longer the children had spent in Romanian orphanages, the worse their outcomes. Even after 4 or more years in an adoptive family, they were more likely to have difficulties forming normal social relationships with their parents and others. Nonetheless, some of the children who had been in Romanian orphanages for more than a year seemed to recover fully after a few years in adoptive homes. It is less clear, however, whether these more fortunate outcomes were due to temperamental differences that made the children especially resilient or to especially effective patterns of child rearing in these adoptive homes or to both.

These studies also suggested that social deprivation can cause a general disengagement from the world that may also impede cognitive development. The Romanian children who had spent at least 8 months of infancy in orphanages had considerably lower intelligence test scores than Romanian children who had been adopted before they were 4 months of age. In one study, Romanian children who grew up in Romania with their parents had cognitive development scores averaging around 103 (on a scale where the mean is 100), while children who were in the orphanages for extended periods had scores averaging around 66 (Smyke et al., 2007; see Figure 6.19). The effects likely arose not only from less interaction of the children with their environment, but also from the lack of engaged adult caregivers to teach them and to support their ability to learn. But the cognitive differences may also have been related to differences in the kinds of children who grew up in families as opposed to those who were put in orphanages, as some of the institutionalized children may have had preexisting cognitive deficits. Nonetheless, the magnitude of the difference and its persistence across studies leaves little doubt that social deprivation has serious effects, not only on social skills, but on a range of cognitive skills as well (Kaler & Freeman, 1994).

Subsequent studies on the same children suggested that even at age 17, some children who had been in orphanages more than 8 months still showed residual cognitive effects, often taking the form of inattention and hyperactivity (Audet & Le Mare, 2011). Other groups of Romanian orphans adopted into British homes had similar arrays of problems related to the amount of time they had spent in institutions. They sometimes showed "disinhibited" attachments, meaning that they did not modulate their emotions well in social interactions, sometimes being overly friendly with strangers, other times being inappropriately unfriendly (Rutter et al.,

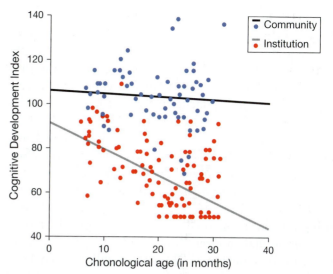

FIGURE 6.19 **Cognitive development and social deprivation.** Children who grew up in Romanian orphanages under conditions of severe social deprivation (labeled "Institution") showed markedly lower scores on tests of cognitive development than did children who grew up with their families in a nearby community (labeled "Community"). Thus, above and beyond the dramatic effects of social deprivation on social development and attachment, there is a strong effect on cognitive development as well. The lines roughly indicate the nature of the correlation between age and cognitive development, with no relationship for the community children and a strong negative one for the children raised in the institution.

2007). Disinhibited attachments appear to be closely related to indiscriminate attachments, mentioned earlier in the chapter, in which children are overly friendly with all adults.

These effects have been replicated in other settings throughout the world. For example, in one large-scale study of 342 children who had been in institutions in Russia, children as old as 18 continued to show cognitive and social problems (Merz & McCall, 2010; St. Petersburg–USA Orphanage Research Team, 2008). A particularly striking feature about the Russian study was that the facility was unusually clean, and the staff made an effort to meet the children's physical needs in terms of food, clothing, and shelter. Social deprivation alone in an otherwise very positive environment was nonetheless associated with much worse developmental outcomes, especially among children who were in the institutions the longest.

Q: What factors are most relevant to the effects of social deprivation on attachment?

Failure to form normal attachments can also have measurable biological consequences. One way of assessing stress is by measuring blood levels of the hormone cortisol, which is released by the adrenal glands in cyclical patterns over the course of each day and is involved in regulating the body's stress response. Unusually elevated cortisol levels generally indicate higher levels of stress. Studies of the relationship between cortisol levels and infants' stress response have found that insecurely attached infants are more likely than securely attached infants to show elevated cortisol levels in situations perceived as threatening (Gunnar, 2000; Gunnar & Vazquez, 2006). Secure attachments may therefore protect infants from mobilizing a stress response too soon. When children in Romanian orphanages were studied, researchers found that their cortisol levels tended to peak during midday as opposed to peaking early in the morning as in normal children (Carlson & Earls, 1997). Lacking secure attachments, the Romanian children may have found their day-to-day routine much more stressful than other children do.

Q: How might security of attachment be related to physiological responses to stress?

Any observational studies on the effects of institutionalization run the risk of confusing correlation with causation. Thus, perhaps children who leave institutions early are selected for adoption because they seem psychologically healthier. Once again, researchers have tried to control for such factors, but it is difficult to do so without an experimental study using random assignment. It is notable, then, that a series of studies that did use random assignment supported the earlier conclusions, reporting strong, unambiguous causal effects of institutionalization (Bos et al., 2010; Nelson et al., 2007; Zeanah et al., 2009). In one study, researchers followed 136 infants who had all initially been in an institution. At about 22 months of age, half of these infants were randomly assigned to home foster care and the other half stayed at the institution. The researchers assessed all the children at around 22 months and then again at 30, 42, and 54 months. Children who stayed in the institution showed higher than normal levels of some disorders, such as high anxiety and depression, whereas children who were assigned to foster homes showed a dramatic drop in levels of anxiety and depression, which continued to decrease toward normal levels over time (Zeanah et al., 2009). A more outward behavioral hallmark of institutionalized children, random repetitive movements, remained high in the institutionalized children, but dropped dramatically in children in the foster homes (Bos et al., 2010). Finally, children assigned to foster homes showed markedly better cognitive outcomes than those who remained in the institution (Nelson et al., 2007; Smyke et al., 2012).

Unfortunately, despite the clear negative effects of institutionalization in which there is marked social deprivation, it remains a reality for many thousands of children worldwide. Every time a family adopts a child from a part of the world where poverty, political crises, or disease cause many parents to give up their children, there is a real chance that the child may have spent much of his or her infancy in such an institution (Hawk & McCall, 2010), potentially causing the child to have both social and cognitive problems and atypical attachment styles. The good news is that, contrary to what might be expected, most children who have suffered badly in institutions make impressive recoveries when adopted or put into a foster care arrangement with warm, responsive caregivers (Van IJzendoorn & Juffer, 2006). Nonetheless, some children do show lasting problems well into adolescence and adulthood (Kumsta et al., 2010; Rutter et al., 2007; Smyke et al., 2012). This wide variation in outcomes between children who show near-complete recovery and others who continue to have major problems is of great interest to researchers, who are seeking to identify the most vulnerable children and devise interventions to give them a better future.

Q: How has random assignment been used to study the effects of social deprivation?

Deprivation Studies in Nonhuman Primates

The earliest work systematically exploring nonhuman attachments was conducted by Harry Harlow and his associates in the 1950s and 1960s (Harlow, 1958; Harlow & Harlow, 1962, 1969; Harlow & Suomi, 1971; Harlow & Zimmerman, 1958). In his classic experiments, Harlow studied rhesus monkeys either in conditions that were analogous to human situations or in conditions that would not be possible or ethical to study in humans. Many of his studies with monkeys involved controlled simulations of the type of deprivation experienced by the Romanian orphans and by the infants Spitz had studied in the foundling home. The effects on Harlow's monkeys were often so devastating that today it would be exceedingly difficult to justify further research that would inflict such suffering on individuals of any species.

Tactile Stimulation and Physiological Needs Initially, Harlow simply wanted to know if severe deprivation had effects on monkeys analogous to those in humans, with the obvious research advantage of being able to conduct true random-assignment experiments from birth. In several studies, Harlow put very young rhesus monkeys into empty wire cages. These monkeys were given all the food they could eat, but they had no contact with any caregiver. After a few months in this environment, the young monkeys began to show behaviors similar to the behavior of deprived human infants: indifference to others and expressionless stares; clutching their heads and bodies, rocking back and forth, and banging their heads; and going into wild rages when approached by strangers. The parallels between the socially deprived monkeys and the infants studied by Spitz and others are striking.

In an attempt to narrow down the causes of these three classes of deviant behaviors, Harlow began to manipulate individual variables that might help the baby monkeys start to form attachments. In one of these manipulations, the infant monkeys were given a choice between a wire-frame "mother" that was roughly the size and shape of an adult monkey and a "mother" that was covered in furry terry cloth. The monkeys invariably preferred the terry-cloth mother and frequently rubbed their stomachs against the front of the terry-cloth mother for tactile stimulation (see Figure 6.20). Quite remarkably, the presence of the cloth-covered mother had a significant positive effect. Relative to the monkeys reared in empty cages or restricted to the wire-frame mother, those with a terry-cloth mother showed less extreme repetitive behavior and fewer rages, though they still feared strangers. As adults, they did not show normal social behavior with other monkeys, but they seemed to fare better than those reared without tactile stimulation.

Moreover, these monkeys formed a real attachment to the terry-cloth mother, which was evident in their responses when an unfamiliar object, such as a plastic, bug-like toy, was put in the cage. The alarmed monkeys would immediately retreat to the terry-cloth figure for comfort and protection. Although the terry-cloth figure was, of course, unresponsive, Harlow noted that it was at least "infinitely patient" with the frightened infant.

Apparently, a key element in the attachment behaviors that enable the young monkey to form bonds involves the particular sensation of clinging and rubbing against a furry surface. This tactile stimulation does not directly satisfy the infant's physiological needs, but the experience is clearly of vital importance. This study illustrates the idea of prepared attachment behaviors linked to attachment. The infant monkeys looked to the terry-cloth mother for protection, even though they had never been protected by "her" and never could be. Yet, there was a link between the behavior of rubbing against the fur of a monkey-like object and a feeling that the object would provide security and protection. This association could not possibly have been learned. Instead, it represents a connection between two attachment-related behaviors as part of a larger attachment complex.

A

B

FIGURE 6.20 **Bonding with the terry-cloth mother.** **(A)** Infant monkeys in the Harlow studies seemed to form strong bonds to inanimate wire-frame mothers wrapped in a furry terry cloth. Harry Harlow's studies on various deprivation conditions and their effects on attachment behavior served to strongly support the ethological perspective. **(B)** Harry Harlow is pictured here with one of the infant monkeys on the terry-cloth mother.

Harlow then tested the importance of tactile stimulation in a follow-up study by pitting the need for tactile stimulation directly against the infant monkey's need for nourishment. The infant monkeys in this experiment were each reared in a cage with two surrogate mothers: the simple wire-frame mother, which had a plastic tube on its front that supplied milk, and a terry-cloth mother that supplied no nutrition. The infant monkeys quickly learned to feed from the wire-frame model, but they regarded it solely as a food source. They spent most of their time clinging to the terry-cloth figure, scampering to the wire model only when they were hungry (see Figure 6.21). The monkeys clearly formed an attachment to the terry-cloth mother, even though the wire-frame mother was the one that relieved their hunger and thirst. In separate scenarios in which both mothers provided milk, the baby monkeys used the cloth mother exclusively (Harlow & Zimmerman, 1958).

These studies not only illustrate the central role of particular behaviors in forming attachments, but also point out problems with the traditional learning and psychoanalytic viewpoints described earlier in this chapter. The learning theorists attempted to account for attachment in terms of patterns of positive and negative reinforcement, in which receiving food should powerfully reinforce the bond with the food provider; yet, in these studies, the monkeys formed no attachment to the wire-frame figure, even when it served as a food source. The psychoanalytic theorists emphasized the act of nursing and the importance of oral gratification in forming early attachments; yet, the infant monkeys attached to the cloth figure that provided no oral gratification.

Of course, leaping to conclusions about humans based on animal studies poses risks. But Harlow's monkey studies clearly illustrate how some early behaviors might serve to support and maintain contact with caregivers. They also show that these behaviors can affect attachment more profoundly than other behaviors that service fundamental nutritive needs.

> **Q:** How are some attachment behavior complexes "triggered" by certain features of artificial primate mothers?

Peer-Raised Infants In the natural world, infants typically form their earliest and strongest attachments to adult caregivers, which seems to imply that the adult's protective, nurturing role is crucial. In fact, we may have an exaggerated sense of its importance because alternative situations are so rare. As noted earlier in Freud and Dann's study of the group of six children who survived the concentration camp together, attachments to peers may provide much of what is needed for normal social development early in life. To test this idea, Harlow designed a monkey analog of the Freud and Dann study by raising monkeys in groups of six peers, with no older monkeys present (Harlow, 1969; see Figure 6.22). They were deprived of social interactions with adults but interacted freely with each other. These infants developed relatively normally, showing few of the deficits that characterized more deprived monkeys and human infants. They did show some social problems, such as difficulties in mothering new babies and fearfulness of strangers, but overall, their development was surprisingly normal.

Newer and more subtle analyses have illuminated some of the lingering problems in the peer-raised monkeys. These monkeys appear to have reduced levels of the neurotrans-

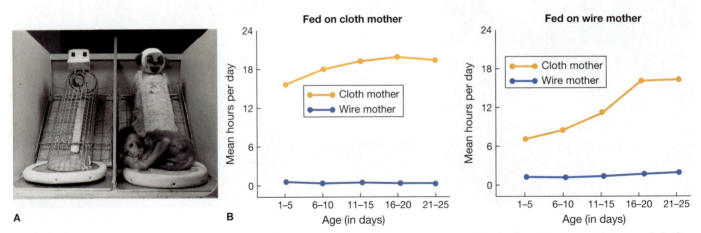

FIGURE 6.21 Contact comfort. (A) When monkeys are given the choice between a wire-frame "mother" and one covered in terry cloth, they not only show a strong preference for the terry-cloth "mom," but also tend to be less devastated by the effects of deprivation. **(B)** The monkeys went to the wire mother only to feed; they went to the terry-cloth mother, whether or not she provided them with milk, for the contact comfort she provided.

FIGURE 6.22 Peer-raised monkeys. Peer-raised monkeys who had no contact with adults developed fairly normally and would play and explore with each other.

mitter serotonin in their brains compared with monkeys raised by adults. Low serotonin levels have been associated with several psychological problems, including aggression and impulsive behavior (Bennett et al., 2002; Higley & Linnoila, 1997). Researchers theorize that the effects of early deprivation may arise largely from changes in two biological systems: a stress-buffering system related to cortisol levels and an impulse control system related to serotonin levels. Cortisol is part of the hypothalamic-pituitary-adrenal axis (HPA), which regulates the body's response to stress as well as regulating other body functions. The neurotransmitter serotonin is involved both in the activation and feedback control of the HPA. Serotonin is thought to play a role in early socialization and attachment by helping to regulate levels of anxiety in stressful social situations, such as separations from caregivers, so that the stress response is neither too extreme nor absent completely.

Perhaps most interesting is the discovery of how individual biological differences interact with environmental experiences. The gene known as *5-HTT*, which regulates serotonin levels, seems to have two alleles: a "long" form and a "short" form. Monkeys who were raised by their mothers showed normal serotonin levels, regardless of which version of the allele they had. But monkeys who were raised by peers—and thus lived in a more stressful environment than the one experienced by monkeys raised by their mothers—had different serotonin levels based on which version of the allele they had. Those with the long version of *5-HTT* fared pretty well when raised by peers, but those with the short version tended to show lower serotonin levels and more impulse control problems, including more aggression (Suomi, 1999). Thus, the form of the

5-HTT gene that a monkey had seemed to predict how he would respond to this nonoptimal social environment (Bethea et al., 2004). We see here one possible biological basis for the individual differences in children's responses to stressful environments.

Of the many studies conducted with monkeys, rats, and humans, the vast majority converge on a finding that the *5-HTT* gene is involved in moderating or exacerbating the effects of stress (Caspi et al., 2003, 2010; Wankerl et al., 2010; but see also Risch et al., 2009). There are two kinds of effects. First, regardless of allele type, severe and very early deprivation leads to lasting differences in *5-HTT* gene expression, which can result in diminished serotonin responses for regulating stress. In effect, these changes can result in greater emotional reactivity to stress (Spinelli et al., 2010). One route for this effect seems to be through a pathway in which stress hormones increase methylation of DNA segments (the pairing of methyl groups to DNA; see Chapter 2), which regulates gene expression and in this case results in diminished serotonin activity (Champagne, 2013; Champagne & Curley, 2009; Ichise et al., 2006; Murgatroyd et al., 2009). Second, in monkeys and humans who have the short version of the *5-HTT* allele, the effects of stress are even more significant, including greater methylation and hence greater reduction in serotonin activity. Even in somewhat less stressful environments, those with the short version may experience epigenetic changes (environmentally induced changes in gene expression that in this case lead to reduced serotonin levels) and greater emotional reactivity, while those with the longer version may not be affected at all. We see here a biological example of a feedback loop in a gene-environment interaction. If an organism has a short version of the *5-HTT* gene, the effects of a stressful environment can be amplified, which in turn causes a higher stress response. This physiological response then causes an even more severe decline in the activity of the relevant gene, leading to even more stress reactivity, and so on, in a downward-cycling feedback loop.

A final interesting twist on the persistence of both short and long versions of the *5-HTT* gene is that the short version may have evolutionary adaptive value in some circumstances, which may be why it has remained in the general population. In a dangerous environment where high levels of vigilance and anxiety may enhance survival, organisms with short versions of the gene will more likely experience enduring epigenetic changes that make them more sensitive responders to potential dangers (Heiming & Sachser, 2010). The short version of the *5-HTT* gene may therefore lead to increased survival in some contexts, though it is now maladaptive for many human infants who are exposed to high levels of stress early in life. As is so often the case with genetic effects, the *5-HTT* gene is likely to be only a small part of the overall genetic story, with comparable gene-environment interactions occurring for several other quite distinct genes (Bogdan et al., 2012).

Critical-Period Effects?

Many early researchers assumed that there was a critical period during which social interactions had to be experienced. Researchers believed that if there was complete social deprivation during this period, the effects were irreversible. Certainly, many of Harlow's monkeys continued to exhibit bizarre behaviors into adulthood and as parents. This view was accepted until one of Harlow's associates, Stephen Suomi, looked more closely at possible ways of "rehabilitating" the monkeys reared in isolation. Using younger monkeys as "therapists," Suomi found that the isolated monkeys could gradually achieve almost full recovery by being taught how to be social (Suomi & Harlow, 1972; see Figure 6.23). In particular, Suomi selected juvenile monkeys that would interact freely with the isolated monkeys without hurting them and that would cling to them gently. Within a few weeks, the isolated monkeys began responding to these overtures by clinging back and approaching the juveniles to interact with them. As they reciprocated in these ways, the symptoms of their deprivation started to disappear.

This successful rehabilitation accords nicely with a major change in views concerning critical-period effects in human infancy. Following Freud's lead, many early theorists were convinced that a child deprived of attachments in the first 2 to 3 years of life was doomed to an "affectionless" life of failing to connect with others or form meaningful relationships (Bowlby, 1951). More

FIGURE 6.23 Monkey therapists. Younger monkeys would comfort monkeys who had been reared in isolation and teach them how to play and be social.

recent evidence seems to point toward some reversible outcomes, although the amount of evidence is not extensive. One longitudinal study of children reared in a socially impoverished institution from birth until 2 years of age or older suggested that having appropriately affectionate adoptive parents could sometimes undo the children's early social problems (Hodges & Tizard, 1989; Tizard, 1977). This is not to minimize the negative effects of an infancy spent in institutions that deprive infants of normal social contact and interactions; the children did appear to be at greater risk for problems. Still, many of the difficulties associated with institutionalization can be reversed, providing that the children are then placed with caregivers who can give them the time, attention, and affection they need (Schaffer, 1990).

At the biological level, there may be an early critical period in utero and during infancy when methylation occurring in response to stress may lead to effects that may be irreversible after infancy (Murgatroyd et al., 2009). Researchers are still asking whether the right kinds of supportive environments could possibly reverse these early effects, perhaps through demethylation (a process through which a methyl group attached to a segment of DNA is removed, thereby often restoring a function). But given that some forms of early methylation in utero have been argued to be irreversible (Le Bouc et al., 2010), there may in fact be a critical period at the biological level. Early changes in *5-HTT* pathways could set a developmental course for certain neural circuits related to emotional regulation. Even so, the existence of a critical period does not mean that an attachment style is fixed. Instead, it means that a child might be at risk for being more emotionally reactive. This might increase the odds of some forms of insecure attachment, but it does not predestine them.

There is intense interest in those cases in which the effects of early deprivation may not be fully reversible even in the most supportive later environments. Thus, while supportive environments do seem to be able to largely reverse withdrawn forms of attachments resulting from adverse early experiences, it seems much more difficult to reverse disinhibited forms of attachment (Smyke et al., 2012). The reasons for this difference are not well understood, but it is possible that the disinhibited cases set up a type of reward circuitry that becomes fixed in the child's brain. One important implication of irreversible effects is that rehabilitation efforts might be more effective if they focused on helping children (and eventually adults with the same problems) learn to better understand how to read and respond to social cues that can lead them into inappropriate behavior rather than trying to eliminate disinhibited social behavior itself (Smyke et al., 2012).

The neurobiological foundations of critical-period effects for attachment styles and other social behaviors are not well understood, partly because the effects themselves are still being uncovered. Researchers suggest, however, that such effects may result from either incomplete genetic coding or miswiring of particular circuits supporting social behavior (Nelson et al., 2011). In the Romanian random-assignment study mentioned earlier, children who were institutionalized had smaller gray matter cortical volumes (which are thought to reflect the degree of interconnectiveness of dendrites) than those who were not institutionalized. While the same study did suggest that white matter volume might be increased by shifts to more socially supportive environments, the declines in gray matter volume may be more irreversible and the possible locus of critical-period effects (Sheridan et al., 2012).

As we have seen, a better understanding of where critical or sensitive period effects might occur for attachment and related behaviors does not lead to "giving up" on a child who is so identified. Instead, such findings might lead to alternative and more effective ways of helping the child learn to develop strategies for avoiding situations that might result in socially dysfunctional behaviors. Or it may be possible to teach the child to develop compensatory strategies that would allow him to thrive in just those situations that normally might pose substantial risks.

> **Q:** What has recent research suggested about the view that there is a critical period for the formation of normal attachments?

Conclusions

Infants construe the social world differently from the way they see the inanimate world. Beyond simply preferring social stimuli, infants expect certain patterns of interactions with other social beings, and their expectations undergird the formation and maintenance of attachments to specific individuals.

The ethological perspective, with its emphasis on the differences and commonalities between humans and other species and the adaptive functions of those differences and commonalities, has repeatedly proved to be the most successful way of understanding the origins of social bonds. Looking at specific social behaviors and their functional roles has revealed that many species' young must solve similar problems, such as signaling a caregiver, maintaining an interaction, and perceiving danger by watching others. These common developmental challenges have fostered different solutions across species. Despite the considerable differences in the details, however, the ethological perspective has yielded important insights about the functional similarities that underlie different species' attachment behaviors.

Forming attachments is not only an aspect of cognitive and social growth, it is essential to normal development. When infants and children are deprived of the opportunity to form attachments, the effects can be devastating for their mental and even physical health. While there are different attachment styles, which are often stable over time and seem to emerge out of a complex set of interactions between the child's own temperament, the ways in which parents and others relate to the child, and even how the culture views appropriate forms of intimacy at different points in development, there is still a large amount of common ground shared by all infants that enables them to form attachments. All infants, regardless of their attachment style, set up and maintain those bonds through an attachment complex consisting of signaling behaviors and proximity behaviors. All infants also have implicit linkages between different attachment components, such as inferring that a highly social and responsive caregiver will be a protector in times of threat.

In the next chapter, we turn to a deeper discussion of several topics touched on in this chapter that relate to attachment and early social relations. As we consider the development of emotions, temperament, and personality, we will ask whether the themes that have emerged from our discussion of the infant's social world, such as evolutionary adaptations, feedback loops, and gene-environment interactions, apply there as well.

STUDY AND REVIEW

SUMMARY

Developing Bonds between Infants and Caregivers

- Human infants and the infants of other species form bonds to those who take care of them and behave in ways that set up and maintain proximity to their caregivers.
- Bonds between infants and caregivers develop out of an ability to pick out and partially understand social beings, with human infants normally developing specific bonds to particular individuals soon after the sixth or seventh month of life.
- Shortly after infants seem to have a bond to specific individuals, they also show marked separation distress (also called separation anxiety) when one of those individuals leaves them alone or with a stranger.

Early Perspectives on Infants' Bonds with Others

- Psychoanalytic views of infant bonds overemphasized the importance of breastfeeding and the centrality of the infant's bond with the mother as opposed to bonds that the infant forms with others. Freud's theory of these bonds emerged out of his account of psychosexual development based on drives, instincts, and sources of pleasure. While many of Freud's specific theories have not held up, he and other psychoanalytic theorists did raise enduring questions about the importance of early experiences, sex differences, and the relevance of an infant's beliefs about others.
- Learning theory approaches to parent-child bonds focused on how environmental contingencies reinforced or discouraged certain behaviors and how infants formed bonds to positively reinforcing stimuli. They neglected possible roles of infants' mental states and beliefs and had difficulty explaining how bonds endured when children are in abusive families.
- John Bowlby's ethological approach has become the dominant perspective for studying how infants form bonds with others. It considers such bonds as part of an attachment complex and focuses on the attachment behaviors that set up and maintain bonds between offspring and caregivers. It also considers analogous systems at work in many other species and examines the similarities and differences in the ways that offspring in other species attach to their caregivers.

The Underpinnings of Attachment

- Attachment behaviors ensure that infants and parents become linked together through strong affectional bonds. They can include signaling behaviors, such as smiling, cry-ing, and merely being cute. They can also include actions, such as following or clinging or touching.
- All the attachment behaviors are embedded in loops of interactions between caregivers and infants that serve to bring them into close proximity and then maintain that proximity.
- Several cognitive systems seem to undergird the ability to form attachments. One particularly important ability is a sensitivity and preference for contingent responding, with parents and children in different cultures having different response routines.
- Social referencing, the use of others' expressions and behaviors to make inferences about how to behave in a situation, is an important way to build bonds between infants and caregivers.
- Joint attention and gaze following, in which a child and another person simultaneously attend to and follow the same object or event, are critical mechanisms for developing a set of shared experiences between children and caregivers, which in turn helps each partner better understand and empathize with the other.

Individual Differences in Attachment Style

- There are striking individual differences in attachment style between infants and their parents that are based on how they relate to each other and on expectations about how they will respond to each other in particular situations. Mary Ainsworth developed a method known as the Strange Situation for measuring differences in attachment style. Four types of attachment styles are most commonly discussed: Type A, or insecure/avoidant attachment; Type B, or secure attachment; Type C, or insecure/resistant (or anxious) attachment; and Type D, or disorganized attachment.
- There are several possible causes of different attachment styles. These include parental behaviors, children's effects on parents, interactions between parent and child effects in various forms of feedback loops, and genetic influences.
- Early attachment styles may have long-term consequences for a child's development. There are associations between early attachment styles and both social and cognitive abilities and tendencies in childhood and adolescence, but the causal account is difficult to untangle. The child's own temperament may elicit certain kinds of responses in others, a constant stressful environment may cause problems at multiple ages, and temperament and environment may interact to amplify or reduce effects.
- There are substantial cross-cultural differences in attachment style as measured by the Strange Situation, but it is difficult to know whether these differences translate directly into dif-

ferences in attachment quality. Interpreting these differences is complex because what is considered a "strange" situation by parents and infants in one culture may be perceived very differently in another culture.

Effects of Early Social Deprivation

- Early deprivation of normal social interactions can have a devastating impact on both humans and other animals, resulting in repetitive motor behaviors and maladaptive patterns of interaction with others. The lack of social interactions early on can result in high mortality rates in infants in settings where such social deprivations are the norm, even if those settings are clean and provide ample food and shelter.

- The effects of deprivation are associated with physiological measures, such as high levels of cortisol and low levels of serotonin. In addition, certain infants may be genetically at risk and particularly devastated by such environments.

- There may be mediating effects in situations of deprivation, however, including the presence of a close group of peers among human infants or "monkey therapists" and tactile stimulation among rhesus monkeys. Although many effects of deprivation can be reversed when children are shifted to more socially rich forms of care, concerns remain about potential long-term effects in at least some children, effects that may be mediated through epigenetic changes in stress regulation systems.

- In some cases, there may be critical-period effects in humans in which severe deprivation may lead to attachment styles and related social deficits that may not be fully reversible in later life, no matter how supportive the environment.

THOUGHT QUESTIONS

1. Difficult life circumstances or more intrinsic personality issues can make some biological parents less able to effectively interact with their children than foster parents. In one series of studies, children were placed in institutions before they were 4 months of age and were then returned to either their original parents or to adoptive parents (Tizard & Hodges, 1978; Tizard & Rees, 1974; Tizard & Tizard, 1971). Both groups showed signs of institutionalization when they first were adopted or reunited, but over the next few years, the adopted children seemed to fare better than those returned to their natural parents. Loving caregivers seemed to undo the effects of deprivation more effectively than biological parents whose lives were otherwise more stressed. Are there

any circumstances in which it would be appropriate for a court to order that children be taken away from biological parents who are not abusive but who are providing grossly inadequate social environments for their children? If so, when would this be justified? If not, why not?

2. Suppose that a pediatrician is concerned about a 1-year-old because the child exhibits a high level of insecure/resistant (anxious) attachment. The pediatrician consults with you as an expert in developmental psychology. What sort of interventions might you devise with respect to modifying parental behavior, the child's environment, and the child's own temperament so as to reduce the level of insecure attachment behavior?

3. Some have argued that males in general are less sophisticated in social cognition than females. How much might such a difference influence the development of attachments in boys and girls?

4. Imagine that you and your partner both have jobs with minimal parental leave policies and that you have to put your 2-week-old infant in full-time day care. Design a plan for evaluating the 16 day care centers in your community that would enable you to choose the one that offers the best opportunity for the social development of your child.

KEY TERMS

anxious attachment (p. 202)

attachment (p. 188)

attachment complex (p. 194)

attachment style (p. 201)

avoidant attachment (p. 211)

dependency (p. 194)

disorganized attachment (p. 203)

indiscriminate attachment (p. 203)

internal working model (p. 208)

insecure/avoidant attachment (p. 202)

insecure/resistant attachment (p. 202)

joint attention (p. 200)

oxytocin (p. 196)

psychosexual development (p. 190)

resistant attachment (p. 202)

secure attachment (p. 202)

secure base (p. 193)

separation anxiety (p. 190)

separation distress (p. 190)

social referencing (p. 199)

specific bonds (p. 189)

still face (p. 199)

Strange Situation (p. 202)

7

The Origins of Emotion, Temperament, and Personality

Emotional Development
- Approaches to Emotional Development
- Differentiation of Emotions in Infancy
- Perceiving and Thinking about Emotions
- Emotional Regulation in Infancy
- Evolutionary Preparedness and Emotional Development

Temperament and the Origins of Personality
- Temperament-Based Components of Personality and Early Development
- Determining Differences in Temperament
- Child-Environment Interactions and Goodness of Fit

Conclusions

Summary

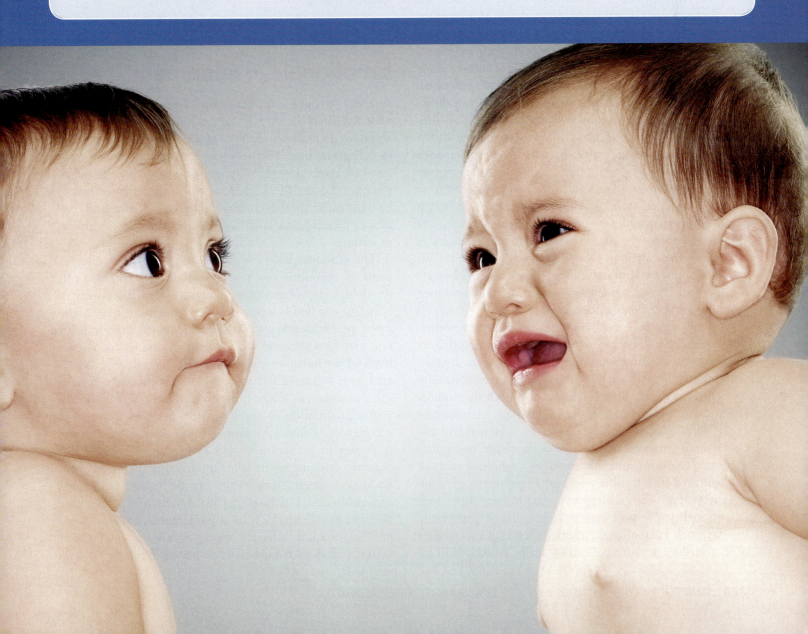

Not long ago, in a supermarket on a busy Saturday morning, I noticed two infants who were showing very different emotions and patterns of interaction with their mothers. Both infants were about 12 months old and were being wheeled about in shopping carts by their mothers. The first infant, a girl, seemed delighted by the visit to the supermarket. As her mother occasionally handed her an item to drop into the cart, she received each one with a smile. She often laughed or looked happily at her mother, and her mother responded positively in return. Likewise, she readily smiled at strangers. The second infant, a boy, seemed angry and upset about being in the supermarket. Scowling at his mother, he either angrily rejected items she handed him or insisted on holding on to them, even though his mother wanted him to put them into the cart or back on the shelves. He avoided strangers' looks and yet also seemed fearful of them. Meanwhile, the boy's older brother, who was around 7 years old, was clearly embarrassed by his sibling's behavior.

Simple interactions like these are repeated countless times a day in different venues around the world and illustrate several phenomena that this chapter explores. Most notably, we will see that young infants show a variety of emotional states as well as individual differences in their emotional responses to the same situation. Looking at infants' early emotional states, as well as the variability in their emotional responses, will help us address the question of how a child's emotional repertoire develops over time. We will also see that there seem to be intrinsic differences in how different infants respond and behave in particular settings. Such individual differences in disposition are known as *temperament* and tend to be quite stable in infancy. Moreover, we will see that when an infant comes to perceive and understand the social world, some of the most salient aspects of that world concern the emotions and personalities possessed by social beings, attributes that make each person a unique individual, distinct from all others. Infants themselves are social creatures, and it is of great interest to know how their emotions and personalities develop.

We will start by considering how an infant's emotions develop in the first couple of years of life, focusing first on the nonverbal measurements of emotions that researchers use with infants. We will ask how many distinct emotions seem to be present shortly after birth and how both the number of emotions and the complexity of emotions increase over time. We will examine how infants learn to perceive and think about emotions in others, how they learn to regulate their own emotions, and how emotions might have evolved. We will then turn to differences in temperament and consider how those early differences relate to later differences in personality. We will look at how behavior patterns in infancy, such as emotionality, activity level, and sociability, may contribute to later personality traits. And we will see how the infant's ability to shift attention and the tendency to be inhibited or uninhibited are related to biological bases for temperament. We will also consider how "goodness of fit" between an infant's temperament and the environment affects the child's development and personality.

This chapter revisits several major themes and introduces some new variations. We will see, for example, how feedback loops often help create and sustain patterns of emotional responding—within the individual, between the individual and the inanimate environment, and between two individuals. On a related note, we will see once again how deeply intertwined cognitive and social/emotional development are and how a full understanding of psychological development requires an understanding of their constant interactions. This chapter also returns to the contrast between the traditional empiricist and nativist views of the developing mind. We will consider the extent to which the newborn infant already possesses characteristic emotions and other components of a full personality and the extent to which emotions and other aspects of personality emerge through experience.

Emotional Development

Anyone who has spent time around a newborn has observed what appear to be displays of emotion, but exactly which emotions do newborns feel? To tackle this question, we need to define emotions precisely—which is a notoriously difficult task, even though everyone has a sense of what emotions are (Izard, 2009). Here we will consider **emotions** to be transient states that correspond to physiological and cognitive processes associated with distinct internal sensations, or feelings.

The physiological, cognitive, and behavioral components of emotions can take several forms. For example, physiological processes may correspond to the effects of hormones on bodily states as well as to changes in the activity of specific neural circuits. Thus, rapid increases in heart rate may be associated with certain emotions, and higher levels of the hormone oxytocin in the brain may be associated with increased feelings of trust and affection. Cognitive processes can range from how an individual appraises a present situation to the influences of memories of past experiences. Behavioral processes can include tendencies to engage in particular actions in particular contexts (for example, cringing when called on in a meeting or crying at weddings). These components can be further subdivided and elaborated, but this brief list is sufficient to illustrate how emotions emerge from a confluence of several components of quite different types. As always, interactions between all these components also occur frequently. Thus, bodily arousal may influence cognitive appraisals, and cognitive appraisals may influence bodily arousal. We will see that this complex web of interactions is often at the heart of understanding specific emotions.

Approaches to Emotional Development

Because infants cannot tell us in words what they are experiencing, we must find ways to infer what they are feeling and thinking. For the most part, researchers have used infants' facial expressions to infer their emotional states. Charles Darwin pioneered this method in the late nineteenth century through careful observations of his own son (Darwin, 1877; see Figure 7.1). Darwin assumed that facial expressions were good indicators of underlying emotional states and that when combined with contextual cues and other infant behaviors, facial expressions could be used to identify several distinct emotions from the beginning of life. Darwin was also deeply committed to the idea that in both humans and other animals, displays of one's own emotions and perceptions of emotions in others serve as adaptations that regulate social interactions. Thus, if a person displayed anger toward someone else, the other person might know to avoid a confrontation that could end up hurting both of them.

While emotional displays may include body posture and vocalizations, Darwin focused heavily on facial expressions, as have most researchers on emotion who came after him. Methods that measure facial expressions are the easiest to

FIGURE 7.1 **Darwin and infant facial expressions.** Charles Darwin took careful observations of the facial expressions of his son William (nicknamed Doddy). This 1842 daguerrotype shows Darwin (age 33) with Doddy (age 3). This is the only known photograph of Darwin with a family member.

use for studying emotions in infants and young children, and they have often been supported with other methods, such as observing body posture. There is now a vast body of research on the use of facial expressions to infer emotional states in both infants and older individuals. Studies of adults have provided a great deal of converging evidence that it is often possible to infer a person's emotional states based on judgments about that person's facial expressions (Ekman & Friesen, 1975; Izard, 1979). The correspondence between expression and emotion is not perfect; some expressions are difficult to interpret, and some people can mask their emotions more effectively than others. But on the whole, we rely heavily on others' facial expressions to infer how they feel (Ekman, 1973). These inferences seem to work the same way in adults, schoolchildren, or toddlers, so most researchers have assumed that infants' facial expressions signify similar emotional states. Although it can be more difficult to tell one emotion from another in young infants, examining infants' facial expressions and the contexts in which they occur (for example, frightening versus comforting situations) can help researchers develop theories about which emotions are present early on and how they change with development.

To study infants' facial expressions, researchers have developed coding systems for scoring the different expressions and assigning them to categories of emotions. Using such coding systems, which are based on analyzing the muscular and anatomical components that vary across facial expressions, they are able to achieve quite high levels of reliability for identifying expressions (Ekman & Friesen, 1978). But it is always a leap to know for sure that the expressions people agree on really do correspond to particular underlying emotional states. Nonetheless, most researchers believe that, combined with other cues, such as the context and infants' vocalizations, these kinds of inferences about infants' specific emotions are warranted.

Based on these observations, infants' emotions appear to show a general pattern of differentiation that progresses from birth onward. One way to describe this differentiation is to classify infants' emotions as either positive or negative and then ask about further divisions into more nuanced emotions within each of those categories. But researchers disagree about the extent to which newborns display particular emotions that go beyond general positivity and negativity. Some maintain that early on, infants simply haven't learned enough about how to use their emotions to guide their expression in more channeled ways (Witherington et al., 2010). This argument is based on the notion that emotions are a kind of communication system that helps regulate interactions with others. In this view, infants' emotional communications are shaped through development as their expressive skills and their needs become more refined.

Others see infants as endowed, largely from the start, with a set of distinct emotions, each of which was selected for through evolution to serve a certain role, such as fear guiding us to avoid danger and joy drawing us to approach something desirable (Ekman, 1992; Izard, 1994). Although it might be difficult to discern different facial expressions for a full set of emotions right at birth, scholars from this tradition still hold that the different emotions emerge largely as a function of physiological maturation rather than primarily through learning. This approach leaves open the questions of whether infants' expressions directly indicate the full variety of emotions they feel and whether expressions that emerge later are nonetheless largely innate (Izard, 1994).

Though emotions are usually thought to arise without conscious effort, they can be thought of as ways of mobilizing ourselves to take action toward a goal (Campos et al., 2003; Saarni et al., 1998). This is the **functionalist approach** to emotion, and it stresses the function of emotional responses. Table 7.1 describes four emotions. Each involves particular kinds of dynamics that elicit the emotion and maintain it. Each emotion serves clear functions, both for our own internal regulation and for regulating and managing social situations. Feeling anger, for example, can get you to channel your resources in a different direction as well as warn others not to get in the way. Sadness conserves energy and encourages nurturance from others. In this view, emotions are elicited not by an event itself but by our own "appreciation" of how the event relates to our personal goals (Campos et al., 2003; Saarni et al., 1998).

One important way that emotions help us achieve goals is by signaling information—that is, communicating—to others. Thus, we tend to treat people who appear to be angry quite differently from the way we treat those who seem to be sad. This signaling function can enable infants to achieve goals that would otherwise be unattainable given their limited physical abilities and restricted mobility. An infant who is afraid of another person and wants to avoid him can convey fear through facial expressions and body postures. In many cases, that conveyed emotion will affect a caregiver's

behavior—for example, leading the caregiver to pick up the infant and carry him away or to hold him protectively—which will enable the infant to avoid the perceived danger. Thus, it is highly adaptive for infants to have a repertoire of emotions to communicate in different settings, enabling them to involve others in helping them achieve their goals. In this way, infant displays of emotion can be seen as having strong functional or evolutionary roles.

Differentiation of Emotions in Infancy

Most theorists see the newborn as having undifferentiated emotions, perhaps only having global positive and negative emotional states (Bridges, 1932; Lewis, 2008). Out of this rudimentary distinction, more mature emotion categories gradually differentiate. Figure 7.2 shows one suggested sequence of differentiation (Lewis, 2008). The earliest emotions present at birth may be little more than contentment, interest, and distress. By around 3 months, these become joy, surprise, and distress. At around 4 months, distress becomes further differentiated to include anger, and then at 6 months, fear emerges.

Basic Emotions By the time they are 6 months old, infants show at least six **basic emotions** (sometimes referred to as primary emotions)—joy, sadness, disgust, surprise, anger, and fear (Campos et al., 1983; Campos & Barrett, 1984; Izard, 2007; Izard & Malatesta, 1987; Lewis, 2008; Saarni et al., 1998). These emotions are considered "basic" for two main reasons: (1) they appear very early in development, and (2) they are considered human universals, in part because people in an extraordinary range of cultures are able to infer these emotions consistently from facial expressions (Ekman, 1973, 1994). These basic emotions are considered the foundational components from which the other emotions later emerge (see Figure 7.3).

Parents can usually tell if their infant is in a positive or negative emotional state. Infants often indicate their posi-

Emotion	Goal	Action
Disgust	Avoid contamination or illness	Prevent substances from entering the body or coming into close contact with the body.
Fear	Maintain integrity of self	Engage in behaviors (flight or withdrawal) that enable us to avoid danger, monitor danger, or escape from danger.
Anger	Any end state that the child wants	Communicate desires or display power or dominance.
Sadness	Any end state that the child wants	Conserve energy by disengaging or withdrawing.

TABLE 7.1 Emotions and goals. Emotions can be thought of as ways of mobilizing ourselves to achieve certain goals. Here four basic emotions—disgust, fear, anger, and sadness—are described in terms of the kinds of goals and actions involved when we feel each emotion. Adapted from Saarni et al. (1998).

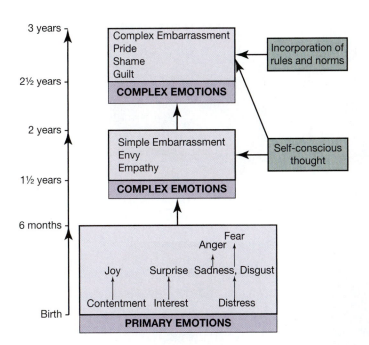

FIGURE 7.2 The differentiation of emotions in the first 3 years of life. According to one model of development, very young infants may start out with little more than the emotions of contentment, interest, and distress. Sadness and disgust may emerge at around 3 months, followed by anger at around 4 months, and fear at about 6 months. Other more complex emotions emerge in the following 2½ years. Embarrassment takes an extended time to develop, with simpler versions based on self-consciousness emerging earlier than more complex versions based on violation of rules. Adapted from Lewis (2008).

tive states through smiles, which can be interpreted as happiness, contentment, or satisfaction with the current state of affairs. As we will see, very early smiles may relate most often to internal states, such as feeling full, warm, and comfortable. As mentioned in Chapter 6, the stimuli that elicit the most smiles change with development, from mostly internal cues in newborns, to general social stimulation in the first few months, to the smile of recognition of specific individuals at around 6 months.

Infants' positive emotions can vary from gentle contentment to exuberant joy. These emotions can be expressed when an infant achieves a simple form of mastery, like shaking a rattle to make a sound, or engages intensely with another person, leading to a rapt state of focused attention. In each of these situations, the infant's smile may show subtle variations, such as an open or closed mouth and a strong or weak raising of the cheeks (Messinger, 2002), so consistently coding each of these variations of smiles and linking them to particular forms of happiness is a challenge for even the most careful researchers. Even in adults, different forms of happiness seem to fade gradually into each other rather than being sharply defined. In contrast, negative emotions are often seen as more clearly distinct from each other in adults, but less differentiated in infants.

Just as it is usually obvious when an infant is in a positive emotional state, it is also clear when an infant experiences negative emotions. Initially, however, it is difficult to distinguish specific negative emotions, as all negative emotions in infancy seem to be variations of distress (Camras & Shutter, 2010; Matias & Cohn, 1993). In fact, some researchers argue that negative emotions, such as fear, sadness, and anger, cannot truly be distinguished in newborns and very young infants because these infants actually experience

something more like general negative emotion (Camras et al., 1993, 2007; Oster et al., 1992). If a newborn receives a shot from a doctor, becomes uncomfortably tangled up in bedding, or is simply hungry, a negative facial expression, often accompanied by crying and postural cues to discomfort, is an unmistakable sign of distress. Caregivers usually feel strongly compelled to respond, and in that sense, even a general, undifferentiated negative emotional state fulfills a signaling function.

By age 2 months or so, general negative emotions start to differentiate into at least the categories of sadness and anger (Izard et al., 1995). Sometimes the same situation may elicit different emotions in different infants. One infant who is frustrated may display anger and may attempt to change the environment to attain her goal, whereas another infant may show sadness and give up. As infants encounter more and more situations in which they have goals and desires that are not instantly met, they come to show both sadness and anger responses more frequently. An infant can also oscillate quickly between sadness and anger in the same situation or may show ambiguous negative states that are hard to tell apart (Camras & Shutter, 2010).

Fear, which will be discussed more extensively later in this chapter, does not seem to be clearly evident until around the sixth month of life, typically several months after sadness and anger (Izard, 2007). Infants around 6 or 7 months old most often show fear in response to strangers, and it can be quite a shock for parents to find their infant suddenly terrified when someone unfamiliar drops by. Infants at this age also typically show fear when faced with other kinds of unknown things, such as an unusual zoo animal or even an unfamiliar toy (Bronson, 1972). They may also begin to display fear in laboratory settings, such

FIGURE 7.3 Facial expressions of basic emotions in infants. Facial coding systems have identified emotions based on infants' facial muscular movements and the positioning of their forehead, eyebrows, eyes, cheeks, and mouth as they are experiencing particular emotions. Facial expressions are social signals to others that enable infants to communicate what they are feeling. Pictured here are infants showing **(A)** joy (indicated by narrowed eyes and widened mouth with corners raised), **(B)** anger (indicated by brows drawn together and lowered and wide-open square mouth), **(C)** sadness (indicated by brows raised and angular, narrowed eyes, downturned mouth, and protruding lower lip), **(D)** disgust (indicated by gaping mouth and lower lip and flattened protruding tongue), **(E)** surprise (indicated by raised and prominently arched brows, widened eyes, and gaping mouth in an O shape), and **(F)** fear (indicated by raised and straightened brows, widened eyes with tense lower eyelids, and horizontally retracted lips).

as when they are on the visual cliff, although this usually emerges at somewhat older ages (Campos et al., 1978; Hiatt et al., 1979; see Chapter 6).

Why would fear appear later than anger and sadness? The answer is not yet clear. One possibility is that figuring out that a situation is potentially threatening may require more complicated mental representations compared with simply noticing feelings of discomfort or recognizing that a goal is being blocked. Assessing the threat level that a situation poses may involve interpreting it in some detail, which may be beyond the ability of a very young infant.

Interestingly, the developmental sequence in which the basic emotions appear in infancy roughly corresponds to the order in which these emotions are thought to have evolved. Thus, using the terms in Figure 7.4, the most primitive kind of emotion might simply be arousal that is neither positive nor negative. Even the emotions of human newborns do not seem to be this undifferentiated, but some very simple organisms, such as insects, might just be experiencing different levels of arousal. Figure 7.4 then shows a split between positive arousal, or excitement, and negative

arousal, or apprehension, which can be seen as an initial emerging divide between the positive and negative emotions (Nesse, 2004). From this point, the positive emotions, or those based on desire, differentiate into narrower categories, such as physical pleasure and acquisitive pleasure derived from material gains, as well as love, friendship, and pride. The negative emotions, or those based on fear, similarly differentiate into pain, sadness, grief, anger, and shame. Although these are not precisely the same categories of emotion normally identified in infants, and their order of emergence is a bit different from the developmental sequence in infants (fear may have appeared earlier than anger and sadness in evolutionary history), the broad parallel between development and evolutionary history is clear.

When a developmental progression corresponds to the course of evolution in this way, the common sequence is often explained by considering how the earliest-emerging components are necessary for the organism's survival. This kind of explanation can easily be applied to both the development of basic emotions at the individual level and to the evolution of these emotions at the level of a

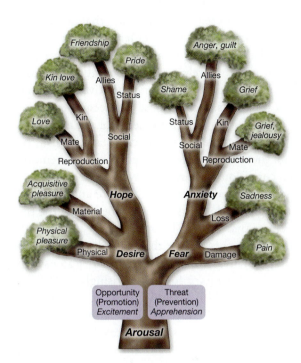

FIGURE 7.4 Evolution and development of emotions. Depicted here is one researcher's phylogeny of emotions. The emotions that appear first in development may have been those that were functionally the most important in evolution and therefore the most conserved across species. From Nesse (2004).

whole species. Even the simplest organisms need to know when to seek out opportunities through positive, exploratory behavior and when to avoid threats through more wary, guarded behavior. Perhaps these two fundamental responses then differentiate into more nuanced types of emotions in more sophisticated organisms. The basic tendency toward apprehension and caution gives rise to fear, pain, and sadness, while the basic tendency toward excitement and approach differentiates into different forms of desire and pleasure. Over the course of this process, as emotions become more subtle and specific, they become increasingly useful in guiding behaviors toward desired goals and away from feared threats. For complex organisms that interact in sophisticated social systems, more elaborate emotions such as guilt and pride help maintain stable relationships and therefore help promote the organism's survival and reproduction.

Complex Emotions Emotions that build on and occur developmentally later than the basic emotions are known as **complex emotions**. They emerge from various combinations of basic emotions and through the introduction of more complex supporting cognitions about a situation. For example, the complex emotion of shame involves *sadness* at losing the respect of another, combined perhaps with *anger*

at oneself for doing so and some degree of *fear* about the consequences. Complex emotions develop later than the basic emotions because they involve more complex kinds of goals, such as maintaining a level of standing among peers. Such goals are at least partly socialized and vary across cultures more than basic emotions do. It may seem implausible that six basic emotions could give rise to the full emotional range. But all the possible combinations of those six basic emotions, each of which can be felt at different intensities, can yield thousands of complex emotions. Thus, this theory has the power to describe the course of emotional development, from a small set of basic emotions in infancy to the rich emotional experience of adults.

One key difference between basic and complex emotions is that many complex emotions are also **self-conscious emotions**, meaning that the emotional experience itself requires some degree of self-awareness (Lewis, 1993). Guilt, shame, embarrassment, and pride are all self-conscious emotions, as are jealousy, envy, and empathy. In each case, the emotion seems to require a sense of self in relation to others, whether it involves feeling superior to others (pride), feeling that something private about us has been exposed to others (embarrassment), or feeling that others are more fortunate than we are (envy). Young children first show self-conscious emotions at around age 1½ or 2, at around the same time they are developing other aspects of a more sophisticated self-awareness. Around this same age, children first begin to sense that they should abide by certain social standards, and they begin to become aware of others' mental states and concerned about what others think of them (Lagattuta & Thompson, 2007). The emergence of self-conscious emotions is closely related to this increasingly elaborate sense of self. Complex emotions may also use different neural circuitry from basic emotions. Basic emotions seem to be more closely linked to the **amygdala**, a brain structure that, among other functions, is known to be involved in forming memories of emotional events. Complex emotions seem to involve other brain regions in interaction with the amygdala (LeDoux, 1996).

It is useful to consider some complex emotions in more detail so as to understand how they differ from each other and can reflect the particular culture in which a child develops. Consider, for example, shame, the feeling of wanting to hide from others' view, or to be invisible. Shame can be intensely painful and uncomfortable, and it primarily leads to inactive behaviors aimed at being less noticeable (Lewis, 1993).

Guilt, in contrast, is a more specific feeling of having failed and wanting to remedy the situation (Lewis, 1993). We might regret having carelessly broken someone else's toy or having been cruel to a vulnerable friend. It is an emotion that tends to lead to actions to try to reduce the guilt—perhaps trying to compensate someone who was wronged (being especially nice to a recent victim) or deciding to act in a more upright way to demonstrate our good character to ourselves and others after causing harm. It has been argued for some time that some cultures tend to socialize children primarily through feelings of shame, while others do so through feelings of guilt (De Vos, 1973). One such proposal argued that Japan was a "shame culture" and that many Western cultures were "guilt cultures" (Benedict, 1946), but such a simple dichotomy is now viewed as an oversimplification. People in both kinds of cultures invariably feel both shame and guilt in different situations (Creighton, 1990). Nonetheless, the general point is that cultures may bias their members over the course of development to interpret situations in ways that lead to a preponderance of one emotional response over another (Tang et al., 2008).

As a final example of a complex emotion, consider embarrassment, an emotion that typically occurs when we realize that we stand out because we have violated a social convention or simply are receiving unwanted attention. It may often be expressed in an attempt to restore social relations after violating a norm or in an attempt to reduce the unwanted attention (Keltner & Anderson, 2000). Embarrassment may be one of the earliest complex emotions to emerge (Lewis, 1993), and, in contrast to shame, it is not always negative. Thus, excessive praise can evoke embarrassment even though the situation is far from shameful. Embarrassment has been experimentally induced in this way in children as young as 2 years old by "overcomplimenting" them on their appearance or abilities, and presumably it is felt because the children feel that they are receiving unwanted and perhaps undeserved levels of attention (Lewis et al., 1989). In addition, at about the age at which children first seem to understand that mirror reflections are representations of themselves rather than of a separate individual (see Chapter 13), they are also easily induced into embarrassment. This suggests that the developing ability to think about the self might relate to the emergence of this emotion.

While full-fledged complex emotions seem to develop from combinations of basic emotions, intriguing precursors to some complex emotions may appear in young infants. Thus, some early "emotions" may reflect evolutionarily prepared ways of influencing others (for example, a coy smile eliciting interaction), while not necessarily meaning that the infant is experiencing the emotion as an adult might. These early emotions may be present early on and serve certain functional roles but may not yet have the supporting cognitive structures found in older infants and children.

Adults often express **Machiavellian emotions**, which are meant to influence others and not simply to reflect an internal state. It may be that young infants are evolutionarily prepared to display certain Machiavellian emotions to caregivers so as to elicit a response from an adult, even if the infants are not really feeling what seems to be expressed

(Campos et al., 2003; Griffiths, 2003). Thus, Machiavellian emotions can serve as "shortcuts" that don't require the infant to actually have a particular feeling in combination with certain cognitions about the self and others. Instead, the infant might merely need to know that a certain facial expression or posture has brought positive results in certain kinds of situations, such as those that seem threatening. The infant may need to have some sense of the emotion's function in terms of what it can elicit or accomplish, but perhaps not the complex interplay between a basic emotion and various cognitions. Many dog owners will confess to being easily manipulated by a certain posture and a baleful look, even though the dog may not really be having the thoughts and feelings that seem to be present.

Other researchers argue that several complex emotions, including shyness, coyness, shame, and jealousy, may be present in rudimentary forms surprisingly early in infancy (Campos et al., 2010; Draghi-Lorenz et al., 2001; Hart & Carrington, 2002; Reddy, 2000; see also Hart, 2010; Hart et al., 1998, 2004). Consider the case of jealousy. In one study, infants as young as 5 months seemed to show distinct jealousy. The infants in the study watched their mother expressing great affection either to another infant or to an adult. On seeing their mother attending to another infant, more than half the infants in the study showed marked distress; yet when their mother expressed affection to an adult, only 10 percent became upset (Draghi-Lorenz, 2000). Similarly, and perhaps even more surprisingly, 6-month-old infants showed greater negative responses when they saw their mother pay positive attention to a lifelike baby doll than when their mother showed the same attention to a book (Hart & Carrington, 2002; see also Hart et al., 1998, 2004).

How can we explain these very early displays of such a complex emotion as jealousy? One possibility is that although infants do not have a complex understanding of social roles, they may still make the simpler distinction between interactions that only involve adults and those that take place between adults and infants—and view the latter as a threat to their own goals of social interaction (Draghi-Lorenz et al., 2001). Thus, the infants' expressions of jealousy may mostly reflect anger that someone else is getting a resource (adult attention) that they desire. Another possibility is that jealousy is a less complex emotion than it initially seemed, since it serves the adaptive function of ensuring that babies are not deprived of the adult affection and other resources that they need.

The accounts of emotional development described so far tend to omit the role of social and cultural contexts in further differentiating and shaping emotions, for even if those accounts advocate a great deal of predetermined structure, they must also recognize significant experiential effects as well (Camras et al., 1990, 1991, 2007; Malatesta et al.,

1989). Infants appear to gradually become "tuned" to the general sets of emotions they see most often around them—for example, in their parents' expressions and actions. We have all seen remarkable similarities between infants (or older children) and their parents and caregivers, not only in their expressions but also in their particular ways of experiencing emotions. Thinking of this process as a tuning of a preexisting system to particular sets of inputs is one way of capturing the important social and cultural influences. These processes can continue throughout the lifespan. One particularly intriguing case is whether certain types of personal failings are experienced in terms of shame versus guilt, depending on the culture. As we noted earlier, members of Western cultures may be more likely to react to certain experiences by feeling guilt, whereas those in some Eastern cultures may be more likely to feel shame in comparable situations. This difference might well reflect how a common and shared shame/guilt complex becomes tuned to particular cultural and social expectations (Crystal et al., 2001; Wong & Tsai, 2007).

Moral Emotions? Psychologists used to think that the ability to judge right from wrong developed fairly late in childhood as a preschooler or young elementary school student became immersed in the values of his or her culture. Such cultural factors are certainly important (we will consider them when we look closely at moral development in Chapter 12), but recent studies suggest that some facets of morality may emerge as part of an infant's emotional repertoire. The idea that emotions are part of moral judgments is actually an old one (Hume, 1739–1740/2000) that has seen a major rebirth in recent years (Haidt, 2003). These studies are part of a new wave of research on the "moral lives of babies" (Bloom, 2010; Wynn, 2008). Scholars in this area are quick to caution that these "moral emotions" in infants are not the same as mature moral reasoning and judgment. Still, this research suggests that preverbal infants may have some intuitive sense of right and wrong—that some core moral intuitions may emerge very early, guided by emotional likes and dislikes toward social agents (Hamlin & Wynn, 2011; Hamlin et al., 2011).

It appears that infants react to "mean" and "nice" social agents in much the same way as older children and adults. One study that investigated these capacities built on the classic study described in Chapter 5, in which infants watched a cartoon showing a triangle that "helped" a ball move up a hill while a square "hindered" its attempts (see Figure 7.5). The researchers then measured the infants' reactions to other cartoons in which the ball approached either the triangle (the helper) or the square (the hinderer; Heider & Simmel, 1944). When the ball approached the hinderer, infants as young as 10 months looked significantly longer (Hamlin et al., 2007; Kuhlmeier et al., 2003). This response suggests that the infants were surprised to see the ball approach the shape that had been "mean" to it as opposed to the one that had been "nice."

When the task was changed so that infants watched an enactment on a display stage of the cartoon event with small geometric solids (with eyes attached to make them look more animate) and then were allowed to choose to play with either the triangle helper or the square hinderer, even 6-month-olds more often chose the helper. By repeating the experiment with different shapes in the various roles, the researchers determined that infants seemed to like the helper more than the hinderer based solely on their actions, not their appearance (Hamlin et al., 2007). Ongoing research is asking if infants have comparable emotional reactions to "friends" and "punishers" of mean and nice agents and whether infants seem to extend these reactions to members of the social groups to which the agents belong (Bloom, 2010).

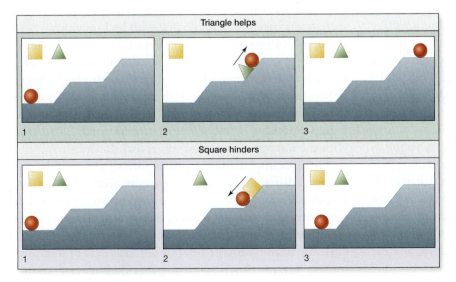

FIGURE 7.5 Helping and hindering. When video clips were shown in which geometric shapes either helped or hindered another geometric shape (here, a ball) climb up a ramp, 12-month-old infants looked longer when a later video clip showed a ball "choosing" to approach the hinderer (here, the square) rather than the helper (here, the triangle). Adapted from Kuhlmeier et al. (2003).

Perceiving and Thinking about Emotions

We have seen that within the first few months of life, infants display several distinct emotions and that many more emotions emerge in the next couple of years. From very early in life, emotions also play an important role in social interactions, and infants not only have and display emotions, but they soon become able to perceive and think about emotions in others. These abilities are critical to infants' and young children's social and cognitive development as well as to their capacity to regulate their own emotions.

Recognizing Emotions in Others In many ways, even young infants seem sensitive to others' emotions, and they often respond to expressions of emotion in appropriate ways. Long before being able to understand a parent's sentences, infants seem to understand the emotions conveyed in her tone of voice. Thus, certain intonations of alarm in a mother's voice will make an infant more cautious (Fernald, 1992). Using both visual and auditory cues together, infants as young as 4 months are able to respond differently to several different emotions, such as happiness, sadness, and surprise (Walker-Andrews, 2008). Even when listening to unfamiliar languages, infants as young as 5 months will respond differently, depending on the tone of voice (Fernald, 1993). By 7 months, infants' brains respond more strongly in the right inferior frontal cortex when they hear a happy intonation than when they hear a neutral tone (Grossmann et al., 2010). Around this same age, infants are also able to distinguish between others' expressions of several basic emotions, such as happiness, sadness, anger, and fear (Hoehl & Striano, 2010; Leppänen & Nelson, 2006).

Infants can also use visual and auditory signs of others' emotions to guide their own behavior (Hertenstein & Campos, 2004). If a 1-year-old infant at the edge of a visual cliff notices alarm in his parent's voice or face, the infant will be less likely to venture out on the cliff (Sorce et al., 1985). Similarly, if an infant is shown a novel toy and his parent, or even a stranger, reacts with fear, an infant as young as 10 months will clearly avoid the toy (Mumme et al., 1996; Mumme & Fernald, 2003). As described in Chapter 6, watching the expressions and actions of others who know more about an unfamiliar or potentially dangerous circumstance is called *social referencing*. Infants use their parents' reactions as cues to interpret ambiguous situations, and the effect of social referencing in these situations can be quite pronounced. In these circumstances, infants show a strong tendency to respond more powerfully and consistently to negative emotions than to positive ones, a phenomenon called the **negativity bias** (Vaish et al., 2008). The negativity bias may occur because there is a larger cost to ignoring or misinterpreting negative emotions than positive ones. If someone misses another person's expression of anger or fear, there is a good chance of experiencing harm, whereas the stakes are lower for overlooking an expression of joy or pleasure. This bias may be seen as an early-developing aspect of the human tendency to be risk averse (Rozin & Royzman, 2001).

It is not hard to spot young children actively using social referencing to look for clues from a parent about how to interpret an unfamiliar scenario. I was keenly aware of this behavior in one of my children when we were riding a gondola up the hill at a ski area when he was an infant. As the swinging gondola rocked and bumped, he looked mildly anxious, but he frequently glanced at my face and calmed when he saw that I was relaxed. Then the gondola stopped unexpectedly for a long period, and the ski area staff warned that because of an equipment breakdown, we might have to be lowered from the gondola to the ground by emergency rope. In the middle of that conversation, the gondola slightly lurched and I jerked; my son instantly began crying inconsolably. Infants and young children can be extremely sensitive to the smallest of cues. (Fortunately, they fixed the gondola, but it felt like a very long trip up and down the mountain.)

By the age of 9 months, infants not only use others' emotional states to gauge whether they themselves should be cautious in a particular situation, they also use this information to make inferences about other people's future behaviors. In one study, infants observed a person gazing unhappily at an unfamiliar object in one experimental condition, and they saw another person gazing happily at the same object in another experimental condition. They then saw a person's hand holding the object, but the face was obscured so the infants couldn't tell which person it was. Finally, the person's face was revealed, and the infants looked longer when the person they saw was the one who had previously been unhappily gazing at the object (Barna & Legerstee, 2005). Thus, by 9 months, infants use the emotional states of others to infer how they will likely interact with novel objects. When they saw the person with an obscured face holding the object, they assumed it must be the person who had the happy expression, and they were surprised when the person with the unhappy expression was revealed instead.

These examples illustrate that infants can clearly perceive the difference between a generally positive or negative emotional reaction. But it is not yet known whether they can perceive the subtle nuances that emotional expressions communicate, such as distinguishing disgust from fear, or curiosity from fondness. Yet, just as in the case of interpreting ambiguous situations, it appears that at least around the first year of life, infants more heavily weigh negative information in making attributions and inferences about others (Vaish et al., 2008). For example, when infants see adults show either positive or negative reactions to toys, their choice of toys to play with is driven much more by negative reactions than by positive reactions (Hertenstein & Campos, 2004). Nonetheless, when prior attention to an object is pitted against having shown a negative emotion to an object, 14-month-olds will often assume that the actor will still act on the object that had been attended to even though it was accompanied by a negative reaction (see Scientific Method box). Thus, inferring actions engaged in by others from their emotions can be difficult for older infants when attentional cues are also involved. When an infant expects that an actor will act on an object that the actor had both attended to and regarded positively, that task is easier since both cues work in the same direction. When they are in conflict, prior attention seems to drive expectations.

Emotional Contagion Perceiving what others are feeling often influences the observer's own emotional states, in some cases involving the transmission of the same emotion to the observer. One of the most basic forms of this transmission of emotions is known as **emotional contagion** (Hatfield et al., 1994), and it takes place when someone around us feels a particular emotion and we subsequently seem to "pick it up" and feel the same way ourselves. By 6 months of age, infants, too, seem to pick up emotional states from others and show those emotions at a similar level of intensity (Haviland & Lelwica, 1987; Hay et al., 1981). The cliché is that "laughter is contagious," but emotions such as happiness, sadness, and fear can all be contagious. Perhaps because of the negativity bias, infants seem especially sensitive to distress, both in adults and other infants. Even newborns show distress at hearing other newborns in distress, with distress continuing to be especially contagious throughout the first year of life (Geangu et al., 2010). In fact, infants' early ability to notice and understand others' emotional states may be closely tied to this ability to "catch" others' emotions.

Although we do not fully understand the mechanisms underlying emotional contagion, it may be related to empathy, which is a sensitivity to the emotional states of others. Andrew Meltzoff and Keith Moore (1998) speculated that social imitation in newborns may be a critical component of learning how to sense the emotional states in others. In Chapter 4, we considered studies (including pioneering work by Meltzoff and Moore) showing that newborns who are only a few weeks old are surprisingly capable of imitating facial expressions. These abilities to imitate not only require remarkable perceptual-motor integration, as described earlier, but may also reflect some of the earli-

est ways in which emotional contagion spreads from one person to another. The act of making a facial expression may be closely related to the emotions associated with that expression (Niedenthal et al., 2010). Several researchers have suggested that this process may be mediated by *mirror neurons*. Recall that these neurons fire when an individual either engages in a particular action or observes someone else performing that action, as described in Chapter 4. Mirror neurons may play a role in emotional contagion by linking action and perception such that the same neurons fire when a person either expresses an emotion or observes that emotion in others. Thus, when someone perceives a particular facial expression—say, an expression of sadness—mirror neurons may be activated that enable the perceiver to immediately express that emotion as well and, in doing so, potentially convey that emotion to yet another individual. Nonetheless, there is considerable controversy about exactly what cognitive and emotional processes correspond to mirror neuron activity in humans and whether they actually support the processes involved in emotional contagion (Decety, 2010).

> **Q:** What is emotional contagion, and how might it first emerge in development?

Emotional Regulation in Infancy

We all have done or said something in a heated moment that we later regret. Anger, sadness, fear, and many other emotions can seem to "take over," and if unchecked, they can cause great difficulties. In their daily lives, most adults manage to keep the swings of their emotions within a fairly moderate range, but infants and young children are far less adept at avoiding outbursts or getting their surging emotions under control. Infants can work themselves into a state of uncontrollable distress that seems to feed on itself until they eventually cease crying from pure exhaustion. Children may fly into tantrums or become inconsolably sad. What is different about infants and young children that makes it more difficult for them to regulate their emotions, and how does the ability to regulate emotions develop?

Through processes of **emotional regulation**, we influence the emotions we experience, when and how we experience them, and how we reveal our emotions to others (Gross, 1998). Emotional regulation includes conscious processes, such as actively and deliberately suppressing emotions, as well as unconscious processes, such as automatic actions or habits that reduce the intensity of an emotional experience. We

Hypothesis:

Preverbal infants can use the emotional states of others to infer their actions.

Method:

1. In a familiarization trial, 14-month-old infants sat on their mother's lap and watched an actor repeatedly show either a joyous reaction or a disgust reaction to one of two cups.

2. Infants then saw the actor with a neutral face either reach into the cup (attended cup) the actor had looked at on prior trials or reach into the other cup (unattended cup) he had not looked at before.

3. Experimenters recorded how long infants looked at the events when the actor's hand went into the attended cup and when it went into the unattended cup.

Results:

Infants looked longer whenever the actor reached into the cup that was not attended to before, regardless of whether the actor showed a joyous reaction or a disgust reaction.

Conclusion:

Even older infants seem to have difficulty inferring actions of others from their emotional states and instead seem to assume that people will act on things that they have previously attended to, even if they showed negative emotions while attending.

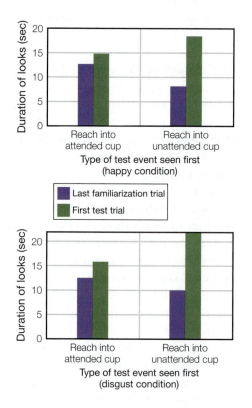

Source study: Vaish & Woodward (2010).

regulate positive emotions as well as negative ones. You might, for example, attempt to dampen your joy at winning a contest when you realize that your best friend lost and is terribly disappointed. Finally, emotional regulation can involve external factors, such as a parent soothing an infant, or internal factors, such as an infant purposely shifting his attention away from a frightening image (Eisenberg et al., 2010; Fox & Calkins, 2003; Thompson, 1994). These facets of emotional regulation, among others, have been explored extensively in adults (Gross, 1998). From a developmental perspective, three aspects of emotional regulation are especially important in infants: situational factors, attentional deployment, and response modification. In addition, for younger infants, the parents play an especially important role in regulating infants' emotions, as infants under 6 months have a relatively limited repertoire of ways to regulate their own emotions.

Situational Factors One way of regulating infants' emotions is to change the situation in which they are immersed, a method called **situation modification**. The change may be caused by a parent or other caregiver, and early in development, these adult-driven modifications will usually predominate in soothing the infant, such as when a parent removes a frightening toy or takes the infant out of her crib. Even young infants, however, can modify a situation themselves. Once infants are able to move about, they can sometimes modify a situation by moving away from something they find unpleasant—perhaps crawling away from the deep side of the visual cliff. They can also modify a situation with a facial expression, vocalization, or gesture. If an infant is frightened by a loud stranger, she might show an alarmed face, causing the stranger to become quieter and more soothing, thereby changing the nature of the situation. An infant who is distressed at being unable to reach a desired object may also modify the situation by gesturing to a caregiver, who then makes the object attainable. Young infants, too, may elicit parental help through crying, but this situation is somewhat different from the others, as the infants may be unable to calm themselves without parental intervention (Kopp & Neufeld, 2003).

Early on, infants are usually better able to modify the situation they find themselves in than to select the situation they prefer, as they are very often plopped into a setting by their caregivers with little chance of escape. In the early years, a responsive adult is more likely to notice an infant's negative reaction to a situation and then select a different situation on the infant's behalf. Once they can crawl, infants may be able to select a situation themselves, perhaps moving from one room to another to stay close to their mother or to avoid a frightening dog. Over the course of development, the **situation selection** method of regulating emotions becomes increasingly important as the infant becomes able to take actions that enable her to approach pleasant situations or avoid unpleasant ones.

Attentional Deployment Our attentional skills are closely related to our emotional experiences. Someone who finds it difficult to disengage from upsetting stimuli may become increasingly distressed and unable to regulate that emotion. When we use **attentional deployment** to regulate our emotions, we direct our thoughts in a way that makes a situation feel less emotionally charged. This is generally done through distraction, focusing our attention on a less adverse aspect of a situation or thinking about something else completely (see Figure 7.7A). Among all the methods of regulating emotions, infants are thought to use attentional deployment most actively. For example, they will sometimes change the focus of their attention by looking away from an unpleasant stimulus to a more neutral one. In the still-face procedure discussed in Chapter 6, infants will sometimes look away from the mother's impassive face,

apparently in an effort to keep it from making them feel unhappy (Mesman et al., 2009; Striano & Liszkowski, 2005). Twelve-month-olds use similar attentional strategies to regulate their emotions in the Strange Situation (Braungart & Stifter, 1991).

Following from the infant's rudimentary skill of looking away in contexts like the still-face procedure, the ability to regulate emotions by redirecting attention develops significantly throughout infancy and early childhood, resulting in an increasing ability to avoid overexposure to negative stimuli and to achieve an optimum amount of exposure to positive stimuli. For example, a preschooler might become more skilled at not just looking away from a troubling sight, but also at purposely focusing on something else to more actively distract himself (Zelazo & Cunningham, 2007). As we will see in Chapter 17, attentional deployment strategies continue to be used throughout the lifespan.

Response Modification Another method of emotional regulation is **response modification**, which involves managing an emotional reaction by directly influencing the physiological response itself—for example, relaxing muscles or slowing the heartbeat—or by engaging in an activity that indirectly leads to a change in the expression of an emotion. The conscious use of strategies to manipulate the bodily state may be relatively late emerging, but self-soothing behaviors, such as thumb-sucking, can begin quite early (Stifter & Braungart, 1995; see Figure 7.7B). Later in infancy, at around 1 year, infants start to learn to inhibit motor movements associated with either extreme distress or overexcitement (Fox & Calkins, 2003). Over time, children learn increasingly subtle response modification techniques to handle strong emotions, such as counting to 10, taking a deep breath, or eating a favorite snack. As with attentional deployment, our response modification strategies continue to develop over the lifespan as we learn how to engage in behaviors that either reduce anxiety or increase arousal.

One form of response modification, namely the suppression of certain emotions, seems to be heavily influenced by culture. Many studies have shown how adults socialize children not to display certain emotions even when they are feeling them strongly, and these **display rules** governing what kinds of emotional expressions a particular group considers appropriate can vary dramatically across cultures (Hofer & Eisenberg, 2008; Thompson, 2011). For example, Iranian children are socialized to suppress their emotions more than Dutch children, especially when in the presence of family members. On the other hand, when Dutch children do suppress their emotions, they tend to do so more in the presence of peers (Novin et al., 2009). As another example,

The Effect of Parenting on Emotion Processing in Children

Early interactions between parents and their children may have a major influence on how children interpret what others are feeling. Important recent research is investigating whether growing up with abusive or emotionally inappropriate parents influences children's ability to perceive and interpret the emotions of others. One study examined the ability of 9-year-olds to detect emotional facial expressions, comparing the emotional sensitivity of children of abusive parents with that of children whose parents were not abusive. To test the children's sensitivity to even the earliest traces of particular expressions, the researchers showed them a digitally altered series of images of the same face, with the images gradually transforming from a face with a neutral expression to a face with a strong emotion, such as extreme anger (Pollak et al., 2009). When viewing the photo series that progressed from neutral to angry faces (see Figure 7.6), children of abusive parents identified anger at an earlier point in the series than the children whose parents were not abusive. But the abused children and those in the control group were equally sensitive to sad, fearful, happy, and surprised expressions. These findings suggest that abused children are especially prone to identifying ambiguous expressions as angry ones and therefore are more likely to interpret other people's expressions as being angry in real-life situations.

In another study, researchers looked at the kinds of facial and vocal emotional expressions produced by mothers who were either abusive or nonabusive (Shackman et al., 2010). When researchers rated their expressions, the abusive mothers showed facial expressions that were less typical of anger (for example, showing less intensity in lowering and contracting their eyebrows, which are typical expressions of anger) than did nonabusive mothers when they were angry. Even more important, the children of abusive mothers showed corresponding deficits in their ability to process their mother's angry expressions, having more difficulty in sensing their mother's anger. Moreover, the children of abusive mothers were more likely to be anxious, depressed, and aggressive than were the children of nonabusive mothers, possibly because of the greater uncertainty about their mother's emotional state. Other scholars have likewise found relationships between mothers who are chronically depressed and their children's abilities to identify and describe the emotions of others (Raikes & Thompson, 2006). Measures of children's neural activity associated with interpreting emotion also show differences related to their early experiences. In one study, infants and toddlers who had been institutionalized in orphanages in Romania viewed emotional faces while researchers monitored the electrophysiological activity in their brains. Compared with children who grew up in normal homes, they showed much less response in a component of electrical waves called P1 (Moulson et al., 2009). It also appeared that leaving the institution and spending time in foster care could gradually lessen these effects (see Chapter 6). Several researchers are now documenting a diverse set of such biomarkers (ranging from electrophysiological to hormonal measures) that are associated with particular social experiences with caregivers and the ability to process emotions (Strang et al., 2012).

As in so many other cases, it is difficult to be sure if abusive or depressed parents actually cause the changes in how children perceive and think about emotions. An alternative expla-

contrast the emotional expressions of children who grow up in agrarian farming families in the Nso culture in northwest Cameroon with those of urban, middle-class children growing up in northern Germany. In the Nso culture, children are socialized early to suppress any signs of negative emotions. By comparison, German children are socialized to express emotions readily, especially positive emotions that may be seen as markers of their autonomy and individuality (Keller & Otto, 2009). Yet, while some forms of response modification, such as a general suppression of negative emotions, may begin to be instilled during infancy in many cultures, the more nuanced ways of following cultural display rules in specific contexts continue to develop well into middle childhood.

Thus, well before the first year of life, situational selection, attentional deployment, and response modification each play a role in regulating infants' emotions. All three processes are present early on, and they become more sophisticated in the months and years that follow. In addi-

nation is that some of the same factors that cause parents to be abusive or depressed may also affect their children's abilities to perceive and understand emotions. For example, some abusive parents may have genetically predisposed biases in how they perceive and understand emotions that contribute to their abusive behavior. If so, their children may inherit these predispositions and show similar problems perceiving and interpreting what others feel. Another possibility is that some kinds of environments are so stressful that they can cause both parents and children to perceive and understand emotions differently. Such alternatives need to be explored more fully, but the finding that abused children are sometimes *more*

sensitive to negative emotions suggests that these children have fairly complex differences in emotional processing, rather than simple deficits.

It is critical that we learn how early such emotional processing differences appear in these children's behavior in order to understand whether interacting with emotionally dysfunctional parents is a root cause. That research, in turn, will help researchers determine when negative effects of abusive parenting first appear. Taken together, these future research findings will help guide practitioners in their decisions concerning how to better intervene and help children who grow up in such environments.

 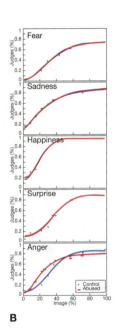

A   **B**

FIGURE 7.6 Abused children and emotion perception. (A) The faces shown here range from neutral to more and more emotional for fear, sadness, happiness, surprise, and anger. **(B)** The accompanying graphs show when control children and abused children recognized emotional expressions. Abused children tended to see anger earlier, as expressions varied from neutral to angry faces (bottom panel), but they showed no higher sensitivity for fearful, sad, happy, or surprised expressions (top four panels). Adapted from Pollak et al. (2009).

tion, these processes interact from a very early age. An infant may modify a response in a way that also deploys her attention in a different manner and that consequently modifies her situation. As each of these processes becomes more sophisticated and interacts with the others, they collectively offer many ways for cultures to exert their own influences and create culturally unique patterns of emotional modulation that go beyond these early forms. Finally, as children grow older, they develop new emotional regulation processes. One example involves cognitive reframing

or reappraisal (Gross, 1998), which consists of rethinking a situation to interpret its negative aspects in less upsetting or more positive ways. There is not yet any evidence that infants are able to use this kind of cognitive reframing, but such a process may yet be shown to have precursors in infancy. Interestingly, the neural circuits involved in distraction and reappraisal during emotional regulation have several distinct components, which may help explain why these two forms of regulation have different developmental trajectories (McRae et al., 2010).

A   **B**

FIGURE 7.7 Emotional regulation. All infants learn to regulate both unpleasant and pleasant emotions, a process that involves several components that can take many years to fully develop. **(A)** Infants can use attentional deployment and learn to redirect their attention elsewhere if an aversive event (for example, a competitor with a toy) is troubling them. **(B)** Infants can also use response modification. For example, self-soothing, by putting a hand or a thumb in one's mouth, can be a surprisingly effective technique for some infants.

> **Q:** In what ways are infants less able to regulate their emotions than older children and adults?

Evolutionary Preparedness and Emotional Development

In some cases, the developmental paths of emotions may be strongly constrained because the child is *prepared*, in the evolutionary sense, to experience distinctive emotions in certain well-defined situations. As described in Chapter 4, many species learn some associations more readily than others because they involve behaviors that are especially important to the species' survival in its natural environment. Likewise, humans might be prepared, even in infancy, to more quickly learn to feel disgust toward certain things and fear toward other things because of the ways that certain responses promoted our ancient ancestors' survival. For example, it is much easier to develop a fear of snakes or spiders—which posed real threats to our forebears—than a fear of rocks or fish. To see why some emotional responses are thought to be prepared in this way, we will look more closely at fear and disgust responses and then briefly turn to other possible cases of prepared emotions.

Preparedness for Acquiring Certain Fears One kind of fearful reaction that is especially salient involves **phobias**, which are extreme, often irrational fears of specific things

or situations. Some people have quite distressing and disruptive phobias of such things as going outdoors, flying in airplanes, or eating food cooked by others, but it is a mistake to think of all phobias as maladaptive. All humans and some other species may share fears of particular kinds of events and objects, and for good reason. This chapter does not consider the development of clearly irrational and maladaptive phobias, which are forms of psychopathology. The focus here is on the ways in which some fears are influenced by prepared learning.

An upsetting experience is much more likely to become associated with the fear of some objects than with the fear of others. A clinical observation of a 4-year-old girl who saw a snake in a park while she was on an outing with her family nicely illustrates this aspect of prepared learning of phobias (Marks, 1977). On seeing the snake, the girl had examined it with interest but no apparent fear. Then, a little later, she accidentally hurt her hand on the door of her family's car. If she was to develop any phobia following this outing, it seems likely that she would come to fear car doors or perhaps cars. Instead, she developed a lifelong fear of snakes. She strongly associated the experience of pain and trauma with the snake she had recently encountered, even though she had seen the snake *before* the car door accident. Learning to associate a painful or unpleasant experience with something encountered much earlier runs counter to the principles of classical conditioning, which predicts stronger learned associations between events that happen closer together in space and time. But a more evolutionary or ethological perspective easily explains the girl's experience and the resulting phobia. Instead of focusing on whether her experience with the snake and her injury happened very close together in time, these approaches emphasize the adaptive survival value of being highly sensitive to learning fears of natural dangers, such as snakes (Seligman, 1971).

If humans are indeed prepared to learn certain fears, it should be possible to show these biases in young children and perhaps even in infants. Just as infants have biases for more easily learning about human speech and human faces, infants may also have biases for quickly learning about evolutionarily threatening stimuli in the environment, such as snakes and spiders (LoBue et al., 2010; Rakison & Derringer, 2008). If humans are prepared to develop fears of snakes and spiders, it might make adaptive sense for these fears to emerge very early and to become easily associated with threatening stimuli (see Figure 7.8).

The most compelling argument that prepared fears have a strong genetic component (rather than developing mostly through experience) comes from studies in which the developing organism is afraid of particular "naturally" feared objects without having been previously exposed to them, either directly or culturally. Because such studies require subjects to be socially and culturally isolated, they are not ethical to do with humans, but they can be done with rhesus monkeys. In one study, researchers showed monkeys who had been raised in isolation videotapes of other rhesus monkeys exhibiting extreme fear to different sorts of stimuli (Cook & Mineka, 1989). Through clever editing of the tapes, some monkeys saw videos that seemed to depict model monkeys showing fearful reactions to harmless items, such as flowers or a toy rabbit, while other monkeys saw videos of model monkeys showing fear of a toy snake or a toy crocodile. Although the monkeys who watched the videos had not seen any of the feared objects before or had any opportunity to learn about them, they nonetheless developed a strong fear of snakes and crocodiles and no fear of rabbits or flowers. Thus, without any experience of the kinds of fearful events they watched, they developed fears in response to certain prepared stimuli simply by seeing others respond to them fearfully.

Like the rhesus monkeys, young children often show a strong prepared fear of snakes before they have had any negative experiences with them—or any experiences with them at all. In one set of studies, children between the ages of 3 and 5 years were asked either to find a picture of a snake among eight "distractor" pictures of harmless objects, such as flowers, or to find a flower picture among eight snake pictures (see Figure 7.9). Similar studies used pictures of frogs or caterpillars for distractors, both of which have some snakelike features. In all cases, even the 3-year-olds identified the snake picture among the distractors much faster than they could find another object among pictures of snakes (LoBue & DeLoache, 2008). Equally important, the children who had no prior experience with snakes were just as likely as those with substantial experience to detect snakes more quickly. Apparently, even without any direct experience with snakes, young children are much more vigilant for snakes than for other objects and notice them much more quickly (LoBue, 2013).

Further evidence shows that young children not only notice snakes especially quickly, but also are prepared to learn to fear them. In a second line of studies, researchers showed infants as young as 7 months a short video, either of snakes or some other exotic animal, while the infants listened to either a fearful voice or a happy voice (DeLoache & LoBue, 2009; see Figure 7.10). Even 7-month-olds looked longer at the snakes when the snakes were paired with the fearful voice, indicating that they were especially prepared to associate fear with snakes. Nonetheless, they did not look longer at the snakes when there was no sound accompanying the videos or when still pictures were used. Apparently, in young infants, one trigger for the fear of snakes involves associating the fear with an animated display. Infants also seem to show a similar prepared fear of spiders in the first 6 months of life. Infants as young as 5 months show a preference to visually track spider stimuli over other

FIGURE 7.8 **Prepared fears.** The preparedness model suggests that a toddler will be much more prone to develop a fear of snakes than to develop a fear of neutral objects.

The Causes and Consequences of Problems in Emotional Regulation

Some young children seem to lose control of their emotions whenever they get upset, spiraling into fits of despair, anger, or both. These children are not just touchy or easily distressed; instead, their emotions seem to run away from them.

Some children who have difficulty regulating their emotions seem to have problems in the domain of *emotional intelligence*. That is, they have difficulty inferring others' emotional states from their expressions and behavior, and they do not seem to understand how specific situations are likely to lead to certain emotions (Salovey & Sluyter, 1997; see also Chapter 11). These difficulties also seem to extend to their perceptions of themselves. They have difficulty recognizing and understanding their own emotions (Shields et al., 2001). As a result, they may have trouble keeping their feelings in check as a highly emotional situation starts to ramp up. A child with low emotional intelligence may fail to notice his own emotional response early enough to regulate it effectively.

Difficulties with emotional regulation can begin to cause other problems for these children quite early. Thus, young children who have trouble keeping their own emotions in check or understanding their own emotions and those of others tend to have more difficulty than their peers adjusting to the first year of preschool (Shields et al., 2001). Despite the challenge of precisely defining and measuring emotional regulation problems (Cole et al., 2004; Eisenberg & Spinrad, 2004), research suggests that toddlers and young children who have an unusually difficult time regulating their emotions seem to be more likely than other children to experience behavioral problems later in life, including having greater anxiety, depression, and difficulty interacting with peers.

Nonetheless, not all children with emotional regulation problems go on to have these difficulties. Rather, the level of stress in the child's environment seems to influence the outcome. We have seen this kind of interaction between a child's own tendencies and his environment in other domains of development as well; this is another instance in which a group of infants or children are not *predetermined* to have a particular kind of problem, but are at risk for doing so if they also have certain kinds of experiences. For example, one study compared two groups of children who were determined to be genetically at risk for emotional regulation problems but had experienced different kinds of parenting styles. One group of at-risk children who had a short form of a serotonin-related gene (see Chapter 6) grew up with parents who were not fully responsive and sensitive to their needs, and these children did indeed develop poor emotional regulation skills (Kochanska et al., 2009b). The other group of at-risk children had the same genetic allele associated with emotional regulation problems, but the children in this second group had more responsive parents. Interestingly, the children in this second group did not develop any more emotional problems than children who showed no genetic risks.

Much as in our discussion of parenting styles and attachment in Chapter 6, we should not assume that parenting styles directly

objects such as flowers, suggesting an early-emerging bias to monitor certain kinds of potential threats (Rakison & Derringer, 2008). Finally, at least one study suggests that female infants may be more predisposed than male infants to associate fear with snakes and spiders, a pattern that is also found in adults (Rakison, 2009) and that raises questions about origins of sex differences in some phobias.

The evolutionary roots of phobias serve to remind us that although the same situation can elicit different emotions in different people, the relation between situations and emotions is not arbitrary (Ohman & Mineka, 2001). We easily learn to fear potentially dangerous natural stimuli like snakes, and we find it hard to extinguish those fears. Moreover, we can even acquire those fears in cases where snakes are presented so briefly that we are not even aware of them (Mineka & Ohman, 2002b; Ohman & Mineka, 2003). These patterns of fear conditioning follow some of the usual laws of associative learning, but they also go beyond them in ways that reflect strong preparedness effects (Mineka & Ohman, 2002a). In short, many species seem to share evolutionarily ancient predispositions to develop fears of snakes, spiders, and even heights and other categories of stimuli (Barrett, 2005).

Preparedness and the Development of Disgust We have seen that some fears are rooted in prepared learning and do not depend purely on experience. Is the development of other emotions also influenced by adaptive prepared-

caused emotional regulation problems in the first group of children, since many other genetic and environmental factors were also involved. But such a study does offer a plausible account of how one aspect of a child's environment (parenting style) potentially might interact with emotional regulation problems and influence the child's emotional development. Similarly, another study showed how insecurely attached children and coercive parents could get into vicious negative-feedback loops in which the parents' increased coercive behaviors seemed to exacerbate poor emotional regulation skills in their children, which in turn led to more coercive behaviors by the parents (Kochanska et al., 2009a). More generally, researchers may refer to "emotional availability" in parent-child relationships, where emotional availability includes effective emotional communication between parent and child, mutual emotional understanding, and emotional accessibility of each partner in an interaction. High levels of emotional availability in parent-child relationships are associated with good emotional regulation skills in infants (Bornstein et al., 2012).

One way that parental influence can work is by affecting the strategies that children develop for coping with emotional regulation. For example, infants of depressed mothers seem to cope with their distress differently than infants whose mothers are not depressed. Researchers examined the reactions of two groups of 5-month-olds—those whose mothers were depressed and those whose mothers were not—to the still-face procedure, in which the mother shows the infant a frozen, unresponsive, neutral expression. Infants whose mothers were clinically depressed were more likely to deal with the still face by using behaviors such as thumb-sucking to soothe themselves. In contrast, infants of nondepressed mothers were more likely to use attentional deployment strategies, such as looking away from the still face (Manian & Bornstein, 2009). One interpretation of these results is that infants of depressed mothers felt a

stronger need to remain engaged with their mothers, who are often nonresponsive. Rather than looking away, even though the still face was upsetting, they kept looking at their mothers and tried to comfort themselves in other ways.

Children's emotional regulation problems raise a number of difficult questions. First and foremost, what can be done to help these children with their emotional struggles? One common therapeutic approach is to focus on specific behaviors, such as tantrums associated with excessive anger. In this case, a therapist might work with a child and his parents to develop strategies for modifying the child's tendency to throw tantrums (Kazdin, 1997). The therapist might teach the child an alternative behavior that more effectively regulates anger, such as deep breathing, and show him how it is more rewarding in the long run than throwing a tantrum.

A different approach attempts to expand on the child's ability to understand his own emotional states and those of others, assuming that such an increased awareness will lead to enhanced abilities to arrest an emotional surge before it gets out of control (Slaby et al., 1995). In addition, because parents of children with emotional regulation problems often discourage talk about emotions, developing strategies for having more extensive discussions between parent and child about emotional states may also be a way to give children some insight into how to manage their emotions (Suveg et al., 2005). With these approaches and a number of others, many children who have trouble regulating their emotions may be able to develop appropriate skills and see real, long-term improvements. Ideally, we would like to intervene earlier in infancy, when these problems may start to emerge, but the challenge is to design effective interventions for infants. Training parents to be more responsive and less coercive to their infants may well be the best strategy with younger infants.

ness? Disgust may well be another emotion that occurs in response to particular stimuli within the constraints of prepared learning. This idea dates back to Charles Darwin (1872/1975), who noted that disgust seems to consist of the specific emotion and facial expression that relate to potentially ingesting something offensive (see Figure 7.11). Emotional responses that are universal to humans are the ones most likely to have roots in evolutionarily prepared reactions. In the case of disgust, prepared reactions seem most likely in response to ingesting either living things or their by-products (hair, body excretions, and the like). In addition, there is a universal bias toward reactions of disgust to food that is physically connected with something offensive (for example, a long string connecting a plate of food

to a disgusting substance), even when there is no way the physical connection could contaminate the food. Similarly, if an object has previously come into contact with offensive material, such as feces, people often react to that object with disgust, as if it has been contaminated, even if there is no rational way that any contamination could survive.

Although disgust, like some fears, shows evidence of preparedness, its development shows different patterns of change and cross-cultural variability than we saw with prepared fears. For example, disgust toward feces appears to be universal to adults in all cultures (Rozin et al., 1986, 2000, 2008), but it is not usually present in toddlers in any culture, at least not until the children are toilet trained. Instead, it typically develops sometime between 3 and

FIGURE 7.9 Threat detection. Preschool children tend to more quickly detect snakes than flowers. This may be because humans have evolved a bias to see snakes, but not flowers, as threatening. This boy is shown eight pictures of snakes and one picture of a flower on a computer monitor and asked to touch the flower. It takes him longer to identify the flower than it would to identify one snake in the midst of eight flowers. From LoBue & DeLoache (2008).

7 years of age (Rozin et al., 1986, 2000). Disgust seems to develop from a response to a very narrow range of stimuli, such as disgusting tastes (typically bitter ones early on), to a much broader range of stimuli. One view suggests that humans' earliest disgust reactions to bitter substances may be shared with many other species. As children grow older, however, the emotion of disgust becomes more general, as it is applied to items that could cause disease, such as animal body products. It then becomes further generalized to things and events that more broadly threaten the integrity

of the body, such as death, wounds, bad hygiene, or sex. These extensions of disgust beyond taste seem to be unique to humans (Rozin et al., 1986, 2000, 2008).

Finally, all humans seem to develop culturally specific extensions of disgust to strange or undesirable people and to certain moral offenses, both of which pose potential threats to the social order. This ability to rely on culture for broadening the disgust category may have its roots in early infancy. Thus, while infants may not show stable disgust reactions to much beyond bitter tastes, by at least 11 months they do take note of adults' disgust reactions and avoid the objects of those responses (Hertenstein & Campos, 2004). Later in development, by at least 5 years of age, children are able to extend disgust reactions to immoral actions (Danovitch & Bloom, 2009).

Disgust therefore develops differently from fear in the sense that an early, specific disgust reaction becomes extended beyond a narrow range of stimuli to a much broader set of stimuli. Even in those extensions, however, humans show evidence of preparedness to associate disgust with particular types of things and situations, such as contaminants that threaten the integrity of the body or that potentially cause disease (Oaten et al., 2009). That notion of disgust may then become extended to certain sexual practices or moral transgressions that may contaminate the social system either by reducing reproductive success or by violating social norms (Tybur et al., 2009). Interestingly, even these broader extensions of disgust may be evolutionarily constrained, such that adults show disgust pertaining to three major domains: disease contamination from invisible things, such as microbes; certain

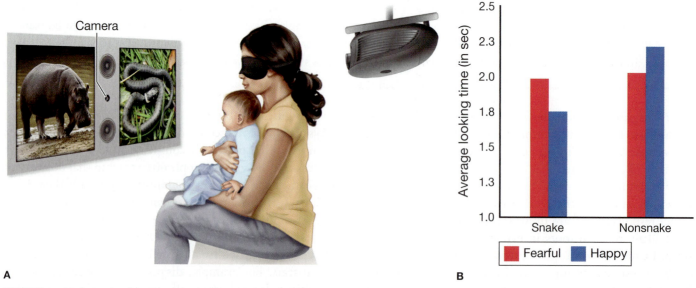

FIGURE 7.10 Learning to associate snakes with fear. (A) In this experiment, infants sit on their mother's lap and watch videos showing hippos and snakes accompanied by fearful or happy voices. **(B)** Infants as young as 7 months will look longer at a brief video of a snake when they hear a fearful voice, but not when they hear a happy voice. They look equally long at brief videos of hippos when they hear a happy voice as when they hear a fearful voice (the nonsnake differences shown are not statistically significant). Adapted from DeLoache & LoBue (2009).

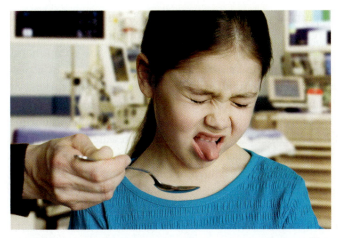  

FIGURE 7.11 Preparedness for disgust. As these photos illustrate, disgust reactions are easy to observe in people of all ages. One component of the reaction seems to be a reflexive set of movements that serve to block any additional offending substances from entering the mouth.

types of immoral actions; and choice of sexual partners and behaviors. One major remaining challenge is to understand how and why people seem to develop a common emotional reaction to offenses within these particular diverse domains. Other questions that are still being investigated have to do with the reasons women tend to react more strongly than men to most disgust-provoking stimuli (Björklund & Hursti, 2004; Haidt et al., 1994; Marzillier & Davey, 2004, 2005).

> **Q:** How might irrational thought related to disgust be evidence for disgust as a biologically prepared emotion?

Preparedness and the Development of Other Emotions The idea of preparedness may explain some aspects of the development of most emotions, but the details of these explanations await further work. For example, smiling may be a prepared response to a particular set of situations, which in turn helps give rise to feelings of joy. (The situation may give rise to joy itself, but the smiling response may enhance that feeling.) As mentioned earlier, the idea that emotions are rooted in prepared, adaptive responses to particular situations fits well with the view that emotions involve responding to situations in goal-directed ways. That is, certain emotions may be prepared to be associated with certain specific *combinations of goals and situations*. Thus, you are much more likely to be angry when a goal is blocked intentionally by others than when the obstacle is caused by natural events. Anger is surely more effective when it is expressed to another being who can respond to it than when it is displayed to something inanimate. For that reason, natural selection may have favored a prepared anger response to obstacles purposely raised by others.

We have seen that certain kinds of emotions seem to be linked, quite possibly through natural selection, to particular kinds of stimuli and to certain response routines. Over and above these deeply rooted linkages, emotional development involves constant refinement, fine-tuning, and extension of prepared emotions to broader classes of situations, resulting in more sophisticated and nuanced responses. Ultimately, our understanding of these prepared emotional systems needs to be integrated into broader accounts of how all emotions and our ways of regulating them develop. In addition, such an integration may bring new developmental insights into the close relationship between emotions and personality.

Temperament and the Origins of Personality

Any parent who has more than one child quickly realizes that different infants tend to react differently to similar situations. What frightens one infant might interest another. Some infants greet a challenge with anger, others respond with sadness, and still others show renewed effort. An infant's tendency toward particular emotional and behavioral responses to specific situations is known as **temperament**. An individual's temperament emerges early in life and remains relatively stable over time and can also involve individual differences in self-regulation (Goldsmith & Campos, 1982; Goldsmith et al., 2000; Rothbart & Bates, 2006; Zentner & Bates, 2008).

Temperament describes, roughly, an infant's personality. But most researchers use the term *temperament* when describing an infant's disposition because behavioral differences among infants are not the same as those that distinguish older children or adults. Because temperament describes infants' emotional tendencies, features of adult personality centering around emotions and moods seem to be among the most likely aspects of personality to have clear roots in infant temperament. But even in these domains, infants certainly do not show the richness or complexity of personality that older children and adults do. Moreover, personality includes many other aspects of human variation, such as intelligence, creativity, and self-monitoring ability, to name a few, that seem highly implausible—or at least unmeasurable—in infants. These considerations have led researchers to talk about temperament as a more biologically rooted and hence earlier-emerging part of personality (Allport, 1937; Buss & Plomin, 1984). Hence, the vast majority of research on the origins of personality in infancy has focused on studying infant temperament.

> **Q:** What is the difference between temperament and personality? How are they related?

As we will see, a major challenge arises in trying to understand how differences in temperament among infants are part of the larger story of personality development. As part of that challenge, we will ask how differences in temperament that are present in infancy contribute to later patterns of personality and how certain types of social experiences and cultural practices influence this process.

Temperament-Based Components of Personality and Early Development

The notion that the richness and diversity of personality might develop from different combinations of a relatively few biologically based values actually dates back thousands of years. The ancient Greek physician Hippocrates was the first to offer a detailed version of this theory (Arikha, 2007; Smith, 1979). He believed that there are four different personality types, which reflect different balances of the body's four humors (derived from the Latin *umor*, meaning "fluid"): blood, phlegm, yellow bile, and black bile. For example, he thought that people who are social, outgoing, and optimistic show those traits because they have a relatively large amount of blood, whereas melancholic, introspective, and morose people have an abundance of black bile.

Although there is no physiological basis for Hippocrates's theory, it shares some important elements with the modern understanding of both temperament and personality. For example, many researchers hold that the vast variety of personality differences—over 10,000 terms in English refer

to aspects of personality (Allport, 1937; Goldberg, 1982)—emerge from far fewer critical components, such as fearfulness and agreeableness. In this view, these few components interact with one another and with other aspects of a person and her experiences, yielding all the traits and types of personality (Cattell, 1978). Perhaps surprisingly, the four personality types that Hippocrates described resemble some of the categories presently described by researchers who study infant temperament and the development of personality.

Modern views of temperament integrate biological views with psychological processes. One influential line of work with a strong biological emphasis focused on the early emergence of temperament and its high degree of heritability—that is, how much genes contribute to individual variation—as its critical attributes (Buss & Plomin, 1984). These approaches are sometimes called *trait approaches* for their emphasis on behavior patterns as heritable traits. Over the years, this view evolved into an account that focused on three fundamental trait-like categories—emotionality, activity level, and sociability—which were thought to make important contributions to later personality traits. These three categories have become prominent for several interrelated reasons. First, each has been associated with significant heritabilities across a wide range of studies, suggesting important influences of genetic pathways. Second, several neural circuits and structures are associated with these categories. For example, amygdala activity is associated with both emotionality and sociability and more broadly with approach and withdrawal tendencies. The amygdala and its associations with temperament have also been linked to genetic variations. Thus, in young primates, a particular variation of the central amygdala gene *Ce* has been linked to anxious temperaments through a pathway that involves decreased receptor production and activity in the central amygdala (Fox et al., 2012). The same gene and its variants are present in humans. Other physiological correlates of emotionality, sociability, and activity level can involve variations in heart rate, cortisol levels, and the degree of involvement of the frontal lobes (Henderson & Wachs, 2007; Zentner & Shiner, 2012). Finally, there seem to be analogous temperamental variations in a variety of social species, including some primates and dogs, suggesting an adaptive role for these dimensions of temperament that occurs robustly across several species.

As always, the involvement of both genetic and biological influences should not be interpreted as genes and biology predetermining an infant's temperament. Instead, these factors interact with particular kinds of environments to create differences in temperament. These environmental influences include parent-child interaction patterns and the degree to which an infant's environment is predictable and nonthreatening.

Other researchers on temperament focus on individual differences in infants' tendencies to express and regulate basic emotions (Goldsmith & Campos, 1982, 1986, 1990). Consider basic emotions such as sadness, happiness, anger, surprise, and fear. Temperament would be interpreted here as tendencies to show either high or low levels of such emotions. We can see how differences in emotionality, activity level, and sociability could all lead to different tendencies to express basic emotions. Hence, even though these two approaches to temperament seem quite different, they may both be related to regulation of emotions. Indeed, if emotions are seen as having functional roles concerned with mobilizing oneself and eliciting reactions in others, emotional regulation can be seen as intrinsic to variations in the tendency to express emotions.

Determining Differences in Temperament

To identify different characteristics of infant temperament, researchers have used reports by caregivers, observations of infants in natural settings, and observations of infants in the laboratory. In the earliest studies on temperament, researchers used parents' reports about their infants and then coded the behaviors into a set of general characteristics. In all these approaches, stability of a temperamental classification over time and a range of situations was an important concern. Thus, a quick emotional reaction by an infant to a threatening situation is interesting to the extent that it appears repeatedly in similar contexts. Researchers also had to find ways to distill from thousands of highly specific observations of infant behaviors much broader characterizations of individual differences that enabled them to talk usefully about different temperamental types and dimensions. Moreover, the entire approach was also mindful of the long-term goal of ultimately connecting these broader factors to personality types in older children and adults.

The New York Longitudinal Study A major milestone in temperament research came in a large-scale longitudinal study conducted by Alexander Thomas and Stella Chess (Thomas et al., 1963, 1968; Thomas & Chess, 1984). Recall that a longitudinal study involves assessing each child repeatedly over an extended period of time to explore what remains constant and what changes in the child. The children in Thomas and Chess's New York Longitudinal Study were studied from infancy to middle age. As seen in Chapter 1, the central questions in this approach and in most other longitudinal studies on individual differences are whether what is measured at one age shows a similar value across all ages, observers, and situations (reliability) and whether the measure predicts the more naturalistic and intuitively compelling behaviors that are thought to underlie the temperamental measures (validity).

Among its most important contributions, the New York Longitudinal Study suggested some patterns in the development of temperament that became a basis for later research. Based on extensive interviews with the mothers at the beginning of the study in which each mother was asked to provide a detailed description of her infant's daily activities and routine rather than explicit information about the infant's personality or temperament, the researchers described nine dimensions of temperament: activity level, approach/withdrawal (from novel objects, people, or situations), adaptability (ease of changing responses to situational influences), mood (positive or negative feelings), threshold of responsiveness (when an infant starts to respond to a stimulus), intensity of reaction, distractibility, rhythmicity (regularity of biological functions), and attention span/persistence. Each baby was then scored and classified into one of three categories: (1) *Easy babies* (roughly 40 percent of the group) were happy and adaptable, generally showed a positive attitude, did not overreact to situations, and had regular daily routines. (2) *Difficult babies* (roughly 10 percent of the group) were often unhappy, did not adjust well to new situations, had irregular eating and sleeping patterns, and tended to show intense reactions. (3) *"Slow to warm up" babies* (roughly 15 percent of the group) were initially negative in mood, less active, reacted with relatively low intensity, and adapted slowly to new situations. The remaining 35 percent of the participants were called *average babies*, and they tended to have intermediate values on these scales.

Over the years, Thomas and Chess examined how these categories of infant temperament might relate to different patterns of behavior in later life, and they suggested some longer-term relationships. For example, they believed that a difficult baby who is also highly reactive to situations and shows a low attention span might be less likely to do well in highly structured elementary school settings and more likely to have hostile relations with peers (Rubin et al., 2003; Thomas et al., 1968). Moreover, children considered to be slow to warm up might tend to become more isolated from peers and would rarely become central members of social groups.

In several ways, the New York Longitudinal Study laid a crucial groundwork for later studies. First, it looked at infant behaviors in their own right rather than conceiving of them as infant versions of adult behaviors and qualities. Second, it suggested that infants' behaviors could be coded into temperament categories that might have some degree of developmental continuity, at least into the school years. Finally, it started to reveal how the specific circumstances of a child's development could strongly modify a child's temperamental disposition. Although the study has been criticized for failing to meet various criteria of reliability and validity, this frequently happens for studies that develop the first systematic measures in an area (Rothbart &

Bates, 2006). It usually takes time and considerable trial and error to work up optimal measures. Moreover, in longitudinal designs, it may be difficult to change a measure at later ages, even when its shortcomings are fully realized, as a changed measure might prevent direct comparisons with results at earlier ages.

Modern Approaches to Studying Temperament

Researchers have now developed more sensitive and accurate ways of measuring infants' temperament in terms of their behavior in particular settings. One especially promising measure, the Infant Behavior Questionnaire-Revised (IBQ-R) describes temperamental differences between infants in terms of three major dimensions: surgency/extroversion (such as exuberance, sociability, and approach, as well as impulsivity), negative affectivity (such as sadness, fearfulness, and irritability), and orienting/regulation or effortful control (such as effective shifting of attention, ability to focus on tasks, and behavioral inhibition). This questionnaire involves asking various caregivers specific, detailed questions about the infant's behavior. For example, where an older questionnaire might ask parents to rate their agreement with the statement "Child is very energetic" on a five-point scale (Buss & Plomin, 1984), the IBQ-R might ask, "When put in the bathwater, how often does the baby splash or kick?" and require caregivers to rate the frequency in the past week (Hwang & Rothbart, 2003). The second questionnaire leaves less room for different interpretations of what is being asked and over what time period. Questionnaires like this one, which ask about more focused, concrete behaviors, produce more reliable and valid results.

Thus, by focusing on specific behaviors and incorporating responses from several adults who regularly spend time with the infant, the IBQ-R helps reduce the influence of parents' subjective judgments. As a result, there is typically good agreement among an infant's different caregivers (Gartstein & Rothbart, 2003). In addition to questionnaires on temperament and the kinds of interviews with parents that Thomas and Chess used, researchers also observe children directly in their homes and in laboratory settings (Rothbart & Goldsmith, 1985; Rothbart et al., 2000). These converging methods help researchers focus on those aspects of temperament that are more consistently found across many situations (Goldsmith et al., 1999).

Researchers are also examining how the development of the brain's networks that regulate attention may relate to the emergence of individual differences in temperament (Posner & Rothbart, 1981; Rothbart et al., 1995, 2008). As the brain systems underlying attention (for example, the prefrontal cortex and anterior cingulate gyrus) mature, infants and young children develop the ability to focus and shift their attention, becoming increasingly able to direct their attention away from unpleasant aspects of a situation to focus on more pleasing ones. As a result, they become better able to inhibit and control their actions and perceptions (see Chapter 4; see Jackson, 1865/1958), which also significantly influences their ability to regulate their emotions and other aspects of their social development.

Because differences in attention play a role in early-emerging variations in temperament, researchers have started to ask whether variations in growth rates of the brain's attentional systems might help explain how some temperamental differences unfold over time. In fact, children appear to show different rates of maturation of these attentional systems, which may give rise to differences in temperament (Morales et al., 2005; Posner & Rothbart, 2009). A child who is less able to shift attention away from an unpleasant situation or thought might well develop a different kind of responsiveness to everyday situations (such as a crying younger sibling, an angry parent, or a frightening dog) and might sometimes develop more serious problems controlling attention that could lead to anxiety and depression (Racer & Dishion, 2012). Researchers are also finding that the development of the different neural networks that support specific attentional abilities—like purposefully shifting attention or ignoring distractions—seems to be influenced by different genetic pathways. Thus, one way that genes may contribute to variations in temperament is by fostering different developmental patterns in specific attentional capacities (Posner et al., 2010).

> **Q:** How can studying the development of infants' attentional systems help us understand their individual differences in temperament?

Another approach to studying temperament focuses on the temperamental differences between infants who appear inhibited and those who seem uninhibited (Kagan, 1994, 2008). Inhibited infants and young children are more likely to be fearful and tentative in novel surroundings, such as a trip to a new store or meeting new neighbors, whereas uninhibited infants show more positive emotions and exploratory behavior in these settings and enjoy the novelty. Distinguishing between inhibited and uninhibited behavior might seem to describe a single dimension of behavior, related to how eagerly the infant engages with her world. But a leading researcher in this area, Jerome Kagan, believes that infants' inhibited behaviors actually have different biological bases than their uninhibited behaviors (Kagan, 2008). In addition, these two tendencies toward either wariness (inhibited behavior) or ready engagement (uninhibited behavior) can affect other aspects of temperament, because these tendencies interact with the degree to which certain kinds of emotions are expressed. In particular, uninhibited infants are more likely to express positive emotions, such as happiness, and inhibited infants are more likely to express negative emotions, such as fear.

Kagan suggests that the development of inhibited and uninhibited behaviors in infancy shows some significant patterns that seem to be human universals. For one, children throughout the world show increasingly inhibited behaviors in response to unexpected or unfamiliar events during the first two years of life. Kagan has argued that these kinds of inhibitions were important adaptive behaviors that promoted safety and survival by inducing the child to pay attention to stimulus discrepancies and not to approach or get involved in unfamiliar events (McCall & Kagan, 1970). If a child was not old enough to know how to interpret the world's real dangers, the best strategy might be to prefer what has been safe in the past and to be wary of novelty. Infants' tendency toward inhibition could also trigger distress sounds, like crying, that attracted caregivers' attention to potentially dangerous situations.

This wariness of novelty has also been documented in other species as an important behavioral strategy. For example, as some frustrated homeowners know, rats are notoriously "bait shy"; they have an enormous aversion to switching from a familiar diet to a substance with a new taste (Garcia et al., 1972). Similarly, one of the most powerful ways to contrast breeds of dogs is in terms of their different, genetically rooted levels of inhibition, or fearfulness (Mahut, 1953; see Figure 7.12). Although these differences might be influenced by the way owners interact with their dogs, different breeds' tendencies toward inhibited (fearful) or uninhibited (bold) behaviors are robust enough to demonstrate that these temperament-like differences can have a strong genetic component (Jones & Gosling, 2005; Saetre et al., 2006). More broadly, these comparative studies of genetic differences in animals' temperament-like traits can shed light on how we view the origins of human temperament. Because a wide range of organisms with quite modest cognitive and attentional skills show genetic variations in behaviors such as boldness, wariness, and fearfulness, some facets of human temperament may also not require the kinds of sophisticated cognitive appraisals and attentional processes that have been invoked elsewhere. Thus, some of the oldest evolutionary roots of human temperament may not depend on sophisticated information processing (Gosling, 2001).

Kagan argues that inhibition can have considerable value in protecting young children from the hazards of the world, but only in moderation. Excessive inhibition, which can give rise to inappropriate levels of shyness, can cause problems for children if it leads them to be overly fearful and avoidant of new people and situations. Kagan and his coworkers have found that children who were very inhibited at age 2 continued to show high levels of inhibition and shyness several years later, in elementary school (Kagan, 1994). Similarly, infants who showed notably uninhibited behavior remained more uninhibited and exuberant into elementary school. More recent studies of these same children are finding that these patterns continue into adolescence and adulthood (Kagan et al., 2007; Schwartz et al., 1999, 2003).

> **Q:** What are some evolutionary arguments for inhibited behaviors across species?

More than most approaches to temperament, the research focusing on inhibition tries to tell a coherent story of how an early trait becomes manifested in later personality differences such as shyness. Indeed, this research has documented reliable correlations between early behaviors in infancy and behaviors that emerge over the course of later childhood and into young adulthood. Kagan developed

A   B

FIGURE 7.12 Temperaments in dog breeds. Different dog breeds, such as **(A)** the border collie and **(B)** the terrier, tend to have different temperaments. A shyness/boldness dimension is one of the strongest contrasts among breeds.

his approach from an evolutionary perspective, asking about the potential adaptive value of both inhibited and uninhibited behavior, and he has repeatedly emphasized the importance of cross-cultural data for showing that the developmental courses of both inhibited and uninhibited behavior patterns are universal. Finally, he has advocated a move away from describing children by using traditional emotion terms ("a fearful child") toward describing how they respond to specific situations ("a child who shows inhibited behavior when encountering a stranger in a store"). Studies of differences in inhibition therefore provide an excellent demonstration of how one facet of infant temperament projects forward through childhood and beyond. One major reason for the success of this approach may be that it focuses on an evolutionarily ancient and foundational aspect of temperament that has an important adaptive role throughout development. We now turn to other aspects of temperament that are more richly integrated with higher-level cognitive and attentional processes and in which the links between infant temperament and personality are more subtle and complex.

Linking Temperament to Personality Development

Ultimately, researchers who study infant temperament and those studying personality in older children and adults want one smooth, integrated account showing how temperament develops into personality from infancy to adulthood (Caspi, 1998). Though there is not yet a single account of this process, we can say, in broad terms, that initial aspects of temperament likely interact with each other, contributing in complex ways to the development of personality traits throughout childhood and adulthood (see Figure 7.13). For an example of

how these interactions might work, consider the personality trait of conscientiousness, which can refer to being meticulous and careful or to acting in accord with one's conscience. Conscientiousness is not present in infancy, as it develops out of the interaction of specific components of early temperament. Thus, as Figure 7.13 illustrates, this trait slowly develops as a result of the interplay between activity level and persistence/attention span. A highly conscientious individual needs relatively high levels of both attentional monitoring and activity to remain vigilant as to her progress toward her goals and to be able to act quickly and efficiently. An excess of either vigilance or activity, however, could lead to distractibility and impulsivity, so the most conscientious people may be at the high, but not extreme, ends of these temperamental dimensions. These interactions between aspects of temperament are also influenced by culture and social experiences, so that infants with very similar temperaments can develop remarkably different personalities. In the next section, we will address how such environmental influences on temperament and personality take shape.

Child-Environment Interactions and Goodness of Fit

In thinking about the role of a child's environment and experiences in the development of personality, we need to keep in mind that different sorts of environments, cultures, and parents might "fit" much better with some sorts of infants than with others. Thomas and Chess, who conducted the New York Longitudinal Study discussed earlier, referred to

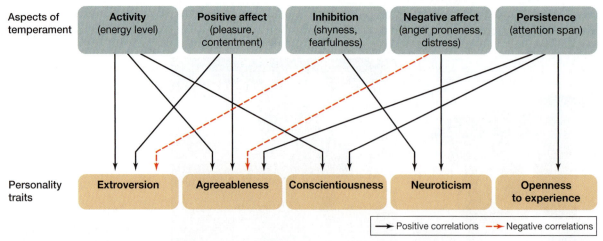

FIGURE 7.13 Linking infant temperament to personality. Linking measures of infant temperament to later personality measures is difficult. This figure illustrates one proposal about how such linkages might be organized, where black lines represent positive correlations and dashed red lines represent negative correlations. The multiple effects and possible negative and positive influences help illustrate why it is so difficult to translate infant measures into adult ones. Adapted from Caspi (1998).

this idea in terms of the **goodness of fit** between the child and the environment. In essence, the notion of goodness of fit maintains that the same environment is not optimal for all children and that an environment that could devastate some children might have little or no negative effects on others. This idea also implies that most children can flourish if they experience an environment well suited to their temperament.

The idea of goodness of fit helped launch a major shift in how we view infants and children, both within the study of development and at large. Many earlier views of development were based on the notion that children were passive recipients of whatever the environment threw at them. In contrast, the idea of goodness of fit stresses the ways in which children are active agents, whose interactions with caregivers and with their environment help to shape their development (Sameroff & Chandler 1975). The broad influence of goodness of fit has changed our ideas about the formation of personality, differences in children's learning styles in the classroom (Cronbach & Snow, 1977; Snow, 1989), and many other aspects of development. As a result, we now see children as actively seeking the best-fitting environment (for example, the environment best suited to their intellectual development; Scarr & McCartney, 1983) and parents and others (such as gifted teachers) as altering the environment to better fit each child. In the strongest terms, this concept also suggests that some environments might even have opposite effects on different types of children, helping some and hurting others. As we will see, there is now evidence to support these claims.

Q: How does the idea of goodness of fit relate to the notion of infants and children as active participants in their environment?

Environments for "Squeaky Wheels"

A little reflection on the different aspects of temperament discussed so far suggests ways in which these features might enhance or diminish outcomes, depending on the infant's environment. For example, the saying "the squeaky wheel gets the grease" means that those who complain loudest fare better than others. This adage also suggests how some babies' temperaments might confer an advantage in environments involving competition for scarce resources.

In particular, we might expect "difficult" babies to show better developmental outcomes than "easy" babies in impoverished environments. A study of infants born in parts of East Africa during a drought confirmed that the "difficult" infants, although certainly not thriving, had better health outcomes and lower mortality rates than the "easy" infants

(Devries & Sameroff, 1984). It is easy to imagine how a stressed, undernourished parent would find it difficult to monitor whether all of her children were receiving equal resources and instead might simply respond to the children who appeared most distressed.

Undoubtedly, difficult children also gain an advantage in other kinds of environments of scarcity. For example, we might predict that the worse the ratio of caregivers to children in a day care setting, the more likely that difficult children will get a greater share of attention, as overburdened caregivers are reduced to responding to the children who are most obviously upset. Similarly, children of impoverished families, especially larger families in which there is much competition among children for attention and resources, might fare better by being difficult (Garmezy, 1993). The outcomes associated with being a difficult infant or child also differ cross-culturally. One source of these differences has to do with how parents in a particular culture perceive the vulnerability of children and how those perceptions interact with their own child's temperament. Thus, parents who view infants as vulnerable to the influences of evil spirits and other negative forces are likely to be quite responsive to children who show high levels of distress because they are likely to perceive the distress as a sign of real danger. In contrast, parents from a culture that views young children as less vulnerable might see the same kind of behavior as whining and try to discourage it (Cervera & Mendez, 2006).

Q: Under what conditions might difficult and irritable temperaments in infants actually work to their advantage?

Parental Influences on Temperament

In talking about interactions between a child's environment and her temperament, it is easy to overlook the ways that parents themselves affect a child's environment. In fact, even in identical settings, different parents can create very different experiences. For example, if a new mother is frequently distracted from what is going on around her because she is depressed, an "easy" baby might suffer from neglect because he would not call attention to his needs, whereas a more "difficult" baby who cried frequently for attention might receive adequate, if not cheerful, attention. In terms of goodness of fit, then, it seems unfortunate that children of depressed parents are often more inhibited than their peers (Kochanska, 1991). But as this example shows (and as we will continue to see), it is difficult to draw conclusions about causality based on these kinds of correlations between parents' and children's behaviors. A correlation that seems to show a parent's behavior affecting a child may really be more strongly influenced by the genes that the parent and child share, manifesting in different ways in children and adults. Thus, we can ask: To what extent is the child of a depressed parent more inhibited because of the kind of parenting she experienced? And to what extent are her inhibitions related to genetic factors that she has in common with her depressed parent?

Because birth parents and their infants share genes that might put them both at risk for certain behaviors and interaction patterns, adoption studies look at adoptive parents, who do not share any genes with their children, to find a way to ask about parental effects that are solely environmental and that do not also arise from shared genotypes. For example, one study of adopted infants and their adoptive parents asked how the adoptive parents' dispositions (in this case, their tendency to be anxious or depressed) affected infants with different temperaments, despite the fact that the infants and adoptive parents did not share any genes (Leve et al., 2010). In the study, 9-month-old infants were allowed to play with an attractive toy for a while and then were separated from the toy by a clear plexiglass barrier, which clearly induced frustration in the infants. The critical measure was how long the infants continued to stare at the barrier, the source of their frustration, rather than disengaging from the upsetting event. Infants considered at genetic risk for emotional regulation problems (because their biological parents had such problems) were more likely to stay fixated on the barrier when they also had adoptive mothers who showed high levels of anxiety and depression. This study illustrates two closely related points. First, it shows the importance of gene-environment interactions for developmental outcomes. At-risk infants do not invariably become fixated on frustrating barriers; they only do so when they experience specific kinds of parenting. Similarly, infants who are not genetically at risk for emotional regulation problems may not develop such problems, even when they experience parenting that might well promote these kinds of difficulties in at-risk infants. Second, this study shows how research designs that help to rule out particular influences can provide insight into development. Thus, the adoptive parents' behaviors influenced their children's temperament in ways independent of a shared genotype.

Q: How might a pair of monozygotic twins nonetheless develop different temperaments in infancy as a result of being reared by different adoptive parents?

As a result of their own personalities, particular caregivers mesh better with some sorts of infants than with others, and the best matches, or "fits," depend on both partners in the interaction. Recognizing that the development of early aspects of temperament are inherently interactive helps us understand why accurate measures of temperament are very difficult to develop. The interaction patterns between an infant and a caregiver form a dynamic system that is constantly changing based on the responses of both people involved. Consider a baby who, early on, is difficult—often fretful or crying and rarely content—perhaps because of an undetected earache. Some parents will find this difficult behavior extremely hard to handle, and they may begin to think about the baby in ways that reduce affection, leading to less patient behavior on the parents' part and, in turn, even more difficult behavior from the infant. The infant's increase in difficult behavior then causes more negative parental reactions, and the ensuing feedback loop can escalate negative behaviors on both sides, as shown in Figure 7.14.

Different parents might see the same early behaviors in a more positive light, interpreting them as an indication that their child is strong-willed. Or perhaps the parents would observe the infant's behavior in other situations before drawing conclusions. In such cases, the initial behavior might enter into a different feedback loop that channeled both parental and infant behavior in a much more pleasant direction, as shown in Figure 7.14. As we will see again in Chapter 16, clinicians may suggest that parents who are having difficulties with their children try to "reframe" how they construe the children's behavior (and likewise that the children reframe how they construe their parents' behavior). In some cases, such a change in interpretation can interrupt a dysfunctional feedback loop and lead to a cycle of interactions that gradually promotes more positive behaviors from both parents and children.

Several years ago, I came to know a family that used skillful reframing to deal with a challenging child. From birth onward, this boy had exhibited many "difficult" characteristics. He was extremely overreactive to change, flying into unpredictable rages even at minor problems. To most, these behaviors were enough to label the child as impossible, and he soon was setting records in his community for expulsions from preschools. One preschool director even went so far as to declare him a "juvenile delinquent" at the age of 3 (he lasted a very short time in that preschool)! These problem behaviors continued as he grew older, and by elementary school, he seemed to spend more time in the principal's office than in the classroom. Despite these negative behaviors, the boy's mother never framed his temperament purely in negative terms. She showed serious concern about her son's emotional problems and inappropriate behaviors, but rather than seeing him only as "unstable" or "impossible," she viewed these qualities as tradeoffs that come with a

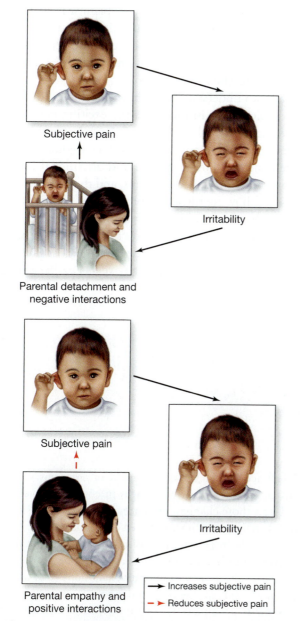

FIGURE 7.14 Interaction patterns. Two different parents might have dramatically different interactions with an infant who has an earache. A parent who finds the infant's irritability aversive may withdraw and react negatively, exacerbating the subjective pain of the earache, which increases the infant's irritability, causing even more negative reactions from the parent in a downward spiral. A different parent might react in a manner that reduces (dotted red line) the infant's subjective pain and the level of irritability.

(Labels within figure:)
Subjective pain
Irritability
Parental detachment and negative interactions
Subjective pain
Irritability
Parental empathy and positive interactions
→ Increases subjective pain
- ▶ Reduces subjective pain

"fiery" and "spirited" disposition. In countless subtle but important ways, she helped to channel these aspects of her son's temperament into behaviors that were inspirational and exciting rather than antagonistic—and that boy is now a successful, charismatic adult. The kinds of behavior that caused such problems early on were turned into passion, enthusiasm, and, as his mother always saw it, "fiery" and "spirited" behavior.

Of course, not all behavior problems can be addressed by reframing, and there are many dangers in seeing one's children as incapable of wrongdoing. But when parents can strike a balance between taking behavior problems seriously and creating a "best-fit" environment for the child, the results can help to guide the child's temperament toward a very positive adult personality. To some extent, this influence undoubtedly involves helping the child to seek out environments and situations in which his best traits can flourish. The degree to which parents can influence or change a child's personality remains a controversial question, a topic to which we will return in Chapter 14. Even if the child's basic personality structure is not subject to much direct parental influence, however, parents may well influence the positive or negative ways in which that personality is seen.

Conclusions

While the focus on the early development of emotions and personalities may seem very different from the discussion in previous chapters of how we perceive and think about the world, strikingly similar themes emerge here as in earlier chapters. Research on the development of emotions, temperament, and personality is undergoing dramatic change. Infants are increasingly viewed as active seekers and creators, not only of their environments, but also of their own emotions, temperaments, and personalities. Rather than simply responding emotionally to a particular event or having features of temperament and personality impressed on them from the outside, they are constantly interpreting the world and using those interpretations to act on it. These interpretations and actions give rise to emotions and also contribute to aspects of temperament and personality.

Emotions also have an adaptive value that allows infants to regulate their own responses and their interactions with others. Along these lines, different personalities and temperaments have different advantages and drawbacks, depending on the environment. This has fostered the idea of goodness of fit—namely, that individual infants and children may flourish optimally in quite different environments. There is no such thing as a standard, ideal environment in which to raise children. The adaptive orientation has also led to a shift toward describing infants' behaviors, thoughts, and emotions in terms of their goals and how they perceive their ability to pursue those goals in specific situations, which is a key part of both the functional and evolutionary perspectives on emotions.

Emphasizing the adaptive value of early emotions and traits also leads developmental researchers to consider the extent to which emotions and temperamental styles might be targets of natural selection, preparing humans and other species to link specific emotions to certain kinds of stimuli or situations. Similarly, some dimensions of temperament, such as inhibition and wariness, may help infants learn the subtle tradeoffs between being cautious and exploring new opportunities.

There seem to be more and more suggestions that cognitive and attentional factors play a central role in evoking and possibly even forming many emotions as well as qualities of temperament and personality. Along these lines, developmental changes in cognition and attention may help to explain many aspects of the development of emotion, temperament, and personality. Exploring these cognitive and attentional contributions may bring insights into the distinctly human aspects of temperament and personality, as opposed to those shared across many species. They can also help us to understand how the more complex emotions might emerge from the basic ones present in early infancy. Moreover, cognitive

and attentional factors can help to explain why many facets of an individual's early temperament do not translate directly into later personality traits but instead interact with many developing cognitive and attentional skills that affect the individual's developing personality.

Finally, an understanding of how emotions and temperament develop early in life offers the exciting possibility of uncovering relationships between various components of emotions and personality in adults. Developmental studies can demonstrate how cognitive and attentional strategies can powerfully influence emotions, and they may help us to understand how sophisticated processes of emotional regulation, such as reframing and reappraisal, work in adults. Similarly, developmental research that reveals the order in which particular emotions emerge can also suggest what kinds of situations elicit the later- versus earlier-emerging emotions in adults.

STUDY AND REVIEW

SUMMARY

Emotional Development

- Emotions are transient states that correspond to physiological and cognitive processes associated with distinct internal sensations, or feelings. They have been studied in terms of facial expressions and evolutionary signaling, physiological arousal, situational appraisal, and goals.
- We all share the same range of emotions, even as we vary dramatically in the extent to which we express particular types of emotions. Young infants, even newborns, also seem to show distinct emotions, as indicated by their varying facial expressions and behaviors in different contexts.
- Newborns initially experience positive and negative states that gradually differentiate into joy, surprise, and distress at 3 months, as well as anger at 4 months, and then fear at around 6 months.
- Infants do not show the full range of emotions that older children and adults do. One way of explaining this developmental change is to consider how cognitive interpretations of goals, situations, and their resolutions combine with basic emotions to create more sophisticated emotions.
- Complex emotions include shame, guilt, embarrassment, pride, jealousy, envy, and empathy, many of which are self-conscious emotions that require some degree of self-awareness. Social and cultural contexts play a role in differentiating and shaping emotions, including the moral emotions.

- A full account of the development of emotions will likely involve an integration of changes in cognitive development and how those changes influence the appraisals of situations and thereby create more nuanced emotional states.
- Even young infants seem sensitive to others' emotions and can distinguish basic emotions based on tone of voice. They are especially sensitive to negative emotions such as fear or anger, which helps them avoid danger.
- In some social situations, one individual's emotions can be readily transmitted to others. This phenomenon of emotional contagion seems to emerge very early in development as an intrinsic part of human social interactions.
- Through processes of emotional regulation, even infants can influence the emotions they experience and how they experience them. Emotions can be regulated through situation modification and selection, attentional deployment, and response modification. Initially, caregivers help infants regulate their emotions, but over time, infants begin to regulate their own emotions to a greater and greater extent.
- Some emotions, most notably phobias, seem evolutionarily prepared to be associated with certain stimuli. Fear of snakes is one such prepared association. Infants may have an early-emerging bias to track potential threats like snakes and spiders rather than flowers. Other emotions, such as disgust, may be similarly linked to special situations and kinds of stimuli with major adaptive significance, although cultural

factors may also play an important role in channeling and honing these prepared responses. This evolutionary perspective on the functional role of emotions may shed light on how emotions develop.

Temperament and the Origins of Personality

- Variations in emotions and other responses to stimuli contribute to differences in temperament among infants and young children.
- There is considerable evidence for temperamental differences among young infants, which gradually develop into personality differences. These developmental paths involve complex patterns of interactions between children and their physical and social environments, in concert with their biological predispositions.
- The New York Longitudinal Study classified infants into easy babies, difficult babies, and "slow to warm up" babies. Later studies measured infants' temperaments based on their behavior in particular settings and also found major dimensions on which they differed, including surgency/extroversion, negative affectivity, and orienting/regulation.
- Researchers have studied brain structures and neural circuits to understand differences in temperament. They have found that attentional structures and the ability to inhibit and direct attention may play a role in temperamental differences. Moreover, reactivity to novel situations may also play an important role in temperamental differences between inhibited and uninhibited infants.
- Different kinds of parents, environments, and cultures may "fit" better with some infants than with others. This idea of a goodness of fit between the child and the environment stresses that children are active agents who help shape their own development.

THOUGHT QUESTIONS

1. In some cultures, people may be more prone to feel the emotion of guilt, while in other cultures, they may be more prone to feel the emotion of shame. How might cultural practices influence a child to adopt a guilt versus a shame way of experiencing emotions? How might the cognitive components of these emotions differ?
2. How might a child's own actions make her a more active partner in the construction of her personality? Think of some specific actions and how they might influence particular aspects of her personality.
3. Would emotional contagion be more likely among those who are more like you—that is, members of your in-group? Would children and even infants also show such in-group effects?
4. How might certain forms of attentional training improve the emotional regulation skills of children? Design such a training program and consider the feasibility of actually implementing it.
5. The notion of goodness of fit argues that children with certain temperaments and personality traits may thrive in very specific environments and not in others. In what environment might a painfully shy child show an advantage over other children?

KEY TERMS

amygdala (p. 233)

attentional deployment (p. 239)

basic emotions (p. 230)

complex emotions (p. 233)

display rules (p. 239)

emotional contagion (p. 237)

emotional regulation (p. 237)

emotion (p. 228)

functionalist approach (p. 230)

goodness of fit (p. 253)

Machiavellian emotions (p. 234)

negativity bias (p. 236)

phobias (p. 242)

response modification (p. 239)

self-conscious emotions (p. 233)

situation modification (p. 239)

situation selection (p. 239)

temperament (p. 247)

PART III
Developing Competencies

8

Language Development

The Structure and Complexity of Language
- Components of Language
- Universal Constraints on Language

Acquiring a First Language
- Developmental Patterns
- Child-Directed Speech

Theories of Language Acquisition
- Behaviorist Approaches
- Connectionist Approaches
- Statistical Learning Approaches
- Nativist Approaches

Discovering the Meanings of Words
- Linking Words to Concepts
- Constraints on Word Meanings
- Developmental Changes in Word Meanings

The Growth of Grammar

Effects of Age on Language Acquisition
- Acquiring Language after the Critical Period
- Acquiring American Sign Language after the Critical Period
- Inventing a New Language

The Domain Specificity of Language
- Neural Dissociations
- Species Specificity

Language and Thought
- Linguistic Relativity and Linguistic Determinism
- Language as an Amplifier of Thought
- Influences of Cognitive Development on Language

Language and Communication

Conclusions

Summary

A few years ago, I spent a long train ride sitting behind a young toddler and his mother in a nearly empty car, which made it quite easy to hear the mother and her son talking. In the course of those few hours, their communication revealed many of the patterns and tendencies that drive one of the most intricate and impressive developmental processes: language acquisition.

Even without attending closely to what the mother and child were saying, it was clear that a real conversation was occurring. The mother would say a sentence or two and then the child would respond, so that their exchanges maintained a tempo with active turn-taking on both sides. The child sometimes mislabeled things, such as calling a huge office building a house, and he often constructed statements in grammatically incorrect ways—for example, saying "I seed boat!" or "No take nap!" The mother, in turn, rarely pointed out these mistakes, although she sometimes responded to the child by using the corrected form, saying, for example, "I saw a boat, too." In addition, the mother spoke differently with the child than with the conductor, using shorter sentences, a higher-pitched voice, and slower, more careful pronunciation.

How did this child, at barely 2 years of age, become able to utter systematic, meaningful streams of words, when a year earlier he may have not been speaking at all? How can we explain the error patterns in this early speech, which are common and reliable, but are not the kinds of mistakes ever made by mature speakers? And what role do parents and other adults play as young children's guides to language learning?

Nearly all children proceed from showing no evidence of language use in the first year of life to producing and comprehending complex constructions in their third year. Few other patterns of developmental change are more clear and dramatic. Language acquisition is not an intentional intellectual achievement, like learning to play chess; language is acquired automatically, and apparently effortlessly, by almost all children in the first few years of life (see Figure 8.1). A language that emerges in this way is known as a **natural language**, which typically refers to any language spoken on a daily basis by a community. It is so uncommon for a child not to acquire any language (including sign languages, which are full-fledged languages like spoken languages) that most of us will never meet or hear of anyone who is completely language free. Acquiring language is an achievement that is so commonplace that it is easy to overlook the extraordinary complexity of language itself, which makes children's language development so impressive.

One indication of the complexity of language acquisition is the great difficulty this process poses for computers. Even though computers far outperform humans at many

A

B

FIGURE 8.1 Learning language versus learning to play chess. The rules and computational complexities underlying the language of a preschooler far outstrip those of learning to play chess, and yet virtually all 3-year-olds seem to effortlessly learn language, while only a small handful of preschoolers learn to play chess, and only then with a large amount of explicit instruction and deliberate effort. Indeed, many would regard this chess photo **(A)** as implausible and probably staged, while seeing the chatting preschoolers **(B)** as perfectly natural.

other complex tasks, humans are unmatched in the ability to learn and use languages. For example, several chess-playing computer programs that run on a standard personal computer can beat all but a few thousand humans, but it is much more difficult for computers to learn the nuances of language. There are a great many ways that a chess game can unfold, and as with language processing, the chess-playing program has to analyze complex, novel structures and patterns and interpret them to compute a response. What makes chess so easy for computers, while language learning and processing is so difficult?

To begin to answer these questions, we will briefly consider some general properties of all languages before examining how children acquire language. We will consider the developmental changes in the kinds of things children say as their language develops, as well as changes in how others speak to children as they grow older. We will consider several theoretical models—behaviorist approaches, modern connectionist approaches, statistical learning approaches, and nativist approaches—each offering a different explanation of how language acquisition takes place.

We will then turn to how children decipher word meanings and how such meanings might change with development. We will discuss how children develop the ability to put together words in ways that follow the rules of a particular language, asking in what ways the ability to acquire a grammar might be constrained and whether children could create a new grammatical language largely on their own. Building on these discussions, we will ask about the extent to which linguistic abilities constitute a separate domain of cognitive development and whether these abilities seem to be uniquely human.

The relationships between language and thought also raise a host of fascinating developmental questions, such as whether specific languages guide thought in particular ways and whether language development amplifies the power of thought as the child matures. We will also ask how the child's cognitive development might, in turn, influence her language abilities. Finally, we will consider language as part of a broader social, communicative system that involves phenomena such as metaphor and irony. Our first step is to get a better sense of the workings of language itself.

The Structure and Complexity of Language

All languages allow us to constantly produce novel sentences that were never uttered before. Using a relatively small number of basic linguistic components and rules, we can create a boundless variety of unique expressions. This characteristic of language, known as its **generativity**, is surprisingly powerful. By one calculation, the number of possible English sentences of 20 words or less is 10^{20}—that's 100 billion billion sentences (Pinker, 1994)! If it takes roughly 5 seconds to hear a sentence, it would take 100 trillion years to hear all those sentences if you listened for 24 hours a day.

Using a finite system, our brain, we can comprehend and produce an infinite set of utterances. It is likely that no sentence in this paragraph has ever appeared in print before, and yet, as you read these novel sentences, you can easily and automatically judge whether they make sense and are well formed. Researchers in linguistics aim to specify the kind of human knowledge that allows us to make such judgments and to make them in distinctive ways for each

of the world's languages. The related task for developmental psychologists is to explain how this mastery of language emerges in childhood.

Components of Language

To get a clear picture of language acquisition, we need to understand the main components that make up language's multilayered structure. The most common distinctions have been between *phonology*, *semantics*, *syntax* (a major component of grammar), and *pragmatics*.

Phonology is concerned with the sound patterns of a language and the rules for combining sounds into words. Thus, a phonological rule in a Boston dialect of English states that "r" in the final syllable position should be omitted; hence, "Harvard" is pronounced "Harvad." Similarly, in some dialects of African-American English, if a consonant is in an unstressed syllable, it cannot be followed by either an "r" or an "l"; hence, "protection" is pronounced "potection." Within a language, the smallest units of sound that create differences in meaning are called **phonemes**. For example, in the words "pin" and "thin," the differences are /p/ and /th/, and these sound units (or phonemes) change the meaning of the two words. In normal speech, more than 800 distinct phonemes are rushing by each minute. By age 3, most children can track almost all of these phonemes. Most 3-year-olds can also use phonetic rules to segment these sounds into words, allowing them to easily identify most of the words they hear in spontaneous speech. To understand the difficulty of this task, listen to a burst of speech in an unfamiliar language and try to determine the number of words. Then compare your guess with a native speaker's tally. To most adults the task seems impossible on first exposure to a new language; yet young children master it with apparent ease.

Semantics tells us not only the meanings of individual words but also how words combine to convey larger meanings. Thus, semantic analysis tells us why the sentence "Every arrow hit a target" has two potential meanings (*each arrow hit its own target* or *all the arrows hit the same target*). The set of words that a person knows is often called her **lexicon**. As children gain semantic knowledge, they develop more extensive and elaborate conceptual knowledge of categories (though it is also possible to understand some conceptual categories without having words for them).

In the context of language development, **syntax** traditionally refers to a set of rules concerning how words are combined into sentences. Knowledge of syntax is sometimes equated with knowledge of a language's **grammar**, but grammar also refers to knowledge of other rules beyond those governing relations between words, such as relations between elements inside words (for example, how words are constructed from roots). Because of the rules of English syntax, "Venetian blind" means something quite different from "blind Venetian," and saying that "surgeons are butchers" is different from saying "butchers are surgeons."

Finally, **pragmatics** is concerned with how we use language to convey our intended meaning within a particular social context and how we figure out others' intended meanings. Pragmatics, for example, helps us understand if an utterance is meant literally or sarcastically. Thus, pragmatics involves taking into account the inferred goals and motivations of a speaker, the status of those involved in the speech act, and other nonlinguistic cues to intended meaning, such as situational constraints, gestures, and tone of voice.

Each of these aspects of language has an extraordinary richness and complexity. Our ability to understand and use these components of language results in a single, unified language competency. Here we will focus primarily on syntax and semantics, largely because those are the two areas in which most of the experimental research has been conducted.

> **Q:** What are some key components of language?

Universal Constraints on Language

One of the most interesting discoveries in the study of language in recent decades is that all languages show some of the same **universal constraints** on their structural patterns. These constraints take the form of consistent rule patterns across all languages, which result in specific structural features that all languages share (Bouma et al., 2001; Crain & Lillo-Martin, 1999; Maratsos, 1998; Richards, 2001). Consider one example. The sentence "Mary was amazed at how quickly she wrote the paper" has two possible meanings. "Mary" and "she" could refer to the same person (if Mary was surprised by her own speedy writing), or they could refer to different people (if Mary was surprised by another woman's quick work). Yet in the sentence "She was amazed at how quickly Mary wrote the paper," "she" and "Mary" cannot be the same person. This pattern of relating pronouns to noun phrases is not just a facet of English; it occurs in all known languages, and it arises from a quite abstract constraint on how pronouns are structurally embedded within sentences. A rich repertoire of similar constraints applies to all known languages, and the most fascinating thing about them is that *everyone honors them* without being told that they should. Universal constraints may play a pivotal role in guiding the acquisition of a first language. Thus, if a child already "knows" such constraints or somehow learns them very early on, she will be able to greatly narrow down the possible meanings of sentences that she hears. In addition, in her attempts to figure out the particular grammatical rules of her language, she can use the universal constraints to narrow down the possible rules quite dramatically, tacitly knowing that certain structures would never occur.

Acquiring a First Language

Language acquisition reflects a wide range of developmental changes, from the growth of a child's vocabulary to mastering intricate sentence structures. As we begin to explore language acquisition, it is useful to start with a broad overview of some of the major developmental patterns that shape the process. Later in this chapter, we will look more closely at how those patterns occur. Throughout this chapter, we will keep in mind that there is more than one way to measure and describe language abilities. In general, children tend to be able to comprehend what others say before they develop the ability to produce language themselves. Thus, while this chapter often describes the emergence of a particular language skill in terms of children's speech production, it is important to be aware that when this same skill is measured in terms of children's comprehension, it may appear earlier than their ability to display that skill in production.

Developmental Patterns

Although the age at which children show their first linguistic accomplishments varies considerably between individuals, there are some general patterns for the emergence of various aspects of language (see Brown, 1973; Clark, 2009; de Villiers & de Villers, 1978; Guasti, 2004; Pinker, 1995). Between the ages of 1 and 6, the average length of children's utterances (roughly the number of words), their vocabulary, the number of syntactic constructions (combinations of words to form primitive sentences), and their use of embedded sentences (relative clauses within sentences) all increase dramatically. But these different aspects of language often show their own distinct patterns of change. For example, the length of children's utterances starts to increase rapidly around age 3, long before they show a sharp rise in their use of embedded clauses, around age 5. In the following sections, we will see how these different patterns unfold over the course of acquiring a first language.

Prelinguistic Perception and Communication Long before children start to say intelligible words, they are paying attention to and producing aspects of language. As we saw in Chapter 3, very young infants actually perceive a larger number of distinct speech sounds than adults do. But with more exposure to their native language, infants stop perceiving phonemic differences that are not meaningful in their language. For example, the Japanese language does not require speakers to differentiate between "r" and "l" sounds. Consequently, Japanese infants can distinguish between those sounds more easily than Japanese adults. Long before they speak, infants learn which phonemes matter in their own language and which ones they can ignore. This process of learning to *categorically perceive* meaningful differences between sounds helps infants to begin making sense of the full range of speech sounds in their language. Clustering sounds into categories (such as all "ba" sounds or all "pa" sounds) allows many of the language's nuanced, intermediate sounds to be treated as equivalent. As a result, these sound categories make it much easier to learn the language's other rules for combining sounds. (Without categorical perception, every minor variation on a speech sound could seem to require its own rules.)

Although infants produce a variety of **prelinguistic vocalizations** in the first few months, ranging from lip smacking to cooing and squealing, consonant-like sounds do not normally appear until infants begin **babbling**, sometime after the fourth month of life. Babbling infants do not appear to be trying to express word meanings; rather, they are exploring the sounds in their language to get a feel for them (Pinker, 1994). Deaf infants babble aloud at a later age and with less frequency than do hearing babies, but if they are exposed to a sign language, they soon begin "babbling" with their hands, trying out the basic components of a sign language much as hearing babies do with sounds (Petitto & Marentette, 1991). Brain activity during babbling seems to occur largely in the left hemisphere, the region that typically supports language abilities, which suggests that babbling may be an important precursor of the brain's language system (Holowka & Petitto, 2002).

Babbling is also a way to start mastering a language's phonemes, which, as we have said, are the smallest units of sounds that cause contrasts in meanings (as in the initial sounds of "bin" and "thin"). As infants learn to combine phonemes in ways unique to each language, they begin to build up their language's **morphemes**, which are its smallest units of meaning. Morphemes can be individual words or parts of words that carry distinct meanings, such as prefixes (for example, "anti-" or "re-") or suffixes (like the "-s" that indicates a plural). Throughout the first year, infants are also mastering the rising and falling pitch patterns that are central to identifying and using words in all languages. For example, in English, a rising pitch at the end of a sentence can indicate a question. In tonal languages, such as Chinese, the meaning of a word may depend on whether the speaker's tone rises or falls at the end. Well before they can say recognizable words, infants start to produce the pitch changes that characterize their language (Davis et al., 2000).

As children start acquiring language, they also increasingly show joint attention, the ability to interact with another person about an object of common interest (see Chapter 6). Thus, as children begin acquiring words, they already are able to establish a shared point of focus with another person and to know what a speaker is talking about. Joint attention may even be essential for normal language acquisition (Bruner, 1995; Tomasello, 1999).

One-Word Utterances At about age 1, most children utter one word at a time, typically referring to concrete objects (for example, "doggie," "teddy," "Mommy") but also to actions ("up") and properties ("hot"). The predominant one-word utterances are sometimes referred to as **holophrases**. A holophrase can stand for a whole sentence that the child has in mind as a linguistic entity but simply cannot produce (Bloom, 1970). By this account, a child who raises both arms toward a parent and says "up" doesn't just mean the action but means for the word to stand for a sentence such as "I want you to pick me up" (see Figure 8.2).

A

B

FIGURE 8.2 **One-word utterances.** Even in complicated situations in which a young child clearly seems to be trying to describe an entire event, such as **(A)** a dog chasing a stick or **(B)** wanting to be picked up by her mother, she may only be able to utter one-word sentences to describe what she means, such as saying "stick" or "up."

Multiword Utterances At around 1½ years of age, many children start to put together strings of words in utterances of two or more words. Typically, these several-word sequences take the form of rote, inflexible phrases. For example, at around this age, our youngest son began saying "time to go now," but he didn't leave words out ("time to go") or insert new words ("time to go right now") until several months later. It is rare for children this young to combine words creatively.

At this point in the language acquisition process, children show dramatic individual differences. Some seem to hold off any attempts at multiword constructions until they have reached a high level of proficiency. Though the story is likely an exaggeration, the British historian and author Lord Macaulay supposedly spoke his rather surprising first words to a party guest of his mother's. After the guest apologized for spilling hot tea on him, the young Macaulay is said to have responded, "Thank you, Madam, the agony is sensibly abated" (Pinker & Bloom, 1990). Stories like this one help illustrate that children's ability to understand language can develop well before they begin using words in combination. The first words children speak may provide only a rough indication of their underlying linguistic abilities.

> **Q:** Describe three different aspects of language that change during the first few years of life.

Children's initial multiword utterances are typically two words long, which is why children at this point are said to be in the "two-word stage." (This limit is not absolute, however; occasional three- and even four-word combinations are also possible.) In the two-word stage, children's utterances show highly consistent patterns. They tend to convey certain kinds of relationships, such as connecting an agent with the object of an action (agent-object) or linking a possessor with a possessed object (see Table 8.1). In addition,

children at this stage very often express these relationships using the same word order that is most common in the language that they are trying to acquire (Braine, 1976; Brown, 1973). In English, for example, an agent who performs an action (agent-action) is typically named before the action.

After the two-word stage, children begin to vary their sentence length, up to about 10 words. These long sentences can appear as early as age 2, although there is usually a gradual lengthening of the average utterance length over several years. When children first start to combine words into phrases, they usually drop out words that are less important to convey meaning, such as articles and prepositions. Thus, instead of saying "The man picked up the brush," a child might say "Man pick brush," a speech pattern called **telegraphic speech**. Like the senders of telegrams, who had to pay by the word, children seem to face huge processing "expenses" associated with using many words in a single utterance—so they use only the words needed to communicate the gist of what they mean. In more modern-day parlance, we might refer to this as "texting speech."

Linguistic Rules Over the preschool years, children undergo extraordinary changes in grammatical competence as they master many more levels of language's complexity (Pinker, 1994; see also Crain & Lillo-Martin, 1999; Ingram, 1989). These changes suggest that even very young children's use of language involves rich, abstract mental rules. For example, many young children initially indicate questions by simply making a statement with a different tone of voice. Thus, a child might ask if he can ride a train by simply saying "I ride train?" with the rising intonation pattern of a question. Later, he might ask a question by putting a "wh-" word at the beginning of a sentence, as in "When I go home?" Only much later do children master the more subtle nuances involved in forming correct questions (Klima & Bellugi, 1966). During the preschool years, children also gradually master the ability to use a pronoun to refer to a proper name in a distant part of the same sentence (for example, "John knew it was important to wash

Conceptual Relationship	Word Orders Found	Word Orders Not Found
Agent-object	"Daddy book" "doggie sock"	"book Daddy" "sock doggie"
Agent-action	"Mommy read" "Daddy break"	"fall Mommy"
Action-object	"eat dessert" "bounce ball"	"dessert eat"
Possessor-possessed object	"dog tail" "Mommy tea"	"tea Mommy"
Object-location	"sweater chair" "man car"	"chair sweater" "car man"
Object-recurring	"more cookies" "more juice"	"milk more" "cookies more"

TABLE 8.1 Early two-word utterances. Even though young children may rarely produce utterances longer than two words, they still honor word orders that conform to those that adults normally use in their language.

himself before making dinner") and to use complex sentence structures, such as one sentence embedded within another (for example, "Mary saw the dog that ran across the street after the cat").

In short, children learn the rules of their language even though their understanding of those rules may be largely tacit and based on abstract principles that they are not aware of. This enables them to have reliable intuitions about novel constructions, an ability that was vividly demonstrated in a classic study by Jean Berko-Gleason (Berko-Gleason, 1958). Berko-Gleason examined three different English noun endings that make plurals: an "es"-sounding ending, as in "glasses," "matches," and "patches"; a "z"-sounding ending, as in "dogs," "caves," and "tubs"; and an "s" sound, as in "books," "hats," and "caps." A rule is considered generative if it creates novel patterns never heard before but that still honor the rule based on familiar patterns. Berko-Gleason's clever insight was to ask children to complete sentences that used novel, artificial words that nonetheless strongly obeyed the three plural patterns. A child would be shown a picture of two creatures (see Figure 8.3) and would be told, "This is a wug. Now there is another one. There are two of them." Then the researcher would say, "Now we have two_____" and look expectantly at the child. Most children immediately offered "wugs" as an answer. Like adults, they automatically inferred that the ending would be pronounced like a "z."

This kind of generalization may seem obvious, but consider the minimal sort of knowledge a child would have to possess to be able to consistently make such judgments. Since the child has never heard any of the words before, she could not simply have memorized what plural endings went with what specific words. Instead, she might be using a more abstract principle concerning how certain consonants are combined with other consonants and vowels to make plurals. One such rule would be roughly of the form: All nouns ending in unvoiced stop consonants are pluralized by adding an "s" sound. If the rule were precisely of this form, the child would know an abstract rule that most adults are not consciously aware of. This rule would be immediately available to the young child to guide judgments in the wug task. Alternatively, a child might represent the regularities in a simpler way that only gives the appearance of having rules. For example, she might remember a large array of words in both singular and plural forms and create networks of associations between the word forms she has already encountered that allow her to generalize to novel cases without having an explicit rule (Zapf & Smith, 2007). Perhaps simply noting how often certain forms occur and co-occur in speech for familiar words would be enough to use as a basis for generalizing to novel words. Later in this chapter, we will look at different theoretical approaches that try to explain how young children are able to generalize word forms.

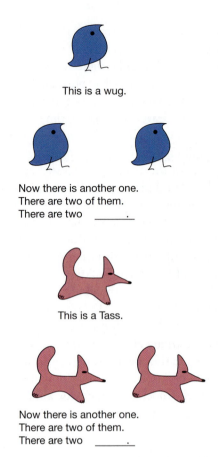

This is a wug.

Now there is another one.
There are two of them.
There are two _____.

This is a Tass.

Now there is another one.
There are two of them.
There are two _____.

FIGURE 8.3 Rules for plurals. In this classic Berko-Gleason task, young children seem to know a productive rule of pluralization, as they quickly and effortlessly know which of several possible plural forms go with novel words that they have never heard before. They know that the plural of *wug* is *wugs* and that the plural of *tas* is *tasses*. From Berko-Gleason (1958).

One other rule-related developmental phenomena is repeatedly encountered in language acquisition studies and is often called **overregularization**. Consider the ability to form the past tense for English verbs. Children often go through three distinct stages in their acquisition of this ability. Early on, they may make a number of mistakes but also frequently show some apparent mastery of the past tense forms of both regular and irregular verbs. Thus, a 2-year-old might be heard to say "kicked" and "liked" (regular past tenses) as well as "went" and "saw" (irregular past tenses). One might therefore conclude that the child is well on her way to mastering the subtle contrasts that adults use for past tense forms of verbs. Then, however, a curious thing happens: older children sometimes start to make more mistakes. They now take the regular form of the past tense (adding "-ed") and use it for some irregular verbs. This incorrect use of the regular form leads to such utterances as "John goed home yesterday" or "I seed it." These mistakes can persist for quite some time, even years, before the child once again starts to use the correct past tense of irregular verbs.

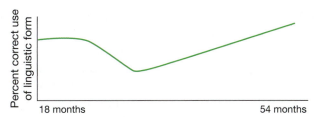

FIGURE 8.4 An idealized U-shaped developmental curve. These are some of the most intriguing patterns found in the developing child. They are often interpreted as reflecting the emergence of a new cognitive structure or a new rule that, in its initial stages, is used too crudely, and then becomes more carefully tuned. In the case of past tense forms, the emergence of a general "past = verb + ed" rule was thought to be initially overused with some irregular verbs and then gradually narrowed down to the right set. Later approaches tried to argue that U-shaped patterns could be modeled in distributed networks in which no specific rules were represented. Adapted from Marcus et al. (1992) and Marcus (1993).

Figure 8.4 shows an idealized version of this pattern, which holds true for other forms as well, such as regularizing irregular plurals (for example, "foots," "sheeps"; see Marcus, 1995). This kind of *U-shaped developmental curve* is one of the most intriguing and classic findings in developmental psychology (see Chapter 3). Such patterns have launched many debates about the underlying changes occurring in the child's mind (Strauss, 1982).

To understand this pattern, keep a few points in mind. First, the input does not change radically when children start to overregularize. Children of all ages are hearing essentially the same distributions of verbs and tenses. Second, irregular verbs are among the most frequently used in English, with the consequence that the majority of past tense verbs heard by children in normal speech are irregular ones with idiosyncratic past tense forms. When they start to overregularize the past tense "-ed" rule, they are therefore taking a pattern observed in a minority of instances and applying it to a broader range of cases. Third, parents rarely provide feedback to children about the correctness of such forms. They may laugh from time to time at the mistakes, but parents are generally unlikely to correct ungrammatical early utterances (Braine, 1971; Brown & Hanlon, 1970). Fourth, children usually have never heard these incorrect overregularizations in the speech of others, so they are producing novel, incorrect forms on their own.

Given these considerations, this particular U-shaped curve has been said to represent children's discovery of the past tense "-ed" rule. Younger children may only be remembering individual verbs and their different forms on a case-by-case basis. Children might hear verbs such as "go" and "went" and store them separately in their mental dictionary (Ullman, 1999; Ullman et al., 2005), perhaps even noting that "went" is used more in situations talking about the past. As they grow older, however, children

discover the "-ed" rule, and even though it may occur in a minority of utterances, it is at least a clear rule. The discovery of this rule apparently suggests a broader pattern of use to the children than is seen in adult usage. Only with time and new insights into exceptions to the rule are the irregular forms once again mastered. The extent of the dip in this curve is often exaggerated, but even a small dip illustrates the classic developmental pattern.

When children as a group show a drop in performance, it is often taken as a strong sign of a developmental reorganization and the emergence of a new psychological system. We saw several clear cases in perceptual development; use of the past tense seems to be a case in language. This effect can occur in several other areas of language acquisition as well. The pattern is so compellingly explained by the notion of discovery and initial overuse of a rule that it is difficult to imagine that the children are not mentally representing abstract categories such as verb and past in a rule-like manner. As we will see later, however, this interpretation has been challenged by theories of learning that try to avoid any representations of abstract rules.

> **Q:** What have U-shaped developmental patterns traditionally been assumed to represent?

Child-Directed Speech

Adults do not talk to young children in the same way they speak to older children or adults. This special type of speech, which was previously called **motherese** (Newport et al., 1977) and is now known as **child-directed speech** or infant-directed speech, differs from other speech in many ways. When talking to young children, parents tend to enunciate their words very clearly and to speak more slowly and at a higher pitch. These differences tend to accentuate the boundaries between individual words and between phrases. Child-directed speech also uses simpler words and fewer words per sentence, and it tends to be more grammatically correct (Snow & Ferguson, 1977; see also Golinkoff & Alioto, 1995). When speaking to children, parents more often repeat and expand on the child's previous utterance, or respond by **recasting**, in which they paraphrase what the child has said (Bohannon & Stanowicz, 1988). In recasting, adults are unlikely to directly correct a child's utterance by saying it is wrong, but will use the correct form of a verb or noun in their responses. In general, child-directed speech is modified in many ways that highlight critical elements in the language.

Infants in all cultures prefer to listen to speech that has the characteristics of child-directed speech (Fernald, 1985; Werker et al., 1994; see Chapter 3). Yet, there is no evidence that children who hear more child-directed speech than others learn any language faster or better. Cultures vary considerably in the extent to which parents modify their speech to young children, yet the course of language acquisition does not seem to vary in a corresponding fashion (Ingram, 1989). Child-directed speech probably helps attract the child's attention, and it may make some aspects of language processing, such as word segmentation, easier (Thiessen et al., 2005; see also Fernald & Hurtado, 2006; see Figure 8.5). Even accounting for these influences, however, many intriguing questions remain about how children learn their first language.

> **Q:** How does child-directed speech differ from talk between adults?

Although differences in child-directed speech do not seem to affect how quickly children learn language, some other aspects of parent-child interactions may play a role. In one longitudinal study, mothers were videotaped while freely playing with their child. Researchers then examined the tapes to rate aspects of the mothers' responsiveness, such as their playfulness with their child or how often they imitated their child's utterances. Later, the children's milestones of language acquisition were tracked, including when each one spoke his first word, acquired his first 50 words, and first talked about the past. When the two types of measures were compared, the children of more responsive mothers tended to reach language development milestones at an earlier age (Tamis-LeMonda et al., 2001). Similarly, children whose mothers are more sensitive to their emotional states tend to achieve language milestones earlier (Nicely et al., 1999). Parents' interaction patterns may contribute to the considerable individual differences seen in the rate of language acquisition. As with the case of child-directed speech, however, these influences cannot fully explain children's basic ability to learn language. Using the right kinds of words can also have an apparent effect on vocabulary growth above and beyond simply using a lot of words. Even when controlling for socioeconomic levels and previous vocabulary levels, 3-year-old children who hear a more diverse and sophisticated vocabulary from their parents have larger vocabularies 1 year later (Rowe, 2012). Parental effects on language development may resemble the effects of fertilizer and water on plant growth; they are more helpful for explaining individual differences in growth rates than for describing the basic developmental pathway.

FIGURE 8.5 Child-directed speech. Parents adjust their speech in many ways when speaking to young children. These adjustments may help make some aspects of language structure more apparent to the child, but they do not explain how the child acquires language.

Theories of Language Acquisition

Over the years, there have been many competing models offering starkly different accounts of how children acquire language. Perhaps the most intuitively appealing model is that children simply imitate the language that they hear. As we saw in Chapter 4, even very young infants are capable of imitation. But there are two reasons why language is not simply learned through imitation. First, if what we mean by imitation is reproducing bits of what we hear, as a parrot does, then imitation clearly will not work as a model. Children are not at all like parrots or other animal mimics. If they were, they would not show the common problem of overregularization, and they would not be able to produce sentences they had not already heard. In fact, they would not be able to produce novel sentences at all if they simply stored parts of utterances and played back the most appropriate ones later.

Second, if we suggest that imitation is more flexible and that rather than imitating specific strings of words, infants imitate intentions, goals, and perhaps even rules, this explanation adds little to a model of language acquisition. If the infant is not imitating the speaker's actual spoken language but something much more abstract, such as underlying intentions or rules, then imitation only explains a general motivation. It leaves unexplained how a child discovers the rules or intentions that she imitates, since neither is directly observable. The question therefore remains how young children can learn linguistic rules from what they hear.

Moving beyond the superficially appealing but ultimately uninformative imitation account, we can consider several more detailed proposals about how language acquisition occurs. One major contrast between some of the most influential models concerns whether children acquire language through general learning mechanisms such as associations that work in essentially the same way as for acquiring many other forms of information (such as spatial or numerical knowledge) or whether children acquire important aspects of language through a learning mechanism specialized for linguistic information. This theme regarding general versus specific learning systems occurs in other areas of cognitive development, but it is especially salient in language acquisition. Here we will consider behaviorist models of language acquisition that favor the association-based general learning explanation and then related, more recent views known as connectionism and statistical learning. We will then turn to the nativist accounts, which tend to favor specialized learning systems, often those with specializations for abstract rules. As proposed earlier, young children may not be able to acquire language unless their language learning system "knows" some structural regularities of all natural languages from the start. Understanding the nature of what is already known, or what kinds of linguistic patterns are favored from the start, is the most central question of language acquisition. A child's ability to imitate may help him fine-tune some speech sounds or practice complex constructions (Speidel & Nelson, 1989), but it cannot explain the truly creative abilities that all children show as they master their mother tongue.

Behaviorist Approaches

Some theories about how children acquire language are based on broader accounts of learning that have been well known to psychologists for many years. As described in Chapters 1 and 4, these learning theories are meant to apply to all kinds of information. They are based on the idea that a few general principles, such as reinforcement to shape behaviors or the tendency to associate events that occur together frequently, are meant to explain all forms of knowledge and skill acquisition. Behaviorism, which stresses the ways that reinforcement shapes responses, dominated much of psychological research for the first half of the twentieth century. The prominent behaviorist B. F. Skinner believed that the same laws of learning that apply to rats and pigeons also apply to humans in their acquisition of language (Skinner, 1957). Skinner argued that parents and other caregivers gradually shape infants' linguistic response patterns, which gradually become more like adult language. For example, a child's babbling might initially appear random. Parents and others then respond more positively to babbles that resemble adult speech sounds and more negatively to those that do not, guiding and shaping the child's speech to become more like a mature speaker's. Moreover, it was thought that parents have the same effect on children's use of grammatical rules, reacting more positively as children utter strings of words that come closer and closer to adult grammatical patterns. To behaviorists, language acquisition seems to consist of learning the appropriate verbal "responses" in a variety of circumstances, making it a seemingly straightforward, easily measured object of study. Moreover, behaviorists never required any analysis of what goes on inside the mind of an infant or child; to them, all that mattered were environmental contingencies (see Chapters 1 and 4).

At first glance, the behaviorist account seems plausible. Children clearly learn the languages they hear spoken by those around them, and child-directed speech can influence patterns of acquisition. But a closer look at what is actually happening between adults and children during language acquisition reveals major problems with the behaviorist account. The most penetrating and influential criticisms of behaviorist models of language learning came from the linguist Noam Chomsky (Chomsky, 1959). Among his critiques, Chomsky pointed out that behaviorists assume that the learner needs direct, specific feedback, but he noted that parents rarely correct or compliment children's grammar in early utterances. Instead, parents devote most of their attention to the meaning that the child conveys (Brown & Hanlon, 1970). Consider a 2½-year-old who toddles up to her mother and says, "Mommy mostest pretty tonight." Virtually all parents would smile warmly—not explain to the child how her sentence was grammatically incorrect. Likewise, most parents would respond negatively to a rude, but grammatically perfect, statement by a child.

Behaviorist approaches would also predict that acquiring two or three languages at once should take a child much longer than learning just one language, since it would take more time for the child to experience enough positive and negative reinforcements for their speech in each language. In fact, bilingual and even trilingual children tend to acquire all their languages together at about the same rate as a monolingual child. They may experience minor early delays, but these seem to disappear just a few months into the learning process (Petitto et al., 2001).

Connectionist Approaches

Behaviorist approaches rely on simple learned associations between reinforced behaviors, but such simple associations have been insufficient to explain many aspects of language acquisition. In the 1980s, researchers introduced **connectionism**, a way of representing networks of associations based on computer simulations with multiple levels of associations. In at least some cases, the computer simulations can mimic what looks like the use of a rule even though the rule was never explicitly stated in the simulation. Connectionist approaches rely on associative mechanisms, but they are vastly more powerful than the early behaviorist explanations. Their power arises primarily from two innovative explanations of how language processing occurs. First, connectionist approaches propose that language acquisition depends on the brain's massive capacity for parallel processing—that is, handling many kinds of information simultaneously. Second, connectionism incorporates hidden layers of processing that go beyond overt associations learned through reinforcement. More broadly, connectionist approaches to language acquisition argue that the human brain operates like a computer. They emphasize that the brain can process vast amounts of information simultaneously and that it is made up of separate processing units that share information across networks of connections.

Most connectionist approaches fall within the empiricist tradition. They assume that cognition is built up from learned associations based on input from the environment and experience. But unlike the behaviorist approaches, which make this same assumption, connectionism also seeks to understand the mental processes, and even the neural structures, that underlie language acquisition. Thus, many connectionist theorists refer to brain anatomy and patterns of neural functioning to support their views (Rumelhart, 1989).

The computer models that are built by connectionist researchers test language acquisition theories by simulating the language learning process. When the two key ideas of parallel processing and hidden layers are supplemented with some general learning algorithms and rules, these software-based systems can often engage in surprising patterns of learning. They can, for example, represent several developmental patterns described earlier, including overregularization and the appearance of learning "rules." Thus, connectionist models have attempted to simulate the child's acquisition of past tense verb forms, including a pattern of learning that follows a U-shaped curve. Rumelhart and McClelland (1986) decomposed words into strings of phonemes and then presented them one at a time to a computer network. The computer was apparently able to learn the past tense, showing the same pattern of overregulariza-

tions typical of young children, without ever learning or explicitly representing the past tense "rule" anywhere in the system.

These results were criticized for several reasons, however, including concerns that the strings of phonemes input into the computer models were unrealistic (they differed from what a child hears) and that the computers were too powerful to provide a good model of children's language learning (Pinker & Prince, 1988). Later studies tried to rectify these concerns (Plunkett & Marchman, 1991) but had other shortcomings (Marcus et al., 1995). Currently, there is no consensus among language acquisition researchers about whether a connectionist model using a single associative process provides a better representation of the child's language development than a dual-process model consisting of both rules and associations (Bandi-Rao & Murphy, 2007; Marshall & van der Lely, 2006; Takac et al., 2012).

> **Q:** What is the associative versus rule-based learning debate?

Statistical Learning Approaches

Language learning can also be examined in terms of **statistical learning**, which is learning based on the probability of events occurring both at the same time and in sequences over time. In recent years, researchers have given renewed attention to statistical learning to study the early roots of language development, using statistical learning to investigate the relative roles of linguistic rules and associations in language acquisition in infants. Statistical learning approaches are often allied with connectionist approaches, which are computational models that rely on statistical patterns of inputs. In statistical learning approaches, researchers have asked how infants can distinguish words out of streams of continuous sounds. They have examined whether infants can recognize the probability of sounds co-occurring within words (that is, the likelihood that one sound follows another within a word) or occurring at the end of one word and beginning of another. In one study, 8-month-olds listened to uninterrupted strings of phonemes in which particular sets of sound patterns were repeated, suggesting words. For example, the string "bidakupadotigolabubidak . . ." would continue for several minutes, during which time the sound sequences "bidaku" and "padoti" each occasionally repeated, interspersed with other phonemes. After listening for just a few minutes, infants seemed to learn which groups of sounds in this string reliably occurred together as "words." When the recording stopped and was replaced by either familiar sound sequences ("bidaku" and "padoti") or unfamiliar ones (such as "dakupa"), the infants looked longer toward the speakers when the novel sequences played (Saffran et al., 1996). This result excited researchers because it seemed to show that infants have a rapid, powerful statistical learning ability for acquiring language and learning other nonlinguistic sounds (Bates & Elman, 1996).

Subsequent research found that young infants could also learn sequences of tones that recurred together within a stream of other tones but that did not sound like any language (Aslin et al., 1998; Saffran et al., 1999). In addition, after hearing particular sound sequences, such as "bidaku," recur within a stream of phonemes, children are more likely to later learn word labels that use those same sound sequences than they are to learn sequences using other sounds, such as "dabiku" (Graf-Estes et al., 2007). Apparently, the brief exposure to recurring sound patterns helps prime young children to learn that such recurring sound sequences can represent meaningful words that are associated with objects and categories (Lany & Saffran, 2010; Shukla et al., 2011). Statistical learning theorists suggest that young infants' ability to rapidly extract and use such complex recurring patterns from a continuous stream of sounds reflects not a language-specific system, but a much more general learning system that calculates conditional probabilities (that is, probabilities that a given event will occur given the occurrence of another event).

Can infants go beyond recognizing language's recurring sound patterns to learning its rules? To explore this question, another research team (Marcus et al., 1999) presented infants with phoneme sequences much like those described in the previous study (Saffran et al., 1996), except that the sequences that the infants heard taught them a rule rather than a relation between specific groups of sounds (see Figure 8.6). Rather than simply repeating the same elements in the same three-syllable order, the researchers presented the infants with different elements that followed a similar rule-based pattern. For example, to teach an ABA rule, the recording would repeat the same element before and after an intervening one, so the infants might hear "ga ti ga" or "li na li" and the like for about 2 minutes. In another condition that taught an ABB rule, infants would hear sequences like "ti ga ga" or "na li li." In the test phase, infants heard new sound sequences that either followed the old rule (for example, "wo fe wo" for ABA) or did not (for example, "fe wo wo"). In the test condition, the infants looked longer at the novel patterns that violated the rule, indicating their awareness of the rule and their surprise that the rule had not been followed. Moreover, infants who were only 7 months old (that is, 1 month younger than infants tested in the original study of phoneme sequences) recognized when a rule had been violated. A later rule-learning study showed the extra power gained

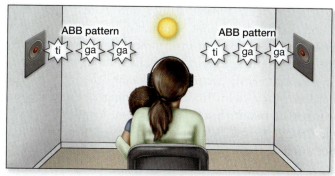

A Training condition

B Test condition

FIGURE 8.6 Learning abstract rules. In the Marcus et al. study, 7-month-old infants learned to recognize abstract rules such that a sound pattern that they had never heard before but that corresponded to an old rule was seen as familiar. The infants sat in a booth on their parents' laps (their parents wore headphones so that they could not influence their children) listening to sound patterns coming from side speakers. **(A)** During the training condition, after the center yellow light flashed, the infant was familiarized with the sound pattern (here ABB) coming from speakers behind red bulbs on both the right and left. **(B)** During the test condition, the infant was presented with different sound patterns coming from the speakers on the right and the left. A novel ABB sound pattern came out of one side speaker and a novel ABA pattern came out of the other side speaker. The researchers found that the infants looked longer at the speaker emitting the new ABA pattern that at the new ABB pattern that resembled the one they had heard during training, indicating their recognition of the rule and their surprise that it had been violated.

when information is combined across sensory modalities. When 5-month-old infants were presented with visual patterns that were associated with each syllable they heard in a speech stream, the infants looked longer at the shapes on the screen when they were presented with new syllables that corresponded to a new rule as opposed to an old one (Frank et al., 2009). Thus, with adequate support, well before the first half year of life, infants can learn abstract rules that are distinct from any specific sound sequences (see also Frank & Tenenbaum, 2011).

One challenge for statistical learning models concerns cases in which the syllable strings that infants hear vary in length from, say, one syllable to four. Can infants still learn to segment these syllable strings into words? One study found that neither 5- nor 8-month-olds could do so, even though they could do it easily when "word" lengths were the same (Johnson & Tyler, 2010). Even though the "words" of different lengths recurred predictably, the infants could not learn them. This finding is puzzling, because the real words that infants hear clearly vary in length (for example, "doggy," "ball," "banana"). It may be that infants need both to hear certain falling and rising pitch patterns associated with some word beginnings and endings and to see visual cues associated with objects to learn words of varying lengths. There may also be other statistical patterns, such as overall distributions of sound patterns, that are integrated together with conditional probabilities to help solve this learning problem (Thiessen et al., 2013).

Statistical learning approaches are becoming ever more diverse as researchers consider new patterns of frequencies, correlations, and contingencies in language learning, and formal ways of processing that information. One powerful technique is based on Bayes's rule, which provides a formal way of updating beliefs in light of new evidence. In terms of language learning, it is a way of confirming that certain rules hold. Based on new pieces of evidence, a child can become more or less certain of those rules, a process that is continuously repeated as the child encounters more and more evidence (Griffiths et al., 2012). Bayesian learning models provide ways of exploring how children of different ages, even when presented with the same evidence, might adjust the strength of a rule to differing degrees because younger and older children bring different kinds of prior knowledge to that learning event. In contrast to most connectionist models, in which rules are only tacitly present in a network, Bayesian learning models can apply statistical learning to the strength of explicit rules (Frank & Tenenbaum, 2011).

Before we close our discussion of behaviorist, connectionist, and statistical learning approaches to language acquisition, let's consider again the question of empiricism versus nativism. Empiricist systems are specialized to handle specific kinds of information *only* at the earliest parts of the learning process. As previously described, many statistical learning theorists view infants' ability to identify statistical patterns as evidence for a general learning system rather than a language-specific one. Connectionists have also noted that the basic features of a connectionist system—neural networks capable of parallel processing—make up almost all animals' brains. Thus, connectionists argue that humans acquire language and other species do not mostly because humans have a bigger, more powerful brain—not because the human brain is somehow tailored for the complexities of language. To understand this view, consider that relatively simple computers cannot run the complex software that runs easily on a more powerful computer. But if you look inside both computers, you will not necessarily find anything about the more sophisticated one that is tailored for that software. More likely, it just has sufficient memory and a fast enough processing speed to execute the intricacies of the program without crashing.

A different analogy is also possible, however. The two computers might differ not only in size and power, but also in their specific components. If the more powerful computer is able to run the software because it has a set of chips dedicated to processing graphics, while the other computer lacks such a device, then the first computer gains its unique capabilities from a specialized system. This second case is more like the nativist view of language acquisition, which we will turn to now.

It is important to acknowledge, however, that statistical learning approaches need not be squarely in the empiricist tradition. For example, a Bayesian learning model might grant that certain types of rules are so improbable that they can virtually never be favored based on new evidence, while other types of rules are so probable as to virtually never be discounted based on new evidence. If those rules and their probabilities are relevant only to language, then they can be seen as language-specific learning constraints.

Nativist Approaches

Nativist approaches emphasize the idea that humans are endowed with a specific brain system specialized for acquiring any natural language. That system would not work well for learning about spatial layout, number, or moral principles. But it must be able to acquire all natural languages, even though those languages vary widely at the surface level in terms of their grammatical rules and many other features. The nativists do not claim that the system specifies details, such as particular grammatical rules. Instead, they say that it includes abstract principles that guide learning about the structural patterns common to all languages. This specialized system, which is often called the **language acquisition device** (Chomsky, 1965), is thought to embody a great deal of implicit linguistic knowledge about all languages. Thus, it must be specialized for learning the kinds of abstract grammatical patterns all languages share, while remaining flexible enough to learn any particular language.

Over the years, Noam Chomsky has made a number of proposals about the nature of the language acquisition device. For example, he pointed out that the linguistic information that young children receive from other speakers is full of false starts, interruptions, and unfinished sentences. (Listen to any casual conversation, and you'll see how frequently sentences are interrupted or ill formed.) Because young children hear imperfect speech, Chomsky argued that what they hear is not a sufficient basis for learning language. This view, known as the **poverty of the stimulus argument**, holds that since children couldn't possibly learn language only by listening to others talk, they must already have some knowledge of the language's structure. (Even though adults often address young children with simplified, child-directed speech, the amount of this kind of speech that a child hears does not seem to predict how easily he acquires language.)

Nativists point out that in behaviorist theories of learning, the learner's incorrect responses must be corrected in order for the learner to make progress. But children receive only very rare, minimal feedback about their many early errors. This small amount of negative feedback seems insufficient to shape their many ungrammatical sentences into the correct, mature use of the language. Nonetheless, while children make many mistakes early on (such as "goed" instead of "went"), they still manage to correct themselves as they get older.

More generally, nativist approaches about the nature of the language acquisition device attempt to figure out how such a system might learn language effectively from only a few relatively simple, minimal inputs. Along these lines, they embrace the idea that the language acquisition device can use a few key bits of information, such as differences in intonation, as richly meaningful cues to linguistic structures.

Discovering the Meanings of Words

The speaking toddler seems like an utterly different creature from the preverbal infant. As the child labels objects and events, asks questions, and comments on situations, we gain new insights into his mental life. How do children learn word meanings as they transition out of a preverbal state to become more fluent users of language? How do children's language development and other emerging cognitive capacities influence each other? How do children learn to use language to communicate in ways that go beyond the literal, as in the use of metaphor or irony? Many researchers believe that in trying to answer these questions, we can come closer to understanding what makes us human. To begin to address these issues, we examine how children begin to learn word meanings.

Linking Words to Concepts

When a child learns a new word, she doesn't simply link that word onto a single object in the world. Instead, she links the word onto a concept, which then enables her to

apply the new word to various objects that correspond to the concept at hand. For example, a child who learns the word "doggy" doesn't just learn that a particular sound sequence is associated with the dog she has just encountered. Instead, she learns that "doggy" names a concept or class of things—roughly, furry, four-legged creatures that bark. This process of linking sounds that form words onto concepts is known as mapping. **Semantic development**, or the emerging understanding of word meanings and their interrelationships, requires linking words to concepts, which in turn often correspond to real-world phenomena. (There is not always a correspondence of words to real-world concepts, however, as we can learn words such as "unicorn" or "kryptonite" even though neither is real.) First, we will consider a few basic patterns concerning the growth of the child's lexicon, or the set of words he knows.

During the first year of life, many children speak no words at all and probably understand just a few. After about age 1, words start to enter the child's productive vocabulary (that is, the words that the child can produce or say) at the gradually increasing rate shown in Figure 8.7. The child initially starts acquiring words at a slow rate, but then that rate increases continuously over the next few years, hitting a peak rate somewhere around 4 years of age. By age 5, many children have vocabularies as large as 10,000 words (Anglin, 1993; Bloom, 2000).

The contents of words also change with increasing age. Many children's first words refer to concrete objects, although this pattern is subject to large individual differences. Early

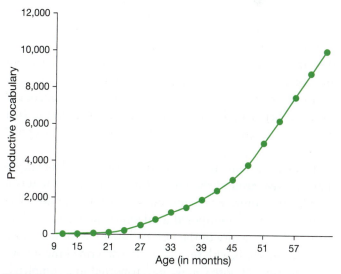

FIGURE 8.7 Vocabulary growth. The child's vocabulary initially grows at a slow rate, but then rapidly accelerates in later years. The actual vocabulary size can vary considerably across children. This example would be for a fairly precocious child. For most children, the rate gradually increases with age with no sharp spurts. Adapted from Bloom (2000) and Ganger & Brent (2004).

words for actions, such as "up" (for being lifted up) or "open" are also common. A child's first words also tend to be at an intermediate level of generality. Thus, a child is much more likely to first learn "dog" than either "collie" or "mammal." Levels of generality are predicted from the frequencies with which terms at the different levels are used by adults, and young children tend to linguistically encode the world at the level most often used by adults (Anglin, 1977; Brown, 1958a, 1958b; Horton & Markman, 1980; Mervis & Crisafi, 1982; Rosch et al., 1976).

Children do not require explicit training to increase their vocabularies. Sometimes parents do correct a child's mistaken word usage or point to a novel object or event and label it. But parents rarely provide children with full definitions, such as "A dog is a mammal that has four legs, a tail, and makes a barking noise. It is a social animal and has litters of roughly six puppies." For many words, such a complete definition would involve words that are beyond the young child's comprehension. The extraordinary speed with which young children seem to map words onto the correct concepts, sometimes as fast as 500 new words a month, is often called **fast mapping** (Carey & Bartlett, 1978). Fast mapping is thought to be possible because out of the universe of possible word meanings, children are somehow biased to infer only a relatively small subset, making the learning problem much easier, given the child's cognitive abilities.

> **Q:** What sorts of words are more common in the early stages of word learning?

These developmental patterns are fascinating because they reveal an extraordinary ability to learn words without any apparent explicit instruction. How is such a rapid and seemingly effortless process explained at the psychological level? To better understand this process, it is useful to first consider the nature of the challenge in more conceptual terms.

To a large extent, all the patterns in the growth of vocabulary revolve around the most central question: How is it possible to acquire word meanings at all? The philosopher Willard Quine (1960) posed a dilemma that can help illuminate the difficulty of the task children face as they learn to associate words with meanings. He described the following scenario: Suppose you were transported to a completely unfamiliar culture in an unexplored rain forest. You have been dropped off by helicopter and are standing alone in a clearing when a native of this culture comes along. At the same time, a rabbit hops into the clearing and the native gestures toward it and says "gavagai" (see Figure 8.8). How

A

B

FIGURE 8.8 Riddle of reference. (A) Quine's example of a person from a radically different culture uttering "gavagai" while pointing to a rabbit illustrates the riddle of reference. There is no way to know for sure whether the person means rabbit, rabbit parts, or any number of other meanings that cannot be distinguished by merely pointing. **(B)** The young child also seems to face this problem every time she encounters a new word (here "rabbit" as spoken by her father) and yet narrows down the set of possible meanings to a much smaller set that makes the learning of word meanings feasible.

can you tell what the native is talking about—that is, how can you translate the word correctly?

We will refer to this dilemma as the **riddle of reference**. It is impossible to tell whether "gavagai" applies to rabbits, the set of connected rabbit parts, or a rabbit-related event or action. Quine argues that we assume that "gavagai" means rabbit (and not rabbit event or parts) just because we share with the other speaker a common way of carving up the world into meaningful units. The scenario Quine describes is especially dramatic because no amount of experience could ever make you certain that you had understood what "gavagai" means. The information available from both the environment and experience is too ambiguous to ever distinguish between "set of connected rabbit parts" and "whole rabbit." Moreover, the learning process is complex even when the environment does enable you to clearly distinguish between meanings. If "gavagai" means "rabbit head," it would take a specific set of highly unusual events with incomplete rabbits to figure this out. Similarly, recognizing the meaning of the words for "rabbit fur" or "hopping rabbit" would require quite particular encounters.

The "gavagai" example bears directly on the challenge facing a young child as she begins to connect words with meanings. The child resembles the traveler in the clearing, except that in some ways the child's dilemma is more difficult. The traveler arrives with one language, which can be used to attempt to translate the unfamiliar terms. In contrast, the young child has no other language, so her task involves both translating the sounds into concepts and building new concepts to correspond with speakers' meanings.

> **Q:** How do theoretical problems with language translation lead to questions about the acquisition of word meaning?

Constraints on Word Meanings

The only solution to the riddle of reference is to assume that the child's choices among possible word meanings are limited somehow. Many types of **constraints on word meanings**, or ways of limiting the number of possible meanings that could be assigned to a given word, have been proposed. Researchers suggest that infants and young children have certain biases that guide them in determining what a word is referring to (Markman, 1989, 1992). Our purpose here is to consider how these different types of constraints help to solve the problem of connecting words with meanings. As Quine's dilemma illustrates, if a child entertained all possible meanings every time she encountered a new word, she would never be able to begin building a vocabulary. If, on the other hand, most possible meanings are ruled out from the start, word learning becomes feasible. In this way, constraints on word meanings do not really constrain the child; they liberate her by reducing the number of possible meanings (Keil, 1979). We will consider three types of constraints on word meaning: *perceptual*, *conceptual*, and *pragmatic* constraints. For this

system of constraints to help the child learn the meanings intended by others, the child must share the same sets of constraints with the speakers around her.

> **Q:** Why are constraints on word meanings considered essential to explanations of word learning?

Perceptual Constraints The first kinds of constraints on word meanings are perceptual constraints, which are biases toward certain interpretations of words that arise from the way our perceptual system naturally carves up the world into distinct objects and events. This process can involve all the senses, but most researchers have focused on vision. One example of a perceptual tendency that constrains word meanings is the **shape bias**, according to which objects of roughly the same shape are assumed to have the same name (and objects with different shapes are assumed to have different names). Toddlers show this bias in the lab when, having learned the name of a novel object, they are asked to pick something else with that same name from a pair of unfamiliar objects. Children as young as 18 months will choose the object with the same shape as the first object, rather than choosing an object that shares its same colors or textures. This attention to shape over the object's other properties suggests a bias to think that things with the same shape will have the same label (Landau et al., 1988).

> **Q:** How might an object's shape help word learning?

Conceptual Constraints Our perceptual biases are not the only influence on our choices of which things to name. We are also guided by conceptual constraints that make some kinds of categories or relationships seem more "natural" to label. Thus, even when there may be equally compelling perceptual features, some conceptual slices of the world are more easily mapped onto words (Arunachalam & Waxman, 2010a). For example, the **whole-object bias** describes our preference for labeling whole, bounded objects—rather than objects' parts or their relationships to other things (Macnamara, 1982; see Figure 8.9). For example, if 3-year-olds are presented with several unfamiliar tools, and each has one very noticeable part, they will still assume that the labels associated with these tools apply to the whole tool, not just to the part. More broadly, when

FIGURE 8.9 The whole-object bias. This bias assumes that novel words refer to whole bounded individuals and not to their parts, colors, textures, or other component attributes.

young children encounter a label for an unfamiliar object, they tend to assume that it applies to the object as a whole (Markman, 1989; Markman & Wachtel, 1988). This has the potential to greatly simplify first guesses about the referents of novel terms. Infants also assume that a novel word refers to a whole object as opposed to a property such as color or texture.

Infants also appear to make taxonomic assumptions, such that they prefer to attach labels to objects of the same kind (for example, five dogs or five balls) and not to relationships between objects (for example, five dogs chasing balls) (Markman & Wachtel, 1988). Moreover, children may also use Bayesian inference to acquire word meanings. Thus, it has been argued that when a child hears an individual label three dogs with the same label, she may infer that it is very unlikely that the speaker meant "animal" with the label and not "dog" because it is implausible that the speaker would have repeatedly picked just dogs and no other animals with a label meaning "animal" (Xu & Tenenbaum, 2007).

SCIENTIFIC METHOD: Early Use of Syntax to Guide Learning New Words

Hypothesis:

Even very early in syntactic development, children are able to use syntactic information to infer word meanings.

Method:

1. Seventy-two 19-month-olds were given practice watching videos with background narrations and choosing videos in response to questions.

2. In a test condition, children saw side-by-side videos in which an actor performed a novel action while another person stood by (intransitive action) or in which an actor performed some action on another actor (transitive action).

3. While looking at the videos, children heard either a two-noun sentence ("She is gorping her"), a one-noun sentence ("She is gorping"), or a neutral sentence ("Look here").

4. Experimenters scored the proportion of looking time for the two-participant event (transitive action).

Results:

Infants looked longer at the transitive video after hearing a sentence with two nouns. They had no strong bias to prefer either video in the neutral condition without nouns.

Conclusion:

Well before 2 years of age, infants will use the presence of one versus two syntactic categories (nouns) in a sentence to infer the meanings of novel verbs.

Source study: Yuan et al. (2012).

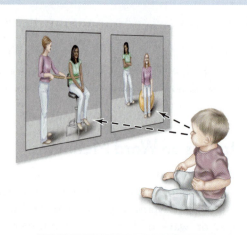

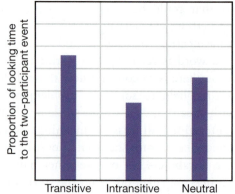

Finally, the surrounding sentence frame can give conceptual clues to new word meanings. Thus, if a speaker says "John flugged that Bill lives next door," we can constrain the meaning of "flug" to a class of verbs involving beliefs and attitudes (for example, "thought," "believed"), which generally are not understood until relatively late in development (Lidz et al., 2001). This is known as "syntactic bootstrapping" (Chierchia, 1994), early versions of which may be present when the infant is as young as 19 months (Yuan et al., 2012; see Scientific Methods box), but which is clearly evident by the time infants are 24 months (Arunachalam & Waxman, 2010b).

Pragmatic Constraints

Along with perceptual and conceptual constraints, the goals and beliefs attributed to a speaker may guide a child's understanding of what a word means. Such pragmatic constraints on word meaning come into play when the child infers what the speaker is referring to, thereby limiting where the child directs his attention (Tomasello, 2000). One pragmatic constraint, known as **mutual exclusivity**, refers to the assumption that each object in a language has only one label (Clark, 1988; Markman, 1989; Markman & Hutchinson, 1984; Markman & Wachtel, 1988; Merriman & Bowman, 1989). That is, if something is called a "hammer," then it is unlikely to be called by another name as well. To study how children use this constraint, researchers presented children with two objects—one that they were already able to name and one that they could not yet label (see Figure 8.10). While looking at both objects, the experimenter asked the child for an object by using an unfamiliar label. In this scenario,

FIGURE 8.11 Using the speaker's gaze. Children younger than 18 months old know that the direction in which a speaker is looking provides information about what she is speaking about. In this study, the experimenter used a mirror to covertly watch where the child was looking while the experimenter looked into a bucket and declared "It's a blicket." Even though the child did not know she was being observed, she checked the direction of the speaker's gaze to decide what the person was calling a "blicket."

children as young as 2 years old tended to choose the object whose name they did not already know. They apparently assumed that each object had only one label, so that the new label did not refer to an object whose name they already knew.

Other kinds of pragmatic cues also help children narrow down possible word meanings. For example, where parents look and the emotions they show influence how children interpret the things parents say (see Chapters 6 and 7). A series of elegant experiments examined how children as young as 1 year use the direction of an adult's gaze to help them understand what is being talked about (Baldwin, 1991, 1993). In one setup, at the same time that the child was looking at a toy, the experimenter would look into a bucket and utter "It's a blicket" (see Figure 8.11). The child would often look away from the toy to focus on the adult to see where his gaze was directed. Later, when the child was shown both the toy she had been looking at and the object that was in the bucket and asked to "point to the blicket," she would point to the object that had been in the bucket. These results argue strongly against the notion that children merely associate the words they hear with whatever they are looking at. Instead, even the youngest children took into account where the adult was looking. Children also rely on a speaker's mental and emotional state. Thus, if a speaker says, "Let's find the blicket" and frowns while looking at and touching two objects, but smiles while looking at and touching a third object, a 2-year-old will assume that the third object is the "blicket" (Tomasello & Barton, 1994).

FIGURE 8.10 Mutual exclusivity. This bias associates new words with objects that do not already have labels. If the child is confronted with two objects and knows the name of only one ("key"), she will assume that a new name ("magnifier") applies to the other object.

The Nature of Constraints on Word Meanings We have seen several examples of constraints on word meanings. Although the nature of these constraints remains controversial, it appears that they may reflect broad cognitive biases that extend beyond the process of word learning (Bloom, 2000). Consider the whole-object bias, for example—children's strong preference to attach new words to whole objects rather than to objects' parts or properties (Woodward & Markman, 1998). This same bias is also involved in tasks that have nothing to do with word learning (Bloom, 2000). In counting, for example, children show a strong bias to count whole objects as opposed to objects' properties (Dehaene, 1997). Like words, numbers are typically associated with whole objects.

The mutual exclusivity bias may also have a much broader basis. We do tend to think that if one object already has a label, then a new label must apply to something else. But more broadly, when we are engaged in conversation, we assume that the speaker will indicate shifts in topic. Thus, if the speaker introduces a new label rather than using a familiar one, we tend to assume that the label must apply to an object not yet named and that the new label is serving as a topic-shifting device (Clark, 1995).

Children could not learn word meanings without powerful ways of limiting the number of possible meanings. Several different combinations of constraints provide these limiting guidelines, and they appear to apply not just to words but to many aspects of cognition and communication. If there is a language acquisition device, it does not seem to be specialized for learning most word meanings. Instead, children usually acquire specific word meanings through using more general learning strategies (Bloom, 2000).

Developmental Changes in Word Meanings

Beyond the constraints that enable children to narrow down the vast number of possible word meanings, children's understanding of word meanings seems to change in fundamental ways over the course of development. Researchers have investigated this process for more than a century, exploring whether the changes in children's mental representations of words occur gradually or in distinct, qualitatively different stages.

Overextensions and Underextensions The studies of developmental changes in children's understanding of word meanings have focused on two common patterns that children show as they acquire new words. The first of these tendencies, called **overextension**, involves applying a word too broadly. For example, a toddler who calls any large, four-legged animal a "cow" has extended this label far beyond its true boundaries. A child might happily use this label for horses, pigs, and large dogs, and on a trip to the zoo might call zebras, elephants, and antelopes "cows" as well. This pattern is especially apparent in observational studies in which caregivers or other observers write down children's notable utterances each day. Those records often document overextensions because they are obvious and often amusing—as when a toddler starts calling all men "Daddy." On the other hand, the related pattern of **underextension**, in which a child incorrectly applies a word too narrowly, is much less noticeable, though also very common (Anglin, 1970). A child who underextends the word "doggie" by applying it only to dogs that look like the family pet might say "doggie!" when he sees a Labrador retriever or another kind of large dog but might say nothing in the presence of small dogs (see Figure 8.12). This underextension would probably go undetected by his parents and others.

Linking Features with Meanings One way to think about semantic development focuses on the features associated with word meanings. In particular, most researchers assume that people use certain perceptual and conceptual features of objects and events to help link words to relevant objects and events. For example, the meaning of "dog" is typically said to rely on both perceptual features of dogs, such as certain sizes, textures, and shapes, as well as conceptual features of dogs, such as being an animal, a living thing, and a physical object. Researchers who are studying semantic development have investigated how these semantic links between features and words develop, and they have asked: Are the developmental changes in children's understanding of word meanings linked to changes in the way they think about semantic features?

Overextension   Underextension

FIGURE 8.12 Overextensions and underextensions. While overextensions of word meaning are often easier to notice (and were more commonly recorded in early diary studies of children), underextensions also occur. The child might comment on something without realizing that a familiar name applies to it, or the child might say nothing at all.

One proposal suggests that the types of features children use to represent word meanings change with development. For example, younger children may focus on perceptual features, such as color, size, and surface texture, rather than functional or conceptual features, such as an object's use or whether it is dangerous. This view assumes that younger children are either unable to use some kinds of features or, at the least, have a strong bias against using them (Gentner & Rattermann, 1991; Landau et al., 1998; Nelson, 1973).

A second view suggests that the ways that children internally represent semantic features change. For example, younger children might take note of as many features of an object as possible to determine what its name means, whereas older children weigh only the few features they have determined are central to the meaning. To see how these theoretical approaches are translated into experimental studies, we will take a closer look at an example of this second type of proposal.

One way of envisioning how mental representations of word meanings develop is based on the idea that word meanings are made up of two kinds of features (Smith et al., 1974). **Characteristic features** are the properties most typically associated with members of a category. For example, characteristic features of jails include that they have bars on the windows and are highly secure. **Defining features** are the properties that pertain to what the word really means and how adults would tell whether it applies in a particular case. Thus, a defining feature of jails is that they are places where criminals are held. Not all words' characteristic and defining features can be easily distinguished, but for those that can, a possible developmental model emerges (Keil, 1989; Keil & Batterman, 1984). Perhaps younger children initially rely on characteristic features as the basis for word meanings, and then, as they get older, they shift to understanding word meanings in terms of defining features. Thus, they may undergo a shift from relying on characteristic features to emphasizing defining features for learning word meanings. This characteristic-to-defining shift could also help

explain younger children's greater use of over- and underextensions of word meanings. If a younger child puts a greater emphasis on the characteristic features of the most typical jails, she might call a well-fortified bank a "jail" (overextension), while not recognizing a more upscale jail as such (underextension).

In an experiment designed to discover whether children considered characteristic or defining features more important to various word meanings, researchers told preschoolers and elementary school children several pairs of descriptive stories created to pit an object's characteristic features against its defining features. For example, in one story, the children were told:

> There is a beautiful building with columns. Mr. Johnson lives there, but he has a big problem. There are these cracks in his floors and walls. So, he covers them with paintings and statues, and he never lets anyone see them. Could that be a museum?

This building has several characteristic features of a museum (it is beautiful, has columns, and is filled with art), but it lacks an important defining feature: no one is allowed to see the art inside. In contrast, the second story in this pair describes a building with the defining features of a museum, but not its characteristic features:

> There is this small wooden shack in the countryside. People come from all over and pay 50 cents to get inside and see the interesting display of dirty shirts with rings around the collar and spots and stains. Could that be a museum?

If younger children understand word meanings only in terms of characteristic features, they should identify the first example as a museum, but not the second. And if older children and adults base word meanings on defining features, they should do the opposite.

The results suggested that preschoolers more often base their notions of word meanings on characteristic features, and elementary school children more often use defining features. Nonetheless, this characteristic-to-defining shift does not occur for all words at the same time. Rather, depending on the words involved, it can extend from the preschool years on into adulthood. Words in some domains, such as terms for moral actions (lying, stealing, cheating) shift in the preschool years, while words in other domains, such as terms for kinship (uncle, aunt, grandmother) shift much later (Keil, 1989). Interestingly, the shift does not occur for each word separately; instead, clusters of closely related words shift at the same time, probably because the words have closely interconnected meanings. It is very hard, for example, to know the defining features of a husband without knowing those of a wife.

In short, children initially use characteristic features to understand word meanings, and over the course of development, they increasingly focus on defining features. Adults, too, show this pattern of semantic development as they progress from novice to expert in a particular area (Chi et al., 1981).

> **Q:** Give an example of a characteristic-to-defining shift in the development of word meaning.

The Growth of Grammar

We have seen that as children acquire word meanings, they seem to draw on general learning strategies and constraints that extend far beyond the domain of language. Learning grammar, however, may depend on much more specific mechanisms and constraints that are unique to language. The grammar of a language principally contains the syntactic rules for combining words, prefixes, and suffixes into well-structured sentences. In the first few years of life, the child's syntactic abilities develop rapidly, which has drawn many researchers to explore how these impressive changes unfold.

One theory that aims to explain how children come to use and understand syntax, known as the **principles and parameters approach,** was advanced by Noam Chomsky (Chomsky, 1975, 1981). This approach suggests that a common set of principles governs the internal structure of all languages—for example, the principle that all sentences must have a verb. In addition, because specific languages also vary in many ways, this view also holds that early in life, the child's mind contains a large number of possible linguistic forms or alternative parameters that become fixed, or set, according to the specific language the child learns—for example, whether the language requires that a sentence explicitly includes a subject or if it can be dropped and represented implicitly. Thus, while all languages share certain kinds of grammatical categories—for example, subject, verb, object—individual languages differ in terms of other factors that have to be set for each language—for example, how clauses are embedded within sentences or word order.

By analogy, consider the process of installing a new scanner. All scanners share basic features and use similar methods for transferring data, but they differ in the details of their resolution settings, error-checking routines, and the like. To set up a new scanner, you have to make a number of choices to make it compatible with your computer, printer, and perhaps other devices. Similarly, researchers following Chomsky hypothesized that the young child does not have to "start from scratch" to figure out most aspects of language structure. Instead, she has to figure out a relatively small number of "settings" appropriate to her own language.

One example of a language parameter is its **branching direction**, which refers to the order in which ideas typically occur in a sentence. English is a right-branching language, which is evident in the sentence "I saw the man who taught the child who had a broken arm." The embedded clauses in this sentence ("who taught the child" and "who had a broken arm") branch out after, or to the right of, the main verb ("saw"). Japanese, by contrast, is a left-branching language, so the ideas in this same sentence would typically occur in a different sequence, "Had a broken arm child taught man I saw," with clauses branching out before, or to the left of, the main verb. Children seem to learn very early whether their language is right or left branching and then "set" that parameter, which then guides additional learning about syntax.

Interestingly, the early-acquired parameter of branching direction has close connections with the rhythm ingrained in the sentences spoken to a child. Left- and right-branching languages are each associated with particular intonation patterns. As very young children listen to their native language being spoken, they may use these patterns to "set" the parameter for right or left branching even before understanding much of the syntax (Mazuka, 1996, 1998). Thus, children may get their earliest clues about grammatical forms from the **prosody** of the speech they hear—that is, its acoustic properties, such as intonation, rhythm, and pitch (Hirsh-Pasek & Golinkoff, 1996).

The branching direction of a language is just one of many possible parameters on which languages differ and that need to be "set" by the young language learner (Valian, 1994, 2009). In fact, one drawback of the principles and parameters approach is the difficulty of determining how many parameters are involved in the world's languages and how many "settings" or variations are possible for each language. This approach also leaves researchers with the significant challenge of understanding precisely *how* parameters become set in the mind of a young language learner. Nonetheless, the principles and parameters approach to syntactic development is appealing in many ways. It describes how languages' universals might occur in conjunction with their many differences. It offers a theory about how children might learn syntactic structures and patterns that are specific to their own language by setting a parameter, rather than having to start from scratch.

In short, learning syntax and grammar seems to require rich mental capacities to support children's ability to master the specific, elaborate rules of their native language using only the relatively simple cues that they hear. When it comes to finding clues to their language's complex underlying structures, children are good detectives, even if their detective work occurs largely outside of awareness.

> **Q:** What is parameter setting and how is it relevant to language acquisition?

Effects of Age on Language Acquisition

In addition to the overall constraints on syntactic structures that we have discussed, there are limitations on the periods during which syntax and phonology are acquired with ease. We can understand these limits by considering several kinds of evidence for such *critical periods*, including what happens when language acquisition occurs after such periods. Many of us have noticed that young children seem able to learn languages much more easily than adults. Such a pattern suggests a critical period for language acquisition—although, as we have seen, references to critical periods do not usually imply that learning becomes impossible after a certain point. Instead, critical-period effects usually refer to the way that certain behaviors or types of information, such as fusing visual information from the two eyes, singing a species-specific birdsong, or following one's parent rather than another moving object, become more difficult to learn after a certain point in development.

Some of the strongest evidence for critical periods for language acquisition concern our ability to learn a second language. Adults who move to a community where a language that is new to them is spoken will often speak the new language with an accent, even after speaking only that

language for decades. Yet, young children who grow up in bilingual communities become fluent (and accent-free) in both languages. This change in language learning ability typically occurs during the onset of puberty. These critical-period effects on language acquisition can show up clearly in siblings who emigrate to a new country at the same time—for example, at the ages of 8 and 16—and must learn its language. Even 40 years later, when the siblings are 48 and 56, the older one will probably still show traces of an accent, while the younger one will likely sound like a native speaker. Although some especially talented or hardworking individuals learn to speak new languages without an accent into adulthood, this is rare.

The language abilities of non-native speakers also differ in more subtle ways that reflect critical-period effects. Much like the issue of accents, our ability to learn the more complex aspects of a second language's grammar partly depends on the age at which we learn the new language. Researchers had bilingual adults listen to sentences recorded in English (their second language), then tested their ability to detect subtle grammatical errors in these sentences. These studies showed a gradual, continuous drop in the adults' English grammatical skills, depending on the age at which they began learning the language (Newport, 1990; Figure 8.13). Adults who had been introduced to English when they were under 5 showed grammatical abilities equivalent to native speakers, whereas those who learned English as older children or as adults did not perform as well. Thus, someone exposed to English for 30 years, between the ages of 20 and 50, might well show poorer command of subtle grammatical forms than someone exposed to the language for only 10 years, from age 8 to 18.

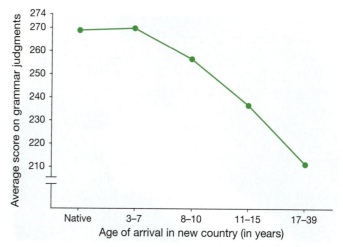

FIGURE 8.13 The critical-period effect for grammatical ability. When an average score is constructed for each person on a set of subtle grammar judgments in that person's second language, there is a clear decline in scores as the age of first arrival in the country of their second language increases. Adapted from Newport (1990).

Acquiring Language after the Critical Period

The most striking demonstration of a critical-period effect on language development would involve complete deprivation of exposure to any language until the critical period was over. This would enable researchers to find out whether language learning would still be possible beyond the critical period. Of course, deliberately depriving a human child of language would be immoral, but over the years, some relevant cases have emerged from the enormous variety of human childhood experiences.

For centuries, there have been reports of **feral children**— that is, "wild" children who spent infancy and childhood out of contact with other humans. The first well-documented case occurred in 1800, when a French doctor, Jean Marc Gaspard Itard, began studying Victor, "the wild child of Aveyron," who apparently had spent much of his youth roaming the forests of southern France without any human contact (see Figure 8.14). When Victor was discovered at the age of 12, he was reported to possess no language.

Itard attempted to carefully document the child's psychological development and particularly his abilities to learn new linguistic, cognitive, and social skills. Despite Victor's early promise, however, he never developed much

FIGURE 8.14 Feral child and language. Jean Marc Gaspard Itard studied Victor, "the wild child of Aveyron," a child who had lived in the woods without human contact until he was about 12 years old. When he was found, Victor could not communicate in words. Despite progress in understanding language, Victor never acquired more than a rudimentary ability to speak.

language ability, and Itard eventually grew discouraged (Itard, 1932/1962; Lane, 1976). It seemed as if there was a critical period for language and that by the time he was discovered in early adolescence, Victor had missed it.

More recently, another tragic case of a "wild" child occurred in the United States, which yielded more specific information about a possible critical period for language development. In 1957, Genie was born to parents who grossly maltreated her, at least partly because they regarded her as defective. She was born with a dislocated hip that required a cast (which her father prematurely removed), and she was improperly diagnosed as retarded because of her slow performance in an early pediatric examination—while ill with a high fever. Genie spent most of her childhood strapped to a potty or in a crib within an isolated room in a large house. During those years, she never heard another human utter a word (her parents only grunted and growled at her), and she was beaten for vocalizing any sounds (Curtiss, 1977; Rymer, 1992). When Genie was 13, her condition was discovered, and she was immediately moved to a foster home, and psychologists, social workers, and linguists worked to help her overcome her massive cognitive, social, and linguistic deficits (see Figure 8.15A). Finally, it was decided that the benefits of a more private life outweighed those of continued instruction and assessment, so her treatment was gradually discontinued.

Reports of Genie's language skills, compared with her cognitive and social skills, revealed a specific language learning difficulty. Even after 4 years of instruction and care (Curtiss, 1977), Genie differed most from other children with respect to language. While her nonlinguistic cognitive abilities had reached or surpassed the levels expected for an 8-year-old, showing that she had gone through rapid cognitive changes, her language skills lagged far behind.

With respect to language, Genie readily acquired new words, at least those for concrete objects, and her vocabulary continued to expand throughout the time she was studied. Genie also could perform adequately when she could rely on pragmatic cues to understand a speaker's intentions. For example, if someone in a room with her looked toward the open window and asked, "Genie, would you please close the window?" she would nod and go close it. (It is tempting to conclude that she understood the request. But if the person had instead looked toward the window and said, "Window" or "Don't close the window," Genie would likely have responded in the same way, simply assuming that the other person wanted the window to be changed somehow.)

Genie had much more trouble, however, when the task required her to understand linguistic structure. She entered the two-word stage rather easily, but then her progress slowed enormously. Although she did quite well at developing her vocabulary and in other areas of cogni-

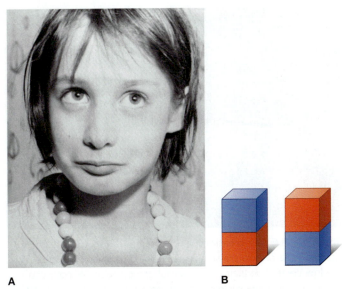

A   **B**

FIGURE 8.15 Genie and language acquisition. (A) A photo of Genie, who had been abused and not exposed to language until she was 13 years old. **(B)** After Genie was finally exposed to language, she rapidly learned many words but was never able to master syntax. For example, when she was shown two sets of colored blocks like the ones shown here and asked to either "give me the one that blue is on" or "give me the one that is on blue," she had great difficulty choosing correctly. This sort of task, which requires careful attention to syntax, was easy for much younger typically developing children.

tive development, Genie had considerable difficulty mastering aspects of syntax. For example, as a teenager, Genie did not perform as well as a typical 4-year-old at answering questions about the spatial relationships between two pairs of colored blocks, despite having had much more explicit instruction by that time than most 4-year-olds would have experienced (see Figure 8.15B). She also had not mastered the structures of negations, questions, or embedded sentences. Her grammatical development seemed far more impaired by her early experiences than other aspects of her cognition.

It therefore seems that, in those few well-documented cases, children who grow up without the benefit of human communication struggle to learn the grammatical structure of a first language at a later age. Domain specificity is implicated because in many other areas of knowledge acquisition they seem to progress rapidly and often become indistinguishable from other children of the same age.

Acquiring American Sign Language after the Critical Period

A different line of work on learning a language after the critical period has passed has looked at a group of people who experience relatively normal early cognitive and social envi-

ronments in all other respects: congenitally deaf children acquiring American Sign Language (ASL). About 90 percent of deaf children are born to hearing parents, and the time of these children's first exposure to ASL varies widely, usually occurring when the children enter a residential school that teaches ASL as the main language. Being exposed to ASL at an earlier age results in clear advantages at mastering some aspects of its structure (Newport, 1990). Even decades of immersion in ASL among congenitally deaf adults was not enough to make up for starting to acquire it a few years later than one's peers (see Emmorey et al., 1995; Mayberry, 2010). Many health agencies require regular screenings for deafness starting at birth, and the evidence for critical-period effects suggests that it is most beneficial to start ASL instruction as soon as the child is identified as being deaf.

The most common explanation of such critical-period effects is that an underlying capacity specific to language learning declines with age (Borer & Wexler, 1987; Lenneberg, 1967). We saw in Chapter 4 that some critical-period effects in other species, such as songbirds and barn owls, are rooted in the changes that take place in the brain as it matures. Similarly, in humans, there is evidence that critical-period effects on language learning are associated with brain maturation. People who learn another language later in life seem to rely on different brain regions for their second-language grammatical processing than do people who learn the additional language early on (Bloom, 2000; Kuhl, 2010; Mayberry et al., 2011; Wartenburger et al., 2003)—and comparable brain differences have been found for learners of ASL as a second language (Newman et al., 2002). Other explanations of the critical-period effects on language development have not been fully ruled out, however. For example, rather than causing a decline of a language-specific ability, maturation may cause a more general learning capacity to diminish, affecting language acquisition as well as other abilities (Greenfield, 1991). Although some controversies remain about critical periods for language (Birdsong & Molis, 2001; Hakuta et al., 2003), the effects have been found often enough to suggest that they are real, even though they are not yet fully understood (Clahsen & Felser, 2006).

Inventing a New Language

Perhaps the strongest test of whether the child comes into the world with a bias for a rich array of highly structured abstract linguistic patterns would involve demonstrations that children could invent languages on their own that honored the universal patterns of all languages. We have seen that this will not occur in cases where children are reared in total isolation, but perhaps the results would be different in settings where communicative partners are available.

One dramatic case of language creation involves deaf children. In some cultures that considered spoken language intrinsically superior to signed language, deaf children were never exposed to signs; they were only spoken to, with the assumption that they eventually would acquire spoken language through lip reading or other means (Neisser, 1990). Tragically, very few of these children could easily use even a dozen spoken words. Fewer still had much success with lip reading, a medium in which many of language's meaningful distinctions (for example, the difference between the sounds "pa" and "ba") remain ambiguous. In these situations, deaf children have sometimes developed their own unique signed languages, either with their speaking family members or covertly with other deaf children if the surrounding culture discouraged signing. These invented sign languages clearly show the essential core features shared by all the world's other languages (Feldman et al., 1978). When these children created a new language, they seemed to be implicitly guided by a set of universal principles shared with all other known languages. They may have arbitrarily chosen certain parameters to set because there were no clues from a surrounding language, but they were still guided by a skeletal set of universal constraints on syntactic forms.

Nicaraguan Sign Language is a recent, more detailed example of a language created virtually from scratch by deaf children (Kegl, 2002; Kegl et al., 1999; Senghas, 2010). Because deafness was stigmatized in Nicaragua, most deaf people there spent their time largely in their homes or those of relatives. They had few opportunities to meet other deaf people, and they rarely married or had children. Thus, over many generations, deaf children typically had hearing parents and grew up with no exposure to sign language and no peer group within which to develop it.

Groups of deaf children were brought together for the first time in Nicaragua when the government set up new schools for the deaf in 1979. Initially, the children had no common language, just their own individualized signs. But they soon started to share their signs and adapt them into shared ones (see Figure 8.16). Together, they invented new signs, and their language developed a richer, more elaborate structure. Researchers observed that younger children had more complex and more fluent forms of the new language than the older children (Kegl, 1994, 2002, 2008; Kegl et al., 1999), suggesting a possible critical-period effect in which the ability to create a new language from scratch is more powerful in younger children. The language, which is now called Idioma de Signos Nicaraguense (Nicaraguan Sign Language), was created entirely out of the minds of the first deaf children in Nicaragua to be educated together.

As amazing as the story of Nicaraguan Sign Language is, it is not unique. Deaf children have repeatedly been shown to spontaneously create full-fledged languages of signs (Brentari & Coppola, 2013; Goldin-Meadow & Mylander,

FIGURE 8.16 The creation of a new sign language. These children in Nicaragua are signing fluently in a language that deaf children created on their own. A social group seems necessary to trigger the language system, but not input from others who already know a language.

1998; Meir & Sandler, 2008; Senghas & Coppola, 2001). In addition, when parents of deaf children make a concerted effort to use a standard sign language such as ASL, the richness and complexity of the children's ASL quickly surpass that of their parents. Again, because children deprived of all language input are able to create languages from scratch when they grow up with peers, we see support for the idea that hearing children bring to the task of learning their native tongue a tacit knowledge of those aspects of their language that are universally shared with all other languages. It is presumably the same tacit knowledge that guides deaf children to create new languages despite not having any external input.

Q: Why is sign language repeatedly used as evidence for the creation of new languages?

The Domain Specificity of Language

To what extent do young children start language learning already endowed with cognitive capacities that are tailored specifically for learning language? If those capacities are truly used only for the acquisition of language and nothing else, then they would constitute strong evidence for the domain specificity of a language acquisition device. As we saw in Chapter 1 and in our discussion of perceptual development (Chapter 3), these questions about domain specificity are closely linked to debates between empiricists and nativists. In addition, the debates often focus on whether domain specificity occurs only at the initial stages of language processing or whether some higher-level thought processes are also language specific. Thus, many empiricists might argue that some aspects of humans' sensory or perceptual abilities are especially sensitive to speech-like stimuli (domain specific), but that more abstract representations, like a language's meaning or structure, depend on cognitive abilities that also contribute to other, nonlinguistic skills (domain general). Nativists endorse domain-specific specializations at those more abstract levels as well. The most passionate debates about language focus on whether humans use a language-specific ability to learn some aspects of grammatical rules or whether they can fully learn grammatical rules through a more general set of cognitive skills that enable them to also learn other patterns beyond grammar.

In this section, we will take two different approaches to these questions. One strategy for assessing whether language is a domain-specific skill is to ask whether it can be dissociated, or distinguished as separate, from other cognitive functions. This approach involves looking closely at neural dissociations between brain functions that support language and those involved in other areas of cognition. If brain damage or congenital disorders can selectively affect aspects of language while sparing other functions (and vice versa), then those particular linguistic skills may be domain specific. We then ask whether other species can acquire human-like languages and what such findings suggest about domain specificity. In particular, if other species that have never shown any use of human-like languages in the wild can nonetheless learn such languages with a reasonable level of competence in captivity, it would seem that they must be using learning systems that are not specialized for language. It would, after all, be quite mysterious for them to have a language-specific learning system if they had never had to learn such languages in their evolutionary history.

Neural Dissociations

To examine whether language learning is domain specific, we will discuss neural dissociations in which language and other cognitive skills are affected differently by strokes or other damage to specific brain regions and neural circuits. We will discuss a kind of brain damage in which language is affected but other cognitive skills are not. We will also look at genetic disorders in which language skills are preserved but other cognitive skills are not. Finally, we will examine specific language impairment in which there are specific inherited syntactic deficits in language but not in other cognitive abilities.

Aphasias In adults, the dissociation between language and other cognitive capacities has most often been studied in **aphasia**, a type of neurological deficit in which localized damage to the brain causes language impairments. In some cases, often in a region in the left inferior frontal gyrus known as Broca's area, syntactic abilities are damaged while semantic skills remain more intact, often leading to especially salient deficiencies in producing language and labored speech. In other cases, often in a region in the posterior part of the temporal lobe known as Wernicke's area, semantic abilities are impaired and syntax seems to remain largely intact, often resulting in problems understanding speech while still being able to produce rapid speech (even though it is now made up of combinations of words that do not make sense). Moreover, other patterns of brain damage, such as those that severely impair spatial skills, often have little impact on language skills (Goodglass, 1993; Swinney, 1999). These patterns of deficits in adults may provide evidence for built-in language-processing regions and circuits in the brain. But it is also possible that areas of neural tissue with no specializations for language in young infants could nonetheless end up becoming specialized for language in older children and adults because they become organized in that way over the course of learning.

Williams Syndrome A new wave of developmental studies with populations of children who, because of genetic anomalies, either have intact language with impaired cognition or impaired cognition with intact language are of great interest to researchers studying whether language is domain general or domain specific. If these children show evidence for a dissociation of language from other cognitive skills at the earliest stages of language learning, this would provide compelling evidence for domain-specific language specialization within the brain. Thus, researchers ask if certain unusual alleles enable some children to learn language relatively well even if they are more generally learning disabled and if other alleles enable different children to learn nonlinguistic information well, but not language.

The genetic disorder known as **Williams syndrome** may provide one example of the "compartmentalization" of language relative to other cognitive abilities (Pinker, 1994). Although Williams syndrome is rare, it affects approximately 1 out of 10,000 children. It is caused by the deletion of a series of 26 genes from chromosome 7 and is characterized by an unusual set of physical and behavioral traits (Bellugi & Wang, 1998; Martens et al., 2008; Mervis & Velleman, 2011). Physically, these children are said to have similar facial features, including small upturned noses, long upper lip lengths, full lips, and small chins (see Figure 8.17). They are generally cheerful and extremely sociable. Overall, they score below normal on intelligence tests and especially on tests of visual-spatial and mathematical skills. Children

FIGURE 8.17 Williams syndrome and language. Children with Williams syndrome share a genetic disorder that seems to largely spare language abilities while impairing other areas of cognition. The defect also results in a facial expression, as shown here, in which the child has a small upturned nose, a long upper lip length, full lips, and a small chin.

with Williams syndrome may lag behind other children in the earliest stages of language acquisition (Bates, 2004). But by age 3, their expressive language skills seem relatively intact (Bellugi et al., 1993; Marini et al., 2010), and they chatter away rapidly in relatively fluent sentences. As adults, they still speak quickly, using many idiomatic phrases and an advanced vocabulary, but their speech often involves little meaningful content.

Many questions remain about the abilities and deficits of people with Williams syndrome. For example, those with Williams syndrome have often been reported as being quite musical. Perhaps there is a specific ability that is preserved in Williams syndrome, but it may not be as specific as language. It could be a somewhat broader cognitive ability based on differences in the volumes of particular brain regions and on dendritic connections (Eckert et al., 2006). As research in this area intensifies, it will likely provide a clearer account of the links between Williams syndrome and models of domain specificity. At present, however, the dissociation seems likely and points toward a separate language acquisition skill. In particular, the evidence suggests that children may have a special brain-based ability to acquire aspects of language that can work relatively independently of other cognitive skills, such that a child with obvious deficits in general cognitive skills can still reach relatively high levels of linguistic proficiency with little evident effort.

Q: Which cognitive capacities seem most affected in Williams syndrome and which ones seem to be spared?

Specific Language Impairment (SLI) The best evidence for dissociation of cognitive abilities comes in the form of *double dissociations*. Establishing a double dissociation between two cognitive abilities requires showing that either ability can be impaired while the other one remains intact. To show a double dissociation between language and other kinds of cognition would require two types of evidence. In addition to people who have broad cognitive problems and relatively intact language abilities (like those with Williams syndrome), you would also need to show the reverse—people with largely intact cognition and impaired language. Researchers seem to have discovered this second pattern in cases of specific language impairment.

Specific language impairment (SLI) first came to light in a single family. Members of this family were generally bright and successful. Over several generations, however, they showed highly specific problems using particular syntactic structures, including noun-verb agreement, verb tenses, and the proper use of articles (such as "a" and "the") and prepositions (Gopnik, 1990a, 1990b, 1994; Gopnik & Crago, 1991; van der Lely & Christian, 2000). Within members of the family, these language problems showed a distinct pattern of inheritance that suggested that the deficits were genetic. Moreover, the problems seemed to be linked to a specific rare mutation of an allele on a gene that was associated with these particular aspects of linguistic performance; the rest of their cognitive skills seemed completely unaffected.

Later studies have examined whether SLI is truly specific to these narrow linguistic deficits or whether it might reflect broader cognitive problems, such as difficulty perceiving rapid sequences of stimuli (Bates, 2004; Thomas & Karmiloff-Smith, 2005; Ullman & Pierpoint, 2005). Thus far, SLI does seem to involve some language-specific deficits. Although individuals with SLI struggle to process rapid speech sounds, they do not have this problem with rapid visual stimuli (Archibald & Gathercole, 2006). It also now appears that several genetic defects may contribute to SLI, including some that are language specific and others that have broader, more domain-general effects (Bishop, 2006; Graham & Fisher, 2013; Newbury et al., 2011).

Studies of language skills and deficits in special populations—such as in people with aphasia, Williams syndrome, or SLI—are still in their early stages, but they promise exciting insights into whether, or to what extent, language skills are domain specific. Current evidence suggests that a

A Language Gene?

For some time, researchers have suspected that certain locations on the human genome might be closely and specifically related to language abilities. In fact, many spoken and written language abilities seem to have genetic components. And different aspects of language, such as lexical versus syntactic abilities (that is, knowledge of words versus understanding of how to put words together into meaningful sentences), seem to be associated with distinct genetic loci (Stromswold, 2001). The most powerful evidence for genes related to language abilities comes from studies designed to pinpoint specific genes associated with language deficits. The findings point to a gene known as FOXP2, which is located on chromosome 7 and produces a protein that affects the formation of brain regions and circuits associated with motor control. In humans, it also affects brain regions associated with planning and ordering in speech and language.

This finding emerged during a study of three generations of the KE family in England (Fisher et al., 1998; Fisher & Scharff, 2009; Lai et al., 2001, 2003; Vernes & Fisher, 2011). Roughly half the family members showed significant spoken language difficulties, while the other half were unaffected. The affected relatives had severe articulation problems, so that their speech seemed extremely effortful. They also had enormous difficulty producing ordered speech sounds and could barely be understood. Overall, these individuals seemed to show severe disruptions of the planning processes and movements necessary for clear speech. A closer look revealed that the affected members also had difficulties interpreting some grammatical aspects of language.

It was clear that there was a genetic component to the KE family's language disorder, so the researchers started to look for a mutation that may have led to the disorder (Lai et al., 2000). Because relatives share more of their genes than strangers do, it was not easy to isolate the relevant gene that might have led to the mutation by comparing the family members' genetic sequences. A major advance occurred when researchers discovered a boy with highly similar language problems who was unrelated to the KE family (Lai et al., 2001). When his genetic sequence was compared with that of the KEs, it corresponded to the genetic sequence in every one of the affected family members—but not in the unaffected members—in a crucial way. Like the genes of the affected KEs, his genes showed a distortion of 1 amino acid out of the 715 produced at the site of the FOXP2 gene. Other studies have since found that other abnormalities in the FOXP2 gene are also associated with language deficits (Fisher & Scharff, 2009; MacDermot et al., 2005; Peter et al., 2011; Zhao et al., 2010) and with abnormal patterns of functioning in language-related brain areas (Liegeois et al., 2003; Vernes & Fisher, 2011).

Do these findings provide evidence for a "language gene"? One critical question concerns whether the gene's effects are language specific or whether its mutations actually affect a broader range of cognitive functions. The affected members of the KE family scored below normal on intelligence tests, but so did the unaffected members. This pattern suggests that the affected relatives' genetic difference at the FOXP2 site was not necessarily a factor in their low scores. Even so, testing all the family members to compare their performance on more linguistic and nonlinguistic tasks would help clarify whether their deficit really is restricted to language-related learning and skills.

A second finding also relates to the question of whether FOXP2 specifically affects language. This same gene is found in many species as a regulatory gene that activates other genes involved in the formation of brain structures and circuits during the embryonic period and in learning to sequence movements. The chimpanzee FOXP2 gene differs from the human version in only 2 of the 715 amino acids it produces. The version in mice differs by 3. Moreover, the best estimates of when in evolution humans and chimpanzees diverged—that is, when the uniquely human gene emerged—point to between 120,000 and 200,000 years ago (Enard et al., 2002). Thus, around 10,000 generations ago, a very small mutation in FOXP2 may have spread quickly and conferred a strong selective advantage on a human-like species, possibly leading to the ability to rapidly articulate strings of speech-like sounds.

Even if the FOXP2 gene in humans turns out to be involved only in language abilities (and deficits), the mechanism underlying its effects still remains unclear, and the current evidence in no way suggests a single "language gene" or even a single gene for a particular component of language (Marcus & Fisher, 2003; Vargha-Khadem et al., 2005). It remains to be seen whether FOXP2 is necessary for language, but it is clearly not sufficient. A full account of how humans are able to acquire a natural language with all its astonishing complexity will depend on the interaction of many genes with an elaborate set of environmental inputs.

domain-specific language acquisition system is present from the start, but more research will be needed before we can say that there is definitely such a system. More broadly, it is becoming clear that different aspects of language may yield different answers to questions about domain specificity. These answers in turn will inform questions about what sorts of cognitive abilities all normal children use to learn language and will help explain how such a complex body of knowledge and skills emerges so quickly in the first few years of life.

> **Q:** What aspects of language seem to be affected in the disorder known as specific language impairment?

FIGURE 8.18 Comparing language acquisition abilities. The chimpanzee Gua and the human child Donald were raised together as if they were sister and brother in one of the first naturalistic studies comparing language acquisition in a human and a chimpanzee.

Species Specificity

Humans appear to be unique in their ability to acquire and use language, and yet researchers have wondered whether other animals, especially our closest primate relatives, might learn language more successfully under carefully tailored circumstances. If other species could acquire language, this would have important implications for understanding how young children's linguistic abilities develop. For example, if chimpanzees were able to learn and use language, despite never having shown such a rich communication system of their own, they would presumably have to rely on learning mechanisms that were not innately tailored for language. If this achievement were possible, it would show that the capacity for language does not require language-specific brain areas or cognitive abilities. Rather, it would suggest that more general systems, tailored for learning and using a broader variety of information, could be sufficient to acquire language.

Chimp as Child In the 1930s, psychologist Winthrop Kellogg and his wife Luella attempted to raise a 7½-month-old chimpanzee named Gua along with their own 10-month-old infant son, Donald, treating the two very similarly in order to compare their development (Kellogg & Kellogg, 1933/1967; see Figure 8.18). The Kelloggs called Gua by name and regularly encouraged her to talk but did not try to tutor her. Instead, Gua experienced the same sort of environment in which human children acquire language. Although Gua and the Kelloggs bonded and did communicate in some ways, Gua soon lagged behind Donald in the ability to speak. When the study ended, after about 9 months, Donald was already outpacing Gua at acquiring language. Interestingly, when the Kelloggs compared Gua and Donald's other cogni-

tive abilities, Gua often outperformed Donald. She could skillfully manipulate objects, such as a door latch or a spoon, at an earlier age, and she could solve more complex spatial problems. Thus, Donald's much greater success with language suggested a bias for language learning that was specific to humans, given that he was not merely a better learner than Gua in all respects. Because the Kelloggs' study supported the notion that language is a specifically human ability, it also lent support to the possibility that linguistic abilities show domain specificity. If primates perform well in nonlinguistic cognitive tasks, then domain-general cognitive abilities are apparently not sufficient for learning language. Instead, some other cognitive component is needed that may be tuned to process and learn linguistic information.

Nonhuman Primates and Sign Language Several decades later, researchers tried a different approach to teaching apes human language. Around this time, a new, landmark account of the evolution of linguistic abilities argued that humans' unique specializations for language included not only mental capacities but also the structure of the anatomy that allows humans to articulate a wide variety of nuanced sounds (Lenneberg, 1967). Although the structure of the mouth, throat, vocal cords, and voice box in nonhuman primates prevents them from speaking, researchers wondered if chimps and great apes might be able to acquire a nonspoken sign language. This idea that nonhuman primates might be able to learn language using their hands converged with an increasing awareness that human sign languages were as natural and complex as spoken languages (Klima & Bellugi, 1979; Neisser, 1990).

Initial studies in which researchers attempted to teach chimpanzees to use American Sign Language (ASL) seemed to show some success (Gardner & Gardner, 1969, 1980).

The chimps appeared to master using signs to refer to specific classes of things, as well as combining signs in ways that suggested an understanding of syntax. These findings were met with tremendous interest and raised many questions. If the chimpanzees could learn signs, why didn't they ever invent them on their own? Did the chimps' "language," which they mostly used to request things, really resemble human language? And critically, how different were the chimps' conditions of language instruction from the experience of a young child learning a language?

If the chimps' manner of learning is quite different, we must be cautious in deciding whether the skill they have learned (and the cognitive capacities it involves) truly resembles that of humans. Consider the old observation that although a dog can learn to walk on its hind legs, dogs, unlike humans, do not have a predisposition to do so. The dog requires continued, intentional instruction to maintain the behavior, whereas the child simply develops the skill without guidance or reinforcement. If other species can only acquire language in a manner that resembles the dog learning to walk on its hind legs, this shows a profound difference between other species' language capacities and those of humans. For nonhumans, the only path to learning and maintaining language seems to be through intensive effort and continuous reinforcement.

Aside from the way they learned language, a closer look at other primates' rudimentary language abilities is also revealing (Seidenberg & Pettito, 1979; Terrace et al., 1979). Under scrutiny, the chimps trained to use ASL mostly seemed to be imitating signs that humans modeled for them, rather than spontaneously producing new phrases. More broadly, other primates, whether gorillas or chimpanzees, did not appear to have the capacity to use language in a flexible, generative way to form new, spontaneous expressions. There is, after all, a large difference between memorizing symbol sequences and being able to generate an indefinitely large number of new, meaningful, and well-formed sequences.

> **Q:** In what ways are chimpanzees most similar and most dissimilar to the young child with respect to the ability to acquire a first language?

Bonobos and Joint Attention Criticisms of the early ASL studies with chimps bolstered the view that nonhuman primates' linguistic abilities fell far short of those of humans. But as the study of primate communication continued, researchers started to ask whether some primates might show partial language abilities—and which specific skills might be involved. As described in Chapter 5, one essential component of learning language is the ability to use joint attention to focus, along with a communication partner, on the same thing in the environment (Tomasello, 2005; Tomasello & Call, 1997). Primatologist Sue Savage-Rumbaugh and her colleagues (1998) sought to investigate whether bonobos, a rare species of primates that seems relatively more capable of joint attention than other nonhuman primates, would also do better than other primates at learning language. An opportunity arose when, in the course of teaching a language system to an adult bonobo, the researchers noticed that her adopted son, Kanzi, seemed to be picking up the language by observing her lessons—and without direct training (see Figure 8.19).

Kanzi's spontaneous learning was impressive, and the group quickly directed its efforts to him. He was paired with a 2-year-old child, and both were exposed to spontaneous speech and simple geometric shapes called *lexigrams* that were used to represent words. Kanzi's ability to understand syntax appeared to far surpass primates in earlier studies, but his ability to produce language lagged considerably behind the ability of a human child. More generally, bonobos seem to be capable of learning some relations between categories. But it is difficult to know whether their learning is truly based on understanding how syntax works (like the relation between a subject and a verb) or whether they are relying on a more concrete, conceptual understanding (such as the relationship between an agent and an action). Based on her studies, Savage-Rumbaugh concluded that it may be more accurate to think in terms of a continuum when comparing humans' language acquisition skills with those of other primates, rather than a sharp distinction (Savage-Rumbaugh et al., 1998).

FIGURE 8.19 Communicating with nonhuman primates. Kanzi, a male bonobo, learned language using lexigram symbols and appeared to be able to produce genuinely novel structures.

Indeed, it seems likely that the most sophisticated and social primates may have some abilities that are important to learning language and that these abilities may form the foundation on which our own abilities to acquire languages evolved. Evolutionary debates continue on the extent to which humans evolved broad, cognitive abilities that supported changes in many domains, including language (Hauser et al., 2002)—or whether the evolution of a capacity for language was more domain specific (Bickerton, 2007; Fitch, 2011; Pinker & Jackendoff, 2005; Stromswold, 2010).

Language and Thought

As language emerges in children, the question arises as to how it interacts with other aspects of thought. Does language come to structure thought and knowledge in ways that would otherwise be impossible without language? Does language make possible different kinds of cognitions? And do the particular properties of the specific language a child learns come to exert any unique guiding influences on the way she thinks about the world? Conversely, do changes in the child's cognitive development influence the way she uses language? Many strong claims, running in both directions, have been made about powerful influences between thought and language. We will start with the question of how language might structure thought.

Linguistic Relativity and Linguistic Determinism

Are our ways of seeing and understanding the world framed by the language we speak? This idea, that thoughts and perceptions are influenced by our native language, is termed **linguistic relativity**. The stronger version of this notion, **linguistic determinism**, holds that the language we speak actually determines the nature of our thoughts. Counter to both of these views, some argue that differences in communication merely reflect cultural differences between groups and that they can still exist even if the groups speak the same first language but have radically different cultures. These issues have interested developmental researchers, who have sought to understand whether these linguistic influences exist and how they might take shape as children come to master their native tongue.

The Sapir-Whorf Hypothesis The idea that specific languages powerfully mold thought is known as the **Sapir-Whorf hypothesis** after the anthropologist and linguist Edward Sapir and his student Benjamin Lee Whorf. In this view, all speakers of a language acquire a way of perceiving and understanding the world that is unique to that language and a direct consequence of special aspects of that language (Whorf, 1956). Thus, the words of a language can influence the categories that the speaker uses for objects and ideas, and the grammar of a language can affect how the speaker perceives events. In this view, all prelinguistic children might think in terms of similar conceptual schemes, but as each child acquires a specific language, their conceptions of the same events would increasingly diverge (see Figure 8.20).

The Whorfian view is generally in line with empiricist traditions. It assumes that prelinguistic children have essentially no strong predispositions in how their minds "carve up" the world—or that if they do have predispositions, such biases are easily overridden by the specifics of each language. Yet, such an assumption seems increasingly questionable, given all that we have learned about the highly structured ways in which infants perceive and understand their world. It is still possible, however, that language exerts many new cognitive influences beyond those present in infancy.

Some of the most famous claims for language structuring our thoughts involve different levels of nuanced meaning across languages. You may well have heard the claim that children growing up in the Arctic learn far more words for snow than other children do and that this rich vocabulary allows them to perceive subtle differences between types of snow that other speakers cannot see. Although this example has become a classic, it is fraught with problems. First, it illustrates the problem of disentangling experience and language. If people living in the Arctic can discriminate between more kinds of snow, perhaps it is simply because they have a great deal of experience with it and more opportunities to see different types. Language would then simply mirror these conceptual distinctions rather than creating them. Second, speakers of other languages might well be able to make all the same distinctions by describing them with compound nouns and phrases rather than single words. Third, the analyses of Eskimo-Aleut languages that gave rise to the initial claim may have been inaccurate. Many languages' grammar includes rules for adding chains of prefixes and suffixes to a single root word, such that a whole complex sentence might appear to an outsider as one long word (Baker, 1996). Thus, the many "words" for snow may really be descriptive phrases, much like those that speakers of many other languages would use (Woodbury, 1991). In fact, the snow example itself may be little more than an urban myth that was never actually proposed by a serious scholar (Pullum, 1991).

In short, children who grow up in the Arctic are undoubtedly familiar with more types of snow than those in the tropics, but this difference may be completely inde-

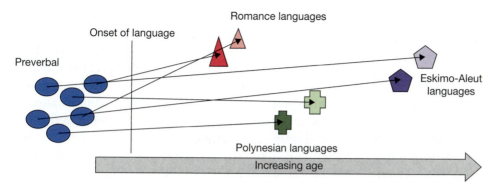

FIGURE 8.20 Linguistic relativity. According to Whorf, prior to the onset of language (indicated at the vertical line), children from different cultures have very similar conceptual schemes (indicated by same-shaped ovals), but after they become immersed in specific language families, their conceptual schemes diverge (indicated by different geometric shapes and different locations in conceptual space).

pendent of the languages they speak, resulting instead from varying experiences. It is clear that irrefutable support for the Sapir-Whorf hypothesis will require more powerful and carefully collected evidence. More recent research examining linguistic influences on thought has focused on more subtle effects that are often only evident in carefully controlled experimental settings. We now turn to a few such cases.

Color and Number If two languages' color words divide the spectrum of light differently, perhaps speakers of those languages actually perceive different sets of color categories. Because infants show categorical perception of color many months before any language skills (see Chapter 3), we know that language is not necessary for categorical perception effects. Nonetheless, color words might subtly tune color perceptions in ways that resemble the effects of spoken language on categorical perception of speech sounds. Some linguistic influences have indeed been found in languages that require two different color words for a category that has only one color word in English. For example, Russian speakers use different words for dark blue and light blue, while English speakers can simply use "blue" for both. Native Russian speakers do seem to show a subtle advantage over English speakers in the ability to discriminate between blues that take different labels in Russian (Winawer et al., 2007). Apparently, their need to constantly monitor different hues of blue to know which label to use may sharpen perceptual processes related to the discrimination of those colors.

Language development may also affect where in the brain categorical perception of color is processed (Kay & Regier, 2006; Regier & Kay, 2009). Preverbal infants are better at discriminating between color categories when the colors are presented to the left visual field, and therefore processed primarily in the brain's right hemisphere. In contrast, children and adults show better color discrimination when the colors are presented to the right visual field, and processed primarily in the left hemisphere. Moreover, toddlers who are just beginning to learn color words seem to process color category names in the right hemisphere, whereas those who

show more mastery of the same color terms do so in the left hemisphere (Franklin et al., 2008).

Even in adults, learning new terms for unfamiliar color categories can quickly redirect which parts of the brain are dedicated to color processing, shifting the processing of the new categories from the right to the left hemisphere (Clifford et al., 2010; Zhou et al., 2010), but it is not yet understood how this change happens. Researchers are also exploring whether learning the names of objects might exert comparable effects on the way the brain processes objects. Along these lines, one study found that when 1-year-olds view objects for which they have learned labels, they show increased levels of visual object processing than they do while viewing equally familiar objects for which they do not have labels (Gliga et al., 2010). Certainly, not all cross-language labeling differences directly affect object perception and cognition (Barner et al., 2010), but there are some indications that language can modulate and redirect the way children process some aspects of colors and perhaps objects.

Specific languages also appear to affect mathematical thought, as demonstrated in one remarkable study of bilingual children who spoke both Welsh and English fluently (Ellis & Hennelly, 1980; see also Baddeley et al., 1975). The researchers utilized the fact that there is a difference in the length of the words that each language uses for numbers. Welsh number words are longer, and as a result, they make greater demands on memory and cause more difficulty in timed calculations like those on intelligence tests. Thus, the researchers found that the same child who was fluent in both languages took longer to do some mathematical calculations in Welsh than in English. Similar effects have been found when comparing mathematical calculations done in other languages with those done in English (Chan & Elliott, 2011; Pixner et al., 2011). Thus, a child's specific language may modestly influence the development of her mathematical thought. These effects may also be quite specific. For example, if Russian-English bilinguals learn to do a particular calculation in one language, they will later be able to do that calculation more quickly in that language than in the other language in which they are equally fluent (Spelke & Tsivkin, 2001b).

Other Influences of Language on Thought Another possible influence of language on thought involves subtle differences in how categories are understood. For example, when a term is masculine in one language and feminine in another, subtle differences may arise in how other properties are associated with the object that the term refers to (Boroditsky et al., 2003). Thus, "key" is masculine in German and feminine in Spanish. German speakers tend to use more stereotypically masculine terms to describe keys (for example, jagged, hard, awkward), while Spanish speakers tend to use more stereotypically feminine terms (for example, shiny, intricate, yellow). Another study suggests that a child's native language may also affect how early the child learns his or her own gender. When a language requires speakers to specify the gender of others extensively—as Hebrew does, requiring gendered words for "you"—its young speakers seem to learn their own gender almost a year earlier than children learning a language such as Finnish, which has very sparse gender markings. Children learning English, which is in between Hebrew and Finnish in its gender markings, learn their own gender about 6 months earlier than the Finnish speakers (as described in Boroditsky, 2011). Thus, constantly marking a particular contrast in words may accelerate children's learning about it.

Some of the most intriguing claims about linguistic relativity arise from studies of how languages encode orientation (Levinson, 1997; Majid et al., 2004). Some languages guide their users to encode directions in terms of an external set of reference points (for example, north, south, east, or west) or particular geographical points ("It is in the down-mountain direction"). Other languages, including English, guide their users to encode directions relative to the speaker ("It is to the right of me"). Thus, Canadians and Europeans tend to say, "The boy is to the right of me," but speakers of Australian languages of the Pama-Nyungan group say, "The boy is north of the table" or "The boy is up-island from the table." Similarly, the Tzeltal language in Mexico uses both absolute terms of reference ("down mountain" or "across mountain") and intrinsic terms ("at the front side of an object"), but it has no words for terms relative to the self, such as "left," "right," and "behind."

These linguistic differences seem to affect cognitive schemas and performance on spatial reasoning tasks. Consider, for example, the two tasks shown in Figure 8.21. Adults are shown several objects arranged on a table. The adults are then rotated 180 degrees, taken to another table, and asked to reproduce the arrangement using a new, duplicate set of objects. Tzeltal speakers will set up the objects in the same orientation as the first set relative to external points of reference (for example, placing the same object in the northernmost part of the display). By contrast, Dutch speakers will arrange the objects in the same orientation relative to themselves (for example, placing the same object in the part of the display closest to themselves). These and many other spatial tasks illustrate that the spatial terms a speaker uses seem to cause different ways of representing spatial information (Levinson, 1997).

Developmentally, these influences of language on spatial representations can occur quite early. For example, when children who are around age 8 in the Netherlands (where self-referential terms are primarily used) and in Namibia (where external referential terms are generally used) perform a wide range of spatial reconstruction tasks, they show differences very much like those found in adults (Haun et al., 2011). Their languages seem to have already set up strong default modes of spatial thought. Moreover, when the experimenters prompted the children to switch to the other type of spatial reasoning, the children found it very difficult, suggesting that by age 8, if not earlier, these modes of spatial thought are quite entrenched.

With the current revival of more subtle versions of the Sapir-Whorf hypothesis, we cannot yet know the extent to which language variations might influence cognitive development, but any such differences that have been documented in adults have strong developmental implications. In any areas where language exerts an influence on cognition, children can be expected to take different cognitive developmental paths from the time they begin learning a language, branching off in subtle ways from a common, preverbal path.

Language as an Amplifier of Thought

Even as controversies continue about whether differences in language cause differences in thought, there is another way in which language might shape thought that is independent of the differences between languages. This view focuses on the universal properties that all languages share as formal systems of symbols. The key question is whether language acquisition in general, regardless of the particular language acquired, might have a dramatic influence on the nature of thought, making thought in the presence of language profoundly different from thought in the absence of language. In fact, many suppose that human thought differs profoundly from thought in other animals precisely because of the way language amplifies and structures thought. In this view, as children acquire language, their thoughts are dramatically restructured through the common properties shared by all languages.

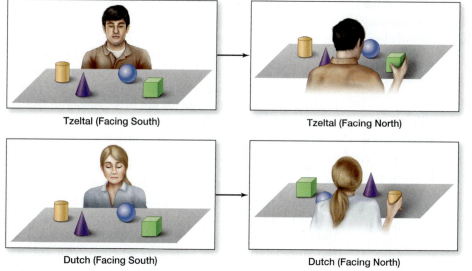

FIGURE 8.21 Spatial relative versus spatial absolute languages. Speakers of spatial relative languages (Dutch and English) and spatial absolute languages (Tzeltal) seem to perform nonlinguistic spatial tasks in different ways, re-creating displays in sharply contrasting formats that correspond to underlying spatial schemes. Adapted from Levinson (1997).

Tzeltal (Facing South)

Tzeltal (Facing North)

Dutch (Facing South)

Dutch (Facing North)

One of the most eloquent and forceful proposals about how the emergence of language reshapes thought came from the Russian developmental psychologist Lev Semyonovich Vygotsky (Vygotsky, 1934/1962, 1978). Vygotsky's approach to development was wide-reaching and influential, and we will consider other aspects of his approach later in the book (see Chapters 9 and 11). In this chapter, we will discuss his view of the influence of language on thought. Vygotsky believed that over the course of early development, the child internalizes his own language, making it a true vehicle or tool for thinking about the world. He held that before language is internalized, the child's thoughts are entirely concrete and tied to the here and now. Language, Vygotsky claimed, liberates the child's thoughts by making them more abstract and therefore a more powerful, principled way of understanding meanings and categories. Vygotsky described phenomena very much like the characteristic-to-defining shift that we discussed earlier in the chapter, and he assumed that such shifts are a consequence of internalizing language. He believed that language enables the child to formulate mental definitions instead of mere associationistic impressions. Others have since argued that when children begin talking themselves through difficult tasks, this is evidence that they have internalized their language as a vehicle of thought (Sokolov, 1972).

In Vygotsky's view, language may facilitate thought in both children and adults. It can provide additional memory and attentional support for complex tasks and can sometimes foster more analytical problem solving. Sometimes the effects of language may result from the ways in which grammatical structures and interpretations of words focus thought in particular domains like number (Carey, 2009) and theory of mind (Astington & Baird, 2005; de Villiers & de Villiers, 2009). Other times language may help integrate domains of thought. These general influences of language on thought may be analogous to the influences of gesture on thought, where nonverbal gestures often provide critical additional support to children to focus their memory and attention in complex tasks, boosting cognitive performance above levels found with language alone (Goldin-Meadow, 2011).

Several scholars have converged on the idea that the emergence of language allows the child to bring together different domains of thought and to combine them in novel ways (Carey, 2009; Carruthers, 2002, 2004; Gentner, 2003; Inagaki & Hatano, 2003; Mithen, 1996; Spelke, 2003; Spelke & Tsivkin, 2001a). They argue that preverbal children might understand concepts in separate domains but might need language to bring them together. Some examples include using language to unite knowledge of an environment's geometric features with its landmarks, to unite number estimations with more precise numerical knowledge, and to unite the domains of plants and animals into a common domain of living things. Language is considered a domain-general common ground within which to combine elements from separate domains. A key challenge for this proposal is to demonstrate that language is the dominant vehicle for these integrations, rather than just one of many ways of uniting elements of thought (Atran, 2002; Hampton, 2002). To resolve this question, researchers are increasingly conducting experiments to carefully contrast linguistic influences with those of other kinds of representations, such as symbols and pictures.

In the end, some effect of emerging language use on thought seems inevitable, if only because speaking our thoughts aloud so often brings new insights. But even after years of intensive research on how verbalizing while thinking relates to basic cognitive skills, many aspects of the relationship are still not understood (Bloom & Keil, 2001). At present, we simply do not know how much of an effect language has on developing thought. It most likely does not cause a global, stage-like shift, but it may well have interesting effects on more focused aspects of thought and knowledge.

Q: What is some recent evidence that language may facilitate specific aspects of thought?

Influences of Cognitive Development on Language

We have considered ways in which acquiring particular languages, as well as language in general, might influence the way a child thinks. We can also turn the tables and ask if changes in a child's cognitive development can influence his language. There is surprisingly little evidence that differences in cognitive development have a strong influence on the development of grammar (Snedeker et al., 2012), but cognition may have more of an influence on how language is effectively used. Jean Piaget, whose theories of infant cognition were described in Chapter 5, was especially influential in this area. Recall that Piaget was a proponent of developmental stages; he claimed that children experience distinct, qualitative changes in their ways of thinking and understanding. In his view, language is just one part of a much larger system of thought, and a child's progress through the stages of cognitive development has profound effects on his use of language (Piaget, 1926/1959).

Piaget observed, for example, that in experimental studies, young children had trouble understanding the full range of possible perspectives on a situation. More specifically, he concluded that children younger than about 7 years old were unable to take more than one perspective on a scene or to free themselves from their own viewpoint. He assumed that this **egocentrism** represented a general cognitive deficit that would also be manifested in young children's language. To examine how children's egocentrism affected their ability to communicate with others, Piaget set up an experiment in which children were told a story, then asked to repeat it to someone else. Here is one of the stories, followed by a typical repetition by an 8-year-old child:

> Original version: Once upon a time, there was a lady who was called Niobe, and who had 12 sons and 12 daughters. She met a fairy who had only one son and no daughter. Then the lady laughed at the fairy because the fairy only had one boy. Then the fairy was very angry and fastened the lady to a rock. The lady cried for 10 years. In the end she turned into a rock, and her tears made a stream which still runs today. (Piaget, 1926/1959, p. 83)

> An 8-year-old's version: Once upon a time, there was a lady who had 12 boys and 12 girls, and then a fairy a boy and a girl. And then Niobe wanted to have some more sons. Then she was angry. She fastened her to a stone. He turned into a rock, and then his tears made a stream which is still running today. (Piaget, 1926/1959, pp. 102–103)

Clearly something was lost in the repetition! Younger children seemed to neglect whether the people they were addressing would be able to make sense of their retelling. By using personal references and unclear pronouns, they thoroughly confused listeners who did not already know the story. Rather than providing listeners with the relevant background and details, it was as if the children were recounting the story to themselves or to someone else who knew as much as they did. Their problems in retelling the story are especially interesting because the children knew perfectly well what had happened. They could answer Piaget's specific, detailed questions about what took place, but they apparently did not know how to communicate their understanding.

In a similar study by Piaget and his colleagues, a researcher told young children how a device worked, then asked them to explain it to others. The researchers did their best to ensure that the children understood how the device—perhaps a syringe or steam engine—worked. Nonetheless, even children who seemed to fully understand the mechanism still regularly failed to explain it to someone else because they did not take the other person's viewpoint into account.

One of the most dramatic demonstrations of children's egocentric speech uses a **referential communications task** (Krauss & Glucksberg, 1969), in which two children (or a child and an adult) sit on opposite sides of a table, separated by a large vertical panel (see Figure 8.22). One child, designated the "communicator," is charged with telling the other child, "the listener," how to stack a sequence of patterned blocks. As the communicator takes each block out of a dispenser on his side of the panel, he instructs the listener to select the same block from her set, then put it on a stacking peg.

There are two reasons why children younger than roughly 6 years of age often fail spectacularly as communicators in these tasks: (1) Their descriptions are often too vague. They might say, for example, "Take the red one" when there is more than one red block. (2) Their descriptions often are too idiosyncratic and personal to be helpful to the listener. They might say, "Get the one that looks like Mommy's favorite hat" or "Take the one that looks like the tree in our yard" without understanding that these references are unfamiliar to their partner.

But is the egocentric use of language really a developmental stage, as Piaget supposed? Figuring this out requires addressing two questions: (1) Are there similar tasks at which adults also fail? If so, the cognitive ability in question may change in a slower, more incremental way over time, rather than showing a distinct shift into a new stage. (2) Are there similar tasks at which much younger children succeed? If there are, this raises the possibility that children may fail at particular versions of these tasks because they require more advanced abilities for completing the particular tasks—perhaps in terms of memory or conceptual understanding—that are separate from the overall cognitive ability being studied. In the case of the egocentric use of language, the evidence suggests that the answer to both questions is yes. Rather than a general stage of cognitive development, egocentrism seems to be a view that people revert to in the midst of difficult communicative tasks.

Adults often communicate egocentrically in unfamiliar settings, such as while traveling abroad. In especially blatant instances, tourists assume that everyone living in the foreign place they are visiting knows the tourist's own language. In slightly more subtle cases, someone in the host country makes a polite, tentative attempt to speak the tourist's native language—and the tourist replies with a rapid barrage of speech, forgetting that this is clearly a second language for the host. Egocentrism is therefore a factor in communication even in adult life (Keysar, 2008). But at the other end of the continuum, even very young children are not always egocentric communicators. Interestingly, very young children make the same adjustments to their vocabulary and speech patterns as adults do when they are talking to even younger children (Shatz & Gel-

man, 1973). Moreover, the specific ways that they change their language suggests that they are not just imitating what adults do. They seem to recognize that the younger child needs to have things made simpler. One way of understanding developmental change is to see children getting better and better at overcoming egocentrism as their executive functioning gradually increases and they become more skilled at inhibiting their own point of view so they can more easily take into account other perspectives. Thus, there is evidence that increasing executive skills are related to increasing performance in referential communication tasks (Nilsen & Graham, 2009).

Q: What is egocentrism, and how does it relate to language development?

This kind of debate, about whether particular developmental changes are stage-like or more continuous, is a classic one in developmental psychology. When evaluating claims that there are stages of development characterized by qualitative changes to a cognitive or social ability, consider the alternative. The ability may be manifested along a continuum, in which even the youngest children can succeed at the easiest levels and even mature adults might fail at the hardest levels. If this kind of pattern emerges among adults and children, and if all the different levels of the task are indeed tapping into the same basic ability, then the existence of developmental stages becomes less likely.

Language and Communication

As our discussion of egocentrism in communication shows, the development of language skills goes beyond semantics and grammar. Another important aspect of language development involves the ability to convey and interpret additional layers of meaning in an utterance, depending on its context. That context can include the surrounding sentences, the physical situation, and the listener's inferences about the speaker's (and other listeners') mental state. Adults can use and understand metaphors, irony, and sarcasm (Gibbs, 1994, 1999). They can decide when to discount a speaker's credibility, and they can understand the unstated norms of conversation. These *pragmatic* aspects of language—ways of using language to relay and infer meanings within a particular context and to understand and use indirect language—have roots early in the preschool years, but they can take many years to fully master.

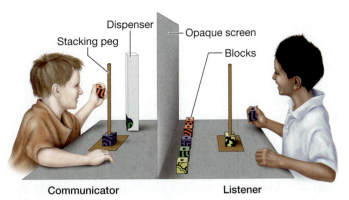

FIGURE 8.22 The referential communication task. Children fail to realize what the communicative common ground is and make highly idiosyncratic references to the blocks in front of them. These references make it difficult or impossible for the listener to know which block the communicator is referring to. As a result, the listener is unable to pick out the blocks described by the communicator to stack them on the peg. Adapted from Krauss & Glucksberg (1969).

The Cognitive Effects of Bilingualism

Early views of bilingualism seemed to suggest that children who faced the "chore" of learning two or more languages would certainly fare worse—in both linguistic and cognitive skills—than their peers who learned just one language (Haugen, 1956). But these early studies almost always confounded the effects of bilingualism with the effects of specific social disadvantages. They frequently involved the bilingual children of poor, immigrant families who were often enrolled in inferior schools. Within a few decades, however, a series of landmark studies led to a major turning point in our understanding of the effects of bilingualism on cognitive development.

Consider the situation in Montreal, Canada. Montreal is in the province of Quebec, which is officially French speaking, but where many people are bilingual. For the first half of the twentieth century, the city's wealth and power were largely concentrated in certain English-speaking groups, such that those who only spoke English often had an economic advantage over bilingual speakers of both French and English. Not surprisingly, the children from economically disadvantaged backgrounds, many of whom were bilingual, often performed worse than monolingual children on a variety of cognitive tasks. The breakthrough on the effects of bilingualism occurred when Wallace Lambert and his colleagues conducted much more careful studies of children from Montreal, balancing the socioeconomic status of the monolinguals and bilinguals (Lambert, 1975, 1985; Lambert & Tucker, 1972).

Lambert's results were striking. The bilingual children performed at least as well on intelligence tests and in academic settings as the monolingual children, and in several cases they performed better. Being immersed in two languages seemed to help the bilingual children become more aware of language itself as a system of arbitrary symbols. They developed this awareness earlier than the children who spoke just one language, and it seemed to also make them more aware of their other cognitive skills, such as their memory abilities. Since Lambert's studies, hundreds of other studies worldwide have documented a similar pattern: speaking more than one language is associated with several possible cognitive advantages and no known deficits (Bialystok & Barac, 2012; Diaz, 1983, 1985; Hakuta, 1986).

Bilingual and multilingual individuals consistently show advantages in tasks that require a more objective understanding of language and its structures. In one group of studies, monolingual and bilingual children were shown drawings of objects with word labels below them. Although the children could not yet read, some of them had a sense that words carried meaning. And when the labels were moved to accompany different pictures, these children also knew that the words retained their meanings, despite being placed under different objects. The bilingual children understood at much earlier ages than the monolingual children that words have fixed meanings and that words' physical characteristics are not linked directly to objects—that is, that bigger words do not necessarily correspond to bigger objects (Bialystok, 1997). Moreover, the awareness of language as a

Some forms of indirect language (language that is not literal, such as complicated metaphors, sarcastic or ironic comments, or double entendres) may hinge critically on cognitive capacities that develop during the school years, such as the child's understanding of the intricacies of others' mental states. (We will look more closely at these abilities in the next few chapters.) For our purposes here, the key point is that preschool children may have difficulty going beyond a literal understanding of utterances that depend on a rich interpretation of the speaker's beliefs and desires. Younger children might not have a sufficiently developed model of other people's mental states and how they interact with situations to be able to go beyond the literal. Moreover, even adults who are, for example, oblivious to the underlying hostility in a situation may not notice sarcasm or irony that would

be obvious to people familiar with the circumstances. Examples like this make it clear that some aspects of indirect speech take years to understand and require that children become more knowledgeable about social situations and the mental states that specific situations elicit in the people involved. Thus, while a young child may easily understand metaphors such as "The car is hungry" (for a car that needs gas) or "The dog is talking" (for a barking dog) or "The house needs a new hat" (for a house that needs a new roof), that same child may have great difficulty understanding a wry comment about someone's mental abilities when phrased as "not the sharpest tack in the box." Understanding this metaphor requires knowing what it means to be a "sharp tack in a box" as well as inferences about relative mental states in others. Children are able to understand metaphors when they link domains

system in itself (and not just as a means of communication), which bilingualism seems to foster, may also be critical to learning how to read. In comparisons of carefully matched groups of bilingual and monolingual children, the bilingual children often seem to master initial literacy skills earlier than the monolingual children (Bialystok, 1997). By fostering a more developed awareness of how language works, bilingualism may indirectly promote earlier literacy.

We began with the question of how learning more than one language early on might affect other cognitive abilities; it appears that there are only benefits. But these issues are quite different from the more often politicized questions about whether public schools should offer bilingual education for children whose first language is different from the region's official language. When bilingual education initiatives were first introduced across the United States in the 1960s, they were hailed as a major advance in educational opportunities for children who were not native English speakers. Although such initiatives came in several versions, one of the most common proposals in the United States was to offer instruction in both Spanish and English, especially to children for whom only Spanish was spoken in the home. Advocates argued that failing to provide bilingual education amounted to discrimination against immigrants. They held that children should learn to read and develop a knowledge base in their native tongue before learning English—so that they would not have to face learning to read in an unknown language. It also seemed that giving immigrant children the chance to initially learn in their native language would boost their self-esteem, whereas having to learn in an unknown language could cause a string of initial academic failures. Supported by this reasoning, bilingual education became a major program in school districts across the country. The need for these programs quickly increased as the percentage of new students who spoke little or no English rose rapidly in the 1990s and in the first decade of the twenty-first century.

Despite the broad reach of bilingual education programs, several reports comparing them with English-immersion programs have shown little or no advantage of bilingual programs (Glenn, 1997; Gersten et al., 1992; Rossell & Baker, 1996). By the late 1990s, these problems led California businessman Ron Unz to campaign for a new law to make English-only immersion programs the default for California's public schools and to offer bilingual public education only in specific districts where parents requested it. Interestingly, many members of California's Hispanic and Latino communities supported the proposal, which was approved in 1998. Since that time, a series of studies have argued that when we take a longer-term perspective, there may well be benefits from bilingual education because it enables children to achieve more rapid mastery of language and general-knowledge skills by initially exposing them to instruction in their native tongue (Christian, 2011; Collier & Thomas, 2007; Oades-Sese et al., 2011). But others ask if there may be delays in second-language development and whether those delays offset gains in other areas (Conger, 2010; Tong et al., 2008). The debate continues with great passion and emotion on both sides. We can only hope that the next decade will resolve the debate as more long-term and comprehensive studies on English-immersion and bilingual programs are compared. Nonetheless, the cognitive benefits of bilingualism still hold regardless of the way a second language is learned.

that they understand (for example, linking vehicles with eating), but they don't understand metaphors in which they don't understand one of the domains (Keil, 1986).

We also learn when to doubt what others say. We are, for example, often cynical about politicians' seemingly self-serving statements. More broadly, we are inclined to doubt a statement when it seems that the speaker is making it merely for personal gain. Although this cynicism seems like a fairly sophisticated interpretive skill, young elementary school children actually seem to know when to take a statement with a grain of salt. In one study, children were told about a race in which two runners finished so close to each other that it was hard to tell who won. When children as young as 7 years old were told that one of the runners said he had won the race, they thought he was less likely to be telling the truth than a runner who said that he had lost (Mills & Keil, 2005). Apparently, children take people's intentions and motivations into account when they are quite young as a way of judging their truthfulness.

> Q: What are some reasons why indirect speech might take longer to learn to understand than direct speech?

A different aspect of the social uses of language involves learning how to be a conversational partner—how to create a clear narrative and how to use and interpret the pragmatic devices that enhance communication. Research suggests two broad patterns in the development of these skills. First, even the youngest speakers usually have some sensitivity to pragmatic devices and other conversational practices. Second, full mastery of such devices and skills takes many years, and young children often miss the more subtle nuances of communicative practices (Thompson, 1997). We will consider a few examples to illustrate children's early but incomplete awareness of these conventions: turn-taking skills, collaborative repair, politeness mechanisms, and narrative skills.

Turn-taking is a key aspect of learning to converse with others. Each speaker must be able to sense when the other has reached the end of a thought or a reasonable pause point. Almost all children sometimes interrupt inappropriately, but these turn-taking failures, while very noticeable, seem to be fairly uncommon. Even the youngest children rarely engage in simultaneous speech when someone is speaking to them (Garvey, 1984; Garvey & Berninger, 1981). In addition, young children are sensitive to pragmatic cues, such as the length of a speaker's pause, that serve as signals for turn-taking (Miura, 1993).

In the course of speaking to conversational partners, miscommunications may sometimes arise, necessitating collaborative repairs. The repair is completed when the speaker who was misunderstood realizes what was missing from the unclear utterance and repairs it by providing the necessary details to her communicative partner. Even very young children show some rudimentary forms of collaborative repair in their play. In one observational study, a group of 2- and 3-year-olds talking among themselves at nap time worked together to resolve miscommunications in very much the same way that adults do (Aviezer, 2003). Moreover, bilingual children as young as 2½ engaged in repairs while talking to someone who spoke only one of their languages. In these cases, if the listener asked the child to clarify a miscommunication, the child would switch to the listener's language (Comeau et al., 2007). On the other hand, despite their early, basic understanding of collaborative repairs, younger children show a limited ability to monitor the context of a conversation and understand when clarifications are needed (Loukusa et al., 2007).

Finally, it is important to keep in mind that conversational norms vary significantly across cultures—and even among supposedly similar peoples. Thus, even though the Swedes are considered quite reserved by international standards, a cross-cultural comparison of mealtime conversations revealed that they are chatterboxes compared with the Finns (Tryggvason, 2006). Every mealtime was an opportunity to instill in children this very noticeable difference in conversational style. Thus, the tempo of conversational exchanges, the time intervals that are perceived as "uncomfortable silences," and the amount of time that any one speaker talks before relinquishing control of the conversation are not simply reflections of general cogni-

tive styles of information processing constraints. Instead, they can evolve over the years to have their own form in each culture and then be passed down from generation to generation.

Politeness mechanisms also vary considerably between languages and cultures; some languages, such as Japanese, have subtle conventions of politeness that may take until adulthood to master (Brown & Levinson, 1987; Holtgraves, 2002; Watts, 2003). Politeness serves complex social functions, including acknowledging differences in status or power, or softening the impact of a request (Clark & Schunk, 1980). Thus, when adults want someone else to do something, whether it is as simple as passing the salt or as onerous as jump-starting a car, they do not just issue directives. Instead, they embed the request in a frame of politeness. They also tend to be more polite with strangers than with close friends or family. Learning all these subtleties of politeness takes children several years. Early on, they often use simple direct commands like "Pass the salt!" (Bates, 1976). Not until age 7 or 8 do they begin to frequently make the kind of indirect requests that are culturally considered polite ("Could you pass the salt, please?"). By around age 9 or 10, children can easily recognize the inappropriateness of direct requests made by others (Axia & Baroni, 1985; Baroni & Axia, 1989).

Narrative skills involve the ability to describe an event in a coherent, organized way that conveys its key themes. Fully developed narrative skills normally consist of devices that convey the story's structure, including a brief summary or "title" telling the listener what the story is about, an introduction that is often quite conventional (such as "once upon a time . . ."), descriptions of the story's time and place, its characters, and the problem or challenge they face, the resolution, and an ending that, like the introduction, is often stylized. In addition, narrative skills include a kind of interpretation of the story's events, such as signaling the speaker's point of view through emphasis (Uchikoshi, 2005, see also Chang, 2004). Finally, narratives should order a sequence of events clearly in time, leaving out unimportant details.

Although children as young as 3 years old have a sense that events should be described in temporal order, children do not develop most narrative skills until they are about 6 years old. Younger children often omit key events from their narratives, giving incomplete accounts in which the events are not connected. Even 5-year-olds often end their stories at the high point rather than continuing through to the resolution (Peterson & McCabe, 1983). Thus, narrative skills develop and grow increasingly elaborate from the early preschool years into the first grade and beyond. In addition, there may be some gender differences, with girls starting to use context and make evaluative comments earlier than boys (Haden et al., 1997).

Narrative skills do not develop in the same way the world over. Their structure depends in important ways on the child's culture, including, for example, the extent to which the child experiences bedtime stories (Fivush et al., 2006; Heath, 1986). In one study, when 5- and 6-year-olds engaged in reading experiences that encouraged dialogues about the content of a storybook, they showed a substantial increase in narrative skills compared with children who received phoneme-awareness training, a common technique for early literacy teaching (Lever & Sénéchal, 2011). Given that the development of narrative skills enhances some forms of memory and may help to foster some reading skills (Fivush et al., 2006), it is impressive that narrative skills can even be imparted by mass media in relatively simple ways. For example, in one study, kindergarten children watched one of two television shows regularly for 1 year: either a program with a strong narrative structure or one that focused on verbal skills and vocabulary. By the end of the year, the group that had watched the show with a strong narrative structure showed markedly better narrative skills than the other group (Uchikoshi, 2005). Even though certain ways of describing events may seem obvious and automatic, it is clear that children's narrative skills improve when they are exposed to certain approaches to storytelling modeled in the broader culture.

This survey of conversational skills reveals that mastering them takes more time than almost any other aspect of language development. Very early on, children show awareness of turn-taking, collaborative repairs, politeness, and narrative skills. But in most cases, mastering these skills depends on developing an ability to read the social and cultural context of a conversation as it is unfolding, a skill that does not always come easily, even to adults.

Conclusions

Language is among humans' most distinctive abilities. Almost all people share this capacity. By contrast, after years of intensive and sophisticated instruction, even the most talented primates are far less linguistically competent than young children who receive no explicit language instruction at all. The capacity to acquire language is apparently so powerful that children who learn two or even three languages simultaneously do not seem to learn them more slowly than those who acquire only one (Gleitman & Bloom, 1999). And regardless of the number of initial languages, no one remembers trying to learn a language as a young child—it *just happens*.

We have seen substantial support for the view that we are endowed with a set of cognitive capacities that seem to be specifically tailored for language. That endowment

is assumed to be the basis behind universals in linguistic structure throughout the world. Many cognitive and perceptual universals might well arise from stable environmental regularities, but such accounts are difficult to make in the case of language. Nonetheless, even with such an endowment, a great deal else is required for successful language acquisition. Thus, we might also have a much larger general learning ability than all other species that enables us to handle larger informational bundles much more easily and that supplements any language-specific mechanisms to make human language especially rich and complex. We might also have distinctive cognitive skills that are essential not just to language acquisition but also to a range of other cognitive activities that are distinctively human, such as joint attention, hierarchical embedding, and logical thought. These skills might again support any language-specific mechanisms in powerful ways.

At the same time, it would be too strong an interpretation to try to account for the human capacity for language solely in terms of general cognitive skill or in terms of other nonlinguistic cognitive capacities. A child's general cognitive abilities seem to have only a modest influence on his language acquisition. In some areas of thought, mature primates approach the competence levels of a 3-year-old child; yet with respect to language, they seem vastly worse off. In addition, while it is certainly true that we have other apparently distinctive capacities besides language, such as the production of art, those abilities do not seem to be obviously based on language. At present, there are no compelling demonstrations of cognitive capacities that are larger in scope than language and that can completely explain language acquisition.

Yet, aspects of language acquisition still draw on other domains of cognitive development as well. Thus, word meanings do not seem to be acquired in the same manner as the grammar of a language. Words are acquired through more general cognitive learning mechanisms, ones that are especially sensitive to the intentions of speakers. A rich network of constraints is needed to explain how word learning ever gets off the ground, but none of those constraints may be specific to language.

That all but the tiniest fraction of humans effortlessly acquires natural languages with all their remarkable complexity is one of the great wonders of cognitive science. It is all the more remarkable that this occurs without any explicit instruction and usually without any explicit formulation of rules. We also see in language acquisition a reprise of many of the key themes that have appeared in earlier chapters and that will appear again in later chapters. These include the importance of constraints, of social and cultural context, of the interplay between both domain-specific and domain-general faculties, and of the ways in which structures become fine-tuned through interactions with the environment. Language is also an intrinsically social enterprise, and yet its acquisition depends on the cognitive and representational capacities of each individual that make learning possible. Finally, we have seen that language is not just one thing with one pattern of acquisition.

Grammar, word meanings, and pragmatics each have their own distinctive developmental stories and mechanisms, and while they do intersect in interesting ways, it is clear that no one overall account of learning works for these areas collectively.

STUDY AND REVIEW

SUMMARY

The Structure and Complexity of Language

- Language has generativity, which means that an unlimited number of novel expressions can be created by combining basic linguistic structures and by using basic rules.
- The main components of language are phonology (the sound patterns and rules for combining sounds into words), semantics (word meanings), grammar (including syntax—the rules for the structural relations of words), and pragmatics (how intended meaning is conveyed or understood in context).
- Universal constraints on possible grammatical structures may apply to all languages.

Acquiring a First Language

- Infants initially perceive more phonemic differences than the ones that they hear in the language spoken around them, but they soon come to perceive only the phonemes (or sounds) that are used in their native language.
- Infants begin babbling at about 4 months old. They go on to one-word utterances when they are about 1 year old and then to multiword utterances when they are around 1½ years old.
- Infants start to acquire language rules that are largely tacit and can generalize from words that they know to plural words and regular and irregular past tenses that they have never encountered before and do not know. As they grow older, however, they may overregularize plurals and past tenses until they finally are able to again use both regular and irregular constructions, thus showing a U-shaped developmental curve in language acquisition.
- Adults often use child-directed speech when talking to infants, speaking slowly and loudly, using a high-pitched voice, and accentuating the boundaries between words. As children start to incorrectly put together words, adults will often respond with recastings of what the child has said to show the child a correct grammatical form without specifically indicating that he was mistaken or giving him a rule for the correct form.

Theories of Language Acquisition

- Behavioral approaches maintain that language is learned through reinforcement and associations. But since parents rarely correct a child's grammar, this does not seem the most likely way that children learn to speak.
- Connectionist approaches use computer modeling of language acquisition to argue that humans use parallel processing and large multilayered networks of associations to learn to speak.
- Statistical learning approaches focus on language learning based on the probability of sounds co-occurring or following after each other in the speech stream. They examine how infants recognize recurring sound sequences within words or between words when they hear streams of sounds. Bayesian approaches are one way of tabulating statistical patterns, and they allow for straightforward integration of both statistical information and rules.
- Nativist approaches claim that infants are born with a language acquisition device (LAD) that enables them to recognize patterns common to all languages but that is flexible enough for the acquisition of particular words and constructions in specific languages. The LAD is dedicated to the learning of linguistic structures and not other forms of knowledge.

Discovering the Meanings of Words

- Children link words to concepts, which enables them to apply the words to the corresponding objects, properties of objects, or relations between objects. This linkage is a mapping of the words to the concepts and occurs without specific training and so quickly that it is often referred to as fast mapping.
- Constraints on word meanings, based on biases for interpreting words, limit the number of possible meanings that can be linked to a given word. There can be perceptual constraints (for example, the shape bias), conceptual constraints (for example, the whole-object bias), and pragmatic constraints (for example, that each object has only one mutually exclusive label) that help children more easily learn what words stand for.

- As children grow older, their understanding of word meanings changes. For example, they tend to both overextend word meanings (broadly applying meanings to many words) and to underextend (applying meanings too narrowly). For some kinds of words, there is also a shift from meanings based primarily on characteristic features (properties typically associated with members of a category) to defining features (properties that are necessary and specific to category membership).

The Growth of Grammar

- Common principles govern the internal structure of all languages, all of which have such categories as subjects, verbs, and objects, and certain abstract structural relations among these categories when they occur in sentences, while at the same time allowing for other structures that are unique to each language.
- Different parameters apply to specific languages, including the language's branching direction, which is the way that linguists describe different patterns of hierarchical embedding of syntactic elements in a sentence.

Effects of Age on Language Acquisition

- There may be a critical period for language acquisition, such that a language's grammar is more easily learned, as is its pronunciation without an accent, before a certain age (approximately puberty).
- Feral children may never easily learn a language's syntax if they are returned to human contact after they reach puberty.
- American Sign Language is more easily learned before puberty, just as is spoken language.
- Children who are born deaf and not exposed to language have been shown to invent their own sign language, complete with a rich, elaborate syntactic structure. This invention process occurs before the critical-period window closes.

The Domain Specificity of Language

- Aspects of language may be domain specific, with cognitive capacities tailored specifically for language, or domain general, with general cognitive abilities leading to language skills as well as to other cognitive achievements.
- Neural dissociations, such as aphasias, Williams syndrome, and specific language impairment, seem to indicate that some aspects of language are domain specific. Some cognitive structures used for the acquisition of syntax, but not semantics, may be specific to the domain of language. Despite intriguing genetic markers of language processing difficulty, the precise nature of these domain-specific structures remains a matter of active debate.
- Humans seem to have a special ability to acquire languages that is not shared with any other primates. Although chimpanzees have been taught sign language and bonobos have been taught to communicate with lexigrams, no nonhuman primate has even approached the linguistic abilities of any normal human child.

Language and Thought

- The Sapir-Whorf hypothesis held that language influences thought. But this classic view of language as dramatically changing thought in ways that are strikingly different across families of languages has not been shown to be true. In more subtle ways, however, specific languages do seem to influence the availability of certain cognitive schemas that can in turn cause differences in task performance.
- Researchers also doubt older views that languages in general cause a new stage of cognitive development by dramatically amplifying the powers of thought. At the same time, there are many smaller ways in which the emergence of language may foster the growth of cognitive skills.

Language and Communication

- Children constantly refine their abilities to understand the real meanings behind utterances. These abilities start, in more limited ways, very early with young children showing some sense of metaphor and of the ways in which speakers' motivations are relevant to the truth of their utterances. Children also show marked increases in conversational and narrative skills during the preschool and early school years.

THOUGHT QUESTIONS

1. In what ways does bilingualism seem to confer cognitive benefits? Would those benefits be reduced if the second language were acquired as an adult? Why or why not?
2. When we write out our ideas, we often find that we can create more complex thoughts and arguments than when we merely try to do so orally. In what ways might the cognitive benefits of writing be analogous to the cognitive benefits that oral language confers on nonverbal thought? In what ways are those benefits different?
3. Given that the vast majority of children rapidly acquire their first language without any explicit instruction, some argue that it is odd to grade language courses in college in the same manner used to grade other types of coursework. They believe that language competency in college should instead be treated more like passing a swimming test. Consider the pros and cons of this position and state your own view.
4. How is the acquisition of birdsong, as described in Chapter 4, similar to the acquisition of human language? How is it different?

KEY TERMS

aphasia (p. 285)

babbling (p. 264)

branching direction (p. 280)

characteristic feature (p. 279)

child-directed speech (p. 267)

connectionism (p. 270)

constraints on word meanings
(p. 275)

defining feature (p. 279)

egocentrism (p. 294)

fast mapping (p. 274)

feral child (p. 282)

generativity (p. 262)

grammar (p. 262)

holophrase (p. 264)

language acquisition device
(LAD) (p. 272)

lexicon (p. 262)

linguistic determinism
(p. 290)

linguistic relativity (p. 290)

morpheme (p. 264)

motherese (p. 267)

mutual exclusivity (p. 277)

natural language (p. 261)

overextension (p. 278)

overregularization (p. 266)

phoneme (p. 262)

phonology (p. 262)

poverty of the stimulus
argument (p. 273)

pragmatics (p. 263)

prelinguistic vocalization
(p. 264)

principles and parameters
approach (p. 280)

prosody (p. 280)

recasting (p. 267)

referential communications
task (p. 294)

riddle of reference (p. 274)

Sapir-Whorf hypothesis
(p. 290)

semantic development
(p. 273)

semantics (p. 262)

shape bias (p. 275)

specific language impairment
(SLI) (p. 286)

statistical learning (p. 270)

syntax (p. 262)

telegraphic speech (p. 265)

underextension (p. 278)

universal constraints
(p. 263)

whole-object bias (p. 275)

Williams syndrome (p. 285)

9

The Growth of Knowledge

Dimensions of Cognitive Development

- Qualitative versus Quantitative Development
- Global versus Local Patterns of Development
- Foundational versus Emergent Constraints

A Closer Look at Piaget's Theory

- The Preoperational Period

- The Concrete Operational Period
- The Formal Operational Period
- Alternative Explanations of Piaget's Theory and Results

Domains of Knowledge

- Spatial Relations
- Number
- Biology
- Other Domains of Thought

Sociocultural Views of the Development of Knowledge

- Vygotsky's Views

Conclusions

Summary

For over a century, researchers have interviewed children at different ages to see how they conceptualize and talk about the world around them. As children age, their understanding of the world changes. These changes seem apparent even if the vocabulary they use is not different. Something about their thought patterns themselves seems to change with development. Consider two brothers, ages 5 and 9 years old, overhearing adults discussing various family relationships, including siblings and parent-child relations, between people that the children do not know. At one point, the 9-year-old interrupts to say that one person must be another's uncle. The adults nod in agreement, while the 5-year-old looks surprised, then confused. "How did you know that?" he asks his brother. Just such a conversation happened between two of our sons when they were young, and it illustrates a clear contrast in how they drew inferences from what was said in the overheard conversation. Our older son understood kinship terms in such a way as to realize that one must be an uncle. Our younger son could not grasp that such a relationship was logically implied by what was said.

When children talk about the world, you can quickly guess their approximate age, even when the vocabulary they use at different ages is about the same. At a deeper level than word choice, their thought patterns seem to mature with development. As a result, children of different ages sometimes interpret the same conversation in quite disparate ways.

This chapter explores how age differences affect the way that children think about and understand the world. Our goal here is to characterize the changes in cognition that occur with age. We will see right away that these changes do not just affect children's language. Instead, they take place at the level of children's conceptual knowledge, which is then reflected in their language. We will want to understand how the changes in children's knowledge and thoughts are manifested in the things children say and do. To this end, we will look at how they reason about simple real-world situations, ranging from pouring liquids into containers, to animals' life cycles, to the occurrence of day and night. We will then see how researchers use that information to infer what is changing in the child's mind.

In all these cases, we will ask how a child's understanding of the world changes with age. Does the older child simply know more facts about the world? Is the older child simply faster or endowed with a larger memory that somehow makes him see events and relations differently? Does the older child have certain ways of thinking, such as an understanding of certain logical relationships, that are unavailable to the younger child? Studying the ways that children come to know and understand the world has yielded some extremely ambitious, broad theories about psychological development. These theories have captivated professionals in many fields who work with children, affecting many aspects of their work, from school curriculum designs to psychotherapy techniques.

This chapter also explores some of the differences between the best-known theories of the growth of children's knowledge. We will consider how these approaches differ on each of three dimensions used to describe developmental changes: (1) Are changes considered qualitative or quantitative? (2) Are developments viewed as global or local? (3) Is the process of change limited and directed by foundational constraints, which are present from the start (often allied with "nature" views), or by emergent constraints, which arise over the course of development and reflect the influences of experience (often allied with "nurture" views)?

The first theorist we will discuss is the highly influential Jean Piaget. Then, as we have in other chapters, we will consider the research that has followed from his work and challenged many of his ideas. As we will see, many decades after Piaget's initial studies, researchers continue to test children with variations on his experimental tasks, and many of the phenomena he uncovered remain topics of intense interest. Along the lines of the recent work on infant cognition, which we discussed in Chapter 5, this more recent research on childhood cognition suggests that young children are far more capable than Piaget thought possible. Much as was the case with infant cognition, apparent failures by young children on some Piagetian tasks have been reinterpreted in ways that reveal that young children actually have a range of impressive cognitive abilities that serve as building blocks for later conceptual growth.

We will then turn to how children develop basic knowledge and understanding within several broad nonsocial domains that are relevant to life in all cultures, such as spatial relations, number, and the biological world. By looking into these culturally universal domains, we will be focusing on intuitive forms of knowledge and taking the perspective of the child trying to understand the structure of the world around her.

Finally, we will consider the broad social and cultural contexts within which cognitive development occurs. Children do not develop as isolated individuals trying to make sense of the world alone. Instead, they grow up in particular cultural and social settings, which are critical components in understanding their cognitive development. We will see that something as basic as living in a rural setting versus an urban setting can strongly influence how children think about the living world and that a culture's emphasis on individualism as opposed to collectivism can influence how children interpret simple events. We will consider the sociocultural perspective put forth by the Russian psychologist Lev Semyonovich Vygotsky, who believed that children are guided by the frameworks of knowledge and ways of thinking that prevail in their own culture and that they eventually come to internalize them. More generally, we will consider how parents and teachers can provide support that enables children to perform at much higher cognitive levels than they otherwise would.

In the next chapter, we will look at the child from a different perspective, one that focuses on specific cognitive skills like memory, attention, and reasoning, which enable the child to process information and negotiate the world. There, we will also examine a few specific skills—reading, arithmetic reasoning, and using symbolic representations—in which individuals' levels of accomplishment can differ significantly. The perspectives on cognitive development discussed in these two chapters are closely related, and treating them separately runs the risk of setting them artificially apart. Although they represent different aspects of cognitive development, the three dimensions of change that begin this chapter (qualitative versus quantitative change, global versus local development, and foundational versus emergent constraints) will be relevant to both discussions.

Dimensions of Cognitive Development

One of the greatest challenges in developmental psychology is to specify how a young child's mind differs from the minds of older children and adults. No one doubts that a 10-year-old knows different things about the world than a 5-year-old does. The difficulties arise in trying to carefully specify the nature of those differences. Three themes that have recurred throughout this book can provide some helpful bases for comparing and contrasting theories of cognitive development (see Figure 9.1). Each of these three dimensions can help refine our questions regarding what it is about the child's conceptual thought and understanding that changes and why.

Qualitative versus Quantitative Development

One of the oldest and most persistent issues in developmental psychology concerns whether particular patterns of cognitive change that affect the way children mentally represent or process information are best described as qualitative or quantitative. At first, the distinction seems easy enough. Recall that *quantitative development* involves smooth, continuous changes without the kind of abrupt transitions that

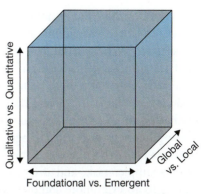

FIGURE 9.1 Three dimensions describing theories of cognitive development. Developmental theories place different amounts of emphasis on issues of qualitative versus quantitative change, global versus local change, and foundational versus emergent constraints. These three contrasts can be imagined as the dimensions of a cube that contains the full range of developmental theories. As illustrated in this chapter, most spaces within the cube are occupied by different theories, and each one's location within the cube depends on which dimensions and values it emphasizes.

would suggest a wholly new process or structure. *Qualitative development*, on the other hand, involves distinct and dramatic changes in structure. In cases of qualitative development in cognitive ability, the child has an entirely different kind of understanding or mental capacity than before. Although the differences between quantitative and qualitative development seem fairly straightforward, these contrasts can be difficult to apply to actual developmental changes. As an analogy, consider the problem of describing the change that occurs between day and night. While there are obvious qualitative differences between daytime and nighttime, the shift between these two states happens continuously and gradually. Each moment in which the light changes slightly seems extremely similar to the previous one.

Likewise, over the course of development, small incremental changes can create large qualitative differences. Viewed from another angle, this means that most qualitative changes can be broken down into a series of tiny steps—which can make the change look much more continuous and quantitative. These problems have led some developmental psychologists to abandon any attempts to distinguish between qualitative and quantitative changes. But to deny this contrast runs the risk of overlooking everyday intuitions about how children's knowledge of the world changes—as well as key differences between the theories that seek to explain these changes.

Given that qualitative changes can often be viewed as a series of many tiny quantitative changes, what does it really mean to call a cognitive change "qualitative"? A qualitative change in a child's way of thinking often means that his thinking changes dramatically. For example, imagine showing a child a bouquet of red carnations mixed with white carnations and asking, "Which is larger—the number of red carnations or the number of carnations?" If 4-year-olds seem unable to reason that there must be more carnations overall than red carnations, while 8-year-olds understand this logic immediately, we can say that a qualitative change in logical reasoning happens between the ages of 4 and 8. By contrast, if 4-year-olds can understand this kind of logic in the context of a simpler task, and if 8-year-olds fail to grasp the reasoning in an even more complex version of the task, we might say that there is a quantitative change in logical reasoning between these ages. In this scenario, the change would be considered more continuous and incremental because children's success would depend largely on the task's level of complexity rather than on the development of a completely new reasoning capacity sometime after age 4. As we consider the theories that aim to explain how knowledge develops over the course of childhood, this distinction between quantitative and qualitative change will remain important.

Global versus Local Patterns of Development

Developmental changes in knowledge can occur either globally, across all domains of knowledge, or locally, on a domain-specific basis (Wellman & Gelman, 1998; see Figure 9.2). Accounts of global cognitive development describe changes to broad mental capacities that are thought to be used in all

kinds of thinking. Thus, when this kind of **domain-general** cognitive capacity improves, it should lead to advancements in each and every domain of knowledge. For example, imagine that humans' cognitive capacity to reason about all kinds of cause-and-effect relationships is a single, broad, global ability. If this were the case, then a young child who does not understand that causes must precede effects would make errors in understanding the sequence of all sorts of events—including biological events (for example, claiming that having an infection could cause you to get germs), physics (for example, claiming that thunder could cause lightning), social interactions (for example, claiming that scolding the class caused the teacher to be displeased), and events in other domains. In contrast, in accounts of local, **domain-specific** cognitive development, children are seen as going through a series of changes in knowledge and reasoning that are unique to each domain. In this view, a child's ability to reason about causes and effects in the biological world would progress largely independently from her causal reasoning about physical mechanics or social interactions.

Several questions about the growth of knowledge directly pertain to the contrast between global and local cognitive development. A recurring issue focuses on whether the learning processes that adults use to acquire specialized skills differ substantially from the ways that young children acquire general knowledge about the world. One difference between children and adults may revolve around the idea that children are universal novices, while adults are only novices in more restricted areas (Brown & Campione, 1994). We will want to keep these issues in mind as we consider the development of thought in different domains and how conceptual development in children might be different from adult conceptual learning.

Q: What sorts of domains have most often been invoked in accounts of domain specificity in cognitive development?

Foundational versus Emergent Constraints

As we have seen, development always involves interactions between genetic and environmental factors. Keeping this perspective in mind, however, it is also increasingly clear that the role that each of these factors plays varies greatly between different aspects of development. One way to think about these influences is in terms of how and when the developmental path is narrowed, or constrained, toward a particular outcome (see Figure 9.3). Thus, some kinds of knowledge seem to emerge in ways that are innately con-

FIGURE 9.2 Global versus local patterns of change. When young children like those at this fountain undergo a change in their concepts about animals, do their other concepts—such as how to count the number of ducks or boats in the water or the way the stick they are holding can act as a lever—also change in roughly the same ways? Or does their intuitive understanding of biology, number, and physics each show distinct developmental patterns?

FIGURE 9.3 Foundational versus emergent constraints. When a young child starts to understand how solid objects collide with one another and cause movement, is that understanding largely guided by intuitions about physical mechanics that are present in infancy (foundational constraints) or by the knowledge the child gains from experience, such as watching billiard balls smacking together, then rolling away (emergent constraints)?

strained to follow roughly the same developmental path across a wide range of environments. For example, as we saw in Chapter 3 in the perceptual realm, binocular vision develops in much the same way in the vast majority of children. Only in extreme cases of visual deprivation or brain damage do children fail to develop the ability to mentally integrate the visual information from both eyes. The outcomes of these developmental paths (within a wide range of normally experienced environments) are limited from the outset by **foundational constraints**, which are usually thought of as genetically rooted.

Other forms of knowledge can show more variation in their developmental paths in response to environmental influences. We will refer to the limitations on these kinds of developments as **emergent constraints** because of the way their effects emerge—and come to shape thought and behavior—as a result of specific experiences. One cognitive skill that is significantly influenced by emergent constraints is the ability to recognize the symbols of a particular writing system. This ability requires extensive exposure to a specific set of symbols, and cultures vary greatly both in their uses of writing symbols and in which of those symbols children learn. A child's experiences with her own culture's writing system gives rise to the emergent constraints that guide the processes of learning to read and write in a particular language. For example, when children learn to read Hebrew or Arabic they must not only learn

to encode different kinds of symbols for sounds, they must also adopt the practice of reading from right to left. This pattern can become so deeply ingrained that it also affects their automatic visual scanning patterns and can change the way dyslexia, a language-based learning disability, is manifested (Ziegler & Goswami, 2005).

In light of the understanding that genetic and environmental influences together contribute to all aspects of development, it remains valuable to consider their relative contributions to particular developmental paths. In doing so, we can contrast the cases in which foundational constraints dominate with the cases in which emergent constraints are more central. Couching this contrast in terms of foundational versus emergent constraints (rather than as a contrast between "nature" and "nurture" or between "innate" and "learned" behaviors) captures the interactional nature of development while also representing the contrast between biologically determined learning frameworks and those that arise through experience.

In many areas of cognitive development, psychologists continue to debate the relative roles of foundational constraints (arising from genetic factors) and emergent constraints (arising from environmental factors). Consider, for example, the vigorous debates presented in Chapter 8 about how children come to know a language. Some theorists believe that the language learning process must be supported by powerful foundational constraints. They argue that young children's experiences with language are insufficient to explain how children learn complex systems of grammar and that the process must be guided by a rich set of foundational constraints. In contrast, other theorists contend that there are few foundational or genetic constraints on language learning. They propose that the child is able to extract rich information about language from the environment, using a more general (less foundationally constrained) learning system that is highly attuned to sound patterns and correlations. In this view, as the child gradually acquires linguistic knowledge, this knowledge establishes the emergent constraints that guide further learning.

Most major theories of cognitive development can be understood in terms of where they lie along each of the three dimensions we have considered: qualitative versus quantitative development, global versus local change, and foundational versus emergent constraints on development. As we explore how children's knowledge and understanding change, we will want to keep these dimensions in mind. Each can provide a useful way of clarifying what kinds of changes are taking place and how they are occurring. We will focus initially on Piaget's theory of cognitive development from the toddler years into early adolescence, referring back to these dimensions to better understand how Piaget's theory contrasts with other theories (see Figure 9.4).

FIGURE 9.4 Piaget and young children. Piaget is best known for his work on cognitive development that occurs as preschoolers, who are in the preoperational stage, develop into school-age children and enter the stage of concrete operations.

A Closer Look at Piaget's Theory

Jean Piaget is as central to the study of children's cognitive development as he is to the study of infant cognition (see Chapter 5). Although his theory has been challenged and reevaluated in many ways, it has remained a foundational point of reference for many researchers. As described in Chapter 5, Piaget believed that the child is born with a bundle of built-in sensorimotor reflexes. As the infant learns about the world from experience, these reflexes are modified and transformed into new *schemes*, which, as we have seen in our discussion of infant cognition, are patterns of understanding and interacting with the world. These schemes are the basic building blocks in Piaget's theory of the young child's mental life. As the child gains more experience, his schemes combine, interact, and grow more elaborate. For Piaget, these changes in the schemes' structure and complexity explained the child's progress through later periods of cognitive development.

In this view, the child's acquired knowledge exerts a broad influence on future learning. When the child masters certain knowledge, this change enables him to make a qualitative transition into a new way of thinking and of understanding the world. Piaget also viewed these transitions largely as domain general, affecting all domains of knowledge. For example, Piaget argued that when the preschooler develops a sufficient understanding of the concepts of "greater than" and "less than," this enables the emergence of a new form of logic known as **transitive reasoning**. Tran-

sitive reasoning (also known as transitive inference) involves reasoning about known relationships of stimuli to infer a relationship between the stimuli that were not initially directly related to each other (for example, if A is taller than B, and B is taller than C, then A must be taller than C). As a result, children who can use transitive reasoning perform qualitatively differently from children who cannot on many tasks that involve comparing unequal sizes or amounts. In Piaget's view, children develop a whole new cognitive ability or structure; the child's learning experiences foster the development of the new cognitive structure, but it is the new structure itself that, once it reaches a certain degree of complexity, launches the development of the next new structure or cognitive ability.

Piaget's theory posits four major periods of cognitive development: the *sensorimotor period*, the *preoperational period*, the *concrete operational period*, and the *formal operational period* (see Table 9.1). The discussion in Chapter 5 focused on the sensorimotor period, which, in Piaget's view, makes up the first 2 years of cognitive development. This chapter focuses on the next two periods: the preoperational and concrete operational periods, and particularly on the shift from preoperational to concrete operational thought. Piaget believed that during these two periods, children initially grasp the structure of the world and begin to substantially elaborate and flesh out that understanding over time.

> **Q:** Where along each of the three dimensions of cognitive development would Piaget's theory be situated?

The Preoperational Period

According to Piaget's theory, children emerge from the sensorimotor period at about age 2, having gained a crude ability to think in terms of simple symbols, which Piaget believed enables them to mentally represent ideas that are not completely driven by action and perception. The emergence of language is the most obvious hallmark of this new ability. They then enter the **preoperational period** (approximately ages 2 to 7), during which they lack the capacity to think about the world abstractly. Instead, Piaget held that preoperational children, while having learned symbols such as the words of their language, are unable to use those symbols in flexible ways that help them to break down a task into its critical components and represent it as a set of lawfully interacting elements. Thus, a preoperational child might remark that a ball of dough gets wider under a rolling pin. However, Piaget found that the same child could not

Period of Cognitive Development	Age	Characteristics	Relevant Cognitive Skills
Sensorimotor	Birth–2 years	The infant represents the world in terms of her own sensations and reflexes.	Object permanence
Preoperational	2–7 years	The child is egocentric, ignores all but one aspect of a problem, fails to use basic operators such as compensation, reversibility, and identity.	Symbolic representations
Concrete operational	7–12 years	The child can apply operators to concrete information, but fails to apply them to abstract or hypothetical information.	Classification, conservation, seriation, transitive reasoning
Formal operational	12 years on	The child is able to think logically about things that are not immediately present and can engage in hypothetico-deductive reasoning.	Scientific reasoning tasks

TABLE 9.1 Piaget's four periods of cognitive development. According to Piaget's theory, transitions between these periods involve sweeping, across-the-board transformations in the nature of thought. Although children show reliable patterns of failures and successes on the experimental tasks that Piaget devised, psychologists are still debating how accurate he was in interpreting what kinds of cognitive changes underlie these patterns.

isolate the relationship between the ball's width and its other physical properties. Thus, the child could not understand that the increase in its width must be accompanied by a corresponding decrease in its height. More generally, because the preoperational child lacks the ability to think about relations between concrete properties such as height and width, he cannot see how a change in one property might necessarily imply a change in another property. By contrast, older children realize that the ball must logically become shorter in a way that compensates for its increasing width.

Piaget's theory predicted that children in each period except the last one are largely unable to grasp the kinds of concepts and problems that require cognitive abilities developed only in the next period. In his research, Piaget observed how children of different ages fared on specific types of tasks, and he made strong claims about their abilities based on their performance on these tasks. The most famous and best studied of these tasks are the **conservation tasks**, in which children are asked to judge whether certain physical properties of an object, such as its size or amount, are "conserved" (remain unchanged) when the object is transformed along different sorts of dimensions. Our ball of dough is one such example—that is, an increase in width must be associated with a decrease in height because the amount of dough remains the same.

To make the concept of conservation more explicit, consider one of the tasks used to test whether children have mastered the conservation of number. In this type of conservation task, an experimenter shows the child two rows of objects: let's assume they are coins. Initially, as shown in Figure 9.5, the coins are arranged in two identical rows, with each row having the same number of coins with equal spaces between them. The experimenter then asks the child whether both rows have the same number of coins or if one row has more coins. When the child responds that they have the same number of coins, the experimenter asks the child to watch carefully, then spreads out one row so that the coins in that row now form a much longer line. Again, the experimenter asks the child whether one row has more coins or if they both have the same number. Many preschoolers will now answer that the longer row has more coins.

Part of Piaget's genius lay in his ability to devise similar tasks to test children's understanding of conservation with many different kinds of quantities, such as number, liquid volume, mass, and length (see Figure 9.6). Piaget argued that children fail at conservation tasks because they lack the critical mental **operators**, or formal mental tools, needed to consider the relations between sets of properties. Operators are therefore logical, rule-based ways of comparing mental representations of situations before and after transformations.

In particular, Piaget believed that preoperational children lack the logical operators of *compensation*, *reversibility*, and *identity*. The operator of **compensation** involves noting that a change in one dimension compensates for a change in another dimension. In the example of the two rows of coins, the children notice that one row is longer than the other after the experimenter spreads out one of the rows of coins. But if they lack the operator of compensation, they do not understand that the increase in length is due to an increase in the space between the coins. The operator of **reversibility**

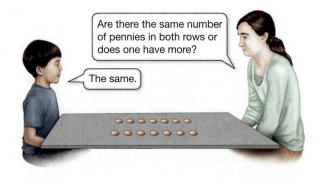

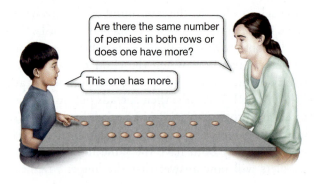

FIGURE 9.5 Piaget's number conservation task. Children in the preoperational stage seem to see the change in the length of a row of coins as relevant to the number of coins in the display, therefore failing to "conserve" number.

focus excessively on one dimension of a transformation (for example, length) while ignoring other relevant dimensions (for example, density), a phenomenon called **centration**. But he said that once children gain new mental computational and representational tools that enable them to solve one conservation task, they begin gradually learning to use these operators on a wider range of conservation tasks.

> **Q:** Provide three specific examples of different conservation tasks.

Piaget expanded his theory to explain the difficulties that preoperational children have with many other kinds of tasks besides conservation. One such task is the **seriation** of objects, the ability to order objects according to a shared property, such as length or size. A seriation task might involve taking a pile of sticks of different lengths and putting them in order from longest to shortest. This ability requires an understanding of the transitive ordering relationships among the objects on a particular dimension, such as length—for example, if A is greater than B, and B is greater than C, then A must be greater than C on that dimension. Piaget also applied his theory to children's performance on **classification** tasks, which involve sorting objects according to a consistent criteria, such as color, shape, or size.

Most relevant to this chapter, however, are the ways in which Piaget used the same fundamental principles to

involves noting that a change can be reversed or "run backward" to return things to their initial condition. Thus, children who lack the operator of reversibility fail to notice that the longer row—which they believe has more coins—can easily be transformed back to the length of the shorter row without removing any coins. The operator of **identity** involves noting that values on a dimension are the same. In the case of the rows of coins, this means noting that the critical dimension of numerical value does not change—it remains constant despite the other changes. But children lacking the operator of identity do not realize that the number of coins remains the same. Piaget argued that in the preoperational period, children do not have these operators and, as a result, are unable to conserve in any area. He also believed that preoperational children's lack of mental operators lead them to

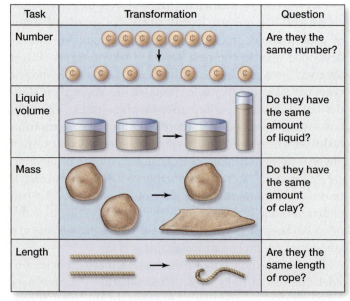

Task	Transformation	Question
Number		Are they the same number?
Liquid volume		Do they have the same amount of liquid?
Mass		Do they have the same amount of clay?
Length		Are they the same length of rope?

FIGURE 9.6 Conservation tasks. Piaget found that children in the preoperational stage (about age 2 to 7) seemed to fail to conserve across many kinds of changes. These examples show some of the transformations Piaget used to test children's ability to conserve number, liquid volume, mass, and length.

explain how preoperational children understand concepts in such diverse domains as number, space, time, biology, and physical mechanics. He believed that there are no a priori mental processes or structures that are specifically suited for particular domains. In his view, a child's success in understanding each domain of knowledge follows directly from how well she can pick up on that domain's important patterns using broad, general cognitive capacities. As the child gains knowledge, her cognitive structures modify themselves somewhat to fit what she has learned about the environment (see the discussion of *accommodation* in Chapter 5). But these changes are constrained in important ways by the child's stage, or period, of cognitive development.

The Concrete Operational Period

According to Piaget, at roughly age 7, most children enter the **concrete operational period**. The child moves into this period by acquiring the same mental operators that he previously lacked, such as reversibility, identity, and compensation. During the concrete operational period, from about age 7 to 12, children gradually expand their use of these mental operators by applying them to a broader range of problems (see Figure 9.7). As a result, concrete operational children start to respond correctly on conservation, seriation, and classification tasks. It may take several years, however, before they can smoothly use identity, compensation, and reversibility across all tasks and situations.

The mechanism of change that enables a child to progress from preoperational thought to concrete operations is one of the less clearly explained aspects of Piaget's theory. In general terms, Piaget suggested that the knowledge structures of one stage, such as preoperational thought, become progressively elaborated to a critical point, where they become a launching platform for the next stage. The child's mental structures at the end of one stage start to lay the groundwork for the structures of the next stage, and through accommodation and assimilation, there is a qualitative restructuring of the child's thought. Concrete operational thought, however, is not the final stage for most children, for this period also has significant limitations that bind children to the here and now. Although concrete operational children use concepts such as compensation and transitivity to reason about concrete situations, Piaget argued that they cannot reason about what would happen if a situation were different from the way it is. For example, they might have difficulty reasoning about how the United States would be different if it were a mirror image of itself (with San Francisco on the East Coast and New York on the West Coast). Such reasoning about hypotheticals was said to require an ability to generate a range of hypotheses and explore the implica-

FIGURE 9.7 Concrete operations. Recycling objects by sorting them into different types is a form of classification activity. Piaget argued that only in concrete operations do children fully understand how to consistently classify objects and understand the relationships among classes, such as superordinate-subordinate relations.

tions of each one. Piaget held that this kind of thinking requires a set of more abstract mental operators that the child acquires only in the final stage: formal operations.

The Formal Operational Period

Formal operational thought has not been studied as much as preoperational and concrete operational thought, and we will discuss it only briefly here. The **formal operational period** was thought to emerge around age 12, and its hallmark was the ability to engage in **hypothetico-deductive reasoning**, the ability to think systematically about different possibilities that might depart from the current reality (Inhelder & Piaget, 1958). According to Piaget, this form of reasoning is supported by new mental operators that enable adolescents to propose hypotheses, mentally explore their logical consequences, and rule out alternative hypotheses. Thus, an important aspect of a child's advancement into the formal operational period is the ability to reason logically without reference to the immediate surroundings (which constitute the concrete world of the concrete operational child). Tests of formal operations have often involved giving a child a physical system, such as a set of pulleys, and seeing whether he can figure out how the system works by systematically testing different hypotheses. Piaget believed that a younger child would try to learn how the system works by trial and error, often failing to explore critical components of the system.

The child's achievements during the formal operational period were often thought to represent the emergence of "scientific thinking skills," the ability to plan and perform experiments by isolating individual variables and seeing how they change when they are systematically manipulated one at a time (Klahr, 2000; Kuhn & Angelev, 1976; Kuhn & Brannock, 1977; Kuhn et al., 2009). In contrast, children who are not yet in the formal operational period would simply tinker with different possibilities rather than thinking them through and applying them one by one. Indeed, one group of researchers has described the developmental transition from the concrete operational period to the formal operational period as going from an engineering model (how can I get this to work?) to a scientific model (how does this work, and what are its critical causal features?) (Schauble et al., 1991).

Piaget and Inhelder's best-known studies of the development of formal operations focused on a task in which children had to figure out how to change the length of time it takes a small pendulum to swing back and forth. The children could vary the length of the pendulum's string, the weight of the pendulum bob, and the height from which they dropped the bob to see what would cause the pendulum to swing back and forth more quickly (see Figure 9.8). Children in the concrete operational period often failed to carefully test the effects of changing a single variable while holding everything else constant. For example, these younger children typically did not compare the effects of using different bob weights with the same string length and drop height, or using different string lengths with the same bob weight and drop height. These younger children rarely realized that the string length was critical and that the bob weight and drop height did not matter. Younger children also failed on a number of other tasks that required making systematic changes to a system to isolate the critical variables.

The formal operational period differs from earlier periods in Piaget's theory in the sense that not all children achieve it. During normal development, the vast majority of children eventually progress well into concrete operational thought, but Piaget and Inhelder maintained that a significant number of people never attain formal operations, even in adulthood. In addition, there seems to be considerable cultural variation in the proportion of a population that achieves formal operations (Dasen, 1977). These variations raise questions about whether formal operations really represents a natural period of cognitive development that emerges when concrete operational thought is sufficiently developed.

Piaget was not unique in proposing that the major patterns of developmental change involve across-the-board reorganizations of children's internal representational and computational capacities. Several other thinkers also

FIGURE 9.8 Formal operations. In Piaget's pendulum task, children try to figure out what variables (length of the string, weight of the ball, or height from which the ball is dropped) determine the rate of swing. In the diagram, the boy is timing how long it takes for each ball to go through one complete swing cycle. Piaget argued that children must be in the formal operations stage to be able to systematically control variables so as to unambiguously isolate length as the only critical variable influencing periodicity.

embraced this view of cognitive development. For example, we will see that Vygotsky's (1978, 1986) sociocultural view of cognitive development also proposed broad, sweeping changes in children's modes of thought, even though Vygotsky hypothesized quite different mechanisms of change. As we evaluate Piaget's theory, we should keep in mind that some criticisms of the domain-general patterns of change he proposed may extend to other domain-general theories of development as well.

Q: What are some cognitive operations that, according to Piaget's theory, are common to success in conservation tasks during the period of concrete operations?

Alternative Explanations of Piaget's Theory and Results

Piaget's theory of cognitive development covers an extraordinarily broad range of phenomena, including language, space, number, time, causality, logic, and dreams (for overviews, see Brainerd, 1978; Flavell, 1963; Ginsburg & Opper, 1988). This breadth arises naturally from his theory of domain-general qualitative changes in the ways that children represent information. According to Piaget, these global changes should have predictable effects on almost any cognitive domain, including children's thinking about physical, social, and abstract phenomena. In addition, Piaget was extraordinarily creative in designing empirical studies that would uncover ways in which younger children's thinking differs from that of older children.

If Piaget's account were even roughly correct, it would offer a truly unified theory of cognitive development—and the vast majority of his many studies and observations do yield essentially the same results when they are repeated today. The more controversial question, however, is whether these studies truly provide an accurate test of his claims. Researchers have subjected his work to intense scrutiny over the past few decades (Brainerd, 1978; Fischer & Bidell, 1998; Gelman & Baillargeon, 1983). New studies have raised many questions about Piaget's account and have also revealed new patterns of evidence, leading to the emergence of important new theories about children's cognitive development.

One way to test a theory like Piaget's is to assess it experimentally using carefully designed variations of his tasks to determine whether alternative explanations for children's task performance might be more plausible than Piaget's account. In doing so, researchers follow a method similar to the one discussed in Chapter 8 for testing whether egocentrism affects early language development. They ask whether much younger children can succeed at simpler versions of the task that still tap into the specific ability of interest—and whether even older children fail at more sophisticated versions of the tasks.

Researchers set up studies with variations on Piaget's tasks to examine the bases for children's failure or success on the tasks (see Figure 9.9). For example, 5-year-old children might fail a conservation task for any of the following reasons: (1) As Piaget proposed, they might lack the critical cognitive structures or abilities. (2) Even if they are capable of the type of reasoning or understanding that the task is designed to test, a particular version of the task might require other kinds of cognitive skills that are beyond the reach of most 5-year-olds. For example, the task might require remembering more information than most 5-year-olds can, or it might impose demands on attention that make it too difficult for 5-year-olds. (3) When the children are presented with the task, they might not realize which aspects are most important to keep in mind and so they might fail to encode the problem correctly. If they were shown

FIGURE 9.9 Why do young children fail on Piaget's conservation tasks? Following Piaget's early studies in which children failed on conservation tasks like this one examining conservation of liquid in different-sized glasses, researchers have proposed alternative reasons for why children fail on these tasks, raising questions about Piaget's theory of cognitive developmental stages.

how to encode it, however, they would do fine. (4) If some aspect of the task seems to imply a particular kind of response, the children might be responding based partly on how they believe the experimenter wants them to answer. Piaget's theory would be supported only if the children consistently fail on the conservation task for the first of these reasons.

Another way to empirically assess alternative explanations for Piaget's results would be to conduct a similar set of studies with adults. In such studies, the experimenter could slowly increase the task's demands on encoding, attention, and memory to make it more difficult. The experimenter could also set up the tasks to subtly imply that a particular (incorrect) response is desired. The alternative explanations for Piaget's findings would gain support if the adults fail at the more difficult or unclear versions of the tasks in ways that resemble young children's failures. Since most adults would be considered cognitively mature in Piaget's view, their failures would help clarify how factors other than those that Piaget aimed to test could influence performance on the tasks he designed.

As we consider specific Piagetian tasks in detail, we will see several studies in which children seem to fail at Piaget's tasks for reasons 2 through 4. This evidence seems to undermine Piaget's own explanation for the children's failures (reason 1). Other studies have shown that, contrary to Piaget's theory, much younger children can sometimes show elements of formal operations, the most advanced level of cognitive development in his theory (Klahr, 2000; Klahr et al., 1993; Zimmerman, 2000). In addition, when the tasks are very complex in ways that tax memory and attention, even adults frequently make errors in formal operational thinking, such as failing to explore all the necessary manipulations of variables in a scientific experiment. All of these

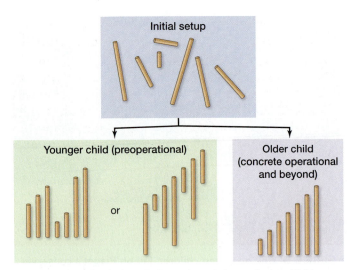

FIGURE 9.10 Seriation. In Piaget's seriation task, the child is asked to arrange a set of rods in order from shortest to longest. Preoperational children fail at this task. They often line up the rods as increasing in length at one end, but ignore the other end, or they correctly order a few rods at a time but are unable to arrange the whole set continuously. Piaget thought that children younger than about 7 typically fail at this task because they lack the mental operator that supports transitive reasoning.

patterns of behavior lend support to the alternative explanations for Piaget's results.

In the studies designed to test the alternative explanations for the patterns of failures and successes on Piaget's tasks, young children typically still make errors. But in many cases, their performance also vastly improves in ways that would be difficult to explain if the children truly lacked certain cognitive structures, as Piaget suggested. Consider, for example, the cases of seriation, thinking about classes, and conservation.

Seriation Piaget developed classic seriation tasks, in which a group of objects must be ordered according to a shared property, such as size or height. One of these tasks is to order rods according to their length, which is difficult for children younger than roughly 7 years of age (see Figure 9.10). Their failures at these tasks have often been cited as clear evidence that they lack the ability to use transitive reasoning to understand the relationships between several pairs of inequalities (for example, to understand that if Adam is taller than Bill, and Bill is taller than Chris, then Adam also must be taller than Chris). Piaget claimed that preoperational children's cognitive structures do not allow them to use transitive reasoning when they attempt seriation tasks (Halford et al., 1998).

If the younger child truly lacks the ability to use transitive reasoning, then it should be possible to show clear differences between younger and older children on any task that requires this skill. But consider for a moment how Piaget's classic seriation tasks actually test a child's transitive reasoning. A child is shown a series of rods of different lengths and asked to order them from shortest to longest. Doing so correctly

requires careful attention to the way each rod's length relates to the others. If you can remember all those relationships, you will quickly know that if rod A is longer than rod B, and rod B is longer than rod C, then rod A is also longer than rod C. You must also remember to look at both ends of the rods and not be swayed by what looks like constant length increases along the tops if the bottoms are also changing relative to each other.

The key question about Piaget's seriation task is whether children younger than around 7 fail because they are incapable of transitive reasoning or because of other elements of the task. For example, younger children may have trouble remembering how the length of each rod relates to the lengths of the others. If so, perhaps solving the memory problem would make transitive reasoning easy for them. Peter Bryant and Tom Trabasso conducted an elegant study to figure out whether young children might be failing at seriation tasks because of the tasks' memory demands (Bryant & Trabasso, 1971). This study clearly illustrates how carefully designed experiments can tease apart the reasons that children fail at Piagetian tasks.

Using the setup shown in Figure 9.11, Bryant and Trabasso extensively trained young children to compare pairs of colored rods to determine which was longer. The children learned the length relationships for pairs of rods by associating the lengths with the color of the rods and memorizing the inequalities in the lengths of these different-colored

FIGURE 9.11 Memory and transitive reasoning. In Bryant and Trabasso's study, researchers trained children by pulling pairs of colored rods out of a holder and showing the children the size differences between the rods. The children memorized the length inequality relationships (E>D, D>C, C>B, B>A) so that they were able to correctly report size inequalities when just looking at the rods inserted in the box. They were then asked about several new inequalities, which they could only determine through transitive reasoning (for example, D>B). In this scenario, in which they were trained on the memory component of the task separately, preoperational children could use transitive reasoning to figure out the novel inequalities. This finding suggests that young children had failed at Piaget's original seriation task because of problems with memory or attention, not because they were incapable of transitive reasoning.

rod pairs. They then were presented with pairs of rods that they had never directly seen side by side. To determine those length relationships, the children had to use transitive reasoning. The memory training had striking effects on the children's performance. Once the younger children had demonstrated reliable memories for the length relationships they were taught, they could easily make judgments about the new inequalities, presumably by using transitive reasoning (for example, recognizing that if rod D is longer than rod B, and B is longer than A, then D also must be longer than A). The transitive reasoning component of the task did not seem to cause them any problems.

Bryant and Trabasso's study suggests that by devising the right experimental task, such as training children to memorize a set of length inequalities before using those inequalities in transitive reasoning, researchers can disentangle transitive reasoning skills from memory capacity. Moreover, their findings suggest that children younger than about 7, whom Piaget considered preoperational, may not have problems with transitive reasoning itself. Rather, they are more likely to fail at transitive reasoning tasks because those tasks make larger memory demands than young children can manage (see Chapter 10). To defend Piaget's account, you would have to show that the new version of the task is too different from the original one to serve as a true test of transitive reasoning (Halford, 1993). Such accounts would have to show that reducing the children's memory load by training them to remember some inequalities somehow does away with their need to use real transitive reasoning to determine the novel length relationships. (This is not an easy thing to show about Bryant and Trabasso's study.)

Q: Why might children who actually understand transitive reasoning fail on most transitive reasoning tasks?

Thinking about Classes Seriation is just one of many tasks that Piaget used to support his theory. He also considered how children reason about classes when they are thinking about categories of objects. Because Piaget's model was based on domain-general (global) changes, he believed that all of a child's mental processes, including her understanding of classes, are limited in similar ways by the child's stage of cognitive development. Thus, he held that a preoperational child lacks the logical operators necessary to understand certain kinds of relationships, including **class-inclusion relations**—that is, how different classes in a hierarchy relate to each other and how broad superordinate categories can encompass

narrower, subordinate categories. These operators include transitivity (recognizing that supersets contain categories directly subordinate to them as well as objects that are subsets to those subordinate categories) and equivalences (realizing that two things are the same in some critical respect even as they vary in another respect). For example, a child who has these operators would understand that if *toy poodles* are a subset of the category *poodles*, and *poodles* are a subset of the category *dogs*, then *toy poodles* must also be a subset of *dogs*. Similarly, a child would understand equivalence in a case where a set of blue and red triangles forms a class that is distinct from one formed by a set of blue and red squares. In Piaget's view, the limitations on preoperational children's understanding of these kinds of relationships keep them from realizing how hierarchically arranged categories relate to each other (Inhelder & Piaget, 1958, 1964).

In line with his theory, Piaget documented preschool children's striking failures to understand classification. In one of Piaget's tasks, a preschooler was shown a bouquet of flowers consisting of nine daffodils and three daisies and then was asked whether there were more daffodils or more flowers (see Figure 9.12). Many preschoolers responded that there were more daffodils—which was logically impossible. Of course, even if there are more daffodils than any other kind of flower, the daffodils still must be a subset within the set of all flowers. Piaget interpreted this failure in reasoning about class-inclusion relations as evidence that the children lacked the appropriate mental operators to infer transitivity and hierarchical relations between classes.

FIGURE 9.12 Classification in preschool children. When asked, "Are there more daffodils or more flowers?" in a mixed bouquet of nine daffodils and three daisies, a preoperational child may say that there are more daffodils. Piaget argued that preoperational children cannot reason about two classes at different levels (in this case, daffodils and flowers). In his view, this limitation explains why they seem to mistake the fact that there are more daffodils than daisies for evidence that there are more daffodils than flowers.

Piaget also believed that preoperational children have difficulty understanding how classes are defined. He argued that they do not recognize that once a class is set up and defined by a set of properties, such as all red things, that criteria have to remain constant throughout all subsequent uses of the class. Rather, Piaget found that when sorting things into classes, preschoolers frequently abandon one criterion and switch to another. A 4-year-old might begin sorting things into a class based on the criterion of color and, before finishing, end up switching to the criterion of texture. Piaget also noted that instead of grouping objects based on a single criterion, such as having four legs, preschoolers sometimes sort objects based on their thematic relationships. For example, imagine an exercise in which a child is shown pictures of three barnyard animals (a cow, a horse, and a sheepdog), three animal areas (stables, a dairy barn, and a doghouse), and three kinds of animal food (oats, hay, and dog food). A researcher then asks the child to "put the ones together that go together." A 4-year-old might put the horse, the stables, and the oats together; might group the cow, the barn, and the hay; and then might put together the dog, the doghouse, and the dog food. Because there are no logical common criteria uniting the items in each group, the groups are not true classes in the logical sense. In contrast, at around 7 years of age, a child would form true class-based clusters of animals, dwellings, and foods. Piaget believed that the younger child fails because he does not yet have the mental operators necessary to understand the logical bases of classes.

The developmental changes that Piaget described for reasoning about classes have been subject to the same concerns as his accounts of transitive reasoning and seriation: Could factors other than the ones Piaget proposed be responsible for these changes in performance? Apart from Piaget's view that domain-general limits constrain children's reasoning abilities, other possible factors include the tasks' demands on memory and attention, the arbitrariness and meaninglessness of the tasks for younger children, and potential misunderstandings of the experimental situation or the experimenter's intentions. Consider, for example, how children's performance on classification tasks changes when the classes are made less arbitrary and more meaningful (Rosch et al., 1976).

The **basic level of categorization** falls at an intermediate level of specificity. It is narrower than the very general, superordinate categories, such as animals, furniture, and clothing, but broader than highly specific subordinate categories, such as collies, kitchen chairs, and T-shirts. As Figure 9.13 shows, the basic level corresponds to such things as horses, dogs, tables, chairs, pants, and shirts. At the basic level, all category members are both maximally similar to each other and maximally distinct from members of other categories. At the superordinate level, such as the category *animals*, members need to have only a few common features to belong to the category. On the other hand, within a basic-level category like *horses*, there are few obvious differences between members, such as Arabian horses and quarter horses. Children's earliest word labels also tend to fall at the basic level of categorization, and these words tend to be among the shortest and most frequently used words in a language (Murphy, 2002; Murphy & Lassaline, 1997; Rosch et al., 1976).

There are many distinctive features of basic-level categories that reinforce the idea that this is the most cognitively natural level of categorization and perhaps therefore the easiest to think about (Murphy, 2002; Murphy & Lassaline, 1997; Rosch et al., 1976). The question therefore arises: Could young children reason about classification more easily using basic-level categories? Eleanor Rosch and her colleagues explored this possibility by asking young children to sort or group together items that resembled each other at either the basic level of categorization or the superordinate level (Rosch et al., 1976). Thus, a child might be given four kinds of toy *vehicles* and four different kinds of *clothing* and asked to group the items that go together (superordinate categories), or they might be given four kinds of toy *cars* and four kinds of *shirts* to sort (basic-level categories). The same preschoolers who failed to sort based on superordinate categories showed no problems sorting based on basic-level

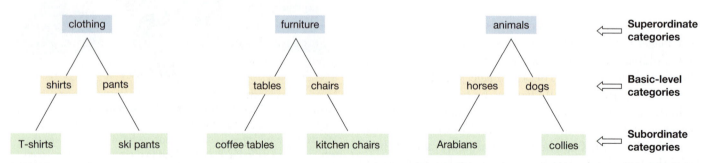

FIGURE 9.13 Basic-level categories. The basic level is an intermediate level of categorization that seems to be especially salient, psychologically natural, and easy to think about. Preschoolers are much better at sorting objects into basic-level categories than they are at using other category levels. This finding suggests that young children's failures at class-inclusion reasoning may have more to do with their difficulties thinking about the relevant categories than with missing the mental operators pertaining to classification.

categories; they easily put all the shirts together and all the cars together. Thus, younger children are capable of the kind of feature-based, logical classifications that they fail at in Piaget's sorting tasks.

If their mental abilities only allowed them to sort items thematically, preoperational children would be unable to sort by class regardless of the categories. Their much better performance with basic-level categories raises the serious possibility that they fail to sort by superordinate categories either because it requires processing larger amounts of information than the children can keep in mind at once or because the categories themselves are unfamiliar or arbitrary. In fact, Rosch's studies were just the start of a line of research showing that young children can think about categories in surprisingly sophisticated ways, especially at the basic level. If young children have a good understanding of how a category relates to other familiar information, this knowledge also seems to help them reason about the category.

Children also seem to be more capable of class-inclusion reasoning than Piaget thought. For example, if preschoolers are shown a group of five "boy" frogs and two "girl" frogs and then asked whether there are more boy frogs or more frogs, they will make the usual class-inclusion mistake—claiming that there are more boy frogs. But if they are asked instead if there are more boy frogs or more in the "family" of frogs, then they will correctly say that there are more in the family (Markman & Siebert, 1976). The label "family" may help the child solve this problem by drawing her attention to relationships organizing the whole "collection." This pattern of findings raises questions about Piaget's original account, given that such a small change in the question can significantly change children's performance (McGarrigle & Donaldson, 1974). More broadly, researchers have found that young children are able to think about categories in ways that suggest not only an appreciation of class inclusion but also the advantages of learning about categories as a whole as opposed to merely learning about the individuals that make up those categories (Cimpian & Park, 2013; see Scientific Method box).

> **Q:** What are some ways of making classification tasks easier for preschoolers?

Conservation Hundreds of studies have reexamined Piaget's conservation tasks from different perspectives to see whether his explanations for children's failure to conserve hold up under scrutiny. The full story of this research is complex (see Brainerd, 1978; Gelman & Baillargeon, 1983),

but we only need to examine a few studies to see that some of the findings deeply challenge Piaget's theory.

Consider, for example, preschool children's apparent inability to conserve number. In the number conservation task, children are asked to compare the number of coins in each of two equal lines and then to compare them again after the experimenter has spread the coins in one line farther apart. Does the child fail, as Piaget supposed, because she cannot think in terms of principles such as reversibility (what would happen if the spread-out coins were moved closer together again) and identity (no coins were added or removed in the transformation, so there must be the same number before and after it)? Alternatively, does she have all the cognitive capacities necessary to answer correctly, but simply misunderstands what the researcher is asking?

A pioneering series of studies by Margaret Donaldson and her colleagues raised serious questions about how children in the preoperational age range (about 2 to 7 years old) interpret Piaget's number conservation tasks. As we saw in Chapter 8, in interactions with others, even very young children take into account pragmatic factors, such as others' actions and intentions as well as aspects of the social context, to infer meaning and to guide their interpretations of what is wanted in a task. Perhaps these factors can also influence young children's performance on conservation tasks.

Donaldson and her colleagues suggested that the traditional number conservation task is confusing for children because it is so pragmatically unusual (Donaldson, 1978, 1983; McGarrigle & Donaldson, 1974). How often does someone ask how many things there are in a display, then purposely manipulate those things and ask about the number again—unless the questioner thinks it likely that the number of things has changed? Repeating the same question may suggest to the child that the experimenter is asking again because she has changed the number. To explore this possibility, Donaldson modified the task in a simple way that significantly changed the pragmatics of the interaction—that is, the intentions that the child attributed to the experimenter.

In one of Donaldson's variations, which we will call the "clumsy experimenter" variation, the experimenter pretends to slip and accidentally change the length of one row of objects, so that it becomes either longer or shorter than the other row. In a different variation, the child sees a "naughty teddy bear" mess up the display, making one of the rows either shorter or longer than the other, before being scolded and sent away. In both of these variations on number conservation tasks, preschoolers succeed much more often than they do in Piaget's original version. In these variations, they frequently say that the number of objects has not changed, despite the change in the row's length.

Hypothesis:

Young children are motivated to learn about kinds (or categories) of objects from reliable sources and prefer to learn new information about kinds of objects than to learn new information about particular instances, even though the instances are more concrete.

Method:

1. There were 48 children having an average age of 4 years 9 months who participated in the study.

2. There were 24 children in the knowledgeable-adult condition and 24 children in the ignorant-adult condition.

3. In the knowledgeable-adult condition, the experimenter told the child that she knew a great deal about a set of four pictures and, for each picture, invited the child to choose whether he wanted to learn from the experimenter about an individual novel animal ("the one *pangolin* in this picture") or the kind of animal ("this kind of animal, *pangolins*").

4. In the ignorant-adult condition, the experimenter told the child that she knew nothing about the set of pictures and invited the child to choose whether he wanted the experimenter to guess something about "the one *pangolin* in this picture" or about "this kind of animal, *pangolins*."

Results: With the knowledgeable adult, children strongly preferred to learn about the kind of animal. With the ignorant adult, children showed no significant preferences but some tendency to prefer guesses about the individual animal. The preference for learning about kinds with knowledgeable adults therefore is not simply because children generally prefer to hear information about kinds; they do so only when they think that the information is likely to be of high quality.

Conclusion: Even though young children might be thought to prefer to first learn about single concrete instances of categories, in fact they prefer to learn high-quality information about entire kinds at a more abstract level.

Source study: Cimpian & Park (2013).

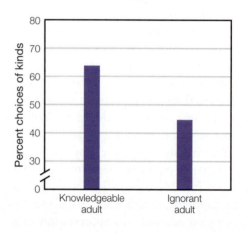

It seems that in Piaget's original task, the child might be thinking, "I just told him the number of coins in each row is the same. Why is he asking me the same question again? He must have changed the number somehow, and he wants to see if I can tell. Since one row is longer than it was before, I guess he must have added something and that's why he is asking." In Donaldson's pragmatically different variations, however, the experimenter never intentionally changes the rows of objects and seems to be asking the question a second time simply to make sure nothing has changed (see Figure 9.14). Donaldson's claim that young children often fail at the original task because they misinterpret the experimenter's intentions gained further support from another task variation. In this variation, the younger children often answer correctly when the question about number is asked only once, which avoids any pragmatic confusion (Rose & Blank, 1974; Samuel & Bryant, 1984).

Donaldson's critique of pragmatically odd components in Piaget's number conservation task that might mislead young children can also be extended to Piaget's other conservation tasks (Donaldson, 1985; Gelman & Baillargeon, 1983). All of the classic versions of these tasks, whether they test conservation of number, weight, liquid volume, or another property, involve the odd practice of asking a child the same question twice, before and after intentionally manipulating the materials. Donaldson's studies show that young children

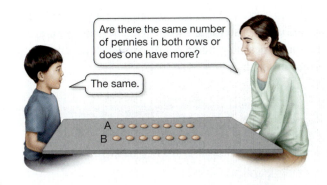

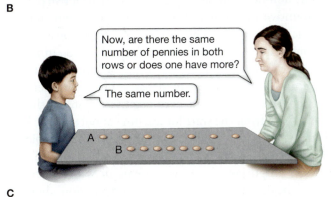

FIGURE 9.14 Changing pragmatics and conservation of number. In variations on Piaget's number conservation task, either a clumsy experimenter or a "naughty teddy bear" seem to accidentally change the length of one row. Because the child does not see the experimenter intentionally change one row and then ask about number a second time, the pragmatics of the task are changed dramatically. In these altered tasks, preoperational children become much more likely to conserve number. Adapted from McGarrigle & Donaldson (1974).

do not have the kind of central cognitive deficits for understanding conservation that Piaget proposed. Nonetheless, even in the modified tasks that reduce pragmatic demands, younger children still make more mistakes than older children. This pattern suggests that the odd pragmatic cues in the original tasks do not fully explain young children's failures. What other sorts of factors might be at work?

One type of influence on children's performance has to do with complexities of the task that make it more difficult, even though they are irrelevant to the type of reasoning that the task is designed to test. Suppose, for example,

that a child fails a conservation of number task because the task uses numbers that are too large for the child to track. After all, if an adult observed two equal-sized piles of 324 coins and then saw an experimenter move one pile around so that it took up more space, even the adult might fail to conserve—responding to the question "Which has more coins?" by simply picking the pile that seemed larger. To test whether this kind of complexity is a factor in children's conservation task performance, researchers can simplify the tasks by using fewer objects. For example, a child might be asked to compare a row of three objects with a row of two objects. In addition, the question "Which has more?" may be ambiguous. The child may think that this is a question about which overall size or length is greater, rather than a reference to the number of objects. To avoid this problem, an experimenter could teach the child that the "winner" of two displays is the one with more objects and then ask, "Which is the winner?" With these changes to the number conservation tasks, even preschoolers often succeed on the tasks (R. Gelman, 1969, 1972).

Children still do not perform perfectly on these modified tasks, however, which raises questions about where the additional difficulties lie. Given the substantial improvements that young children achieve on the simplified tasks, it is likely that their remaining problems have to do with the tasks' demands on memory and attention, and the need to interpret the pragmatics of the experimental situation, rather than with the kind of global, qualitative differences in reasoning that Piaget theorized.

Although children's mental abilities are not strictly limited across-the-board by the constraints that Piaget described, children may still undergo some global developmental shifts in the biases and strategies that guide their thinking. That is, when younger children take stock of a problem, they may focus on different kinds of information than older children do. This difference in focus may lead younger children to answer incorrectly, even though they are capable of using the kind of logic required to solve the problem. For example, younger children might focus on compelling perceptual features of displays and discount recent history. Thus, when they are asked whether the volume of water in a display has changed when it is poured from a short container into a tall one, they might focus on the tall beaker's height and disregard the fact that the same water was recently in a shorter, wider beaker. This failure appears similar to the one Piaget described, but it may actually reflect a lapse in attention or memory of the sort that even adults sometimes show, rather than an inability to use certain logical operators. In a related vein, younger children might remember the last piece of information they received (for example, that the water is now in the tall beaker) and weigh that information more heavily than their knowledge of what happened earlier. Either of these biases could explain many of children's conservation errors.

These mistakes are easier to understand if you consider that even adults are susceptible to perceptual illusions about quantity. Most adults will assume that a tall, thin glass holds more than a shorter, fatter one unless they see the liquid poured from one glass into the other. Adults also tend to underestimate the volumes of spheres and cubes and overestimate the volumes of elongated shapes. (This bias is common knowledge in retail sales: candy bars, cereal boxes, and shampoo bottles are often elongated to give an illusion of larger volume.) Children are subject to the same perceptual biases. Now suppose that they also tend to find the end state of a transformation much more salient than the past states before the transformation. In this case, children would be taken in by the perceptual illusion that the taller container, where the liquid ends up, seems to have a larger volume than the prior, shorter container. They would fail the conservation task, but not necessarily because they lack the necessary mental operators.

Piaget was aware of many of these possible pitfalls in his theory. He acknowledged that young children seem to focus excessively on beginning and ending states and ignore the transformations themselves, especially their reversibility and how one dimension compensates for another. He also relied on the notion of centration, arguing that young children have great difficulty focusing on more than one dimension of a task, such as both height and width in the case of liquid volume. But he assumed that this happens because younger children lack the mental operators that enable them to understand transformations. More recent findings indicate that younger children do not seem to show qualitative differences from older children in terms of their ability to understand and reason about seriation, classification, and conservation. Instead, researchers have found that younger children sometimes seem to be overloaded by the tasks' demands on memory and attention, and they tend to focus on different aspects of the problems than older children.

Beyond his research on seriation, classification, and conservation, Piaget also studied children's understanding of many real-world concepts, including their thoughts about dreams, living things, aging, spatial relations, and causality. In all of these areas of knowledge, he tried to explain children's errors in terms of qualitative differences in children's cognitive capacities at different ages. In each of these cases, challenges to Piaget's explanations have been raised that resemble the critiques of his theories about seriation, classification, and conservation. Although younger children do fail at Piaget's experimental tasks, follow-up studies have shown how difficult it is to point to global, qualitative differences in the ways that preschoolers and elementary school children mentally represent information. Younger and older children certainly differ in what they know and what they can do, but describing those differences as qualitatively different stages of general cognitive development has proved quite difficult.

> **Q:** How might pragmatic factors make a child who understands conservation fail on conservation tasks?

Domains of Knowledge

One consequence of the research that challenges Piaget's domain-general theory has been a surge of interest in how development proceeds in specific domains of knowledge. It appears that the domains of psychology, physics, spatial layout, number, and biology each show distinctive patterns of cognitive development guided by their own domain-specific constraints. The nature of those constraints—whether they are largely foundational and innate or emergent and developing over time within each of these domains—is more open to debate. Thus, children may approach the world with core cognitive systems that are constrained from the start for learning about specific kinds of input, such as spatial relationships, number, or biological patterns. Alternatively, children may start with more general, all-purpose learning systems in which they take in and begin to interrelate bits of information about the world over time, putting this information together into larger structures of knowledge that start to take on a life of their own and exert emergent constraints that are unique to that domain. When scholars envision a domain as being constrained by foundational and innate constraints, they often refer to such domains as **core domains**, suggesting that these are basic universal cognitive components shared by all infants throughout the world and which then become elaborated on and combined in more powerful ways over the course of development (Carey & Spelke, 1996; R. Gelman, 2009; Spelke & Kinzler, 2007).

As is so often the case in development, this distinction between the roles of foundational and emergent constraints is not an either/or situation. Both types of constraints always work together, even as one type may constrain the developmental process to a greater degree at particular times. For example, domain-specific foundational constraints may provide a necessary "foothold" for initial learning in a given area. Then, as the child learns more, this new knowledge may contribute to emergent constraints that guide later learning and the knowledge structures that are created. In each of these domains, we will see how the child's knowledge emerges in ways that challenge the older views of global, stage-based change, favoring instead the idea of domain-specific knowledge "journeys" that are quite distinct to each area of knowledge. Thus, we will see how children's understanding of space, number, and biology each takes on a life of its own with unique developmental patterns.

Spatial Relations

We saw in Chapter 5 that infants can track an object's location in a small space and that, on a larger scale, young toddlers can sometimes find their way back to a starting point in a novel setting. Mentally representing the spatial layout of an environment, however, is a more complex task. This ability becomes increasingly important in the preschool and elementary school years, as children come to navigate more extensive environments independently. This more complex ability raises similar issues to those that we considered in the earlier discussion of infants' spatial abilities: How do children know where they are relative to where they started, and how do they keep track of desired objects?

As a child's increased mobility allows her access to larger and more cluttered environments, it becomes more difficult for her to see all the terrain she has covered at once. A child must internally represent the space to keep track of where she is and where she wants to go. If a child loses track of her location, she needs to be able to reorient herself using familiar aspects of the environment and their relationships to each other. For many years, psychologists have known that humans and other animals use **cognitive maps** by which they mentally represent the spatial layout of their environment to infer distance, direction, and ways of navigating (Tolman, 1948). But the research tradition examining how nonhuman animals learn the layout of an environment has only recently merged with the study of humans' spatial and navigational skills to explore how humans develop an understanding of spatial layout. Taken together, these lines of research are suggesting new ways of addressing some of the phenomena that Piaget examined.

Piaget made a number of proposals about how children develop the ability to mentally represent the layout of an environment and other spatial relationships (see Chapter 5 for the discussion of Piaget's views about infants' spatial knowledge). One of Piaget's ideas that was especially relevant to cognitive maps was his notion that young children can think about and remember spatial layouts and relations only in terms of their own point of view (that is, egocentrically) and not in terms of independent coordinates, like the longitude and latitude on a map (Piaget, 1936/1953, 1954). (This idea is closely tied to Piaget's theories that young children use language egocentrically, as described in Chapter 8.) In line with this idea, Piaget found that young children responded egocentrically in several tasks testing spatial orientation.

In one of Piaget's best-known tasks, the three mountains task, he constructed a scene made out of three papier-mâché mountains, each with distinctive colors and landmarks. The three mountains were placed on a board in clear and unambiguous spatial relation to each other (see Figure 9.15). Children were asked to describe what a doll who was sitting at a different spot than the child would see and to choose what the doll would see from among pictures of four different vantage points of the scene. The researcher then asked the child to reconstruct the scene from each of the four points of view by placing the three mountains on an empty surface and then putting a doll in such a position that the doll would see that view. In each case, children younger than about 7 years old responded in a manner that was interpreted as spatially egocentric. Thus, they often thought that the doll (who was in a different position than they were) would still see just what they saw, and they had enormous difficulty understanding how the scene would look from a point of view other than their own. Piaget concluded that younger children are unable to take more than one perspective on a scene and are unable to free themselves from their own particular point of view. He assumed that this behavior represents a very general cognitive deficit that reflects being in the preoperational stage.

In other tasks related to the child's sense of object location, if a young child initially learned that an object was in a corner of the room that was to her left, she would still look to her left for the object later, even if she had turned around so that the object was now to her right. Older children would not make this mistake, since they would use the object's relationships to other features of the environment to guide their search, rather than the object's relationship to their own body orientation.

Other studies suggested, however, that even young children could sometimes think about spatial relationships in less egocentric ways. For example, consider what happened when children were instructed to place a doll where it could "hide" from a policeman. In this situation, even 3-year-old

FIGURE 9.15 Piaget's three mountains task. A classic demonstration of apparent egocentrism in young children. Egocentrism was thought to influence the child's understanding of spatial relations.

children were more successful at overcoming their egocentric perspective to take the doll's "viewpoint," presumably because the task seemed more familiar and accessible to them (Hughes, 1975). Given the conflicting findings about whether young children think about spatial relations egocentrically, researchers began to wonder if egocentrism is really a consequence of being in a preoperational period of cognitive development. Another possibility, as we saw in Chapter 8's discussion of egocentric language, is that many children, and even adults, may resort to egocentric thinking when cognitive tasks become very challenging.

A separate line of animal research gave rise to a new perspective on spatial cognition that had strong implications for humans (Gallistel, 1990; see also Pick, 1983). The animal research helped clarify two crucial points about spatial cognition: (1) An organism can use many kinds of information to track its spatial location, and (2) the type of spatial information that an organism relies on depends partly on the particular task and setting. Thus, the animal might draw on one kind of information in one context and another kind in a second context. These animal studies also suggested why young children perform so differently on various types of spatial tasks. For example, a small enclosure may be mentally represented differently from the way a large room is represented, which in turn may be represented differently from the way a village is represented (Acredolo, 1990; Learmonth et al., 2002). Additional cognitive abilities may be involved in grasping the spatial relations in maps and scale models and determining how they correspond to their real-world counterparts (DeLoache, 1987, 1989). Yet another set of spatial abilities may be involved in manipulating small objects such as tools (Newcombe et al., 2013; Spelke et al., 2010). To understand how humans' spatial knowledge develops, we first need to consider a few of the many ways in which an organism keeps track of its location.

Landmarks can provide one source of spatial information by serving as consistent reference points (see Chapter 5). Both people and other animals can navigate by estimating distance and direction in relation to these salient objects in the environment. Of course, for landmarks to be useful, we must note how they appear from different angles. Then, based on our viewpoint, we can figure out an approximate sense of direction and location relative to the landmark. If we also know the landmark's actual size, then its perceived size can convey an approximate sense of how far away it is.

A second method of locating ourselves in space is highly reliable but involves little attention to local landmarks. This method makes use of the **geometric information** in an environment. That is, we construct a mental representation of the environment's overall shape. Most natural scenes have an asymmetrical outline (see Figure 9.16). Recognizing this outline and knowing where we are relative to its edges and

FIGURE 9.16 Navigating with contour information. The asymmetrical terrain in natural environments creates contours that allow an organism to identify its unique location within that environment. This sense of place, which occurs largely outside of awareness, appears to be one of the earliest-emerging capabilities in humans and one that is shared with many other animals. The orange line illustrates how this location has a kind of shape, or contour, that is defined by the larger surfaces on the perimeter of the clearing.

overall shape can become a powerful means of knowing our location. This way of representing location works well even when local landmarks or other small features of the landscape change. It can also work well in low light or with limited visual acuity (Gallistel, 1990).

Using geometric information only fails in perfectly symmetrical artificial environments. For example, in a rectangular room, geometric information will always be ambiguous. Because the enclosure is symmetrical, every point in the room corresponds to a second point where the available geometric information is exactly the same. Imagine yourself in the room shown in Figure 9.17. Based

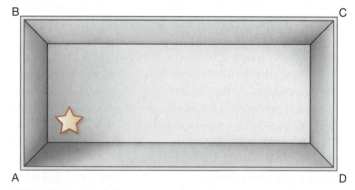

FIGURE 9.17 Ambiguous contour information in an artificial environment. What would happen if you were located at the star and used only contour information to remember this location? You would recall facing the corner with a long wall on your left and a short wall on your right. In this kind of artificial, symmetrical environment, however, this set of contour information also matches a second location: corner C. Rats, young children, and even adults (if they are kept from using landmark information) will incorrectly choose C about as often as they correctly recall A, even if there is a vivid distinguishing landmark at A.

on geometric information, you recall that when you are facing the walls, an object in the room is near the corner where a long wall on your left meets a short wall on your right—but that relation specifies two locations in the room, not just one. Researchers have made use of this potential problem, which applies specifically to using geometric information in symmetrical environments, to test whether subjects are using this geometric information to recall locations. They may ask subjects to return to a particular spot in a symmetrical room and pay attention to the types of errors they make. If the subjects choose both of the corresponding locations equally often, even when other available information specifies the one correct location, then it can be inferred that they are primarily using geometric information (the contours of their environment) to remember where objects are.

> **Q:** What are two different ways of navigating through space?

When rats' spatial abilities are tested in artificial rectangular enclosures, they show errors suggesting that they often rely heavily on geometric information and ignore other forms of information on location (Cheng, 1986; Cheng & Gallistel, 1984). Imagine that a rat is put into a rectangular box, where it discovers food in a particular location. The rat is then briefly moved to another enclosure, where it is spun around in the dark so that it is fully disoriented. When it is put back into the first box, it correctly locates the spot where it previously found food only half of the time, even when there are unique landmarks in the box that correspond to where the food is hidden. The rat's error during the other half of the trials reveals its use of geometric information. It mistakenly chooses the mirror-image location that corresponds to the original location of the food. Thus, the rat seems to learn the location in terms of the overall shape of the environment.

The animal research raised the question of whether, in some circumstances, young children might show the same pattern of mistakes. Remarkably, when young preschoolers were disoriented and put in small, symmetrical enclosures, they behaved very much like the rats (Hermer & Spelke, 1994, 1996). They seemed to rely exclusively on geometric information, and roughly 50 percent of their searches incorrectly led to the second, mirror-image location suggested by geometric relations. Like the rats, they made these mistakes despite the salient landmarks that pointed to the correct location. Nonetheless, even though this strategy of orienting by geometric information leads to errors when it is used in symmetrical enclosures, it is an excellent strategy in the natural world, where environments are almost never perfectly symmetrical. In natural environments, the shape of an area can almost always serve as a unique guide to location (Lee et al., 2012).

As suggested earlier, the type of spatial information that is used depends in part on the setting. Children and other animals seem to rely on geometric information in small rooms (say, 4 feet by 6 feet). In considerably bigger rooms, however, both children and animals rely less on geometric cues and may use landmark information along with simple spatial relations, remembering, for example, that the object is a bit to the left of one side of a landmark (Burgess, 2006; Learmonth, et al., 2002; Lourenco & Huttenlocher, 2007). They may use geometric information less often in large rooms because it is harder to see the whole room at once to determine its shape (Lavenex & Banta Lavanex, 2006). Other studies have shown that even in small enclosed spaces where geometric cues are uninformative, such as square rooms, children can still reorient themselves if the cues are not wall colors or landmarks, but surface textures such as gradients of raised dots that vary in density (Lourenco et al., 2009; Nardini et al., 2008).

As children grow older, they become increasingly able to use other sources of information, such as landmarks, to orient themselves and to find hidden objects. They usually start successfully using landmarks at about age 5, which is also the age at which they increasingly refer to objects in terms of relative spatial locations (for example, "to the left of"). Some researchers argue that language helps children to integrate different forms of spatial information, such as landmarks and layout, into one coherent representation of space (Shusterman et al., 2011; Spelke, 2003; Spelke & Lee, 2012).

Others counter that although children begin using more spatial language at the same time that they become increasingly able to use multiple sources of spatial information, these linguistic changes do not actually *cause* new spatial abilities to emerge (Newcombe et al., 2013; Sovrano et al., 2002; Twyman & Newcombe, 2010). This question is still being debated. Either way, the earlier, Piagetian view of younger children's spatial knowledge as being purely egocentric has not held up, as newer evidence has shown how and in what circumstances children use different types of spatial information (Acredolo, 1978, 1990; Hughes, 1975).

We have seen that younger children rely more on geometric information in smaller environments, while older children can more easily integrate other kinds of spatial information. Nonetheless, the development of navigational skills is not a matter of replacing one way of mentally representing layout with another way. Older children and adults certainly still use geometric information as a guide to location. In some circumstances when adults are distracted, they will even favor geometric information over other kinds of spatial information, even ignoring landmarks and other local cues. Similarly, in some kinds of simplified navigation tasks, younger children and even infants as young as 6 months can be guided to increase their use of landmark information and other local cues (Learmonth et al., 2002; Lew et al., 2004; Newcombe, 2002).

Taken together, the evidence from research suggests that, at all ages, people can use a navigational system that keeps track of geometric information as a source of spatial knowledge. But recent studies suggest that they do not use all the available geometric information and instead tend to encode such things as "long wall to the left of the short wall" rather than precise angles between walls (Hupbach & Nadel, 2005; Spelke et al., 2010). As children grow older, they become better able to flexibly use and integrate many different sources of spatial information and to use more of the available geometric information, such as angles. They also become better at coordinating geometric cues with other forms of information, such as landmarks, for orienting or locating objects.

It is not yet clear just how distinct the brain systems that use geometric information are from those that use other forms of spatial information (Cheng & Newcombe, 2005; Lew, 2011). But there is an emerging consensus that navigation, orientation, and object manipulation ultimately involve a complex interplay of several different forms of information. Many of these appear to have roots or simpler forms that are evident even in infancy but that can take years to become fully integrated into an efficient and flexible system of spatial cognition.

Q: What facets of geometric information are not fully grasped by younger children and infants?

Number

Along with spatial and navigational skills, another area of intuitive knowledge that young children acquire through experience is their understanding of number. Every culture uses some system of mathematics in everyday life. Most adults are able to count groups of items and use addition and subtraction to compute changes to those groups. As described in Chapter 5, even young infants seem to be sensitive to number. In this chapter, we focus on the intuitive knowledge of number that seems to be spontaneously acquired in the real world in early childhood, outside formal instruction in school. For example, some of the most important aspects of quantifying the world involve identifying what sorts of things to count in the same set or class (see Figure 9.18), how to assign numbers

FIGURE 9.18 **Understanding counting.** Knowing how to count requires understanding what sorts of things are sensible to count as one group. In this market scene, we might choose to count individual food items, types of foods, people, males or females, sellers or buyers, or human-made versus natural things, among many other choices. These choices require a grasp of meaningful categories and of which kinds of things are countable, an understanding available even to very young children but not to any computer.

to groups of things, and how numbers relate to each other. (We will look at aspects of school-based instruction of mathematics in Chapters 10 and 11.)

We saw in Chapter 5 that infants seem to have some sense of numerosity of small displays and some intuitive arithmetical skills that give them a sense of what changes when small amounts are added or subtracted. But even with all their impressive achievements, infants' understanding of number is very different from that of preschoolers, who in turn differ from older children in this area of knowledge. Take, for example, the case of counting aloud. Because preverbal infants obviously cannot count this way, researchers can only infer that they can somehow extract information about quantities from small displays. For example, one study found that 18-month-olds, but not 15-month-olds, look longer at a video in which a hand points successively to each of six objects while a voice in their own language counts up to 6 than they look at a video in which the hand moves back and forth between the same two objects while the voice counts to 6 (Slaughter et al., 2011). They do not show any difference in looking, however, if the voice counts in another language or if they hear different beeps instead of spoken numbers.

Researchers have hypothesized that preschool children have implicit knowledge of the counting principles of one-to-one correspondence (one number label per object), stable order (numbers are always counted in the same order), cardinality (the last number counted is the total number of objects in a group), abstraction (anything can be counted), and order irrelevance (it doesn't matter which object is counted first or in which order), although the young children do not always count accurately (Gelman & Gallistel, 1978). Toddlers show their first attempts at counting at about age 2, and their early attempts at counting show strikingly consistent patterns. Children around this age seem to know that counting always involves using the same labels in the same order ("1, 2, 3 . . ."), even if the labels they use are idiosyncratic. Thus, a 2-year-old might consistently count, "1, 2, 3, 5, 6, 11" (Gelman & Gallistel, 1978). Toddlers also seem to know that counting involves using just one label per object. By age 3½, children can easily tell when others violate this one-to-one correspondence principle (Gelman & Meck, 1983). Knowledge of these counting principles suggests that preschool children have a relatively sophisticated understanding of numbers and how they are used. As we have seen, some inkling of the one-to-one correspondence principle may emerge even before children are able to count.

Yet, in other ways, very young children have been found to show some serious limitations in their understanding of numbers. Even though they understand that they can begin to count with any one of the objects, they do not usually understand—sometimes until as late as age 10—that a count can proceed in any order whatsoever—for example, from left to right or right to left (Kamawar et al., 2010). More significantly, for a young child, the counting routine often does not serve as a way of figuring out how many things there are. A 3-year-old might correctly count a group of seven objects aloud, but still not realize that this means that there are seven objects present (see Figure 9.19). Early on, counting is simply a verbal routine performed with objects, but it may be somewhat disconnected from mathematical understanding (Wynn, 1990, 1992).

> Q: Which counting principles are typically mastered by preschool children, and which counting principles take longer to develop?

Researchers disagree on how young children's counting routines become integrated with other aspects of their mathematical knowledge during the preschool and early elementary school years. Some psychologists argue that children's numerical knowledge is closely linked to the quantity of number labels in their language (Le Corre et al., 2006). Supporters of this view point to early evidence that languages with very few number labels may deprive speakers of counting ability. For example, the Piraha, a small Amazon tribe whose terms for numbers

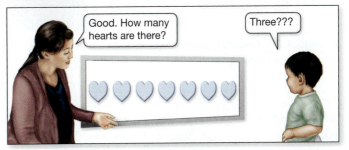

FIGURE 9.19 Limitations on counting by preschoolers. Although young children seem to master counting routines quite well early on, they often do not realize the relation between the last number of the count and the number of objects counted.

include only "one," "two," and "many," seem unable to count or to use any of the counting principles (Gordon, 2004). According to this view, the counting principles cannot emerge as basic insights without significant support from language.

The supporters of an alternative view argue that the development of counting skills and early mathematical knowledge does not depend so much on language for their growth and elaboration. Instead, they hold that numerical knowledge is largely separate from language, both in terms of the brain areas that support these two types of knowledge and the ways they develop (Gelman & Butterworth, 2005). These researchers point out that cultures with few number terms actually show much greater numerical competencies when they are examined more closely. Other support for this second view comes from studies of children with specific language impairment (SLI), a condition described in Chapter 8. Children with SLI show significant delays in language development, which also affect their counting-out-loud routines. Nonetheless, they seem able to learn basic principles of arithmetic in ways that are independent of their struggles with language (Donlan et al, 2007). Thus, this second view considers young children's counting routines to be based on an implicit, domain-specific understanding of number and to develop without major influences from the particular language that a child speaks (see Figure 9.20). In addition, young children's nonlinguistic abilities to estimate quantities may relate to the development of an understanding that the last number counted indicates the quantity of items in the set. Preschoolers

FIGURE 9.20 Counting across cultures. Children all over the world engage in counting but vary considerably in their counting patterns and how they link counting to other forms of mathematical knowledge.

who are especially good at estimating gain that insight about counting at an earlier age (Wagner & Johnson, 2011).

A more nuanced perspective arises from work on the understanding of number by Nicaraguan home-signers, deaf people who use systems of invented hand gestures to communicate with hearing friends and relatives (see Chapter 8). They grow up in a culture where number is clearly important, but their home-created language has no number symbols, and they have difficulty thinking about precise number values much higher than 3 (Spaepen et al., 2011). Thus, even though they know numbers are important and understand discrete numbers up to 3, they tend to switch to a more approximate estimation system when they encounter even modestly large numbers. Above and beyond the debate about how much language contributes to understanding number, however, it is clear that preschoolers' numerical abilities surpass what Piaget envisioned, since he argued that real numerical understanding was not present until the transition to concrete operational thought around age 7 (Piaget, 1952).

Developmental research on number skills has also raised questions about how children's intuitive concepts of number change between infancy and middle childhood (Carey, 2009; Wynn, 1995, 1998). Older children develop a new system that is responsible for more sophisticated mathematical thought and complex computations, and as the study of the Nicaraguan home-signers suggests, language may be central to this second system. A child may take several years, from age 3 to roughly 7, to fully benefit from the subtle but powerful clues that language can provide about more sophisticated aspects of mathematics. This gap of several years between the point when a child can first use number terms to count and the time she is able to talk about mathematical relationships may help explain why early counting often doesn't result in knowing how many things there are.

One line of research suggests that children's increasing understanding of number words and plural forms helps them to see more complex and systematic numerical relationships (Carey, 2001, 2009). Somehow, children with "number-rich" languages manage to learn that numbers above 3 continue to each have a discrete value (Huang et al., 2010). In addition, the more parents talk to their children about number-related topics in these languages, the earlier the children make the transition to understanding that the number 4 corresponds to exactly four things, even when socioeconomic factors and other aspects of parents' language use are controlled (Levine et al., 2010). Children may achieve this insight by noticing patterns in the way small numbers are used in their language, and then seeing how those patterns apply to larger numbers as well. In this form of learning, which is often called **bootstrapping**, children appear to build on their early insights about small numbers, using these patterns as a foundation for understanding new and quite different kinds of number concepts (Carey, 2009; Negen & Sarnecka, 2012; Slusser & Sarnecka, 2011).

As with spatial knowledge, research on the development of mathematical thought suggests several important themes about how this area of knowledge begins to take shape in childhood. Three of these themes are most prominent:

1. The principles that govern our ways of thinking about numbers and mathematical relations share some common properties across all cultures. In particular, almost every culture's number system shares fundamental assumptions about what numbers are, how they are connected to countable objects, and what sorts of operations can be performed on the numbers derived from counting representations.

2. The development of mathematical thought involves changes in several kinds of knowledge systems, including a system for estimating large numbers and a system for precise operations on small number values, such as 1 and 2. Some forms are nonverbal and relatively inflexible, like the information handled by the estimation sys-

tem. Other forms can be easily stated in language, such as mathematical rules and principles. This language-related type of mathematical knowledge creates a foundation for more powerful and abstract mathematical thought and helps transform the very concept of number.

3. A final pattern concerns the distinction between knowing how to do something and being able to succeed at it consistently at all levels of complexity. One group of mathematics researchers has related competence to mathematical skills by describing three components of competence and applying them to the progression of mathematical development (Gelman & Greeno, 1989; Greeno et al., 1984). They distinguish between knowing abstract mathematical principles, like the principles of counting mentioned earlier (conceptual competence), knowing how to perform the behaviors that fit with particular principles (procedural competence), and being able to figure out which principles to use for a particular task (utilizational competence). These researchers argue that competence with the principles comes first, but that being able to apply the principles to real problems requires both of the other facets of competence in order to plan and perform mathematical operations. In this view, young children can keep the counting principles in mind fairly easily, but using them is more difficult and requires further mathematical development. The principles become more applicable to the real world as the child develops performance skills and an increasing awareness of which skills to use for specific tasks.

Which dimensions of cognitive development best characterize the emergence of intuitive mathematical thought? In terms of the three dimensions introduced at the beginning of this chapter, number exhibits a rich interplay of several distinct processes. Early number skills during the preschool years may draw heavily on local, number-specific forms of cognition that are guided strongly by foundational constraints, such as estimation skills and possibly some counting principles. During this period, change may be largely quantitative. Then, a qualitative shift in number concepts seems to take place, when numerical skills seem to become subject to more emergent constraints. This change may be facilitated by experience with a number-rich language. As we will see in Chapter 10, more domain-general cognitive skills like memory and attention become critical as we consider higher levels of mathematical reasoning and computation. Across the full sweep of development, numerical cognition draws on all the different dimensions that describe cognitive development. Thus, it illustrates how a developing system can have many interacting components, which make developmental change quite different at various ages.

Q: How is linguistic input related to the emergence of mathematical thought?

Biology

Young children seem to develop naive, or intuitive, theories about broad slices of the natural world that we might loosely associate with domains such as biology, physics, and psychology. Their collections of beliefs are thought to resemble theories because they are about abstract causal patterns in the world, have some degree of connectedness or coherence, serve as a basis for making predictions, and seem to evolve over time (Gopnik & Wellman, 1994, 2012). They are not like scientific theories in that they are often very sparse in terms of details (Keil, 2012), but they do reflect ways in which children and adults develop intuitive beliefs about areas of the natural world that they may never have learned about through formal instruction. These intuitive areas are often known by such labels as folk physics, folk psychology, and folk biology. We start here with a discussion of the development of folk biology, which is an intuitive understanding of living things and biological processes that occur in the natural world. We will be asking whether young children start off very early with an understanding of the living world as a distinct realm or whether folk biology only emerges as a distinct form of intuitive theory several years later in development.

Over the course of childhood, we develop a great many beliefs about the biological world, many of which we come to take for granted. These include ideas about birth, growth, death, and the inheritance of traits in plants and animals. They also include ideas about disease, contagion, and healing, as well as a host of beliefs about how living things function and how they are adapted to their environments.

Cross-cultural research suggests that several aspects of intuitive biological thought are universal (Atran & Medin, 2008). For example, people in all cultures share the following biological beliefs: (1) Groups of animals and plants can be organized taxonomically—that is, systematically in hierarchical categories based on how they naturally relate to each other. (2) Animal and plant types have distinct essences—that is, their observable properties arise from crucial, defining, deeply rooted qualities. (3) Organisms have properties that are adapted to their needs within their niches—that is, the physical environments they inhabit (Atran, 1995, 1999; Berlin, 1992; Medin & Atran, 1999). For example, people throughout the world believe that a local bird is (1) part of a hierarchy of different kinds of animals, (2) a member of its category because it shares essential

Sputnik and Intuitive Science

On October 5, 1957, U.S. citizens were shocked to learn that the Soviet Union had launched Sputnik, the world's first artificial satellite (see Figure 9.21). In response to this achievement, the United States undertook an all-out effort to make its children more scientifically literate. Large resources were devoted to enhancing science education at all levels, from elementary school to graduate school, with the National Science Foundation playing a particularly central role (Atkinson, 1999). The program succeeded in some respects; technological and scientific innovation in the United States continues to outpace that of many other countries. Yet, on tests of scientific knowledge and reasoning, U.S. children continue to be outperformed by children in other countries. In the late 1990s, the Third International Math and Science Study revealed that after the fourth grade, children in the United States started to fall dismally behind students in other industrialized countries (Schmidt et al., 1997, 1999). In response to these findings, congressional hearings examined the weaknesses in U.S. science education, and President Clinton vowed to address the crisis head-on. Yet, a similar 2009 study by the Program for International Student Assessment (PISA) showed that U.S. students ranked no higher than 17th in the world in their knowledge of science (National Center for Education Statistics,

FIGURE 9.21 Sputnik. The launching of the world's first artificial satellite by the Soviet Union in 1957 set off a wave of initiatives focused on improving science education in the United States.

2009). But it is not clear what the U.S. students' persistently poor performance on science-related standardized tests really means for the future of science education and innovation in the country. In short, we don't know which aspects of science education matter most for increasing the number of leading scientists

---

properties with all the category members, and (3) particularly suited for the environment in which it lives. All adults therefore come to appreciate many of the distinctive properties and relations that distinguish living things from everything else. Thus, their biological thought comes to have its own special properties that make it distinct from other domains of knowledge (Hull & Ruse, 1998; Sterelny & Griffiths, 1999). Furthermore, because these core biological beliefs seem to be universal, all children must come to know them at some point in development (see Figure 9.22).

In addition to these core principles, children learn a host of more specific ways that the living world differs from the nonliving world, as well as many biological distinctions, such as that between plants and animals. They learn that living things reproduce, grow, and die, and that living things must ingest food and water to be able to grow and reproduce. They learn that members of the same plant or animal category can change their shape and appearance radically over the course of development: a baby becomes an adult, a tadpole becomes a frog, and a caterpillar becomes a butterfly.

FIGURE 9.22 The living world. As fancifully depicted in the painting *Tropical Forest with Apes and Snakes* (1910), by Henri Rousseau, the living world includes a fantastically diverse array of organisms. How do children come to understand that all these organisms are in the domain of biology?

in a country. Although the average citizen has only a rudimentary understanding of many natural phenomena, such as the changing seasons, it is not clear whether this broad lack of knowledge influences how scientists are trained in universities or how children end up choosing a scientific career path. There is a clear need to link public policy questions about investment in science education to studies of whether such investments really make a difference for the state of science in a country.

Over the past few decades, research in cognitive development has started to influence beliefs about how to teach science. For example, a report issued by the National Research Council called *Taking Science to School* emphasized two themes that should underlie the instruction of science in the schools (National Research Council, 2007). First, science instruction should focus on the gradual growth and accumulation of knowledge that builds on earlier knowledge learned over several years, as opposed to providing snapshots of unrelated topics over various years. Second, children bring to elementary school some basic intuitions about domains such as space, number, biology, and physical mechanics. Because these areas of scientific inquiry, called *privileged domains* of science, have roots in children's very early intuitions about the world, science teachers can build on students' rudimentary understanding in these areas, rather than seeing students as limited by Piagetian stages in which certain kinds of reasoning and knowledge are impossible.

As we have seen, children's intuitions in these domains are sometimes mistaken, but their early knowledge can still serve as a foundation for future learning rather than being dismissed as a useless bunch of misconceptions. Unfortunately, past instructional programs have too often focused primarily on children's failings and ignored their powerful ways of tracking the important relations they encounter in the world. As researchers uncover more details about how children's intuitive understanding of privileged domains emerges, science education will be able to build on this understanding in powerful ways that make sense to students.

This new approach emphasizes continuities over time rather than stages and limitations in both cognitive development and science education. It will, however, require major efforts from schools and teachers to develop coherent instructional programs in science in which each year's coursework systematically revisits core ideas in deeper and deeper ways, building on what was taught in prior years. Ideally such an approach could be adopted across many schools, so that children who change schools would still share their classmates' scientific knowledge base, which their teacher could continue to build on. To achieve such an integrated science curriculum across schools and districts, however, will require a team effort among schools, government officials, and citizens.

How do children develop these biological beliefs, and what mistakes do they make as they acquire adult knowledge?

> **Q:** What are some universal core biological beliefs?

Here we will consider in detail two different sets of proposals that describe how children learn about living things. The first set of views, which we will refer to as late-emerging biology views, assumes that even very young children's impressions of living things are embedded within larger explanatory systems that provide them with a sense of why those things are the way they are. In these views, children use a theory for explaining the social world called *naive psychology* and a theory for explaining the physical world called *naive physical mechanics*. Thus, these views propose that young children can interpret and explain things only in psychological terms or in terms of simple physical inter-

actions between objects. Applying these ideas to children's biological knowledge, proponents mostly assume that children explain animal properties in psychological terms and explain plant properties in simple physical terms (Carey, 1985, 1995). According to these views, as children develop, they come to realize that neither the psychological nor the physical system of explanation is fully adequate for explaining the properties of living things, and they begin to develop a new, specifically biological system of explanation. This biological explanatory system is based on the idea that living things are systems made up of smaller systems, such as the muscles and the digestive system. Their biological thinking also takes into account the ways that these smaller systems serve specific functional roles that help an organism survive in its environment.

The second set of views, which we will call early competence accounts, holds that even very young children think of biological things as different from other kinds of things and accordingly explain their properties and actions as distinctive, too. According to these views, most developmental change in biological thinking consists of becoming more capable of applying biological explanations to specific phenomena and different kinds of situations and gaining more detailed knowledge of biological mechanisms (Hatano & Inagaki, 1999; Inagaki & Hatano, 2002, 2004, 2006; Kalish, 1997; Keil, 1992; Keil et al., 1999). These views are often blends of views that emphasize enrichment of core domains, increasing access to these domains for more and more tasks, and shifting biases in terms of which kind of explanatory system first comes to mind. They all share the idea that living things have so many distinctive features that very young children start to see the living world as a distinct domain long before they understand how biological systems work.

As we did in the discussions of spatial navigation and number sense, we will use Piaget's views as a point of departure here. Piaget documented several ways in which preschoolers seem to use **animism**—the tendency to imbue inanimate things with psychological motivations such as desires and beliefs—to explain the physical mechanics of objects, the movements of the sun and clouds, and the behavior of plants in intentional terms. For example, young children may think that the sun moves because "it wants to" and that the bridge broke because "it was angry" at the person on it. Piaget argued that young children are incapable of reasoning in purely physical, causal, and mechanical ways. He saw young children as having great difficulty disentangling explanations about animate things from more mechanical, inanimate explanations—that is, they seemed unable to separate the world of the mind from the world of the physical (Piaget, 1926/2007).

Some of Piaget's other notions about young children's cognitive limitations also strongly suggest constraints on early biological thought. According to Piaget, a young child, who is presumably egocentric, would likely assume that other animals think as she does. Thus, she might freely apply human mental states to other animals. In Piaget's view, children in the preoperational period, who presumably have difficulties with conservation, would therefore also have great difficulty understanding biological processes like digestion that involve any kind of physical transformation. In some ways, Piaget's account sounds very much like the late-emerging biology view in which much of early biological thought is believed to be embedded within a naive psychology. Unlike that view, however, Piaget suggested that young children very often confuse psychological and physical thought, rather than using each of them as a distinct explanatory system.

As we have seen in other domains, the patterns in children's responses that Piaget documented have been replicated in other studies, but later researchers have interpreted those patterns in new ways and drawn different conclusions about children's understanding of biology. In addition, researchers have clearly shown that preschoolers are fully capable of reasoning in physical, causal, and mechanical ways (Bullock et al., 1982; Koslowski, 1996; Shultz & Kestenbaum, 1985). One of the most extensive critiques of Piaget's interpretation came in a series of studies by Susan Carey, who sought to reconcile the findings about preschoolers' capabilities with Piaget's earlier observations (Carey, 1985). After examining the young children's responses in Piaget's animism studies, Carey argued that these children were not really mixing psychological explanations with physical, mechanical ones, as Piaget had claimed. Instead, she interpreted the animism data as showing that young children tend to use psychological interpretations too broadly, especially in applying them to living things. The children's occasional uses of psychological explanations for occurrences in the inanimate physical world does not, in Carey's view, undercut the wealth of evidence that preschoolers can reason easily about physical causality.

To test her view, Carey developed several methods for studying how children attribute biological properties to animals and nonliving things. To compare how children's prior knowledge influences their thinking about biological questions, Carey asked children questions about whether some familiar biological terms, such as *heart*, and some unfamiliar terms, such as *omentum* (a tissue covering the intestines), could apply to various living and nonliving things. For example, she might tell a child that humans have an omentum and ask the child if dogs have an omentum. If the child believed that dogs are living beings, he would say that dogs do have an omentum. Thus, in such a property induction task, the child would induce which other entities have a property based on a known example. This **property attribution** method assumes that the kinds of guesses a child makes about what properties apply to living things can reveal the underlying conceptual system that the child is using to think about living things.

Consider another example from Carey's research. A 4-year-old might be asked whether the following biological properties apply to humans: Do people eat? Do people sleep? Do people breathe? Do people have babies? Do people have bones? Most 4-year-olds will answer "yes" to each question about humans. The interesting part of the task concerns how young children answer similar questions about other animals and about nonliving things. Here, children's errors are sometimes dramatic and surprising. Consider this interchange with a 4-year-old:

Interviewer: Do worms eat?
Child: No.
Interviewer: Do they have babies?
Child: No, they just have little worms.

Like this child, preschoolers are often reluctant to attribute many basic biological properties to simpler animals such as worms and insects. How can this be? How can a child have roughly the correct idea about what biological properties like eating and having babies mean and fail to apply them to virtually all animals? If a child has even the crudest idea of the real biological purposes of such properties, surely she would realize how essential they are to all living things.

This pattern was so compelling that Carey concluded that younger children must not really understand those properties in a true biological sense. That is, they do not understand the essential functions that these properties serve. Carey proposed that this lack of understanding arises because the children have no broader biological system of explanation within which to embed these specific properties. The children in Carey's study were not responding to the questions randomly, however. Instead, they were interpreting those basic biological properties by embedding them within a psychological mode of explanation. In such a psychological explanatory mode, we sleep "because we feel tired and want to rest"; we eat "because we feel hungry and know that food will taste good and make us feel full"; we have babies "so that we can cuddle them and take care of them." Thus, Carey's approach suggests a "biology-out-of-psychology" view of the development of biological understanding, in which biology emerges relatively late as an independent theory. Children seem to interpret basic biological properties entirely in terms of the human psychological motivations that are associated with them.

If children understand these biological properties only in a psychological way, it makes sense that they would not apply them to simple animals that do not have mental states like ours. Young children believe that since worms do not have rich thoughts and desires, they do not eat, sleep, or have babies *in the psychological sense* in which children seem to think about these properties. Thus, in deciding whether these properties apply to other animals, children largely focus on the extent to which the animals seem behaviorally and psychologically similar to humans (see Figure 9.23). Because dogs show some psychological sophistication, young children believe that they are much more likely to have these basic biological properties than are "simpler" animals.

This late-emerging biology view suggests that early on, children understand biological ideas only in psychological terms. Then, over time, they experience a major conceptual revolution in the way they attribute properties to living things. They replace the early psychological interpretations with a distinct set of biological explanations. These new ideas allow the child to see for the first time that eating serves a general biological function—it allows all animals to get the nutrients they need to move, function, and grow.

Carey's model differs from a Piagetian approach in important ways. For one, Carey described a local, or domain-specific, revolution in conceptual understanding. This change reflects the emergence of a specific theory of biology, rather than the kind of underlying global change in cognitive structures that Piaget proposed. In addition, the more detailed patterns of reasoning that Carey documented are quite different from what Piaget might have predicted. Young children's reluctance to attribute psychologically interpreted properties to simpler animals, for example, runs contrary to the animism that Piaget interpreted in children's responses.

Carey's late-emerging biology model is not the only way to explain this pattern of results, however. Indeed, another line of research suggests an alternative account that stresses children's early competence in biological knowledge. This alternative view becomes apparent upon a closer inspection of Carey's property attribution method. Are preschoolers completely unable to interpret properties in a biological sense and therefore limited to explanations that fall within a psychological explanatory system? Or could they simply be misunderstanding which of their several explanatory systems is relevant to the task? As adults, we often shift between different kinds of interpretations. For example, if I hear that someone has a "big brain," I might interpret that either as a figurative statement about intelligence or a literal one about a biological organ, drawing very different inferences in each case. Perhaps children can also shift between different types of interpretations.

To test this possibility, researchers can try to pose the questions about biological properties in a way that signals which explanatory system is relevant without providing any details about it. For example, the researcher might tell

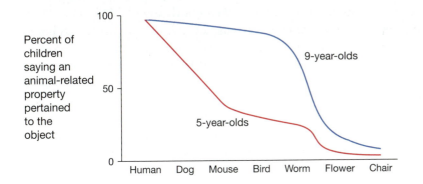

FIGURE 9.23 **Attributing biological properties.** In Carey's original studies, younger children seemed to decide whether animal-related biological properties pertained to different categories of living and nonliving things based on the extent to which those things seemed behaviorally similar to humans.

a child, "When I ask about whether worms eat, I am asking about eating in the sense that it helps the body move and grow." If the child then correctly attributes eating to worms, this could indicate that she understood the concept all along, but didn't know the researcher was asking about that particular concept. Another approach is to engage the child in a brief, general conversation about how animals can be like machines in some ways, with inside parts that serve specific functions for the animals. After having this discussion, the researcher then asks the child the same questions about applying biological properties. The same younger children who made many errors in the original property attribution task may now respond much like the older children in Figure 9.23 (Gutheil et al., 1998).

These studies raise the strong possibility that even young preschoolers may not lack biological thought. Instead, the broader context seems to strongly influence whether they choose biological explanations over psychological ones. In some contexts, even young children will use biological explanations and apply them in generalized ways that indicate a far-reaching application of biological ideas. Cross-cultural research has provided evidence for this early competence view. One study focused on Mayan children living in traditional agricultural communities in Mexico's Yucatán Peninsula. Even very young children showed no tendency to apply biological traits exclusively to humans and animals that were psychologically similar to humans. Instead, the children applied biological properties to all animals in generalized ways that reflected a true naive biology, rather than the absorption of biology into psychology (Atran et al., 2001).

It may be that the human-centered bias emerges only in certain cultures, around age 5. One study showed that in a wide range of cultures, 3-year-olds do not show a bias to apply biological traits only to humans. This tendency only seems to emerge in 5-year-olds when they are raised in urban environments, which apparently stress a human-centered view of nature (Herrmann et al., 2010). Related studies also show that the human-centered view is not a universal feature of children's biological reasoning. It depends on several aspects of culture, including the kinds of conversations parents have with their children about the living world (Medin et al., 2010). Thus, in cultures in which people live closer to nature, young children may have a much earlier bias toward relying on biological explanations.

The same theme arises in several other lines of research on the development of biological thought. Psychologists have studied children's beliefs about how properties are passed down to offspring (Hirschfeld, 1996; Springer & Keil; 1989; Waxman et al., 2007), about disease and contagion (Keil et al., 1999), about how biological things adapt to their environments (Greif et al., 2006), about the kinds of essences inside living things (S. Gelman, 2003), and about the coherence of causal mechanisms underlying biological

processes (Erickson et al., 2010). All of these studies seem to indicate that preschoolers show an early competence with biological thought. They understand the category of *living things* to which both animals and plants belong, and they have a cluster of beliefs about how living things differ from other sorts of things.

> **Q:** How do late-emerging biology views of the development of biological thought differ from early competence accounts?

If even young children show some early competence with biological reasoning, how does their thinking about biology develop over the course of childhood? The evidence suggests that children do not build up biological knowledge by first learning specific, concrete bits of information, then eventually progressing to abstract rules and principles. Instead, they seem to learn some initial, abstract patterns and then gradually fill in all the concrete details and mechanisms that fit with those patterns. This "abstract-to-concrete shift" in children's mastery of biological concepts has been documented in several cases. One example is the way children come to understand the concept of "insides." Preschoolers expect animals to have insides, and they think that insides play a critical role in influencing the animals' outsides as well as affecting their behavior (R. Gelman, 1990; S. Gelman, 2003). They also think about animal insides differently from the way they think about machine insides: animal insides help the animal survive, whereas machine insides help meet the needs of the machines' users (Keil, 1995). In this case, preschoolers show a relatively abstract causal understanding about what insides are for—but this conceptual understanding is not necessarily based on any knowledge of specific, concrete details. In fact, preschoolers may know little or nothing about what insides actually look like (see Figure 9.25).

Any description of how biological knowledge develops will have to explain how children's understanding of abstract patterns and causal relationships can emerge before they know anything about the relevant concrete details. Young children seem to be able to extract some rough sense of what makes living things different from nonliving things without needing a fully worked-out theory (Au & Romo, 1999). This learning process suggests that the popular metaphor of children as "little scientists" testing specific theories about the world may be flawed. At least in the biological domain, children often seem to have powerful hunches, but no more than a vague knowledge of the details.

By at least age 3, children seem to be aware of some of the distinctive patterns that characterize the biological world, especially its more abstract principles and causal relationships. They can use this early knowledge to begin

Biological Knowledge and Exposure to Nature

Most developmental studies assume that the outcome or "end state" of development is the level of knowledge common among college students or other adults in mostly urban, technological societies. But what happens when that end state is neither the normal state of mature knowledge nor especially sophisticated? This is arguably the case with the development of biological knowledge (Wolff et al., 1999). After all, the most salient living things that the average city dweller encounters are probably other humans. By contrast, an inhabitant of a rural area experiences a much broader range of biological forms (see Figure 9.24). In the realm of naive biological thought, people who grow up in urban cultures may have a relatively impoverished understanding.

Work with children in "biology-deprived" environments and with children in "biology-enriched" environments suggests that lack of experience with nature affects biological understanding (Atran et al., 2001, 2004; Herrmann et al., 2010; Medin & Waxman, 2007; Ross et al., 2003). Compared with adults who regularly encounter many diverse forms of nature, adults in biology-deprived environments show greater difficulty attributing biological properties, categorize the living world at less specific levels, reason in less sophisticated ways about biological problems, and think about biological essences differently. Their children also show comparable difficulties (Atran et al., 2004). The influence of specific cultures on this domain of thought seems to emerge around age 5, suggesting a more universal, common framework in younger children (Herrmann et al., 2010).

Different amounts of exposure to nature may play a role, as may the different ways that members of a culture talk about humans and other living things (Anggoro et al., 2010; Taverna et al., 2012). Cultures may also differ in how they expose children to animals, both in real life or indirectly through various media. When children from urban, rural, and Native American communities were asked to name all the animals they could, urban children more often named exotic animals they had learned about from picture books and other media (such as lions, tigers, and elephants) than common examples from their urban environments (such as squirrels and pigeons). Rural children, and to a greater extent Native American children, named more local animals (Winkler-Rhoades et al., 2010). Thus, while young children often benefit from learning through others (S. Gelman, 2009; Keil et al., 2008), direct experience is also important.

Because urban adults may have such limited knowledge of biology, examining urban adults to learn about the development of biological knowledge may produce a skewed account. In most cultures, the normal developmental path may lead to the early emergence of rich biological knowledge. Younger children in urban or suburban areas may tend to interpret biological properties in psychological ways because they have grown up in a biology-deprived culture. More broadly, the study of how knowledge develops in any domain risks telling a distorted story if the mature state of knowledge is measured according to cultural norms that do not represent most cultures (Medin et al., 2010; Waxman et al., 2007).

FIGURE 9.24 Developing biological thought in urban and rural youth. It now appears that urban children may have a different and simpler set of beliefs about biological properties than children raised in rural environments.

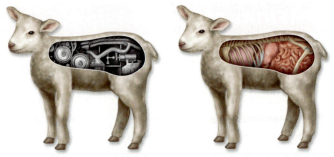

FIGURE 9.25 Ignorance of insides. Children younger than 5 frequently confuse what sorts of "insides" belong in machines and animals. Thus, many young children will not be able to choose which kind of insides shown here goes with a lamb or with a car. Yet, at a more abstract level, the same children have a reliable understanding of differences between the categories of machines and animals. Adapted from Simons & Keil (1995).

reasoning about living things—so, in that sense, they do have a distinct biological knowledge. At the same time, they do not know much about the specific mechanisms of how living things work. In this area, children show dramatic developmental changes during the preschool and elementary school years.

Young children may adopt certain broad assumptions about the living world that enable them to see some of its distinctive patterns without knowing the details. One such assumption may be **vitalism**, the belief that living things are distinctive because of a vital force inside them that is responsible for growth and movement (Inagaki & Hatano, 2002, 2004). Vitalism is in fact a very old idea that dates at least as far back as ancient Greece. It seems vague and unscientific to most adults in industrial cultures today, but it helps us understand something about children's early biological thought.

Figure 9.26 shows the child's vitalist beliefs. Some young children hold the view that food and water instill a force in animals that enables them to move and be active (without this force, the animals become increasingly inactive and tired). They believe that if there is a surplus of this vital force beyond these needs, the surplus is used for growth and health. Younger children do not always understand the direct link from food and water to growth and health, but older children come to see food and water as having a more direct influence. Along with vitalism, children also show a naive **essentialism**, in which they assume that living things have inner essences that are responsible for their surface properties (S. Gelman, 2003). Together, the general theories of vitalism and essentialism may be the most critical components of early biological thought.

A final feature of children's biological thought seems to be a tendency to interpret animals' and plants' properties in terms of the functions they serve. Thus, children may want to know what the parts of animals and plants "are for" more often than they would ask this question about the parts of nonliving natural objects, such as rocks (Greif et al., 2006; Keil, 1992). They use functional explanations more broadly than older children by extending them more often to nonliving natural objects (Kelemen, 1999). Yet, adopting functional explanations more strongly toward the living world early on may help children begin to understand its distinctive nature. Interestingly, preschoolers also seem to know that while it makes sense to ask what the parts of an animal are for (for example, the claws, the stripes, the fangs), it makes less sense to ask what the animal as a whole is for—even though it would be a reasonable question to ask about a tool (Greif et al., 2006).

> **Q:** What are vitalism and essentialism, and what roles do they play in early biological thought?

Other Domains of Thought

We have examined how children's intuitive knowledge develops in the domains of spatial layout, number, and biology. Here we will briefly consider how early understanding emerges in a few other domains: physical mechanics, substance beliefs, and cosmology. Comparing the ways that knowledge develops across all of these domains reveals an interesting commonality: in the preschool years, children start to develop some structured hunches about patterns in the world. Over the course of childhood, they develop more detailed beliefs about the specific mechanisms that give rise to these patterns in each of the domains.

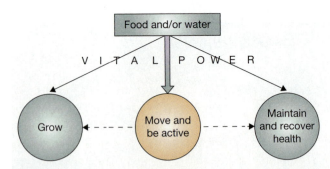

FIGURE 9.26 Vitalism in young children. As captured in the diagram, young children believe that food and water provide a vital force that enables animals to become active (as indicated by the thick arrow). When there is a surplus of this vital force, it acts as an impetus for growth and for maintaining and recovering health (as indicated by the dashed arrows). As children grow older, the direct links between food and growth and health are more clearly understood (as indicated by the thinner arrows). Adapted from Inagaki & Hatano (2004).

Beliefs about Physical Mechanics The domain of physical mechanics concerns beliefs about solid objects' behaviors, such as trajectories and collisions (Riner et al., 2000). In Chapter 5, we saw that infants seem to be aware of a few mechanical principles: (1) They seem to understand *continuity*—the idea that objects exist continuously and move on connected paths and are unable to jump from one place to another without occupying the intervening space. (2) They appear aware of the principle of *solidity*—the idea that solid objects cohere as bounded wholes and cannot interpenetrate. (3) They seem to understand the *contact* principle—the idea that objects cannot influence other objects without touching them; they must make contact. Infants also develop very different expectations about how inanimate objects behave compared with social beings. We can think of this early intuitive understanding about physical objects as the beginnings of "naive physics," or folk physics. As children leave infancy and enter the toddler and preschool years, they refine and elaborate on these broad patterns.

Many early childhood beliefs about physical objects are the legacy of these intuitions from infancy. Preschoolers know that unsupported things must fall and that even supported objects will fall over when set off-balance (Baillargeon, 2002; Dan et al., 2000; Keil, 1979). They pay more attention to patterns that conform with underlying mechanistic notions, assuming, for example, that a certain configuration of blocks is likely, but not certain, to fall over (Griffiths et al., 2004). Preschoolers also show further elaborations on intuitions from infancy about how inanimate objects differ from animate or social beings. When they are asked to explain the behaviors of simple devices, such as a box with levers, they clearly prefer mechanical causal explanations over social or biological explanations (Bullock et al., 1982; Gelman & Lucariello, 2002). Similarly, they explain violations of physical norms (such as an object floating in the air) in very different causal terms from moral violations (such as stealing) and from transgressions of social conventions (such as driving on the wrong side of the road; Lockhart, 1981).

During the elementary school years, children begin to understand in more detail how physical mechanics works. For example, while younger children think of physical forces as intrinsic characteristics of objects, older children come to see forces as "acquired properties" that affect objects because of the ways they interact with other objects, such as by being given a push—that is, objects have no forces until they acquire them by being influenced by other objects (Ioannides & Vosniadou, 2002). Elementary school children also come to understand how an object's length and weight can affect its balance, which is part of the general process of realizing how levers work (Siegler, 1981).

Though children show many early capabilities in understanding physical mechanics, they do hold some misconceptions, as do infants (see Chapter 5). For example, younger children tend to adopt oversimplified rules that can lead them astray. Thus, shortly after infancy, they seem to use a gravity rule that unsupported things must fall straight down regardless of how the support is removed (Hood et al., 2006). They predict that an object that rolls off a table will continue moving straight out from the edge for a moment, then drop straight down in a cartoon-like way. By the time children are 5 or 6 years old, they start to understand that an object rolling off a table will fall in a curved path, but they still make errors—which persist into adulthood—about the paths of objects dropped from moving carriers.

When children who are younger than about 3½ years old see a ball dropped into a curved tube, as shown in Figure 9.27, the "straight-down" rule is so strong that it often seems to cause them to see the ball come out of the wrong tube, the one whose bottom is directly below the dropping point (Hood, 1995). When children are made more familiar with the tubes, they predict more correctly where the ball will emerge (Bascandziev & Harris, 2011), but their initial mistakes indicate their difficulty inhibiting the "straight-down" rule without such training (Hood et al., 2006).

The more salient finding, however, is the extent to which some traces of these early ways of thinking about physical objects persist into adulthood. Thus, the belief sometimes persists even when the physical constraints of the task make such a straight-down path impossible (Caramazza et al., 1981; Krist, 2000; White, 2012).

In addition, both children and adults make incorrect predictions about trajectories, movements after collisions, and the natures of forces on objects (Bertamini et al., 2004; Clement, 1993; Espinoza, 2005; Proffitt & Gilden, 1989: White, 2012). Many aspects of physical mechanics remain

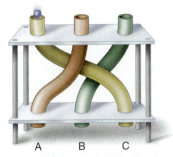

FIGURE 9.27 The straight-down rule. Until about age 3½, children often assume that an object dropped in a solid tube must emerge from the tube directly below where it was dropped. Older children and adults clearly expect the ball to emerge from the bottom of the tube into which it was dropped. Adapted from Hood et al. (2006).

Brown and Campione's second theme, fostering *meta-cognitive awareness*, translates into classroom practice by using methods that encourage students to pay attention to their own cognitive states. The method of "reciprocal teaching" can foster this kind of awareness, as each member of a group of roughly six children and a teacher takes turns leading the discussion. By requiring each student to present ideas, explain them, and answer questions about them, this method encourages children's awareness of the nature of their own knowledge. When children can develop their own areas of expertise, they can act as resources to the whole community of learners. In some cases, students who have trouble learning certain computational or reasoning skills when they are taken out of context can excel at learning to apply these same skills within a particular domain or context. Each child can take pride in his own area of expertise, and as the children learn to rely on each other, this distribution of knowledge fosters interactive learning and interdependence.

Clearly, these techniques for improving metacognitive awareness are closely tied to Brown and Campione's third theme, the importance of *domain-specific learning*. In addition to its metacognitive benefits, allowing students to develop some individualized areas of expertise also allows teachers to observe how each child acquires knowledge in different domains at different rates. These insights can help teachers carefully diagnose each student's proficiency in order to determine a zone of proximal development for each child in a particular domain. Such domain-specific assessments allow teachers to see, for example, that a child has not yet mastered the concept of the number line. In

that case, he should not yet be taught mathematics that relies on that concept (Bruer, 1997). Domain-specific assessments of preparedness are crucial here, since a child who is cognitively well prepared for learning may still need more help understanding specific concepts within a particular domain.

Q: How is the zone of proximal development concept useful to education?

Implementing Cognitive Science Ideas in the Classroom Cognitive science is offering many new approaches for teaching (Bruer, 1993a; Duit & Treagust, 2003; Klahr & Li, 2005; Klahr et al., 2011; Metcalfe & Kornell, 2007; Richland et al., 2005; Wieman, 2010), some of which are now making their way into the classroom. To see how their results measure up, consider Figure 11.19, which compares test performance among three groups of students: those taught with the Community of Learners program methods for a full year, those exposed to these methods for half a year and normal instruction for the other half, and those taught all year in a regular classroom. The Community of Learners methods had dramatic impacts on the amount of knowledge that students acquired and retained. As the second-semester graphs show, the program's impact increased over the months, such that children immersed in it for a full year learned much more than children who learned the same material in a more traditional format.

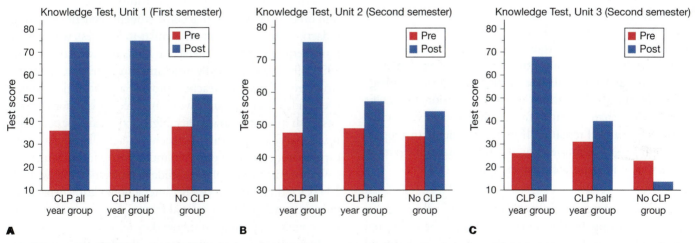

FIGURE 11.19 Effects of the Community of Learners program of instruction. The first group (CLP all year) was exposed to the Community of Learners program methods for a full year. The second group (CLP half year) was taught with these methods during the first semester, then switched to regular instruction for the second semester. The third group (no CLP) had regular classroom experience all year. The Community of Learners program clearly enhanced student test performance. **(A)** Unit 1 test results during the first semester when both the CLP all year group and the CLP half year group did research, but the no CLP group did not do research. **(B)** Unit 2 test results during the second semester when only the CLP all year group did research. **(C)** Unit 3 test results during the second semester when again only the CLP all year group did research. Adapted from Brown (1992).

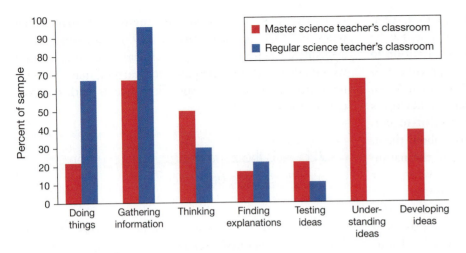

FIGURE 11.20 **Teaching children how to think about science.** When sixth grade students taught by a master science teacher were compared with students taught by a regular science teacher, there were striking differences in the sorts of questions the students asked in discussions about science. For example, among the master teacher's students, metacognitive questions— that is, questions about the thought processes involved in doing science—were seven times more common than they were among the regular science teacher's students (the comparison classroom). By contrast, more descriptive questions were three times more common in the comparison classroom. Adapted from Smith et al. (2000).

Q: How has cognitive science started to influence educational practice?

It is especially encouraging that teachers do not need to be immersed in the latest cognitive science research to implement many of its messages in the classroom. Master teachers often use these principles on a daily basis. In a small parochial school in Wisconsin, a teacher known as Sister Mary Gertrude Hennessey taught science to the same group of children for most of their elementary and middle school years (Smith et al., 2000). She used many of the principles that Brown and Campione advocate, and her students' progress was remarkable (see Figure 11.20). Like many master teachers, Sister Gertrude also deeply understood her discipline. Moreover, she also had earned a doctorate in philosophy, which she felt greatly enhanced her teaching of science. Her great success demonstrates that after several years in an extraordinary teacher's classroom, ordinary middle school students can show patterns of scientific reasoning and conceptual understanding that typically do not emerge until late in high school or in college (Smith et al., 2000). Stories of such exceptional teachers provide more than encouragement; they also serve as critical cases for careful research. If master teachers can support such high levels of achievement, it is important to help more instructors to incorporate their methods.

Aptitude-Treatment Interactions Not all students approach learning in the same way. Even when children have very similar levels of intelligence and background knowledge, their most effective ways of learning will vary. Therefore, the methods that a teacher uses to help one child blossom may not work well for another child. Looking at this relationship in the inverse: a learner's specific strengths (her aptitudes) and weaknesses impact the effectiveness of

a particular teaching method (the treatment) (Cronbach, 1975; Cronbach & Snow, 1977). This reciprocal relationship is known as **aptitude-treatment interactions**. Aptitude-treatment interactions provide an educational example of the idea of "goodness of fit" that we encountered in Chapter 7. There we considered how an infant's temperament fits with that of his caregiver, affecting their interactions and thereby helping to shape development. Here the idea of "fit" is narrower, focused on the interaction between a student and a particular manner of instruction.

Many studies have documented aptitude-treatment interactions involving a broad range of cognitive factors, often called "learner characteristics." Some people learn better when they adopt *holistic strategies*, considering many aspects of a problem at once. Others may do better by using *local strategies*, breaking down the problem into small, distinct components. Some people learn more effectively from visual imagery, while others may do better with verbal approaches (Riding & Cheema, 1991). Still other studies show that some students benefit more from didactic forms of instruction (similar to lectures), while others learn better from more interactive kinds of instruction (Snow, 1989, 1992). More broadly, teaching situations that are highly structured—in which teachers provide a great deal of control over student activities and give clear, direct instructions—work best with students of low ability, high anxiety, and/or poor organizational skills. But this approach can actually hinder highly capable students, who often do much better in less structured environments that emphasize student exploration (Snow, 1989, 1992). Optimal student-teacher interactions clearly depend not only on social and motivational factors, but also on both people's cognitive aptitudes and how they relate.

Aptitude-treatment interactions illustrate the importance of recognizing that children are individuals with different cognitive strengths, since what works well for one child might be a disaster for another (Pakarinen et al., 2011). The challenge, of course, is to develop more sensitive ways of assessing and understanding these differences and adjusting instruction to take them into account. The concept of aptitude-treatment interactions may be particularly useful when devising instructional programs for children who have special needs or who are especially gifted. As children depart from cognitive norms, it becomes more likely that their ideal learning environment will differ from that of most children. For example, when developmentally delayed children experience different educational settings, the most delayed children tend to benefit more from highly directive instruction, whereas somewhat less delayed children benefit more from instruction that involves more interaction (Dale et al., 2005).

> **Q:** Provide a specific example of how two groups of children might thrive optimally in quite different educational settings.

Creativity

Aptitude-treatment interactions demonstrate that people vary cognitively in far more ways than IQ subscores can measure (Riding & Cheema, 1991; Sternberg & Zhang, 2005). One widely described pattern of variation that is distinct from intelligence is **creativity**, the ability to come up with novel insights and new ways of solving problems. We all know of people with impressive analytical abilities and extensive practical knowledge, but who never seem able to escape conventional ways of thinking. We also know of people who seem less analytical and informed, but who frequently devise powerful new ideas and solutions. Such creativity is valuable and can lead to great advances in such fields as industry, medicine, and teaching. For these reasons, most researchers believe that creativity varies independently from intelligence—that is, the two measures are only weakly correlated or not correlated at all (Furnham & Nederstrom, 2010; Kaufman, 2009; Runco, 2007). But creativity is extremely difficult to measure. When you ask people to define creativity in testable ways, they express a wealth of opinions about the ability's core nature. Does it primarily depend on the ability to draw new analogies, to defy conventions, to think "laterally" instead of "vertically," or to break old patterns of thought and to be open to new ones? Such questions have generated a great deal of research; several thousand studies of creativity have been published in the last 10 years alone. We will highlight several themes that have emerged from this work and consider a couple of common ways of assessing creativity.

One controversy about creative ability concerns whether people are creative largely because of their intrinsic qualities or whether there are certain kinds of situations that make virtually anyone highly creative (Kasof, 1999). Both kinds of influences on creativity are relevant, but here we will focus more on the internal, or dispositional, influences. In Chapter 13, we will see how socialization affects creativity.

Measures of Creativity

One classic approach to defining and measuring creativity is based on the idea of achieving a novel perspective on a problem. People can often become trapped in a particular perspective on a problem. Creative people seem more able to break that focus on the conventional way of looking at a task to adopt a novel perspective (Eysenck, 1994). A variety of methods have been used to measure this aspect of creativity:

- *Nonverbal tests*—for example, drawing lines to elaborate on a simple shape (Torrance, 1974).
- *Category generation*—for example, listing as many things as possible that have gears or listing things that get smaller over time (Wallach & Kogan, 1965).
- *Generating consequences*—for example, imagining what would happen if all laws were abolished (Guilford, 1954).
- *Alternative meanings test*—for example, writing as many meanings as possible for ambiguous words such as *cut* or *duck* (Getzels & Jackson, 1962).
- *Alternative uses*—for example, generating as many alternative uses as possible for familiar objects such as bricks or paper clips (Getzels & Jackson, 1962; Guilford, 1962).

Alternative uses have been studied extensively in overcoming **functional fixedness**—that is, the bias to use an object or tool in a conventional rather than a novel way to solve a problem. Creative people are not as likely to stay "fixated" on an object's standard function. For example, in a classic study by Karl Duncker (1945), participants were asked to attach a candle to a wall and were given a box of matches, a box full of tacks, and a candle. The solution (see Figure 11.22) required a novel way of using the tacks and the melted wax from the candle. It was thought that only creative people could break out of the familiar uses of each component and come up with the solution.

All these ways of measuring creativity have allowed researchers to investigate two closely related developmental questions: Can creativity be taught? And do people's levels of creativity remain stable as they age (for example, are kindergartners who are considered creative more likely to also be viewed as creative in adulthood)? These two questions are linked because, to the extent that creativity can be taught (and thereby increase over time), it is likely to be less stable over the lifespan.

Computers and e-Learning in the Schools

Computers have had a dramatic impact on many cultures. Many children in industrialized countries spend more time looking at computers or cell phone screens than they do watching television (Taylor & Keeter, 2010). Using the Internet to search for information, play online games, or interact on social networks has become a commonplace event. But before these uses became commonplace, children were using computers in schools. Today, the vast majority of schools in developed countries make Internet-linked computers available to their students (see Figure 11.21).

The use of computers in the schools on such a large scale since the 1980s raises questions about how they affect education. Do they support more efficient learning? Are they more helpful in some academic disciplines than in others? Does access to the wealth of information on the Internet contribute to children's conceptual growth, or does it overwhelm them with too much information, much of it dubious? Computer use in the schools varies so widely that there are no easy answers to these questions, and so controversy remains regarding their academic value (Cuban, 2001; Hew & Brush, 2011; Joshi et al., 2010; Sandholtz & Reilly, 2004; Tamim et al., 2011). Nonetheless, some general messages are emerging about the most effective ways of using computers to enhance learning.

The cognitive science approach to educational practice has helped promote the use of computers to further educational goals (Roschelle et al., 2000). Rather than simply providing positive and negative reinforcements in automated drills, computers can be used to improve students' access to information, to further communication, and to provide some domain-specific assessments of the child. Computers can be most effective in the classroom when teachers have clear, specific goals for incorporating them into lessons and evidence that these goals are feasible. Too often, school districts buy a large number of computers, set them up in the classrooms, and then are dismayed to find that they have little impact on learning. But when computers have been used in the context of cognitive theories of learning, there have been some striking successes (Sandholtz & Reilly, 2004; Tamim et al., 2011). Brown and Campione's Community of Learners program used computers to help teachers hone in on students' zones of proximal development (see Chapter 9). Software designed for classroom use can help teachers get more precise moment-to-moment snapshots of a child's progress on an academic task. This can help teachers determine which new topics would be challenging but still within the student's capability.

Computers and other modes of Internet access can also enhance education by supporting collaborative learning. With computer networks, students can collaborate over long distances and large time frames by posting their work in a com-

FIGURE 11.21 Computers in the schools. Although computers are now used in virtually all schools in developed countries, controversy remains concerning their usefulness as supplements to more traditional forms of education.

In fact, an individual's performance on common creativity tests remains fairly stable over time, but there is less consistency on creativity tests than on intelligence tests (Simonton, 2000). To the extent that creativity test performance is less stable than intelligence test performance, it supports the view that anyone can become at least somewhat more creative by learning and practicing specific ways of thinking (Murdock, 2003; Sternberg et al., 2004). These techniques include using mental images to explore new possibilities (Smith et al., 1995), exploiting the power of analogies (Holyoak & Thagard, 1995), and radically reframing problems (Polanyi, 1966). In addition, simply focusing on developing task-relevant cogni-

munal space on a server or on a social networking site. Cognitive science researchers have shown considerable interest in trying to understand the special nature of learning and thinking in groups where intellectual resources are shared (Hutchins, 1996). Internet access allows children in one classroom to develop collaborative working groups that span several continents. Web 2.0 software and supporting hardware enable children to create content and evaluate content created by others (Kitsantas & Dabbagh, 2010). Children may not always use social networking sites, wikis, and other Web 2.0 technologies in productive ways (Carr, 2010), but the potential for increased information access and evaluation is there. At the same time, there may be some unintended cognitive effects of having information easily accessible through search engines. Thus, when individuals bookmark search results, they are much more likely to forget those results than when they do not click on a bookmark (Sparrow et al., 2011). Thus, while search engines can greatly increase access to knowledge, they may also sometimes result in individuals' knowing less on their own.

As computers become more powerful, flexible, and easier to use, they have the potential to become collaborative partners in the learning process and not just passive tools (Linn & Hsi, 2000). Advances in artificial intelligence already allow computers to interact in increasingly conversation-like ways with students and to be sensitive to students' cognitive and emotional states (Graesser et al., 2007; Song et al., 2004). We do not understand how this kind of "collaboration" will enhance learning or which sorts of students are most likely to benefit, but many education researchers are exploring the benefits of these forms of learning (Bransford et al., 1999). An important component of the success of computer-supported collaborative learning seems to be the awareness of the knowledge and areas of expertise of other group members and the presence of software tools to help optimize that awareness (Janssen & Bodemer, 2013).

One recurring problem is that computers are often in special resource rooms and only used sporadically by students, sometimes as little as 1 hour a week (Cattagni & Ferris, 2001). That sort of limited access may largely thwart the most effective ways in which computers can be used. Those limitations, however, are rapidly changing. Many schoolchildren can now access the Web any-where with their smartphones, and some school districts are providing all the students in a classroom with tablet computers. These devices enable children to have continuous portable access to the Internet and to simple computer programs (Hu, 2011). These changes may facilitate collaboration, information access and transmission, and more rapid feedback. Before school districts rush to invest in such new technologies, however, they must take care not to repeat the mistakes of prior failed computer implementations. Large-scale pilot studies should be run to ascertain the potential benefits and efficacy of smartphones and tablets, thereby avoiding any unnecessary expense for information technology in the classroom (Hu, 2011). In making the decision as to whether to commit limited resources to purchasing tablets and other devices, school districts, especially poorer ones, will need to know how this new generation of computers affects educational experiences. They will also need to ask hard questions about cognitive tradeoffs of Internet access. Some critics suggest that continuous Internet access can reduce attention span under the guise of "multitasking" and create what some call an "Internet-induced ADD" (Carr, 2010). Texting, Web surfing, and interacting with peers in an unsupervised manner on social networking sites are not always positive educational experiences. Throughout the world, the issue for schools will soon not be whether children have personal computers in the form of smartphones (they almost all will, even in the least developed countries); it will be when it is educationally effective for them to use those devices in the classroom.

E-learning in all of its forms is becoming a central part of the modern classroom. If designed efficiently, e-learning can save money rather than increase expenses because it allows children to practice certain kinds of problems, such as math exercises or vocabulary drills, with less direct teacher involvement. Indeed, some charter schools have relied heavily on blending traditional teaching with e-learning to meet their budgets (Abramson, 2011).

As computers get better at tracking each child's individual strengths and weaknesses, there is the potential for tailored instruction that may not always be possible in a traditional classroom. Computers and their software programs are increasingly being designed as "pedagogical agents," helping children to build on their skills in an optimal fashion (Graesser & McNamara, 2010; Graesser et al., 2012).

tive skills and heuristics can lead to more creative thought (Hennessey & Amabile, 2010).

These kinds of training do seem to improve certain aspects of creative thinking, but it is not clear whether similar experience-dependent effects account for most people's creativity. Certainly, many people like to think that there is an intrinsic component as well. Some researchers suggest that because creativity appears to run in families, there may even be a substantial genetic contribution (Eysenck, 1995). It is difficult, however, to disentangle genetic effects from those that might occur from growing up in an environment fostered by highly creative parents.

Wall

A   B

FIGURE 11.22 Functional fixedness. In this classic problem studied by Karl Duncker in 1945, creativity was measured by the extent to which participants could avoid being fixated on **(A)** the standard functions of matches, candles, and thumbtacks and **(B)** come up with novel and creative uses. Adapted from Duncker (1945).

The Development of Extraordinary Creativity

Howard Gardner (1994, 1997), whose theory of multiple intelligences was discussed earlier in the chapter, has advocated a different approach to studying creativity. Gardner argues that the common psychometric approaches to defining and measuring creativity have yielded several important insights, but they largely fail to truly identify the people who are most creative in everyday life. Instead, Gardner advocates studying extraordinarily creative people as a way to uncover creativity's critical components.

Two approaches best capture Gardner's proposals for how to study creativity. The first of these, the **idiographic approach**, involves studying case histories of highly creative individuals to see whether they seem to cluster into different types. The second method, known as the **nomothetic approach**, involves comparing the lives of especially creative individuals to look for common patterns or principles (Simonton, 2000). Thus, we might ask if extraordinary creativity typically emerges late in life, or we might ask whether more highly creative people tend to live during times of dramatic cultural change.

Gardner has often taken the idiographic approach, studying in detail the lives of creative geniuses. He used several criteria to choose these individuals. First, he sought out people who exemplified creativity in seven of the eight multiple intelligences he had defined in his earlier research: linguistic, logical/math, musical, spatial, bodily/kinesthetic, interpersonal, and intrapersonal intelligence. As Table 11.4 shows, each kind of intelligence lends itself to particular professions, and Gardner studied creative geniuses in each one.

Gardner emphasized that most outstanding people spent many thousands of hours of practice or sustained effort in their chosen domain. Thus, creativity rarely just appeared without a passion to invest time and effort in a domain (Ericsson, 1996). In each area, Gardner chose people who had continually excelled in their domain by solving problems, fashioning products, or raising issues. Moreover, their contributions had to be recognized as new and different and yet be broadly accepted in a way that had dramatic influence on the culture at large. Thus, the recognition of extraordinary creativity must always be seen as a social judgment relevant to a particular cultural group. People are not creative in isolation, but only in terms of how their accomplishments relate to the society in which they live (Csikszentmihalyi, 1997; Harrington, 1990). This observation also resonates with Vygotsky's ideas about how children come to internalize the sociocultural context in which they grow up. Similarly, creativity emerges as an individual becomes embedded within a set of cultural and social structures.

Although Gardner's sample of seven people is too small to form strong conclusions about how creativity develops, he was nevertheless struck by the many ways in which these people's life experiences differed from what we might expect from a random sample of the population. Taking a nomothetic approach, Gardner looked for similarities between their lives and began to uncover some common principles. The following patterns hold true for most, if not all, of the seven geniuses:

1. Most were born near great cultural centers or cities.
2. Most came from middle-class backgrounds, rather than from the intellectual elite, wealthy families, or poor families.

TABLE 11.4 Creativity in different domains. Gardner originally suggested that there are seven separate intelligences and that each one can result in its own form of creative genius. (Naturalistic intelligence was later added as an eighth kind of intelligence. Charles Darwin would be a creative genius in naturalistic intelligence.)

Kind of intelligence	Profession	Creative geniuses
Linguistic	Poet, writer	T. S. Eliot
Logical/mathematical	Scientist, mathematician	Albert Einstein
Musical	Composer, musician	Igor Stravinsky
Spatial	Sculptor, painter, sailor	Pablo Picasso
Bodily/kinesthetic	Dancer, athlete, choreographer	Martha Graham
Interpersonal	Teacher, salesperson, leader	Mahatma Gandhi
Intrapersonal	Counselor, psychologist	Sigmund Freud

3. Their families were usually intact and had strong work ethics.
4. Most experienced no pressure to achieve in a particular profession, just to work hard at whatever was chosen.
5. Most had strong emotional ties to nonfamily members, such as caregivers and early mentors.
6. Most did not choose which profession to pursue until around the age of 20. Few were child prodigies.
7. At around age 20, most moved to major centers of culture.
8. Most sought out like-minded people and immersed themselves in groups of literary companions, artists, scientists, and so on.
9. The older they got, the more their work became an all-consuming part of their lives.
10. Most had an unusual combination of intellectual talents, not just the one in their domain of endeavor.

These common patterns are fascinating, but they do not neatly coalesce into a sensible account of what makes a person creative. Gardner also uncovered other factors in these people that seem to more directly relate to the manifestation of great creativity. For example, most of them went to greater-than-average lengths to promote themselves and to advance their own reputations. Even the most modest, Einstein, was careful to make sure that others were aware of his work and that it was presented in the right way. They also tended to have difficult relationships with those close to them, ranging from Einstein's near total disregard for others to Picasso's sadistic behavior. Gardner felt that to some extent, all of these people sacrificed their relationships in service of their work.

> **Q:** Describe two different approaches to the study of creativity and the merits and problems of each.

Bringing similar approaches to bear on the developmental factors associated with creative genius, researchers have repeatedly found that highly creative adults often have adverse childhoods. It appears that, in many cases, a difficult childhood that runs against the normal social grain, as well as a childhood experience persevering in the face of adversity, may be important (Simonton, 1994, 2000). But remember that these early experiences themselves do not necessarily enhance creativity (or do so alone). Even if these experiences are formative, the real cause may be genetic. That is, parents of creative children may also be somewhat rebellious individualists, likely to create nonstandard environments for their children that pose unique challenges.

These parallels among the lives of some of the best-known creative minds in recent history suggest many hypotheses about what creativity is and how it develops. We know that creativity is expressed in diverse domains, from the symbolic worlds of literature, art, and mathematics to the world of human understanding. Some masters, like Mozart, exhaust an existing art form, making way for new ones to emerge. Others, like Beethoven, invent a new style or come up with other novel creations. But we are still left with the mystery of why one person becomes so much more creative than another.

One possibility is that these extraordinary people are the way they are not from an excess of creativity but from other aspects of their character and experience. These other aspects may have helped them project their creativity far more than other, equally creative people. Thus, being a strong self-promoter, being able to tolerate catastrophic interpersonal relations with intimates, and being able to neglect all else in their lives except their creative pursuits may have set these people apart from countless others with as much creative spark.

Conclusions

One key theme of this chapter is that intelligence is tightly intertwined with social and cultural contexts. Intelligence tests assess a particular kind of cultural adaptation, and test performance is often closely linked to a person's social class or status in a society. Moreover, intelligence tests seem to assess only a small subset of the cognitive abilities that allow some people to thrive in school or at work. Social intelligence, creativity, and certain kinds of cognitive flexibility seem to be of equal importance. Even more broadly, we once again see how cognitive abilities are intertwined with social domains and how factors such as social attributions, motivation, and other emotions can interact with cognitive abilities. Because we do not yet have well-developed measures for these other sorts of cognitive abilities, intelligence tests remain the best tool for predicting academic and workplace success. But this may change as new assessment tools become more refined and standardized.

The social aspects of intelligence are especially apparent when we consider large group differences that have not been well accounted for by other kinds of explanations, such as genetic explanations. In addition, birth order effects, in which IQ scores gradually drop for each later-born child, are likely to have social explanations. Similarly, the Flynn effect, the gradual rise of IQ in many populations worldwide, is likely to be almost fully explained by social and cultural effects. In the chapters that follow, we will examine some of these social influences on the mind and behavior in much greater depth.

Schooling provides the most vivid example of how social and environmental factors can influence intelligence. Not only do children with high IQ scores tend to stay in school for more years, but the longer children of various IQ levels stay in school, the more their intelligence rises on a wide variety of fronts, ranging from transitive reasoning to storytelling and comprehension skills. As schools bring children within the framework of the dominant culture, the effects on patterns of thought and cognitive performance can be profound.

Schools need to be sensitive to the individual child and the ways in which a child's particular aptitude interacts with instructional techniques. Consideration of such "learner characteristics" also reinforces the view of development as an active exploratory process and not simply one of the child acting as a passive recipient of experiences. More broadly, as the rate of technological change accelerates, schools must confront the problem of teaching only a fixed set of skills. Rather, students must hone the ability to acquire new sets of skills as the world around them changes. If the curriculum becomes focused on training students for high-stakes standardized tests, teachers may not have the chance to prepare students to be adaptive, flexible learners. The problem is not with the tests themselves, but with designing tests that go beyond simply assessing factual knowledge and that do not cause high levels of test anxiety.

Clearly, the research on the development of intelligence draws together several familiar developmental themes. With respect to the nativist/empiricist debate, the links are more remote than they first appear. The classical nativists and empiricists debated about human nature and how people acquire knowledge. They rarely, if ever, were concerned with the kinds of individual differences that are a major focus of intelligence testing. (Unfortunately, the term *nativist* has sometimes been used to describe those who believe that differences in intelligence have a strong genetic basis. This sense of the word, which focuses on how people differ from each other, is completely separate from the meaning we have been using in this book, which is instead concerned with what is common to all humans in comparison with other species. The two meanings should not be confused.) More commonly, controversies about how differences in intelligence develop are referred to as the nature/nurture debate, where differences among people are seen as largely a consequence of their intrinsic natures or of how they are nurtured. By contrast, both sides of the nativist/empiricist debate have classically focused on how to characterize patterns of development that are common to all people.

In several places in this chapter, we have discussed the advantages of viewing developmental psychology as the study of emerging competencies and abilities rather than the gradual disappearance of cognitive deficits that plague the younger child. Likewise, this perspective has been valuable in thinking about intelligence in relation to models of education. It is far less helpful to ask what younger children are "missing" with respect to intelligence and creativity than to explore the nature of the earliest roots of cognitive abilities—roots that can stretch back to infancy. We have seen that schooling is more effective when it focuses on abilities that children bring to the classroom and works on developing those abilities further while linking them to other skills in an integrated fashion. Fortunately, this kind of focus on early competencies is what the best teachers do naturally.

STUDY AND REVIEW

SUMMARY

What Is Intelligence?

- Despite frequent, widespread references to intelligence, there is relatively little consensus on what it really means to be intelligent. Traditionally, researchers have focused on a psychometric approach, using tests that attempt to quantify intelligence in terms of analytical intelligence, the ability to engage in computations and abstract comparisons.

- Psychometric tests of intelligence reliably show a positive correlation among their subtests, including those for language, mathematical, and visual/spatial abilities. Some researchers have argued that these correlations indicate that there is a single underlying factor, a general intelligence, or *g*, which affects performance on all intellectual tasks.

- Other explanations for the positive correlations among components of intelligence tests either do not require a *g* factor or see it as only a part of overall intelligence. Carroll's hierarchical three-stratum theory of intelligence is an influential approach that describes how different cognitive abilities might be distinct components of intelligence occurring at three levels: narrow abilities, broad abilities, and a part that corresponds to *g*. However, through computer modeling, it is possible to show enough simulated intersections of cognitive abilities over time that a "virtual" *g* materializes in a cognitive system where no real *g* component was originally present. Developmental cognitive neuroscience may help ascertain the degree of utility of *g* as it pertains to intelligence.

- Alternative approaches to intelligence consider how and why people excel at a wider range of contexts and situations. These theories have been used to measure forms of intelligence quite different from those measured by IQ tests. Gardner's theory of multiple intelligences and Sternberg's theory of successful intelligence are two examples that do not map neatly onto traditional notions of intelligence. Researchers are also exploring broader notions, such as social and emotional intelligence.

- IQ tests tend to predict school performance and even job performance better than most other available measures, but by no means with great accuracy. As new ways of assessing intelligence become more widespread, they may be better predictors than traditional IQ tests in many settings.

Origins of Intelligence

- All forms of intelligence undergo dramatic changes during childhood and adolescence. The speed at which infants habituate to novel displays partially predicts analytical intelligence many years later, a finding that poses new challenges for accounts of how intelligence develops.

- Intelligence test scores show a substantial heritability, meaning that in most populations, a substantial proportion of the individual differences in intelligence is due to genetic differences. At the same time, there is still a significant amount of variance that is due to environmental factors. Furthermore, no matter how large the heritability is, it does not mean that any differences *between groups* are due to genetic factors. This is an important misconception that has led to much confusion in the popular understanding of intelligence research. The search for a gene or small number of genes that might represent the essence of intelligence has been fruitless. It is now clear that despite a high heritability, genetic causal pathways are likely to involve large numbers of genes in complicated nets of interactions with other genes and the environment. In addition, any model of the genetic influences must explain why heritability increases quite dramatically with age from young childhood well into adolescence.

Group Differences and Intelligence Tests

- On average, overall intelligence test scores are equal between men and women, partially because the tests' components are weighted to equalize the overall scores across genders. Nonetheless, there are reliable sex differences on sections of most intelligence tests. The sexes also differ in their distributions of scores. There are more men than women among the extremely high scorers and the extremely low scorers.

- There are large group differences in overall intelligence test scores between ethnic groups, but no compelling evidence has emerged showing that those differences arise from biological factors, as opposed to social and cultural ones.

- Stereotype threats are a powerful sociocultural influence that affects some groups more than others. People do less well on tasks when they fear that their poor performance will confirm negative stereotypes about them. A strong awareness of stereotypes develops during the elementary school years. Among children who perceive stereotypes about intellectual ability as relevant to themselves, this awareness is linked to declining performance.

Environmental Influences on Intelligence Test Scores

- A wide variety of environmental influences, ranging from malnutrition to parental involvement and birth order, can influence intelligence test scores. One of the most important influences is schooling, where time in school is clearly related to performance on intelligence tests.

- Preschool programs, especially Head Start, can have long-term positive effects on a child's intelligence and prospects in life.

Schooling

- Schools provide far more than the education that fosters analytical intelligence. As socializing agents, schools teach children how to behave in large, controlled settings. As cultural institutions, they expose children to the dominant culture. As vehicles of values, schools often aim to instill self-discipline and encourage students to be sensitive to others' needs. Whether and how schools should explicitly teach particular values has been a topic of controversy.

- Cognitive science has made major advances in understanding what kinds of educational practices help children learn. Studies have shown that focusing on students' metacognitive awareness and using Vygotsky's theory of the zone of proximal development to guide students' progress can enhance their learning. But educators should be aware of aptitude-treatment interactions, the finding that different sorts of learners thrive in different sorts of teaching environments.

Creativity

- Creativity, the ability to devise novel insights and solutions, is one of the most valued human traits and one that can vary greatly among people with similar levels of analytical and practical intelligence. Although there is only a weak consensus on how best to measure creativity, most creativity tests attempt to measure the ability to take novel points of view or come up with novel solutions to familiar situations or problems.

- Researchers using the idiographic approach to studying creativity have examined the lives of creative geniuses and tried to understand what made them different. This approach suggests that creativity may flower in different ways that correspond to different kinds of intelligences. The nomothetic approach has explored broader principles concerning when and how creativity is likely to emerge in development. These different approaches suggest some commonalities among highly creative people; perhaps the most surprising is that they seem unusually likely to have experienced significant adversities in childhood.

THOUGHT QUESTIONS

1. Some scholars have argued that the trend of rising intelligence test scores, or the Flynn effect, is starting to level off, while others think that it is still rising and will continue to rise for several decades to come. Which view do you favor? Support your view by examining possible mechanisms underlying the Flynn effect.

2. An early Head Start program in a small town proposes to have all pediatricians conduct a standardized habituation test of all infants in the town at age 10 months so as to identify those infants who might be most at risk for having lower intelligence test scores later on. The goal is to then to be able to intervene more effectively to help those infants early on. Do you consider this proposal to be a good idea?

3. In an attempt to improve the quality of education in a school district, the school board is evaluating two proposals: to lengthen the school year by 3 weeks or to lengthen the school day by 2 hours. It can only afford to implement one of these two options. Which do you think would be more educationally effective? Do you think the best option might vary as a function of the age of the child?

4. To address budget cutbacks, an elementary school principal proposes doing away with recesses, which require additional supervisory staff and playground maintenance. A parent objects that this change will discriminate against boys and will cause an increase in ADHD diagnoses in boys in that school because some boys will simply not be able to sit still in a classroom for an entire school day. State your reasons for agreeing or disagreeing with the parent.

KEY TERMS

aptitude-treatment interaction (p. 416)

bell curve (p. 389)

creativity (p. 417)

crystallized intelligence (p. 392)

emotional intelligence (p. 395)

fluid intelligence (p. 392)

Flynn effect (p. 406)

functional fixedness (p. 417)

general intelligence, *g* (p. 390)

idiographic approach (p. 420)

intelligence quotient (IQ) (p. 387)

interpersonal intelligence (p. 395)

intrapersonal intelligence (p. 395)

multiple intelligences (p. 393)

nomothetic approach (p. 420)

normal distribution curve (p. 389)

perceptual reasoning index (p. 388)

platoon school (p. 410)

processing speed index (p. 388)

psychometric approach (p. 387)

social intelligence (p. 395)

standard deviation (p. 389)

stereotype threat (p. 404)

verbal comprehension index (p. 388)

working memory index (p. 388)

PART IV

The Self and Others

12

Morality in Thought and Action

The Development of Moral Thought
- Debating the Origins of Moral Thought
- Evolutionary and Cultural Psychology and Morality
- Characterizing the Basis of Moral Thought

Piaget's Theory of Moral Development
- Piaget's Stages of Moral Reasoning
- Evaluating Piaget's Account

Kohlberg's Theory of Moral Reasoning
- Kohlberg's Stages of Moral Reasoning
- Evaluating Kohlberg's Theory

Alternative Theories of Moral Development
- Gilligan's Theory of Moral Development
- A Pluralistic Approach to the Development of Moral Thought

The Development of Moral Behavior
- Consistency of Moral Behavior
- Antisocial and Prosocial Behavior
- Temperament, Personality, and Moral Behavior
- Social Influences on Moral Behavior

Conclusions

Summary

On April 11, 2013, Emil Kapaun was posthumously awarded the U.S. military's highest honor, the Medal of Honor, even though he never fired a shot or engaged in any form of aggression toward others. Indeed, he showed kindness and compassion to his enemies. During the Korean War, Kapaun served as a chaplain in the army. When his battalion was encircled by the Chinese army in a battle in North Korea, he dodged heavy enemy fire to drag many wounded and dying soldiers to safety. Although he could have retreated with the army when combat conditions worsened, he chose to stay behind and care for the wounded soldiers. Kapaun and others were captured and forcibly marched 87 miles to a brutal prison camp under extremely harsh conditions. On the march and in the camp, many men died of starvation, extreme cold, lack of medical attention to their wounds, and from disease. Throughout his incarceration, Kapaun engaged in repeated heroic acts of sacrifice for his fellow prisoners. He gave them his own clothes for warmth, he stole food from the guards to give to those who were starving, and he shared his own pitiful food rations with the other prisoners, even as he himself was wasting away. He scavenged for rags to use as bandages to prevent infection from wounds and thereby saved many soldiers from death. He stood between a captor and a wounded fellow soldier who was about to be shot, saving the soldier's life by carrying him away. Kapaun died of pneumonia while he was still incarcerated, even as his last known acts were attempts to help his fellow prisoners. In an interview in April 2013, one of his fellow prisoners who survived said: "People had lost a great deal of their civility. . . . We were stacking the bodies outside where they were frozen like cordwood and here is this one man—in all of this chaos—who has kept his principles." (Robert Wood, quoted in the *Washington Post*, April 11, 2013).

Kapaun grew up in modest conditions on a farm in rural Kansas and had an unremarkable childhood. He was known to be a good student and a polite but somewhat shy child, but there are no records that indicate that he showed the kind of extraordinary moral behavior that would come to distinguish his later life. It is not known how a seemingly ordinary farm boy grew up to adhere to the highest moral principles while under conditions of extreme duress, nor is it known how those principles emerged in the course of his development.

Kapaun's life illustrates the complexity of moral thought and behavior. We may all have strong intuitions about the morality of actions, yet we vary greatly in how those intuitions become organized into larger systems of beliefs that motivate us toward action. Where do those intuitions come from? On what basis do we make our judgments of morality? How does the ability to make those judgments emerge in childhood? How does it lead to actions? How can a boy who grows up having an apparently normal childhood become

such a remarkable moral individual while other boys growing up in highly similar environments and families end up with very different moral convictions and behaviors? How can a group of individuals all believe they are acting correctly and morally but nonetheless do very different things in the same situations?

In this chapter, we will examine the origins of moral thought, theories about moral development and moral reasoning, and the imperfect link between moral thought and moral action. With respect to moral thought, we will explore whether young children have qualitatively different ways of thinking about what is right and wrong, and we will once again discuss Piaget as well as another classic scholar in the field, Lawrence Kohlberg. We will then turn to more recent views of moral judgment and ask about the extent to which moral judgments should be thought of like the rest of analytical cognition or whether they require more intrinsic roles for emotion.

After examining moral judgment and reasoning, we will discuss moral actions, asking about the ways in which moral thoughts might be related to tendencies to actually act in good and bad ways. We will see that the links between thought and action are far more complex than they might appear to be at first. We will then consider actions more directly in their own right. We will ask whether there are biological bases for individual differences in morality and will also discuss social and cultural influences on moral behavior. In addition, we will look at different kinds of punishment and modeling and will ask how they can affect moral behavior. Finally, we will consider the development of conscience and its possible relations to parent-child interactions.

The Development of Moral Thought

Examining the development of moral thought raises questions about its origins, its evolutionary and psychological bases, and its degree of domain specificity. Do children across the world develop some common moral principles, or are cross-cultural differences so broad that there are no moral universals? What kinds of psychological processes contribute to moral thought, and how do these processes change with age? And is moral reasoning truly a separate realm of thought with its own special characteristics and developmental patterns? We will consider all of these questions in this section, but first we need to take note of how moral thought relates to moral actions.

Having beliefs about what is right and wrong is quite different from behaving well or badly. We all assume that moral thoughts are related to moral behavior, but as we will see, the relations are intricate and often difficult to predict. It is common to say that people often act against their better judgment, which implies that a person can have a clear intuition about how he should behave but not be able to do so because of other impulses. This lack of a clear link between moral thoughts and actions raises interesting developmental questions. Is the link even more tenuous in younger children because they have even less ability to formulate clear moral judgments and then stick to them? In addition, are even the most analytical moral judgments ever really free of the influences of emotional impulses, and are such influences stronger in younger children?

Debating the Origins of Moral Thought

For hundreds of years, philosophers and other scholars have debated about the moral characteristics of young children and how morality develops. Two broad views have characterized much of that debate: (1) the idea that young children have some kind of inherent moral nature, and (2) the contrasting notion that they have no inherent moral characteristics and must learn about morality from their social and cultural experiences. Within these views there can also be strong variations.

Consider the view that the young child comes into the world with certain moral propensities. The eighteenth-century French philosopher Jean-Jacques Rousseau, for example, proposed that young children are intrinsically good. He believed that infants and young children are pure in heart and mind and would always behave in morally appropriate ways if not for the corrupting influences of society. In this view, a primary goal of child rearing should be to shield children from society's corrupting influences so that their intrinsic moral sense has time to mature and become less vulnerable to such influences. The French physician Jean Marc Gaspard Itard undertook a dramatic and disturbing "test" of this premise by administering random beatings to Victor, the "wild child" discussed in Chapter 8. Itard wanted to see whether Victor would show outrage at the abuse, even though he had spent much of his childhood alone and isolated from social rules and norms. When Victor did show outrage, Itard reasoned that this response revealed the boy's deep-seated, unlearned sense of justice.

Others who believed in an inherent moral nature took a darker perspective. They saw children as selfish creatures who need to be civilized by society. The same negative view persists today in more subtle forms. For example, William Golding's classic novel *Lord of the Flies* describes how a group of children stuck on a deserted island become unmoored from society's social and moral constraints and descend into antisocial and even violent actions (see Figure 12.1).

FIGURE 12.1 Are children inherently antisocial? In his novel *Lord of the Flies*, William Golding suggested a view of morality in which children, once removed from the constraints of society, develop into cruel antisocial beings. Shown here is a film still from the 1963 film based on the book.

This account suggests that children are filled with base impulses that need to be controlled and suppressed by civilization.

The other view of moral development sees no moral capacity and no inclination toward either good or bad in infants and young children. Many who hold this view argue that very young children are no more moral than animals because they lack the cognitive capability to have a moral sense. They hypothesize that young children are initially amoral and that they learn morality as a consequence of development. In general, proponents of this view believe that infants and young children are not cognitively and emotionally capable of moral thought, so they are not fit to be judged as either good or bad. In this view, it makes no more sense to think of a young child as good or bad than it does to judge a tiger's morality in its behavior toward prey.

In short, there is a long history of thinking about children's moral development as if they were primarily bad or good from the start, or as if they only gradually acquired moral capabilities after being exposed to the values of their society. The views favoring an inherent moral nature did not ignore society's effects; they just saw them as interacting with preexisting moral natures. The views that saw children as amoral held that society's effects are largely responsible for children's morality, much like the empiricists' view of the child as a blank slate.

More recently, these two types of views have been complemented by perspectives arising from evolutionary and cultural psychology. Although these modern perspectives acknowledge many kinds of influences on the development of moral thought, they often disagree about which influences

Evolutionary and Cultural Psychology and Morality

In recent years, morality and its development have been major areas of study in both evolutionary psychology and cultural psychology. These two approaches share the assumption that children are not intrinsically good or bad. But they differ in the extent to which they see biological constraints as shaping the nature of moral thought.

Evolutionary psychology considers morality from the standpoint of how certain moral behaviors and patterns of thought might have been selected in the course of evolution. This perspective is committed to the idea that humans have a certain moral sense because it has had adaptive value in the emergence of the human species (Cosmides & Tooby, 2013; Levy, 2004; Pinker, 2002; Singer, 2005; Wright, 1994, 2010).

Many evolutionary psychologists argue that emotional empathy and the tendency to consider fairness and sharing conferred a selective advantage among our species' ancestors, as in cases where primates engage in mutual grooming (see Figure 12.2). Individuals with these traits may have had fewer enemies, more success finding mates, or a better ability to work together in social groups (Haidt, 2007, 2008; Hauser, 2006). As a result, they had more offspring—and more chances to pass on their genes. Similarly, a tendency to ramp up aggressive or self-protective behavior in threatening situations could also convey a selective advantage.

FIGURE 12.2 Reciprocal altruism. Many primates, such as these Japanese macaques, engage in mutual grooming even when they are not related. Evolutionary psychologists suggest that these kinds of cooperative behaviors may be related to prosocial behaviors in humans.

Such behaviors, which may be related to moral behaviors labeled as hurtful or selfish, could also promote an individual's survival and the ability to pass on his genes. According to this account, some aspects of morality are universal because all humans share the biologically based core morals that have been selected over many generations.

Even though views based on evolutionary psychology clearly favor inherent biological constraints on moral behavior, these views do not conclude that young children have inherent moral natures. These views see evolved constraints on moral thought as the basis for a survival function and not as the basis for judging an agent as bad or good. Thus, views from evolutionary psychology allow for mixtures of all sorts of basic moral components, including sharing, hoarding, deception, aggression, intimidation, and compassion. In addition to the idea that there must be a core morality that all people share, evolutionary psychologists also acknowledge that learning and culture significantly influence these universal aspects of morality.

By contrast, the field of **cultural psychology** approaches the study of moral thought and behavior by focusing on how cultures instill ways of thinking and fostering certain behaviors. This approach recognizes that there may be some basic universal moral concerns, but it argues for more powerful influences of culture on various aspects of morality. Richard Shweder, for example, shows that different cultural groups have dramatically different patterns of moral reasoning, ruling out a single dominant moral belief system. He does, however, recognize three clusters of basic moral values related to justice, community, and spirituality within which specific moral rules in each culture fall (Shweder, 1982; Shweder et al., 1987, 1997; Shweder & Haidt, 1993). Shweder offers examples of moral judgments and behaviors in some Eastern societies that, on the surface at least, seem almost incomprehensible to Westerners (see Figure 12.3). In U.S. history, the explorers Lewis and Clark reported a comparable bewilderment when they encountered Native Americans who held very different views than their own about the nature of possessions and whether people were entitled to take something that someone else was using (Ambrose, 1996).

The evolutionary and cultural perspectives on moral development offer distinctive emphases and interpretations, illustrating just how different the current psychological views of morality can be, even when all sides have access to the same data. Together these perspectives help to frame a wide range of accounts of moral development (Turiel, 1998) that seek to account for the influences of culture and of universal, biological constraints (Miller, 2006). Indeed, more recent accounts blend these two perspectives by arguing that evolution provided a basic set of intuitive moral "building blocks" that then got combined in different ways by cultural influences (Haidt, 2013; Haidt & Kesebir, 2010).

FIGURE 12.3 Moral beliefs across cultures. In many areas of India, cows are revered and granted nearly unlimited rights to go where they wish and when they wish, as in this street scene. Many Westerners, who do not understand the moral and religious beliefs leading to such practices, can have great difficulty understanding them.

Q: How do evolutionary and cultural views of morality differ in regard to the young child?

Characterizing the Basis of Moral Thought

To reach a better understanding of how the development of moral thought might fit with both evolutionary psychology and cultural psychology, it is useful to consider different ways of characterizing the psychological basis of moral thought. What sorts of psychological processes and structures seem to lead to judgments of right and wrong?

One view argues that there is really no reason to consider moral thought and that moral thoughts are largely window dressings that come to bear long after we commit to an action, perhaps as a way of justifying or rationalizing the action. According to this view, moral thought is a non-essential side effect rather than an important part of understanding moral behavior. This view asserts that other forces, such as positive and negative reinforcements, give rise to and control our actions, based on the tradeoffs between benefits and detriments (Skinner, 1971). Reinforcement-based views, which are part of the classical learning tradition, have largely disappeared in recent years as researchers have uncovered highly systematic and richly structured sets of moral intuitions, often about novel scenarios for which we could never have experienced reinforcements.

More recent views see emotions as intrinsically interwoven with moral thought in a complex web of interactions (see

Figure 12.4). Emotions such as empathy, anger, shame, and fear may often provide our most rapid moral intuitions, with rational judgments coming into play only afterward (Haidt, 2003; Prinz, 2004, 2007; Singer, 2005). Historically, many philosophers, such as the British empiricist David Hume (1739/2007), have seen emotions as the basis for moral action. Of course, emotions themselves may have cognitive components (see Chapter 7), but the moral emotions view shifted the focus from complicated moral deliberations about harm and benefits to simpler and quicker emotion-driven intuitions. Variations of the view of emotions as the basis for moral actions are very much in evidence today (Eisenberg, 2000; Haidt, 2012; Hoffman, 2000; Kagan, 1994). Indeed, some argue that deliberate, well-thought-out consideration of moral situations is simply too slow and requires too much thought to govern the daily rush of situations that call for action; they believe that we need faster, noncognitive means to respond "on the fly" (Haidt, 2001, 2003; Haidt & Kesebir, 2010). We often act so quickly and impulsively that it is difficult to see the basis of such actions as lying in well-thought-out moral reasoning.

The claim that cognition about moral situations is slow, however, assumes that we do all our moral computations only after entering a situation and appraising it. Instead, we may consider various types of situations in advance, building up elaborate moral schemas ready to be enacted in an instant response that requires little real-time thought. All of us have entered situations to which we have given much thought in advance and to which we can respond very rapidly based on our prior cognition. For example, if your roommate repeatedly fails to take her turn doing the dishes, you may have a prepared, readily available response the next time she shirks the job. This view suggests that there is a constant dynamic interaction between emotional and cognitive factors in the determination of most actions. Emotions may make certain patterns of reasoning more salient or available, and patterns of reasoning may trigger certain emotions. Thus, one type of moral thought does not necessarily cause the other; rather, both types continuously elaborate and inform each other, especially in complex social situations (Dunn, 2006).

In addition, patterns of reasoning can help encode or frame an action as being part of the moral realm or belonging to a particular sphere of morality, such as a concern with purity (Cushman & Young, 2011). Some researchers talk about a process of "moralization," in which cultural beliefs and customs and certain networks of causal beliefs can cause a pattern of behaviors to enter the moral realm. The act of smoking may be one such example of an action initially seen as a custom that became moralized in many areas of North America (Rozin, 1999; see Figure 12.5). More broadly, cultures can expose children to certain schemas and causal interpretations that can powerfully shape whether actions even elicit moral emotions (Sachdeva et al., 2011).

FIGURE 12.4 **Cognitions versus emotions as the basis for moral judgments.** For centuries, scholars have disagreed as to whether moral judgments are grounded in rational thought about principles, as in **(A)** *Star Trek*'s fictional Spock, or in moral emotions, as in **(B)** the obvious empathy shown by St. Francis of Assisi. Related questions ask about the relative roles of emotions and cognition at various points in a child's development.

B

Most of the foundational work on children's moral development emphasizes the cognitive component of moral thought and the child's growing understanding of rules and principles for guiding moral reasoning. These views often carry the developmental implication that moral judgment is the highest form of morality and that the most virtuous people are those most able to rely on cognitive factors and not on other factors in making judgments (Kohlberg, 1984). In these early theories, moral development consists of increasingly being able to act on the basis of reasoned moral judgments, with the youngest children being most ruled by other factors, such as their emo-

tions. These early views include stages of moral development in which children's thinking about rules and moral judgments changes with age; they were first proposed by Jean Piaget in his theory of moral development, followed by the stages proposed by Lawrence Kohlberg and Carol Gilligan. We will discuss each of these theories in turn and ask how they differ. Recent research has stressed a pluralistic approach in which an individual draws on different forms of moral thought in different contexts at all ages and may not pass through stages as such. Moreover, today scholars have shown that emotions continue to have a central role throughout development.

Q: What are three different views of the importance of emotions in moral thought?

Piaget's Theory of Moral Development

As in many other areas, we start by looking at Piaget's work on cognitive development. In considering the development of moral thought, we encounter many familiar issues. For example, we consider whether children progress through qualitatively distinct stages of moral reasoning, and if so, whether those stages resemble the developmental stages proposed in

FIGURE 12.5 **Moralization.** Certain behaviors, such as smoking, can shift from being seen as merely unhealthy to entering the moral sphere, as seen in this antismoking ad.

other domains. We also ask whether moral thought should be considered as a single, unified domain or as a collection of narrower domains with their own distinct properties and developmental patterns. Finally, we consider some of the ways that the development of moral thought varies across individuals and whether some core components of moral thought might be common to all cultures.

When Piaget devised his theory of moral development, he intended to incorporate it into his broad, comprehensive theory of the stages of cognitive development (Piaget, 1932/1965). He argued that moral thought is not a separate cognitive domain with its own patterns of reasoning and developmental course. Instead, he believed that moral development shares the same broad features that he attributed to other areas of cognitive development, including the notion of stages. Thus, according to Piaget, some patterns of moral reasoning are simply unavailable to children until they reach the relevant stage of moral development.

Piaget studied moral development from several perspectives. Most notably, he examined children's understanding and use of rules, their judgments of culpability and guilt, and their understanding of justice. Each of these lines of investigation has spurred extensive moral development research by others.

> **Q:** How did Piaget's broad theory of cognitive development relate to his perspective on moral development?

Piaget's Stages of Moral Reasoning

Piaget began his study of young children's morality by observing how they play simple games. Specifically, he saw a close link between children's moral beliefs and the way they use a game's rules. Based on their behaviors at play, Piaget inferred links between children's use of rules and the stages of moral reasoning they had attained. Piaget proposed three stages of moral development, roughly corresponding to his stages of preoperational, concrete operational, and formal operational thought (see Table 12.1).

Stage 0: Premoral Development Until around 4 years of age, children's play seems to be simply for the fun of the activity, without any apparent use of rules. Piaget saw the child in this stage as unaware that rules exist and treating games like any other social activity. A child in the premoral stage might imitate older children playing the same game, but without understanding that set guidelines govern the way the game is played. Children at this age supposedly do not assess culpability or have intuitions about justice.

Stage 1: The Heteronomous Stage Piaget believed that children spend the years from about age 4 to 10, after toddlerhood and throughout the preoperational period and much of the concrete operational period, in the **heteronomous stage**. *Heteronomous* means governed by an external set of laws or control, and in Piaget's view, children in this stage see rules as inviolate and unalterable and having a kind of external reality like the laws of nature.

At the same time, Piaget observed that children in the heteronomous stage show evidence of egocentrism in their use of rules. They attempt to use standard rules and think that they are using them in consistent ways, but in fact, their use of rules is often highly idiosyncratic. They often modify or even make up rules, which they then assume are the general rules of the game. Anyone with a younger sibling can remember frustrating attempts to play a game with the younger brother or sister who adopted idiosyncratic rules, often to his or her own advantage, while seemingly remaining unaware that these rules differed

Stage	Name of Stage	Approximate Age	Reasoning about Rules
0	Premoral development	Up to 4 years	There is no explicit awareness of rules, no use of moral principles or notions of justice.
1	Heteronomous stage	4 to 10 years	Rules are seen as unchanging and external, like physical laws. Judgments of culpability are based on the act's consequences rather than the actor's intentions. There is little sense of what punishment is appropriate for what degree of transgression.
2	Autonomous stage	10 to 11 years and older	Rules are seen as human agreements that can be changed if all parties consent. Judgments of culpability are based in part on intentions, and punishment should be appropriate to the severity of the transgression.

TABLE 12.1 Piaget's stages of moral reasoning. In Piaget's theory of moral development, children progressed through three stages of moral reasoning, with the first stage supposedly devoid of any awareness of moral rules, principles, or ideas of justice.

from the standard ones. The heteronomous stage is particularly striking because the same 5-year-old child who frequently breaks the rules or makes them up also believes that the rules are immutable and fixed for all time. The combination of these features creates the central phenomena of Stage 1.

Piaget believed that the way children think about the rules of a game resembles their thinking about moral principles, which could be construed as rules for behavior. In some of his best-known studies of moral development, a researcher described a series of moral scenarios to a child and asked the child to judge the culpability of the child in the story and to decide whether the main character had acted badly. The most interesting manipulation involved scenarios in which the character's intentions did not match the magnitude of consequences resulting from his actions. Consider the following pair of stories that Piaget used in his studies (see Figure 12.6):

Neutral Intentions, Major Negative Consequences: A little boy who is called John is in his room. He is called to dinner. He goes into the dining room. But behind the door there was a chair, and on the chair there was a tray with fifteen cups on it. John couldn't have known that there was all this behind the door. He goes in, the door knocks against the tray, bang go the fifteen cups and they all get broken! (Piaget, 1932/1965, p. 118)

Negative Intentions, Minor Negative Consequences: Once there was a little boy whose name was Henry. One day

when his mother was out he tried to get some jam out of the cupboard. He climbed up on to a chair and stretched out his arm. But the jam was too high up and he couldn't reach it and have any. But while he was trying to get it, he knocked over a cup. The cup fell down and broke. (Piaget, 1932/1965, p. 118)

Thus, in some stories a character's good or neutral intentions had quite bad consequences, while in others a character's bad intentions brought only slight negative consequences.

Most adults listening to Piaget's stories focused on the characters' intentions and decided that the child with the most negative intentions was guiltiest, even though the consequences of his behavior were much less severe. In contrast, children in the heteronomous stage seemed to ignore intentions and focus only on the consequences. They believed that the well-intentioned child who broke many cups was guiltier and more deserving of punishment than the ill-intentioned child who broke only one cup.

Here, for example, are responses by a 6-year-old named Geo to questions that were asked by an interviewer in that classic study:

Interviewer: What did the first boy do?
Geo: He broke eleven cups.
Interviewer: And the second one?
Geo: He broke a cup by moving roughly.
Interviewer: Why did the first one break the cups?
Geo: Because the door knocked them.

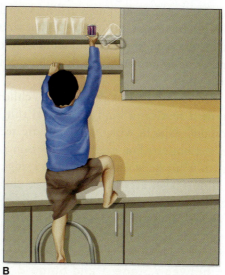

A　　　　　　　　　　　　　　　　　　**B**

FIGURE 12.6 Scenarios used by Piaget to elicit children's moral reasoning. In the heteronomous stage, children tend to judge consequences as more important than intentions. Thus, they judge **(A)** a child who accidentally causes 15 glasses to break as more guilty than **(B)** a child who accidentally causes 1 glass to break, despite the fact that the first child did not intend to do anything wrong, but the second child did have a negative intention (reaching for jam that was deliberately placed out of his reach).

Interviewer: And the second?

Geo: He was clumsy. When he was getting the jam the cup fell down.

Interviewer: Is one of the boys naughtier than the other?

Geo: The first is because he knocked over twelve cups.

Interviewer: If you were the daddy, which one would you punish most?

Geo: The one who broke twelve cups.

Interviewer: Why did he break them?

Geo: The door shut too hard and knocked them. He didn't do it on purpose.

Interviewer: And why did the other boy break a cup?

Geo: He wanted to get the jam. He moved too far. The cup got broken.

Interviewer: Why did he want to get the jam?

Geo: Because he was all alone. Because his mother wasn't there.

Interviewer: Have you got a brother?

Geo: No, a little sister.

Interviewer: Well, if it was you who had broken the twelve cups when you went into the room and your little sister who had broken one cup while she was trying to get the jam, which of you would be punished most severely?

Geo: Me, because I broke more than one cup.
(Piaget, 1932/1965, pp. 120–121)

Piaget further argued that children in this stage reason the same way in making moral judgments about lies. Thus, after hearing similar stories, the children judged making a very false claim without intending to deceive (for example, being mistaken) as worse than purposely telling a small lie to deceive. To Piaget, these patterns suggested that younger children are unable to take into account intentions in evaluating the morality of actions, making them incapable of mature moral reasoning.

Piaget was also concerned with younger children's beliefs in **immanent justice**, a kind of magical thinking in the heteronomous stage in which accidents are seen as cases of divine retribution. For example, a person steals an apple, and then while he is walking home a bridge collapses beneath him. Piaget argued that younger children are much more likely to see the collapse of the bridge as a kind of justice caused by God or spirits, rather than as a mere accident.

The Transition between Stage 1 and Stage 2 Piaget described a transition in children's thinking about both game rules and morality that occurs between the ages of about 7 and 11. He saw children as becoming more concerned with winning games and realizing that maintaining uniform rules is central to that goal. Thus, they start to honor standard rules and feel that others should as well. In this transition period from Stage 1 to Stage 2, children also start to weigh intentions more in judging culpability, and they become more aware of what is fair and how the severity of a punishment should relate to the transgression. Even so, their behavior in this period remains somewhat inconsistent. Piaget observed that they do not follow the rules perfectly, and their thinking still shows elements of Stage 1 moral reasoning as well.

Stage 2: The Autonomous Stage Finally, when children reach the **autonomous stage** at around age 10 or 11, they see rules as human conventions. Thus, children come to understand that people create rules for the purpose of organizing an interaction and that people can change the rules as well. According to Piaget, when children reach this stage, they begin to realize that moral principles are not a set of external laws. They come to understand that morals arise from group norms and from convictions based on individuals' beliefs and that intentions are central to judgments of culpability and consequences are of less importance. Piaget believed that by this stage, children have well-developed notions of fairness and appropriate justice. They understand that a punishment should be appropriate to a transgression, not arbitrarily harsh. Children's belief in immanent justice also diminishes, as they realize that bad things happen to good people (and vice versa) and that accidents should not be interpreted as punishments or rewards from an external agent.

Evaluating Piaget's Account

Piaget launched an important and highly active area of research on moral reasoning. In the process, he invented the influential technique of presenting children with moral situations and asking them to evaluate guilt. His account of moral development captures some of the important patterns of change in children's use and understanding of rules. Research has shown that once children become aware of rules, they often become excessively rigid in how they apply them. In many studies, children at around 7 years of age latch on to rules as inviolate and unchangeable, only to later understand how and why they might be malleable. Some of Piaget's observations about children's moral judgments also pick up on real-world developmental phenomena. Younger children do sometimes fail to take intentions into account in their moral judgments, and they can have difficulty calibrating the appropriate level of punishment for an action, but neither of these abilities is as limited in young children as Piaget thought. More generally, Piaget pioneered a truly cognitive approach to the development of morality, and in doing so, he helped all later researchers explore the limits of a purely cognitive approach uninfluenced by emotions. At the same time, however, there are concerns about whether several of his studies were really focusing on the moral domain and its unique properties.

Distinguishing Morality from Conventions

One possibility that corresponds to discussions in earlier chapters is that young children have more difficulty thinking about the kind of arbitrary patterns and rules typical of most games than they do about nonarbitrary functional patterns such as putting on their socks before their shoes. For example, whether card players deal from the deck clockwise or counterclockwise has no inherent meaning and little to do with which rules would be "most sensible"; both alternatives work equally well. Even so, the chosen rules must be honored to make the game work. Learning such arbitrary rules may be more difficult for young children, as the rules have little real-world significance to help explain them.

But Piaget's attempts to link children's understanding and use of game rules to morality also faces a deeper problem. Moral laws are very different from **social conventions**, which are arbitrary rules jointly agreed to by a group or a society to facilitate interaction and coordinate activity. The philosopher David Lewis has pointed out that social conventions have a different structure from moral laws, including the critical distinction that conventions are arbitrary and moral laws are not (Lewis, 1969). Take the convention of driving on the right side of the road in the United States, which is fully arbitrary; in other countries, such as Great Britain, drivers get along fine on the left side (see Figure 12.7). In contrast, the moral principle that people should be honest is not arbitrary, and it would be difficult to do business or even converse in a society where lies were the norm.

Because game rules are largely arbitrary, they seem much closer to social conventions than to moral laws.

Interestingly, when researchers directly examined young children's ideas about social conventions, moral laws, and inviolable physical laws (like gravity), even preschoolers seemed to understand the essential differences (Lockhart et al., 1977). In one series of studies, preschoolers were told about situations in which a person violated either a social convention (drives on the wrong side of the road), a moral law (steals from others), or a physical law (floats in the air). Preschoolers tended to explain these transgressions in different ways, describing violators of social conventions as being "crazy," violators of moral laws as being "bad," and violators of physical laws as using "magic" (Lockhart, 1980). It therefore seems that Piaget overinterpreted younger children's difficulties with arbitrary game rules by assuming that they reflected broad problems using rules, including moral laws. In fact, children understand the differences between different kinds of rules at an early age, and they seem to have a sense of how moral laws differ from arbitrary rules (Turiel, 1983, 1998).

Q: In what ways does children's understanding of game rules differ from their understanding of social conventions?

Accounting for Intentions

Piaget may have underestimated younger children's ability to account for people's intentions in evaluating actions. If, as Piaget claimed, children younger than about 10 could not take intentions into account in their moral judgments, they would be unable to see the difference between an accidental harm and a deliberate injury. We have seen, however, that even preverbal

FIGURE 12.7 Social conventions versus moral laws. Driving on a particular side of the road is an arbitrary social convention established by a society, as shown by **(A)** British drivers, who drive on the left side of the road, and **(B)** American drivers, who drive on the right side of the road. **(C)** Prohibitions against stealing would be considered moral laws in all societies.

infants seem acutely sensitive to others' intentions and goals (see Chapter 5). It would therefore be surprising if young children were so attentive to intentions early on, yet unable to use them to evaluate malice and culpability.

A closer look suggests that the differences in the ways that younger children and adults think about intentions may be more nuanced than Piaget believed. Researchers have thoroughly investigated the claim that younger children cannot take intentions into account, using a much wider range of stories and story formats than Piaget did. These studies have repeatedly uncovered cases where even preschoolers are fully capable of considering intentions, especially if intentions are described at the end of a story rather than at the beginning (Karniol, 1978; Keasey, 1978). If children are told to pay attention to intentions or if intentions are stressed in some way, young children often take them into account (Costanzo et al., 1973; Farnill, 1974; Keasey, 1978; Nelson, 1980). These findings suggest that varying the experiments might reveal circumstances in which young children would consider intentions. If there are no distracting differences in consequences, children might base their judgments on which intentions are better. Similarly, if positive consequences are pitted against neutral ones, the intentions might also become more salient. Finally, if researchers use videotapes or cartoons that make the differences in characters' intentions clearer, young children might be more likely to factor them into their moral judgments (Chandler et al., 1973). Thus, an extensive literature shows that in some situations, young children do have a clear awareness of intentions and their relation to morality (Baird & Astington, 2004).

Children may weigh consequences more than adults, but it may not be because of a marked developmental difference in moral understanding. Rather, younger children may be less skilled at discerning intentions or at keeping several aspects of a story in mind at once. Nonetheless, these differences do not mean that younger children reason about moral situations in fundamentally different ways than older children and adults. There are parallels here to Piaget's claims as to why young children fail at conservation tasks. As we saw in Chapter 9, rather than lacking certain logical reasoning skills that make conservation impossible, younger children simply may have more difficulty remembering the entire sequence of events and may focus too much on the final components of a chain of events.

Although preschool-age children are sometimes able to consider intentions, the question remains as to why, with increasing age, children can more easily take intentions into account. One possible explanation is based on **information integration theory**, which examines how children integrate different dimensions of a problem to gain understanding and make decisions. This theory argues that younger children often focus on one dimension of a problem (in the case

of moral judgments, this could be either intentions or consequences), while older children are capable of integrating several dimensions at one time (both intentions and consequences in the case of moral judgments; Anderson, 1980; Anderson & Butzin, 1978).

Experimental tasks that involve manipulating several dimensions of moral judgment have supported this explanation of how children become increasingly able to take intentions into account (Baird & Astington, 2004; Zelazo et al., 1996). Nonetheless, these predictions cannot apply to all sorts of thinking and reasoning because, as we saw in Chapters 9 and 10, younger children sometimes have difficulty zeroing in on the critical dimension of a problem and instead will consider several at once. But at least in some cases, the developmental effects of information integration are evident, presumably in situations where the child has to weigh several dimensions against each other to reach an optimal decision.

> **Q:** Why might young children have trouble taking intentions into account in judging the culpability of others?

Immanent Justice across Cultures Piaget's claim that younger children are more inclined toward magical thinking about rewards and punishments has also been challenged. Cross-cultural studies suggest that this may not be the best characterization of how moral thought develops. For example, more than 70 years ago, the renowned anthropologist Margaret Mead studied the development of magical thinking in traditional people in Papua New Guinea by asking them about the reasons for natural events (Mead, 1932). Contrary to some popular claims, younger children did not invoke more magical thinking than adults. Instead, they offered simple, concrete causal explanations, whereas adults tended to also invoke supernatural explanations involving spirits and gods. For example, if asked why a canoe floated away, a child might explain that it was not properly tied to a dock, while the elders might also say that certain spirits caused it to happen. In fact, when the younger children were offered metaphysical explanations instead of the more practical, mechanical ones, they rejected them. Sometimes it takes years of training in a culture's belief system before an individual will readily offer causal explanations that go beyond the physical, mechanical ones.

> **Q:** What is Piaget's notion of immanent justice, and why has its developmental status been questioned?

Building on his research on children's use of rules, Piaget offered a general model of moral development that says that younger children do not take intentions into account in their moral judgments. Although his model no longer seems tenable, the idea of stages of moral reasoning remains influential, especially as it pertains to the work of Lawrence Kohlberg.

Kohlberg's Theory of Moral Reasoning

Lawrence Kohlberg approached the study of moral development with close attention to Piaget's work. Kohlberg believed that one mistake that trapped both Freudians and behaviorists was to not think seriously about what morality itself is. There was, for example, almost no attention from either of those camps to thousands of years of philosophical discourse as to what constitutes true virtue. For Kohlberg, beliefs about what is moral are not incidental, but rather central to the proper study of moral development and how children become moral thinkers—or what he called "moral philosophers."

Kohlberg believed that children construct morality by developing a system of beliefs about concepts like justice and individual rights. He thought that it takes a long time for children to develop accurate beliefs and reasoning patterns about morality and that early on, they confuse moral issues with other issues, such as power, coercion, and authority. This process of discovering which issues are truly moral formed the basis for Kohlberg's model.

Kohlberg's Stages of Moral Reasoning

Kohlberg initially proposed six stages of moral development to describe how children's basic concept of virtue changes. He then clustered these six stages into three larger levels of moral reasoning—preconventional, conventional, and postconventional reasoning—which loosely resonate with the stages of moral development that Piaget proposed. Both of their theories capture the idea of the child moving through stages of being unaware of rules, of using rules too literally, and of engaging in more abstract thought.

Kohlberg assessed children's level of moral development by using a method that he devised known as the **moral dilemma**. Kohlberg's moral dilemmas were short descriptions of morally ambiguous situations in which a character must make a difficult moral choice. After hearing the dilemma, the study participant is asked which course of action is morally superior and why. Piaget and earlier researchers had also used stories to pose moral questions and elicit children's judgments, but Kohlberg's key innovation was to focus on the child's pattern of reasoning about the situation rather than on the judgment itself. Kohlberg's dilemmas also featured difficult situations about which morally sophisticated people could honestly disagree.

The most famous dilemma concerns a sad figure named Heinz, who had to decide whether to steal a drug to save his wife's life:

> In Europe, a woman was near death from a special kind of cancer. There was one drug that the doctors thought might save her. It was a form of radium that a druggist in the same town had recently discovered. The drug was expensive to make, but the druggist was charging ten times what the drug cost him to make. He paid $200 for the radium and charged $2,000 for a small dose of the drug. The sick woman's husband, Heinz, went to everyone he knew to borrow the money, but he could only get together about $1,000 which is half of what it cost. He told the druggist that his wife was dying and asked him to sell it cheaper or let him pay later. But the druggist said: "No, I discovered the drug and I'm going to make money from it." So Heinz got desperate and broke into the man's store to steal the drug for his wife. Should the husband have done that? (Kohlberg, 1963, p. 19)

For this dilemma, many arguments could support moral approval or disapproval of Heinz's action. According to Kohlberg, certain kinds of arguments, both for and against his choice, typify each stage of moral development.

In Kohlberg's first level of moral reasoning, the *preconventional level* (Stages 1 and 2), a child believes that someone is virtuous if she is not punished much for her actions or does not suffer much compared with her gains. Thus, a child in Stage 1 might say that it is not appropriate to steal the drug because Heinz will be punished harshly for theft. Another child in Stage 1 might say that it is appropriate to steal the drug because Heinz will get a much worse punishment if he lets his wife die. Both responses are considered typical of Stage 1, regardless of the particular moral choice, because in both cases avoiding punishment is the key concern. Children in Stage 2 might say that it is acceptable to steal the drug because it is worth spending some time in jail to keep your wife alive. Or they might say that it is not acceptable to steal the drug because the jail time would not be worth it given that his wife is so sick that she might die anyway.

To a child in the *conventional level* of moral reasoning (Stages 3 and 4), being virtuous means doing what we are told or conforming to group norms. Children in Stage 3 might say that it is acceptable to steal the drug because a nice person does not let his wife die, or they might say that it is not acceptable because only bad people steal things.

Stage 4 involves reference to law and order. The Stage 4 argument against stealing the drug is simply that Heinz is wrong to break the law, whereas arguments in favor would allude to following implicit, natural laws about not letting others die.

People who reach the final, *postconventional level* (Stages 5 and 6) believe that being virtuous means adhering to a "higher" principle of justice or fairness than either society or the individual's own interests dictate. Stage 5 arguments appeal to group norms, such as a group belief that it is acceptable to steal to save a life—or a society's belief that theft cannot be tolerated, no matter the cost. Finally, Stage 6 reasoning refers to the individual's own internal moral standards. Thus, a Stage 6 reason for stealing the drug is that the individual will not be able to live with himself if he lets his wife die. And a Stage 6 argument against stealing the drug is that stealing violates the individual's own beliefs about never stealing. Table 12.2 shows Kohlberg's three levels of moral reasoning divided into six stages.

Evaluating Kohlberg's Theory

Kohlberg's theory has been extremely influential in the field of moral development. His ideas served as the basis for hundreds of studies exploring how children and adults reason about complex moral problems. By considering people to be "moral philosophers," Kohlberg helped researchers focus on the reasoning processes related to moral thought rather than the specific moral choices. In addition, as researchers examined moral development across cultures, they often found support for the developmental patterns Kohlberg proposed. Younger children do tend to focus on immediate consequences, such as punishment, while older children and adults tend to focus more on principles governing the social interactions in a community, such as the Golden Rule (Gibbs et al., 2007).

As in Piaget's theory, Kohlberg's stages of moral development were supposed to be an invariant sequence in which each stage necessarily built on the one before. He contended

Level	Stage	Approximate Ages	Moral Principle	Kinds of Reasoning
I. **Preconventional morality:** Arises from basic needs and drives.	1	2 to 10 years	Obedience and punishment orientation	Moral judgments are driven by a need to avoid punishment.
	2	2 to 10 years	Instrumental-relativist orientation	Moral judgments are driven by the desire to meet personal needs.
II. **Conventional morality:** Arises from conforming to expected roles and pleasing others.	3	9 years and older	"Good boy/good girl" orientation	Moral judgments are driven by a need to be accepted by others as a good person.
	4	9 years and older	Law and order orientation	Moral judgments are driven by a desire to adhere to the letter of the law or to authorities.
III. **Postconventional morality:** Arises from abstract principles that transcend individual circumstances and local cultural contexts.	5	12 years and older	Social contract orientation	Moral judgments arise from adherence to laws that are set up as social contracts for the common good.
	6	12 years and older	Principled conscience-driven orientation	Moral judgments arise from adherence to personal principles, such as the Golden Rule.

TABLE 12.2 Kohlberg's stages of moral development. Each of Kohlberg's three levels of moral reasoning is divided into two stages. Kohlberg argued that each of these six stages shows distinctive patterns of moral reasoning. Although Kohlberg later revised his theory to add and later eliminate a stage, we present here his original six stages, which are the most widely known version of his theory. Adapted from Kohlberg (1976).

that a child has to progress through each stage to reach the next one. Yet, if you look closely at the reasoning at each stage, it is not clear how each stage logically forms the basis for the next one. Why, for example, should a concern with avoiding punishment (Stage 1) lead to a concern with how to meet personal needs (Stage 2)? These issues and several others have led to three types of criticisms of Kohlberg's theory: unclear stages, cross-cultural variations, and possible gender biases.

Unclear Stages The stages in Kohlberg's model are less clear-cut than they might initially seem. Kohlberg and his associates developed a long, complex test manual and set up training sessions to teach other psychologists the nuances of the scoring procedure. The indeterminacies in their scoring system led to many controversies and even to some revisions to the theory. Kohlberg later added a new Stage 7 and a partial Stage 4.5, then still later combined Stages 5 and 6, reducing the total number of stages to five (Colby & Kohlberg, 1987). The elaborate scoring system raised concerns about the extent to which most researchers could reliably agree on assigning judgments to specific stages (Krebs & Denton, 2005; Kurtines & Greif, 1974).

Researchers have also found that responses to moral dilemmas vary more than Kohlberg's model suggests. According to his theory, a typical kindergartner can evaluate a moral choice only in terms of how much he might suffer for his actions. In fact, even the youngest children do not show these strict limitations and sometimes reason at the highest levels. In addition, it is not uncommon for a child to respond to Kohlberg's moral dilemmas with judgments that span several stages. Because children's answers do not consistently fall into one or two of Kohlberg's stages (Krebs & Denton, 2005), it is difficult to use his model to classify or compare people's levels of moral development. This problem would be easier to handle if most children's responses clustered in one stage despite a few responses from other stages, but in many cases a child's responses span four stages or more.

Kohlberg made an important advance by raising the possibility of several different modes of moral reasoning and by asking how those modes might vary with development. Subsequent studies suggest, however, that instead of a strict progression of stages, there may be a more diverse set of moral reasoning styles even in quite young children that vary as a function of context and culture. There may still be developmental changes in terms of which forms of reasoning are most salient or cognitively accessible, but children do not seem to be trapped exclusively in one stage at a time.

Cross-Cultural Variations Kohlberg claimed that his stages of moral development are universal across cultures throughout the world. Yet, researchers who evaluated Kohlberg's system were surprised to find that different cultures show quite different proportions of the population having reached the higher moral levels. For example, when researchers used Kohlberg's model to evaluate moral development in Turkey in the 1970s, the results seemed to suggest that most of the Turkish adult population never moved beyond Stages 1 and 2. According to the findings, only a tiny percentage reached Stage 6 (Kurtines & Greif, 1974). Kohlberg never showed evidence of having a political agenda or other ulterior motives for raising some cultures morally above others. Unfortunately, his scales seemed to do this anyway in that people in Western developed cultures tended to show higher average scores than did people in non-Western cultures.

There may also be a relationship between modes of moral reasoning and the different roles that people occupy in a culture. For example, in one classic study in a rural African community in western Kenya, two groups of men were studied who were similar in age, religion, education, and income but who differed in the extent to which they were called upon by their neighbors to settle disputes (Harkness et al., 1981). Those who were often chosen to settle disputes made more moral judgments at conventional levels, such as the law and order level, whereas those who were not called upon to settle disputes tended to give more judgments at the instrumental-relativist level. Thus, even when people are matched in age and a wide range of socioeconomic indicators, they may give different moral judgments as a function of the social roles that they typically occupy. When cultures are more heterogeneous in terms of such roles, there is a greater possibility of variation in kinds of moral judgments (Edwards, 1987).

> **Q:** To what extent are the developmental patterns uncovered by Kohlberg found in other groups and cultures?

Possible Gender Biases When Kohlberg developed his moral reasoning scales in the 1950s, he based the stages on data he collected from middle-class boys. At first no one considered the consequences of not including data from girls. Matters changed dramatically in 1977, however, when Carol Gilligan argued that different kinds of moral reasoning might be more dominant in girls and women than in boys and men (Gilligan, 1977). In contrast to Kohlberg's stages, which emphasize justice, Gilligan believed that girls and women more commonly stress empathy and caring in their moral judgments. By failing to consider this gender difference, she argued, Kohlberg's scales make females look less morally developed than males. Gilligan contended that when this care-oriented dimension of morality is taken into account, girls and women show much more sophistication in their moral reasoning and males show less developed moral thought (Gilligan, 1979, 1982). We now turn to a discussion of Gilligan's theory of moral development to get a better sense of her views.

Alternative Theories of Moral Development

Concerns about Kohlberg's theories led to two other approaches. One, based on Gilligan's theory, preserved the idea of stages but shifted the focus away from justice and rights to care. Another, arising from several researchers, started to question the strength of stage effects and proposed that children of all ages might have multiple ways of construing moral situations; we will call this the pluralistic approach.

Gilligan's Theory of Moral Development

Gilligan proposed her own three-stage sequence of moral development in which females tend to progress more rapidly than males. Children start in a preconventional stage in which their own personal welfare is all that matters. They then move into a conventional stage in which empathy and care for others motivates a belief that self-sacrifice is an intrinsic good. Finally, in a postconventional stage, children combine care about themselves and care for others into an integrated moral reasoning system that takes into account both factors (see Table 12.3).

Here is how Gilligan described one of the main gender differences underlying her model:

> The moral imperative that emerges repeatedly in interviews with women is an injunction to care, a responsibility to discern and alleviate the "real and recognizable trouble" of this world. For men, the moral imperative appears rather as an injunction to respect the rights of others and thus to protect from interference the rights to life and self-fulfillment. (Gilligan, 1982, p. 100)

Gilligan believed that for women, moral rights and responsibilities occur in terms of relationships. Yet, despite her emphasis on care, concern, and empathy in women's moral thought, Gilligan did not put emotions at the center of her theory. Rather, like Kohlberg, she believed that there is a critical cognitive component to morality that is related to thinking about moral principles. For Gilligan, the fundamental organizing principle is that people should help others who are in need or distress, whereas for Kohlberg, the central principle is that people should treat each other fairly. Thus, both theories emphasize moral rules or laws that elicit a particular form of reasoning about many interconnected principles.

Like Kolhberg's system, Gilligan's system has been scrutinized for evidence of consistent gender differences in moral development and for indications as to whether empathy or caring might be a more dominant mode of moral thinking in some non-Western cultures. Despite Gilligan's suggestion of a major gender bias in Kohlberg's work, in almost 90 percent of roughly 100 studies of Kohlberg's stages of moral reasoning, no gender differences were found. In the remaining studies, sometimes males scored higher on moral reasoning, and sometimes females did (Walker, 1991, 2006).

The data on possible gender differences in the morality of caring is less clear, because few major studies of large samples have been conducted (Turiel, 1998). Over several studies, it appears that the vast majority of people use both care-oriented and justice-oriented forms of moral reasoning, relying on them for different questions and in different contexts. The evidence suggests that on average, females tend to use care-oriented reasoning more often, and males tend to use justice reasoning more often, and there are some indications that females can switch between the two forms of reasoning more easily (Haste & Baddeley, 1991; Jaffee & Hyde, 2000). But such differences in the frequency of use are quite modest and do not seem to represent a fundamental difference in males' and females' moral reasoning styles (Hyde, 2007).

If most people show both kinds of reasoning, further questions arise about how patterns of reasoning vary as a function of context. Perhaps males and females differ because they tend to be exposed to somewhat different types of situ-

TABLE 12.3 Gilligan's stages of moral reasoning. Gilligan's theory of moral development endorsed the idea of stages but shifted the focus to care.

Stage	Form of Reasoning
Preconventional	Individual survival is all that matters.
Conventional	Self-sacrifice is good in its own right and is driven by care for others.
Postconventional	Care about others and care about the self are integrated.

ations. Almost all moral judgments require an appraisal of the situation. If someone commits a questionable action, it may matter greatly to know more about whether he was compelled to do it, what others who were involved did, and so on. Even the same action, when interpreted by different people, can lead to contrasting judgments.

Finally, just as Kohlberg has been criticized for collecting data primarily from middle-class boys, Gilligan has been criticized for basing her theory on data collected from women attending elite colleges such as Harvard University. Studies that included women from a broader spectrum of socioeconomic groups, including women from various disadvantaged minorities, found much smaller differences between men and women in care-based and justice-oriented moral reasoning than Gilligan did. In these studies, justice-oriented reasoning often dominated among both sexes (Stack, 1986, 1990). In addition, in some cultures, care-based reasoning seems to take on a quite different way of thinking from that proposed by Gilligan. For example, in both Japan and India, when children talk about care, they talk less about interpersonal feelings and more about duties arising from various societal roles (Miller, 2006; Shimizu, 2001). Moreover, the care focuses more on communities and groups than on individuals (Jensen, 2008).

A Pluralistic Approach to the Development of Moral Thought

One consistent theme has emerged from recent research on moral development: the same person comes to rely on different patterns of moral thought, depending on the context. We will call this theme the "pluralistic approach," meaning that each individual is not bound to one or two forms of moral thought but instead may switch between several different forms as a function of the situation in which that person is embedded and how the situation is viewed. In this pluralistic view, moral development is not a simple linear progression through stages but rather an elaboration of several different modes of moral thought that are available at a given age as well as shifts in which ones are dominant in certain situations. Thus, some possible modes of moral thought might be reasoning about sharing, helping others, modesty, defeat, or privacy (Smetana, 1997). This theme draws heavily on ideas in two subfields of psychology: personality psychology, which emphasizes how situations influence behavior, and cultural psychology, which emphasizes the social construction of belief systems.

Contributions from Personality Psychology One major focus in modern-day personality psychology is the study of person-situation interactions (Bem & Allen, 1974; Bem &

Funder, 1978; Mischel, 1968), which also affect moral thinking. In personality psychology, person-situation interactions reveal that personality traits such as shyness can vary dramatically as a function of the situation in which a person is embedded. Various studies have shown that, like adults, children switch between different styles of reasoning, depending on the context. In one study, for example, stressing interpersonal relationships caused more care-based reasoning as opposed to justice-based reasoning (Smetana et al., 1991). Thus, if children heard stories in which a moral transgression was described as occurring between siblings, care-based reasoning was more prominent than when the same transgression was described as occurring between more casual acquaintances. The notion of group and individual differences in moral reasoning must therefore take into account theories of how moral reasoning interacts with social contexts. Just as it has become common to talk about how personality traits vary across situations and contexts, styles of moral reasoning may be similarly linked to situations and contexts.

Contributions from Cultural Psychology The modest differences in moral reasoning across sexes and the more notable variations across cultures have led some researchers to suggest that, contrary to Piaget's and Kohlberg's theories, moral universals may be exaggerated if they are understood to be the same stepwise progression of moral reasoning in all cultures. In some cases, moral systems may be culturally specific in ways that outsiders find difficult to understand. Thus, those who view moral development as more culturally relative consider the highest levels of Kohlberg's stages as too culture specific and simply irrelevant to many non-Western cultures (Shweder, 1982).

One major cultural difference that can affect moral reasoning involves the way that cultures prioritize the rights and well-being of individuals versus the rights and well-being of groups. In **individualist cultures**, the rights of the individual are supreme and favored over group rights, whereas in **collectivist cultures**, the rights of the group are central and the individual's rights are subordinate to those of the group. In general, Western societies are considered more individualist, and American culture is often seen as the most extreme example. In contrast, non-Western societies (and some Western societies with socialist political systems) are considered more collectivist (Bronfenbrenner, 1970; Shweder & Bourne, 1982). These differences in emphasis between, say, the United States and Japan or between Australia and China are not disputed, but their implications for patterns of moral reasoning are less clear. Shweder and his colleagues argue that the contrast can lead to cultural differences in morality: in individualist cultures, morality is based on notions of individual rights; in collectivist cultures, morality is based on duties to the larger group (Shweder et al., 1987).

One systematic analysis of the development of moral reasoning in four countries, including two individualist cultures (the United States and Canada) and two collectivist cultures (China and India) suggests that the broad individualist versus collectivist contrast may not fully capture the cross-cultural variations in children's and adolescents' moral reasoning (Neff & Helwig, 2002). When they were asked to judge moral situations, the children and adolescents in these four cultures did show cultural differences in their moral judgments. But they also took situational features into account, which affected the patterns of cultural variation. For example, Indian boys were more likely to judge a husband's actions in individualist terms and a wife's actions in collectivist terms, while boys in other cultures showed less of a gender bias. Yet, the Indian boys still made individualist interpretations for wives in some situations. In a different context—moral decisions about the rights of children to have a say in their own course of academic instruction—the cultural differences went against the broad predictions of a collectivist versus individualist account, with Chinese adolescents putting more weight on the individualist rights of students and Canadian adolescents putting more emphasis on the larger system of education and the importance of deferring to authority. Rather than an individualist/collectivist contrast, the cultural differences in children's patterns of moral judgment supported a **constructivist approach** to moral reasoning, in which the child evaluates the situation and the actors and takes into account culturally specific meanings in order to construct an interpretation specific to that context (Turiel, 2002).

This evidence suggests that, just as sex differences in moral reasoning seem better understood in terms of the influences of social context, some cultural differences can also be better understood in terms of situational influences. Unfamiliar cultures may rely on similar underlying patterns of moral reasoning but express them in different ways, depending on the culture's particular distribution of social contexts.

Rather than there being no moral universals, it may be that we all share a universal set of moral reasoning patterns that manifest in different ways, depending on cultural and social contexts. Indeed, in a revision of his theory, Shweder suggested that all cultures may share three fundamental moral values—autonomy, community, and divinity—with each culture placing a different emphasis on each. Autonomy refers to notions of harm, rights, and justice as they bear on an individual's ability to meet his or her own needs. Community refers to notions of duty, social hierarchy, and mutual dependency as they bear on an individual's role and standing in a community. Finally, divinity refers to notions of natural and sacred orders, sanctity, sin and purity, and how they bear on the ability of a person to maintain spiritual integrity.

This view suggests that people in all cultures are capable of the same general moral reasoning patterns, but each person expresses them according to his or her own culture-bound contexts and ways of interpreting situations. For example, Americans are thought to emphasize autonomy most heavily and to de-emphasize community and divinity, whereas many groups in India seem to emphasize community and divinity most heavily and de-emphasize autonomy. Nonetheless, each of these three aspects of morality can be manifested in any culture, given the appropriate context (Shweder et al., 1998). More generally, it is difficult to support the claim that any particular culture completely lacks a certain form of moral reasoning, as opposed to just using it in fewer types of situations (Turiel, 1998).

The influence of social context on morality also bears on moral development. As Kohlberg's early work showed, a specific child's patterns of moral reasoning can span as many as five distinct stages (Kurtines & Greif, 1974). It has since become clear that children, like adults, take situational factors into account as they choose from a wide range of reasoning patterns. But this is not to say that moral reasoning does not change with development. Reasoning undoubtedly becomes more complex with age, and the higher stages typical of adolescents and adults often involve more complex reasoning than the early stages. Nonetheless, simple versions of fairness and the "Golden Rule," normally considered fairly sophisticated moral reasoning (corresponding to Kohlberg's Stage 6), seem to be within the grasp of young children.

> **Q:** Describe how patterns of moral reasoning might vary across different social contexts.

Domain-Specific Moral Reasoning Piaget, Kohlberg, and Gilligan devised theories of moral development that generated enormous amounts of research. Still, their approaches have not exhausted the range of developmental paths to mature moral reasoning. Each of their approaches describes a progression of stages intended to apply to moral thought in all kinds of situations. More recently, some theorists have suggested models of domain-specific moral reasoning, in which moral reasoning is thought to occur in quite distinct modes that may be related to evolved systems governing self-protection and interpersonal interactions. The domain-specific approach is also quite compatible with the pluralistic perspective, in which different situations invoke different moral domains.

For example, William Damon believes that there may be a specific moral domain for reasoning about sharing and the justice of distributing resources to others and that it includes several stages that follow a developmental progression (Damon, 1980, 1990). Whether this progression really reflects a complete incompetence of younger children to think about sharing in certain ways or whether some kinds of reasoning tend to be more complicated and, when simplified, might still have cores that are accessible to much younger children remains to be studied. But Damon suggests that young children often neglect the extent to which one person might be more deserving in judgments about sharing. Above and beyond the details of the particular developmental progression, Damon's central idea is that development in the realm of sharing and resource distribution takes its own trajectory that is markedly different from the developmental path in other domains, such as those involving harm or lying.

Another domain-specific theory of moral reasoning focuses on prosocial reasoning—that is, how children think about cases of **altruism**, where an individual acts for the benefit of another at her own personal expense. Nancy Eisenberg has proposed that children's reasoning about altruistic actions includes a set of developmental stages that are roughly analogous to Kohlberg's (Eisenberg, 1986, Eisenberg et al., 2005). Eisenberg's stages of reasoning about altruism consist of a concern with immediate self-interest, seeking approval of others, and appealing to internalized principles. Yet, the stages are not presented as a rigid developmental sequence, but rather as a collection of forms of reasoning, most of which are available to an individual. In this view, the form of reasoning an individual uses to decide whether to act altruistically depends more on situational factors than on the person's age. In addition, prosocial reasoning seems to develop quite independently from reasoning about what is wrong (Eisenberg, 2000; Robinson et al., 1994). We will revisit prosocial morality later in this chapter when we consider how emotions such as empathy can guide behaviors differently than moral reasoning alone.

There may not be any particular type or stage of moral reasoning that is inherently so complex that it is fully unavailable to preschoolers. In fact, even very young children are able to access and appropriately use advanced forms of moral reasoning when the scenario is sufficiently simple and heavily linked to familiar contexts. This ability suggests that children may not actually undergo the kind of developmental progression through a series of moral stages that many theorists of moral development have described. Instead, children may show early difficulties with some kinds of moral reasoning because young children generally have more trouble reasoning about complex ideas—not because they are unable to understand the concepts at stake in these "higher" levels of moral reasoning (Gibbs et al., 2007).

In addition to being influenced by social contexts, moral thoughts of various forms are also linked to moral emotions, to automatic nonconscious thought, to neuroscience, and to primatology (Haidt, 2008). In many cases, moral intuitions seem to bypass slow deliberative thought (see box on moral dumbfounding). One version of these non-deliberative processes is shown in Table 12.4 (Haidt & Joseph, 2004). In this

Moral Modules	Harm/Care	Fairness/ Reciprocity	Ingroup/Loyalty	Authority/ Respect	Purity/Sanctity
Adaptive challenge	Protecting and caring for young, vulnerable, or injured kin	Reaping benefits of mutual cooperation with nonkin	Reaping benefits of group cooperation	Negotiating hierarchy, deferring to authority	Avoiding microbes and parasites
Proper domain (adaptive triggers)	Suffering, distress, or threat to kin	Cheating, cooperation, deception	Threat or challenge to group	Signs of dominance and submission	Waste products, diseased people
Actual domain (commonly encountered triggers)	Baby animals, cartoon characters	Marital fidelity, broken vending machines	Home sports teams	Bosses, respected professionals	Taboo ideas (communism, racism)
Characteristic emotions	Compassion	Anger, gratitude, guilt	Group pride, belongingness, rage at traitors	Respect, fear	Disgust
Relevant virtues [and vices]	Caring, kindness [cruelty]	Fairness, justice, honesty, trustworthiness [dishonesty]	Loyalty, patriotism, self-sacrifice [treason, cowardice]	Obedience, deference [disobedience, uppitiness]	Temperance, chastity, piety, cleanliness [lust, intemperance]

TABLE 12.4 Moral modules. One way of presenting the pluralistic view of morality argues that humans have five distinct moral modules that are shared with evolutionary ancestors. Human cultural and cognitive processes have elaborated on these basic modules, giving rise to moral emotions and to our notions of virtues and vices. Adapted from Haidt & Joseph (2007).

model, moral intuitions arise from **moral modules**, which are forms of moral reasoning that have evolved to deal with specific kinds of moral problems encountered by individuals and groups. Separate modules give rise to harm/care concerns, fairness/reciprocity issues, in-group/loyalty tensions, authority/respect perceptions, and purity/sanctity problems. Several kinds of primates show behavior consistent with these moral modules because of the ways they meet adaptive challenges. Likewise, humans have applied these same modules to modern-day contexts and have elaborated on them as the bases for moral virtues. This account of moral thought and behavior blends together evolutionary psychology, cultural influences, cognitive factors, and a clear sense of domain specificity. Domain specificity is indicated by the idea that different forms of moral thought are elicited by specific kinds of situations or domains. Haidt's approach also suggests a model of development in which the domains for which the module was initially evolved become extended into more culturally modern domains and become culturally interpreted in terms of virtues. In Table 12.4, these are shown as a shift from "proper domains" that are triggered because of evolutionary adaptations to "actual domains" that are triggered by more recent cultural factors as well.

The Development of Moral Behavior

A full theory of how moral judgment develops is many years off, but even the present, partial theories make it clear that moral judgments do not lead directly to moral behaviors. We can all bring to mind things that we have done despite knowing they were wrong, and extensive evidence supports this intuitive sense that we do not always act as we think we should (Tangney et al., 2007). Moral behaviors are determined by many other factors besides moral reasoning and judgment. In this section, we will focus on the development of moral behavior in its own right and also consider its relationship to moral thought.

We start by considering whether individuals typically behave consistently in moral or immoral ways across situations. This discussion leads to a consideration of the extent to which moral judgments predict moral behaviors. We then consider some temperament and personality factors important to moral development and reflect how they relate to the emergence of antisocial and prosocial behavior. This discussion raises controversial questions about whether individual differences in morality may have biological bases. We then consider social influences on moral development, including the role of parents in the early development of conscience, and both the punishment and modeling approaches to guiding moral development.

Consistency of Moral Behavior

If a child cheats regularly in the classroom, does he also cheat on the playground? If so, at least the behavior is potentially consistent with an admittedly nonstandard set of beliefs about what is right. But if classroom cheaters are rarely also playground cheaters, this discrepancy suggests a weaker link between moral judgment and action and a significant influence of situational factors.

In the early twentieth century, researchers studying cheating in the classroom and cheating on the playground were surprised to find that cheating in one context did not seem to indicate cheating in another (Hartshorne & May, 1928; Hartshorne et al., 1930). Children who were scrupulous about classroom work might be the worst offenders at recess, and vice versa (see Figure 12.8). It appeared that, given the right range of contexts, almost any child could be observed to cheat, but hardly anyone cheated consistently in all situations. In addition, when these children were asked about right and wrong behaviors, they usually disapproved of the same acts, even as they violated these judgments in their actions.

This classic study had two crucial implications: (1) it ruled out simple accounts of moral development that linked moral judgments directly to moral actions, and (2) it supported the theory that all personality traits (including those related to moral choices) are situation specific. Although later reanalyses of Hartshorne and May's data suggested more consistency than originally reported—especially when social conventions were distinguished from moral principles (Grusec & Lytton, 1988)—the general conclusion of some moral inconsistency for individuals across situations has endured. One scholar has argued that it is misleading to describe someone as brave or caring in general and that it makes much more sense to describe a person as brave in certain circumstances (such as when a close friend is being threatened by someone with a gun) or caring in specific contexts (such as when seeing someone in pain; Doris, 2002). In a different situation, that same person may not appear to be either brave or caring. A particular type of person might well show a strong tendency to behave in a particular way in a certain well-described set of situations, but would not always behave in this way and would not show a completely consistent moral character across all situations (Funder, 2006).

Another difficulty in predicting actions from judgments is that several different patterns of judgments may lead to the same actions. This is especially evident in Kohlberg's system, in which several different levels of moral reasoning can lead to each of the two possible choices in a moral dilemma. A study of one of the first campus political actions of the turbulent 1960s, the Berkeley Free Speech Movement, revealed this slippage between levels of reasoning and action among students confronted with a real-life moral dilemma (Haan et al., 1968). In 1964, the

A

B

FIGURE 12.8 **Consistency of cheating.** A classic study by Hartshorne and May (1928) suggested that children who cheat in the classroom **(A)** are not necessarily those who cheat on the playground **(B)**.

university administration became unhappy that students were distributing leftist political pamphlets on-campus, and it attempted to ban these materials, claiming that the tables set up to distribute them were slowing campus traffic. In response, the students conducted a traffic flow study documenting no such problems. When the administration did not back down, the incensed students insisted that their civil rights had been violated and eventually held a sit-in at one of the university buildings—a highly provocative act in which participants risked not only their academic standing but their future careers (see Figure 12.9).

Was it possible to predict who engaged in the sit-in based on their stages of moral reasoning? Haan and her colleagues assessed many of the demonstrators, using Kohlberg's moral dilemmas to determine their levels of moral reasoning. We might expect that only students at the highest levels would have engaged in an action that would put them at such risk solely on the basis of a relatively abstract principle such as free speech. In fact, students at several levels of moral reasoning were well represented. Although there were proportionally more protesters at Kohlberg's two highest levels of moral reasoning (Stages 5 and 6) than in the student body at large, there were also some protesters who were at Stage 2. Even as some students were demonstrating as a way of honoring principles, others were doing so apparently for purely hedonistic reasons. These students saw the sit-in as great fun, and their enjoyment outweighed the risks.

Thus, many decisions and actions can be justified at various levels of moral reasoning or in terms of several different moral belief systems, making it quite difficult to use beliefs to predict behaviors (Keniston, 1970). People who consciously want their moral beliefs to be consistent with their actions may show more consistency (Blasi, 1980), but even this desire does not always result in consistency. Predicting moral behavior from beliefs may also be possible in studies that set up situations in which certain forms of

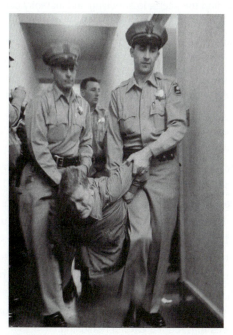

FIGURE 12.9 **Moral judgments and moral actions.** Although students who participated in the Free Speech Movement on the Berkeley campus in the 1960s were more likely to show higher levels of moral reasoning on Kohlberg's stages, there were still many other protesters from lower stages and many who did not participate from higher stages, revealing that there is no simple mapping from levels of moral reasoning to kinds of moral behaviors.

Q: Why might it be problematic to use someone's tested level of moral reasoning to predict his moral behavior?

Moral Dumbfounding: Judgment or Intuition?

The idea that moral intuitions might be rooted in emotions is an old one, going back at least as far as the eighteenth century. Recently, researchers have proposed a new view of the role that emotions play in moral thought, spurred by the phenomenon of **moral dumbfounding**. This term refers to the finding that for some moral situations, people have strong convictions about what is right and wrong but are unable to explain why. The phenomenon of moral dumbfounding builds on an apparent disconnect between having strong "gut feelings" about what is right and being able to justify those feelings with higher-order reasoning. The phenomenon does not exist for all moral situations, only for certain ones that most people immediately consider wrong, although they cannot explain why.

In many cases, moral dumbfounding reactions fit within an evolutionary psychology perspective. One such scenario describes an adult brother and sister who have consensual sex (Haidt, 2003). The scenario painstakingly describes how the brother and sister decided to do it only once, used contraceptives, and had no adverse emotional reactions. The vast majority of adults find the scenario shocking and instantly condemn it as wrong. Yet, when asked to explain why they think it is wrong, most adults either give incorrect reasons (for example, "the couple might have a child with genetic defects," even though they know the couple used contraceptives) or say they don't know why. People judge quite a large number of scenarios in this way. For example, even if they are not religious, people think it is wrong to use sacred articles to, say, clean out a toilet bowl, whether or not anyone else even knows about it, and yet they are "dumbfounded" when asked to explain why (Haidt & Bjorklund, 2008; Haidt & Joseph, 2004).

Moral judgments of this sort may be like judgments of aesthetics. Most people who find a sunset beautiful would be hard pressed to explain why it is more beautiful than any other. People seem to perceive the beauty directly. Similarly, some moral intuitions may be triggered by emotional reactions rather than being a result of deliberative rational thought. These cases that rely on gut feelings about what is right might be quite distinct from cases that require careful reasoning.

One way researchers have studied these kinds of situations is by presenting participants with two moral situations, only one of which draws on emotion-based intuitions. For example, imagine that you are at a trolley stop, and you see that a runaway trolley is about to kill five people on the track. You can pull a switch that will send the trolley onto a different track on which there is just one person who will be killed (see Figure 12.10). Is it right to throw the switch? Most people say it is, and they give thoughtful explanations about sacrificing one person to save five people. Now consider a second situation that is similar to the first, except that instead of throwing a switch, you can shove a large, curly-haired man with glasses from a footbridge onto the tracks in front of the trolley, knowing that sacrificing this one man's life will save the other five people, as the large man's body will stop the trolley before it reaches the other five people.

Most people find the second action unacceptable. But what is the difference? The first scenario describes an **impersonal moral situation**, one that is abstract and does not directly involve specific individuals. In this case, it is relatively easy to distance yourself from the situation and consider the tradeoffs involved in either throwing the switch or not. The second scenario describes a **personal moral situation** because it involves the individual in the situation in a direct, immediate way (Greene et al., 2001; Singer, 2005). Thus, in the switch-throwing (impersonal) case, it is relatively easy to distance yourself from the situation and consider the tradeoffs in abstract terms. In the shoving (personal) case, it is impossible not to encode the effects of this action on a specific person (which is why the description includes personal characteristics), and it is difficult not to be horrified at the thought of harming an innocent person.

Moral intuitions in impersonal versus personal situations appear to show different patterns of activation in the brain (Cushman et al., 2010). In fMRI studies of increased blood flow in brain regions that occurs while engaging in judgments about the two kinds of situations, different sets of brain regions become activated; for example, areas associated with emotional processing are significantly more activated in the personal moral situations than in the impersonal moral situations (Greene et al., 2001, 2004). In addition, people who suffer brain damage to the prefrontal cortex, a key region associated with personal moral intuitions, tend to make "utilitarian" moral judgments in which they treat both trolley scenarios as a simple weighting of the total number of lives saved (Greene, 2007; Koenigs et al., 2007; Young & Koenigs, 2007).

Moral dumbfounding arises from powerful emotions; there is an immediate sense of knowing what is right and wrong without reflection, based on a link between an emotion and a moral evaluation (Dwyer, 2009). The **social intuitionist model** of moral judgment suggests that in these cases, emotions like anger or contempt can be triggered automatically by perceived violations of norms and rights. Thus, people can have moral intuitions about a scenario without considering abstract moral principles (Haidt, 2001; Haidt & Joseph, 2004).

In this view, violations of the community's ethical norms can provoke contempt, violations of individual rights can provoke anger, and violations of sacred relations can provoke disgust (Rozin et al., 1999). According to the social intuitionist view, critical cultural experiences during late childhood affect the ways that these basic moral emotions become associated with particular situations. Thus, people in different cultures will sometimes have different moral reactions to the same situation. More specifically, the theory holds that children are especially sensitive to the way that expressions of anger, disgust, or contempt correlate with moral transgressions (of social norms, individual rights, or sacred relations) in their own cultures. Cultural psychologist Jonathan Haidt (2001) has suggested that there may be a sensitive period in late childhood during which time culture helps form links between basic emotions and certain kinds of culturally specific situations. Early moral emotions may also help spur the development of moral reasoning in the more cognitive realm. Thus, children who suffer brain lesions in a region critically associated with personal moral thought (which is often emotion linked) tend not to progress as far in terms of Kohlberg's stages (Young & Koenigs, 2007).

One criticism of the social intuitionist model of moral development is that it may overemphasize the role of emotions at the expense of cognition. As noted earlier, people can reason in advance extensively about a type of moral situation, building up cognitive schemas that can guide rapid moral judgments when the situation arises. Similarly, the effects of culture may be mediated by rich cognitive structures that lead to highly automatic and reflexive modes of responding, even if it took considerable time to build up those routines. Even if the moment of making a moral judgment does not involve extensive explicit reasoning, this kind of thought over the course of past experiences may have laid the groundwork for rapid responses (Pizarro & Bloom, 2003). In addition, the phenomenon of feeling certain but being unable to explain why may not be unique to moral dumbfounding. People who are confident that they know how common everyday items work are often shown to be clueless (Rozenblit & Keil, 2002; see Chapter 10). Even with these concerns, however, the social intuitionist approach is charting an important new direction for moral development research by challenging researchers to consider precisely why and when emotional reactions rather than explicit reasoning guide moral judgments.

A

B

FIGURE 12.10 Moral dumbfounding. (A) In the first scenario, there is a runaway trolley and five people are on one track and one person is on another track. Participants are asked if they would throw a switch that would shift the trolley from the track on which five people would be killed to the track on which one person would be killed. **(B)** In the second scenario, participants are asked if they would push one person onto the track to save the five people on the track.

reasoning are likely to suggest specific kinds of responses. For example, in situations where respected authority figures urge participants to do something morally questionable, participants whose moral reasoning is more authority based are more likely to go along with the authority. You may have read about social psychologist Stanley Milgram's study of obedience, in which subjects were urged to give increasingly powerful shocks to a "learner" each time he made a mistake on an experimental task (Milgram, 1963). Although the learner was actually a confederate of the experimenter and no real shocks were administered, the participants in Milgram's study did not know this, and the majority of them followed the experimenter's instructions, despite believing that they were causing the learner great pain. In another version of this classic study, Kohlberg and Candee (1984) found that 75 percent of the people who were at Stage 6 in Kohlberg's stages of moral reasoning refused to increase the amount of shock as the experimenter ordered, whereas only 13 percent of subjects at lower levels of moral reasoning refused. This finding has been interpreted as showing that Stage 6 people are less inclined to make moral judgments and take action based on appeals to authorities. They may feel less obligated to follow the instructions of authorities, or they may not view the experimenters as being authoritative, or they may not be as intimidated in general by the views of others.

The conclusion from these sorts of studies is that simply examining someone's beliefs or judgments about what behavior is right in a given situation is not a reliable way to predict behavior. It is often possible to explain the reasons for a behavior after the fact, but predicting behavior is much more difficult. In addition, there is no evidence that the weak link between beliefs and behavior is more (or less) straightforward among young children (Hardy & Carlo, 2011; Kang & Glassman, 2010; Walker, 2004). Nonetheless, this complexity does not indicate that beliefs are completely separate from behaviors. The links between them are likely to be both intricate and powerful, but they are hard to predict because so many influences affect behavior and because many situations are ambiguous.

These features of moral behavior in older children and adults raise a central question about development: Do younger children tend to show more behaviors that are considered immoral than older children and adults do? Do children gradually engage in more morally appropriate behaviors as they mature? To be sure, younger children may have more difficulties resisting some temptations, may not always be as sensitive to how their actions influence others, and may be less prone to shame and guilt. But for all these differences, their behaviors do not show a general trend toward becoming increasingly moral.

Antisocial and Prosocial Behavior

To find out whether different types of moral and immoral behaviors show developmental patterns, we first need a way of classifying such behaviors. A good classification system should clearly distinguish moral acts from immoral ones, and it should include subtypes within the category of immoral and moral acts to help distinguish which ones, if any, show developmental changes. Any such classification of moral and immoral behaviors is difficult. It raises problems concerning differences in morality across cultures, as well as difficulties in evaluating actions alone without full information about intentions.

Despite these complexities, research in moral development has focused on two broad categories of behavior: prosocial behavior and antisocial behavior. **Prosocial behavior**, or altruism, normally refers to actions performed for the benefit of others and at some cost to the person performing the action. **Antisocial behavior** consists of acts that harm another individual or a group. It includes not only physical violence, but also verbal assaults and attacks on society and norms, such as cheating and stealing. In considering antisocial behavior, we will sometimes use the term *aggression* to describe hostile acts that are detrimental to others, rather than referring to the personality trait of an aggressive personality. This distinction is important because some people may be seen as having highly aggressive personalities but not as behaving immorally.

> **Q:** Describe several different examples of prosocial and antisocial behaviors.

Antisocial Behavior There are no obvious developmental trends in the tendency to cheat. A surprising number (some say more than 50 percent) of elementary school children cheat at some time in their grade school days (see Figure 12.11). Interestingly, the incidence does not seem to drop as they grow older. It continues in secondary school and beyond (Davis et al., 1992; Evans & Craig, 1990; Houser, 1978; Jensen et al., 2002). Some estimates suggest that as many as 75 percent of college students cheat at one point or another. Moreover, cheating does not stop at the end of college. Estimates of people who cheat to some degree on their income tax returns run very high. And there are many people who do not tell a cashier when they are mistakenly undercharged. In short, there is no evidence that people cheat less as they get older.

Similarly, there is no evidence of developmental trends for stealing, lying, and disloyalty. These behaviors may take a different form with age, as transgressions become increasingly sophisticated and subtle. Still, it is not clear

FIGURE 12.11 **Cheating by children in school.** As shown in this photo of rural schoolchildren in Tibet, cheating occurs throughout the world. Although cheating may become more subtle and sophisticated, there is no evidence that cheating becomes less prevalent with increasing age.

that once a child has reached toddlerhood, there is a developmental change in the prevalence of any of these types of immoral acts. Of course, it can be difficult to compare and measure the immoral behavior of people at different ages. But young children are typically much less capable than adults of inflicting harm, regardless of their intentions, and adults are often much more capable of concealing antisocial behaviors or casting blame on others. Once those factors are accounted for, it is much more difficult to know whether the rates of *purposeful* antisocial behaviors change with age.

Most children do become better able to control their impulses and delay gratification of their immediate desires as they grow older. Hence, moral transgressions related to such difficulties often occur less often with age. Nonethe-

less, many transgressions are not based on an inability to delay gratification.

Prosocial Behavior The same lack of a clear developmental trend occurs in analyses of cooperation and competition. Although many Western cultures encourage competition, experimenters studying cooperation and competition generally consider cooperative behavior more morally desirable and reward cooperative behavior much more strongly. Figure 12.12 shows a game that has been used for studying cooperation and competition among children in many cultures. First, a marble is put in a container, which is in the middle of a table. Two children sit on opposite sides of the table, and each one takes one of the strings attached to the sides of the container. The object of the game is to pull on the string to move the container close enough to reach in and get the marble. The children are told that they will receive a reward for every marble each of them gets (Kagan & Madsen, 1972). Every time one child gets a marble, the container is put back in the middle of the table, and a new marble is put in it. The container is held together by magnets, and if both children pull hard on the strings, the container will come apart and the marble will roll away, so that neither child will get it. The only way to get the marble is to agree to cooperate by taking turns, such that first one child pulls the container close enough to take out the marble while the other child holds the string lightly and does not pull, and then the other child pulls the container and takes out the marble.

In practice, many children never seem to reach a level of mutual trust that allows them to cooperate by taking turns, and therefore neither wins any marbles. Rather than finding a general developmental trend of increasing cooperation in all children, this research points to individual differences, with some children being much more cooperative than others. These findings have held up across many kinds of assessments of cooperation and competition, ranging from observational studies of free play to more structured games and scenarios. Research in this area also shows strong

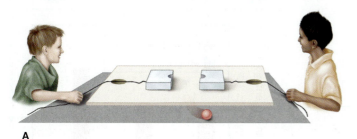

A   B

FIGURE 12.12 **Cooperation versus competition.** Shown here is an apparatus used to measure cooperation and competition among children. The goal is for each child to retrieve a marble from within the container. Competitive participants simply pull on the strings, causing the breakup of the container (which is held together by magnets), and thereby causing the marble to roll away, so that neither child gets the marble. Cooperative participants agree to let each other get a marble on successive terms. Adapted from Madsen & Connor (1973).

cross-cultural differences. For example, in one classic study, children in a small Mexican town cooperated considerably more on the marble task than did children from an American town (Madsen, 1971).

> **Q:** Describe how cooperation and competition might be measured in two children.

Some studies have found gradual developmental increases in prosocial behaviors such as sharing and helping (Eisenberg & Mussen, 1989; Eisenberg et al., 2006). But it can be difficult to distinguish between a child's emerging grasp of socially approved behaviors (such as holding a door open for others) and an increase in a genuine desire to engage in more altruistic behaviors. Recent studies suggest, however, that if the situation is set up appropriately, very young children can be strikingly altruistic and prosocial, both in

SCIENTIFIC METHOD: Instrumental Helping in Toddlers

Hypothesis:

When a situation clearly shows that a person is in need of help to achieve a goal, even young toddlers will behave altruistically.

Method:

1. Twenty-four 14-month-old toddlers participated in the experiment.
2. All the children saw an experimenter (1) drop a clothespin while hanging up clothes and then try to retrieve it, (2) drop a marker while making a drawing and then try to retrieve it, and (3) try to pick up paper balls with tongs when the balls were out of reach for the experimenter but not for the child.
3. In a control condition, the experimenter intentionally threw away the clothespin/marker or did not try to move the paper balls to a new spot.
4. The researchers recorded the incidence of instrumental helping by the toddlers.

Results:

In all three tasks, but especially the paper ball task, toddlers helped more in the experimental condition.

Conclusion:

In tasks that involve instrumental helping of another person to achieve a goal, very young children will altruistically offer assistance at no benefit to themselves.

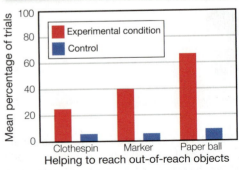

Helping to reach out-of-reach objects

Source study: Warneken & Tomasello (2007).

terms of helping others and in terms of wanting to be fair about the distribution of resources (Shaw & Olson, 2012; Warneken et al., 2011). One line of work depicts adults struggling to do some task in which assistance would help them greatly (such as trying to open a cabinet while carrying several things or trying to obtain an out-of-reach object; see Scientific Method box). Even infants as young as 14 months old will spontaneously act to help when they see someone in need (Warneken & Tomasello, 2006, 2007). Younger children may have difficulty inferring complex goals and coordinating helping actions, but when the task is as simple as providing objects that another person is trying to reach, even 14-month-olds do offer to help when there is no obvious benefit to themselves or any expected reward from the person they are helping.

This form of prosocial behavior is called **instrumental helping**. It involves perceiving someone who is unable to achieve a goal and acting altruistically to help that person, even when there are no obvious benefits to the helper (see Figure 12.13). Thus, even when 18-month-olds are presented with physical obstacles to climb over to help another, they readily do so, suggesting a desire to act even at considerable

Out-of-reach

A person accidentally drops an object on the floor and unsuccessfully reaches for it.

Physical Obstacle

A person wants to put a pile of books into a cabinet, but she cannot open the closed doors because her hands are full.

Wrong Result

A book slips from a stack as a person attempts to place it on top of the stack.

Wrong Means

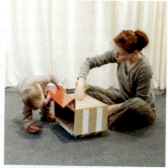

An object drops through a hole into a box and the person unsuccessfully tries to grasp it through the small hole, ignorant of a flap on the side of the box.

FIGURE 12.13 Early altruism. Children who are at least 18 months old will help adult strangers, even when there is no obvious benefit or reward for helping. From Warneken & Tomasello (2009b).

personal cost (Warneken & Tomasello, 2009a). This is different from prosocial behavior based on sharing or comforting, both of which may appear somewhat later in development.

Slightly older children will help even when it costs them the opportunity to play with extremely attractive toys. These children are clearly not motivated by rewards; indeed, they will help just as often when the person who needs the help does not reward them as when the person does. In fact, in some cases, external rewards can actually reduce the desire to help in the future for reasons discussed more extensively in Chapter 13.

The evolutionary roots of instrumental helping seem quite old. Chimpanzees, whose common ancestors with humans go back several million years, will help caregivers who are trying to reach for an object and will do so in situations where no rewards are present (Warneken & Tomasello 2009a). Chimpanzees may not show helping in as wide a range of situations as young humans, but there is clearly a common drive to help others in ways that reflect true altruism.

Recent research has also shown that young children can be quite sophisticated and prosocial in their sharing behaviors as well. Although children may not seem to engage in much sharing until around 5 or 6 years of age, some situations will elicit genuine sharing at considerably earlier ages. For example, when children engage in collaborative efforts, even 3-year-olds will share fairly in the fruits of those efforts (Warneken et al., 2011). They will also adjust their allocations so as to provide more resources to those who work more productively (Kanngiesser & Warneken, 2012).

One theory of the development of altruistic helping is that younger children are more indiscriminately helpful in cases where they clearly perceive a person in need of help. As they get older, however, they start to be more selective in whom they choose to help, and they become more influenced by such factors as whether they see the individual as belonging to the same social group as themselves and whether they see the person as worthy of help (Warneken & Tomasello, 2009b). Because of their lack of discrimination, younger children may actually be more altruistic than older children.

Yet, in other contexts, young children may be less altruistic, at least in situations where their lack of fairness is unlikely to be detected by others. Thus, young children who are asked to allocate resources for another child who is not yet present and who will not know of their actions will often allocate more resources to themselves even when older children and adults would think it only fair to allocate them equally (Sheskin, 2013). Other studies show that between roughly 6 and 11 years of age, children want to appear to be fair in allocating resources when others will witness the allocation, but will still be more unfair when it won't be detected (Shaw et al., 2013). More generally, when considerable rewards are at stake and a salient audience is not present, young children may have more difficulty behaving fairly and prosocially and may be less generous (Leimgruber et al., 2012). The cases of spontaneous helping by much younger children are not an exception to this pattern because there is no competing strong reward. Empathy for others who are in trouble may be very early emerging, but fair allocation of rewards may be much more situationally sensitive and often difficult for young children.

Above and beyond any possible development patterns, there are huge differences among individuals. Even if people are not fully consistent across situations, individuals still show clear differences in the way they act in moral situations. Perhaps only 1 person out of 1,000 would dive into the sea to save a drowning stranger 100 yards away (see Figure 12.14); only a handful of people would walk past an old lady who has fallen in the street without offering help; only a small number of people would try to verbally and physically intimidate others to gain material resources.

These differences across individuals raise the compelling question of why some people act in more morally appropriate ways than others. Situational factors can be enormously compelling, but how can we explain the clear individual differences that exist over and above situational influences? We have already seen that differences in moral judgments are fairly poor predictors of differences in moral behavior, so what are other factors that might cause such individual differences? At the broadest level, two other factors lead to individual differences in moral behavior—and by this point, they will be familiar as sources of individual differences in other areas of development as well: (1) temperament and personality, and (2) differences in social influences. It is in these two areas that most of the research on prosocial and antisocial behavior has occurred. This research tends to ask why some individuals show more (or less) of a behavior than do others, rather than seeking universal patterns of moral development.

Temperament, Personality, and Moral Behavior

Most researchers who investigate individual differences in moral behavior do not consider some children to have inherently better or worse moral judgment than others. They do, however, ask whether particular psychological mechanisms could make some people more likely than others to commit immoral acts. These mechanisms could range from differences in impulse control to the degree of empathy someone experiences. Even when the right thing to do is clear, some people might find it easier than others to resist temptation or to delay gratification. Similarly, people who have difficulty empathizing with another's pain or need would likely have trouble using the Golden Rule or care-based forms of moral reasoning. It is critical to keep in mind the difference between psychological processes that often lead to moral (or immoral) actions and the ability to make moral judgments.

> **Q:** How are psychological processes that might help foster immoral behaviors different from psychological processes that underlie moral judgments?

Self-Regulation One of the most frequently discussed sets of processes associated with prosocial and antisocial behavior is **self-regulation**, the ability to control our impulses by managing our emotional states and our reactions to others and to situations and to delay gratification of desires rather than always acting on them immediately (see Figure 12.15). An impulsive person with poor self-regulation will not necessarily engage in immoral behaviors, but he may engage in actions that are considered morally inappropriate since they often spring from an inability to suppress a desire or impulse.

Studies examining differences in immoral behavior more often focus on adults than on how this kind of behavior develops. One reason for this is that immoral behaviors are difficult to document until later in life, when infractions such as school suspensions and criminal convictions make this kind of behavior easier to identify and measure. For that reason, the study of self-regulation in adults is closely con-

FIGURE 12.14 Altruistic behavior. Prosocial reasoning about altruism—helping others at a possible expense to the helper (here a person is jumping into the water to save strangers who are drowning)—may include stages in which there is a concern with self-interest, a desire to seek the approval of others, and an appeal to internalized principles. Researchers ask if reasoning about altruism should be considered a distinct domain with its own trajectory.

FIGURE 12.15 Self-regulation. A lack of self-regulation—such as drawing on the wall of a formal living room—can be interpreted as immoral behavior if the child is thought to be old enough to know better.

nected to morality, while these topics have more often been studied separately in children. We will discuss the development of self-regulation in more depth in Chapter 13, which concerns the child's awareness of the self and others. Here we discuss self-regulation more narrowly in the context of its links to the study of moral behavior.

Self-regulation in the broadest sense is concerned with modulating our emotions in ways that help us accomplish a goal (Eisenberg et al., 2004). It can often involve inhibiting an impulse, but it can also involve initiating an emotional state, such as consciously working up our courage to do a difficult act. In all its forms, this kind of effortful control of behavior is more difficult for young children, perhaps because the ability to self-regulate is heavily related to the maturation of the prefrontal cortex.

Children with poor self-regulation or low impulse control may be unable to wait long enough before they act to consider the consequences of their actions. Thus, they may act on their impulses before they realize that their actions may hurt others or violate social rules (Dunn & Hughes, 2001). Poor impulse control can also lead to a tendency to give in to temptation, even while knowing that it is better to do otherwise. On the other hand, when a child has better impulse control, even a small delay before doing something questionable may provide the child with enough time for reason to exert an influence.

Self-regulation is also related to the ability to delay gratification. **Delay of gratification** simply refers to the ability

to hold off engaging in an action that will bring a desired reward. Some individuals seem to need positive experiences immediately and are unable to wait for what they want. They might well choose to get a small reward for minimal sacrifice over the option of working longer at an unpleasant task to earn a much larger eventual reward. Despite the common assumption that antisocial children and adults have difficulty with impulse control and delay of gratification, few studies convincingly show a biological predisposition for such difficulties.

Personality variables also seem to influence the extent to which a particular environment leads to behavior problems. One analysis of very low income families asked which children in those families showed more **resilience**—that is, the ability to adjust or recover from adverse events or situations—in the harsh environment (Buckner et al., 2003). Children with higher levels of self-regulation, as measured by emotion management and executive functioning skills, were also more resilient. It should be noted, however, that these children also had more actively involved parents, raising the possibility that both parental effects and common, genetically driven temperamental components contributed to their higher levels of self-regulation and resilience.

Problems with self-regulation and delay of gratification have been suggested as a partial cause of extreme antisocial behaviors that can lead to criminality. There have been repeated suggestions that criminality is higher among individuals who are more closely related genetically (Eysenck, 1996; Gabrielli & Mednick, 1983; Wilson & Herrnstein, 1985). Several studies have found higher concordance rates among MZ twins than among DZ twins, but these findings on their own cannot easily rule out the fact that MZ twins also experience more similar environments (Joseph, 2001). More compelling are adoption studies in which environmental and genetic differences are more neatly separated. In one adoption study in Denmark, adopted children whose genetic fathers had criminal records were twice as likely to have criminal records as were adopted children whose genetic fathers did not have criminal records (Hutchings & Mednick, 1977; Mednick et al., 1984). These findings have been criticized, however, on the grounds that the placement of adopted children is not random, which means that environment as well as genetic background could be influencing criminality (Joseph, 2001). Nonetheless, the research in this area tends to support a partial genetic basis for individual differences in antisocial behavior (Rhee & Waldman, 2002; Viding, 2004).

In addition to being related to self-regulation, genetic factors may also help make a child especially resilient to environmental stressors (such as child neglect) or especially vulnerable to those stressors. Thus, the strongest genetic influences are seen in particular kinds of environments and their interactions with particular alleles (Moffit, 2005). Moreover, it seems that genetic factors are more likely to influence the emergence of physical aggression than **social aggression**, which includes such behaviors as malicious teasing, social exclusion from a group, and humiliation (Brendgen et al., 2005).

Early antisocial behavior also tends to predict similar later behaviors. One way this connection has been documented is that children with conduct disorders are more likely to engage in criminal behavior as adults. Children who are diagnosed with a **conduct disorder** regularly transgress in ways that impinge on others' rights or in ways that violate social norms. In most cases, children who routinely steal, bully others, or cheat would qualify for this diagnosis, as would those who show a callous insensitivity in social interactions (Frick et al., 2003; Lahey et al., 2003). Children who consistently show these behaviors tend to exhibit them for extended periods, well into adulthood. As adults, they are more likely to be physically abusive toward both intimates and others. They are also more likely to violate the law and become criminals (Kazdin, 1995; Lahey et al., 2003; Loeber, 1996; Robins & Rutter, 1990; Zoccolillo et al., 1992).

The strong link between childhood conduct disorders and adult rates of antisocial and criminal behavior is not necessarily evidence of a temperamental or personality basis for antisocial behavior, however, since environmental influences are constantly at work as well. But the consistency that individuals' antisocial behavior patterns often show over much of the lifespan, combined with such traits as emotional insensitivity, does make it somewhat more plausible that underlying psychological differences may put some children more at risk for such behaviors.

In addition, theories about the genetic bases of more extreme immoral behavior, such as crime, may not fully apply to people who are prone to more moderate or mundane immoral actions. Most of the available statistics on conduct disorders and their links to adult behaviors examine only one extreme end of the continuum between moral and immoral behavior. But only a very small percentage of children are diagnosed with conduct disorders, and an even smaller percentage of them commit crimes as adults.

At present, many researchers believe that less extreme cases of antisocial behavior involve the same processes as cases of conduct disorder and criminality, but to lesser extents. Chapter 16, which deals with childhood psychopathology, discusses the dangers of assuming continuity between behavior associated with psychopathology and similar behaviors that are more common and less detrimental. Moreover, as we will see, genetic influences on criminality may extend far beyond the processes of emotional regulation and delay of gratification.

Arousal Level and Positive Emotionality Most people have a similar range of typical arousal levels. This means that they are typically alert and moderately reactive to normal stimuli. Arousal levels have been linked to moral behaviors on the assumption that they influence emotional reactions to stimuli and situations. Unusually low ranges of arousal have been of special interest. The notion of underarousal is widely invoked in explanations of adult criminality. For psychopaths, who feel neither empathy nor remorse, the arousal problem is largely emotional (see Chapter 16). Because they do not feel normal levels of anxiety about committing transgressions, they cannot learn from negative emotional feedback (Eysenck, 1964). For individuals with ADHD, the arousal problem is considered to be more attentional, leading to a decreased ability to maintain attention and to track what happens in their environment. This problem might include difficulty tracking various clues that an action is likely to be considered inappropriate or upsetting. Developmentally, each of these arousal deficits can become especially evident when parents and society try to instill a system of morality. If a child is emotionally underaroused, parents will have greater difficulty teaching moral lessons or instilling feelings of guilt about transgressions. If a child is attentionally underaroused, parents will have trouble ensuring that the child listens to moral explanations and understands the reasons for not engaging in certain behaviors. In addition, underarousal may be related to an inability to feel empathy, a correlation found in children as young as 2 years old (Young et al., 1999).

In addition to general arousal level, a child's temperament (see Chapter 7) is also related to prosocial behaviors. Studies have repeatedly found that children with sunnier dispositions—those who are temperamentally predisposed to show positive emotions—tend to have more frequent and stronger feelings of empathy than less upbeat children, and children who show more positive emotions are more likely to engage in prosocial behaviors (Eisenberg et al., 2000). One possible explanation for this link is that positive emotions may make it easier to think more about others' feelings rather than being more self-focused (see Figure 12.16). Research on the development of empathy has examined these issues and others in more detail.

Empathy We saw earlier that empathy plays an important role in Eisenberg's theory of the development of prosocial behavior. Her theory claims a close link between reasoning and behavior and emphasizes prosocial behaviors and empathy. Feelings of empathy are often thought to lead to appropriate prosocial behavior (Hoffman, 1990). Considering the wide range of individual differences in prosocial behavior, do some people simply have less capacity to feel empathy for others? Can someone with normal social and cognitive abilities nonetheless be unable to feel empathy? This question leads back to psychopathological popula-

FIGURE 12.16 Empathy. Children differ in the extent to which they feel empathy and act on those feelings, in this case comforting another child in distress. Young children who show high levels of empathy and empathy-motivated behaviors are more likely to show similar behaviors in later years.

tions, particularly psychopaths, who rarely feel intense emotions of any kind. In the case of empathy, this deficit leads to an inability to emotionally put themselves in another person's shoes. In addition, there is some evidence that genes contribute to differences in the ability to feel empathy (Frick et al., 2003; Zahn-Waxler et al., 2001). Such a genetic contribution may help explain why young children who show prosocial behaviors, such as sharing toys, are more likely to make substantial charitable contributions as adolescents or young adults (Eisenberg, 2005; Eisenberg et al., 1983, 1991, 2002). The strong, immediate empathy that leads a 3-year-old to share a favorite doll may, in a more mature form, lead her to make regular donations to a homeless shelter.

In their first year of life, children may share others' distress mostly as a form of imitation. Shortly thereafter, their imitation seems to become full-fledged empathy, leading children not only to feel another's distress but in some cases to try to alleviate it (Cole et al., 1992; Eisenberg, 2000; Meltzoff, 2002; Zahn-Waxler et al., 1992). Empathy in young children also enables them to engage in moral actions without having to rely on moral reasoning. Thus, just seeing someone else's distress may trigger a desire to comfort that person separate from forming a judgment about how that person has been treated. A strong sense of empathy alone, however, does not guarantee that a child will engage in a

moral action, as other influences can also come into play. For example, a child might witness a classmate's humiliation in front of a large group and fully feel her classmate's pain but be unable to intervene because she is too shy to act in front of the group.

Of course, feeling empathy and acting on it can take many forms. There are different levels of empathy that correspond to different levels of cognitive, perceptual, and emotional complexity. For example, empathy-related phenomena across various species can range from simple agitation that an animal may feel when a member of its species is in pain, to imitation, to purposefully taking another's point of view (as do humans), to fully experiencing another's suffering (Preston & de Waal, 2002). In evolutionary terms, the ability for groups with shared genotypes to cooperate can provide members with a selective advantage, since this can make them more likely to survive and reproduce, making it more likely that they will pass on their genotype to a new generation. This logic may help explain why many organisms have developed behaviors that enable them to be sensitive to the emotional states of others (Sober & Wilson, 1998).

Similar to the notion that there are different degrees of empathy and that empathy-related behaviors can take many forms, psychologists often distinguish between emotional empathy and cognitive empathy (Losoya & Eisenberg, 2001). Experiencing **emotional empathy** involves witnessing another's emotional state and, in a relatively immediate and direct way, feeling the same emotion. It appears to be a more basic and earlier-emerging form of empathy. **Cognitive empathy**, which involves understanding and representing the emotional and mental points of view of others, requires social cognitive skills and the ability to take another's perspective. Cognitive empathy is often thought to develop later than emotional empathy and to be evolutionarily more recent. The finding that emotional empathy and cognitive empathy seem to activate different brain regions has led some researchers to suggest that people with autism have a deficit in cognitive empathy but not emotional empathy, while psychopaths may have the opposite deficit (Blair, 2005, 2008; Saxe, 2006; see Chapter 16). More broadly, fMRI studies of children suggest that emotional empathy appears early in development and involves activation of the amygdala and related regions and then later becomes integrated with more frontal cortical areas that involve more cognitive forms of empathy (Decety et al., 2011).

A third form of empathy, called **motor empathy**, is usually described as being elicited either as part of the process of pure physical imitation or by simply observing and feeling an action that we might be able to reproduce. As discussed in Chapter 4, it may be mediated by mirror neurons, which are the neurons in specific brain regions that fire either when a specific action is performed or when we see another person engaging in that action (Blair, 2005; Decety & Lamm, 2006). These three forms of empathy very often interact with each other. Thus, motor empathy may often trigger emotional empathy, and emotional empathy in turn requires at least some sense of cognitive empathy to understand how "the other" relates to the self (Losoya & Eisenberg, 2001).

Empathy seems to be closely linked to emotional regulation as well (Eisenberg, 2005; Eisenberg et al., 2006). If a child is overwhelmed by negative emotions triggered by another child's distress, that flood of emotions may lead the child to focus on his own feelings rather than on those of the other child. To recognize emotional states in others, children must be able to pull back and modulate their own emotions. Thus, children who are found to have higher levels of emotional regulation seem to feel more emotional and cognitive empathy for others. Across several studies that asked teachers and parents to rate elementary school students' emotional regulation skills, the children who were rated as having higher levels of emotional regulation were found to also be more likely to show feelings of empathy for others (Eisenberg, 2005).

Empathy is also influenced by the social context in which an individual is immersed (de Vignemont & Singer, 2006; Dovidio et al., 2006; Lanzetta & Englis, 1989). For example, in situations that promote cooperative efforts, people are prone to feel empathy toward others in their group. But in competitive situations, they may actually feel sadness at others' happiness and joy at others' misfortunes, a phenomenon that has been called *counterempathy* (Lanzetta & Englis, 1989). The classical notion of *schadenfreude*, or "pleasure from the misfortune of others," may well predominate in situations when the other person is construed as a rival. Developmentally, we can see how differences in children's cooperative and competitive tendencies could interact with aspects of the situation that promote either feelings of empathy or feelings of counterempathy. In some tasks, children show more joy in succeeding in a difficult task when another child does worse and more envy and antagonism in failing when another child does better. This version of *schadenfreude* is stronger in younger children (age 7) than in older children (age 13) and may be related to reduced sharing behavior in younger children (Steinbeis & Singer, 2013).

In summary, many factors related to temperament or personality can influence moral behavior, but they do not directly make a child behave morally or immorally. A child can be impulsive or emotionally volatile without showing a high incidence of immoral behaviors. Similarly, a child with great empathy for others may still not act on those feelings in prosocial ways especially in some competitive situations. Even when we examine the strongest links between a temperamental factor and a moral behavior, the influences of socialization and other environmental factors on behavior are potentially very large. We turn to those effects in the next section.

Social Influences on Moral Behavior

All children engage in inappropriate behaviors from time to time. Most children lie, cheat, or steal at least a few times during their childhood. Moreover, it seems that parents, peers, and society at large all influence children's tendencies to engage in antisocial and prosocial behaviors. In fact, the vast majority of research on moral development in children has asked how various social factors influence moral behavior. In this section, we will consider how such factors can influence both antisocial and prosocial behaviors; in essence, we will begin examining how children are socialized. In later chapters, we will more systematically consider how families (see Chapter 14) and the community at large (see Chapter 15) socialize children. Here we will focus specifically on the social influences on moral behaviors.

We would all like the next generation of children to be virtuous—to refrain from lying, cheating, stealing, and using physical and verbal aggression to intimidate and unfairly gain resources from others. Antisocial behaviors can be learned in several ways, and there are several ways to discourage such behaviors. Many of these types of social influences follow traditional theories of development.

A number of theories have set out to explain how social influences affect children's moral behavior. Learning theorists think in terms of positive and negative reinforcements, using rewards and punishment to change children's behavior (Gershoff, 2002; Parke, 2002; Parke & Asher, 1983; Parke & Walters, 1967). Another classic theory of socialization, which is known as modeling theory, argues that people will reproduce behaviors that they see others performing. Regarding the development of moral behavior, this theory argues that when children see adults acting in prosocial ways, they are likely to curb antisocial behavior and engage in prosocial behavior (Bandura, 1971; Bandura & Walters, 1963). Many contemporary approaches take a more cognitive perspective on these social influences, asking how parenting practices, among other influences, help to instill a conscience in the child. As we will see, these different approaches offer a set of tradeoffs, in which each approach partially explains how parents and society might help make a child behave more morally, but no single approach provides a comprehensive account.

Punishment and Learning Theories Learning theory accounts of moral development tended to focus on the effects that positive and negative reinforcements, delivered in various patterns, have on children's behavior. These theories tended to dominate the psychological literature

At What Age Should an Offender Be Treated as an Adult?

Several high-profile cases of prosecuting juveniles as adults have raised questions about the age at which children should be held morally responsible for their actions. No one would think that a 4-year-old who kills an older sibling with his parent's gun should be held as responsible as an adult, but what about an 11-year-old or a 14-year-old?

Consider the case of Nathaniel Abraham, who in 1997, at the age of 11, shot and killed a stranger with a .22 caliber rifle. Nathaniel, who was 13 at the time of his trial, was prosecuted in court as an adult. Many observers were shocked at the thought of a 13-year-old being treated as an adult, but the prosecutors insisted that Abraham was no ordinary 13-year-old (see Figure 12.17). At the time of the crime, he had a long history of problems with the police, many of them involving violence against others (Bradshaw, 1999). Convicted of second-degree murder, he avoided imprisonment in an adult facility only because the law grants judges the discretion of sentencing children younger than 14 to juvenile facilities.

FIGURE 12.17 Treating youthful offenders as adults. Nathaniel Abraham, shown here in court at age 13, was tried as an adult for murder. A recent surge of such trials in several countries raises profound questions about how scientific research on the moral development of children should be used to evaluate the appropriate age at which juveniles might be tried as adults.

How does research on the development of moral reasoning and moral behavior bear on the question of trying a 13-year-old killer as an adult? Despite the thousands of studies on moral development, the implications are unclear. Given the difficulties of demonstrating clear stages in the development of moral reasoning, it is not an easy matter to declare that children at a given age simply lack a certain level of moral reasoning. Moreover, even if it were possible to create a scale of moral maturity, it would be difficult to ensure that the courts applied it consistently to all offenders. We know that a fair number of adults show moral reasoning patterns that seem to be more common among children. Should those people, who are not necessarily mentally deficient, be held less responsible for their actions than other adults?

A second issue concerns whether the justice system should be more concerned with protecting the safety of others or with punishing wrongdoers. It would be possible to make the case that a child who has committed a violent crime is likely to commit other violent acts in the future, but this does not necessarily mean that the child should be punished as an adult. In fact, imprisoning the child with adult criminals, who may exert an even more antisocial influence on him, may increase (rather than diminish) the chance that he will commit future violent crimes when he is released from prison. Instead of putting the child in prison, another approach might be to find a way to monitor the child so as to minimize his risk to others without treating him like an adult offender in other respects.

At present, perhaps the most that developmental research can offer is evidence for the wide variety of ways in which moral reasoning and judgment develop. Even if there are no clear moral stages, the many documented developmental differences in such areas as emotional regulation, forms of empathy, and understanding of consequences all support arguments for treating children differently from adults in the criminal justice system (Whaley & Koenen, 2001). We all believe that young children differ from adults in their abilities to appreciate the consequences of their actions and to inhibit their impulses. Still, we need to better understand how these abilities emerge before developmental differences should be brought to bear on public policy decisions.

in the middle of the twentieth century and have become less prominent in recent decades. They examined the efficacy of punishment in instilling moral behavior in a child. Among their findings, learning theorists documented that it is not the severity of punishment alone that most clearly predicts internalization of moral values. Instead, many factors interact with the way the punishment is delivered. One of the strongest factors concerns the timing of the punishment.

Theories about the role of timing in delivering an effective punishment were inspired by pioneering studies of the effectiveness of punishment with dogs (Solomon, 1964; Solomon et al., 1968). Imagine an experiment in which a hungry beagle is led into a room that has two bowls of food: an attractive bowl of the tastiest, freshest dog food and a bowl of a clearly inferior dry product. An experimenter sits between the two bowls of food with a rolled-up newspaper (see Figure 12.18). Naturally, the beagle starts to approach the bowl of tastier food.

At this point, the situation breaks into two experimental conditions. In one condition, the beagle is punished with a swat of the newspaper as soon as he merely touches the fresher food with his nose. The dog is not punished for touching the inferior food, however, and eventually, he eats that food instead. In the second condition, the beagle is allowed to begin eating the preferred food before he is punished, and he is then restricted to eating the inferior food. If the dog is later led into the room that has both bowls of food, will he be more likely to continue to avoid the bowl with the tasty food and eat the dry food in the other bowl?

FIGURE 12.18 Early and late punishment. In a classic study with beagles, the experimenters either **(A)** punished the beagles immediately upon detecting their intent to eat a preferred food (early punishment), or **(B)** punished them as they were eating some of the desired food (late punishment). Although both groups of dogs learned to eat the inferior food in the immediate training task, the delay of punishment had a very different effect on later behavior. Adapted from Solomon et al. (1968).

It might seem that the punishment delivered after the dog began to eat would be more effective than a punishment delivered while the dog was merely initiating the action. In fact, punishment delivered early was much more effective. Beagles punished early continued to avoid the desired food, even when they were alone in the room with no experimenter present. They would enter the room, cast a seemingly forlorn look at the better food, and then unenthusiastically eat the inferior food. By contrast, beagles punished later would sneak over to the favored food and eat it rapidly and nervously, sometimes seeming to look apprehensively toward the door where the experimenter might appear. In short, punishing early seemed to cause a lasting avoidance of the superior food, whereas punishing late caused the dogs to be more furtive about eating the superior food.

> **Q:** How does timing of punishment seem to interact with the internalization of a desired behavior?

Because a beagle's intelligence obviously differs markedly from that of a child, the punishment-induced inhibition is not thought to involve a cognitively rich sense of guilt. Instead, it is assumed that with early punishment, the dog is conditioned to have a negative arousal so early in the action that he changes his behavior. By contrast, if the negative arousal is conditioned after starting the behavior, it occurs too late to inhibit the behavior. Instead, late punishment often results in behavior that is focused on avoiding getting caught.

You might think that children, with their more sophisticated levels of thought, might not show the same pattern of responses to the timing of punishments. Yet, in a series of studies modeled closely after the Solomon studies with dogs, early punishment was shown to be much more effective for children as well (Parke, 1969; Parke & Walters, 1967). In this study, kindergartners were taken to a classroom where there was an appealing toy (such as a bright red truck) and an unattractive "toy" (such as some small drab toy dishes). Children in the early punishment condition were scolded for approaching the attractive toy, whereas children in the late punishment condition were rebuked only after they began playing with it. The children were then left alone in the room with the toys while the experimenters watched them covertly. Like the beagles, the children punished early reluctantly trudged over to the unattractive toy and played with it while looking wistfully at the attractive toy. By contrast, the children punished late were much more likely to play with the attractive toy while watching the door anxiously in case an adult appeared.

Children, of course, are much more complex creatures than dogs, which is evident in the many other factors that interact with the timing of children's punishment to make it maximally effective. Social development researcher Ross Parke found that punishment is likely to be most effective if (1) it is delivered consistently, (2) it is delivered by a person whom the child likes and sees as warm and caring, and (3) it is accompanied by a reasoned explanation. These three guidelines may seem easy to implement in theory, but they can be surprisingly difficult to honor in reality. Most caregivers show at least some inconsistency in administering punishment or they sometimes fail to provide full explanations. For example, if a father is completely exhausted after a rough day at work and his 4-year-old daughter is making a fort in the yard with her bed linens, he may just sigh and let it happen rather than going to the trouble of scolding the child, explaining why the behavior is wrong, and then dealing with the resulting tears and sadness. He may know full well that it is important to be consistent and to explain precisely why the behavior is wrong and why punishment is occurring, but it is not always easy to follow through with that knowledge.

The greater effectiveness of warm and caring punishers may seem surprising, given the folklore about children behaving like angels around the cold, heartless schoolmaster. But Parke's findings suggest that such harsh taskmasters may only be effective in ensuring compliance when they are present. Such strictness may not prompt children to internalize the appropriate behavior so that they comply with it even when they are alone. This principle leads to an important point: punishment should be used sparingly. If it occurs too frequently, the child may no longer perceive the adult as warm and caring, which is what makes the adult so effective with the child.

Finally, in the real world, an adult cannot always be present when the child is just beginning an immoral action. But when punishment has to be administered long after a transgression, several cognitive techniques can be used to help the child bring to mind the misbehavior that occurred hours earlier. One intriguing technique involves "reliving" the act. For example, if a child put glue in a classmate's winter hat just before it was worn during recess, the parent cannot be there to impose punishment at the beginning of the action. But that evening, the parent can remind the child of what was happening at the time of the misbehavior, asking him to think through his earlier motivations and actions, and then administer the punishment. For example, a dialogue of the following sort might occur:

Parent: Johnny, do you remember when you snuck off to the coatroom today with that jar of glue from Ms. Stebbin's desk?
Child: Yes.

Parent: And do you remember how you thought it would be funny to put the glue in Susie's hat so that it would get all over her hair during recess?
Child: Yes.
Parent: Do you remember thinking how Susie would look and how everyone would laugh at her?
Child: Yes.
Parent: Well, it was very wrong to want to do that to Susie, and it was a terrible way to treat her. The glue was painful to get out and made her feel embarrassed. You should be ashamed of yourself [followed by more scolding and revocation of privileges].

In short, much is known about how to deliver effective punishments that can help children develop the internal ability to inhibit certain behaviors. The learning theorists' work on punishments may not lead to a better understanding of the nature of guilt and conscience, but it does provide an understanding of the cognitive repertoire that can be used in punishing the child, including both the explanations that should accompany punishments and the methods for helping the child "relive" an experience so as to make the punishment coincide with things the child thought and felt at the beginning of the misbehavior.

It is important to remember, however, that even when punishments are delivered in an ideal way, they can have negative side effects over time. Children may come to avoid the punishing adults, thus weakening emotional bonds with caregivers when they are most needed. Even worse, children may start to imitate the patterns of punishment themselves, using them aggressively and inappropriately on others. Certainly children who have experienced a great deal of excessive physical punishment are much more likely to be physically abusive as adults, both with their spouses and with their children. Indeed, one extensive **meta-analysis**—statistical analysis of the data from many studies—examined the relationship between physical punishment and several other variables (Gershoff, 2002). Despite repeated claims that physical punishment might have an important place in child rearing, the meta-analysis revealed no positive effect beyond an association with higher rates of immediate compliance. In all other respects, physical punishment was consistently related to negative outcomes, such as increased aggression against others and a weaker internalization of moral values. Table 12.5 shows these patterns of associations with physical punishment.

Q: What are some of the negative side effects of using physical punishment on children?

Not all studies paint a uniformly negative picture of physical punishment. For example, a light spanking,

TABLE 12.5 Associations between physical punishment and various measures in childhood and adulthood. Experiencing more physical punishment is associated with various kinds of effects during both childhood and adulthood. All of the associations are statistically significant, but they vary in degree. A small association means that physical punishment has a significant but modest correlation with a measure, whereas a large association means that the correlation is quite high. Adapted from Gershoff (2002).

Type of Effect	Size of Association
In childhood	
More immediate compliance	Large
Greater likelihood of suffering physical abuse	Medium to large
More antisocial behavior	Medium
Poorer mental health	Medium
More aggression	Small to medium
Less internalization of morals	Small
In adulthood	
More aggression	Medium
More antisocial behavior	Small to medium
Poorer mental health	Small
Greater likelihood of abusing one's child or spouse	Small

accompanied by both a reason and a genuine concern for the child's welfare, may not have worse effects than non-physical forms of punishment (Benjet & Kazdin, 2003; Larzelere & Kuhn, 2005). In addition, the negative effects of physical punishment may vary across cultures and even among subgroups within a culture (MacKenzie et al., 2011). The negative associations with physical punishment summarized in Table 12.5 tend to hold for European-American families in the United States, but physical punishment does not always show such undesirable associations in African-American families. Indeed, careful, appropriate physical punishment is more associated with positive outcomes than with negative outcomes in certain cultures (Lansford et al., 2004; Larzelere, 2000).

Examining punishment across a wider range of cultures, including those of China, India, Italy, Kenya, the Philippines, and Thailand, reveals quite substantial variations in the amount of physical punishment parents use (Lansford et al., 2005). For example, parents in Thailand are much less likely to use physical punishment than parents in Kenya. Moreover, in cultures where physical punishment is common, it is not nearly as strongly related to childhood behavior problems as it is in cultures where physical punishment is less common (Lansford et al., 2005).

Even in relatively similar cultures, there are substantial variations in the acceptability of physical punishment. For example, its acceptability varies quite dramatically within the countries of the European Union, and in general it is considered less acceptable in countries whose govern-

ments have made prominent efforts to raise public awareness of the effects of physical abuse on children (Gracia & Herrero, 2008). Socioeconomic strain and the lack of social support structures can also cause very substantial variations in the prevalence of physical punishment within a culture (MacKenzie et al., 2011). For example, in the state of Kentucky, physical punishment in the school is more prevalent in counties that have higher incidences of families living in poverty and lower incidences of involvement in community groups such as churches (McClure & May, 2008). In addition, males, single parents, and those associated with some fundamentalist religions are more likely to use physical punishment (Xu et al., 2000). These patterns of variation make it clear that social policies designed to ameliorate the negative effects of physical punishment must be very sensitive to the social contexts in which it occurs.

Modeling Theory and Moral Behaviors We have so far largely focused on the punishment of antisocial behaviors. It is more difficult and rare to punish a child for not being especially altruistic. There is, however, another form of social influence on morality that seems to apply equally to both antisocial and prosocial behaviors. Known as **modeling theory** (or **social learning theory**), it relies on the likelihood that people tend to reproduce behaviors that they see others performing (Bandura, 1971).

Hundreds of studies have shown that both children and adults become more likely to perform a wide variety of antisocial behaviors after seeing someone else engaging in the behavior. In the most famous studies of this phenomenon, conducted by Albert Bandura and his associates, children observed an adult being physically aggressive toward an inflatable toy called a Bobo doll (Bandura et al., 1961). The adult modeled a series of aggressive acts toward the Bobo doll, including hitting, kicking, and sitting on it (see Figure 12.19). After the children patiently watched this rather strange adult behavior, they were left alone with the Bobo doll and were covertly observed by the experimenter to see what they would do. As Figure 12.19 shows, the children often copied the adult's violent behavior with frightening intensity and specificity.

Of course, the Bobo doll study presents children with a bizarre experimental setting in which they may have thought they were taking part in a game rather than really being aggressive. But an extensive series of follow-up studies by both Bandura and others suggests that in real-life situations, too, seeing others modeling aggressive and antisocial behaviors can increase the prevalence of similar behaviors in those who observe the aggressive behaviors (Bandura, 1971; Bandura & Walters, 1963). Moreover, because the behavior that is imitated is often highly specific, it is difficult to explain the modeling effect as simply a general loosening of inhibitions. Even without any reinforcement, children become more likely to steal, cheat, lie, hit, or tease after observing models doing so.

At one level, modeling theory seems to offer a full account of how both antisocial and prosocial behaviors emerge, suggesting that children will reproduce either type of behavior after seeing it modeled by others. Moreover, Bandura and his colleagues have shown numerous ways in which modeling can be made more effective. A child is more likely to copy the model's behavior if she likes and respects the model, if the actions are clear and salient, and if the model frequently performs actions that are easy to imitate. Anyone who masters the research on modeling can use that knowledge to change children's behavior. Yet, at the same time, modeling theory has little to say about why children copy models. Instead, it often focuses on the variables that make children more likely to imitate them. To explain why children copy some people's actions and not the actions of others, however, requires a broader theory of identification, respect, and affiliation with others. To explain why children find some actions more salient than others requires an account of how children perceive and encode social actions. The modeling approach has provided a framework, but there is still a need for more comprehensive theories in each of these areas.

In the realm of prosocial behavior, we have seen that young children often engage in actions that suggest an intent to benefit others rather than themselves. We have also seen that children and adults vary a great deal in the extent to which they act prosocially. Many researchers have turned to modeling theory to explain these individual differences, in part because it offers a clear explanation of how caregivers might encourage prosocial behavior. If you have a warm relationship with your child, and your child respects and identifies with you, then the stage is set for effective modeling. When the child sees you engage in a prosocial behavior that she can easily understand and reproduce, she will more likely reproduce the behavior. This pattern of influence has been supported both in studies in which adults and children who

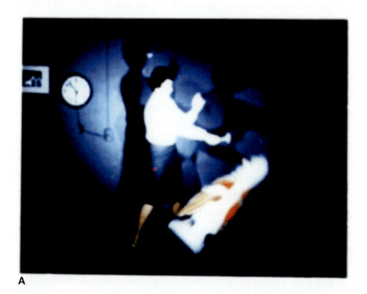

A

B

FIGURE 12.19 Modeling aggressive behavior. Children have repeatedly been shown to reproduce quite specific behaviors modeled by adults, whether it is the somewhat bizarre act of physically assaulting a Bobo doll or the verbal assault of younger, more helpless individuals. From Bandura (1971).

act altruistically are interviewed later and in experimental studies examining the effects of prosocial modeling on children (Eisenberg & Fabes, 1998; Hoffman, 1977).

Q: What form of socialization seems to be most natural for prosocial behavior?

Parent-Child Interactions and the Development of Conscience Although it might seem that more cognitive views of how parenting instills a sense of morality are quite recent, the earliest version of this approach was proposed by Sigmund Freud (1923/1960). Like much of Freud's work, this theory was based on Freud's idea that the mind is composed of three parts: the id, the ego, and superego. The **id** appears first in development and represents basic desires and drives. The **ego** appears next and enables the child to channel and direct the id. Finally, the **superego** appears last, when true morality is thought to emerge. According to Freud, younger children are unable to be truly moral because they are governed solely by the id, which responds only to impulses and lacks any moderation or controls that make it possible to delay gratification. Only later, in toddlerhood, does the ego start to emerge as the regulator of the id's instinctual passions. But the ego merely keeps these passions in check until they can be satisfied. It has no sense of right or wrong. Only the superego, which is not fully formed until around age 6, is capable of providing an internal moral sense. Freud believed that before the superego develops, only external controls, such as punishments and reinforcements from parents, can guide a child toward moral behavior.

Freud's theory of moral development is marred by many problems. It emphasizes the growth of the superego out of Oedipal and Electra conflicts, in which children subconsciously resent their same-sex parent out of jealousy for the other parent's affection. Freud's ideas about these conflicts led him to make a variety of predictions, including the erroneous claim that women are less "moral" than men because the resolution of the Oedipal conflict by boys more strongly promotes the development of the superego than does the resolution of the Electra conflict by girls. Moreover, Freud's claim that guilt and conscience do not develop until age 6 is suspect, given reports that children as young as 2 or 3 clearly show guilt and remorse (Hoffman, 1982). And his more detailed predictions about the effects of various parental styles and dispositions on children's emerging superegos also fail to hold true (Hoffman, 1970). Let us therefore consider more contemporary approaches to how parents and other caregivers might socialize children to have a moral sense.

Parents do not merely "instill" their values in the child. Rather, the child also plays a role in his or her own moral development. Just as older views of cognitive and perceptual development saw the child as an empty vessel or a blank slate that passively receives knowledge, so do many views of moral socialization see the parents and society as providing the child with the right sorts of values. Yet, there is every reason to think that such a passive model of the child works no better for morality than it does for cognitive and perceptual development in general. Indeed, it is important for caregivers and developmental researchers alike to be sensitive to the ways in which children actively construct their own moral sense and behaviors, and not always by simply imitating those of adults (Grusec & Goodnow, 1994). As parents, especially, we must recognize that our children will not always reason morally as we do, nor will they always come to precisely the same conclusions that we do. But we can hope that they will become moral individuals in a rich, deep, and self-constructed sense. Moreover, different children take very different pathways to achieving a conscience, and the same style of parenting that is effective with one child may be ineffective with another (Kochanska, 1997).

The development of conscience is often linked to the emergence of feelings of shame and guilt (see Figure 12.20). These feelings often motivate people to act on their conscience. Young children show intriguing individual differences in their tendencies to react to problems with either shame or guilt. In one study, children between 2 and 3 years old were allowed to play with toys belonging to the experimenter, and during the play session, they were led to believe that they had broken a toy (Barrett et al., 1993). The children were classified according to their reactions to the broken toy. The "avoiders," who seemed motivated by shame, avoided the experimenter when she returned to the room. They also did not tell the experimenter of the mishap and were very slow to try to fix the situation. The "amenders," who seemed motivated by guilt, did not avoid the experimenter and were quick to tell her that the toy was broken and to try to repair it themselves. Clearly, children with these different styles might respond very differently in similar real-life situations.

Shame orientations generally seem to have more adverse psychological correlates, such as higher rates of depression, in older children and adults (Kim et al., 2011; Tangney et al., 2007). Shame is considered more painful because it negatively impacts the self more directly, creating feelings of being helpless and worthless as well as exposing a person's flaws. In contrast, guilt is thought to focus a person's thoughts and feelings on a specific behavior rather than on the core sense of self and is generally less painful and devastating to a person. The early emergence of individual differences in the tendency to experience shame versus guilt raises important questions about the extent to which parents might be able to gently guide the child more toward a guilt orientation, and indeed, there are suggestions that different

FIGURE 12.20 Guilt versus shame. (A) Children who are motivated by guilt often focus on a particular behavior rather than on core feelings about themselves, whereas **(B)** children who feel shame often feel helpless and worthless.

parental interaction styles might lead to different self-conscious moral emotions (Lagattuta & Thompson, 2007).

Parents can also influence how sensitive their children are to different aspects of moral behaviors and their consequences. One study examined these effects by asking mothers of 4-year-olds to talk about their child's good and bad actions in the prior week. The researchers then analyzed the mother's comments to determine how often she referred to the child's feelings and intentions, rules, or the consequences of the child's actions. The extent to which the mother made comments focusing on such themes predicted the child's conscience development, which was measured in terms of compliance and internalization of certain values (Laible & Thompson, 2000). In other words, the way a mother talks about her child's actions, both to the child and to others, may affect the way the child thinks about moral issues and acts on them (Grusec et al., 2000). More generally, parents who adopt a noncoercive, highly interactive, and sensitive parenting style that is infused with positive emotions and that uses very gentle discipline strategies tend to foster an earlier development of conscience in their children (Kochanska & Aksan, 2006).

Developmental psychologists have learned a great deal about how patterns of child rearing and socialization can affect a child's moral development (Bugental & Goodnow, 1998; Eisenberg, 2000; Kochanska & Aksan, 2006; Shweder et al., 1997). Much of that research is also closely connected to the broader issues of socialization discussed in Chapters 14 and 15, concerning how the child becomes part of a family and society. Throughout these discussions, one important caution to keep in mind is that correlations between parenting styles and children's behaviors are just that, correlations. Explaining these patterns requires a careful investigation of whether shared genetic factors, similar environments, and the children's effects on their parents may

also contribute to the correlation—instead of, or in addition to, parents' effects on their children. We will return to these issues in more detail in Chapters 13 through 16.

Conclusions

Morality is a complex, multifaceted aspect of being human. We reason in moral ways that are distinct from reasoning about such things as social conventions and physical laws, and these distinctive ways of reasoning seem to appear quite early in development. Within the realm of morality itself, there are further differences. When we are quite young, we can empathize with others in need, and yet that empathy relates only indirectly to altruistic reasoning and to prosocial actions. Similarly, aggressive feelings are related to antisocial reasoning and behaviors, but they are not the same thing. We can have hostile and aggressive feelings but not necessarily act on them. Moreover, the reasoning associated with such feelings may change over development with the emergence of more sophisticated ways of understanding situations and other agents. We can reason about many moral domains, including sharing resources, fairness and justice, and care, in ways that show their own developmental trajectories and that can be relatively compartmentalized (Killen, 2007). Finally, all kinds of moral reasoning are linked in subtle and complex ways to behavior, although there is no easy, straightforward way of translating moral beliefs into actions.

Despite this pluralism and the rapid state of change in research on moral development, some general themes in this area do emerge and reflect themes we have discussed in earlier chapters. First, the idea that the child as an active constructor of morality rather than a passive recipient is intrinsic to Kohlberg's approach and to many other theories of moral reasoning, such as Gilligan's, Damon's, and Eisenberg's. It is less intrinsic to many older theories of socialization and to current political arguments about instilling moral values in children. But most current, sophisticated views of socialization do seem to recognize that the child is an active participant in the socialization process.

A second familiar theme is that patterns of moral reasoning and behavior show less dramatic developmental shifts than were formerly assumed to be the case, and many aspects of moral development are significantly influenced by situational factors. Of course, in some situations, older children tend to use more complex patterns of moral reasoning than do young children, but even younger children can grasp these patterns when they are carefully simplified and made relevant to them.

On a related note, cross-cultural research suggests that there may not be universals of moral reasoning in the sense of everyone everywhere evaluating certain kinds of moral dilemmas in the same way. At the same time, however, cultures do not differ so dramatically that we cannot find common ground with other groups. There may be a universal collection of moral reasoning systems, and cultures may emphasize (or downplay) different moral components, depending on which situations and social structures are most pervasive in those cultures.

Finally, as we look back to the two views of morality introduced at the beginning of this chapter, it is now clear that young children are not amoral in the manner we assume holds for most animals. Within their first 2 years, children show compassion, selfishness, and a range of other behaviors indicating an early moral sense. It is also clear that young children are neither primarily moral nor immoral. At all ages, children show both prosocial and antisocial behaviors. Children share with adults a tension between good and bad impulses.

STUDY AND REVIEW

SUMMARY

The Development of Moral Thought

- One classical view of how children come to be moral beings sees the young child as having an inherently moral nature, sometimes of good, sometimes of evil. A different view sees the young child as essentially amoral and too immature to be considered capable of either moral judgment or culpability for actions.

- Evolutionary psychology and cultural psychology have each offered more recent views of the origins of moral thought. The evolutionary perspective emphasizes moral universals that are part of humans' biological heritage, and cultural psychology focuses on the influence of culture on moral values.

- Although moral thought and moral action are intimately related, it is clear that they are not the same thing and that one does not always predict the other. For that reason, it has been most natural as a research strategy to focus on either moral judgment in its own right or on factors that influence the emergence of moral and immoral behaviors.

- Piaget formulated his theory of the development of moral thought based on observations of how children come to understand game rules. He proposed a series of three stages of moral reasoning (premoral, heteronomous, and autonomous stages) based on the child's developing concepts of rules, of culpability, and of appropriate justice.

- As with much of cognitive development, a closer look at the evidence for stage theories has revealed serious problems. Rather than an early inability to engage in certain kinds of moral thought, developmental differences in moral reasoning seem more related to a wide variety of variables not directly linked to morality, such as social conventions and an inability to remember an entire sequence of events. In addition, Piaget's attempts to draw inferences about moral judgment from studying children's conceptions of game rules are problematic because children's understanding of social conventions develops quite differently from their understanding of morality.

- Lawrence Kohlberg's work largely superseded Piaget's theory. Kohlberg advocated a theory of moral development with six numbered stages divided into three levels (preconventional, conventional, and postconventional). He used moral dilemmas to uncover forms of moral reasoning that he believed revealed children's beliefs about what morality really is. As later researchers more extensively probed Kohlberg's stages, however, it became clear that they do not represent an invariant sequence across cultures and genders.

- Carol Gilligan proposed three stages of moral development (preconventional, conventional, and postconventional) that emphasize care, concern, and empathy. According to Gilligan, females progress through the stages more quickly than males. Later research did not consistently find a gender difference, however, in moral reasoning.
- Findings showing that the same individual can use several distinct forms of moral reasoning, depending on the situation, gave rise to a pluralistic view of moral thought. In this view, children and adults have several systems of moral interpretation available to them. Different kinds of interpretations predominate among different people and groups, but all interpretations are potentially available to most groups, given the right context. Moral development looks less like a progression through stages of moral reasoning and more like shifts in terms of what forms of reasoning are used in specific situations. Younger children have trouble understanding some complex moral situations, but these difficulties may be largely due to the complexity of the description rather than differences in moral reasoning ability.

The Development of Moral Behavior

- A different research tradition has focused more on the development of moral behavior itself. Adults and children may not be morally consistent across situations. A moral offender in one situation may be a moral upholder in another. It is not at all easy to reliably predict moral behaviors from moral reasoning patterns. People of any age may know what is right, but still fail to do it.
- Antisocial behavior does not show obvious developmental trends, and there is no evidence that people cheat, steal, or lie less as they age. Nonetheless, the particular forms of the antisocial behaviors may change with age as the person becomes more sophisticated. Prosocial behavior does seem to become more common with age, although even very young children can show some forms of altruism, such as instrumental helping. There are, however, powerful individual differences among children (and adults) in the incidence of moral behavior. Scholars have attempted to explain these differences both in terms of underlying differences in temperament and personality and in terms of social influences.
- Temperamental and personality differences in moral behavior have focused not on morality itself but on psychological components that can influence immoral behavior. Problems with impulse control, difficulties delaying gratification, deficits in the ability to feel empathy, and low levels of arousal have all been associated with the development of antisocial behaviors. Some behavior problems have significant heritabilities, so there is some reason to believe that psychological components may have some biological basis related to genetic variation. Children who show very early behavioral problems in preschool are also statistically more likely to have more serious

behavioral problems later in life, which some have argued supports the notion that these behaviors have a genetic basis.

- Correlations between early behavioral problems and later ones may also be caused by a constant adverse environment or manner of parenting. Albert Bandura's research into modeling theory showed that children will reproduce quite closely the actions of models like parents and other older individuals around them, including antisocial and immoral behaviors.
- Some forms of punishment can cause long-term changes in behavior, but the timing of the punishment is extremely important, as is making sure the child understands the rationale for the punishment. Other forms of punishment can be ineffective or cause negative side effects in many situations, as in the case of physical punishment.
- Children may develop moral consciences that are either driven largely by guilt or shame. Children who feel guilt are more likely to try to repair a wrong in the presence of an adult than those who feel shame.
- It still remains to be seen whether differences in parenting styles cause differences in children's morality or whether, for example, the similar genotypes and/or environments that parents and children share are the true causes of any links between parents' and children's behaviors.

THOUGHT QUESTIONS

1. Adults will often rationalize a moral transgression after the fact in an attempt to justify it or reduce its perceived severity. Discuss how the ability to engage in such rationalizations might develop in childhood. Would it be possible for some form of rationalization to be present even in preschoolers? How might early emerging rationalizations differ from later ones?

2. Under what circumstances, if any, do you think it is acceptable to use physical punishment with a 7-year-old child? How do you justify that choice in terms of the research literature?

3. Under what circumstances might rapid emotionally driven moral judgments result in more ethical decisions than slow, deliberative, and more cognitively based ones? Are there useful rules of thumb that emerge from your analysis? Are there developmental implications?

4. Some politicians have suggested that having children read stories about historical figures who show great moral character will lead to more moral children. Consider the feasibility of such an approach and how it might have unanticipated consequences.

KEY TERMS

altruism (p. 443)	cognitive empathy (p. 455)
antisocial behavior (p. 448)	collectivist culture (p. 441)
autonomous stage (p. 434)	conduct disorder (p. 454)

constructivist approach (p. 442)

cultural psychology (p. 429)

delay of gratification (p. 453)

ego (p. 462)

emotional empathy (p. 455)

evolutionary psychology (p. 429)

heteronomous stage (p. 432)

id (p. 462)

immanent justice (p. 434)

impersonal moral situation (p. 446)

individualist culture (p. 441)

information integration theory (p. 436)

instrumental helping (p. 451)

meta-analysis (p. 459)

modeling theory (p. 460)

moral dilemma (p. 437)

moral dumbfounding (p. 446)

moral modules (p. 444)

motor empathy (p. 455)

personal moral situation (p. 446)

prosocial behavior (p. 448)

resilience (p. 453)

self-regulation (p. 452)

social aggression (p. 454)

social convention (p. 435)

social intuitionist model (p. 446)

social learning theory (p. 460)

superego (p. 462)

13

Knowing Ourselves, Knowing Others

Self-Concepts and Self-Representations
- Senses of Self
- The Mirror Test and Self-Concept
- Gender Identity

Developing a Sense of Self-Worth
- Self-Esteem
- Self-Efficacy

Self-Regulation
- Brain Maturation and the Development of Self-Regulation

- Contextual Influences on Self-Regulation

Developing a Theory of Mind
- Early Aspects of Theory of Mind
- Comparative Perspectives on Theory of Mind
- Understanding False Beliefs
- A Theory of Mind Module?
- Beyond False Beliefs

Making Attributions about Ourselves and Others
- Emerging Explanations of Behavior

- Traits and Optimism
- Attribution, Motivation, and Creativity

Conclusions

Summary

When you come across your baby pictures or watch a video from your childhood, what kind of connection do you feel to the person in the pictures? If you have no memory of these particular early experiences, the images can evoke a sense of great distance from your younger self, along with some feeling of being less connected to that self. But when you see a recent photo of yourself or encounter your reflection, you almost always recognize and identify with this self-image automatically.

Many years ago, as we were looking through an old album, our 3-year-old became fascinated with a series of pictures showing him riding a pony in Yosemite National Park. Before we had even mentioned the pictures, he pointed to them and excitedly said, "That's me! That's me!" Somehow, either from contextual cues or from the resemblance between the child in the photograph and himself, he recognized that the photo showed him and not another child. This seemingly simple act requires not just having a sense of self, but also being able to use certain cues to recognize our own image. These abilities are just the beginning of a much richer awareness of the self, along with the ability to think about our own mind and the minds of others and an understanding of how people's beliefs and traits are linked to behaviors.

A great deal of complex development occurs as children come to understand themselves as well as the minds and emotions of others. In this chapter, we will consider how children gain this social understanding of themselves and others and how this understanding relates to motivation and actions. Chapter 14 considers how children, as socially aware individuals, become parts of families. Chapter 15 broadens the discussion further to explain how children take part in ever larger social communities, from their peer group to their whole culture.

We will begin this chapter by focusing on how children develop concepts and representations of themselves. We will see that there is no single sense of the self. Rather, there are several different senses that emerge at different times to eventually create a more integrated mature sense of self in middle childhood. Then we will turn to the classic "mirror test," in which the child recognizes that he is the person in the mirror, and we will ask how this ability to recognize himself in a mirror relates to the various senses of self and their developmental courses. From there we will consider how children value and regulate themselves and their behaviors. Next we will see that the relation between self-esteem and various developmental outcomes is more complex than some popular accounts might suggest. We then consider the relation between self-esteem and self-efficacy—namely, the sense of having an influence on the world. While revisiting the topic of self-regulation, we will address broader questions regarding senses of self and self-awareness.

We build on these ideas to discuss how children develop an understanding of the minds of others and how they come to have insight and control with respect to their own mental and emotional states. People in all cultures think not only about their own minds but also about other people's minds. This ability to think about other people's beliefs and desires and how those beliefs and desires predict and explain behavior is referred to as **theory of mind**. It is critical to mature social interactions. We have seen in Chapters 5 and 6 that even infants are aware of social entities as being distinct from nonsocial ones, and by 18 months of age, these children are clearly able to make inferences about a person's behavior in terms of his or her goals. But these social skills, impressive as they might be, are only a small part of what comes to be a full-fledged theory of mind. Lastly, we will consider how this understanding of the mind unfolds in childhood, becoming ever more important in social interactions, and how individuals make attributions about themselves and others. The first place to start, however, concerns thoughts about the self.

Self-Concepts and Self-Representations

The developmental psychology of the self has several components, including the different ways of thinking about and being aware of who we are. It also involves an understanding of the ways in which external devices, such as mirrors, videos, or photographs, can represent us. Finally, it involves the linkage of larger sociocultural roles, such as being a boy or a girl, with knowledge of our own sex.

Senses of Self

One way to understand the development of the child's ability to think about minds and behavior is to look first at how the child develops a **sense of self**—the various ways an individual thinks about himself and has distinct kinds of self-awareness. It is tempting to think that the development of a sense of self is a single psychological event—something like consciously thinking, "I am different from others in a special way." Looking more closely, however, it is apparent that people sense the self in several ways that have their own developmental pathways, rather than forming one monolithic sense of self.

Neisser's Five Senses of Self The idea that people have several senses of self has been around for some time. In 1890, the great American psychologist and philosopher William James described four senses of self: the physical self, the mental self, the spiritual self, and the ego (Gallagher, 2000; James, 1890/1950). One of the many researchers who have elaborated on this view is the psychologist Ulric Neisser. His perspective touches on many of the developmental studies we have examined in earlier chapters. Neisser argued for five senses of self: *ecological, interpersonal, extended, private*, and *conceptual* (Neisser, 1988; Neisser & Fivush, 1994).

These different senses of self emerge at different points in development, but it is important to realize that the sense of self continues to develop over the years. Thus, earlier senses of self are not simply serving as building blocks for later ones, as we have seen in many stage theories. Rather, all the different senses of self coexist in adults. We will consider each of Neisser's five senses of self in a bit more detail.

The **ecological self** is our sense of where we are as we move through the world (see Figure 13.1). Humans and many other species have this perceptual and motor sense of self. The ecological self utilizes what our senses perceive, calculating and responding to where we are relative to objects in the external world. It is automatic, immediate, and nonverbal. To use a term coined by the psychologist James J. Gibson, it is also "directly perceived," meaning that the newborn has an ecological sense of self instantly, from the first moment that she perceives the world. This sense of self is evident when, for example, an infant flinches at the approach of a looming object, clearly showing a sense of the self being threatened as the object approaches on a collision course (Ball & Tronick, 1971; Schmuckler & Li, 1998; see Chapter 3). The ecological self becomes more sophisticated as the child's motor and perceptual skills develop.

The **interpersonal self** is the sense of interacting with other intentional agents. It arises automatically and without reflection. This inherently social sense of self includes a sensitivity to the reciprocal nature and the timing parameters of social interactions. It is roughly the immediate sense of

FIGURE 13.2 The interpersonal self. When interacting with other social agents, even infants appear to have a sense of the interpersonal self.

"I" and "you" that arises when we first encounter and interact with another. Humans share this sense of self with many other social species and it does not, in its early forms, require the ability to think about how another person's beliefs and desires explain that person's actions. It, too, may have its earliest origins shortly after birth (see Figure 13.2). We saw evidence for an early emergence of the interpersonal self in Chapter 6. Infants under 2 months of age become distressed when their mothers do not interact in a manner that fits the natural timing of back-and-forth social interactions (Adamson & Frick, 2003; Bertin & Striano, 2006; Cohn & Tronick, 1988, 1989; Field, 1977; Gunning et al., 2013; Nadel et al., 1999; Tronick, 1989; Murray & Trevarthen, 1985).

The **extended self** is our sense of ourselves as progressing along an autobiographical timeline. We think of ourselves as linked to the past (through memories) and to the future (through beliefs about what will likely happen next). As we saw in Chapter 10, the development of this sense of self in the preschool years may be an important factor in explaining the point at which infantile amnesia ends (Fivush & Schwarzmueller, 1998; Nelson & Fivush, 2004).

The **private self** is our sense that we have certain privileged experiences that no one else has access to unless we choose to communicate those experiences to others. The private self includes our dreams, the unique perspectives and background knowledge that we bring to any situation, and our unique knowledge of how it feels to move our body in a certain way (see Figure 13.3). These different aspects of the private self may not all develop at the same time, but they typically emerge in the later preschool years. The emerging private self may be seen when preschool children start to appreciate that their own point of view may differ from those of others. We have seen evidence of the development of this sense of self in circumstances where children do not show

FIGURE 13.1 The ecological self. When a child is moving through her environment, such as traveling down a train track as the world flows by, she experiences a sense of self-presence and movement in the environment.

FIGURE 13.3 The private self. At some point during the late preschool years, children start to understand that dreams are part of the private self.

egocentrism, including the development of narrative skills (see Chapter 8) and their understanding of spatial relations (see Chapter 9). We will see later in this chapter that children's developing understanding of mental lives can include a sense that different people will have different mental states and privileged experiences.

The **conceptual self** includes our sense of the roles that we occupy in broader social and cultural contexts. It can include notions of gender roles, family roles (as a child or parent or sibling), tribal or ethnic or national roles, or roles as a person in contrast to other living creatures. This may be the most sophisticated sense of self and the one most influenced by other people and the surrounding culture. In short, the conceptual self includes the various ways in which high-level cognition helps articulate who we are relative to others. In Chapter 14 and especially Chapter 15, we will see several ways in which children begin learning these roles in the preschool years and continue through elementary school, adolescence, and young adulthood.

Neisser's five senses of self, summarized in Table 13.1, represent some of the different facets of the self that have been uncovered by the large and diverse body of research on perceptual and cognitive development. The same developmental phenomena potentially could be more finely divided into six senses or collapsed into four, and whether these particular senses of self are precisely the right ones will continue to spur investigations for many years to come. (For alternative models, see Damon & Hart, 1988; Harter, 1998.) The key point is that the sense of self is not based on a single insight that children have at some point in development, nor is it acquired by gradually developing one kind of understanding. Rather, there are qualitatively different senses of self. Each one follows its own developmental journey, even as it interacts with other senses of self and contributes to an even higher-order self-concept.

Sense of Self	Time of Emergence	Characteristics
Ecological self	Birth onward	Sense of where we are as we move through the world Perceptual and motor awareness Automatic, immediate, nonverbal
Interpersonal self	Shortly after birth onward	Interacting with other intentional agents Automatic, without reflection Inherently social
Extended self	Age 4 onward	Autobiographical timeline Understanding that we are linked to the past and having the ability to think about the future
Private self	Age 4 onward	Understanding that we have privileged experiences no one else has Knowledge, dreams, perspectives
Conceptual self	Age 4–5 onward, with major growth in middle childhood and beyond	Most influenced by others and by ambient culture Social roles (gender roles, family roles) Able to articulate who we are relative to others

TABLE 13.1 Neisser's five senses of the self. Neisser (1988) argued that there are five distinct senses of the self rather than a single unitary concept.

The Mirror Test and Self-Concept

One of the most studied aspects of the sense of self concerns our ability to recognize ourselves in a mirror. Experimenters have tested this self-recognition ability in young children and various animals using a technique called the **mirror test**. This method involves putting an artificial mark on the subject and testing whether, when faced with a mirror, the subject realizes that the mark seen in the mirror is actually on the self and not on another individual (Gallup, 1970). When this test was first used with chimpanzees, a bright red mark was placed on a chimp's forehead when it was under anesthesia. The chimp was put in front of a mirror, and when it awoke, researchers observed whether the animal's behavior suggested awareness that the mark it saw in the mirror was on its own head.

Data from the mirror test have been vigorously debated, but those debates tend to converge on some common conclusions (Anderson, 1984; Heyes, 1998). Even though many animals can be taught to use mirrors to find hidden objects, only humans, some of the great apes (chimpanzees, bonobos, orangutans, and possibly gorillas; see Figure 13.4A), elephants, and bottle-nosed dolphins have passed the mirror test (Boyson & Himes, 1999; Plotnik et al., 2010). In one study, bottle-nosed dolphins that had already become accustomed to mirrors on one side of their tank clearly passed the mirror test (see Figure 13.4B). The researchers used a waterproof marker to make a visible mark on the heads of some of the dolphins, and as a control, they used invisible ink to make the same mark on the other dolphins. Those with the visible marks spent much more time in front of the mirrors examining themselves than the dolphins whose marks were invisible. They also seemed intent on turning and positioning themselves in front of the mirror to get the best views (Reiss, 2011; Reiss & Marino, 2001).

Most children first pass the mirror test at around 18 months (see Figure 13.4C), but some children do not pass it until age 2 (Anderson, 1984; Lewis & Brooks-Gunn, 1979; Lewis et al., 1985). Before that time, they do not touch the mark on their own foreheads when they see it in a mirror, although they might touch the odd-looking mark on the "other child" in the mirror. Given that so few species pass the mirror test and that most of those species are either closely related to humans or otherwise thought to have high-level cognitive capacities, it is perhaps not surprising that creatures who pass the test have been credited with a sophisticated **self-concept**—namely, a conscious sense of the self as an independent agent in the world. In addition, some researchers have argued that the psychological processes that enable creatures to pass the mirror test are the same processes that enable a creature to have empathy for others (Gallup, 1998).

Variations on the Mirror Test It is difficult to say whether passing the mirror test reflects a full self-concept. Instead, it may tap into a child's more specialized ability to notice that a visual image moves in perfect synchrony with his own body and that the synchronized image corresponds to himself. With this kind of sensitivity, which has been called a **kinesthetic self-concept**, the child senses

A   B   C

FIGURE 13.4 The mirror test. In the mirror test, a visible mark is put on a participant's face and is only visible in a mirror. When the participant sees the mark in the mirror, the critical question is whether he will touch the mark on the mirror or the mark on his own body. The relative rarity of this behavior across species has led some to argue that it is evidence for a true concept of self as well as the ability to put oneself in others' shoes empathically (Gallup, 1998). But it may be that the ability to pass the mirror test is only one part of the full self-concept. Pictured here are mirror tests with **(A)** a chimpanzee, **(B)** a bottle-nosed dolphin, and **(C)** an 18-month-old human infant.

a link between himself and the synchronous display without a deeper understanding that the display *shows an image of himself* (Mitchell, 2002). The kinesthetic self-concept resembles Neisser's ecological self, concerned with perceptual and motor awareness (Neisser, 1993).

Studies that substituted a video display for the mirror have supported this more conservative speculation on what it means to pass the mirror test. The video display was either synchronous with what the child was doing or there was a delay—sometimes as brief as 2 seconds—between what the child was doing and what she saw in the video. When the display was synchronous, the children would sometimes notice the dot in the video and then touch their own foreheads. But when the video was even slightly delayed, they did not touch their foreheads (Povinelli & Simon, 1998). They noticed the "other" child and sometimes called it by their own name, but they did not seem to recognize it as their own image. Not until they were almost 4 years old did children respond to the dot in the delayed displays by examining the same spot on their own bodies.

Based on these results, some have argued that the extended sense of self must emerge toward the end of the third year, allowing children to pass the delayed mirror test, and that passing the test in the synchronous condition shows only the earlier, kinesthetic sense of self. Interestingly, no other animals are known to pass the delayed mirror test (Povinelli, 1998). Children who are 2 and 3 years old also fail the test much more often with the simultaneous video than with mirrors (Suddendorf et al., 2007). This "video deficit" remains even when the video image is life-size and reversed, just as it would be in a mirror. For those reasons, the video studies cannot offer conclusive evidence that toddlers who pass the mirror test are relying on synchronicity alone.

Quite a few young children and many monkeys do seem to have some sense that mirror images of themselves are special, even though they may not know that the image is actually of themselves. Thus, infants as young as 4 months old behave differently in front of mirror images of themselves than in front of images of others mimicking them (Rochat & Striano, 2002). Similarly, capuchin monkeys behave differently in front of mirror reflections than in front of images of other monkeys (de Waal et al., 2005). Although neither the young infants nor the monkeys could pass the mirror test with the mark, they do have some rudimentary sense that self-images are different.

Researchers have also found that passing the mirror test does not simply require the child to be able to recognize an anomaly on his face, a plausible possibility given the special salience of faces. In a variation on the mirror test, researchers covertly put a sticker on a toddler's leg where the child could not directly see it. When the child was then put into a high chair in front of a mirror so he could see his legs reflected, he would reach for the sticker on his own body.

The toddlers touched the leg stickers at the same age that they touched stickers on their faces.

This line of research also showed that toddlers rapidly update their self-representations. When a new pair of pants was attached to the high chair, such that the child could be slipped into them unknowingly, the child would not reach for the sticker when seeing his legs in the mirror (Nielsen et al., 2006). In contrast, if the toddlers could see the new pants as they were put into the high chair, they would touch the sticker on their leg after seeing it in the mirror. Apparently, when they did not realize they had on new pants, they thought that the legs might belong to another child; but with a brief cue that new pants were on their own legs, they passed the mirror test. Thus, when toddlers can pass the mirror test, they can do so for all parts of their bodies, and they readily update their sense of what those parts look like.

These results of the various versions of the mirror test reinforce the idea that the self-concept has many facets, each with its own developmental journey. The facets may interrelate and even form critical foundations for later-emerging ones. Thus, the kinesthetic or ecological sense of self may be a necessary step for the child to develop the extended self, even as all the facets persist and continue to develop.

> **Q:** What are the limitations of the mirror test for providing a full account of the development of the self-concept?

Gender Identity

One facet of the self that seems quite closely anchored to the self-concept is **gender identity**, which means having a clear sense of being either male or female. Children seem to first learn their own gender category, as well as some of the surface trappings of gender (clothing, hair, and so on) at around 2 years of age. At about the same time, they also start to learn about gender-typical activities (for example, shaving versus putting on makeup) and gender-typical toys (for example, vehicles versus dolls; Halim & Ruble, 2010; Poulin-Dubois et al., 2002; Serbin et al., 2001). Finally, a sense of a deeper essential nature of gender—that there is something intrinsic and inside the body determining gender—starts to emerge at around 4 years of age (Gelman et al., 1986; Gelman & Taylor, 2000; Kohlberg, 1966). Interestingly, 5- and 6-year-olds view gender-related properties as just as intrinsic as animal species properties. In contrast, between age 10 and adulthood, individuals start to differentiate the two kinds of properties, seeing gender identity as more influenced by the environment and socialization (Taylor et al., 2009).

It seems obvious that at some point, children's ideas about gender are heavily influenced by noticing anatomical differences between their own sex and the other sex and then, over time, adopting the culture's views about how each gender should act. Thus, gender identity (perceptions of the self as a girl or a boy) and **gender roles** (how I should behave as a girl or a boy) have often been assumed to develop as one integrated complex. But this assumption is problematic, because some individuals who have a clear sense of their gender might still, for a variety of reasons, adopt nonstandard gender roles (for example, men who identify as males but dress as women). Despite these exceptions, however, it was assumed until the last decade or so that children learned both gender identity and gender roles by observing others in their culture (Lytton & Romney, 1991).

For that reason, for much of the twentieth century, if a genetically male infant was born with ambiguous or missing genitalia, doctors and psychologists often advised parents to raise the child as a girl (Money, 1975). Based on the idea that an individual's gender identity and sense of gender roles developed simultaneously, researchers believed that the child would assume that "her" anatomy was that of a girl and would therefore develop the gender identity of a girl. In many cases, if the genitalia were atypical or missing, additional surgery would be performed to make the infant appear more like a girl, the assumption being that this would make it even easier for the child to adopt a female gender identity.

One dramatic case involved identical twin boys, one of whom, as an infant, had his penis accidentally severed in a mishandled circumcision in 1966. John Money, a psychologist and expert on gender identity and sexual reassignment at Johns Hopkins University, was presented with the case and argued that the boy with the missing penis should be raised as a girl. This was reportedly the first time that sex-reassignment surgery was done on a boy who had neither genetic nor hormonal abnormalities. This case was widely discussed for years as an example of how either male or female gender identity could be imposed on genetically identical individuals based on how they were raised. Because the two boys were identical twins, they not only shared the same genomes, but also had experienced the same intrauterine environment. The prevailing view at the time was that a person's gender identity merely reflects how the person is labeled and how he or she is raised. Researchers believed that if you give a genetic male a female name and raise the child as a girl in all respects, the child will adopt the gender identity of a girl (see Figure 13.5).

Over the years, however, the assumption that gender identity is entirely learned and completely malleable has been severely challenged—and strong evidence against the original view came from this twin's case. That individual, who was raised as Brenda and never informed of "her" genetic maleness, nonetheless resisted being raised as a

FIGURE 13.5 Gender identity. Gender identity was thought to be completely a result of socialization practices, such as dressing girls and boys in distinctive colors, which might encourage children to feel similar to others of their own sex and different from those of the opposite sex from a young age. But there are some indications that children have a biologically determined sense of their sex that may overcome socialization practices.

girl (see Figure 13.6). Despite extreme efforts to socialize Brenda as a girl, she rebelled against this socialization and was desperately unhappy (Colapinto, 2000). When she was informed at age 14 that she was born a genetic male, she chose to reverse all feminizing medical procedures and hormonal treatments and started living as a male called David. David later married a woman and became the father of several adopted children. Tragically, at the age of 38, David killed himself.

The extent to which gender identity is biologically determined has been studied more systematically in a large

FIGURE 13.6 Biological sex and gender identity. Although biologically male, Bruce Reimer was raised as a girl (and renamed Brenda) after a botched circumcision. Despite major attempts to socialize Brenda as a girl, which also involved feminizing hormones, the child never felt comfortable with that gender identity. As an adult, she changed her name to David, had male reconstruction surgery, and lived as a male, as shown here.

number of genetic males who, like Brenda, were raised as females—in these cases, because of atypical genitalia at birth (Reiner, 1997, 2005; Yang et al., 2010). Quite remarkably, a large majority of these genetic males, even after being raised as girls for many years and not knowing their genetic sex, stated that they felt themselves to be male. Other studies also support the idea that biological gender, as specified by X and Y chromosomes and the hormonal environments they typically induce, has an important influence on gender identity (Bao & Swaab, 2011; Savic et al., 2010). Nonetheless, as we will see in Chapters 14 and 15, socialization can have a strong influence as well (Cohen-Kettenis, 2005; Meyer-Bahlburg, 2005).

The fascinating question that arises is how the genetic and hormonal differences between males and females can cause such cognitive differences. What physiological differences can lead a child who is told that "she" is a girl and is made to look like a girl and act like a girl still feel comfortable only as a boy? Two possibilities arise. One is simply that the child prefers certain activities that are associated with boys, despite his parents' attempts to instill other preferences. Perhaps the child is more aggressive and prefers more rough-and-tumble activities. Perhaps the child prefers focusing on physical objects, such as blocks and vehicles, rather than on social interactions and conversations. The child might then notice that boys prefer the same activities and come to identify with them. We could call this the similarity explanation. An alternative explanation is that aspects of the concept of being male or female are genetically and hormonally predetermined. This second view may seem implausible, but the first explanation has problems as well, since we all know of young girls or boys who prefer activities associated with the opposite gender and yet identify strongly with their own gender. In addition, the first explanation depends on actively debated assumptions that sex chromosomes do cause differences in such behaviors as rough-and-tumble play or interest in social interactions. As is the case with so many developmental phenomena, gender identity almost surely involves a rich interplay of biological influences (genetic and hormonal) and socialization. Here we have focused more heavily on the biological influences. In Chapters 14 and 15, we will focus more on socialization, although such socialization influences tend to involve gender roles as opposed to gender identity.

> **Q:** How have views changed about the role of socialization in the emergence of gender identity?

It is important to keep in mind that gender identity is not the same as gender role or gender object choice. Catego-

rizing oneself as a boy or a girl (*gender identity*) is usually associated with preferring activities and appearances that are correlated with that category (*gender roles*). In addition, sexual attraction to a particular gender category (*gender object choice*) is also typically correlated with an attraction to the opposite gender category. But each of these aspects of gender can be independent of each other. A boy can strongly identify as a male, prefer typically feminine things, and be attracted to girls. Every permutation is possible. For that reason, the development of gender identity is discussed in this chapter, while gender roles and attractions are discussed in Chapters 14 and 15, which deal more with social interactions and influences.

> **Q:** What are the differences between gender identity, gender roles, and gender object choice?

Developing a Sense of Self-Worth

Beyond simply having a sense of themselves as individuals, children also develop feelings about their own worth and about their ability to accomplish goals. Over the course of childhood, they also improve control over their impulses and over the actions necessary to achieve their goals. During this time, children become more sophisticated interpreters of behavior, observing the effects of particular situations and individuals' dispositions to make inferences about themselves and others. This section explores these different facets of the self, which all bear on the question of how children's developing views of themselves relate to their behavior.

Self-Esteem

The child's self-concept and self-esteem are intricately intertwined, and it is difficult to discuss one without the other (Damon & Hart, 1982, 1988). As a first approximation, however, we can think of **self-esteem** as the value-related aspect of thinking about ourselves (Blascovich & Tomaka, 1991; Harter, 1998). In particular, self-esteem involves an assessment of our own worth and the emotions that accompany such an assessment. Self-concept, on the other hand, is a somewhat broader term with two major aspects. One facet of the self-concept is relatively judgment free and involves knowing facts about ourselves (*I am a boy. I live in Springfield. I like peppermint ice cream.*). The other facet evaluates aspects of the self, often by comparing ourselves to others (*I am the best runner. I am very smart. I am handsome.*). We will therefore consider the development of self-esteem in conjunction with the development of social comparison skills. If the younger child has only limited social comparison skills, then the kinds of social comparisons he is able to make should relate to the nature of his self-esteem.

Between the preschool years and adolescence, self-esteem normally undergoes several significant changes, which fall into roughly four periods (Harter, 1998). The first period, during the preschool years, involves excessively positive views of the self on all dimensions. These views are not only unrealistic, but also comically extreme at times. Who hasn't heard a 3-year-old boast that she is the strongest, fastest, or bravest person anywhere and that she can do anything? At these early ages, children ignore negative feedback that contradicts these inflated views of the self. This pattern seems to be related to their excessive optimism, discussed later in this chapter. It may be highly adaptive for the young child to overestimate her abilities so that she is not discouraged by the inevitable failures involved in becoming a more mature, skilled individual (Lockhart et al., 2002; Shin et al., 2007).

In the second period, during the early school years, the positive attitude remains but is not as extreme and unrealistic. Children around this age start to make social comparisons, mostly by comparing their current selves with the way they were at earlier ages (Oosterwegel & Oppenheimer, 1993; Ruble & Frey, 1991). Thus, a child might notice that she is now taller, stronger, or faster than she used to be. Conveniently, those comparisons to her younger self tend to reinforce a positive attitude about getting better and better (see Figure 13.7). Although some older accounts see the child as simply incapable of making other sorts of social comparisons in the early school years, the reality is more complex. At one level, preschoolers clearly make social comparisons, which can be evident in their jealousy when a peer has the object or approval they feel they deserve. But in the early school years, these social comparisons may not significantly affect the way the child views himself. That is, they may not lead the child to consider himself intrinsically worse than another child in some way—just deprived of something he deserves. Thus, the conscious sense of being deficient in comparison with others may not emerge until later, although it may be rooted in the same factors that induce jealousy. Similarly, even though 3-year-olds show shame at failing an easy task and pride in excelling at a hard one (Lewis et al., 1992), the effects of those feelings are limited to the situation at hand, not translated into a change in self-esteem.

In the third period, middle childhood, the child is able to break down her self-image into many components and evaluate each separately. As a result, she has a larger number of negative self-evaluations than in earlier years. During this period, social comparisons seem to more directly

FIGURE 13.7 Change in self-esteem. Younger children are more likely to have high levels of self-esteem, which tends to drop with increasing age.

influence how the child values herself on various dimensions (Frey & Ruble, 1990). A child might observe, over several episodes, that he does not do as well as others at certain activities (for example, sports that involve large body movements such as running). Across these experiences, he may conclude that he is uncoordinated and that this is a trait-like property in him.

In the fourth period, during later periods of adolescence and young adulthood, social comparisons become more complex and context dependent. Adolescents learn to more carefully decide whom to compare themselves to, and their inferences about their own traits and dispositions become more refined. In addition, individual differences in interpreting social comparisons tend to become more pronounced during this period. Some now see their poor performances as evidence of enduring, unchangeable faults, whereas others view their weaknesses as areas where they need to devote more effort.

As Table 13.2 shows, self-esteem starts off unreasonably high and gradually becomes more realistic. As children enter adolescence, however, some characteristic ways of interpreting their own behavior (for example, believing that failure is due to stable, internal factors that affect all aspects of the self) may lead to the opposite extreme, resulting in unrealistically negative views of the self and low self-esteem. Those individuals can be at risk for serious depression (Bos et al., 2010; Buhrmester et al., 2011; Crocker & Wolfe, 2001; Harter, 1999).

As adolescents move into adulthood, self-esteem may appear to drop more than it really does. Some research shows that as people get older, they get better at the art of false modesty; that is, they learn how to act modestly even while maintaining a very high self-image (Baumeister & Ilko, 1995). This developing ability to manage public image must also be factored into many studies that involve changes in self-evaluations with age (Orth et al., 2011).

Period	Time of Emergence	Characteristics
1	Preschool years	Extreme positive views of self-esteem on all dimensions
		Related to preschoolers' general tendency toward excessive optimism
		Overestimates of abilities may serve an adaptive function by reducing discouragement when failures occur
2	Early school years	Still positive, but less extreme than in earlier years
		Begins to make social comparisons, but only by comparing to himself at younger age
3	Middle childhood	Begins to break down self-image into components
		Sees clear negative attributes in self
		Social comparisons begin to influence self-worth
4	Adolescence	Social comparisons become more complex
		Social comparisons depend more on context
		Individual differences in ways of interpreting social comparisons become more pronounced

TABLE 13.2 Developmental changes in self-esteem. As children grow older and engage in more sophisticated social comparisons, their level of self-esteem tends to drop from early overconfidence to a more realistic level, as well as becoming more intricately structured.

Q: How does the nature of children's self-esteem change from the preschool years to adolescence?

Self-Efficacy

Self-esteem is closely related to self-efficacy, a notion largely developed by the social learning theorist Albert Bandura (1977). **Self-efficacy** refers to people's beliefs about how capable they are of achieving their goals. It has a more moment-to-moment quality than self-esteem, as a person of stable, high self-esteem may, in some contexts, feel that she has little self-efficacy. When visiting another culture, for example, this person may realize how little she knows about its social norms and, consequently, how ineffective she would be at achieving immediate goals. Nonetheless, she may maintain high self-esteem because she realizes that this difficulty applies only to that local context. Similarly, a person of low self-esteem may have feelings of high self-efficacy in some circumstances, even if he does not act on his relatively limited or fragile confidence. This person might believe that he could easily play the lead in the school musical because he knows he can sing all the songs well, but he might not even try out because he feels that "losers" like him never get picked.

Self-esteem and self-efficacy are often tightly linked. One reason is the tendency to devalue or distance ourselves from those aspects of the self in which we have low self-efficacy. If, for example, someone who values athleticism discovers after many painful failures that he is unlikely to ever excel in most sports, he might have very low self-efficacy in that domain. Yet, if he devalues athleticism and comes to see it as irrelevant to his ideal self, this appraisal might not have much impact on self-esteem. Conversely, individuals trapped in a mire of low self-esteem may discount their areas of competence. Self-esteem tends to be global and domain general, while assessments of self-efficacy can be highly specific to tasks and contexts (see Figure 13.8).

FIGURE 13.8 Self-efficacy. Although feelings of self-efficacy can sometimes be exaggerated, such feelings are normally a more focused way of motivating behavior than much broader feelings of self-esteem.

This feature of self-efficacy has made it particularly interesting to clinical psychologists and educators. Because self-efficacy is more focused on specific situations, it has more potential for change than self-esteem, which tends to remain fairly stable across situations. Many psychologists believe that our self-efficacy can be powerfully shifted by the outcomes that we experience (Bandura, 1986). Imagine two individuals with the same initial appraisals of self-efficacy in mathematics and the same level of math ability. They could end up with very different feelings of self-efficacy if the first person attempts a very difficult problem and fails, while the second person takes on an easier mathematical task and succeeds. These results illustrate the usefulness of the concept of self-efficacy for teasing apart the related but distinct notions of self-esteem and true ability in particular areas. Only by realizing that self-esteem, self-efficacy, and true ability can each function and affect the self independently is it possible to account for behaviors.

One intriguing facet of self-efficacy is that it can change even without a direct experience of failure. Following other work by Bandura (1977), researchers have shown that when children observe peers (acting as models) experience success or failure, the peers' experiences can affect the self-efficacy of the observers (Schunk, 1987). This potential "contagiousness" of self-efficacy appraisals can be either unfortunate or encouraging. Imagine, for example, a girl in a classroom who observes two other girls whom she admires doing terribly on math tasks. If she identifies strongly with those girls, she might come away feeling low self-efficacy in math, even if she is very skilled in that area. If, however, she observes those two girls doing better at math than the other students, she might adopt related feelings of high self-efficacy.

The links between self-efficacy beliefs and behaviors also seem to become stronger with development. Young schoolchildren are more likely to have efficacy beliefs that do not strongly predict actual behaviors. As we will see later in this chapter, one reason for this disconnect arises from unrealistically high levels of optimism that young children often have about their current and future abilities. In contrast, older schoolchildren show a tighter relation between self-efficacy beliefs and behaviors related to those beliefs, and this holds across diverse domains. For example, compared with younger children who hold similar beliefs, older children who feel a higher efficacy about either their math ability or their ability to be aggressive are more likely to show higher levels of math achievement or aggression (Davis-Kean et al., 2008). Thus, programs designed to change self-efficacy beliefs may have greater consequences in older children.

In the end, the idea of self-efficacy is useful because it suggests a different type of intervention from those focused on self-esteem. The domain specificity of self-efficacy suggests that children who are doing poorly in one area should not be encouraged with broad statements about how wonderful they are. Specific praise is also likely to be less effective than actual *experiences* of self-efficacy. Even if praise can convince a child that he is highly talented in a specific area, that heightened self-esteem is fragile and can be shattered easily by experiencing a negative outcome. Instead, the most effective and beneficial way to intervene is to find a situation in which the child can experience a genuine, positive outcome and legitimately feel competent. For a child just beginning to learn a new skill, this approach would involve starting with relatively easy tasks in which success is likely (Bandura, 1997). This approach is similar to Vygotsky's ideas about how adults' supportive scaffolding and attention to a child's zones of proximal development can provide rewarding, hands-on learning experiences (see Chapter 9).

Q: Compare and contrast the notions of self-efficacy and self-esteem.

Self-Regulation

Along with the value-driven facets of the self, our sense of self includes our emotional states together with *self-regulation*—our ability to control our emotions and actions and behave in ways that are appropriate for various circumstances. Most parents and teachers would agree that young children do not always have their emotions under full control. Young children also have difficulty delaying gratification, even when doing so would pay off for them (see Figure 13.9). Older

FIGURE 13.9 Delay of gratification. Younger children have more difficulty delaying gratification, often because they are unable to use strategies to divert their attention.

Potential Drawbacks of Self-Esteem

The influence of self-esteem on behavior has become increasingly controversial in the realm of social policy (Twenge, 2006). For years, the conventional wisdom was that the more self-esteem that could be instilled or encouraged in children, the better. In addition, some argued that children from some disadvantaged groups might not be doing as well in school and on standardized tests because of lower self-esteem. Many schools in inner-city neighborhoods put enormous efforts into treating self-esteem problems under the assumption that raising self-esteem would solve problems of academic underachievement (Jackson, 2009).

Yet, the empirical data has not been so clear on the link between belonging to a disadvantaged group and having low self-esteem. An extensive analysis of 261 studies, which included a combined total of over half a million participants, concluded that self-esteem scores for African-American children were not lower, but actually slightly higher, than those for European-American children (Gray-Little & Hafdahl, 2000). In particular, compared with their European-American peers, African-American children under age 10 had slightly lower scores, while those over age 10 had higher scores. However, when children of all ages were taken together in a single comparison, the African-American children had higher self-esteem scores than the European-American children. This difference has appeared in subsequent analyses as well (Eccleston et al., 2010) and raises questions about whether efforts to raise self-esteem would be effective ways to close academic achievement gaps between disadvantaged groups and more advantaged groups.

In retrospect, these findings should not be that surprising. Children tend to compare themselves with the peers they typically encounter in order to build up norms on which to make a self-esteem judgment. Most African-American children are therefore going to compare themselves with other African-American children in the same situation. While far more African-American children live in poverty than European-American children (by some estimates the likelihood that an African-American child lives in poverty is almost four times greater (U.S. Bureau of the Census, 2010), that difference would not affect self-esteem judgments nearly as much as how well-off each child perceives himself relative to his immediate peers.

The strong influence of immediate peers is borne out by a related finding that wealthy African-American children who live in upscale suburban communities, typically among even more affluent European-American children, do tend to show lower self-esteem ratings than European-American children in the same communities, presumably because they are comparing their situation to their even more affluent neighbors (Gray-Little & Hafdahl, 2000). The implications of this research are complex. Group identification seems to help minority children's self-esteem when it focuses their comparisons on children living in similar circumstances. However, it can hurt their self-esteem when their group is juxtaposed with another group that is better off.

Contrary to earlier ideas, low self-esteem may also not be among the main reasons that some individuals transgress against society. Low self-esteem was, for a time, a popular

children often prey on their younger siblings' inability to delay gratification by dangling in front of them an immediately available toy or snack as an alternative to a much more desirable one that requires waiting. What 3-year-old can resist an older brother's offer of a pretty good toy that is here *now* in exchange for a much better one due to arrive by mail in a few days?

Self-regulation and the ability to delay gratification are recurring topics in this book. We saw early elements of these processes in infants in Chapter 7, and we also considered them in Chapter 12 in the context of how they might contribute to antisocial behavior. In this chapter, we want to focus on how the processes of self-regulation and the ability to delay gratification change over the course of normal child development. We will address how they are related to

developmental changes not only in cognition and attention but also in the structure and functioning of the brain.

Many studies have examined which factors influence the ability to self-regulate and thereby delay gratification. In one classic study, 4-year-olds were asked which snack food they preferred: marshmallows or pretzels. The experimenters then told the children that they could have the less preferred food immediately, or if they waited for a longer time (up to 15 minutes), they could receive the preferred food (Mischel & Ebbeson, 1970; Mischel et al., 1972). Despite the relatively short wait time, younger children clearly had great difficulty delaying gratification, opting instead for the readily available, smaller gain.

One variable influencing the ability to wait was whether the children were left alone during the 15-minute delay

explanation for why people "act out" against others; yet some of the most antisocial individuals, whether they are members of the Ku Klux Klan or violent killers, actually have unusually high self-esteem (Baumeister et al., 1996). Similarly, it used to be thought that bullies were driven by low self-esteem when in fact their self-esteem is comparable to other children's (Baumeister et al., 2005; see Figure 13.10). Low self-esteem undoubtedly has bad effects, but high self-esteem should not be considered uniformly positive. Indeed, in some cross-cultural comparisons, a high level of self-criticism, which would correspond to lower self-esteem, is often regarded as a positive personality trait because it encourages people to better themselves by addressing their faults (Heine et al., 1999). A more critical self-appraisal may be linked to an individual's viewing his traits as more modifiable, although the direction of influence here is unclear.

Actively pursuing higher self-esteem also generally has negative consequences. If people see certain aspects of themselves as crucial to their self-esteem and then try to ensure that they are doing well in those areas, they are likely to become frustrated and unhappy. Even when they do well, there is always a higher-level or a new, more impressive group to compare themselves against. Focusing directly on raising their self-esteem may cause brief increases in happiness, but not sustained ones (Crocker & Knight, 2005; Crocker & Park, 2004). Simply enjoying the process of developing an ability, without seeing it as essential to your worth, is much more likely to bring satisfaction. In addition, efforts to raise self-esteem to improve academic performance can backfire. In one study, college students experiencing academic difficulty actually did worse in their studies when their self-esteem was elevated (Forsyth et al., 2007). The researchers suggested that this drop in performance

FIGURE 13.10 **Bullying.** It has often been claimed that people who aggress against others, such as these school bullies, do so because they suffer from low self-esteem. But that claim seems to be mostly a myth, as such people often have higher levels of self-esteem.

might have been because the weak students, in an effort to maintain or elevate self-esteem, actually reduced their academic effort.

In short, how people value themselves is certainly central to understanding behavior, mood, and motivation. Yet, the links between self-esteem and these facets of the self are more complex than previously thought. They involve the ever-growing ability to make social comparisons (both as an individual and as a member of a group), to believe that personal traits are changeable, and to use self-critical appraisals. The implications for social policy are correspondingly complex, calling into question any seemingly straightforward remedies based on raising self-esteem (Baumeister et al., 2003).

with the reward in front of them, which made it harder to resist immediate gratification than when the reward was not present. This result is not surprising; adults, too, are much more tempted by visible rewards. A subtler finding is that the ability to delay gratification may involve an attentional component that changes over the course of development (Mischel & Ebbeson, 1970; Mischel et al., 1972, 1973). As children grow older, they seem more able to direct their attention to things other than the immediately appealing object by focusing on either the other things in the room or various things in memory as a purposeful distraction. As adults, we use these strategies so automatically that we may not realize how common they are. (They are perhaps more obvious in attempts to deal with pain.) To overcome immediate impulses in favor of longer-term gains, children

develop a wide range of strategies, from verbally reminding themselves of the long-term goal, to diverting their attention, to changing their attitude toward the various reward factors (Mischel, 1996).

A common method of distancing ourselves from temptation involves mentally replacing desired objects with symbols for those objects. In one study of this strategy, researchers showed 3- and 4-year-olds two piles that contained different numbers of jelly beans: a pile of three and a pile of eight (Carlson et al., 2005). They were taught that if they pointed at one pile, a puppet would get to take that pile, and they would receive the other pile. Although they clearly understood the instructions, the children had trouble learning to inhibit pointing to the pile that they wanted. They often pointed to the larger one and then unhappily received the smaller one for themselves. However, when the piles were replaced with symbols for larger and smaller amounts (for example, a picture of an elephant and a picture of a mouse) and the researchers explained the relationships between the symbols and jelly beans, the children could much more easily point to the mouse symbolizing the smaller amount in order to receive the larger pile. The symbols distanced the children from the temptation and allowed "cooler heads" to prevail over the immediate desire (Garon & Moore, 2007). The effects of symbols suggest that the abilities to inhibit responses and delay gratification are linked to both attentional abilities and the ability to use mental representations to regulate behaviors (Garon et al., 2008). This complex interplay of factors, some of which continue to develop throughout childhood, helps explain why the ability to delay gratification continues to improve gradually for many years after the preschool period.

Children show substantial individual differences in the ability to delay gratification. Some 4-year-olds could wait much longer than others for the snack they badly wanted. Interestingly, when the researchers followed up with those same groups of children more than 10 years later, they found that the ability to delay gratification at age 4 was correlated with many later aspects of cognitive and social behavior, including SAT scores (Mischel et al., 1989). Some researchers have also argued that a strong ability to delay gratification, or exercise "effortful control," as a toddler is a personality trait that remains stable for several years, and it manifests in such areas as having a stronger conscience (Kochanska & Knaack, 2003).

Q: How can strategies influence the development of self-regulation?

Brain Maturation and the Development of Self-Regulation

Along with the cognitive strategies for delaying gratification that emerge with development, there are good reasons to suspect that some patterns of brain maturation also contribute to this ability. When a child chooses to eat pretzels immediately rather than wait for the marshmallows she really wants, it may be because the child is unable to inhibit the desire for the pretzels long enough to wait for the larger reward. Whenever the notion of inhibition is raised, the brain's frontal lobes are potentially involved. As discussed in Chapter 2, the frontal lobes, which are part of the frontal cortex, lie behind the forehead at the front of the brain. Among their many capacities, one key role involves executive functions, the cognitive activities involved in goal-directed tasks and problem solving. These abilities allow us to optimize not just immediate payoffs but also long-term benefits (see Chapter 10).

One of the most famous cases in neuropsychology, which involved massive frontal lobe damage, began to reveal these structures' crucial contributions to self-regulation, especially emotional regulation. Phineas Gage, a 25-year-old railroad worker, was a victim of an unfortunate accident in 1848 in which a large iron rod entered his head at such an angle that it caused massive damage to the frontal lobes (see Figure 13.11). Quite remarkably, Gage survived the trauma and lived for 12 more years, but his personality had changed dramatically. He no longer seemed to have much control over his emotions; he had become impulsive and more prone to unnecessary risks. The injury impaired his ability to inhibit many aspects of his behavior. The relationship between frontal lobe damage and difficulties in self-regulation has been repeatedly documented for over 150 years (Heatherton, 2011).

FIGURE 13.11 Damage in the frontal lobes and difficulties in self-regulation. (A) The metal spike that went through Phineas Gage's head is shown vividly in this diagram. The damage to Gage's frontal cortical regions caused profound changes in his ability to control his impulses. It has been argued that young children, who have frontal lobes that are less developed than the rest of their brain regions, are in effect developmental versions of Phineas Gage. They are subject to similar neurological deficits that cause difficulties in delay of gratification, impulse control, and planful behavior. (B) A photo of Phineas Gage.

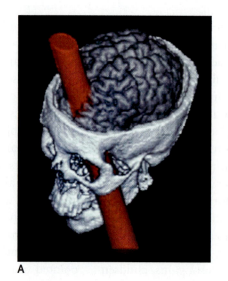

A

B

In recent years, researchers have found intriguing evidence supporting a link between frontal lobe maturation and the development of self-regulation (Posner et al., 2012; Rothbart et al., 2011). One such study recorded event-related potentials (ERPs) occurring in children's brains as they engaged in tasks requiring self-regulation (Lewis et al., 2006). (ERPs are electrophysiological patterns of brain activity that can be monitored and recorded by electrodes placed on the scalp. Over the years, researchers have learned that specific ERP patterns are closely correlated with certain psychological events and can be used to infer when those events occur.) In this study, certain frontal lobe ERP patterns associated with inhibition declined with increasing age, decreasing in activation level in a manner that was closely related to improvements in self-regulation. It seems that older children become more efficient at inhibiting responses, allowing them to inhibit more effectively with less effort. This finding fits the common observations of experimenters and parents alike: Young children sometimes grimace with great effort to resist temptation, as many did in the pretzel-or-marshmallow task, but they often eventually succumb. Similarly, when children of the same age group (for example, toddlers) were studied, differences in the degree of self-regulation among those children were also correlated to measures of frontal lobe circuit activation (Morasch & Bell, 2011). For our purposes, it is important to note that the frontal lobes, as well as other associated brain regions involved in regulation of the emotions, are among the latest brain regions to mature (Heatherton, 2011; Sowell et al., 1999). As always, it is difficult to infer causal relations between behaviors and the many ways in which any brain area matures. However, it seems likely that the developing ability to regulate emotions and behaviors depends not only on learning but also on an increasing capacity for this kind of regulation as the frontal lobes and other brain areas mature (Garon et al., 2008; Posner et al., 2012; Rothbart et al., 2011).

Another provocative example of how biological factors are critical to the development of self-control comes from a study of two adults, both of whom had suffered substantial damage to the prefrontal cortex before they were 16 months of age (Anderson et al., 1999). Both were raised by middle-class, college-educated, married parents who seemed fully committed to supporting their children both materially and emotionally. Yet, despite these advantages, both adults had a long history of poor self-regulation. They regularly lied and stole, and, typical of patients with frontal lobe damage, had little concern for the future. They did not make plans or consider future events. Equally interesting was their apparent deficit in the expression of guilt or regret. This sort of pattern suggests that the development of self-regulation is linked to moral reasoning, not just moral behaviors.

As we saw in Chapter 12, one way to think about moral reasoning is as a cognitive system that develops but may not always be implemented because of difficulties in self-regulation. Another possibility is that difficulties in self-regulation could themselves influence the development of moral reasoning. If someone with poor self-regulation is not motivated to feel and engage with moral dilemmas, she may spend little time even thinking about them and instead simply act on her own desires. The two adults in this study also showed little empathy, a factor that would also limit their tendency to rethink or inhibit their actions out of concern for the suffering they cause in others.

> **Q:** What are some biological factors that have been implicated in the development of self-regulation?

Contextual Influences on Self-Regulation

Self-regulation in young children can be modulated by the surrounding context in ways that are also seen in adults. For example, when a situation increases self-awareness, there is a tendency to show higher levels of self-regulation. An especially striking version of this effect occurs when people perform a behavior in front of a mirror. The mirror creates a feeling of self-consciousness and increases self-regulation in adults (Diener & Wallbom, 1976). The same mirror effect occurs in young children. For example, 3- and 4-year-olds showed higher levels of self-regulation (such as not looking in a box) when behaving in front of a large mirror than when the mirror was not present (Ross et al., 2011). Thus, contextual factors can have a strong influence even on young children who may have much more difficulty regulating their behaviors. Context is not a gradually "added on" modulator as development proceeds; rather, it is an important influence from an early age.

Context also bears on questions of school readiness and cultural variation. In earlier chapters, we saw several challenges to theories of cognitive development that argue for qualitative changes in concepts or reasoning. These challenges make such accounts difficult to use in arguments about school readiness. More plausible arguments may be made about self-regulation skills needing to reach a certain level of competence for children to thrive in schools (Blair, 2002; Blair & Razza, 2007; McClelland & Cameron, 2012). On average, it appears that at some point in the fifth or sixth year of life, most children have sufficient attentional flexibility (both staying on tasks and shifting as needed) and inhibitory control to be able to sit in a classroom and move through various tasks as the school day unfolds. These skills gradually improve to a threshold that is sufficient for success in the classroom and do not seem to represent a qualitative shift. Yet, children vary considerably in when they achieve such levels of self-regulation, with boys typically developing later than girls (Mathews et al., 2009).

There are many ways to measure the different dimensions of self-regulation, but one simple task, known as the Head-Toes-Knees-Shoulders (HTKS) task, offers an integrated assessment of many components of self-regulation, including attention, memory, executive skills, and impulse control. The task involves having children initially touch the body part mentioned with their hand. It then progresses to asking the children to touch "the opposite" body part (for example, the toes when the child hears "head" or the shoulders when the child hears "knees"). This second part of the task requires attention, working memory, and response inhibition—all components of self-regulation (McClelland & Cameron, 2012; Wanless et al., 2011). Moreover, the task is easy to use in real-world settings and predicts success in the classroom. In addition, it has been used cross-culturally and lends further support to findings of cross-cultural differences in the development of self-regulation skills. Research using the HTKS task has shown repeatedly that children from Asian countries tend to have higher levels of self-regulation early on than children from Western countries, such as the United States (Oh & Lewis, 2008; Sabbagh et al., 2006; Wanless et al., 2011; see Figure 13.12). The reasons for the cross-cultural and gender differences are unclear, but there are correlations with differences in socialization across the cultures. For example, teachers in Asian cultures tend to give more instructions concerning behavioral regulation (Lan et al., 2009). Thus, a child's local cultural context may help accelerate the development of self-regulation skills.

Our discussion of self-regulation has focused on the child's cognitive and emotional states and the interactions between them. These factors are critical for understanding how self-regulation develops, but it is in no way sufficient for a full understanding of self-control and moderation of children's behavior. Parents, peers, and the culture at large also affect how children internalize norms, attitudes, and ways of expressing emotions. These topics, however, are better discussed in Chapters 14 and 15, which deal with the influences of the family and of the larger culture.

Developing a Theory of Mind

In the course of a day of running errands, working, and interacting with family members, a typical adult makes many inferences about his own mind and the minds of others. Consider a middle-aged father arising at 6:00 a.m. As the alarm goes off, he wakes and momentarily considers what a strange dream he was having. His wife starts to stir, and he waits to ask her a question until she sits up in bed. He then asks her if she should pick up pizza on the way home that evening. She replies that she will be coming home early that day and will have time to do some shopping. He nods. Eating breakfast, he hears a radio commentator railing against a politician he has not heard of before. He assumes that the criticism is probably suspect. His teenage son sits down to breakfast and says, "Great, I love eating Brand X cornflakes five days in a row." The father acknowledges that he has been too busy to go shopping recently. Driving to work, the father notices a street sign that was struck by a car the night before and is now pointing the wrong way. He realizes that drivers who do

A

B

FIGURE 13.12 Cross-cultural differences in self-regulation. Numerous studies have reported that **(A)** 5-year-olds in Asian cultures have higher average levels of self-regulation than **(B)** 5-year-olds in North American cultures. Such differences may arise from differences in socialization practices.

not know the area will be surprised when they do not arrive at the destinations they intended. At work, he notices a coworker avoiding eye contact with the boss and assumes that person has just missed a deadline.

This example covers only the first few hours of the day, but this man has already revealed many facets of a mature theory of mind. That is, he has a well-developed set of untaught, intuitive beliefs about others' mental states and processes and an understanding of how to use those beliefs to infer others' goals to explain their actions. He can distinguish real from internally generated mental events such as dreams. He understands the cognitive differences between conscious and unconscious states. He knows why someone—in this case, his wife—would answer a question with a seemingly unrelated statement. Hearing the radio commentator, he uses a theory about how strong emotions can cloud judgment. He understands cues to irony or sarcasm and infers his son's true message. He realizes how a misplaced sign can cause false beliefs, with surprising results for those who act on them, and he knows how individuals who have irritated or disappointed someone typically act.

We make inferences based on our theory of mind so automatically that, much like our use of language, we often take for granted its complexity and sophistication. It may seem that there is no alternative to interpreting the social world this way. But consider the same morning from the perspective of someone who lacks a sound theory of mind. He wakes up wondering how he has suddenly, seemingly by magic, moved from being in a battle (his dream) to lying in bed. He immediately starts speaking to his wife, who is still groggy and misses most of what he says. When she awakens, he repeats himself, telling her to get pizza (asking is too subtle a concept, as it requires expecting the other person to consider the question and respond in a particular way). Her reply about coming home early mystifies him, because it is unrelated to pizza. Upon hearing the radio commentator, he assumes that the politician is bad. He is pleased to hear that his son likes Brand X cornflakes. He makes no inferences about the consequences of the reversed street sign, and he makes no assumptions about his coworker, whose behavior seems arbitrarily a bit different.

This second man is almost completely unable to make inferences involving beliefs, desires, and other mental events, not only in others' minds but also in his own. This scenario may seem far-fetched, yet some people with autism exhibit such cognitive deficits. And as mentioned in Chapter 6, some who have less extreme theory of mind deficits (among other differences) may be diagnosed with Asperger's syndrome, a related disorder on the autistic spectrum of developmental disorders (Baron-Cohen & Wheelwright, 2004; Klin et al., 2000). These individuals have tremendous difficulties negotiating the social world, even though they often do quite well in situations that do not require thinking about either their own minds or those of others. It is provocative to consider that both young children and autistic adults lack certain abilities to understand others' minds. Whether they share this behavior for the same cognitive reasons remains unknown.

We now turn to the question of how children develop a theory of mind. Building on topics from Chapters 5 and 6, we will start with a brief look at the early roots of theory of mind in very young children's inferences about social beings. We will then consider when and how children come to understand the consequences of holding false beliefs. These findings can help us address the question of whether theory of mind develops as a **module** (a relatively autonomous, specialized cognitive system) or whether this ability reflects the growth of a much broader cognitive skill, such as the ability to think about abstract representations of any kind. We will then consider the many ways in which the development of a full comprehensive theory of mind continues into late childhood and adolescence, involving forms of social understanding that go far beyond those measured by false-belief tasks.

> **Q:** How is an intuitive theory of mind important for getting by in everyday life? Provide examples.

Early Aspects of Theory of Mind

As discussed in Chapters 5 and 6, even young infants treat social beings differently from nonsocial ones. They attend to eye gazes from other people in the first few months of life and become increasingly sophisticated at using eye gaze to infer another person's goals, perceptions, and mental states. For example, 9-month-old infants assume that eye gaze is an important cue to an object of interest. They will look longer at objects in locations that are in the direction of an eye gaze than at objects that are in the opposite direction from an eye gaze (Senju et al., 2008). They will even do so when the objects appear and reappear such that the objects are never on the screen at the same time as the face depicting eye gaze. Thus, the infants seem to be making inferences about what an agent is interested in, and they maintain such inferences over time. This ability in 9-month-olds appears to build on an earlier-developing, specialized neural circuit that responds to object-directed gazes. The brain activity of 4-month-old infants shows a distinctive pattern of event-related potentials (ERPs) when they are looking at someone else's object-directed gaze. This ERP pattern differs from the pattern measured when the infants are looking at a non-object-directed gaze (Hoehl et al., 2008). These results fit with the finding that adults show unique brain responses to gazes toward objects versus people (Pelphrey et al., 2003, 2004). Remember also that after 1-year-olds "interact" with a furry blob-shaped object that seems to respond to their vocalizations by beeping back at them, the infants will then make assumptions about gaze based on this semblance of a social interaction. When the blob then rotates toward one side, the infants will turn their heads the same way to see what the blob is "gazing" at (Johnson et al., 1998; see Chapter 5).

Many researchers are now investigating the early components of our ability to use relatively simple perceptual cues to make social inferences. As described in Chapter 5, by 10 months of age, children observing objects in motion interpret certain kinds of cues, such as self-propelled movement that seems to take into account changing conditions, as strong indicators of social agents with goals (Meltzoff, 1995; Woodward, 1998). A key question in these studies focuses on whether these early components form a critical foundation for a later, more complex theory of mind.

One proposal about the development of theory of mind suggests that the first step involves learning to attribute goals to other social beings (Leslie, 1994; Leslie et al., 2004). In this view, the learning process is driven by our interpretations of various perceptual cues, most notably direction of gaze (Baron-Cohen, 1995). In light of this possibility, it is interesting that humans are the only species whose eyes have dark pupils and irises against a clearly visible, bright white background, which makes discerning the direction of another's gaze much easier (see Figure 13.13 and Scientific Methods box). There may be some evolutionary cost if the whites of human eyes are more visible to predators, but the benefits for those who can more efficiently use gaze direction to infer others' goals may well be worth it (Tomasello et al., 2007).

By 18 months or so, infants begin to master the second step toward developing a full-fledged theory of mind. They become able to infer an actor's intention and imitate that goal rather than simply reproducing every action (Meltzoff, 1995). However, if they see cues indicating that the actor purposely chose an unusual or inconvenient way of doing something, such as turning on a light with his forehead even though his hands were free, they will imitate the precise action instead. If the actor's hands were full, they will imitate the goal (Gergely et al., 2002). The infants seem to infer that the hands-free actor must have chosen the more difficult action for a reason. (Chimpanzees also make this kind of inference while watching human actors in a nearly identical task, suggesting that this facet of the theory of mind is not unique to humans; Buttelman et al., 2007.) These are just a few of the various forms of evidence that indicate that well before age 1, infants make inferences that attribute rationality to social beings (see Chapters 5 and 6).

Comparative Perspectives on Theory of Mind

Just how much does a creature need to understand about the mind to be capable of rich social interactions? We know, for example, that many other species' social interactions go far beyond their mating and aggression rituals. Several primate species, for example, maintain elaborate **dominance hierarchies**, networks of social relations based on the ranking of group members. The structure of the hierarchy often involves a single powerful individual at the top and increasingly large groups of subordinates as social status decreases. These networks have powerful consequences for individuals and how they interact with one another (see Figure 13.14). More dominant members of a group usually have better access to mates, food, and shelter. When new members join a primate group, they are remarkably adept at observing interactions and inferring the whole hierarchy of relationships, such that establishing dominance relations with just one or two members allows them to know how they stand with everyone else. In addition, subordinate monkeys sometimes form coalitions that can change the group's power relationships, which implies a sophisticated understanding of rank and power (Barrett et al., 2007).

Considerable controversy remains over the extent to which the social reasoning skills of nonhuman primates psychologically resemble those of humans (Penn & Povinelli, 2007; Santos et al., 2007). Even the most sophisticated nonhuman primates, such as chimpanzees, sometimes fail spectacularly at tasks that seem to depend on social cognition. For example, Japanese and rhesus macaque monkeys will alert their offspring to the presence of a predator even when the offspring clearly knows about the predator already and the alerting call will put the parents at risk (Cheney &

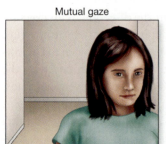
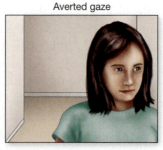

Mutual gaze   Averted gaze

FIGURE 13.13 Direction of gaze. When participants watched a virtual person pass by who looked directly at them, they showed a different neural response than when the person's eyes were averted. These results suggest an early-emerging neural system specialized for processing gaze. Adapted from Pelphrey et al. (2004).

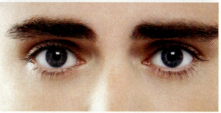

FIGURE 13.14 Social dominance and cognition. This juvenile rhesus monkey is showing a stereotypical expression of submission to an approaching dominant male. Primates can be very sensitively tuned to the social dominance relations that hold in quite large groups, performing what seem to be complex computations about others; yet they also can show glaring deficiencies in other theory of mind tasks.

Seyfarth, 1990, 1991). Similarly, chimpanzees will ignore gaze cues telling them where food is hidden, looking just as long at a container that a human is not looking at as at one that the human is staring at (Call et al., 2000).

But when primates are put into competitive situations, such as competing for food, they seem to show much more sophisticated forms of social cognition (Santos et al., 2007). In a situation where a known competitor can see one cache of food but not another, a chimpanzee will first get the food from the concealed location (Tomasello et al., 2003). In fact, across a wide range of competitive settings, several different classes of primates seem to take into account others' knowledge, using inferences about what their competitors are perceiving as a cue to what they know.

Do these successes in competitive circumstances mean that primates think about the social world in similar ways to humans? It is far too early to tell, but many researchers think that nonhuman primates' social understanding is likely to be more limited (Call & Tomasello, 2008; Tomasello et al., 2003). In particular, there may be some

Theory of Mind in Dogs?

Most research comparing social cognition in humans and other species has been with nonhuman primates, such as chimpanzees, gorillas, and various species of monkeys, since their genomes are most closely related to that of humans (chimpanzee DNA shares 96 percent of its sequence with human DNA). Yet, from an evolutionary perspective, it does not make sense as a research strategy. While primates vary dramatically in their degree of sociability—some species are loners and others are "groupies"—some nonprimate species are also highly social, sometimes in ways that are closely linked to human activities. It is especially interesting to ask how these other species—which do not share as many broad cognitive abilities with humans—might nonetheless have sophisticated social cognitive skills. Such a focus starts to reveal just how important general cognitive capacities might be to the development of social skills in humans (as opposed to more specific adaptations for social cognition).

Few groups are more appropriate for such questions than dogs (see Figure 13.15). Dogs started to differentiate from wolves roughly 15,000 years ago (Savolainen et al., 2002), and certain traits were selected for as these animals adapted to a special social niche with humans. Dogs may have been selected for their ability to partially perceive mental states in humans and work with them cooperatively rather than competitively in ways that maximize mutual benefit (Hare & Tomasello, 2005), and to excel at social as opposed to causal thinking (Brauer et al., 2006; Miklósi & Topál, 2012). Thus, although dogs do far worse than chimpanzees at using nonsocial cues to find the location of hidden food, they do better than chimpanzees in locating food on the basis of pointing gestures made by humans (Brauer et al., 2006).

Developmental studies have been particularly informative as to how dogs might differ from wolves. When dogs and wolves are both hand reared in equivalent socially rich human environments, young puppies show more advanced social cognition skills than young wolf pups. When hand-raised dogs and wolves were given pointing tasks, older wolves could use pointing cues to find hidden food, but younger ones (4-month-olds) could not, while 4-month-old puppies did just fine (Gácsi et al., 2009). Young dogs actually prefer human companions to other dogs, while young wolves do not (Morell, 2009). Dogs seem prepared to think more adeptly about social states, especially those in humans. Wolves can be gradually trained to be more social, but they do not seem to have the head start that dogs do.

There is active debate on just how rich a theory of mind to grant to dogs, but it does seem that they are adept at following

FIGURE 13.15 Dog social cognition. Recent evidence suggests that dogs may have been selected for a set of specific perceptual and cognitive skills for detecting social information and intentions in humans, often in ways that exceed those found in great apes. These findings are important for understanding the origins of our own species' abilities to negotiate our social world.

eye gaze and sensing human goals (Miklósi & Topál, 2012). The fascinating question revolves around how simple the "seed" social cognitive skills need to be in young dogs to enable them to later be such adept social companions to humans. Answering this question will help us better understand what might be the minimal amount of social learning biases we might want to grant to human infants. It is impressive that higher-order social cognitive behaviors, such as the human tendency to "overimitate" the intentional acts of others (Lyons et al., 2011), are also found in dogs but not in apes (Miklósi & Topál, 2012).

Dogs and humans may also provide an example of convergent evolution of a set of social skills. Because dogs are in many ways more socially skilled and socially perceptive than most nonhuman primates, it seems that they developed these skills long after any common mammalian ancestor to both dogs and primates. Thus, they must have developed their social skills independently from those adaptations that humans may have acquired to be socially skilled. That convergence raises two questions: Have dogs adapted to the social niche in subtly different ways than human infants? Do dogs use different mechanisms than humans in developing social skills, or is there only one straightforward way to build social skills, such that both species independently evolved essentially the same building blocks of social cognition and perception?

limitations to how nonhuman primates think about beliefs. They may lack an ability to consider the beliefs of others across a wide range of situations where there are clear benefits to being aware of such beliefs, such as whether or not relatives are aware of predators; and they may have particular difficulties with understanding when others have beliefs that are not true reflections of reality. In more narrowly defined areas, such as competitive tasks, we may need to grant primates some notion of beliefs (Santos et al., 2007). At the least, those who do not want to grant beliefs to primates must come up with an alternative explanation of what mental processes make possible their success in competitive tasks.

In comparison with other primates, humans' more sophisticated abilities to think about intentions can sometimes lead young children astray. In one task, for example, both chimpanzees and preschoolers were presented with transparent containers that they had to manipulate to get at a desired object inside (Horner & Whiten, 2005; Lyons et al., 2007, 2011). The containers had several movable knobs and handles, only some of which were mechanically useful. Both chimpanzees and children watched an adult manipulate all of the knobs and handles, including the useless ones, before removing the object from its container. When the chimpanzees were then allowed to try to get the object out of the container, they omitted the unnecessary actions and efficiently removed the object, copying only the model's goals, not each action. In contrast, the children reproduced all the actions, including several blatantly unnecessary ones. Other studies have revealed that children who see an adult act on an object to achieve a goal assume that all the adult's actions must be causally relevant (Lyons et al., 2007, 2011). Thus, the children's sensitivity to the usual relationship between intentions and actions temporarily blinds them to the irrelevance of some actions. Complex social intuitions are an important part of understanding such cases where children "overimitate" (Over & Carpenter, 2013). The chimpanzees have no such problem.

In short, a rich body of evidence supports the idea that infants and young toddlers have some sense of the ways in which the goals and perceptions of social agents can influence those agents' actions. Furthermore, they seem to share many aspects of these abilities with other primates. Even some social nonprimates, such as dogs, can show surprising sophistication in some of these abilities (see New Directions box). Given this remarkable precocity, it is perhaps surprising that many researchers have also claimed that one central aspect of theory of mind, the ability to understand how beliefs influence behavior, may not be fully functional until well into a child's third year. These claims are based on a set of classic experimental tasks for investigating children's understanding of false beliefs.

Understanding False Beliefs

Normal adult functioning requires near-constant use of sophisticated capacities for thinking about other minds. Yet, researchers have repeatedly argued that young children have specific problems in thinking about some aspects of other minds. The most studied method for examining what children understand about others' beliefs has come to be known as the **false-belief task**. There are a number of variations on the task, all of which aim to assess a person's ability to understand how others might behave when they hold inaccurate beliefs (Wellman, 1990; Wimmer & Perner, 1983).

One of the most common false-belief tasks has been called the "Smarties task" (Perner et al., 1987), after a popular British candy similar to M&M's. The experimenter first shows the child a container with the familiar Smarties logo and asks what is inside. The child says it contains Smarties candy—but when the researcher opens the container, the child sees that it actually contains pencils. The researcher then asks what is really in the container, and the child replies, "Pencils." Up to this point, all children answer the same way, regardless of their age.

The child is then asked what another person seeing the container for the first time would think was inside of it. This question elicits very different answers depending on the child's age. Children who are approximately 3½ years and younger say that the new person would think there were pencils in the container. Children who are older than about 3½ respond like adults do, saying that the new person will think that the container contains Smarties (see Figure 13.16). Younger children do not seem to understand that beliefs do not simply mirror reality; rather, they represent a person's subjective understanding of reality (Cassidy, 1998; Perner et al., 1987). Consequently, they cannot see how someone could hold a belief contrary to what they, themselves, know to be true.

Hundreds of studies have documented younger children's apparent inability to understand the nature of false beliefs (Bloom & German, 2000; Flavell, 1999; Scholl & Leslie, 1999; Wellman et al., 2001). Some of them use tasks known as *unexpected contents tasks*, which closely resemble the Smarties task. Another type of false-belief task, sometimes known as *unexpected locations tasks* or "Sally–Anne tasks," after the best-known version, involves shifting objects to other locations. In this task, the experimenter verbally describes and visually depicts a person (Sally) who puts an object in a covered basket and then leaves the room. While Sally is gone, Anne enters, moves the object from the basket to a covered box, and leaves the room. Sally then returns, and the child is asked where Sally will look for the object (see Figure 13.17). Most children under age 3½ say that Sally will look in the box. Most children over 4 years of age say that Sally will look

FIGURE 13.16 Understanding false beliefs. The Smarties task is one of several false-belief tasks in which children younger than between 3 years 6 months and 3 years 10 months tend to equate another person's beliefs with what is true in the world and not with their prior experiences and beliefs. The upper panels show a child who is 3 years 4 months first looking at a closed box of Smarties and then at an open box that says Smarties but contains pencils. In the lower panels, the child who is 3 years 4 months now thinks that another child would believe that pencils are in the closed box, but a child who is 3 years 11 months would think that another child would believe that Smarties are in the closed box.

Step 1

Step 2

Step 3 for a child at 3 years 4 months

Step 3 for a child at 3 years 11 months

in the basket (Frith & Frith, 1999). Thus, across the different types of false-belief tasks, children younger than about 3½ fail to see how a person's beliefs might cause them to act in a way that is contrary to the facts. These younger children seem to view human beliefs as if people were all-knowing (Barrett & Driesenga, 2001).

> **Q:** Describe two different types of false-belief tasks.

How, then, do younger children understand beliefs if they are unable to see them as fallible? One proposal is that before about age 3½ children tend to think about beliefs as if they were desires (Wellman, 1990). To understand this frame of mind, consider that when we observe simpler animals, explanations based on drives (internal physiological states like hunger or thirst) are sometimes the most plausible way of explaining their behaviors. We do not think of a fly as having beliefs, but we can imagine it having something that might be construed as a desire in the sense of a drive or

behavioral orientation toward reducing an uncomfortable physiological state or increasing a pleasant one. This kind of drive or "desire" is much simpler and more immediate than a goal-driven behavior. For example, a fly lands on sugary soft drink residue because it "wants" to eat sweet things. Of course, the sense of "want" that we attribute to the fly is not the same as our understanding of what it means for a 4-year-old to want another child's toy. In the child's case, we rely on our own mature theory of mind and assume that the child's wanting is associated with a rich set of beliefs about what the toy is like, who owns it, and what owning it would be like. On the other hand, a child who has not yet passed the false-belief task may not have that level of insight about the kinds of thoughts and feelings a playmate associates with wanting a toy and may see other people's behaviors in ways that more closely resemble how we see the fly.

> **Q:** How might a 2-year-old's theory of mind be different from a 4-year-old's theory of mind?

This is Sally.   This is Anne.

Sally puts her ball in the basket.

Sally goes away.

Anne moves the ball to her box.

Where will Sally look for her ball?

FIGURE 13.17 The Sally–Anne task. Most children under 3½ years of age will say that Sally will look in the box. Most children over 4 years of age will say that Sally will look in the basket.

Evaluating the False-Belief Task At first glance, it seems that a failure to understand how false beliefs predict behaviors is an indication that a child has not yet developed a theory of mind. But there are troubling aspects to the false-belief tasks, leading some to suggest that it should be abandoned as a measure of the theory of mind (Bloom & German, 2000). Proponents of this argument offer two

main criticisms of the tasks. First, succeeding at false-belief tasks may require abilities that have little to do with the theory of mind, such as a more general ability to inhibit judgments driven by salient knowledge. Thus, in the Sally–Anne task, children must inhibit their own knowledge of the object's true location and consider instead where the object might seem to be to another person.

This kind of inhibition has been studied separately in experiments that can perhaps shed some light on findings from false-belief studies. One example involves the **false-photograph task**. In this task, a child is shown a camera on a tripod with an object—say, a rubber duck—in front of it on a stand. The experimenter presses a button on the camera and declares that the camera has taken a picture. The duck is then replaced with a different object—for example, a teddy bear. The child is then asked what picture the camera took when the experimenter pressed the button. Three-year-olds had difficulty saying that the camera had taken a picture of the duck if the new object, the bear, was in front of the camera when the researcher asked the question (Zaitchik, 1990). Because reporting what happened with the camera does not require thinking about others' minds, this finding suggests that around age 3, children show a more general difficulty inhibiting responses driven by present displays. More precisely, young children's struggles with the false-photograph task seem to indicate that early on, it is difficult for them to inhibit a default response in which beliefs correspond to what presently appears to be true (Leslie, 2000; Leslie & Polizzi, 1998; Leslie et al., 2005). In most real-world situations, this is a good default strategy, since we usually think that our beliefs reflect reality (Birch & Bloom, 2007).

Other evidence supports the possibility that young children fail false-belief tasks, at least in part, because of difficulty inhibiting a default, present-oriented response. Older children with autism can pass the false-photograph task, but they fail the false-belief tasks intended to test for a theory of mind (Leekam & Perner, 1991; Leslie & Thaiss, 1992). Children with autism, like typically developing children, develop inhibitory skills that enable them to pass the false-photograph task. However, autistic children continue to have a specific deficit in thinking about beliefs. This pattern suggests that younger children without autism may fail false-belief tasks not because they cannot think about beliefs, but because of problems with inhibition common to all very young children. In sum, there are at least two possible explanations for young children's failures on false belief tasks. They may have less ability to inhibit a present-oriented response (a problem that is not specific to false beliefs), or they may have a problem thinking about others' false beliefs in particular.

The studies on children with autism raise the possibility that the developmental changes associated with passing false-belief tasks may be more associated with inhibitory abilities than with abilities to think about false beliefs per se. In this regard, it is interesting that the elderly, who show declines in executive functioning and inhibitory skills, can also show increased errors in the false-belief task—even though they clearly have not lost the ability to think about beliefs (German & Hehman, 2006). Other studies with children also support the idea that beyond issues related to theory of mind, some combination of deficits in planning, working memory, action awareness, and inhibition contributes to young children's failures on the false-belief task (Sabbagh et al., 2006a, 2006b).

The second objection to using false-belief tasks to measure theory of mind is closely tied to our earlier discussion about the ways that very young children think about social agents. In several respects, young children show at least some awareness and understanding of others' mental lives. In fact, there is some evidence that children may even show the ability to reason about false beliefs much earlier than age 3½ if the social reasoning is not embedded in a task that relies on verbal descriptions. In one study described more fully in Chapter 5, 15-month-olds saw an actor place an object in one location and then saw the actor go behind a screen, which blocked his view while the object was moved to a new location. When the actor returned and looked for the object in the new location, the infants looked longer than when the actor looked for the object where he left it (Onishi & Baillargeon, 2005). In a similar study, researchers showed 13-month-old infants animated movies in which a caterpillar-like creature either had visual information indicating the location of a hidden object or did not. When the creature had a visual cue, infants expected it to be more successful at finding the object (Surian et al., 2007). The nonverbal violation of the expected behaviors has also been used to show success by 2½-year-olds in both unexpected contents and unexpected locations tasks (He et al., 2011). Even in verbal tasks very much like the classic false-belief task, it is possible to get many 2½-year-olds to succeed if the experimenter looks up at the ceiling and seems to ask herself where the protagonist will look (He et al., 2012). In the classic task, when the experimenter looks at the child and asks the same question, 2½-year-olds will fail. Directly eliciting a response from the child seems to increase processing load and result in failure. More generally, the development of theory of mind and the ability to understand false beliefs now appear to develop in a more continuous manner after infancy and not as a dramatic qualitative shift at around 3½ years.

Further research is needed to know whether the infants are really thinking in terms of false beliefs or whether a simpler kind of understanding enables them to pass these tasks (Perner & Ruffman, 2005). Still, the fact that they can pass them at all makes the meaning of the original false-belief tasks less clear. One possibility is that the nonverbal violation of expectations tasks draw on a more implicit, nonverbal sense of the relationship between perception and knowledge, while the classic false-belief tasks tap into a more explicit, verbal sense of how beliefs can be at odds with reality (Sodian, 2011; Sodian & Thoermer, 2008).

Tracking of beliefs at a more implicit level has been found in infants as young as 7 months. For example, if infants see an animated agent watch an object go behind a barrier, they seem to automatically encode the agent's beliefs and, as a result, look longer when the object reappears in a manner that violates that agent's false beliefs (Kovács et al., 2010). Infants and adults alike seem unable to avoid encoding belief states of others and having those belief states influence their own responses to situations.

Well before children pass classic false-belief tasks, in some cases as young as 18 months, they can also reason about others' pretend play (Leslie, 1987b, 1992, 1994; Schwebel et al., 1999). The early emergence of this ability may seem surprising, since it, too, seems to involve reasoning about mental states that are contrary to reality. There is, however, a crucial difference between these forms of play and false beliefs. Pretend play does not require deliberately suppressing a belief about something that is true; rather, the game often involves making it clear to all players that the real object is not the same as the object it represents. The child who pretends to use a banana as a phone means for all to know that it is not really a phone, just a pretend phone. The pretend "belief" does not directly conflict with reality like the false belief does. Pretend play may therefore be one of the earliest ways in which children can think about alternative views of reality and be aware that those alternatives are mentally created.

> **Q:** What are some limitations of the false-belief task as a measure of the child's developing theory of mind? What other factors might be influencing performance on the task?

A Theory of Mind Module?

Several theory of mind researchers have concluded that the ability to reason about the mental states of others is a special cognitive adaptation that was selected for in the course of evolution. According to these views, theories of mind do not simply arise from learning about the social world; they get a powerful head start from a dedicated cognitive system that is strongly influenced by our genes. This type of specialized mental system for understanding the beliefs and mental state processes of other people is sometimes described as a **theory of mind module** (**TOMM**). It is based on the proposal of philosopher Jerry Fodor (1983) that part of human cognitive makeup consists of specialized, autonomous systems for processing distinct kinds of information, such as spatial layout, syntactic structure, and number. Our abilities to reason about the minds of other people may be a module in the same sense (Scholl & Leslie, 1999). Such modules need not be present in fully functional forms at birth. They may take time to mature or may need certain environmental experiences to trigger them (Scholl & Leslie, 2001). In the debates about whether theory of mind constitutes a module, different scholars' meanings of "module" vary somewhat (Butterfill, 2007; Coltheart, 1999), creating challenges in comparing their claims.

The most prominent issues revolve around two main questions. First, does theory of mind constitute a separate cognitive domain—a cognitive system tailored for one kind of information? Second, do theory of mind abilities show informational encapsulation—that is, is the module influenced only by other information that is processed within the module (Fodor, 1983)? This latter question is based on the idea that once a module begins to process information, its operations are not influenced by other external information. Informational encapsulation is an appealing explanation for optical illusions, in which, for example, you cannot help but see that one line is shorter than another despite knowing that they are identical in length. Some argue that theory of mind functions similarly, as a domain-specific, informationally encapsulated module (Scholl & Leslie, 1999). One form of evidence for this possibility resembles the optical illusion example. If circles and triangles moving about on a screen appear to "interact" in certain ways, most people cannot help but interpret them as animate, social agents, as if their movements trigger a theory of mind module. We saw in Chapter 5 how even quite young infants seem to have similar social agent inferences triggered by simple geometric forms.

The proposal that theory of mind abilities form a module is perhaps most dramatically illustrated by the specific deficits of some individuals who are diagnosed with autism (see Figure 13.18). Autism is a developmental disorder marked by language problems and extraordinary difficulties with social interactions. Yet, some autistic individuals also show normal proficiency or even exceptional skill in other cognitive domains, including math, music, drawing, or reasoning about complex devices. Even so, the same person who excels at some cognitive tasks may still fail at false-belief tasks (Baron-Cohen, 1995). By contrast, some individuals without autism may not do as well on cognitive tasks but may pass false-belief tasks easily. This pattern is compatible with the claim of a biologically determined distinct system

FIGURE 13.18 **Autism and theory of mind.** Although this child diagnosed with autism may show meticulous attention to objects and their relations, such as making this neat ordered progression of ducks, the same child may have great difficulty thinking about the mental states of other people, a deficit that some researchers construe as evidence for a theory of mind module.

for processing beliefs and other sophisticated aspects of mental lives—processing that can be notably difficult for people with autism (Leslie, 1994; Leslie & Thaiss, 1992). This claim is compelling to the extent that the difficulty with beliefs is bounded (that is, confined to that one sphere) and most evident in socially rich environments where other children would develop complex understandings of others' minds.

The idea of a theory of mind module is controversial, however, and other scholars believe that it may be possible to explain the sense of social agency in simple animations, the autism findings, and related phenomena in other ways. In this view, there is no module for thinking about beliefs. Instead, this ability emerges from a combination of lower-level perceptual abilities and higher-level, domain-general cognitive mechanisms (Stone & Gerrans, 2006). In particular, there may be dedicated neural systems for processing gaze, processing vocal intonations, and recognizing emotions. All this perceptual information could then feed into a domain-general set of cognitive mechanisms. One frequently emphasized domain-general skill known as *meta-representation* is concerned with the ability to understand and think about the sense in which a representation—like a mental image or an idea—stands for something else. Understanding representations at this level is necessary for understanding beliefs. A critical question for future research is whether theory of mind tasks require the same meta-representational skill as other kinds of tasks unrelated to thinking about beliefs.

Finally, any discussion of the modularity of theory of mind must also consider the correlation between poor language skills and autism. The implications of this correlation are unclear, in part because as a child develops language skills and theory of mind, each ability can influence the other. That is, some aspects of language acquisition, such as the ability to learn words, may be intimately related to the ability to think about the mental states of other people (Bloom, 2000; see Chapter 8). At the same time, language development may help foster a more sophisticated theory of mind. For example, developmental changes in the ways that children use verbs about mental states, such as "think" and "know," correlate with success on traditional false-belief tasks (Astington, 1993, 1999; Bartsch & Wellman, 1995). Children may have to master these verbs and the syntactic constructions they require in order to reason more explicitly about false beliefs (de Villiers & de Villiers, 2000). As research on both directions of influence are understood in more detail, they will inform the debates about whether there is a theory of mind module.

Beyond False Beliefs

Beyond the study of false beliefs, much remains to be understood about theory of mind development. As mentioned earlier, it is clear from studies of infants and animals that both are capable of specialized reasoning about social entities, and this reasoning occurs in infants long before they can succeed on the standard false-belief task. It is also clear that much of this social reasoning may occur automatically, which makes the "theory" part of "theory of mind" a misnomer. (We do not describe the processes of object perception as requiring a "theory" of three-dimensional objects.) Indeed, if theory of mind functions largely automatically, as an informationally encapsulated module, it becomes less theory-like.

At the more sophisticated end of the developmental continuum, the ability to reason about others' minds is certainly not complete when the first explicit false-belief task is solved. A host of other, later-emerging cognitive skills support more nuanced social inferences, and there are correspondingly complex false-belief tasks that children solve only at later ages (Perner & Wimmer, 1985; Stone et al., 1998; Wellman & Liu, 2004). Later in this chapter, we will look more closely at some of these more advanced social skills, such as the ability to make attributions about behaviors in others and in ourselves.

Like false-belief tasks, certain kinds of humor—which do not necessarily involve false beliefs—can reveal the limits of children's abilities to make inferences about states of mind. It is not uncommon to see a bright 10-year-old staring at a cartoon or comic strip without understanding why it is funny. To be sure, humor is sometimes based on adult knowledge that the child simply has not acquired. But sometimes the child is mystified because of missing insight into the nuances of social interactions and others' mental states. Consider the cartoons in Figure 13.19. The idea of a "guilt trip" that a parent might put on a child involves complex inferences about both parties' beliefs, goals, and conflicting internal states. Similarly, the silliness of the "precious gift of hindsight" is based on understanding that it is always easier to speak authoritatively about the recent past than about the future. Humor, one of the least understood of human behaviors (Provine, 2000), very often involves sophisticated reasoning about the mental states of others.

Theory of mind is also critical to sharing information. Almost all forms of communication are incomplete and rely on the two parties' assumptions about their common ground of understanding (Clark, 1996). For example, when I tell someone that there is a bathroom on the second floor, we both immediately assume a rich arena of unstated common knowledge (I mean the second floor of the building we are in; I mean a bathroom that is working; if we are in

FIGURE 13.19 Humor and theory of mind. In both of these cartoons, relatively subtle aspects of our beliefs about other minds are needed to see the intended humor. These examples serve to illustrate how theory of mind skills continue to develop long past middle childhood and suggest that the developmental patterns seen in toddlers should perhaps be seen as part of a much longer continuum of developmental change than as the a critical period in which a mature theory of mind emerges.

"We must never take for granted the precious gift of hindsight."

public, I mean different bathrooms for men and women). Likewise, using and appreciating human artifacts, whether they are books, signs, or art, critically involve thinking about the creator's goals, beliefs, and desires. The simplest acts of communication would be incredibly difficult without a rich theory of mind that helps us to decide what the speaker likely knows already and what is new. Full mastery of such communicative nuances takes many years to develop (Birch & Bloom, 2004; Matthews et al., 2007).

Making Attributions about Ourselves and Others

Closely linked to the ability to infer another person's goals is the ability to attribute or ascribe particular reasons for behaviors. This, too, is a critical part of understanding people's actions. If the person in front of you in line is impatient with the cashier, is he generally a rude, inconsiderate person, or is he just running late? More generally, how and when do we interpret someone's behavior as evidence for what kind of person he is? We make similar attributions to explain past experiences and to predict how we and others might do on future tasks. Furthermore, the nature of those predictions changes over the course of our development. In addition, our attributions about our own behavior, including why we engage in certain activities, seem to strongly influence how we go about them and how much we enjoy them.

Emerging Explanations of Behavior

Most people engage in particular actions either because of some intrinsic fact about them (they love chocolate) or because of some degree of environmental pressure (they want to be like their friends who love chocolate). We can all recognize both kinds of factors, but most Western cultures tend to overemphasize **dispositional factors**, those influences on behavior that have to do with a person's intrinsic nature, at the expense of equally important **situational factors**, aspects of a situation that influence the way a person acts. Thus, a researcher might be able to show empirically that performance on a math test is influenced by both situational variables (noise, anxiety, and fatigue) and dispositional variables (math ability, motivation, or speed of processing). Nonetheless, when most Westerners observe someone else doing poorly or well in math, they are much more likely to attribute the failure or success to internal, dispositional variables than to situational ones. This bias in observing others is known as the **fundamental attribution error** (Ross, 1977; see Figure 13.20).

Interestingly, this bias does not occur to the same extent across cultures, occurring more frequently in individualist cultures than in collectivist ones. (As described in Chapter 12, individualist cultures consider the rights and autonomy of the individual to be paramount, whereas collectivist cultures place more value on the rights of the group and the connections between people.) Members of individualist cultures more often attribute a person's behavior to dispositional factors—aspects of her personality or disposition. On the other hand, members of collectivist cultures tend to

A

B

FIGURE 13.20 The fundamental attribution error. The fundamental attribution error leads people to **(A)** attribute negative behaviors in others to internal trait-like dispositions but **(B)** the same behavior in themselves to situations. Researchers have asked how the relative emphases on dispositions and situations change with development.

understand behaviors as arising from situational factors—aspects of the specific circumstances or situation (Brewer & Chen, 2006; Miller, 1984; Nisbett, 2003; Oyserman & Lee, 2008; Peng et al., 2001). Social psychologists refer to the study of the theories people use to explain their own behavior and that of others as **attribution theory**. Indeed, one of the originators of attribution theory, Fritz Heider, referred to it as the study of "naive psychology" (Heider, 1958).

How do these different aspects of attribution develop? Early researchers suggested that younger children tend to take a situational view of behavior and only switch toward a dispositional view with increasing age (Higgins & Bryant, 1982; Ruble et al., 1979). But these claims were made before the strong cross-cultural differences were known. It now seems much less plausible that a dispositional orientation is the mature, adult state, since we know that the majority of adults in the world do not end up with that orientation.

More recently, many studies have shown that children do not uniformly use situational attributions. For example, in one study, children ranging in age from 4 to 7 years of age were told about an individual's traits and asked to predict that person's behavior (for example, "Sally is really mean. Will she share her cookies?"). By at least age 5, the children could use the trait information as evidence to predict behavior (Yuill & Pearson, 1998). We saw in Chapter 12 that when children reason about moral decisions or guilt, they sometimes focus exclusively on the situation and neglect the mental states of others, especially if the scenario is described in a way that does not emphasize mental states. However, the tendency to neglect those internal or dispositional factors in moral decisions unless they are made salient does not amount to an *inability* to think about them.

In fact, even young children sometimes assume that other people's internal qualities help explain their behaviors (Gelman, 1992, 2003; Gelman & Wellman, 1991). For example, a child who repeatedly observes a friend's room in disarray might conclude that the friend is a messy person. That sort of *essentialist bias* toward explaining a person's behavior in terms of his unchanging, inner essence seems to suggest that children would rely too much on dispositional factors early on, something that is also claimed to contribute to some forms of prejudice. Thus, young children will sometimes assume that if a person with a different skin color than her own does something wrong, the tendency to do things wrong may be intrinsic to everyone with that skin color (Hirschfeld, 1996).

The observation that young children can use trait information to explain behavior raises the interesting question of whether they use this information in the same way as older children and adults. **Trait-based reasoning**, which is more common at older ages, is a nuanced way of considering individual qualities or traits in relation to specific circumstances. For example, a good person's trusting nature may make him overly gullible, which could lead to reckless or harmful behavior in some situations. In this way of thinking, traits themselves are not necessarily good or bad; the outcome depends on the situation. In contrast, research suggests that younger children are more likely than older ones to use **evaluative reasoning**, which involves viewing a person as entirely good or bad, and predicting his future behaviors based on that view (Alvarez et al., 2001). Someone who engages in evaluative reasoning may notice a specific trait, such as selfishness, and then evaluate the person as wholly good or bad based on it (see Figure 13.21). When 5- and 6-year-olds were compared with 9- and 10-year-olds, the younger children were much more likely to rely on broad, evaluative judgments in predicting behaviors and to be less attentive to trait-specific ones (Alvarez et al., 2001). This tendency in young children may also shed light on the earlier idea that they do not consider dispositional factors. Some traits, such as being shy or outgoing, are relatively free of evaluative components. If a young child is primarily using evaluative reasoning, she might find it more difficult to use these neutral traits to predict behavior.

While evaluative and trait-based reasoning may seem like qualitatively different types of understanding, a more conservative interpretation is that simplified versions of trait-based reasoning may be as salient as evaluative ones. Young children may be most aware of the global, evaluative aspect of traits, and perhaps attend to it first, because

FIGURE 13.21 Evaluative versus trait-based reasoning. When preschoolers make attributions and judgments about others, they may have a tendency to make more global evaluative judgments than more trait-specific ones.

Q: How do young children's attributions about others' behavior differ from those of older children and adults? How might these developmental patterns vary across cultures?

it suggests some very simple, useful behavioral guidelines, such as avoiding people with "bad" traits and interacting with those who show "good" traits. Thus, developmental changes may reflect more intrinsic complexity of some attributions than it does a qualitative shift. There are indeed subtle traits that lead to complex behavioral predictions that may escape a young child, but there are even subtler aspects of traits and their expressions in situations that can similarly elude many adults. If you observe someone behaving shyly on a date, you would be hard-pressed to predict whether he would be shy about giving a speech. Indeed, we may underestimate how often as adults, especially in times of stress, we gravitate toward the same holistic, evaluative attributions. This tendency is related to the fundamental attribution error, in that both involve an essentialist bias. But they differ in that evaluative reasoning involves characterizing someone as entirely good or bad based on a particular trait, whereas the fundamental attribution error involves relying too much on dispositional factors (which need not be especially positive or negative) to explain behavior.

If younger children are sometimes able to reason about specific traits, why did the earlier studies suggest otherwise? One possibility is that even though the children understood the traits, they may have struggled with the way that the traditional experimental tasks asked about links between traits and behaviors. In many older studies, the child would hear a description or watch a video of an individual doing something. A researcher would then ask the child to choose which of two other behaviors was more likely for that person based on the first one. For example, a child might watch a video of a boy sharing a toy (a trait-relevant behavior). Then an experimenter would ask the child whether the boy was more likely to help a friend clean his room or not help and just stand by idly. In these studies, children often would not make correct inferences until age 8 or older (Rholes & Ruble, 1984).

These sorts of tasks, however, require a more complex reasoning process than a single trait-based prediction of behavior. The child has to make an inference from one behavior to a trait (from sharing a toy to kindness) and then link that trait to a second behavior (helping clean a room). But what would happen if the task were broken into two parts: one that requires making an inference from a behavior to a trait and another that involves making an inference from a trait to a behavior? And would children's performance improve if the trait-behavior relationships were made clearer and more salient, perhaps by providing several example behaviors for each trait? With these methodological changes, even 4-year-olds can easily reason about specific traits (Liu et al., 2007). Therefore, what develops may not be an ability to think about specific traits as much as an ability to combine behavior-to-trait inferences with trait-to-behavior inferences. This ability may be supported by the child's language development as she improves at using labels for traits (Liu et al., 2007). It also seems that when children are thinking about personal attributes in areas where they are particularly well practiced (such as figuring out which adults are the most expert informants about how to label things or which adults give the clearest instructions), they can make quite focused attributions about reliable versus unreliable informants without extending such attributions in a more global, evaluative manner (Einav & Robinson, 2011; Fusaro et al., 2011; Jaswal et al., 2010; Lutz & Keil, 2002).

> **Q:** What is evaluative reasoning, and what is its purported role in the development of the ability to make attributions about others?

Although recent evidence calls into question the earlier claims that children simply describe behavior and neglect internal states, it is difficult to discern an overall developmental pattern in terms of when (and whether) children show a dispositional or a situational bias. Thus far, researchers have used very different methods to examine how children make attributions at different ages. As a result, it is difficult to generalize across studies to say whether children start with either a situational or a dispositional bias and how their attributions change depending on the culture around them. The most conservative interpretation of the research at present is that at least by the age of 5, and possibly quite a bit earlier, children can take into account both situational and dispositional factors in their attributions. It is possible that infants and toddlers show no early bias between the two styles before adopting the one that prevails in the surrounding culture. To see how attributional differences across cultures develop, we need a more systematic set of studies that uses similar methods but controls for possible age effects on how children make attributions.

Beyond situational versus dispositional biases, children at least as young as 5 years of age take into account how traits emerge when they make inferences about traits and evaluate individuals with those traits. For example, in one set of studies, children were told about traits that emerged in individuals either naturally, through sustained effort, through extrinsic rewards, or through artificial medical enhancement. Even though all traits were manifested to the same extent in the described individuals, children tended to see the naturally emerging traits as persisting over longer time periods and under more challenging conditions. In addition, they evaluated those who acquired traits naturally more positively than those who acquired them through extrinsic means or through some kind of medicine (Lockhart et al., 2013). This bias for naturally emerging traits therefore appears early and persists into adulthood; and it represents one way in which the causal story of a trait's emergence influences subsequent inferences and evaluations about that trait. Even young children do not simply evaluate a trait in terms of its current surface characteristics; they are strongly influenced by information about how that trait originated.

Traits and Optimism

Your view of yourself clearly influences your view of your future. If you believe you are a powerful, competent person, you are inclined to think the future bodes well for you. If you see yourself as helpless and incompetent, you will more likely believe that uncontrollable events are in store and that you will not manage them well. Two key questions help frame these issues with respect to development: (1) Are there any general patterns concerning how children at different ages view the future? (2) What kinds of individual differences develop among children in this respect?

Regarding general developmental patterns, younger children seem to be more optimistic about the future than older ones (see Figure 13.22). In one set of studies, each child was told about another child of his or her same sex and age who had a negative attribute that was either physical (such as an allergy) or psychological (such as being messy) or a blend of the two (such as being physically aggressive; Lockhart et al., 2002). Table 13.3 shows several sample attributes. The

Type of Negative Trait	Examples
Biological	Missing finger
	Allergy
Blend of biological and psychological	Aggression
	Attentional problems
Psychological	Messy
	Fearful

TABLE 13.3 **Youthful optimism about negative traits.** This table shows the three types of negative traits that children and adults were asked about in the study of children's optimism about the future. The younger the child, the more likely he was to see negative traits as likely to improve. Adapted from Lockhart et al. (2002).

child was then asked what the child in the story would be like at various times in the future, up to young adulthood. Even the youngest children expected more positive change in psychological attributes than physical ones. But remarkably, they also expected that the physical traits, some as permanent as a missing finger, would dramatically improve in the future.

This youthful optimism reflects a positive attitude toward others' traits and presumably toward their own, since the protagonists were of the same age and sex as the participants. Younger children's optimism may help protect them from getting discouraged by the inevitable failures that come from being unskilled in so many areas (Lockhart et al., 2002). Interestingly, a study comparing young Japanese children's and adults' responses to the same type of stories about children found the same general pattern as in the original U.S. study: the Japanese children showed much more optimism about improvement of negative traits than did the adults (Lockhart et al., 2008). However, the Japanese data suggested a somewhat different developmental trajectory, in which Japanese adults tended to be more optimistic about some scenarios than were American adults.

This research reveals that young children can be quite sensitive to others' traits and can differentiate between different types of traits. They also tend to see negative traits as more likely to eventually change for the better. As children grow older, this optimism starts to fade, and in middle childhood, individual differences in attributional style become more prominent. As we will see in Chapter 16, the children who become most pessimistic may also struggle with depression in adolescence (Cole et al., 2008).

Alongside these general developmental patterns, children's individual differences in optimism and attributional styles have become a major area of research in their own right. The most prominent view describes two contrasting

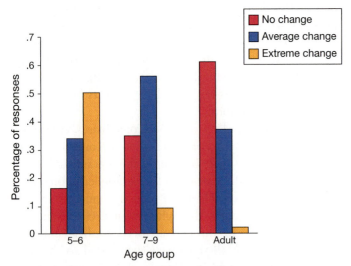

FIGURE 13.22 **Younger children as more optimistic.** There is a dramatic developmental change between kindergarten and second grade in the extent to which traits are seen as changing in a positive direction with increasing age. Adapted from Lockhart et al. (2002).

ways that children come to regard their own traits and consequently their prospects for future success. The first type of children, known as **fixed-trait theorists**, think of their traits as unchangeable, or fixed, aspects of themselves. If they fail at something, they assume they must be permanently deficient in that area. The other type of children, **incremental theorists**, see their traits as changeable with enough work. They therefore may have a more positive view of the future and be more likely to sustain their efforts (Dweck, 1986, 2006, 2012; Dweck & Leggett, 1988). Given the finding that younger children are more optimistic than older ones about traits improving in the future, we can view younger children as tending toward incremental theories and, in some cases, developing fixed-trait theories in middle childhood. It seems likely that the children who shift toward fixed-trait attributions do not change their attributions for all traits across the board. However, the specificity of those changes still needs further research.

Q: How do young children differ from older children in terms of their optimism about traits? Why might such a difference exist?

Attribution, Motivation, and Creativity

Although children who develop a fixed-trait attribution style tend to be more pessimistic about the possibility of self-improvement, they do not necessarily maintain an unalterable level of self-esteem. In fact, the nature of fixed-trait attributions can be changed somewhat by valuing the traits differently. Thus, simply praising a group of schoolchildren for doing well on a task *because of their intelligence*, which emphasizes a fixed trait, instead of praising them for doing well *because of their efforts*, can reduce their intrinsic motivation for the task. Emphasizing a fixed trait this way may make the possibility of failure much more threatening—since failure could then reflect a fixed lack of intelligence rather than an easily addressed lack of effort. Such trait-oriented feedback may unintentionally encourage children to choose rote, easy tasks in which success is virtually guaranteed (Dweck, 2006; Mueller & Dweck, 1998). Moreover, if a child views a particular negative trait that he possesses as fixed, he may give up on developing skills related to that trait. Such differences in attributional style have been used to explain why some children give up when faced with failure, while others persevere (Dweck, 2012; Dweck & Leggett, 1988).

A related effect involving attributions about motivation does not arise from individual differences; instead, it reflects ways in which all children—and, in fact, people of all ages—can have intrinsic motivation and even creativity undermined based on attributions they make about themselves. A set of landmark studies vividly demonstrated this effect by showing how a previously enjoyable activity can come to seem like a chore (Condry & Chambers, 1978; Deci, 1971, 1972; Lepper et al., 1973; Lepper & Greene, 1975).

At the outset of one study, all the children in a preschool classroom were given some new play materials: a set of magic markers and some drawing paper (Lepper et al., 1973). The researchers pointed out the markers and paper to the children and then measured how long each child spent playing with the markers compared with the other available toys. Children who showed some intrinsic interest in drawing by playing with the markers for more than a certain amount of time were selected for the experiment. They were then randomly assigned to one of three conditions: the expected-reward condition, the unexpected-reward condition, or the no-reward condition.

Each child was then taken individually to a separate room. Children in the expected-reward group were shown an ornate certificate called a "Good Player Award" and told that they would receive it if they helped the experimenters by drawing pictures for them. The children in the unexpected-reward and the no-reward conditions were simply asked to play with the materials and draw some pictures. In all three conditions, the children were given the same amount of time to draw. Children in the expected-reward condition were all given the expected award for playing well. Children in the unexpected-reward group were told, after they had spent their time drawing, that because they drew so well they were going to be given a "Good Player Award" (which was identical to that in the expected-reward condition). Finally, children in the no-reward group were returned to their classroom without any mention of rewards. A week or two after these one-on-one sessions, a new group of researchers, who had no information about which experimental condition each child had experienced, observed the children drawing with markers in the classroom, just as they had when their intrinsic interest was first assessed. Figure 13.23A summarizes this procedure.

This study's findings, which are summarized in Figure 13.23B, are impressive. Children in either the unexpected-reward condition or the no-reward condition played with the materials more than they had at the outset. In contrast, the children who drew pictures for the expected reward showed a marked drop in spontaneous play with the drawing materials. This drop has been explained in terms of several factors that blend ideas about the self with attributions about a person's own motivation. More specifically, after the children in the expected-reward condition heard about the "Good Player Award," they apparently came to attribute their own interest in drawing to the expectation of being rewarded for it. Attributing their behavior to that extrinsic factor (the reward)

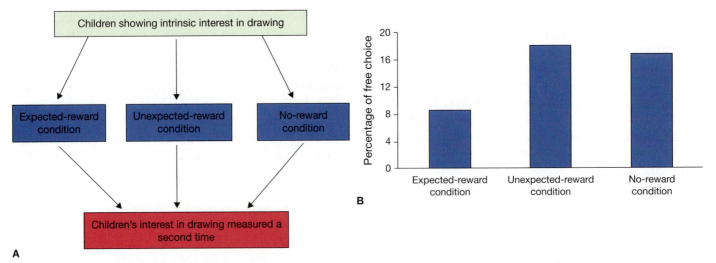

FIGURE 13.23 The effects of reward on intrinsic motivation. (A) The 1973 study by Lepper and colleagues assigned children to three distinct groups and then used a common assessment to determine the percentage of time that children later chose to play with toys that they had played with during the experimental session. **(B)** This bar graph shows the mean proportion of time that children chose to play with the target activity in postexperimental sessions. Adapted from Lepper et al. (1973).

made them discount their earlier, intrinsic motivation for it, a phenomenon called the **overjustification effect**. After drawing to earn the certificate, they seemed to say to themselves, "I was doing this because I knew I'd get a reward, not because I liked doing it." Thus, their self-concept mediated the way the reward influenced their behavior.

Later studies have shown that if a child simply knows that an adult is carefully watching her behavior, it can be enough to reduce intrinsic motivation for the behavior (Lepper & Green, 1975). In at least some situations, a child who knows she is being monitored may reframe the situation in such a way that she believes that her behavior is motivated by an external factor. Even the simple act of praising a child's actions can have a similar effect, undermining motivations for those actions (Henderlong & Lepper, 2002). Yet, not all praise has negative effects; praising internal factors like effort, rather than actions, is less likely to decrease motivation.

These kinds of interactions and individual responses are cognitively complex. The child must assess her own mental and motivational states, take into account the context in which she is acting, weigh the external conditions influencing her actions, and then reassess the relationships between the situational and dispositional factors that drive her behaviors. Thus, the presence of the overjustification effect in preschoolers suggests that they clearly can take into account both situational and dispositional factors when interpreting their own behaviors.

One of the most insidious ways that extrinsic rewards can influence self-perception and motivation comes from how children change their approach to a task when the rewards are still present. In the example of drawing with markers, if the children who initially expected (and received) a reward

for drawing were later asked to draw to earn a reward, they tended to make a larger number of drawings that were of lower quality. Some children even set up little assembly lines to churn out lots of drawings that were each much simpler than the ones they produced before being rewarded. This new approach to the task fit their interpretation of working for the reward (Loveland & Olley, 1979).

Nonetheless, some have argued that extrinsic rewards need not undermine creativity if they are handled carefully. These researchers suggest that if you fine-tune the system to reward only high-quality work and explicitly convey this criterion, the rewards can enhance creativity (Eisenberger & Cameron, 1998). Yet, these manipulations can be subtle and difficult to implement with young children. In the long run, the rewards may still subtly undermine motivation and creativity if they are removed. For example, one study on educational video games that teach mathematical skills found that games designed around intrinsic motivational factors (such as embedding math problems in the most exciting parts of the games) were seven times as likely to be played in the future as those that were designed around extrinsic factors (such as embedding math problems in tests at the end of the game, where achieving a good score was the reward; Habgood & Ainsworth, 2011).

In research that rewarded children with stickers for eating vegetables they disliked, the studies reported an increased preference for the rewarded vegetables more than 3 months later (Cooke et al., 2011). The success may be because the vegetables were initially strongly disliked, and by being rewarded for eating them, the children learned that they were not so bad. On the other hand, if the children's initial dislike for the vegetables had been mild, the result of reinforcement could have been negligible. Thus, when there is less of an initial negative bias, it may be harder to instill a shift toward the more positive.

The findings that external rewards, mediated by children's self-perception, can undermine intrinsic motivation strike a clear blow to behaviorist models of learning. According to the behaviorists, reinforcing a behavior in any organism, whether it is a human or a rat, should increase the propensity for the behavior. Yet, the drawing studies (and many other studies that followed) showed the opposite pattern. Although some have contended that this large set of studies was flawed and have argued that the effect does not exist (Eisenberger & Cameron, 1996), more recent, extensive analyses strongly indicate that these overjustification effects are real and substantial (Deci et al., 1999; Lepper et al., 1999, 2005). These interactions may be far more complex than originally envisioned, and it may be possible to craft effective, beneficial patterns of external reinforcement by attending carefully to the child's mental states. Most interesting, however, is the evidence that the overjustification effect provides rich social cognitions that influence behavior, even in the preschool years.

In practical terms, this research shows that extrinsic rewards should be used with caution in educational and other structured settings. Extrinsic awards extend far beyond the classroom to include medals for athletic competitions, prizes for artists, and salary bonuses in the workplace. In a broader sense, the critical issue seems to be giving people the sense of having a choice in decisions about their lives and daily activities, or what is sometimes called **self-determination** (Ryan & Deci, 2000). If people feel that they have had an important role in determining their behaviors, they will be more motivated to engage in those behaviors. This effect seems even stronger in children, for whom tangible rewards seem to have the most negative consequences (Patall et al., 2008). The importance of choice, however, also suggests ways to mitigate the negative effects of rewards. For example, if people are given a choice among several rewards, that element of choice can often reduce the feeling of being coerced by the reward (Patall et al., 2008; see Figure 13.24). Thus, introducing a genuine opportunity for choice and self-determination into a reward system, such as allowing children in a task to use their "earnings" to choose which of several rewards to purchase, can often mitigate the negative effects of rewards and can sometimes maintain their positive effects on immediate performance.

A second practical issue concerns whether the harmful effects of extrinsic rewards might vary across cultures and groups. It has been reported, for example, that extrinsic motivations may be less detrimental in some non-Western settings, such as China, where conformity to group norms is often valued more than autonomy (Iyengar & Lepper, 1999). But a closer look suggests more commonalities than differences in this respect between Western and Chinese children

FIGURE 13.24 **Choice among rewards.** When children are given a choice among rewards, the choice can reduce the degree to which intrinsic motivation is undermined.

(Bao & Lam, 2008). For example, if Chinese children have strong social and emotional connections to those providing rewards, their negative effects are somewhat reduced. However, when there is no such close connection, the rewards tend to decrease intrinsic motivation, just as they do in the West (Bao & Lam, 2008). One interpretation of this finding is that the Chinese children have internalized the goals and needs of those to whom they are closely attached, such that the intrinsic motivation of someone like a parent is, by extension, their own intrinsic motivation. This view suggests that children in the West might also be insulated from the negative effects of extrinsic rewards if they see the reward givers as part of their own close-knit, supportive group, such as a family with strong shared values and goals (Bao & Lam, 2008; Lepper et al., 2005).

Q: Describe how it is possible to turn play into work, even for preschoolers. What mechanism seems to explain this transformation?

Conclusions

The ability to understand our own mental states and those of others is an essential part of being a mature person. Contrary to earlier views, it seems that young children and even infants do have some sense of self, but it may be based largely on their perceptions and actions, without involving conceptual or autobiographical ways of construing themselves. Each of these senses of self have early versions, or competencies, that become more sophisticated over time, again supporting a recurring theme in this book of the value of focusing on emerging abilities as opposed to disappearing deficits. In addition, the different facets of the self interact and support growth in each other over the course of development. Thus, an increasing sense of the private self supports the development of the extended self, and the conceptual self interacts with the autobiographical self. In fact, there are interactions between almost every pairing of the dimensions of self that reinforce each other and that may ultimately help create a more integrated sense of self.

In the development of self-esteem and self-efficacy, which add an evaluative component to self-knowledge and understanding, we see once again how basic cognitive skills influence a child's social interactions and emotional states. Contrary to popular accounts, however, low self-esteem may not be the prime cause of various acting-out behaviors, and overly high self-esteem can pose its own set of problems. Thoughts about the self are also related to emotional intelligence and self-regulation. The ability to regulate ourselves by deferring gratification may heavily involve attentional skills that enable us to focus on other objects rather than the most salient goal. Self-regulation ability is also influenced by context: whether those influences are local, such as the presence of a mirror, or cultural, reflecting the way a culture values strong self-regulation skills early on. In this way, we see that self-regulation can be amplified or reduced by the environment in which a child develops.

The child's understanding of other people's minds shows several major developmental changes. Based on the much-studied false-belief tasks, earlier researchers believed that children younger than about 3½ cannot think of others as having false beliefs about a current situation. But more recent studies suggest that young children's failures on false-belief tasks tell only part of the story of how theory of mind develops. More recent research is beginning to link simple patterns of goal attribution in infancy to more complex patterns of thought about second-order beliefs in late childhood. It is therefore misleading to think that there is a particular age at which a child acquires a theory of mind. Instead, it makes more sense to think of infants and young children as using a rich array of cognitive and perceptual tools to gain insight into the behaviors of social agents. Even an understanding of false beliefs now seems to be within the conceptual reach of infants, at least at an implicit level. Again, emerging competencies is a powerful theme. Younger children and infants do not have as many of these tools, and they use some of them in more limited ways. Nonetheless, they are sensitive from a very early age to some special properties of social agents, and they benefit from ways in which all these tools work together to help them think about the minds of others.

A critical part of thinking about others involves inferences about dispositions and traits and how they might vary or stay the same over time. Children, much more than adults, tend to believe that negative traits in younger people will improve and that positive traits will endure. This youthful optimism may be a way of protecting themselves against the failures that younger children inevitably experience as they mature. These attributions are critical, as well, to understanding motivation and creativity in the young child. More broadly, these developmental patterns and the related idea of self-determination reinforce the theme that for optimal development, children need to be active agents in their own developmental journeys and not just passive recipients of environmental inputs and contingencies. Of course, external inputs and encouragement are important, but they should always occur in ways that are sensitive to a child's intrinsic interests and curiosities.

STUDY AND REVIEW

SUMMARY

Self-Concepts and Self-Representations

- In the first few years of life, there are dramatic changes in how children come to view themselves. These changes are best understood by realizing that there may be at least five distinct senses of self that emerge at quite different times and in different ways: the ecological self, the interpersonal self, the extended self, the private self, and the conceptual self.
- An important dimension of knowing ourselves is gender identity, a form of knowledge that may be far more subject to biological constraints than was originally thought. The sense of gender identity, however, is quite distinct from culturally provided sex roles, which can vary independently, as an individual can firmly believe that he or she has a certain gender while engaging in many roles typically associated with the other gender.

Developing a Sense of Self-Worth

- Self-esteem, a sense of our own value, changes dramatically during childhood, generally progressing from extremely high views of the self to more realistic assessments based on increasingly complex social comparisons.
- Self-efficacy, the belief about our capacity to achieve goals, is a more focused kind of assessment often tied to a particular situation. Feelings of low self-efficacy are often easier to change in a child than low self-esteem.

Self-Regulation

- Younger children are more likely to show difficulties in self-regulation and hence have problems in delaying gratification. Difficulties may frequently arise from inadequate strategies for diverting their attention from a desired object or from an inability to think of ways to make the desired object less salient or accessible. Some of these problems may arise from relatively late maturation of regions of the frontal lobes. Damage to these regions in adult brains can also cause self-regulation problems. Self-regulation levels vary across both genders and cultures. They seem to be influenced by surrounding cultural and local contexts as well as socialization practices.

Developing a Theory of Mind

- Young children are certainly aware of the distinctive nature of social beings, but at first they may understand other social beings' behavior only in terms of their goals and desires.

Even after young children come to explicitly appreciate that others have beliefs (usually around 2 years of age), it isn't until about 3½ years of age that they stop having difficulty reasoning about other people having *false* beliefs. The ability to understand false beliefs is not the same as having a full-fledged theory of mind, but it is an important component. At a more tacit level, however, and in tasks that pose lower loads on executive processing, even infants may have rudimentary senses of false beliefs.

- There is some evidence that nonhuman primates can grasp a rudimentary sense of others' false beliefs, although this kind of understanding may become uniquely rich and nuanced in humans.
- These patterns raise questions about whether the child's theory of mind develops as a cognitive module that is domain specific, informationally encapsulated, and strongly determined by biological factors. Some proponents of a theory of mind module have proposed that disruptions in the development of theory of mind skills may underlie some forms of autism.

Making Attributions about Ourselves and Others

- The ability to make attributions that explain others' behaviors is critical to functioning as a social individual. Younger children have rudimentary attributional skills, but they often seem to miss the subtler connections between traits, situations, and behaviors. They may be more likely to use evaluative reasoning, making global evaluations of others as good or bad and missing the more subtle aspects of how traits can predict behaviors.

  Younger children show greater optimism than older children and adults, leading them to believe that negative traits change for the better as people age. This optimism may have adaptive value if it shields the child from discouragement when she faces failures associated with being young and inexperienced.
- Attributions about the self can powerfully influence motivation and creativity. Even for preschool children, an intrinsically interesting form of play can become much more like work if they perceive that they are doing it merely to earn external rewards.
- It is possible to motivate children without undermining intrinsic motivation. This can be done by reminding children of the intrinsic values of their actions as well as enabling feelings of choice and control when using more external forms of reinforcement.

THOUGHT QUESTIONS

1. We have seen that people have at least five distinct senses of self that emerge at different times in the first few years of life. To what extent do you think these different senses of the self start to become integrated into a more unitary sense of self as a child grows older? If you do think such an integration occurs, speculate on how it might happen. If not, explain why you think the senses stay separate.

2. How might an extremely low level of self-esteem have very different consequences for a young child, a schoolchild, an adolescent, and an adult?

3. Describe a situation in which a typical 7-year-old would fail to reason adequately about the mental states of others, but a typical 16-year-old would succeed. What is different about the cognitive capacities of the two age groups that would explain the failure of the younger child and the success of the teenager?

4. An elementary school has been using extrinsic rewards in an attempt to motivate its students to achieve at higher levels in mathematics. The program is not working well, as the students are starting to regard mathematics as unpleasant work. The school is not willing to stop using the rewards but asks you for advice on what else they might do to diminish the negative side effects of the rewards. What do you recommend?

KEY TERMS

attribution theory (p. 494)

conceptual self (p. 470)

dispositional factor (p. 493)

dominance hierarchy (p. 484)

ecological self (p. 469)

evaluative reasoning (p. 494)

extended self (p. 469)

false-belief task (p. 487)

false-photograph task (p. 489)

fixed-trait theorist (p. 497)

fundamental attribution error (p. 493)

gender identity (p. 472)

gender role (p. 473)

incremental theorist (p. 497)

interpersonal self (p. 469)

kinesthetic self-concept (p. 471)

mirror test (p. 471)

module (p. 483)

overjustification effect (p. 498)

private self (p. 469)

self-concept (p. 471)

self-determination (p. 499)

self-efficacy (p. 476)

self-esteem (p. 474)

sense of self (p. 468)

situational factor (p. 493)

theory of mind (p. 468)

theory of mind module (TOMM) (p. 491)

trait-based reasoning (p. 494)

14

Becoming Part of the Family

Parenting
- Parenting Styles
- Parenting Contexts
- Interventions to Improve Parenting
- Parent Effects in Relation to Other Influences
- The Interactionist Approach to Family Dynamics
- Gender Socialization in the Family: A Web of Interacting Influences

Siblings and Family Dynamics
- Birth Order Effects
- Sibling Relationships and Socialization

Changes in the Family
- Changes in Parents' Age
- Changes in Family Size
- Working Parents and Child Care
- Changes in Family Structures

Child Abuse
- Effects of Abuse
- Explaining the Cycle of Abuse
- Foster Care

Conclusions

Summary

When Bill Clinton rose to prominence on the American political stage, people naturally wanted to know about his family background. When attention turned to his younger half-brother, Roger, it seemed that Roger could not be more different from Bill (see Figure 14.1). Roger had drifted from job to job, and his career as musician never got off the ground. He became increasingly involved in drug use, which in turn led to drug dealing. For these activities, Roger served 2 years in prison. Meanwhile, his brother Bill earned a scholarship to Georgetown University, then a prestigious Rhodes Scholarship to Oxford. He attended Yale Law School before returning to his home state of Arkansas, where he was elected governor at age 32, making him the youngest governor in the country. After nearly 12 years as governor, he was twice elected to the presidency of the United States.

Given such dramatically different outcomes for these two boys born to the same mother, many people assumed that the sharp contrasts in their lives must have been caused by their different fathers, presumably because of different genetic predispositions. Others pointed to birth order and argued that Bill Clinton, being the firstborn, was bound to be less rebellious and more driven to achieve. In fact, developmental studies that consider large numbers of families tell a more complicated and more interesting story (Conley, 2004). For example, one major influence on children appears to be the economic status of the family as a whole. When a family is wealthy, siblings tend to turn out more alike. When a family is poor, as was the case with the Clintons, parents have to choose how to allocate their limited resources, often devoting most of them to the child who shows the earliest promise, which is frequently the

FIGURE 14.1 **Sibling differences.** Even though they grew up in the same family and have a physical resemblance, Bill and Roger Clinton had markedly different life courses. Recent research is beginning to offer explanations for why siblings turn out to be similar or very different.

firstborn. Because there are many other possible sources of influence, we cannot know for sure whether the Clintons' economic situation contributed significantly to the differences between Bill and Roger, but we do know that these effects are much more common in less advantaged families. As this chapter describes, the family is a site of numerous interacting influences on development, from socioeconomic and cultural factors, to the effects of parents and children on one another, to the consequences of sibling relations, to the importance of shared genetic predispositions.

For most of us, the most important social unit in our lives is our family. We explain our preferences in relation to family traditions (either aligned with them or against them); we relate powerful, formative family experiences, from moments of shared understanding to horrific fights; and we refer to our family role, such as the scapegoat, the leader, the joker, or even the black sheep. We do these things because we assume that many aspects of who we are can be understood in terms of what our family is like. In this chapter, we will consider how the many facets of the family contribute to a child's development. We will start with views of parenting, then consider siblings, and finally explore how changes, conflict, and physical and psychological abuse in the family might be understood in light of the wide range of possible influences that can arise between the child and the other members of the family.

Studies on families employ an enormous range of methods, many of them quite different from the experimental approaches encountered in earlier chapters. To study the effects of parents on children, of children on parents, or of siblings on each other, it is not often feasible to experimentally assign groups of children to different parenting conditions. Instead, researchers usually have to examine interactions in real families as they unfold. They then infer causal patterns from the intricate networks of correlations between family members' behaviors, their personality traits, and many types of family environments. Striking correlations often emerge, but it is difficult to uncover an unambiguous causal pathway or cycle that explains those correlations.

It is important to keep these methodological challenges in mind as we address several questions about families. First, we will focus on the parents and ask how different kinds of parenting can influence a child's development. For example, does a rigid and overly controlling style of parenting tend to affect children's personality traits, perhaps by making the children more submissive? We will also consider how different contexts, whether cultural or socioeconomic, can interact with the effects of different kinds of parenting (see Figure 14.2). We will ask about other possible causes of correlations between parental behaviors and those in their children. In particular, we will discuss research regarding children's effects on their parents, effects of shared genotypes

FIGURE 14.2 Parents and families. Throughout the world, families are considered the primary social unit of a child's life and where many of the strongest emotional bonds are formed. It is therefore not surprising that families, and parents in particular, have been thought to be the primary agents behind a child's personality and value system. That view, however, has become highly controversial, as other factors beyond the family are shown to have influence as well.

between parents and their children, and the effects of different environments on both children and their parents. We will also explore how all of these factors interact in contributing to long-lasting characteristics in children.

We will then consider the relations between siblings, including whether a child's position relative to other siblings has a systematic effect on development: Does birth order matter, and does it matter more in some kinds of families than in others? We will also examine whether siblings try to differentiate themselves from one another. And we will consider the other social and cognitive effects that sibling relationships may have on the children themselves and within the family system.

We will then turn to the developmental consequences of changing family demographics. In the United States and many other developed countries, the trends in recent decades point toward older parents, smaller families, and more families in which both parents work full-time outside the home. Each of these trends can change the family dynamic, influencing both parents and children. We will also consider some of the changes to family structure that have become more prevalent in recent decades, including single-parent families, families with same-sex parents, and families in which parents divorce and perhaps remarry, blending two previously separate families. There is now extensive research on what kinds of effects these different family structures have on children and how, in some cases, they seem to vary, depending on the children's age and gender.

Finally, we will consider the prevalence and effects of child abuse. Such cases can range from physical and verbal abuse to incest. These tragedies raise significant concerns about the long-term consequences for children. In addition, they demonstrate potential effects across generations, as abused children become abusive parents themselves, creating a "cycle of abuse." We will also ask about the potential effects of foster care on children. For example, what are the potential tradeoffs associated with placing children in foster care as opposed to keeping them in their own problematic home setting?

In all of these cases, it is important to carefully monitor the kinds of methods that researchers use and the extent to which these methods can support clear conclusions about causal patterns. We will also want to keep in mind the cycles of interactions that can happen in a family and the challenges of disentangling causes from effects. At the broadest level, we will consider families in terms of two complex webs of interactions, one that occurs among family members and another that occurs between the family and the larger culture in which it is situated. Our goal will be to discern some reliable patterns that hold across these two webs of interactions.

Parenting

Parenting can take several forms that serve different functions for the child. One review described seven important components of parenting that guide a child's development (Brooks-Gunn & Markman, 2005). Each of these components forms a continuum with positive and negative forms of parental behaviors at opposite ends. The positive and negative behaviors show dramatic differences in their prevalence and their effects across different socioeconomic and cultural groups, and these patterns are correlated with different outcomes for children.

- *Nurturance* involves showing children warmth and responding to their needs and changing emotions (see Chapter 6). When parents fail to nurture, they may be either disengaged or inappropriately intrusive.
- *Discipline* methods that attempt to explain the reason for a punishment are generally considered more effective than

punishments that are coercive, physical, or insufficiently explained (see Chapter 12).

- *Teaching* a child ideally involves questioning a child carefully to find out where she is coming from cognitively. Parents who are less effective teachers may instead take over the task for the child without considering the child's own mental state, or they may not offer any help.
- The *language* that parents use to engage the child can be adjusted to suit his age and situation, and it can include questions, expansions of the child's utterances, and a rich narrative structure (see Chapter 8). Alternatively, a parent may talk to the child only rarely or may talk "at the child" without encouraging interaction.
- The *materials* that parents provide to foster creative play—like books, toys, and games—enable a child to imagine, explore, and interact more fruitfully with others. Other parents may provide minimal support or prefer materials more useful for "managing" the child, such as sitting him in front of a television for long periods.
- *Monitoring* includes being aware of a child's activities throughout the day, such as where the child is and what she is reading or playing with or watching on television. A low-monitoring parent may be barely aware of a child's activities and may not really have any sense of how a child spends her time.
- Parents *manage* their children's time by arranging play dates or other recurring activities that give a child's life structure and regularity. Parents who fail to adequately manage a child's time might not plan for the days or weeks ahead, leaving the child with no routines and no sense of what is coming next.

Across these seven dimensions of parental behavior, some common aspects distinguish the more positive, balanced ways of interacting with children from the negative ways, which can be either quite rigid or disengaged. In particular, parents tend to vary in the level of warmth and responsiveness they show to their children and in the level of demands or control they place on them. Variations in these broader aspects of parental behavior form the foundation for one of the most influential theories about parenting effects.

Parenting Styles

For several decades, researchers have examined parenting styles and the possible influences of such styles on children. We define **parenting styles** as the ways in which parents engage in behaviors and have attitudes toward their children that create a particular parenting environment or climate. As already noted, the most prominent theory of parenting styles is based on two main ways that parental behaviors vary: the warmth and responsiveness of parents toward their

children and the level of parents' demands or control. This theory holds that a parent can be either high or low on each dimension and that a parent's particular combination of warmth and control ends up setting the tone for most interactions between parent and child. Simplifying each of these dimensions into high and low values yields a two-by-two table showing the four most commonly discussed parenting styles (see Table 14.1).

Table 14.1 reflects one of the most active areas of research on parenting (Maccoby & Martin, 1983). The *authoritative*, *permissive*, and *authoritarian* styles were originally proposed by developmental psychologist Diana Baumrind in 1966 (Baumrind, 1966). (The fourth style, *neglectful/uninvolved*, logically results from a low level of both warmth and control, but it was not a major component of Baumrind's original account.) Although threads of these ideas extend back though earlier studies (Grusec, 2011; Hess & Shipman, 1965; Lewin, 1946; Sears et al., 1957), Baumrind initially developed these categories after observing preschool and school-age children in school, in lab settings, and interacting with their parents at home. She also interviewed the parents about how they interacted with their children. The parenting styles that Baumrind proposed appeared quite distinct and were associated with different behaviors and traits in the children.

Over several decades of research and analysis, Baumrind's parenting styles have endured remarkably well (Baumrind, 1991). Given that versions of these types do seem to exist, at least among middle-class North American parents, the obvious question is whether they directly influence aspects of the child. Researchers have frequently addressed this question by looking for correlations between parenting styles and aspects of children's behavior and personalities (see Figure 14.3). Any significant correlations were then assumed to result from the parenting style—the classic fallacy of equating correlation with causation. This is an important concern to keep in mind as we look at each parenting style and the patterns of correlation with developmental outcomes and consider what sorts of causal influences are suggested. Our first examples are limited to middle-class, white, North American children. They mostly pertain to children in early and middle adolescence, as many researchers assume that parenting effects may be the most dramatic after several years of parenting.

	High Control	Low Control
High Warmth	Authoritative	Permissive
Low Warmth	Authoritarian	Neglectful/uninvolved

TABLE 14.1 Parenting styles. Each of the four parenting styles involves a different combination of warmth and control.

A   **B**

FIGURE 14.3 Links between parenting styles and children's behavior. Parents can differ quite dramatically in their typical patterns of interactions with their children, ranging from authoritarian parents to permissive ones. Such differences in parenting styles have been found to correlate with personality differences in children, suggesting to some that the styles cause the differences. Other factors, however, such as shared genotypes and children's effects on parents, may be equally if not more important in shaping personality types.

Authoritarian parents are low in warmth and high in control and typically order their children around, expecting compliance with no questioning or discussion. Their parenting is often described as harsh, partly because they generally do not try to change a child's behavior through discussion, positive remarks, or rewards. Instead, they tend to use punishment and coercion. In Baumrind's initial description, many authoritarian parents believed they were enforcing behavioral standards based on fundamentalist religious doctrines (Baumrind, 1996). In public places, such as playgrounds or supermarkets, authoritarian parents can sometimes be quite conspicuous—yelling at their children, spanking them, or refusing to put up with any of the children's comments.

Children of authoritarian parents tend to be more dependent and to lack social competence in dealing with peers. They often seem relatively withdrawn and passive and especially compliant to authority figures. In adolescence, they tend to show lower self-esteem and to be more depressed than other children (Baumrind, 1991; Karavasilis et al., 2003). Relative to their peers, boys with authoritarian parents tend to show more hostility, whereas girls tend to set lower goals for achievement. Certainly, this constellation of traits gives the impression that the parents' demanding, overcontrolling approach created passive, withdrawn children who have had little opportunity for independence, self-expression, or initiative.

Quite the opposite of authoritarian parents, **permissive parents** are high in warmth and low in control. They make few demands of their children and rarely attempt to monitor or control their behavior. Instead, they are highly tolerant of their children's behaviors and desires. Their focus as parents is on helping to meet their children's needs and desires rather than on moderating their children's actions. They are often very sensitive to their children's emotions and motivations and try to respond to them without imposing any restrictions. They rarely discipline their children, and when they do, it may be inconsistent: the same behavior is punished on one occasion and tolerated on the next.

Children of permissive parents tend to seem more immature than their peers and to have trouble controlling their impulses or setting limits on themselves. In Baumrind's observations, they are less likely to accept responsibility for their own actions. They also tend to act less independently than other children, which may seem surprising given that they have had so few constraints. As adolescents they are more likely than their peers to exhibit problem behaviors. However, they also show relatively high self-esteem, relatively low rates of depression, and better social skills.

Authoritative parents are high in both warmth and control, but here it is important to take a more nuanced view than the simple two-by-two table suggests. Authoritative parents' "high control" is more balanced and less rigid and overbearing than that of authoritarian parents. Authoritative parents set guidelines for their children's behavior, but they are also flexible and will listen to children's concerns and needs. They favor positive feedback and rewards as opposed to punishment or coercion. Discipline is consistent, and the parent usually explains the reasons for punishment, along with requesting that the child make amends for the transgression. (If an older brother takes a younger sibling's toy, he might be asked to apologize, return the toy, and perhaps loan his brother one of his own toys for a while.) Authoritative parents are warm and sensitive to children's mental states, but they do not simply capitulate to their children's desires. They encourage their children's autonomy while upholding guidelines for appropriate behavior.

Children of authoritative parents seem to fare best among Baumrind's groups. They tend to be relatively independent and self-reliant and have good self-control. They do well in high school relative to the other groups and often take the initiative in various matters. Compared to their peers, boys with authoritative parents tend to be more socially responsible, while girls tend to be more independent. A child with authoritative parents seems to be his or her own person, having internalized standards of self-restraint and achievement.

Like authoritarian parenting, authoritative parenting also involves a form of control over children, but it is important to closely consider what kind of control. Several researchers have stressed that psychological control differs in several ways from behavioral control (Barber, 1996, 2002; Barber et al., 2005; Steinberg, 1990, 2005; Steinberg et al., 1989, 1994). *Psychological control* involves attempting to regulate a child's behavior by manipulating his feelings. These manipulations can include withdrawing affection from the child or inducing guilt or shame. Psychological control can include a parent's intrusions into a child's deeply personal domains, in which she feels she should have autonomy, especially as an adolescent (Steinberg, 2005). Psychological control, which is more typical of authoritarian parents, is often associated with more depressive and anxious symptoms in children (Steinberg, 2005). *Behavioral control*, in contrast, involves attempting to regulate a child's behavior by setting guidelines that follow the norms and values of the family or society—perhaps by requiring certain homework hours, a set bedtime, or appropriate ways to speak to older adults. Compared with psychological control, behavioral control is more common among authoritative parents and is generally associated with fewer negative outcomes in children.

Finally, while Baumrind's initial focus was not on the fourth cell, it is important to mention the *neglectful/uninvolved parents*, who seem to ignore and not care about their children. They do not interact much with their children, which makes their style almost a form of nonparenting. They might be oblivious to the child's hopes, desires, and fears and uninterested in monitoring the child's behaviors. This category is less discussed than the others, but may be more likely among parents who struggle with many problems of their own, making them unable to function well as parents. Imagine, for example, a single mother who is deeply clinically depressed. She has little motivation to do anything more than the bare minimum required to get through the day. Her child is largely irrelevant to her. In other cases, a parent may actually develop feelings of hostility toward a child that consequently contribute to a tendency to be neglectful and uninvolved.

Children of neglectful/uninvolved parents tend to fare badly. One especially clear pattern is their tendency to be especially susceptible to peer pressure and therefore to engage more often in behaviors that do not conform to adult norms (Bednar & Fisher, 2003; Durbin et al., 1993; Shucksmith et al., 1995). Some studies have suggested that girls with neglectful/uninvolved parents are more likely than other girls to become involved in peer groups whose norms are clearly different from those of the dominant adult culture (Brown et al., 1993; Lamborn et al., 1991). Table 14.2 summarizes the features of each parenting style and some of the associated developmental outcomes.

Q: What are Baumrind's three parenting styles, and how are they associated with psychological differences in children? When and how is gender of the child relevant?

Parenting Contexts

Many of these differences among children seem to fit with causal explanations of how parents might influence their children. But accounting for cross-cultural and social class differences inevitably complicates those causal stories because the associations between parenting styles and children's behaviors differ across cultural and socioeconomic groups.

Parenting across Cultures Even when a parenting style appears to be the same across several cultures, it can

	Parents	All Children	Boys	Girls
Authoritarian	Low warmth, high control (overbearing, rigid, psychological control)	Dependent, low social competency, look to authority	Hostile	Set low goals
Permissive	Low warmth, low control	Immature, low impulse control, not inclined to take responsibility or act independently	No obvious gender differences	No obvious gender differences
Authoritative	High warmth, high control (balanced, flexible, behavioral control)	Self-reliant, self-controlled, willing to explore	Responsible	Independent and socially responsible
Neglectful/uninvolved	Low warmth, low control	Strongly influenced by peers		May show a greater tendency to join peer groups that depart from adult norms

TABLE 14.2 Effects of parenting styles Four different parenting styles have been consistently associated with particular kinds of behaviors and traits in middle-class North American children.

nonetheless mean very different things—and be associated with different outcomes—depending on each culture's social norms. Contrast, for example, Chinese-American children and European-American children. A parenting style with many authoritarian components is associated with much better outcomes among Chinese-American children than among American children of European descent. Part of the explanation for this difference may lie in the different meanings that highly similar parental behaviors can have across cultures. Although Chinese-American parenting practices superficially resemble those of authoritarian parents in North America, many Chinese parents are driven more by a philosophy of training than one of domination and control (Chao, 1994, 2001). That attitude in turn is undoubtedly linked to cultural differences in the extent to which people's abilities are thought to result from training and hard work as opposed to being fixed and intrinsic. (Many Asian cultures regard traits such as intelligence to be much more dependent on training than North American cultures do.) Thus, many East Asian children may interpret authoritarian-looking parenting styles as concerned with training rather than as overbearing or intrusive.

A specific culture may therefore provide a radically different way of understanding an action than the way a child from another background would understand it (Darling & Steinberg, 1993; Hatano & Wertsch, 2001). At the same time, Chinese-American children do seem to sense a tension between the typical levels of parental warmth and control of the broader culture and the warmth and control shown by their parents. They often have internalized the norms of the broader culture and thereby see their own parents as being less warm than normal (Wu & Chao, 2011). In this way, they have a different experience from children in China, where that tension does not exist, while also having a different experience from European-American children. More broadly, children acculturate in different ways and to different extents than their parents, and those differences can be sources of tension in the family (Telzer, 2011).

Parenting across Socioeconomic Groups Parenting styles not only differ across cultures, but they also differ across socioeconomic groups within cultures. Thus, it has been repeatedly found that families of higher socioeconomic status (SES) use authoritative parenting styles more often (and use authoritarian styles less often) than working-class or poor families. The differences can be substantial. In one study, upper- or upper-middle-class parents talked with their children twice as much as those in the most impoverished class. They also used only half as much language forbidding actions and used far less physical coercion. Perhaps most dramatically, the high-SES parents gave their children six times

more positive feedback than parents from the most impoverished groups (Hart & Risley, 1995). Similar patterns have been found across many studies and a variety of cultural settings. Economic hardship and other life stressors are strongly associated with a drop in both parental social responsiveness and parents' warmth and empathy toward their children (Huston & Bentley, 2010).

These patterns can also shift as life circumstances change. Thus, mothers who leave welfare support and escape poverty are less likely to use authoritarian child-rearing patterns than those who leave welfare but remain poor (Smith et al., 2001). Parenting styles can even vary from day to day, depending on the parent's stress level. In one study, air traffic controllers who were monitored at work and at home were less involved, less effective, and more negative as parents on days when their work was highly stressful (Repetti, 1994). The same pattern holds for parents who have stressful days in other work settings (Crouter & Bumpus, 2001; Repetti & Wood, 1997; Repetti et al., 2009).

One interpretation of the relationship between hardship and certain forms of parenting suggests that more controlling styles may be appropriate in times of risk and threat (Fischer et al., 2010; Harrison et al., 1990). If a child's safety is jeopardized by not obeying his parents, then the parents will need to be as firm as possible, especially in a chaotic and distracting environment. Poverty can bring enormous stresses for parents, as well as increased risks to children's well-being, whether through higher crime rates, more hazardous home environments, or more competition for scarce resources. One study found that simply reminding parents of terrorist incidents resulted in more authoritarian parenting behavior toward their children (Fischer et al., 2010). In stressful, risky environments, it is possible that an authoritarian parenting style would be adaptive. Along similar lines, most parents become more authoritarian in moments of high stress and danger. You probably recall a time when, spurred by an immediate threat, a caregiver suddenly shifted from warm and interactive to urgent, dictatorial, and controlling. Indeed, the situational specificity of parenting styles is an important topic that has received relatively little research attention.

Although authoritarian styles might sometimes be more adaptive and appropriate for groups at risk than for those who are well-off, this is not always true. Sometimes the differences do not benefit the child and instead merely reflect the demands of a difficult life. Imagine, for a moment, that you are a single parent with three young children. While you work long hours in an exhausting, menial job, you have to leave your children in substandard day care because there is no better alternative that you can afford. You live in a crowded, rundown apartment building with only intermittent heat and electricity. You return from work with the children in tow and have to cook dinner, change their diapers (which were neglected at day care), and help the oldest child with his homework. It is hardly surprising that this parent would lack the energy to have rich, interactive conversations with the children. It would be easier, at least at first, to give clear orders and back them up with threats of punishment. In the short term, authoritarian parenting styles can often produce quick behavioral changes more easily. In the long term, however, those styles may become less effective, resulting in the range of negative behaviors more commonly seen among children of authoritarian parents.

The Ecological Systems Approach The influence of context has been described in a broader sense as the **ecological systems approach** to families, which emphasizes that contextual factors, including culture and social class, among others, are crucial to understanding the child's development within a family (Bronfenbrenner, 1977, 1979, 1986). This approach, which was devised by developmental psychologist Urie Bronfenbrenner, considers the child's environments at several scales, ranging from the family itself, to the school, to the larger culture. In addition, other environments, such as the parents' workplaces, may indirectly affect the child by limiting the parents' time for interacting with the child or through the child's experiences in day care. According to ecological systems accounts, attempts to characterize how families are important to a child's development must consider the child's role in each of these "social ecosystems" and how that role interacts with other participants in the systems. Ecological approaches attempt to shed light on the influences of a child's many social contexts by drawing parallels to the ways that organisms interact in biological systems. We will return to Bronfenbrenner's ecological systems approach in Chapter 15 as part of our consideration of children's roles in social systems outside the family. These other systems include peer relationships, social groups, the media, and the larger culture in which a child develops.

> **Q:** How do different parenting contexts like culture and SES affect the associations between parenting styles and children's psychological outcomes?

Interventions to Improve Parenting

Over the past few decades, researchers in North America and elsewhere have offered courses in parenting skills, specifically targeting groups that are more likely to show authoritarian or neglecting/uninvolved parenting styles (Cowan et al., 1997). These interventions are based on the belief that even in stress-ridden families, the authoritarian style is still not best for either the children or the parents. A number of these interventions have shown positive effects for both parents and children. The most compelling studies randomly assigned parents to either a group that received instruction on parenting skills or a control group that was involved in an activity unrelated to parenting (Cowan & Cowan, 2002). This experimental approach enabled the researchers to disentangle mere correlations from causal influences. In several such studies, the children of parents who were coached to be less coercive and more interactive showed corresponding improvements in behavior (Spoth et al., 2001). Training generally focused on creating opportunities for positive family interactions, establishing appropriate expectations about children and appropriate monitoring and discipline, teaching parents how to coach their children to resist peers when needed, reducing and managing instances of family conflict, and emphasizing the value of displaying positive emotions.

The issue of parenting interventions becomes especially important in the context of large-scale programs such as Head Start. As described in Chapter 11, Head Start targets millions of lower-income children throughout the United States in an effort to increase school readiness. A related program, Early Head Start, focuses on children between birth and 3 years. One facet of both programs is to teach parenting skills to lower-income disadvantaged parents. It was assumed that such interventions might also promote school readiness by fostering more learning-rich interactions between young children and those around them. There have been many analyses of the outcomes of such programs, and a consensus seems to be emerging that parenting skills can be successfully taught in such large-scale programs (Brooks-Gunn & Markman, 2005; Zhai et al., 2011); and, in at least some cases, interventions in random assignment studies have been linked to higher levels of school readiness (Sheridan et al., 2011). Thus, parents can, with guidance, become more attentive, less coercive, and more interactive with their children. Interestingly, the effectiveness of these interventions differs, depending in part on the parents' race. These interventions tend to have a large effect with African-American parents, but they often show no effect with European-American parents (Sheridan et al., 2011). The reasons for these group differences are not yet clear.

Will the parents who undergo training maintain a warmer, more interactive parenting style in the face of continuing life stresses? And do the effects on children's behavior with their parents have a positive influence on relationships with other adults or with peers? These questions are essential to understanding whether the considerable public funds expended on programs to improve parenting skills are well spent. It may be that these interventions, focused on directly reaching the affected individuals, are the most powerful approach, especially as they become more carefully tailored to specific groups of parents and children at risk (Hutchings & Lane, 2005; Shonkoff & Meisels, 2000). Unfortunately, such approaches can also be the most labor and skill intensive.

More broadly, most studies have found modest, but enduring positive effects of Head Start and Early Head Start interventions, especially with respect to measures such as grade repetition and behavioral problems in school (Deming, 2009; Joo, 2010; Ludgwig & Phillips, 2008; Sheridan et al., 2011; Zhai et al., 2011). However, test scores and other academic measures tend to show diminishing effects with increasing age, and some scholars have concluded that long-term benefits in academic achievement are rare (Gibbs et al., 2011). If interventions involving parental training are one of the key routes to having a positive influence, it may make sense that long-term benefits of such programs are more associated with broad behavioral measures than with more narrowly defined academic outcomes.

Parent Effects in Relation to Other Influences

It is tempting to see parenting as the primary influence on a child's personality, but some scholars have argued that the correlations we have examined between parenting styles and children's behaviors have been mistakenly interpreted. Rather than studying how parents affect their children's behaviors and traits, they have largely focused on child effects—the ways that children influence their parents' behavior—as well as on genetic factors that could influence parents and children similarly (Bell & Harper, 1977; Harris, 1998; Rowe, 1994). While the correlations between parenting styles and developmental outcomes are statistically significant, they are often relatively small, making it easier to argue for these alternative accounts. Nonetheless, the evidence for child effects and common genetic influences does not reduce or exclude parent effects. In many cases, these factors interact with patterns of parenting.

Child Effects Whenever the child's traits or behavior causes the parents to act in a certain way in response, **child effects** are at work (see Figure 14.4). Consider, for example, an inhibited, shy child whose parent tends to encourage him to be cautious. Does this correlation suggest that the parent is fostering the child's timidity, or is the child's timidity eliciting more protective behavior from the parent? First impressions might suggest a dominant role for parents, but the child can have major effects as well. In one study of 125 U.S. 3-year-olds and 100 Korean 3-year-olds, researchers carefully coded videotapes of the more inhibited children, recording whether parents encouraged the children to approach or withdraw from novel threatening stimuli and how often they discouraged the children's tendencies to withdraw (Belsky et al., 2000). In this case, the children were largely driving their parents' behaviors, especially that of their mothers. In particular, the more inhibited children elicited a wider range of parental responses: the more a child withdrew from interactions, the more the parents tended to

A

B

FIGURE 14.4 Child effects. Although researchers traditionally tended to emphasize the effects of parental behavior on children, the children themselves may have a powerful influence on their parents. For example, **(A)** a child who repeatedly throws tantrums may elicit very different behaviors in his parents than **(B)** a child who is excessively shy.

Epigenetics and Families

As described in Chapter 2, epigenetic regulation is one way that environmental influences can affect the activity of genes. This kind of gene regulation occurs when the chemicals surrounding a particular cell type affect which of the cells' genes are active or inactive, such that when the cells divide, the genes of all the cells that they create can have the same pattern of active and inactive genes. As epigenetics becomes an increasingly important aspect of the study of development, it is beginning to illuminate some of the surprisingly strong ways that parents, children, and siblings influence each other.

For some time, researchers have been able to demonstrate powerful epigenetic effects in animals, most notably in rats and mice. For example, when a rat pup is frequently licked by its mother, chemical changes to a certain gene related to hippocampal function cause other genes to trigger the production of higher levels of neurotransmitters, such as serotonin, in the young rat (see Figure 14.5). That increase in neurotransmitter levels in turn seems to bias the rat pup to be less fearful and less reactive in stressful environments. Rat pups whose mothers lick them less often do not undergo these genetic changes, which results in lower levels of neurotransmitter production and more fearful and reactive behavior (Caldji et al., 1998; Meaney, 2001; Meaney & Szyf, 2005; Weaver et al., 2004). Thus, early maternal behavior can affect the activation or deactivation of a particular set of genes, resulting in a long-term effect on the offspring's physiological and psychological responses to stresses. This kind of effect initially was thought to be irreversible after

FIGURE 14.5 Epigenetics and parental care. When rat mothers lick their offspring more, that increased care can turn on gene pathways that produce more neurotransmitters involved in reducing anxiety. Thus, a rat mother who is not stressed and who is able to devote more extensive care to her offspring can cause the genes correlated with lower anxiety to switch on in her offspring.

gene expression was "fixed" early in life. However, follow-up studies have shown that these maternal effects on offspring's genetic activity can be reversed through drug treatments in adult rats (Champagne et al., 2008; Weaver et al., 2005, 2006).

It is, of course, a great leap from mother rats licking their pups to the possibility of epigenetic effects of parenting in humans. But researchers in both animal systems and human development have drawn parallels, and work with nonhuman primates has strengthened those parallels. In some studies, an important manipulation has been to compare peer-raised and mother-raised monkeys (Suomi, 1997, 2005). As mentioned in Chapter 6,

either encourage approach and discourage withdrawal—or, on other occasions, encourage the inhibition. The child's shyness affected the parents by making his interaction with (or withdrawal from) peers a more central issue in parent-child interactions (Rubin et al., 1998).

The clearest way to study child effects is to set up an interaction that can be repeated by many parent-child pairs. Researchers can experimentally "manipulate" the child's behavior by randomly assigning children to behave in particular ways and then compare the effects of the child's behavior on parents' responses. In one study, children were randomly assigned to be either compliant and cooperative or resistant and noncooperative while performing a task with an adult stranger (Bugental et al., 1980).

In general, the same adult would much more likely slant toward an authoritarian style with a less cooperative child. A more naturalistic, longitudinal study of children with conduct disorders found similar patterns: when difficult children misbehave, that bout of misbehavior triggers more authoritarian behavior in parents, who then exercise more control and use more negative coercions (Dodge, 2002). Other studies suggest that negative temperaments in children cause negative reactions in their parents, although these studies are not experimental and depend on complex statistical analyses to infer child temperament effects on parenting as opposed to effects in the opposite direction (Ganiban et al., 2011; South et al., 2008). At least one study has shown that difficult temperament-related behavior in

rhesus macaques raised in a peer group without adult macaques do develop attachment bonds with their peers, but they are also more fearful than those raised by adults. More importantly for the epigenetic hypothesis, the peer-raised macaques show neurological differences. They have less developed neural networks using the neurotransmitter serotonin, especially in brain areas related to inhibitory control and emotions (Ichise et al., 2006). These similar patterns across monkeys and rats have led some researchers to suggest that a similar epigenetic effect may hold in humans as well (Branchi, 2009).

In humans, the activities of genes involved in producing the neurotransmitters oxytocin (discussed earlier in Chapter 6), serotonin, and dopamine are related to feelings of interpersonal trust and intimacy and behaviors associated with sensitive parenting (Bakermans-Kranenburg et al., 2003; van IJzendoorn et al., 2011). When parents whose genes trigger lower levels of oxytocin, serotonin, or dopamine are exposed to stress or daily hassles, they are more likely to show less sensitive parenting. That is, parents with certain genotypes seem to be at greater risk than other parents to resort to insensitive parenting when they are put under stress.

Building on these findings as well as the epigenetic studies in nonhuman animals, researchers are now asking whether experience-induced regulation of genetic activity could also influence such behaviors as parenting. Based on the animal work showing how stressful environments can alter gene pathways, and based on the work showing how neurotransmitter levels in humans can influence behaviors related to parenting (Domes et al., 2007; Feldman et al., 2007; Kosfeld et al., 2005), it now seems plausible that stressful social situations experienced early in life could have far-reaching epigenetic effects. Stressful experiences during childhood could downregulate gene pathways, altering neurotransmitter levels and potentially making these individuals less sensitive as parents (Champagne & Curley, 2008; Ogren & Lombroso, 2008). Some of these chemical changes involved in gene regulation could last a lifetime and even be passed on to offspring (Ogren & Lombroso, 2008), although, as noted earlier, such effects have been reversed in animal studies. It is not yet clear just how common such cases of transgenerational epigenetic inheritance are for psychological traits in humans (Grossniklaus et al., 2013).

It is too early to develop full-fledged epigenetic explanations for the variations in interactions between parents and children, but there is a strong possibility that epigenetic influences are significant (Szyf et al., 2008; van IJzendoorn et al., 2011). More generally, the epigenetic perspective goes beyond analyses of genetic effects to show how, even at a molecular level, genotypes and environments continuously interact. Consider, for example, how one study has shown a link between human parenting and epigenetic changes in children (Essex et al., 2013). Parents were interviewed about the levels of stress in their own lives when their adolescent children were infants or young children. Reports of high levels of parental stress, especially in mothers, were then related to increased levels of methylation of DNA in cells scraped from the inside of the cheeks of their adolescent children. (Methylation is thought to be the primary way in which specific genes are turned off and, less commonly, turned on.) Future research will have to demonstrate comparable methylation effects on neurons and then link those changes to neurotransmitter levels and behavior. Such pathways of influence seem increasingly likely in humans, especially given their presence in other species.

children may have a causal influence on higher levels of physical mistreatment and neglect by the parents (Schulz-Heik et al., 2009).

Other studies have shown that parents' perceptions play as important a role in child effects as children's behavior does. When researchers experimentally manipulate parents' perceptions of whether or not their children's misbehavior was intentional, those who perceive their children as acting out on purpose respond with harsher, more intense discipline (Slep & O'Leary, 1998). Parents' perceptions can also interact with child effects. For example, parents who perceive themselves as having little control over children tend to react more strongly and harshly when children are uncooperative (Bugental et al., 1993, 1999, 2000).

> **Q:** How is the study of child effects relevant to the study of parenting?

Genetic Effects We have considered how parents influence children via parenting styles and how children influence parents via child effects. But in some cases, correlations between parents' and children's behavior may be best explained by a third factor—the genes that parents and children share. Thanks to substantial advances in behavioral genetics, researchers are beginning to disentangle some of the interactions between genes and behaviors that pertain to parenting.

Although some behavioral geneticists have focused on understanding genetic influences on either the parent's behavior or the child's behavior, another approach offers an account distinct from parental influences and child behavior. Instead of a one-way influence of the child on the parent (or vice versa), the parent and a child might share a genetic disposition toward a particular trait, such as shyness or irritability. That shared disposition could then cause a strong correlation between a particular style of parenting and a particular kind of behavior from the child. Likewise, if withdrawn parents tend to have withdrawn children, it may not be the parents' behavior or the children's behavior that causes the correlation, but the third factor of their shared genotype. It is important to remember, however, that even with shared genotypes, phenotypic expressions of those genotypes may be quite different in young children and adults. Thus, a toddler who has a genotype that makes him irritable and therefore prone to crying fits and physical tantrums when frustrated is not likely to have a parent who behaves in the same way, even if the genotype for their irritability is shared. That parent may be volatile and reactive but is unlikely to plop down on the grocery store floor, burst into tears, and have a physical tantrum.

Behavioral genetic studies cover more than shared genotype effects and accounts of how certain genotypes are related to child and parent effects. In animal studies, researchers are also making headway in understanding the epigenetic mechanisms through which some parental behaviors can affect genetic activity in offspring (see the New Directions in Developmental Research box). As more sophisticated techniques emerge for studying the entire human genome and looking at complex interactions between sets of genes, a much more diverse set of causal pathways between behaviors and genes is likely to be part of any discussion of parenting.

> **Q:** How can a behavioral genetic approach explain correlations between parents' and children's behavior without primarily relying on either parent effects or child effects?

The Interactionist Approach to Family Dynamics

Genetic effects and child effects do not necessarily diminish the effects of parenting on children. Instead, taken together, the three types of effects suggest a much more complex, interactional way of understanding family dynamics (Dodge & Pettit, 2003; LaFreniere & MacDonald, 2013; Maccoby, 2000; Parke, 2004). A particular kind of parenting may benefit some kinds of children much more than others, and for some it may even be detrimental. Similarly, some parenting effects may depend on aspects of the child that change over the course of development, initially exerting little immediate sway, then strongly influencing the child for a period of time before waning.

Consider one example of how an interaction pattern between parent and child might change with development because of both parent and child effects. A parent who is prone to ordering children about might do so to a greater extent with smaller and less vocal children who cannot respond adequately to this behavior. Thus, authoritarian parenting might wax and wane as a child develops. This case illustrates how more subtle differences in temperament and personality of children and parents can create quite intricate patterns of interaction. There are now "biopsychosocial" approaches that see certain combinations of biological disposition, psychological tendencies, and sociocultural contexts as likely to either increase or decrease children's risk of some adverse outcomes (such as becoming aggressive toward others) early in life. These approaches also seek to account for ways that experiences with parents, peers, and the broader social world either increase or reduce that risk (Dodge & Pettit, 2003). Figure 14.6 shows one model of the ways these interactions could contribute to conduct disorder, which is a behavior pattern in children and adolescents that involves repeated incidents of actions that infringe on the rights of others. It is often called "antisocial behavior."

The interactionist approach is valuable for its broad yet nuanced view of the many influences affecting both parents and children, but its critics have cited one serious

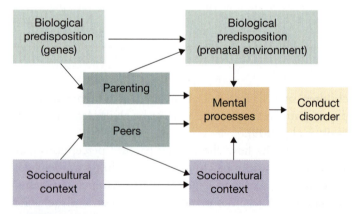

FIGURE 14.6 Interactionist models. As this sample interactionist model shows, interactionist views of parenting incorporate many kinds of effects, including biological (both genetic and toxic prenatal environment), sociocultural, and peer influences, that may moderate or exaggerate parents' effects on children (here operationalized as children with conduct disorders). These models, however, can be frustrating to test because it is often unclear what kinds of outcomes they would predict. Adapted from Dodge & Petit (2003).

drawback: it is almost always possible to explain a set of observations in terms of the many complex interactions that likely influenced the outcome. It is much harder to use an interactionist model to predict such effects in advance and then test those predictions as a way of evaluating the model. Moreover, these models are especially tough to test because they depend on intricate webs of interactions in which it is difficult to disentangle causal relationships from mere correlations. The interactionist model is clearly a more comprehensive approach to studying parenting and effects on children. At the same time, it highlights the challenges for future researchers in developing more complex and sophisticated methods of accounting for the influences at work in parent-child dynamics.

Despite the clear merits of the interactionist view, there is also a need for further research documenting which parental behaviors contribute the most to these systems of interactions. For example, a great deal of traditional research has asked how parenting practices might affect a child's personality traits, but personality is invariably the result of a host of interactions in which parenting is just one component. Other aspects of the child, however, may relate more indirectly to parents' behavior. By choosing where a family lives and what elementary school a child will attend, parents greatly influence the pool of potential friends and teachers that a child will have. Parents might affect a child's hobbies by simply exposing her to certain activities. Similarly, children's knowledge of etiquette or specific cultural practices depends significantly on how their parents live.

A final point concerns the implications of the interactionist model for parenting. If a wide variety of interacting influences are at work in all parent-child dynamics, the most effective parents would need to be sensitive to the child's nature and be able to adjust parenting strategies accordingly. Not all parents tailor their approach to their children as individuals, instead tending toward one style for all their children. By acknowledging a wide variety of influences on family members, the interactionist approach suggests that parents and children who are able to respond to one another's individual natures will have the most positive relationship (Grusec et al., 2000; Kochanska, 1997b, 1998). Indeed, the long-term pattern of interactions between a particular child and parent may be far more important for understanding parenting effects than a number of brief, specific parent-child interactions, since the same pattern of parental behavior may be interpreted very differently at different times, depending on the long-term context of the relationship.

Q: What are the strengths and weakness of the interactionist approach to studying parenting?

Gender Socialization in the Family: A Web of Interacting Influences

Boys and girls tend to behave differently on many dimensions, ranging from favorite activities to patterns of social interactions. These differences raise questions about the relative contributions of parents, children, social/cultural context, peers, and genes in influencing those behaviors. We will see that the development of gender-typical behaviors vividly illustrates the interactionist perspective in which all of these factors influence each other rather than simply making independent contributions. The massive amount of research on parenting and children's gender supports the common sense intuition that parents treat children of the two sexes differently (Leaper, 2002, 2011; Lundberg, 2005; Lytton & Romney, 1991; Raley & Bianchi, 2006). Parents tend to offer children sex-stereotyped toys, such as giving trucks to boys and dolls to girls; and they tend to interact with their children in ways that reflect their notions of the differences in girls' and boys' behavior, inviting boys to be involved in more physical activities and girls in more social and conversational ones. Table 14.3 summarizes some of these differences. It is important to keep in mind, however, that while these differences are reliable, they are usually surprisingly modest, especially with children younger than 6 years of age (Maccoby, 2003; Maccoby & Jacklin, 1974; Russell & Saebel, 1997).

One way of explaining gender socialization focuses on the ways that parents' gender schemas affect children. **Gender schemas** are cognitive systems for interpreting gender-related activities and roles (Bem, 1981). They are shaped in parents by the norms and stereotypes that exist for each gender in a parent's culture. For example, when parents were asked to teach their grade school children how to perform three tasks involving physical science, computer programming, and hypothetical interpersonal dilemmas, the language the parents used varied, depending on the sex of the child, the content the parent was teaching, and the parent's gender schema (Tenenbaum & Leaper, 2003). Fathers used more cognitively demanding speech when asking questions about science problems with their sons than they did for similar problems for their daughters. Similarly, when children ask about why some natural phenomenon occurs or how a device works, parents tend to offer more complex and cognitively deeper explanations to boys than to girls (Crowley et al., 2001; Tennenbaum & Leaper, 2003; Tennenbaum et al., 2005). One study found that parents also are three times as likely to offer scientific explanations to boys as to girls in everyday conversations, even though both boys and girls ask for such explanations to roughly equal degrees (Crowley et al., 2001). Parents can also influence their children's choices about courses of study in middle school, selecting more math and science courses for their sons than for their daughters (Tenenbaum, 2009).

	Conversational Interactions	Manner of Play	Reactions to Emotions
Boys	Both parents talk to boys somewhat less and focus more on nonpersonal or intrapersonal topics.	Both parents play more roughly with boys and offer them toy vehicles and sports equipment to play with.	Fathers react negatively to crying, fearfulness, or other expressions that could signify weakness in boys.
Girls	Mothers talk to girls more overall and specifically about emotions.	Both parents play more gently with girls and offer them dolls and props for playing house.	Both parents are more tolerant of displays of distress and fear-related emotions in girls.

TABLE 14.3 Some differences in how parents socialize boys and girls. The effects of parental socialization vary as a function of the gender of the parent and that of the child; usually, same-gender pairs have the strongest influence. Nonetheless, these differences are often more modest than expected, especially when children are younger than 6 years of age. From Maccoby (2003).

Gender biases in adults also seem to be more tolerated by children than other forms of biases. Thus, in one study in Denmark, when children were asked to make judgments about exclusion from activities based on gender as opposed to ethnicity, they thought that exclusion based on ethnicity was less acceptable and more morally inappropriate (Moller & Tenenbaum, 2011). This pattern follows earlier studies in the United States showing a greater willingness to tolerate exclusion based on gender than on ethnicity (Killen, 2007). Thus, parents may get less negative feedback or resistance when they show gender bias as opposed to other forms of group biases.

In general, even though parents interact differently with their sons and their daughters across a wide spectrum of behaviors and situations (see Figure 14.7), like so many other aspects of socialization, it is difficult to show how these gender-related differences in parenting actually affect the children. Even when there are strong associations between parents' behaviors and gender-related differences in children, it is difficult to prove that parenting actually *caused* the differences in children. To understand why it is so hard to show a causal effect, we will now consider some models of parenting influence.

Even though studies of parent effects have tended to dominate the research on parenting and gender, children's behaviors can also strongly influence their parents. For example, girls and boys often have strong toy preferences well before 2 years of age, before they experience gender-stereotyped toys or related interactions with their parents (Maccoby, 2003). That is, they bring to their early interactions certain behavioral patterns that may lead the parent to conclude that the child prefers one kind of toy to another and then offer what the child seems to want. This pattern sometimes surprises parents who avoid gender-stereotyped toys so as not to impose gender roles on their children. More formally, researchers have long known that even when we factor out differences in parents' behaviors in terms of the types of toys they provide or offer to their sons and daughters, the children still show gender-based differences in toy preferences (Calders et al., 1989). If parental socialization cannot fully account for young children's early gendered preferences, what other explanations are possible?

One alternative approach suggests that children have biologically determined biases that influence their preferences in ways that are initially independent of socialization, biases that may have counterparts in other primates. It may seem implausible that a child's biological sex might somehow directly bias him or her toward gender-stereotyped toys, but several studies have supported that possibility. For example, the extent to which a female fetus is exposed to testosterone seems to relate to the likelihood that she will later show a tendency to like toys that boys normally prefer. This association has been shown in rare cases where a female fetus has the inherited adrenal gland disorder known as congenital adrenal hyperplasia (CAH). CAH results in exposure to higher than normal levels of masculinizing hormones, such as testosterone, in utero. Girls born with CAH show increased preferences for playing with gender-atypical toys (Berenbaum & Beltz, 2011; Cohen-Bendahan et al., 2005;

A   B

FIGURE 14.7 Gender and parenting. There are modest but consistent differences in how parents of each sex interact with children of each sex. The impact of these differences on the children is less clear.

Hines, 2013; Pasterski et al., 2005). Even when two girls are born to the same family, the girl born with CAH shows more of a preference for gender-atypical toys than her sister born without CAH (Pasterski et al., 2005). Girls with CAH also tend to show a higher preference as teenagers for future occupations involving "things" (such as auto mechanic or jet pilot) than those involving "people" (such as social worker or teacher; Beltz et al., 2011).

Because girls with CAH often have more masculine genitalia, it is possible that their parents notice these differences and behave differently toward their two daughters, influencing their toy preferences (Cohen-Bendahan et al., 2005: Jordan-Young, 2011). Additional indirect effects could occur through the intensive medical and psychiatric attention that girls with CAH receive and expectations by parents and others that their daughters will be "masculine" (Jordan-Young, 2011). Such indirect effects, however, are not likely to provide a full explanation for the different behaviors in girls who have higher prenatal levels of masculinizing hormones. In fact, when mothers of girls with CAH are studied, they do not treat their daughters in ways that favor masculine behaviors and, if anything, show more of a bias toward feminine behaviors (Hines, 2010).

Some researchers have examined testosterone levels in the mother's blood during pregnancy and then analyzed their children's behaviors, including toy preferences (Auyeung et al., 2009; Hines et al., 2002; see Figure 14.8). They found that the higher the testosterone levels, the greater the children's tendency to play with stereotypically male toys. Thus, there was a "dose-dependent" relationship between levels of testosterone and the extent to which male activities were preferred. The mothers in these studies were unaware of their own testosterone levels, making parental attitude and behavior effects less plausible in this case. In addition, some studies show that "antiandrogen" compounds that reduce prenatal testosterone levels in boys are associated with decreased levels of masculine play (Swann et al., 2010). At the same time, it is important to note that, in statistical terms, variations in testosterone levels in these studies could account for only part of the variation in toy preferences, leaving room for parental influences as well (Jordan-Young, 2011).

The effects of prenatal testosterone could still be interacting with differences in parenting if parents notice subtle differences in body shape or activity level in girls who have been exposed to more testosterone and then treat them differently. But this account cannot explain the striking findings of toy preferences in other primate species that show no parental socialization related to toy preferences. Studies have repeatedly found that young male monkeys prefer playing with trucks instead of dolls or plush animals, and the females sometimes show the opposite preferences

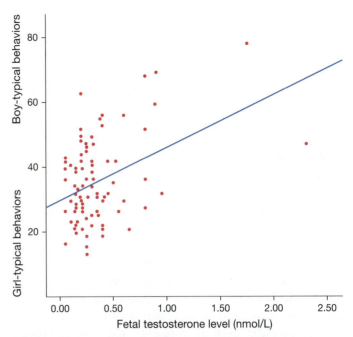

FIGURE 14.8 **Prenatal testosterone levels and sex-stereotyped behaviors.** Higher levels of prenatal testosterone in girls are associated with greater frequencies of childhood behaviors favored by boys. Adapted from Auyeung et al. (2009).

(Hassett et al., 2008; Hines & Alexander, 2008; Williams & Pleil, 2008; see Figure 14.9). It is not yet known which features of the toys drive these preferences, as monkeys clearly have no evolved tendencies to interact with any of these objects. Future studies that carefully and systematically vary the perceptual features of different categories of toys will help researchers understand the real nature of the effect.

FIGURE 14.9 **Toy preferences and gender in vervet monkeys.** For reasons that still need to be understood, even vervet monkeys, which have no reason to play with toy trucks or dolls, show gender-based toy choices.

Parental socialization practices can certainly influence toy preferences in boys and girls. Yet, it now seems clear that parents' behaviors are likely to interact with aspects of toy preferences that are present before the occurrence of socialization. In some cases, these presocialization toy preferences can even compete with parental biases. Most of the time, however, parents' gender socialization behaviors and children's early biases probably reinforce each other.

If we take a wider view of familial influences on gender, siblings, too, seem to influence one another's gender role qualities. One study examined families over a 3-year period to determine how siblings' and parents' gender role qualities interacted. To learn whether children influenced the extent to which their siblings adopted gender-stereotyped views and roles, the researchers analyzed the effects of siblings on leisure activities, toy preferences, and ways of approaching social situations (McHale et al., 2001). They found that older siblings' gender role qualities predicted similar qualities in younger siblings 2 years later, even when parents' and younger siblings' initial roles were controlled for statistically. Moreover, the older siblings influenced younger siblings' gender role qualities more than parents did, and their influence was significant in both same-sex and mixed-sex sibling pairs. The older siblings, in contrast, were most influenced by their parents. Thus, parents seem to influence gender roles most strongly in their firstborn children, who then propagate those roles with younger siblings. This may also interact with the finding, noted earlier, that children are more tolerant of gender biases shown by parents and peers than they are of other sorts of biases, such as those involving ethnicity (Killen, 2007; Moller & Tenebaum, 2011). By acquiescing to, or even endorsing, such biases, siblings and peers may reinforce parental behaviors.

> **Q:** Describe at least three different interacting influences that contribute to children's gender socialization.

Siblings and Family Dynamics

We have all heard people explain the behavior of another on the basis of that person's place in the family. Firstborn children, at least early on, frequently have the undivided attention of both parents, whereas later-borns always have to compete for parental resources. In other respects, though, later-born children may have the advantage. They benefit from more experienced parenting, they tend to experience parental tensions less intensely, and they can learn much from their older siblings.

In examining sibling effects, the critical question is whether these kinds of differences in family structure actually influence development. Like the debates about parenting effects, there has been considerable contention, in recent years, as to whether sibling effects are real and substantial (Harris, 2000). The true debate, however, seems to have more to do with the degree of sibling effects than with their existence. When considered in detail, family structure seems to have a modest but broad, multifaceted influence on children.

Birth Order Effects

Of the many factors proposed to be influenced by birth order, the most heavily studied has been intelligence. In 1975, a provocative paper was published showing what seemed to be a correlation between intelligence, as measured by intelligence tests, and birth order. The data indicated that firstborns had the highest intelligence and that intelligence consistently dropped the later a child's position was in the birth order (Zajonc, 1976; Zajonc & Markus, 1975; see Figure 14.10). The documented drop in scores is very modest, sometimes as little as 1 percent of the score of the next oldest sibling, and large population samples are usually needed to find a significant, reliable effect (Kristensen & Bjerkedal, 2007).

This pattern immediately raises the question of whether the birth order effect actually *causes* the difference in scores. One objection is that larger families tend to be more common in lower socioeconomic classes, who also, for a variety of other reasons, tend to score lower on intelligence tests. But when socioeconomic status is held constant, the birth order effect on intelligence remains significant in some populations. More subtle statistical issues have kept debates over the magnitude of the effect alive (Armor, 2001; Rodgers et al., 2000; Wichman et al., 2007; Zajonc, 2001). But despite these disagreements, the current consensus still favors an effect (Black et al., 2011; de Haan, 2010). Moreover, another analysis has suggested that firstborns also tend to complete more years of schooling (Black et al., 2005).

Two potential causes for the birth order effect on intelligence have been frequently discussed. The first, **resource theory**, holds that the more children in the family, the less attention parents can devote to each child. The second explanation, **confluence theory**, argues that as families get larger, their average overall intellectual climate drops (Zajonc & Markus, 1975). Thus, the firstborn child is more likely to be exposed to the parents' more adult-centered discourse, while a fourth-born will more likely be exposed to conversations about toilet training and various cartoon characters.

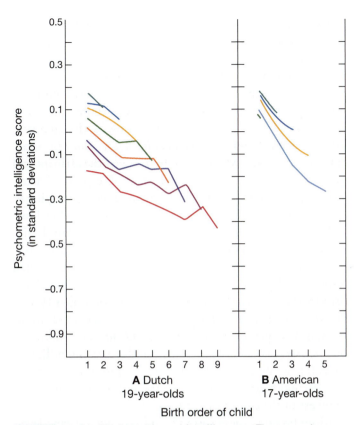

FIGURE 14.10 Birth order and intelligence. These graphs are from very large samples of children in the Netherlands and the United States. They show consistently modest relations between birth order and intelligence. Each curve represents the data for families of the size indicated by the rightmost number on the x-axis for that curve (thus, 1 indicates a family with 1 child, 2 indicates a family with 2 children, and so on through 9, which represents a family with 9 children). Studies of children from other populations showed more mixed results. Adapted from Zajonc (1976).

Detailed statistical analyses have supported the confluence theory. For example, this theory predicts that as later-born children get older, they should show fewer negative effects of birth order than they do when they are younger. (As their older siblings become more adult-like, the intellectual climate in the family is bolstered, which is predicted by the confluence theory.) In fact, analyses have shown that birth order effects do tend to decline as younger siblings age (Zajonc, 2001). It is important to stress, once again, that although they do seem reliable in very large data sets, these birth order effects are quite small, and it is not possible to predict intelligence differences on this basis in any single family.

Q: Describe two different models for the apparent relation between birth order and intelligence.

More surprising and striking than the potential impact of birth order on intelligence is the claim that birth order also predicts a personality trait related to rebelliousness, respect for authority, and conscientiousness. This link was first proposed by a historian of science, Frank Sulloway, who stumbled on what seemed to be a pattern among historical revolutionaries, in which firstborns were more likely to defend the status quo and reject radical change. By contrast, the later-born children were more likely to question and overturn traditions and norms (Sulloway, 1996). One study of 700 brothers who played professional baseball found that younger brothers were more than 10 times as likely to attempt to steal bases than were the firstborns. This observation is interpreted as a sports-related measure of risk taking, as attempts to steal bases are thought to more broadly reflect a tendency toward more radical behaviors (Sulloway & Zweigenhaft, 2010).

The effects in Sulloway's analysis are impressive and provocative—making other failures to find comparable personality effects in hundreds of birth order studies all the more puzzling (Harris, 1998, 2000, 2006). Some have argued that birth order influences on personality are highly context specific, affecting the way children behave toward their parents and siblings, but not generalizing to other situations as a broader personality trait would (Harris, 2006). Two arguments form a reply. One is that many studies that show no effects measure personality traits with self-report data, which may be less reliable than other types. Thus, some people who say they are "open to new experiences" or "welcome change" may really mean that they welcome change within the existing paradigm. The most telling data come from people's willingness to take real revolutionary action, as rated by judges who know neither the hypothesis nor the birth order of the individuals involved.

Such data are very rare outside of Sulloway's studies, but those that focus on real acts of rebellion seem to support his birth order prediction. One study examined 17 college students who had participated in civil disobedience as part of an ongoing labor dispute (Zweigenhaft, 2000). This small sample showed a significant relationship in which later-borns were more likely to have been arrested previously (and more frequently) for civil disobedience. A much larger study of 1,022 families in California and British Columbia found that siblings tended to describe firstborns as high-achieving and conscientious, while later-borns were called most rebellious, liberal, and agreeable (Paulhus et al., 1999). To see whether the participants were merely reflecting popular stereotypes about birth order, the researchers varied whether they emphasized birth order at the beginning of the questionnaires or whether it went unmentioned. This manipulation should have had large effects if the descriptions were based on popular stereotypes, but it made little difference in respondents' descriptions.

If the claimed birth order effects on personality do exist, on average, across large population samples, how might these effects come about? Sulloway and later authors (Paulhus et al., 1999) offered a model that closely resembles evolutionary notions about how different species compete for a particular biological niche. When a species takes over a particular habitat or food source within an ecosystem, it can force other closely related species to adapt to different niches. Similarly, these authors argue, firstborn children might tend to occupy certain typical family roles, thereby forcing their later-born siblings to seek out different niches. In their view, the firstborn is more likely to engage in behaviors that imitate parents (such as caring for the younger sibling) and will often be rewarded for it if those behaviors help the parents. They further argue that the firstborn is more likely to find that his acts of dominance and aggression against his siblings succeed, since the firstborn is physically bigger early on. These factors and others could make firstborns more likely to embrace their parents' values and more strictly uphold norms. By contrast, the later-born children, having been forced out of that niche, may tend to be more rebellious as well as more agreeable (since they are weaker at first).

Of course, such stories are easy to tell after the fact and difficult to test experimentally; but the notion of siblings forcing others to seek out contrasting niches is a powerful one that seems to fit many siblings' personal experiences. Recent studies of this phenomenon often use the term **sibling differentiation** to describe children's process of seeking out activities that resonate with their abilities and also reduce their competition with older siblings. Interestingly, siblings tend to get along better as they see themselves as occupying different roles in the family, rather than being in direct competition (Feinberg et al., 2003).

Q: What is sibling differentiation? How can it be used to explain the socialization patterns in a family?

An Interactionist Approach to Birth Order Effects
Even if these theories of birth order effects tend to hold true on average across large population samples, they undoubtedly interact with many other aspects of family life, producing enormous variations. As just one example, we saw at the beginning of this chapter that siblings' development can vary considerably depending on the socioeconomic status of the family (Conley, 2004). That is, siblings' future outcomes will be more similar when they grow up in families of high socioeconomic status, where parents do not have to make difficult choices about resource allocation (Conley & Glauber, 2005).

Parents from higher socioeconomic classes also tend to have more social capital, and this knowledge of social structures and professional contacts provides another advantage for their children. This might include knowledge about what sorts of schools and programs best prepare children for competitive colleges or what sorts of summer jobs offer an adolescent the best future opportunities (Furstenberg, 2005). Such differential social capital effects may be accelerating in societies where the gaps between the affluent and poor are increasing. These issues may have particular relevance to societies that have implemented policies trying to reduce family size (see Development and Social Policy box).

Parental resources can interact not only with family size but also with gender of children. For example, one study in South Korea found that when families have limited resources, there is an effect of family size on educational investments in girls, but little or no impact on boys (Kang, 2010). This gender difference was discovered by examining family expenditures on private tutoring for children, a practice seen as essential in many South Korean families for educational advancement. This finding presumably reflects the parental belief in South Korea that it is more important to invest in the educational future of sons.

More broadly, these sorts of findings suggest new levels of complexity to interactionist views. Researchers must consider how factors such as sibling spacing, birth order, sex, and family size interact with socioeconomic status of the family, cultural beliefs and practices, and whether that family belongs to a group that is stigmatized by the larger culture. By accounting for socioeconomic and cultural influences on sibling dynamics, researchers hope to predict more precisely when factors such as family size will significantly influence development.

Sibling Relationships and Socialization

Aside from birth order effects, which remain somewhat controversial, several other patterns of sibling interactions, including siblings' jealousy and conflict but also their degree of social understanding, may have long-term developmental outcomes. These interactions often involve parents and other important figures in a child's life as well.

Jealousy and Conflict between Siblings The birth of a new child can be especially upsetting to firstborns who are close in age to the new baby. This effect makes sense, given that parents do tend to devote less attention to the firstborn after the new arrival, try as they might to do otherwise (Dunn & Kendrick, 1982). Firstborns tend to react to this change by becoming more demanding of their parents. Sibling jealousy is also common and seems to vary in degree, depending on the children's age and their temperament. Among younger children, a reactive temperament is associated with more jealousy, whereas older children show more jealousy if they have poor emotional understanding (Volling et al., 2002). Moreover, siblings who perceive that parents treat them differently in terms of the resources they offer tend to have more difficult relations with one another and with their parents (Kowal et al., 2004; Reiss, 2001, 2003; Volling, 2012; Volling et al., 2010). A major goal for future research is to gain a better understanding of the circumstances that increase jealousy and competition between siblings and to find the best way to foster cooperation instead.

Conflict between siblings is not always based on jealousy, and it can be one of the most stressful aspects of family life. Although a moderate level of conflict can actually force siblings to negotiate more and increase their theory of mind skills (Howe et al., 2002), an excessive level exacts a toll on all family members. Many parents identify sibling conflicts as their worst family problem (Smith & Ross, 2007). Fortunately, parents can be trained to mediate sibling conflicts, and the training may also affect the children, who are more likely to learn how to resolve conflicts in constructive as opposed to destructive ways (Smith & Ross, 2007; see Scientific Method box). For example, after parents of 5- and 10-year-olds received mediation training, children of both ages compromised more often and seemed to understand their sibling's point of view better than a control group of children of untrained parents (Smith & Ross, 2007). Conflict resolution is a complex cognitive and social skill in which training can have strong, multifaceted, and long-lasting effects. In addition to conflict resolution, parental training and socialization of children should be concerned with prosocial behaviors in their own right (Kramer, 2010). It is an oversimplification to focus on sibling conflicts as the central dynamic among children in a family when in fact there are many positive dimensions of successful sibling relationships that can be influenced by parents as well.

Siblings and Social Understanding

A positive effect for siblings, especially when they are close in age, is the development of more advanced theory of mind skills. Compared with only children or with those whose siblings are much younger or much older, siblings who are close in age are more likely to have practice thinking and talking about the mental states of others. This practice in turn may facilitate their understanding of the nuances of complex social interactions and the mental states of others (Jenkins & Astington, 1996; McAlister & Peterson, 2007; Peterson, 2000; Ruffman et al., 1998). Moreover, the more child-aged siblings a child has, the more theory of mind skills seem to be enhanced (McAlister & Peterson, 2013); thus, even if a large number of siblings may have some minor negative effects on intelligence test scores, it can have positive effects on social cognition. In a clear illustration of the intricate links between social and cognitive development, the early, consistent presence of others with similar interests and aptitudes apparently promotes the ability to think about other minds.

Sibling Relationships within the Family

Besides the direct effects that siblings have on one another, their relations can involve the entire family in a web of interactions. For example, several studies have now shown that parents sometimes form expectations based on the firstborn child that strongly influence their interactions with later-born children (Brody, 2004; Whiteman & Buchanan, 2002). This has been called "the first child as the first draft" effect (Whiteman et al., 2003). Thus, a difficult first child may set up parental expectations that result in stricter parenting with younger siblings. These effects can even extend beyond the family when teachers make assumptions about how a child will perform academically based on how the child's older siblings performed (Georgiou, 2008; Rubie-Davies et al., 2006). On the other hand, parents' positive expectations can sometimes benefit later siblings. One study showed that when older siblings are both academically and socially skilled, parents tend to show higher self-esteem and better psychological functioning that translate into better parenting practices with later children (Brody et al., 2003). Intricate statistical analyses suggest that the older sibling actually *causes* changes in the parents that affect how the parents interact with younger siblings However, it is difficult to rule out other possible causes, such as shared genetic influences on parents' and children's personalities.

Much like the interactionist approaches to parenting research, studies examining the effects of siblings and family structures on development are becoming more sophisticated by increasingly taking contextual factors (such as relationship quality) into account. Consider, for example, the effects of sibling relationship quality on parents, parenting, and other siblings (Brody, 1998). As noted earlier, many parents identify sibling conflicts as the worst problem in their family (Smith & Ross, 2007). And when siblings are constantly at odds with each other, the likelihood of those siblings having problems with peers, poor performance in school, and general hostility increases (Smith & Ross, 2007). These correlations must be treated with caution, since a number of other factors could cause both the sibling conflicts and the other problems; but there is the real possibility that the conflict itself is corrosive to other relationships. Interestingly, siblings with similar temperaments tend to have fewer conflicts (Munn & Dunn, 1989). This finding was not immediately obvious, as some might think that siblings who play distinct, complementary roles in a family would be most compatible.

China's One-Child Policy

Children who are "only children" and have no siblings have been stereotyped in a variety of ways, some of them contradictory. They are sometimes seen as spoiled, unusually mature (or unusually immature), dependent, selfish, and socially incompetent (Silverman & Silverman, 1971). But are they really at greater risk for developing these largely negative traits? Although some early studies suggested problems in only children that accord with stereotypes, later reviews of the body of research found that only children show no systematic deficits (Falbo & Polit, 1986). This finding is reassuring given that in developed countries, many more families are now choosing to have just one child compared to a decade ago (Frejka & Sardon, 2007).

But what about cases where having an only child is not a voluntary decision but a nationwide decree? In 1979, the People's Republic of China laid down a set of regulations known collectively as the "one-child policy" (see Figure 14.11). These laws stated that every family was to have not more than one child. The goal was to prevent the widespread famines that had resulted in the past when China's food supplies fell short of its large population. Some exceptions to the one-child policy were granted, especially in more rural areas, but it generally accomplished its goal: China's birth rate fell and its incidence of single-child families greatly increased (Doherty et al., 2001). From 1980 to 2000, China's birth rate declined from roughly 35 children per 1,000 people each year to roughly 16 children per 1,000 people.

Have such dramatic and rapid changes in the structure of Chinese families caused developmental changes in children and young adults? This question has been of great concern to Chinese politicians and social planners, and many articles in the popular press have expressed worries about a new generation of "little emperors"—terribly spoiled, overindulged only children (Dean, 1992). Even in recent years, employers have posted job openings with the restriction that single children need not apply (Chang, 2008). In addition, 75 percent of China's urban couples reported that they would have preferred to have larger families, more like the ones they grew up in, and that they regard the one-child policy as a considerable sacrifice. Parents also worried that their children would be lonely without siblings and would miss out on critical social interactions (Tao & Chiu, 1985; Tung, 1997). A Chinese version of *Sesame Street* even included special segments aimed at teaching only children how to get along with peers (Tung, 1997).

Early studies of China's new generation of only children reported differences that followed the "little emperor" stereotype. Only children were said to be more spoiled and demanding (Jiao et al., 1986). These studies, however, were challenged by later ones that found no major differences in the behaviors or personalities of only children and other children (Chen et al., 1994; Falbo & Poston, 1993). Whether a child was the firstborn of several siblings or later-born, that child did not seem to differ in any systematic way from only children. In fact, in some studies, only children were found better adjusted than other children (Liu et al., 2010). Incidentally, these children with siblings were quite easy to find in China because certain regions were permitted fairly widespread exceptions to the one-child policy.

One explanation for this shift in research findings is that parents and grandparents concerned about having spoiled children

FIGURE 14.11 China's one-child policy. As can be seen from **(A)** a family photo taken in 1934 and **(B)** a recent family photo, family size in China has changed dramatically over the years as a result of China's one-child policy to manage a burgeoning population. Several commentators have argued that a nation of only children will grow up to be adults that are very different from those of earlier generations.

A

B

might have changed their child-rearing patterns (Rosenberg & Jing, 1996). In addition, as more Chinese children of the current generation spend increasing amounts of time in community day care from an early age, their interactions with peers may re-create some of the effects of siblings.

Although this second wave of studies did not show one-child effects, some effects may well exist, despite being difficult to pinpoint among the effects of other cultural and economic changes unfolding in China. In the last two decades, the one-child policy has brought a population shift in the cities from roughly 20 percent only-child families to 95 percent only-child families. Over the same period, the ways children spend their time has shifted from mostly being at home around relatives in the extended family to mostly being in day care. China has also seen improvements in the health and well-being of most of its people and a marked change in the political system and institutions of education. Any of these changes—let alone all of them at once—would likely affect children's social behavior regardless of our theory of socialization. The challenge for developmental researchers is that these large-scale changes have been so numerous and nearly simultaneous, making it difficult to untangle their cause-and-effect relationships without much larger and more systematic studies.

Some researchers argue that one-child effects can be found in behaviors other than those revolving around erroneous stereotypes of only children (Mancillas, 2006). For example, one study in the United States found evidence of a reduced ability to manage conflict with peers, perhaps because of less practice dealing with similar conflicts with siblings (Kitzmann et al., 2002). Comparable studies in China have yet to be done. As only children grow older, they may also have greater anxiety about having to be the sole caregiver of their aging parents, an obligation that is taken especially seriously in some Eastern cultures (Mancillas, 2006).

As the example with aging parents suggests, it may be that some of the effects of being only children take many years to manifest and may only be found in adults. This was the argument of one large-scale study of 412 Chinese adults who were born just a year or two before or after the one-child policy was implemented in 1979 (Cameron et al., 2013). The adults were studied in experimental tasks designed to assess trust, risk, and performance in competitive tasks. Children born in the first year of the one-child policy performed in these tasks in ways that were less trusting, less trustworthy, and less willing to take risks. Of course, the presence of such traits in laboratory tasks might not translate into real-world behaviors. Somewhat more naturalistic questionnaires after the experiments, however, also found strong effects,

most notably less optimism about the future, less conscientiousness, and more neuroticism.

Demographically, one effect of the one-child policy is unmistakable, namely, a huge shift in the ratio of boys to girls in the general population. As seen in Figure 14.12, in rural areas there are roughly 25 percent more male than female births, the highest male-to-female sex ratio in the world, with some rural regions having 40 percent more male births (Zhou et al., 2011). A strong cultural bias toward boys has led to a reduction in the number of girls through abortion and infanticide. The psychological and social consequences of such uneven sex ratios are unclear, but they seem to cause many rural men to feel "useless, aimless, hopeless, miserable, sad, distressed, angry and lonely" (Zhou et al., 2011, p. 1426) as they consider their small chance for a future marriage. (To make matters worse, many rural men watch as their female peers leave for more affluent areas to find mates and "marry up.") These attitudes may start to emerge in late childhood and color the perspectives of many boys, especially those from more rural regions (Zhou et al., 2013).

The full effects of the one-child policy will require many more years to fully understand, but the situation helps to illustrate, once again, the critical importance of an interactionist perspective, where a huge confluence of factors must be considered to understand socialization effects and interventions that change traditional family structures. Regardless of the long-term effects of the one-child policy, it must ultimately be considered against a larger backdrop of a country burdened with overpopulation and a history of famines and other population-related disasters. Even the worst alleged psychological consequences of such a policy may pale when considered against the alternatives.

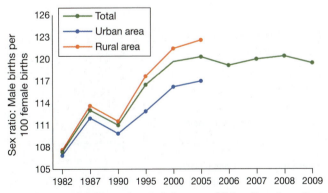

FIGURE 14.12 Sex ratios and the one-child policy. One effect of the one-child policy, especially in rural areas, is a huge shift in the ratio of boys to girls, which may well have a profound impact on social relations among peers. Adapted from Hvistendahl (2010).

SCIENTIFIC METHOD: Training Parents to Moderate Sibling Conflicts

Hypothesis:

Training parents to use formal mediation procedures helps them intervene in sibling conflicts between their children and reduce the intensity of those conflicts.

Method:

1. Forty-eight families with children ranging in age from 5 to 10 years old were randomly assigned to either mediation or control groups.

2. In the mediation group, parents were trained in a series of formal mediation techniques.

3. In the control group, parents were told that the study examined sibling conflict and parental interventions and were told to intervene normally.

4. Parents' reports of subsequent conflict episodes between siblings were recorded.

Results:

Siblings whose parents were assigned to the mediation group showed better conflict resolution strategies, compromised more frequently, and managed the outcomes of conflicts better. They also showed less negativity in recurrent conflicts, more nuanced assessments of blame, and greater ability to appreciate their siblings' points of view (see table).

Conclusion:

Training parents in well-proven mediation strategies for adults can reduce the intensity and tone of sibling conflicts both in terms of behaviors and in terms of social cognitive styles.

1. Let's set some ground rules about how to resolve your disagreements.

2. Each of you should say what you think was happening and how you disagree or agree.

3. Each of you should say what you want and how you feel.

4. You should both try to find a way to resolve your disagreement and check to see if your solution is feasible.

Frequencies of Conflict Resolutions

	Mediation Condition	Control Condition
Resolutions		
Compromise	74	40
Win/lose	6	27
Reconciliation	18	9
No Resolution	10	52
Who Resolves?		
Parent	11	74
Children	46	30
Children with parent's help	50	26

Source study: Smith & Ross (2007).

The interactionist approach to sibling dynamics sheds light on many developmental patterns and variations and suggests countless new research questions. Equally important, it is also powerfully relevant to practical developmental issues. For example, when children have to be removed from their parents' care and placed in a foster home following a crisis (such as serious child mistreatment), social agencies are often anguished about whether to compromise the quality of the foster care placement in order to keep all the siblings together.

Research on children in foster homes suggests an answer: siblings should only be kept together when they have a low-conflict relationship. In one study, siblings with significant behavior problems prior to placement in a foster home fared better after 18 months if they were placed in separate foster homes. In contrast, siblings who had positive relationships prior to placement did better if they were placed together in the same foster home (Linares et al., 2007). Clearly, policies that keep siblings together in foster home placements at all costs should be made more sensitive to the context and quality of sibling relationships.

Changes in the Family

We have a tendency to think that "family" has had the same meaning throughout history. In fact, it is among the most dramatically changing concepts in the social sciences. Today's families differ in many respects from families in 1959, which were in turn different from families in 1910. From a psychological viewpoint, how have these differences influenced children's development? In this section, we will consider different kinds of families, including one- and two-parent families,

small nuclear families and large extended ones, families with older versus younger parents, and families in which both parents work outside the home.

Changes in Parents' Age

Most people assume that the average age of parents in two-parent families has been gradually increasing over the last 100 years, but this assumption depends partly on the frame of reference. To be sure, the median age of marriage in the United States—which is closely related to parents' age when their first child is born—has risen in the past several decades. But as Figure 14.13A shows, looking at the median age of marriage over a longer time frame reveals that the recent rise is less marked than the striking drop that occurred right after the Second World War (Cherlin, 2005). This is a useful reminder that as dramatic as recent trends might seem, they should always be considered in terms of broader historical contexts. Nonetheless, in recent decades, maternal age at the birth of a married couple's first child has increased significantly throughout North America, Western Europe, and Japan (Cliquet, 2003; Mathews & Hamilton, 2009; see Figure 14.13B).

It is not completely clear why parents of newborns are getting older in many areas of the world, but one factor seems to relate to finances (Gustafsson, 2005). Many couples are postponing marriage until they have more economic resources, so that they will be able to support a child without having to cut back on their normal levels of consumption. As we will see shortly, older parents also tend to have smaller families.

What are the effects of delaying the childbearing years until the late 30s or even 40s? Although this question

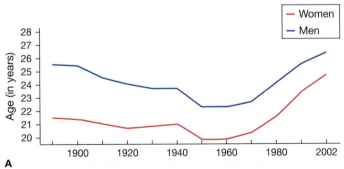

A

FIGURE 14.13 Median age of marriage and birth of first child over the last century. (A) The age of parents, which is related to the age of marriage, has risen dramatically in the past 40 years, but much of that rise is related to a return from a dramatic drop in the age of marriage that occurred after World War II. Adapted from Cherlin (2005). **(B)** Over the past four decades, however, whether the parents are from North America, Europe, or Japan, the mean age of mothers at the time of the birth of their first child has increased dramatically. Adapted from Mathews & Hamilton (2009).

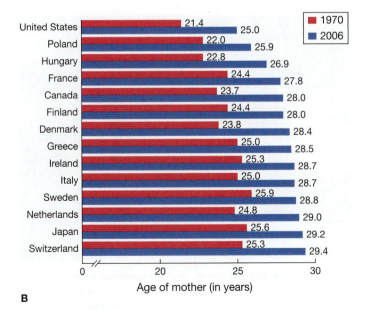

B

has only recently been extensively studied, some provocative suggestions have come to light. One analysis suggests that older parenting brings tradeoffs for the children (see Figure 14.14). There is likely greater economic security for the family, but perhaps some negative social costs, such as greater psychological distance between parents and children (Martin, 2004). In general, scholars have emphasized the benefits of delaying marriage and childbearing, including more stable marriages, more elaborate networks of social support for the family, and parents' ability to provide more resources for the children (Gustafsson, 2005; Martin, 2004; Miller, 2011). Older parents also tend to interact with their children verbally in more sophisticated ways and to be less reactive. As always, though, it can be difficult to distinguish these effects from socioeconomic ones, since older parents are more likely than younger ones to be of higher socioeconomic status.

The downside of delayed childbearing is less apparent, but some effects seem likely. First, many children of older parents may have grandparents so old that they play only a marginal role, if any, in their lives, depriving these children of the benefits of a close relationship with their grandparents. These families may also be deprived of the kind of support that grandparents can provide to a family, such as providing day care, helping out in times of crisis, or simply being a mentor and source of expertise (Hayslip & Kaminski, 2005). Second, children report that they identify less with older parents, see them as more remote from their own lives, and feel less in tune with them. Research also suggests that older parents have less energy and more limited ability to engage in physical activities with their children (Martin, 2004). Finally, as seen in Figure 14.15, there are clear biological factors to consider, as the incidence of fertility and

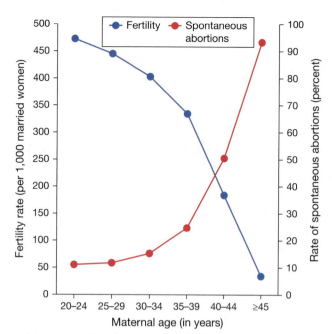

FIGURE 14.15 Age and motherhood. When women choose to have their first child at later and later ages, fertility rates and spontaneous abortions can change dramatically. Adapted from Heffner (2004).

pregnancy complications increases greatly in the third and fourth decades of a woman's life (Heffner, 2004). This, in turn, can have a huge influence on family planning as well as creating additional stressors. In short, it will be important for future studies to systematically investigate the negative effects of late childbearing, as the answers concern increasing numbers of families.

Older parents are only part of the story of the changes in parental age in the last several decades. At the same time that parents in two-parent families are getting older, there has been a substantial increase in the number of single-parent families (U.S. Census Bureau, 2012a). Some of these single-parent families are headed by teenage mothers, although the rate of teenage pregnancies and the percentage of young teen mothers has decreased since the 1990s (Hamilton et al., 2012; Martin et al., 2012; see Figure 14.16). The net effect of these changes regarding parent age is to create an increase in two kinds of parents: those who are young and single and those who are older and have a partner.

What are the developmental effects of having very young parents—what some call the phenomenon of "children having children"? Several studies have reported that very young teenage mothers are at greater risk for depression, and their children are more likely to have academic and behavioral problems, such as acting out in school (Beers & Hollo, 2009; Pogarsky et al., 2006; Shaw et al., 2006; Sullivan et al., 2011). In these cases, however, disentangling causation from correlation is difficult. Very young mothers tend to be from lower income brackets than older mothers, are more likely

FIGURE 14.14 Older parents. In many countries, parents are older when they have their first child. Being an older parent presents a number of tradeoffs in terms of its impact on children.

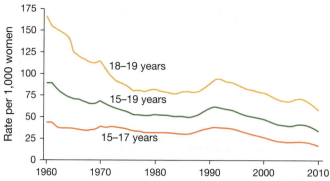

FIGURE 14.16 **Teen pregnancy rates.** Teen pregnancy and birth rates have been steadily declining for the last four decades. Adapted from Martin et al. (2012).

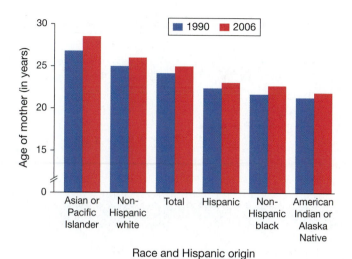

Race and Hispanic origin

FIGURE 14.18 **Average age of mother at first birth for various groups.** For a diverse set of groups, the average age of mothers has increased in recent years. Adapted from Mathews & Hamilton (2009).

to be single parents, and tend to be less educated (see Figure 14.17). When researchers try to account for these other correlated influences, the effect of being a teenage mother per se often becomes smaller. However, when these other factors are controlled, children—especially boys—of teenage mothers still face a greater risk of negative outcomes (Olausson et al., 2001; Pogarsky et al., 2006). In many other cases, factors such as the mother's education level are so strongly linked to maternal age that it is difficult to examine the effects of maternal age separately from these associated factors.

Although the incidence of teenage pregnancy has declined in recent years in the United States and other countries, the statistics vary widely among racial and socio-economic groups. The mean age of U.S. mothers when they first give birth ranges from roughly 29 for Japanese Americans and Chinese Americans to roughly 22 for African Americans, Mexican Americans, and Native Americans (see Figure 14.18). This increasing age for first births has been found in many parts of the world. In some groups, a younger mean age reflects a disproportionate number of

teenage mothers. In short, although the number of very young mothers may be dropping overall, they still represent a large proportion of parents in some groups.

Changes in Family Size

In countries where the average parental age is rising, one consequence is a decline in family size. In addition, in many countries, factors independent of parents' age also contribute to smaller family size. Parents are choosing to have fewer children partly because of the economic burden of supporting more children and because the demands of caring for larger families is more likely to impinge on the parents' career aspirations (Miller, 2011). Average family size varies considerably in different countries, as Figure 14.19A shows. Most developed countries have seen a pattern of decreasing family size over the years. Yet even countries that are culturally very similar can show striking differences, both in average family size and in family size trends over time (see Figure 14.19B). In addition, within any given country, family size can vary considerably as a function of race and ethnicity (see Table 14.4). For these reasons, any statements about the developmental influence of changing family sizes have to consider the local cultural context.

It might seem that children in larger families would tend to have worse outcomes. After all, the more children there are in a family, the less economic resources and parental time and energy can be spent on each child, an argument that has been used to explain some sibling and birth order effects. On the whole, children from larger families do tend to receive fewer years of education and earn less money, and they are more likely to have disciplinary problems (Loeber & Stouthamer-Loeber,

FIGURE 14.17 **Teenage mothers.** One major challenge, being met here by these teenage mothers in Brazil, is to continue schooling.

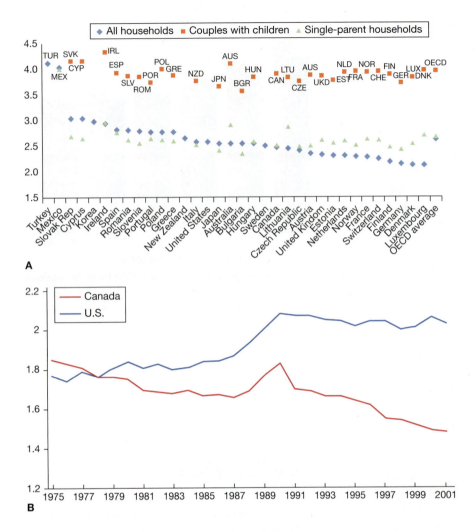

FIGURE 14.19 Family sizes in different countries. (A) Family size varies considerably across countries of similar levels of economic development. The graph depicts family size in the early and mid-2000s. Adapted from OECD Family Database (2010). **(B)** Despite the many similarities between the United States and Canada, these two nations are diverging rapidly with respect to average family size, as revealed by the mean total fertility rates from 1975 to 2001. Adapted from Eberstadt & Torrey (2005).

1986). But a closer look at these statistics reveals that family size is unlikely to be the main reason for these patterns. Family size is generally correlated with socioeconomic status: poorer families tend to have more children. Thus, in many cases, negative outcomes associated with large families may also be due to socioeconomic status. As mentioned earlier, family size may have negative effects primarily on poor families. For families that are not so poor, family size does not seem to negatively influence educational outcomes (Black et al., 2005). At the other end of the continuum, growing up as an only child does not seem to make children more spoiled or demanding, despite popular stereotypes (Chen et al., 1994; Falbo & Posten, 1993; Mancillas, 2006).

Another way of thinking about family size and structure involves the difference between nuclear families and extended families. **Nuclear families** generally consist of the mother and father as heads of the household, along with their children. **Extended families** reach across generations and sometimes incorporate aunts, uncles, and cousins. Often a grandfather or grandmother may be head of the extended

	Total Number of Households (millions)	Average Household Size	People under 18 in Household	People over 18 in Household
All	80.5	3.13	0.90	2.23
Hispanic	1.6	3.78	1.38	2.40
White	65.4	3.08	0.86	2.23
Black	10.0	3.31	1.16	2.15
Asian	4.3	3.40	0.92	2.48

TABLE 14.4 Family size and ethnicity in the United States. From U.S. Census Bureau (2012b).

family household. In many parts of the world, including much of Asia, extended families are the norm. Older parents may also have more of an impact on family dynamics in such cultures because if the parents are old enough, the grandparents may be too old to participate effectively.

Both kinds of family structures can have different positive and negative effects on children. Members of the extended family, and especially grandparents, can provide extremely important support to parents; in nuclear families, the sole responsibility for child-care arrangements more often falls to the parents. But extended families may encounter more disruptive transitions than nuclear families as grandparents age and family structure changes.

Working Parents and Child Care

Sometimes, cultural influences on families reflect changing socioeconomic realities. In Chapter 6, we considered the ways that day care arrangements might influence a child's attachment to his parents. In many countries, this issue is part of a much larger change in the number of families in which both parents work full-time outside the home. The incidence has increased in several Western countries over the past few decades (see Figure 14.20). For example, in the United States in 2012, 58 percent of mothers with a child under 2 years of age were employed outside the home (Bureau of Labor Statistics, 2013). In contrast, in the early 1950s, only 18 percent of mothers with a child under age 6 were employed outside the home (Halpern, 2005). The shift has primarily occurred among married women with a husband present in the household, as single mothers have worked at higher levels all along.

How has such a dramatic shift influenced the children in those families? Mothers who work outside the home might be spending less time with their children, which could have some negative effects. A few researchers have reported negative socioemotional effects, such as more difficulty in interpersonal relationships (Belsky, 2002; Belsky & Johnson, 2005; National Institute of Child Health and Human Development, 2003), but the vast majority of studies do not find any consistent effects, and when effects are found, they tend to be small.

In short, the shift to working outside the home by mothers does not seem to have had any consistently measurable negative impact on their children (Gottfried & Gottfried, 2006; Halpern, 2005). At least one study has shown that children of mothers working outside the home have no differences in educational achievements or in social or behavioral problems (Kalil & Ziol-Guest, 2008). One long-term study followed children up to the age of 24 and found no differences in occupational status at that age (Gottfried & Gottfried, 2006). Likewise, there is little reliable evidence

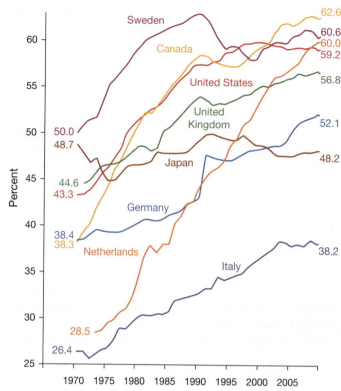

FIGURE 14.20 The rise of women in the workplace. Over the past three decades, there has been a sharp rise in the percentage of women in the workplace, although differences between countries remain very large. Adapted from the Bureau of Labor Statistics (2011).

that children's cognitive development suffers when mothers work outside the home (Burchinal & Clarke-Stewart, 2007).

There are several reasons why the effects of having two working parents seem small or nonexistent. Although some researchers found that employed mothers spend less time with their children (Gottfried & Gottfried, 2006), others found that by sacrificing leisure time, working mothers usually manage to spend just as much time with their children as those who are not employed. One line of research, in which mothers recorded their activities in detailed diary entries, carefully documented how these working mothers engaged in more multitasking and cut back on time doing housework in order to spend as much time with their children as mothers did in prior generations (Bianchi, 2011).

Indeed, one study found that working mothers during the period from 2003 to 2008 spent an hour *more* per week with their children than did stay-at-home mothers in 1975 (Bianchi et al., 2006; Fox et al., 2013). In addition, fathers are spending more time with their children as mothers spend more time working outside the home. As a result, today's children may actually spend more time with their parents than children did in prior generations (Halpern, 2005). Another reason why children of working mothers fare as well as other children may relate to the consistent finding that poverty negatively influences child development: when both parents work, their children are less likely to grow up in poverty.

Sometimes when both parents are working, there are negative effects on children. When mothers have nonstandard work hours, such as night shifts or erratic schedules, their children are somewhat more likely to show substantial delays in cognitive development (Han, 2005). One reason for such an influence is that parents who work nonstandard schedules have far more limited child-care options. High-quality center-based care, which has consistently been shown to benefit young children, is often unavailable to parents who need care in the middle of the night or on unpredictable schedules.

Finally, there are some suggestions that working women are often stretched to the limit more than working fathers (Porter, 2006). Many working mothers are using up every available nonwork hour, and they sleep almost 4 hours less per week than mothers who stay at home (Bianchi et al., 2006). Although no negative effects of such busy lives have been found, it is possible that for some working mothers, fatigue and burnout take a toll.

Changes in Family Structures

There are as many traditional family structures as there are cultural traditions, but in general, the recent changes in family structure in many developed countries include increases in single-parent families, families with same-sex partners, and families in which parents divorce and sometimes remarry.

Single-Parent Families Much attention has been focused on single-parent families, usually those with single mothers, since they are far more common than families headed by single fathers. Throughout the world, the percentage of single-parent families has been increasing over the past two decades (see Table 14.5). Because single-parent families are more common in lower socioeconomic groups and some minority groups, it can be difficult to know whether any adverse outcomes for children of single parents truly arise from having only one parent or whether they are largely due to other factors, such as economic hardship, and the ways they interact with other influences of single parenthood.

Low-income single parenting, for example, is strongly correlated with problems for children. One study examined differences between three groups of low-income parents: those who were single, those who were unmarried and living with a partner, and those who were married. Among these low-income groups, the single parents showed higher levels of mental and physical illness and drug abuse than those with other family structures, but these correlations are not evident for single parents with high incomes (McLanahan, 2004).

Thus, financial stresses may be exacerbated by being a single parent, and vice versa.

Other studies examining a wider range of economic groups have found associations between single-parent families and children's educational and economic outcomes. On average, children of single parents tend to get fewer years of schooling and to earn lower incomes (Björklund et al., 2004). One intriguing analysis of African-American families suggests that single parenting is not associated with problems for children as long as another individual is also acting as an invested caregiver. For example, in many African-American families headed by a single mother, a grandmother serves as a second caregiver, providing critical support that reduces or prevents any negative effects of single parenthood (Simons et al., 2006), although later studies show that the positive effect of grandparents seems to vary as a function of contexts that are not yet fully understood (Arnold et al., 2011). In short, having a single parent need not have negative consequences for a child, but if that parent is also poor and lacks social support, there are increased risks for adverse effects.

In addition, the rates of single-parent families have varied dramatically across countries, over time, and across ethnic groups (Ellwood & Jencks, 2004; McClanahan, 2004). For example, a child born in the United States in 1995 was five times more likely to grow up with a single parent than a child born in Italy in 1995. Even larger differences exist within the United States: a child born into poverty or a disadvantaged minority group is seven times more likely to grow up with a single parent than a child born into affluence or in a more advantaged ethnic group (Hummer & Hamilton, 2010). The broad range of family structures that exist within many different cultural contexts therefore makes it difficult to generalize about the impact of family structures on children. More detailed and context-sensitive analyses are needed.

Same-Sex Parents A different kind of family structure involves same-sex caregivers (see Figure 14.21). There has been a marked increase in the number of gay and lesbian adults raising children over the past two decades. In 2005, approximately 300,000 children in the United States were living in families with two same-sex parents (Romero et al., 2007). When single gay and lesbian parents were included in a 2013 analysis, almost 2 million children in the United States were being raised by gay and lesbian parents (Siegel et al., 2013). These estimates are likely to increase considerably in future years in the United States and other countries where there is increasing social acceptance of same-sex couples and marriages.

One reason for increasing approval of adoptions by same-sex parents is that no negative outcomes have ever been consistently found for children of gay and lesbian couples when compared with children of heterosexual couples (Anderssen

Country and Year	Percent of All Households with Children	Country and Year	Percent of All Households with Children
United States		**Germany**	
1980	19.5	1991	15.2
1990	24.0	1995	18.8
2000	27.0	2000	17.6
2008	29.5	2008	21.7
Canada		**Ireland**	
1981	12.7	1981	7.2
1991	16.2	1991	10.7
2001	23.5	2002	17.4
2006	24.6	2006	22.6
Japan		**Netherlands**	
1980	4.9	1988	9.6
1990	6.5	2000	13.0
2000	8.3	2009	16.0
2005	10.2		
Denmark		**Sweden**	
1980	13.4	1985	11.2
1990	17.8	1995	17.4
2001	18.4	2000	21.4
2009	21.7	2008	18.7
France		**United Kingdom**	
1982	10.2	1981	13.9
1990	13.2	1991	19.4
1999	17.4	2000	20.7
2005	19.8	2008	25.0

TABLE 14.5 Single-parent families across cultures. The number of single parents has been increasing throughout the world to a degree that far exceeds the rate of population growth in those countries. Source: U.S. Census Bureau (2012b).

et al., 2002; Chan et al., 1998; Patterson, 1992, 2013; Perrin, 2002; Siegel et al., 2013; Tasker, 2002, 2005). Children who grow up in gay and lesbian families do not differ from other children in their cognitive and social development or their incidence of behavioral problems. They also show the same profiles of sexual preferences, gender identities, and gender role behaviors. Some reviews suggest that children in gay and lesbian families may have more negative experiences than their peers associated with others' homophobia and stigmatizing of their parents, but even these negative experiences do not appreciably change child outcomes (Tasker, 2005). Indeed, at least one study reports higher levels of cognitive and social functioning and lower levels of behavioral problems among children of lesbian parents (Gartrell & Bos, 2010). One factor to keep in mind is that

for most same-sex couples, the process of giving birth to or adopting a child is necessarily quite deliberate and involved, so same-sex parents have fewer unplanned or unwanted children. Moreover, same-sex couples, like all other couples who adopt children, have to pass assessments by adoption agencies and other social service organizations of their fitness as parents before they are allowed to adopt. Finally, many lesbian partners exercise choice in their selection of donors for insemination and may therefore be selecting for certain positive behavioral traits in fathers that are passed on to their children.

In short, although there are many popular stereotypes about problems associated with single-parent families and same-sex parents, the negative effects of growing up in either of these kinds of families are usually nonexistent. In

FIGURE 14.21 Same-sex parents. Same-sex parents have become more common in many parts of the world. Children of same-sex parents do not seem to have different psychological outcomes from children of different-sex parents.

the case of single-parent homes, negative outcomes for children more likely relate to other variables, such as poverty, that are not inherent to family structure.

Divorce Over the past few decades, the incidence of divorce has increased in several countries. In 1958, there were roughly 2 divorces per 1,000 individuals in the United States. This number rose rapidly in the following decades and peaked at approximately 5.5 divorces per 1,000 individuals in the 1980s, more than double the earlier rate. It has declined a modest amount since that time to roughly 3.6 divorces per 1,000 people (Centers for Disease Control and Prevention, 2013; Fields, 2003; Fields & Casper, 2001).

Approximately 40 percent of all children in the United States will experience a divorce and a transition to a single-parent family by the time they are 18 years of age

(Amato, 2000; Cherlin, 2010; Kennedy & Bumpass, 2008). In the United States, over 1 million children are affected by a divorce every year (U.S. Census Bureau, 2012a). Beyond formal marriages and divorce, there also changes in cohabitation arrangements that may have similar effects. Such effects may be especially strong in the United States, where mothers are much more likely to change their cohabitation partners than are mothers in most European countries (Bianchi, 2011; Cherlin, 2010; Kennedy & Bumpass, 2008).

Divorce rates also vary as a function of social class and education, with increasingly higher rates among those who have fewer years of education (Bramlett & Mosher, 2002; Martin, 2006; see Figure 14.22). The reasons for this difference are complex but may be related to the average earlier age of marriage of those with fewer years of education. It is possible that younger couples are less experienced at dealing with the conflicts that can arise within relationships. Divorce rates also vary considerably across race and ethnicity. In the United States, the highest rates occur for non-Hispanic whites, followed in decreasing order by African Americans, Hispanics, and Asians, who get divorced at roughly one-third the rate of non-Hispanic whites. Again, the reasons for such differences are complex and are related to such factors as the overall rate of marriage, which is quite a bit higher, for example, for non-Hispanic whites than for African Americans (Fischer & Hout, 2006).

Divorce rates also vary considerably between countries. As Figure 14.23 shows, the U.S. rate is almost seven times that of Italy and considerably higher than that of several other countries, including Canada. These patterns often reflect cultural norms, which can also be reflected in laws and regulations designed to discourage divorce. They should not be taken as evidence that, for example, unhappy marriages are seven times more frequent in the United States than in Italy. These differences do show that the study of divorce and its

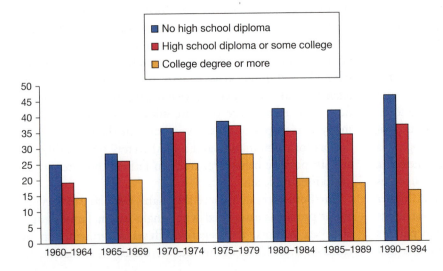

FIGURE 14.22 Divorce rates and educational level. Less educated parents are more likely to be divorced, a trend that has become more pronounced in recent years. Adapted from Martin (2006).

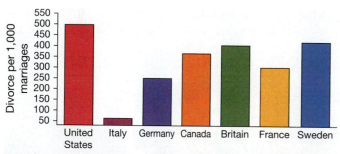

FIGURE 14.23 Divorce rates across different countries. Divorce rates can vary dramatically across different countries. Divorce rates reflect, among other things, the degree to which a culture's laws and moral norms oppose divorce, so a country's relatively high rate does not necessarily indicate that marital dissatisfaction is more common in that society. Adapted from Cherlin (2005).

impact on families must take into account many cultural settings rather than simply drawing universal conclusions from the preponderance of studies conducted in the United States. Nonetheless, because most major studies have been U.S. based, they will form the bulk of our discussion.

The central message here is that divorce patterns vary greatly across nations as well as socioeconomic classes and ethnic and racial groups within nations. Since there are so many divorce patterns, it is difficult to make many generalizations about the effects of divorce on children.

Q: Describe ways in which divorce rates vary across historical time periods in one culture and across cultures within the same time period.

Research on divorce has primarily focused on understanding its impact on children. This issue raises questions about differences in impact on boys and girls and on younger and older children. It also raises questions about whether different kinds of families (for example, extended versus nuclear families) and children (for example, only children versus those with several siblings) fare differently in divorce. Finally, it raises questions about tradeoffs. Is it better for the children of an unhappy marriage for the couple to stay together? Is it better for a child of divorced parents to spend equal time with each parent or to live primarily with one parent? Thousands of studies, not only by psychologists but also by sociologists, economists, anthropologists, legal scholars, and even evolutionary biologists, have examined divorce and its consequences. Many controversies remain, but a few fairly reliable patterns emerge, several of which may run counter to popular lore about divorce (Amato, 2010; Hetherington & Kelly, 2002; Hetherington & Stanley-Hagan, 2002).

First, the effects of divorce and their magnitude vary across studies, but divorce is generally associated with increased problems for children, potentially including declining school performance, delinquency, depression, aggression, and even increased health problems (Amato, 2010; Ellis, 2000; Grych & Fincham, 1992; Hetherington et al., 1985; Oldehinkel et al., 2008). One large-scale study of almost 1,500 families documented a wide range of behavioral problems reported by parents, teachers, and the children themselves (Furstenberg et al., 1983). Across many studies, it seems that the incidence of problem behaviors ranges from slightly more to almost double the rate for children of married parents. These increases are concerning, but their overall magnitude should not be exaggerated. Even doubling the average incidence of problematic behaviors means that only a relatively small minority of children in divorced families struggle with serious behavioral or emotional problems.

Q: What are some of the associations between divorce and behavioral problems in children?

Are the effects of divorce more detrimental for boys or for girls? The answer depends on the children's age and the particular problems in question. Among younger children of divorced parents, boys tend to show more behavioral problems than girls (Fauber et al., 1990). This is especially true when the child lives with a single mother, the most frequent post-divorce outcome in most countries. In these circumstances, young boys show more intense behavior problems than girls, and the problems arise sooner (Hetherington et al., 1985; Wallerstein, 1985a, 1985b; Warshak, 1992). For girls, the negative effects seem more pronounced later, during adolescence. They are more likely to be delinquent from school or excessively sexually promiscuous, in some cases even when the divorce occurred in early childhood (Allison & Furstenberg, 1989; Hetherington, 1991; Slater & Haber, 1984).

One difference between girls' and boys' responses to divorce, at all ages, is inherent in their trends for specific styles of coping reactions. Girls tend to show **internalizing problems**, which are largely within the individual, such as depression and loss of self-esteem. In contrast, boys tend to show **externalizing problems**, which are expressed by acting out in antisocial ways, such as bullying, underage drinking, and disruptive behavior in the classroom (Peterson & Zill, 1986).

Part of the complexity of the findings concerning different impacts on the sexes may also have to do with the gender of the single parent who remains with the child. This is yet another example of how, in any discussion of the effects of gender in families, the gender of both the parent and the child contribute to developmental outcomes. In most cases, living with a parent of their same sex seems to be better for the child; boys tend to fare better in single-father homes, while girls typically do better with single mothers (Camara & Resnick, 1988; Clarke-Stewart & Hayward, 1996). But this finding is complicated by the relative rarity of single fathers with custody of their children. These cases are roughly one-tenth as frequent as mothers with child custody. In fact, a large number of fathers interact very little with their children after the divorce. In one study, 20 percent of fathers interviewed reported not having seen their children at all in the prior year, and another 50 percent reported not seeing their children more than a few times a year (Seltzer, 1994). Thus, the relatively rare cases where fathers become the custodial parent may reflect the effects of atypical fathers rather than fathers in general.

The long-term nature of the effects of divorce runs counter to some commonly held views, which suggest that the effects taper off after a year or two. Even as adults, however, children of divorced parents are more likely to experience divorce in their own marriages (Amato, 1996, 2010; Amato & Booth, 1996; Cherlin et al., 1998; Hetherington & Kelly, 2002; Wallerstein et al., 2000). In some cases, and more commonly among women, divorce in childhood is associated with increases in depression and relationship difficulties when those children are adults (Kim, 2011; Wallerstein et al., 2000). In addition, parent-child relationships can suffer over the long term, with more deleterious effects usually occurring with fathers (Kalmijn, 2013). The mechanisms behind such long-term effects are unclear. They range from continued family stress to the power of early experiences to genetic predispositions shared with parents.

FIGURE 14.24 Parental conflict. Overt conflicts between parents can have negative psychological effects on their children. Less overt tension or marital dissatisfaction does not seem to impact children as severely.

> Q: How is divorce related differently to behavioral problems in boys and girls?

What is it about a divorce that causes the most problems for children? Several studies now suggest that explicit conflict between parents is especially problematic for children. It is often said that it is always better for the children if unhappily married parents divorce; but several studies suggest a more nuanced view that depends on the circumstances of individual families (see Figure 14.24). If the parents' difficulties do not erupt into overt verbal or physical conflict, there is some evidence that the children may fare better if the parents stay married, even if they are uncomfortable around each other or fairly detached from each other (Amato, 2006, 2010; Amato & Booth,

1996; Buchanan et al., 1991, 1996; Camara & Resnick, 1988; Emery, 1988; Katz & Gottman, 1993). As one extensive review points out: "Living in a marriage marked by mutual disengagement is a less-than-satisfying experience for parents. But . . . in these families, children have ready access to both parents, a standard of living based on both parents' income, and a predictable and stable home environment. Divorce in these cases appears to increase the risk of a number of problems for offspring" (Amato, 2006, p. 199).

A stable family situation for the child can often be more important than parents first realize (Amato, 2010). But if the parents cannot avoid overt conflict, then the picture changes and the children are better off with one parent, providing that the post-divorce situation reduces the conflict (Amato, 2006, 2010). Of course, these conclusions cannot provide clear guidelines to a couple contemplating divorce. It may, for example, be difficult for parents to tell whether their disengagement from each other is stressful for their children. In addition, if parents' disengagement causes one or both of them severe distress, even if there is no overt discord, their distress may influence their parenting skills in other ways.

As divorce is usually a powerful, painful experience, it is natural to assume that the parents' divorce directly causes any associated problems in the children. But in many cases, a third factor, related to parents' and children's shared genetic disposition, may contribute to the difficulties that result in divorce and to the children's difficulties afterward. In the past decade, researchers have become increasingly interested in the genetic contributions to divorce and to the problems that affect some children of divorced families. One study of 398 adoptive and biological families with divorced parents found an intriguing interaction between genetic and environmental effects (O'Connor et al., 2000). The adopted children all had been adopted in the first few weeks of life. When the children were 12 years old, they and their families were extensively interviewed, and the children were assessed for a range of potential problems stemming from their parents' divorce. Based on these interviews and other assessments, the researchers examined five categories of potential effects of the divorce: changes in self-esteem, social competence (positive assertiveness and social responsibility), academic achievement, psychopathology, and substance abuse.

Notably, the differences in these categories were small between the adopted children of divorced parents and the children of divorced biological parents. Nonetheless, the children who were biologically related to their divorced parents seemed to show more negative effects from the divorce than did the adopted children. In particular, children of divorced biological parents showed more severe impacts on self-esteem, social competence, and academic achievement. The groups showed no differences with respect to more severe psychopathology.

These results support the idea that biological children and their parents share a genotype that both contributes to the difficulties that lead to divorce and makes the children more susceptible to problems as a result of the divorce. However, we should not regard our genetic heritage as strongly predicting our marital future. Indeed, some scholars have argued that shared genotype has a very limited role in explaining causal links between parental divorce and adverse outcomes in children (Amato, 2010).

Q: How can behavioral genetic models potentially help to explain associations between divorce and problems with children in divorced families?

Blended Families Given the high incidence of divorce and remarriage in countries like the United States, it is not surprising that there has also been a corresponding rise in blended families, created when parents remarry. **Blended families** consist of the parents and all children from their current relationship as well as children from prior relationships (see Figure 14.25). There are few reliable statistics on stepfamily configurations, but given divorce and remarriage statistics, it is safe to say that well over 10 percent of children live with at least one stepparent and that stepmothers are more common than stepfathers. Some estimates run as high as 30 percent if we include parents'

FIGURE 14.25 Blended families. Many children grow up in blended families in which all members thrive. In some cases, however, there are tensions with stepparents and stepchildren. In addition, some studies show that stepparents can be less invested in stepchildren.

cohabitation with new partners after a divorce (Bumpass et al., 1995; Radhakrishna et al., 2001). The increase in the incidence of these new kinds of families raises questions about how stepparents and stepchildren interact differently from the way parents and their biological children interact. Popular lore often condemns stepparents, and the theme of the cruel stepmother or stepfather is a frequent storyline in literature and folktales. Could there be any truth to the claim that stepparents favor their own children over their spouse's?

Although there are millions of stepparents and stepchildren who have strong, loving relationships, the research shows some modest differences, on average, in the expected direction. Children tend to have more conflicts with their stepparents and less intimate relationships with them than with their biological parents (Furstenberg, 1987; Hetherington, 1999; Hetherington & Jodl, 1994). There is also a great deal of variation, though, and some studies find that children of divorced mothers who remarry fare just as well as those of divorced single mothers (Demo & Acock, 1996).

Other research, much of it spawned by claims from evolutionary biology, has argued that there are significant differences in how stepparents treat their spouse's children compared with their own biological children. One widely cited study reported that stepfathers abuse their stepdaughters more than 8½ times more often than biological fathers abuse their daughters (Russell, 1984). These findings and similar ones have been interpreted as showing that stepparents treat stepchildren more poorly because they have no genetic investment in them. According to this evolutionary argument, stepparents are less committed to their stepchildren's well-being because, unlike a parent's biological children, stepchildren will not grow up to pass along the stepparent's genes to the next generation.

These explanations have been a source of controversy (Adler-Baeder, 2006; Temrin et al., 2000), but most studies do suggest that stepparents tend to behave less positively toward stepchildren than toward their own children (Anderson, 2011; Gardiner & Björklund, 2007). Some of the more interesting analyses of parental investment concern the subtle ways that parents treat children differently. One analysis of investments in college education in two-parent families found a difference in relative financial contributions between households with two biological parents and those in which one or both parents also had stepchildren. Stepparents started college savings accounts later, put less money aside, and expected to pay less than biological parents did for the first year of college (Zvoch, 1999). This pattern occurred even when stepparents and biological parents were of equal socioeconomic status and income level. Other researchers have found similar patterns (Anderson et al., 1999a, 1999b).

Another study found that stepchildren tended to be physically shorter than biological children (Flinn et al., 1999), a finding that gains some plausibility from other evidence that stressful environments can affect a child's height (Eiholzer et al., 1999). Even doubts about paternity can have an effect. A father's degree of confidence that he is the biological father of a child has been related to how much time he spends with that child (Anderson et al., 2007). At the same time, the effects in these studies are generally small. Many interacting influences bear on a child's development, and most stepparents by themselves do not exert a dominant effect on a stepchild's future.

There also seem to be some sex differences in the effects of stepparents on children's emotional development. Boys sometimes benefit from the presence of a new father figure, while girls, especially adolescents, often seem to have an increase in problems with the arrival of a new father in the house (Hetherington, 1989; Hetherington et al., 1985; Hetherington & Stanley-Hagan, 2002; Zimiles & Lee, 1991). Both boys and girls tend to have more difficult relationships with stepmothers (Hetherington, 1999). One possible reason for the problem with stepmothers is that fathers in such families often expect the stepmothers to take over the role of the more "full-time" parent, while mothers do not tend to have similar expectations of stepfathers. Children may resent it when a new stepparent suddenly becomes the more dominant parenting figure (Hetherington, 1999).

Q: Describe at least two distinct forms of evidence that stepparents may treat their children differently than biological parents.

Child Abuse

Sadly, parents do not always provide healthy, or even benign, environments for their children. Throughout the world, some parents inflict serious harm, which can take the form of physical abuse, psychological abuse (usually in the form of verbal attacks), or sexual abuse. The abuse may involve taking physical action against a child, but neglect of the child's physical or emotional needs can also constitute abuse. The question of which psychological factors can lead a parent to commit abuse is more suited to a discussion of adult psychopathology than to developmental psychology. Here the central question concerns the impact of abuse on children.

First, consider some statistics about the prevalence and patterns of child abuse in the United States. One data collection reported that almost 750,000 children were victims of maltreatment each year, a rate of roughly 10 per 1,000 children in 2011. In this group, roughly 20 percent suffered from physical abuse, approximately 10 percent from sexual abuse, and almost 60 percent from various forms of neglect (U.S. Department of Health and Human Services, Administration for Children and Families, 2012). These numbers come from cases that were reported and officially recorded by an agency. It is widely assumed that many cases of abuse are never reported, as parents fear being prosecuted and children often fear both parental retaliation and abandonment.

Abused children are generally young—most are less than 3 years old—and the incidence of physical and verbal abuse is roughly equal between the sexes, although girls are four times more likely than boys to be sexually abused. Moreover, abuse is highly likely to recur. Children who are reported as abused once are much more likely than other children to be reported as abused in the future, even when agencies attempt to monitor the situation and prevent recurrences. Victimization rates in the United States differ across ethnic groups, most likely because poverty and other stresses on disadvantaged groups greatly increase the likelihood of abuse and neglect. Overall, roughly 60 percent of the people who abuse children are female, usually the mothers. In the case of sexual abuse, however, the abuser is much more likely to be male and the father. These, then, are the raw statistics. The critical developmental questions concern how these patterns of abuse are set up and maintained and how they affect children. Another key question is what sorts of interventions can reduce the incidence of abuse.

> **Q:** Describe some examples of how child abuse patterns seem to vary across population groups. How might these differences be explained?

Effects of Abuse

There is an extensive body of research investigating how abuse affects children, both in the short term and later on in their adult lives. In general, all forms of abuse have substantial negative effects on children of both sexes, but the size of these effects varies enormously across studies (Dallam et al., 2001). The field is emotionally charged to an extraordinary extent, as most adults find child abuse, especially child sexual abuse, to be so morally repugnant that they find it difficult to remain neutral about claims that seem to minimize its long-term negative effects. Indeed, the gut feeling against abuse is so strong that it may be subject to moral dumbfounding of the sort described in Chapter 12. A similar outrage in many scientists makes it difficult to objectively design and interpret studies. Even with those cautions, however, most studies do point to the same kinds of negative effects.

The effects vary somewhat across the aforementioned categories of abuse: physical abuse, psychological abuse (usually in verbal forms such as sarcastic and demeaning remarks), and sexual abuse. A fourth category is neglect. For infants and toddlers, all forms of abuse are associated with insecure attachments. Older children who are physically and psychologically abused show more aggression starting as early as preschool. The aggression continues throughout adolescence, often becoming increasingly severe (Aber et al., 1989; Allesandri, 1991; Beitchman et al., 1991, 1992; Boney-McCoy & Finkelhor, 1995; Gross & Keller, 1992; Hart & Brassard, 1987; Kendall-Tackett et al., 1993; Malinosky-Rummell & Hansen, 1993).

Children who are sexually abused show different patterns. Those who have been chronically, severely sexually abused show insecure attachments early on, followed by a spectrum of both internalizing problems, like depression and anxiety, and externalizing problems, such as substance abuse (Bouvier et al., 1999; Browne & Finkelhor, 1986; Finkelhor et al., 1990; Fleming et al., 1999; Mullen et al., 1994). There is some controversy over the relative impact of childhood sexual abuse on boys and girls when they become adults, but the evidence suggests perhaps a more prolonged and severe impact on girls. An important caution to keep in mind, however, is that much of the data are collected by interviewing adults about their psychological status. If men are less willing than women to disclose psychological problems to an interviewer, the data on sex differences will be skewed. Most of these studies have also been done with college students. But there is good reason to believe that many of the individuals most severely affected by abuse would never make it to college; consequently, they would not be included in the samples, thus reducing the apparent effects (Dallam et al., 2001).

One major problem in child abuse research involves appropriate ways of controlling for factors in abusive families, other than the abuse itself, that affect children's development. Abuse of all forms is more common in families that also show other dysfunctional patterns, making it difficult to distinguish the effects of abuse from those of other forms of dysfunction (Boney-McCoy & Finkelhor, 1996). Moreover, if common genetic predispositions influence such traits as low impulse control, then the same traits that lead parents to abuse may also lead their children to act out impulsively or show other kinds of behavior problems.

> **Q:** What are some of the challenges in trying to understand the psychological effects of abuse on children?

Explaining the Cycle of Abuse

These issues come to the fore in considering different theoretical approaches to the causes and consequences of child abuse. All of these approaches try to address one of the most tragic aspects of child abuse: its tendency to recur in ensuing generations of the same family line, often known as the **cycle of abuse** (Egeland et al., 1988). One possible explanation for the cycle of abuse builds on attachment theory, suggesting that abuse creates insecurely attached children who, as a result of being insecurely attached, grow up to behave toward their own children in a way that fosters insecure attachments. This attachment style could then increase the odds of negative parent-child interactions and abuse (Egeland et al., 1988). Other explanations invoke a social learning perspective, arguing that children learn to model their parents' behaviors. In this view, abused children go on to re-create, in their own families, the abuse they have observed and experienced (Bandura, 1971).

Environmental explanations argue that the stress of living in poverty, along with the attendant risks of crime and drug abuse, sets up a context in which parents are more likely to abuse their children. This effect might be further exacerbated in single-parent homes, where a second parent is not around to buffer the occasional lapses of the other. Thus, the immediate household environment and the larger-scale community in which a child lives may both increase the chances of abuse. In addition, some argue that a culture that emphasizes corporal punishment might make it easier for parents to cross the line from physical punishment to abuse (Gershoff, 2002; see Figure 14.26).

In contrast, a behavioral genetic view would argue that a cycle of abuse continues because both parents and children have genetic tendencies to be aggressive, impulsive, or likely to commit some other behavior that creates a climate of abuse. The most extreme version of this view claims that these inherited tendencies will express themselves regardless of experience. The more nuanced and more common genetically based view holds that some genetic factors put individuals at high risk of becoming abusive if they are exposed to certain stressful or aversive environments that would be much less harmful to others.

It is critical to note that any and all of these factors interact; they are not mutually exclusive. Even so, understanding which factors are most influential would have a huge impact on attempts to break the cycle of violence and abuse. Currently, programs throughout the world attempt to solve the problem by focusing on improving the attachment relationship, by modeling more positive behaviors for parents and children, and by alleviating environmental stresses that might make abuse more likely. Applying the behavioral genetic approach is a more complex proposition because it requires theories about the

ways that specific genes interact with other variables to increase the risk of abuse.

Studies show that the variety of interventions that attempt to reduce child abuse have mixed results. There are some significant success stories, but many other cases show little reduction in violence. More systematic research on the factors that contribute to the cycle is essential to develop reliable, highly effective interventions.

Q: How do cycles of abuse perpetuate abuse across generations?

Foster Care

When children are considered to be at serious risk of abuse, they are often removed from their parents and assigned to live with a foster family. Children in foster care may have a series of foster families, either until they reach maturity or until it is considered safe for them to return to their biological family. In the United States, the number of children in foster care grew from approximately 276,000 in 1985 to 568,000 in 1999 (Swann & Sylvester, 2006). This estimate has since declined somewhat to roughly 424,000 in 2009 (Child Welfare Information Gateway, 2011). The proportion of children in foster care is not evenly distributed across ethnicities, with disadvantaged minorities having a larger proportion in foster care (see Figure 14.27).

It is difficult to measure the extent to which foster care influences children's development (see Figure 14.28). In addition to the tremendous range of foster care situations, most of the children in foster care are there because they have suffered some sort of trauma. It is therefore not surprising that children in foster care tend to have more psychosocial problems than children who grow up in their birth family homes. Children also commonly move in and out of foster care. Roughly half the time, they end up reuniting, at least temporarily, with their birth families (Chipungu & Bent-Goodley, 2004), making it difficult to estimate the effects of foster care itself.

One provocative study conducted in Minnesota looked at three groups of children: 46 children who entered foster care primarily because of child maltreatment, 46 who endured maltreatment but remained at home with the maltreating caregiver, and 97 who were not maltreated and not put into foster care (Lawrence et al., 2006). All three groups of children were from poor families with young mothers. At the beginning of the study (and before any of the children were placed in foster care), all of the children were assessed for attachment quality, self-control, and emotional health.

FIGURE 14.26 Corporal punishment and child abuse. Although many cultures endorse some degree of physical punishment as part of child rearing, some researchers regard corporal punishment and physical abuse as running along a continuum on which the appropriate line can be difficult to draw.

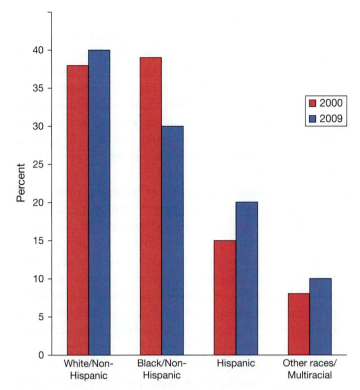

FIGURE 14.27 **Race and ethnicity of children in foster care.** The incidence of children in foster care in the United States has increased over the past decade in all groups except African Americans, who have shown a substantial decline. Adapted from Child Welfare Information Gateway (2011).

FIGURE 14.28 **Foster care families.** Throughout the world, many children spend part of their childhood growing up in foster care families, which may consist solely of foster children or be a blend of the foster parents' biological children and foster children. Foster care families vary greatly in terms of the kind of environment they provide, and there is ongoing concern for those children being raised in substandard foster care settings.

At this point, both groups of maltreated children—those who would enter foster care and those who would remain at home—showed similarly high levels of many kinds of behavior problems compared with the control children. After spending time in foster care, that group of children showed more behavioral problems than the children who remained with a maltreating parent. These problems continued for many years after the children left foster care and as they became young adults.

This study has its limitations, however, even with the considerable methodological care taken by the researchers. For example, when maltreated children stayed in their parents' homes rather than entering foster care, there was likely something about their home life or their family relationships that convinced social workers that they could safely stay in their homes—something that was not true of the families whose children were placed in foster care. The preplacement data showed comparable levels of problems between the two groups of maltreated children, but these more subtle family differences may still have affected the children's development.

As seen earlier in this chapter, the effects of foster care also interact with how siblings get along with each other, such that low-conflict siblings should be kept together in foster placements, but high-conflict siblings are better off

when placed in different foster homes (Linares et al., 2007). Several additional, carefully designed studies will be needed to understand when it is better to place a child in foster care rather than allowing him to stay in a problematic home. Clearly, another central issue in this area of research is the need to develop better ways of characterizing different kinds of foster care situations to understand which types will more often lead to developmental problems and how those situations interact with the internal dynamics of the families at risk.

Conclusions

An understanding of the child's role in the family seems to invoke a different sort of approach from those used in earlier chapters. Many different theoretical approaches can be used to examine the associations between behavioral and psychological patterns in children and those in their parents and siblings. The focus of these theories ranges from social learning effects, to behavioral genetic forces, to attachment-based dynamics, to environmental influences. As we have seen, in many cases, all of these factors are at work, making the job of sorting out causes from mere correlations extraordinarily complex. Given the numerous interacting influences that affect family dynamics, we cannot simply ask a question such as how much parents matter. Instead, we must ask how parental influences interact with the child's disposition, the local environment, and the particular aspects of child development under investigation. The surrounding culture can be critical as well. What constitutes harsh, unyielding parenting in one culture may be seen as a normal, caring style in another.

This complex web of interactions can be difficult to disentangle, but the best work manages to conceptualize and empirically uncover stable, widely applicable patterns. These patterns often take the form of interactions between types of parents, types of children, and types of behaviors. For example, we saw that research on the effects of divorce points to a pattern of effects that interacts with the gender of both the parents and the children. That same pattern of effects is also influenced by the children's age—both when the divorce occurred and the age of the child when the potential effects of the divorce are studied. From this set of interactions, reliable patterns have emerged that can be used to make interventions more effective for children struggling to cope with their parents' separation. Similarly, some studies suggest that teaching parenting skills can have positive outcomes for children, although it is not always easy to obtain long-term positive effects from such interventions. Finally, research on foster care is starting to help social workers and other professionals understand when and why it is important to keep siblings together in foster family placements and when it is better to keep them apart.

The social policy implications of research on the family are far too important to let larger patterns of cause and effect go unexplained. We see once again how viewing development as an active exploratory process is so important for understanding many aspects of the role of the child in the family. For example, the idea of child effects as explaining links between parenting and children's behaviors is closely linked to a perspective that sees the child as an active, influential participant in the process of socialization in the family (Grusec, 2011). It also fosters a view of parents and children as frequently becoming intertwined in interactive feedback loops, rather than seeing the child as a passive recipient of parental influences. We also see in many ways how social, cognitive, and personality development are interwoven in understanding many causal patterns within the family. For example, gender roles are related to children's beliefs about themselves and others, to interaction patterns between parents and children, and to the particular personalities of all participants. Similarly, sibling conflicts and jealousy within the family can only be understood by considering cognitive capacities, social interactions, temperament, and personality in all their interactive richness. As research models become better able to take all these causal patterns into account, social policy decisions will be correspondingly better informed.

STUDY AND REVIEW

SUMMARY

Parenting

- Parenting involves many different kinds of behaviors that support a child's development, including nurturance, discipline, teaching, language use, providing toys and educational materials, monitoring children's behavior, and time management. All of these behaviors vary, depending on the family's culture and socioeconomic status.
- Parents in Western cultures show quite distinct parenting styles. Diana Baumrind and her successors described four styles—authoritarian, permissive, authoritative, and neglectful/uninvolved. These styles differ in terms of the level of warmth and responsiveness that parents show to their children and in their level of demands or control.
- The authoritative style is more strongly correlated with positive outcomes in children, leading many to draw the conclusion

that parenting style causally influences the child's personality and other factors. Although some studies have suggested a causal role for parenting style, that conclusion must also be tempered by other influential factors, such as child effects, shared genotypes between parent and children, and the influences of local environments and peers.

- The influences of particular parenting styles seem to be highly culturally specific. Children in different cultures may interpret the same parental behaviors very differently, resulting in very different outcomes for the children.
- Interventions to improve parenting seem to help both parents and children with their relationships when the programs are designed carefully and with sensitivity to the particular group of children at risk.
- Parenting is not the only way to explain a child's personality and behavior. Children themselves produce effects in parents and others, which set up feedback loops of interaction

between parents and children. In addition, parents' and children's shared genetic bases for some behaviors may account for some similarities in ways that go beyond the influence of parenting practices. Parenting may be less important to understanding how a child's personality takes shape than it is in understanding the kinds of experiences to which a child has had access, such as sports teams, clubs, and shopping venues.

- In the end, an interactionist view of parenting seems most useful as a way of understanding the variety of influences that guide children in development.

- Gender socialization is a complex process involving a web of interacting influences. Parents tend to offer gender-stereotyped toys and to engage boys in more physical activities and girls in more conversational ones. Yet, children themselves also affect this process, often showing strong gender-stereotyped toy preferences before the age of 2. One facet of these early biases has been linked to hormone exposure before birth. For girls, a higher level of testosterone exposure in utero correlates with preferences for more stereotypically male toys. Research into sibling effects on gender role qualities suggests that parents' influence is strongest on older siblings, who then propagate those roles to younger siblings.

Siblings and Family Dynamics

- In families with more than one child, each child's position in the family may have developmental effects. Firstborn children appear to have richer and more stimulating environments. This may give them a slight edge in intelligence even when other factors are controlled. Other indications suggest that later-born children may be more rebellious and willing to challenge the status quo, although it is unclear whether these effects are reliable and whether they apply only in specific circumstances.

- Siblings can also affect one another more directly. Jealousy and conflict between siblings can take a toll on the whole family, but when parents are trained to mediate these conflicts, children often show a corresponding tendency to resolve the conflicts constructively. Siblings who are close in age may accelerate one another's development of theory of mind. There is less clear evidence that being an only child has distinctive effects, despite popular claims of negative effects.

Changes in Families

- Families are changing in many ways. On average, parents are having children at an older age and are having fewer children, and in many cases, both parents work full-time outside the home. Over the last few decades, a number of changes in the family structure have also become more common, including single-parent families, families with same-sex parents, and families in which parents have divorced and perhaps remarried. These patterns vary dramatically, both across cultures and across socioeconomic and ethnic groups.

- Children may be affected by family size and by living with single parents or working parents. But these effects are often subtle and interact with factors such as a child's socioeconomic status.

- Divorce does seem to increase the odds of problems for children, ranging from internalizing problems (such as depression) to externalizing problems (such as increased aggression or sexual promiscuity).

- When parents remarry and families become blended, other problems may emerge as well. Evolutionary theory predicts more problems between stepparents and their nonbiological offspring. There is some evidence in support of that prediction.

Child Abuse

- Physical, psychological, and sexual abuse of children occurs at alarming rates; recent data show that approximately 10 per 1,000 children were victims of some form of abuse in 2010, and most abused children are younger than 3. Abuse is more common among the poor, most likely because the stresses of poverty increase the chances of child maltreatment.

- The effects of abuse on children vary considerably between studies. One consistent pattern is that physical abuse and psychological abuse seem to have different effects than sexual abuse.

- Cycles of abuse, in which children of abusive parents go on to abuse their own children, may be caused by multiple factors. These factors range from the children replicating parenting practices, to the effects of adverse environments, to shared genotypes between parents and children that are correlated with abusive behavior phenotypes.

- Children are usually put into foster care when the situation in their own biological family has high levels of abuse and when no other placements with relatives seem feasible. Foster care arrangements vary widely, with some being associated with adverse consequences for children. This is especially true when there is little long-term stability and sibling relationships are not taken into account.

THOUGHT QUESTIONS

1. Should future parents be asked to get parenting licenses? In most of the world, a teenager who wants to drive a car must pass a test of driving proficiency before he or she is allowed to drive. Some have argued that societies should also have "parenting" licenses wherein a prospective parent must take a course and pass a test to receive such a license, as the consequences of being a poor parent are much worse than those of being a poor driver. Evaluate such a view in light of research on parenting.

2. Foster home care has mixed results because the quality of care varies so greatly and because some foster children have no stable home. Sometimes foster children shift between more than a dozen homes as they grow up. Should local or

state governments greatly increase the size of public facilities where children might spend their time growing up in the same residence and surrounded by the same people?

3. Many states have required waiting periods for couples contemplating divorce. Imagine that a state legislator proposes doubling the waiting period for couples with children under the age of 21. Consider the pros and cons of such a proposal.

4. How might the socialization of a young child be different when that child grows up in a household in which both sets of grandparents are living in the house as well as the parents? Consider how that child might have differing experiences from a child who grows up in a household with no grandparents present.

KEY TERMS

authoritarian parent (p. 507)

authoritative parent (p. 507)

blended family (p. 535)

child effect (p. 511)

confluence theory (p. 518)

cycle of abuse (p. 537)

ecological systems approach (p. 510)

extended family (p. 528)

externalizing problem (p. 533)

gender schema (p. 515)

internalizing problem (p. 533)

nuclear family (p. 528)

parenting style (p. 506)

permissive parent (p. 507)

resource theory (p. 518)

sibling differentiation (p. 520)

15

Becoming Part of the Community

Levels of Affiliation
- The Changing Nature of Social Interactions
- Developing Relationships
- Social Groups
- Developmental Patterns in Levels of Affiliation
- Social Network Effects

Media Influences on Development
- Television
- Video Games, Computers, and the Internet

Roles in the Larger Culture
- Distinctive Cultural and Subcultural Roles
- Gender Roles and Stereotyping

Conclusions

Summary

On December 7, 1941, the day Japan launched a surprise attack on Hawaii's Pearl Harbor, 11-year-old Rahn Taoka watched as her Japanese father was arrested in their San Francisco home. He was one of the first Japanese citizens arrested by the U.S. government because it was feared they were spies. The government would soon initiate a nationwide program to round up and incarcerate over 100,000 Japanese Americans and Japanese nationals in the "war hysteria."

Rahn, her sister, and their English mother avoided incarceration, but they had to agree to move to a small town in northern Minnesota where they would stay with their father's European-American business partner. Though Rahn was initially apprehensive, her life in this small town suddenly brightened when she met Marilou. The girls were inseparable and spent endless hours together both in school and out. This friendship transformed Rahn's frightening, strange experience in which she was surrounded by many suspicious peers into a year and a half that she later remembered as one of the happiest times of her life.

When her father was released to Japan in a prisoner exchange, Rahn and the rest of the family went with him, even though his wife and daughters did not speak a word of Japanese. They suffered severe hardships in Japan in the waning days of the war. The daughters were treated as social outcasts by their peers and struggled to adapt to their new cultural community. After many years, they finally managed to move back to the San Francisco Bay Area in 1955.

Finally, 64 years after they had last seen each other, Rahn and Marilou were reunited through the efforts of their children. Within minutes, they were interacting as if they had never been separated. As Rahn reflected, "Don't you find that with any true friend, you can be apart for years and pick up where you left off?" (Lagos, 2007).

What is it about childhood friendships that can make a seemingly impossible situation into one of the best periods of one's life? How do such friendships help protect children when their status in a peer group is of poor quality or when they are making a difficult transition? Some have argued that a special kind of "best friend" relationship in early adolescence is an essential part of healthy development. How might friendships benefit a child, and does having a best friend offer unique benefits? How do friendships change from early childhood through middle childhood and adolescence? Finally, how do girls' friendships and other social relationships differ from those between boys?

Friendships are part of a larger complex of environments outside the home that influence children's development. We can think of the moderate effects of occasional interactions with others as well as the more pronounced effects of sustained relationships, either with friends, enemies, or even with bullies. One other especially influential sustained relationship that emerges in adolescence can be the romantic relationship. Expanding further, we can look at larger peer groups to see how social status relationships work at the level of a clique, a classroom, or a school. Finally, we can consider the broadest cultural communities and their influences on children through the media, especially television, video games, and the Internet.

In Chapter 14, we introduced Bronfrenbrenner's *ecological systems approach* to development as a way of understanding the different social contexts that affect the family. The ecological approach stresses the importance of the environments in which a child develops and the need to consider these environments at several scales, ranging from the family itself, to groups of friends, to the school, to the larger culture. We saw how researchers consider the child's role in each of these "social ecosystems" and how that role interacts with the roles of all other players in those systems. In this chapter, we will see how this approach can be extended beyond the family and consider the kinds of social niches that children occupy in an ever-widening web of social relationships and communities. Socialization processes can occur at each level of grouping, often with quite different patterns of influence, depending on how the child's disposition interacts with her specific niche.

This chapter focuses on these influences of broader groups beyond the family. We will start with the group closest to the family, the friends in the immediate community, and then expand the circle to eventually consider media influences and differences across cultures. Finally, we will consider how gender and other sociocultural roles emerge in these contexts.

Levels of Affiliation

Developmental psychologists have been interested in the influences of peers since the earliest days of psychology (Renshaw, 1981), but research in this area gained significant momentum following two striking findings about the effects of peers on attachment. As described in Chapter 6, both Freud and Dann's (1951) studies of groups of children who relied on one another for support in concentration camps and after their liberation and Harlow's studies of peer-raised monkeys (Meyer et al., 1975; Suomi & Harlow, 1972) showed that peers could alleviate some of the consequences of otherwise dreadful social environments. More recently, the field of evolutionary psychology has stressed that peer relations might be an especially powerful realm of social influence.

The power of peers never ceases to amaze parents. At certain points in development, it certainly seems that peers are more important to children (and especially to adolescents) and more influential than almost anyone else. Some researchers have suggested that, in general, peers are far more influential than parents (Harris, 1998), but most researchers see peers and parents as operating in different spheres of influence. Peers seem especially influential on such things as personal taste, clothing, and hairstyles, while parents hold more sway over such things as career choices and broad social values (Smetana et al., 2006).

To gain a better sense of peer influences, we need to first think about the different ways in which peers might interact. These interactions can be categorized into three distinct levels of affiliation, which apply to other animals as well as to humans: interactions, relationships, and groups (Hinde, 1987, 1997; Rubin et al., 1998). *Interactions* can be prosocial if they facilitate social engagement, antisocial if they discourage social engagement, or withdrawn as in cases of shyness. *Relationships* consist of a progression of interactions over time. Particular relationships then become associated with predominant emotions, such as love or hate, and different degrees of commitment. Finally, *groups* arise from sets of relationships, and they can be evaluated in terms of their cohesiveness, dominance relations, diversity, and local norms. In this system, relationships build on interactions in much the same way that groups build on relationships (Rubin et al., 1998). The developmental study of peer relations involves all levels, but most often focuses on groups.

FIGURE 15.1 Early social interactions. Although infants are aware of other social beings, such as other infants, their patterns of interactions may be largely limited to contagion of the emotional states of others.

> **Q:** What are three different levels of affiliation between peers?

The Changing Nature of Social Interactions

Infants' and toddlers' interactions are very simple and not so different from those seen in other animals. They often experience joint arousal (see Figure 15.1). When one child is excited and happy, that state can induce a comparable feeling in another child, which can then cause a positive-feedback loop of increasing arousal. Moreover, sadness and despair in one child can also cause a drop in arousal in the other child, as very young children apparently feel empathy. As seen in Chapter 6, infants and young toddlers are exquisitely sensitive to social agents and the timing of back-and-forth social interactions, such as smiles between mother and child. That sensitivity is only the beginning of an ability to manage smooth, reciprocal interactions with peers.

Preschoolers show considerably richer and more varied repertoires in their interactions than do infants. They show gen-

uine instances of sharing and have some sense of reciprocity, or cooperative exchange. They play pretend games with others, often playacting imagined episodes with each other. Their levels of conflict decrease somewhat with age, and more notably, the kinds of conflicts they experience show developmental changes. In one study, 400 children at ages 2, 3, and 4 years were videotaped as they engaged in routine activities in their preschool classrooms. The experimenters later scored the first conflict episode that occurred during a set observation period (Chen et al., 2001). In most cases, at least one conflict occurred, with several typically occurring at all ages.

What changed with age, however, were several key factors relating to what triggered the conflicts and how they were resolved. The 2-year-olds had more conflicts about the distribution of physical resources, such as vying for a coveted toy (see Figure 15.2). The 3- and 4-year-olds had more conflicts around ideas, such as which superhero is stronger, or around play, such as who gets to be "it" in tag. In addition, the younger children showed less willingness to back down and higher levels of insistence, often prolonging the conflict until an adult intervened, while the older children were better able to resolve conflicts on their own. Dealing with conflict seems to be an essential part of social development from an early age, and children have much to learn to understand what is a reasonable conflict and how to resolve disputes (Chen et al., 2001; Rubin et al., 2003).

> **Q:** How does the nature of conflict interactions tend to change during the preschool years?

FIGURE 15.2 **Negative interactions.** When 2-year-olds get into fights, they most often fight about toys. When older preschoolers fight, the conflicts are more often around ideas, such as which superhero is stronger, or around games, such as who gets to go first.

In the elementary school years, children experience a huge surge in social interactions. The networks beyond the family, arising from sports teams, the school, and the neighborhood, for example, enable children's social lives to flourish. Peer group sizes increase throughout this period, going from groups of two or three early on to social circles of a dozen or more. During this period, children require less and less adult supervision and can sometimes be found playing in the neighborhood or on school grounds for hours with little or no adult oversight. During this period, most children also shift markedly toward interacting with peers of their own sex. Suddenly, sometimes seemingly inexplicably, girls and boys who have played together for years sort themselves into same-sex groups and engage in predominately single-sex interactions (Fabes et al., 2003; Martin & Fabes, 2001; Strough & Covatto, 2002). According to the psychoanalytic approach to development, this takes place during what is referred to as the **latency period** of middle to late childhood, when sexuality is said to be largely dormant and does not overtly influence interactions. During this period, children also show a decline in pretend play and become more likely to use verbal or physical aggression in conflicts, sometimes with great cruelty. In a similar vein, gossip about others also increases (Crick et al., 2001; Crozier & Dimmock, 1999).

Q: How do patterns of play between the sexes change during early and later childhood, and what classic construct in psychology has been used to explain these changes?

As children enter adolescence, their interactions seem to change yet again. Peer interactions come to predominate over interactions with parents or teachers. Finally, in many cultures, cross-sex interactions emerge as a critical part of most adolescents' social lives. Teenage dating is for many parents one of the most salient and nerve-wracking behaviors of children in this age group.

Developing Relationships

All relationships serve essential functions for the developing child. They serve to transfer information between individuals and help set up stable, enduring patterns of interaction, whether those interactions are between friends and mentors, or bullies and enemies. Relationships can allow individuals to provide mutual support for each other—both social and physical support. In other, more harmful relationships, there may be patterns of dependency and control between individuals. All kinds of relationships, however, can serve to create stable social links, and structured sets of links that are larger than individuals.

Friends With respect to the earliest relationships, infants show unique, repeated interaction patterns with certain individuals, such as with a parent or a sibling, but these interactions are not true friendships. **Friendships** are ongoing, positive reciprocal relationships with chosen companions. As described in Chapter 6, infants have particular expectations of certain specific interactional partners, but these interactions largely lack the reciprocal exchanges (for example, sharing toys or projects) that are essential to friendships. In addition, these relationships develop largely as a matter of convenience, depending on who is accessible, and less because of a desire to be with a specific peer. Some infants are naturally more friendly and outgoing than others and seem to enjoy being around others as opposed to being on their own, but they still do not seem to build structured social connections with others.

Toddlers, on the other hand, develop clear friendships (Howes, 1996; Newcomb & Bagwell, 1995), which seem to consist mostly of animated, positive interactions while playing (Gifford-Smith & Brownell, 2003). Toddlers purposefully choose their friends, usually picking the children most like themselves. They begin to show more prosocial behaviors—for example, sharing and empathy—with friends during this period, but they also begin showing more hostility than before with both friends and enemies.

School-age children develop more sophisticated notions of friendship. For example, they gain a clearer idea of reciprocity, understanding that friends do not just get benefits from each other; they also provide benefits (Hartup, 1999; Selman, 1980, 2003). As their theory of mind skills improve, children start to use their increasing social cognitive capacities to make more elaborate inferences about their friends' mental states and to adjust their behaviors accordingly. In short, they become increasingly adept at putting themselves in their friends' shoes (Rubin et al., 1998). Unfortunately, school-age children also develop some less positive relationship styles, such as bullying and verbal aggression.

Gender differences in friendships become more dramatic with increasing age. By the time they enter elementary school, boys tend to play in larger groups than girls and are more likely to have clear dominance hierarchies within those groups. Girls tend to show more prosocial behavior and empathy in relationships, while boys show more rough-and-tumble play and focus on goals, such as achieving dominance (Hartup, 1996; Rose & Rudolph, 2006). Late school-age children and young adolescents show clear differences in the fragility of friendships. Girls tend to have fewer long-lasting very close friendships than boys and to be more distressed at the thought of losing their friends (Benenson & Christakos, 2003; MacEvoy & Asher, 2012). One possible reason for this gender difference in the length of close friendships may be that girls have more intimate relationships that result in more intense reactions during conflicts, reactions that can cause irrevocable breaks. Greater intimacy may also provide girls with more ability to hurt each other during a conflict, as they may divulge private information that was shared in confidence. Finally, because girls tend to have relationships in the absence of groups, they may not have the benefits of a group to buffer conflict (Rose & Rudolph, 2006). During this period, girls and boys tend to act out against friends in different ways. Girls tend to victimize their friends in social ways, such as conspicuously excluding them from an activity, a form of antagonism known as **relational aggression** (Benenson et al., 2011). In contrast, boys more often victimize friends physically (Crick & Nelson, 2002).

School-age children also tend to try to control their friends' other friends and can become jealous when a close friend develops new, close friendships with others. Although this pattern can exist in older children and adults (Heider, 1958), it is more common in younger adolescents (Parker et al., 2005; Selman, 1980). In early adolescence, jealousy over friends is also more common among girls than among boys (Parker et al., 2005). Friendship jealousy seems to peak in late childhood or early adolescence, which has been explained in two main ways: (1) Younger children may be less sophisticated at engaging in social comparisons, and so they may not consider whether a friend's new close connec-

FIGURE 15.3 Chums. Harry Stack Sullivan proposed that in late childhood, a special form of close friendship forms in which there is a favored best friend. Sullivan called these best friends "chums."

tion implicitly suggests that their friend values them less; older children and young adolescents are generally better at making these social comparisons. (2) Older adolescents may be better able to understand objectively that they cannot meet all of their friend's needs and that other friends can meet different needs without posing a threat to their own relationship (Selman, 1980; Selman & Schultz, 1990). The increase in friendship jealousy in early adolescence may also be related to a proposal made many years ago that a pattern of *chumships* emerges in late childhood in which many children have one favored best friend (Sullivan, 1953; see Figure 15.3). As a former best friend's favored status wanes in early adolescence, jealousy may be more common.

Q: What are some of the ways boys' and girls' patterns of friendship differ?

As adolescence proceeds, friendships become closer and more intimate, and friends form deeper loyalties (Rubin et al., 1998). Adolescents develop more specific standards about how they expect their friends to behave, coming to expect loyalty, support, and discretion (Furman & Buhrmester, 1992; Johnson, 2003). More generally, they see friendships as entailing high levels of self-disclosure to each other, with corresponding confidentiality. The rise in online communication methods and cell phone texting has provided adolescents with dramatic new ways to communicate confidential information and make self-disclosures to close friends, even when those friends are not physically present. Shy adolescents may be especially prone to using these new methods (Reid & Reid, 2007; Subrahmanyam &

Greenfield, 2008; Underwood et al., 2012). The developmental changes in self-disclosure are often thought to reflect increasingly sophisticated social cognitive skills that enable friends to share more information and build stronger trust with each other (Gifford-Smith & Brownell, 2003; Rubin et al., 1998).

Friendships can provide several advantages to children. They can foster social skills, such as the ability to sense and empathize with the thoughts and feelings of others. Being someone else's preferred companion may also reaffirm a child's sense of self-worth. Friendships can help motivate children to acquire new skills, such as a sport or hobby, and they can help instill in children a sense of their culture's norms (Bukowski, 2001). And it has been repeatedly suggested that friendships can buffer children from life's stresses, whether those stresses arise from moving to a new school or neighborhood or from a family crisis such as divorce (Gifford-Smith & Brownell, 2003; Hartup, 1996; Hartup & Stevens, 1999).

As is often the case, however, causality can be difficult to pin down in studies of friendship effects. Although it certainly seems plausible that friendships directly alleviate the effects of some kinds of stressors, another possibility is that children who have more difficulty forming friendships are also more reactive to stressors. It is obviously unethical to do an experiment in which children are randomly assigned to have friends or to be deprived of them and then subjected to the same kind of stress. Sometimes, however, situations can approximate these conditions, providing more compelling evidence of whether friendships can truly protect children from the effects of stress. For example, if two groups of families with children have to relocate to new, faraway communities, and they are randomly assigned either to neighborhoods with no children or to neighborhoods with many children, the case for causal effects of friendship can be more carefully explored.

Friendships can also have detrimental effects on children, although the positive effects generally far outweigh the negative effects. We have seen that friendships can lead to feelings of jealousy and even aggression toward those who threaten a relationship. In addition, especially among girls, friendships can sometimes foster a tendency toward *co-rumination*, a type of interaction in which friends tend to repeatedly discuss and mull over negative events and emotions in ways that may exacerbate a problem or increase anxiety, despair, and depression (Rose, 2002; Rose et al., 2007; Schwartz-Mette & Rose, 2012). Friendships can also sometimes foster undesirable behaviors. If, for example, a child has some aggressive tendencies, there is evidence that associating with friends who share these tendencies will increase the child's own inclinations toward aggression (Dishion et al., 1995). Finally, the quality of friendships can vary dramatically. Some

friendships consist largely of supportive prosocial behaviors, while others involve strong components of envy, rivalry, and bursts of conflict. Those negative interactions can, in some cases, outweigh the positive interactions (Berndt, 1996, 2002; Salvas et al., 2011).

For the most part, however, friendships are a critical, positive aspect of development. They help provide a sense of worth and a set of social skills that can serve as a buffer against a variety of negative experiences. The specific benefits of friendship change with age, but its positive effects persist throughout development, while its few negative aspects pale by comparison.

Imaginary Companions Children may develop relationships with **imaginary companions**—that is, fantasized characters that they make up or objects that they treat as if they were alive. Having an imaginary companion is neither unusual nor a sign of distress in a child. Although popular media have sometimes portrayed children with imaginary companions as deviant or mentally ill, in fact, there are no indications that having imaginary companions is correlated with any sorts of childhood problems. It might seem, for example, that children with imaginary companions are especially lonely or shy, but neither of those conjectures appears to be true (Taylor, 1999). Rather, imaginary companions are a sign of a vivid imagination. And for many years, it has been known that a vivid imagination in a young child is associated with positive outcomes, such as higher levels of creativity (Singer, 1961).

Imaginary companions are quite common, even in children in the elementary and middle school years. In one survey of 1,795 British children between 5 and 12 years of age, 46 percent of the children reported having had an imaginary companion, with a somewhat greater incidence (52 percent versus 48 percent) among girls than boys (Pearson et al., 2001). When children of all ages are considered, some estimates suggest that 65 percent of children have had an imaginary companion at some point (Taylor, 1999; Taylor et al., 2001; see Figure 15.4).

Imaginary companions may enable many young children to try out their developing ability to have social relations outside of the family. One reason that researchers talk about imaginary "companions" as opposed to just imaginary "friends" is that imaginary companions can fill very different social roles for children. In addition to being playmates, they may be older mentors, babies to care for, or animals, among others. In many cases, they may be invisible; in other cases, they may be partially embodied in a doll or stuffed animal (Taylor et al., 2001). This rich variety of social roles can be useful to children as they experiment with different forms of relationships. Imaginary companions can therefore provide the child with an opportunity to safely enter a world with a wide range of social possibilities, in which the child can try out many forms of social interactions different from those she typically experiences.

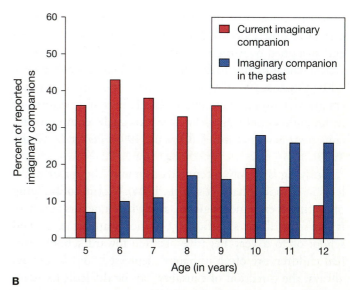

FIGURE 15.4 Imaginary companions. (A) Imaginary companions are quite common, not only in elementary school but even in middle school. When the entire span of childhood is taken into account, the majority of children report having had an imaginary companion sometime during that period. **(B)** The graph shows how the incidence of having an imaginary companion changes with age. In this study, over 50 percent of children at certain ages reported either having an imaginary companion or having had an imaginary companion. Older children either forgot having had an imaginary companion earlier or chose not to disclose that fact. Adapted from Pearson et al. (2001).

Imaginary companions also serve several other purposes for children. They may allow the child to act out various social scenarios in a nonthreatening manner, they may alleviate loneliness or boredom that occasionally afflicts virtually all children, and they may allow children to deal with frightening situations or work out problems. In almost all cases, however, children do realize that their imaginary companions are not real (Taylor, 1999). They may attribute to their imaginary companion a personality, as well as beliefs, desires, and other emotions, but they do all of this with full knowledge that their imaginary companion is not really "there" in the sense that other people are.

Children with imaginary companions tend to have somewhat higher levels of some cognitive and social skills. They tend to be less shy and are more able to consider situations from another's point of view, a valuable skill in many social situations (Taylor, 1999; Taylor et al., 2004). Sometimes, the imaginary companion can be a vehicle for a child to tell his parent about a problem he is encountering. For example, a child might tell a parent that his imaginary companion is being picked on at school as a way of relating his own experience. (This practice is not so different from the adult technique of broaching an awkward topic by saying, "I have a friend who [has the following problem].") An imaginary companion also enables a relatively helpless child to feel more powerful or competent as he acts out roles with his companion that might not yet be feasible in daily life. More generally, imaginary companions increase social skills and social understanding (Taylor et al., 2004) and provide a better sense of self-knowledge (Davis et al., 2011). They also have been shown to increase children's referential communication skills—that is, the ability to direct others' attention to objects or tasks (Roby & Kidd, 2008). Thus, children with imaginary companions tend to show more advanced communication skills in experimental tasks in which they have to communicate to someone behind a screen how to identify the correct picture from a set. (They are not better at understanding instructions in these tasks, just at giving them.)

Why do imaginary companions disappear as the child grows older? One likely reason is that, as the child experiences a wider range of real relationships, the imaginary ones become less necessary. Many cultures also stigmatize adults with imaginary companions, and children may choose to censor their own imaginations as they become aware of this stigma. It is interesting to note that imaginary companions become much more acceptable for adults when they are in extreme isolation. Consider, for example, the main character in the 2000 film *Cast Away*, who is marooned on a desert island and develops an imaginary friendship with a volleyball. The ball acquires a distinct character that is deeply missed when it is lost at sea. It is easy to empathize with the need for a companion in times of isolation, suggesting that, even as adults, we retain vestiges of the cognitive and emotional roots that give rise to children's imaginary companions.

Bully-Victim Relationships Some relationships have decidedly negative consequences for one or both of the individuals involved. One especially vivid and much-studied case involves relations between bullies and victims of bullying. **Bullying**, which is also known as **peer victimization**, generally consists of making verbal or physical threats or attacks against a victim. This form of aggression is repeated and sustained over time and is typically directed against a victim who is unable to defend himself (Espelage & Swearer, 2003; Olweus, 1993). Most of the time, it occurs when others are watching. These characteristic bullying patterns of intimidation and aggression are extremely common and consistent across cultures (Olweus, 1993; Pepler & Craig, 1999).

Bullying is widely recognized as one of the major problems in schools (Sharp & Smith, 1994). Victims of bullying often find it extremely painful, and when it occurs at school it can contribute significantly to not wanting to attend school or to a very negative attitude toward school. Bullied children are often unhappy, depressed, and lonely. As always, the direction of causality can be difficult to ascertain. Depressed, unhappy, and lonely children may be more prone to being bullied, but many think that being bullied contributes to these states. One chilling recent finding was that 60 percent of 41 children who engaged in shooting sprees in schools were reported by neighbors, friends, and teachers as having been victims of bullying (Vossekuil et al., 2002). This is far higher than the typical rate of roughly 10 percent of children having been bullied (Kumpulainen et al., 1999).

Do bullies and victims have characteristics that make it possible to predict who will bully and who will be victimized? In each case, some common tendencies have been repeatedly reported. The most central characteristic of victims seems to be conveying the impression that they will not answer aggression with retaliation (see Figure 15.5). The victim may be physically smaller or weaker, but in some cases, behavioral clues can indicate a victim's docility or submissiveness, even if the individual is physically quite large. In short, what seems to matter most is that the victim appears to be a safe target to aggress against (Olweus, 1997). Victims frequently

do not have popular or powerful friends, apparently reinforcing the sense that aggression against them will not provoke a response from anyone who could pose a threat. In addition, victims often tend to interpret provocative behaviors, such as teasing, as more aggressive than they actually are, thus indicating to bullies that they are liable to respond with fear and psychological pain (Sullivan, 2000).

In other respects, however, victims can be quite a diverse group. While some are timid, withdrawn, and nonaggressive, others are extroverted and even aggressive (Olweus, 1997; Sullivan, 2000). If the extroverted, aggressive child is nonetheless seen as weak and unable to retaliate effectively against violence, that child may still be victimized. Victims also tend to show high levels of anxiety around bullies, which seems to fuel the bully's aggression. In a sense, this picture of victims leaves room for optimism for reducing bullying, because victims' behaviors, which are potentially changeable, seem to be more important triggers of bullying than more permanent physical traits.

Bullies also have a number of distinguishing characteristics. Bullies are not generally individuals of low self-esteem who are compensating for their feelings of inferiority by dominating others. Although this is a popular way of characterizing bullies, there is little evidence to support it (Batsche & Knoff, 1994; Baumeister et al., 1996; Olweus, 1993). In fact, inflated self-esteem may facilitate and empower bullies. Bullies often have siblings who engage in bullying or even parents who sometimes bully others. These correlations could result both from children modeling the behaviors of these family members and from their shared, genetically rooted dispositions. Bullies usually do not choose their victims out of **reactive aggression**, which would involve retaliating for an offense the victim committed against them. Instead, they tend to act out of **proactive aggression**, abusing the victim because it helps them achieve a goal, perhaps taking something the victim owns or simply making the victim miserable (Dodge, 1991).

FIGURE 15.5 Bullying. The effects of bullying can be highly negative in the long run for both victims and bullies.

Q: Describe three distinct forms of aggression shown by children, and characterize how they might vary across the sexes and across bullies and nonbullies.

Bullying tends to be most prevalent early in adolescence, during middle school, and tends to decline in high school (Pellegrini & Long, 2002). The reasons for this decline are unclear, but one factor may be peers' increasing intolerance of bullying and the social ostracism of those seen as aggressors. Bullies seem to be angrier than other children, having higher sustained levels of anger and being more prone to temper flare-ups (Espelage & Swearer, 2003). They are also more likely to have criminal convictions later in life (Olweus, 2011). One popular view of bullies is that they have certain deficits in processing social information that lead them to make incorrect attributions about others (Crick & Dodge, 1994). Specifically, they are thought to have deficient theories of mind that lead them to make more hostile attributions about the actions of others than are warranted. This view, however, does not fit those cases in which a bully has a precise awareness of the victim's mental state and uses it to maximally humiliate or antagonize the victim (Sutton et al., 1999a, 1999b).

There are three main types of interventions to curb bullying: (1) regulating the bully's behavior through external means, such as punishment; (2) having the bully regulate his own behavior internally; and (3) changing the victim's behavior. It is quite clear that external regulation of bullies works. If teachers or other adults closely monitor bullying and punish it, it will decrease (Ttofi & Farrington, 2011). It is also possible to improve a bully's empathy and make him feel more uncomfortable mistreating others (Olweus, 1993, 1994). One way to increase empathy might be to get a bully to imagine the situation from the victim's viewpoint or to think through the consequences of bullying (Caravita et al., 2009; Cirillo et al., 1998)—but these internal changes are less effective than external ones. They do not bring about as much of an immediate cessation of bullying. Some researchers suggest that bullies do not have a general problem feeling empathy; they just do not feel it when they initially engage in bullying in a particular instance (Espelage & Swearer, 2003). Overall, despite many studies of interventions designed to reduce bullying by increasing the aggressors' social skills, such as their empathy and perspective-taking, these programs have been, at best, only modestly effective (Vreeman & Carroll, 2007).

Less research has focused on techniques for changing the victim's behavior, which is unfortunate, since this behavior can easily make the individual vulnerable in new situations. Training in assertiveness and self-confidence sometimes helps victims (Sharp, 1996), but it is challenging to convince anxious, fearful children to stand up for themselves in a manner bullies will find convincing. This is an important area of future research, as the child who gives off certain signals, such as high social anxiety, will be detected by bullies in many situations, and adults will not always be around to punish tormentors at the mall, at summer camp, or at the movie theater.

Research on bullying illustrates how dynamic interaction patterns can become self-perpetuating and more intense over time. It also illustrates the challenge of intervening, given the interconnected set of factors that contribute to and sustain bullying. A clear goal of future research is to identify the most effective points in such interactive patterns in

which to engage in interventions. The group contributions to such effects will be more apparent when we consider the group level of affiliation.

Enemies Some negative relationships go in both directions, which is the case when two children become enemies, either after a friendship ends or in a relationship that is negative from the start. The pattern of **mutual antipathies**, in which two children intensely dislike each other, can occur between bullies and victims (Card & Hodges, 2007), but it can also occur between two children who are each aggressive and dominant (Abecassis, 2003; Abecassis et al., 2001). In contrast to bully-victim relationships, **inimical relationships** are more symmetrical, in that the children are equally hostile and aggressive toward each other and consider each to be the other's enemy (Card, 2007). Interestingly, preschoolers very rarely have enemies, with incidences usually under 2 percent (Abecassis, 2003; Card & Hodges, 2007). Starting in elementary school, however, far more children have enemies—well over 30 percent according to one study (Abecassis et al., 2001). And in later childhood, there is a marked increase in enemy relationships (Berger et al., 2011; Hodges & Card, 2003). These relationships often cause both parties to avoid each other, but in some cases they are both drawn into a cycle of mutual aggression and retaliation in which revenge becomes a kind of social bond. Having enemies is stressful, and children with enemies can show many of the same symptoms as victims of bullying (Abecassis, 2003; Abecassis et al., 2001; Card & Hodges, 2007).

Aggression between enemies usually takes one of two forms. Boys, especially at early ages, engage in more physical aggression, while girls tend to show more relational aggression (see Figure 15.6). This latter type of hostility involves efforts to damage an individual's social relationships through rumors, gossip, and ridicule, potentially causing the person to be excluded from a desired peer group (Crick & Nelson, 2002). Some researchers have found gender differences in physical aggression but equal incidences of relational aggression among girls and boys (Espelage et al., 2003). Antipathy also often seems to arise between members of groups representing different interests and backgrounds, such as between students who receive very high grades and those who are more focused on sports. There certainly can be mutually aggressive relationships between members of the same group, but more often it may be that "opposites detract" (Laursen et al., 2010).

In short, mutually aggressive relationships are stressful and related to a wide range of negative developmental outcomes in terms of children's social adjustment, depression, and more general acting out and misbehavior. Again, however, the direction of causality is unclear. Perhaps the same personality factors that make a child more prone to

FIGURE 15.6 **Relational aggression.** Relational aggression can cause great discomfort in others through gossip or rumor, with effects that can be just as devastating as those from physical aggression.

mutually aggressive relationships also lead to other social difficulties.

Dating and Romantic Relationships As children enter adolescence, a new form of relationship becomes more and more common: romantic relationships between pairs of individuals. We will define **romantic relationships** as mutually recognized voluntary interactions that are seen as more intense than other relationships. These relationships are also distinguished by displays of affection, either with actual sexual behavior or with the anticipation of such behavior occurring (Collins et al., 2009). As seen in Figure 15.7, the rate of romantic relationships doubles from age 13 to age 17, from an incidence of 36 percent in 13-year-olds to 54 percent in 15-year-olds to 70 percent in 17-year-olds (Collins et al., 2009). It was commonly thought that such a rise was closely linked to the maturation of sexual gonads and sex-related hormones such as testosterone and estrogen, but closer analysis tends to show that the rise is more closely related to age norms for dating in various cultures (Carver et al., 2003; Collins et al., 2009; Dornbusch et al., 1981). Similar age-related norms seem to be found in both different-sex and same-sex relationships, with somewhat later rates of incidence for same-sex relationships, perhaps because such relationships are not endorsed by many cultures (Floyd & Stein, 2002). In adolescence, girls are somewhat more likely to have both boys and girls as partners or as potential partners than do boys (Collins et al., 2009).

Sexual orientation tends to remain quite stable across adolescence and young adulthood among those who initially identify themselves as primarily preferring different-sex or same-sex partners (Savin-Williams et al., 2012). Those who identify themselves as bisexual tend to show more change, with women showing a shift to mostly heterosexual

relationships and men more equally distributing themselves among the categories of bisexual, homosexual, and heterosexual relationships. Individuals who are involved primarily in homosexual or bisexual romantic patterns unfortunately often suffer from stigma, prejudice, and discrimination from others who disapprove of same-sex relationships. It is particularly tragic that the more stigma and prejudice a same-sex couple experiences, the more likely it is that their own relationship quality will be negatively affected. Fortunately, at least some same-sex couples are able to shield, and sometimes even strengthen, their relationships in the face of such prejudice. Researchers are trying to better understand the strategies that more successful couples use to respond to stigma and prejudice (Frost, 2011).

Compared with other kinds of relationships with peers, adolescent romantic relationships tend to have more conflicts. This may seem surprising, given that those relationships are more intimate, but they are also more intense and are typically of relatively short duration (about 18 months or less), with the breakups often laced with conflict. Sexual relationships are seen by girls as more appropriately occurring in romantic relationships than in more casual relationships, a perception that is not as strong among boys (Collins et al., 2009). As seen from the perspective of evolutionary psychology, this difference in perception follows from the argument that men seek diverse mates to maximize procreation, whereas women seek mates who will show longer-term loyalty during pregnancy and child rearing (Buss & Shackelford, 2008).

What factors predict which pairs of individuals tend to form romantic relationships? With heterosexual adolescent couples, males tend to choose same-age partners where possible and females often choose somewhat older males. Despite some claims that opposites attract, adolescents generally choose partners who are similar to themselves in level of physical attractiveness, popularity, and even mood—for example, a depressive orientation (Collins et al., 2009).

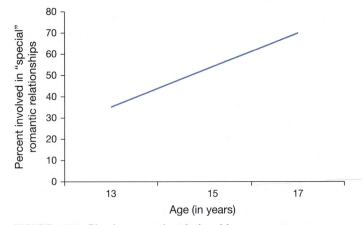

FIGURE 15.7 **Rise in romantic relationships among teenagers.** The incidence of romantic relationships reported as "special" doubles between ages 13 and 17. Adapted from Collins et al. (2009).

Developmentally, romantic relationships have often been described as shifting in their nature over the course of adolescence. Older adolescents tend to see their significant others as more supportive, close, and interdependent. The shift seems to be most dramatic between ages 15 and 17 years (Collins, 2003). During that period, the rate of dating goes up from roughly 25 percent to 75 percent. The length of relationships also increases, with those younger than 15 rarely having relationships lasting more than 11 months and the majority of those older than 17 having relationships that last longer than 11 months. Younger adolescents tend to choose partners for reasons that are often superficial, including clothing style and standing of the potential partner in a peer network. But fortunately, older adolescents tend to focus on partner traits that are more related to fostering intimate relationships and longer-term compatibility. Older adolescents are also more likely to resolve conflicts through compromise. In short, it appears that the ability to form romantic relationships is a skill that develops over the course of adolescence into a more durable and rewarding form.

Researchers argue that adolescent romantic relationships and dating are important because the developmental trajectory of such relationships is related to the quality of relationships later in life (Collins et al., 2009; Simpson et al., 2011). Difficult romantic relationships in adolescence have been linked to difficulties in later romantic experiences (Grello et al., 2003). Moreover, simply having romantic relationships may increase the risk of experiencing later depressions, given that a breakup of those early relationships is likely. Overall, however, adolescents who shift to deeper, more meaningful relationships as they progress through adolescence seem to have a better chance of having sustainable rewarding relationships as young adults. One revealing line of work suggests that it is not just conflicts themselves that matter to long-term relationship quality, but how couples recover from such conflicts. Thus, couples who recover from conflicts well in adolescence are more likely to later have more stable, positive relationships that provide greater satisfaction to both members of the relationship (Salvatore et al., 2011).

Social Groups

Infants and young toddlers do not form groups of their own making, probably because they lack the cognitive complexity needed to manage a group. Preschoolers do form groups, but they are often temporary, forming briefly around a particular activity and then dissolving. Preschool girls tend to play in smaller groups of the same sex, and in those groups they tend to be cooperative, engage in conversation, and show concerns about relationships. Preschool boys tend to play in larger groups of the same sex, and in

those groups they tend to compete, engage in more physical roughhouse play, and show concerns about dominance relations (Maccoby, 1998; Parker et al., 2006).

Dominance hierarchies start to appear between group members, and these networks of social status relationships resemble those of many other species (see Chapter 13). These hierarchies can reduce aggression within groups, as subordinate members tend to reserve aggression for those of even lower status, and dominant members only rarely have to show aggression to assert their higher position (Sluckin & Smith, 1977). One interesting aspect of preschoolers' dominance hierarchies is that even though such hierarchies can be quite stable over time, the children are usually not consciously aware of their own status in the hierarchy (Strayer & Santos, 1996). The mental mechanisms that maintain the social structure appear to be largely implicit. This finding may sound improbable, but in fact, we have seen very similar cognitive patterns in young children in other domains. Just as young children are unaware of some properties of their language or their memory, even though they use them both heavily, they show little awareness of their own social position within a group, even as they honor that position in their behavior.

Cliques and Crowds Among elementary school children, groups have a very different character. Much more stable **cliques**, which are small groups of peers who voluntarily spend a great deal of time together and seem to actively exclude others, start to emerge (see Figure 15.8). Cliques play an important role by providing the child with a sense of belonging as well as helping form a group identity. Being popular becomes a powerful social goal of many children. By this time, children can be acutely, and often painfully, aware of their own status within groups, knowing full well when they are unpopular or viewed as outsiders. Being rejected by peers and not included in a group is linked to problems of psychological adjustment (Ladd, 2006), but it can be difficult to tell if rejection causes such problems or if children with such problems tend to be rejected, or both.

In a related vein, children in this age group show a marked increase in **social comparison**, evaluating others relative to themselves or their group, such as assessing who is smarter, richer, more athletic, or better looking. Even preschoolers engage in some social comparison (Butler, 1998; Rhodes & Brickman, 2008; Yee & Brown, 1992), but it becomes much more frequent and intense during the later elementary school years. Presumably, during this time, children become more sophisticated at noticing and interpreting differences between their own group and other groups—for example, becoming aware of social rules that might be special to a group. One consequence of these group comparisons is that children tend to evaluate their own group more positively and other groups more negatively, even when group assignments are random (Bigler et al., 1997). With respect to majority and minority

A   B

FIGURE 15.8 Social groups in early adolescence. (A) Cliques appear in middle childhood and reach their peak in the early teens, declining in high school. **(B)** In a group of children such as these, often the most popular children are the most physically attractive.

groups, there are indications that children as young as 7 years old reflect the adult pattern of showing stronger out-group biases when they are members of a majority group as opposed to a minority group (Newheiser & Olson, 2012).

> **Q:** When, in the course of development, do cliques tend to first appear? Why might they not appear until that age?

Finally, in adolescence, cliques start to decline in importance. Although some adolescents still try to maintain cliques and reap the benefits of belonging to an exclusive group, most adolescents are less focused on cliques (Adler & Adler, 1998). The makeup of social groups also changes, shifting toward more mixed-sex groups in which both sexes interact and collaborate. There is also a rise in what are sometimes called "crowds" in adolescence, where stereotyped identities, values, and activities tend to define a particular crowd and where a particular adolescent might get a reputation (perhaps not fairly) that links him to one crowd. Thus, in high school, it is common to talk of groups such as nerds, jocks, Goths, stoners, punks, and preppies. For many high schoolers, affiliations with such crowds can have enormous influences on their friendships and daily activities (Brown & Klute, 2003).

Any careful observer of children at different ages would notice many of these patterns. The more challenging research questions center around the different ways that children come to occupy specific niches or social roles within groups. As we examine the wide variety of social roles that children occupy in groups, we will also keep in mind questions about how developmental change interacts with the different social roles children play in their peer groups and

with the broader social patterns in these groups. To do this, we will consider a wide range of research that measures children's social status in groups. Many of these studies investigate the factors that lead children to hold certain social positions and what the developmental consequences might be of occupying these positions.

Sociometric Status and Social Interaction For more than 75 years, researchers have been interested in devising a typology that describes how peers interact with each other, which could then be used to classify children into different kinds of roles within groups. In 1934, the psychiatrist Jacob L. Moreno developed a method of discussing social status in groups known as *sociometry*. Moreno believed that analyzing a group's internal structures and the particular position that an individual occupies in these structures—that is, the person's **sociometric status**—could help predict the person's psychological well-being (Moreno, 1951). Moreno determined sociometric status based on how much peers liked or disliked others in their group. Moreno's sociometric method has become a common tool for understanding children's development within the context of social groups. Over the years, a typology of five types of children has developed: *popular children, rejected children, controversial children, average children,* and *neglected children* (Newcomb et al., 1993).

The most common sociometric method for determining sociometric status and sorting a group of children into these five types is the **peer nomination** technique. Each child in the group is individually asked to name the children in the group whom they like the most and those they would most like to play with (Coie et al., 1982). They are also asked to nominate the children whom they like the least and those they would least like to play with. Computing the "like" and "dislike" ratings enables researchers to create the five status types, which have proved to be associated with different behaviors and kinds of abilities.

Popularity is a topic of great concern to older children and teenagers and is frequently talked about (Adler & Adler, 1998). In sociometrics, **popular children** are nominated as being liked by most children and disliked by few children, often as a result of both appealing physical attributes and social skills. For example, popular children may be liked by other children because they are often smiling or because they are friendly, helpful, and sensitive to others. But well-liked children are not necessarily the same children as those who are perceived as popular by their peers. Perceived popularity (which is not always the same as true popularity) is more influenced by perceived power and dominance within a group than by factors such as kindness and trustworthiness (Parkhurst & Hopmeyer, 1998).

Physical attractiveness is one attribute that is often related to popularity (Berscheid & Walster, 1974; see Figure 15.8B). Even preschoolers who are rated as more physically attractive are more likely to be popular among their peers (Vaughn & Langlois, 1983). Later on, near puberty, early physical maturation is related to popularity. Moreover, as seen in Chapter 3, even in infancy there seems to be considerable consensus on what makes someone attractive. Thus, some children would seem to have, simply by accident of birth, a better chance than others at being popular. (There is a large literature also suggesting that physically attractive people continue to enjoy a number of advantages in both their private and professional lives; see Berscheid & Walster, 1974; Snyder et al., 1988). At the same time, physical attractiveness is not a completely fixed attribute. A child's attractiveness can vary considerably as a function of demeanor, hair and clothing style, and mood. Besides physical attractiveness, athletic ability and performance may also be physical factors that contribute to a child's popularity. But athletic performance tends to be more associated with popularity in boys than in girls (Closson, 2009; Lease et al., 2002a, 2002b).

Beyond physical attributes, many psychological attributes are correlated with popularity and unpopularity. There seem to be different sets of attributes that make children popular to different sets of peers. One study with 452 grade school boys (fourth to sixth grades) found two quite distinct types of children that were highly popular within their respective peer groups (Rodkin et al., 2000): popular prosocial "model" children and popular antisocial "tough" children. The model children were athletic, adept at leadership, cooperative rather than competitive, studious, outgoing, "cool," and nonaggressive. Moreover, kindness was also a common trait in model children (Estell et al., 2003; LaFontana & Cillessen, 2002). The tough children were "cool," athletic, aggressive, and generally antisocial toward authorities and social norms. These traits were noticed not just by independent observers but also by peers. Both groups of popular children were "cool," which seems to reflect a kind of social adroitness and awareness, but beyond that trait, they displayed sharply contrasting types of personalities. This contrast has been found in other studies with both boys and girls. The causal relation is not always obvious, however. A behavior may make a child popular, but it is also possible that being popular may help cause certain behaviors to emerge.

The social adroitness of popular children has been examined more systematically in studies of the social cognitive capacities of popular children. One review of the sociometric literature concluded that popular children are more adept at navigating a wide range of social situations, including perceiving actors' intentions, developing social problem-solving strategies, and focusing on interpersonal relations—that is, how to get along with other children or adults—in addition to attaining concrete instrumental goals, such as obtaining a desired object or mastering a task (Gifford-Smith & Brownell, 2003). The connection between social cognitive skills and peer acceptance may appear quite early, with some studies showing associations between higher theory of mind and peer acceptance in preschoolers (Slaughter et al., 2002).

One facet of popularity occurs in the cliques that appear in late childhood, usually around the sixth grade, and that continue into early adolescence, usually starting to decline after the eighth grade (Crockett et al., 1984). These small, exclusive peer groups can cause pain for those who are excluded, as well as sometimes causing anxiety for group members concerned about maintaining their status. It is interesting that cliques are rarely stable beyond a few months (Adler & Adler, 1995). They are frequently forming and dissolving or adding and dropping members, so that the composition can vary dramatically over time. Cliques may be especially sought out during the middle school years because children see them as a way to catapult themselves into an elite status group (Schrum & Cheek, 1987). As children grow older, they may start to realize that membership in such transient groups does not really confer lasting positive status and that members of cliques can also be targets of considerable resentment and distrust, especially by former friends who have now been excluded by a child who has recently joined a clique (Adler & Adler, 1995). They may also start to realize that they themselves may likely be dropped from a clique and accountable to former friends that they excluded upon joining the clique.

There is a huge literature on a group of children known as **rejected children**. These children receive the highest number of nominations as peers who are most disliked. When this group is studied more directly, these children seem much more likely than other children to interpret ambiguous actions by others as hostile (Dodge et al., 2003).

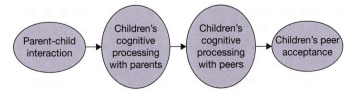

FIGURE 15.9 A causal model of peer acceptance. Several researchers have suggested that specific parent-child interaction patterns help instill certain social cognitive processing skills in children that then influence social cognitive processing of interactions with peers, which in turn influences peer acceptance. In practice, it is difficult to tell if such links are causal as opposed to correlational, mediated by other variables. Adapted from Rah & Parke (2008).

This pattern of thought in rejected children is often known as the **hostile attribution bias** (Nasby et al., 1979).

How might something like a hostile attribution bias appear in development? Some scholars have argued that certain kinds of social cognitive styles emerge out of parent-child interaction patterns and then come to influence peer interactions (Rah & Parke, 2008). This kind of model is shown in Figure 15.9. In particular, these researchers believe that parents' manner of interaction with their children can lead to changes in three kinds of social cognitions in children: goals, strategies, and attributions (Crick & Dodge, 1994). Thus, if a parent is constantly berating and coercing a child, that child might focus on instrumental goals—for example, obtaining a good grade—rather than relational goals—for example, developing a better relationship with the parent. Instrumental goals might in turn lead to strategies that neglect the parents' feelings and interests, which in turn could lead to attributions about the hostile intent of the parents. The social cognitions that are learned from parent-child interactions are then transferred to interactions with peers, with the child now continuing to make hostile attributions about ambiguous situations, attributions that often lead to peer rejection.

There are many studies suggesting associations between parent-child interaction patterns and certain kinds of cognitive styles, as well as many studies showing associations between children's social cognitions and peer acceptance or rejection (Crick & Dodge, 1994; Dodge et al., 2003). Certain longitudinal studies suggest that the patterns of correlation point toward the causal model shown in Figure 15.9, in which parental behavior ultimately causes patterns of peer acceptance or rejection (Rah & Parke, 2008). But because these studies are not experimental in nature, it is still possible that the patterns of association do not indicate causal relationships. For example, children and their parents might share common genotypes that might predispose them toward more hostile attributional styles, which in turn might influence interactions between the children and their parents and between the children and their peers. Similarly, growing up in a harsh and threatening environment may increase hostile attributional styles in both parents and children, which in turn may carry over and contaminate relations with peers. Longitudinal designs are meant to be able to tease apart such alternatives, but in practice it is difficult to make a definitive conclusion.

As researchers examine popularity in more subtle and detailed ways, they start to see how particular kinds of interactions might relate over time to particular kinds of aggression. For example, among children from ages 10 to 14, especially girls, relational aggression predicts, and seems to cause, a form of "perceived popularity," in which a child is seen as one of the most popular; but this perceived popularity does not seem to lead to "sociometric popularity," in which the child is the one whom children most want to have as their friend (Cillessen & Mayeux, 2004; Cillessen & Rose, 2005). Sadly, this causal link between relational aggression and perceived popularity may provide an incentive for some children to gossip and slander others.

When peer group acceptance is explained in terms of social cognitive capacities, this is known as the **social information processing** approach (Crick & Dodge, 1994). This approach is often broken up into five steps (see Figure 15.10): (1) The child must encode social cues and the setting in which they occur (for example, *Joe bumped into me in a crowded hallway*). (2) The child must make sense—that is, interpret the cause and intent—of the cues in that situation (for example, *Joe bumped into me because he is out to get me*). (3) The child must set up goals for responding to the situation (for example, *I have to figure out a way to retaliate against Joe*). (4) The child must access a set of possible responses to attain that goal (for example, *I could go up and bump into Joe right away, or I could*

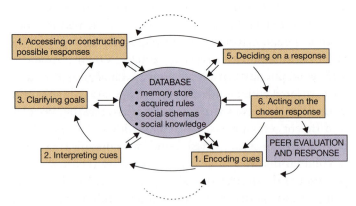

FIGURE 15.10 Social information processing model of attributions in children. Crick and Dodge (1994) proposed that the child processes social information in five steps that lead to a final behavioral response. In the model shown here, the process is seen as a repeating cycle that can lead a child to have a hostile attributional style and to be a rejected child or to have a more positive attributional style and be a popular child. Adapted from Crick & Dodge (1994).

spill food on him in the cafeteria). (5) Finally, the child must decide which of the possible responses is the best one to use.

Rejected children seem to have deficits in every one of these five steps (Crick & Dodge, 1994), although most research has focused on the second step, in which the child constructs an interpretation of the cues. Studies repeatedly find that rejected children tend to be both aggressive and more inclined to make hostile attributions about the actions of others (Orobio de Castro et al., 2002). At the same time, rejected children do not automatically make a hostile attribution about an ambiguous event. If a rejected child feels positively toward a peer, the same ambiguous action is much less likely to result in a hostile attribution than when it is carried out by a peer for whom the child has negative feelings (Peets et al., 2008). Thus, the hostile attribution bias is strengthened by the extent to which a child feels a general dislike for another child. Since many rejected children have at least some friends (Cairns et al., 1988), they show quite different attributional patterns when settings include primarily their friends as opposed to other groups of peers for whom they have either neutral or negative feelings. The finding of increased deficits in all five steps means that rejected children may initially make mistakes in encoding critical features of an event, as well as generating a nonoptimal set of response strategies and then choosing an option that is especially aggressive and usually counterproductive.

Rejected children tend to have difficulties in adjustment in childhood and adolescence, with higher rates of emotional problems (for example, anxiety and depression) and behavioral problems (for example, being disruptive in class, getting into fights, and substance abuse; Bierman, 2004; Rubin et al., 2005). There are also indications that children who exhibit high levels of demanding behaviors at a younger age are more likely to become rejected children in later childhood (Dodge et al., 2003). Unfortunately, when a child is classified strongly as being in the rejected group, that classification can remain quite stable over much of childhood and adolescence (Rubin et al., 2005).

Yet, aggression does not always lead to rejection. Roughly half the children who are seen as aggressive are not rejected by their peers (Coie et al., 1991). It appears that children who respond to an unambiguously aggressive action in an aggressive way are not as likely to be rejected as those who use aggression to achieve a particular goal. In other words, if aggression seems to be a reasonable response to a clear provocation, other children do not seem to take that behavior as a basis for rejection.

Children who are classified as controversial score high on both the like and the dislike scales. In many ways, they are the opposite of the neglected children (discussed shortly), as they are noticed by everyone, just in different ways. **Controversial children** are seen as sociable and as leaders, but they are also more likely to be seen as aggressive and arrogant, with boys showing more of a propensity for aggression and girls for arrogance (Gifford-Smith & Brownell, 2003). Controversial children do not seem to have negative developmental outcomes. In addition, the classification of being a controversial child shows less stability over time than being either a rejected child or a popular child. Moreover, during adolescence, controversial children may become more popular with peers who value a certain degree of rebelliousness (Gifford-Smith & Brownell, 2003).

Children who have average values on the like and dislike scales have not been studied much in their own right because they are generally assumed to have unremarkable behaviors and psychological problems. They may also be quite mobile in that they can move in and out of the popular groups. There is no evidence that average children fare any worse than popular children in the long run.

Neglected children seem to be largely ignored by their peer group and do not appear to be high on either the like or dislike scale. These children go through their days without much notice, and they do not seem to fare much worse than average children (Asher & Wheeler, 1985; Gifford-Smith & Brownell, 2003). Neglected children seem to be just as happy and no more lonely than peers who are classified as average. They do seem to be more shy and withdrawn (Coie & Dodge, 1988), but this behavior does not seem to be associated with any negative outcomes. There is also some evidence that being in the neglected category is less stable than categories such as rejected and popular, suggesting that neglected children might move in and out of other categories, such as average and popular, at different times in development (Gifford-Smith & Brownell, 2003; Newcomb et al., 1993).

Overall, the sociometric method has been useful for classifying relationship patterns among peers. The classifications with the most stability over time, rejected and popular, are also the most divergent in terms of developmental outcomes. Children who are well liked and not disliked tend to have happy lives with relatively low anxiety and relatively few behavioral problems. Children who are strongly disliked and not liked tend to have unhappy lives tainted with depression, anxiety, and a large number of behavioral problems. Children who are labeled as neglected, controversial, or average do not seem to have any obvious problems. It is tempting to draw causal inferences here, but a more cautious interpretation is more appropriate. It may be that certain attribution patterns cause peer rejection or acceptance, but it may also be that peer rejection or acceptance greatly amplifies a particular attributional style. In addition, it may be that other variables, such as a difficult home life, may causally influence both attributional styles and attitudes of peers. In reality, it seems likely that all these factors, among many others, interact in a complex web of cycles and feedback loops, making any simple causal chain implausible.

Longitudinal studies are now also revealing that peer relations can have effects on quite subtle social cognitions, which in turn can feed back on social interaction abilities. For example, difficulty understanding faux pas—social blunders such as violating a local culture's rules of etiquette—can be linked to peer rejection over time. In younger children (5 to 6 years old), peer rejection predicts more difficulty in understanding faux pas in later years, while difficulty in understanding faux pas in older children (8 to 9 years old) predicts higher levels of peer rejection in even later years (Banerjee et al., 2011). On the other hand, early theory of mind understanding (for example, at 5 years old) tends to predict more adept social relations, higher peer acceptance, and lower rejection rates a few years later (Caputi et al., 2012). Thus, both directions of influence—from social cognitive capacities to peer relation quality and from peer relation quality to social cognitive capacities—may be at work at all ages, depending on the particular social capacities studied.

Developmental Patterns in Levels of Affiliation

Research on interactions with peers and other people beyond the family constitutes one of the largest areas of developmental psychology. Moreover, that research is increasingly being connected to other areas of research—such as the development of social cognition, theory of mind, and perspective taking, as well as to attachment patterns emerging from infancy. Individual differences loom large in much of this research and for very understandable reasons. We all are interested in the factors that made some children, including ourselves, popular or unpopular during childhood and adolescence and in whether there are long-lasting consequences of occupying one of those social roles. We have seen that questions about causes and consequences are extremely difficult to disentangle, even as researchers repeatedly document strong associations between some sociometric categories and a host of social, emotional, and cognitive factors.

It is important, however, to step back and remind ourselves that above and beyond the sometimes striking individual differences that are found, there are also very general patterns of development for peer interactions, relationships, and social groups that apply to virtually all children. We return to those patterns here as a way of keeping in mind this broader developmental perspective. Table 15.1 summarizes the major developmental findings for peer interactions that have been found over thousands of studies using the perspective of levels of affiliation (Rubin et al., 1998). It

is only within the context of these broader developmental changes that we can understand how peer status categories emerge in childhood, change over time, and then gradually dissipate in later adolescence.

Social Network Effects

A different research tradition has begun to make important contributions to the study of the developmental effects of groups on behaviors. This line of work examines formal and quantitative properties of social networks to see if a person's position in the structure of a social network influences that person's nature. Social network effects were first documented most dramatically in terms of health patterns and group relationships. For example, one study found that the more obese friends you have, the more likely you are to be obese. More strikingly, if the friends of your friends are obese, those links can make it more likely for you to be obese. Finally, and most dramatically, even the level of obesity of the friends of your friends' friends can influence whether you are overweight (Christakis & Fowler, 2007). Over a period of 32 years, it was possible to predict the spread of obesity in a large social network based on friendship links that had as many as three degrees of separation from the person who was affected. In general, same-sex mutual friends tended to have the strongest influences on each other in terms of obesity, while different-sex friends did not have any measurable influence on each other in terms of obesity. Interestingly, at four degrees of separation, no significant effects were noticed. These results indicate that people who you do not know or may never meet can still influence your life through a form of social contagion of habits, lifestyles, or health-related behaviors.

More recent work has documented that such effects can also spread through social networks in adolescence (Ali et al., 2012; de la Haye et al., 2010; Fletcher et al., 2011; Fowler & Christakis, 2008; Valente et al., 2009). Thus, obesity in adolescents can be predicted from the prevalence of obesity among those who are as many as three links away from them in social networks. Similarly, eating habits strongly reflect network relations (Fletcher et al., 2011). There is every reason to suspect that such network effects start much earlier in childhood. Consider, for example, the ways that fads can spread wildly among schoolchildren in a neighborhood.

Subsequent studies have found three-link effects in social networks for a wide variety of behaviors, including smoking, alcohol use, exercise habits, and academic achievement, with many such effects now being demonstrated in adolescents and school-age children (Haas et al., 2010; Macdonald-Wallis et al., 2011; Mundt, 2011; Veenstra & Dijkstra, 2012). One strong effect occurs for happiness, with clusters of happiness appearing in networks (Fowler &

Level of Affiliation	0–2 years	2–5 years	5–11 years	11 years and older
Interactions	Not really social; more simply joint arousal Little reciprocal give-and-take High conflict	More elaborate patterns of play Increase in sharing, pretense, and orderly interactions	Large increase in frequency of social interactions Increase in size of peer groups Less adult supervision More single-sex interactions More interactions outside the home More verbal aggression and gossip; less pretend play	Peer interactions more influential and more frequent More cross-sex interactions
Relationships	Unique patterns of sustained interactions between pairs, but not really friendships	Children purposefully picking friends, usually choosing those most like themselves More prosocial with friends but also more hostile	Bullying Broader view of friendship, allowing for a more diverse range of friends and friendships	Recognition of nonexclusivity of friendships and granting of more autonomy to friends; thus, less jealous of friends' other relationships Increased intimacy with friends
Groups	Little evidence of group behavior	Dominance hierarchies; less overall aggression, but little explicit awareness of own status in hierarchy	Stable cliques; popularity hierarchies Social comparison more frequent and influential	Decreasing importance of cliques Increasing importance of integration of sexes

TABLE 15.1 Developmental changes in social affiliations. Children's social relations show distinct patterns of change during different developmental periods and across various levels, from interactions to relationships to groups. Adapted from Rubin et al. (1998).

Christakis, 2008; see Figure 15.11), and it is also possible to predict loneliness based on how peripheral versus central a person is to a particular network. These studies also show how happiness in a few individuals can spread through a network over time, with some fortunate indications that happiness spreads more robustly than sadness (Fowler & Christakis, 2008).

This new approach to group influences in development has great promise and offers the potential for major advances in the study of peer relations and groups. For example, it allows more formal analysis to be undertaken, which in turn enables quite precise predictions about effects. In addition, it illustrates for the first time how there can be effects at three degrees of separation from an individual and by people never encountered face-to-face in the person's lifetime. Finally, whether a person is central or peripheral in a network or has a dense versus a sparse set of connections may lead to interesting predictions about both social contagion and likely psychological states such as loneliness.

Media Influences on Development

Moving beyond face-to-face peer interactions and relationships, we now consider how the media come to have a socializing effect on children. The media can be intimately related to peer influences, suggesting how peers supposedly look and behave in a wide range of circumstances. The media can provide a large, albeit distorted, database for social comparison, suggesting, for example, typical levels of affluence and typical hobbies and styles. Media also can portray morally laden norms, such as appropriate ways to act both prosocially and aggressively. Television has long been thought to be the most influential medium, but in recent years, Internet communities and video games have also come to exert major influences on children. All of these influences in turn feed back on how peers interact with each other, whether it

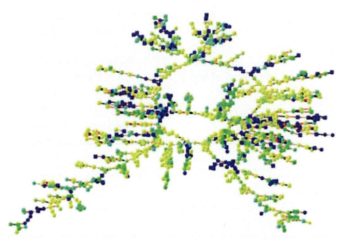

FIGURE 15.11 Social networks and happiness. Friendship relations in a social network can predict many facets of health and psychological states. This graph depicts "happiness clusters" by showing squares for males and circles for females and showing the connections of individuals with friends, spouses, and siblings. Siblings are shown as connected by black lines, and friends and spouses are connected by red lines. Yellow indicates happiness; blue indicates sadness; shades of green indicate moderate levels of happiness. Such graphs can be constructed for both adults and adolescents. People who are surrounded by other happy people tend to be happy. The researchers in this study found that happiness spreads through the network rather than simply occurring because of associating with other happy people. In addition, a peripheral (as opposed to a central) location in a network can predict loneliness. From Fowler & Christakis (2008).

is through social networking sites or through adopting the styles and values of a popular television show.

Television

Although television is prevalent, it varies dramatically in its content and how it influences children across their development. Any discussion of the possible influences of television on children must consider how influences vary both as a function of content and of age. Television can influence children in various ways, ranging from the cognitive to the emotional to the social. And these influences can be either positive or negative. On the positive side, television has the potential to teach children about the world, to encourage them to engage in prosocial behaviors, to give them practice in various forms of reasoning, and to facilitate language acquisition. On the negative side, television has the potential to hinder cognitive development, to impair prosocial behavior, and to foster antisocial and aggressive behavior.

Obviously, the effects must depend at least partially on the kinds of programs that children watch. Because educational programs make up only a small fraction of the television shows that most children watch, we need to ask about the overall effects of television in which entertain-

ment programs dominate. In the discussions that follow, we will consider both the potential of television programming to have positive and negative effects when experimenters have children watch particular kinds of shows in experimental settings, and also the most common effects given the actual viewing habits of most children. But it is important to keep in mind the tradeoffs between experimental designs and naturalistic studies. Experimental studies, in which children are randomly assigned to one of two conditions, such as viewing violent versus nonviolent television, have the virtue of uncovering causal effects. They are also, however, often faulted for extrapolating from a situation in which children watch television for a few hours in a laboratory to real-life influences of television that may happen over thousands of hours and years of watching. Naturalistic studies have the obvious advantage of looking at real-life viewing habits that occur over appropriate time frames and viewing situations, but they have real limitations as well. If a correlation is found between, for example, viewers of violent television and higher levels of aggressiveness toward friends, it could be that television is causing the effect or it could be that aggressive children prefer to watch violent programming.

The Pervasiveness of Television Watching Watching television occupies a very substantial part of children's time in almost all cultures. Although the majority of studies of television viewing have occurred in North America, Japan, and Europe (since those regions were the first to have televisions in most households) television viewing has now spread throughout the world (see Figure 15.12). In the United States, there is at least one television in almost every home, and roughly 75 percent of those households subscribe to cable or satellite feeds, thus guaranteeing a huge variety of viewing options (Anderson et al., 2003). Moreover, in many households, television watching is the dominant activity in the home. Far more homes have the television on for several hours a day as opposed to 1 or 2 hours a week. An elementary school child in the United States typically spends 4 hours each day watching television. Counting weekends and summers, a child may spend far more time watching television than attending school, playing sports, or engaging in activities with the family (Comstock & Scharrer, 2006; Roberts et al., 1999). In addition to watching television shows, children also watch an enormous number of commercials, with a typical child seeing over 40,000 commercials a year (Kunkel, 2001).

Given the extraordinary prominence of television programming and advertising in children's lives, it is natural to assume that it must be having an influence on their development. Researchers have asked about the potential negative and positive effects of watching television. On the positive side, we can ask whether television can enhance cognitive skills such as attentional strategies, problem-solving

FIGURE 15.12 Television watching throughout the world. Although television was initially found primarily in the homes of those living in more developed countries, it is now a fixture in the lives of children in most areas of the world, even when there is no direct electrical service to a home.

routines, and literacy. We can also ask if television can improve prosocial behavior, such as sharing or resolving disputes. On the negative side, there has been extensive work asking if exposure to violence on television leads to both a greater tolerance of violence by children and an increase in violent behavior. Other studies have asked if television can impair aspects of cognitive development, such as attention, reading skills, and comprehension of complex narratives. Television does not simply reflect the culture at large. It is often a distortion of that culture, which may help create a distorted image of reality. In this discussion, we will try to give a modest sense of those other influences as well.

Q: Describe, in quantitative terms, the incidence of television watching by children in North America.

Changes in Television Watching with Age To understand how television might influence various aspects of a child's mind and behavior, it is helpful to first examine how a child develops the ability to extract information from television. Observe a child under 1 year of age in a room with a television. Even if older children and adults in the room are watching the television with rapt attention, the baby is unlikely to spend much of her time staring at the television screen. While quite young infants can extract some information from video monitors and even imitate facial expressions displayed on a monitor, imitation of complex actions takes more time to develop. For example, one study of 24- and 30-month-olds found that while they would imitate

an action demonstrated by a television actor even after a 24-hour delay, they showed a considerably higher incidence of imitation when the actor was live as opposed to televised (Hayne et al., 2003). Another study found that 12-month-olds had considerable difficulty reproducing actions they had observed on a video monitor but could easily reproduce these actions when they saw them performed by a live actor (Barr & Hayne, 1999). The relative inability of younger children to learn as effectively from video as from live demonstrations is often called the **video deficit** and is repeatedly found across a wide range of studies (Anderson & Hanson, 2010; Kirkorian et al., 2008). In addition, it appears that infants younger than 12 months have difficulty telling the difference between coherent content and incoherent content in videos, such as the difference between a sequence that has logically ordered clips versus clips that are shuffled randomly (Anderson & Pempek, 2005; Kirkorian et al., 2008; see Figure 15.13). Thus, the narrative structure of most programs is not likely to be understood by infants younger than 12 months old. Detailed analyses of eye movements show that 1-year-olds have much more difficulty tracking changes from one scene to another, often requiring several seconds to orient to the new scene; as a result, they are unable to follow the unfolding narrative (Kirkorian et al., 2012). Similarly, 1-year-olds often have difficulty connecting what they see in videos with what is occurring in the real world, even when the relationships are very obvious to older children (Troseth, 2010).

FIGURE 15.13 Very young television viewers. Before 1 year of age, infants do not seem to be able to understand the narrative structure of programs and have difficulty telling the difference between randomly ordered clips and those that follow a thematic progression.

After infancy, children become much more dedicated television viewers, and the typical toddler spends several hours a day in front of a television. At approximately 30 months of age, a much larger range of programming may become comprehensible to the child and therefore of interest (Anderson & Hanson, 2010; Anderson & Pempek, 2005). Audiovisual presentations that are especially tailored to younger audiences—for example, "baby videos" that are marketed as enrichment materials—may well be of interest to children as young as 12 months, especially when adults are present who direct the infant's attention to critical actions and actors (Barr et al., 2008). The vast majority of commercial programming on cable television or networks, however, is usually only of interest to children older than 30 months. Obviously, highly complex plots and actions will continue to elude the understanding and imitative abilities of younger children, but at least by the time they are 3 years old, children can pick up on and reproduce relatively elaborate televised actions, often after considerable delays.

> Q: How does the child's ability to absorb the content of television change with age?

Positive Effects of Television Television can transmit a great deal of beneficial information to children that can help them in their development. Such positive effects usually occur when children watch educational or other sorts of shows specifically designed to teach children—programs usually shown on nonprofit television channels. Children who watch prosocial and academic programming are somewhat more likely to perform better academically and to have better social skills (Calvert & Kotler, 2003). A major problem with evaluating the findings, however, is achieving true random assignment of viewers to watch different forms of television content. When studies show that children who prefer prosocial and academic television have positive outcomes, it is difficult to tell if there is another factor causing the children both to want to watch those forms of programming and to show better academic and prosocial skills. Far more compelling are studies that approximate experimental designs in which children are randomly assigned to watch different kinds of programming or to be part of groups that either have unrestricted television watching or limits to the programs they can watch. Nonetheless, such studies are less frequent than correlational studies because of the practical difficulties in carrying them out in naturalistic settings.

In terms of cognitive skills and learning, there are positive links to watching educational television. Children can learn vocabulary by watching television and video programs (Rice et al., 1990; Wright et al., 2001a), but the effects interact with programming content. In one study, when children viewed educational television between the ages of 2 and 3, they subsequently scored higher on vocabulary tests at 4 and 5 years, but when children between 2 and 3 watched more entertainment-oriented programs, their vocabulary was subsequently lower at 4 and 5 years than children who had watched less of such programming. This was not an experimental study with random assignment, but it did try to demonstrate statistically the causal effect of television viewing on vocabulary. Studies with experimental designs have also shown such effects. Yet, when children are younger than 2 years old, they often may not learn words from television that they can easily learn from live models (Krcmar et al., 2007; Zimmerman et al., 2007), even when they are viewing television and video programs targeted for children under 2 years of age. Thus, they still show the video deficit that is found in younger children. In general, there is little evidence that videos designed for children under 2 years of age actually teach them anything (Anderson & Hanson, 2010; Kirkorian et al., 2008).

Some educational television programs also appear to have positive effects on other cognitive skills, such as problem solving. For example, one popular program, *Blue's Clues* (see Figure 15.14), posed a problem at the beginning of each episode and then presented a story containing a series of clues; the viewer was then invited to see how the clues might be used to solve the problem. When children lived in a community that had *Blue's Clues* in its programming, they showed cognitive advantages on problem-solving tasks in comparison to children from a demographically comparable community that did not have the programming (Anderson et al., 2000). Viewing educational television that

FIGURE 15.14 Educational programming for young children. Television shows with a clear and well-designed educational mission, such as *Blues Clues*, which posed a problem to be solved through a series of clues, is associated with improved cognitive skills in younger viewers.

specifically aims to promote literacy also can have a positive effect with younger children (Moses, 2008).

The overall message about the positive cognitive effects of television is clear. If the content has a well-designed educational mission, it can have a positive effect on many aspects of cognitive development in children over 2 years old, perhaps especially for children from disadvantaged backgrounds (Huston & Wright, 1998). Children from low socioeconomic backgrounds may benefit more than advantaged children from watching educational television programs because they may encounter ways of speaking and situations that they are less likely to encounter at home than are advantaged children, and such exposure may help better prepare them for learning in school. If the content is designed primarily for entertainment and commercial value, however, it usually has negative rather than positive effects. This is unfortunate, given that children tend to prefer to watch entertainment programs (Comstock & Scharrer, 2006).

In terms of social effects, the message is quite similar. Educational television can have positive effects on prosocial behavior. There is some evidence suggesting that viewing programs such as *Sesame Street* can help young children gain a better understanding of different emotions and what sorts of factors are likely to give rise to those emotions. In addition, with the right kinds of programming, there may be modest influences on the ability to feel empathy for others (Wilson, 2008).

In general, prosocial behavior is more salient and frequent in educational as opposed to entertainment-oriented television, and the positive effects tend to occur in children who regularly watch educational shows. In experimental studies with random assignment, children assigned to watch prosocial television episodes are more likely to later show altruistic behavior, such as sharing, than are children assigned to watch episodes without obvious prosocial behavior. One meta-analysis of 34 studies found consistent positive effects of television shows that had prosocial content (Mares & Woodard, 2005). Other studies found that children who regularly watched shows such as *Mister Rogers' Neighborhood* or *Barney & Friends* were more likely to help another child with a difficult project than were children who watched programming without prosocial content (Friedrich & Stein, 1975; Singer & Singer, 1998). Across several such studies, it also appears that when parents point out to their children instances of prosocial behavior in educational programming, the act of commenting enhances positive effects in the children, quite possibly because prosocial actions are less salient or less comprehensible than violent actions and are therefore easier to miss without parental commenting (Wilson, 2008).

Even younger children may have some positive benefits of watching prosocial television, despite not fully comprehending it. For example, children between 12 and 18 months who watched *Sesame Street Beginnings* with their parents later had more frequent and higher-quality interactions with their parents in free-play sessions than did control children (Pempek et al., 2011). This indirect effect is not the same as an effect that directly increases prosocial behavior, and it may primarily reflect changes in parents, but it does show how a certain kind of positive interaction pattern between parents and very young children may get promoted if both watch a program that models such actions.

Finally, television may increase children's sensitivity to cultural issues and their acceptance of diversity in others. Educational programming often exposes children to a wider range of ethnic and racial groups than they might encounter in their daily lives, and it often portrays people from other ethnic groups in professional or social roles that might be different from what a child most commonly observes. Children who watch such programming tend to show more positive attitudes toward members of other groups and hold less negative stereotypes (Wilson, 2008). Of course, if a child mostly watches cartoon shows, there may be very little information that could create positive attitudes for diverse groups.

> **Q:** Describe some ways in which television might present distorted impressions of social and cultural patterns in the world.

Negative Cognitive Effects of Television Most of the studies on the effects of television viewing have focused on the negative effects rather than the positive effects in regard to both learning and social behavior. For the most part, the negative effects tend to occur when children watch entertainment programming, which in the elementary school years and later years is by far the most common form of programming watched.

We have already seen some glimpses of the negative cognitive effects of television in our discussion of the positive cognitive effects. In general, when children are exposed to entertainment television instead of educational television, there tend to be negative effects on attention, problem solving, vocabulary, and literacy. For example, the same study that showed positive effects of educational television on attentional skills also showed negative effects of entertainment television on attentional skills (Kirkorian et al., 2008). Similarly, another study showed that 4-year-olds who were exposed to fast-paced cartoon shows for just 9 minutes showed deficits immediately afterward on executive function tasks, such as those involving delay of gratification, compared with children who had watched educational shows or engaged in drawing for the same period (Lillard & Peterson, 2011). Other studies have found a negative relationship between the amount of viewing of commercial television and vocabulary in very young children (Zimmerman et al., 2007).

One major source of concern about the negative effects of television revolves around achievement in school. If children are spending a great deal of time watching television, doesn't that activity take time away from academic activities, such as doing homework? Certainly, this is the message that many parents impart to their children. But the evidence for such effects is not strong. Television tends to displace other leisure activities, such as listening to the radio and going to movies, but not academic activities (Kirkorian et al., 2008). There are negative correlations between the amount of television watching and academic achievement, but closer analyses do not strongly support a causal link. For example, children from disadvantaged backgrounds tend to spend more time watching television, but a host of other factors associated with disadvantaged backgrounds may be influencing academic performance and not television per se. Again, without additional experimental studies, it is difficult to find strong evidence for a causal effect. Similarly, it is difficult to find clear evidence that entertainment television displaces time spent on reading and thereby reduces literacy. Although some older studies seem to suggest that such an effect occurred when television was introduced into one town and not into another, recent studies do not consistently show a causal relation between amount of entertainment television watched and reduced literacy (Moses, 2008). While there is a positive relation, there is no evidence supporting claims by some in the entertainment industry that entertainment television increases literacy.

Negative Social Effects of Television A great deal of violence occurs in television shows, and there are no indications that it is on the decline. One analysis compared the number of antisocial acts per hour on television in contemporary programming with that occurring 25 years earlier (Potter & Vaughan, 1997). There was a slight increase from 40.8 antisocial acts per hour to 42.1 antisocial acts. In addition, the content of violent programming is very different from reality. In the television world, violent acts are punished much less often, and violent actors are often more attractive and heroic than in the real world (Potter et al., 1995). Even the news portrays violence at far higher rates than it actually occurs in most people's daily lives (Anderson et al., 2003; Johnson, 1996; see Figure 15.15). By some estimates, a child at the end of elementary school is likely to have witnessed roughly 8,000 murders and over 100,000 other violent acts on television (Anderson et al., 2003, Condry, 1989; Huston et al., 1992). Ironically, cartoon shows for children show three times as much violence as violent entertainment television for adults (Wilson et al., 2002).

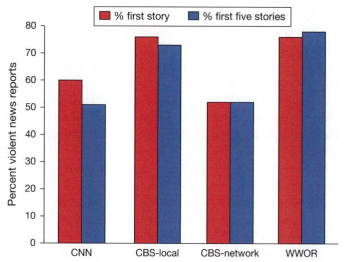

FIGURE 15.15 Violent television programming. News reports are heavily skewed toward reporting violent events. Adapted from Johnson (1996).

Does all this violence matter? Some writers have gone so far as to suggest that the violence in television is actually good because it gets everyday violence out of children's systems through the psychological mechanism of *catharsis*. The **catharsis hypothesis**, which was initially proposed in a much broader and potentially plausible account by Freud, argues that experiencing violence in a pretend setting is a form of release that makes it less likely that aggressive impulses will be released in real life. The catharsis hypothesis for television, however, has been repeatedly discredited (Bushman et al., 1999; Geen & Quanty, 1977). It is safe to say that violent television does not normally reduce aggression in viewers of any age. Moreover, many people believe, on some intuitive level, that violence on television increases aggression.

Q: What is the catharsis hypothesis, and what is the nature of the evidence about the effects of violent television programming on children?

The question of whether violence on television actually does increase aggression has been addressed in experimental ways, as well as in naturalistic studies, with the limitations inherent in both kinds of studies. As the total number of studies on the influences of television is well over 1,000, it is not possible to survey these studies with any degree of completeness. It is possible, however, to describe the overwhelming patterns found in both naturalistic studies and in experimental settings.

In naturalistic settings, the evidence normally must be correlational in nature. It is extremely difficult to make strong inferences about causation when experimental control is

Child TV measures	Adult Composite Aggression		Adult Physical Aggression		Adult Indirect Aggression	
	Men	Women	Men	Women	Men	Women
TV violence viewing	.21	.19	.17	.15	.03	.20
Perceived realism of TV violence	.22	.25	.14	.14	.05	.28
Identification with aggressive female characters	.15	.23	.05	.09	.01	.19
Identification with aggressive male characters	.29	.22	.14	.12	.05	.22

TABLE 15.2 Violent television viewing in childhood and adult aggression. Significant positive correlations are found between various measures of watching and identifying with television violence as a child and displaying both physical and more indirect forms of aggression as adults, with men showing more physical aggression and women showing more indirect aggression. Adapted from Huesmann et al. (2003).

lacking. Nonetheless, the naturalistic studies do show consistent correlations between higher levels of watching violent television and higher levels of aggression. For example, Table 15.2 shows one analysis of how viewing television in childhood was correlated with aggressive behavior 15 years later (Huesmann et al., 2003).

Unlike the experimental studies, naturalistic studies often have the appeal of looking at patterns of television viewing that occur over the course of several years, as opposed to an hour or two in a laboratory. Summarizing across many naturalistic studies, one meta-analysis of 400 studies on the relation between violence and television found a positive correlation of roughly .2 (Paik & Comstock, 1994; see also Hogben, 1998). As we will see shortly, even though a correlation of .2 means that most of the variations in violent behavior are not accounted for by variations in how much violent television is watched, it still represents a strongly significant effect for a population as a whole.

One classic study looked at links between how many hours adolescents spent watching violent television and the degree to which they reported engaging in aggressive behavior (Robinson & Bachman, 1972). Other studies have found correlations between watching violent television in childhood and engaging in aggressive behavior as adults many years later (Huesmann et al., 1984). As we have repeatedly seen, the obvious question in such cases is whether viewing aggression on television is causing children to become more aggressive or whether children who prefer violent television are also those who prefer to be aggressive throughout their lifespan. Thus, it is possible that some intrinsic aggressive tendency, or perhaps one that is socialized into the child by factors other than television, may lead the child to watch more violent television and to exhibit more aggressive behavior, without the television violence actually causing increases in a child's aggression. It is difficult to fully address this concern in nonexperimental studies, but statistical analyses designed to tease out evidence for causal effects do suggest that watching violence on television causes more aggressive behavior (Anderson et al., 2003; Huesmann et al., 2003).

An alarming pattern occurs across all the nonexperimental studies: the correlation between violent television watching and aggression seems to be rising. As seen in Figure 15.16, the rise has been most dramatic since 1995. One possible explanation for the rising correlation is simply that the quality of studies is improving and that the relation is being measured with increasing precision and is coming closer to the correlations found in carefully controlled experimental studies (Bushman & Anderson, 2001). An alternative explanation is that somehow aggression on television is becoming more influential on children's behavior, perhaps as expertise in programming and special effects increases.

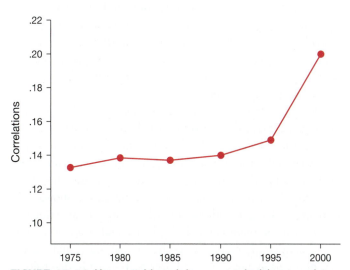

FIGURE 15.16 How watching violence on television correlates with violent behavior. This graph shows the cumulative correlations over the years between watching violent shows and violent behavior. As studies accumulate, the correlation has risen substantially, especially since 1995. Adapted from Bushman & Anderson (2001).

Experimental studies of the relationship between television and aggression allow us to more directly infer causation, even as we lose some of the naturalistic realism of the studies. In general, the experimental studies tend to show stronger effects of watching violent television than do the naturalistic studies. Recall from Chapter 12 the classic studies of children's inclination to model aggressive behaviors of adults after watching film clips showing adults beating up a toy Bobo doll (Bandura et al., 1961). In the years since those early studies, other experimental studies have shown similar relationships between observing violence on film and television and acting aggressively.

Aggressive behavior might increase because children start to accept higher levels of violence as normal, a process often called **desensitization**. One particularly chilling study had 44 fourth-graders watch either violent or nonviolent programming (Drabman & Thomas, 1974). All fourth-graders were then taken to a room where they were led to believe that they were keeping an eye on younger children in another room by observing them on a video monitor linked to a camera in the other room. In fact, the video monitor was not playing a live broadcast of events in the other room, but rather a filmed sequence of staged events in which there were gradually escalating violent physical actions. The children in the room initially played quietly together, but then they became increasingly destructive and engaged in more physical abuse toward each other, with the tape ending as they seemed to destroy the camera. The experimenters measured how long it took for the fourth-graders who were observing the monitors to seek out adult help to respond to the situation and whether they did so when physical abuse between the children was first seen. There was a strong effect from the sort of television programming that the fourth-graders had watched. Those who had watched violent television were much less likely to seek out adults when physical abuse first occurred, and they took much longer to seek out adult help. It appeared that those children had come to regard a much higher level of violence as acceptable.

Desensitization studies of this sort in both television and video game media demonstrate that children, as well as adults, can start to take certain levels of violence for granted if they watch enough of it on television (Carnagey et al., 2007). But desensitization does not in itself lead to increased aggressive behavior. Perhaps viewers of violent television shows stop noticing violence in others but still are just as restrained in committing it themselves. Indeed, it could even be argued that desensitization reduces the chance that individuals see the acts of others as aggressive and overreact—that is, desensitization may make their "fuse" longer and slower. In reality, most experts suspect that desensitization increases the tendency to violence by making the experience of violence a less aversive emotion, but there are not yet any definitive studies showing a link between desensitization and increased violent behavior (Anderson et al., 2003).

There is substantial evidence from a wide range of studies for a link between watching violence on television and increases in violent behavior. One classic laboratory study showed elementary and middle school children programs that varied in levels of violence and then presented them with scenarios in which they were asked to choose between one of two possible actions. For example, a researcher describes a situation to a child in which someone comes up to him and calls him names and then asks the child whether it is better to engage in one of two actions in response, such as hitting the person or telling an adult about the incident. The results clearly indicated that violent actions were chosen more often by viewers of violent episodes (Leifer & Roberts, 1972).

When children are compared with adults, the effects of violent television on children are often longer lasting than the effects on adults. When adults view violent television, they may experience a brief increase in arousal and priming of aggressive thoughts and actions; when children view violent television, it appears that they learn new, long-term methods for dealing with difficult situations, as well as a general desensitization toward violence (Bushman & Huesmann, 2006; Huesmann, 2007). This difference in age effects has important implications for studies that attempt to generalize results from adult studies to children.

> **Q:** Describe the overall findings of naturalistic and experimental studies on the effects of violent television programming on children and describe the tradeoffs of each approach.

It is, of course, difficult to determine just how much violence researchers can ethically elicit in children, especially of the interpersonal sort. Nonetheless, the vast majority of studies indicate that a substantial increase in physical and verbal aggression can be created in laboratory tasks by exposing children to violent programming (Anderson et al., 2003; Bushman & Huesmann, 2012; Comstock & Scharrer, 2006; Wilson, 2008). Despite these repeated results, however, some critics argue that the real-life effects of violent television on individual children are not that large and that researchers make too much out of the negative effects of violence in the media (Freedman, 2002; Gunter, 2008). This criticism is an important one that must be acknowledged. In the research literature, correlations at or near .3 between violent television watching and aggression are on the high end of the measured effects. This means that most of the time there will not be an observable effect of violent television programming on any given child's behavior. Statistically, only 10 percent of the variance in a child's aggressive behavior would be accounted for by a .3 correlation. Thus, even if a child spends every day of his summer vacation watching extremely violent television, the odds are that this experience will not lead to behavior problems in the child.

At the same time, when television violence is viewed as a public health threat in the same way as biological factors, its impact seems quite large (see Figure 15.17). Instead of asking about the likelihood of any given child engaging in violent acts as a result of watching violent television, we can instead ask whether, in a population as a whole, there will be a greater incidence of violence as a result of violent programming. Thus, if we consider a metropolitan area of 10 million people (such as the greater Chicago area), we can ask how many more violent events might occur because of a positive correlation between violent television and aggression. Considered that way, even a correlation of .2 could still mean that hundreds of additional incidents of violent behavior would occur in that region. In this manner, the effects of violent programming are considered in the same way that smoking is considered as contributing to lung cancer. Even among heavy lifelong smokers, the odds are that the smoking will not lead to death from lung cancer. Although the lifelong smoker is much more likely to die from lung cancer than a nonsmoker, the correlation is still far from 1. It is true, however, that a smoker is more than 10 times as likely to die from lung cancer as a nonsmoker. When watching violent television is viewed in this way, the public health threat of violence on television can be construed as one of the largest threats in the United States, second only to that of smoking. There is a stronger correlation between media violence and aggression than there is between condom use and sexual transmission of HIV, exposure to lead and IQ scores, and exposure to asbestos and laryngeal cancer (Bushman & Anderson, 2001). It is striking, especially in the wake of massive legal settlements in areas such as smoking and asbestos exposure, that the effects of media violence have never been adequately addressed. If, for example, studios and networks produced and distributed violent shows while fully knowing that such programming increased violent behavior, others might well hold them accountable for such actions. Indeed, some legal scholars have suggested that television should be treated as a "toxic environment" for children in much the same way that more traditional chemically toxic environments are treated (Woodhouse, 2004).

Q: If violence on television is considered a public health threat analogous to biological threats, how serious a threat does it seem to be relative to those other threats?

Responding to the Influences of Television Violence

Given that violence on television does seem to increase levels of aggression in many viewers, what options are open to parents to limit the effects? One option is to try to limit access to violent programming. In practice, this is difficult to do. Children often watch television in public places or at friends' houses, venues where parents have little or no control. In addition, it is not always obvious from the name of a program that there will be extensive violence in its content. Even in their own home, parents may have difficulty restricting access to violent television. They are certainly not present at all times when their children are watching television, and few parents have the time to carefully censor the content of all shows their children watch.

More official attempts to allow regulation of violence have not been widely implemented. In 1996, the U.S. Congress passed legislation requiring manufacturers to install V-chips in all television sets with screens larger than 13 inches by January 1, 2000 (see Figure 15.18). Despite unfounded opposition based on the claim that the chips would significantly add to the price of television sets, V-chip technology was soon made available in all television sets at virtually no increase in cost. Programs were rated by networks for level of violent and sexual content, and parents could select the level of violence they were willing to have on their televisions. This technological innovation, however, led to little real-life use by parents (Hazlett, 2004). Parents were mostly

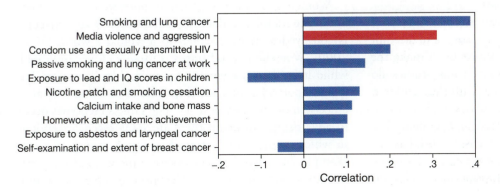

FIGURE 15.17 Television violence as a public health threat. When the correlations (both positive and negative) between various behaviors and outcomes are compared, the correlation between media violence and aggression is larger than all other major public health threats except for the correlation between smoking and lung cancer, which is only modestly higher. Adapted from Bushman & Anderson (2001).

FIGURE 15.18 Filtering out television violence. In 2000, following a recommendation made by President Clinton (shown here holding up a V-chip), the U.S. Congress mandated that all new television sets had to contain a V-chip, which could be set to filter out television shows containing different levels of violence. Even though most televisions soon had such chips, only a tiny percentage of parents ever programmed their televisions to limit their children's access to violent programming.

dren (as well as being aversive if the parents do not enjoy the content!).

In the end, censorship of content by parents or joint watching and commenting by parents may mitigate somewhat the influences of television violence on aggression in their children, but the effects of these interventions are likely to be modest given the practical difficulties involved. A more dramatic effect might occur if viewing of television of any sort were heavily restricted. But to avoid being hypocritical, parents would also need to cut back on their own viewing habits, and most are not willing to do so. Moreover, television acts as a form of "electronic babysitter" for many parents who are unable to engage in more interactive encounters with their children. Children are usually remarkably passive and docile when lounging in front of a television set (Condry, 1989), and this tranquilizing effect is not lost on parents or on car manufacturers, who routinely include small video displays as a highly attractive option in the family minivan.

> **Q:** Describe at least two different approaches to reducing the effects of television violence on children. How effective have these approaches been?

Stereotyping in the Media While the vast majority of research on the effects of television has focused on how violent content increases aggression, the effects of television may also involve gender, racial, and lifestyle stereotyping. Television programming shows young, traditionally attractive women far more often than their representation in the population and more often than it does so for men (Witt, 2000). When couples are shown, the casting director picks women who are considerably younger than the men, even if the ages in the script are meant to be quite close, thus conveying a sense that married women should look younger than they actually are. In addition, the average television or film actress is far more likely to have had extensive cosmetic surgery than is the norm in the general population, again creating a distorted image of body appearance.

Women and girls are generally portrayed as less smart and more submissive than men, and physical attractiveness is conveyed as more essential to a woman's worth (Witt, 2000). Women's marital status is usually clearly indicated, while it is often ambiguous for men. Men are more frequently portrayed in leadership roles or as being pivotal to a decision or change in events. The same stereotypes occur in advertising. Although there are some recent exceptions in which women are portrayed in smart, strong roles (for example, as judges, lawyers, doctors, and even as the president of a country), these are exceptions to a general pattern

unwilling to learn the new techniques for programming their televisions to block violent shows or did not want to deal with the hassles of having to turn the violence filters on and off for different viewers. Some cynical commentators have suggested that the V-chip was largely intended to be a public relations maneuver to placate V-chip advocates without ever threatening the ratings of television networks. That argument gains credibility given the minimal effect of V-chip technology. An additional side effect of censoring television violence in the home, whether by means of the V-chip or some other intervention, may be to make such programs become more desirable ("forbidden fruits") to the children who are not allowed to watch the programs at home. Although there are no systematic studies demonstrating such a possibility, parents do report that their children become especially eager and attentive audiences of forbidden shows when at their friends' houses.

Another option for parents who want to limit the effects of violent television programs is for the parents to attempt to reinterpret the violent content of shows or to make the shows less attractive to their children. Some studies do indicate that when parents watch shows with their children and voice concern over the violent episodes as they occur, children who might otherwise be at risk end up being less violent (Anderson et al., 2003), but extensive work has not yet been done in this area. Moreover, it is difficult for many busy parents to consistently watch television with their chil-

that has been consistent for decades (Collins, 2011). Moreover, across several types of media, there is an increasing trend to portray women, but not men, in explicit sexual roles (Bleakley et al., 2012; Hatton & Trautner, 2011).

It is commonly believed that such depictions give children distorted images of norms of appearance, affluence, and even diet. There are also frequent claims that the media pressures young women to engage in certain behaviors, pushing some into anorexia (Hamilton & Waller, 1993; see also Groesz et al., 2002; Kilbourne, 1994; see Chapter 17). One particularly dramatic suggestion of such influences arose from a study on the introduction of television into a rural community in Western Fiji in 1995 (Becker, 2004; Becker et al., 2002). In 3 years, exposure to prime-time soap operas featuring young female characters who were all attractive and thin was associated with a rise from almost no weight-conscious behaviors to 15 percent of adolescent girls reporting using induced vomiting to control weight and 69 percent reporting having been on diets (see Figure 15.19). Roughly half the girls thought that they were too fat. It certainly appeared that television had ushered in a new set of views of the preferred female body.

Television may also influence perceptions of norms of affluence and consumerism. The protagonists in most shows tend to be more affluent than most people in North America, let alone in other parts of the world (Taylor, 1989; Yang et al., 2008). Moreover, the activities of the protagonists are often consumer based, including shopping and attending events and clubs, and rarely show activities such as doing homework, household chores, or working at a desk (Anderson, 1995). In many ways, this bias is hardly surprising, as much of real life does not make good entertainment. But it may convey an

impression to viewers that their lifestyles are out of line with the "norms" presented on television. Given frequent claims of how television might distort children's perceptions of various norms (Woodhouse, 2004), there is a clear need for more focused experimental research on such issues.

Video Games, Computers, and the Internet

One of the most dramatic changes in recent years has been the surge in the use of video games, computers, and the Internet by children in developed countries and, increasingly, in developing and undeveloped regions. In addition, because the Internet and games can now be accessed not just through computers, but also through tablets and smartphones, many children are connected and playing games almost every waking hour and in every possible location. The patterns of usage are now so extensive that they have led researchers to initiate a wave of studies on the effects of these forms of media on children. Although the studies and effects are quite similar in many ways to research on television, there are important differences related to intrinsic properties of these forms of media, most notably their interactive features.

Video Games Playing video games now rivals the time children spend watching television (Rideout et al., 2010). The emerging literature on video games generally suggests that the effects of video games can be both more positive and more negative than the effects of television, in essence amplifying influences when a child is an active participant in a game as opposed to a passive viewer. In addition, as video games become ever more realistic and engrossing, their effects may increase as well (Greitemeyer, 2011). Finally, just as with television, the content of the video games is critical to whether they have positive or negative effects.

One surprising positive change that differs from the effects of television viewing involves improvements in attention skills, such as noticing objects and avoiding distractors (Green & Bavelier, 2003; Powers et al., 2013). Moreover, people with extensive experience playing video games can have a distinct advantage in learning laparoscopic surgical techniques that involve manipulations of robotic arms via joysticks and other computer interfaces (Rosser et al., 2007). This is hardly to say that aspiring surgeons should devote more energy to video games than to traditional academic experiences, but it is intriguing that, as surgical techniques increasingly use video and robotic interfaces, those techniques may come to draw on skills derived through extensive experience with video games. In many areas of expertise, it can take several thousand hours of practice to reach high levels of proficiency (Ericsson & Charness, 1994). Comparable effects of video

FIGURE 15.19 The introduction of television into rural Fiji. One study documented a close association between the introduction of U.S. network television programming into rural areas of Fiji and a very substantial rise in weight-conscious behaviors, ranging from dieting to eating disorders. The associations were primarily found for girls in late childhood and the teenage years.

Free Speech and Children's Rights

A discussion of children and the media should consider not just the media that children are exposed to but also the media that children produce. One of the most controversial topics in social policy concerning children involves restraints on what children are able to say and write. This topic brings into play issues concerning the moral development of children, the development of impulse control, and peer aggression, among many others. It also raises questions about whether children should be restricted in their own speech so as to protect others from that speech, and it thereby again introduces issues concerning the influence of media on children, even when it is produced by peers.

In many countries, free speech is one of the most cherished rights of its citizens. It may therefore seem ironic that free speech is not guaranteed for children and adolescents in some contexts, most notably in the schools. The legal rationale against granting free speech to children is based on theories about children's cognitive and social development as well as ideas of promoting the educational mission of schools. In 1988, the U.S. Supreme Court decided in *Hazelwood School District et al. v. Kuhlmeier et al.* that a group of high school students who were members of the Hazelwood East High School, in St. Louis County, Missouri, did not automatically have the protection of free speech and that the high school's principal was allowed to forbid publication in the school newspaper of items that he thought might embarrass members of the school community (for example, the effects of divorce on families) or that might be inappropriate for younger readers of the paper (for example, discussions of birth control and sexual activity).

Why was free speech not guaranteed in a high school newspaper, given that it is usually allowed on college campus newspapers? Why should high school students be forced to "shed their constitutional rights to freedom of speech or expression at the schoolhouse gate" (*Tinker v. Des Moines Independent Community School District,* 1969)? Some cases are related to concerns that the school newspaper might contain material that would be inappropriate for younger readers at the school, but many other cases simply involve speech that is uncomfortable for the faculty and administration of a school or that is perceived as "disruptive to the educational mission of the school" (Garnett, 2008). The notion of disruption, however, can be difficult to define and often seems to involve assumptions about how the immaturity of minors makes them more easily influenced. In one highly publicized case (*Morse v. Frederick,* 2007), a student in a public high school in Juneau, Alaska, was suspended from

---

game experience are now being found in other domains as well, such as learning how to remotely operate drone aircraft (McKinley et al., 2011).

Given that many children start playing video games before they even enter school, the cognitive effects of playing such games that are seen in adolescents may be building on many years of prior experience. Any adult without video game experience who tries to learn a new game along with a child rapidly realizes how much he is at a disadvantage as a learner. Children may have years of expertise gained from playing a wide variety of video games that gives them a huge head start even for learning a completely novel game.

Many video games are designed to teach specific skills, such as mathematics skills (Lopez-Morteo & Lopez, 2007) and various science topics (Minton, 2008). When the games are well designed, they usually have strong educational benefits (Swing & Anderson, 2008). In addition, video games have successfully been used to facilitate instruction in military strategy and operations, disease management, and of course airplane piloting. There are few popular video games that focus on prosocial behavior and even fewer studies of the positive effects of such games. But based on findings about the effects of prosocial television shows, researchers expect to find comparable if not even stronger effects of video games that reward prosocial, nonaggressive behavior (Wilson, 2008). In fact, such effects are now being uncovered by researchers. For example, one study randomly assigned college students either to a prosocial video game in which their goal was to take care of small creatures or to a neutral game involving falling shapes (Tetris). Later, the experiments staged an aggressive encounter between people in the laboratory and measured the likelihood of the game players to intervene. Those who had previously played the prosocial version intervened more than half the time, while those who had played the neutral game intervened only one-fifth of the time (Greitemeyer & Osswald, 2010). Other studies have shown that even when playing violent video games, if the players form cooperative teams, some prosocial

school when he held up a banner with the phrase "BONG HiTS 4 JESUS" as an Olympic torch was being carried down the street (see Figure 15.20). Even though the student did not display the banner on school grounds, the U.S. Supreme Court ruled that the

FIGURE 15.20 Freedom of speech and minors. When a group of high school students unfurled a provocative banner on a public street while a parade passed in Juneau, Alaska, a student from an area high school was suspended for holding up the banner. The case, which was heard by the U.S. Supreme Court, raised fundamental questions about why the developmental status of minors should curtail some rights concerning free speech.

suspension was constitutional. The Court ruled that the banner's message had the potential to be disruptive to the school because it might encourage students to engage in illegal drug use. The same behavior by a college student or a town resident would be protected under the First Amendment to the U.S. Constitution. What is it about younger children that suggests that they should be treated differently?

The challenge here is knowing what is appropriate in terms of constraints on what children are allowed to say or have access to (Hudson, 2004). Some, for example, have argued that in the post-Columbine era, students' rights, free speech among them, are being trampled through such actions as censorship in attempts to ensure their safety (Calvert, 2000). It would seem that the only way to have informed opinions about when to curtail such rights would be to have better research on a host of developmental questions. In particular, is there something about younger children that requires that they need protection from certain kinds of information while older youth do not? In what ways are the taste and judgment of younger children deficient and in need of monitoring? Are aspects of children's ability to engage in moral reasoning relevant to their entitlement to free speech? As children and adolescents have ever-increasing access to public forums through such means as Internet websites, blogs, and social networking, the challenges of constraining their free speech appropriately are also increasing. Scholars are now asking how developmental psychology might inform debates about the boundaries of free speech for children and adolescents (Levesque, 2007).

behaviors may also be promoted in later tasks (Greitemeyer et al., 2012). The authors of these studies strongly suggest that such positive effects of prosocial games should also be found in quite young children, but large-scale experimental studies still need to be done with younger populations.

When video games contain violence, they may facilitate aggression even more than television programs, as video games foster and train active aggression as part of the experience rather than offering passive viewing, as is the case with television. A child learning to play a video game becomes more and more skilled at killing, maiming, and brutalizing other agents, many of which can look like normal humans. Although the body of research on video games and aggression is less extensive than that on television, most reviews of the research conclude that, similar to the findings with television, there is a relation between the time spent playing violent video games and increased levels of aggression. Moreover, the relation is found in both naturalistic studies, where causation is more difficult to infer, and experimental studies,

where the causal influence is much clearer but the effects are more likely to be measured only on a short-term basis (Anderson & Bushman, 2001; Gentile & Anderson, 2006; Sherry, 2001; Swing & Anderson, 2008). Researchers suggest that the same clusters of factors that mediate the influence of violent television on aggressive behavior are at work in video games as well, including desensitization, arousal, priming of certain actions and response tendencies, and learning new ways to aggress (Anderson et al., 2010; Swing & Anderson, 2008). In addition, researchers have argued that video games have properties that may cause greater effects than television. These properties include increased identification with the aggressor (in many games the player can pick an aggressor that he identifies with), active participation, rehearsal of aggressive actions from start to finish, direct rewards for engaging in violent behavior, and a much higher incidence of violent episodes per hour. Heavy involvement in aggressive role-playing games on the Internet may have similar effects (Holtz & Appel, 2011; Krahé et al., 2011; Lee et al., 2010). In some experimental studies with children, simply playing violent video games for a few hours can increase levels of both aggressive cognition (speed of accessing violent concepts) and aggressive behavior, such as deciding on harsh punishments for opponents in games (Anderson et al., 2007). Playing violent video games also results in decreased empathy and prosocial behavior, with these effects apparently equally strong in both males and females (Anderson & Hanson, 2010).

In short, although video games have great potential for positive effects, ranging from well-documented influences in cognition and learning to effects in the prosocial realm, they also can have well-documented negative effects, depending on the content of the games. In particular, when the games contain violence, as the vast majority of popular video games do, they increase aggressive thoughts and behaviors in children at least as much as watching violent television shows does and quite possibly a good bit more.

Internet Communities In a relatively brief period of time, a whole new kind of community has emerged that children and adolescents, as well as adults, have joined in droves: social networks on the Internet (Subrahmanyam & Greenfield, 2008). Although social network sites such as MySpace and Facebook officially prohibit users younger than 14 or 13 years of age, assessments of real users suggest that many of the users are quite a bit younger (Rosen et al., 2008). By some estimates, almost 40 percent of children between 9 and 12 years old use Facebook (Livingstone et al., 2011). In addition, while many children and young adolescents are using social network sites to create communities of friends and role-playing groups, and while parents report that they are concerned about what goes on in such Internet communities, in practice most parents are unaware of what their children are actually doing when logged onto such communities (Rosen et al., 2008). More broadly, in developed countries, and increasingly in developing countries, many children are using the Internet by the fourth grade, through e-mail, instant messaging services, chat rooms, and other ways that connect individuals (Blais et al., 2008; Lenhart et al., 2001). When simple access to the Internet of any type is examined, even 25 percent of 5-year-olds have some access (see Figure 15.21). In addition, use of the Internet for such activities as chat rooms, instant messaging, and role-playing games occurs widely across the entire socioeconomic spectrum (see Table 15.3).

Scholars have been divided over the effects of Internet activity on social development. Some suggest that social interactions on the Internet are a poor substitute for real-world social interactions and result in weakened real-world social relationships and loneliness (Kraut et al., 1998). Others propose that the Internet provides opportunities for maintaining, enriching, and discovering new social relationships and thereby enhances social relationships, intimacy, and a sense of belong-

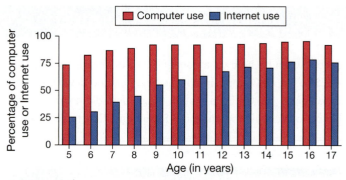

FIGURE 15.21 Percentage of computer use or Internet use by age. In the United States, the use of computers and the Internet has become widespread. Even 25 percent of 5-year-olds in 2001 used the Internet. From DeBell & Chapman (2003), based on data from the U.S. Census Bureau (2001).

ing to a community of peers (Valkenburg & Peter, 2007). One possible consequence is that children and adolescents are likely to disclose personal details about themselves to relative strangers far more quickly online than in person (Bargh et al., 2002; Gross et al., 2002), with the possible effect of forming much more intimate friendships in a shorter period of time while not really having those people as normal friends.

A closer look at Internet use patterns by children and adolescents suggests how proposals for both negative and positive effects may be true in specific contexts. In particular, we can partition social interactions on the Internet into two kinds: those that continue relationships developed in the real world, taking them into the Internet via e-mail, instant messaging, and status updates, and those that involve meeting strangers online via chat rooms and social networking sites (Blais et al., 2008). The use of the Internet to support already formed real-world relationships generally seems to have positive social benefits, with children and adolescents experiencing stronger and more satisfying social relationships in ways that seem to build and enhance friendships and romantic relationships (Manago et al., 2012; Reich et al., 2012). In contrast, those who form new relationships with strangers online generally find them to be less satisfying and experience increased alienation and lower-quality friendships. While it does appear that the majority of children use the Internet to build on existing real-world relationships, as many as a quarter of those in some age groups may focus on developing friendships with strangers (Blais et al., 2008). Moreover, in some cases, patterns of online media usage are related to negative social outcomes. For example, one study of over 3,000 girls between the ages of 8 and 12 found that girls who showed high use of Internet media, especially online videos, experienced increased negative social interaction (they had trouble making friends or engaging in social activities and disapproval by their par-

Internet activity	Family Income				
	Less than $20,000	$20,000–$34,999	$35,000–$49,999	$50,000–$74,999	$75,000 or more
Completing school assignments	63.5	65.8	68.7	73.2	78.2
E-mail or instant messaging	45.6	54.3	61.6	68.3	75.8
Playing games	58.1	61.4	65.3	63.7	62.6
News/weather/sports	32.2	33.8	33.0	38.9	42.3
Finding information on products	24.0	28.7	30.2	34.7	41.6
Chat rooms or listservs	20.1	17.4	19.5	20.6	22.5
Watching/listening to TV, movies, radio	19.3	18.1	19.4	18.5	20.4
Making purchases	5.9	6.1	6.7	10.5	16.8
Phone calls	4.5	3.3	3.3	2.6	3.0
Taking a course online	1.5	0.7	1.2	0.7	0.9
Other	1.7	1.7	1.3	2.0	1.7

TABLE 15.3 Internet use patterns (shown as percentages) and socioeconomic status. Usage patterns of the Internet are quite similar across various socioeconomic groups, with a tendency toward higher usage rates in most categories for more affluent children. Adapted from DeBell & Chapman (2003), based on data from the U.S. Census Bureau (2001).

ents of their friends). In contrast, higher levels of face-to-face communication were associated with more positive social well-being (Pea et al., 2012).

Other studies suggest that a primary focus with online friends can lead to a form of "Internet addiction" in which children of both sexes seem to become intensely preoccupied with online activities as opposed to face-to-face interactions (Smahel et al., 2012). Most children, however, seem to use the Internet in a manner that helps promote and maintain offline relationships. In addition, only a relatively small number of children seem to engage in Internet activities that are unsafe with respect to exposure to either inappropriate content or individuals (Valcke et al., 2011). For parents who are concerned about the time their children are spending on the Internet, it is clearly important to get a sense of what activities their children are engaging in to assess whether they might be harmful. As noted earlier, the vast majority of parents find it difficult to monitor Internet activity at that level of detail. Fortunately, the early fears of children being exposed to nearly continuous hazards seem to be heavily exaggerated.

One troubling pattern in Internet activity among children and adolescents is known as **cyberbullying**, a form of aggression over the Internet, often by a group against an individual (Li, 2007; Ybarra & Mitchell, 2004, 2008). Cyberbullying can occur in real time as users gang up on one another in an instant message board or chat room. It can also occur over longer periods by posting hurtful messages or graphics on Web pages or bulletin boards. Cyberbullying raises concerns because of the ways it departs from real-world bullying (Menesini & Spiel, 2012). Cyberbullies can be anonymous, they can search out a wider range of vulnerable targets, and they can more easily find willing accomplices. The potential to embarrass or humiliate another person can be greatly exacerbated by having a much larger audience to witness the event. In addition, cyberbullying tends to be even less monitored by adults, who may be largely oblivious to harsh bullying that would be noticed in the real world. This may be a particularly acute problem because incidences of bullying can spiral out of control in a community when parents and school authorities have little or no awareness that it is happening. Finally, any feelings of empathy that might be triggered when a victim is being bullied face-to-face are not likely to be triggered on the Internet (Li, 2007; see also Blais, 2008; Patchin & Hinduja, 2006; Smith et al., 2008, for related discussions of the unique aspects of cyberbullying). Moreover, cyberbullies report lower feelings of remorse for their actions than do bullies in the physical world (Slonje et al., 2012).

It appears that bullies on the Internet are often the same individuals who engage in bullying in the real world (Blais, 2008; Gradinger et al., 2009; Olweus, 2012; Vazsonyi et al., 2012). The effects of cyberbullying seem quite similar to those of real-world bullying, with victims showing decreased levels of social belonging and a worse quality of social life at school. In addition, because cyberbullying is usually a form of relational social aggression, it appears to be practiced more by girls than by boys (Blais, 2008; Smith et al., 2008; Sourander et al., 2010). Taken together, the research on cyberbullying suggests that parents and other authority figures need to maintain their own presence on the Internet and a level of Web literacy if they are to have some influence in stopping inappropriate aggressive behavior between peers on the Internet.

The effects of cyberbullying can be so devastating as to compel a victim to commit suicide. In a widely publicized case in 2006, Megan Meier, a 13-year-old girl, was befriended by a "Josh Evans" on MySpace. But Josh Evans was a fictitious name invented by the mother of a former friend of Meier who was worried about what Meier was saying about her daughter online. After initially sending Meier friendly messages, the mother and others had "Josh Evans" turn on Meier and reject her on the website. The rejection was seen as leading to Meier's suicide. This case also illustrates how bullying of a child can sometimes not just come from peers but from adults as well when they think their identities can be concealed. In short, cyberbullying has the potential to amplify the effects of offline bullying in devastating ways. But it is important to also understand that its prevalence is far less than traditional bullying, that the extreme sensationalized accounts are very rare, and that very often the same individuals are involved in cyberbullying and traditional bullying (Olweus, 2012).

> Q: How might the greatly increased presence of computers, Internet access, and video games influence the social development of children?

Roles in the Larger Culture

In addition to the influences of various specific factors on children, such as television, video games, and peers, the broader culture as a whole can exert its own influences on children, influences that may largely be invisible to those within that culture but obvious to those outside it. These influences can be seen as setting up certain roles that all members of that culture are expected to play in social interactions. We will consider roles that apply similarly to all members of a culture or subculture, as well as roles that seem to be organized around gender. Throughout this book we have considered cultural and gender differences in specific contexts as they arise, but it is useful in this chapter to consider cultural and gender roles more directly. A major theme

of this chapter is the influences of ever-widening communities on the developing child. We therefore will ask how cultures and subcultures can cause children to come to adopt certain "lenses" on reality that result in their interpreting situations and adopting values quite differently from those who come from different backgrounds. In addition, we will see how socialization of attributional styles, as discussed earlier this chapter, can be a mechanism of immersing a child in a cultural role.

Distinctive Cultural and Subcultural Roles

One example of the role played by culture is seen in how children who grow up in the southern United States react to insults as opposed to how children in the rest of the country react to them. The culture in the South has been labeled a **culture of honor** in that many people in the South endorse greater levels of violence in certain situations, most notably when they have been insulted or perceived threats to their home or property (Nisbett & Cohen, 1996; see Figure 15.22). Adult southerners show higher levels of anger responses, including greater testosterone and cortisol levels, to threats that northerners might shrug off as inconsequential. Similarly, acts of violence in response to insults or threats to home and property are viewed as more acceptable by southerners. This difference is confined to violent responses of the sort just described, not to violence of all sorts. The culture of honor is sometimes compared with cultures that emphasize "dignity" or "keeping face," with each culture having particular ways of perceiving and reacting to social situations (Leung & Cohen, 2011).

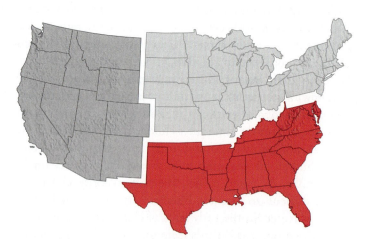

FIGURE 15.22 The culture of honor in the South. Children who are brought up in the southeastern United States tend to adopt a "culture of honor" in which acts of violence in response to insults or threats to property are seen as more acceptable than in other areas of the United States. Similar cultures of honor have been found in other regions of the world where children are socialized in ways that teach accepted forms of response to aggression and insult.

Adherence to this culture of honor seems to take place by middle childhood, and it may be partly learned through different patterns of child rearing in which violent responses to perceived insults are often seen as a legitimate way of socializing children. It may also be mediated by how the culture, parents, and peers shift the social attributional styles of children. Thus, as discussed earlier in this chapter, children vary in the attributions they make about ambiguous situations. Attitudes produced by different cultures may cause group differences in how ambiguous situations are interpreted and what the thresholds are for considering an act as aggressive (Dodge, 2006). These differences can appear very early in development. For example, one study showed behaviors and social categorizations that are typical of a culture of honor appearing earlier and more robustly in young Spanish children than in young Dutch children (Rodriguez Mosquera et al., 2000). Cultures also vary in the extent to which their children are guided toward making either compliant or defiant responses, with the result that different scripts are activated in difficult situations (Chen & French, 2008). Thus, in rural Nepal, children from the high-status Brahman caste are not rebuked for using anger to solve problems in difficult situations, while children from the low-status Tamang caste are strongly discouraged from doing so (Cole et al., 2002, 2006).

> Q: What is the "culture of honor"? In what ways might it influence how children from such a culture react in certain situations?

A different cultural contrast discussed earlier in this book (see Chapters 1, 12, and 13) is between collectivist and individualist cultures (Triandis, 1995). Individualist cultures, which include most Western cultures, stress the rights of the individual as the most important consideration in a society. The United States is often said to have one of the most individualist cultures. Collectivist cultures, which exist throughout the world, tend to emphasize the rights of the group relative to those of the individual. It is not simply the case, however, that a particular culture produces only one kind of orientation. When researchers examine parenting styles cross-culturally, they find that both forms of cultural values are taught to young children in all cultures, even if these cultures are normally labeled collectivist or individualist (Wang & Tamis-Lamonda, 2003). But within a particular culture, a child's social status may influence what values are expressed in what contexts. Thus, dominant and powerful members of a culture often find it easier to embrace moral reasoning from an individualist perspective (Turiel, 2002). Moreover, there are also some gender differences in patterns of socialization across cultures, leading to differences in what values are expressed by girls and boys.

Allowing for these variations within cultures as a function of social status and gender, it has still repeatedly been observed that children in individualist societies are strongly socialized to act as individuals who are self-directed and have their own personal styles. Children in collectivist societies are strongly socialized to identify with a group and to think about the common good (Chen & French, 2008). This also seems to be reflected in play. Children from individualist cultures show increased tendencies to engage in "sociodramatic" play, meaning that they tend to act out more fantastical scenarios, often with superheroes or other exotic actors, playing dramatic and unrealistic roles in which they personally save the day. In contrast, children from collectivist cultures tend to act out more mundane, everyday situations that involve family members. Children from these two cultures also tend to resolve conflicts differently. Thus, when groups of four 7-year-olds from China and groups of four 7-year-olds from Canada played with a single highly desirable toy, the Chinese children tended to respond more positively to requests by peers for possession of the toy. Moreover, passive and reticent behaviors were treated with more group acceptance by the Chinese children than by the Canadian children. It was also common for Chinese children to defer to one or two children as group "leaders" who coordinated actions of the group with respect to the toy. Canadian children, on the other hand, referred more to norms of sharing and were more likely to spontaneously give the toy to a peer (French et al., 2011). This study, which had several subtle cultural contrasts, illustrates how in a specific setting and task, cultural differences can manifest themselves in unique and complex ways.

Socialization differences are also seen in parental views of how children should control themselves under stress and how they should handle conflicts with peers. Parents in collectivist cultures are less tolerant of overt conflicts among children, while parents in individualist cultures see merit in some level of disagreement and in defending one's own views. Similarly, parents in collectivist cultures highly value self-regulation skills in difficult situations or conflicts and place a higher priority on the importance of preserving harmony, even if it is at some expense to individual rights (Chen & French, 2008).

These cultural differences have also been interpreted in terms of Bronfenbrenner's ecological systems approach to development, which has been used to interpret many patterns in this chapter (Chen & French, 2008). Children adapt to the niches in which they grow up, finding ways to fit their talents and natures within the culture around them. The dynamic nature of such adaptation is vividly seen in cases where cultures change dramatically over time. One of the first documented instances occurred in the 1930s when the great Soviet psychologist Alexander Luria went to central Asia to study what happened as rural peasants became assimilated into a town and the emerging Soviet culture

(Luria, 1974). Although Luria's investigations largely focused on cognitive factors, they showed how, as peasant children and their parents learned to read, write, and function within Soviet culture, their cognitive styles and ways of interpreting situations began to change and they became better able to fit into the radically changing social structures around them. Later studies have applied this analysis of historical change to the collectivist/individualist contrast. For example, parents in traditional cultures in Turkey shifted away from collectivist ideals to individualist ones concerning their views on child rearing when they moved into cities and became more affluent (Chen & French, 2008). Similarly, as China went through revolutionary changes toward a market economy in the 1990s, researchers found shifts in the traits that parents and peers valued in children. For example, during the early 1990s, childhood traits that were compatible with group harmony, such as shyness, were perceived positively and were related to peer acceptance. But by the end of the decade, those same traits were perceived negatively and associated with peer rejection, as the ability to excel and stand out became increasingly prized (Chen et al., 2005; Chen & French, 2008).

The message of the collectivist/individualist contrast may extend to other supposed contrasts between cultures. Cultures are rarely, if ever, exclusively dedicated to one cognitive style or value system. Instead, most children in most cultures can be thought of as being exposed to most variations. As they grow older, children start to master nuances of how different styles and value systems are likely to be favored in local cultural contexts. Overall, this can amount to broad differences between cultures, but the subtleties and contextually induced variations should always be kept in mind as well (Conry-Murray & Turiel, 2012; Rentfrow et al., 2008).

> **Q:** What are some general ways in which cultures vary in their perspectives of the social world? Are these perspectives better thought of as fixed limitations or as default biases?

Gender Roles and Stereotyping

As we saw in Chapter 14, quite young children are aware of their gender. But how do they learn to map certain activities and objects onto their gender so as to conform to their culture's stereotypes? Although there are arguments that some preferred activities and toys may arise from children's own dispositions, it also seems clear that the culture at large provides considerable information about what it considers to be gender-typical behaviors and preferences. It is thought that children first identify themselves with a gender, then observe what behaviors, preferences, and beliefs are associated with both genders, and then usually adopt the gender behaviors, preferences, and beliefs that are typical of their own gender (Bigler & Liben, 2007; Martin & Halverson, 1981; Ruble & Martin, 1998).

While gender-based toy preferences emerge quite early, at least by 2 years of age (Weinraub et al., 1984), inferences about complex roles and activities take considerably longer to develop, with a majority of children not matching activities to gender until late preschool or early elementary school (Campbell et al., 2004). For example, while a 2-year-old boy might prefer playing with trucks to playing with dolls, not until 4 or 5 years of age might he actually know that certain activities are stereotypically done by boys or girls. Such activities can include hobbies, careers, and even intellectual pursuits, such as mathematics. For example, by second grade, many children, especially boys, see math as an especially appropriate activity for boys (Cvencek et al., 2011). Although these particular stereotypes may vary from culture to culture, it does appear that in all the cultures that were studied, gender-based stereotypes are picked up on at roughly the same time (Knobloch et al., 2005). Thus, the cognitive factors involved in adopting cultural stereotypes involve both universal processes and those that are specific to a particular culture (Kohlberg, 1966).

If cultures can influence perceptions of gender-appropriate activities, can they also affect positive and negative attitudes toward the work typically done by different genders? Unfortunately, there appears to be a widespread effect of how society values different kinds of work associated with different genders, and it seems to be difficult to change. Consider one series of studies looking at how children perceive the relative status of pink- and blue-collar jobs (Liben et al., 2001). Children at ages 6 and 11 years were asked to judge the status of various jobs and their own personal interest in the jobs. First, they were asked to judge familiar jobs, such as doctor, farmer, dentist, plumber, truck driver, auto mechanic, and scientist (culturally masculine jobs), and fashion model, librarian, nurse, secretary, teacher, and bank teller (culturally feminine jobs). Girls and boys at both ages judged the masculine jobs to have a higher status (as measured by questions such as "How hard do you think it is to learn to be a(n) ____?" or "How important is the job of being a(n) _____?"), while saying that they would be more interested in actually doing the jobs that corresponded to the stereotypes associated with their gender.

This pattern of results, however, does not make it clear how the linkage between gender, status, and occupation gets set up in the first place. Perhaps children see the higher status accorded to people in specific jobs and then note the dominant gender. Alternatively, they might form a stereotype that men's work is of higher status, regardless of what it is, simply because it is performed by the "higher-status" gender. To test this second alternative, Liben and her colleagues created novel occupations to which children could not have had any prior exposure and described them to a child either with all males engaging in the occupation or all females, as shown in Figure 15.24. The researchers asked younger and older children the status questions and interest questions. The older children showed a clear gender-linked status rating, judging exactly the same occupation as being of higher status when modeled by males. The younger children showed no significant difference in their ratings based on whether the job was modeled by a male or female; there were no differences in their interest in doing the jobs, and the gender of the children did not influence how they judged the status of the jobs (Liben et al., 2001).

The results suggest that for familiar jobs, gender stereotypes emerge quite early and that jobs typically associated with males are valued more highly. Apparently, this value structure then becomes an interpretive schema for prejudging the status of totally novel occupations as a function of the gender that models that occupation. One obvious question for future research is whether there might be dramatic cross-cultural differences in the extent to which occupations gain or lose status merely as a function of which gender typically holds that kind of job.

One intriguing finding on the emergence of gender stereotypes is that as younger children learn and consolidate a stereotype and before they learn to be more flexible, they may hold stronger stereotypes than older children (Martin & Ruble, 2004). It seems that initially, at around age 3, they struggle to learn a stereotype and that during that period, they apply it unevenly to a sex. Then, when they clearly master the stereotype, they tend to apply it far too rigidly as an essentially all-or-none statement about appropriateness of an activity for males or females. Thus, a 5-year-old might be observed to vehemently insist that police officers can only be men, even if that child has regularly observed female police officers in his neighborhood. This rigidity may be related to an early tendency to see gender roles as closely linked to biological essences (Taylor et al., 2009). As the stereotype is mastered in later childhood and becomes easy to deploy, children tend to become increasingly flexible in the way they use it (see Figure 15.23). Even younger children, however, can show some flexibility when they think about the context in which a gender norm is observed, such as when it occurs in a different culture (Conry-Murray & Turiel, 2012). This may provide ways of helping younger children abandon rigid stereotypes.

The general process of forming group-based stereotypes has been examined within the framework of what is known as **developmental intergroup theory** (Bigler & Liben, 2007). According to this theory, at least as early as age 4, children start to notice perceptually salient group differences and attach these to stereotypes. (This especially happens in regard to "minority groups," groups that are proportionally smaller in an overall population.) The salience of such

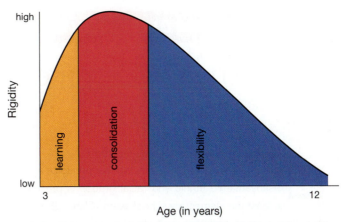

FIGURE 15.23 Gender stereotype rigidity and age. The rigidity of gender stereotypes, as learned from a culture, reaches a peak at roughly 5 years of age. Adapted from Martin & Ruble (2004).

groups is further enhanced when the culture at large tends to label them, as when a teacher says, "Good morning *boys* and *girls*." Quite remarkably, negative attitudes toward a group can be produced in just a matter of a few weeks. In one study, researchers randomly assigned children as young as 6 to either a blue-colored T-shirt group or a green-colored T-shirt group, and teachers had the children form lines or be seated or do other tasks based on whether they were wearing a blue or green T-shirt. Even though both groups were treated equally, within a few weeks, the children in each group had increased negative attitudes toward the members of the other group (Bigler et al., 1997). If bias can be found in such artificial cases with no real differences in treatment, it is easy to see how much stronger the effects can be in the real world. Later studies have shown that 5-year-olds will quickly adopt negative biases to an out-group that is set up on clearly arbitrary grounds and will distort information so that it is positively construed for the in-group and negatively construed for the out-group (Dunham et al., 2011; see Scientific Method box). More naturalistically, even preschoolers show group favoritism at an implicit level that is just as strong as it is in later childhood and adulthood. The preschool children seem to be "prepared" to develop such implicit prejudices and to quickly adopt them at full strength (Dunham et al., 2013).

Biases can also emerge from other superficial markers of out-group status, such as accent. For example, when two novel speakers were observed by 2-year-olds, both U.S. and French children preferred to give a "present" to the individual who was a native speaker as opposed to giving it to someone who was speaking with a foreign accent (Kinzler et al., 2012). Even younger infants (10-month-olds) preferred toys that were modeled by people with native accents as opposed to foreign accents. Children also preferred to associate with those who had their same native accent (Kinzler et al., 2009).

The use of stereotypes to predict the behaviors of others does not require a rich sense of the mental lives of others, which is part of the reason stereotypes are so pernicious.

The Development of Racial and Ethnic Occupational Stereotypes

For many years, it has been known that prejudice against disadvantaged ethnic and racial groups is present by at least the elementary school years (Clark, 1955). The nature of prejudice and discrimination has changed in the past few decades, however, from explicit and willful attacks on other groups to more implicit forms of discrimination in which the actor often believes that he is not prejudiced (Dovidio et al, 1997; Fazio & Olson, 2003; Wittenbrink et al., 1997). Interestingly, the attitudes of parents and peers do not always predict those of children (Aboud & Doyle, 1996; Stephan, 1999). Children seem to be most influenced by those peers and adults whom they most respect and who discuss prejudice in ways that touch on topics that the children care most about (Aboud & Fenwick, 1999). In addition, some forms of prejudice may arise from observations of how the culture at large seems to treat and value different groups. In the United States, it has repeatedly been shown that both European-American and African-American children tend to develop negative stereotypes regarding African Americans (Aboud, 1988; Spencer & Markstrom-Adams, 1990), assuming that positive traits, such as being intelligent or nice, are more likely to be seen in European Americans and that negative traits are more likely to be seen in African Americans.

One line of work asks how children's views of occupations might be influenced by these ethnic and racial stereotypes (Bigler et al., 2003). This research follows the same approach as that used in studies of gender stereotypes and children's evaluations of occupations (Liben et al., 2001). African-American children from the first and sixth grades and from higher and lower socioeconomic status (SES) groups were asked about the status of familiar and novel occupations and also about their interest in engaging in those jobs themselves. For the familiar jobs, even the first-graders had already learned from their culture stereotypes about the relation of job status to the dominant ethnic and racial groups, assuming that European Americans were more likely to dominate in the higher-status jobs and African Americans in the lower-status jobs. This difference was just as strong in African-American children whose parents were from high-SES backgrounds and thus occupied high-status jobs. Evidently, counterexamples from their own family were not sufficient to block the cultural stereotype. At the same time, and contrary to gender results, the children all indicated a preference to have the higher-status jobs, even though they perceived such jobs as being dominated by a racial group different from their own.

The most compelling result, however, came in a study modeled closely after the gender study described in Figure 15.24. Novel occupations were pictured with either European-American models or African-American models doing the same jobs. For exactly the same occupation, the race of the models had a large impact on status ratings by both first- and sixth-graders, with the occupation being granted higher status when modeled by European Americans. The children also tended to show a tendency to have a greater interest in pursuing a job when it was modeled by European Americans. This result has been echoed by other findings, including the finding that children in South Africa tend to associate racial groups with social class (Olson et al., 2012).

This constellation of results illustrates the challenges of reducing stereotypes about occupations and roles and reducing the use of those stereotypes to drive prejudices about types of peoples. Sadly, it seems that even if an underprivileged group makes great strides by moving into a profession previously populated by a dominant group, unless those strides are made in many fields at the same time, those advances may be undercut by a reduction of the perceived status of the profession.

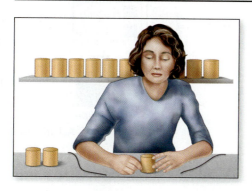

FIGURE 15.24 Job status and gender. Illustrations based on a study in which a novel occupation (here called "a clipster") was described to children with either all-male or all-female workers. At age 11, children accorded the same job much higher status when it was modeled by males. Adapted from Liben et al. (2001).

Hypothesis:

By age 5, assignment to a clearly arbitrary group can cause immediate biases against members of another group.

Method:

1. Sixty-four 5- and 6-year-olds were randomly assigned either to a group that wore green T-shirts or to a group that wore blue T-shirts, with assignment based on the children choosing a coin from the experimenter's closed hand.

2. Children heard one story about a child in a picture who wore the same-colored T-shirt as the participant and another story about a child who wore the other-colored shirt. Both stories assigned an equal number of positive and negative behaviors to the child in the picture (four each).

3. All children were asked to recall details of the stories and to choose which child protagonist they wanted to play with.

4. Researchers coded memory of positive and negative behaviors and playmate choice.

Results:

Participants recalled significantly more positive behaviors about in-group characters than about out-group characters and showed a tendency to recall more negative behaviors about out-group characters. They also strongly preferred in-group characters as potential playmates.

Conclusion:

Even though membership in the group was clearly arbitrary, children as young as 5 processed information differently about characters that matched their in-group versus those in an out-group.

Source study: Dunham et al. (2011).

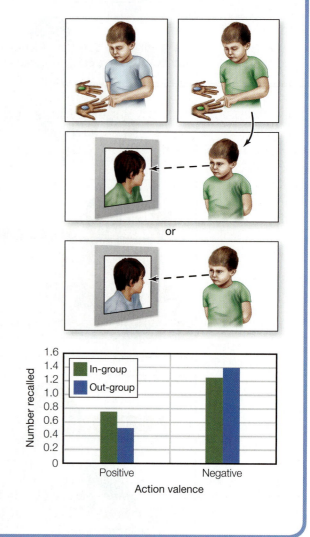

We only need to associate negative behaviors with a certain group to predict how they will behave. Those predictions may be more wrong than right, but they are often made in cases of racist and gender-based stereotypes. Because we do not need to take into account another's beliefs and desires when using a stereotype to predict behavior, even individuals with autism can use stereotypes even though they are unable to pass traditional theory of mind tasks (Hirschfeld et al., 2007). It could be that sophisticated insight into another person's mind would lead to empathy and thereby blunt the bias. But unfortunately, sophisticated insight into other minds does not guarantee open-mindedness toward other groups. In fact, in one study, elementary school children who were less egocentric and more aware of how an out-group's preferences might differ from their own also showed more

negative bias toward those out-groups. Apparently, having additional information on how the two groups potentially differed enabled children to build up stronger reasons for their biases (Abrams, 2011).

As children begin to enter middle school, they start to realize the inappropriateness of holding negative stereotypes. This emerging awareness can in some cases cause older children to do worse than younger children on tasks that would be most easily solved by explicitly acknowledging race. For example, when 8- and 9-year-olds were shown pictures of 40 faces that varied on several dimensions, including race, and had to guess which one the experimenter had in mind, they solved the task more quickly and with fewer questions than 10- and 11-year-olds (Apfelbaum et al., 2008). The older children were more reluctant to use explicit references to race to solve the task even when it would clearly have helped them to do so, whereas the younger children were relatively oblivious to the social discomfort of talking about others in terms of their race.

Parental behavior is related to racial bias in their children, but perhaps not in ways that you might think at first. For example, one study of European-American mothers and their children found that virtually all the mothers in the study used "color-blind" language in reading race-themed books to their children, and thus the way they referred to other races in that context did not predict racial bias in the children. However, those children whose mothers had a higher proportion of non-European-American friends showed considerably less racial bias than those children whose mothers had fewer non-European-American friends (Pahlke et al., 2012). Apparently, children are more influenced by their parents' actual relationships with people from other ethnic groups than by how they talk about them.

> **Q:** Describe some parallels and differences in the development of gender and racial stereotypes.

Conclusions

The child's life outside of the family clearly matters. At times in development, the influences of peers can be truly dramatic and can seem to overwhelm the influence of parents. In addition, the culture at large, through its media and simply through daily encounters with its rituals, institutions, and workers, communicates a host of beliefs, attitudes, and stereotypes to young children. For the most part, these influences are implicit, occurring outside of awareness; indeed, those who hold certain prejudices and stereotypes are often shocked when those mental views are revealed to them. The cognitive components of social interactions and of cultural influences remain a largely unexplored area but one that is gaining a great deal of attention in recent research. The challenge for the future is to integrate these cognitive components with the social and motivational factors that govern the interactions between children, their peers, and their larger culture. Many of these issues can also be fruitfully informed by taking a social ecological perspective on development in which we ask how children end up fitting into social ecosystems.

Although all areas of developmental psychology must confront the tradeoffs between naturalistic observational studies and experimental paradigms, this dilemma is especially vivid in studies of how larger communities influence a child's development. Whether the research is focusing on the media, cultural groups, or peers, the difficulty of making random assignments to experimental designs can pose a special challenge for making unambiguous causal conclusions. Thus, it can be difficult to truly randomly assign children to groups that experience different kinds of media in different ways or that are immersed in different kinds of peer relationships. Almost always, other factors—including the child's own disposition and background environment—are also involved in whether a child is in one situation or another.

Moreover, the rapid rise of Internet communities, social network sites, and new forms of communication, such as texting, all raise questions about how these new forms of relationships might have qualitatively different kinds of influences on children. It is too soon to tell whether an increasingly wired world really will change the nature of social and cognitive development or whether developmental patterns will remain robust across these dramatic technological changes. The only way to know is to constantly conduct well-designed studies that track each new technology and its possible influences. We also see that these new social technologies and the rich trails of interactional data that they leave behind can lead to new forms of analysis, such as the rapidly growing formal and computational studies of social network effects. Without such tools, we might never have known the extent to which individuals we have never met, but who are three friendship links away from us, may influence our health, our values, and our lifestyles.

STUDY AND REVIEW

SUMMARY

Levels of Affiliation

- Children grow up in several levels of communities, starting with their own families, then moving on to peers, local subcultures, and finally the culture at large in which they live.
- Peers have a critical influence, especially in middle childhood and early adolescence. Indeed, some have argued that, as humans mature, they have an evolutionary bias to attend more to peers than to parents.
- Peer relations can be thought of as occurring at three levels: interactions, relationships, and groups.
- Interactions are the simplest forms of relations, ones that may well be transient. In younger children and infants, interactions may be little more than mutual arousal of excitement or distress. Older children show notions of reciprocity and sharing and start to engage in play and pretense.
- Relationships are unique and repeated patterns of interactions between two people, such as a child's relationships with peers, parents, or siblings. Infant relationships may include strong bonds of affection and expectations of classes of behaviors, but they do not contain the reciprocal give-and-take found in toddlers and older children and which is so essential to friendships. As children approach and enter adolescence, friendships take on more intensity, and gender differences in friendship patterns become more prominent.
- In addition to real friends, many children also have imaginary companions. They may also have enemies. Children also can become involved in bully-victim relationships. Bullies often have an inflated sense of self-esteem rather than low self-esteem, contrary to popular lore. The victims of bullies tend to be repeated targets of bullying who suffer considerably from the experience.
- While friends and even imaginary companions are usually associated with positive outcomes, enemies and both parties in bully-victim relationships are associated with negative outcomes.
- Because the formation of groups may require somewhat more cognitive complexity, groups are not voluntarily formed by human infants. Preschoolers form ad hoc groups, but in elementary school, children start to form groups that are more stable, often exclusive cliques.
- Sociometric status is a measure of a child's standing in a group. It is usually measured by asking peers which children in the relevant group are the most liked and which ones are the least liked. There seem to be five different kinds of children as revealed by such ratings: popular children, rejected children, controversial children, average children, and neglected children. The most negative developmental outcomes are associated with rejected children, who are the most heavily studied group as well.

Media Influences on Development

- As a person moves beyond peers to the larger culture, one of the most powerful influences worldwide is that of television, which has become a major part of the daily lives of people, not just in the developed world but also in the developing world. Many children in developed countries spend more time watching television than doing any other activity, including time spent learning in school.
- While infants may not be influenced much by the content of television, by 2 years or so, children start to become engrossed with the content of television that is age appropriate.
- Educational programming has been shown to have both positive cognitive and positive social effects on children. Unfortunately, it is not the most frequently watched form of television.
- Entertainment television tends to contain high levels of violence, levels that have remained equally high for decades. The vast majority of research on the influences of television on children has focused on the question of whether violence on television leads to aggression in children. Across several hundred studies, both of a naturalistic and experimental nature, it is clear that exposure to violent programming is correlated with higher levels of aggression and probably causes it.
- The correlation between violent television watching and aggression is not massive, and it is certainly not able to predict a high likelihood of aggression by any child based on her viewing habits, but when taken for a population as a whole, the risk of increased aggression as a result of viewing violent television may represent a health hazard of a magnitude close to that of the relation between smoking and lung cancer. It has been difficult to address this potential health problem through public policy. A large array of other potential effects of television is increasingly receiving attention.
- As computers become ever more prevalent in the home and video games become more complex, comparable questions have arisen about their influences. Although a smaller number of studies have been conducted in this area, the effects appear to be similar to those produced by television, at least in the area of violence. Nonetheless, positive cognitive benefits can be found for educational video games, and even prosocial effects may be found for the right kinds of games.

- As interactive technologies improve on the Internet, the very nature of social interactions may be shifting as well and may reflect a new form of cultural socialization of children. Internet communities can have positive influences when they serve to maintain and enhance relationships that started and continue in the real world. There is greater concern about relationships that start on the Internet.
- One worrisome new trend is the occurrence of bully-victim relationships on the Internet, often known as "cyberbullying." Cyberbullying may be more severe than real-world bullying because it can occur more easily without adult monitoring and has the potential to put vulnerable children into painful circumstances with much larger audiences.

Roles in the Larger Culture

- Cultures as a whole can also convey styles of thought and kinds of roles that the actors may never explicitly know that they play. These may include a culture of honor in the American South and different attitudes in individualist and collectivist cultures. The most reasonable view of all these effects may be that most people in most cultures have access to several of these roles and cognitive styles, but use them to different extents in different contexts.
- Distinctive roles for the two sexes can also be communicated by cultures, not just in terms of favorite toys, but in terms of expectations about gender-appropriate occupations and hobbies. Those expectations are abstracted from familiar instances, allowing generalizations about novel instances in which men and women are seen as more likely to be in certain occupations.
- Just as there is gender stereotyping, there is also racial stereotyping. Racial stereotypes are typically first seen in young schoolchildren and become stronger during the elementary school years even as older children become better at masking overt bias. There are strong tendencies to build negative impressions of out-groups that can easily fuel racial and ethnic stereotypes and biases.

THOUGHT QUESTIONS

1. Imagine that you are a principal of a high school in a diverse but fairly affluent community. The PTA comes to you with concerns about controlling the content of the student-run high school newspaper. What regulations would you put in place, and how would you justify them to the students?
2. Children often tease each other in ways that are playful forms of affection. Yet, other forms of teasing can be highly destructive and can even be considered bullying. Is it feasible to develop an intervention program for children that could sanction playful teasing but stop harmful teasing, or is it better to try to stop all forms of teasing?
3. Many middle schoolers and young high schoolers spend countless hours texting to each other when it is equally possible to talk on a phone or even chat face-to-face. What factors motivate this preference for texting, and how might these factors change during the high school and college years?
4. It has been argued that extensive use of social networking sites can lower children's self-esteem as they encounter inflated, sculpted, and unrealistically positive portrayals of peers and feel that they are inferior in comparison. Consider whether this claim is plausible and whether children might be much more at risk to such influences than young adults.

KEY TERMS

bullying (p. 549)

catharsis hypothesis (p. 564)

clique (p. 553)

controversial child (p. 557)

culture of honor (p. 574)

cyberbullying (p. 573)

desensitization (p. 566)

developmental intergroup theory (p. 577)

friendship (p. 546)

hostile attribution bias (p. 556)

imaginary companion (p. 548)

inimical relationship (p. 551)

latency period (p. 546)

mutual antipathy (p. 551)

neglected child (p. 557)

peer nomination (p. 554)

peer victimization (p. 549)

popular child (p. 555)

proactive aggression (p. 550)

reactive aggression (p. 550)

rejected child (p. 555)

relational aggression (p. 547)

romantic relationship (p. 552)

social comparison (p. 553)

social information processing (p. 556)

sociometric status (p. 554)

video deficit (p. 561)

PART V
Broader Developmental Context

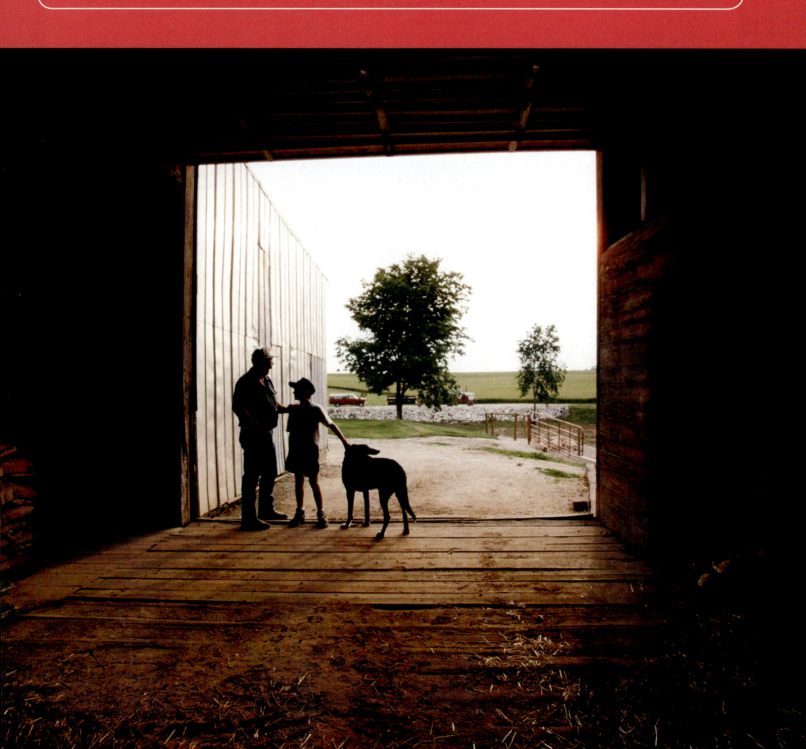

16

Psychopathology in Childhood

Autism
- Features of Autism
- Diagnosis of Autism
- Incidence of Autism
- Causal Factors

Anxiety Disorders
- Incidence of Anxiety Disorders
- Causal Factors
- Obsessive-Compulsive Disorder

Eating Disorders
- Anorexia Nervosa
- Bulimia Nervosa

Depression
- Unipolar Depression
- Bipolar Disorder

Conduct Disorder: The Case of Psychopathy
- Features of Psychopathy
- Diagnosis of Psychopathy
- Causal Factors

Schizophrenia
- Features of Schizophrenia
- Causal Factors
- Early-Onset Schizophrenia

Treatment of Childhood Psychopathologies
- Behavioral Therapies
- Cognitive-Behavioral Therapy
- Psychoanalytic Therapies
- Family Therapies
- Pharmacological Treatments
- Evaluating Therapies

Conclusions

Summary

Sometimes parents have dramatically different outcomes with their children, despite treating them very similarly. Imagine a family with two boys, Adam and Bill, who are fraternal twins. Born at the same time and seemingly experiencing pretty much the same childhoods, they nonetheless take very different trajectories. Adam is an easygoing child who develops along a normal path in virtually all respects. He is a popular, outgoing boy who does somewhat above average in school and enjoys a wide variety of extracurricular activities. In high school, he dates frequently, plays second-string quarterback on the football team, and does well enough to be admitted to one of the regional state universities.

Bill is not an easygoing child, and he seems to gradually decline into his own private hell. His parents do not remember anything unusual about his infancy, but by the time he is in preschool, problems start to emerge. Bill is told that it is important to wash his hands before eating or else he might ingest germs. Very soon, hand washing becomes a dominant part of his life. He washes his hands dozens of times a day, often for more than 30 minutes at a time. His hands are bright red and cracked and sometimes bleed. His parents tell him that the washing is excessive, and at one level he seems to recognize the problem, but he cannot seem to help himself.

As he grows older, Bill's problems compound themselves. He continues to wash obsessively, but now he also spends excessive time in the bathroom wiping himself, usually with the result of completely filling the toilet bowl with toilet tissue. His parents give him a house key when he is 12 so that he can enter and leave the house when they are not home. Soon he finds himself going back to the house as much as a dozen times to make absolutely sure that he has really locked the door. Often, after checking that the door is locked, he rushes into the house to make sure he hasn't left the faucet running, which in turn might trigger another bout of hand washing. As Bill cycles through these routines, he is often late for school.

Bill's problems continue to plague him throughout his life. His parents try a wide variety of therapies to little avail, often because they don't seem to be designed for children. For example, his parents put him on medications to reduce his symptoms, but there is no evidence that the medications are safe when used by children. As an adult, Bill takes a medication that helps control his rituals, but the side effects are aversive, creating a constant battle between the effects of the medication and those of the disease.

This example raises several questions that frame much of this chapter. What sorts of psychological problems commonly afflict children and adolescents? What are the distinguishing features of such problems and what are their causes?

Finally, how do developmental issues affect these psychological disorders? Is it even meaningful to use the same label to classify a mental illness in a 7-year-old child and in a 37-year-old adult? More broadly, all of these questions relate to the question of what counts as psychopathology and how those criteria might change with age. In most cases, psychopathology is considered present when an individual reveals behaviors, thoughts, or emotions that are unusual and that make it difficult for the individual to function or that cause difficulties for others (Nolen-Hoeksema, 2011). Psychopathology can manifest itself in the despair of depression, the disabling feelings of anxiety, or the disordered thoughts of a person with schizophrenia. In all disorders, however, we have to keep in mind that deviance at one age may not be deviance at a younger age. We may think that an adult who throws tantrums by dropping down on his stomach and pounding on the floor of a supermarket is severely emotionally disabled, but we may accept such behaviors as within the range of normal for a toddler. Thus, it is important to put behaviors in a developmental context when considering whether they are likely indications of psychopathology. Psychopathology from a developmental perspective therefore poses several unique challenges. First, we need to reinterpret behaviors in terms of whether they are symptoms of psychopathology. Second, we need to ask if some forms of psychopathology require a certain level of psychological development to manifest themselves. For example, the forms of depression that seem to be driven by ruminative cognitions (repeated thoughts that won't go away) might not be present in young children. Third, there is the challenge of knowing how to treat psychopathology when it is present. For example, will therapies designed around a certain form of self-awareness or "mindfulness" be effective in a kindergartener?

In this chapter, we will consider several mental and behavioral disorders, starting with those that tend to emerge earliest in development and progressing to those with the latest typical age of onset: autism, anxiety disorders, obsessive-compulsive disorder, eating disorders, mood disorders, conduct disorders, and schizophrenia. As we work through these disorders, we will revisit the questions just raised and see how the answers vary across different types of disorders. Finally, we will consider how clinicians treat these problems and how the science of developmental psychology, as discussed in earlier chapters of this book, contributes to a better understanding of the disorders.

Q: What are some general questions that arise in considering psychopathology in children?

Autism

Some children seem to have severe problems in socially interacting and communicating with others (autism) or substantial problems in social intelligence (Asperger's syndrome). In Chapter 13, we mentioned that autism may provide evidence for a theory of mind module that may be defective, perhaps for genetic reasons, in people with autism and Asperger's. Behaviorally, however, autism is associated with a wide range of other problems as well. In the clinical psychology literature, disorders in which such a broad spectrum of problems occurs have often been called **pervasive developmental disorders**, presumably because they affect so many aspects of a person's life.

Features of Autism

Autism was first diagnosed by Leo Kanner in the 1940s (Kanner, 1943), when it was often known as Kanner's syndrome. Before Kanner's work, individuals with autism were often lumped together with children who were labeled "retarded." Kanner noticed a set of problems that occur together and that are now considered the central features of autism: emotional aloneness or remoteness, obsessions with preservation of sameness, and a tendency toward **elective mutism**, in which children capable of speaking seem to have no desire to do so, especially in a communicative manner. Children diagnosed with autism can range from those who show massive cognitive deficits in all areas and require assistance with even the simplest daily functions to those who, in rare cases, can exhibit remarkable skills in specific areas. For that reason, any description of the features of autism must be understood as only approximate for a given child with that diagnosis. Indeed, it is common to talk of "autism spectrum disorders" so as to make clear how much the various deficits and atypical behaviors can vary (Klin et al., 2004; Lord & Jones, 2012; Rapin & Tuchman, 2008a; Volkmar et al., 2007). For the same reason, most current researchers tend to think that there is not just one cause of autism and that, instead, different kinds of "autisms" may arise through different causal pathways (Betancur, 2011; Rapin & Tuchman, 2008b).

One set of symptoms revolves around problems with social skills. Children with autism may not respond to social overtures by others. For example, they may not respond when spoken to, sometimes even if their own name is called. They often seem to lack empathy for others (see Chapter 12) and seem to have trouble understanding the mental states of others, such as their beliefs or feelings (Rapin & Tuchman, 2008a; Volkmar et al., 2007). A related set of problems concerns difficulties in "reading faces." One sign of this is shown in the very different ways in which people with autism scan

faces during a social interaction. Most people keep referring back to another person's eyes as the most significant source of social information, but people with autism often seem to focus primarily on the mouth (perhaps because it moves the most) or even on other salient objects in the environment, such as a moving hand. Figure 16.1 shows how eye-scanning patterns in toddlers with autism differ from the patterns seen in typically developing toddlers.

A

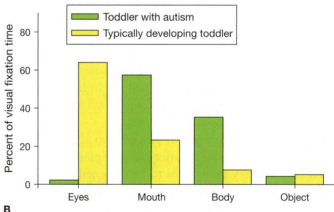

B

FIGURE 16.1 Visual fixations by toddlers with autism and toddlers without autism. Toddlers with autism and typically developing toddlers watched a video of an adult, and researchers tracked where the toddlers directed their eyes. **(A)** Stills of the video indicate the eye scan patterns and show striking differences between the scans of typically developing toddlers (in yellow) and the scans of toddlers with autism (in green). Note in particular how typically developing toddlers focus on the eyes to a vastly greater extent. **(B)** The graph shows the percent of visual fixation time on different body parts by the toddler with autism and the normally developing toddler. Adapted from Jones et al. (2008).

A second set of symptoms revolves around language and communication skills. Children with autism frequently show significant delays in the emergence of language, sometimes never acquiring language at all. Even when they do have some language, they may have difficulty with such linguistic devices as irony. They may also engage in *echolalic speech*, in which they repeat back the words and phrases of others verbatim or repeat certain set scripts. Above and beyond language deficits, they may also show communicative difficulties when engaging in or understanding such activities as pretend play (Rapin & Tuchman, 2008a; Volkmar et al., 2007). They also may show difficulties in adjusting their gaze appropriately in communicative tasks involving pointing and gesturing, often taking an excessively long time to shift their gaze (Falck-Ytter et al., 2012).

A final set of symptoms involves stereotyped movements that are often repeated many times, such as a particular manner of waving the hands. Children with autism may show such repetitive movements and marked resistance to any change in routine as well as a tendency to make the world orderly in ways that other children do not, such as sorting all the toys in a room by color. They may also focus on an extremely narrow area of interest, such as having a particular fascination with airplanes. And they may sometimes show rigidity and perseveration—that is, the continuing repetition of a behavior over an extended period of time (Leekam et al., 2011; Rapin & Tuchman, 2008a; Volkmar et al., 2007).

Diagnosis of Autism

Although the age of onset of autism remains unclear, the first diagnoses typically are made no earlier than about 18 months of age, often in association with language delays. There are some suggestions that even in infancy, autistic children do not connect well socially to their caregivers, leading researchers to wonder whether it might be possible to base a diagnosis on symptoms that are present even before language delays are evident (Barbaro & Dissamayke, 2009; Macari et al., 2012; Yirmiya & Charman, 2010). But the low incidence of autism makes it very difficult to collect enough data to support firm conclusions about symptoms in the first few months of life. (After a child is diagnosed with autism, retrospective reports from caregivers can be colored by their current perceptions of the child, making such reports less useful than observational data gathered before a problem is suspected.) One recent strategy involves **baby sib studies**. Such studies are based on the finding that younger siblings of children with autism are at far greater risk for the disorder themselves, presumably because of shared genetic risk factors. Researchers are therefore starting to intensively study younger siblings from early infancy on the assumption that some percentage of the siblings will develop full-

fledged autism and possibly reveal early precursor behaviors. It is still too early to know what the full set of precursor behaviors might be, but there are indications of some subtle problems with social engagement during the first year of life (Caronna et al., 2008; Macari et al., 2012). At 1 year, there seem to be delays in early language skills, ranging from difficulties in joint attention (the ability to understand a social interaction in which both parties are meant to attend to the same thing; see Chapter 6) to delays in babbling.

Another method for investigating early signs of autism relies on parents' videotapes of their children's earliest birthday parties, which can give researchers a window into a child's social interactions as early as 1 year of age. In one such study, judges used birthday party videos to score 20 children later diagnosed with autism and 20 children who were not later diagnosed with autism on various communicative measures, including the degree to which they responded when called by name and the extent to which they seemed to engage in joint attention. The judges who scored the children's behaviors in the videos were not informed about which children were later diagnosed with autism, but they found less social interaction, less joint attention, and less responsiveness to their own name in the children who were later diagnosed with autism (Osterling et al., 2002). Researchers who watched videotapes of infants in other situations (not birthday parties) claim to have found anomalies in gaze and affect perhaps as early as 6 months in infants who would later develop autism (Clifford & Dissanayake, 2008). Even so, these results pertain to older infants, and it remains much less clear whether signs of autism are already present in the first few months of life.

Incidence of Autism

Autism was initially reported to occur in roughly 3 to 5 out of every 10,000 children. But the incidence has been reported to be rising, with some studies finding rates as high as 1 per 150 children, and over 1 per 100 children when the less severe Asperger's disorder is also included (Elsabbagh et al., 2012; Fombonne et al., 2011; Rapin & Tuchman, 2008b). Some prenatal factors (such as viruses or maternal illnesses or substance abuse or environmental toxins) or some postnatal environmental experiences may account for some of the increase in autism (Kaye et al., 2001; Taylor et al., 1999). But most of the increase is probably illusory and reflects more extensive screening in all social groups and more accurate diagnosis as well as diagnosis at earlier ages (Rapin & Tuchman, 2008b).

There has been some recent controversy as well over whether autism is overdiagnosed as a result of other cognitive and social disabilities being swept into the category inappropriately. This controversy crystallized around the revision of the *Diagnostic and Statistical Manual of Mental Disorders* (DSM), the manual used by clinical psychologists and psychiatrists to diagnose mental disorders. In May 2013, the DSM-V revision replaced prior versions that had appeared in 1994 (DSM-IV) and 2000 (DSM-IV-TR). DSM-V listed the same diagnostic features of autism as earlier manuals, but it increased the strictness of the diagnostic criteria (for example, requiring more symptoms for a diagnosis), which may result in the exclusion of less severe cases. As part of the changes, it also combined autistic disorder, Asperger's disorder, childhood disintegrative disorder, and pervasive developmental disorder not otherwise specified (PDD-NOS) into one larger category called autism spectrum disorder, or ASD, arguing that the divisions into four related disorders had been artificial and that the disorders occurred in more of a continuum. It is not yet clear how much the changes will affect the number of diagnosed cases of autism, but some researchers project quite substantial drops in those receiving ASD diagnoses, especially among those who were formerly diagnosed with Asperger's or PDD-NOS (McPartland et al., 2012). More generally, however, the shifting boundary of criteria for diagnosis with ASD is not likely to influence psychological theories of autism as much as debates about availability of resources for people with disabilities and conclusions as to whether there is a true "autism epidemic."

Autism is diagnosed four times as frequently in boys as in girls. This is a pronounced sex difference, but this kind of disparity is not unusual for incidences of mental illness. The difference may be even larger for milder cases of autism, such as Asperger's disorder, which has been reported to have a male to female ratio of 8:1 (Auyeung & Baron-Cohen, 2008). One hypothesis aimed at explaining why autism is more common in boys suggests that the psychological features of autism resemble an extreme version of the male social brain (Baron-Cohen, 2003; Baron-Cohen et al., 2005). According to this theory, the sexes have different ways of viewing the social world, which can be imagined as opposite ends of a continuum. In particular, females are said to be more sensitive to emotional and mental states in others and to be more skilled socially and more empathic, while males have a tendency to be less socially aware, empathic, and adroit and to also have more of a tendency to analyze and systematize objects and events (Lai et al., 2012). The ability to systematize is more explicitly defined as "the drive to analyze a system in terms of the rules that govern the system, in order to predict the system" (Baron-Cohen et al., 2005, p. 820).

Causal Factors

As we have noted, autism has been hypothesized to involve a severe impairment of the ability to empathize and the related ability to "read" others by engaging in theory of mind

reasoning (see Chapter 13). At the neural level, some fMRI studies have suggested that individuals with autism show less activity in brain regions associated with social cognition (Philip et al., 2012). The theory suggests that without these social skills, people with autism tend to rely on other more analytical and systematized ways of understanding, which is an extreme form of the usual male analytical tendency. This observation also fits with the tendency for many individuals with autism to have an intense interest in orderly routines, arrangements of objects, and the like. It may also explain why autism has been found to be more common in families of physicists, engineers, and mathematicians, groups that tend to represent stereotypical male cognitive styles (Baron-Cohen et al., 1998). Yet, it is not clear how such sex differences are affected by biological mechanisms—that is, how the presence of a Y chromosome could lead to behavioral differences related to autism. There are some indications of links of subsequent autistic traits (such as reduced eye contact, less empathy, and more systematizing) to fetal testosterone levels (see Figure 16.2). Higher levels of fetal testosterone in either sex are correlated with reduced social skills and increased systematizing tendencies (Auyeung & Baron-Cohen, 2008; Auyeung et al., 2009, 2010; Mills et al., 2007). Normally, of course, higher fetal testosterone levels are much more common in males. Somewhat more surprisingly, even in adults, testosterone can have an influence on empathy-related brain regions that presumably had been influenced prenatally by sex hormones. Thus, when

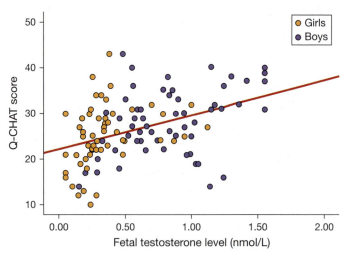

FIGURE 16.2 **Fetal testosterone and subsequent autism.**
For both boys and girls, there is a significant positive relationship between the amount of fetal testosterone and later diagnosis of autism-related symptoms. On the graph, the y-axis is a measure of degree of autism symptoms, known as Q-CHAT (Quantitative CHecklist for Autism in Toddlers), in which higher scores represent more symptoms. The x-axis depicts the amount of fetal testosterone as measured in the mother's amniotic fluid. Higher levels of testosterone are related to higher Q-CHAT scores, especially in boys. Adapted from Auyeung et al. (2010).

adult women are given low doses of testosterone, they experience temporary impairments in their ability to perform on subtle empathy tasks (van Honk et al., 2011). Such effects of testosterone and other hormones on social-emotional states, however, are complex and often only occur in specific contexts (Bos et al., 2012).

> **Q:** What is the sex difference with respect to the incidence of autism, and what is an explanation for this difference?

Another biological explanation for autism focuses on the genes. While there is substantial evidence for a genetic predisposition to autism, the specific genetic influences are complex, involving several distinct gene locations and intricate patterns of gene interactions (Devlin & Scherer, 2012; Folstein & Rosen-Sheidley, 2001; Freitag, 2007; Geschwind, 2008; Hu, 2013; State & Levitt, 2011). Nonetheless, the rates of autism in monozygotic and dizygotic twins provide a clear illustration of a genetic influence at work (Geschwind & Spence, 2008). Each member of a pair of monozygotic twins is substantially more likely to have autism if the other twin has the disorder. One study that used fairly strict diagnostic criteria found a concordance rate (the likelihood that two individuals share the same trait) among monozygotic twins of roughly 60 percent, with a concordance of roughly 20 percent among dizygotic twins. If the diagnostic criteria are broadened to include a spectrum of cognitive and social abnormalities, the concordance is almost 80 percent for monozygotic twins and roughly 30 percent for dizygotic twins (Hallmayer et al., 2011). In a related study, researchers gave a difficult theory of mind task both to siblings of people with Asperger's disorder and to a control group of nonrelatives. They found higher concordance rates for difficulty in understanding others' states of mind among the siblings than among the nonrelatives (Dorris et al., 2004).

Genetic influences for autism may also arise as a result of mutations to the mother's eggs or the father's sperm later in the parent's life. The risk of some disorders, such as Down syndrome, are related to the mother's age, and maternal age was often thought to be more associated with the development of most disorders in the child than paternal age. This is because the same set of eggs is present throughout much of the mother's life and has more time to accumulate mutations than sperm cells, which are constantly being produced. Yet, some researchers have suggested that the age of the father may be related to the incidence of autism in the child (Kong et al., 2012). This is because sperm cells arise from dividing precursor cells, and they acquire new mutations each time they divide as a result of errors occurring

during cell division. Thus, the older the father, the more errors and possible mutations that may have occurred in his sperm and therefore the greater the risk of the child having new mutations in his or her genome related to autism that were not present in either parent's genome, a relationship that was borne out through whole-genome analyses of fathers in Iceland. The increase in risk is not massive, and autism still does not have a high probability of occurring in children of older fathers, but it may help explain the increase in the incidence of autism in many developed countries, where the age of fathers has also been increasing.

> **Q:** What is the evidence for a genetic basis for autism and related disorders?

There was an early environmental theory of autism, commonly called the "refrigerator mother" scenario (Bettelheim, 1972), a socialization theory that has since been discredited. Clinicians had thought that autistic children were disproportionately from middle- and upper-class families, and they hypothesized that the mothers in those families were often cold and disengaged from their children, creating such a violation of the normal attachment sequence as to cause autism. One problem with the greater incidence of cases of autism in children of better-educated parents, however, may be that those parents are more likely to refer the children to specialists who diagnose autism, creating a **sampling bias**. Consequently, the refrigerator mother theory has not held up over time. There is no evidence that a colder, more dispassionate parent causes a child to develop autism. Nonetheless, there may be a modest correlation between socially nonresponsive parents and autistic children because they share a genetic tendency to be emotionally limited in social interactions.

> **Q:** Describe a socialization theory of the origins of autism, and comment on its limitations.

Other environmental factors have been found to be associated with autism, although the direction of causality is often unclear. Researchers have found that various infections in early infancy or prenatally are associated with higher levels of autism (Atladottir et al., 2010, 2012). For example, children with autism are likely to have higher levels of antibodies associated with having had various viral and bacterial infections (Hornig & Lipkin, 2001; Patterson, 2011). This pattern is often interpreted as indicating that children with autism (or their mothers) have had a higher incidence of various infections early in development, although it is also possible that they may have more active immune responses to infections or that autism early on could lead to greater susceptibility to infections. Other work suggests that autistic individuals may have more immune-related diseases, such as autoimmune disorders (Patterson, 2011; Trottier et al., 1999). Indeed, one view suggests that as many as one-third of the cases of autism may result from problems of immune system regulation in the mother, sometimes as a side effect of an infection, but other times simply because a poorly regulated immune system results in inflammatory disease that influences fetal brain development (Velasquez-Manoff, 2012).

More broadly, a wide array of environmental factors, ranging from infectious diseases to exposure to insecticides, has been seen as potentially related to the onset of autism. In addition, when such effects do occur, they may be produced through gene-environment interactions. For example, a particular kind of environmental exposure might influence a genetic mechanism regulating a specific aspect of neuronal development (Pessah & Lein, 2008). Environmental factors on their own may not be sufficient to trigger the onset of autism in most individuals, but these factors may have such effects in a special subset of individuals who are at risk because they have a certain genotype. Such gene-environment interaction patterns are often described in terms of the **diathesis-stress hypothesis**, which proposes that some individuals have a genetic or biological vulnerability (a "diathesis") that causes them to be more likely to show a disease when immersed in a stressful, negative environment. At the present time, however, the research community has not achieved much consensus on the links between specific environmental factors and autism spectrum disorders.

Anxiety Disorders

We all have observed children who are more fearful and anxious than others. Within the normal spectrum, we can simply attribute variations of anxiety and fearfulness to different personality types. Similarly, the different attachment styles that we considered in Chapter 6 do not in themselves indicate psychopathology. But in some cases, anxieties can become so strong and persistent as to be debilitating for the child, interfering with the child's normal functioning and thereby becoming a form of mental illness known as an **anxiety disorder**. Anxiety disorders can cover a wide spectrum of problems, ranging from severely insecure attachment styles to phobias to obsessive-compulsive disorders. In this section, we will focus on generalized anxiety disorder, separation anxiety disorder, and social anxiety disorder,

having briefly discussed phobias in Chapter 7 in the context of prepared fears. We will then discuss obsessive-compulsive disorder as an anxiety-related disorder that has some distinctive components that do not affect all people with anxiety problems.

Incidence of Anxiety Disorders

Considered collectively, anxiety disorders are the most prevalent mental illness in children, with incidences approaching 15 percent of children between ages 9 and 17 (Cartwright-Hatton et al., 2006; Costello et al., 2005; Muroff & Ross, 2011; Southam-Gerow & Chorpita, 2007; Velting et al., 2002). Anxiety disorders seem to be about equally common among boys and girls in childhood, but they become more common among girls in adolescence (Kashani & Orvaschel, 1990; Kubarych et al., 2008; Nielsen et al., 2000). Anxiety disorders are among the earliest psychopathologies to emerge, with patterns of anxious behavior in infancy predicting social anxiety many years later—probably even in adulthood. Moreover, when anxiety problems are identified in children, they are highly likely to be predictive of long-term problems. For example, the child who is excessively anxious about school tests, parties, and athletic events is more likely to have severe anxiety problems as an adult, and often depression as well (Bernstein et al., 1996; Brady & Kendall, 1992; Southam-Gerow & Chorpita, 2007).

> **Q:** Describe the prevalence of anxiety disorders in children.

Anxiety and fearfulness can first manifest themselves in the young infant. We saw in Chapters 6 and 7 that preverbal infants can vary considerably in the degree to which they become alarmed or upset by novel or mildly threatening stimuli. Moreover, some infants seem much more inhibited than others around novel stimuli, exhibiting fearfulness and withdrawal, as seen in Chapter 7. Infants who are highly inhibited in infancy are more likely to show social anxiety disorder and generalized anxiety disorder as adolescents (Chronis-Tuscano et al., 2009; Khalid-Khan et al., 2007; Schwartz et al., 1999, 2003; Trentacosta et al., 2008; White et al., 2011). **Social anxiety disorder** tends to involve fears and anxiety about social situations or situations in which a person is being evaluated by another (see Figure 16.3). This disorder can lead to either avoidance of such situations or to high levels of discomfort when the person is in those situations (Muroff & Ross, 2011). **Generalized anxiety disorder** involves excessive levels of worry about a wide range of

FIGURE 16.3 **Social anxiety disorder.** Most people feel some anxiety in front of groups, but when the anxiety becomes so strong that the individual cannot even look at others, it may be a sign of social anxiety disorder. Social anxiety disorder often becomes most salient when children are in middle school.

situations. A child with such a disorder might worry excessively about an upcoming trip to the zoo, whether she will have to use the toilet at school, and whether her school bus will crash on a field trip. If the worries are more focused on just social situations, the disorder is a social anxiety disorder. If the worries are primarily about a particular fear, such as a fear of large dogs, the disorder is a phobia.

Developmentally, the earliest signs of anxiety are seen in the form of separation anxieties (discussed as separation distress in Chapter 6), with some children showing excessively fearful and anxious responses upon separation from a parent or other adult caregiver. Specific phobias are usually the next disorder to appear, often before 7 years of age. Generalized anxiety disorder doesn't usually appear until around age 9 or 10 (Muroff & Ross; 2011; Southam-Gerow & Chorpita, 2007). Social anxieties tend to become more prominent around age 12, while panic disorder (a disorder in which panic attacks occur frequently and for no obvious reason) doesn't usually occur until around age 15 (Southam-Gerow & Chorpita, 2007). With the exception of children with panic disorder, children who show one kind of anxiety disorder are more likely to show other kinds of anxiety disorders as well, suggesting some shared underlying causes (Muroff & Ross; 2011; Wood et al., 2003).

Taking a closer look at the anxiety disorders, we observe that anxiety manifests itself differently throughout development. Most notably, for both normal and abnormal cases of anxiety, the objects that produce anxiety tend to change with age. Younger children tend to worry more about physical objects or threats to their person (will they fall off a bridge, will a trip to the dentist be painful), whereas older children might worry about behavioral performance (will they do well on a test, will they be able to remember their way home) or about social and psychological threats (will they be disliked by others, will they be too nervous to speak in front of the class) (Gullone, 2000; Westenberg et al., 2004; Wood et al., 2003).

> **Q:** How do anxiety disorders tend to change with increasing age?

Causal Factors

There have been several theories about how and why anxiety disorders emerge in children, ranging from those that focus on the biological components, like the genetic basis for cortical circuits that inhibit behaviors (see Chapter 7), to accounts that refer to a child's early experiences, such as patterns of parenting (see Chapter 6). Freud described cases of anxiety arising out of internal conflicts. In one of his most colorful accounts, he described the case of "Little Hans," who supposedly acquired a phobia of horses because of an Oedipal conflict in which he saw the horse as proxy for a castrating father (Freud, 1909). By contrast, we saw in Chapter 4 how John Watson instilled anxiety in a child through classical conditioning, a technique that tried to deny any value to considering mental states in the child (Watson & Rayner, 1920). Here, however, we focus mostly on generalized anxiety disorder, in which a child seems to be anxious about a wide range of events and possible futures and not about a highly specific object, as in the case of phobias.

Insecurely attached infants and children are more likely to show anxiety problems later on (Brumariu & Kerns, 2011; Cassidy & Berlin, 1994; Colonnesi et al., 2011; Esbjørn et al., 2012; Thompson, 2001). As is often the case with attachment-related research, however, it is difficult to assess causal directions. While it might be that parents who are insensitive to children's needs may cause children to become more anxious, it is also possible that anxious children cause parents to behave in ways that make the parents appear to be insensitive. Moreover, there are associations between depression in mothers and increased anxiety in children (Feng et al., 2008; Pilowsky et al., 2006). Such associations may reflect the influences of unresponsive mothers or the modeling of anxiety by depressed mothers (Gerull & Rapee, 2002). In fact, researchers have shown in experimental studies that when parents are told to model anxiety-reducing behaviors, children show less anxiety toward potentially anxiety-inducing stimuli (Egliston & Rapee, 2007). In addition, when mothers go into remission from depression after treatment, their children show improved mental health, with one measure involving reduced levels of anxiety (Wickramaratne et al., 2011). Thus, beyond any shared genotype effects, parental behavior seems to also influence a child's level of anxiety, at least in specific contexts.

Cognitive Factors Children with anxiety disorders tend to be apprehensive about the present and to worry a great deal about the future. They tend to engage in **catastrophizing**, assuming the worst possible outcome for future events, even when those outcomes are highly unlikely or implausible. These features are considered central to diagnoses of anxiety disorders (American Psychiatric Association, 1994). Researchers looking for ways in which children with anxiety disorders might be cognitively different from children who do not have anxiety disorders have therefore asked whether anxious children show a higher preponderance of some kinds of cognition as opposed to children who are not anxious.

A range of studies suggests that there are more negative cognitions in anxious children. For example, when researchers asked children to describe the cognitions they had had during a previously taken test, anxious children tended to report higher numbers of negative cognitions (thoughts like "I did not do well on the test" or "I incorrectly answered most of the questions") than children who were not anxious (Hogendoorn et al., 2012; McDonald, 2001; Prins & Hanewald, 1997). The same pattern emerged when researchers presented children with ambiguous stories about social situations and asked the children to say when they thought the story started to be "scary" and how they themselves would feel if they were the protagonist in the story (Muris et al., 2002a). Socially anxious children ages 8 to 13 tended to hear fewer sentences of the stories before they decided they were scary—that is, they formed a judgment of the story as socially threatening earlier than children who were not socially anxious. In addition, the socially anxious children showed a higher overall incidence of labeling stories as threatening and displayed higher levels of negative feelings and cognitions as a result of listening to the stories than did children who were not anxious. It therefore appears that socially anxious children form different cognitive interpretations of social situations, even when they are bystanders, and that these interpretations result in higher perceptions of threats and higher levels of negative emotions (Gregory et al., 2007; Muris & Field, 2008). In addition, socially anxious children tend to perceive their own bodily indications of anxiety in more dramatic and public terms. For example, in socially stressful situations, they perceive their heart rate as faster and more noticeable to others than do children with low social anxiety who have the same actual heart rate (Schmitz et al., 2012).

Q: How might a child's cognitions be involved in precipitating or maintaining generalized anxiety or social anxiety?

Anxious children appear to have cognitive biases that contribute to anxiety in several different ways. They have attentional biases that lead them to pay more attention to aversive and distressing stimuli, and they have greater difficulty disengaging from such stimuli. They have interpretation biases that lead them to make more negative interpretations of ambiguous situations that other children might see as neutral or even positive. Finally, they have memory biases that lead them to recall more negatively charged aspects of prior events. These different biases can be integrated into a single model, as shown in Figure 16.4 (Muris & Field, 2008).

Children who are socially anxious may have less developed social intelligence, making it more difficult for them to understand the nuances of delicate social situations (Sood & Kendall, 2007; Southam-Gerow & Kendall, 2000). Their anxiety may arise from difficulty in understanding their own emotional states as well as those of others. Or it may result from particular difficulties in understanding the relation between cognition and action and between different emotional and cognitive states that may co-occur in the same mind at the same time. These difficulties may create a default bias to assume that when in doubt, the social

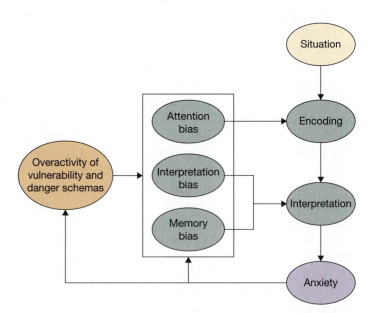

FIGURE 16.4 Cognitive and attentional biases contributing to anxiety disorders in children. Children with anxiety disorders show (1) more attention to and more difficulty disengaging from disturbing stimuli, (2) a tendency to interpret ambiguous events in more negative ways, and (3) selective recall of memories of events that are more negatively charged. Adapted from Muris & Field (2008).

situation is a threatening one. A better understanding of all children's abilities to grapple with multiple simultaneous emotions and cognitions may therefore be essential to understanding how social anxiety disorder develops and changes as the child develops (Choe et al., 2005).

We discussed phobias briefly in Chapter 7. The main point here is that individual differences in the tendencies to form phobias may be related to generalized anxiety disorder in children. Thus, the child who always imagines worst-case scenarios and who cannot disengage from thinking about all that could go wrong in a present or future situation may well be more likely to develop and maintain phobias than less anxious children. All children can develop phobias, and the phobias are constrained by preparedness phenomena of the sort discussed in Chapter 7, but anxiety may help exacerbate the process.

Biological Factors Across many twin and adoption studies, researchers have consistently found evidence for genetic influences on anxiety (Gregory & Eley, 2007; Rapee et al., 2009; Sakolsky et al., 2012). Most studies have focused on genes associated with the production and regulation of the neurotransmitter serotonin, but other studies have suggested links to genes associated with other neurotransmitters, such as dopamine, and genes associated with stress-related hormones. In addition, the association between genes and anxiety disorders can be stronger in some environments than in others (Fox et al., 2005; Sakolsky et al., 2012). For example, variations in genes that regulate serotonin show significant relations to anxiety when children are in families

that have low levels of social support. In families with high levels of support, however, the same patterns of variation are not related to anxiety. This is a gene-environment way of understanding the notion of being "at risk"—namely, some children may be genetically predisposed to show a disorder but only in a certain range of environments.

In general, genetic factors don't just act on their own; rather, they interact with both environmental and cognitive factors. Thus, genetic influences on attention and memory might in turn influence some forms of anxiety. Similarly, some kinds of family environments might make a child more susceptible to genetic influences. Finally, environments might even trigger the turning off or on of a genetic regulatory pathway.

Obsessive-Compulsive Disorder

As seen at the beginning of this chapter, some children can develop a series of behaviors that involve a high level of anxiety as well as high incidences of checking various things, persistent, intrusive thoughts that cannot be ignored or set aside, and highly repetitive behaviors (American Psychiatric Association, 2000; Leckman et al., 1997). This pattern of behaviors is known as **obsessive-compulsive disorder (OCD)**.

Types of Obsessive-Compulsive Disorder Let's consider in more detail the four main types of obsessive-compulsive disorder that researchers have repeatedly proposed (Bloch et al., 2008; see Figure 16.5). One cluster of behaviors revolves

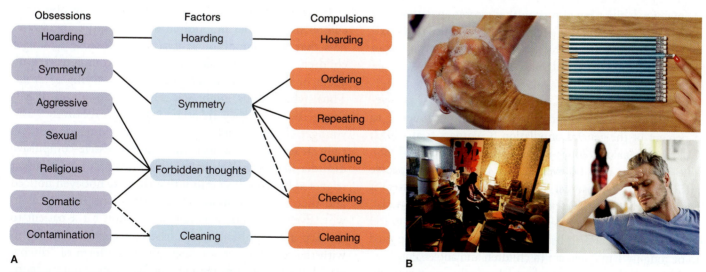

FIGURE 16.5 Clusters of symptoms in obsessive-compulsive behaviors. Obsessive-compulsive behaviors are often classified into four types or factors, with characteristic obsessions and compulsions, which can overlap somewhat: cleaning and contamination fears, a desire to order things, hoarding of objects, and forbidden thoughts (usually aggressive, blasphemous, or sexual).The diagram shows solid lines for links between obsessions or compulsions and factors that can be found in both adults and children, and dashed lines for links between obsessions or compulsions and factors found only in children. Adapted from Bloch et al. (2008).

around fears of contamination and is accompanied by compulsive cleaning. A person might obsess about dirt, germs, or other forms of contamination and might engage in compulsive cleaning and washing to reduce anxiety about the contamination.

A second cluster revolves around an obsession with order and symmetry and is accompanied by compulsive ordering, repeating, and counting behaviors. A person with this cluster might repeatedly line up a set of objects in a precise and symmetrical manner, or a child might take all of his toys and carefully arrange them in a neat geometric pattern.

A third cluster revolves around an obsession with losing things that may be of importance and is accompanied by hoarding behavior in which a person is extremely reluctant to throw anything away for fear it might be needed someday. People can hoard everything from used pieces of aluminum foil to old magazines to bottle caps.

Finally, a cluster revolves around unwanted aggressive, sexual, or religious/blasphemous thoughts or excessive somatic (bodily) worries about catching severe illnesses, such as cancer or AIDS. A person with this cluster might be plagued with highly unwelcome thoughts about assaulting another person or engaging in a horrible transgression of his or her religion. Attempts to reduce the anxiety associated with such thoughts might often take the form of compulsive checking behavior, such as going back to make sure the apartment is locked a dozen times or looking both ways 20 times before crossing a street.

These four clusters are found repeatedly when we look across cultures (Matsunaga et al., 2008; Pallanti, 2008; Torresan et al., 2009). In addition, there are reports that each cluster involves somewhat different brain structures (Maia et al., 2008). Across all types, however, there is a common theme of a debilitating obsession that creates anxiety and of compulsive behaviors that are attempts to reduce that anxiety. In addition, some individuals can show symptoms from more than one cluster (Calamari et al., 2012).

Incidence of Obsessive-Compulsive Disorder

Obsessive-compulsive disorder is estimated to occur in about 2 to 3 percent of the general population (Calamari et al., 2012; Gilbert & Maalouf, 2008; Jenike, 2004; Karno et al., 1988). The incidence may be even higher because many people afflicted with the disorder go to great lengths to conceal it from others because they sense how irrational it is. By contrast, younger children are less self-conscious and less likely to feel the need to conceal their behaviors. The incidence is reported to be roughly 1 to 2 percent in children and adolescents.

Although obsessive-compulsive disorder has been reported in 2-year-olds (Rapoport et al., 1992), it is normally first noticed in children between 6 and 15 years of age (Gilbert & Maalouf, 2008). When the disorder appears in young children, it is more likely to be seen in boys, but by adolescence the distribution between the sexes becomes more even. There is a second, later period, between ages 20 and 29, in which another wave of onsets of the disorder is seen. This later period, combined with the shifting gender ratios, leads some to suggest that early-emerging obsessive-compulsive disorder may have a somewhat different basis than the disorder that first emerges in young adults (Taylor, 2011).

Diagnosis of Obsessive-Compulsive Disorder

The diagnosis of obsessive-compulsive disorder relies on several converging forms of evidence. Although there are no simple genetic markers or other physiological markers of the disorder, there are some physical signs that can indicate some variants of the disorder. Thus, simple examination of the red hands of a compulsive hand washer or the bleeding gums of a compulsive tooth brusher can help confirm a diagnosis. Behaviorally speaking, we can ask if engaging in the behavior seems to reduce anxiety but is not enjoyable in its own right (for example, washing hands may reduce anxiety but may not be at all pleasurable). These behaviors can be quite time-consuming, often taking well over an hour each day. More cognitively, the obsessions, in addition to falling into categories such as contamination, loss of objects, and ordering, also tend to consist of unrealistic concerns. The obsessions are usually unwelcome and intrusive thoughts that adults, at least, will often regard as not making any sense and will frequently regard with fear and disgust. Diagnosis in children is the same as in adults except that, unlike adults, who normally are aware of the irrationality of their compulsions and/or fears but cannot stop doing them, the children may not have such an explicit awareness (American Psychiatric Association, 2000).

It is interesting that the diagnostic criteria for obsessive-compulsive disorder in children do not require any awareness that the compulsion is irrational. Moreover, younger children with the disorder often do not consciously think about or discuss the threats that they are trying to avoid. Thus, while adults might say that they are afraid of getting germs when they are asked why they excessively wash, younger children might simply say that things do not feel right. It seems as if, in its early stages, obsessive-compulsive disorder involves self-protective behavior programs that get triggered by stimuli so minor that they are not even noticed and then are set in motion with little or no thought as to why. Even in adults, it is not uncommon for a patient to develop a compulsion before having a good reason for it, with the reason emerging later, often as a form of "discovery." For example, one patient who had a set of compulsions around contagion and contamination for many years learned about AIDS and declared that the compulsive behaviors had always been to avoid getting AIDS, even though the behaviors began before AIDS was publicly known (Rapoport, 1989).

Causal Factors Compulsions may originate in the normal levels of ritual and repetitive behavior in young children (Leckman & Bloch, 2008; Leonard et al., 1990; Thomsen, 1998). Children younger than 3 years old often engage in such behaviors, which then gradually die out in toddlerhood. It may be that obsessive-compulsive disorders lead to the retention and elaboration of such behaviors rather than the normal course of decay.

> **Q:** What are some examples of obsessive-compulsive behaviors in young children?

Many behaviors associated with OCD, including cleaning and checking, may be part of a **security motivational system** that is part of many animals and is built to recognize and respond to very subtle and indirect cues to danger, including cues to predators, toxins, and other possibly harmful changes in normal routines (Szechtman & Woody, 2004). Such a system is thought to be a separate module that is akin to modules for language and spatial cognition and that may have four distinctive features: (1) risk detection of potential dangers, (2) easy activation and slow deactivation, (3) orientation toward action designed to reduce the likelihood of future dangers (such as checking behavior), and (4) orientation toward prevention of future events as opposed to avoidance of present ones.

The security motivational system recognizes a "feeling of knowing" that appropriate protective actions have been taken, which serves as a signal for the system to shut down. In normal circumstances, a person appraises his actions, concludes that he has taken all reasonable precautions, and reduces his levels of threat prevention. According to this theory, cases of obsessive-compulsive disorder seem to involve blocking information that prevents a person from feeling that he has taken all reasonable protective actions. As a result, the person continues trying to protect himself because "things just don't feel right," even though at a more rational level he knows full well that his hands must be clean, the oven must be off, or the house must be locked. Here the problem of OCD is less a cognitive issue and more related to emotion—namely, getting the feeling of assurance or "satiation" in the activity that causes the person to feel that he has done enough and can stop his self-protective behaviors (Szechtman & Woody, 2004). The process is thought to be analogous to cases of physiological satiation. For example, if someone is thirsty, the awareness of having just drunk a lot of water can induce a feeling of satiation long before the water is absorbed into the body.

> **Q:** How has the presence of a security motivational system been used to explain the emergence of obsessive-compulsive disorder?

In short, obsessive-compulsive disorder may arise from a relatively modular threat anticipation/avoidance system that, while involving a high level of anxiety, works quite differently from the system leading to other fears. Its modular nature allows compulsions to be set up and maintained largely outside of conscious control. Most models of the disorder in adults put a heavy emphasis on cognitive factors, assuming that obsessional thoughts help trigger and maintain the compulsions. But in young children, and by some accounts perhaps in adults as well (Szechtman & Woody, 2004; Woody & Szechtman, 2011), the obsessions may not precede the compulsions as much as follow them. Development may promote a growth of unwanted obsessive thoughts that enhance the already present compulsions and that ultimately can take on a life of their own, leading to new forms of compulsions (for example, counting words in sentences or the number of streetlights passed) that may depart more and more from those evolutionary ancient ones (for example, excessive washing to avoid contamination). At all ages, the compulsions tend to be more common in times of stress, suggesting again that a relatively automatic vigilance system gets put into action trying to discover subtle and often nonexistent cues to threats and ways to avoid them. Developmental differences in the manifestation of obsessive-compulsive disorder (such as a higher incidence of checking behaviors with increasing age) may be critical to understanding the different cognitive and emotional components of this disorder (D. Geller et al., 2001).

Problems identifying the source of their memories (see Chapter 10) may also contribute to the incidence of compulsive behavior in children, who may have more difficulty knowing whether they have really performed an action or just thought that they did and therefore perform it again. Because younger children in general have greater difficulty identifying the sources of their memories (for example, whether the memories come from a dream or from a real-life experience), a child concerned with contamination may have more difficulty accurately remembering whether he washed his hands or just thought about doing so.

Why do some children develop obsessive-compulsive disorder and others do not? There are several distinct models of etiology, many of which could mutually contribute to the disease. There are clear indications of a genetic basis, as the incidence of OCD in MZ twins is roughly twice that in DZ twins (approximately 80 percent versus 40 percent concordance rates), with far higher concordance rates for OCD than for most other anxiety disorders (Carey & Gottesman, 1981; Pauls, 2008, 2012; Pauls et al., 1995; Rasmussen, 1993). Alleles linked to higher levels of OCD are often involved in serotonin-related pathways (Abudy et al., 2012; Taylor, 2013). In addition to a genetic basis, adverse neurological events in infancy and early childhood may cause the disorder. These may include birth difficulties, responses to various infections such as meningitis, autoimmune reactions, or even brain damage from an accident (D. Geller et al., 2008; Jenike et al., 1998).

In contrast to the strong evidence for biological factors causing obsessive-compulsive disorder, there is far less evidence for psychological models, such as the Freudian idea that failures to progress normally through toilet training and the anal stage lead to disorders of control (Sears et al., 1957). There simply doesn't seem to be any good reason to believe that a particular type of parenting causes the emergence of obsessions and compulsions. In a sense, this may be a bit surprising. It might seem that a parent who constantly worries about potential future threats and models endless checking behaviors might well instill such behaviors in the child, and such associations between parental overprotectiveness and childhood OCD have been found (Wilcox et al., 2008). But when the genetic commonality is taken into account, it is difficult to find an independent contribution from patterns of child rearing. One final route for parental and broader environmental influences might simply be one where increased stresses cause a rise in obsessive-compulsive behavior in children who are already at risk for the disorder. Thus, if a child with a tendency for obsessive-compulsive behavior is repeatedly put into circumstances that raise anxiety, that heightened anxiety may trigger obsessive thoughts and compulsive behaviors.

> **Q:** What are the most likely causes of obsessive-compulsive behavior in children?

Eating Disorders

One of the most striking developmental phenomena in psychopathology is the emergence of certain eating disorders in early adolescence, with a significant preponderance of the disorders appearing in girls. There is an immense literature on eating disorders that normally divides the disorders into anorexia nervosa, bulimia, and binge eating, while also allowing for other rarer forms of eating disorders, such as fixations on the "right" foods (Brownell & Foreyt, 1986; Keel et al., 2012). These disorders can have devastating health consequences. For example, girls with anorexia nervosa are 12 times as likely to die in a given year as girls who do not have the disorder (Smink et al., 2012; Sullivan, 1995).

The incidence among teenage girls of all forms of eating disorders is estimated to be as high as 3 percent (Favaro et al., 2003; Hoek, 1995; Hsu, 1996; Smink et al., 2012). The age of onset of anorexia nervosa and bulimia nervosa appears to be decreasing in younger generations, although still occurring in the teen years. This earlier onset is associated with earlier age of menstruation, a reduction in number of siblings, and higher levels of socioeconomic status, although the specific causal relations among these factors remain unclear (Favaro et al., 2009). The incidence among girls younger than 9 years old is vastly lower, usually reported at well under 1 percent for anorexia nervosa, bulimia, and binge eating (Nicholls & Bryant-Waugh, 2009; Smink et al., 2012). Anorexia nervosa occurs less than one-tenth as often among boys than girls in all age groups, and bulimia occurs in boys at about one-hundredth the rate among girls (Hoek & van Hoeken, 2003; Levine & Piran, 2005; Smink et al., 2012). It should be noted, however, that the prevalence may be underestimated because so many people afflicted with these disorders go to great lengths to conceal them.

Eating disorders in general have several common properties: they are more common in girls, often much more common; they usually first emerge in adolescence; and they are often associated with nonoptimal family structures. Their absence in younger children is probably not due to a limitation imposed by younger children's cognitions as much as it is a function of the sorts of physical and social changes that are associated with entering puberty and how the child, her family, and the culture at large relate to those changes. The two most commonly discussed eating disorders are anorexia nervosa and bulimia nervosa. A brief summary of the contrasting diagnostic criteria of these two eating disorders is given in Table 16.1. We will discuss each in turn.

Anorexia Nervosa

Anorexia nervosa is distinguished by a person's intentional refusal to eat anything beyond minimal amounts of food. It may be a way for an achievement-driven girl to demonstrate her own form of control in situations in which she

Anorexia Nervosa	Bulimia Nervosa
Body weight voluntarily maintained at below normal level	Large uncontrolled eating binges at least twice weekly
Intense fear of gaining weight or becoming fat	Inappropriate compensatory behavior (e.g., vomiting)
Amenorrhea (in females)	Self-esteem closely linked to body weight/shape

TABLE 16.1 Key diagnostic features of anorexia nervosa and bulimia nervosa. While both eating disorders are much more common in females than males, they have distinct characteristics. In addition to the diagnostic features described here, anorexia nervosa has a slightly earlier age of onset than bulimia nervosa and has been a more consistent disorder both historically and cross-culturally. It also has been more closely associated with genetic influences. From Walsh & Devlin (1998).

feels powerless. Adolescents with anorexia nervosa tend to have extremely low body weights, and their self-esteem is based on an excessive concern with being thin rather than on their intellectual skills, personality, or physical skills (see Figure 16.6). A preoccupation with a high level of exercise is also often observed. Anorexia is also associated with **amenorrhea**, the absence of a menstrual period in women who are of menstrual age. Anorexia in a child is frightening for parents because they feel powerless to stop their child from wasting away.

Incidence of Anorexia As indicated earlier, this disorder shows the strongest bias toward girls, occurring at least 10 times as frequently in girls as in boys. The disorder is very rarely seen before middle school, although a very small number of cases of what seems to be the disorder have been reported in girls under age 10 (Bostic et al., 1997; Rhodes et al., 2009; Watkins & Lask, 2002). It typically appears around age 12, reaches its height in adolescence and college, and then gradually wanes, although it may continue to be seen in middle age (Keski-Rahkonen et al., 2007; Smink et al., 2012). Anorexia often co-occurs with other forms of psychopathology, especially depression and anxiety-related disorders.

The disorder has been reported in various forms for centuries (Vandereycken & Van Deth, 1994). But given some of the popular press on the topic, it might seem as if there has been a surge of anorexia cases in recent years, perhaps even an epidemic. A closer look at historical patterns, however, suggests only a modest rise over the course of the twentieth century, with drops sometimes occurring in recent years (Currin et al., 2005; Keel & Klump, 2003; Keel et al., 2006;

Smink et al., 2012). The contemporary media's emphasis on the desirability of very thin bodies may have helped contribute to that modest increase, but the more important pattern is that, for centuries, in the context of religious fasting or simply worrying about being thin, anorexia nervosa has occurred in a higher proportion of girls than boys, with the huge sex difference remaining relatively constant over that period (Brumberg, 1988).

It had long been held that anorexia nervosa was a disorder that was more common among those in the upper socioeconomic classes and among those in advantaged groups that had more achievement-driven girls trying to assert control. While there is some support for this view (Levine & Piran, 2005; Pate et al., 1992), analyses of reports of the disorder do not always show a preponderance of cases in the upper ranges of the socioeconomic spectrum (Forman & Goodman, 1999; Gard & Freeman, 1996). Rather, there are reports of higher incidences of anorexia in more technologically advanced societies that tend to have an abundance of food for their citizens (Miller & Pumariega, 2001). It may be that cultural factors are becoming more important than socioeconomic factors as all members of a culture, rich and poor, start to adopt standard images of the ideal body shape for that culture (Lake et al., 2000; see also Kayono et al., 2008; Keel & Klump, 2003).

We saw in Chapter 15 how the introduction of Western television programming into traditional communities in Fiji was related to an increase in eating disorders based on an "idealization of thinness" as depicted in the Western programs. Even this commonly reported cross-cultural finding, however, needs to be supported by large-scale

FIGURE 16.6 Anorexia in young adults. In 2010, the highly successful French model and actress Isabelle Caro died from complications related to anorexia. For many unfamiliar with the disease, it was baffling that such a successful and popular figure could actually die from the eating disorder.

rigorous comparisons of different cultures that use the same assessment instruments in the same way. For example, one problem is that some cultures may have much higher stigma attached to the disorder and therefore may have higher levels of underreporting by children to their families and by the families to their physicians. One extensive analysis of cross-cultural differences in anorexia found that while there may be some cultural variation in anorexia as a function of a culture's "idealization of thinness," anorexia is found in every culture in the world where the numbers and methods are adequate for reporting it (Keel & Klump, 2003).

> **Q:** How does anorexia vary across gender and across cultures?

Cognitive Distortions in Anorexia A person with anorexia may report that she sees herself as fat and needs to be thinner, while others would say that she already appears to be extremely thin. Thus, there seems to be a form of distorted cognition in which a girl who by any objective account is incredibly thin still sees herself as fat or overweight. This distorted perception of one's body has been documented many times in the literature (Cash & Deagle, 1997; Exterkate et al., 2009; Keizer et al., 2012). The most common method to assess an individual's body image is to take a photo of the individual and then stretch the image on either a horizontal or vertical axis and ask the individual to adjust the image on those two dimensions until it fits with how she thinks she looks. Compared with participants who do not have eating disorders, an individual with anorexia or bulimia is more likely to adjust the image so that it portrays an individual as considerably heavier than she actually is. To make these simulated images more realistic, researchers have used software that allows participants to adjust several dimensions of their body image. In one study, participants were asked to adjust an image of themselves that showed their real weight and body shape, then to adjust the image to correspond to their ideal weight. As seen in Figure 16.7, participants with anorexia and bulimia were more likely to depict themselves as heavier than they really were. In addition, the participants with anorexia set up a considerably thinner ideal image (Tovee et al., 2003).

Many clinicians and researchers believe that such distorted images help set up and maintain anorexic behavior, and indeed many therapies are designed around the idea of shifting the distorted perception (Exterkate et al., 2009; Rosen, 1997). Nonetheless, the causal link between distorted body image and anorexic behavior remains largely speculative. For example, one issue is whether people with

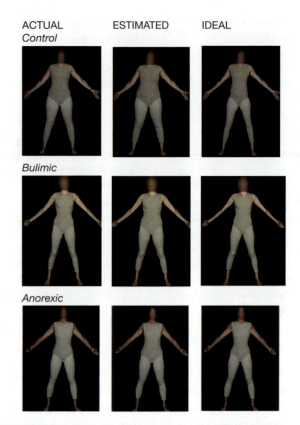

FIGURE 16.7 Body distortions by those with anorexia and bulimia. When computer software is used that simulates accurately how weight gets added to the body, individuals with both anorexia and bulimia will adjust the images in ways that show a distortion of their body image to higher weights than they really are. In addition, individuals with anorexia have an ideal body image that is thinner than the ideal shown by normal participants. From Tovee et al. (2003).

anorexia really "perceive" their bodies differently or whether they actually have the same perceptions as everyone else but respond differently because they want to convince others, and perhaps even themselves, that they are fat. One way to explore this issue is to develop more tasks that tap into very rapid perceptual processing of images that might not be as influenced by conscious response biases. For example, consider a set of photographs of an individual with anorexia in a natural setting, including head shots, full body shots, and partial body shots, where some of the shots were accurate and others were distorted to make the individual look heavier (as the person with anorexia normally seems to perceive her body). If those images were then embedded in a much larger set of images of other women of roughly the same age and the woman with anorexia was asked to identify herself as rapidly as possible when the images were presented in rapid succession, would the woman with anorexia actually be faster at identifying her "fat" self than her real self? This is just one example of the sorts of studies that researchers might conduct to assess how much anorexia is a problem in actual perception as opposed to response biases.

Genetic and Environmental Causal Factors There is evidence of a genetic component for anorexia, with a higher concordance rate both for monozygotic twins and dizygotic twins (Bulik et al., 2000, 2007; Devlin et al., 2002; Klump et al., 2001; Thornton et al., 2011). Heritability estimates are at roughly 50 percent, which indicates a substantial genetic contribution. Specific genes also seem to be emerging as especially relevant to the disorder (Bulik et al., 2007; Grice et al., 2002). The causal pathways for genetic influences, however, remain unclear, although at least some scholars have wondered if there might be a link to certain cognitive styles related to obsessional thought, as described earlier.

Although 50 percent is an impressive degree of genetic influence, this still allows for substantial environmental influences as well. One theory of environmental influence, which also tries to explain the gender difference, focuses on the physical and physiological changes that happen in girls during puberty (see Chapter 1). As girls approach puberty, their bodies increase dramatically in certain dimensions, such as hip and breast size, and there is normally a considerable increase in the proportion of body fat. They also start to menstruate. Boys undergo quite different patterns of changes, often losing body fat and developing a body shape that is thinner than their prepubertal form. Given these differences, it has been repeatedly suggested that girls are more at risk for being upset with these body changes, especially in a culture that embraces thinness. Moreover, many girls may feel apprehension over the body changes associated with becoming a woman because of the increased sexuality that is implied and reinforced by the monthly recurrence of menstruation.

These speculations lead to an interesting prediction. In those who will develop anorexia, girls who mature earlier physically should show an earlier onset for the disorder than those who mature later. This prediction is borne out (Swarr & Richards, 1996). The effect of puberty itself, however, seems to be more modest when other factors, such as peer group and culture, are considered (McCabe & Ricciardelli, 2003; Tremblay & Lariviere, 2009). Moreover, the actual influence of body changes on anorexia may be caused more by the buildup of fatty tissue that occurs in puberty rather than by the actual onset of puberty itself. Thus, when the proportion of fatty tissue and the age of menstruation are looked at independently of each other, large increases in fatty tissue seem to be the primary predictor of body dissatisfaction (Lynch et al., 2008; Stice & Whitenton, 2002). To the extent that physical and physiological changes in girls' bodies are related to genetic factors, these genetic factors may also be indirectly related to the onset of anorexia. That is, if genetic factors cause a more rapid increase in fatty tissue in some girls, those changes may also put the girls at higher risk of developing anorexia.

Family influences have often been thought to be an important factor in anorexia. Indeed, one family therapist, Salvador Minuchin, coined the term **anorexic families** to describe families in which particular patterns of interactions may be related to the emergence of anorexia in the child (Minuchin et al., 1978). Minuchin hypothesized that the parents in anorexic families have difficulty allowing their daughter to become more independent from the family in which she is enmeshed and to become an individual in her own right. In particular, anorexic families were said to have the following traits:

1. **Enmeshment.** A family structure in which everyone is so intertwined in their relationships and responsibilities that it is difficult for each member to emerge as an individual.
2. **Overprotectedness.** A family structure in which parents worry too much about a child's safety and tend to overreact to minor threats, resulting in not allowing the child to learn to cope in a more autonomous fashion.
3. **Rigidity.** A family structure in which there is an unwillingness to change the dynamics that constitute the dysfunctional family, including a tendency to stick to old patterns, no matter how painful they might be.
4. **Conflict avoidance.** A family that is unable to ever deal with conflicts or have useful confrontations. Parents avoid the conflict by withdrawing, refusing to respond, or otherwise escaping interactions over the conflict.

Collectively, these four factors were thought to drive some children toward seeking a way to exercise control and have autonomy. Supposedly, one of the few ways for them to do so is to exercise extreme control over their own bodies by refusing to eat, as this is the one pattern of behavior that the enmeshed, rigid, protective family environment cannot control.

Minuchin's hypotheses about the interactions of anorexic families were later tested in studies that compared the interaction patterns within families that had children with anorexia with the patterns of families that did not have children with anorexia (Casper & Troiani, 2001; Humphrey,

1989). In some studies, there are indications of different family dynamic patterns roughly similar to those proposed by Minuchin, but even in those cases, the causal argument does not follow directly, as parents may simply be manifesting a shared genotype with their children. Even Minuchin is careful to state that family factors might not initially cause anorexia, but rather they might maintain and perhaps exacerbate the disorder once it emerges. As is so often the case, the real causal pattern most likely involves a complex interaction of many social factors, with particular emphasis on genetic predispositions (Lacy & Price, 2004).

> Q: Describe how family interaction patterns have been thought to be involved in the causation or maintenance of anorexia.

Bulimia Nervosa

Bulimia nervosa is an eating disorder that is quite different from anorexia. A person with bulimia will engage in huge bouts of excessive rapid eating two or more times a week and then follow those episodes of overeating with some way of purging the food, usually by self-induced vomiting. A person's anxiety and stress may trigger a bout of eating that is often accompanied by feelings of disgust toward her own body, with the purging then bringing a form of relief from the stress and negative feelings. In contrast to individuals with anorexia, those with bulimia tend to be of normal weight and can even be quite overweight.

Incidence of Bulimia As already noted, bulimia is much more common in girls than in boys (Carlat et al., 1997; Keski-Rahkonen et al., 2009; Smink et al., 2012). Bulimia is more common than anorexia, and it is observed at least twice as often (Favaro et al., 2003). Moreover, the disorder seems to have been documented more recently than anorexia, as it has been widely reported for only a few decades (Gotestam & Agras, 1995). This recent rise of bulimia fits with the observation that its prevalence also varies more dramatically across cultures than anorexia does, being essentially absent in some cultures while relatively common in others, such as in North America (Keel & Klump, 2003). As with anorexia, bulimia is virtually nonexistent in young children and then shows a significant rise in adolescence (see Figure 16.8).

Causal Factors While there is some evidence for a genetic component to bulimia, the strength of the evidence and the possible genetic conclusion is not as strong as it is for anorexia (Kaye et al., 2004; Keel & Klump, 2003; Waller & Sheffield, 2008). Bulimia may therefore be more strongly influenced by cultural and familial factors. In particular, cultures that put tremendous emphasis on thinness and stigmatize obesity may have higher levels of bulimia. One interesting indication of the power of cultural effects is found in a study of 9- and 11-year-old girls who were either in schools with considerably older children or in schools with children around their own age (Wardle & Watters, 2004). Being exposed to older girls in school was associated with the participants feeling more obese and being more concerned with dieting. Because the girls were essentially randomly assigned to the schools and the body weights did not differ between girls assigned to the different schools,

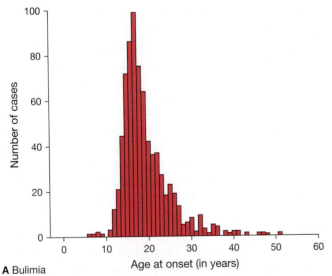

A Bulimia

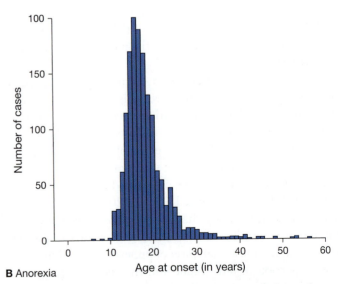

B Anorexia

FIGURE 16.8 Age of onset of bulimia and anorexia. Despite being quite distinct diseases with different etiologies, the typical age of onset for bulimia is very similar to that for anorexia. Adapted from Favaro et al. (2009).

this study shows how a relatively small difference in school environment can create some of the psychological differences thought to be associated with eating disorders, especially bulimia.

Family influences have also been explored extensively. Mothers of girls who are bulimic tend to have a variety of traits that are different from the traits of other mothers. In one study, mothers of girls with bulimia were more unhappy about how their families functioned, more likely to have eating disorders themselves, had atypical patterns of dieting, and were more likely than other mothers to think that their daughters should lose weight. They were also more likely than other mothers to judge their daughters as less attractive than the girls judged themselves (Pike & Rodin, 1991). Parents of children with bulimia are also more likely to be depressed and to show less affection and more hostility and belittling in interactions with their children (Humphrey, 1989). Moreover, there seems to be a linkage between parental concerns about their children becoming obese and the children's eating behaviors long before the typical onset of bulimia in adolescence. In one study of infants and toddlers of mothers who had eating disorders (mostly bulimia), the mothers were more concerned about the baby's eating habits and the babies themselves were described as being more avid eaters, as if a fixation with eating had been set up very early in their lives (Agras et al., 1999). Again, however, claims of family influences need to be evaluated in the context of the alternative of a common genetic contribution to problems in both parents and children. The weaker evidence for genetic factors does at least initially lend more support for family and cultural influences in the case of bulimia.

Q: How do the most likely causes of bulimia seem to differ from the most likely causes of anorexia?

Depression

Everyone feels sad or blue from time to time, but some people fall into more sustained states of sadness and despair that become pathological. In adults, depression is a kind of affective (mood) disorder that has two prominent subtypes: unipolar depression and bipolar disorder. Each has its own course of progression. In children, the incidence of both types was long considered to be rare until at least some time in adolescence, raising profound questions about what factors protect most children from these potentially debilitating disorders.

A large set of adult studies suggests that these two types of depression are quite distinct clusters that occur in different groups of people (Angst & Marneros, 2001; Forty et al., 2008; Winokur et al., 1995; see Table 16.2). **Unipolar depression** is a severe and sustained drop in affect that is often accompanied by agitation, feelings of sadness and worthlessness, insomnia, and loss of appetite. It tends to be roughly twice as common in women as in men (6 percent of women versus 3 percent of men), a ratio that is present from early adolescence (Nolen-Hoeksema & Girgus, 1994). The most typical age of onset is in the 20s (American Psychiatric Association, 1994).

Bipolar disorder is a distinct affective disorder characterized by swings between periods of lethargy and low affect and periods of high activity, or "mania," in which the person often

Symptoms	Unipolar	Bipolar	Statistical Significance of Difference
Incidence of psychoses during depression	Half as common as in bipolar	Twice as common as in unipolar	Large
Number of lifetime episodes of depression	Somewhat less frequent	Somewhat more frequent	Moderate
Longest episodes of depression	Much longer	Much shorter	Large
Excessive self-reproach	More extensive	Less extensive	Large
Difficulty sleeping	Less difficulty	More difficulty	Large
Loss of energy	Greater loss	Less significant loss	Large
Diminished libido	More diminished	Less diminished	Large

TABLE 16.2 **Bipolar disorder versus unipolar depression.** Even in their depressive periods, people afflicted with unipolar depression have different symptoms and time courses than those with bipolar disorder. People with bipolar disorder have more frequent incidences of psychoses, more frequent episodes of depression, and shorter episodes of depression, among other differences. From Forty et al. (2008).

has inflated self-esteem, grandiose plans, increased talkativeness, and a diminished amount of sleep (American Psychiatric Association, 2013). It affects men and women equally (roughly 1 percent of the total population) and has an earlier average age of onset than unipolar depression, typically during late adolescence. People with bipolar disorder may have difficulty sleeping, but they are also more likely to have difficulty waking up in the morning. The genetic basis for bipolar disorder is considerably stronger than for unipolar depression. Loss of appetite is less common and may oscillate with binge eating. In the depressive phase, people with bipolar disorder are likely to be very slow in motor movements and not agitated as in the unipolar case. People with unipolar depression are more likely to display anger than those with bipolar disorder. Because of these differences, it is useful to think about the development of the two forms of depression separately.

Q: What are some differences in how depression is manifested in people with bipolar versus unipolar versions of the disorder?

Unipolar Depression

It was traditionally held that young children simply didn't get depressed. More recently, there seems to be a consensus that young children can develop true depressions that are similar to both the unipolar and bipolar types in adults (Coyle et al., 2003). This opinion is based on the ability to reliably use assessment questionnaires for childhood depression and because of convergences between what parents say about the behaviors of their children and the children's own self-reports (McClellan & Werry, 2000). The childhood assessments focus on factors that tend to be more behavioral in nature, such as problems in school and in social interactions and the presence of behaviors that are disruptive and aggressive. There are also indications of unpleasant or uncomfortable moods and an undervaluing of the self relative to others (Carle et al., 2008). Some children do seem to enter sustained periods of reduced affect and have some of the other symptoms found in adults, such as feelings of hopelessness about the future, excessive rumination about negative events, and suicidal thoughts. It is far less clear, however, that these children experience the full range of adult or adolescent symptoms. In fact, the recent flurry of attention to the presence of depression in young children runs the risk of overlooking much more dramatic developmental facts: the incidence of unipolar depression skyrockets during adolescence and swings from an even distribution among the sexes to a huge preponderance among females (see Figure 16.9). Unipolar depression, with its somewhat muted forms of negative affect

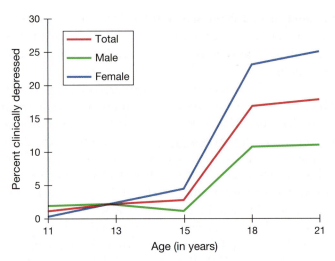

FIGURE 16.9 **Rise of depression in adolescence.** The incidence of clinical depression rises dramatically during the teenage years, especially among females. Adapted from Hankin et al. (1998).

with reduced intensity, increases markedly after 15 years of age (Hankin et al., 1998; see also Ge et al., 1994; Lakdawalla et al., 2007; Petersen et al., 1993).

Why is there such a dramatic increase in the rate of depression after puberty? Several possible reasons have been proposed: more stressful life events during and after puberty (Ge et al., 2001), increased interpersonal vulnerability (Gotlib & Hammen, 1992), physiological changes produced by puberty, and changes in cognition (Lakdawalla et al., 2007; Lockhart et al., 2002; Rutter, 1987). These accounts also attempt to explain why the surge in incidence coincides with the quite sudden onset of a large gender difference. Each of these factors is considered in exploring the etiology of childhood and adolescent depression.

Biological Causes Unipolar depression and its weaker variants tend to run in families, suggesting a genetic component. Indeed, in one study of severe depression among monozygotic and dizygotic adolescent twins, the much higher concordance rate among MZ twins suggested a heritability of roughly 40 percent (Glowinski et al., 2003; Lau & Eley, 2010; Rice & Thapar, 2009). Thus, even in cases of relatively early onset of the disorder, the heritabilities are as high as in adults, suggesting that the biological basis in adolescence may be similar to that found in older individuals. Moreover, if one individual in a family experiences depression in adolescence, the likelihood that a relative will also experience depression in adolescence increases based on how closely related the two individuals are (for example, MZ twins, DZ twins, non-twin siblings, or cousins), suggesting that genetics plays an important role in the onset of the disorder.

Genetic factors may often work in combination with daily life stressors, such that adolescents who have a particular genetic vulnerability may be much more likely to be plunged into depression when encountering a series of stressful life experiences, even though they may not fall into depression in less stressful environments (Hyde et al., 2008; Wichers et al., 2009). These extensive interactions with environmental influences may help explain why, despite high heritabilities, it continues to be difficult to isolate specific genes that are consistently associated with unipolar depression (Cohen-Woods et al., 2012). Such interactions also provide a good example of the diathesis-stress model of the development of psychopathologies, in which some individuals are seen as vulnerable to a specific psychopathology when exposed to stress.

> **Q:** How does the incidence of depression change with development?

Genes can code for a wide variety of developmental changes, ranging from hormonal to cognitive changes, which has led researchers to investigate possible connections between hormone levels and depression. In particular, some studies have focused on whether the rapid changes in the levels of hormones circulating through the body during puberty, which differ between the sexes, could be related to girls' much higher rates of depression in adolescence. Despite the intuitive appeal of this hypothesis, however, the idea of a direct connection between adolescent hormone levels and depression has not been borne out by the research (Brooks-Gunn & Warren, 1989; Brooks-Gunn et al., 1994; Buchanan et al., 1992). In short, despite the popular idea that teenagers are being overwhelmed by "raging hormones," circulating levels of hormones in their blood have not been shown to directly affect their emotional states.

Nonetheless, there are good reasons to believe that there are indirect relations between hormones and emotions as a result of other processes. One possible influence may be that girls tend to mature earlier than boys and that those who mature especially early are put under social stresses at an earlier age owing to their changing bodies and appearance (Ge et al., 1996; Hyde et al., 2008). The 13-year-old girl who looks like a fully grown woman may encounter more social stresses than the 13-year-old who continues to look like a young girl for a few more years (Graber et al., 1997). By contrast, for boys, maturing early, when it does happen, may actually be a positive event. There is some evidence to support the idea of increased social stresses both for early-maturing girls and late-maturing boys (Angold & Rutter, 1992; Ge et al., 1996; Kaltiala-Heino et al., 2003). According to this account, the hormones themselves do not have a direct effect on depression, but they do bring about physical changes that, in turn, can cause depression-inducing stress. Yet, while indirect effects through the social consequences of early and late maturity are more feasible, these explanations, too, remain controversial. This is because hormones and physical maturation, while related, are not the same, as the initial spurt of hormones may happen for quite a while before the physical maturation is evident, thus making it important to ask about the independent contributions of these two factors. Hormones may also have other indirect physiological effects, such as increased levels of estrogen, which influence levels of the neurotransmitter serotonin, which in turn is related to depression (Hyde et al., 2008; Naninck et al., 2011).

Social Causes Social factors may also play a role in their own right. Certainly children in most cultures tend to experience major changes in their life experiences as they enter puberty. Such dramatic social changes influence both sexes, hence explaining the rise of depression in both sexes. Still, some researchers have argued that the influence is greater for girls, which can help explain the sex differences as well. For example, gender role socialization may be more intense and constraining for girls than for boys during this period (Hill & Lynch, 1983). In one study of 12,000 Norwegian adolescents, the onset of depression in girls seemed to be more closely related to perceptions about sex roles than it was in boys (Wichstrom, 1999). On a smaller scale, parenting styles also have a relation to the onset of depression in children. For example, the adolescent children of mothers who unconditionally accept their children for who they are have lower incidences of depression, while the adolescent children of mothers who are highly controlling (through such means as criticism, negative comparisons, and "guilt trips") have higher incidences of depression (Barber, 2002; Garber et al., 1997; Mandara & Pikes, 2008; see also Blatt et al., 1979, for a different view of parenting effects). The higher incidences of depression are thought to be partially produced through feelings of low self-worth in the children, but again having a shared genotype may also produce these results. The same genotype that causes girls to be depressed may cause a combination of depression and excessive control in their mothers. Surely, any social factors influencing the development of depression in childhood interact in important ways with both biological and cognitive factors.

> **Q:** What are some explanations for gender differences in depression?

Cognitive Causes The role of cognitive patterns is one of the most intriguing explanations for the emergence of depression in adolescence and for the gender differences. For some time, researchers have proposed that people with major depression have different cognitive schemas for thinking about the world and interpreting events. For example, Aaron Beck proposed that depressed individuals have a negative style of thought that leads them to make different sorts of attributions than nondepressed individuals and that this difference in attribution style leads to depression (Beck, 1967). Beck hypothesized that depressed individuals have a mutually reinforcing set of negative beliefs about themselves, about the world, and about their future that causes a negative schema to automatically be used in most situations. A key part of Beck's approach was the idea that various biological factors, such as a certain genotype, place a child at risk and then a particular kind of stressful environment triggers the negative cognitive style. Thus, not all children with a genetic vulnerability to depression will become depressed and not all children growing up in highly stressful environments will become depressed, but when the two factors are both present, depression may emerge.

> **Q:** How might stress and genetic factors interact to create depression?

A related theory proposes that depression grows out of feelings of hopelessness that are usually engendered by specific life experiences (Hyde et al., 2008; Rose & Abramson, 1992). A child might be ill treated, and in her attempts to figure out why, she might develop a cognitive style in which she assumes that her misfortune is because of something about her rather than about the world. When she starts to see this negative feature in global terms (that is, across many different contexts) and as stable over time, she may fall into a state of cognitive hopelessness in which her future looks very bleak. This is because she thinks that something intrinsic about her, which is very wide ranging in effects and which will always be present, will doom her to a future of negative events. This view evolved out of a theory known as **learned helplessness**, in which animals (including humans) are put in a series of uncontrollable negative situations from which they cannot learn a way to escape, leading them to "learn to be helpless." For example, a rat might be put into a cage in which it receives shocks that it can neither escape nor have any control over. When animals or people are put in these situations, they seem to learn a helpless style that is thought to be closely related to depression (Seligman, 1975).

Yet, neither of these cognitive approaches on their own can explain either the huge surge of depression in adolescence or the sex differences. We can argue that transitions during puberty result in changes in learning experiences in school, peer groups, and the like, and that girls have more stressful transitions. This links the social influence

arguments mentioned earlier to tendencies to appraise many life events in more negative terms. But it is not always the case that the environments faced by teenagers are that much more stressful than those encountered a few years earlier. In fact, as seen in Chapter 15, bullying and other forms of peer aggression often reach their peak before puberty. Nonetheless, adolescence may pose its own uniquely stressful challenges, and with respect to sex differences, there are consistent reports that girls both report and actually experience more negative life events in late childhood and adolescence (Hyde et al., 2008).

We can also look beyond the impact of stressful life events on cognition and instead directly consider the child's cognitive development. Are there more general changes in how children think about the world that might be related to the surge of depression in teenagers? Such a change does seem to occur in the extent to which children are optimistic about whether current negative traits will change into more positive versions of those traits in the future. As described in Chapter 13, there is a major shift during the elementary and middle school years in how children regard the malleability of negative traits (Lockhart et al., 2002). Younger children assume that negative traits, even physical ones like missing a finger, are likely to change for the better with maturity. Older children and adults think that such change toward the positive is much less likely. In addition, younger children tend to see more of a role for their own efforts in bringing about change, hence inoculating them from learned helplessness. Children's views of the role of effort also seem to vary across cultures, which may explain the lower rates of depression in cultures such as Japan, where traits are seen as more changeable through effort (Lockhart et al., 2008).

Although a decrease in cognitive optimism may offer insight into the increase in depression in adolescence, it does not in itself explain sex differences. Future studies need to examine more systematically whether children's diminished optimistic bias as they age coincides with the onset of depression on an individual basis. As with other models, some interaction with a biological risk factor or social experiences more common to girls is also needed to explain why some individuals develop depression and others do not. It is also important to keep in mind that changes during puberty do not seem to be correlated with the rate of cognitive development during the same period (Litt, 1995). Thus, cognitive development is likely to make an independent contribution to depression that is above and beyond any direct or indirect effects of puberty (see also Lakdawalla et al., 2007).

> **Q:** How might patterns of cognitive development explain the increase in depression with age?

Sex differences in depression during adolescence may also be related to another cognitive difference known as **rumination**. While some people respond to negative situations by problem solving or simply by distracting themselves, a third response style is to continue to think about the negative problem. People with a ruminative response style tend to mull over negative events both in the present and in the past in a manner that helps set up and maintain depressive states. That style is more common both among depressed individuals and among women than in the population at large. Women may have a stronger tendency than men to ruminate, partly because of their socialization, as girls are more likely to be encouraged to think through a situation thoroughly, whereas boys are often encouraged to problem-solve or to fix negative situations (Nolen-Hoeksema, 2003). For those who get used to this cognitive style, it can be quite difficult to change. Thus, if a group of people who tend toward depression and another group who do not are asked to think positive thoughts about themselves, the more depressed individuals are more reluctant to do so on the grounds that they are still gaining insight into themselves through the negative ruminations (Lyubomirsky & Nolen-Hoeksema, 1993). Moreover, there seem to be reciprocal negative-feedback loops in female adolescents in which rumination increases depression, which in turn increases ruminative thinking, leading to a kind of downward spiral (Nolen-Hoeksema et al., 2007). In addition, those adolescents who show more rumination about negative events are more likely to later show severe major depressive episodes than those who show lesser amounts of rumination about comparably negative events, a pattern that has led some researchers to conclude that rumination may serve to amplify the effects of negative events in ways that lead to depression (Abela & Hankin, 2011).

Even if girls are more likely to be socialized to ruminate than are boys, this still does not explain the surge of depression in the teenage years. Rumination would seem to be present in elementary school children just as much as it is in adolescents. But in adolescence, parental socialization recedes and peer influences rise, and ruminative tendencies among peers may be mutually reinforcing and rise to higher levels than at earlier ages (see New Directions in Developmental Research box).

While the etiology of all mental disorders involves an interaction of multiple factors, unipolar depression may well involve the most factors in the most complex web of interactions. Figure 16.10 illustrates one model of how affect, biology, and cognition interact over the course of development to create depression, and in particular gender differences in depression (Hyde et al., 2008). In this model, some individuals are more vulnerable, either cognitively, biologically, or emotionally in terms of temperamental traits, but in many cases the individuals may be more vulnerable in all three ways at the same time. When these vulnerabilities interact with negative life events, they together lead to what is called **depressogenic vulnerability**, which represents the convergence of all the separate factors to create depression. Unfortunately, these factors tend to be stronger in girls, and they therefore collectively contribute to the large sex difference in depression during adolescence, as shown in Figure 16.10.

Bipolar Disorder

As described earlier, bipolar disorder is marked by two distinct phases, a depressive phase and a manic phase. Although earlier views tended to see the depressive behaviors of unipolar and bipolar depression in similar ways, more recent approaches point toward some behavioral differences, including more lethargy and sleeping in bipolar disorder, as well as more changeable mood and perhaps less ruminative cognition (Bowden, 2005; Forty et al., 2008; Goldberg et al., 2008; Hantouche & Akiskal, 2005). The same approximate range of behaviors is used in the diagnosis of

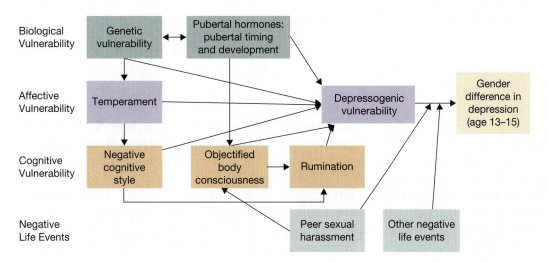

FIGURE 16.10 Factors contributing to the emergence of depression in adolescence. It now appears that biological, affective, and cognitive factors can create a high level of "depressogenic vulnerability" that interacts strongly with negative life events to create depression in adolescence and that seems to converge more strongly for girls. Adapted from Hyde et al. (2008).

Co-rumination, Gender, and Depression

As researchers attempt to explain the large gender difference in depression and its onset in puberty, one new variable of interest is that of **co-rumination**. Co-rumination occurs when a group tends to dwell on negative events in a mutually reinforcing manner. Like rumination, it seems to maintain and perhaps exacerbate depression, and it occurs more frequently among girls and women than among boys and men. Yet, it may seem paradoxical that girls, who are known to have generally closer and more extensive social relationships than boys, are more depressed, as social bonds are thought to normally alleviate depression (Bukowski et al., 1996). But if co-rumination is often a consequence of those bonds, it may help to explain the higher rates of depression among girls.

Co-rumination is more socially dynamic and interactive than rumination. As we first mentioned in Chapter 15, co-rumination is the excessive discussion of personal problems in one-on-one interactions with friends. These discussions may include going over the problem again and again, speculating about future problems, being encouraged by others to engage in such discussions, and focusing on negative emotions. Such discussions might be about whether a potential boyfriend is about to break up with a girl or whether a comment made by another girl is really a veiled insult (Rose, 2002). The constant discussion of problems and negative emotions might prevent vulnerable girls from thinking or acting more positively and hence might lead to or maintain depression.

When a co-rumination scale was developed, it did indeed demonstrate more co-rumination among third, fifth, seventh, and ninth grade girls than among boys, with the gender difference much larger among the adolescents in the group (Rose, 2002). Questions still remain about why co-rumination occurs more among girls in the first place. Is it simply a natural outgrowth of girls' tighter social relations and higher levels of self-disclosure? Is it a side effect of socialization differences that tend to push girls toward thinking more about internal states and personal attributions? Or does it reflect something deeper about the cognitive styles of girls and boys? Whatever the answers, the co-rumination hypothesis does suggest that girls who are depressed might be helped by interventions that focus on the social groups in which they are embedded and how the members of those social groups interact. More broadly, the social interaction patterns that distinguish boys and girls, especially shortly before and during adolescence, may be critical to understanding the emergence of gender differences in psychopathology (Crick & Zhan-Waxler, 2003).

Co-rumination may have costs by inducing depression. But it also may have benefits by promoting close friendships and networks of social support, which may help explain why it persists even with some negative consequences. Studies of adolescent girls do indeed suggest such a dual role in which co-rumination levels are associated both with higher levels of depression and with tighter social bonds (Rose et al., 2007; Starr & Davila, 2009). In addition, co-rumination seems to facilitate contagion of depressive emotions among friends (Schwartz-Mette & Rose, 2012), illustrating how the positive effects of friendships may also have negative side effects in vulnerable groups prone to co-rumination. The study of co-rumination represents a new direction of research because it takes the process of rumination beyond that of a lone individual. In considering how a social network might cause a kind of positive feedback that increases the depressive effects of rumination while also being reinforced by the ways in which it builds social bonds and mutual support, researchers can seek ways to break the loop and reduce depression.

bipolar disorder in both children and adults, except that it is necessary to adjust the ratings of such factors as "grandiose plans" for what is normal for a child of that age (Leibenluft, 2008; Leibenluft & Rich, 2008). Thus, it might not be that unusual for a fourth-grader to think that he might really become an NBA star, despite having limited athletic skills, but it would be unusual for a fourth-grader to think that he could study hard and get a college degree over the next few months.

In addition to the behavioral differences, bipolar and unipolar affective disorders tend to occur in different family groups and are reliably distinguished by different assessment instruments and by different developmental time courses, with bipolar disorders tending to emerge earlier (Leibenluft & Rich, 2008; Moreno et al., 2012). Unlike unipolar depression, bipolar disorder is not characterized by any difference between the sexes. Finally, the heritability of bipolar disorder seems to be a good deal higher than the heritability of unipolar depression. In some studies, the heritability of bipolar disorder is as high as 85 percent and averages around 65 percent (Craddock & Jones, 1999; Edvardsen et al., 2008; McGuffin et al., 2003; Potash & DePaulo, 2000; Taylor et al., 2002; Wray & Gottesman, 2012).

Causal Factors Although there is a strong genetic component to bipolar disorder, it is not so strong as to rule out other important influences. As in unipolar depression, there seems to be an important contribution from stressful life events that can both trigger the initial onset of the disorder and launch a new series of mood cycles (Post & Leverich, 2006; Rush, 2003). One study of 2.1 million Danes found clear evidence for a genetic influence based on family relatedness and a possible environmental trigger caused by the death of a parent, although the authors acknowledge a possible confound in that parents who have bipolar disorder have a higher mortality rate, and thus it could be the genetic factor that is actually at work (Mortensen et al., 2003). Children and adolescents who show deficits in the ability to label facial emotions and emotions in vocalizations may also be at greater risk for bipolar disorder (Brotman et al., 2008; Deveney et al., 2012), perhaps because such deficits lead to more stressful social interactions.

Diagnosis of Bipolar Disorder One major problem in uncovering the cause of bipolar disorder is the difficulty in diagnosing the disorder in younger children as distinct from diagnosing attention deficit hyperactivity disorder (ADHD), conduct disorders, and even schizophrenia (Weller et al., 1995). Children and young adolescents in general seem to have far more variable mood states than older individuals, and when those mood states are embedded in other disorders, they can sometimes be mistaken for symptoms of bipolar disorder. Over the last decade or so, there has been a substantial increase in the diagnosis of children, and even preschoolers, with bipolar disorder. In some cases, these may be misdiagnoses in which difficult behaviors in a child are confused with the more specific symptoms associated with pediatric bipolar disorder. If the strict criteria of the DSM-IV-TR system are used with age-appropriate adjustments for some symptoms, however, it appears that bipolar disorder can be clearly identified in quite young children, although probably not at the high levels that are often reported (Leibenluft, 2008, 2011; Leibenluft & Rich, 2008). A related diagnostic problem is that children with bipolar disorder often have several other disorders at the same time, and so the overall suite of symptoms of a bipolar child can overlap with those of children who have no bipolar component. This can create agony for parents who may hear multiple diagnoses from different professionals, each of which might lead to radically different treatments and medications. For example, if a genuine case of bipolar disorder is misdiagnosed as ADHD, several of the medications for ADHD might help launch a bipolar child into a manic episode rather than be therapeutic.

Bipolar disorder is likely to have its own developmental trajectory that is quite distinct from unipolar depression, with bipolar disorder emerging earlier and with different symptoms even in the depressive state. The developmental trajectory does not seem to surge as dramatically at a particular age, and the disorder has even been seen in preschoolers (Blumberg, 2007; B. Geller et al., 2004), suggesting that the relatively strong genetic predisposition toward bipolar disorder may result in early manifestations in childhood instead of late manifestations in adolescence or adulthood as a function of environmental stresses. Moreover, because the cases that are diagnosed very early often do show all the symptoms of a full-fledged disorder several years later, there is good reason to believe that the same disorder is involved (B. Geller et al., 2008; Wozniak et al., 2011). Indeed, in studies that develop careful assessments to distinguish the mania of bipolar disorder from other high levels of activity in children, misdiagnoses were quite uncommon (Wozniak et al., 2011). The challenge is to instill the same level of care in frontline clinicians. Finally, treatment with lithium and other mood stabilizers seems to be equally effective at all ages (Weller et al., 2004).

> **Q:** How are the etiology and developmental trajectory of bipolar disorder different from those of unipolar disorder?

Conduct Disorder: The Case of Psychopathy

There is a huge area of developmental psychopathology that focuses on **conduct disorder**, which can be diagnosed in terms of a set of behaviors that are both aggressive and antisocial (Baker, 2009; Kazdin, 1995; Loeber et al., 2009). As seen in Table 16.3, the critieria fall into four categories: aggression against people and animals, destruction of property, theft or other violations of trust, and breaking major rules. For a child to be diagnosed with conduct disorder, he or she must show at least three of these behaviors over the course of a year. Because we have considered aggression and antisocial behaviors in other chapters and because the full scale of conduct disorders is so vast, this discussion will focus on one particular subtype—that of psychopathy, or sociopathy. We will not discuss antisocial behaviors in which there is evidence of empathy, regret, guilt, and other

Behavior Category	Specific Behaviors
Aggression against people or other animals	1. Bullies or threatens others.
	2. Becomes easily engaged in or initiates physical fights.
	3. Uses a weapon, such as a knife or large stick, to threaten or hurt another.
	4. Is physically cruel to people or animals.
	5. Has robbed another person through force or intimidation.
	6. Has forced another into some form of sexual activity.
Willful destruction of property	1. Sets fires intentionally, hoping to cause damage.
	2. Intentionally destroys others' property in ways other than fire.
Theft or violation of trust	1. Has broken into or entered (without permission) another's home, car, or place of business.
	2. Uses lies for personal gain, such as lying about needs or obligations.
	3. Has stolen items in ways that don't involve direct confrontation with the owner, such as shoplifting or using another's credit card.
Violation of major rules	1. Stays out late at night as a preteen even though parents may have strict rules against doing so.
	2. Is truant from school as a preteen.
	3. Has run away from home overnight at least twice.

TABLE 16.3 Diagnosing conduct disorder. Conduct disorder is diagnosed when at least three of these behaviors are present within a 1-year time interval. Adapted from American Psychiatric Association (2000).

emotions, since a different basis for these inappropriate behaviors has been hypothesized (Blair & Blair, 2009). In addition, when we consider conduct disorders as a whole, the primary focus will be on treatment methods.

Features of Psychopathy

Psychopathy is one of the most chilling disorders, and adults afflicted with this disorder often arouse highly negative reactions in those around them. For centuries, historians and writers have discussed individuals who seem to be cold, calculating, and remorseless. In 1941, Hervey Cleckley crystallized these observations in a compelling account of the disorder entitled *The Mask of Sanity* (Cleckley, 1941), which described the adult with psychopathy as having no guilt, shame, or emotional attachments, and as highly manipulative and intelligent. In essence, this characterization remains the same today, with somewhat less emphasis on intelligence as a critical factor. A person with psychopathy can be described as someone who is driven by the pursuit of goals but who does not feel the impediments of morality or empathy toward others. As such, to get to a desired end, a skilled person with psychopathy will manipulate a victim through lies, deception, and distortions.

Imagine a teenager, Harry, who "befriends" George, one of the least popular but most academically talented students in a class. Harry gives George small gifts and flatters him heavily. He finds out about George's secret crush on Mary, one of the girls in their class, and he tells George that he knows Mary. He then shows George some alleged excerpts from Mary's diary that he says he accidentally found and which say nice things about George. A few days before a critical take-home final examination, Harry asks George for help on the exam, a clear violation of the honor code. When George objects, Harry downplays the moral issues and reminds George that he did look at Mary's diary. In a veiled threat, he asks George if helping on the exam would be as embarrassing as everyone knowing that George looked at Mary's diary and had a secret crush on her. George ends up helping Harry on the exam. Since Harry has no further use for George, he stops interacting with him and, to relieve boredom, writes an anonymous e-mail telling the entire class about George's crush on Mary. When George confronts Harry, Harry denies involvement in a completely compelling manner that also casts George's one true friend in the class under a pall of suspicion.

It is difficult to imagine that people could behave so callously and ruthlessly to others and without any pangs of conscience, but the abundant case reports of such individuals suggest that they constitute roughly 1 percent of the general population and a much higher proportion of inmate populations. Some of the most successful people with psychopathy are so adroit at manipulating others that they are rarely recognized as having caused the pain that they inflict. It might seem that psychopathy is a disorder that could not emerge until adolescence or adulthood because of the manipulative skills involved. As seen shortly, however, the roots of this disorder appear very early, and a core deficit may well be shared between young children with psychopathy and adults with the disorder.

Diagnosis of Psychopathy

Specific assessments for psychopathy have been developed relatively recently, as the disorder was originally lumped into a much larger category of antisocial personality disorders in the DSM diagnosis system. When a specific screening device for psychopathy was developed, it became possible to recognize a highly specific disorder that differed from disorders in which people transgress against society for a wide variety of other reasons (Harris et al., 1994). There are reliable assessment instruments for diagnosing psychopathy in both adults (Hare, 1991) and children (Corrado et al., 2004; Das et al., 2009; Frick et al., 2000). Table 16.4 lists the features of psychopathy that are looked for in the most widely used child assessment, the Psychopathy Checklist: Youth Version (PCL:YV), which is used to assess psychopathy in adolescents between 13 and 18 years of age. The adult version is quite similar. One critical aspect of psychopathy is that the disorder is distributed fairly evenly among all socioeconomic groups, which tends to argue against the theory that psychopathy is completely a product of socialization (Pitchford, 2001; Rutter et al., 1998). More specifically, it has proved difficult to use differences in parenting practices to explain why some children appear to be callous and unemotional (Wootton et al., 1997).

> **Q:** Describe some typical symptoms of psychopathy.

Item	Description
1. Impression management	Exhibits superficial charm and presents positive attributes to gain trust of others.
2. Grandiose sense of self-worth	Is opinionated and domineering and shows inflated sense of self.
3. Stimulation seeking	Is prone to boredom, seeks novelty and excitement, and enjoys taking risks.
4. Pathological lying	Lies easily and often.
5. Manipulation for personal gain	Deceives, manipulates, and cons people.
6. Lack of remorse/guilt	Does not feel guilty or care about hurting others.
7. Shallow affect	Does not feel deep emotion, but pretends to feel emotion and to care about others.
8. Callousness	Lacks empathy, views others as objects, and does not care about others' feelings and needs.
9. Parasitic orientation	Exploits others by taking their money and possessions or by manipulating others to do his work.
10. Poor anger control	Is easily offended and provoked to violence.
11. Promiscuous sexual behavior	Has many casual sexual encounters, often involving threats and coercion.
12. Early behavioral problems	Lies, steals, and sets fires before age 10.
13. Lacks goals	Has no interest in education and has unrealistic future goals.
14. Impulsivity	Acts out, may quit school or leave home on a whim, and does not consider consequences of his actions.
15. Irresponsibility	Engages in reckless behaviors and does not fulfill obligations or pay back debts.
16. Failure to accept responsibility	Blames others for his problems and does not take personal responsibility for his actions.
17. Unstable interpersonal relationships	Does not show commitment or loyalty to others and has volatile relationships.
18. Serious criminal behavior	Engages in many instances of criminal activity.
19. Serious violations of conditional release	Commits two or more violations (for example, crimes or drug or alcohol abuse) when released on probation from juvenile correctional facilities.
20. Criminal versatility	Engages in at least six kinds of criminal behavior.

TABLE 16.4 Symptoms of psychopathy. The Psychopathy Checklist: Youth Version rates individuals on 20 items that collectively are quite effective in identifying adolescents with psychopathy. Adapted from Dolan (2004).

The early roots of psychopathy are a matter of some controversy. Adults with psychopathy often have a history of various antisocial behaviors in childhood (Lynam et al., 2007), although some children who behave this way grow up to be normal adults (Hill, 2003; Saltaris, 2002). Are there more specific precursors to developing psychopathy? Among aggressive or antisocial children, some seem to lack a moral sense that guides their actions, show no genuine affection, and are unusually self-centered (Lynam, 1997). These children, who also tend to form weak attachments to their caregivers and peers, seem to be more likely to develop psychopathy (Saltaris, 2002). Some scholars have identified callous or unemotional traits that are indicators of psychopathy in young children (Barry et al., 2000; Frick & Ellis, 1999). Indeed, one review suggests that stable indicators of aberrant empathy and guilt can be found in children as young as 3 years old (Loeber et al., 2009). Moreover, even children under 2 years old who show disregard and lack of concern for others are more likely to show some antisocial and psychopathic characteristics in middle childhood (Rhee et al., 2013). Another study followed young children who showed strong antisocial patterns to see whether they later developed psychopathic tendencies. These children were compared to another group of children who first showed antisocial behavior as adolescents. In adolescence, the two groups' antisocial behaviors were quite similar. But as 26-year-olds, those who had been antisocial as young children were far more likely to show adult psychopathic tendencies (Moffitt et al., 2002).

> **Q:** How might the first signs of psychopathy emerge in children?

Causal Factors

At all ages, those with psychopathy seem to share a core deficit: an inability to have empathy for the emotional states of others. While a skilled, successful person with psychopathy might be able to feign interest and pretend to care for another so as to attain some goal, the real ability to empathize and perceive others' emotional states may be severely impaired. Using the Psychopathy Checklist (youth and adult versions) and other measures, researchers have assessed whether children and adults who score high on the checklist also have specific deficits pertaining to empathy. They have found that both adults and children with high psychopathy scores seem to have a selective impairment in the ability to process sad and fearful expressions (Blair et al., 2001;

Sylvers et al., 2011; see Scientific Methods box). Children as young as 9 years old who score high on psychopathy have been shown to have difficulty detecting sadness and fear in both facial expressions and verbal tones, but no difficulty in detecting happy or angry facial expressions or tones (Blair & Coles, 2000; Blair et al., 2001). Other studies, however, suggest that the deficits in emotion recognition may be broader than just for fear and sadness and may cover a wider range of emotions in both facial and vocal expressions (Dawel et al., 2012). Children with high psychopathy scores have also been shown to have greater difficulty distinguishing moral principles from social conventions (Blair, 1997), a distinction that comes very naturally to much younger children who do not score high on psychopathy (Lockhart, 1981; Turiel, 1983).

Adults with psychopathy appear to have a particular deficit in the amygdala, a brain region associated with emotional responding (Blair, 2008; Dawel et al., 2012; Laakso et al., 2001; LeDoux, 1998). Recall from Chapter 7 that the amygdala is a central part of a brain circuit concerned with processing emotional stimuli and generating emotions in response to those stimuli. For example, when adults who score high on psychopathy are asked to remember words with negative connotations, they show less activation in the amygdala than individuals who do not score high on psychopathy, as revealed by fMRI studies, but they do not show this difference when remembering neutral words (Kiehl, 2006; Kiehl et al., 2001; see Figure 16.11). Similar physiological measures also seem to be present in children who score high on psychopathy. When electrodes are used to record skin responses from high-scoring and normal-scoring children, both groups responded similarly to neutral stimuli. But when they were exposed to threatening stimuli, the high-scoring children showed much smaller skin responses than did the normal-scoring children (Blair, 1999). Using functional neuroimaging techniques (fMRI), researchers have shown that children as young as 10 years old who are callous and unemotional show reduced activation levels of the amygdala when viewing fearful facial expressions, but not when viewing angry or neutral expressions. The results suggest that children who show signs of early psychopathy may have a specific deficit at the neural level in the ability to process information related to perceiving distress in another (Jones et al., 2009; Marsh et al., 2008). A similar finding has been found in adults (Kiehl, 2006).

These neural deficits are presumably related to difficulties in emotional regulation that are often noticed in children and adults who exhibit psychopathic behaviors. Not only is there less activation in the amygdala for those scoring high on psychopathy, there is also reduced connectivity with frontal brain regions that can regulate and

Hypothesis:

Children with psychopathic traits display fear-recognition deficits when engaging in automatic visual processing outside of their attention and awareness.

Method:

1. Researchers included in the study 88 boys, ages 7 to 11, who had often been in trouble at home or at school.

2. All boys were administered the Antisocial Process Screening Device (APSD), which detects psychopathic tendencies. Higher scores indicated more psychopathy.

3. All boys sat at a monitor while wearing goggles that quickly flashed different images to each eye. One eye saw an abstract pattern in motion that faded; the other eye saw a face (either fearful, happy, disgusted, or neutral) that also faded. The abstract pattern made it difficult to notice the faces.

4. Children were asked to press a button on the monitor as soon as they saw the face.

5. Researchers measured how quickly the boys pressed the button.

Results:

Children who had lower APSD scores noticed the fearful faces before other kinds of faces, but children who had higher scores (and more signs of psychopathy) did not.

Conclusion:

Children who score high on psychopathy screening tests take longer to notice fearful faces when they are automatically processing visual stimuli that are outside of their awareness. This may be because they are not as sensitive to potential threats in their environment when they are engaged in preattentive processing of the world around them. This early automatic deficit may make it difficult to train them to be more sensitive to such expressions.

Source study: Sylvers et al. (2011).

inhibit emotions (Glenn et al., 2009; Motzkin et al., 2011; Verona et al., 2012). EEG studies of children who exhibit psychopathy-related behaviors when they are as young as 8 years old show that these children have similar difficulties in modulating negative emotions (Granic et al., 2012). Thus, it may be that early difficulties in appropriately modulating and regulating emotions interact with difficulties in empathy and emotion perception to create psychopathic behaviors.

It has also been hypothesized that there is a specific gene variant in mice that results in reduced amygdala volume and increased aggressive behavior and that it may have a counterpart in humans (Blair, 2003; Meyer-Lindenberg et al., 2006; Monaghan et al., 1997; Raine, 2008). While the heritability of psychopathy has not been studied in as much detail as the heritability of other mental disorders, there are consistent indications of genetic influences on two distinct factors, one that is concerned with impulsivity and antisocial behavior (especially of a proactive as opposed to a reactive sort) and another that is associated with callousness and "interpersonal detachment" (Bezdjian et al., 2011; Larsson et al., 2006; Liu et al., 2002; Taylor et al., 2003; Viding et al., 2008, 2012). It is not yet clear if one of these factors is more primary and tends to lead to the other or whether both contribute relatively equally to the emergence of psychopathy, but there is some sense in the literature that callousness and interpersonal detachment may be more central to the emergence of psychopathy.

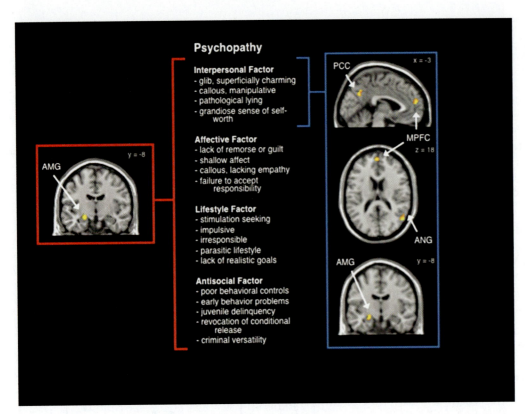

In short, problems in empathy and concern for others may appear very early in development and may predict psychopathy in childhood and adulthood. Children who are unrelentingly cruel to animals and do not show any signs of remorse and who show callous disregard for others are likely to later develop psychopathy (McPhedran, 2009). One learning theory view of how this deficit results in full-fledged psychopathy works as follows: Pain or distress in others will not be a negative stimulus to a child with an empathy deficit. Because the negative event of empathizing with distress in others will not be paired with acts by the child that cause that distress, the child will not learn moral rules or other guidelines to inhibit behavior that is hurtful to others (Blair, 2003). The possibilities for intervention are discouraging. It may be that children who really cannot tap into negative emotional states of others will be exceedingly difficult to socialize in ways that build a conscience. But there may still be elements of empathy that can be identified in even the most extreme children that can then be used as targets of socialization. In addition, full-fledged psychopathy may also involve problems in inhibiting impulses and low anxiety, and these problems might be addressed through other means, including medication.

Q: What is the evidence for neurophysiological and genetic causes of psychopathy?

Schizophrenia

In many ways, **schizophrenia** captures the most popular assumptions about madness, and the earliest discussions of it often focused on the bizarre thoughts and behaviors of those with the disorder (Bleuler, 1911/1950; Kraepelin, 1919). From a developmental perspective, it is an especially intriguing disorder because it seems to occur in only a very small number of children and teenagers. Instead, it usually first appears in a person's 20s. One of the most publicized cases of a normal young adult succumbing to schizophrenia was that of John Nash, who later won the Nobel Prize in economics and was the subject of the film *A Beautiful Mind* (see Figure 16.12).

Features of Schizophrenia

Schizophrenia in adults is distinguished by a large set of symptoms that are usually sorted into three types: positive, disorganized, and negative symptoms. Positive symptoms refer to distortions or excesses of normal sensations, thoughts, beliefs, or behaviors. These may include hallucinations, usually abnormal auditory or thought patterns that are often revealed through stretches of incoherent speech, and grossly false beliefs known as **delusions**. Collectively, such patterns of positive behavior are frequently referred to as evidence of **psychosis** and often involve loss of contact

FIGURE 16.12 The emergence of schizophrenia in young adulthood. John Nash, whose brilliant work in mathematics and economics led him to be awarded a Nobel Prize, led a normal childhood and adolescence but was diagnosed with schizophrenia as a young adult and had to cope with the disease for the rest of his life.

with reality. Disorganized symptoms include more chaotic forms of speech and behavior that either make no sense or are inappropriate for a situation (such as going to the grocery store in pajamas).

Negative symptoms refer to an apparent loss of normal behaviors and traits. These may include a restricted range of emotional responses, flat affect, a lack of social responsiveness, and poor eye contact. They may also include difficulty in communicating, such as problems in answering simple questions. Finally, negative symptoms can include a loss of motivation or desire to engage in activities. A person may appear listless and may sit for long periods without any apparent desire or interest in doing anything.

Q: What are the differences between positive, disorganized, and negative symptoms of schizophrenia?

Many researchers are convinced that the core of the disorder concerns the cognitive deficits, perhaps most critically in working memory and attention (Elvevag & Goldberg, 2000; Whitfield-Gabrieli et al., 2009; Whitfield-Gabrieli & Ford, 2012). These core cognitive deficits are thought to result in positive, disorganized, and negative symptoms. There are also often motor problems and tics, unusual jerky movements, or lack of coordination. As with so many mental disorders, schizophrenia may be a cluster of several related disorders that have overlapping symptoms and causes rather

than one cleanly defined deficit. In fact, Eugen Bleuler, when he initially labeled the disease, called it the "group of schizophrenias" in recognition of this possibility (Bleuler, 1911/1950).

The lifetime prevalence of schizophrenia is approximately 4 out of 1,000 (Bhugra, 2005). The disease is quite rare in children; roughly 1 out of every 40,000 cases occurs in a child under 13 years of age (Gochman et al., 2011), and most cases do not appear until late adolescence or early adulthood (Eaton et al., 1995). The obvious question is: What causes the dramatic rise in the late teens and early 20s, and why does it occur during that age period in particular? This question still puzzles researchers, as do the rare cases of clear schizophrenia that emerge much earlier in some children.

There may be two different populations of children who develop schizophrenia after childhood: those who throughout childhood seemed somehow odd, and those who seemed completely normal and were suddenly afflicted with the disease (Brennan & Walker, 2000; Neumann et al., 1995). The children who show more sudden onset are in the group that seems to be especially affected by changes in puberty. However, even in the rare cases of child-onset schizophrenia, there appears to be a catastrophic series of brain events occurring during puberty that greatly exacerbates the disease.

Unlike in cases of eating disorders and depression, it is more difficult to argue that the unique social pressures of adolescence or patterns of cognitive development are responsible for the emergence of schizophrenia during late adolescence or early adulthood. Nevertheless, stress has certainly been implicated as a possible factor in precipitating the disorder, perhaps through the effects of cortisol released on at-risk brain circuits (Corcoran et al., 2003; Walker et al., 1996, 2008). Adolescence can pose unique stresses, but a more detailed and plausible account of how such stresses could spur such a significant increase in the incidence of the disorder remains elusive. Moreover, schizophrenia tends to surge more in males than in females, a finding that is at odds with the more rapid rise in females of depression and eating disorders, both of which are thought to be related to females' experience of greater stresses in puberty (Eme, 1979; Zahn-Waxler et al., 2008).

In short, the reasons for the surge of schizophrenia in adolescence remain a mystery. No straightforward biological, social, or cognitive story has yet been well supported. More indirectly, we can look for explanations by considering the full developmental history of children who develop schizophrenia during or after puberty. Are there developmental precursors to this disease that can give us some insight into its occurrence? Although there may be different subpopulations of children who manifest the disease in different ways, this account will focus on a few general patterns that seem to hold for most cases.

Because of the low incidence of schizophrenia, it is not very practical to closely observe a large group of children knowing that only 1 percent will end up being the group of interest. It would be much easier to take a group of people who have the disease and somehow observe what they were like as children. This idea seemed impossible until researchers realized that with the rise of video cameras and home movie systems, it has become a ritual for many families to record their children at each birthday party and other events (Grimes & Walker, 1994; Schiffman et al., 2004; Walker et al., 1993). Could information in these home movies suggest precursors of schizophrenia? Once the idea emerged, the general method was clear. A group of judges watched large collections of these home movies of children, some of whom later developed schizophrenia and some of whom did not (usually siblings of the first group). The judges, who were blind as to the children's future outcomes, coded a wide range of behaviors in the children. There were unmistakable indications of differences. In particular, children who developed schizophrenia showed more **affective blunting**—that is, less pronounced emotions as well as less frequent displays of responses indicating either strong positive or negative emotions. Thus, while those diagnosed with schizophrenia may not show the symptoms of the disorder as children, a significant number do tend to show precursor behaviors having to do with social responsiveness that may reflect social and cognitive deficits that continue to gradually accumulate throughout adolescence and beyond (Algon et al., 2012; Cannon et al., 2002; Welham et al., 2009).

Beyond social responsiveness deficits, we can also find communicative and language difficulties and some cognitive and attentional deficits (Erlenmeyer-Kimling et al., 2000; Kates, 2010; Reichenberg et al., 2010). Moreover, when at-risk children and adolescents show higher levels of unusual thought content, greater tendencies of suspicion/paranoia, and a history of substance abuse (for example, heavy use of marijuana), they are substantially more likely to later exhibit psychosis and other symptoms of schizophrenia (Cannon et al., 2008). The association of later schizophrenia with earlier marijuana use does not mean that heavy marijuana use early on causes schizophrenia, but some researchers do suspect that it may play a role in aggravating or precipitating symptoms (Anglin et al., 2012).

Other potential early signs may involve motor movement difficulties, with children who show a certain class of motor movements more likely to later develop symptoms of schizo-phrenia. In addition to simple delays in motor development, the unusual motor patterns include writhing and jerky movements of the limbs, unusual postures with the arms, and tics and spasms (MacManus et al., 2012). Such motor abnormalities have even been reported in infants (Walker et al., 1994).

None of these predictors, however, means that we can foretell the future of any individual child. Many children with these symptoms will not develop schizophrenia, and many people who are diagnosed with the disorder as adults do not seem to have had any history of these predictive behaviors in childhood. This raises challenges for interventions, for even if a child exhibits many predictive behaviors, we would not want to intervene in too radical a way to try to reduce the possibility of schizophrenia if the intervention itself was potentially harmful (for example, using strong medications that might have harmful side effects).

Causal Factors

The genetic basis for schizophrenia has been extensively studied, and a clear relation exists between the likelihood of developing the disorder and how closely one is related to another relative who has the disorder (Cannon et al., 1998; Jablensky & Kalaydjieva, 2003). The genetic story is complex, involving several different genes and their interactions and cases where some of the genes may be present but not expressed (Claes et al., 2012; Gejman et al., 2011; Gottesman & Bertelsen, 1989).

The strong genetic component of the disease is unmistakable and might seem to suggest a purely biological explanation. But another equally dramatic finding raises further questions: roughly half of MZ twins in which one twin is diagnosed with schizophrenia do not share the disorder, even though they have identical genomes, a genetic effect that is weaker than that for obsessive-compulsive disorder (see Figure 16.13). Thus, although researchers repeatedly find higher heritabilities for schizophrenia in relatives of those with schizophrenia than in the general population, it is important to keep in mind that many adults with schizophrenia have never had any relatives who were diagnosed with the disorder (Gottesman & Erlenmeyer-Kimling, 2001). In addition, the same study that found that higher paternal age is linked to higher rates of autism in children also found a link between higher paternal age

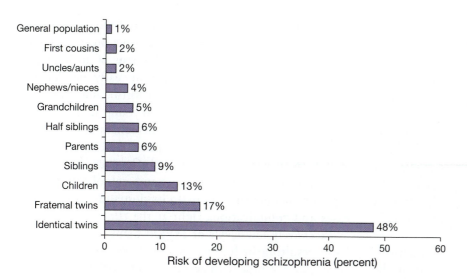

FIGURE 16.13 Genetics of schizophrenia. If an individual has schizophrenia, the odds of a relative also having the disease are closely related to the degree of genetic overlap between the two relatives. Thus, if one identical twin has schizophrenia, the odds of the other having the disease are essentially 50 percent, whereas for siblings who are not identical twins, the odds are around 10 percent. From Williams et al. (2009), based on data from Gottesman & Wolfgram (1991).

and higher rates of schizophrenia in children, apparently resulting from mutations being introduced into the child's genome when precursors of sperm cells repeatedly divided, and not because of the inheritance of mutations in either parent's genome (Kong et al., 2012).

The lack of a complete genetic predetermination for schizophrenia was most dramatically revealed in a highly unusual case of four sisters born in the 1930s. Known as the Genain quadruplets, they first came to the attention of researchers in the 1950s because one of them was showing the symptoms of a full-blown case of schizophrenia. They were all monozygotically related—hence, they had identical genes—yet they varied strikingly in the extent to which they manifested the disorder, and they continued to differ from one another at age 66, almost 40 years after they were first studied (Rosenthal, 1963; see also Mirsky et al., 1995, 2000). One sister, known as Myra, had symptoms of schizophrenia, but she was able to manage with them quite well, and she married, had children, and successfully raised a family. At the other extreme, a sister known as Hester was never able to make it on her own outside of a sheltered environment such as an institution or a home with extensive care. The other two sisters, called Nora and Iris (all are pseudonyms to protect privacy), showed moderate levels of symptoms between Myra's and Hester's.

Q: Describe evidence showing how genetic factors cannot provide a full explanation of schizophrenia.

The glaring question was: How could four genetically identical individuals have such a wide range of outcomes with a disorder that is often thought to be biologically based? The answer may lie in the details of how the dis-

order emerges. One account suggests that children with the at-risk gene carried by the Genain sisters will be much worse off if they contract certain infections while in the womb or shortly after birth (Rentakallio, 1997; Torrey, 1988). Since even Myra had some schizophrenic symptoms, it appears that all four sisters were equally at risk, but that differences in the severity of an early infection resulted in a difference in the extent to which the schizophrenic effects were amplified. A prenatal infection seems more plausible than a postnatal one, because that is the period during which the brain is especially susceptible to trauma (see Chapter 2).

Support for the infection theory was found after the massive 1918 worldwide influenza epidemic. Following the epidemic, children whose mothers had been victims of the epidemic when they were pregnant with the child showed a higher incidence of schizophrenia (Yudofsky, 2009). In addition, the incidence of schizophrenia shows a seasonal variation based on when children are born, with schizophrenia tending to be more likely in those born in winter or spring months, shortly after periods when infectious diseases are more common (Mortensen et al., 1999). Of course, many pregnant mothers contract influenza and have children who never develop schizophrenia. Thus, some researchers have suggested that the disorder develops because of the combination of being genetically at risk and contracting an infection by a particular type of virus—sometimes called a "schizovirus"—that amplifies the genetic effects. In some cases, a particularly bad infection on its own, such as toxoplasmosis, a disease often passed to pregnant mothers by house cats, may cause schizophrenia in those who are not genetically at risk (Torrey & Yolken, 1995, 2003).

The infection theory remains controversial. Higher levels of antibodies for some viruses have been found in those with schizophrenia, but not for other viruses that are also thought to be agents that cause schizophrenia (Brown et al., 2004; Karlsson et al., 2001). Because some viruses have been known to be dormant for many years before flaring up, the infection account has also been used to explain the surge of schizophrenia in adolescence, but the mechanism remains unclear. From a cross-cultural viewpoint, some striking differences in the incidence of the disease, such as a rate that is four times higher in some regions of Ireland, have also been cited to support a model based on local disease epidemics. Taken as a whole, there seems to be an emerging consensus that exposure to influenza in the womb probably can be a contributing factor to developing the disorder (Brown et al., 2004; Yudofsky, 2009).

An alternative account argues that stress and maltreatment early on can amplify the disorder, and once again the Genain sisters may offer hints. There is some evidence that the sisters' abusive father was considerably kinder to Myra and Nora than to Iris and Hester, leading some to argue that while stress alone cannot cause schizophrenia, it can greatly amplify the symptoms (Mirsky et al., 2000). There is also the possibility, however, that Hester and Iris were treated worse because they were more impaired.

The most plausible model is one that suggests strong interactions between biological factors, such as genes and infections, and environmental ones, such as stress (Walker & Diforio, 1997; Walker et al., 2008). This "neurodevelopmental model," which emphasizes the critical influence of a biological factor during prenatal development that then gradually unfolds for many years after birth, may offer the best explanation of how the disorder gets initially launched, especially when combined with a genetic factor that makes some fetuses more vulnerable to the effects of those pre-

natal events (Marenco & Weinberger, 2000). One neurodevelopmental account posits three distinct times when there may be influences that increase the odds of an individual developing schizophrenia: conception, early development (prenatal and during and soon after birth), and later development (childhood, adolescence, and young adulthood).

As seen in Figure 16.14, the influences at conception are largely genetic factors that put a developing human at risk (Karlsgodt et al., 2011). Influences during early development involve both prenatal complications arising from factors such as malnutrition and maternal diseases and complications right at the time of birth, such as excessively low levels of oxygen being supplied to the baby, resulting in brain damage. These early complications may combine with certain genetic risk factors to create abnormalities in several brain regions, especially those involving the frontal and temporal lobes, the limbic system, and the hypothalamic-pituitary-adrenal axis. Later developmental factors may involve genetic abnormalities that cause excessive pruning of gray matter in frontal and temporal lobes and diminished development of white matter tracts that connect regions concerned with attention and memory. These later developmental factors are likely to be exacerbated by environmental stresses. A series of detailed MRI structural studies looking both at gray matter volume and white matter connectivity between brain regions has shown that deterioration resulting from excessive pruning of neurons and synapses and decreased connectivity often precedes the onset of full-blown symptoms of schizophrenia, strongly suggesting a causal role of these changes—that is, they are not just consequences of having the disorder (Karlsgodt et al., 2011).

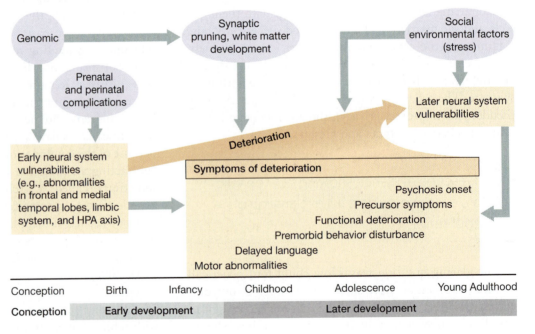

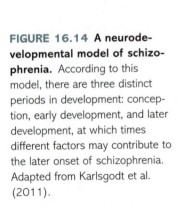

FIGURE 16.14 A neurodevelopmental model of schizophrenia. According to this model, there are three distinct periods in development: conception, early development, and later development, at which times different factors may contribute to the later onset of schizophrenia. Adapted from Karlsgodt et al. (2011).

Early-Onset Schizophrenia

For some time, scholars dismissed the presence of true schizophrenia in children. Indeed, there are serious problems distinguishing the distorted and unrealistic thoughts of a person with schizophrenia from the occasional lapses seen in many children. But as more careful measures have been introduced, including ones that look closely at cognitive abilities and distortions, researchers have identified a genuine form of schizophrenia in children (Asarnow et al., 2004; Kim-Cohen et al., 2003; Kumra & Schulz, 2008; Rapoport & Frangou, 2012; Vyas & Gogtay, 2012). Moreover, that form of the disorder shows strong developmental continuity with adult forms of the disorder, since positive, negative, and disorganized symptoms all seem to be present (Poulton et al., 2000). When schizophrenia occurs in children, it seems to particularly involve a loss of cortical gray matter in the neocortex (Rapoport et al., 1999; Thompson et al., 2001). One study compared the brains of children who had early and sustained psychosis, a hallmark of childhood schizophrenia, with the brains of both children with no signs of the disorder and children who had transient psychosis—namely, a relatively brief episode of hallucinations and other delusional behaviors. Only those in the group with sustained psychosis showed the loss of cortical gray matter, a pattern of loss that is not seen in those with late-onset schizophrenia (Gogtay et al., 2004). More focused analyses of these declines suggest that as the temporal lobes lose gray matter, there is a rise of positive symptoms, such as auditory hallucinations, and as the frontal lobes lose gray matter, there is a rise of negative symptoms, such as withdrawal. The early-onset cases are thought to end up being more severe disorders in adults and to have a stronger genetic predisposition as well as a higher incidence of relatives with the disorder (Kumra & Schulz, 2008).

In summary, schizophrenia remains a puzzling disorder with a host of causal factors that have been implicated, including genetic influences, infections, environmental stressors, and distinct periods in development when different contributing factors may dominate. The neural consequences of the disorder are, in some cases, quite dramatic and suggest that a combination of excessive pruning and diminished connectivity of brain regions may be responsible for the huge surge of the disorder in late puberty, especially among those who have already been put at risk by earlier developing factors. In the future, more sophisticated pattern recognition analyses of MRI structural information, combined with newer fMRI studies, may enable clinicians to identify with some confidence teenagers who are highly likely to soon show symptoms of the disorder (Karlsgodt et al., 2011).

> **Q:** Compare early-onset schizophrenia with the more common case of late-onset schizophrenia.

Treatment of Childhood Psychopathologies

If this were a text on childhood psychopathology, it would be natural to discuss the treatment strategies for each disorder in turn, since they have to be tailored to the particular properties of each disease. In the context of developmental psychology as a whole, however, it is more useful to consider the general issues arising with treatment of children and to see how they apply to specific cases. The primary issue is how changing patterns of development interact with treatment. The issue concerns both normal developmental patterns and the specific patterns of development associated with psychological disorders. With respect to normal patterns of development, we can ask how, for example, cognitive development might relate to the efficacy—that is, the effectiveness—of various therapies that assume some level of information processing. With respect to the development of a disorder, we can ask whether the disorder progresses in a way that requires treatments for young children that are different from those used for adolescents or adults. These are complex issues. In this overview, we will consider some common methods of treatment in adults and whether they need to be modified for use in children, and then we will consider techniques used only with children. Some of the most common adult treatment strategies are behavioral, cognitive-behavioral, psychoanalytic, family systems, and pharmacological treatments, with frequent combinations of one or more of the first four techniques with pharmacological treatments.

Behavioral Therapies

Behavioral therapies seem to be applicable to all ages, as they are based on behaviorist principles that should work on a wide variety of animals, including people. Behavioral therapies have three major forms: classical conditioning, operant conditioning, and modeling.

Classical conditioning approaches attempt to create or extinguish a relationship between a stimulus and a response. For example, if a child has developed a fear of dogs, the therapist might attempt to expose the child repeatedly to dog images, toy dogs, and eventually real dogs in a manner that extinguishes any fear response that may have originally arisen because of a highly negative encounter with a dog (Marks, 1987; Wolpe, 1958). This technique can be effective, but it has its limitations as well. It works best for problems that have clear external triggers, such as phobias. Moreover, increased exposure to the threatening stimulus can sometimes result in a heightened fearful response to the stimulus, as opposed to extinction of the response (Zinbarg et al., 1992). More broadly, it now appears that fear conditioning may have its own unique properties and associated neural circuits that make it different from other kinds of classical conditioning, as well as from the conditioning of more general anxiety disorders (Mineka & Oehlberg, 2008). This, in turn, suggests that treatments for specific phobias might work differently from treatments for generalized anxiety, or at least that treatments might need to take into account several distinct processes that combine in different ways to contribute both to specific fears and to more general anxiety (Beckers et al., 2013).

Operant conditioning techniques, modeled after Skinner's methods, seek to shape a child's behavior in the appropriate direction through rewards and punishments (Patterson et al., 1982). These techniques have often proved successful in treating a child with a conduct disorder—for example, in treating a child who acts out frequently in the classroom or throws tantrums in supermarkets in ways that are highly disruptive and that go beyond normal childhood outbursts. A number of therapeutic programs try to use some sort of reward system with tokens that provide benefits for good behavior (Sulzer-Azaroff & Mayer, 1977, 1991). One problem concerns the finding that reinforcement schedules, while changing a behavior, can often turn the newly shaped behavior into a form of work (Lepper et al., 1973), thereby removing any intrinsic reasons to engage in the behavior and increasing the probability of it disappearing when the rewards disappear (as seen in Chapter 13, this problem often occurs when extrinsic motivations are frequently used).

A final behavioral technique uses social learning, or modeling approaches (Bandura, 1971). As we have seen in earlier chapters on socialization, this technique can effectively instill behaviors that are otherwise difficult to develop through operant conditioning. Modeling approaches have been used to reduce aggression, increase social skills, foster feelings of self-efficacy, and inhibit fear reactions, among many other targeted behaviors. For example, if young toddlers watch their mothers model positive reactions to potentially fearful stimuli, such as toy spiders and snakes, they are less likely to develop specific phobias to those stimuli when they later observe others reacting in a more aversive manner to the same stimuli (Egliston & Rapee, 2007).

Yet, all three of these approaches are affected by developmental considerations. With modeling, for example, the effectiveness of the modeling intervention is heavily dependent on a large number of variables that may in turn depend on the child's cognitive and social development. A child must be able to mentally represent the adult model's action at an appropriate level of cognitive complexity and must have a positive social relation with the model for the modeling to be effective. In tweaking all the variables of modeling to make it most effective, the therapist has to take into account every facet of social and cognitive development and thereby use very different modeling interventions as the age of the child varies.

> **Q:** What are three different versions of therapy that are based on traditional learning theories? What are their limitations?

Cognitive-Behavioral Therapy

Cognitive-behavioral therapy (CBT) is based on the idea that a person's problems stem from how she sees and thinks about the world and how abnormal perceptions and cognitions can cause problem behaviors. Consequently, the way to change the behaviors is not simply to shape the behaviors themselves but to try to change the way the person processes and encodes information—that is, to change the way she interprets and thinks about the world around her. CBT has become the most widely used of all therapies, and it is used to treat a wide range of disorders, including depression, anxiety, obsessive-compulsive disorder, eating disorders, and even schizophrenia (Butler et al., 2006; Rector & Beck, 2001; Spangler, 1999).

First introduced by Aaron Beck as a way of treating depression (Beck, 1967; Beck et al., 1979), cognitive-behavioral therapy has a variety of techniques for helping people change their cognitive schemas. Beck identified certain patterns of thinking that were associated with depression and developed his therapy around trying to alter those cognitions. Cognitive-behavioral therapy requires active engagement and effort on the part of the patient as well as a clear goal that the patient wants to address. This alone can make it difficult to use with young children, who may not be able to identify a complex behavioral goal or who may find it hard to grasp techniques intended to change thought patterns. Cognitive-behavioral therapy tries to make a patient aware of "automatic" thought patterns that are maladaptive and tries to get the patient to recognize how changing these thought patterns would be desirable. In that sense, it requires a certain degree of metacognitive ability, the capacity to think about one's thoughts. For example, if a college student feels that he is a complete loser when he fails an exam or doesn't make a team, a CBT practitioner will try to help him see that such an extreme conclusion is not warranted and will try to guide him toward more reasonable interpretations, which will presumably make him less depressed. This technique of pointing out the irrationality of a thought or way of thinking in order to motivate change is one of the most common methods of CBT. Cognitive-behavioral therapy does not try to go as deep as psychoanalytic approaches and instead seeks to find the more immediate cognitive causes of specific behaviors and to attain specific behavior change through changing those particular cognitive causes.

> **Q:** How does cognitive-behavioral therapy differ from more psychoanalytic approaches in the way it explores cognitive states in an individual?

CBT was designed for use with adults, so its methods need to be adjusted for use with children. Adult CBT patients are often asked to do specific "homework" exercises in which they are to try out new cognitive schemas in everyday situations. They may be asked to keep a detailed journal of their day, recording adverse situations as they arise, which increases their awareness of a problem. They may also be asked to explain or justify their distorted beliefs, and in doing so, they may recognize their inherent contradictions. Obviously, these techniques would be ineffective or impossible to use with young children.

There are several techniques to make CBT more workable with younger children. One is to engage the parents as full partners and have them work closely with their children to make them aware of alternative cognitive interpretations and to gently remind them of the problems with their distorted cognitions. By helping their children think through these issues, parents can reduce the cognitive complexity of the children's task (Albano & Kendall, 2002; Kendall et al., 2002). Therapists can also simplify the representations of thoughts by drawing cartoons for the children or by accompanying them in a difficult situation and rehearsing alternative cognitive strategies with them. The huge wave of cognitive developmental research in recent years has shown that there is far more cognitive capacity in young children when tasks are structured at their level. This can mean that if CBT is done in a developmentally sensitive manner, it can be made more easily accessible to children. As we move beyond the older views of young children as limited by stages of pre-logical thought or concrete reasoning, it seems more viable to use developmentally sensitive CBT with children (Cartwright-Hatton & Murray, 2008; Derisley, 2004).

> **Q:** What are some challenges of using cognitive-behavioral therapy with young children?

Because anxiety disorders are one of the most frequent forms of psychopathology in young children, most CBT studies with children have focused on anxiety-related disorders. As researchers start to adjust CBT in developmentally appropriate ways, there are indications of its increasing effectiveness as a way of treating anxiety disorders in school-age children, although young children do tend to show a larger remission rate for the disorder than do older children and adults (Barrett et al., 2001; Cartwright-Hatton & Murray, 2008). CBT is now being used more broadly to treat other forms of psychopathology in children (Brent & Maalouf, 2009; Creswell & O'Connor, 2011; Hofmann et al., 2012). The challenge for the future is to more fully integrate the rapid pace of basic research on cognitive development, especially those areas related to metacognition and reasoning skills, with the techniques of CBT (Erickson & Achilles, 2004). There may also be a convergence of methods based on recent advances in using CBT to treat adults with intellectual disabilities. Traditionally, it was thought that CBT would not work with people who scored very low on intelligence tests and that classical and operant techniques would have to dominate. But with carefully tailored therapies analogous to some changes made for children, CBT can have good treatment effectiveness with that population as well (Taylor et al., 2008).

Psychoanalytic Therapies

Psychoanalytic approaches to therapy with children have a long history that goes back as far as Freud. That history has been a checkered one, however, as the efficacy of psychoanalytic approaches has been challenged by newer approaches, such as CBT. Several of the psychoanalytic approaches build on the ideas of Freud, his daughter Anna, and many others, but the area is too vast and complex to discuss in detail here. It is impressive that despite many years of sustained attacks by alternative approaches, psychoanalytic approaches retain a considerable following and are increasingly being subjected to careful experimental tests for their efficacy as well as being connected to recent research on cognitive development and attachment (Fonagy & Adshead, 2012; Fonagy & Target, 2002; Fonagy et al., 2002). One meta-analysis of almost 40 years of studies concluded that long-term psychoanalytic therapy does consistently produce positive effects in many adults (de Maat et al., 2009). Given what seems to be an emerging consensus that this form of therapy has an important role to play in treating adults, there is renewed interest in how it might be modified to be effective with children.

Family Therapies

We briefly discussed family-based approaches in the context of anorexia, when we presented Minuchin's bold ideas on the role of dynamic systems in families that fall into abnormal interaction patterns (Minuchin & Fishman, 1981). These approaches are notable because they require far more than a one-on-one therapist-child relationship; they focus on engaging the entire family. In many cases, it seems to make sense to view the child's problem as part of a full family system that has dysfunctional interaction patterns that need to be treated. Family therapy approaches have been shown to be effective on problems ranging from infant sleep patterns, to conduct disorders, to obsessive-compulsive behaviors, to depression, to substance abuse (Asarnow et al., 2001; Carr, 2009). In some cases, treating the family as a whole seems to produce larger and more enduring results. For example, in one study comparing treatments for teenagers with substance abuse problems, researchers found that while both CBT and family therapy had similar short-term effects, family therapy had better long-term outcomes, as well as being more effective for more severe forms of abuse (Liddle et al., 2008). Simply treating the child alone may not be as effective in the long term if the parents are also engaging in behaviors that tend to aggravate or even promote drug use—for example, belittling a child's competence or not providing opportunities for rich and rewarding social interactions with the rest of the family.

One major challenge of family therapy is that many members of the family often do not want to acknowledge their role in creating the underlying problems. It is all too common for parents to drop their children off at the therapist and assume that all of the child's problems are within the child and simply need to be fixed by the therapist. Even if there is some sense of a larger context for the problem, parents and therapists may not agree as to what it is. For example, in one study, researchers asked children, parents, and therapists to identify the fundamental problem or problems that they should be working on. More than 75 percent of the child/parent/therapist triads began therapy without any agreement on even a single problem that they were supposed to be working on. Even when the problem was put in the broadest terms, such as aggression or anxiety/depression, only half of the triads mutually agreed as to what the problem was (Hawley & Weisz, 2003). It is easy to see the challenges of family therapy approaches in such cases. In addition, it can take especially skilled therapists to draw a young child into a conversation rather than simply having

the family and the older siblings talk about the younger child (Rober, 2008). Like so many other forms of therapy, the sensitivity and competency of the therapist is critical to the success of the therapy.

> **Q:** What are some of the challenges of using family therapy techniques?

Pharmacological Treatments

In addition to the wide range of therapies based on interpersonal interactions, there are, of course, attempts to treat disorders directly through various medications. The steady increase in the use of drugs to treat childhood psychopathology in recent years is a vast and controversial topic (see Development and Social Policy box). Drug treatment tended initially to be for children with disorders related to ADHD and most often consisted of doses of methylphenidate (trade name Ritalin). As described in Chapter 10, the use of methylphenidate and related drugs for ADHD with ever younger children has soared, but in many cases, such drug treatment may be overused, even as it seems to have clear benefits for children who are correctly diagnosed with the disorder. At present, a much wider range of drugs is being used to treat adolescents and children (Figure 16.15 illustrates the increase in use of both stimulants and antidepressants in children and adolescents over the past few decades). In addition to drugs for ADHD, antidepressants such as fluoxetine

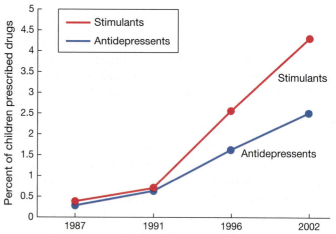

FIGURE 16.15 The rise of psychiatric drug use in children. The use of both stimulants and antidepressants by American children younger than 20 rose dramatically in the last part of the twentieth century. Although the rate of increase has slowed somewhat in more recent years, it continues to stay high. Adapted from Whitaker (2010).

Prescribing Psychoactive Medications to Young Children

Although most childhood psychopathologies have been treated through different sorts of therapies, in recent years drugs have emerged as a frequent form of treatment as well, a phenomenon that has generated enormous controversy (Morris & Stone, 2011; Whitaker, 2010). There has been an extraordinary rise in the use of various psychoactive medications with children, with the age for prescribing such medications decreasing to the point where even preschoolers are being given medications originally developed for adult forms of psychopathology. In fact, the fastest-growing rate of prescriptions for antidepressants is in preschoolers, with the rates of prescriptions for some groups of children tripling in the last decade (Brown, 2003; Zito et al., 2003). Over one recent 4-year period, prescription rates for preschool girls rose 65 percent (Delate et al., 2004; Warner et al., 2004), and the rates have continued to rise significantly (Parens & Johnston, 2008). It is true, of course, that these increases were from an initially very low rate, but the increases are nonetheless dramatic.

There is a lack of critical information about the risks of using such medications to treat very young children, especially over the long term. In most cases, young children are prescribed drugs that have had little or no testing of their effects in children (Brown, 2003; Hsia & Maclennan, 2009). Children are being given medications based on the results of studies conducted on adults and based on doctors' best guesses about the likely impacts and best dosages for children. But children absorb medicine at different rates than adults, and children may metabolize psychoactive medications differently than adults, which could change the drug concentrations that would be harmful in the target tissues of children. Moreover, young children might have difficulty expressing whether they are experiencing side effects from too large a dosage of a drug. All of these factors make guessing at doses a risky procedure.

When a psychological disorder is diagnosed in preschoolers, it is exceedingly difficult to know whether its causes might resemble those in an adult or older teenager, raising even more doubts about whether a particular medication designed for those groups would work in young children. Of special concern is the effect of medications taken over the long term on a child's developing brain. We have seen that there are exquisitely sensitive feedback loops between various neural circuits in development that help regulate aspects of brain growth (see Chapter 2). How might elevated levels of neurotransmitters and certain firing patterns caused by psychiatric drugs influence brain growth? At present, the answers to these questions are unknown. And even if psychoactive drugs do improve the short-term mental health of some children, it will be years before the long-term developmental implications are fully understood.

Some researchers are concerned that the welfare of children may be in conflict with the profit motive of some pharmaceutical companies (Harris, 2004). In that context, it is notable that the United Kingdom, which has a more socialized form of medicine than the United States, has much more stringent rules against prescribing antidepressants to children (Satel, 2004). The contrast between the two countries reveals how economic factors have the potential to interact with the health interests of children. These issues have become especially salient, given reports of higher levels of suicide among children taking antidepressants as opposed to placebos (Brent & Maalouf, 2009; Jureidini et al., 2004). It has even been argued that giving extended high doses of medications such as Ritalin to young children could increase the risk of tipping some children into psychotic states (Whitaker, 2010).

Some have argued that opposition to using such medications with children is "misguided resistance to appropriate treatment" (Koplewicz, 2004), on the grounds that any increased risks posed by the medications for depression, psychosis, and conduct disorders are offset by the larger risks associated with harm to the child, such as in adolescent and child suicide, or to others through violence by the child. Consider the case of depression. If it could be reliably demonstrated that prescribing antidepressants to children and adolescents does reduce the incidence of suicide, it would make it easier to evaluate the costs and benefits of such prescriptions, but no such demonstration is available (Jureidini et al., 2004; Tsapakis et al., 2008).

Parents must consider all of these concerns when deciding if their child should take psychoactive medications. When children are in a state of clear psychological distress and at great risk to themselves or others, it is inevitable that parents will have to consider the use of medications that are at least sometimes effective in bringing short-term improvements in a child's condition. Given these considerations, there is a clear need for more long-term studies of the efficacies and side effects of using psychoactive drugs in children (Rapoport, 2009).

(trade name Prozac) are commonly used for children who are either depressed or anxious, and antipsychotic drugs such as risperidone (trade name Risperdal) are used for children who have severe conduct problems and emotional outbursts as well as for some children diagnosed with ADHD (although this latter use is highly controversial).

The patterns of usage can be troubling. First, the drugs are often used "off-label," meaning that while they may have been approved for treatment of a specific disorder in adults, they may not have been approved for treatment of this disorder (or any other disorder) in children, as their effectiveness and safety in children may not have been established. Off-label usage can result in either overdosing or underdosing children and does not take into account potential long-term developmental effects (Mehler-Wex et al., 2009). Second, there are enormous variations in prescribing drugs among different populations, raising questions about the right level of use and the dangers of overprescribing. For example, prescribing antipsychotics, antidepressants, and stimulants to children is much higher in the United States than it is in the Netherlands and Germany (Mehler-Wex et al., 2009). Within the United States, children in foster care are almost four times more likely to receive ADHD-related drugs, antidepressants, and antipsychotics than children in the same socioeconomic group who are not in foster care (Zito et al., 2008). While it is true that children in foster care do have a higher incidence of diagnosed psychopathologies, it is not clear if the level of drug use is appropriate or if it reflects attempts to "manage" difficult children through medication because more social therapeutic means are less available. Comparable higher rates have also been found for children on welfare (Raghavan et al., 2012).

In many cases, it appears that psychoactive drugs in combination with one or more forms of therapy can be much more effective—especially over the long term—than any single approach used alone (Keller et al., 2000). These "multimodal" approaches may try to produce rapid change through drug treatment and then maintain the change through other forms of therapy. Such approaches do require, however, that the health practitioners involved be open to a range of techniques and not be wedded too strongly to any one method in which they may have received their training.

Evaluating Therapies

Researchers are very concerned about the need for **evidence-based therapy** with children (Kazdin & Weisz, 2003). This phrase, as well as "outcome-based therapy," is a way of simply asking that studies have been conducted showing that the therapies have proven effectiveness when used with children. It is clearly important to determine if a therapy is beneficial for children or if a drug is working

at a particular level when prescribed to a child. In practice, this is much more difficult than it sounds. Many of the therapies that we have considered may be vastly more effective in the hands of a highly skilled and experienced therapist. Attempts to design large-scale experiments with such therapies frequently end up in the hands of relatively unskilled research assistants, who are often fairly young graduate students using "manualized" versions of the therapy, meaning that they try to follow what is almost a procedural cookbook. It is easy to see how much can be lost in the implementation and how flexibility and on-the-spot fine-tuning may be missing in such studies, potentially undermining an approach (Connor-Smith & Weisz, 2003). Without great care, the research could show the effectiveness of just those therapies that are the easiest to mindlessly implement without much therapist skill. No one thinks that such results would shed the best light on what really works and why. There are, however, strong economic incentives to manualize therapies as much as possible so that they can be delivered by less extensively trained, and therefore less expensive, therapists.

Despite these cautions about evidence-based approaches, it is clear that all of health care should focus on treatments with proven effectiveness and that treatment for psychological disorders should be no different. Fortunately, there are now extensive studies of evidence-based treatments, especially of CBT, that go beyond simply asking if certain programs can be easily implemented (Weisz & Kazdin, 2010). The emphasis on evidence-based treatments has resulted in welcome increases in studies with true random assignment to conditions that compare different treatments or that contrast a treatment with a no-treatment condition, and there has been more attention to replicating these studies (Kazdin, 2011). Clinicians can now employ treatments with good confidence that there is research supporting their effectiveness. There are now even several studies of such treatments' effectiveness with preschoolers (Njoroge & Yang, 2012). One remaining challenge is the need to conduct longitudinal studies of various treatments. Evidence-based studies often favor treatments that do not take extended periods, as it makes it much easier to conduct efficient studies if the researchers do not have to wait several years to assess the effectiveness of a treatment. But it seems likely that as more long-term studies are conducted, there will be some cases where more extended treatments are shown to be equally if not more effective for specific disorders. In addition, as clinicians are increasingly blending together several therapies in one program of treatment, such as combining drugs, CBT, and family therapy, there is still a need to carefully examine the effectiveness of all of these approaches in various patterns of combination, including evaluating the therapies both when used at the same time and when used one after the other.

Conclusions

The field of childhood psychopathology is so vast that it has often been viewed as a separate domain only loosely affiliated with the rest of developmental psychology. The goal of this chapter has been to familiarize readers with common childhood psychopathologies and how they emerge in development as well as to provide some basic information about possible ways to treat these disorders. As each disorder was considered, it became clear how issues in neurobiological development, social development, and cognitive development are central to understanding how and when a disorder initially emerges and how it changes over time. In turn, the problems in psychopathology pose questions that will drive future research. What sorts of cognitive capacities are needed to see contradictions and inconsistencies in one's own beliefs, and how do these capacities develop? What are the socialization patterns that might cause parents to guide girls toward more intrapersonal introspection and boys toward more problem-solving strategies? Why do these patterns exist, and how might they be related to gender differences in depression? How does the child's buoyant cognitive optimism change into the pessimism that might be responsible for the surge of depression in adolescence? These and countless other questions are coming into much sharper focus as a result of attention to psychopathology in children and adolescents. There is potential for enormous advances if the interactions of findings in these two traditional areas of psychology—developmental psychology and abnormal psychology—are explored more and more in the future.

Neuroscience is also taking on a larger role both in our understanding of the causes of psychopathology over the course of development and in devising therapeutic interventions. From an etiological viewpoint, several new technologies may start to provide converging insights. High-resolution MRI studies are uncovering changes both in gray matter, suggesting local change through excessive pruning of neurons and synapses, and in white matter, suggesting impaired connectivity between brain regions. These structural brain changes are, in turn, being linked to advanced genomic analyses that are able to track how genetic variants might be related to and even predict such changes. Epigenetic factors are also now being explored more fully, with factors ranging from stress, to infections, to use of various medications as all potentially being involved in turning certain gene pathways on or off. Neuroscience will not replace psychological models of psychopathology, but it will inform and constrain them just as psychological models will guide neuroscientific investigations.

STUDY AND REVIEW

SUMMARY

- Studying psychopathology from a developmental perspective means evaluating unusual behaviors, thoughts, and emotions that cause difficulties in functioning in terms of whether they are symptoms of psychopathology in children or symptoms that will appear as an individual grows older. It means establishing criteria for diagnosing and treating psychopathology at different ages. A developmental approach not only illuminates problems that occur in childhood, but it can help explain the nature of psychopathology in adult populations as well.

Autism

- Autism has early origins and seems to involve deficits in reasoning about the mental states of others, deficits that can have a cascade of other consequences. Usually diagnosed at 18 months, those with autism may exhibit even earlier precursor behaviors, including subtle problems with social engagement, language delays, and difficulties with joint attention. It is diagnosed four times as often in boys as in girls.

- Genetic predispositions and environmental factors, such as infections or disease either prenatally or in early infancy, have been implicated in the etiology of autism, but not certain forms of socialization.

Anxiety Disorders

- Anxiety disorders are some of the most common mental disorders in children and, in addition to specific phobias, can take the form of generalized forms of anxiety or social anxieties. Negative cognitions seem to predominate in children with these disorders and have been thought to play a causal role, interacting with genetic predispositions to anxiety. Anxiety problems in childhood generally predict long-term anxiety problems, although the source of the anxiety generally changes with age.

- Obsessive-compulsive disorder is a special form of anxiety disorder that seems to have its own distinct etiology and a strong genetic basis. The four main types of this disorder cluster around obsessions about dirt and contamination; order and symmetry; losing things and hoarding; and unwelcome violent, sexual, or blasphemous thoughts. This is a quite early-emerging disorder that may reflect a defect in an evolved safety vigilance system.

Eating Disorders

- Eating disorders emerge relatively late in development, usually in early adolescence, and tend to be far more common in girls than in boys. The three eating disorders are anorexia nervosa, bulimia, and binge eating. Adolescents with anorexia tend to be extremely thin because they intentionally refuse to eat more than minimal amounts of food, and they base their self-esteem on their thinness. Those with bulimia tend to be of normal weight or even overweight and engage in bouts of excessive eating followed by purging.

- Anorexia seems to have a more powerful genetic component than bulimia, while bulimia may be more culturally influenced. Several theories attempt to account for the gender difference and late onset but none have yet been conclusive. There does seem to be a major cognitive component to anorexia that involves distorted cognitions and/or perceptions. Some children in overprotective, conflict-avoiding families may develop anorexia as a way of exercising control and autonomy.

Depression

- Depression shows a later onset in the vast majority of cases, although clear cases of depression in early childhood have also been observed. The two different forms of depression, unipolar and bipolar, have quite different symptoms and patterns of development. Unipolar depression increases markedly in females after puberty. Bipolar disorder, which consists of shifts between depressive and manic phases, tends to occur equally in males and females, and generally emerges in late adolescence.

- The late emergence of most cases of unipolar depression may be related to changes in cognitive development, including a reduction of an optimistic bias that colors the thoughts of younger children and an increase in various forms of rumination. Unipolar depression tends to run in families, as does bipolar disorder, which has an even higher genetic heritability.

Conduct Disorder: The Case of Psychopathy

- Conduct disorder is a broad class of behavioral problems, but one severe form, known as psychopathy, is normally not diagnosed until adolescence or adulthood. People with psychopathy are extremely self-centered, are superficially charming, and do not have guilt or shame or emotional attachments that prevent them from manipulating or hurting others.

- There may be much earlier precursors of psychopathy in childhood, including difficulties in detecting sadness and fear in others' facial expressions and verbal tones. The disorder may be related to deficits in certain capacities for emotions of caring and empathy.

Schizophrenia

- Schizophrenia does not normally occur until late adolescence or early adulthood. The reasons for its late onset remain a mystery but may be related to the consequences of excessive pruning of neurons and synapses and impaired connections between brain regions that occur during adolescence.

- A very small number of cases of early-onset schizophrenia have now been documented and have been shown to be related to loss of gray matter in the neocortex. It is thought that early-onset schizophrenia, with its more devastating prognosis, may provide insights into late-onset cases as well.

- Although there are clear genetic contributions to schizophrenia, there are also striking cases where individuals with identical genes manifest the disease to dramatically different extents, making it clear that environmental factors, ranging from disease to stress, are also at work.

Treatment of Childhood Psychopathologies

- There are many ways to treat mental illness in children, ranging from classical and operant conditioning, to modeling, to cognitive-behavioral techniques, to psychoanalytic methods, to methods that work with family systems. All of these forms are still used, although cognitive-behavioral treatments, often in conjunction with medications, have become much more widespread in recent years.

- All of the treatment approaches must be sensitive to the developmental status of the child. Cognitive development, in particular, interacts heavily with the ways in which various forms of treatment might be implemented. For example, therapies that ask children to think about their own beliefs must take into account metacognitive development, and therapies that focus on family dynamics must adjust for the social and communicative abilities of the youngest members of those families.

THOUGHT QUESTIONS

1. There are several reported cases of identical (monozygotic) twins who experience very different outcomes with respect to psychopathology. Discuss a hypothetical pair of twins where one develops a serious mental illness and the other lives a life without any apparent mental illness. Consider at least three different causal factors that could be responsible for these different outcomes.

2. The onset of puberty may be related to increases in certain forms of psychopathology. Consider a form of psychopathology in which the incidence might be most related to the onset of puberty and one in which the incidence might be most unrelated. Explain your predictions in terms of potential underlying mechanisms.

3. Imagine that a 6-year-old and a 26-year-old are both referred to a clinical psychologist because of a crippling generalized anxiety disorder that is most often manifested in terms of intense anxiety when in public places. The psychologist devises two treatment programs within the cognitive-behavioral therapy (CBT) framework. Describe in detail how the treatment programs would both be compatible with CBT but at the same time be quite different because of the two ages involved.

4. A boy enters kindergarten as the youngest boy in his class and soon appears to have problems sitting still and paying attention. The teacher and the school psychologist conclude that the young boy has ADHD and strongly urge the parents to see a specialist who will prescribe Ritalin for their son. The specialist whom they recommend, a psychiatrist, agrees and suggests a medication schedule. Given that this is a very young age to start a child on Ritalin, how would you evaluate the costs and benefits of these recommendations in terms of what is best for the child? What alternatives might you consider?

KEY TERMS

affective blunting (p. 616)

amenorrhea (p. 599)

anorexia nervosa (p. 598)

anorexic family (p. 601)

anxiety disorder (p. 592)

autism (p. 588)

baby sib study (p. 589)

bipolar disorder (p. 603)

bulimia nervosa (p. 602)

catastrophizing (p. 594)

cognitive-behavioral therapy (CBT) (p. 620)

conduct disorder (p. 609)

co-rumination (p. 608)

delusion (p. 614)

depressogenic vulnerability (p. 607)

diathesis-stress hypothesis (p. 592)

elective mutism (p. 588)

evidence-based therapy (p. 624)

generalized anxiety disorder (p. 592)

learned helplessness (p. 606)

obsessive-compulsive disorder (OCD) (p. 595)

pervasive developmental disorder (p. 588)

psychopathy (p. 610)

psychosis (p. 614)

rumination (p. 607)

sampling bias (p. 591)

schizophrenia (p. 614)

security motivational system (p. 597)

social anxiety disorder (p. 592)

unipolar depression (p. 603)

17

Development after Childhood and Adolescence

Physical and Physiological Changes in Adulthood

Cognitive Changes in Adulthood
- Reaction Time and Speed of Processing
- Memory, Higher Cognitive Functions, and Reasoning
- Daily Activities and Cognitive Aging
- Circadian Rhythms, Cognition, and the Lifespan

Changes in Personality in the Lifespan: Individual and Group Changes
- Changes in Individuals
- Stressful Life Events
- Group Changes

Stages of Life?
- Erik Erikson's Approach

- Understanding Stages of Adult Development

What Does It Mean to Be Old?
- Stereotypes and Ageism
- Cultural Variation in Stereotypes and Ageism?

Conclusions

Summary

n 1968, the U.S. Democratic Party nominated a charismatic representative from the state of Georgia, Julian Bond, as its candidate for vice president. A short while later at the party's national convention, Mr. Bond stood up and withdrew his name from consideration. At age 28, he was younger than the minimum age required for the presidency of the United States (see Figure 17.1). Based on the age restrictions for serving in the British Parliament, the U.S. Constitution states that the vice president and the president of the United States must be at least 35 years of age. Other age restrictions are placed on members of the Senate (30 years old) and the House of Representatives (25 years old). Such requirements are not unique to the United States and Great Britain. They are written into constitutions of countries throughout the world, some of which require even older ages, such as 40, for the head of state.

Why should country after country set up age restrictions for its leaders, often extending them well into middle age? In most cases, the reasons revolve around a conviction that people older than 35 or 40 years of age have better psychological qualifications for leadership roles than those who are younger. This view may seem a bit surprising at first. In many areas of cognitive functioning, there is a gradual decline after people reach their mid-20s; in tasks that measure processing speed and working memory capacity, for example, people in their 20s often outperform those who are older. But older adults may outperform younger adults in tasks requiring experience and expertise as well as more emotional regulation. Are the alleged superior psychological qualifications of people in their 40s and 50s a myth,

perhaps perpetuated by older people trying to hold on to power, or are there real advantages that occur with age?

In this chapter, we will explore psychological changes that occur after adolescence, recognizing that psychological development is a lifelong process that is not arbitrarily cut off at the end of adolescence. We will also consider a somewhat different approach known as the life course perspective, which emphasizes key transitions that occur in various social contexts. More broadly, we will explore how we change physically and psychologically after young adulthood and how others view and respond to those changes. We will also ask what factors can explain these changes and whether individual differences in personality and intelligence stay relatively stable with increasing age. We will consider whether age groups as a whole shift in the degree to which they exhibit certain kinds of personalities, but we will also examine the enormous variation in how people age, ranging from **successful aging**, in which people seem to thrive until very late in life, to **pathological aging**, in which people decline very rapidly starting in their mid-60s. In a related vein, we will consider whether certain lifestyles and daily activities might influence the quality of aging. Finally, we will ask if there are adult "stages" of development and, to the extent that there are, whether they reflect internal changes in the maturing individual or changes dictated by the individual's changing role in society. We will also consider whether cultural influences can change the whole meaning of what it means to be old. One key message throughout the chapter is that despite clear signs of the decline of some basic physical capacities, many cognitive capacities do not decline with age and can even develop further in the elderly. Similarly, when personality changes do occur, such as a greater ability to inhibit impulsive behavior with increasing age, they often are changes that would widely be considered desirable.

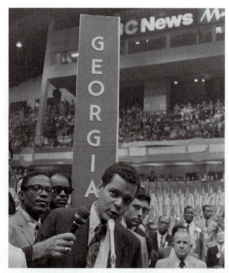

FIGURE 17.1 **Age limits on certain jobs.** On August 29, 1968, at the Democratic National Convention in Chicago, 28-year-old Julian Bond had to decline the nomination to be vice president of the United States because, according to the U.S. Constitution, a candidate must be at least 35 years old to be suitable for the presidency or vice presidency.

Physical and Physiological Changes in Adulthood

The health and lifestyle of older adults continue to improve as researchers discover more about the process of aging and find medical treatments and adaptive strategies that enable people to cope with age-related changes more effectively. People born in the mid-nineteenth century were considered old when they were in their 50s, and most people of that age had chronic disabilities. People born in the 1920s mostly lived past 60 without developing serious or chronic diseases, but they then showed a marked increase in disease and infirmity starting in their 60s. People born in the 1980s, however, are considered to have a 50-50 chance of living to 100 and being highly active, fit, and healthy into their 70s (Fogel, 2005). In addition, there is more variation than ever in aging patterns as people engage in behaviors that result in either highly successful aging or unsuccessful aging. Positive behaviors include healthier diets and eating patterns, physical and cognitive exercise, building networks of social support, and avoiding excessive amounts of stress (Jeste et al., 2010). For these reasons, discussions of patterns of aging are a moving target, and most readers of this text are likely, with appropriate behaviors, to live longer and be healthier than even those born in the 1980s.

Despite the many ways in which older adults are healthier and living more vigorous lives than ever before, most physical and physiological measures show a continuous pattern of decline from the mid-20s onward. Muscle mass and strength gradually decline throughout middle age, and the rate of decline accelerates in later years. From age 45 on, muscles decrease roughly 15 percent in strength each decade (Frontera et al., 1991; Hughes et al., 2001). A typical, active 25-year-old may have a total muscle mass equal to 30 percent of body weight, while a typical 75-year-old may have a total muscle mass equal to only 15 percent of body weight, with men losing muscle at a considerably faster rate than women (Murton & Greenhaff, 2009). At the same time, however, muscle endurance—that is, the ability to repetitively engage in a task over a long period of time—declines much more slowly. This is evident in the much longer careers of long-distance runners and cyclists as opposed to sprinters, whose performance is more dependent on strength (see Figure 17.2). Fast-twitch, or type 2, muscles also tend to decline more quickly than slow-twitch,

or type 1, muscles. The loss of endurance is also thought to reflect loss of mitochondria—the "energy factories" of the cell—in muscle cells (Holloszy et al., 1995). At the same time, however, the effects of muscle atrophy can be reduced to a remarkable degree by increased levels of exercise, especially in resistance training (Koopman & van Loon, 2009; Yarasheski, 2003).

> **Q:** What aspects of muscle function decline most with age?

People decrease in height as they age, as the vertebrae in their backs become more compressed (Rothman & Simeone, 1982). The skin becomes less taut and consequently more wrinkled, apparently becoming thinner and losing fat and collagen content (Newcomer & Young, 1989). Aging adults may also show osteoporosis, in which calcium depletion in bones leads to a drop in bone density and some skeletal deformities after age 50, especially in women. The onset of menopause and the sharp drop in related hormones cause the accelerated decline in bone density in women. Interestingly, humans seem to be one of the very few species that undergo menopause, leading to speculation that there may have been evolutionary pressure to stop fertility in older females because of their increased risk of dying in childbirth, which would then make them unavailable to care for older children and grandchildren (Diamond, 1996).

Almost all organ systems show some degree of decline. The kidneys show a decline in the ability to filter blood and excrete urine. The heart muscle weakens and loses capacity, and there is a drop in peak heart rate. The ability to circulate blood also declines as the arteries become more clogged. The lungs lose some capacity. The basic rate of metabolism also tends to decline, and as many middle-aged people painfully notice, their dietary intake must be cut back accordingly or their weight will increase (Cristofalo & Adelman, 2002; Tallis & Fillit, 2003).

> **Q:** Describe three different patterns of physical change in the body that occur later in life.

FIGURE 17.2 Relative sparing of endurance-related muscles. While muscles related to sprinting and other explosive rapid movements tend to decline quite noticeably throughout the 20s, muscles related to longer-lasting activities can be highly effective for many more years, as seen when 37-year-old Meb Keflezighi finished fourth in the 2012 Olympic Marathon.

Just as their organ systems decline with age, older adults also experience a pattern of decline in aspects of their brain and sensory receptors. The actual size of the brain decreases with age, losing as much as 10 percent of its weight and volume by the time a person reaches roughly 70 years (Cristofalo & Adelman, 2002; Scahill et al., 2003; Tallis & Fillit, 2003). There are also decreases in volume in many

Why Do We Age and Why Do We Live as Long as We Do?

A basic fact of human life remains a mystery: Why do we age? Why don't we reach a peak adult form and then simply maintain that form for perpetuity, constantly replenishing damaged tissue in the same manner that a salamander regrows its tail? One long-accepted theory argues that aging is an evolved trait in which organisms are programmed to gradually die after they have created viable offspring so that they can make resources available for the next generation (Weismann, 1889). More recently, the idea of evolutionarily programmed aging and death has been discounted as implausible when considered in detail (Kirkwood & Cremer, 1982; Sutphin & Kennedy, 2009), but the original proposal illustrates how the overall question of how and why we age is one of the most central questions in biology and one that is still not well understood. More current views argue that aging is a side effect of the lack of natural selection for repair mechanisms of tissue damage occurring later in life (Partridge, 2010).

Average lifespans vary considerably across organisms and are certainly related to their genetic makeup. It has been possible, for example, to selectively breed species of worms (Kenyon, 2001) and fruit flies (Landis et al., 2004) to obtain "Methuselahs" with far greater lifespans (for example, 75 days in fruit flies rather than 40 days). Such a genetic involvement, however, should not be taken as evidence for a genetic program that specifically triggers aging. It simply means that the factors that contribute to aging are partially related to an organism's genetic makeup.

Several distinct theories of aging remain under debate. One posits a gradual accumulation of negative random events, most often as a product of metabolic processes such as oxidation, which can leave by-products that decrease the efficiency of proteins and metabolic structures such as mitochondria.

A second view argues that cells can divide only a limited number of times, roughly 50 in many cases. This cell division limit is known as the **Hayflick limit** (Hayflick, 1965, 1998). It is thought to be related to DNA sequences called **telomeres**, which are located at the ends of chromosomes and protect the chromosomes from deteriorating and from fusing with other chromosomes. Telomeres prevent the loss of critical base pair sequences at the ends of the chromosomes during cell division by acting as protective caps to these base pairs. Because duplication of base pairs cannot occur at the extreme end of the chromosome, essential base pairs would be lost if the base pairs of the telomeres were not there. But some of the base pairs of the telomeres are not reproduced, and so the telomeres become a bit shorter with each division, sacrificing themselves to save the more critical base pairs. Ultimately, they will become too short and will lose their functional roles, although at least some cells in the body, as well as cancer cells, seem to have a mechanism for re-extending the telomeres through an enzyme known as **telomerase** (Hastings et al., 2004; Klingelhutz, 1999; Rubin, 1998). Recent work also suggests that high-stress environments, either physiologically in terms of poor nutrition or psychologically in terms of adverse events, may accelerate the rate of telomere shortening (Effros, 2009, 2012; Epel, 2009). More optimistically, some hypotheses suggest that more benign environments may halt and even reverse the effect and cause telomere lengthening and slower aging (Effros, 2009; Epel, 2009). This work has led to proposals that telomere length might be seen as a **psychobiomarker**—a biological feature that serves as an indicator of psychological functioning—of the quality of aging (Epel, 2009).

We can also see how the full life cycle becomes relevant to the effects of shortened telomeres. Thus, it may be that stress very early in life starts to prematurely shorten telomeres. One study of chick embryos showed that injecting the eggs with hormones related to stress responses resulted in shortened telomeres when the chicks were born (Haussmann et al., 2012). In humans, children who suffer from maltreatment also show shortened telomeres compared with controls (Price et al., 2013). There are even reports that children from lower socioeconomic groups have shortened telomeres compared with more affluent children, with calculations that the shortening is "roughly equivalent to 6 years of additional aging" (Needham et al., 2012). If supported by further research, these reports suggest that without amelioration later, earlier negative life experiences could have negative effects on aging half a century later.

A third view suggests that the genetic material itself, the animal's DNA, becomes slowly degraded over time through mutation and other events, such that it becomes more and more likely to produce nonoptimal proteins. If this third view is correct, the greater longevity of some species, such as humans, may be related to the higher incidence of redundant strings of DNA, which can provide a kind of backup production of critical proteins (Morrish et al., 2002).

Why do women live longer than men? The difference is quite dramatic, and ever more so with increasing age, as seen in Figure 17.3. There are a host of potential proximal causes, such as differences in hormonal influences on various body tissues, but the larger question remains whether there is any sort of adaptive reason for women to have longer lives. One evolutionary theory is based on the idea that women have more certain knowledge that their offspring are truly theirs, and therefore they have more reason to be fully invested in their offspring for the long haul so as to maximize the transfer of their genetic material to future generations (Perls & Fretts, 1998). Men, especially in societies of thousands of years ago, had far less certainty about paternity of any potential offspring and thus less of an investment in continuing care.

Genetic breeding studies with species such as worms and fruit flies may provide powerful new insights into questions of why we age and why there are sex differences in that process. These species are used because their life cycles are relatively short, allowing for relatively quick breeding. As the genomes of these species become available and as researchers come to better understand the precise roles of genes and gene pathways, the reasons for differences in aging may become clearer, as well as the possibility, someday, of gene therapy for aging humans. Unfortunately, those species that are optimal for this kind of research because of their short life cycles tend to be very different from humans, making implications for humans highly tentative and speculative. As discussed earlier, one finding that seemed to hold across a diverse range of species is that dietary restriction tends to increase longevity, and there are even some indications of such effects in humans (Partridge, 2010). Nonetheless, given the failure to find such

FIGURE 17.4 **Grandparents and the transmission of human culture.** About 30,000 years ago, grandparents may have begun to play a critical role as reservoirs of human cultural practices that they passed down to their grandchildren, thereby amplifying the effects of culture for future generations.

effects in rhesus monkeys, the consequences for human aging are less clear.

The flip side of asking why people age is to ask why we should survive much past the age when our own offspring are able to reproduce. In traditional hunter-gatherer societies that have existed for much of human evolution, parenthood comes in the early teenage years. Why should parents need to live much past their 30s? For hundreds of thousands of years, they may not have survived much longer than that, but comparison of the teeth of fossil populations from four successive time periods suggests that a radical shift occurred in the demographics of ages in a population about 30,000 years ago. Through careful analyses of the teeth of humans and hominins over these different time periods, it is possible to estimate the distribution of ages in a population through the degree of wear in the teeth (Caspari, 2011; Caspari & Lee, 2004). Such analyses reveal a dramatic surge in the population of older adults about 30,000 years ago. In a relatively short time interval, there were more than four times as many people living into old age. This surge in the elderly coincided with simultaneous bursts in populations and cultural complexity. There may have been a mutual symbiosis between cultural complexity and the proportion of older individuals. Cultures were able to grow in size and complexity to the extent that the collective information of that culture could be retained and passed down to the next generation. Especially in preliterate societies, the best repository of that knowledge was almost surely the elder members of those populations. Thus, the elderly served as a source of essential information that more and more complex societies could use as a foundation for further advancements (see Figure 17.4). In turn, as these cultures became more advanced, they were better able to protect and care for their elderly, thus completing the symbiotic circle. It is fascinating that this sort of dramatic change may have occurred over such a relatively recent time in the history of humans.

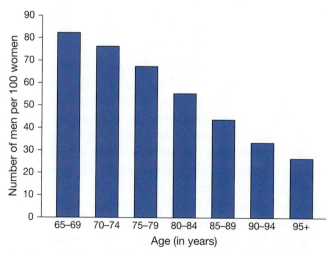

FIGURE 17.3 **Sex ratios and aging.** As is quickly evident at any retirement home, women vastly outnumber men in elderly populations. Adapted from the U.S. Census Bureau (1996).

local brain regions (in the hippocampus, for example, which affects memory; see Driscoll et al., 2003; Jernigan & Gamst, 2005; Ystad et al., 2009), in cortical thickness, and in neurotransmitter functioning. Moreover, there are increases in incidences of brain metabolites and neurofibrillary tangles, which are signs of Alzheimer's disease but not limited to those with the disease, as such increases appear in other elderly populations as well (Salthouse, 2009).

With respect to perception, there are usually substantial declines in vision and audition with age. Acuity drops off, even with corrective lenses. One of the most pervasive and commonly noticed changes is a decline in the ability to change the shape of the eye lens to focus on near objects. The need for reading glasses and bifocals is inevitable for most people at some point in their 40s. Even the most ardent health addict who defies aging in most other respects cannot avoid the need for corrective lenses for reading. Later in life, the disorder known as macular degeneration may occur, a condition in which the central area of the retina becomes pigmented and develops thinning layers; these changes eventually cause a dramatic drop in acuity. The lens of the eye also deteriorates with age, becoming yellow and filtering out some wavelengths of light. Night vision also tends to decline, as does the ability to quickly adapt to changing levels of illumination (Hyman, 1987; McMurdo & Baines, 1988).

There are also reliable patterns of decline in hearing. As the hair cells of the inner ear, or organ of Corti, become damaged, fragile, or simply die, there is a decline in the ability to hear certain frequencies, especially high frequencies. Nerves from the hair cells also tend to diminish in number. The bones that transmit sounds into the hair cells become more calcified and less able to transmit sounds. Taken together, these factors result in a decline in the overall sensitivity of hearing, which leads many elderly people to be hard of hearing and especially to have problems with hearing higher frequencies. Some entrepreneurs have capitalized on the ability of teens and young adults to hear frequencies that are not heard by older adults by developing devices that emit very annoying high-pitched sounds that discourage teens from loitering (Delaney, 2008).

Declines in taste, olfaction, and touch sensitivity also occur, but they tend to be more modest. Unfortunately, as vision and audition are often most needed in many psychological tasks, these two areas of more extensive decline can influence task performance quite dramatically.

There are several psychologically relevant diseases that occur primarily, although not exclusively, in the elderly. These include Parkinson's disease, Alzheimer's disease, general dementia, and sleep disorders. Parkinson's disease occurs when certain dopamine-producing cells in the midbrain start to die off. Although the best-known symptoms are related to motor skills, such as difficulty walking, shaky hands, and slow movements (Jankovic, 2008), psychological deficits also occur as the disease progresses, ranging from distractibility and difficulty in planning, to memory problems, to sleep disorders, to depression (Chaudhuri et al., 2006). Finally, in still later stages, many patients come to have severe dementia. Most cases start after age 60.

Alzheimer's disease is often first noticed when an individual has difficulty solving problems or remembering recent events or confuses recent memories with earlier ones. As the disease progresses, the affected individual can have substantial mood changes, language difficulty, and loss of long-term memory. The disease develops at different rates in different individuals, but in most cases, once the disease is correctly diagnosed, few individuals live much more than 10 to 15 years. Its cause is not yet known, although it is associated with the buildup of plaques (pathological accumulations of protein fragments that collect between nerve cells) in the cortex and fiber tangles (twisted fibers of protein) within nerve cells (Minati et al., 2009). Most cases start after age 60.

Dementia is a much broader pattern of disease associated with difficulties in problem solving, attention, memory, and language, and those who have dementia may also have late stages of Parkinson's and Alzheimer's disease, as well as many other disorders. While it can occur early in life, dementia is typically found in older individuals. By some estimates, roughly 1 out of 20 people older than 65 have some form of dementia, 1 in 5 people over 80 have it, and perhaps as many as half the people over 100 have it (Mathers & Leonard, 2000). But it appears that the rate of dementia is gradually declining as the elderly engage in more adaptive aging behaviors and as treatments for various disorders improve (Manton et al., 2005; Rocca et al., 2011; Schrijvers et al., 2012).

Many people older than 60 have difficulty sleeping through the night, often waking up several times for extended periods. The reasons for this change are unclear, especially given that there is considerable variation across individuals in the extent to which sleep patterns change. It is not yet known how much of the rise in "sleep fragility" is directly related to aging or how much is due to other age-related changes. One important consideration is that all people who are sleep deprived show cognitive decline, so it may be that some of the cognitive declines that are observed in the elderly might be reduced simply by improving their sleep (Crowley, 2011).

What factors cause some people to age much more successfully than others? The answer is complex and only slowly unfolding. It might seem that genes would strongly predict longevity, but their contribution, while significant, is certainly not the entire story. Thus, even monozygotic twins can show considerable variation in aging rates, although the rates are more correlated in MZ twins than in strangers (Talens et al., 2012). In addition, it is proving exceedingly difficult to isolate specific genes that may be predominantly responsible for aging effects (Barzilai et al., 2012).

There has also been a great deal of interest in the effects of diet on aging, especially in the effects of restricted diets. In several other organisms, such as rats, a restricted diet far below the normal level of intake (from 10 to 40 percent less) is associated with living substantially longer (Messaoudi et al., 2006). Nonetheless, this finding may not hold for humans—a disappointment to those who have restricted their diet in the hope of living longer. When researchers studied rhesus monkeys, a primate closely related to humans, they found no extension of life as a consequence of caloric restriction (Mattison et al., 2012). Given the large set of studies showing diet restriction effects in other species, it may be that future studies will also start to show stronger effects in primates, including humans. But the failure to find effects in one large-scale study does highlight some of the risks of extrapolating conclusions to humans. And since a large-scale random assignment study in humans is not feasible, it may be many years before there is convincing evidence of how dietary restrictions affect aging in humans.

> **Q:** Describe four different ways in which the sensory capacities and brain structure change in the last two decades of life.

Cognitive Changes in Adulthood

Given all the age-related changes in physiology, sensory systems, and brain architecture, we might expect related declines in psychological capacities. In fact, while there are certainly some declines, there are also many areas of preserved and even improved psychological performance with age. Human cognitive capacities are so flexible and adaptive that they are not that closely tethered to underlying biological changes. We will start, however, with some of the areas of cognitive decline, for these make all the more interesting the areas of preserved and improved performance. The cognitive aspects of aging have been an intensive area of research for many years. There are practical questions about the loss of cognitive capacity in the elderly. But a major problem in such investigations is distinguishing between patterns of decline in diseases that happen to be more frequent in the elderly and patterns of decline that are caused by the aging process itself. For example, Alzheimer's disease tends to occur much more frequently in the elderly, but it would be incorrect to assume that the massive patterns of psychological decline

that occur in those with Alzheimer's disease are comparable to the effects of normal aging. When people in their 40s and 50s begin to forget people's names or where they left their keys, the decline is more likely directly attributed to aging.

Reaction Time and Speed of Processing

Older people appear to slow down with normal aging. It might seem that this change simply reflects aging muscles and the ability to move limbs quickly, but in fact, speed of processing also starts to decline and at a surprisingly early age. First consider reaction time. **Simple reaction time**— namely, the time it takes to respond to a stimulus, such as pressing a computer key whenever an *x* appears on the screen—speeds up from infancy on into young adulthood. But as a person approaches her third decade of life, there is a longer response time, at first quite gradually through midlife and then much more dramatically in the seventh or eighth decade of life (Cerella, 1985, 1990; Finkel et al., 2003). The decline that starts in the late 20s is reflected in those sports where a slower reaction time may mean that an athlete in his 30s is beginning to lose his edge. Tennis may be one such example.

More **complex reaction times**, such as those involving different responses, depending on various spatial and temporal configurations of stimuli, also tend to slow down with increasing age after a person is in her 20s, but this depends on the task. With novel stimuli, there is a standard U-shaped curve (Hommel et al., 2004; Li et al., 2009; see Figure 17.5). By contrast, in areas of high expertise, reaction times and speed of processing may not slow down with increasing age but may hold constant or even get faster. One classic demonstration of increasing speed with age involved a study of the speed at which telegraph operators could type out a message in code (Bryan & Harter, 1899). By chunking sequences of dots and dashes—that is, grouping them into hierarchically organized clusters—expert telegraphers were able to achieve levels of speed that were far more related to their years of experience than to their age. Nonetheless, less expertise-laden measures of processing speed generally do decline with age, with differences in the rate of decline partially influenced by genetics, as shown by research that has found that MZ twins show more correlated rates of decline than DZ twins (Lee et al., 2012).

Memory, Higher Cognitive Functions, and Reasoning

Declines have also been found in higher-level cognitive performance. The declines often start to occur when a person is in his early 20s and then gradually lessen until he reaches

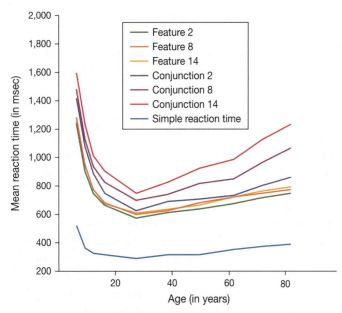

FIGURE 17.5 Complex reaction times. Reaction times in a complex task where expertise is irrelevant follow a pattern of speeding up until about age 25 and then gradually slowing down into late life. In a visual search task, adults are asked to respond as soon as they see a certain combination of features. Adapted from Hommel et al. (2004).

his mid-50s, after which point the drop can be quite a bit more dramatic (Salthouse, 2004, 2009). Figure 17.6 shows curves for four different sorts of general tasks: speed of processing, working memory, long-term memory, and world knowledge. There is a drop on the measures of speed of processing, working memory, and long-term memory. Only world knowledge improves with age, at least until the individual reaches his late 60s, and then there is only a very modest decline (Salthouse, 2004). Between the ages of 20 and 80, the drop in cognitive performance for speed of processing, working memory, and long-term memory is hardly subtle. Adults in their early 20s perform near the 75th percentile in the overall population, while those in their early 70s perform near the 20th percentile (Salthouse, 2004). Moreover, the drop occurs in roughly the same way for all healthy aging adults and is not caused by a small subset of the population afflicted with such age-related diseases as Alzheimer's (Deary et al., 2009). These differences in performance on cognitive tasks have sometimes been described as the difference between fluid and crystallized intelligence (Cattell, 1987), where fluid tasks tend to be those involving reasoning and stimulus processing in novel situations with new information, while crystallized tasks rely more on

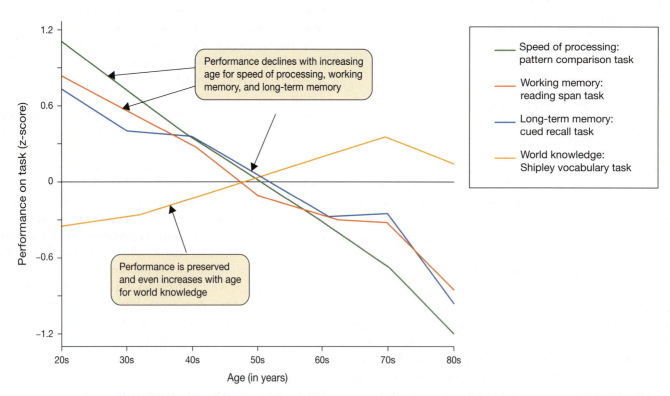

FIGURE 17.6 Fluid versus crystallized intelligence and aging. On most cognitive measures of what is considered "fluid intelligence," there is a marked decline in performance with increasing age. On measures of more "crystallized intelligence," performance can increase until a person is well into his 70s. Tasks involving speed of processing, working memory, and long-term memory clearly show declines in performance, while tasks involving general world knowledge generally show increases in performance. Adapted from Zimerman et al. (2011).

the use of information that is already available and familiar. The continuing strength of task performance relying on crystallized intelligence is a robust finding found across a wide literature (Hertzog, 2011; Palmer & Dawes, 2010; Salthouse, 2010).

In some tasks that are particularly dependent on accumulated knowledge, the hallmark of crystallized intelligence, the advantages of age can be striking. For example, the success rate on difficult crossword puzzles often continues to rise well into a person's 70s (Hambrick et al., 1999; Salthouse, 2004; see Figure 17.7). But even though they show good performance on vocabulary tests and crossword puzzles, we might expect people in their 60s and 70s to do less well on many everyday cognitive tasks, especially since 20-year-olds are in the top quarter of the population on many laboratory tasks and 70-year-olds are in the bottom quarter. Yet, older people generally do retain their competence when doing everyday cognitive tasks. Why is this so?

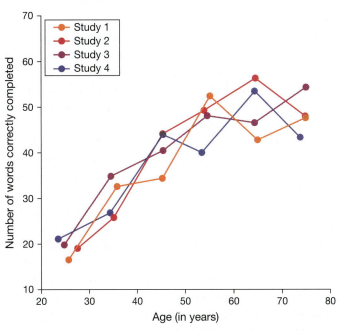

FIGURE 17.7 Consistent cognitive improvement with aging. One of the most robust examples of a cognitive skill that increases throughout the lifespan is that of solving crossword puzzles. This graph shows strikingly similar improvements across four different studies. Adapted from Salthouse (2004).

There are several reasons why people in their 60s and 70s may continue to do well on a wide variety of cognitive tasks. First, many everyday tasks, such as shopping for groceries, preparing a tax return, or assessing a cell phone plan, build on large blocks of familiar knowledge, an area where age can often be an advantage. Second, as seen in the telegraph operator example, many skills can continue to improve over time as individuals develop ever more integrative strategies. For example, even though muscle movements, reaction times, and other speed-related measures all decline starting when people are in their 20s and into their 50s, there is no decline in typing speed among expert typists (Salthouse, 1984, 1999). Indeed, in many cases, there is a continuing increase in speed well into midlife. Many skills can be more and more refined and hierarchically organized in ways that make them more efficient to produce. People often underestimate just how long it takes to become truly expert in a domain. In many areas of complex skills, such as anesthesiology, stock trading, or carpentry, it is estimated that at least 10,000 hours of full, effortful engagement in the task are needed to reach the highest level of expertise (Ericsson & Lehmann, 1996). Assuming that many people in their jobs may not spend more than 20 hours a week actually engaged in a task (such as surgery), it would take roughly 10 years to reach such a level, which after initial qualifying training is factored in, may mean that people do not reach the maximum skill level until sometime in their mid-40s.

Thus, in many areas, as people grow older, they decide to specialize in a manner that optimizes a particular niche of expertise. This means that they choose an area in which they can use the strategy of **optimization**—that is, continuing to practice over many hours to perfect a skill such as manuscript editing—and they select specific goals within that area—for example, building up world knowledge relevant to the topic areas where they do most of their editing by reading extensively about those areas. Although the upper limits of the benefits of such specializations and practice are not yet known, it seems reasonable that, in many cases, a person may be able to continually optimize performance for 20 or even 30 years. Those individuals who cognitively age in a "successful" manner may be those who develop a skill that they can continue to fine-tune and improve in decade after decade.

A different phenomenon that mitigates the effects of aging on performance may be **compensation**—using aids or altering behavior to make up for losses in cognitive or physical abilities. As people age, they may start to realize more clearly the limits of their cognitive systems and may develop ways of working around those limits. This might be as simple as learning to use a notepad to help them remember novel information or as complex as developing new networks of friends and acquaintances who can complement their cognitive shortcomings. An aging person may learn a large array of strategies for dealing with declining facets of cognition and thereby keep her performance at a high level (Bäckman & Dixon, 1992; Dixon et al., 2001; Freund & Baltes, 2002a). A general model of selection, optimization, and compensation has been proposed by Baltes and his colleagues (Baltes, 1997; Freund & Baltes, 2002b; Marsiske et al., 1995), in which successfully aging individuals learn to select tasks at which they will excel, optimize performance in these tasks, and compensate for some deficits with other skills. Baltes and his colleagues describe the particularly compelling case of the aging, brilliant pianist Arthur Rubinstein, who continued to play the piano with enormous skill well into his 80s (see Figure 17.8). When asked how he did it, Rubinstein described in detail how he picked a smaller set of age-appropriate pieces (selection), worked on them with great effort (optimization), and learned to mask loss of finger motor speed with a technique of speed contrast that gave a strong illusion of great speed (compensation).

Q: What are some reasons why certain cognitive functions stay constant or even improve in aging populations?

FIGURE 17.8 Successful aging and motor skills. Arthur Rubinstein continued to dazzle audiences well into his 80s by cleverly compensating for some slowing of his finger movements with other skills.

Skills in selection, compensation, and optimization may play a large role in the increasing ability to remember to do a task or to attain a goal in the future, which is known as **prospective memory**. Prospective memory might include remembering to pick up the dry cleaning on the way home from work or remembering to send in an absentee ballot before an election. Although performance on memory tasks generally tends to decline in the elderly, prospective memory is often preserved until very old age. Thus, as people in their 50s continue to age, their ability to remember to perform future acts may stay constant or even improve in some areas (Einstein & McDaniel, 1990; Einstein et al., 1997). One common explanation of this improvement may be that there is a robust ability for a person to monitor his cognitive performance with metacognitive and executive skills, which may continue to function well with age, perhaps especially as a means of compensating for specific areas of decline (Baltes, 1997; Einstein et al., 1997; Scullin et al., 2011). As older people start to confront the limits of working memory in more novel tasks, they may develop a clear sense of the ways that memory can fail and acquire strategies for working against such failures. Such strategies might be as simple as putting a note on a door as a reminder to do something when leaving the house in the morning or as complex as getting several friends to feel socially obligated to do an important task. These everyday strategies may help explain why older adults may show deficits in laboratory tasks of prospective memory but actually outperform younger adults in many real-life prospective memory tasks (Bailey et al., 2010; Henry et al., 2004).

Not all memory processes that involve strong metacognitive and executive processing continue to function well in the elderly. One area of decline involves failures in source monitoring (Henkel et al., 1998) and in related abilities to distinguish the frequency with which memories have been encountered from the actual instances in which those memories were experienced (Hay & Jacoby, 1999; Jacoby, 1999b). As we saw in Chapter 10, source monitoring involves the ability to tag a memory to the source or situation in which it was learned. Was it learned firsthand, through testimony of another, or through a dream? There is now considerable evidence of source monitoring problems in the elderly (Johnson & Mitchell, 2002; Mitchell & Johnson, 2009). For example, older adults are more likely than younger adults to say that they saw something that was only falsely suggested to them and are more confident of those false memories. Subsequent analyses revealed that older adults were less likely than younger adults to encode or use various cues to source information, such as perceptual cues distinguishing speakers, or context, or temporal (time-related) cues that could place information in a plausible or implausible time frame. Moreover, confidence in the semantic information (knowledge of the facts) of a message often seems to give a false confidence in the episodic information (knowing the experience and situation in which facts were learned; see Mitchell et al., 2003). It seems likely that difficulties in source monitoring are closely related to difficulties with episodic as opposed to semantic memory and with declines in function in some processing areas of the left prefrontal cortex. In a related manner, implicit memories also tend to show much less decline than explicit memories (Chauvel et al., 2012; Fleischman et al., 2004). Thus, an elderly person might learn to remember how to do a new routine in a nursing facility quite easily but not be able to remember ever having been taught the new routine.

A related problem may be a loss of the ability to distinguish a strong sense of familiarity from more episode-specific memories; indeed, some have argued that unscrupulous sales representatives prey on such disabilities to lull the elderly into a false sense of trust (Jacoby, 1999a). For example, a sales representative for a dubious life insurance policy might call up an elderly woman several times and give his name each time. The woman would not initially know his name, but over time she would come to recognize it as familiar. She might not, however, remember the context in which she had acquired that familiarity. Thus, when the salesperson called for the sixth time, she might have a reassuring sense of familiarity but no memory that the familiarity had been built up by repeated calls from a stranger. The salesperson, who would be aware of this deficit, would start to act as if he were an old acquaintance and then would make the sales pitch on that basis. The precise deficit here seems to involve a lack of explicit memories of specific events but a near complete sparing of an implicit memory that provides a strong sense of familiarity.

A different domain of cognition that often seems to be spared in the healthy elderly is that of spatial memory. When tested over brief intervals to determine their memory for at least modest-sized displays of objects in different spatial locations, the healthy elderly showed no obvious decline with age (Olson et al., 2004). Because these sorts of memory traces are often learned incidentally in real life—that is, we build a cognitive map automatically as we move through an environment—it may be that such memories are relatively spared in the same way as much of implicit memory (Pilotti et al., 2003).

In some cases, older adults can show considerably better reasoning skills than younger adults in context-rich everyday decision tasks. For example, younger adults tend to commit reasoning errors because of an **attraction effect** in which their estimates of the value of a good may vary as the result of additional information about other goods, even though that information should be irrelevant. Thus, if I know that a medium-quality radio costs $30 and a high-quality radio costs $60, my choice of which is a better buy should not be influenced by knowing that a poor-quality radio costs $15. Yet, such information does influence younger

adults' decisions. As such, context affects judgments where it should not (Tversky & Simonson, 1993). When the same tasks are given to older adults, however, they make decisions in a more rational and consistent manner that is not buffeted about as much by context (Tentori et al., 2001). Moreover, older adults show this resistance to context influences not only in domains of expertise but also in unfamiliar domains, whereas college students tend to be more limited, showing some immunity to context only in more familiar domains (Kim & Hasher, 2005).

It is not completely clear why older adults should show an advantage over younger adults in decision-making tasks that are prone to attraction effects. But one possible explanation may have to do with a tendency on the part of younger adults to try to adopt analytical strategies in which each alternative is weighed carefully, setting up possible interference effects from new information. Older adults, who use more global heuristics, may not be so "attracted" to discrete new pieces of information (Kim & Hasher, 2005; Peters et al., 2000).

More broadly, it would be misleading to characterize most elderly people as easy marks for unscrupulous predators who are attempting to bamboozle them into making bad decisions. Even though there may be declines in several components of memory processing, attention, and reasoning, elderly people often do well in more complex decision tasks. In some cases, they do so by engaging in the decision-making process in a manner that minimizes the effects of any deficits, such as slowing down the decision task and perhaps writing down key points on a notepad (Yoon et al., 2009). In other cases, as shown in the case of attraction effects, the cognitive abilities of the elderly may confer advantages in certain decision tasks without the need for any real efforts to compensate for deficits (Blanchard-Fields, 2007; Healey & Hasher, 2009: Zimerman et al., 2011). Elderly adults seem to be especially adept at making emotion-laden interpersonal decisions, apparently because they are more sophisticated at regulating their emotions during decision making (Blanchard-Fields et al., 2007). Greater abilities in some of these areas may be why some governments require that elected leaders be above a certain age. In an emotion-laden crisis, a higher level of emotion regulation may be important.

Daily Activities and Cognitive Aging

Although it is clearly a mistake to see aging as a decline on all psychological fronts, most people in their later years would like to slow down, stop, or even reverse the decline of some aspects of their cognitive abilities. It has been assumed for some time that exercise and diet matter, but only recently have experimental studies shown that they affect cognitive functioning. Based on these studies, it is now clear that daily activities can make a difference.

People who exercise regularly in their later years tend to show slower rates of cognitive decline, a finding that was originally based on correlational studies (Spirduso, 1980). But it is difficult to make inferences about causation from such studies. Perhaps people who have high levels of cognitive functioning are more likely to pick exercise activities. Or perhaps people with a more positive mood choose to engage in both more cognitively challenging tasks and more strenuous forms of exercise. The causal effects of exercise become clearer when experimental studies are considered. From a large series of studies, we know that when elderly participants are randomly assigned to exercise groups and control groups, those who engage in regular exercise for as little as a few months will show better levels of cognitive functioning on tasks as diverse as simple speed tasks and complex executive functions such as planning, switching tasks, and inhibiting distracting information, with the strongest effects usually occurring for the higher cognitive and executive functioning tasks (Colcombe & Kramer, 2003; Hillman et al., 2008; Kramer et al., 2006; see Figure 17.9). At the neural level, studies with rats and mice show that regular exercise can have a dramatic effect on structures throughout the brain, not just in the motor cortex (Cotman & Berchtold, 2002; van Praag et al., 2005). In addition, there are improvements in cognitive performance in abilities associated with those brain regions (van Praag, 2009; van Praag et al., 2005). These effects are strong in older animals as well, not just in young adult animals. The mechanism seems to involve the turning on of several gene cascades responsible for nerve growth and synaptic activity (Chae et al., 2009; Cotman & Berchtold, 2002). In studies with humans, it has also been shown that those who are randomly assigned to a group that engages in aerobic exercise will not only have increases in cognitive performance but will also have increased activation levels in brain regions associated with those tasks and increases in gray matter and white matter volume in those brain regions (Bherer, 2012; Colcombe et al., 2004, 2006; Erickson & Kramer, 2009; Hillman et al., 2008; Kramer et al., 2006).

In short, simple physical exercise seems to stimulate and preserve brain systems that support both simple and complex cognitions, and it may actually slow the various forms of neural and cognitive decline that occur with aging. It is important to note, however, that the positive effects of exercise on brain function and cognition occur at all ages, so even college-age populations can show significant cognitive benefits from exercise (Aberg et al., 2009).

Diet can also influence cognitive decline. But the most dramatic influence may not be a function of what we eat as much as a consequence of how much we eat. In particular, a diet that is sharply restricted in total calories has been associated with a slower rate of cognitive decline. Again, the majority of the human studies are correlational. Lean adults tend to have slower rates of cognitive decline than overweight adults, but this may be because people with a certain level of achievement motivation are both more diligent learners and more diligent dieters. Experimental studies with healthy elderly participants more clearly show a causal influence of caloric restriction on cognitive ability. In one study with people whose average age was around 60, the group that had their daily calories reduced by 30 percent showed marked improvement in performance on memory tasks after 3 months (Witte et al., 2009). On some memory tasks, the calorie-restricted group showed a more than 20 percent

A

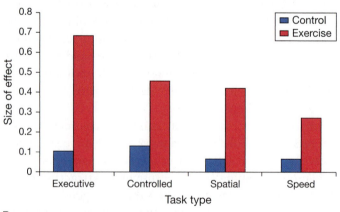

B

FIGURE 17.9 Exercise and cognitive aging. (A) Regular aerobic exercise has been causally linked not just to improved physiological health in the elderly but also to improved cognitive performance. **(B)** In older adults, exercise is strongly associated with higher scores on a variety of cognitive tasks, with the strongest effects occurring on executive tasks and more modest effects occurring on speed-of-processing tasks. These effects are found not only in correlational studies but also in experimental studies that randomly assign elderly individuals to exercise groups and control groups. This graph summarizes a meta-analysis of a large set of such studies. From Hillman et al. (2008).

increase in performance when compared with controls who did not have their diets restricted. The reduced calories may work through changing insulin levels that lead to increases in synaptic connections and protection of neurons in the brain (Witte et al., 2009).

Q: What aspects of cognition are influenced most by daily exercise?

It has long been thought that there is a "use it or lose it" rule that governs cognitive aging, because those who stay more cognitively active show slower rates of cognitive decline (Hultsch et al., 1999; Schaie, 2008). Many older adults who believe in this rule will engage in regular cognitively challenging activities such as word and card games as a form of cognitive calisthenics. Again, random assignment training studies are the best way to make strong inferences about causality. Here the findings are complex but point toward the need for a good deal of specificity in the training. Thus, if a group of elderly people practice daily on a certain activity such as a video game, they will show improvements in that game and in closely related tasks but generally not in other less similar cognitive tasks (Mather, 2010; Rabipour & Raz, 2012).

Some accounts of the sparing of cognitive functions in the elderly refer to the idea of "cognitive reserve" (Stern, 2009). **Cognitive reserve** is the idea that some people have more brain capacity to begin with and thereby have more brain structures "in reserve" to support functioning in the face of aging-associated decline or minor brain injuries. They may also have richer links between memories, thereby allowing the memories to more robustly reinforce each other. There is good evidence that people with above-normal cognitive capacities in college and middle age do tend to show higher levels of cognitive functioning in old age (Stern, 2009), but it is not yet known if cognitive reserve is the primary reason or if people with higher levels of cognitive ability remain active on many fronts and thereby maintain their abilities through activity, not because of reserves.

One study of young and old college professors and young and old people selected from a more general population documented less decline in the older professors than in the general population, but also found interesting differences across tasks. Simple speed tasks, such as tasks involving one-choice reaction times, showed similar patterns of decline in the elderly professors and among the elderly in the general population. With more cognitively complex tasks, however, such as recall of a prose passage, the elderly professors showed almost no decline in performance, while the elderly people from the general population showed a dramatic decline (Shimamura et al., 1995). The finding of a decline in simple speed tasks tends to suggest that a cognitive reserve explanation cannot be the whole story, since the reserve might be expected to reduce decline in those areas as well.

Q: What contrasting roles do implicit and explicit memories seem to play in aging populations?

Circadian Rhythms, Cognition, and the Lifespan

Circadian rhythms—that is, the shifts in biological activity and functions throughout a daily cycle—typically vary in college-aged people and middle-aged people. Most college students seem to be more alert and cognitively functional in the late afternoon or evening, while most middle-aged adults seem to be "morning people" (see Figure 17.10). Interestingly, children also tend to have peak performance earlier in the day, but a shift toward peak performance later in the day happens rather rapidly around puberty. As people

FIGURE 17.10 Time of day and cognitive functioning. Although many college students may find that they study best late in the afternoon or in the evening, older adults tend to be more effective cognitively in the early morning and can show marked drops in performance in the late afternoon, often taking naps on purpose or simply falling asleep unintentionally wherever they are.

progress into middle age and beyond, however, they seem to shift back to the morning as the time of day when they do their most productive and challenging intellectual work. This shift might reflect the ways in which adults take on the habits of the workplace, where productivity in the early hours may be a critical part of a business. Or the causation may operate in the opposite direction, with the workplace hours of middle-aged individuals reflecting the optimal time of day for being most productive. Support for this second interpretation comes from a wide variety of studies in both humans and animals in which the optimal period for complex tasks has been shown to gradually shift toward earlier and earlier times of the day as organisms age (Hasher et al., 1999; Martin et al., 2008; Winocur & Hasher, 2002).

Moreover, the shift does not seem to merely reflect increasing fatigue over the course of the day in older people. Instead, people's daily circadian rhythms, which reflect 24-hour cyclical surges of a large number of hormones, and changes in neurotransmitter functions and physiological patterns, shift with respect to the time of day corresponding to optimal arousal (Ingram et al., 1982; Yoon et al., in press). The shift does not apply to everyone, but it does hold for most people. Thus, roughly 75 percent of older adults find morning to be their peak time, while only about 35 percent of college students feel that morning is their best time (Winocur & Hasher, 2002).

The shift with increasing age to better performance during an earlier time of the day is seen in many other species besides humans. In rats, for example, older members of a population perform better on memory tasks shortly after waking for the day, while younger rats tend to show a surge in their performance later in the day (Winocur & Hasher, 2002, 2004). In addition, in humans at least, the daily rhythms may have different influences on different forms of memory. Thus, older adults seem to do better on explicit memory tasks early in the morning, while younger adults seem to do better on such tasks later in the day; older and younger adults often show the reverse patterns when engaged in implicit memory tasks. Such results suggest that these different memory systems may interact with endogenous circadian cycles in quite different ways (May et al., 2005). Moreover, older adults often use compensatory strategies with respect to time-of-day effects, shifting to the mornings those tasks that are most demanding.

Q: How does the time of day tend to interact with patterns of cognitive functioning in older and younger adults?

Overall, the range and extent of cognitive changes in the elderly are large and often dramatic, making it all the more impressive that before very advanced age (80s and older) we do not see obvious evidence of these deficits in the daily lives of the elderly (see Figure 17.11). We have seen that compensatory strategies, as well as continued building of specialized expertise and adaptive shifts in chosen activities, all work together to compensate for the effects of aging. If the raw components of reaction time, speed of processing, and working memory of novel items were all that mattered to cognitive performance, then everything would be downhill after the early 20s, and there would be little to learn from our elders in college, job internships, and medical residencies. Fortunately for those adults who are well past their 20s, other aspects of cognitive ability, many of which arise from ever more elaborate knowledge bases, allow the older generations to provide added value in their contributions to society. In addition, in some areas, the elderly may actually be prone to fewer errors in reasoning than younger people, especially in interpersonal, emotionally laden reasoning tasks, where the elderly may show more effective emotion regulation than adolescents and young adults.

One major principle concerning aging is that there are enormous individual differences ranging from successful aging, in which a person retains and even improves in some abilities up until the very last months of life, to pathological aging, in which people experience a dramatic decline starting in their late 50s or early 60s (Schaie, 2008). While we have seen that some of these differences are due to genetic predispositions and to the effects of specific diseases, such as Alzheimer's disease and Parkinson's disease, it is also reassuring that for virtually all of us, healthy or ill, exercise and diet can make a substantial difference in the rate of decline of our abilities.

FIGURE 17.11 Cognitive activities and aging. Many elderly people engage in challenging mental activities, such as playing bridge, out of the conviction that one of the best ways to hold off the decline of cognitive skills is by continuing to vigorously exercise their cognitive faculties. Such activities can indeed help to slow or even halt decline, especially in tasks that are closely related to the original activity.

Changes in Personality in the Lifespan: Individual and Group Changes

We have now considered extensive evidence for patterns of change in cognitive functioning from adolescence on into old age. Many of those changes are declines in function, but some are actually improvements in function. Moreover, most of the changes are in skills or bodies of knowledge; there is far less evidence for stage-like changes in the manner of thought. As we saw in Chapters 10 and 11, stage theories of cognitive development in children have undergone serious challenges, and there is even less evidence for such changes in adults. Beyond cognition, however, there are many aspects of personality that need to be considered. These questions can be addressed in two ways. First, we can ask if personality traits remain relatively stable over time. Personality traits are typically thought of as "relatively enduring patterns of thought, feelings, and behaviors that distinguish one person from another" (Roberts & Mroczek, 2008), but such a definition raises the question of whether some traits are more likely to change over time than others. The adage "You can't teach an old dog new tricks" is very often meant to apply to personality. Therefore, it might seem that happy teenagers will be happy seniors, shy teenagers will be shy seniors, and messy children will be messy seniors (see Figure 17.12). Moreover, the strong genetic components for many personality behaviors described in Chapter 7 would seem to support that claim as well. Second, we can ask if an age group as a whole can show a change in personality style that goes beyond individual personality differences within the peer group. For example, do the elderly as a whole become more conservative, more anxious, and more depressed? Both questions have received considerable attention in recent years.

Changes in Individuals

How likely is it that a shy, anxious, and messy teenager will become an outgoing, carefree neat freak as an elderly person? For the most part, such an outcome is unlikely, especially if that person's personality is evaluated relative to his peers. If John was much shier than most teenagers, he is also probably much shier than most of his peers in the retirement home. William James, the great psychologist/philosopher of the late nineteenth and early twentieth century, was convinced that little changed after the college years:

> Already at the age of twenty-five you see the professional mannerism settling down on the young commercial traveller, on the young doctor, on the young minister, on the young counsellor-at-law. You see the little lines of cleavage running through the character, the tricks of thought, the prejudices, the ways of the "shop," in a word, from which the man can by-and-by no more escape than his coat-sleeve can suddenly fall into a new set of folds. On the whole, it is best he should not escape. It is well for the world that in most of us, by the age of thirty, the character has set like plaster, and will never soften again. (James, 1890/1950, p.121)

Continuity in personality type has often been assessed by repeated administration of personality assessment tools over a person's lifespan. One widely cited series of studies conducted in Baltimore, Maryland, argued that few personality traits change at all over much of the lifespan (Costa & McCrea, 1994; McCrea & Costa, 1984, 1994). Not surprisingly, continuity seems particularly strong for those aspects of personality that have been shown to have the strongest genetic components: extroversion, neuroticism, openness to experience, agreeableness, and conscientiousness. Known as the **Big Five** (Goldberg, 1992), these traits repeatedly emerge in a statistical technique known as **factor analysis**, which looks for relatively independent clusters of traits. One developmental version of the continuity view

FIGURE 17.12 Constancy of personality traits. Bill Clinton, shown here at ages 25 and 66, today is notably extroverted compared with his peers. But his outgoing nature was also evident in his 20s compared with his peers.

argues that personality traits arise from primarily biological causes (such as genetic factors) and that personalities evolve and develop in childhood and young adulthood but then become fixed at around age 30, as William James believed (Costa & MacCrae, 1994). More thorough longitudinal and cross-sectional analyses of personality change after age 30, however, suggest that there is continued change into old age, change that is influenced by the environments in which each person spends his life. Contextual perspectives emphasize the influences of social environments, life events, and social roles on personality, with people tending to score higher on conscientiousness when they enter the workforce and higher on agreeableness when they become parents, but lower on openness to new experiences during middle and old age (Roberts & Mroczek, 2008; Srivastava et al., 2003). Thus, the idea that people become rigidly set in personality by around age 30 does not seem to hold up. Rather, there is considerable plasticity throughout adult development (Baltes, 1997). Nonetheless, people tend to occupy the same relationships relative to their peers in terms of how they as individuals score on the Big Five traits—for example, those who are anxious when they are adolescents continue to be more anxious than their easygoing peers throughout life.

Some scholars have suggested that consistency measures have tended to focus on continuity from early life into early middle age and that later in life, as many people move into their 50s, continuity of traits starts to erode for some individuals (Lachman, 2004; Roberts & DelVecchio, 2000). As people start to assess their lives as a whole and often become more self-reflective about their roles, that increased level of introspection may cause some real reorganizations of personality. Even with this caveat, and even taking into account continued plasticity, continuity is probably the dominant pattern for major aspects of personality, especially when an individual's personality is considered in comparison with her peers. The shiest person in a large group at age 30 is likely to still be a very shy person in the same group at age 80.

There is some evidence that there may be more potential for change in individuals who suffer from personality disorders, which are manifestations of psychopathology in personality traits, than for personality change in their peers who do not manifest such psychopathologies (Clark, 2009). Personality disorders can range from paranoia to narcissism to obsessive-compulsive disorder. It now appears that, in cases of severe personality disorder, more change is possible over time. A person who exhibits extreme paranoia may show a much more muted form several years later. The reasons for this greater variability relative to his peers are not yet clear, but one factor may be that, as a person learns to change other aspects of his life to cope with a severe disorder, the disorder itself may become less prominent.

> **Q:** Describe some of the arguments for and against the idea of continuity of an individual's personality over the course of the lifespan.

Stressful Life Events

One possible exception to the stability of personality traits over adulthood may occur in the face of repeated stressful life events. Such events appear to increase the incidence of depression in some at-risk people. Researchers have found several different patterns linking stressful life events and depression in midlife and later years (Kendler et al., 1999; Mazure & Maciejewski, 2003a, 2003b; Monroe, 2008). One pattern involves gender differences and indicates that women seem to be quite a bit more likely than men to become depressed as a result of exposure to stress (Husky et al., 2009; Kendler et al., 2001; Maciejewski et al., 2001; Sandanger et al., 2004; Stegenga et al., 2012). While it is difficult to match stress precisely for men and women (typical stressful events include relationship terminations and work-related stresses such as job loss), there consistently seems to be a pattern in which roughly equivalent stressful events are more likely to influence the lives of women than men, even quite late in life. Some analyses of twin data do suggest that researchers may overrate the influence of stressful life events on depression in middle age and underrate genetic predispositions that are independent of those events (Kendler et al., 1999), but there do seem to be residual effects arising from the stressful events themselves.

It has often been thought that the elderly are less likely to be fazed by life's ups and downs, having learned over the course of their lives that such variations are inevitable and simply must be taken in stride. There does seem to be some truth to this view, as elderly adults overall do not seem to be as susceptible as younger adults to the effects of stressful life events in terms of depression. At the same time, however, there are subgroups of elderly adults who show certain cognitive styles that can make them much more vulnerable to stressful events, with the odds of depression being from 6 to 11 times more likely in people with such cognitive styles and personality types when they encounter stressful events of specific types (Mazure et al., 2002). Thus, people who experience negative interpersonal events (for example, divorce) are much more likely to be influenced by those events if they show a high need for approval and reassurance in interpersonal relationships. In contrast, people who experience negative events pertaining to achievement (for example, being passed over for an important promotion) are influenced by those events to the extent that they put a heavy emphasis on individual success and on control. In this way,

we see that while many elderly adults may have developed adaptive ways of coping with stressors, substantial subsets of elderly adults have cognitive styles that continue to make them quite susceptible. It may also be that there is a connection between cognitive styles and whether stressful events lead to depression in men and women, with more women having cognitive interpersonal styles that make them prone to depression (Mazure & Maciejewski, 2003b).

Group Changes

Above and beyond the question of whether individuals have roughly the same personality relative to their peers over the course of adult life, one can ask if people in an entire age group tend to show certain gradual shifts in personality. One way this might happen is through "cohort effects," where all people who grow up during a certain historical period, such as the Great Depression of the 1920s, have personality shifts as a cohort—for example, the ability to thrive in the face of adversity (Schaie, 1984). Moreover, there may be other ways that people in different age groups show different personality tendencies. In earlier parts of the life cycle, such patterns are largely taken for granted. Young adults and older adolescents are considered much more likely to engage in risky behaviors that may well increase their chances of being seriously injured or seriously injuring others (Steinberg, 2008; see Figure 17.13). There seems to be considerable truth to this stereotype, especially for young adult males. Automobile insurance rates are higher

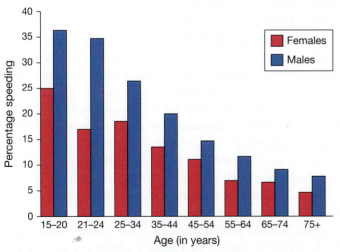

FIGURE 17.13 Speeding in fatal crashes in different age groups. Data on traffic fatalities and age are complex, as elderly people die much more often in car crashes because of their greater frailty. But if car crashes are looked at from a perspective of risk-tasking behavior, as defined by speeding, it is clear that younger drivers are much more prone to die in car accidents because they were engaging in riskier driving—that is, speeding. Adapted from Nell (2002).

for young adults not only because these individuals are less experienced drivers; young people also take more risks when driving. They are more likely to engage in risky sex, unsafe travel, and dangerous patterns of drug and alcohol use both because of increased sensation-seeking behaviors and because of different perceptions of risk (Cohn et al., 1995; Greene et al., 2000; Lightfoot, 1997). In addition, when put into highly stressful situations, older adults tend to slow down and take fewer risks, while younger adults show no such decline (Mather et al., 2009). Such risky behavior by younger adults has been argued to be an important part of demonstrating their fitness in mate competition (Wilson & Daly, 1993), but it is also a bit paradoxical. Why, with most of their lives ahead of them, do young adults put themselves at such risk? Why don't the elderly members of a society, who have relatively short futures ahead of them, choose to take larger risks? As discussed in Chapter 2, the increased risk taking in adolescence may reflect relatively late emergence of frontal lobe circuit feedback on the limbic system, but it is not clear whether brain changes underlie behavioral changes in older adults.

Young adulthood is not the only period in which a group is thought to shift along a personality dimension such as risk taking. There have been many stereotypes about the personalities of the elderly. Are older people more anxious, more conservative, or more irritable than people in younger age groups? Despite negative views about older people, such as the stereotype of "grumpy old men," the best-documented age group changes are generally more favorable (Charles & Carstensen, 2010). For example, one well-studied dimension of personality is that of the **positivity bias** (Carstensen & Charles, 1998; see Figure 17.14). It appears that as adults grow older, they tend to have a more positive view of reality and of their experiences. This positivity bias has been demonstrated in many ways. Compared with younger people, older adults tend to pay less attention to negative events in a variety of experimental settings. In one study, participants were asked to look at side-by-side pairs of faces that depicted neutral and either positive or negative emotions. When the emotion was positive, both young and old adults were more likely to have encoded the positive face, but when the emotion was negative, the people in the two age groups showed sharply contrasting patterns. Younger adults encoded the negative face, while older adults focused their attention on the neutral face (Mather & Carstensen, 2003; see Scientific Method box). This positivity bias has repeatedly been found when older adults engage in perceptual and attentional tasks (Lee & Knight, 2009; Mather & Carstensen, 2005; Samanez-Larkin & Carstensen, 2011).

Older adults also do not remember negative information as well as they remember positive information. One study with 300 nuns looked at their memory of responses on a questionnaire that they had filled out 14 years earlier

A

B

C

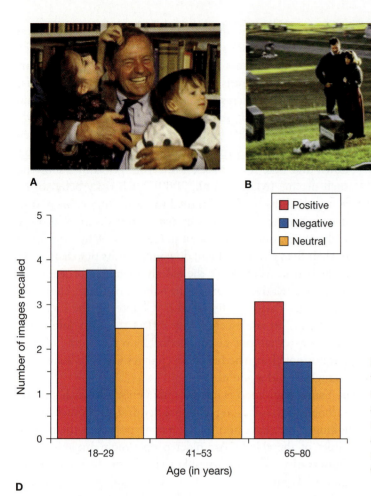

FIGURE 17.14 A positivity bias in memory. Participants of different ages were shown photos of **(A)** positive events, **(B)** negative events, and **(C)** neutral events. **(D)** As shown in this graph, older adults (ages 65 to 80) recalled more positive images than either neutral or negative ones, while middle-aged adults (ages 41 to 53) and younger adults (ages 18 to 29) recalled both positive and negative images more than neutral ones. Adapted from Mather & Carstensen (2005).

D

(Kennedy et al., 2004). The nuns ranged in age from 47 to 102 years at the time of recall. Older nuns showed a strong bias toward recalling items in their questionnaires more positively than they had originally reported them 14 years earlier. Older nuns were seen as more motivated to provide a positive interpretation of past life events, perhaps as a way of regarding their lives, as they neared their ends, as more worthwhile. (Since more than 60 percent of the nuns who had originally filled out the questionnaire had died during this period, the impending end of life was likely to be very salient to the older nuns.) Over shorter time intervals, older people also show a distinctly better memory of positive pictures compared with negative and neutral ones (see Figure 17.14).

Positivity effects also have an influence on decision making. For example, when college students and people in their 60s were asked to list positive and negative features of several common objects (for example, a pen, a mug), those in the older group tended to list more positive features and fewer negative ones. Both groups then got to pick an object to keep, and those in the older group declared more satisfaction with their choice both immediately and after 2 weeks (Kim et al., 2008). This difference in satisfaction occurred only when both groups were asked to evaluate each object

and list positive and negative features. If they were simply asked to pick an object and then rate satisfaction with their choice, there was no difference between the groups. Thus, the positivity bias influences feature choice in the evaluation task, which then influences satisfaction with the choice. There may be real-world implications concerning strategies used to influence decision making in older adults as opposed to younger adults. Having older adults generate a list of pros and cons for a decision is more likely to result in their being satisfied with the decision than it is for younger adults.

At the neural level, this positivity effect has been demonstrated by showing that the amygdala, a brain region heavily involved in emotions, shows markedly less activation in response to negative stimuli than to positive stimuli in older adults, while showing strong responses to both kinds of stimuli in younger adults (Mather et al., 2004). Because negative events do not elicit as strong an emotional response in older adults, they are not nearly as motivated to attend to or remember negative information. It appears that older adults also focus more on emotional regulation and are often better at it than younger adults, being less quick to feel anger in reaction to negative events, reacting less strongly, and letting anger and negative affect

SCIENTIFIC METHOD: The Positivity Bias in Older Adults

Hypothesis:

Older adults are biased to attend more strongly to positively slanted forms of information.

Method:

1. Fifty-two younger adults (18 to 35 years old) and 52 older adults (62 to 94 years old) participated.

2. All participants started by looking at a blank screen across the room.

3. Two faces appeared for 1 second: one with a positive or negative emotion and one that had a neutral expression.

4. A small dot then appeared where one of the faces had been, and participants were asked to say what the emotional expression had been on that face.

5. The researchers measured the speed of the participants' response.

Results:

Positive scores indicated faster responses when the dot appeared after an emotional face than after a neutral face. Negative scores indicated slower responses when the dot appeared after an emotional face than after a neutral face. Younger adults had faster responses for both positive and negative faces than they did for neutral faces. Older adults were much faster in responding to positive faces but slower in responding to negative faces.

Conclusion:

Older adults track information about positive faces more effectively, showing a positivity bias for information.

Source study: Mather & Carstensen (2003).

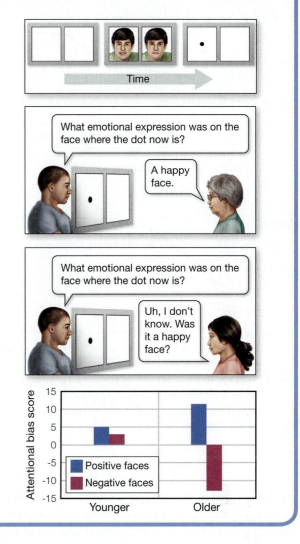

dissipate more quickly. One reason for this shift in focus is the related finding that, as people approach the end of life (including younger people with terminal illnesses), they tend to shift their priorities more to goals related to emotional well-being in the present and less to those related to gaining knowledge for future use (Mather & Carstensen, 2005). Older adults also show an asymmetry in neural processing of anticipated gains and losses compared with younger adults. This, too, may be related to the positivity bias. In particular, when anticipating rewards, individuals from both age groups show equally strong neural responses in reward-related centers. But when they are anticipating losses, older adults show considerably lower levels of activity in both the dorsal striatum and the anterior insula, which are regions related to processing gains and losses (Samenez-Larkin et al., 2007). This pattern may result in older adults having less anxiety associated with worries about potential future losses, which may thereby lead

them to be more optimistic and to show the positivity bias (Samenez-Larkin & Knutson, 2014).

Beyond the preference for noticing and remembering positively construed information, there are other ways in which personality for an entire age group tends to change as people age. Again, while a person may still be disagreeable relative to his same-age peers, he may become much more agreeable in more absolute terms (comparing across all ages) as he grows older. As seen in Figure 17.15, these changes can be very substantial in some areas, such as conscientiousness or agreeableness. Overall, scholars have repeatedly noted that these changes tend to be ones that impartial observers would rate as desirable. Thus, as people grow older, their personalities tend to shift in ways that others would see as making them better people (Roberts & Mroczek, 2008).

Sometimes, apparent age-related shifts in personality may simply reflect changing realities. Older individuals are

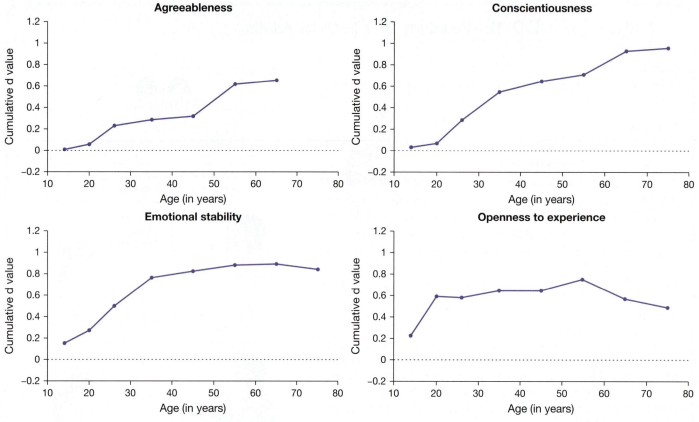

FIGURE 17.15 Group changes in personality. While people tend to show consistency in personality types relative to their same-age peers, age groups as a whole can show quite dramatic changes with increasing age along various personality dimensions. Here we see substantial rises in three dimensions (agreeableness, conscientiousness, and emotional stability) and relative stability in another (openness to experience). From Roberts & Mroczek (2008).

often described as being more anxious, but the increase in anxiety may not be as much an endogenous change in personality as a reflection of the greater likelihood of injury in their lives. People in their 90s, for example, are highly likely to suffer a broken hip from a fall. Their greater anxiety about falling when getting around may simply be a rational appraisal of the ways in which they are more physically at risk, just as younger adults with at-risk conditions, such as asthma or heart problems, might be more anxious.

More broadly, age group effects raise questions about whether there are general life stages that people tend to pass through, stages that might be related to some trends in personality change in different age groups.

Q: What are some ways that older adults as a group tend to shift in terms of their personality characteristics, their views of reality, and their remembered experiences?

Stages of Life?

As seen in Chapters 5 and 10, the notion of stages of cognitive development in infancy and childhood were problematic. It might still be the case, however, that within the broader context of the full lifespan, there are stages of development. For the most part, proposals of such stages have not been about cognitive functioning per se and have been more about social, emotional, and general life perspectives. As mentioned earlier in Chapters 7 and 13, the best-known theory of lifespan stages was put forth by Erik Erikson (see Figure 17.16).

Erik Erikson's Approach

Erikson was initially trained in the psychoanalytic tradition and in fact studied under Anna Freud. At the same time, he had a strong background in anthropology, which led him to take into account the effects of culture to a far greater

FIGURE 17.16 Erik Erikson. Erikson proposed a series of stages of psychosocial development that applies to the entire human lifespan and is marked by a distinctive conflict at each stage that an individual either masters positively or endures negatively.

handled and form a good foundation for the next stage, or it may be unsuccessfully managed and not only form a weak foundation for the next stage but also reappear later, especially in times of stress. Let's consider each stage in more detail.

Stage 1: Trust versus Mistrust As babies start out in life, relationships with the mother are thought to be central. If the mother or other primary caregiver is able to respond to the baby's needs and make him feel safe and secure, the infant is likely to develop a sense of trust in those around him. By contrast, if the mother is unable to meet his needs, the baby is likely to become mistrustful and suspicious of others.

Stage 2: Autonomy versus Shame/Doubt As children start to walk about and explore their environments, their parents need to grant them some sense of autonomy while also making sure that they do not get into too much trouble. Ideally, parents will allow their children to explore and move about in the freest manner that still ensures their safety. But Erikson believed that if the parents are too controlling or too protective, their children will develop doubts about their own abilities and shame at their incompetence.

Stage 3: Initiative versus Guilt Preschool children develop a better and better sense of their own personal responsibility. As their circle of relationships extends to the family as a whole, they become more aware of how their actions influence others. They need to learn to take the initiative as they seek to gain mastery of a wide variety of life tasks, but too much initiative without any guilt may lead to psychopathic behavior, producing a child without

extent than either Freud or his daughter. Erikson proposed eight stages of psychosocial development, as summarized in Table 17.1, with each stage organized around a type of **psychosocial conflict** (Erikson, 1950). These conflicts are the challenges people face in relating to others or to society at large. They occur throughout the lifespan and must be addressed in order to establish an identity within the social world. The challenge at each stage may be successfully

Stage	Approximate Age (in years)	Developmental Period	Psychosocial Conflict	Most Important Relations
1	0–1.5	Infancy	Trust vs. mistrust	Mother/primary caregiver
2	1.5–3	Toddler	Autonomy vs. shame/doubt	Parents
3	3–6	Preschool	Initiative vs. guilt	Family
4	6–12	Childhood	Industry vs. inferiority	Neighborhood/school
5	12–18	Adolescence	Identity vs. role confusion	Peer groups
6	18–30	Young adulthood	Intimacy vs. isolation	Partners, friends
7	30–50	Middle age	Generativity vs. stagnation	Family, coworkers
8	50 and older	Later adulthood	Integrity vs. despair	Mankind /"my kind"

TABLE 17.1 Erikson's stages of psychosocial development. Erikson proposed eight stages of psychosocial development, each marked by a distinctive form of conflict that an individual has to address to help construct his social identity.